Strategic Brand Management

Visit the *Strategic Brand Management: A European Perspective* Companion Website at **www.pearsoned.co.uk/keller** to find valuable **student** learning material including:

- Video cases on IKEA and Electrolux, including interviews with the top management teams
- Links to relevant sites on the web
- An online glossary to explain key terms

We work with leading authors to develop the
strongest educational materials in marketing,
bringing cutting-edge thinking and best
learning practice to a global market.

Under a range of well-known imprints, including
Financial Times Prentice Hall, we craft high-quality print and
electronic publications that help readers to understand
and apply their content, whether studying or at work.

To find out more about the complete range of our
publishing, please visit us on the World Wide Web at:
www.pearsoned.co.uk

Strategic Brand Management

A European Perspective

Kevin Lane Keller
Tony Apéria
Mats Georgson

FT Prentice Hall
FINANCIAL TIMES

An imprint of **Pearson Education**

Harlow, England • London • New York • Boston • San Francisco • Toronto • Sydney • Singapore • Hong Kong
Tokyo • Seoul • Taipei • New Delhi • Cape Town • Madrid • Mexico City • Amsterdam • Munich • Paris • Milan

Pearson Education Limited

Edinburgh Gate
Harlow
Essex CM20 2JE
England

and Associated Companies throughout the world

Visit us on the World Wide Web at:
www.pearsoned.co.uk

_____

First published 2008

© Pearson Education Limited 2008

ISBN: 978-0-273-70632-8

British Library Cataloguing-in-Publication Data
A catalogue record for this book is available from the British Library

Library of Congress Cataloging-in-Publication Data
Keller, Kevin Lane
    Strategic brand management : a European perspective / Kevin Lane Keller, Tony
Aperia, Mats Georgson.
        p. cm.
    Includes bibliographical references and index.
    ISBN 978-0-273-70632-8 (pbk. : alk. paper)   1. Brand name products--Management.   I.
Apéria, Tony. II. Georgson, Mats. III. Title.
    HD69. B7K449 2008
    658.8'27--dc22

                                                            2008003326

10 9 8 7 6 5 4 3 2 1
11 10 09 08

Typeset in 10/12.5 pt Palatino by 73

Printed by Ashford Colour Press Ltd, Gosport

The publisher's policy is to use paper manufactured from sustainable forests.

Contents

Guided Tour

A **Preview** opening each chapter highlights the issues to be covered, enabling you to see at a glance what you will learn from reading the chapter

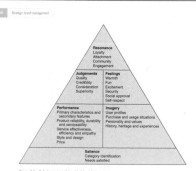

Figure 2.6   Sub-dimensions of brand building blocks

Clear and memorable **Figures** express the models, principles and theories of branding, helping you to visualise the concepts discussed

Strategic brand management

Brand Briefing 3.1

Trying to find some homes for light colas

With consumers turning to healthier options such as water and sports drinks, soft drinks sales have been flat. 'Light' or 'diet' versions have been more successful and represent a growing market segment. Soft drink companies are therefore looking for ways to appeal to calorie-conscious consumers, especially men who are turned off by the taste of diet carbonated drinks or perceive a stigma attached to the word 'light'. And sweeteners, such as Splenda, which appeals to low-carb dieters, create even more options.

The drive to appeal to the health-conscious crowd, however, is making soft drinks a crowded category and success has not come easy for the cola giants. Coca-Cola tried to add Coke Light with Splenda and C2 to its diet cola portfolio as companions to its hugely successful Coke Light brand. In the process, Coca-Cola has been going head-to-head in the light category with Pepsi, which has a reformulated Pepsi One, as well as Pepsi Max.

Although these line extensions are intended to boost sales, some critics point out that they can also backfire if new versions cannibalize sales of a company's existing drinks. Even worse, many feel that Coke and Pepsi run the risk of confusing consumers with endless variants. Despite spending millions on advertising, experts say customers don't always understand the differences between the options.

Introduced in 1998, Pepsi One appropriately has one calorie. Pepsi waited for Food and Drug Administration approval of sweetener acesulfame potassium (Ace-K) and spent more than €68.4 million on marketing the year following the launch. Pepsi positioned Pepsi One as a full-flavoured yet healthy option to regular colas and targeted men aged 20 to 30 who did not like the taste of light colas. Unfortunately, initial advertising, featuring actor Cuba Gooding Jr, failed to describe exactly what Pepsi One was and how it was different from Pepsi Max. Campaigns came and went and, when Pepsi One failed to garner the market share the company hoped for, it was reformulated with Splenda.

With the launch of Coke Zero and Coca-Cola Light with Splenda in 2005, consumers faced an array of low- or no-calorie Coke options, including Coke Light with Lime, Coke Light with Lemon, Light Cherry Coke, Light Vanilla Coke and Caffeine Free Coke Light, Coke Zero, named for its zero calories, was designed to taste more like original Coke than Light Coke. Coke Zero began with the formula of Coca-Cola but used aspartame and acesulfame potassium as sweeteners instead of sugar. Because the company was trying to stay away from the light label, the words 'light' and 'calories' were not mentioned in the initial marketing campaign. As a result, consumers didn't really know what Coke Zero was and the company eventually switched to ads emphasizing its 'Real Coca-Cola taste, zero calories, no compromise.' Coke Zero was launching in the UK, Spain and Germany in the summer of 2006.

Brand Briefings spotlight brand management scenarios as experienced by real-life companies and organisations, showing you how brands are operated

---

Brand positioning

seminars at its Disney Institute on the 'Disney style' of creativity, service and loyalty for employees from other companies.

In some cases, internal branding can both motivate employees and serve to attract customers externally. For example, to help create an expectation of trust with its customers, Midas ran an ad campaign showing its own employees as heroes. Awareness of the Midas corporate brand rose 25 percent as a result.[29] In short, internal branding is a critical management priority. Successful internal branding requires a mixture of resources and processes, all designed to inform and inspire employees to maximize their mutually beneficial contribution to brand equity.

CHAPTER REVIEW

Determining the desired brand knowledge structures involves positioning a brand in the minds of consumers. According to the customer-based brand equity model, deciding on a positioning requires determining a frame of reference (by identifying the target market and the nature of competition) and the ideal points of parity and points of difference brand associations. Determining the proper competitive frame of reference depends on understanding consumer behaviour and the consideration sets consumers adopt in making brand choices.

Points of difference are those associations unique to the brand that are also strongly held and favourably evaluated by consumers. Determining points of difference associations that are strong, favourable and unique is based on desirability and deliverability considerations, which are combined to determine the resulting anticipated levels of sales and costs that might be expected with the positioning. Points of parity, on the other hand, are those associations that may be shared with other brands. Category point of parity associations are those associations that consumers view as being necessary to be a legitimate and credible product offering within a certain category. Competitive point of parity associations are those associations designed to negate a competitor's points of difference. Deciding on these four ingredients will determine the brand positioning and dictate the desired brand knowledge structures.

A broader set of considerations is also useful for positioning, especially for a more developed brand that spans many categories. A mental map accurately portrays in detail all salient brand associations and responses for a particular target market (eg, brand users). Core brand associations are those sets of abstract associations (attributes and benefits) that characterize the five to ten most important aspects of a brand. Core brand associations can serve as an important foundation for the brand strategy. In particular, core brand associations can serve as the basis of brand positioning in terms of how they relate to points of parity and points of difference. Finally, a brand mantra is an articulation of the 'heart and soul' of the brand. Such mantras are three- to five-word phrases that capture the essence or spirit of the brand positioning and brand values. Their purpose is to ensure that all employees within the organization as well as all external marketing partners understand what the brand most fundamentally is to represent with consumers so that they can adjust their actions accordingly.

A **Chapter Review** both summarises the themes and arguments of the chapter, and places it in a broader context, encouraging your own further investigation

---

Strategic brand management

The concepts discussed in this chapter are powerful tools to guide positioning. Once the brand positioning strategy has been determined, the actual marketing campaign to create, strengthen or maintain brand associations can be put into place. Chapters 4 to 7 describe some of the important marketing mix issues in designing supporting marketing campaigns.

Discussion questions

1. Apply the categorization model to a product category other than drinks. How do consumers make decisions whether or not to buy the product, and how do they arrive at their final brand decision? What are the implications for brand equity management for the brands in the category? How does it affect positioning, for example?

2. Pick a brand. Describe its breadth and depth of awareness.

3. Pick a category dominated by two main brands. Evaluate the positioning of each brand. Who are their target markets? What are their main points of parity and points of difference? Have they defined their positioning correctly? How might it be improved?

4. Can you think of any negatively correlated attributes and benefits other than those listed in Figure 3.6? Can you think of any other strategies to deal with negatively correlated attributes and benefits?

5. Think of one of your favourite brands. Can you come up with a brand mantra to capture its positioning?

References and notes

[1] Much of this chapter is based on Kevin Lane Keller, Brian Sternthal and Alice Tybout, 'Three questions you need to ask about your brand', *Harvard Business Review*, September 2002, 80 (9): 80–9.

[2] Phillip Kotler and Kevin Lane Keller, *Marketing Management*, 12th edn, Upper Saddle River, NJ: Prentice Hall, 2006.

[3] Chip Walker, 'How strong is your brand?', *Marketing Tools*, January/February 1995: 46–53.

[4] Chip Walker, 'How strong is your brand?', *Marketing Tools*, January/February 1995: 46–53.

[5] Russell I. Haley, 'Benefit segmentation: a decision-oriented research tool', *Journal of Marketing* July 1968, 32: 30–5.

[6] Also, the demographic specifications given may not fully reflect consumers' underlying perceptions. For example, when the Ford Mustang was introduced, the intended market segment was much younger than the ages of the customers who actually bought the car. Evidently, these consumers felt or wanted to feel younger psychologically than they really were.

[7] Ronald Frank, William Massey and Yoram Wind, *Market Segmentation*, Englewood Cliffs, NJ: Prentice Hall, 1972.

[8] Allan Baldinger and Joel Rubinson, 'Brand loyalty: the link between attitude and behavior', *Journal of Advertising Research*, November–December 1996: 22–34.

[9] A complete treatment of this material is beyond the scope of this chapter. Useful reviews can be found in any good marketing strategy text. For example, see David A. Aaker, *Strategic Market*

Discussion Questions at the end of each chapter can be used to test your understanding as you review what you have read, whilst a full list of **References and Notes** is provided to aid your independent research

Preface

It is useful to answer a few questions to provide the reader and instructor with some background as to what this book is about, how it is different from other books about branding, who should read it, how the book is organized, what is new in this second edition and how a reader can get the most out of using the book.

WHAT IS THE BOOK ABOUT?

This book deals with brands – why they are important, what they represent to consumers and what should be done by firms to manage them properly. As many business executives now recognize, perhaps one of the most valuable assets that a firm has is the brands that the firm has invested in and developed over time. Although manufacturing processes and factory designs often can be duplicated, strongly held beliefs and attitudes established in the minds of consumers often cannot be so easily reproduced. The difficulty and expense of introducing new products, however, puts more pressure than ever on firms to skillfully launch their new products as well as manage their existing brands.

Although brands may represent invaluable intangible assets, creating and nurturing a strong brand poses considerable challenges. Fortunately, the concept of *brand equity* – the main focus of this book – can provide marketers with a valuable perspective and a common denominator to interpret the potential effects and tradeoffs of various strategies and tactics for their brands. Fundamentally, the brand equity concept stresses the importance of the role of the brand in marketing strategies. Brand equity relates to the fact that different outcomes result from the marketing of a product or service because of its brand name or some other brand element than if that same product or service did not have that brand identification. In other words, brand equity can be thought of as the marketing effects uniquely attributable to the brand. In a practical sense, brand equity represents the added value endowed to a product as a result of past investments in the marketing activity for a brand. Brand equity serves as the bridge between what happened to the brand in the past and what should happen to the brand in the future.

The chief purpose of this book is to provide a comprehensive and up-to-date treatment of the subjects of brands, brand equity and strategic brand management.

Strategic brand management involves the design and implementation of marketing campaigns and activities to build, measure and manage brand equity. An important goal of the book is to provide managers with concepts and techniques to improve the long-term profitability of their brand strategies. The book incorporates current thinking and developments on these topics from both academics and industry participants. The book combines a comprehensive theoretical foundation with numerous practical insights to assist managers in their day-to-day and long-term brand decisions. Illustrative examples and case studies are based on brands marketed in Europe, in the United States and all over the world.

Specifically, the book provides insights into how profitable brand strategies can be created by building, measuring and managing brand equity. It addresses three important questions.

1. How can brand equity be created?
2. How can brand equity be measured?
3. How can brand equity be used to expand business opportunities?

In addressing these questions, the book is written to deliver a number of benefits. Readers will learn the following:

- the role of brands, the concept of brand equity and the advantages of creating strong brands;
- the three main ways to build brand equity by properly choosing brand elements, designing supporting marketing campaigns and leveraging secondary associations;
- different approaches to measuring brand equity and how to implement a brand equity measurement system;
- alternative branding strategies and how to devise brand hierarchies and brand portfolios;
- the role of corporate brands, family brands, individual brands and brand modifiers and how they can be combined into sub-brands;
- how to adjust branding strategies over time and geographic boundaries to maximize brand equity.

WHAT IS DIFFERENT ABOUT THIS BOOK?

In writing this book, the objective was to satisfy three key criteria by which any marketing text can be judged.

- *Depth:* the material in the book had to be presented in the context of a conceptual framework that was comprehensive, internally consistent and cohesive, and well grounded in the academic and practitioner literature.
- *Breadth:* the book had to cover all those topics that practising managers and students of brand management found interesting or important.
- *Relevance:* finally, the book had to be well grounded in practice and easily related to past and present marketing activities, events and case studies.

Although a number of excellent books have been written about brands, no book has really maximized these three dimensions to the greatest possible extent. Accordingly, this book set out to fill that gap by accomplishing three things. First, the book develops a framework that provides a definition of brand equity, identifies sources and outcomes of brand equity and provides tactical guidelines as to how to build, measure and manage brand equity. Recognizing the general importance of consumers and customers to marketing (ie, the necessity of understanding and satisfying their needs and wants), this framework approaches branding from the perspective of the consumer and is referred to as *customer-based brand equity*. Second, besides these broad, fundamentally important branding topics, over 30 boxes provide in-depth treatment of cutting-edge ideas and concepts, and each chapter ends with an extended Brand Briefing box that delves into detail on specific, related branding topics such as brand audits, legal issues, brand crises and corporate name changes. Finally, to maximize relevance, numerous examples are included to illuminate the discussion on virtually every topic and many other Brand Briefings are included to provide more in-depth examinations of certain topics or brands.

Thus, this book can help readers understand the important issues in planning and evaluating brand strategies, as well as provide appropriate concepts, theories and other tools to make better branding decisions. The book identifies successful and unsuccessful brand marketers – and why they have been so. Readers will gain a greater appreciation of the range of issues covered in branding as well as a means to organize their thoughts about those issues.

WHO SHOULD READ THIS BOOK?

A wide range of people can benefit from reading this book:

- students interested in increasing both their understanding of basic branding principles and their exposure to classic and contemporary branding applications and case studies;
- managers and analysts concerned with the effects of their day-to-day marketing decisions on brand performance;
- senior executives concerned with the longer-term prosperity of their brand franchises and product or service portfolios;
- all marketers interested in new ideas with implications for marketing strategies and tactics.

The perspective adopted in the book is relevant to any type of organization (public or private, large or small) and the examples provided cover a wide range of industries and geographies. To facilitate understanding of branding concepts across different settings, specific applications to industrial, high-tech, online, service, retailer and small business brands are reviewed in Chapters 1 and 15.

HOW IS THE BOOK ORGANIZED?

The book introduces branding concepts in Chapter 1, then moves on to provide all the specific details of those concepts and ends by summarizing and applying those concepts in various contexts.

Chapter 1 sets the stage for the book by providing the 'big picture' of what strategic brand management is all about. The goal of the chapter is to provide a sense of the content and context of strategic brand management by identifying key branding decisions and suggesting some of the important considerations for those decisions. Specifically, Chapter 1 introduces some basic notions about brands and the role that they have played and are playing in marketing strategies. Chapter 1 defines what a brand is, why brands matter and how anything can be branded and provides an overview of the strategic brand management process.

Chapters 2 and 3 address the topic of brand equity and provide a blueprint for the rest of the book. Chapter 2 introduces the concept of customer-based brand equity, outlines the customer-based brand equity framework and summarizes guidelines for building, measuring and managing customer-based brand equity. These two chapters provide a useful overview of the scope and topics covered in the book. As such, they provide an excellent 'top-line summary' for readers who want to sample the flavour of the book or who do not have the time to read all of the chapters. Chapter 3 develops a conceptual model of brand knowledge and addresses the critically important issue of competitive brand positioning.

Chapters 4 to 7 examine the three major ways to build customer-based brand equity, taking more of a 'single product–single brand' perspective. Chapter 4 addresses the first way to build customer-based brand equity and how to choose brand elements (ie, brand names, logos, symbols, slogans and so forth) and the role they play in contributing to brand equity. Chapters 5 and 6 are concerned with the second way to build brand equity and how to optimize the marketing mix to create customer-based brand equity. Chapter 5 is concerned with product, pricing and distribution strategies; Chapter 6 is devoted to the topic of creating integrated marketing communication campaigns to build brand equity. Although most readers are probably familiar with these '4 Ps' of marketing, it can be illuminating to consider them from the standpoint of brand equity and the effects of brand knowledge on consumer response to marketing mix activity and vice versa. Finally, Chapter 7 examines the third major way to build brand equity: leveraging secondary associations from other entities (eg, companies, geographic regions, persons, other brands and so on).

Chapters 8 to 10 look at how to measure customer-based brand equity. These chapters take a detailed look at what consumers know about brands, what marketers want them to know and how marketers can develop measurement procedures to assess how well they are doing. Chapter 8 provides a big-picture perspective on these topics, introducing the brand value chain and examining how to develop and implement a brand equity measurement system. Chapter 9 examines approaches to measure customers' brand knowledge structures in order to be able to identify and quantify potential sources of brand equity. Chapter 10 examines how to measure potential outcomes of brand equity in terms of the major benefits a firm accrues from these sources of brand equity.

Chapters 11 to 14 address how to manage brand equity, taking a broader, 'multiple product–multiple brand' perspective as well as a longer-term, multiple-market perspective to brands. Chapter 11 considers issues related to branding strategies (eg, which brand elements a firm chooses to apply across the various products it sells) and how brand equity can be maximized across all the different brands and products that might be sold by a firm. Chapter 11 describes two important tools to help formulate branding strategies: the brand–product matrix and the brand hierarchy. Chapter 12 outlines the pros and cons of brand extensions and develops guidelines to facilitate the introduction and naming of new products and brand extensions. Chapter 13 considers how to reinforce, revitalize and retire brands, examining a number of specific topics in managing brands over time, such as the advantages of maintaining brand consistency, the importance of protecting sources of brand equity and tradeoffs between fortifying and leveraging brands. Chapter 14 examines the implications of differences in consumer behaviour and the existence of different types of market segments on managing brand equity. Particular attention is paid to international issues and global branding strategies.

Finally, Chapter 15 considers some implications and applications of the customer-based brand equity framework. It highlights managerial guidelines and key themes that emerged in earlier chapters of the book. The chapter also summarizes success factors for branding, applies the customer-based brand equity framework so as to address specific strategic brand management issues for different types of products (ie, industrial goods, high-tech products, online brands, services, retailers and small businesses) and relates the framework to several other popular views of brand equity.

REVISION STRATEGY FOR THIS EDITION

The overarching goal of the revision of *Strategic Brand Management* was to preserve the aspects of the text that worked well but to improve it as much as possible and add new material as needed. The main objective of the second edition was to again maximize three dimensions: depth, breadth and relevance. The customer-based brand equity framework that was the centrepiece of the first edition was retained but embellished in several significant ways. Given all the academic research progress that has been made in recent years as well as new market developments and events, the book required and was given some substantial updates.

Specifically, there were six objectives to the revision, as follows:

1. overhaul the conceptual thrust of certain chapters;
2. adopt a stronger technological and global perspective;
3. update the Brand Briefings and academic references;
4. streamline chapters;
5. update original cases and introduce new cases;
6. provide better presentation of text material and stronger supplementary support.

Overhaul the conceptual thrust of certain chapters

A number of chapters reflect new thinking and concepts.

- *Chapter 1:* the chapter now formally introduces the strategic brand management process.
- *Chapter 2:* this chapter is now organized around the customer-based brand equity pyramid that describes the four steps (identity, meaning, response and relationships) and six different types of core brand values (salience, performance, image, judgements, feelings and resonance) necessary to build a brand. This detailed framework helps to provide more structure to the consumer brand knowledge topics as well as tie more directly into how to build brand equity, the thrust of the next four chapters.
- *Chapter 3:* new positioning material is included to further develop the book's unique competitive brand positioning model and the key concepts of points of parity and points of difference.
- *Chapter 6:* a new set of criteria is included for how to evaluate integrated marketing communication campaigns.
- *Chapter 7:* a revised framework for brand leverage is used as an organizing device.
- *Chapters 8, 9 and 10:* the material from Chapter 10 of the first edition has been combined with new material on the brand value chain to create a new Chapter 8 that provides a big-picture perspective on the theory and practice of measuring brand equity. The material on research techniques and approaches has been updated and augmented and placed in new Chapters 9 and 10.
- *Chapter 14:* to provide clearer focus, global brand management guidelines are presented in terms of the 'Ten commandments of global branding.'
- *Chapter 15:* new summary comments and future branding priorities are included to provide contemporary perspectives.

Adopt a stronger technological and global perspective

High-tech and online brands and concepts are highlighted throughout the book. Specifically, Chapter 1 introduces both high-tech and online brands as key branding applications. Special attention is paid to URLs and naming websites in Chapter 4; web design and service issues in Chapter 5; and the internet as a communication tool and brand builder in Chapter 6. Finally, Chapter 15 has detailed sections on how to build high-tech and online brands. In terms of global perspectives, besides Chapter 14, a stronger global flavour is found in the text examples and the Brand Briefings.

Update Brand Briefings and academic references

Over half of the examples within the text and the many Brand Briefings have been replaced with more current material. The goal was to blend classic and contemporary examples, so some appropriate examples were retained from the first edition. The academic references throughout the book have also been brought up to date.

Streamline chapters

Lengthy passages and examples have been edited. Each chapter ends with an extended Brand Briefing that includes more detailed material or material that might otherwise disrupt the flow of the chapter. Examples include the history of branding in Chapter 1, brand audit guidelines in Chapter 2, own labels in Chapter 5, crisis marketing in Chapter 6 and corporate name changes in Chapter 13.

Update original cases and introduce new cases

To provide broader, more relevant coverage, the cases have been removed from the back of the book, updated and placed in a separate casebook. Seven new cases that cover even more branding topics have also been included in the casebook: Starbucks, DuPont, Snapple, Accenture, Red Bull, MTV and Yahoo!

Provide better presentation of text material and stronger supplementary support

The text includes more diagrams and figures that help to summarize key conceptual material. All critical figures are reprinted in the instructor's manual. The instructor's manual has been expanded to provide more help for classroom instruction and provide guidance for experiential learning.

HOW CAN A READER GET THE MOST OUT OF THIS BOOK?

Branding is a fascinating topic that has received much attention in the popular press. The ideas presented in the book will help readers interpret current branding developments. One good way to better understand branding and the customer-based brand equity framework is to apply the concepts and ideas that are presented in the book to current events or any of the more detailed branding issues or case studies presented in the Brand Briefings. The Discussion questions at the ends of the chapters often ask readers to pick a brand and apply one or more concepts from that chapter. Focusing on one brand across all of the questions – perhaps as part of a class project – permits some cumulative and integrated learning and is an excellent way to become more comfortable and familiar with the material in the book.

Although it is a trite saying, this book truly belongs to the reader. As with most marketing, branding does not involve 'right' or 'wrong' answers and readers should question things they do not understand or do not believe. This book is designed to facilitate your understanding of what is involved with strategic brand management and present some 'best practice' guidelines. At the end of the day, however, what you get out of the book will be what you put into understanding it and how you blend the ideas contained in these pages with what you already know or believe.

ADDITIONAL COMMENTS ON THE EUROPEAN EDITION

It was a great honour for us to take on the task of making a European version of Keller's *Strategic Brand Management*. Like so many others, we had known, loved the book and used it in our research and teaching many years before we met Kevin, which we did later when we together met his publishers to discuss an adaptation of the third edition.

Having worked internationally with brands of different countries of origin across various markets, we were aware that the so-called brandscape surrounding us, despite globalization, still varies between regions and countries. Depending on where you grow up, be it Ireland, Dubai, Hong Kong, Texas or Addis Ababa, you will have encountered different brands with different established images in those markets, and the brands you know and how you understand them can be much more of a local kind of knowledge than we sometimes think.

The signals from practitioners, students and their professors in Europe were that they loved the book, but that many of the examples centred on the USA's brands, markets and consumer typologies and that some of them did not recognize the brands or the market situations surrounding them. This was the starting point for making this edition of the book.

So in these pages, we have done our best to make Keller's great book more accessible to an international audience, especially Europe. To this end, we have included examples and cases from well-known European brands. We have also included a few more international Asian brands as well. However, certain American examples and cases are very well known internationally and some of them also include data unavailable for other brands and markets, so some of the best American examples remain in this edition. Still we think we have arrived at a good representation of the top international brands, of which the majority should be at least somewhat familiar to the reader.

Our ambition with the Brand Briefings has been to find well-known examples from all industries and use them to illustrate the theoretical points being made. We have, as much as possible, tried to include some depth to these cases as well, trying to capture the decisions, tradeoffs or even mistakes that have been made in the brand management process. We hope you will find them interesting and enlightening.

Beyond the brands and their strategies, fortunes and tragedies that make theory come alive, we have also done our best to make the text reflect a more international perspective, where that is possible. Overall we hope we have contributed to making Keller's book feel more relevant to a geographically wider audience. We hope you will enjoy this as much as we have, whether you are a practitioner, academic or a student aspiring to be a future star of brand management.

Tony Apéria and Mats Georgson
Stockholm March 2008

About the authors

Kevin Lane Keller is the E. B. Osborn Professor of Marketing at the Tuck School of Business at Dartmouth College. Professor Keller has degrees from Cornell, Carnegie-Mellon, and Duke universities. At Dartmouth, he teaches MBA courses on marketing management and strategic brand management and lectures in executive programmes on that topic.

Previously, Professor Keller was on the faculty of the Graduate School of Business at Stanford University, where he also served as the head of the marketing group. Additionally, he has been on the marketing faculty at the University of California at Berkeley and the University of North Carolina at Chapel Hill, been a visiting professor at Duke University and the Australian Graduate School of Management, and has two years of industry experience as Marketing Consultant for Bank of America.

Professor Keller's general area of expertise lies in marketing strategy and planning. His specific research interest is in how understanding theories and concepts related to consumer behaviour can improve marketing strategies. His research has been published in three of the major marketing journals – the *Journal of Marketing*, the *Journal of Marketing Research,* and the *Journal of Consumer Research*. He also has served on the Editorial Review Boards of those journals. With over sixty published papers, his research has been widely cited and has received numerous awards.

Professor Keller is acknowledged as one of the international leaders in the study of brands, branding, and strategic brand management. Actively involved with industry, he has worked on a host of different types of marketing projects. He has served as a consultant and advisor to marketers for some of the world's most successful brands, including Accenture, American Express, Disney, Ford, Intel, Levi Strauss & Co., Procter & Gamble, and SAB Miller. Additional brand consulting activities have been with other top companies such as Allstate, Beiersdorf (Nivea), BlueCross BlueShield, Campbell's, Eli Lilly, ExxonMobil, General Mills, Goodyear, Kodak, Mayo Clinic, Nordstrom, Shell Oil, Starbucks, Unilever, and Young & Rubicam. He has also served as an academic trustee for the Marketing Science Institute. A popular speaker, he has conducted marketing seminars to top executives in a variety of forums.

Professor Keller is currently conducting a variety of studies that address strategies to build, measure, and manage brand equity. In addition to *Strategic Brand Management*, as of the twelfth edition, he is also the co-author with Philip Kotler of the all-time best selling introductory marketing textbook, *Marketing Management*.

An avid sports, music, and film enthusiast, in his so-called spare time, he has served as executive producer for one of Australia's great rock and roll treasures, The Church, as well as American power-pop legends Dwight Twilley and Tommy Keene. He is also on the Board of Directors for The Doug Flutie, Jr. Foundation for Autism. Professor Keller lives in Etna, New Hampshire, with his wife, Punam (also a Tuck marketing professor), and his two daughters, Carolyn and Allison.

Dr Tony Apéria received his PhD from Stockholm University School of Business in 2001 with a thesis focusing on brand management. In 2007 he became a Visiting Professor at Jönköping International Business School Jönköping University in Sweden. Dr Apéria has a background in industry and he has more than 20 years' experience from the marketing and branding field.

In 2003 he founded Nordic Brand Academy, one of the most active academic branding networks in the world. The mission of Nordic Brand Academy is research-based branding. The company, that is partly owned by Stockholm University, acts as a bridge between academics and the world of business. The company operates within three areas: Competence, Insights and Consulting.

Since the beginning, more than 50 respected academics and practitioners have been invited to Stockholm to share their knowledge with the Nordic Brand Academy members. Today, eight of Sweden's largest companies are sponsoring the academy: *Apoteket, Cloetta Fazer, Nordea, Posten, SEB, Svenska Spel, Swedbank and Vattenfall.*

Dr Apéria is actively involved with the industry and has worked with leading brands in Europe and Asia. In 2003 Dr Apéria became the Swedish representative of Reputation Institute a global network focusing on Reputation Management. Every year Nordic Brand Academy measures the reputation of the largest and most visible companies in Sweden.

In 2006 Dr Apéria co-founded Brandjobs. This projective model is designed to explore the emotional side of brands and needs. Brandjobs has become a respected model and today Brandjobs works together with leading companies in Sweden, Northern Europe and Asia.

Dr Apéria has been the author of several books on branding and he teaches at leading Universities in Scandinavia as well as in mainland China and Hong Kong.

He lives in central Stockholm with his wife Lena and his two children, Jakob and Sara. If you want to know more about Nordic Brand Academy or get in contact with the author please visit our website www.nordicbrandacademy.com or tony.aperia@ nordicbrandacademy.com.

Mats Georgson is a consultant, lecturer and Associate Professor within strategy, marketing communication and brand management. He has a Ph.D. from the University of Connecticut and works part time at the University of Stockholm. He has 20 years experience within his fields in the roles as buyer, consultant and educator.

His experiences range from strategy development to implementation in the fields of corporate culture, communication, products, services and design. Mats worked for many years at Ericsson, most recently as the Global Brand Director for Sony Ericsson. He has also worked at several different consultant and advertising agencies in Sweden and USA.

Mats runs the business strategy and brand management consultancy firm *Georgson* out of Stockholm, Sweden. Georgson is a management consultancy firm specialized in business strategy and brand management offering the combination of practical experience from business and consultancy teamed with a sound academic perspective based on extensive knowledge of relevant scientific research. Focus is not only to formulate strategies, but also to make sure they are put into practice and action with measurable results. The clients of the firm vary in size and business type – from small, upcoming entrepreneurs to large multinational corporations. Read more about Mats and Georgson at www.georgson.org.

Authors' acknowledgements

This book has been inspiring to write and I have enjoyed every minute of it from start to finish. Branding is and has always been a journey for me. Over the years I have received a lot of inspiration from Evert Gummesson and Rolf Back. They were part of my thesis committee.

I would like to acknowledge my colleagues, partners and the members at Nordic Brand Academy. Robert Gelmanovski manages the academy together with Karolina Lindberg, Gabriel Montgomery and myself. We all share a strong belief that a Brand is a Promise that has to be Delivered. I would also like to mention Regina Summer who is the Nordic Brand Academy owner representative at Stockholm University.

I would particularly like to mention Tim Ambler, John Balmer, Leslie De Chernatony, Charles Fombrun, Christian Grönroos, Paul Heylen, Jean-Nöel Kapferer, Kevin L Keller, Simon Knox, Larry Percy and Cees van Riel. All of these famous academics have inspired my thinking on branding.

I am also most grateful to all our former and present member companies at Nordic Brand Academy: Apoteket, Bredbandsbolaget, Cloetta Fazer, The Coca-Cola Company, Folksam, Nordea, Pfizer, Posten, SBAB, SEB, Stockholm University, Svenska Spel, Swedbank, Vattenfall, and V&S Group (Absolut).

In addition I would like to give my sincere thanks to Johan Östlund, Senior Planner, DDB London; Lars Friberg, Planner, DDB Stockholm; Niklas Olovson, Sport and Brands; Christian Sandberg, CS Brand Management; Ulf Smedberg, IKEA; Mats Rönne, Electrolux and Stefan Nerpin, Vattenfall; and my Brandjobs colleagues, Fredrik Berggren and Robert Nises.

Tony Apéria

Lots of people have been directly or indirectly involved with this book. First I would like to thank my co-workers at Georgson Strategy: Erika Åhmansson, Malin Anhede, Desirée Brathwaite, Karin Målefors.

Second, thanks to our clients with whom we share all the theoretical and practical challenges of brand management outlined in this book every day.

Third, I would like to thank all my students and co-workers at Stockholm University, as well as my colleagues and inspirators at other universities and companies all over the world.

Fourth, the team at Pearson for being supportive, structured and constructive throughout our two-year grind in this project.

Fifth, I would like to thank my loving and understanding wife Helena for, well, everything. And last but not least, I would like to thank God, psychology and capitalism for making brand management the vast and rich field it is.

Mats Georgson

Publisher's acknowledgements

We are grateful to the following for permission to reproduce copyright material:

Figure 1.6 as summarized in Branding can't exist without positioning in *Advertising Age*, March 14, Crain Communications Inc. (Trout, J. 2005); Figure 1.7 from *Next Generation*, June 20, Forbes (Badenhausen, K. and Roney, M. 2005) reprinted by permission of Forbes Magazine © 2008 Forbes Media LLC; Figure 1.10 from First to market, first to fail? Real causes of enduring market leadership in *MIT Sloan Management Review* Winter, Massachusetts Institute of Technology (Tellis, G. J. and Golder, P. N. 1996); Figure 2.4 from *GfK Roper Reports U.S., 2004*, GfK Roper Consulting (GfK Roper Consulting, 2004); Figure 3.4 from Nokia, Mercator Partners analysis; Figure 4.9 from Measuring the value of corporate and brand logos in *Design Management* Review, Vol. 4, No. 1, Winter, Design Management Institute (Schechter, Alvin H. 1993) courtesy of the *Design Management Review* (Vol. 4, No. 1, Winter 1993) a publication of the Design Management Institute (www.dmi.org). Individual copies of this and other DMI *Review* articles are available for purchase at www.dmi.org/publications. Figure 5.2 adapted with the permission of The Free Press, a Division of Simon & Schuster Adult Publishing Group, from EXPERIMENTAL MARKETING: How to Get Customers to Sense, Feel, Act, and Relate to Your Company and Brands by Bernd H. Schmidt. Copyright © 1999 by Bernd H. Schmidt. All rights reserved. Figure 5.3 adapted with the permission of Simon & Schuster Adult Publishing Group, from PERMISSION MARKETING: Turning Strangers into Friends and Friends into Customers by Seth Godin. Copyright © 1999 by Seth Godin. All rights reserved. Figure 5.4 from *Aftermarketing: How to Keep Customers for Life through Relationship Marketing*, Irwin Professional Publishers, Chicago (Vavra, T. 1995); Figure 5.7 from *Product Management*, Irwin, Burr Ridge, IL (Lehmann, D. and Winer, R. 1994) © The McGraw-Hill Companies Inc; Figure 6.5 and Figure 9.1 from *Introduction to Advertising and Promotion, 3rd ed.*, Irwin, Homewood, IL (Belch, G.E. and Belch, M.A. 1995) © The McGraw-Hill Companies Inc.; Figure 7.10 from Reputation Institute, 2007; Figure 7.6 from Newspix/Rex Features; New Zealand Figure from Rex Features; Figure 7.19 from Marketing Evaluations, Inc., Winter 2004 Performer Q Study with permission of the Q Scores Company; Figure 7.20 from Eddie Mejia/Rex Features; Figure 8.1 from Reputation Institute; Figure 8.4 from Humanistic advertising: A holistic cultural perspective in *International Journal of Advertising* 2, The Advertising Association (Lannon, J. and Cooper, P. 1983), The Advertising Association copyright through World Advertising Research Center, Farm Road, Henley-on-Thames, Oxfordshire, RG9 1EJ; Figure 9.3 from Magne J. Supphellen, Understanding core brand equity: Guidelines for in-depth elicitation of brand associations in

International Journal of Market Research 42, no. 3, The Market Research Society (Supphellen, M.J. 2001); Figure 9.16 from Sipa Press/Rex Features; Figure 11.4 from Rex Features; Figure 11.9 from Managing brand portfolios: How the leaders do it in *Journal of Advertising Research* September/October, The Advertising Research Foundation (LaForet, S. and Saunders, J 1994); Figure 12.14 from Rex Features; Figure 12.24 from *The New Strategic Brand Management: Creating and Sustaining Brand Equity Long Term*, Kogan Page, London (Kapferer, J.-N. 2005); Figure 14.7 from Magnus Torle/Rex Features; Figure 14.13 Reprinted by permission of *Harvard Business Review*. From 'Seven rules of international distribution' by David Arnold, November-December 2000. Copyright © 2000 by the Harvard Business School Publishing Corporation, all rights reserved. Figure 15.3 from Ten lessons for improving service quality in *MSI Report 93–104*, Marketing Science Institute (Berry, L.L., Parasuraman, A, and Zeithaml, V.A. 1993); Figure 4.1 (1) from Kelloggs; Figure 4.1 (2) from McDonald's Restaurants Limited; Figure 4.1 (3) reproduced by kind permission of Michelin; Figure 4.1 (4) image courtesy of Diageo Brands B.V.; Figure 4.1 (5) © Société BIC; Figure 4.1 (6) from WWF – World Wide Fund for Nature; Figure 4.1 (8) from American Express; Figure 4.1 (9) the "Nestlé" name and image is reproduced with the kind permission of Société des Produits Nestlé S.A.; Figure 4.10 supplied courtesy of Intel; Figure 6.2 from Agent Provocateur; Figures 7.7 and 7.8 from Wrigley; Figure 7.9 from www.flickr.com/groups/altoids/pool/courtesy of The Shrike; Figures 7.13, 7.14 and 7.15 from Cycleurope UK Ltd; Figure 9.2 from IKEA Ltd; Figure 12.2 from McDonald's Restaurants Limited; Figure 12.7 courtesy of ICA Banken.

Brand Briefing 1.1 from For new Coke, 'What price success?' in *Advertising Age*, 20 March S1-S2, Crain Communications Inc., New York (Winters, P. 1989); Brand Briefing 1.3 from A roadmap for branding in industrial markets in *Journal of Brand Management* 11 (May) Palgrave Macmillan Ltd (Lane Keller, K. and Webster, F.E. Jr. 2004) reproduced with permission of Palgrave Macmillan; Brand Briefing 1.4 from Branding in high-technology markets in *Market Leader* 22 (Autumn), WARC (Tickle, P., Lane Keller, K. and Richey, K. 2003) © WARC Ltd., www.warc.com; Brand Briefing 5.5 Reprinted by permission of Harvard Business Review. From 'How do you know when the price is right?' by Robert J. Dolan, September-October 1995. Copyright © 1995 by the Harvard Business School Publishing Corporation, all rights reserved. Brand Briefing 8.4 from Scott Davis, Building a Brand-Driven Organization in *Kellogg on Branding*, John Wiley & Sons, Hoboken (Tybout, A.M. and Calkins, T. (eds.) 2005) Copyright © 2005 John Wiley & Sons, Inc. Reprinted with permission of John Wiley & Sons, Inc.; Brand Briefing 9.8 from *Strategic Brand Management*, Kogan Page, London (Kapferer, J.-N. 1992); Brand Briefing 11.4 from Achieving the ideal brand portfolio in *MIT Sloan Management Review* Winter, Massachusetts Institute of Technology (Hill, S., Ettenson, R. and Tyson, D. 2005); Brand Briefing 12.12 from Strategies for leveraging master brands in *Marketing Research*, September 1992: 32–43, American Marketing Association, Chicago (Farquhar, P.H. *et al.* 1992); Brand Briefing 15.12 adapted with the permission of The Free Press, a Division of Simon & Schuster Adult Publishing Group, from BUILDING STRONG BRANDS by David A. Aaker. Copyright © 1995 by David A. Aaker. All rights reserved. Brand Briefing 15.13 from A NEW BRAND WORLD by Scott Bedbury, copyright © 2001 by Scott Bedbury. Used by permission of Viking Penguin, a division of Penguin Group (USA) Inc.

In some instances we have been unable to trace the owners of copyright material, and we would appreciate any information that would enable us to do so.

1 Brands and brand management

PREVIEW

More and more companies and other organizations have come to realize that one of their most valuable assets is the brand names associated with their products or services. In an increasingly complex world, individuals and businesses are faced with more and more choices, but seemingly have less and less time to make those choices. The ability of a strong brand to simplify consumer decision-making, reduce risk and set expectations is thus invaluable. Creating strong brands that deliver on that promise, and maintaining and enhancing the strength of those brands over time, has become a management imperative.

The purpose of this text is to assist those who seek a deeper understanding of how to achieve those branding goals. This advanced text addresses the important branding decisions faced by individuals and organizations in their marketing. Its objectives are:

1. to increase understanding of the important issues in planning, implementing and evaluating brand strategies;
2. to provide appropriate concepts, theories, models and other tools to help make better branding decisions.

Emphasis is placed on understanding psychological principles at the individual or organizational level so as to improve managerial decision-making with respect to brands. This book aims to be relevant to any type of organization regardless of size, nature of activity or profit orientation.

With these goals in mind, this first chapter defines what a brand is. It considers the functions of a brand from the perspective of both consumers and firms and why brands are important to both. It considers what can and cannot be branded and identifies some strong brands. The chapter concludes with an introduction to the concept of brand equity and the strategic brand management process.

WHAT IS A BRAND?

Branding has been around for centuries as a way to distinguish the goods of one producer from those of another. In fact, the word *brand* is derived from the Old Norse word *brandr*, which means 'to burn', as brands were, and still are, the means by which owners of livestock mark their animals to identify them.[1]

According to the American Marketing Association (AMA), a brand is a 'name, term, sign, symbol, or design, or a combination of them, intended to identify the goods and services of one seller or group of sellers and to differentiate them from those of competition'. Technically speaking, then, whenever a marketer creates a name, logo or symbol for a new product, he or she has created a brand.

It should be recognized that many managers, however, refer to a brand as more than that – defining a brand in terms of having created awareness, reputation, prominence and so on in the marketplace.

The key to creating a brand, according to the AMA definition, is to be able to choose a name, logo, symbol, packaging design, etc., that identifies a product and distinguishes it from others. These components that identify and differentiate a brand can be called *brand elements*. As Chapter 4 shows, brand elements come in many forms.

For example, consider the variety of brand name strategies that exist. In some cases, the company name is used for all products (as with Nokia, Ericsson and Samsung). In other cases, manufacturers assign individual brand names that are unrelated to the company name to new products (as with Procter & Gamble and the Ariel, Pampers, Pringles and Pantene products). Retailers create their own brands based on their shop name or some other means (eg, Tesco has its own Healthy Eating, Organic, Kids and Finest brands).

The names given to products come in many forms.[2] There are brand names based on people (eg, Estée Lauder cosmetics, Porsche cars, Lacoste clothes and Björn Borg underwear); places (eg, Amazon, Cisco (short for San Francisco), Fuji (Japan's highest mountain) and Nokia (a town in Finland); animals or birds (eg, Mustang cars, Reebok (an antelope), Dove soap and Greyhound buses); or other things or objects (eg, Apple computers, Shell petrol and Samsung (means 'three stars' in Korean)).

There are brand names that use words with inherent product meanings (eg, Lean Cuisine and JustJuice) or that suggest important attributes or benefits (eg, Duracell batteries and Wash & Go shampoo). There are brand names that are made up and include prefixes and suffixes that sound scientific, natural or prestigious (eg, Intel microprocessors, Lexus cars and Compaq computers).

Similarly, other brand elements, such as brand logos and symbols, may be based on people, places and things, abstract images and so on in different ways. In sum, in creating a brand, marketers have many choices over the number and nature of the brand elements they choose to identify their products.

Brands versus products

It is important to contrast a brand with a product. A *product* is anything that can be offered to a market for attention, acquisition, use or consumption that might satisfy a need or want. Thus, a product may be a physical item (eg, a cereal, tennis racquet or car), service (eg, an airline, bank or insurance company), a shop (eg, a department store, a specialist shop, or supermarket), person (eg, a political figure, entertainer or professional athlete), organization (eg, a charity, trade organization or arts group), place (eg, a city, state or country) or idea (eg, a political or social cause). This book adopts this broad definition of product. It discusses the role of brands in some of these categories in this chapter and in Chapter 15.

Five levels can be defined for a product.[3]

1. The *core benefit level* is the fundamental need or want that consumers satisfy by consuming the product or service.
2. The *generic product level* is a basic version of the product containing only those attributes or characteristics absolutely necessary for its functioning but with no distinguishing features. This is basically a stripped-down, no-frills version of a product that adequately performs the product function.
3. The *expected product level* is a set of attributes or characteristics that buyers normally expect and agree to when they purchase a product.
4. The *augmented product level* includes additional attributes, benefits or related services that distinguish the product from competitors.
5. The *potential product level* includes all of the augmentations and transformations that a product could ultimately undergo.

Figure 1.1 illustrates these levels in the context of air-conditioners and portable MP3 players. Competition within many markets takes place mainly at the product augmentation level because most firms can build satisfactory products at the expected product level. The academic Ted Levitt has argued (1960): 'The new competition is not between what companies produce in their factories but between what they add to their factory output in the form of packaging, services, advertising, customer advice, financing, delivery arrangements, warehousing and other things that people value.'[4]

A brand is therefore a product but one that *adds other dimensions that differentiate it in some way from other products designed to satisfy the same need*. These differences may be rational and tangible – related to product performance of the brand – or more symbolic, emotional and intangible – related to what the brand represents. One marketing observer put it this way:

> More specifically, what distinguishes a brand from its unbranded commodity counterpart and gives it equity is the sum total of consumers' perceptions and feelings about the product's attributes and how they perform, about the brand name and what it stands for and about the company associated with the brand.[5]

So, a branded product may be a physical item (eg, Kellogg's Corn Flakes cereal, Prince tennis racquets or BMW cars), a service (eg, Ryanair, ABN Amro Bank or Allianz insurance), a shop (eg, Harrod's department store, The Body Shop specialist shop or Carrefour supermarket), a person (eg, Richard Branson, Julia Roberts or David Beckham), a place (eg, the city of Rome, region of Provence or country of Australia), an organization (eg, the Red Cross, the Automobile Association or The Rolling Stones) or an idea (eg, corporate responsibility, free trade or freedom of speech).

Some brands create competitive advantages with product performance. For example, brands such as Gillette, TetraPak and others have been leaders in their product categories for decades, due, in part, to continual innovation (see Figure 1.2 for a list

Level	Air-conditioner
1. Core benefit	Cooling and comfort.
2. Generic product	Sufficient cooling capacity (Btu per hour), an acceptable energy efficiency rating, adequate air intakes and exhausts and so on.
3. Expected product	*Consumer Reports* magazine (July 2005) states that, for a typical large air-conditioner, buyers should expect: at least two cooling speeds; expandable plastic side panels; adjustable vents; removable air filter; vent for exhausting air; power cord at least 60 inches long; R-22 HCFC refrigerant (less harmful to the Earth's ozone layer than other types); one-year parts-and-labour warranty on the entire unit; and a five-year parts-and-labour warranty on the refrigeration system.[a]
4. Augmented product	Optional features might include: touch-pad controls; a display to show indoor and outdoor temperatures and the thermostat setting; an automatic mode to adjust fan speed based on the thermostat setting and room temperature; a free phone number for customer service.
5. Potential product	Silently running, completely balanced throughout the room and energy self-sufficient.

Level	Portable MP3 player
1. Core benefit	Musical entertainment on the move.
2. Generic product	Ability to play music downloaded from the web or 'ripped' from CD collections.
3. Expected product	*Consumer Reports* states that, for a typical portable MP3 player, consumers should expect a solid-state device with no moving parts (which eliminates skipping) and 64 to 128 megabytes of memory. Most standard-capacity players have expansion slots to add more memory and software to inter-face with a computer.[b]
4. Augmented product	Optional features might include a colour LCD screen, audio equalizer and the ability to store files other than digital-audio files, including text, image and video files.
5. Potential product	Voice-controlled programming; extended 'infinite life' batteries.

[a]*Consumer Reports*, July 2005.
[b]*Consumer Reports*, Annual Buying Guide, 2004.

Figure 1.1   Examples of product levels

1. Apple	11. Virgin
2. 3M	12. Samsung
3. Microsoft	13. Wal-Mart
4. GE	14. Toyota
5. Sony	15. eBay
6. Dell	16. Intel
7. IBM	17. Amazon
8. Google	18. Ideo
9. Procter & Gamble	19. Starbucks
10. Nokia	20. BMW

Based on poll of 940 senior executives in 68 countries by Boston Consulting Group

Figure 1.2   Twenty innovative companies[6]

Source: Bruce Nussbaum, 'Get creative', *BusinessWeek*, 1 August 2005: 61–8.

of innovative companies). Steady investments in research and development have produced leading-edge products, and sophisticated mass marketing practices have ensured rapid adoption of new technologies by consumers.

Other brands create competitive advantages through non-product-related means. For example, Coca-Cola, Chanel No 5 and others have been leaders in their product categories for decades by understanding consumers' motivations and desires and creating relevant and appealing images surrounding their products. Often, these intangible image associations may be the only way to distinguish different brands in a product category.

Brands, especially strong ones, have a number of types of associations, and marketers must account for all of them in making marketing decisions. The marketers behind some brands have learned this lesson the hard way. Brand Briefing 1.1 describes the problems the Coca-Cola Company encountered in the introduction of New Coke when it failed to account for all of the aspects of the Coca-Cola brand image. Not only are there many different types of associations to link to the brand, there are many different means of creating them – the entire marketing campaign can contribute to consumers' understanding of the brand and how they value it.

Brand Briefing 1.1

Coca-Cola's branding lesson

One of the classic marketing mistakes occurred in April 1985 when the Coca-Cola Company replaced its flagship cola brand with a new formula. The motivation behind the change was primarily a competitive one. Pepsi-Cola's 'Pepsi Challenge' promotion had posed a strong challenge to Coke's supremacy over the cola market. Starting just in Texas, the promotion involved advertising and in-store sampling with consumer blind taste tests between Coca-Cola and Pepsi-Cola. Invariably, Pepsi won these tests. Fearful that the promotion, if taken nationally, could take a big bite out of Coke's sales, especially among younger drinkers, Coca-Cola felt compelled to act.

Coca-Cola's strategy was to change the formulation of Coke to match more closely the slightly sweeter taste of Pepsi. To arrive at a new formulation, Coke conducted taste tests with 190,000 consumers! The findings from this research clearly indicated that consumers 'overwhelmingly' preferred the taste of the new formulation to the old one. Brimming with confidence, Coca-Cola announced the formulation change with much fanfare. Consumer reaction was swift but, unfortunately for Coca-Cola, negative. In Seattle, retired property investor Gay Mullins founded the 'Old Cola Drinkers of America' and set up a hotline for angry consumers. A Beverly Hills wine merchant bought 500 cases of 'Vintage Coke' and sold them at a premium. Meanwhile, back at Coca-Cola headquarters, roughly 1,500 calls a day and literally truck-loads of letters poured in condemning the

Brand Briefing 1.1 *continued*

company's actions. Finally, after months of slumping sales, Coca-Cola announced that the old formulation would return as 'Coca-Cola Classic' and join 'New Coke in the marketplace.

The New Coke debacle taught Coca-Cola a very important, albeit painful and public, lesson about its brand. Coke clearly is not just seen as a drink by consumers. Rather, it seems to be viewed as more of an American icon, and much of its appeal lies not only in its ingredients but also in what it represents in terms of Americana, nostalgia and its heritage and relationship with consumers. Coke's brand image certainly has emotional components and consumers have a great deal of strong feelings for the brand. Although Coca-Cola made other mistakes in introducing New Coke (eg, both its advertising and packaging probably failed to differentiate clearly the brand and communicate its sweeter quality), its biggest slip-up was losing sight of what the brand meant to consumers in its totality. The *psychological* response to a brand can be as important as the *physiological* response to the product. At the same time, the US consumer also learned a lesson – just how much Coke really meant to them. As a result of Coke's marketing fiasco, it is doubtful that either side will take the other for granted from now on.

Source: Patricia Winters, 'For New Coke, "what price success?"', *Advertising Age*, 20 March 1989: S1–S2. Reprinted with permission from the March 20, 1989 issue of Advertising Age. Copyright, Crain Communications Inc. 1989.

By creating perceived differences between products through branding and developing a loyal consumer franchise, marketers create value that can translate into financial profits for a firm. The reality is that the most valuable assets that many companies have may not be tangible assets, such as plant, equipment and buildings, but *intangible* assets, such as management skills, marketing, financial and operations expertise, and, most important, the brands themselves. Thus, a brand is a valued intangible asset that needs to be handled carefully. The next section examines some of the reasons why brands are valuable.

WHY DO BRANDS MATTER?

An obvious question is, why are brands important? What functions do they perform that make them so valuable to marketers? We can look at these questions from a couple of perspectives to uncover the value of brands to both customers and their owners. Figure 1.3 provides an overview of the different roles that brands play for these two parties.

Consumers
- Identification of source of product.
- Assignment of responsibility to product maker.
- Risk reducer.
- Search cost reducer.
- Promise, bond or pact with maker of product.
- Symbolic device.
- Signal of quality.

Manufacturers
- Means of identification to simplify handling or tracing.
- Means of legally protecting unique features.
- Signal of quality level to satisfied customers.
- Means of endowing products with unique associations.
- Source of competitive advantage.
- Source of financial returns.

Figure 1.3 Roles that brands play

Consumers

As with the term product, this book uses the term *consumer* broadly to encompass all types of customers, including individuals and organizations. To consumers, brands provide important functions. Brands identify the source or maker of a product and allow consumers to assign responsibility to a particular manufacturer or distributor. Most important, a brand takes on a special meaning to consumers. Because of past experiences with the product and its marketing over the years, consumers learn about brands. They find out which brands satisfy their needs and which ones do not. As a result, brands provide a shorthand device or means of simplification for their product decisions.[7]

If consumers recognize a brand and have some knowledge about it, then they do not have to engage in a lot of additional thought or processing of information to make a product decision. Thus, from an economic perspective, brands allow consumers to lower search costs for products both internally (in terms of how much they have to think) and externally (in terms of how much they have to look around). Based on what they know about the brand – its quality, product characteristics and so forth – consumers can make assumptions and form reasonable expectations about what they may *not* know about the brand.

The meaning imbued in brands can be profound. The relationship between a brand and the consumer can be seen as a 'bond' or pact. Consumers offer their trust and loyalty with the implicit understanding that the brand will behave in certain ways and provide them utility through consistent product performance and appropriate pricing, promotion and distribution and actions. To the extent that consumers realize advantages and benefits from purchasing the brand, and as long as they derive satisfaction from product consumption, they are likely to continue to buy it.

These benefits may not be purely functional in nature. Brands can serve as symbolic devices, allowing consumers to project their self-image. Certain brands are associated with being used by certain types of people and thus reflect different values or traits. Consuming such products is a means by which consumers can communicate to others – or even to themselves – the type of person they are or would like to be.

Author Daniel Boorstein asserts that, for many people, brands serve the function that fraternal, religious and service organizations used to serve – to help people define who they are and then help people communicate that definition to others. As Susan Fournier notes:

> Relationships with mass [market] brands can soothe the 'empty selves' left behind by society's abandonment of tradition and community and provide stable anchors in an otherwise changing world. The formation and maintenance of brand–product relationships serve many culturally-supported roles within postmodern society.[8]

Brands can also play a significant role in signalling certain product characteristics to consumers. Researchers have classified products and their associated attributes or benefits into three categories: search goods, experience goods and credence goods.[9] With *search goods*, product attributes can be evaluated by visual inspection (eg, the sturdiness, size, colour, style, weight and ingredient composition of a product). With *experience goods*, product attributes – potentially equally important – cannot be assessed so easily by inspection and actual product trial and experience is necessary (eg, as with durability, service quality, safety, ease of handling or use). With *credence goods*, product attributes may be rarely learned (eg, insurance coverage). Because of the difficulty in assessing and interpreting product attributes and benefits with experience and credence goods, brands may be important signals of quality and other characteristics to consumers for these types of products.[10]

Brands can reduce the risks in product decisions.[11] Consumers may perceive many different types of risks in buying and consuming a product.

- *Functional risk:* the product does not perform up to expectations.
- *Physical risk:* the product poses a threat to the physical well-being or health of the user or others.
- *Financial risk:* the product is not worth the price paid.
- *Social risk:* the product results in embarrassment.
- *Psychological risk:* the product affects the mental well-being of the user.
- *Time risk:* the failure of the product results in an opportunity cost of finding another satisfactory product.

Among the many ways in which consumers handle these risks is that of buying well-known brands, especially those with which consumers have had favourable past experiences. This is especially true in business-to-business settings where such risks can have profound implications.

In summary, to consumers, the special meaning that brands take on can change their perceptions and experiences of a product. The identical product may be evaluated differently by an individual or organization depending on the brand identification or attribution it is given. Brands take on unique, personal meanings for consumers that facilitate their day-to-day activities and enrich their lives. As consumers' lives become more complicated, rushed and time-starved, the ability of a brand to simplify decisions and reduce risk is invaluable.

Companies

Brands also provide a number of valuable functions for firms.[12] Fundamentally, they serve an identification purpose to simplify product handling or tracing. Operationally, brands help to organize inventory and accounting records. A brand also offers the firm legal protection for unique features or aspects of the product. A brand can retain intellectual property rights, giving legal title to the brand owner.[13] The brand name can be protected through registered trademarks; manufacturing processes can be protected through patents; and packaging can be protected through copyrights and designs. These intellectual property rights ensure that the firm can safely invest in the brand and reap the benefits of a valuable asset.

As noted earlier, these investments in the brand can endow a product with unique associations and meanings that differentiate it from other products. Brands can signal a certain level of quality so that satisfied buyers can easily choose the product again.[14] This brand loyalty provides predictability and security of demand for the maker and creates barriers that make it difficult for other firms to enter the market.

Although manufacturing processes and product designs can be duplicated, lasting impressions in the minds of individuals and organizations from years of marketing activity and product experience may not be so easily reproduced. In this sense, branding can be seen as a powerful means of securing a competitive advantage.

In short, to their owners, brands represent enormously valuable pieces of legal property, capable of influencing consumer behaviour, being bought and sold and providing the security of sustained future revenues.[15] For these reasons, large sums have been paid for brands in mergers or acquisitions, starting with the boom years of the mid-1980s. The merger and acquisition frenzy during this time resulted in financiers seeking out undervalued companies from which investment or takeover profits could be made. One of the primary undervalued assets of these firms was their brands, given that they were off-balance sheet items. Implicit in this interest was a belief that strong brands resulted in better earnings and profit performance for firms, which, in turn, created greater value for shareholders.

In many instances, the price premiums paid for companies was often clearly justified on the basis of assumptions of the extra profits that could be extracted and sustained from their brands, as well as the tremendous difficulty and expense of creating similar brands. Much of the recent interest in brands from senior management has been a result of these bottom-line financial considerations. For a typical fast-moving consumer goods (FMCG) company, most of its value is made up by intangible assets and goodwill – net tangible assets may be as little as 10 percent of the total value (see Figure 1.4). Moreover, as much as 70 percent of their intangible assets can be made up by brands.

CAN ANYTHING BE BRANDED?

Brands clearly provide important benefits to both consumers and firms. An obvious question then is, how are brands created? How do you 'brand' a product? Although firms provide the impetus to brand creation through marketing and other activities,

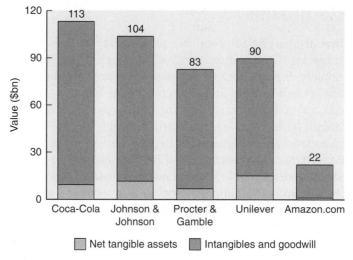

Figure 1.4 Brands on the balance sheet
Source: Interbrand.

ultimately a brand is *something that resides in the minds of consumers*. A brand is a perceptual entity that is rooted in reality but is more than that and reflects the perceptions and perhaps even the idiosyncrasies of consumers.

To brand a product it is necessary to teach consumers 'who' the product is – by giving it a name and using other brand elements to help identify it – as well as what the product does and why consumers should care. In other words, to brand a product or service, it is necessary to give consumers a *label* for the product (ie, 'here's how you can identify the product') and to provide *meaning* for the brand (ie, 'here's what this particular product can do for you and why it is special and different from other brand name products').

Branding involves creating mental structures and helping consumers organize their knowledge about products and services in a way that clarifies their decision-making and, in the process, provides value to the brand owner. The key to branding is that *consumers perceive differences between brands* in a product category. As noted above, brand differences often are related to attributes or benefits of the product itself. In other cases, however, brand differences may be related to more intangible considerations.

Whenever and wherever consumers are deciding between options, brands can play an important role. Accordingly, *marketers can benefit from branding whenever consumers are making a choice*. Given the myriad of choices consumers make each and every day, it is no surprise how pervasive branding has become.

For example, consider how marketers have been able to brand what were once commodities. A *commodity* is a product so basic that it cannot be differentiated in the minds of consumers. Over the years, products that at one time were seen as commodities have become highly differentiated as strong brands have emerged.[16] Some notable examples (with brand pioneers in parentheses) are: coffee (Maxwell House), bath soap (Lux), beer (Heineken), ketchup (Heinz), porridge (Quaker), bananas (Chiquita), chickens (Perdue), pineapples (Dole), synthetic fabrics (DuPont), MP3-type players (Apple iPod), microprocessors (Intel) and even water (Perrier).

These commodity products have been branded. The success factor in each case, however, was that consumers became convinced that products in the category were not the same. In some instances, such as with groceries, marketers convinced consumers that a product was *not* a commodity and could vary appreciably in quality. In these cases, the brand was seen as assuring uniformly high quality in the product category, on which consumers could depend. A recent example of this approach is Intel, which has spent vast sums of money on its Intel Inside promotion to brand its computer chips as delivering the highest level of performance (eg, power) and safety (eg, upgradability) possible.

In other cases, because product differences were almost non-existent, brands have been created by image or other non-product-related considerations, as with Perrier bottled mineral water. One of the best examples of branding a commodity in this fashion has been diamonds (see Brand Briefing 1.2).

Brand Briefing 1.2

Diamond industry creates niches to increase sales

De Beers Group added the phrase 'A diamond is forever' as the tagline in its advertising campaign in 1948. The diamond supplier, which was founded in 1888 and sells about 60 percent of the world's rough diamonds, wanted to attach more emotion and symbolic meaning to the purchase of diamond jewellery. 'A diamond is forever' became one of the most recognized slogans in advertising and helped fuel an industry that was worth nearly €17.1 billion a year in the USA alone by 2004.

Nearly all women who get engaged receive an engagement ring. But that ring may be the only diamond ring they ever own. De Beers has faced the challenge of creating more demand for something that the company once urged customers to think of as a once-in-a-lifetime, 'forever' purchase.

In 2001, De Beers used the tagline 'for your past, present and future' to increase sales of three-stone diamond rings. The company promoted three-stone rings as meaningful anniversary gifts. The goal was to turn engagement ring buyers into repeat customers – and the three-stone ring could work just as well for a 3-year anniversary gift as a 25-year gift. Until then, sales of the three-stone pieces had been only modest but US sales of the rings rose 74 percent in 2002.

Next, De Beers wanted customers to start thinking about their right hand as well as their left. The company aimed to change the perception of diamond rings as limited to engagement rings and wedding bands. It spiced up the stagnant right-hand ring category with fashionable, affordable options.

Industry experts said De Beers wasn't only hoping to expand ring sales but also striving to create a market for the smaller diamonds that manufacturers have in abundance, as consumers favour increasingly bigger diamonds for engagement

The universality of branding can be recognized by looking at some different product applications. Products can be defined broadly to include physical items, services, shops, online businesses, people, organizations, places or ideas. For each of these types of products, basic considerations and illustrative examples are considered below. Some special cases are considered in Chapter 15.

Physical items

Physical items include many of the best-known and most highly regarded consumer products (eg, Coca-Cola, Mercedes-Benz, Nescafé and Sony). As more kinds of products are being sold, or at least promoted directly to consumers, the adoption of marketing practices and branding has spread.

Companies selling industrial products or durable goods to other companies are also recognizing the benefits of having strong brands. Brands have begun to emerge with certain types of physical items that heretofore did not support brands. The remainder of this section considers the role of branding with industrial products as well as technologically intensive or 'high-tech' products.

Business-to-business products

Firms are recognizing the value of having a strong corporate brand in their business dealings with other firms. Business-to-business branding involves creating a positive image and reputation for the company as a whole. Creating such goodwill with business customers is thought to lead to greater selling opportunities and more profitable relationships. A strong brand can provide valuable reassurance to business customers who may be putting their company's fate – and perhaps their own careers – on the line. A strong business-to-business brand can thus provide a strong competitive advantage.

Business-to-business brands are often corporate brands, so understanding branding from that perspective becomes critical. The complexity of business-to-business branding lies in the many people involved, both on the company side and in terms of the many market segment targets. Such complexity requires adjustments to marketing campaigns and marketing communications. One challenge for many business-to-business brands is how to decommoditize themselves to create product and service differences. Brand Briefing 1.3 describes some particularly important guidelines for business-to-business branding.

Brand Briefing 1.3

Understanding business-to-business branding

1. *The role and importance of branding should be tied directly to the industrial marketer's business/profit model and value-delivery strategy.* The starting point for the business model should be the firm's distinctive competence, its target market and customers, its position in the value chain and its strategy for delivering superior value to those chosen customers.

2. *Understand the role of the brand in the organizational buying process.* Use market research to identify the composition of the buying centre and the decision criteria used by the people with the main roles.

3. *Be sure the basic value proposition has relevance for all significant players in the decision-making unit and decision-making process.* There will be many people involved in any buying decision and they all must find the brand promise both relevant and responsive to their needs and concerns.

4. *Emphasize a corporate branding approach.* It is important to remember the importance of the buyer–seller relationship and the central role played by the buyer's corporate credibility and reliability.

5. *Build the corporate brand around intangibles.* Maximize expertise, trustworthiness, ease of doing business and likeability as a way to establish corporate credibility, reputation and distinctiveness.

6. *Avoid confusing corporate communication strategy and brand strategy and carefully manage the relationship to avoid conflict.* The focus of brand strategy should be on the brand as a strategic entity and what it means for the customer, not on the broader issues of corporate citizenship that may or may not be relevant for buyers.

7. *Apply segmentation analysis within and across industry-defined segments, based on differences in the composition and functioning of buying centres within those segments.* Brand positioning within those sub-segments must then be tailored to the unique needs of the individuals in those segments but, just as importantly, must build on and be consistent with the overall corporate brand positioning.

Brand Briefing 1.3 *continued*

8. ***Build brand communications around the interactive effects of media.*** Business-to-business budgets are usually smaller than in consumer marketing and 'mass' media are likely to be limited in terms of reach and availability, so specialized media such as trade shows, educational activities and professional journals may be most effective in reaching specific sub-segments of buyers within customer organizations.

9. ***Adopt a top-down and bottom-up brand management approach.*** *Top-down* brand management involves marketing activities that capture the 'big picture' and recognize the possible synergies between products and markets to brand products accordingly. *Bottom-up* brand management, however, requires that marketing managers primarily direct their marketing activities to maximize brand equity for individual products for particular business units and markets.

10. ***Educate all members of the organization as to the value of branding and their role in delivering brand value.*** Whereas a few individuals may be responsible for developing strategy, the whole organization is responsible for its implementation. Industrial products and brands are likely to have many customer 'touch points', each of which must be managed consistently with the brand image.

Sources: K. Lane Keller and F. E. Webster, Jr 'A roadmap for branding in industrial markets', *Journal of Brand Management*, 11 May 2004: 388–402. P. Mitchell, S. King and S. Reast, 'Brand values related to industrial products', *Industrial Marketing Management*, May 2001, 30 (5): 415–25.

High-tech products

Another example of the increasing realization of the important role that brands play in the marketing equation is with high-tech products (eg, computer-related products). Many technology companies have struggled with branding. Managed by technologists, they often lack any brand strategy and, in the worst case, see branding as simply equal to naming of their products. In many of these product markets, however, financial success is no longer driven by product innovation or by offering the best specifications and features. Marketing skills are playing an increasingly important role in the success of high-tech products.

The rapid nature of the technology product lifecycles causes unique branding challenges. Trust is critical, and companies often buy into companies as much as products. Leaders of technology companies often become a dominant component of the brand (eg, Apple's Steve Jobs and Microsoft's Bill Gates). Marketing budgets may be small, although adoption of packaged goods marketing techniques by companies selling high-tech products has resulted in increased expenditures on mass-market advertising. Brand Briefing 1.4 provides guidelines for marketing managers at high-tech companies.

Brand Briefing 1.4

Understanding high-tech branding

Marketers operating in technologically intensive markets face unique challenges, eg, an accelerated product lifecycle due to continual R&D advances and innovations. Here are ten guidelines that managers for high-tech companies can use to improve their company's brand strategy

1. *A brand strategy should provide a roadmap for the future.* High-tech companies too often rely on the faulty assumption that the best product based on the best technology will sell itself. As the market failure of the Sony Betamax illustrates, the company with the best technology does not always win.

2. *Understand your brand hierarchy and manage it appropriately over time.* A strong corporate brand is vital in the technology industry to provide stability and help to establish a presence in financial markets. Since product innovations provide the growth drivers for technology companies, however, brand equity is sometimes built in to the product name to the detriment of corporate brand equity.

3. *Know your customer and build an appropriate brand strategy.* Many high-tech companies understand that, when corporate customers purchase business-to-business products or services, they are typically committing to a long-term relationship. For this reason, high-tech companies should establish a strong corporate brand that will endure over time.

4. *Building brand equity and selling products are two different exercises.* Too often, the emphasis on developing products leads to an overemphasis on branding them. When a company applies distinct brand names to too many products in rapid succession, the brand portfolio becomes cluttered and consumers may become confused. Rather than branding each innovation separately, a better approach is to plan for innovations by developing an extendible branding strategy.

5. *Brands are owned by customers, not engineers.* In high-tech firms, chief executives in many cases work their way up the ladder through the engineering divisions. While engineers have an intimate knowledge of products and technology, they may lack the big-picture brand view. Compounding this potential problem is the fact that high-tech companies typically spend less on consumer research compared with other types of companies. As a result of these factors, tech companies often do not invest in building strong brands.

6. *Brand strategies need to account for the attributes of the chief executive and adjust accordingly.* Many of the world's top high-tech companies have highly visible leaders, especially compared with other industries. In many cases, the chief executive's identity and persona are woven into the fabric of the brand.

7. *Brand building on a small budget necessitates using every possible positive association.* High-tech companies typically prioritize their marketing mix as follows: industry analyst relations, public relations, trade shows, seminars,

Brand Briefing 1.4 *continued*

direct mail and advertising. Often, direct mail and advertising are discretionary items and may in fact receive no budget.

8. **Technology categories are created by customers and external forces, not by companies.** In their quest for product differentiation, new high-tech companies have a tendency to reinvent the wheel and claim they have created a category. Yet only two groups can create categories: analysts and customers. For this reason, it is important for high-tech companies to manage their relationships with analysts in order to attract consumers.

9. **Rapid change demands that you stay in tune with your internal and external environment.** The rapid pace of innovation in the technology sector dictates that marketers closely observe the market conditions in which their brands do business. Trends in brand strategy and marketing change almost as rapidly as the technology.

10. **Invest the time in understanding the technology and value proposition and do not be afraid to ask questions.** It is important for technology marketers to ask questions in order to educate themselves and build credibility with the company's engineering staff and with customers. To build trust between engineers and customers, marketers must strive to learn as much as they can about the technology.

Source: P. Tickle, K. Lane Keller and K. Richey, 'Branding in high-technology markets', *Market Leader*, 2003, 22 (Autumn): 21–6.

Services

Although there have long been strong service brands (eg, American Express, British Airways, Hilton Hotels, Merrill Lynch and DHL), the pervasiveness and level of sophistication in their branding has accelerated in the past decade. As Interbrand's John Murphy noted: 'In the last 30 years, some of the greatest branding successes have come in the area of services.' Brand Briefing 1.5 describes the ascent of the Ryanair.

One of the challenges in marketing services is that, relative to products, they are more intangible and more likely to vary in quality depending on the particular person or people involved in providing the service. Consequently, branding can be particularly important to service firms to address potential intangibility and variability problems. Brand symbols may also be especially important because they help to make the abstract nature of services more concrete. Brands can help to identify and provide meaning to different services. For example, branding has become especially important in financial services to help organize and label the myriad of offerings in a manner that consumers can understand.

Branding a service can also signal to consumers that the firm has designed a service offering that is special and deserving of its own name. For example, British Airways

Brand Briefing 1.5

Flying high with Southwest Airlines

Southwest Airlines, originally called Air Southwest, was founded by Texans Rollin King and Herb Kelleher in 1967. Southwest started as a commuter carrier with flights between Dallas, Houston and San Antonio, but grew to operate in 55 US cities. Southwest trades on its cheap fares and no-frills service. Seats on its planes are all the same class and the in-flight service offers neither films nor meals.

Southwest knew from an early stage that it could not differentiate on price alone, because competitors could easily muscle into the market with cheaper versions. To promote customer loyalty, the airline sought to create a unique flying experience for its customers. Early flights featured Jet Bunnies – flight attendants dressed in hot pants and go-go boots – who served beverages known as 'Love Potions' and snacks called 'Love Bites'. Southwest encouraged its pilots and cabin crew members to entertain the passengers with jokes and snappy patter during in-flight announcements.

One of the company's early recruitment bulletins specified that applicants should have a sense of humour. Even chief executive Herb Kelleher got in on the act. On occasions, Kelleher donned an Elvis Presley costume to meet passengers at the gate and once served drinks and snacks while dressed in a bunny suit on an Easter flight. Another passenger-pleasing feature of Southwest flights is the first-come, first-served open seating, whereby passengers are given numbered cards that reflect the boarding order based on when they arrive at the gate.

Southwest's advertising has always been informative, yet with humour at the same time. For several years, the airline has used as its tagline a clever play on the standard message from a captain telling passengers they are free to move about the plane's cabin. Southwest's version, which emphasizes its national route coverage, declares: 'You are now free to move about the country.' Recent ads highlighted Southwest's low fares with humorous television spots in which a character commits a social blunder, after which a voiceover asks 'Wanna get away?'

Today, Southwest is the fourth-largest US airline, with 3,000 daily flights to 60 cities in 31 states. It holds the distinction of being the only low-fare airline to achieve long-term success. By offering a low-cost, convenient and customer-friendly option, Southwest has attracted passengers in droves and, after its first profitable year in 1969, achieved profits in each of the next 37.

Sources: Jane Woolridge, 'Baby-boom airline is unknown, cheap', *San Diego Union-Tribune*, 30 December 1984; Katrina Brooker, 'The chairman of the board looks back', *Fortune*, 28 May 2001; Wendy Zellner, 'Holding steady', *BusinessWeek*, 3 February 2003: 66–8.

not only branded its premium business class service as 'Club Class' but also branded its economy service as 'World Traveller', a clever way to communicate to these passengers that they are also special in some way and that their patronage is not taken for granted. Branding has clearly become a competitive weapon for services.

Retailers and distributors

To the retailers or other channel members distributing products, brands provide important functions. Brands can generate consumer interest, patronage and loyalty in a shop, as consumers learn to expect certain brands and products. To the extent 'you are what you sell', brands help to create an image and establish a positioning. Retailers can also create a brand image by attaching unique associations to the quality of a service, their product assortment and merchandising and their pricing and credit policy. Finally, the appeal and attraction of brands can permit higher price margins, increased sales volumes and greater profits. These brand name products may come from manufacturers or other external sources or from the shop itself.

Retailers can introduce their own brands by using their shop name, creating new names or some combination of the two. Thus, many distributors, especially in Europe, have introduced their own brands that they sell in addition to – or sometimes even instead of – manufacturers' brands. These products, referred to as *own label, store brands* or *private label* brands, offer another way for retailers to increase customer loyalty and generate higher margins and profits. In Britain, five or six supermarket chains account for roughly half of the country's food and packaged goods sales, led by Tesco and Sainsbury. Another top British retailer, Marks & Spencer, sells only its own brand goods. Other European retailers also emphasize their own brands. Brand Briefing 1.6 describes some of the branding developments at Wal-Mart. Chapter 5 considers own label, store brands and private labels in greater detail.

Online products and services

In Europe in 2006, the number of internet users varied widely from country to country,[17] with the most developed being the Scandinavian countries with 70–75 percent of its population being connected. The EU average is, at the time of writing, 50 percent. The EU candidate countries, Bulgaria, Croatia, Macedonia, Romania and Turkey average 17 percent. But where the penetration is low, growth rates are very high.

In the pioneering internet countries, the end of the twentieth century revealed an unprecedented head-long rush by new and existing businesses to create online brands. Quickly, these businesses learned the complexities and challenges of building a web-based brand. Such brands came in many different forms, with business models based on selling information, products, experiences and so on.

Many online brand marketers during this heady time made serious – and some-times fatal – mistakes. In general, these marketers seemed to oversimplify the branding process, for example, equating flashy or unusual advertising with building a brand. Although such marketing efforts sometimes caught consumers' attention, more often than not they failed to create awareness of what products or services the brand represented, why those products or services were unique or different and, most important, why consumers should buy the brand.

Online marketers quickly realized the realities of brand-building. First, as with any brand, it is critical to create unique aspects that a important to consumers – such as convenience, price and variety. At the same time, the brand needs to perform satisfactorily in other areas, such as customer service, credibility and personality. Customers

Brand Briefing 1.6

Branding the Wal-Mart way

Wal-Mart, the US retailer that first opened in Rogers, Arkansas, in 1962, is the world's biggest retailer, with more than 5,700 shops, including some 1,350 discount outlets, nearly 2,000 combination discount and grocery shops (Wal-Mart Supercenters in the USA and Asda in the UK) and 550 warehouse shops (Sam's Club). The founder, Sam Walton, sought to build conveniently located shops that offered wide selection, low prices and quality customer service.

Wal-Mart's low prices have always been a key to pleasing consumers. The chain invented the everyday low pricing strategy. The slogan 'We sell for less. Always' illustrates Wal-Mart's dedication to underselling the competition. Its reputation for friendly service is another way the company creates customer satisfaction. At the entrances to its shops, Wal-Mart stations 'people greeters' who welcome and assist customers. The company employs helpful and knowledgeable staff who are positioned throughout the shop to answer questions and help customers find items. These gestures foster trust. According to a company survey that asked 'What does Wal-Mart mean to you?', more customers responded with 'trust' than 'low prices'.

A less well-known contributor to the company's success is its sophisticated logistics. Sam Walton was a visionary when it came to logistics. He realized, as early as the 1960s, that the company growth he was striving for required advanced information systems to manage the volumes of merchandise. By 1998, Wal-Mart's computer database was second only to the Pentagon's in terms of capacity. One business writer recently proclaimed Wal-Mart to be 'the king of store logistics'.

Wal-Mart today bears little resemblance to the Arkansas shop that started it all. The company is an indelible part of the USA's retail landscape and has expanded into South America and Europe. Wal-Mart's annual sales in 2004 reached €175 billion, earning the company the top spot in the Fortune 500 ranking.

Sources: Wendy Zelner, 'Someday, Lee, this may all be yours', *BusinessWeek*, 15 November 1999; 'Will WalMart.com get it right this time?' *BusinessWeek*, 6 November 2000.

began to demand higher levels of service both during and after their website visits. As a consequence, to be competitive, many firms have had to improve their web service by making customer service agents available in real time; shipping products promptly and providing tracking updates; and adopting liberal return policies.[18] Such improvements have been critical to overcoming the low customer service opinions that some consumers hold towards online businesses. Successful online brands were those that were well positioned and found unique ways to satisfy consumers' unmet needs. A classic example is Google.

Founded in 1998 by two Stanford University doctoral students, search engine Google's name is a play on the word googol – the number represented by a 1 followed by 100 zeroes – a reference to the huge amount of data online. Google's stated mission is: 'To organize the world's information and make it universally accessible and useful.' It has become the leader among search engines through its business focus and constant innovation. Google's home page focuses on searches alone and is not cluttered with other services, as is the case with many other portals. By focusing on plain text, avoiding pop-up ads and using sophisticated search algorithms, Google is seen as providing fast and reliable service. By September 2005, Google was the web's most used search engine, with almost half of all searches. Google's revenue was driven by search ads, little text-based boxes that advertiser's only pay for when a user clicks on it.[19]

Online brands also learned the importance of offline activities to draw customers to their websites, and many of the most successful business ventures came from established brands using their strong reputations and marketing muscle online. Web addresses, or URLs, began to appear on all related marketing material. Partnerships became critical as brands developed networks of online partners and links. Online marketers also began to target specific customer groups – often geographically widely dispersed – for which the brand could offer unique value propositions. Website designs have begun to maximize the benefits of interactivity, customization and timeliness and the advantages of being able to inform, persuade and sell at the same time. Brand Briefing 1.7 describes how Amazon.com has built a strong online brand. Chapter 6 examines website and interactive advertising issues.

People and organizations

Brands extend beyond products and services. People and organizations also can be viewed as brands. The naming aspect of the brand is generally straightforward in this case, and people and organizations also often have well-defined images that are understood and liked or disliked by others. This fact becomes particularly true when considering public figures such as politicians, entertainers and professional athletes. Such people compete in some sense for public approval and acceptance and benefit from conveying a strong and desirable image. Take the example of actor Paul Newman.

> Paul Newman has turned his likeable, down-to-earth image into a business. Newman's Own was launched after many of his friends and neighbours wanted more of the salad dressings he gave out as gifts. Since then, the brand has extended into pasta sauce, salsa, steak sauce, lemonade and popcorn. As sole owner, Newman donates all profits and royalties after taxes for educational and charity purposes, totalling €103 million since 1982. He founded the Hole in the Wall Gang Camp to allow children with cancer or serious blood diseases to go to summer camps free of charge. With a corporate slogan of 'Shameless exploitation in pursuit of the common good', it's not surprising that Newman would state on his website: 'It started out as a joke and got out of control.'

That is not to say that you only have to be well-known or famous to be thought of as a brand. Anyone trying to build a career can be thought of as trying to create his or her own brand. Certainly, one key to a successful career is that certain people (eg, fellow workers, superiors or even important people outside the company) know who you are

Brand Briefing 1.7

Building the Amazon.com brand

Jeffrey Bezos left his job on Wall Street as a hedge fund manager in 1994 to return to his home in suburban Seattle and found online retailer Amazon.com, despite the fact that he had no previous retail experience. Bezos did, however, have a vision of making Amazon.com 'the Earth's biggest bookstore'. Within a year, Amazon.com offered a selection of more than one million book titles, which made it the world's largest book broker.

In addition to offering unparalleled selection, Bezos also wanted the website to provide a unique shopping experience and the highest level of customer service. He aimed to be 'the world's most customer-centric company'. To this end, the site was designed so that, when shoppers viewed a book title, a list of related titles that might interest them would appear on the same web page. To customers who submitted information on their favourite authors and subjects, Amazon.com sent periodic recommendations and reviews via e-mail. Another personal touch included the development of personalized front pages that opened whenever registered customers visited the site. Of these customized features, Bezos said: 'We want Amazon.com to be the right store for you as an individual. If we have 4.5 million customers, we should have 4.5 million stores.' To promote goodwill among customers, Amazon.com automatically upgraded many orders to priority shipping at no extra cost. These consumer-focused efforts yielded the desired results: in 1998, over 60 percent of orders were from repeat customers.

Much of Amazon.com's early growth was credited to word-of-mouth sources such as testimonials from satisfied customers and media stories. Before long, Amazon.com had top-of-mind awareness among consumers looking to buy products online. As one industry analyst said in 1998: 'When you think of web shopping, you think of Amazon first.' The company's ad spending was small compared with other dot-coms: in the fourth quarter of 1998, Amazon.com spent €2.5 million, most of which went to radio commercials. The company began advertising more extensively the following year, when it spent €34.2 million on holiday-themed advertisements.

Once the bookselling strategy had proved successful, Amazon.com expanded into CDs, videos and gifts. Between 1998 and 2001, the site added numerous other product categories including baby products, electronics, kitchen and housewares, tools and hardware, toys and even barbecues. During that time, the company established sites in the UK, Germany, France, Japan, Spain and Austria. Bezos declared his company's intention of providing 'the Earth's biggest selection'. With more than 29 million customers and almost €4.8 billion in annual sales by 2004, the Amazon.com brand was stronger than ever.

Sources: www.amazon.com; Alice Z. Cuneo, 'Amazon unleashes $50 million for the holidays', *Advertising Age*, 15 November 1999; Rachel Beck, 'Amazon.com moves beyond books and music with gift shop, video launch', AP Newswire, 17 November 1998; Robert D. Hof, 'Amazon.com, the wild world of e-commerce', *BusinessWeek*, 14 December 1998.

and what kind of person you are in terms of your skills, talents, attitude and so forth. By building up a name and reputation in a business context, a person is essentially creating his or her own brand.[20] The right awareness and image can be invaluable regarding the manner in which people treat you and interpret your words, actions and deeds.[21]

Similarly, organizations often take on meanings through their activities and products. Charitable organizations such as the Green Peace, the Red Cross, Amnesty International and Unicef have increasingly emphasized marketing. National Geographic was a pioneer in this respect.

> Founded in 1888 by 33 US-based scientists, the National Geographic Society is a non-profit scientific and educational membership organization with a mission related to 'the increase and diffusion of geographic knowledge'.[22] The distinctive yellow borders of the brand is one of the world's most recognizable brand symbols. The society's products include *National Geographic* magazine, books, maps, television shows and gift items. The National Geographic Channel, launched in January 2001, ranks as one of the more desirable networks according to viewer surveys. With a tagline, 'Dare to explore', the channel features science, technology and history in addition to its traditional emphasis on natural history and its explorers, scientists and photographers. Its website has won many awards and serves as a companion to the channel. National Geographic Enterprises includes licensing, a catalogue business, travel expeditions, e-commerce and retail. These units oversee the merchandise related to the National Geographic brand worldwide. All National Geographic's net proceeds from licensing support exploration, conservation, research and education activities.

Sports, arts and entertainment

A special case of marketing people and organizations as brands is in the sports, art and entertainment industry. Sports marketing has become highly sophisticated, employing traditional packaged goods techniques. No longer content to allow results on the field to dictate attendance levels and financial fortunes, many sports teams are being marketed through a combination of advertising, promotions, sponsorship and direct mail. By building awareness, image and loyalty, these sports franchises are able to meet ticket sales targets regardless of what their team's actual performance might turn out to be. Brand symbols and logos in particular have become an important financial contributor to professional sports through licensing agreements. Brand Briefing 1.8 describes how Manchester United built a powerhouse football team – and brand.

Branding plays an especially valuable function in the arts and entertainment industries (eg, with films, television, music and books). These offerings are good examples of experience goods: prospective buyers cannot judge quality by inspection and must use cues such as the particular people involved, the concept or rationale behind the project, word-of-mouth and critical reviews.

A film can be seen as a product where the 'ingredients' are the plots, actors and director.[23] Certain titles such as *Star Wars*, *Batman* and *Harry Potter* have established themselves as brands by combining all these ingredients into a formula that appeals to consumers and allows the studios to release sequels (essentially brand extensions)

Brand Briefing 1.8

Building a brand winner with Manchester United

Manchester United, the wealthiest football club in the English league (valued at €513 million) and one of the most popular sport organizations in the world, has a history of winning on the field and in the business world. The club was founded in 1878 and won consecutive English League titles in the 1950s. A tragic plane crash in 1958 that killed seven players brought the club international attention. In 1968, a rebuilt team won another European title. It was not until the 1990s, however, that Manchester United grew into its current role as one of the most popular and lucrative sport franchises in the world. In 1999, a year in which the team won a 'treble' – three English and European soccer titles – its stock market value surpassed €1.37 billion.

Television is credited with much of Manchester United's financial success. With the advent of satellite television, fans all over the world could enjoy live coverage of all the best matches. Football was already a global game played on every inhabited continent, but the game's visibility has never been higher as a result of this increased media coverage. One analyst described Manchester United's recent financial fortunes as follows: 'Basically, they got really lucky. The success on the field has coincided with the success of football as pure media content.' As one of the most successful club teams in the 1990s, the 'Red Devils' received a large share of this burgeoning media coverage.

The club's visibility, combined with its accomplishments, has won it legions of foreign fans. In addition to roughly 7.3 million fans in Britain, Manchester United estimates it has 75 million fans worldwide, with growing interest in Asia. Though football is not as popular in the USA as in other countries – the number of people playing football has held steady at 18 million for a decade – US companies have shown an increased interest in Manchester United. In 2001, the club signed a €342 million, 13-year licensing deal with Nike. But when an American, Malcolm Glazer, purchased the team for €1.02 billion in 2005, a storm of protest from local fans ensued. Their loyalties were further tested later that year when the team failed to qualify for the Champions League or even the UEFA qualifiers.

Sources: Bill Glauber, 'Meet Manchester United marketing', *Baltimore Sun*, 19 March 2001; Andy Dworkin, 'Nike Scores Soccer Sponsorship', *Portland Oregonian*, 7 November 2000; 'Red Devil', *The Economist*, 21 May 2005: 70; Laura Cohn, 'Can Glazer put this ball in the net?' *BusinessWeek*, 30 May 2005: 40.

that rely on the initial popularity of the title. For years, some of the most valuable franchises have involved recurring characters or continuing stories, and many of the successful releases have been sequels. Their success comes from the fact that cinemagoers know from the title and the people involved that they can expect certain things – a classic application of branding.

When *Star Wars* was first shown in 1977, the film licensing industry barely existed. But by the time of the final episode in the series, *Star Wars: Episode III – Revenge of the Sith,* merchandising had generated €6.15 billion in retail sales, almost triple the worldwide box office of €2.32 billion. The force was also certainly with the final film, as Lucas Licensing had deals with about 400 licensees in more than 30 countries covering thousands of products, with expected proceeds of an additional €1.02 billion. This success changed the toy industry, too, making it more focused on television and film entertainment properties.[24]

The existence of a strong brand name in the entertainment industry is so valuable because of the strong feelings that the names engender as a result of pleasurable past experiences.

Geographic locations

Places, like products and people, can be branded. In this case, the brand name is relatively fixed by the name of the location. The power of branding is making people aware of the location and then linking desirable associations to it. Increased mobility of both people and businesses and growth in the tourism industry has contributed to the rise of place marketing. Cities, counties, regions and countries are now promoted. The goals of these types of campaigns are to create awareness and a favourable image of a location that will entice temporary visits or permanent moves from individuals and businesses alike.

Ideas and causes

Finally, ideas and causes have become branded, especially by non-profit organizations. These ideas and causes may be captured in a phrase or slogan and even be represented by a symbol (eg, Aids ribbons). By making the ideas and causes more visible and concrete, branding can provide much value. As Chapter 11 describes, cause marketing increasingly involves marketing to attempt to inform or persuade consumers about the issues surrounding an issue. Brand Briefing 1.9 describes the activities of the World Wildlife Fund.

WHAT ARE THE STRONGEST BRANDS?

It is clear from the examples above that almost anything can be, and has been, branded. Which brands are the strongest, that is, the most well-known or highly regarded? Figure 1.5 reveals *BusinessWeek* magazine's ranking of the world's 25 most valuable brands in 2006 based on Interbrand's brand valuation methodology (see Chapter 10).

RepTrak Pulse 2006 was the first annual ranking of the reputations of the world's largest companies. The study was created by the Reputation Institute to provide executives with a high-level overview of their companies' reputations among consumers. The study is the result of more than 27,000 online interviews with

Brand Briefing 1.9

Branding a cause: World Wildlife Fund

The World Wildlife Fund (WWF), founded in 1961, is the world's largest private organization dedicated to nature conservation. The WWF boasts more than 4.7 million supporters in 100 countries. Its familiar logo, which depicts a panda, represents its enduring efforts to protect that species.

In the USA, its annual budget does not allow for lavish spending on marketing, so the WWF relies on direct marketing to bring its message to the public and solicit contributions. One recent mailing offered recipients a chance to win one of several trips, including an African safari and an Alaskan cruise, in a sweepstake.

The WWF also earns revenue through corporate partnerships. It offers four business partnership options.

1. *Conservation partner:* global sponsorship from multinational corporations. Partners include Canon and Ogilvy & Mather.

2. *Corporate supporter:* financial or in-kind support from medium or large corporations. Supporters include INRA and Delverde.

3. *Corporate club:* support from environmentally aware local businesses. Only offered in Hungary, Russia, Poland and United Arab Emirates.

4. *Product licensing:* agreements to use WWF trademarks. Groth manufactures WWF-branded stamps and coins, and IBTT makes toy animals bearing the WWF panda logo.

To help spread its message, the WWF developed a website. The site contains pages for its national divisions, membership information, updates on environmental issues and information on projects. In 2000, the Web Marketing Association named the site the best for any non-profit organization. In addition to its central website, the WWF developed cause-specific sites, such as its Amazon rainforest relief site (www.worldwildlife.org/amazon), a site dedicated to its clean water campaign (www.panda.org/livingwaters) and a site dedicated to protecting the Arctic National Wildlife Refuge from oil drilling (www.worldwildlife.org/arctic-refuge).

The group changed its name to the Worldwide Fund for Nature in 1986, but is still known by the original World Wildlife Fund name in North America. The original name and the accompanying acronym became a source of controversy when the WWF sued the World Wrestling Federation in 2001 over use of the initials WWF. The main point of contention was the similarity between the website addresses for the two organizations, since the World Wildlife URL was www.wwf.org and the World Wrestling Federation used www.wwf.com. The High Court in London decided in favour of the World Wildlife Fund, giving the wildlife group exclusive rights to the WWF initials and ordering the wrestling group to change its website address.

Source: www.wwf.org; 'World Wildlife Federation loses court case over rights to WWF name', *Dow Jones Business News*, 10 August 2001.

Rank	Brand	Country of origin	Sector	2007 value ($m)	Change in value
1	Coca-Cola	USA	Beverages	65,324	−3%
2	Microsoft	USA	Software	58,709	3%
3	IBM	USA	Computer services	57,091	2%
4	General Electric	USA	Diversified	51,569	5%
5	Nokia	Finland	Telecoms equipment	33,696	12%
6	Toyota	Japan	Automotive	32,070	15%
7	Intel	USA	Computer hardware	30,954	−4%
8	McDonald's	USA	Restaurants	29,398	7%
9	Disney	USA	Media	29,210	5%
10	Mercedes-Benz	Germany	Automotive	23,568	8%
11	Citibank	USA	Financial services	23,443	9%
12	Hewlett-Packard	USA	Computer hardware	22,197	9%
13	BMW	Germany	Automotive	21,612	10%
14	Marlboro	USA	Tobacco	21,283	0%
15	American Express	USA	Financial services	20,827	6%
16	Gillette	USA	Personal care	20,415	4%
17	Louis Vuitton	France	Luxury	20,321	15%
18	Cisco	USA	Computer services	19,099	9%
19	Honda	Japan	Automotive	17,998	6%
20	Google	USA	Internet services	17,837	44%
21	Samsung	Republic of Korea	Consumer electronics	16,853	4%
22	Merrill Lynch	USA	Financial services	14,343	10%
23	HSBC	Britain	Financial services	13,563	17%
24	Nescafé	Switzerland	Beverages	12,950	4%
25	SONY	Japan	Consumer electronics	12,907	10%

Figure 1.5   BusinessWeek/Interbrand ranking of global brands (2007)

Sources: 'Global brands', *BusinessWeek*, 6 August 2007; Interbrand press release 'The *BusinessWeek*/Interbrand annual ranking of the 2006 best global brands', 6 August 2007; www.interbrand.com

consumers in 25 countries on 6 continents measuring the corporate reputations of 700 companies.

There is an industry halo affecting the reputations of companies. Some industries stand out as trustworthy, which benefits individual companies. Other industries struggle to create a positive reputation with the general public and put the companies at risk.

Companies involved in electronics, food production and beverages are trusted and respected for their actions. Companies operating in the telecommunications, utilities, financial services, energy, pharmaceuticals and insurance sectors are all faced with low trust from consumers, a context that makes it harder for individual companies to stand out favourably.

Some of the best-known brands can be found by walking into a supermarket. It is also easy to identify other brands that have been market leaders in their respective categories for decades. According to research by marketing consultant Jack Trout, in 25 popular product categories, 20 of the leading brands in the USA in 1923 can be seen as being still a leading brand today – only five have lost their leadership position (see Figure 1.6).[25]

Product category	Leading brands in 1923	Leading brands of today
1 Bacon	Swift	Swift
2 Batteries	Eveready	Duracell
3 Breakfast cereal	Kellogg's Corn Flakes	Cheerios
4 Cameras	Kodak	Kodak
5 Canned fruit	Del Monte	Del Monte
6 Canned milk	Carnation	Carnation
7 Chewing gum	Wrigley's	Wrigley's
8 Chocolate	Hershey's	Hershey's
9 Crackers	Nabisco	Nabisco
10 Flour	Gold Medal	Gold Medal
11 Mint sweets	Life Savers	Life Savers
12 Paint	Sherwin-Williams	Sherwin-Williams
13 Paper	Hammermill	Hammermill
14 Pipe tobacco	Prince Albert	Prince Albert
15 Razors	Gillette	Gillette
16 Sewing machines	Singer	Singer
17 Shirts	Manhattan	Arrow
18 Soap	Ivory	Dove
19 Soft drinks	Coca-Cola	Coca-Cola
20 Soup	Campbell's	Campbell's
21 Shortening	Crisco	Crisco
22 Tea	Lipton	Lipton
23 Tyres	Goodyear	Goodyear
24 Toilet soap	Palmolive	Dial
25 Toothpaste	Colgate	Colgate

Figure 1.6 Brand leaders in the USA: then and now

Source: Proprietary research by Jack Trout, based on industry share data. As summarized in, Jack Trout, 'Branding can't exist without positioning', *Advertising Age*, 14 March 2005: 28. Copyright, Crain Communications Inc. 2005.

Similarly, many brands that were number one in the UK in 1933 also remain strong today: Hovis bread, Stork margarine, Kellogg's Corn Flakes, Cadbury's chocolates, Gillette razors, Schweppes mixers, Brooke Bond tea, Colgate toothpaste and Hoover vacuum cleaners. These brands have evolved. In many cases, they barely resemble how they started.

At the same time, despite these successes, there are brands that have lost market leadership and, in some cases, their very existence. Winston, after years of dominance in the cigarette category, lost its leadership position to Marlboro in 1975 and now trails that brand by a large margin. Other seemingly invincible brands, such as Levi Strauss, General Motors, Sainsbury's, Polaroid and Xerox have run into difficulties and seen their market pre-eminence challenged or eliminated.

In some cases, these failures could be related to factors beyond the control of the firm, such as technological advances or shifting consumer preferences, but sometimes the blame could probably be placed on the actions or inaction of marketers. Some of these marketers failed to account for changing market conditions and continued to operate with a 'business as usual' attitude or, perhaps even worse, recognized that changes were necessary but were inadequate or inappropriate in their response. Brand Briefing 1.10 provides insights into factors affecting market leadership.

Brand Briefing 1.10

Understanding market leadership

According to a study by Peter Golder, over time, leading brands are more likely to lose their leadership position than retain it. Golder evaluated more than 650 products in 100 categories and compared the category leaders from 1923 with those in 1997. The study found that only 23 of the top brands remained market leaders in 1997. Additionally, 28 percent of the leading brands in 1923 had failed by 1997. The clothing and fashion category experienced the greatest percentage of failures (67 percent) and had no brands that remained leaders in 1997. Leaders in the food and beverage category fared better, with 39 percent of brands maintaining leadership while only 21 percent failed.

One 1923 leader that did not maintain leadership was Underwood typewriters. Underwood's mistake was its lack of innovation. Rather than invest in research and development, Underwood followed a harvesting strategy that sought the highest margin possible for its products. By 1950, several competitors had invested in computer technology, whereas Underwood only acquired a small computer firm in 1952. Subsequent developments in the market damaged Underwood's position. Between 1956 and 1961, lower-priced foreign competitors more than doubled their share of manual typewriter sales. Additionally, sales of electric typewriters, which Underwood did not make, overtook sales of manual typewriters in the early 1960s. Olivetti acquired Underwood in the mid-1960s and the brand name was dropped in the 1980s.

Golder uses Wrigley, which has dominated chewing gum sales for nine decades, as an example of a long-term leader. According to Golder, Wrigley's success is based on three factors: 'Maintaining and building strong brands, focusing on a single product and being in a category that has not changed much.' Wrigley has consistently marketed its brand with high-profile sponsorship and advertising. It also used subsidiaries to extend into categories such as sugarless gum and bubblegum, so as not to dilute the brand. Wrigley's focus on chewing gum enables it to achieve maximum results in what is considered a mature category. During the 1990s, sales of Wrigley's products grew almost 10 percent annually. Finally, the chewing gum market is historically stable and uncomplicated. Still, Wrigley's makes considerable investments in product and packaging to maintain its edge.

Golder and his co-author Gerard Tellis argue that dedication is vital for sustained brand leadership, elucidating five factors for enduring market leadership (see Figure 1.7). They comment:

> The real causes of enduring market leadership are vision and will. Enduring market leaders have a revolutionary and inspiring vision of the mass market, and they exhibit an indomitable will to realize that vision. They persist under adversity, innovate relentlessly, commit financial resources and leverage assets to realize their vision.

Brand Briefing 1.10 *continued*

Tellis and Golder identify five factors as key to enduring brand leadership.

Vision of the mass market

Companies with a keen eye for mass market tastes are more likely to build a broad and sustainable customer base. Though Pampers was not the market leader in the disposable nappy category during the first few years, it spent significantly on research and development to design an affordable and effective product. Pampers soon became the market leader.

Managerial persistence

The 'breakthrough' technology that can drive market leadership often requires the commitment of company resources over a long time. For example, JVC spent 21 years researching the VHS video recorder before launching it in 1976 and becoming a market leader.

Financial commitment

The cost of maintaining leadership is high because of the demands for research, development and marketing. Companies that aim for short-term profitability rather than long-term leadership, as Rheingold Brewery did when it curtailed support of its Gablinger's lager a year after the 1967 introduction of the product, are unlikely to enjoy enduring leadership.

Relentless innovation

Because of changes in consumer tastes and competition, companies that wish to maintain leadership positions must innovate continually. Gillette, both a long-term leader and historically an innovator, typically has at least 20 shaving products on the drawing board at any time.

Asset leverage

Companies can become leaders in some categories if they hold a leadership position in a related category. For instance, Coca-Cola used its success and experience with cola (Coke) and diet cola (Tab) to introduce Diet Coke in 1982. Within a year of its introduction, Diet Coke became the market leader.

Figure 1.7 Factors determining enduring leadership

Source: G. J. Tellis and P. N. Golder, 'First to market, first to fail? Real causes of enduring market leadership', *MIT Sloan Management Review*, 1 January 1996.

Sources: P. N. Golder, 'Historical method in marketing research with new evidence on long-term market share stability', *Journal of Marketing Research*, May 2000: 156–72. See also P. N. Golder and G. J. Tellis, 'Growing, growing, gone: cascades, diffusion, and turning points in the product life cycle', *Marketing Science*, Spring 2004, 23 (2): 207–18; L. Freeman, 'Study: leading brands aren't always enduring', *Advertising Age*, 28 February 2000; G. J. Tellis and Peter N. Golder, 'First to market, first to fail? Real causes of enduring market leadership', *MIT Sloan Management Review*, 1 January 1996.

The study methodology employed the following steps. First, a survey of chief marketing officers and consumers in the USA identified brands that were seen as both growing fast and being innovative. Next, the list was pruned to include only brand-owning companies that beat their peers in earnings growth. The 40 brands remaining were valued using a discounted cash flow model that also factored in the percentage of the business being driven by the brand. The brands whose values increased the most within their respective industries during 2001–2005 are shown below.

	Current ($bn)	Four-year change (%)
1. Apple	5.3	38
2. BlackBerry	1.2	36
3. Google	8.7	36
4. Amazon.com	2.7	35
5. Yahoo!	6.8	34
6. eBay	7.4	31
7. Red Bull	1.7	31
8. Starbucks	3.0	25
9. Pixar	2.9	24
10. Coach	3.9	23
11. Whole Foods	0.7	22
12. EA Sports/Games	6.9	22
13. MTV	7.0	22
14. Samsung	14.3	18
15. Victoria's Secret	6.8	17
16. Nike	7.1	16
17. Toyota	25.8	15
18. Formula One	3.2	14
19. ESPN	9.3	14
20. Harley-Davidson	7.6	12

Figure 1.8   Vivaldi Partners study: next generation growth brands in the USA

Source: 'Next Generation Growth Brands', Vivaldi Partners, June 2005; Kurt Badenhausen and Maya Roney, 'Next Generation', *Forbes*, 20 June 2005: 121–2.

The bottom line is that any brand – no matter how strong – is vulnerable to poor brand management. The next section discusses why it is so difficult to manage brands. Figure 1.8 displays an analysis of fast-growing brands by marketing consultant firm Vivaldi Partners.

BRANDING CHALLENGES AND OPPORTUNITIES

Although brands may be as important as ever to consumers, brand management may be more difficult than ever. Although there has been growing recognition of the value of brands, developments have complicated marketing practices and pose challenges for brand managers (see Figure 1.9), as discussed next.[26]

- Savvy customers.
- More complex brand families and portfolios.
- Maturing markets.
- More sophisticated and increasing competition.
- Difficulty in differentiating.
- Decreasing brand loyalty in many categories.
- Growth of own labels.
- Increasing trade power.
- Fragmenting media coverage.
- Erosion of effectiveness of traditional media.
- Emerging communication options.
- Increasing promotional expenditures.
- Decreasing advertising expenditures.
- Increasing cost of product introduction and support.
- Short-term performance orientation.
- Increasing job turnover.

Figure 1.9 Challenges to brand builders

Savvy customers

Increasingly, consumers and businesses have become experienced with marketing, more knowledgeable about how it works and more demanding. A well-developed media market has resulted in increased attention being paid to the marketing actions and motivations of companies. Consumer information and support exists in the form of consumer guides (eg, *Which?*), websites (eg, pricerunner.com, become.com, zdnet.com), blogs and so on. Consulting firm Brand Keys conducts annual surveys and has found that consumers' expectations are growing two-and-a-half times faster than brands are able to keep up.[27]

In this postmodern marketing world, many believe that it is difficult to persuade consumers with traditional communications.

Other marketers believe that what consumers want from products and services and brands has changed.[28] For example, Kevin Roberts of Saatchi & Saatchi has argued that companies must transcend brands to create 'trustmarks' – a name or symbol that emotionally binds a company with the desires and aspirations of its customers – and ultimately 'lovemarks'.[29] He argues that it is not enough for a brand to be just respected.[28]

> Pretty much everything today can be seen in relation to a love–respect axis. You can plot any relationship – with a person, with a brand – by whether it's based on love or based on respect. It used to be that a high respect rating would win. But these days, a high love rating wins. If I don't love what you're offering me, I'm not even interested.

A passionate believer in the concept, Roberts reinforces the point that trustmarks belong to people and that an emotional connection is critical.

Brand proliferation

Another important change is the proliferation of brands and products, in part spurred by the rise in line and brand extensions. As a result, a brand name may now be identified with a number of products of varying degrees of similarity. Marketers of brands such as Coke, Nivea, Dove and Virgin have added a host of products under their brand umbrellas. With so many brands having introduced extensions, there are few single (or 'mono') product brands around, complicating the marketing decisions that have to be made.

Media fragmentation

Another important change is the erosion or fragmentation of advertising media and the emergence of interactive and non-traditional media, promotion and other communication channels. For several reasons, marketers have become disenchanted with traditional advertising media, perhaps especially television.[30, 31]

- *Cost:* the price of advertising media has risen dramatically in many countries. EU countries had become used to a growth in advertising revenues of 3–10 percent for more than 15 years, the average being nearly 7 percent a year and almost 10 pecent for television.
- *Clutter:* earlier, 30-second TV commercials were the norm. Now there are variations of spot duration, multi-spots or 'duo-spots', 'preferential' sites, billboards (spots of short duration linked to a sponsorship contract) and 'DRTV' (direct response TV spots including referral to a call number or a website).
- *Fragmentation:* in relation to the size of the economy, Europe spends far less on television advertising than the USA. One reason for this is that geography and culture make it hard to use a mass media approach except in certain regions. The growth of cable and digital TV make it far cheaper to broadcast on television and erode the former 'giant' channels' shares.
- *Technology:* the increase in remote controls, video recorders and hard disc digital TV boxes – and the resulting zipping, zapping, grazing and channel surfing – has further reduced TV advertising's effectiveness.

For these and other reasons, the percentage of the communication budget devoted to advertising has shrunk over the years. In its place, marketers are spending more on new and emerging forms of communication such as interactive, electronic media; sport and event sponsorship; instore advertising; mini-billboards on buses and trains, on parking meters and in other locations; and product placement in films.

Increased competition

One reason marketers have been forced to use so many financial incentives or discounts is that the marketplace has become more competitive. Both demand-side and supply-side factors have contributed to an increase in competitive intensity. On the demand side, consumption for many products and services has flattened and hit the maturity stage, or even the decline stage, of the product lifecycle. As a result, sales growth for brands can only be achieved at the expense of competing brands by taking away some of their market share. On the supply side, competitors have emerged due to a number of factors, such as the following.

- *Globalization:* although firms have embraced globalization as a means of opening new markets and potential sources of revenue, it has also resulted in an increase in the number of competitors in existing markets, threatening current revenues.
- *Low-priced competitors:* market penetration of generics, own labels or low-priced 'clones' imitating product leaders has increased. Retailers have gained power and often dictate what happens within the shop. Their chief marketing weapon is price, and they have introduced and pushed their own brands and demanded higher returns from trade promotions to stock and display national brands.
- *Brand extensions:* as noted earlier, many companies have taken their brands and launched products with the same name into new categories. Many of these brands provide formidable competition.
- *Deregulation:* certain industries (eg, telecommunications, financial services, healthcare and transport) have become deregulated, leading to increased competition from outside traditionally defined product–market boundaries.

Increased costs

As competition has increased, the cost of introducing and supporting a product has increased rapidly, making it difficult to match the investment and level of support that brands were used to. By 2000, an estimated 30,000 consumer products were being introduced in the USA each year, however at an estimated failure rate of about 93 percent. Given the millions of dollars spent on developing and marketing a new product, the total failure cost was conservatively estimated by one group to exceed €13.7 billion.[32]

Greater accountability

Finally, marketers often find themselves responsible for meeting ambitious short-term profit targets because of financial market pressures and senior management imperatives. Stock analysts value strong and consistent earnings reports as an indication of the long-term financial health of a firm. As a result, marketing managers may find themselves having to make decisions with short-term benefits but long-term costs (eg, cutting advertising expenditures). Moreover, many of these same managers have experienced rapid job turnover and promotions and may not anticipate being in their current positions for very long. These organizational pressures may encourage quick-fix solutions with perhaps adverse long-term consequences.

THE BRAND EQUITY CONCEPT

As the above discussion points out, the complexity of both brand offerings and marketing communication options has significantly increased in recent years. A number of competitive challenges now exist for marketers. Some critics feel that the reaction by many marketers has been ineffective or, even worse, aggravated the problem. The remaining chapters, present theories, models and frameworks that accommodate and reflect these developments in order to provide useful managerial guidelines and suggest promising directions for thought and research. In particular, a 'common denominator' or unified conceptual framework based on the concept of brand equity is introduced as a tool to interpret the potential effects of brand strategies.

One of the most popular and potentially important marketing concepts to arise in the 1980s was the concept of brand equity. The emergence of brand equity, however, has meant both good news and bad news for marketers. The good news is that it has raised the importance of the brand in marketing strategy, which heretofore had been relatively neglected, and provided focus for managerial interest and research activity. The bad news is that the concept has been defined in several ways for a number of purposes, resulting in confusion and even frustration. Through it all, there hasn't been a common viewpoint that has emerged as to how brand equity should be conceptualized and measured.

> Fundamentally, branding is about endowing products and services with the power of brand equity. Although a number of different views of brand equity may prevail, most observers agree that brand equity should be defined in terms of marketing effects uniquely attributable to a brand. That is, brand equity relates to the fact that different outcomes result from marketing a product or service because of its brand than if that same product or service had not been identified by that brand.

> Branding is about creating differences. Most marketing observers also agree with the following principles of branding and brand equity.

- Differences in outcomes arise from the 'added value' endowed to a product as a result of past marketing activity for the brand.
- This value can be created for a brand in many ways.
- Brand equity provides a common denominator for interpreting marketing strategies and assessing the value of a brand.
- There are many ways in which the value of a brand can be manifested or exploited to benefit the firm (ie, in terms of greater proceeds or lower costs or both).

Fundamentally, the brand equity concept stresses the importance of the role of the brand in marketing strategies. The concept of brand equity clearly builds on the principles of brand management. By virtue of the fact that it adapts theory and research advances to address the challenges in brand management created by a changing marketing environment, the concept of brand equity can provide potentially useful insights.

Chapters 2 and 3 provide an important overview of brand equity and a blueprint for the rest of the book. The remainder of the book addresses in much greater depth how to build brand equity (Chapters 4 to 7), measure brand equity (Chapters 8 to 10) and manage brand equity (Chapters 11 to 14). The concluding Chapter 15 provides additional applications and perspectives. The remainder of this chapter provides an overview of the strategic brand management process that helps to pull all of these concepts together.

STRATEGIC BRAND MANAGEMENT PROCESS

Strategic brand management involves the design and implementation of marketing activities to build, measure and manage brand equity. In this text, the *strategic brand management process* is defined as involving four main steps (see Figure 1.10).

1. Identifying and establishing brand positioning.
2. Planning and implementing brand marketing campaigns.
3. Measuring and interpreting brand performance.
4. Growing and sustaining brand equity.

The remainder of this section highlights each of these four steps, which are examined in much more detail in the remainder of the book.[33]

Identifying and establishing brand positioning

The strategic brand management process starts with a clear understanding as to what the brand is to represent and how it should be positioned with respect to competitors (see Chapter 3). Brand positioning can be defined as the 'act of designing the company's offer and image so that it occupies a distinct and valued place in the target customer's mind'. The goal is to locate the brand in the minds of consumers such that the potential benefit to the firm is maximized. Competitive brand positioning is about creating brand superiority in the minds of consumers. Fundamentally,

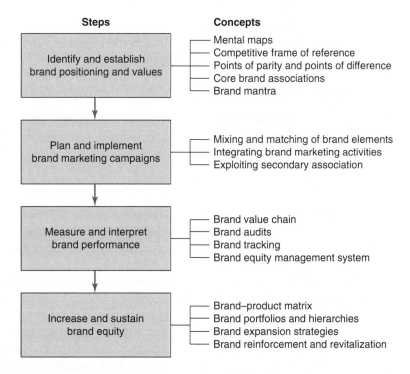

Figure 1.10   Strategic brand management process

Source: © 1996 by Massachusetts Institute of Technology. All rights reserved, Distributed by Tribune Media Services.

positioning involves convincing consumers of the advantages of a brand vis-à-vis competitors (or *points of difference*), while alleviating concerns about any possible disadvantages (establishing *points of parity*).

Positioning also often involves a specification of the appropriate core brand associations and brand mantra. A *mental map* is a visual depiction of the different types of associations that are linked to the brand in the minds of consumers. *Core brand associations* are those sub-sets of associations (attributes and benefits) that best characterize a brand. To focus on what a brand represents, it is often useful to define a brand mantra, also known as a brand essence or core brand promise. A *brand mantra* is a short three- to five-word expression of the most important aspects of a brand and its core brand values. It can be seen as the enduring 'brand DNA' – the most important aspects of the brand to the consumer and the company. Core brand associations, points of parity, points of difference and a brand mantra are thus an articulation of the heart and soul of the brand.

Planning and implementing brand marketing campaigns

As Chapter 2 outlines, building brand equity means creating a brand that consumers are sufficiently aware of and with which they have strong, favourable and unique brand associations. In general, this knowledge-building process will depend on three factors.

1. The initial choices for the brand elements or identities making up the brand and how they are mixed and matched.
2. The marketing activities and supporting marketing campaign and the manner by which the brand is integrated into them.
3. Other associations indirectly transferred to or exploited by the brand as a result of linking it to some other entity (eg, the company, country of origin, channel of distribution or another brand).

Each of the three factors is discussed in turn in Chapters 4–7. Some important considerations are as follows.

Choosing brand elements

A number of options and criteria are relevant for choosing brand elements. As noted above, a brand element is visual or verbal information that serves to identify and differentiate a product. The most common brand elements are names, logos, symbols, characters, packaging and slogans. Brand elements can be chosen to enhance brand awareness or facilitate the formation of strong, favourable and unique brand associations. The best test of the brand-building contribution of brand elements is what consumers would think about the product or service if they only knew about its brand name, associated logo and so forth. Because elements have different advantages, a sub-set or even all of the possible brand elements are often employed. Chapter 4 examines in detail the means by which the choice and design of brand elements can help to build brand equity.

Integrating the brand into marketing activities

Although the judicious choice of brand elements can make some contribution to building brand equity, the primary input comes from the marketing activities related to the brand. Strong, favourable and unique brand associations can be created in a variety of ways by marketing campaigns. This text only highlights some particularly important marketing campaign considerations for building brand equity. Chapter 5 addresses developments in designing marketing campaigns as well as strategy issues of product, pricing strategy and channels. Chapter 6 addresses issues in communications strategy.

Exploiting secondary associations

The third way to build brand equity is to use secondary associations. Brand associations may themselves be linked to other entities that have their own associations, creating secondary brand associations. In other words, a brand association may be created by linking the brand to a memory that conveys meaning to consumers. For example, the brand may be linked to certain source factors, such as the company (through branding strategies), countries or other geographical regions (through identification of product origin) and channels of distribution (through channel strategy), as well as to other brands (through ingredients or co-branding), characters (through licensing), spokespeople (through endorsements), sporting or cultural events (through sponsorship) or other third-party sources (through awards or reviews).

Because the brand becomes identified with another entity, even though this entity may not directly relate to the product or service performance, consumers may *infer* that the brand shares associations with that entity, so producing indirect or secondary associations. In essence, the marketer is borrowing some other associations for the brand to create some associations of the brand's own and so help to build its brand equity. Chapter 7 describes the means of leveraging such brand equity.

Measuring and interpreting brand performance

Determining or evaluating a brand's positioning often benefits from a brand audit. A *brand audit* is a comprehensive examination of a brand involving activities to assess the health of the brand, uncover its sources of equity and suggest ways to improve and exploit that equity. A brand audit requires understanding sources of brand equity from the perspective of both the firm and the consumer. Chapter 3 describes the conceptual foundations of competitive brand positioning and provides guidelines on how to develop such positioning strategies.

Once the brand positioning strategy has been determined, a marketing campaign to create, strengthen or maintain brand associations can be put into place. To understand the effects of such campaigns, it is important to measure and interpret brand performance. A useful tool in that regard is the *brand value chain*. This is a means of tracing the value-creation process for brands to understand better the financial effect of brand marketing expenditures and investments. Chapter 8 describes this planning tool and Chapter 9 and 10 describe a number of measures to operationalize it.

The brand value chain helps to direct marketing research efforts. Profitable brand management requires designing and implementing a brand equity measurement system. A *brand equity measurement system* is a set of research procedures designed to provide timely, accurate and actionable information for marketers so that they can make the best possible tactical decisions in the short run and the best strategic decisions in the long run. As described in Chapter 8, implementing such a system involves two main steps – conducting *brand tracking* and implementing a *brand equity management system*.

Growing and sustaining brand equity

Through the design and implementation of marketing campaigns that capitalize on a well-conceived brand positioning, strong brand leadership positions can be obtained. Maintaining and expanding on that brand equity, however, can be challenging. Brand equity management concerns those activities that take a broader and more diverse perspective of the brand's equity – understanding how branding strategies should reflect corporate concerns and be adjusted, if at all, over time or over geographical boundaries or market segments. Managing brand equity involves managing brands within the context of other brands, as well as managing brands over many categories, over time and across market segments.

Defining the branding strategy

The branding strategy of the firm provides guidelines as to which brand elements to apply across the products it offers. Two tools in defining the corporate branding strategy are the brand–product matrix and the brand hierarchy. The *brand–product matrix* is a graphical representation of all the brands and products sold by the firm. The *brand hierarchy* reveals an explicit ordering of brands by displaying the number and nature of common and distinctive brand components across the firm's products. By capturing the potential branding relationships between the products sold by the firm, a brand hierarchy helps to graphically portray a firm's branding strategy. The *brand portfolio* is the set of brands and brand lines that a firm offers for sale to buyers in a particular category. Chapter 11 reviews issues concerning branding strategies and the concepts of the brand–product matrix, brand hierarchy and brand portfolio. Chapter 12 concentrates on the topic of brand extensions in which an existing brand is used to launch a product in an existing category.

Managing brand equity over time

Effective brand management requires taking a long-term view of marketing decisions. Because consumers' responses to marketing activity depend on what they know and remember about a brand, short-term marketing mix actions, by changing brand knowledge, *necessarily* increase or decrease the success of future marketing actions. A long-term perspective on brand management recognizes that any changes in the supporting marketing campaign for a brand may, by changing consumer knowledge, affect the success of future campaigns. Additionally, a long-term view results in proactive strategies designed to maintain and enhance customer-based brand equity over time in the face of external changes in the marketing environment and internal changes in a firm's marketing goals and activities. Chapter 13 outlines issues related to managing brand equity over time.

Geographic boundaries, cultures and market segments

An important consideration in managing brand equity is recognizing and accounting for different types of consumers in developing branding and marketing campaigns. International issues and global branding strategies are particularly important in these decisions. Chapter 14 examines issues related to broadening of brand equity across market segments. In expanding a brand in this way, it is critical that equity is built by the specific knowledge and behaviours of those market segments.

CHAPTER REVIEW

This chapter began by defining a brand as a name, term, sign, symbol or design or some combination of these elements, intended to identify the goods and services of one seller or group of sellers and to differentiate them from those of competitors. The different components of a brand (ie, name, logo, symbol, packaging design and so forth) are defined as brand elements. Brand elements come in many different forms. A brand is distinguished from a product, which is defined as anything that can be offered to a market for attention, acquisition, use or consumption that might satisfy a need or want. A product may be a physical item, service, shop, person, organization, place or idea.

A brand is a product but one that adds other dimensions that differentiate it in some way from other products designed to satisfy the same need. These differences may be rational and tangible – related to product performance of the brand – or more symbolic, emotional or intangible – related to what the brand represents. Brands themselves are valuable intangible assets that need to be managed carefully. Brands offer benefits to customers and their owners. The key to branding is that consumers perceive differences between brands in a product category. Examples have been provided to show how almost any type of product can be branded by giving the product a name and attaching meaning to it in terms of what the product has to offer and how it differs from competitors. Some branding challenges and opportunities faced by marketing managers were then outlined.

The chapter concluded by introducing the concepts of brand equity and the strategic brand management process and providing an overview of the rest of the book. Brand positioning involves defining and establishing brand vision and positioning. Building brand equity depends on three main factors.

1. The initial choices for the brand elements or identities making up the brand.
2. The way the brand is integrated into the supporting marketing campaign.
3. The associations indirectly transferred to the brand by linking the brand to some other entity (eg, the company, country of origin, channel of distribution, or another brand).

Measuring brand equity requires measuring aspects of the brand value chain and implementing a brand equity measurement system. Managing brand equity concerns those activities that take a broader and more diverse perspective of the brand's equity – understanding how branding strategies should reflect corporate concerns and be adjusted, if at all, over time or over geographical boundaries. Effectively managing brand equity includes defining the corporate branding strategy – by defining the brand hierarchy and brand–product matrix – and devising policy for brand fortification and leverage over time and over geographical boundaries.

Discussion questions

1. What do brands mean to you? What are your favourite brands and why? Check to see how your perceptions of brands might differ from those of others.
2. Who do you think has the strongest brands? Why? What do you think of the *BusinessWeek* list of the 25 strongest brands in Figure 1.5? Do you agree with the rankings? Why or why not?
3. Can you think of anything that cannot be branded? Pick an example that was not discussed in each of the categories provided (services; retailers and distributors; people and organizations; sport, arts and entertainment) and describe how each is a brand.
4. Can you think of yourself as a brand? What do you do to 'brand' yourself?
5. What do you think of the new branding challenges and opportunities that were listed? Can you think of other issues?

References and notes

[1] Interbrand Group, *World's Greatest Brands: An international review*, New York: John Wiley, 1992.
[2] Adrian Room, *Dictionary of Trade Greatest Brands: An international review*, New York: John Wiley, 1992; Adrian Room, *Dictionary of Trade Name Origins*, London: Routledge & Kegan Paul, 1982.
[3] The second to fifth levels are based on a conceptualization in Theodore Levitt, 'Marketing success through differentiation – of anything', *Harvard Business Review*, January–February 1980: 83–91.
[4] Theodore Levitt, 'Marketing myopia', *Harvard Business Review*, July–August 1960: 45–56.
[5] Alvin A. Achenbaum, 'The mismanagement of brand equity', ARF Fifth Annual Advertising and Promotion Workshop, 1 February 1993.
[6] Bruce Nussbaum, 'Get Creative', *BusinessWeek*, 1 August 2005: 61–8.
[7] Jacob Jacoby, Jerry C. Olson and Rafael Haddock, 'Price, brand name and product composition characteristics as determinants of perceived quality', *Journal of Consumer Research*, 1971, 3 (4): 209–16; Jacob Jacoby, George Syzbillo and Jacqueline Busato-Sehach, 'Information acquisition behavior in brand choice situations', *Journal of Marketing Research*, 1977, 11: 63–9.
[8] Susan Fournier, 'Consumers and their brands: developing relationship theory in consumer research', *Journal of Consumer Research*, 1997, 24 (3): 343–73.
[9] Philip Nelson, 'Information and consumer behavior', *Journal of Political Economy*, 1970, 78: 311–29 and Michael R. Darby and Edi Karni, 'Free competition and the optimal amount of fraud', *Journal of Law and Economics*, 1974, 16 (April): 67–88.
[10] Allan D. Shocker and Richard Chay, 'How marketing researchers can harness the power of brand equity', presentation to New Zealand Marketing Research Society, August 1992.
[11] Ted Roselius, 'Consumer ranking of risk reduction methods', *Journal of Marketing*, January 1971, 35: 56–61.
[12] Leslie de Chernatony and Gil McWilliam, 'The varying nature of brands as assets', *International Journal of Advertising*, 1989, 8: 339–49.

[13]Constance E. Bagley, *Managers and the Legal Environment: Strategies for the 21st century*, 2nd edn, St Paul, MN: West Publishing, 1995.

[14]Tulin Erdem and Joffre Swait, 'Brand equity as a signaling phenomenon', *Journal of Consumer Psychology*, 1998, 7 (2): 131–57.

[15]Charles Bymer, 'Valuing your brands: lessons from Wall Street and the impact on marketers', ARF Third Annual Advertising and Promotion Workshop, 5–6 February 1991.

[16]Theodore Levitt, 'Marketing success.'

[17]www.internetworldstats.com; internet usage information comes from data published by Nielsen//NetRatings, by the International Telecommunications Union, by local NICs and other sources.

[18]Lorrie Grant, 'Web sites look to customer service', *USA Today*, Sep 29, 1999.

[19]Julie Schlosser, 'Google', *Fortune*, 31 October 2005: 168–9; Jefferson Graham, 'Google's profit sails past expectations', *USA Today*, 21 October 2005: 1B.

[20]David Lidsky, 'Me Inc.: the rethink', *Fast Company*, March 2005: 16.

[21]University professors are certainly aware of the power of the name as a brand. In fact, one reason why many professors choose to have students identify themselves on exams by student numbers of some type is so that they will not be biased in grading by their knowledge of the student who prepared it. Otherwise, it may be too easy to give higher grades to those students the professor likes or, for whatever reason, expects to have done well in the exam.

[22]Robert P. Parker, 'If you got it flaunt it', ARF Brand Equity Workshop 1994, 15–16 February.

[23]Joel Hochberg, 'Package goods marketing vs. Hollywood', *Advertising Age*, 20 January 1992.

[24]Ben Pappas, 'Star bucks', *Forbes*, 17 May 1999: 53; Gail Schiller, 'Licensed "Star Wars" merchandise to make killing', HollywoodReporter.com, 18 May 2005; Todd Waserman, 'Star Wars: then and now', *Brandweek*, 16 May 2005: 44–6.

[25]Jack Trout, 'Branding can't exist without positioning', *Advertising Age*, 14 March 2005: 28.

[26]Allan D. Shocker, Rajendra Srivastava and Robert Ruekert, 'Challenges and opportunities facing brand management: an introduction to the special issue', *Journal of Marketing Research*, 1994, 31 (May): 149–58.

[27]Kenneth Hein, 'The expectation epidemic', *Brandweek*, 23 May 2005: 34–7.

[28]Alan M. Webber, 'Trust in the future', *Fast Company*, September 2000: 210–20.

[29]Kevin Roberts, *Lovemarks: The future beyond brands*, New York: Powerhouse Books, 2004.

[30]Alvin A. Achenbaum, 'The Implication of price competition on brands, advertising and the economy', ARF Fourth Annual Advertising and Promotion Workshop, 12–13 February 1992. Zipping and zapping refer to the practice of fast-forwarding through ad breaks while watching recorded TV programmes and switching to other channels during commercial breaks while watching live TV programmes. Channel grazing or surfing refers to watching snatches or a few minutes of one programme, then another and so on.

[31]Bruno Liesse, Guy Coeck, Agnès Maqua and Ilse Hendricks, 'Study on the development of new advertising techniques', report for the implementation of the EU directive 'Television without frontiers' for the European Commission, 21 May 2002.

[32]www.bases.com/news/news03052001.html

[33]For discussion of other approaches to branding, see David A. Aaker, *Managing Brand Equity*, New York: Free Press, 1991; David A. Aaker, *Building Strong Brands*, New York: Free Press, 1996; David A. Aaker and Erich Joachimsthaler, *Brand Leadership*, New York: Free Press, 2000; Jean-Noel Kapferer, *Strategic Brand Management*, 2nd edn, New York: Free Press, 2005; Scott M. Davis, *Brand Asset Management*, New York: Free Press, 2000.

2 Customer-based brand equity

PREVIEW

Chapter 1 introduced some basic notions about brands and the role that they have played and are playing in marketing strategies. The chapter concluded by observing that marketers are now faced with an increasing number of tactical options that must be efficiently and effectively applied to an increasing number of product variations for the brand. The concept of brand equity was identified as having the potential to provide guidance to marketers to help them make those decisions. The next few chapters explore brand equity and how to identify and establish an effective brand positioning.

This chapter more formally examines the brand equity concept, introducing one particular view – the concept of customer-based brand equity – that will serve as the organizing framework for the rest of the book.[1] It considers the sources of customer-based brand equity and the outcomes or benefits that result from those sources. The chapter then presents the customer-based brand equity model in detail and discusses the implications of that model. Brand Briefing 2.5 at the end of the chapter provides a detailed overview of the advantages of creating a strong brand. Chapter 3 concentrates on brand positioning.

CUSTOMER-BASED BRAND EQUITY

Two questions often arise regarding brands: 'What makes a brand strong?' and 'How do you build a strong brand?' To answer these questions, this section introduces the customer-based brand equity (CBBE) model. This model incorporates theoretical advances and managerial practices in understanding and influencing consumer behaviour. Although useful perspectives concerning brand equity have been put forth, the CBBE model provides a unique point of view as to what brand equity is and how it should be built, measured and managed.

The CBBE model approaches brand equity from the perspective of the consumer – whether this be an individual or an organization. Understanding the needs and wants of consumers and organizations and devising products and campaigns to satisfy them are at the heart of successful marketing. In particular, two fundamental questions faced by marketers are: 'What do different brands mean to consumers?' and 'How does the brand knowledge of consumers affect their response to marketing activity?'

The basic premise of the CBBE model is that the power of a brand lies in what customers have learned, felt, seen and heard about the brand as a result of their experiences. In other words, *the power of a brand lies in what resides in the minds of customers.* The challenge for marketers in building a strong brand is ensuring that customers have the right type of experiences with products and services and their accompanying marketing campaigns so that the desired thoughts, feelings, images, beliefs, perceptions and opinions become linked to the brand.

Customer-based brand equity is defined as the differential effect that brand knowledge has on consumer response to the marketing of that brand. A brand is said to have positive customer-based brand equity when consumers react more favourably to a product and the way it is marketed when the brand is identified than when it is not (eg, when the product is attributed to a fictitious name or is unnamed). Thus, a brand with positive customer-based brand equity might result in consumers being more accepting of a brand extension, less sensitive to price increases and withdrawal of advertising support or more willing to seek the brand in a new distribution channel. On the other hand, a brand is said to have negative customer-based brand equity if consumers react less favourably to marketing activity for the brand compared with an unnamed or fictitiously named version of the product.

There are three ingredients to this definition:

• differential effect;
• brand knowledge;
• consumer response to marketing.

First, brand equity arises from differences in consumer response. If no differences occur, then the brand name product is essentially a commodity. Competition, most likely, would then be based on price. Second, these differences in response are a result of consumers' knowledge and experience of the brand. Thus, although strongly influenced by the marketing activity of the firm, brand equity ultimately depends on what resides in the minds of consumers. Third, the differential response by consumers that makes up the brand equity is reflected in perceptions, preferences and behaviour related to all aspects of the marketing (eg, choice of a brand, recall of copy points from an ad, actions in response to a sales promotion or evaluations of a proposed brand extension). Brand Briefing 2.5 provides a detailed account of these advantages (Figure 2.1).

The simplest way to illustrate what is meant by customer-based brand equity is to consider some typical results of product sampling or comparison tests. For example, with blind taste tests, one group of consumers samples a product without knowing which brand it is, whereas another group samples the product knowing which brand it is. Invariably, differences arise in the opinions of the two groups even though they are consuming the same product.

For example, Larry Percy reports the results of a beer-tasting that showed how discriminating consumers could be when given the names of the well-known brands of the beer they were drinking, but how few differences consumers could detect when they did not know the brand names. Figure 2.2 displays the perceptual maps – visual

- Improved perceptions of product performance.
- Greater loyalty.
- Less vulnerability to competitive marketing.
- Less vulnerability to crises.
- Larger margins.
- More inelastic consumer response to price increases.
- More elastic consumer response to price decreases.
- Greater trade co-operation and support.
- Increased marketing communication effectiveness.
- Possible licensing opportunities.
- Additional brand extension opportunities.

Figure 2.1 Marketing advantages of strong brands

tools to portray perceptual differences between brands expressed by consumers – that were derived from the two types of responses. As it turns out, even fairly knowledgeable consumers can have difficulty distinguishing different beers (Figure 2.2).

When consumers report different opinions regarding branded and unbranded versions of identical products, it must be the case that knowledge about the brand, created by whatever means (eg, past experiences, marketing activity for the brand or word of mouth), has somehow changed consumers' product perceptions. Examples of branded

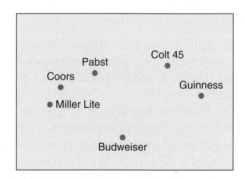

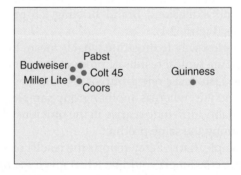

Figure 2.2 Results of blind beer tasting tests: (a) when drinkers are aware of brands used (b) when no brands are mentioned

differences, as with the beer experiment, can be found with most products – conclusive evidence that consumers' perceptions of the performance of a product depend on their impressions of the brand. In other words, clothes may seem to fit better, a car may seem to drive more smoothly and the wait in a bank may seem shorter, depending on the brands involved.

Brand equity as a bridge

So, according to the customer-based brand equity model, the power of a brand lies in the minds of consumers or customers and what they have experienced and learned about the brand over time. Consumer knowledge drives the differences that manifest themselves in terms of brand equity. This realization has important managerial implications. In an abstract sense, according to this view, brand equity provides marketers with a strategic bridge from their past to their future.

Brands as a reflection of the past

Money spent each year on manufacturing and marketing products should not be considered as 'expenses' but as 'investments' – investments in what consumers learned, felt, experienced and so forth about the brand. If not properly designed and implemented, these expenditures may not be good investments, in that the right knowledge structures may not have been created in consumers' minds, but they should be considered investments nonetheless. Thus, the *quality* of the investment is the most critical factor, not necessarily the *quantity*, beyond some minimal threshold. In that sense, it is actually possible to 'overspend' on brand building if money is not being spent wisely. Conversely, as will be evident in this book, some brands that are being considerably outspent by rivals can amass brand equity by judicious spending on marketing activities that create valuable, enduring memories in the minds of consumers.

Brands as a direction for the future

At the same time, the brand knowledge created by these marketing investments dictates appropriate and inappropriate directions for the brand. Consumers will decide, based on their brand beliefs, attitudes and so on, where they think the brand should go and grant permission (or not) to any marketing action or programme. So, at the end of the day, the true value and future prospects of a brand rest with consumers and their knowledge about the brand.

In short, regardless of the definition adopted, the value to marketers of brand equity as a concept depends on how they use it. Brand equity can offer focus and guidance, providing marketers with a means to interpret their marketing performance and help design marketing campaigns. Everything the firm does can enhance or detract from brand equity. Those marketers who build strong brands have embraced the concept and use it to its fullest as a means of clarifying, communicating and implementing their marketing actions. The process of creating such brand power is not without its critics, however, as described in Brand Briefing 2.1. The next section considers the issue of brand knowledge and CBBE in more detail.

Brand Briefing 2.1

No Logo

In her book *No Logo,* Naomi Klein details the aspects of global corporate growth that have led to consumer backlash against brands. She explains the subject of her book as follows:

> The title *No Logo* is not meant to be read as a literal slogan (as in 'No more logos'!), or a post-logo logo (there is already a No Logo clothing line, I'm told). Rather, it is an attempt to capture an anti-corporate attitude I see emerging among many young activists. This book is hinged on a simple hypothesis: that as more people discover the brand-name secrets of the global logo web, their outrage will fuel the next big political movement, a vast wave of opposition squarely targeting those with very high name-brand recognition.

Klein writes about the increasing occupation of free and open space by advertising. The author cites marketing campaigns that exist within schools and universities, among other examples of advertising encroaching on traditionally ad-free space. Klein asserts that as marketers compete for 'eyeballs' using unconventional and unexpected means, fewer ad-free spaces remain and consumer resentment builds. Klein then argues that the vast number of mergers and acquisitions in the past two decades, and the increasing number of brand extensions, has limited consumer choice and engendered consumer resentment. She cautions that an inherent danger of building a strong brand is that the public will be all the more eager to see the brand tarnished once unseemly facts surface.

Klein also details movements that have arisen to protest against the power of large companies and the proliferation of branded space that accompanies this growth. The author highlights such anticorporate practices as 'culture jamming' and 'ad-busting', which serve to subvert and undermine marketing by attacking the marketers on their own terms. Klein also discusses the formation of labour activist organizations such as Essential Action and the International Labour Organization, which perform labour monitoring and hold companies accountable for the treatment of their workers. Klein observes that the issues of corporate conduct are now highly politicized. As a result, Klein notes: 'Political rallies, which once wound their predicable course in front of government buildings and consulates, are now just as likely to take place in front of the stores of the corporate giants.'

Her follow-up book, *Fences and Windows*, reviews newspaper columns written from late 1999 to 2002 covering anti-globalization topics related to corporate behaviour, unions and public protests to summits. *Publishers Weekly* observed:

> The two title images recur throughout: the fences are real, steel cages keeping protesters from interfering with summits, but they are also metaphorical, such as the 'fence' of poverty that prevents the poor from receiving adequate

> ## Brand Briefing 2.1 *continued*
>
> education or healthcare. Klein argues that globalization has only delivered its promised benefits to the world's wealthiest citizens and that its emphasis on privatization has eroded the availability of public services around the globe.
>
> Sources: Naomi Klein, *No Logo: Taking aim at the brand bullies,* New York: Picador, 1999; Naomi Klein, *Fences and Windows: Dispatches from the front lines of the globalization debate,* New York: Picador, 2002; Review, *Publishers Weekly,* 2002.

MAKING A BRAND STRONG: BRAND KNOWLEDGE

From the perspective of the CBBE model, brand knowledge is the key to creating brand equity, because it creates the differential effect that drives brand equity. What marketers need, then, is an insightful way to represent how brand knowledge exists in consumer memory. An influential model of memory developed by psychologists is helpful in that regard.[2] *The associative network memory model* views memory as a network of nodes and links, in which nodes represent stored information or concepts and links represent the strength of association between this information or concepts. Any type of information can be stored in the memory network, including information that is verbal, visual, abstract or contextual in nature.

Consistent with the associative network memory model, brand knowledge is conceptualized here as consisting of a brand node in memory with a variety of associations linked to it. In particular, brand knowledge can be characterized in terms of two components: awareness and image. Brand awareness is related to the strength of the brand node or trace in memory, as reflected by consumers' ability to identify the brand under different conditions.[3] *Brand awareness* is a necessary, but not always sufficient, step in building brand equity. Other considerations, such as the image of the brand, often come into play.

Brand image has long been recognized as an important concept.[4] Although there has not always been agreement on how to measure brand image,[5] one generally accepted view is that, consistent with an associative network memory model, *brand image* can be defined as perceptions about a brand as reflected by the brand associations held in consumer memory.[6] In other words, brand associations are the other informational nodes linked to the brand node in memory and contain the meaning of the brand for consumers. Associations come in all forms and may reflect characteristics of the product or aspects independent of the product itself.

For example, consider Apple computers. If someone asked you what came to mind when you thought of them, what might you say? You might reply with associations such as 'user-friendly', 'creative', 'for desktop publishing', 'used at many

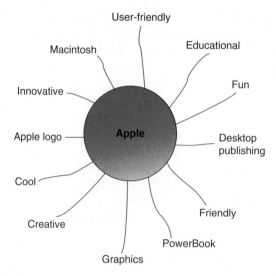

Figure 2.3   Possible Apple computer associations

schools' and so forth. Figure 2.3 shows some common associations for Apple computers among consumers. The associations that came to mind for you would make up your brand image for Apple. Through marketing, Apple has been able to achieve a rich brand image in the minds of some consumers. Different consumers might think of different associations for Apple, although many associations are likely to be shared by a majority of consumers. In that sense, one can refer to 'the' brand image of Apple, but at the same time, it must be recognized that this image may vary, perhaps even considerably, depending on the consumers or market segments involved.

Other brands, of course, will be characterized by a different set of associations. For example, McDonald's marketing campaign attempts to create brand associations in consumers' minds with 'quality', 'service', 'cleanliness' and 'value'. The company's rich brand image probably also includes strong associations to 'Ronald McDonald', 'golden arches', 'for kids' and 'convenient', as well as perhaps potentially negative associations such as 'fast food'. Coca-Cola's marketing campaign strives to link brand associations in consumers' minds with 'refreshment', 'taste', 'availability', 'affordability' and 'accessibility'. Whereas Mercedes-Benz has achieved strong associations with 'performance' and 'status', Volvo has created a strong association with 'safety'. Chapter 3 reviews the types of associations that can become linked with the brand. Chapter 9 outlines research techniques to measure these associations.

SOURCES OF BRAND EQUITY

What causes brand equity to exist? How do marketers create brand equity? Customer-based brand equity occurs when the consumer has a high level of awareness and familiarity with the brand and holds some strong, favourable and unique brand associations in memory. In some cases, brand awareness alone is sufficient to result in a more favourable consumer response – for example, in low-involvement decision settings where consumers are willing to base their choices merely on familiar brands. In most other cases, however, the strength, favourability and uniqueness of the brand associations play a critical role in determining the differential response making up the brand equity. If the brand is perceived by consumers to be the same as a representative version of the product or service in the category, then consumer response to marketing for the brand would not be expected to vary from when the marketing is attributed to a fictitiously named or unnamed product or service. If the brand has some salient, unique associations, then consumer responses should differ.

For branding strategies to create brand equity, consumers must be convinced that there are meaningful differences between brands. The key to branding is that consumers must not think that all brands in the category are the same. Thus, establishing a high level of brand awareness and a positive brand image in consumer memory – in terms of strong, favourable and unique brand associations – produces the knowledge structures that can affect consumer response and produce different types of customer-based brand equity.

Brand awareness

Brand awareness consists of brand recognition and brand recall performance. *Brand recognition* relates to consumers' ability to confirm exposure to the brand when given the brand as a cue. In other words, brand recognition requires that consumers can correctly discriminate the brand as having been seen or heard before. For example, when consumers go to a shop, is it the case that they will be able to recognize the brand as one to which they have been exposed? *Brand recall* relates to consumers' ability to retrieve the brand from memory when given the product category, the needs fulfilled by the category or a purchase or usage situation as a cue. So, brand recall requires that consumers correctly generate the brand from memory when given a relevant cue. For example, recall of Kellogg's Corn Flakes will depend on consumers' ability to retrieve the brand when they think of the cereal category or of what they should eat for breakfast or eat for a snack at the shop (when making a purchase), at home (when making a consumption choice) or wherever.

If research reveals that consumer decisions are made at the point of purchase, where the brand name, logo, packaging and so on will be visible, then brand recognition will be important. If research reveals that consumer decisions are mostly made in settings away from the point of purchase, on the other hand, then brand recall will be more important. As a cautionary note, even though brand recall itself may be viewed as less important when consumer decisions are made at the point of purchase, consumers' brand evaluations and choices will still often depend on what else they recall about the brand given that they are able to recognize it there.

As is the case with most information in memory, it is generally easier to recognize a brand than it is to recall it from memory. The relative importance of brand recall and recognition will depend on the extent to which consumers make product-related decisions with the brand present or not.[7] For example, if decisions are made in the shop, brand recognition may be more important because the product will be present. Outside the shop or in any situation where the brand is not present, on the other hand, it is probably more important that the consumer be able to recall the brand from memory.

For this reason, brand recall is critical for service and online brands: consumers must seek the brand and therefore be able to retrieve it from memory when appropriate.

Consequences of brand awareness

Brand awareness plays an important role in consumer decision-making for three main reasons.

Learning advantages The first way that brand awareness affects decision-making is by influencing the formation and strength of the brand associations that make up the brand image. A necessary condition for the creation of a brand image is that a brand node has been established in memory. The nature of that brand node should affect how easily different kinds of information can become attached to the brand in memory as brand associations. The first step in building brand equity is to register the brand in the minds of consumers, and the choice of brand elements may make that task easier or more difficult, as described in Chapter 4.

Consideration advantages Second, raising brand awareness increases the likelihood that the brand will be a member of the *consideration set*, the handful of brands that receive serious consideration for purchase.[8] Research has shown that consumers are rarely loyal to a single brand but instead have a set of brands that they would consider buying and another – possibly smaller – set of brands that they actually buy regularly. Because consumers typically only consider a few brands for purchase, making sure that a brand is in the consideration set is likely to exclude other brands. Research in psychology on 'part-list cuing effects' has shown that recall of some information can inhibit recall of other information.[9] In a marketing context, that means if a consumer thinks of going to Burger King for a quick lunch, he or she may be less likely to think of going to another fast food chain.[10]

Choice advantages Third, brand awareness can affect choices between brands in the consideration set, even if there are essentially no other associations to those brands.[11] For example, consumers have been shown to adopt a decision rule to buy only more familiar, well-established brands in some cases.[12] Thus, in low-involvement decision settings, a minimum level of brand awareness may be sufficient for product choice, even in the absence of a well-formed attitude.[13] One influential model of attitude change and persuasion, the elaboration-likelihood model, is consistent with the notion that consumers may make choices based on brand awareness considerations when they have low involvement.

Low involvement results when consumers lack either purchase motivation (eg, when consumers don't care about the product or service) or purchase ability (eg, when consumers do not know anything else about the brands in a category).[14]

1. *Consumer purchase motivation:* although products and brands may be critical to marketers, to many consumers in many categories, choosing a brand is not a life-or-death decision. For example, despite the sums spent on TV advertising to persuade consumers of product differences, one survey showed that 40 percent of consumers believed all brands of petrol were about the same or did not know which brand was best. A lack of perceived differences between brands in a category is likely to lead to consumers who are unmotivated regarding the brand choice process.

2. *Consumer purchase ability:* consumers of some products do not have the knowledge or experience to be able to judge product quality. The obvious examples are products with a high degree of technical sophistication (eg, telecommunications equipment involving state-of-the-art features). Yet, there are instances with seemingly less complicated products of consumers still maybe lacking the ability to judge quality. Consider a college student who has not really had to cook or clean before roaming the supermarket aisles for the first time, or a manager forced to make an expensive capital purchase for the first time. The reality is that quality is often difficult to judge without experience and expertise. In such cases, consumers will use whatever shortcut they can come up with to make their decisions. At times, they may end up simply choosing the brand with which they are most familiar.

Establishing brand awareness

In the abstract, brand awareness is created by increasing the familiarity of a brand through repeated exposure, although this is generally more effective for brand recognition than for brand recall. That is, the more a consumer 'experiences' the brand by seeing it, hearing it or thinking about it, the more likely it is that the brand will become strongly registered in memory. Thus, anything that causes consumers to experience a brand name, logo, packaging or slogan can potentially increase familiarity and awareness of that brand element. Examples include advertising and promotion, sponsorship and event marketing, publicity and public relations and outdoor advertising. Moreover, it is important to visually and verbally reinforce the brand name with a full complement of brand elements (eg, in addition to its name, Cadbury's uses its handwritten logo and the colour purple to enhance consumer awareness in many ways).

Although brand repetition increases the strength of the brand node in memory, and thus its recognizability, improving recall of a brand requires linkages in memory to appropriate product categories or other situational purchase or consumption cues. In particular, to build awareness, it is often desirable to develop a slogan or jingle that creatively pairs the brand and the appropriate category or purchase or consumption cues (and, ideally, the brand positioning as well, in terms of building a positive brand image). Additional use can be made of the other brand elements – logos, symbols, characters and packaging.

The manner by which the brand and its corresponding product category are paired (eg, as with an advertising slogan) will be influential in determining the strength of product category links. For brands with strong category associations (eg, Toyota cars), the distinction between brand recognition and recall may not matter much – consumers thinking of the category are likely to think of the brand. For brands that may not have the same level of initial category awareness (eg, in competitive markets or when the brand is new to the category), it is more important to emphasize category links in the marketing campaign. Moreover, as will be discussed in Chapter 11, strongly linking the brand to the proper category or other relevant cues may become especially important over time if the product meaning of the brand changes (eg, through brand extensions or mergers or acquisitions).

Many marketers have attempted to create brand awareness through 'shock' advertising with bizarre themes.[15] For example, at the height of the dotcom boom, online retailer Outpost.com used ads featuring gerbils shot through cannons, wolverines attacking marching bands and toddlers having the brand name tattooed on their fore-heads. The problem with such approaches is that they invariably fail to create strong category links because the product is not prominent enough, so inhibiting recall. They also can generate ill-will in the process. Often coming across as desperate measures, they rarely provide a foundation for long-term brand equity. In the case of Outpost.com, most potential customers did not have a clue what the company did.

In short, brand awareness is created by increasing the familiarity of the brand through repeated exposure (for brand recognition) and strong associations with the appropriate product category or other relevant purchase or consumption cues (for brand recall).[16]

Brand image

A positive brand image is created by marketing campaigns that link strong, favourable and unique associations to the brand in memory. The definition of cus-tomer-based brand equity does not distinguish between the source of brand associa-tions and the manner in which they are formed; all that matters is the resulting favourability, strength and uniqueness of brand associations. This realization has im-portant implications for building brand equity. Besides marketer-controlled sources of information, brand associations can also be created in a variety of other ways: by direct experience; from information communicated about the brand from the firm or other sources (eg, magazine reviews or other media) and word of mouth; and by as-sumptions or inferences from the brand itself (eg, its name or logo) or from the iden-tification of the brand with a company, country, channel of distribution or some particular person, place or event.

Marketers should recognize the influence of these other sources of information by both managing them as well as possible and adequately accounting for them in designing communication strategies. Consider how The Body Shop was able to build its brand equity.

The Body Shop
The Body Shop created a global brand image without using conventional adver-tising. Strong associations with personal care and environmental concern oc-curred through its products (natural ingredients only, never tested on animals, etc.), packaging (simple, refillable, recyclable), merchandising (detailed point-of-sale posters, brochures and displays), staff (encouraged to be enthusiastic and informed about environmental issues), sourcing policies (using small local pro-ducers from around the world), social action (requiring each franchisee to run a local community group) and public relations and activities (taking visible and sometimes outspoken stands on various issues).

Strength of brand associations

Making sure that associations are linked strongly to the brand will depend on how the marketing campaign and other factors affect consumers' brand experiences. Associations will vary in the strength of their connection to the brand node. Strength is a function of both the amount, or quantity, of processing that information receives as well as the nature, or quality, of that processing. The more deeply a person thinks about product information and relates it to existing brand knowledge, the stronger the resulting brand associations. Two factors facilitating such strength of association are the relevance of the information and the consistency with which this information is presented over time. The particular associations that are recalled and salient will depend not only on the strength of association, but also on the context in which the brand is considered and the retrieval cues that are present that can serve as reminders. This section considers the factors that, in general, affect the strength and recallability of a brand association. Chapters 4 to 7 provide more concrete guidelines.

As noted earlier, consumer beliefs about brand attributes and benefits can be formed in different ways. *Brand attributes* are those descriptive features that characterize a product or service. *Brand benefits* are the personal value and meaning that consumers attach to the product or service attributes. In general, the source of information creating the strongest brand attribute and benefit associations is direct experience. This type of information can be particularly influential in consumers' product decisions, as long as consumers are able to interpret their experiences accurately. Word of mouth or other non-commercial sources of information (consumer organizations, the press, etc.) can also create strong associations. Word of mouth is likely to be particularly important for restaurants, entertainment, banking and personal services. Commercial sources of information, such as advertising, are likely to create the weakest associations and thus may be the most easily changed. Figure 2.4 shows how consumers evaluate the importance of different reasons for brand choice.

To overcome this hurdle, marketing communication campaigns attempt to create strong brand associations and recalled communication effects through a variety of means. These include using creative communications that cause consumers to elaborate on brand-related information and relate it appropriately to existing knowledge; exposing consumers to communications repeatedly over time; and ensuring that many retrieval cues are present as reminders. Chapter 6 reviews how integrated marketing communication campaigns can contribute to brand equity. Regardless,

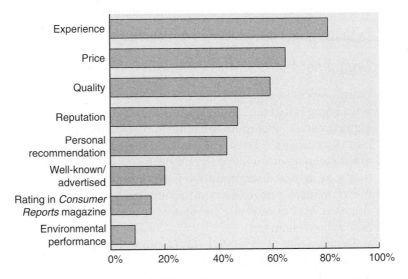

Figure 2.4 Consumer reasons for brand choice in the USA

Source: GfK Roper Reports US, 2004. Figure shows percentage agreement with the statement, 'In deciding whether to buy certain brands of a product, which of the things on this list are most important to you in deciding to buy a brand or not?'

the entire marketing campaign and all activities related to the brand will affect the strength of brand associations. Starbucks, Google, Red Bull and Amazon.com are examples of companies that created rich brand images without intensive advertising.

Favourability of brand associations

Choosing which favourable and unique associations to link to a brand requires analysis of the consumer and competitors to determine the optimal positioning for a brand. Chapter 3 reviews considerations involved in positioning and creating strong, favourable and unique brand associations. In the most basic sense, favourable brand associations are created by convincing consumers that the brand possesses attributes and benefits that satisfy their needs and wants, such that they form positive overall brand judgements. Thus, favourable associations for a brand are those associations that are desirable to consumers and are successfully delivered by the product and conveyed by the supporting marketing campaign (eg, such that the brand is seen as highly convenient, reliable, effective, efficient, colourful and so on).

In terms of desirability, how important or valued is the image association to the brand attitudes and decisions made by consumers? *Desirability* depends on three factors.

- How *relevant* consumers find the brand association.
- How *distinctive* consumers find the brand association.
- How *believable* consumers find the brand association.

Creating a favourable association also requires that the firm be able to deliver on the desired association. In terms of deliverability, the question is: what would be the cost or investment necessary and the length of time involved to create or change the desired association(s)? *Deliverability* also depends on three factors.

- The actual or potential ability of the product to perform.
- The prospects of communicating that performance.
- The sustainability of the actual and communicated performance over time.

Desirability and deliverability are examined in Chapter 3.

Uniqueness of brand associations

Brand associations may or may not be shared with competing brands. The essence of positioning is that the brand has a sustainable competitive advantage or 'unique selling proposition' that gives consumers a compelling reason why they should buy that particular brand.[17] These differences may be communicated explicitly by making direct comparisons with competitors or may be highlighted implicitly. Furthermore, they may be based on product-related or non-product-related attributes or benefits. In fact, in many categories, non-product-related attributes, such as user type or usage situation, may more easily create unique associations (eg, the rugged Western image of Marlboro cigarettes).

The existence of strongly held, favourably evaluated associations that are unique to the brand and imply superiority over other brands is critical to a brand's success. Yet, unless the brand faces no competition, it is likely to share associations with other brands. Shared associations can help to establish category membership and define the scope of competition with other products and services.[18]

Research on non-comparable options suggests that even if a brand does not face direct competition in its product category, and so does not share product-related attributes with other brands, it can still share more abstract associations and face indirect competition in a more broadly defined product category.[19] Thus, although one train service may not compete directly with another, it competes indirectly with other forms of transport, such as airlines, cars and buses. A maker of educational software may be implicitly competing with other forms of education and entertainment, such as books, videos, television and magazines. For these reasons, branding principles are now being used to market a number of different categories as a whole – for example, banks, furniture, carpets, bowling and trains.

A product or service category can also be characterized by a set of associations that includes specific beliefs about any member in the category, as well as overall attitudes towards all members in the category. These beliefs might include many of the relevant product-related attributes for brands in the category, as well as more descriptive attributes that do not necessarily relate to product or service performance (eg, the colour of a product, such as red for ketchup). Certain attributes or benefits may be considered prototypical and essential to all brands in the category, and a specific brand may exist that is considered to be an exemplar and most representative of the product or service category.[20] For example, consumers might expect a running shoe to provide support and comfort and to be built well enough to withstand repeated wear, and they may believe that Reebok or Adidas best represents a running shoe. Similarly, consumers might expect a web retailer to offer easy navigation, a variety of offerings, reasonable shipping options, secure purchase procedures, responsive customer service and strict privacy guidelines, and they may consider Amazon.co.uk to be the best example of an online retailer.

Because the brand is linked to the product category, some category associations may become linked to the brand, either in terms of specific beliefs or overall attitudes. Product category attitudes can be a particularly important determinant of consumer response. For example, if a consumer thinks that all brokers are greedy, then he or she probably will have similarly unfavourable beliefs about and negative attitudes towards any particular brokerage house simply by virtue of its membership of the category. Thus, in almost all cases, some product category associations that are linked to the brand will also be shared with other brands in the category. Note that the strength of the brand associations to the product category is an important determinant of brand awareness.[21]

In short, to create the differential response that leads to customer-based brand equity, it is important that some of the strongly held brand associations are not only favourable but also unique. Unique brand associations are not shared with competing brands. Beliefs about unique attributes and benefits for brands that consumers value more favourably than competitive brands can lead to a greater likelihood of the consumers choosing the former brands.

Not all brand associations will be deemed important and viewed favourably by consumers, nor will they be equally valued across different purchase or consumption situations. Moreover, not all brand associations will be relevant and valued in a purchase or consumption decision. The evaluations of brand associations may be situation- or context-dependent and vary according to the particular goals that consumers have in that purchase or consumption decision.[22] An association may be valued in one situation but not another.[23]

For example, the associations that might come to mind for FedEx, an overnight delivery service, might be 'fast', 'dependable' and 'convenient', with 'purple and white packages and envelopes'. Even though it is a strong brand association, the colour of the packaging may matter little to most consumers when choosing a delivery service, although it may play an important brand awareness function. On the other hand, fast, dependable and convenient service may be more important in consumer choice, but even then only in certain situations. It may be that someone desires those benefits only when meeting an important deadline. If a consumer only needs a delivery 'as soon as possible', then it may be that other less expensive options would be considered.

Chapter 3 considers additional aspects of strength, favourability and uniqueness of brand associations in terms of brand positioning and introduces the concepts of points of parity and points of difference more formally. The next section outlines a more complete version of the customer-based brand equity model.

FOUR STEPS TO BUILDING A BRAND

The previous section considered what makes a strong brand. This section considers how a strong brand is built or created. According to the CBBE model, this can be thought of in terms of a sequence of steps, with each one contingent on achieving the previous step. All the steps involve accomplishing certain objectives with customers, both existing and potential. The steps are as follows.

1. Identify the brand with customers and associate the brand in customers' minds with a specific product class or customer need.
2. Establish the totality of brand meaning in the minds of customers by strategically linking a host of tangible and intangible brand associations with certain properties.
3. Elicit the proper customer responses to this brand identification and brand meaning.
4. Convert brand response to create an intense, active loyalty relationship between customers and the brand.

These steps address fundamental questions that customers invariably ask about brands – at least implicitly if not even explicitly – as follows (with corresponding brand steps in parentheses).

1. Who are you? (Brand identity.)
2. What are you? (Brand meaning.)
3. What about you? What do I think or feel about you? (Brand responses.)
4. What about you and me? What kind of association and how much of a connection would I like to have with you? (Brand relationships.)

There is an obvious ordering of the steps in this 'branding ladder', from identity to meaning to responses to relationships. That is, meaning cannot be established unless identity has been created; responses cannot occur unless the right meaning has been developed; and a relationship cannot be forged unless the proper responses have been elicited.

Brand building blocks

Performing the four steps to create the right brand identity, brand meaning, brand responses and brand relationship is a difficult process. To provide structure, it is useful to think of sequentially establishing six 'brand building blocks' with customers. To connote the sequencing involved, these brand building blocks can be assembled as a brand pyramid. Creating brand equity involves reaching the pinnacle of the CBBE brand pyramid and will only occur if the right building blocks are put into place. The corresponding brand steps represent different levels of the CBBE brand pyramid. This brand-building process is illustrated in Figures 2.5 and 2.6. Each of these steps and corresponding brand building blocks and their sub-dimensions are examined in the following sections.

Brand salience

Achieving the right brand identity involves creating brand salience with customers. *Brand salience* relates to aspects of the awareness of the brand – for example, how often and easily the brand is evoked under various situations or circumstances. To what extent is the brand easily recalled or recognized? What types of cues or reminders are necessary? How pervasive is this brand awareness?

As defined previously, brand awareness refers to customers' ability to recall and recognize the brand, as reflected by their ability to identify the brand. In other words,

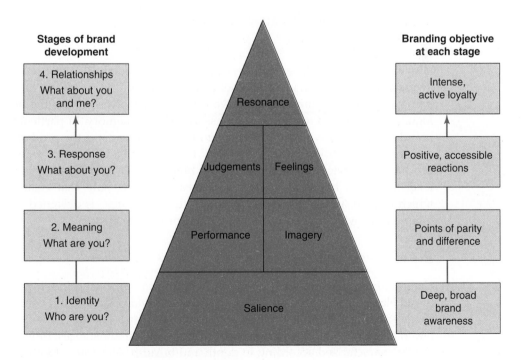

Figure 2.5   Customer-based brand equity pyramid

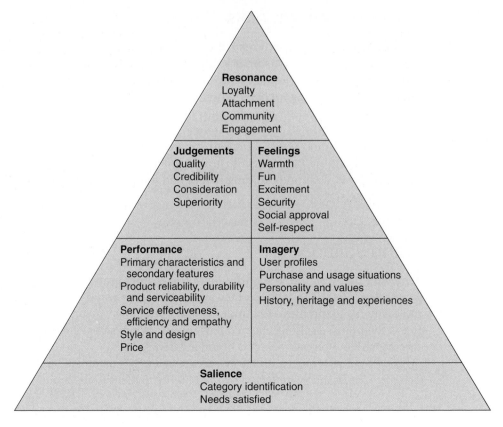

Figure 2.6   Sub-dimensions of brand building blocks

how well do the brand elements serve the function of identifying the product? Brand awareness is more than just customers knowing the brand name and having seen it, perhaps even many times. Brand awareness also involves linking the brand name, logo, symbol and so forth to certain associations in memory. In particular, building brand awareness involves helping customers to understand the product or service category in which the brand competes. There must be clear links regarding what products or services are sold under the brand name. At a broader, more abstract level, however, brand awareness also means making sure that customers know which of their 'needs' the brand, through these products, is designed to satisfy. In other words, what functions does the brand provide to customers?

Breadth and depth of awareness

Creating brand awareness thus involves giving the product an identity by linking brand elements to a product category and associated purchase and consumption or usage situations. From a strategic standpoint, it is important to have high levels of brand awareness under a variety of conditions and circumstances. Brand awareness can be characterized according to depth and breadth. The *depth* of brand awareness concerns the likelihood that a brand element will come to mind and the ease with which it does so. For example, a brand that can be easily recalled has a deeper level of brand awareness than one that only can be recognized. The *breadth* of brand awareness concerns the range of purchase and usage situations in which the brand element comes to mind. The breadth of brand awareness depends to a large extent on the organization of brand and product knowledge in memory.[24] To illustrate some of the issues involved, consider the breadth and depth of brand awareness for Tropicana orange juice.

Tropicana

At the most basic level, it is necessary that consumers recognize the Tropicana brand when it is presented or exposed to them. Beyond that, consumers should think of Tropicana whenever they think of orange juice, particularly when they are considering a purchase in that category. Additionally, consumers ideally would think of Tropicana whenever they were deciding which type of drink to have, especially when seeking a 'tasty but healthy' drink – some of the needs presumably satisfied by orange juice. Thus, consumers must think of Tropicana in terms of satisfying a certain set of needs whenever those needs arise. One of the challenges for any provider of orange juice in that regard is to link the product to usage situations outside of the traditional breakfast usage situation – hence the campaign to boost consumption of orange juice that used the slogan 'It's not just for breakfast any more.'

Product category structure

As suggested by the Tropicana example, to fully understand brand recall, it is important to appreciate *product category structure,* or how product categories are organized in memory. Typically, marketers assume that products are grouped at varying levels of specificity and can be organized in a hierarchical fashion.[25] Thus, in consumers' minds, a product hierarchy often exists, with product class information at the highest level, product category information at the second highest level, product type information at the next level and brand information at the lowest level.

The drinks market provides a good setting to examine issues in category structure and the effects of brand awareness on brand equity. Figure 2.7 shows one possible hierarchy that might exist in consumers' minds. According to this representation, consumers first distinguish between flavoured or unflavoured drinks (ie, water). Next, they distinguish between non-alcoholic and alcoholic drinks. Non-alcoholic drinks are distinguished in consumers' minds by whether they are hot (eg, coffee or tea) or cold (eg, milk, juices or soft drinks); alcoholic drinks are distinguished by whether they are wine, beer or distilled spirits. Even further distinctions are possible. For example, the beer category could be further divided into no-alcohol, low-alcohol and full-strength beers. Full-strength beers can be further distinguished, by variety (eg, bitter or lager), by brewing method (eg, draught, ice or dry), by price and quality (eg, discount, premium or super-premium) and so on.

The organization of the product category hierarchy that generally prevails in memory will play an important role in consumer decision-making. For example, consumers often make decisions in what could be considered a top-down fashion. Based on this simple representation, a consumer would first decide whether to have water

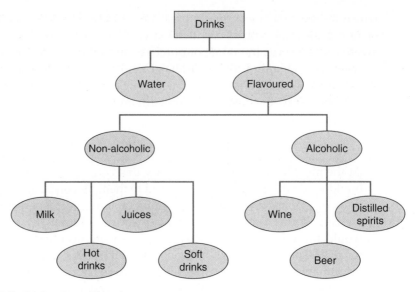

Figure 2.7   Drinks category hierarchy

or a flavoured drink. If the consumer chose a flavoured drink, then the next decision would be whether or not to have an alcoholic or non-alcoholic drink and so on. Finally, consumers might then choose a particular brand within a particular product category or product type in which they are interested. The depth of brand awareness would then relate to the likelihood that a brand came to mind, whereas the breadth of brand awareness would relate to the situations in which the brand might come to mind. In general, soft drinks have great breadth of awareness in that they come to mind in many consumption situations. Other drinks, such as alcoholic ones, milk and juices, have more limited consumption situations.

Strategic implications

Understanding the product hierarchy has implications for how to improve brand awareness, as well as how to position the brand (as will be addressed in Chapter 3). In terms of building awareness, in many cases, it is not only the depth of awareness that matters but also the breadth and linking the brand to various categories and cues in consumers' minds. In other words, it is important that the brand not only be top-of-mind and have sufficient 'mind share', but it must also do so at the right times and places. Breadth is an oft-neglected consideration, even for brands that are category leaders. For many brands, the question is not whether consumers can recall the brand but where and when they think of the brand, and how easily and often they think of the brand. In particular, many brands and products are ignored or forgotten during possible usage situations. As Chapter 13 shows, increasing the salience of the brand in those settings can drive consumption and increase sales volume. For example, US tax returns preparer H&R Block launched a campaign that attempted to establish the company in the minds of consumers as a 'year-round financial services provider' that could provide help with mortgages, insurance, investments, banking and financial planning services at any time.[26]

In some cases, the best route for improving sales is not by improving consumer attitudes towards a brand but by increasing the breadth of brand awareness and situations in which consumers would consider using the brand. Consider the marketing challenges for milk consumption in Europe.

Defending milk sales in Europe

Milk consumption has been in decline throughout the Western world for many years. Northern European countries have traditionally been the heaviest users of milk, while southern Europe has had a larger share of its dairy intake from cheese. Regardless of national differences, the trend has been a steady decline in milk consumption. During these years of decline, many attempts have been made to counter the trend. Typically, these have focused on the health benefits of milk over other drinks – for instance, that milk is high in calcium content which supposedly means it is good for bones. Still, the decline in milk consumption has continued. In more recent years, it seems dairy companies have shifted their focus from creating or reinforcing favourable associations with milk to inventing niche products and different usage occasions. Now, there is milk specifically for expectant mothers in Portugal and Switzerland has a vitamin-enriched, flavoured milk where egg has been added. Another innovation, 'night-time milk' or melatonin-enhanced milk (melatonin is a hormone which in this way supposedly helps you go to sleep), has been introduced in many European markets under different labels. Milk reinforced with Omega-3 exists in Italy and Ireland, effectively making the milk a vitamin supplement rather than a just a drink. Another innovation is flavoured milk for 'on-the-go' consumption, competing with Cola and other soft drinks. Finally, there is milk consumed with cereals and coffee, such as the café latte trend, which helps put milk in the fridges of people who would otherwise have stopped drinking it. Although product innovation and launches are risky, the dairy industry has found that it often pays to invent usage occasions rather than to reinforce an already favourable set of associations.[27]

In other words, it may be harder to try to *change* brand attitudes than to *remind* people of their existing attitudes towards a brand in additional, but appropriate, consumption situations.

Summary

A salient brand is one that has both depth and breadth of brand awareness, so that customers always make sufficient purchases as well as always think of the brand across a variety of settings in which it could possibly be employed or consumed. Salience is an important first step in building brand equity, but is usually not sufficient. For many customers in many situations, other considerations, such as the meaning or image of the brand, come into play. Creating brand meaning involves establishing a brand image and what the brand is characterized by and should stand for in the minds of customers. Although a myriad of different types of brand associations are possible, brand meaning broadly can be distinguished in terms of more functional, performance-related considerations versus more abstract, imagery-related considerations. Thus, brand meaning is made up of two categories of associations that exist in customers' minds related to performance and imagery, with a set of specific sub-categories within each. These associations can be formed directly (from a customer's experiences and contact with the brand) or indirectly (through the depiction of the brand in advertising or by some other source of information, such as word of mouth). The next section describes the two main types of brand meaning – brand performance and brand imagery – and the sub-categories within each.

Brand performance

The product itself is at the heart of brand equity, because it is the primary influence on what consumers experience with a brand, what they hear about a brand from others and what the brand owner can tell customers about the brand. Designing and delivering a product that satisfies consumer needs and wants is a prerequisite for successful marketing, regardless of whether the product is a tangible good, service, organization or person. To create brand loyalty and resonance, consumers' experiences with the product must at least meet, if not surpass, their expectations. As Chapter 1 noted, studies have shown that high-quality brands tend to perform better financially.

Brand performance relates to the ways in which a product or service attempts to meet customers' more functional needs. As such, it refers to the intrinsic properties of the brand in terms of inherent product or service characteristics. How well does a brand rate on objective assessments of quality? To what extent does it satisfy utilitarian, aesthetic and economic customer needs and wants in the product or service category?

Brand performance transcends the ingredients and features that make up the product or service to encompass aspects of the brand that augment these characteristics. Any of these performance dimensions can serve as a means by which the brand is differentiated. Often, the strongest brand positioning involves performance advantages of some kind, and it is rare that a brand can overcome severe deficiencies. The specific performance attributes and benefits making up functionality will vary widely by category. Nevertheless, there are five important types of attributes and benefits that often underlie brand performance.[28]

1. Primary ingredients and supplementary features.
2. Product reliability, durability and serviceability.
3. Service effectiveness, efficiency and empathy.
4. Style and design.
5. Price.

Customers often have beliefs about the levels at which the primary ingredients of the product operate (eg, low, medium, high or very high). Additionally, they may have beliefs as to special, perhaps even patented, features or secondary elements of a product that complement these primary ingredients. Thus, some attributes are essential ingredients necessary for a product to work, whereas others are supplementary features that allow for customization and more versatile, personalized use. These types of attributes vary by product or service category.

As noted earlier, customers can view the performance of products or services in a broad manner. *Reliability* refers to the consistency of performance over time and from purchase to purchase. *Durability* refers to the expected economic life of the product. *Serviceability* refers to the ease of servicing the product if it needs repair. Thus, perceptions of product performance are affected by factors such as the speed, accuracy and care of delivery and installation; the promptness, courtesy and helpfulness of customer service and training; and the quality of repair service and the time involved.

Customers often have performance-related associations that stem from the service interactions they have with brands. Along those lines, *service effectiveness* refers to how completely the brand satisfies customers' service requirements. *Service efficiency* refers to the manner in which these services are delivered in terms of speed, responsiveness and so forth. Finally, *service empathy* refers to the extent to which service providers are seen as trusting, caring and having the customer's interests in mind.

Consumers may have associations with a product that go beyond its functional aspects to more aesthetic considerations, such as its size, shape, materials and colour. Thus, performance may also depend on sensory aspects, such as how a product looks and feels and perhaps even what it sounds or smells like.

Finally, the pricing policy for the brand can create associations in consumers' minds to the relevant price tier or level for the brand in the category, as well as to its corresponding price volatility or variance (in terms of the frequency or size of discounts, etc.). In other words, the pricing strategy adopted for a brand can dictate how consumers categorize the price of the brand (eg, as low, medium or high) and how firm or flexible that price is seen (eg, frequently or infrequently discounted). Consumers often have strong beliefs about the price and value of a brand and may organize their product category knowledge in terms of the price tiers of different brands.[29] (Chapter 5 analyses price associations.)

Brand imagery

The other main type of brand meaning involves brand imagery. *Brand imagery* deals with the extrinsic properties of the product or service, including the ways in which the brand attempts to meet customers' psychological or social needs. Brand imagery is how people think about a brand abstractly, rather than what they think the brand actually does. Thus, imagery refers to more intangible aspects of the brand. Imagery associations can be formed directly (from a consumer's experiences and contact with the product, brand, target market or usage situation) or indirectly (through the depiction of these same considerations as communicated in brand advertising or by some other source of information, such as word of mouth). Many kinds of intangibles can be linked to a brand, but four categories can be highlighted.

1. User profiles.
2. Purchase and usage situations.
3. Personality and values.
4. History, heritage and experiences.

One set of brand imagery associations is the type of person or organization who uses a brand. This imagery may result in a profile or mental image by customers of actual users or more aspirational, idealized users. Associations of a typical or idealized brand user may be based on descriptive demographic factors or more abstract psychographic factors. Demographic factors might include the following.

- *Gender:* for example, Nivea cosmetics and Laura Ashley home decoration have 'feminine' associations, whereas Marlboro cigarettes and Lynx deodorant have more 'masculine' associations.
- *Age:* for example, Pepsi Cola, Puma and Rip Curl position themselves as younger than Coca-Cola, Nike and Patagonia, respectively.
- *Identity:* for example, Gaymobile is a Danish mobile phone operator focused on the gay community.
- *Income:* for example, during the 1980s, Lacoste shirts, Ray-Ban sunglasses and Porsche cars became associated with yuppies – young, affluent, urban professionals.

Psychographic factors include attitudes towards life, careers, possessions, social issues or political institutions. For example, a brand user might be seen as iconoclastic or as more traditional and conservative.

In a business-to-business setting, user imagery might relate to the size or type of organization. For example, Microsoft might be seen as an 'aggressive' company, whereas Patagonia or Timberland might be seen as a 'caring' company. User imagery may focus on more than the characteristics of one type of individual and centre on broader issues in terms of perceptions of a group. For example, customers may believe that a brand is used by many people and therefore view the brand as 'popular' or a 'market leader'.

A second set of associations is under what conditions or situations the brand could or should be bought and used. Associations of a typical purchase situation may be based on a number of considerations, such as type of channel (eg, seen as sold through department stores, specialist chains or through the internet or some other means), specific chains (eg, Habitat and Foot Locker) and ease of purchase and associated rewards (if any).

Similarly, associations of a typical usage situation may be based on a number of considerations, such as the time of the day, week, month or year to use the brand; location to use the brand (eg, inside or outside the home); and type of activity where the brand is used (eg, formal or informal). For example, in terms of usage imagery, advertising for Snickers emphasizes that the bar is 'packed with peanuts' and therefore 'satisfies' as a healthy, filling snack. For a long time, pizza chain restaurants had strong associations with their channels of distribution – Domino's was known for delivery and Pizza Hut for dine-in service – although in recent years each of these competitors has made inroads in the traditional markets of the others.

Brands may also take on personality traits.[30] A brand, like a person, can be characterized as being 'modern', 'old-fashioned', 'lively' or 'exotic.' Brand personality reflects how people feel about a brand as a result of what they think the brand is or does, the manner in which the brand is marketed and so on. Brands may also take on values. Brand personality is often related to the descriptive usage imagery but also involves richer, more contextual information. Five dimensions of brand personality (with corresponding sub-dimensions) that have been identified are sincerity (eg, down-to-earth, honest, wholesome and cheerful), excitement (eg, daring, spirited, imaginative and up to date), competence (eg, reliable, intelligent, successful), sophistication (eg, upper class and charming) and ruggedness (eg, outdoorsy and tough).[31]

How is brand personality formed? Although any aspect of marketing may affect brand personality, advertising may be especially influential because of the inferences consumers make about the underlying user or usage situation depicted. Advertisers may imbue a brand with personality traits through anthropomorphization and product animation techniques (eg, M&Ms), personification through the use of brand characters (eg, Jolly Green Giant), the creation of user imagery (eg, the Oxo family) and so on.[32] More generally, advertising may affect brand personality by the manner in which it depicts the brand – for example, the actors, the tone or style of the creative strategy and the emotions or feelings evoked. Once brands develop a personality, it can be difficult for consumers to accept information that they see as inconsistent with that personality.[33]

Although user imagery, especially in advertising, is a prime source of brand personality, user imagery and brand personality may not always be in agreement. In product categories where performance-related attributes are more central in consumer decisions (eg, food products), brand personality and user imagery may be much less related. Differences may arise in other instances as well. For example, at one time, Perrier's brand personality was 'sophisticated' and 'stylish', whereas its actual user imagery was seen more as 'flashy' and 'trendy'.

In those categories in which user and usage imagery are important to consumer decisions, however, brand personality and user imagery are more likely to be related (eg, for cars, beer, alcohol, cigarettes and cosmetics). Thus, consumers often choose brands that have a personality that is consistent with their own self-concept, although in some cases the match may be based on consumer's desired self-image rather than their actual image.[34] These effects may also be more pronounced for publicly consumed products than for privately consumed goods.[35] On the other hand, consumers who are high 'self-monitors' (ie, sensitive to how others see them) are more likely to choose brands whose personalities fit the consumption situation.[36]

Finally, brands may take on associations with their past and certain noteworthy events in their history. These types of associations may involve distinctly personal experiences and episodes or be related to past behaviour and experiences of friends, family or others. Consequently, these types of associations may be fairly idiosyncratic, although sometimes exhibiting certain commonalties. Alternatively, these associations may be more public and broad-based and therefore be shared to a larger degree by people. For example, there may be associations with aspects of the marketing for the brand – for example, the colour of the product or look of its packaging, the company or person that makes the product and the country in which it is made, the type of shop in which it is sold, the events for which the brand is a sponsor and the people who endorse the brand. In any case, associations with history, heritage and experiences involve more specific, concrete examples that transcend the generalizations that make up the usage imagery. In the extreme case, brands become iconic by combining all these types of associations into what is in effect a myth, tapping into enduring consumer hopes and dreams.[37]

Summary

A number of types of associations related to either performance and imagery may become linked to a brand. Regardless of the type, brand associations making up the brand image and meaning can be characterized and profiled according to three important dimensions – strength, favourability and uniqueness – that build brand equity. Successful results on these three dimensions produce the most positive brand responses, the underpinning of intense and active brand loyalty.

To create brand equity, it is important that the brand has some strong, favourable and unique brand associations *in that order*. In other words, it doesn't matter how unique a brand association is unless customers evaluate the association favourably, and it doesn't matter how desirable a brand association is unless it is sufficiently strong that customers actually recall it and link it to the brand. At the same time, it should be recognized that not all strong associations are favourable and not all favourable associations are unique.

Creating strong, favourable and unique associations is challenging, but essential in terms of building customer-based brand equity. Strong brands establish favourable and unique associations with consumers. Brand meaning is what helps to produce brand responses. Brand responses refers to how customers respond to the brand and all its marketing activity and other sources of information – that is, what customers think or feel about the brand. Brand responses can be distinguished according to brand judgements and brand feelings – that is, in terms of whether they arise from the 'head' or from the 'heart', as the following sections describe.

Brand judgements

Brand judgements focus on customers' personal opinions and evaluations. They involve how customers put together all the different performance and imagery associations of a brand to form kinds of opinions. Customers may make all types of judgements with respect to a brand, but in terms of creating a strong brand, four types of summary brand judgements are particularly important: quality, credibility, consideration and superiority.

Brand quality

Brand attitudes are defined in terms of consumers' overall evaluations of a brand.[38] Attitudes are important because they often form the basis for actions and behaviour by consumers with a brand (eg, brand choice). Such attitudes generally depend on specific considerations concerning the attributes and benefits of the brand. For example, consider Sheraton hotels. A consumer's attitude towards Sheraton depends on how much he or she believes that the brand is characterized by certain associations that matter to the consumer for a hotel chain (eg, location; room comfort, design, and appearance; service quality of staff; recreational facilities; food service; security; prices; and so on).

There is a host of attitudes that customers may hold towards brands, but the most important relate to the perceived quality of the brand. Other notable attitudes related to quality pertain to perceptions of value and satisfaction. Perceived quality measures are inherent in many approaches to brand equity. In the annual EquiTrend survey by Total Research, 20,000 US consumers rate 1,000 brands across 35 categories on 5 dimensions: familiarity, quality, purchase intent, brand expectations and distinctiveness. Total research then creates an Equity Score based on the first three measures.[39]

Brand credibility

Customers may transcend specific brand quality concerns to form judgements with respect to the company or organization behind the brand. As Chapter 11 describes, *brand credibility* refers to the extent to which the brand is seen as credible in terms of: perceived expertise, trustworthiness and likability. Is the brand seen as:

- competent, innovative and a market leader (brand expertise);
- dependable and keeping customer interests in mind (brand trustworthiness); and
- fun, interesting and worth spending time with (brand likeability)?

In other words, credibility concerns whether consumers see the company or organization behind the brand as good at what they do, concerned about their customers or just easy to like.

Brand consideration

Eliciting favourable brand attitudes and perceptions of credibility is important but may be insufficient if customers do not consider the brand for possible purchase or usage. As noted earlier, consideration is more than mere awareness. It deals with the likelihood that customers will include the brand in the set of possible options of brands they might buy or use. Consideration depends in part on how personally relevant customers find the brand – that is, the extent to which customers view the brand as being appropriate and meaningful. Thus, customers often make an appraisal as to whether or not they have any personal interest in a brand and if they would or should ever buy a brand. Brand consideration is a crucial filter in terms of building brand equity. No matter how highly regarded or credible a brand may be, unless it is deemed relevant, customers will keep a brand at a distance and never embrace it. Brand consideration depends in large part on the extent to which strong and favourable brand associations can be created as part of the brand image.

Brand superiority

Superiority relates to the extent to which customers view a brand as unique and better than others. In other words, do customers believe that the brand offers advantages over other brands? Superiority is critical in terms of building intense and active relationships with customers and depends on the number and nature of unique brand associations that make up the brand image.

Brand feelings

Brand feelings are customers' emotional responses and reactions with respect to a brand. They also relate to the social currency evoked by a brand. What feelings are evoked by the marketing? How does the brand affect customers' feelings about themselves and their relationships with others? These feelings can be mild or intense, positive or negative.

Such emotions can become so strongly associated that they are accessible during product consumption or use. Researchers have defined *transformational advertising* as advertising designed to change consumers' perceptions of the actual usage experience with the product.[40] For example, Herbal Essence shampoo has been positioned as offering a revitalizing, sensual experience. In a parody of a famous scene from the film *When Harry Met Sally*, ads show scenes of women reaching heights of pleasure while lathering, exclaiming 'Yes, Yes, YES.' Brand Briefing 2.2 describes how L'Oréal has engendered brand feelings with consumers.

Brand Briefing 2.2

Managing feelings and user images at L'Oréal

In 1907, L'Oréal began in the hair-colour business. The company soon branched out into other cleansing and beauty products. L'Oréal markets 50 brands in 130 countries, 17 of the brands are global, in all sectors of the beauty business: hair colour, perms, styling aids, body and skincare, cleansers and fragrances.

L'Oréal products are found in all distribution channels, from hairdressers and perfumeries to supermarkets, health/beauty outlets, pharmacies and direct mail. Still, the company is active in only one business, cosmetics, which accounts for 98 percent of turnover.

Part of L'Oréal's success is attributed to a strategy diversifing the cultural origins of its brands. They can convey Italian elegance, New York street smarts or French beauty – but this does not mean an 'Italian' brand is aimed at the Italian market. The portfolio consists of 'European' brands like L'Oréal Paris, Lancôme or Giorgio Armani; 'American' brands like Matrix, Redken, Ralph Lauren, Kiehl's, Maybelline and Soft Sheen-Carson; 'Asian' brands such as the Japanese brand Shu Uemura or the Chinese brand Yu Sai Kan. Through this diversity, L'Oréal is reaching out to more people across a bigger range of incomes and cultures than just about any other beauty products company.

Each brand is managed to give the right associations and feelings. L'Oréal used the 'Because I'm worth it' slogan for many years. This has been replaced by 'Because you're worth it' – probably to shift power to the consumer instead of the spokesperson in the advertising. L'Oréal has also systematically looked for the right spokespersons, such as Penelope Cruz and Scarlet Johansson.

In 2006 L'Oréal took over the ethics-based brand The Body Shop, an area where no L'Oréal brands were present.

L'Oréal has a number of guiding values behind the portfolio of brands.

- *Striving for excellence:* 'Perfection is our goal. We are determined to continue enhancing or brand portfolio with innovative products and to meet the most demanding standards of quality and product safety at all times.'

- *A passion for adventure:* 'Our expertise drives our passion for new discoveries and innovation in cosmetics. Each new achievement – each step forward – is in itself a new beginning.'

Brand Briefing 2.2 *continued*

- *Enrichment through diversity:* 'Understanding and valuing each individual is an essential part of our corporate culture. Our staff members come from many different backgrounds and work together to offer a full range of products through varied distribution channels. Our goal is to serve the beauty and well-being of our consumers in all cultures throughout the world.'

- *Valuing individual talent:* 'Just as we are dedicated to enhancing the well-being of our consumers, we also make it a priority to ensure that each employee has the opportunity to develop his or her potential through personal and professional growth.'

- *Leading innovation in beauty:* 'Research is as much a part of our business as marketing, sensitivity to consumer needs is as important as scientific rigor, and know-how and expertise are as essential as intuition. Building on our unrivalled experience and expertise, fundamental research is a specific focus of investment that drives creativity and contributes to developing the cosmetics of tomorrow.'

Sources: Sandra O'Loughlin, 'L'Oréal believes Johansson is "worth it"', *Brandweek*, 9 January 2006; Sandra O'Loughlin, 'Penelope Cruz is natural match for L'Oréal', *Brandweek*, 9 January 2006; www.loreal. com; *BusinessWeek* online, 'L'Oréal: the beauty of global branding', 1999; www.bbc.co.uk, 'Body Shop agrees L'Oréal takeover', 17 March 2006.

The following are six important types of brand-building feelings.[41]

1. *Warmth:* soothing feelings. A brand makes consumers feel a sense of calm or peacefulness. Consumers may feel sentimental, warm-hearted or affectionate about the brand.

2. *Fun:* upbeat feelings. A brand makes consumers feel amused, light-hearted, joyous, playful and cheerful.

3. *Excitement:* a different form of upbeat feeling. A brand makes consumers feel energized and feel that they are experiencing something special. Brands that evoke feelings of excitement may result in consumers feeling a sense of elation, of 'being alive' or being cool or sexy.

4. *Security:* a brand produces a feeling of safety, comfort and self-assurance. Consumers do not experience worry or concerns that they might have otherwise felt.

5. *Social approval:* consumers have positive feelings about the reactions of others – that is, they feel that others look favourably on their appearance or behaviour. This approval may be a result of direct acknowledgment of the consumer's use of the brand by others or may be less overt and a result of attribution of product use to consumers.

6. *Self-respect:* consumers feel better about themselves. They feel a sense of pride, accomplishment or fulfillment.

The first three types of feelings are experiential and immediate, increasing in level of intensity. The latter three types are private and enduring, increasing in level of intensity.

Summary

Although all types of customer responses are possible – driven from both the head and heart – what matters is how positive these responses are. Additionally, it is important that the responses are accessible and come to mind when consumers think of the brand. Brand judgements and feelings can only favourably affect consumer behaviour if consumers internalize or think of positive responses in their encounters with the brand.

Brand resonance

The final step of the CBBE model focuses on the ultimate relationship and level of identification that the customer has with the brand. *Brand resonance* refers to the nature of this relationship and the extent to which customers feel they are 'in sync' with the brand. Examples of brands with high resonance include Harley-Davidson, Virgin, Apple and football clubs. Resonance is characterized in terms of intensity or the depth of the psychological bond that customers have with the brand, as well as the level of activity engendered by this loyalty (eg, repeat purchase rates and the extent to which customers seek out brand information, events and other loyal customers). Resonance can be broken down into four categories.

1. Behavioural loyalty.
2. Attitudinal attachment.
3. Sense of community.
4. Active engagement.

Behavioural loyalty relates to repeat purchases and the amount or share of category volume attributed to the brand – that is, the 'share of category requirements'. In other words, how often do customers purchase a brand and how much do they purchase? To make a profit, the brand must be bought often and in volume. The lifetime value of loyal consumers can be enormous.[42] For example, a loyal General Motors customer could be worth €189,000 over his or her lifetime (assuming 11 or more vehicles bought and word-of-mouth endorsement that makes friends and relatives more likely to consider GM products). Similarly, experts have estimated that the lifetime value of a sophisticated computer user (defined as one who buys a machine and software about every two years) is about €30,700. A user who postpones purchases as long as possible was estimated to provide €17,100 in lifetime value.

Behavioural loyalty is necessary but not sufficient for resonance to occur.[43] Some customers may buy out of necessity, buying because the brand is the only product stocked or the only one they can afford. To create resonance, there also needs to be a strong personal attachment. Customers should go beyond having a positive attitude to viewing the brand as something special. For example, customers with a great deal of attitudinal attachment to a brand may state that they 'love' the brand, describe it as one of their favourite possessions or view it as a 'little pleasure' that they look forward to.

Research has shown that mere satisfaction may not be enough.[44] Xerox found that if customer satisfaction was ranked on a scale of 1 (completely dissatisfied) to 5 (completely satisfied), customers who rated their products and services as '4' – and thus were satisfied – were six times more likely to defect to competitors than those customers who provided ratings of '5'.[45] Similarly, Frederick Reichheld points out that although more than 90 percent of car buyers are satisfied or very satisfied when they drive away from the dealer's showroom, fewer than half buy the same brand of car the next time.[46] Creating greater loyalty requires deeper attitudinal attachment, which can be generated by developing marketing, products and services that fully satisfy consumer needs.

A brand may also take on broader meaning to the customer in terms of a sense of community.[47] Identification with a brand community may reflect an important social phenomenon whereby customers feel a kinship or affiliation with other people associated with the brand. These connections may involve fellow brand users or customers or may involve employees or representatives of the company. They may also occur online.[48] Brand Briefing 2.3 profiles three ways to help build brand communities. A stronger sense of community among loyal users can engender favourable brand attitudes and intentions.[49]

Brand Briefing 2.3

Building brand communities

Apple

Apple encourages owners of its computers to form local user groups. By 2005, there were 700 groups, ranging in size from fewer than 25 members to more than 1,000. The groups provide Apple owners with opportunities to learn more about their computers, share ideas and get product discounts, as well as sponsor special activities and events and perform community service. A visit to Apple's website helps customers find nearby user groups.

Harley-Davidson

The motorcycle company sponsors the Harley Owners Group (HOG), which by 2005 had 900,000 members in groups all over the world. They share a simple mission: 'To ride and have fun.' The first-time buyer of a Harley-Davidson motorcycle gets a free one-year membership. HOG benefits include a magazine, *Hog Tales*, a touring handbook, emergency road service, insurance, discount hotel rates and a programme enabling members to rent Harleys while on holiday. The company also maintains a website devoted to HOG, which includes information on groups and events and features a special members-only section.

Brand Briefing 2.3 *continued*

Jeep

In addition to the Jeep enthusiast clubs throughout the world, Jeep owners can meet with their vehicles in wilderness areas across America as part of the company's official Jeep Jamborees and Camp Jeep. Since the first camp in 1995, 28,000 people have attended the three-day sessions, where they practise off-road driving and meet other owners. Jeep Jamborees bring owners and their families together for two-day, off-road adventures. Promising to be 'every bit as muddy', Camp Jeep on the Road went to eight cities in 2005 to allow existing and prospective Jeep 4 × 4 owners to put the vehicles through their paces on the road and off.

Finally, perhaps the strongest affirmation of brand loyalty is when customers are willing to invest time, energy, money or other resources in the brand beyond those expended during purchase or consumption of the brand. For example, customers may choose to join a club, receive product updates and exchange correspondence with other brand users or formal or informal representatives of the brand. They may choose to visit brand-related websites, participate in chat rooms and so on. In this case, customers themselves became brand evangelists and ambassadors, so helping to communicate about the brand and strengthen the brand ties of others. Strong attitudinal attachment or social identity or both are typically necessary, however, for active engagement with a brand.

In summary, brand relationships can be characterized in terms of intensity and activity. Intensity refers to the strength of the attitudinal attachment and sense of community. In other words, how deeply felt is the loyalty? Activity refers to how frequently the consumer buys and uses the brand, as well as engages in other activities not related to purchase and consumption. In other words, in how many different ways does brand loyalty manifest itself in day-to-day consumer behaviour?

Implications for building a brand

The importance of the customer-based brand equity model is in the road map and guidance it provides for building a brand. It provides a yardstick by which brands can assess their progress, as well as a guide for marketing research initiatives. With respect to the latter, one CBBE application is in terms of brand-tracking and providing quantitative measures of the success of brand-building efforts (see Chapter 8). Figure 2.8 contains a set of candidate measures for the six brand building blocks. The model also reinforces a number of branding tenets, five of which are particularly noteworthy.

1. Salience

- What brands of product or service category can you think of? (Using increasingly specific product category cues.)
- Have you ever heard of these brands?
- Which brands might you be likely to use under the following situations . . . ?
- How frequently do you think of this brand?

2. Performance

- Compared with other brands in the category, how well does this brand provide the basic functions of the product or service category?
- Compared with other brands in the category, how well does this brand satisfy the basic needs of the product or service category?
- To what extent does this brand have special features?
- How reliable is this brand?
- How durable is this brand?
- How easily serviced is this brand?
- How effective is this brand's service? Does it completely satisfy your requirements?
- How efficient is this brand's service in terms of speed, responsiveness and so forth?
- How courteous and helpful are the providers of this brand's service?
- How stylish do you find this brand?
- How much do you like the look, feel and other design aspects of this brand?
- Compared with other brands in the category with which it competes, are this brand's prices generally higher, lower or about the same?
- Compared with other brands in the category with which it competes, do this brand's prices change more frequently, less frequently or about the same amount?

3. Imagery

- To what extent do people you admire and respect use this brand?
- How much do you like people who use this brand?
- How well do the following words describe this brand: down to earth, honest, daring, up to date, reliable, successful, upper class, charming, outdoorsy?
- What places are appropriate to buy this brand?
- How appropriate are the following situations to using this brand?
- Can you buy this brand in a lot of places?
- Is this a brand that you can use in a lot of different situations?
- To what extent does thinking of the brand bring back pleasant memories?
- To what extent do you feel you grew up with the brand?

4. Judgements

- Quality

  What is your overall opinion of this brand?

  What is your assessment of the product quality of this brand?

  To what extent does this brand fully satisfy your product needs?

  How good a value is this brand?

- Credibility

  How knowledgeable are the makers of this brand?

  How innovative are the makers of this brand?

  How much do you trust the makers of this brand?

Figure 2.8   Possible measures of brand building blocks

To what extent do the makers of this brand understand your needs?

To what extent do the makers of this brand care about your opinions?

To what extent do the makers of this brand have your interests in mind?

How much do you like this brand?

How much do you admire this brand?

How much do you respect this brand?

- Consideration

How likely would you be to recommend this brand to others?

Which are your favourite products in this brand category?

How personally relevant is this brand to you?

- Superiority

How unique is this brand?

To what extent does this brand offer advantages that other brands cannot?

How superior is this brand to others in the category?

5. Feelings

Does this brand give you a feeling of warmth?

Does this brand give you a feeling of fun?

Does this brand give you a feeling of excitement?

Does this brand give you a feeling of security?

Does this brand give you a feeling of social approval?

Does this brand give you a feeling of self-respect?

6. Resonance

- Loyalty

I consider myself loyal to this brand.

I buy this brand whenever I can.

I buy as much of this brand as I can.

I feel this is the only brand of this product I need.

This is the one brand I would prefer to buy/use.

If this brand were not available, it would make a difference to me if I had to use another brand.

I would go out of my way to use this brand.

- Attachment

I really love this brand.

I would really miss this brand if it went away.

This brand is special to me.

This brand is more than a product to me.

- Community

I really identify with people who use this brand.

I feel like I almost belong to a club with other users of this brand.

This is a brand used by people like me.

I feel a deep connection with others who use this brand.

- Engagement

I really like to talk about this brand to others.

I am always interested in learning more about this brand.

I would be interested in merchandise with this brand's name on it.

Figure 2.8   *Continued*

I am proud to have others know I use this brand.

I like to visit the website for this brand.

Compared with other people, I follow news about this brand closely.

It should be recognized that the core brand values at the bottom two levels of the pyramid – brand salience, performance and imagery – are typically more idiosyncratic and unique to a product and service category than other brand values.

Figure 2.8 *Continued*

Customers' own brands

The premise of the CBBE model is that the measure of the strength of a brand depends on how consumers think, feel and act with respect to that brand. In particular, the strongest brands will be those to which consumers become so attached and passionate that they, in effect, become evangelists or missionaries and attempt to share their beliefs and spread the word about the brand. The point to realize is that the power of the brand and its ultimate value to the firm *resides with customers.* It is through customers learning about and experiencing a brand that they end up thinking and acting in a way that allows the firm to reap the benefits of brand equity. Although marketers must take responsibility for their brand-building plans, the success of such marketing depends on how consumers respond. This response, in turn, depends on the knowledge that has been created in their minds about those brands.

Don't take shortcuts with brands

The CBBE model reinforces the fact that there are no shortcuts in building a brand. A great brand is not built by accident. It is the product of carefully accomplishing – either explicitly or implicitly – a series of logically linked steps with consumers. The more explicitly the steps are recognized and defined as concrete goals, the more likely it is that they will receive the proper attention and thus be fully realized, providing the greatest contribution to brand building. The length of time taken to build a strong brand will therefore be directly proportional to the amount of time it takes to create sufficient awareness and understanding so that firmly held and felt beliefs and attitudes about the brand are formed that can serve as the foundation for brand equity.

The brand-building steps may not be equally difficult. In particular, creating brand identity is a step that effective marketing can accomplish in a relatively short time. Unfortunately, this step is the one that many brand marketers tend to skip in their haste to quickly establish an image for the brand (as is evident by the failed dot-com brands whose target market had no inkling as to what they did). As Chapter 3 describes, it is difficult for consumers to appreciate the advantages and uniqueness of a brand unless they have a frame of reference as to what the brand is supposed to do and with whom or what it is supposed to compete. Similarly, it is difficult for consumers to achieve high levels of positive responses without having a reasonably complete understanding of the characteristics of the brand.

Finally, due to circumstances in the marketplace, consumers may actually start a repeat purchase or behavioural loyalty relationship with a brand without having many underlying feelings, judgements or associations. Nevertheless, these other brand building blocks will have to come into place at some point to create true resonance. That is, although the start point may differ, the same steps in brand building eventually must occur to create a truly strong brand.

Brands should have a duality

One important point reinforced by the model is that a strong brand has a duality in that it appeals to both the head and the heart. Thus, although there are perhaps two ways to build loyalty and resonance – going up the left side of the pyramid in terms of product-related performance associations and resulting judgements or going up the right side in terms of non-product-related imagery associations and resulting feelings – strong brands often do both. Strong brands blend product performance and imagery to create a rich, varied, but complementary set of consumer responses to the brand.

By appealing to both rational and emotional concerns, a strong brand provides consumers with many access points while reducing competitive vulnerability. Rational concerns can satisfy utilitarian needs, whereas emotional concerns can satisfy psychological or emotional needs. Combining the two can lead to a formidable brand position. Consistent with this reasoning, a McKinsey study of 51 brands found that having both distinctive physical *and* emotional benefits drove greater shareholder value, especially when the two were linked.[50]

Brands should have richness

The level of detail in the CBBE model highlights ways to create meaning with consumers and the range of possible avenues to elicit consumer responses. Collectively, these aspects of brand meaning and the resulting responses produce strong consumer bonds. The associations making up the brand image may be reinforcing, helping to strengthen or increase the favourability of other brand associations, or may be unique, helping to add distinctiveness or offset some potential deficiencies. Strong brands thus have both breadth (in terms of duality) *and* depth (in terms of richness).

At the same time, brands should not necessarily be expected to score highly on all the various dimensions and categories making up each core brand value. Building blocks can have hierarchies in their own right. For example, with respect to brand awareness, it is typically important to first establish category identification in some way before considering strategies to expand brand breadth via needs satisfied or benefits offered. With brand performance, it is often necessary to first link primary characteristics and related features before attempting to link additional, more peripheral associations. Similarly, brand imagery often begins with a concrete articulation of user and usage imagery that, over time, leads to broader, more abstract brand associations of personality, value, history, heritage and experience. Brand judgements usually begin with positive quality and credibility perceptions that can lead to brand consideration and then perhaps to assessments of brand superiority.

Brand feelings usually start with either experiential ones (warmth, fun and excitement) or inward ones (security, social approval and self-respect). Finally, resonance again has a clear ordering, whereby behavioural loyalty is a starting point but attitudinal attachment or a sense of community is almost always needed for active engagement to occur.

Brand resonance provides important focus

Brand resonance is the pinnacle of the CBBE model and provides important focus and priority for making decisions about marketing. Marketers should use resonance as a goal and a means to interpret their brand-related marketing activities. The question to ask is: to what extent is marketing activity affecting the elements of brand resonance – consumer loyalty, attachment, community and engagement? Is marketing creating brand performance and imagery associations, and consumer judgements and feelings that will support brand resonance? In an application of the CBBE model, the marketing research firm Knowledge Networks found that brands that scored highest on loyalty and attachment dimensions were not necessarily the same ones that scored high on community and engagement dimensions (see Figure 2.9).

Yet, it must also be recognized that it is virtually impossible for consumers to experience an intense, active loyalty relationship with all the brands they use. Thus, some brands will be more meaningful than others, in part because of the nature of their associated product or service, the characteristics of the consumer and so on. When it is difficult to create a varied set of feelings and imagery associations, marketers may not be able to obtain the 'deeper' aspects of brand resonance. Nevertheless, by taking a broader view of brand loyalty, marketers may be able to gain a more holistic appreciation for their brand and how it connects to consumers. By defining the proper role for the brand, higher levels of brand resonance should be obtainable.

Rank	Brand loyalty	Brand attachment	Brand community	Brand engagement
1	Harley-Davidson	Harley-Davidson	Harley-Davidson	Harley-Davidson
2	Hershey's	Hershey's	Lifetime Television	Lifetime Television
3	Campbells	Campbell's	Public Broadcasting Channel	Lexus
4	Clorox	Discovery Channel	Fidelity Investments	Discovery Channel
5	Heinz	BMW	MSN	Public Broadcasting Channel
6	Kodak	Wal-Mart	Lexus	Wal-Mart
7	Kraft	Public Broadcasting Channel	Discovery Channel	BMW
8	Wal-Mart	Kraft	AOL	Dell
9	Duracell	Kodak	Chevrolet	Toyota
10	Discovery Channel	NBC	Hershey's	Fidelity Investments

Figure 2.9   Brand rankings on resonance dimensions (USA, autumn 2001)

CREATING CUSTOMER VALUE

Customer–brand relationships are the foundation of brand resonance and building a strong brand. The importance to firms of adopting a strong consumer and customer orientation has been espoused for years. The CBBE model puts that notion up front, making it clear that the power of a brand resides in the minds of consumers and customers. Brand Briefing 2.4 describes some criteria that point to whether or not a company is consumercentric.

Even so, many firms find themselves paying a price for lacking customer focus. Even the biggest firms, such as Volkswagen, can stumble.

Brand Briefing 2.4

Putting customers first

Most employees don't have any idea what their company's return on invested capital is, let alone the returns on specific customer segments – and even if they knew, they'd be powerless to do anything about it. But according to Selden and Colvin, a few companies, such as Dell, Best Buy and Royal Bank of Canada, have been solid stocks for shareholders because of their customercentric approach. According to these authors, *customercentricity* means that all employees understand how their actions affect share price. They maintain that customercentric companies are a good bet for investors because they hold an advantage that can lead to a jump in share price. To determine if a company is customer-focused, Selden and Colvin suggest customers ask themselves these questions.

1. *Is the company looking for ways to take care of you?* Only a few companies identify customer needs first and then create ways to meet them. Too many try to make customers buy the products and services they already offer. Royal Bank of Canada is an example of a company that found a customer segment with unique needs and met those needs. Many of the bank's customers were Canadians who spent winters in Florida or Arizona. Those customers, who tended to be affluent, wanted to borrow money in the USA for homes and get a US credit rating that reflected their Canadian record. They also wanted to be served by employees who knew the USA as well as Canada. To serve those customers, the bank opened a branch in Florida through its US subsidiary. The results have been exceptional: customers signed up in droves. Opening branches aimed at specific customer segments represented a growth opportunity for the bank's shareholders.

2. *Does the company know its customers well enough to differentiate between them?* True differentiation means knowing what your customer segments are, what each group wants, where the groups are shopping and how to serve customers individually.

Brand Briefing 2.4 *continued*

3. *Is someone accountable for customers?* At most companies, departments own pieces, but no one owns any specific customer segment. But at companies with customercentric approaches, things are different. At Best Buy, for example, an individual is accountable for the 'soccer-mom' segment across its US stores.

4. *Is the company managed for shareholder value?* If a company is managed for shareholder value, employees know about earning a return on invested capital that exceeds the cost of capital, plus investing increasing amounts of capital at that positive spread and maintaining that spread for as long as possible. Customercentric companies apply those criteria to customer segments. They know how much capital they've invested in a segment and how much return they earn on it. They maintain the positive spread by creating and reinventing enduring customer relationships.

5. *Is the company testing new customer offers and learning from the results?* Constant learning about what customers want and a formal process for sharing it are critical to customercentricity. Seven-Eleven Japan does this well. Every week employees from all over Japan meet to discuss hypotheses tested and verified in the stores. Ideas such as changing the lunch menu for the next day based on the predicted weather (like serving hot noodles on a cool day) are heard throughout the company.

Sources: Larry Selden and Geoffrey Colvin, '5 rules for finding the next Dell', *Fortune*, 12 July 2004; Larry Selden and Geoffrey Colvin, *Angel Customers and Demon Customers: Discover which is which and turbo-charge your stock*, The Woodlands, TX: Portfolio, 2003.

Volkswagen

After a remarkable revival in the 1990s when it enjoyed 50 percent growth for 7 years, the turn of the century was not kind to Volkswagen. By 2005, the German carmaker was experiencing stagnant sales and was losing money in the US market. The culprit? According to chief executive Bernd Pischetsrieder: 'The biggest failure in Volkswagen is too little customer-focus.' In his view, the company was paying too much attention to technology and features that he felt customers didn't want to pay for. According to Pischetsrieder: 'The first question is, how does it help the customer and will the customer pay for it? When we have a test drive, the question is not whether I like it. It's will the customer pay for it or will the customer not even notice it?'[51]

VW is not alone in its recognition of the financial value of customer experiences. Many firms are now defining the financial value of prospective and actual customers and using marketing to optimize that value.

CHAPTER REVIEW

Customer-based brand equity is the differential effect that brand knowledge has on consumer response to the marketing of that brand. A brand has positive customer-based brand equity when customers react more favourably to a product and the way it is marketed when the brand is identified than when it is not (eg, when it is attributed to a fictitiously named or unnamed version of the product).

Brand knowledge can be defined in terms of an associative network memory model as a network of nodes and links wherein the brand node in memory has a variety of associations linked to it. Brand knowledge can be characterized in terms of awareness and image. Brand awareness is related to the strength of the brand node or trace in memory, as reflected by consumers' ability to recall or recognize the brand under different conditions. Brand awareness can be characterized by depth and breadth. The depth relates to the likelihood that the brand can be recognized or recalled. The breadth relates to the variety of purchase and consumption situations in which the brand comes to mind. Brand image is defined as consumer perceptions of a brand as reflected by the brand associations held in consumers' memories.

Customer-based brand equity occurs when the consumer has a high level of awareness and familiarity with the brand and has strong, favourable and unique brand associations. In some cases, brand awareness alone is sufficient to result in more favourable consumer responses – for example, in low-involvement decision settings where consumers are willing to base their choices merely on familiar brands. In other cases, the strength, favourability and uniqueness of the brand associations are critical in determining the differential response making up the brand equity.

To create differential response, it is important to associate unique, meaningful points of difference to the brand to provide a competitive advantage and a 'reason why' consumers should buy it. For some brand associations, however, it may be sufficient that they are seen as roughly equally favourable with competing brand associations so that they function as points of parity in consumers' minds to negate potential points of difference for competitors. In other words, these associations are designed to provide consumers with 'no reason why not' to choose the brand. Assuming a positive brand image is created by marketing programmes that link strong, favourable and unique associations to the brand in memory, benefits can result.

The CBBE model maintains that building a strong brand involves a series of logical steps: (1) establishing the proper brand identity, (2) creating the appropriate brand meaning, (3) eliciting the right brand responses and (4) forging appropriate brand relationships with customers. Specifically, according to this model, building a strong brand involves establishing breadth and depth of brand awareness; creating strong, favourable and unique brand associations; eliciting positive, accessible brand responses; and forging intense, active brand relationships. Achieving these four steps, in turn, involves establishing six brand building blocks: salience, performance, imagery, judgements, feelings and resonance.

The strongest brands excel in all six building blocks and so fully execute all four steps in the CBBE model. In the model, the most valuable building block, resonance, occurs when all the other core values are 'in sync' with customers' needs, wants and desires. In other words, resonance reflects a completely harmonious relationship between customers and the brand. With true brand resonance, customers have a high degree of loyalty marked by a close relationship with the brand such that customers look for ways to interact with the brand and share their experiences with others. Companies that achieve resonance and affinity with their customers should reap valuable benefits, such as greater price premiums and more efficient and effective marketing.

Thus, the premise of the CBBE model is that the true measure of the strength of a brand depends on how consumers think, feel and act with respect to that brand. Achieving brand resonance requires eliciting the proper cognitive appraisals and emotional reactions from customers. That, in turn, necessitates establishing brand identity and creating the right meaning in terms of brand performance and brand imagery associations. A brand with the right identity and meaning can result in a customer believing that the brand is relevant and 'my kind of product'. The strongest brands will be those to which consumers become so attached and passionate that they, in effect, become evangelists or missionaries and attempt to share their beliefs and spread the word about the brand.

Brand Briefing 2.5

The marketing advantages of strong brands

Customer-based brand equity occurs when consumers respond differently to marketing activity because they know a brand than when they do not. The actual nature of how that response differs will depend on the level of brand awareness and how favourably and uniquely consumers evaluate brand associations, as well as the marketing activity under consideration. A number of benefits can result from a strong brand, both in terms of greater revenue and lower costs.[52] For example, Ian Lewis from Time-Life (1993) categorizes the factors creating financial value for strong brands into two categories: factors related to growth (eg, a brand's ability to attract new customers, resist competitive activity, introduce line extensions and cross international borders) and factors related to profitability (eg, brand loyalty, premium pricing, lower price elasticity, lower advertising/sales ratios and trade leverage).[53]

This section considers some of the benefits to a firm of having brands with a high level of awareness and a positive brand image.

Greater loyalty and less vulnerability to competitive marketing actions and crises

Research has demonstrated that different types of brand associations – if seen as favourable – can affect consumer product evaluations, perceptions of quality and purchase rates.[54] This tendency may be especially apparent with difficult-to-assess 'experience' goods[55] and as the uniqueness of brand associations increases.[56] In addition, familiarity with a brand has been shown to increase consumer confidence, attitude towards the brand, purchase intention[57] and mitigate the potential damage from a poor trial experience.[58]

Brand Briefing 2.5 *continued*

For these and other reasons, one characteristic of brands with a great deal of equity is that consumers feel great loyalty towards them. For example, as noted in Chapter 1, at least some top brands have been market leaders for years despite significant changes in both consumer attitudes and competitive activity over time. Through it all, consumers have valued these brands – what they are and what they represent – sufficiently to stick with them and reject the overtures of competitors, creating a steady stream of revenues for the firm. Research also has found that brands with large market shares are more likely to have more loyal customers than brands with small market shares, a phenomenon dubbed *double jeopardy*.[59]

Brand loyalty is closely related to equity but is a distinct concept. Brand loyalty is often measured in a behavioural sense through the number of repeat purchases. Yet, a consumer may continually purchase for reasons not related to a strong preference for the brand, such as when the brand is prominently stocked or frequently promoted. Consumers may be in the habit of buying a particular brand without really thinking about it. When confronted by a new or resurgent competitor providing compelling reasons to switch, consumers' ties to the brand may be tested for the first time.

So, repeat buying is a necessary but not sufficient condition for being a brand-loyal buyer in an attitudinal sense: someone can repeat buy but not be brand loyal. Brand loyalty is one of the many advantages of creating a positive brand image and of having brand equity.

Returning to the benefits of equity, a brand with a positive image also is more likely to weather a crisis or downturn in its fortunes.[60] Perhaps the most compelling example of this fact is Johnson and Johnson's Tylenol brand. Brand Briefing 11.12 describes how J&J contended with a tragic product-tampering episode with its Tylenol pain reliever in the early 1980s. The company saw its market share drop from 37 percent to almost zero overnight and was faced with having to write off Tylenol as a brand. However, J&J was able to regain Tylenol's market share through the skillful handling of the crisis and having a good deal of brand equity to draw on.

The lesson from J&J's Tylenol crisis is that effective handling of a crisis requires swift and sincere actions. There must be an immediate admission that something has gone wrong and an assurance that an effective remedy will be put in place. Most important, the greater the brand equity, the more likely it is that these statements will have credibility with consumers, so they will be both understanding and patient as the firm sets out to solve the crisis. Without brand equity, however, even the best-laid plans for recovery may fall short to a suspicious public.[61] Finally, it should also be recognized that, even if there is no crisis, a strong brand offers protection in the case of a marketing downturn or when the brand's fortunes fall.

Brand Briefing 2.5 *continued*

Larger margins

Brands with equity can command a price premium.[62] Moreover, consumers should also have an inelastic response to price increases and elastic responses to price decreases or discounts for the brand over time.[63] Consistent with this reasoning, research has shown that consumers loyal to a brand are less likely to switch in the face of price increases and more likely to increase the quantity of the brand purchased in the face of price decreases.[64] In a competitive sense, brand leaders draw a disproportionate amount of share from smaller-share competitors.[65] At the same time, research has demonstrated that market leaders are relatively immune to price competition from these small-share brands.[66]

An analysis of consumer goods manufacturers from the extensive PIMS database found that, by providing unique and positive messages, a firm could insulate itself from future price competition, as witnessed by less negative future price elasticities. Conversely, they also found that non-unique messages could decrease future differentiation; for example, price promotions for firms that priced above the industry average led to more negative future price elasticities.[67]

The results of a study by the marketing research firm Intelliquest exploring the role of brand name and price in the decision to purchase business computer buyers is enlightening in that regard.[68] Survey respondents were asked: 'What is the incremental dollar value you would be willing to pay over a 'no-name' clone computer brand?' IBM commanded the greatest price premium, followed by Compaq and Hewlett-Packard. Some brands had negative brand equity; they actually received negative numbers. Clearly, according to this study, brands have specific meaning in the personal computer market that consumers value and will pay for.

Chapter 5 reviews pricing strategies and discount policies to build brand equity.

Greater trade co-operation and support

Brand owners often do not sell directly to consumers. Middlemen in the form of wholesalers, retailers and other parties often play an important role in selling a product. The activities of these members of the channels of distribution can thus facilitate or inhibit the success of the brand. If the brand has a positive brand image with consumers, it is more likely to receive favourable treatment from the trade.

Specifically, a brand with a positive image is more likely to have retailers and other middlemen respond to the wishes of consumers and actively promote and sell the brand.[69] Recognizing the likelihood of consumer demand, channel members are also less likely to require any marketing push from the manufacturer and are more likely to be receptive to any marketing overtures that do arise from the manufacturer to stock, reorder and display the brand.[70] Thus, they should be more likely to

Brand Briefing 2.5 *continued*

pass through trade promotions, demand smaller slotting allowances and give more favourable shelf space.

In short, brands with positive customer-based brand equity are more likely to receive greater trade co-operation and support. This treatment might translate into more prominent display, more attractive promotional offers and so on. Given that many consumer decisions are made in the store, the possibility of additional marketing push by retailers is important. Chapter 5 describes how marketers can work with retailers to maximize brand equity.

Increased marketing communication effectiveness

A host of advertising and communication benefits may result from creating awareness of and a positive image for a brand. These benefits can be seen by considering the manner in which a consumer responds to marketing communications and how the marketing communications campaign for a brand with a great deal of equity may be processed differently by consumers as a result. One well-established view of consumer response to marketing communications is hierarchy of effects models. These models assume that consumers move through a series of stages or mental states on the basis of marketing communications – for example, exposure to, attention to, comprehension of, yielding to, retention of and behaving on the basis of a marketing communication.

A brand with a great deal of equity has created some knowledge structures in consumers' minds. These mental associations increase the likelihood that consumers will pass through various stages of the hierarchy. For example, consider the effects of a positive brand image on the persuasive ability of advertising. As a result of having established brand awareness and strong, favourable and unique brand associations, consumers may be more likely to notice an ad, may more easily learn about the brand and form favourable opinions, and may retain and act on these beliefs over time.

Academic research has shown that familiar, well-liked brands are less susceptible to 'interference' and confusion from competitive ads,[71] are more responsive to creative strategies such as humour appeals[72] and are less vulnerable to negative reactions due to repetition.[73] In addition, panel diary members who were highly loyal to a brand increased purchases when advertising for the brand increased.[74] Other advantages associated with more advertising include increased likelihood of being the focus of attention and increased 'brand interest'.[75]

Because strong brand associations exist, lower levels of repetition may be necessary. For example, in a classic study of advertising weights, the US beer company Anheuser-Busch ran a field experiment in which it varied the amount of Budweiser advertising shown to consumers in different matched test markets.[76] Seven expenditure levels were tested, representing increases and decreases from the previous levels: no

Brand Briefing 2.5 *continued*

advertising, 50 percent less, same level, 50 percent more, double the level, 150 percent more, and 200 percent more. These expenditure levels were run for one year and revealed that the 'no advertising' level resulted in the same amount of sales as the current campaign. In fact, the 50 percent cut in advertising expenditures actually resulted in an increase in sales. The experimental results are consistent with the notion that strong brands such as Budweiser do not require the same advertising levels, at least over a short period of time, as a less well-known or well-liked brand.[77]

Similarly, because of brand knowledge structures, consumers may be more likely to notice sales promotions, direct mail offerings or other sales-orientated marketing communications and respond favourably. For example, studies have shown that promotion effectiveness is asymmetric in favour of a higher-quality brand.[78] Chapter 6 outlines how to develop integrated marketing communication campaigns to build and capitalize on brand equity.

Licensing opportunities

A strong brand often has associations that may be desirable in other product categories. To capitalize on this value, a firm may choose to license its name, logo or other trademark item to another company for use on their products and merchandise. Traditionally, licensing has been associated with characters such as Tintin, Smurfs, James Bond and Mickey Mouse, or celebrities and designers such as J-Lo, Giorgio Armani, Pininfarina. Recently, more conventional brands such as Ferrari, Harley-Davidson, Coca-Cola, and others have licensed their brands.

The rationale for the company obtaining the rights to use the trademark is that consumers will pay more for a product because of the recognition and image lent by the trademark. For example, one marketing research study showed that US consumers would pay €41 for cookware licensed under a TV cook's name as opposed to €27 for identical cookware bearing a shop's name.[79]

The rationale for the licensor relates to profits, promotion and legal protection. In terms of profits, a firm can expect an average royalty of about 5 percent of the wholesale price of each product, ranging from 2 percent to 10 percent depending on circumstances. Because there are no manufacturing or marketing costs, these revenues translate directly to profits. Licensing is also seen as a means to enhance the awareness and image of the brand. Linking the trademarks to other products may broaden its exposure and potentially increase the strength, favourability and uniqueness of brand associations. Finally, licensing may provide legal protection for trademarks. Licensing the brand for use in certain product categories prevents other firms or potential competitors from legally using the brand name to enter those categories. For example, Coca-Cola entered licensing agreements covering radios, glassware, toy trucks and clothes, in part as legal protection. As it turns out,

Brand Briefing 2.5 *continued*

its licensed products were so successful it has introduced a catalogue sent directly to consumers that offers a myriad of products bearing the Coca-Cola name.

Despite the potential benefits from licensing related to profitability, image enhancement or legal protection, there are risks too. A trademark can become overexposed if marketers adopt a saturation policy. Consumers do not necessarily know the motivation or marketing arrangements behind a product and can become confused or even angry if the brand is licensed to a product that seemingly bears no relation. Moreover, if the product fails to live up to consumers' expectations, the brand name could become tarnished. Chapter 7 discusses licensing and its effect on brand equity in more detail.

Additional brand extension opportunities

A *brand extension* is when a firm uses an established brand name to enter a new market. Extensions can be classified into two general categories. A *line extension* is when a brand name is used to enter a new market segment in the existing product class (eg, with new varieties, new flavours and new sizes). For example, Colgate introduced varieties of toothpaste with different flavours (eg, Winterfresh gel), that have different ingredients (eg, with baking soda) or provide a specific benefit (eg, tartar control). A *category extension* is when a brand name is used to enter a different product class. For example, the Swiss Army brand capitalized on the precision image of its knives to introduce watches, sunglasses, writing instruments, travel gear and cutlery.

A brand with a positive image allows the firm to introduce appropriate products as brand extensions. There are many advantages to this strategy. An extension allows the firm to capitalize on consumer knowledge of the parent brand to raise the awareness of and suggest possible associations for the brand extension. Thus, extensions can provide the following benefits to facilitate new product acceptance: reducing the risk perceived by customers and distributors, decreasing the cost of gaining distribution and trial, increasing the efficiency of promotional expenditures, avoiding the cost (and risk) of developing new names, allowing for packaging and labelling efficiencies and permitting consumer variety-seeking.

Besides facilitating new product acceptance, extensions can also provide 'feedback' benefits to the parent brand and the company. Extensions may enhance the parent brand image by improving the strength, favourability and uniqueness of brand associations and by improving perceptions of company credibility (in terms of perceived expertise, trustworthiness or likeability). Extensions may also help to convey the broader meaning of the brand to consumers, clarifying the core benefit proposition and business definition of the company. Finally, extensions may also bring new customers into the brand franchise and increase market coverage.

Academic research has validated many of these assumptions. Studies have shown that well-known and well-regarded brands can extend more successfully and into

Brand Briefing 2.5 *continued*

more diverse categories than other brands.[80] In addition, the amount of brand equity has been shown to be correlated with the highest- or lowest-quality member in the product line for vertical product extensions.[81] Research has also shown that positive symbolic associations may be the basis of these evaluations, even if overall brand attitude itself is not necessarily high.[82]

Brands with varied product category associations through past extensions have been shown to be especially extendable.[83] As a result, introductory marketing campaigns for extensions from an established brand may be more efficient than other such campaigns.[84] Studies have indicated that extension activity has aided (or at least did not dilute) brand equity for the parent brand. For instance, brand extensions strengthened parent brand associations, and 'flagship brands' were highly resistant to dilution or other potential negative effects caused by negative experiences with an extension.[85] Research has also found evidence of an ownership effect, whereby current owners generally had more favourable responses to brand line extensions.[86] Finally, extensions of brands that have both high familiarity and positive attitudes have been shown to receive higher initial stock market reactions than other brands.[87]

Chapter 12 provides a conceptual model of how consumers evaluate brand extensions and presents guidelines for marketers to maximize extension success and its effect on brand equity.

Other benefits

Finally, brands with positive customer-based brand equity may provide other advantages to the firm not directly related to the products themselves, such as helping to attract better employees, generate greater interest from investors and garner more support from shareholders. In terms of the last point, studies have shown that brand equity can be directly related to corporate stock price.[88]

Discussion questions

1. Pick a brand. Attempt to identify its sources of brand equity. Assess its level of brand awareness and the strength, favourability and uniqueness of its associations.
2. With which brands do you have the most resonance? Why?
3. Can every brand achieve resonance with its customers? Why or why not?
4. Pick a brand. Assess the extent to which the brand is achieving benefits from brand equity.
5. Can you think of any other benefits of creating a strong brand? What might they be?

References and notes

[1] Kevin Lane Keller, 'Conceptualizing, measuring, and managing customer-based brand equity', *Journal of Marketing*, January 1993: 1–29.

[2] John R. Anderson, *The Architecture of Cognition*, Cambridge, MA: Harvard University Press, 1983; Robert S. Wyer Jr and Thomas K. Srull, 'Person memory and judgment', *Psychological Review*, 1989, 96 (1): 58–83.

[3] John R. Rossiter and Larry Percy, *Advertising and Promotion Management*, New York: McGraw-Hill, 1987.

[4] Burleigh B. Gardner and Sidney J. Levy, 'The product and the brand', *Harvard Business Review*, March–April 1955: 33–9.

[5] Dawn Dobni and George M. Zinkhan, 'In search of brand image: a foundation analysis', in *Advances in Consumer Research*, Vol. 17, eds. Marvin E. Goldberg, Gerald Gorn and Richard W. Pollay, Provo, UT: Association for Consumer Research, 1990: 110–19.

[6] H. Herzog, 'Behavioral science concepts for analyzing the consumer', in *Marketing and the Behavioral Sciences*, ed. Perry Bliss, Boston, MA: Allyn and Bacon, 1963: 76–86; Joseph W. Newman, 'New insight, new progress for marketing', *Harvard Business Review*, November–December, 1957: 95–102.

[7] James R. Bettman, *An Information Processing Theory of Consumer Choice*, Reading, MA: Addison-Wesley, 1979; Rossiter and Percy, *Advertising and Promotion Management*.

[8] William Baker, J. Wesley Hutchinson, Danny Moore and Prakash Nedungadi, 'Brand familiarity and advertising: effects on the evoked set and brand preference', in *Advances in Consumer Research*, Vol. 13, ed. Richard J. Lutz, Provo, UT: Association for Consumer Research, 1986: 637–42; Prakash Nedungadi, 'Recall and consumer consideration sets: influencing choice without altering brand evaluations', *Journal of Consumer Research*, December 1990, 17: 263–76.

[9] For example, see Henry L. Roediger, 'Inhibition in recall from cuing with recall targets', *Journal of Verbal Learning and Verbal Behavior*, 1973, 12: 644–57; and Raymond S. Nickerson, 'Retrieval inhibition from part-set cuing: a persisting enigma in memory research', *Memory and Cognition*, November 1984, 12: 531–52.

[10] In an interesting twist, it is also the case that consumers would be more likely to recall closely related brands in the category, for example, McDonald's. See Prakash Nedungadi, 'Recall and consumer consideration sets'.

[11] Rashmi Adaval, 'How good gets better and bad gets worse: understanding the impact of affect on evaluations of known brands', *Journal of Consumer Research*, December 2003, 30: 352–67.

[12] Jacob Jacoby, George J. Syzabillo and Jacqeline Busato-Schach, 'Information acquisition behavior in brand choice situations', *Journal of Consumer Research*, 1977, 3: 209–16; Ted Roselius, 'Consumer ranking of risk reduction methods', *Journal of Marketing*, January 1977, 35: 56–61.

[13] James R. Bettman and C. Whan Park, 'Effects of prior knowledge and experience and phase of the choice process on consumer decision processes: a protocol analysis', *Journal of Consumer Research*, December 1980, 7: 234–48; Wayne D. Hoyer and Steven P. Brown, 'Effects of brand awareness on choice for a common, repeat-purchase product', *Journal of Consumer Research*, September 1990, 17: 141–8; C. W. Park and V. Parker Lessig, 'Familiarity and its impact on consumer biases and heuristics', *Journal of Consumer Research*, September 1981, 8: 223–30.

[14] Richard E. Petty and John T. Cacioppo, *Communication and Persuasion*, New York: Springer-Verlag, 1986.

[15] 'Advertisers often take bizarre approaches', *Newsday*.

[16]Joseph W. Alba and J. Wesley Hutchinson, 'Dimensions of consumer expertise', *Journal of Consumer Research*, March 1987, 13: 411–53.

[17]David A. Aaker, 'Positioning your brand', *Business Horizons*, May/June 1982, 25: 56–62; Al Ries and Jack Trout, *Positioning: The battle for your mind*, New York: McGraw-Hill, 1979; Yoram Wind, *Product Policy: Concepts, methods and strategy*, Reading, MA: Addison-Wesley, 1982.

[18]Dipankar Chakravarti, Deborah J. MacInnis and Kent Nakamoto, 'Product category perceptions, elaborative processing and brand name extension strategies', in *Advances in Consumer Research*, Vol. 17, eds. M. Goldberg, G. Gorn and R. Pollay, Provo, UT: Association for Consumer Research, 1990: 910–16; Mita Sujan and James R. Bettman, 'The effects of brand positioning strategies on consumers' brand and category perceptions: some insights from schema research', *Journal of Marketing Research*, November 1989, 26: 454–67.

[19]James R. Bettman and Mita Sujan, 'Effects of framing on evaluation of comparable and noncomparable alternatives by expert and novice consumers', *Journal of Consumer Research*, September 1987, 14: 141–54; Michael D. Johnson, 'Consumer choice strategies for comparing noncomparable alternatives', *Journal of Consumer Research*, December 1984, 11: 741–53; C. Whan Park and Daniel C. Smith, 'Product level choice: a top-down or bottom-up process?', *Journal of Consumer Research*, December 1989, 16: 289–99.

[20]Joel B. Cohen and Kanul Basu, 'Alternative models of categorization: toward a contingent processing framework', *Journal of Consumer Research*, March 1987, 13: 455–72; Prakash Nedungadi and J. Wesley Hutchinson, 'The prototypicality of brands: relationships with brand awareness, preference and usage', in *Advances in Consumer Research*, Vol. 12, eds. Elizabeth C. Hirschman and Morris B. Holbrook, Provo, UT: Association for Consumer Research, 1985: 489–503; Eleanor Rosch and Carolyn B. Mervis, 'Family resemblance: studies in the internal structure of categories', *Cognitive Psychology*, October 1975, 7: 573–605; James Ward and Barbara Loken, 'The quintessential snack food: measurement of prototypes', in *Advances in Consumer Research*, Vol. 13, ed. Richard J. Lutz, Provo, UT: Association for Consumer Research, 1986: 126–31.

[21]Nedungadi and Hutchinson, 'The prototypicality of brands'; Ward and Loken, 'The quintessential snack food.'

[22]George S. Day, Allan D. Shocker, and Rajendra K. Srivastava, 'Customer-oriented approaches to identifying products-markets', *Journal of Marketing*, Fall 1979, 43: 8–19.

[23]K. E. Miller and J. L. Ginter, 'An investigation of situational variation in brand choice behavior and attitude', *Journal of Marketing Research*, February 1979, 16: 111–23.

[24]Elizabeth Cowley and Andrew A. Mitchell, 'The moderating effect of product knowledge on the learning and organization of product information, *Journal of Consumer Research*, December 2003, 30: 443–54.

[25]Mita Sujan and Christine Dekleva, 'Product categorization and inference making: some implications for comparative advertising', *Journal of Consumer Research*, December 1987, 14: 372–8.

[26]Thomas A. Fogarty, 'A company for all seasons', *USA Today*, 13 January 2000: B3.

[27]Pat Brophy 'The future for liquid milk: a southern perspective', report published by *Teagasc*, 2002. See also dairy product news at www.nutraingredients.com

[28]David Garvin, 'Product quality: an important strategic weapon', *Business Horizons*, May–June, 27: 40–3; Philip Kotler and Kevin Lane Keller, *Marketing Management*, 12th edn, Upper Saddle River, NJ: Prentice Hall, 2000.

[29]Robert C. Blattberg and Kenneth J. Wisniewski, 'Price-induced patterns of competition', *Marketing Science*, Fall 1989, 8: 291–309.

[30]Joseph T. Plummer, 'How personality makes a difference', *Journal of Advertising Research*, December 1984/January 1985, 24: 27–31.

[31]See Jennifer Aaker, 'Dimensions of brand personality', *Journal of Marketing Research*, August 1997, 34: 347–57.

[32]Aaker, 'Dimensions of brand personality'; Susan Fournier, 'Consumers and their brands: developing relationship theory in consumer research', *Journal of Consumer Research*, 1997, 24 (3): 343–73.

[33]Gita Venkataramani Johar, Jaideep Sengupta and Jennifer L. Aaker, 'Two roads to updating brand personality impressions: trait versus evaluative inferencing', *Journal of Marketing Research*, November 2005, 42: 458–69.

[34]M. Joseph Sirgy, 'Self concept in consumer behavior: a critical review', *Journal of Consumer Research*, December 1982, 9: 287–300; Lan Nguyen Chaplin and Deborah Roedder John, 'The development of self-brand connections in children and adolescents', *Journal of Consumer Research*, June 2005, 32: 119–29.

[35]Timothy R. Graeff, 'Consumption situations and the effects of brand image on consumers' brand evaluations', *Psychology & Marketing*, 1997, 14 (1): 49–70; Timothy R. Graeff, 'Image congruence effects on product evaluations: the role of self-monitoring and public/private consumption', *Psychology & Marketing*, 1996, 13 (5): 481–99.

[36]Jennifer L. Aaker, 'The malleable self: the role of self-expression in persuasion', *Journal of Marketing Research*, 1999, 36 (2): 45–57.

[37]Douglas B. Holt, *How Brands Become Icons*, Cambridge, MA: Harvard Business School Press, 2004.

[38]William L. Wilkie, *Consumer Behavior*, 3rd edn, New York: John Wiley & Sons, 1994.

[39]www.harrisinteractive.com/productsandservices/equitrend.asp

[40]William D. Wells, 'How advertising works', unpublished paper, 1980; Christopher P. Puto and William D. Wells, 'Informational and transformational advertising: the differential effects of time', in *Advances in Consumer Research*, Vol. 11, ed. Thomas C. Kinnear, Ann Arbor, MI: Association for Consumer Research, 1983: 638–43; Stephen J. Hoch and John Deighton, 'Managing what consumers learn from experience', *Journal of Marketing*, April 1989, 53: 1–20.

[41]Lynn R. Kahle, Basil Poulos, and Ajay Sukhdial, 'Changes in social values in the United States during the past decade', *Journal of Advertising Research*, February/March 1988: 35–41.

[42]Greg Farrell, 'Marketers put a price on your life', *USA Today*, 7 July 1999: 3B.

[43]Arjun Chaudhuri and Morris B. Holbrook, 'The chain of effects from brand trust and brand affect to brand performance: the role of brand loyalty', *Journal of Marketing*, April 2001, 65: 81–93.

[44]Thomas A. Stewart, 'A satisfied customer is not enough', *Fortune*, 21 July 1997: 112–13.

[45]Thomas O. Jones and W. Earl Sasser Jr, 'Why satisfied customers defect', *Harvard Business Review*, November–December 1995: 88–99.

[46]Fredrick Reichheld, The loyalty effect: the hidden force behind growth, profits and lasting value, Boston, MA: Harvard Business School Press, 1996.

[47]James H. McAlexander, John W. Schouten and Harold F. Koenig, 'Building brand community', *Journal of Marketing*, January 2002, 66: 38–54; Albert Muniz and Thomas O'Guinn, 'Brand community', *Journal of Consumer Research*, March 2001, 27: 412–32.

[48]Gil McWilliam, 'Building stronger brands through online communities', *MIT Sloan Management Review*, Spring 2000, 41 (3): 43–54.

[49]Rene Algesheimer, Utpal M. Dholakia and Andreas Hermann, 'The social influence of brand community: evidence from European car clubs', *Journal of Marketing*, July 2005, 69: 19–34.

[50]Nikki Hopewell, 'Generating brand passion', *Marketing News*, 15 May 2005: 10.

[51]Joseph B. White and Stephen Power, 'VW chief confronts corporate culture', *Wall Street Journal*, 19 September 2005: B2.

[52]Brand Briefing 2.5 is based in part on Steven Hoeffler and Kevin Lane Keller, 'The marketing advantages of strong brands', *Journal of Brand Management*, 10 (6): 421–45, August 2003.

[53]Ian M. Lewis, 'Brand equity or why the board of directors needs marketing research', paper presented at the ARF Fifth Annual Advertising and Promotion Workshop, 1 February 1993.

[54]Peter A. Dacin and Daniel C. Smith, 'The effect of brand portfolio characteristics on consumer evaluations of brand extensions', *Journal of Marketing Research*, May 1994, 31: 229–42; George S. Day and Terry Deutscher, 'Attitudinal predictions of choices of major appliance brands', *Journal of Marketing Research*, May 1982, 19: 192–8; W. B. Dodds, K. B. Monroe and D. Grewal, 'Effects of price, brand and store information on buyers' product evaluations', *Journal of Marketing Research*, August 1991, 28: 307–19; France Leclerc, Bernd H. Schmitt and Laurette Dube, 'Foreign branding and its effects on product perceptions and attitudes', *Journal of Marketing Research*, 1994, 31 (5): 263–70; Akshay R. Rao and K. B. Monroe, 'The effects of price, brand name and store name on buyers' perceptions of product quality: an integrative review', *Journal of Marketing Research*, August 1989, 26: 351–7.

[55]B. Wernerfelt, 'Umbrella branding as a signal of new product quality: an example of signaling by posting a bond', *Rand Journal of Economics*, 1988, 19 (3): 458–66; Tullin Erdem, 'An empirical analysis of umbrella branding', *Journal of Marketing Research*, 1998, 35 (8): 339–51.

[56]Fred M. Feinberg, Barbara E. Kahn and Leigh McAllister, 'Market share response when consumers seek variety', *Journal of Marketing Research*, May 1992, 29: 227–37.

[57]Michel Laroche, Chankon Kim and Lianxi Zhou, 'Brand familiarity and confidence as determinants of purchase intention: an empirical test in a multiple brand context', *Journal of Business Research*, 1996, 37: 115–20.

[58]Robert E. Smith, 'Integrating information from advertising and trial', *Journal of Marketing Research*, May 1993, 30: 204–19.

[59]Andrew S. C. Ehrenberg, Gerard J. Goodhardt and Patrick T. Barwise, 'Double jeopardy revisited', *Journal of Marketing*, July 1990, 54: 82–91.

[60]Rohini Ahluwalia, Robert E. Burnkrant and H. Rao Unnava, 'Consumer response to negative publicity: the moderating role of commitment', *Journal of Marketing Research*, May 2000, 37: 203–14; Narij Dawar and Madam M. Pillutla, 'Impact of product-harm crises on brand equity: the moderating role of consumer expectations', *Journal of Marketing Research*, May 2000, 37: 215–26.

[61]Susan Caminit, 'The payoff from a good corporate reputation', *Fortune*, 10 February 1992: 74–77.

[62]Deepak Agrawal, 'Effects of brand loyalty on advertising and trade promotions: a game theoretic analysis with empirical evidence', *Marketing Science*, 1996, 15 (1): 86–108; Chan Su Park and V. Srinivasan, 'A survey-based method for measuring and understanding brand equity and its extendability', *Journal of Marketing Research*, May 1994, 31: 271–88; Raj Sethuraman, 'A model of how discounting high-priced brands affects the sales of low-priced brands', *Journal of Marketing Research*, November 1996, 33: 399–409.

[63]Hermann Simon, 'Dynamics of price elasticity and brand life cycles: an empirical study', *Journal of Marketing Research*, November 1979, 16: 439–52; K. Sivakumar and S. P. Raj, 'Quality tier competition: how price change influences brand choice and category choice', *Journal of Marketing*, July 1997, 61: 71–84.

[64]Lakshman Krishnamurthi and S. P. Raj, 'An empirical analysis of the relationship between brand loyalty and consumer price elasticity', *Marketing Science*, Spring 1991, 10 (2): 172–83.

[65]Greg M. Allenby and Peter E. Rossi, 'Quality perceptions and asymmetric switching between brands', *Marketing Science*, Summer 1991, 10: 185–204; Rajiv Grover and V. Srinivasan, 'Evaluating the multiple effects of retail promotions on brand loyal and brand switching segments', *Journal of Marketing Research*, February 1992, 29: 76–89; Gary J. Russell and Wagner A. Kamakura, 'Understanding brand competition using micro and macro scanner data', *Journal of Marketing Research*, May 1994, 31: 289–303.

[66]Albert C. Bemmaor and Dominique Mouchoux, 'Measuring the short-term effect of in-store promotion and retail advertising on brand sales: a factorial experiment', *Journal of Marketing Research*, May 1991, 28: 202–14; Robert C. Blattberg and Kenneth J. Wisniewski, 'Price-induced patterns of competition', *Marketing Science*, Fall 1989, 8: 291–309; Randolph E. Bucklin, Sunil Gupta and Sangman Han, 'A brand's eye view of response segmentation in consumer brand choice behavior', *Journal of Marketing Research*, February 1995, 32: 66–74; K. Sivakumar and S. P. Raj, 'Quality tier competition', *Journal of Marketing*, July 1997, 61 (3): 71–84.

[67]William Boulding, Eunkyu Lee and Richard Staelin, 'Mastering the mix: do advertising, promotion and sales force activities lead to differentiation?' *Journal of Marketing Research*, May 1994, 31: 159–72. See also Vinay Kanetkar, Charles B. Weinberg and Doyle L. Weiss, 'Price sensitivity and television advertising exposures: some empirical findings', *Marketing Science*, Fall 1992, 11: 359–71.

[68]Kyle Pope, 'Computers: they're no commodity', *Wall Street Journal*, 15 October 1993: B1.

[69]Peter S. Fader and David C. Schmittlein, 'Excess behavioral loyalty for high-share brands: deviations from the Dirichlet model for repeat purchasing', *Journal of Marketing Research*, 1993, 30 (11): 478–93; Rajiv Lal and Chakravarthi Narasimhan, 'The inverse relationship between manufacturer and retailer margins: a theory', *Marketing Science*, 1996, 15 (2): 132–51.

[70]David B. Montgomery, 'New product distribution: an analysis of supermarket buyer decisions', *Journal of Marketing Research*, 1978, 12 (3): 255–64.

[71]Robert J. Kent and Chris T. Allen, 'Competitive interference effects in consumer memory for advertising: the role of brand familiarity', *Journal of Marketing*, July 1994, 58: 97–105.

[72]Amitava Chattopadyay and Kunal Basu, 'Humor in advertising: the moderating role of prior brand evaluation', *Journal of Marketing Research*, November 1990, 27: 466–76; D. W. Stewart and David H. Furse, 'Effective television advertising: a study of 1000 commercials', 'Lexington, MA: D.C. Heath, 1986; M. G. Weinburger and C. Gulas, 'The impact of humor in advertising: a review', *Journal of Advertising*, 1992, 21 (4): 35–60.

[73]Margaret Campbell and Kevin Lane Keller, 'Brand familiarity and ad repetition effects', *Journal of Consumer Research*, September 2003, 30 (2): 292–304.

[74]S. P. Raj, 'The effects of advertising on high and low loyalty consumer segments', *Journal of Consumer Research*, June 1982, 9: 77–89.

[75]Ravi Dhar and Itamar Simonson, 'The effect of the focus of comparison on consumer preferences', *Journal of Marketing Research*, November 1992, 29: 430–40; Karen A. Machleit, Chris T. Allen and Thomas J. Madden, 'The mature brand and brand interest: an alternative consequence of ad-evoked affect', *Journal of Marketing*, October 1993, 57: 72–82; Itamar Simonson, Joel Huber and John Payne, 'The relationship between prior brand knowledge and information acquisition order', *Journal of Consumer Research*, March 1988, 14: 566–78.

[76]Russell L. Ackoff and James R. Emshoff, 'Advertising research at Anheuser-Busch, Inc. (1963–1968)', *Sloan Management Review*, Winter 1975: 1–15.

[77]These results should be interpreted carefully because they do not suggest that large advertising expenditures did not play an important role in creating equity for the brand in the past

or that advertising expenditures could be cut severely without adverse sales consequences in the future.

[78]See Robert C. Blattberg, Richard Briesch and Edward J. Fox, 'How promotions work', *Marketing Science*, 1995, 14: G122–G132. See also Bart J. Bronnenberg and Luc Wathieu, 'Asymmetric promotion effects and brand positioning', *Marketing Science*, 1996, 15 (4): 379–94. This study shows how the relative promotion effectiveness of high- and low-quality brands depends on their positioning for both price and quality.

[79]Frank E. James, 'I'll wear the Coke pants tonight; they go well with my Harley-Davidson ring', *Wall Street Journal*, 6 June 1985.

[80]David A. Aaker and Kevin Lane Keller, 'Consumer evaluations of brand extensions', *Journal of Marketing*, 1990, 54 (1): 27–41; Kevin Lane Keller and David A. Aaker, 'The effects of sequential introduction of brand extensions', *Journal of Marketing Research*, February 1992, 29: 35–50; A. Rangaswamy, P. R. Burke, and T. A. Oliva, 'Brand equity and the extendibility of brand names', *International Journal of Research in Marketing*, 1993, 10 (3): 61–75.

[81]Taylor Randall, Karl Ulrich and David Reibstein, 'Brand equity and vertical product line extent', *Marketing Science*, 1998, 17 (4): 356–79.

[82]Srinivas K. Reddy, Susan Holak and Subodh Bhat, 'To extend or not to extend: success determinants of line extensions', *Journal of Marketing Research*, 1994, 31 (5): 243–62; C. Whan Park, Sandra Milberg and Robert Lawson, 'Evaluation of brand extensions: the role of product feature similarity and brand concept consistency', *Journal of Consumer Research*, 1991, 18 (9): 185–93; Susan M. Broniarcysyk and Joseph W. Alba, 'The importance of the brand in brand extension', *Journal of Marketing Research*, 1994, 31 (5): 214–28.

[83]Peter A. Dacin and Daniel C. Smith, 'The effect of brand portfolio characteristics on consumer evaluations of brand extensions', *Journal of Marketing Research*, May 1994, 31: 229–42; Keller and Aaker, 'The effects of sequential introduction of brand extensions'; Daniel A. Sheinin and Bernd H. Schmitt, 'Extending brands with new product concepts: the role of category attribute congruity, brand affect and brand breadth', *Journal of Business Research*, 1994, 31: 1–10.

[84]Roger A. Kerin, Gurumurthy Kalyanaram and Daniel J. Howard, 'Product hierarchy and brand strategy influences on the order of entry effect for consumer packaged goods', *Journal of Product Innovation Management*, 1996, 13: 21–34.

[85]Maureen Morrin, 'The impact of brand extensions on parent brand memory structures and retrieval processes', *Journal of Marketing Research*, November 1999, 36: 517–25; John Roedder, Barbara Loken and Christopher Joiner, 'The negative impact of extensions: can flagship products be diluted?' *Journal of Marketing*, January 1998, 62: 19–32; Daniel A. Sheinin, 'The effects of experience with brand extensions on parent brand knowledge', *Journal of Business Research*, 2000, 49: 47–55.

[86]Amna Kirmani, Sanjay Sood and Sheri Bridges, 'The ownership effect in consumer responses to brand line stretches', *Journal of Marketing*, January 1999, 63: 88–101.

[87]Vicki R. Lane and Robert Jacobson, 'Stock market reactions to brand extension announcements: the effects of brand attitude and familiarity', *Journal of Marketing*, 1995, 59 (1): 63–77.

[88]D. A. Aaker and R. Jacobson, 'The financial information content of perceived quality', *Journal of Marketing Research*, 1994, 31 (5): 191–201; D. A. Aaker and R. Jacobson, 'The value relevance of brand attitude in high-technology markets', *Journal of Marketing Research*, November 2001, 38: 485–93; M. E. Barth, M. Clement, G. Foster and R. Kasznik, 'Brand values and capital market valuation', *Review of Accounting Studies*, 1998, 3: 41–68.

3 Brand positioning

PREVIEW

The first two chapters have provided some perspective on branding and described the concept of customer-based brand equity. This was defined as the differential effect that brand knowledge has on customer response to the marketing of that brand. According to this definition, brand knowledge in consumers' minds is central to the creation and management of brand equity. Brand knowledge was conceptualized in terms of a brand node in memory with brand associations, varying in strength, connected to it. Brand equity is then a function of the level of brand awareness and the strength, favourability and uniqueness of brand associations.

The customer-based brand equity (CBBE) model lays out a series of steps for building a strong brand: establish the proper brand identity; create the appropriate brand meaning; elicit positive brand responses; and forge strong brand relationships with customers. The model maintains that six brand building blocks – brand salience, brand performance, brand imagery, brand judgements, brand feelings, and brand resonance – provide the foundation for successful brand development.

As outlined in Chapter 1, the first step in the strategic brand management process is to identify and establish brand positioning. Accordingly, this chapter builds on the notions introduced in Chapter 2 to first consider how to define desired or ideal brand knowledge structures in terms of how to position a brand. Positioning involves identifying and establishing points of parity and points of difference to establish the right brand identity and to create the proper brand image.[1]

With positioning, it is important to associate unique, meaningful *points of difference* to the brand to provide a competitive advantage and 'reason why' consumers should buy it. For some brand associations, however, consumers only need to view them at least as favourably as competitors. That is, it may be sufficient that some brand associations are seen as roughly equal in favourability with competing brand associations, so they function as *points of parity* in consumers' minds to negate potential points of difference for competitors. In other words, these associations are designed to provide 'no reason why not' for consumers to choose the brand. Assuming that other brand associations are evident as points of difference, more favourable brand evaluations and a greater likelihood of choice should then result.

The chapter reviews how to identify and establish core brand associations and a brand mantra. Chapters 4 to 7 describe marketing actions that a firm can take to build brand equity.

IDENTIFYING AND ESTABLISHING BRAND POSITIONING

The CBBE model provides a blueprint for building a strong brand. To use the model, strategic decisions must be made about the specific nature of the brand building blocks involved. To guide those decisions, it is necessary to define the brand positioning, described in this section, as well as a brand mantra, described in the next section.

Basic concepts

The CBBE model describes the way brand knowledge structures should be built to create brand equity. Critical to this view is the creation of strong, favourable and unique brand associations as part of the brand meaning. This section considers how marketers might determine *desired* brand meaning or positioning – that is, what they would like consumers to know about the brand as opposed to what they might currently know. Determining the desired brand knowledge structures involves positioning a brand.

Brand positioning is at the heart of marketing strategy. Brand positioning is the 'act of designing the company's offer and image so that it occupies a distinct and valued place in the target customer's mind.'[2] Positioning, as the name implies, involves finding the proper 'location' in the minds of a group of consumers or market segment so that they think about a product or service in the 'right' or desired way. Positioning is all about identifying the optimal location of a brand and its competitors in the minds of consumers to maximize potential benefit to the firm. A good brand positioning helps to guide marketing strategy by clarifying what a brand is all about, how it is unique and how it is similar to competitive brands and why consumers should purchase and use the brand.

According to the CBBE model, deciding on a positioning requires determining a frame of reference (by identifying the target market and the nature of competition) and the ideal points of parity and points of difference brand associations. In other words, it is necessary to decide: who the target consumer is; who the competitors are; how the brand is similar to these competitors; and how the brand is different from these competitors. These four ingredients are each discussed in turn. Brand Briefing 3.1 describes some of the positioning problems that the cola companies have had in finding good positions for their diet soft drinks.

Target market

Identifying the target consumer is important because people may have different brand knowledge structures and thus different perceptions and preferences for the brand. Without this understanding, it may be difficult to be able to state which brand associations should be strongly held, favourable and unique. A number of considerations are important in defining and segmenting a market and choosing target market segments. A few are highlighted here.

Brand Briefing 3.1

Trying to find some homes for light colas

With consumers turning to healthier options such as water and sports drinks, soft drinks sales have been flat. 'Light' or 'diet' versions have been more successful and represent a growing market segment. Soft drink companies are therefore looking for ways to appeal to calorie-conscious consumers, especially men who are turned off by the taste of diet carbonated drinks or perceive a stigma attached to the word 'light'. And sweeteners, such as Splenda, which appeals to low-carb dieters, create even more options.

The drive to appeal to the health-conscious crowd, however, is making soft drinks a crowded category and success has not come easy for the cola giants. Coca-Cola tried to add Coke Light with Splenda, Coke Zero and C2 to its diet cola portfolio as companions to its hugely successful Coke Light brand. In the process, Coca-Cola has been going head-to-head in the light category with Pepsi, which has a reformulated Pepsi One, as well as Pepsi Max.

Although these line extensions are intended to boost sales, some critics point out that they can also backfire if new versions cannibalize sales of a company's existing drinks. Even worse, many feel that Coke and Pepsi run the risk of confusing consumers with endless variants. Despite spending millions on advertising, experts say customers don't always understand the differences between the options.

Introduced in 1998, Pepsi One appropriately has one calorie. Pepsi waited for Food and Drug Administration approval of sweetener acesulfame potassium (Ace-K) and spent more than €68.4 million on marketing the year following the launch. Pepsi positioned Pepsi One as a full-flavoured yet healthy option to regular colas and targeted men aged 20 to 30 who did not like the taste of light colas. Unfortunately, initial advertising, featuring actor Cuba Gooding Jr, failed to describe exactly what Pepsi One was and how it was different from Pepsi Max. Campaigns came and went and, when Pepsi One failed to garner the market share the company hoped for, it was reformulated with Splenda.

With the launch of Coke Zero and Coca-Cola Light with Splenda in 2005, consumers faced an array of low- or no-calorie Coke options, including Coke Light with Lime, Coke Light with Lemon, Light Cherry Coke, Light Vanilla Coke and Caffeine Free Coke Light. Coke Zero, named for its zero calories, was designed to taste more like original Coke than Light Coke. Coke Zero began with the formula of Coca-Cola but used aspartame and acesulfame potassium as sweeteners instead of sugar. Because the company was trying to stay away from the light label, the words 'light' and 'calories' were not mentioned in the initial marketing campaign. As a result, consumers didn't really know what Coke Zero was and the company eventually switched to ads emphasizing its 'Real Coca-Cola taste, zero calories, no compromise.' Coke Zero was launching in the UK, Spain and Germany in the summer of 2006.

Brand Briefing 3.1 *continued*

Coke and Pepsi also introduced options with half of the calories of other soft drinks that were marketed as 'mid-calorie' colas. With 50 calories, Pepsi Edge had half the sugar, carbohydrates and calories of original colas. Pepsi Edge was geared towards calorie-conscious customers who vacillated between original and diet colas, but preferred the sweeter version. But, after failing to find a lucrative niche in the market, Pepsi announced in May 2005 that it would phase out Pepsi Edge by the end of the year.

Coca-Cola's mid-calorie drink, C2, also experienced slower sales than expected after its 2004 launch in Japan and the USA. Some experts maintain that both of these brands were caught in 'no man's land', offering an unsatisfactory compromise between taste and calories. In other words, people either want the taste and calories of a cola or they don't – there is not much middle ground.

It should be noted that both Coca-Cola and Pepsi have product portfolios that vary significantly across Europe. Also, most international markets use 'light' instead of the US designation 'diet' for low-calorie products.

Sources: Marilynn Marter, 'Zero a hero to pop makers, drinkers', *The Philadelphia Inquirer*, 6 July 2005; Kenneth Hein, 'Positioning: desperately seeking men with extra pounds to shed', *Brandweek*, 22 August 2005; Caroline Wilber, 'Coke Zero had identity crisis', *The Atlanta Journal-Constitution*, 12 August 2005; www.coke.com; www.pepsi.com; Chad Terhune, 'Do real men drink Diet Cola? Pepsi and Coke duke it out', *Wall Street Journal*, 2 July 2004: B1, B4; Heather Todd and Jeff Cioletti, 'A balanced diet', *BeverageWorld*, June 2005: 24–8.

A *market* is the set of all actual and potential buyers who have sufficient interest in, income for and access to a product. In other words, a market consists of all consumers with sufficient motivation, ability and opportunity to buy a product. *Market segmentation* involves dividing the market into distinct groups of consumers who have similar needs and consumer behaviour and thus require similar marketing mixes. Defining a market segmentation plan involves tradeoffs between costs and benefits. The more finely segmented the market, the greater the likelihood that the firm will be able to implement marketing campaigns that meet the needs of consumers. The advantage of a more positive consumer response from a customized marketing campaign, however, can be offset by the greater costs from a lack of standardization.

Segmentation bases

Figures 3.1 and 3.2 display possible segmentation bases for consumer and industrial markets, respectively. In general, these bases can be classified as descriptive or customer-orientated (related to what kind of person or organization is the customer) versus behavioural or product-orientated (related to how the customer thinks of or uses the brand or product).

Behavioural	Demographic
User status.	Income.
Usage rate.	Age.
Usage occasion.	Sex.
Brand loyalty.	Race.
Benefits sought.	Family.
Psychographic	**Geographic**
Values, opinions and attitudes.	International.
Activities and lifestyle.	Regional.

Figure 3.1   Consumer segmentation bases

Nature of goods	Demographic
Kind.	SIC code.
Where used.	Number of employees.
Type of buy.	Number of production workers.
Buying condition	Annual sales volume.
Purchase location.	Number of establishments.
Who buys.	
Type of buy.	

Figure 3.2   Business-to-business segmentation bases

Behavioural segmentation bases are often most valuable in understanding branding issues because they have clearer strategic implications. For example, defining a benefit segment makes it clear what should be the ideal point of difference or desired benefit with which to establish the positioning. Take the toothpaste market. One study uncovered four main segments.[3]

1. *The sensory segment:* seeking flavour and product appearance.
2. *The sociables:* seeking brightness of teeth.
3. *The worriers:* seeking decay prevention.
4. *The independent segment:* seeking low price.

Given this market segmentation scheme, marketing campaigns could be put into place to attract one or more segments. For example, Close-Up initially targeted the first two segments, whereas Crest primarily concentrated on the third segment. Leaving no stone unturned, Beecham's Aquafresh went after all three segments, designing the toothpaste to have three stripes to dramatize each of the three product benefits. With the success of multipurpose toothpastes such as Colgate Total, most brands now offer products that emphasize several benefits. Brand Briefing 3.2 describes a segmentation plan for Nokia customers.

Brand Briefing 3.2

Segmenting mobile phone users at Nokia

As mobile phones became a mass market product, people more or less asked for the same thing: smaller phones that were easier to use. The best brand at improving these aspects won sales. But, as the phones approached the size we are used to today, size was no longer as important. Sleeker designs and replaceable covers became important. As the number of needs and wants in mobile phones grew, manufacturers developed more sophisticated segmentation models.

Segmentation became so crucial to the market leader, Nokia, that, in 2002, it broke its then €16.4 billion mobile phone division into 9 business units, each one focusing on different parts of the market.

In recent years, the segmentation has been based on two dimensions. The first is receptive or belonging versus individualistic and focused on self-esteem; and relaxed and pleasure-orientated versus restrictive, rational and confined. Through the combination of these dimensions, Nokia identified six segments for mobile phone users (Figure 3.3).

The product categories at Nokia were aligned with the consumer segmentation model with categories such as 'classic', 'expression', 'fashion', 'premium', 'basic' and 'imaging'. Segmentation like this has helped Nokia create many models and led to the success of its mobile phone portfolio as a whole.

However, segmenting high-tech products is sometimes not as easy as it might seem. Nokia has at times been criticized for overengineering the segmentation thinking, creating many designs and products that seemed superfluous and complex, such as some of its fashion phones without keypads. Meanwhile, category needs passed Nokia by, such as the sudden popularity of flip phones of the 'clam-shell' variety, which Nokia was slow to introduce.

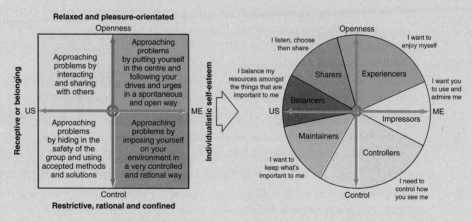

Figure 3.3 Nokia's six segments

Source: Nokia; Mercator Partners' analysis.

Brand Briefing 3.2 *continued*

Perhaps because of the need to balance analysis with simplicity, Nokia expanded its 2005–2006 consumer study to include 42,000 interviews with consumers in 16 countries, which provided the insights for Nokia's category renewal. 'The category renewal will be fundamental to the way Nokia approaches its customers and consumers, and addresses their needs. Having the best consumer understanding in the industry is vital to our whole business – from initial product designs through to sales and customer care', said Robert Andersson, executive vice-president of customer market operations at Nokia. The revision resulted in 11 segments, but with only 4 product categories to serve them: 'Live', 'Connect', 'Achieve' and 'Explore'. The Achieve and Explore product categories also forgot their own sub-brand designations in the product naming system, so they would stand out more clearly as distinct product families.

Andersson was quoted in the press as understanding that customers wanted simplicity even if at the same time the market was definitively not a 'one size fits all'.

Sources: Juha Pinomaa, 'Nokia mobile phones – extending the product range', 27 August 2003, www.nokia.com; Mercator Partners, 'Effective mobile marketing with needs-based segmentation', www.mercatorpartners.com; Russell Beattie, 'Nokia: innovate on the inside', 16 June 2004, www.russellbeattie.com; Nokia press release: 'Nokia connection 2006: extending leadership in mobility', 19 June 2006, www.nokia.com

Other segmentation approaches focus on brand loyalty in some way. For example, the conversion model measures the strength of the psychological commitment of consumers to brands and their openness to change.[4]

To determine the ease with which a consumer can be converted to another choice, the model assesses commitment based on factors such as consumer attitudes towards and satisfaction with current brand choices in a category and the importance of the decision to select a brand in the category.

The model segments users of a brand into four groups based on strength of commitment, from low to high, as follows.

- *Convertible:* on the threshold of change; highly likely to switch brands.
- *Shallow:* not ready to switch, but may be considering options.
- *Average:* comfortable with their choice; unlikely to switch in the future.
- *Entrenched:* staunchly loyal; unlikely to change in the foreseeable future.

The model also classifies non-users of a brand into four other groups based on their openness to trying the brand, from low to high, as follows.

- *Strongly unavailable:* strongly prefer current brand.
- *Weakly unavailable:* preference lies with current brand, although not strongly.
- *Ambivalent:* as attracted to the 'other' brand as to current choice.
- *Available:* prefer the 'other' brand but have not yet switched.

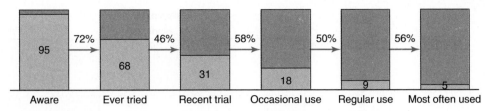

Figure 3.4 Hypothetical example of funnel stages and transitions

Another loyalty perspective, the 'funnel' model, traces consumer behaviour in terms of initial awareness through brand most often used. Figure 3.4 shows a hypothetical pattern of results. In terms of brand building, it is important to understand both the percentage of target market that is present at each stage as well as factors facilitating or inhibiting the transition from one stage to the next. In the hypothetical example, a bottleneck appears to be converting 'ever tried' consumers to those who have 'recently tried'. To achieve more active consideration, marketing may need to be put in place to raise brand salience or make the brand more acceptable in the target consumer's repertoire.

Often, the rationale for descriptive segmentation bases involves behavioural considerations. For example, marketers may choose to segment a market on the basis of age and target a certain age group, but the underlying reason why that age group may be an attractive market segment may be because they are particularly heavy users of the product, are unusually brand loyal or are most likely to seek the benefit that the product is best able to deliver. In some cases, however, broad demographic descriptors may mask important underlying differences.[5] A fairly specific target market of 'women aged 40 to 49' may contain a number of segments that may require different marketing mixes.

The advantage of demographic segmentation bases is that the demographics of traditional media vehicles are generally well known from consumer research; as a result, it has been easier to buy media on that basis. With the growing importance of other media and forms of communication, as well as the capability to build databases to profile customers based on behavioural and media usage, however, this advantage has become less important. For example, US websites can now target such previously hard-to-reach markets as African Americans (NetNoir.com), Hispanics (Quepasa.com), Asian Americans (AsianAvenue.com), college students (Collegeclub.com) and gays (PlanetOut.com).

Criteria

A number of criteria have been offered to guide segmentation and target market decisions, such as the following.[6, 7]

- *Identifiability:* can segment identification be easily determined?
- *Size:* is there adequate sales potential in the segment?
- *Accessibility:* are specialized distribution outlets and communication media available to reach the segment?
- *Responsiveness:* How favourably will the segment respond to a tailored marketing campaign?

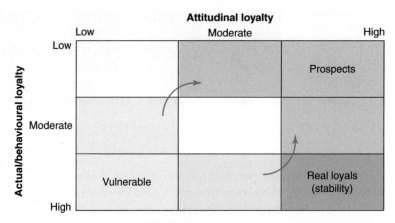

Figure 3.5   Brand loyalty segmentation

The overriding consideration in defining market segments is profitability. In many cases, profitability can be related to behavioural considerations. For example, Baldinger and Rubinson analyzed the implications of a brand loyalty segmentation. In their comprehensive study they mapped the relation between attitude and behaviour. Respondents were interviewed twice, the second interview a year after the first. The study comprised 27 brands in 5 categories.[8]

Traditionally, the procedure for measuring loyalty has been to study the behavioural dimension. However, Baldinger and Rubinson believe that buyers who are loyal to a certain brand are also expected to judge the brand more favourably than brands that they never or seldom buy. They call such customers 'true loyals', while loyal customers who lack this 'true' loyalty to the brand are termed 'vulnerables'.

Their hypothesis was that a higher percentage of 'true loyal' customers remain loyal than 'vulnerable' ones. The respondents were asked about their attitudes towards the brand and then grouped in an attitude–behaviour matrix (Figure 3.5). It became clear that the attitude professed in the first interview had a great effect on the brand's ability to convert low-loyalty customers to high-loyalty customers and on its ability to keep the high-loyalty customers.

The analysis showed that, for 18 of the 27 brands studied, the market share increased over the year if the relationship between the 'prospects' and 'vulnerables' was positive (ie, more 'prospects' than 'vulnerables'). A healthy brand should thus strive to obtain a higher proportion of 'true loyals' compared with competing brands and more 'prospects' than 'vulnerables'. Baldinger and Rubinson suggest that many market-leading brands lack the level of positive attitude that is needed for long-term, continuous consumer loyalty.

Nature of competition

It is difficult to disentangle target market decisions from decisions concerning the nature of competition for the brand because they are often so closely related. In other words, deciding to target a certain type of consumer often, at least implicitly, defines the nature of competition because certain other firms have also decided to target that segment or because consumers in that segment already may look to certain brands. Other issues can be raised, however, in defining the nature of competition and deciding which products and brands are most likely to be seen as close substitutes. For example, the nature of competition may depend on the channels of distribution chosen. Competitive analysis considers a host of factors – including the resources, capabilities and likely intentions of various other firms – to choose markets where consumers can be profitably serviced (see also Chapter 11).[9]

One lesson stressed by many marketing strategists is not to be too narrow in defining competition. Often, competition may occur at the benefit level rather than the attribute level. Thus, a luxury item with a strong hedonic benefit (eg, stereo equipment) may compete as much with a holiday as with other durable goods (eg, furniture).

Unfortunately, many firms define competition narrowly and fail to recognize the most compelling threats and opportunities. For example, sales in the clothing industry have been stagnant as consumers decided to spend on home furnishings, electronics and other products that better suited their lifestyle.[10] Leading clothing makers may be better off considering the points of differences of their offerings not so much against other clothing labels but as against other discretionary purchases.

As noted in Chapter 2, products are often organized in consumers' minds in a hierarchical fashion such that competition can be defined at a number of levels. Take Fanta (a fruit-flavoured soft drink) as an example. At the product type level, it competes with non-cola, flavoured soft drinks; at the product category level, it competes with all soft drinks; and at the product class level, it competes with all drinks. The target and competitive frame of reference chosen will dictate the breadth of brand awareness and the situations and types of cues that should become closely related to the brand. Recognizing the nature of different levels of competition has important implications for brand associations, as described next.[11]

Points of parity and points of difference

Once the appropriate competitive frame of reference for positioning has been fixed by defining the customer target market and nature of competition, the basis of the positioning itself can be defined. Arriving at the proper positioning requires establishing the correct points of difference and points of parity associations.[12]

Points of difference associations

Points of difference (PODs) are strong, favourable and unique associations for a brand. They may be based on almost any type of attribute or benefit association. All that matters for an attribute or benefit association to become a point of difference is that it becomes a strong, favourable and unique association in the minds of consumers. That is, PODs are attributes or benefits that consumers strongly associate with a brand, positively evaluate and believe that they could not find to the same extent with a competitive brand.[13] Although a myriad of brand associations are candidates to become points of difference, according to the CBBE model, such associations can be classified in terms of either functional, performance-related considerations or abstract, imagery-related considerations.

The concept of PODs has much in common with other marketing concepts. For example, it is similar to the notion of the *unique selling proposition* (USP), a concept pioneered by Rosser Reeves and the Ted Bates advertising agency in the 1950s. The idea behind USP was that advertising should give consumers a compelling reason to buy a product that competitors could not match. With this approach, the emphasis in designing ads was placed on communicating a distinctive, unique product benefit (ie, the ad message or claims) and not on the creative (ie, the ad creative or execution). In other words, USP emphasized what was said in an ad as opposed to how it was said.

A related positioning concept is *sustainable competitive advantage* (SCA), which relates, in part, to a firm's ability to achieve an advantage in delivering superior value in the marketplace for a prolonged period of time.[14] Although the SCA concept is somewhat broader than points of difference – SCAs could be based on business practices such as human resource policies – it also emphasizes the importance of differentiating products in some fashion. Thus, the concept of points of difference is closely related to unique selling proposition and sustainable competitive advantage and maintains that a brand must have some strong, favourable and unique associations to differentiate itself from other brands.

Consumers' actual brand choices often depend on the perceived uniqueness of brand associations. Creating strong, favourable and unique associations is a challenge to marketers, but essential in terms of competitive brand positioning. Swedish retailer Ikea took a luxury product – home furnishings and furniture – and made it a reasonably priced option for the mass market. Ikea supports its low prices by having customers serve, deliver and assemble the products themselves. Ikea also gains a point of difference through its product offerings. As one commentator noted, 'Ikea built their reputation on the notion that Sweden produces good, safe, well-built things for the masses. They have some of the most innovative designs at the lowest cost out there.'[15] As another example, consider Subaru.

Subaru

By 1993, Subaru was selling only 104,000 cars annually in the USA, down 60 percent from its peak. Cumulative US losses approached €684 million. Advertised as 'Inexpensive and built to stay that way', Subaru was seen as a 'me too' car that was undifferentiated from Toyota, Honda and all their followers. To provide a distinct image, Subaru decided to sell only all-wheel-drive in its passenger cars. After upgrading its luxury image – and increasing its price – Subaru sold over 187,000 cars by 2004. The following year, it launched an ad campaign in the USA that reflected its global brand positioning and broadened its brand meaning. The ad slogan, 'Think. Feel. Drive' was also used in Japan and the UK.

Points of difference may involve performance attributes (eg, the fact that Hyundai provides six front and back seat 'side-curtain' airbags as standard equipment on all its models for increased safety) or performance benefits (eg, the fact that Magnavox's US electronic products have 'consumer-friendly' technological features, such as television sets with 'smart sound' (keeps volume levels constant while flipping through channels and commercial breaks) and 'Smart Picture' (to automatically adjust picture settings to optimal levels). In other cases, PODs involve imagery associations (eg, the luxury and status imagery of Louis Vuitton or the fact that British Airways is advertised as the 'world's favourite airline'). Many top brands attempt to create a point of difference on 'overall superior quality', whereas a positioning strategy adopted by other firms is to create a point of difference for their brands as the 'low-cost provider' of a product or service. Thus, many PODs are possible.

Points of parity associations

Points of parity (POPs), on the other hand, are associations that may be shared with other brands. These types of associations come in two forms: category and competitive. *Category points of parity* are those associations that consumers view as being necessary to be a legitimate and credible offering within a certain product or service category. In other words, they represent necessary – but not necessarily sufficient – conditions for brand choice. In terms of the discussion of product levels from Chapter 1, these attribute associations are minimally at the generic product level and most likely at the expected product level. Thus, consumers might not consider a bank truly a 'bank' unless it offered a range of current and savings accounts; provided safety deposit boxes, travellers' cheques and other such services; had convenient hours and automated cash machines; and so forth. Category POPs may change over time because of technological advances, legal developments and consumer trends, but the attributes and benefits that function as category POPs can be seen as the 'greens fees' to play the marketing game.

Note that category POPs become critical when a brand launches a brand extension into a new category. In fact, the more dissimilar the extension category, the more important it is to make sure that category POPs are well established. The implications of this realization for the introductory marketing campaign for an extension are clear. In many cases, consumers might have a clear understanding of the extension's intended point of difference by virtue of its use of an existing brand name. Where consumers often need reassurance, however, and what should often be the focus of the marketing, is whether or not the extension also has the necessary points of parity.

Nivea

Nivea became a leader in the skin cream category by creating strong points of difference on the benefits of 'gentle', 'protective' and 'caring'. As it used its brand equity to expand into categories such as deodorants, shampoos and cosmetics, Nivea found it necessary to establish category points of parity before it could promote its brands' points of difference. Nivea's points of difference of gentle, protective and caring were of little value unless consumers believed that its deodorant was strong enough, its shampoo would produce beautiful hair and its cosmetics would be colourful enough. Once points of parity were established, Nivea's heritage and other associations could be introduced as compelling points of difference.

Competitive points of parity are those associations designed to negate competitors' points of difference. In other words, if in the eyes of consumers the brand association designed to be the competitor's point of difference (eg, a product benefit of some type) is as strongly held for the target brand as for competitor's brands *and* the target brand is able to establish another association as strong, favourable and unique as part of its point of difference, then the target brand should be in a superior competitive position. In short, if a brand can 'break even' in those areas where their competitors are trying to find an advantage and can achieve advantages in some other areas, the brand should be in a strong – and perhaps unbeatable – position. For example, consider the introduction of Miller Lite beer.[16]

Miller Lite

When Philip Morris bought Miller Brewing in the USA, its flagship High Life brand was not competing well, leading the company to decide to introduce a light beer. The initial advertising strategy for Miller Lite was to assure parity with a necessary and important consideration in the category by stating that it 'tastes great' while at the same time creating a point of difference with the fact that it contained one-third less calories (96 calories versus 150 calories for a standard-sized, full-strength beer) and was thus 'less filling'. As is often the case, the point of parity and point of difference were conflicting, as consumers tend to equate taste with calories. To overcome potential consumer resistance to this notion, Miller employed credible spokespeople, primarily popular former professional athletes who would presumably not drink a beer unless it tasted good. These people were placed in amusing situations in ads where they debated the merits of Miller Lite as to which of the two product benefits – 'tastes great' or 'less filling' – was more descriptive of the beer, creating valuable points of parity and points of difference. The ads ended with the clever tagline 'Everything you've always wanted in a beer . . . and less.'[17]

Points of parity versus points of difference

To achieve a point of parity on a particular attribute or benefit, a sufficient number of consumers must believe that the brand is 'good enough' on that dimension. There is a 'zone' or 'range of tolerance or acceptance' with POPs. It does not have to be the case that the brand is *literally* seen as equal to competitors, but consumers must feel that the brand does sufficiently well on that particular attribute or benefit so that they do not consider it to be a problem. Assuming consumers feel that way, they may then be willing to base their evaluations and decisions on other factors potentially more favourable to the brand. Points of parity are thus easier to achieve than points of difference, where the brand must demonstrate clear superiority. Often, the key to positioning is not so much in achieving a point of difference as in achieving necessary or competitive points of parity.

POSITIONING GUIDELINES

The concepts of points of difference and points of parity can be invaluable tools to guide positioning. A number of considerations come into play in conducting positioning analysis and deciding on the desired PODs and POPs and the resulting brand image. Two issues in arriving at the optimal competitive brand positioning are:

defining and communicating the competitive frame of reference; and choosing and establishing points of parity and points of difference.[18]

Defining and communicating the competitive frame of reference

A starting point in defining a competitive frame of reference for a brand positioning is to determine category membership. Membership indicates the products or sets of products with which a brand competes. Choosing to compete in different categories often results in different competitive frames of reference and thus different POPs and PODs (see Brand Briefing 3.3 on FedEx).

Brand Briefing 3.3

Competitive frames of reference for FedEx

Consider the history of FedEx, the US pioneer in the overnight delivery service (ONDS) category. Within this category, FedEx created strong, favourable and unique associations with the consumer benefits of being the fastest and most dependable delivery service (as reinforced by its slogan, 'When it absolutely, positively has to be there overnight'). This association provided a point of difference from the usual postal service (which would typically take two or more days depending on the destination), as well as other overnight carriers that found it difficult, at least initially, to match FedEx's high level of service quality.

Companies like FedEx used to build success from securing the transfer of important documents between companies and individuals. However, since offices are now full of fax machines, e-mail-enabled computers and phones, 'speed and reliability' seems obsolete.

When faced with this situation, FedEx had several options. It could cater itself to the occasions when an e-mail or a fax seems insecure. In business, there are many occasions where absolute reliability and confirmation are very important and worth a premium. Even though there is some opportunity there, that market is less than FedEx was used to.

But what about internet commerce? As people on the one hand started buying things on the web, to be delivered to their doorsteps, there was, on the other hand the globalization process and the economic boom in Asia. All of these factors increased the need for fast delivery of packages.

UPS has been a tough competitor due to its aggressive pricing and good ground delivery capabilities. FedEx had to improve its ground delivery offers as well as market the package delivery offer more heavily. Still, the strength of the FedEx position, 'Speed and reliability', is very strong, both in the case of the individual buying stuff on the web and for someone running a manufacturing business in China promising fast deliveries.

Brand Briefing 3.3 *continued*

FedEx was succesful in expanding from its basic positioning. After 2004, the volume of goods FedEx delivered over its international network soared 40 percent, with much of the growth from Asia, and the value of the company more than doubled between 2003 and 2006.

Sources: David Field, 'FedEx not ready to abandon shipping', *USA Today*, 20 October 1999: B3; Dean Foust, 'The ground war at FedEx', *BusinessWeek*, 28 November 2005; Vivian Mannin-Schaffel, 'UPS and FedEx compete to deliver', www.brandchannel.com, 17 May 2004; Dean Foust, 'FedEx taking off like a "rocket ship"', *BusinessWeek*, 3 April 2006.

Communicating category membership informs the consumer about the goals that they might achieve by using a product or service. For established products and services, category membership is not a focal issue. Target customers are aware that Coca-Cola is a leading brand of soft drink, that Kellogg's is a leading brand of cereal, McKinsey is a leading strategy consulting firm and so on.

There are many situations, however, in which it is important to inform consumers of a brand's category membership. Perhaps the most obvious situation is new products, where the category membership is not always apparent. This uncertainty can be especially true for high-tech products.

Personal digital assistants

When personal digital assistants (PDAs) were introduced, the product could have been positioned as either a computer accessory or a replacement for an appointment book. Motorola Envoy's failure could be attributed in part to the lack of a clearly defined competitive set. By contrast, Palm Pilot, a product that performed many of the same tasks as Envoy, achieved success by claiming membership in the electronic organizer category. More recently, BlackBerry has extended that category to encompass e-mail while offering a more traditional keyboard, thus serving as a substitute to some extent for laptop computers. As these handheld devices continue to offer new features and services, their competitive frames of reference will continue to evolve.

Situations also exist in which consumers know a brand's category membership but may not be convinced that the brand is a true, valid member of the category. In such cases, alerting consumers to a brand's category membership is warranted. For example, consumers may be aware that Sony produces computers, but they may not be certain whether Sony computers are in the same 'class' as IBM, Dell and Compaq. In this instance, it might be useful to reinforce category membership.

Brands are sometimes affiliated with categories in which they do not hold membership rather than with the one in which they do. This approach is a viable way to highlight a brand's point of difference from competitors, provided that consumers know the brand's actual membership. For example, Bristol-Myers Squibb ran commercials for its Excedrin aspirin in the USA acknowledging Tylenol's perceived consumer acceptance for aches and pains, but touting their brand as 'The headache medicine'. With this approach, however, it is important that consumers understand what the brand stands for, and not just what it is *not*.

The preferred approach to positioning is to inform consumers of a brand's membership before stating its point of difference in relation to other category members. Presumably, consumers need to know what a product is and what function it serves before assessing whether or not it dominates the brands against which it competes. For new products, separate marketing campaigns are generally needed to inform consumers of membership and to educate them about a brand's point of difference. For brands with limited resources, this implies the development of a marketing strategy that establishes category membership before one that states a point of difference. Brands with greater resources can develop concurrent marketing campaigns in which one features membership and the other the point of difference. Efforts to inform consumers of membership and points of difference in the same ad, however, are often not effective.

Occasionally, a company will undertake to straddle two frames of reference.

BMW

When BMW made a strong competitive push into the USA in the early 1980s, it positioned the brand as being the only car that offered both luxury and performance. At that time, US luxury cars were seen by many as lacking performance and performance cars were seen as lacking luxury. By relying on design, its German heritage and other aspects of a well-designed marketing campaign, BMW was able to simultaneously achieve: a point of difference on luxury and a point of parity on performance with respect to performance cars. The slogan 'The ultimate driving machine' effectively captured the newly created umbrella category – luxury performance cars.

Although a straddle positioning often is attractive as a means of reconciling potentially conflicting consumer goals, it carries an extra burden. If the points of parity and points of difference with respect to both categories are not credible, the brand may not be viewed as a legitimate player in either category. Many early PDAs that unsuccessfully tried to straddle categories ranging from pagers to laptop computers provide a vivid illustration of this risk.

There are three ways to convey a brand's category membership: communicating category benefits, comparing with exemplars and relying on the product descriptor.

To reassure consumers that a brand will deliver on the fundamental reason for using a category, benefits are frequently used to announce category membership. Thus, industrial motors might claim to have power, and analgesics might announce their efficacy. These benefits are presented in a manner that does not imply brand superiority but merely notes that the brand possesses these properties as a means to establish category POPs. To provide supporting rationale so that consumers believe a brand has the benefits that imply membership in a category, performance and imagery associations can be used. A cake mix might attain membership in its category by claiming the benefit of great taste and might support this benefit claim by possessing high-quality ingredients (performance) or by showing users delighting in its consumption (imagery).

Exemplars – well-known, noteworthy brands in a category – can also be used to specify a brand's category membership. When Tommy Hilfiger was an unknown designer, advertising announced his membership as a great American designer by associating him with Geoffrey Beene, Stanley Blacker, Calvin Klein and Perry Ellis, who were recognized members of that category.

The product descriptor that follows the brand name is often a compact way of conveying category origin. For example, USAir changed its name to USAirways, according to chief executive Stephen Wolf, as part of the airline's attempted transformation from a regional one with a poor reputation to a strong national or even international brand. The argument was that other major airlines had the word 'airlines' or 'airways' in their names rather than air' which was felt to be typically associated with smaller, regional carriers.[19] Consider the following examples.

- Cars have been introduced in recent years that combine the attributes of a four-by-four, an MPV and an estate, eg, the Honda CR-V and BMW X3. To communicate this unique position, the vehicles have been designated a 'sports wagon' in the USA.[20]
- When Campbell's launched its V-8 Splash drinks line, it avoided including the word 'carrot' in the brand name despite the fact that it was the main ingredient. The name was chosen to convey healthful benefits but to avoid the negative perception of carrots.[21]
- California's prune growers and marketers attempted to establish a different name for their product, 'dried plums', because prunes were seen by the target market of women aged 35 to 50 as 'a laxative for old people'.

The product descriptor is often critical for technology products. When IBM rebranded its server product line as the eSeries, it created four sets of brands and products within the line. Although three of the series had clear designations – zSeries mainframe servers, pSeries Unix servers and xSeries Intel servers – some critics felt that the designation for their iSeries integrated application servers (formerly the highly successful AS/400) did not necessarily provide clear category membership either within the IBM product line or with respect to its server competitors.

Although it is important to establish a brand's category membership, it is usually not sufficient for effective brand positioning. Although such efforts can help to expand the category, if many firms engage in category-building tactics, the result may be consumer confusion. For example, at the peak of the dot-com boom, a host of websites advertised their category membership. In the USA, Ameritrade, E*Trade, Datek and others advertised that they had lower commission rates on stock trades than conventional brokerage firms; Pets.com, Petopia and other pet food suppliers promoted their vast array of pet supplies; and so on. A sound positioning strategy requires the specification not only of the category in which a brand holds membership, but also how a brand dominates other members of its category. Developing compelling points of difference is thus critical to effective brand positioning.

Choosing points of parity and points of difference

Points of parity are driven by the needs of category membership (to create category POPs) and the necessity of negating competitors' PODs (to create competitive POPs). In terms of choosing points of difference, broadly, the two most important considerations are that consumers find the POD desirable and believe that the firm has the capabilities to deliver on it. If both of these considerations are satisfied, the POD has the potential to become a strong, favourable and unique brand association. Both of these broad considerations have a number of specific criteria, as follows.

Desirability criteria

As noted in Chapter 2, there are three desirability criteria for PODs – relevance, distinctiveness and believability – that must be assessed from a consumer perspective. Only by satisfying these will the POD be sufficiently desirable to consumers to have the potential to serve as a viable positioning alternative.

- *Relevance:* target consumers must find the POD personally relevant and important. Relevance considerations can be easily overlooked. For example, in the early 1990s, a number of brands in different product categories (colas, dish washing soaps, beer, deodorant, petrol, etc.) introduced clear versions of their products to differentiate themselves better. Although 'clear' perhaps signalled natural, pure and lightness to consumers initially, a proliferation of clear versions of products that did not reinforce these other associations blurred its meaning. The 'clear' association has not seemed to be of enduring value or to be sustainable as a point of difference. In many cases, these brands have experienced declining market share or disappeared.
- *Distinctiveness:* target consumers must find the POD distinctive and superior. When entering a category in which there are established brands, the challenge is to find a viable basis for differentiation. A frequent occurrence is that the point of difference selected is one on which a brand dominates its competition and not one that is important to consumers. So, several analgesic brands have found limited demand for the claim that their brand was long-lasting or that infrequent dosing was required. Most consumers place more importance on fast relief than long-lasting relief. Indeed, long-lasting may imply slow-acting – just the opposite of what is desired.
- *Believability:* target consumers must find the POD believable and credible. A brand must offer a compelling reason for choosing it over the other options that might be considered. Perhaps the simplest approach is to point to a unique attribute of the product. Thus, Mountain Dew may argue that it is more energizing than other soft drinks and support this claim by noting that it has a higher level of caffeine. On the other hand, when the point of difference is abstract or image-based, support for the claim may reside in more general associations to the company that have been developed over time. Thus, Chanel No 5 perfume may claim to be the quintessential elegant, French perfume and support this claim by noting the long association between Chanel and haute couture.

Deliverability criteria

Chapter 2 also highlighted three deliverability criteria: feasibility, communicability and sustainability. If these are satisfied, the positioning has the potential to be enduring.

- *Feasibility:* the product must perform at the level stated. In other words, it must be feasible for the firm – in terms of affordability, resources necessary, time horizon involved and so forth – to actually create the POD. The product and marketing must be designed in a way to support the desired association. Does communicating the desired association involve real changes to the product itself or just perceptual ones as to how the consumer thinks of the product or brand? It is obviously easier to convince consumers of some fact about the brand that they were unaware of or may have overlooked than to make changes in the product and convince consumers of these changes.
- *Communicability:* the current or future prospects of communicating information to create or strengthen the desired associations. The issue here is consumers' perceptions of the brand and the resulting brand associations. It is very difficult to create an association that is not consistent with existing consumer knowledge or that consumers, for whatever reason, have trouble believing. The communicability of a brand association can depend on many things, but perhaps the most important is whether or not consumers can be given a compelling reason why the brand will deliver the desired benefit. In other words, what factual, verifiable evidence or 'proof points' can be given as support so that consumers will believe in the brand and its desired associations?
- *Sustainability:* the actual and communicated performance over time. Is the positioning pre-emptive, defensible and difficult to attack? Is it the case that the favourability of a brand association can be reinforced and strengthened over time? If these are the case, the positioning is likely to last for years. Sustainability depends on internal commitment and use of resources as well as external market forces. Applebee's strategy for leadership in the casual dining restaurant business, in part, is to enter smaller towns where a second major competitor might be unlikely to enter. Although there are downsides to the strategy – potentially smaller volume and lethal word of mouth from any service problems – competitive threats are minimal.[22]

Establishing points of parity and points of difference

Creating a strong brand positioning requires establishing the right points of parity and points of difference. The difficulty in doing so, however, is that many of the attributes or benefits that make up the POPs or PODs are negatively correlated. That is, if consumers mentally rate the brand highly on one particular attribute or benefit, they also rate it poorly on another. For example, it might be difficult to position a brand as 'inexpensive' and at the same time assert that it is 'of the highest quality'. Figure 3.6 gives some other examples of negatively correlated attributes and benefits. Moreover, individual attributes and benefits often have positive and negative

Low price v high quality.   Powerful v safe.
Taste v low calories.   Strong v refined.
Nutritious v good tasting.   Ubiquitous v exclusive.
Efficacious v mild.   Varied v simple.

Figure 3.6   Negatively correlated attributes and benefits

aspects. For example, consider a long-lived brand that is seen as having a great deal of heritage. Heritage could be seen as a positive attribute because it can suggest experience, wisdom and expertise. On the other hand, it could also be easily seen as being old-fashioned and not cutting-edge.

Unfortunately, consumers typically want to maximize both of the negatively correlated attributes and benefits. The challenge is that competitors often are trying to achieve their point of difference on an attribute that is negatively correlated with the point of difference of the target brand. Much of the art and science of marketing is how to deal with tradeoffs, and positioning is no different.[23] The best approach is to develop a product or service that performs well on both dimensions. Thus, the ability of BMW to establish their straddle positioning image of 'luxury and performance' was due in large part to product design and the fact that the car was considered both luxurious and high-performance. Similarly, Gore-Tex was able to overcome the seemingly conflicting product image of 'breathable' and 'waterproof' through technological advances.

There are other ways to address the problem of negatively correlated POPs and PODs. The following three approaches are listed in increasing level of effectiveness – but also increasing level of difficulty.

Separate the attributes

An expensive but sometimes effective approach is to launch two marketing campaigns, each devoted to a different brand attribute or benefit. These campaigns may run concurrently or sequentially. For example, Head & Shoulders shampoo met success in Europe with a dual campaign in which one ad emphasized its dandruff removal efficacy while another emphasized the appearance and beauty of hair after its use. The hope was that consumers would be less critical when judging the POP and POD benefits in isolation because the negative correlation might be less apparent. The downside to such an approach is that two strong campaigns have to be developed. Moreover, by not addressing the negative correlation head-on, consumers may not develop as positive associations as desired.

Exploit equity of another entity

In the Miller Lite example discussed earlier, the brand 'borrowed' or leveraged the equity of well-known and well-liked celebrities to lend credibility to one of the negatively correlated benefits. Brands can potentially link themselves to any kind of entity that possesses the right kind of equity – a person, other brand, event and so forth – as a means to establish an attribute or benefit as a POP or POD. Self-branded ingredients may also lend some credibility to a questionable attribute in consumers' minds. Borrowing equity, however, is neither costless nor riskless. Chapter 7 outlines the pros and cons of leveraging equity.

Redefine the relationship

Finally, another potentially powerful but often difficult way to address the negative relationship between attributes and benefits in the minds of consumers is to convince them that in fact the relationship is positive. This redefinition can be accomplished by providing consumers with a different perspective and suggesting that they may be overlooking or ignoring certain factors or other considerations.

Apple

When Apple launched the Macintosh, its point of difference was 'user-friendly'. Although many consumers valued ease of use – especially those who bought computers for the home – one drawback with this association was that customers who bought computers for business applications inferred that, if it was easy to use, then it also must not be powerful – a key consideration in that market. Recognizing this potential problem, Apple ran a clever ad campaign with the tagline 'The power to be your best' in an attempt to redefine what a powerful computer meant. The message behind the ads was that, because Apple was easy to use, people in fact did just that – they used them! – a simple but important indication of 'power'. In other words, the most powerful computers were ones that people actually used.

Although difficult to achieve, such a strategy can be powerful because the two associations can become mutually reinforcing. The challenge is to develop a credible story with which consumers can agree.

Updating positioning over time

The previous section described some positioning guidelines that are especially useful for launching a brand. With established brands, competitive forces often dictate shifts in positioning strategy over time. Brand Briefing 3.4 describes the positioning of the European Union. The credit card wars provides another illustration.

Visa and American Express

Visa's POD as a credit card is that it is the most widely available card, which underscores the category's main benefit of convenience. American Express, on the other hand, has built the equity of its brand by highlighting the prestige associated with the use of its card. Having established their PODs, Visa and American Express now compete by attempting to blunt each other's advantage to create POPs. Along these lines, Visa offers gold and platinum cards to enhance the prestige of its brand and advertises 'It's everywhere you want to be' in aspirational settings that reinforce exclusivity and acceptability. On the other hand, American Express has substantially increased the number of

Brand Briefing 3.4

Positioning of the European Union

The European Union has from the start been dependent on public opinion in its member states. Since the union is made up of democracies, every member state (and the nations interested in joining the union) has found itself with 'pro-EU' and 'anti-EU' camps, which all aim to position themselves.

Since 1973, the European Commission has been monitoring the evolution of public opinion in member states, thus helping the preparation of texts, decision-making and the evaluation of its work. The surveys and studies address topics concerning European citizenship: enlargement, social situation, health, culture, information technology, environment, the euro, defence, etc.

Overall, the most EU-positive citizens in a July 2006 study were Ireland, The Netherlands and Spain (where more than 70 percent of the population was positive), while the UK, Finland, Latvia and Austria were the most negative (with around 40 percent of the population positive). A face-to-face study gave interesting results. The debates in the different countries have resulted in different spontaneous associations (brand associations) to the EU.

For 38 percent of the Dutch and 29 percent of the Spanish, the EU is synonymous with co-operation between member states, while 25 percent of Germans and 27 percent of Italians mentioned the euro as the main symbol of the EU (versus 15 percent on average) and 18 percent referred to mobility. About 39 percent of French citizens saw the EU first and foremost as a series of institutions (ie, 20 points higher than the average). The Irish rated the EU as good at fighting unemployment and for 23 percent of Polish citizens the words 'European Union' have a positive connotation, such as progress or a better future (ie, 8 points higher than on average). The majority of Austrians can be qualified as Eurosceptics; 18 percent of them spontaneously mentioned inflation and 13 percent mentioned the potential negative consequences of immigration.

What this all means is that, while there is only one EU, its brand image differs from country to country, not only on the positive–negative scale but also in position. This comes from the long political history in each country where EU issues have been mixed in with national political issues. So, in branding terms, in one country a party could position EU membership as having certain points of difference (such as higher mobility) while also holding points of parity against the alternative (for instance, holding EU membership as democratic, thus negating the opposing sides arguments). Another country could have the EU advocates holding up other points of difference and points of parity to better suit the national agenda. Since political agendas have been different in the different countries, the EU does not have a clear, common brand image across its member states.

Still, the conclusion of the 'Eurobarometer' is that the EU has a positive image: 'It is above all perceived as democratic, modern and protective. However, that does not

Brand Briefing 3.4 *continued*

prevent its main and loyal supporters from criticising its technocratic and to a certain extent inefficient character.' Even if we agree with this conclusion, Euroscepticism continues to be a problem for advancing the union. In 2000 the Danes and in 2003 the Swedes in referenda voted against adopting the euro, and in 2005, French (29 May) and Dutch (1 June) voters in referenda rejected the treaty establishing a constitution for Europe, leaving the future for that initiative uncertain. Setbacks like these coupled with low participation in EU elections could be signs of unclear positioning of what a 'yes' or a 'no' means, nationally and on the European level.

Margot Wallström, vice-president of the European Commission, responsible for institutional relations and communication strategy, said about the survey: 'The only way for the European Union to regain trust of its citizens is by delivering results: security, better opportunities in the labour market and better quality of life. These are the issues on which we should focus . . . Citizens expect also that the union leaders explain better benefits of enlargement.'

Sources: TNS, 'The future of Europe', for the European Commission, May 2006; Standard Eurobarometer 65: Spring 2006, http://ec.europa.eu/public_opinion; 'Treaty establishing a Constitution for Europe', www.wikipedia.org

vendors that accept American Express cards and created other value enhancements through its 'Do more' and, later, 'Make life rewarding' and 'A world of service' campaigns to reduce Visa's advantage on this dimension.

Updating positioning involves two main issues. The first is how to deepen the meaning of the brand to tap into core brand associations or other, more abstract considerations (*laddering*). The second is how to respond to competitive challenges that threaten an existing positioning (*reacting*).

Laddering

Although identifying PODs to dominate competition on benefits that are important to consumers provides a sound way to build an initial position, once the target market attains a basic understanding of how the brand relates to other products in the same category, it may be necessary to deepen the meanings associated with the brand positioning. It is often useful to explore underlying consumer motivations in a product category to uncover the relevant associations. For example, Maslow's hierarchy maintains that consumers have different priorities and levels of needs.[24] From lowest to highest priority, they are the following.

1. Physiological needs (food, water, air, shelter, sex).
2. Safety and security needs (protection, order, stability).

3. Social needs (affection, friendship, belonging).

4. Ego needs (prestige, status, self-respect).

5. Self-actualization (self-fulfillment).

According to Maslow, higher-level needs become relevant once lower-level needs are satisfied.

Marketers have recognized the importance of higher-level needs. For example, means–end chains have been devised as a way of understanding higher-level meanings of brand characteristics.[25] A means–end chain takes the following structure: attributes (descriptive features that characterize a product) lead to benefits (the personal value and meaning attached to product attributes), which, in turn, lead to values (stable and enduring personal goals or motivations).[26] In other words, a consumer chooses a product that delivers an attribute (A) that provides benefits or has certain consequences (B/C) that satisfy values (V). For example, in a study of salty snacks, one respondent noted that a flavoured crisp (A) with a strong taste (A) would mean that she would eat less (B/C), not get fat (B/C) and have a better figure (B/C), all of which would enhance her self-esteem (V).

Laddering thus involves a progression from attributes to benefits to more abstract values or motivations. In effect, laddering involves repeatedly asking what the implication of an attribute or benefit is for the consumer. Failure to move up the ladder may reduce the strategic options available to a brand. For example, P&G introduced Dash detergent to attract US consumers who used front-loading washing machines. Many years of advertising Dash in this manner made this position impenetrable by other brands. Dash was so associated with front-loaders, however, that when this type of machine went out of fashion, so did Dash. This occurred despite the fact that Dash was among P&G's most effective detergents and despite significant efforts to reposition the brand.

Some attributes and benefits may lend themselves to laddering more easily than others. For example, the Betty Crocker brand appears on baking products and thus is characterized by the physical warmth associated with baking. Such an association makes it relatively easy to talk about emotional warmth and the joy of baking or the good feelings that might arise from baking for others. Similarly, Nivea skin cream has well-entrenched benefits of being 'caring', 'gentle' and 'protective' for the skin. Such a product foundation makes it easier to associate these same values with family relationships or friendships.

Thus, some of the strongest brands deepen their points of difference to create benefit and value associations – for example, Volvo and Michelin (safety and peace of mind), Intel (performance and compatibility), Marlboro (Western imagery), Coke (Americana and refreshment), Disney (fun, magic and family entertainment), Nike (innovative products and peak athletic performance) and BMW (styling and driving performance). As a brand becomes associated with more and more products and moves up the product hierarchy, the brand's meaning will become more abstract. At the same time, it is important that the proper category membership and POPs and PODs exist in the minds of consumers for the particular products sold. After a consideration of how to react to competitors' actions, the following section discusses the related topic of core brand associations. Chapter 13 addresses issues in changing the meaning of brands over time.

Reacting

Competitive actions often aim to eliminate points of difference to make them points of parity or to strengthen or establish new points of difference. Often competitive advantages exist for only a short time before competitors attempt to match them. For example, when Goodyear introduced its Run-Flat tyres (which allowed tyres to keep going for up to 50 miles at a speed of 55 mph after a puncture or blowout), Michelin quickly responded with its Zero Pressure tyre, which offered the same consumer benefit.

When a competitor challenges a POD or attempts to overcome a POP, there are three main options for the target brand – from no reaction to moderate to significant reactions.

- *Do nothing:* if the competitive actions seem unlikely to recapture a POD or create a new POD, the best reaction is probably to just stay the course and continue brand-building efforts.
- *Go on the defensive:* if the competitive actions appear to have the potential to disrupt the market, it may be necessary to take a defensive stance. One way to defend the positioning is to add some reassurance in the product or advertising to strengthen POPs and PODs.
- *Go on the offensive:* if the competitive actions seem potentially quite damaging, it may be necessary to take a more aggressive stance and reposition the brand to address the threat. One approach may be to launch a product extension or ad campaign that fundamentally changes the meaning of the brand.

Deciding the severity of the competitive threat and the appropriate competitive stance can benefit from a brand audit, as described below. Essentially, the intent of the audit in this case would be to assess competitive actions in terms of how they would affect POPs and PODs according to the desirability and deliverability criteria listed previously.

DEFINING AND ESTABLISHING BRAND MANTRAS

Brand positioning describes how a brand can compete against a specified set of competitors in a particular market. In many cases, however, brands span product categories and therefore may have several distinct – yet related – positionings. As brands evolve and expand across categories, it is often useful to define a set of core brand associations to capture the essence of the brand meaning and what it represents. It is also often useful to synthesize the core brand associations to a core brand promise or brand mantra that reflects the essential 'heart and soul' of the brand. Both concepts are described next.

Core brand associations

Core brand associations are abstract associations (attributes and benefits) that characterize the five to ten most important aspects of a brand. Core brand associations can serve as a foundation for the brand strategy. In particular, such associations can serve as the basis of brand positioning in terms of how they relate to points of parity and points of difference.

Core associations can be identified through a structured process. The first step is to create a detailed mental map of the brand. A *mental map* portrays in detail all salient brand associations and responses for a particular target market (eg, brand users). Mental maps must reflect the reality of how the brand is actually perceived by consumers in terms of their beliefs, attitudes, opinions, feelings, images and experiences. The CBBE brand pyramid from Chapter 2 helps to highlight the types of associations and responses that may emerge in a mental map. Chapter 9 describes research techniques that can be used to construct a mental map. One of the simplest means to get consumers to create a mental map is by asking them for their top-of-mind brand associations (eg, 'When you think of this brand, what comes to mind?')

Next, brand associations are grouped into categories according to how they are related, often with two to four associations per category. Each category is labelled to be as descriptive as possible as a core brand association. For example, in response to a Nike brand probe, consumers in the USA may list LeBron James, Michael Jordan, Tiger Woods, Roger Federer or Lance Armstrong, which could be summarized by the label 'top athletes'. There may be as few as 3 to 5 or as many as 10 to 12 core brand associations. In assembling such associations, the challenge is to maximize the coverage of the mental map to include all relevant associations while making sure each one is as distinct as possible. Figure 3.7 displays a hypotetical mental map for MTV and Figure 3.8 lists the core brand associations for the music TV channel.

Brand mantras

To focus on what a brand represents, it is often useful to define a brand mantra.[27] A brand mantra is highly related to concepts such as 'brand essence' or 'core brand promise'. A *mantra* is an articulation of the 'heart and soul' of the brand. Brand

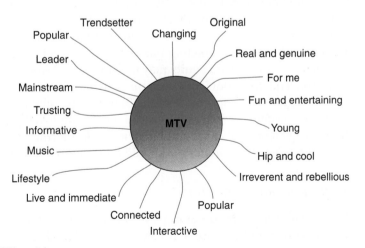

Figure 3.7   MTV mental map

- **Music**
  What's hot and what's new.
- **Credibility**
  Expert, trusting, reality.
- **Personality**
  Irreverent, hip, cool.
- **Accessibility**
  Relevant, for everyone.
- **Interactivity**
  Connected and participatory.

- **Community**
  Shared experience (literally and talk value).
- **Modern**
  Hip, cool.
- **Spontaneity**
  Up-to-the-minute, immediate.
- **Originality**
  Genuine, creative.
- **Fluidity**
  Always changing and evolving.

Figure 3.8   MTV core brand associations

mantras are three- to five-word phrases that capture the irrefutable essence or spirit of the brand positioning. Their purpose is to ensure that all employees within the organization and all external marketing partners understand what the brand fundamentally is to represent to consumers so that they can adjust their actions accordingly.

Brand mantras are powerful devices. They can provide guidance as to what products to introduce under the brand, what ad campaigns to run, where and how the brand should be sold and so on. The influence of brand mantras, however, can extend beyond these tactical concerns. Brand mantras may even guide the most seemingly unrelated or mundane decisions, such as the look of a reception area and the way phones are answered. In effect, they are designed to create a mental filter to screen out inappropriate marketing activities or actions that might hurt customers' impressions of a brand.

Mantras are important for a number of reasons. First, any time a consumer or customer encounters a brand – in any way, shape or form – his or her knowledge about that brand may change and, as a result, the equity of the brand is affected. Given that a vast number of employees, either directly or indirectly, come into contact with consumers in a way that may affect consumer knowledge about the brand, it is important that employees' words and actions reinforce and support the brand meaning. Many employees or marketing partners (eg, ad agency members) who potentially could help or hurt brand equity may be far removed from the marketing strategy formulation and may not even recognize their role in influencing equity. A brand mantra signals the importance of the brand to the organization and an understanding of its meaning as well as the crucial role of employees and marketing partners in its management. It also provides a memorable shorthand as to what are the crucial considerations of the brand that should be kept most salient and top-of-mind.

Writing a brand mantra

What makes for a good mantra? McDonald's philosophy of 'Food, folks and fun' captures its brand essence and core promise. Two high-profile examples of brand mantras come from two powerful brands, Nike and Disney, as described in Brand

	Emotional modifier	Descriptive modifier	Brand functions
Nike	Authentic	Athletic	Performance
Disney	Fun	Family	Entertainment

Figure 3.9   Writing a brand mantra

Briefings 3.5 and 3.6. Brand mantras must economically communicate what the brand is and what the brand is *not*. The Nike and Disney examples show the power and utility of having a well-designed brand mantra. They also help to suggest what might characterize a good mantra. Both examples are structured the same way, with three words, as in Figure 3.9.

Brand Briefing 3.5

Nike's brand mantra

A brand with a keen sense of what it represents to consumers is Nike. The company has a rich set of associations with consumers, revolving around such considerations as its innovative product designs, its sponsorship of top athletes, its award-winning advertising, its competitive drive and its irreverent attitude. Internally, Nike marketers adopted a three-word brand mantra of 'authentic athletic performance' to guide their marketing efforts. Thus, in Nike's eyes, its entire marketing campaign – its products and how they are sold – must reflect the values conveyed by the mantra.

Nike's mantra has had profound implications for its marketing. In the words of ex-Nike marketers Scott Bedbury and Jerome Conlon, the mantra provided the 'intellectual guard rails' to keep the brand moving in the right direction. From a product development standpoint, the mantra has affected where Nike has taken the brand. Over the years, Nike has expanded its brand meaning from 'running shoes' to 'athletic shoes' to 'athletic shoes and clothing' to 'all things associated with athletics' (including equipment). Each step of the way, however, it has been guided by its mantra. For example, as Nike rolled out its clothing range, one important hurdle for the products was that they could be made innovative enough through material, cut or design to benefit top athletes. At the same time, the company has been careful to avoid using the Nike name on products that do not fit with the mantra (eg, casual 'brown' shoes).

When Nike has experienced problems with its marketing, it has often been a result of its failure to figure out how to translate the mantra to the challenge at hand. For example, in Europe, Nike experienced disappointments until realizing that 'authentic athletic performance' has a different meaning in Europe and, in particular, has to involve soccer in a major way, among other things. Similarly, Nike stumbled in developing its All Conditions Gear outdoors shoes and clothing sub-brand in translating the mantra into a less competitive arena.

Brand Briefing 3.6

Disney's brand mantra

Disney's development of its mantra was in response to its incredible growth through licensing and product development during the mid-1980s. In the late 1980s, Disney became concerned that some of its characters (Mickey Mouse, Donald Duck, etc.) were being used inappropriately and becoming overexposed. To investigate the severity of the problem, Disney undertook an extensive brand audit. As part of a brand inventory, it compiled a list of all Disney products that were available (licensed and company manufactured) and all third-party promotions (complete with point-of-sale displays and relevant merchandising) from shops all over the world. At the same time, Disney launched research – a brand exploratory – to investigate how consumers felt about the Disney brand.

The results revealed some potentially serious problems: the Disney characters were on so many products and marketed in so many ways that in some cases it was difficult to discern what could have been the rationale behind the deal to start with. The consumer study only heightened Disney's concerns. Because of the broad exposure of the characters, many consumers had begun to feel that Disney was exploiting its name. In some cases, consumers felt that the characters added little value to products and, worse yet, involved children in purchase decisions that they would typically ignore.

Because of its aggressive marketing, Disney had written contracts with many of the 'park participants' for co-promotions or licensing arrangements. Disney characters were selling everything from nappies to cars to hamburgers. Disney learned in the consumer study, however, that consumers did not differentiate between all of the product endorsements. 'Disney was Disney' to consumers, whether they saw the characters in films, records, theme parks or consumer products. Consequently, *all* products and services that used the Disney name or characters affected Disney's brand equity. Consumers reported that they resented some of these endorsements because they felt that they had a special, personal relationship with the characters and with Disney that should not be handled so carelessly.

As a result of the audit, Disney moved quickly to establish a brand equity team to manage the brand franchise and carefully evaluate licensing and other third-party promotional opportunities. One of the mandates of this team was to ensure that a consistent image for Disney, reinforcing its key brand associations, was conveyed by all third-party products and services. To encourage this supervision, Disney adopted an internal brand mantra of 'fun family entertainment' to serve as a screen for proposed ventures. Opportunities that were not consistent with the mantra – no matter how appealing – were rejected. For example, Disney was approached to co-brand a mutual fund in Europe that was designed for families as a way for parents to save for the college expenses of their children. The opportunity was declined despite the consistent 'family' association because Disney believed that a connection with the financial community or banking suggested other associations that were inconsistent with their brand image (mutual funds are rarely intended to be entertaining).

These mantras can be broken down into three terms. The *functions* term describes the nature of the product or service or the type of experiences or benefits that the brand provides. This may range from concrete language, where the term just reflects the product category itself, to more abstract notions, as with Nike and Disney, where the term relates to higher-order experiences or benefits that may be delivered by a variety of different products. The *descriptive modifier* is a way to circumscribe the business functions term to clarify its nature. Thus, Nike's performance is not just any kind (eg, not artistic performance) but only *athletic* performance; Disney's entertainment is not just any kind (eg, not adult-orientated entertainment) but only *family* entertainment. Combined, the brand function term and descriptive modifier help to delineate the brand boundaries. Finally, the *emotional modifier* provides another qualifier in terms of how the brand delivers these benefits. In other words, what is the qualitative nature of what the brand does? How exactly does it provide benefits and in what way? This term provides further delineation and clarification. To provide distinctiveness, for example, the Disney mantra could add the word 'magical'.

Such mantras don't have to follow this structure, but whatever structure is adopted, it must be the case that the brand mantra clearly delineates what the brand is supposed to represent and therefore, at least implicitly, what it is not. Several additional points about brand mantras are worth noting.

First, mantras derive their power and usefulness from their collective meaning. Other brands may be strong on one, or perhaps even a few, of the brand associations making up the mantra. For the brand mantra to be effective, no other brand should singularly excel on all dimensions. Part of the key to both Nike's and Disney's success is that for years no other competitor could really deliver on the promise suggested by their mantras as well as those brands.

Second, these mantras typically are designed to capture the brand's points of difference. Other aspects of the brand positioning – especially the brand's points of parity – may also be important and may need to be reinforced in other ways. Finally, for brands facing rapid growth, a brand function term can be critical to provide guidance as to appropriate and inappropriate categories into which to extend. For brands in more stable categories, the mantra may focus on points of difference as expressed by the functional and emotional modifiers, perhaps not even including a brand functions term.

Implementing a brand mantra

Brand mantras should be developed at the same time as the brand positioning. As noted earlier, such positioning typically is a result of an in-depth examination of the brand through some form of audit or other activities. Mantras may benefit from the learning gained from those activities but, at the same time, require more internal examination and involve input from a wider range of employees and marketing staff. Part of this internal exercise is to determine the means by which each and every employee affects brand equity and how he or she can contribute in a positive way to a brand's destiny.

Procedurally, the brand positioning can often be summarized in a few sentences or a short paragraph that suggests the ideal core brand associations that should be held by consumers. Based on these core brand associations, a brainstorming session can attempt to identify combinations of words as brand mantra candidates. A number of characteristics seem to distinguish brand mantras. To arrive at the final mantra, the following considerations should come into play.

- *Communicate:* a good mantra should both define the category (or categories) of business for the brand to set the brand boundaries and clarify what is unique about the brand.
- *Simplify:* an effective mantra should be memorable. As a result, it should be short, crisp and vivid. In many ways, a three-word mantra is ideal because it is the most economical way to convey the brand positioning. There are times, however, when more words – in the form of clarifying the business functions or the nature of the modifiers – may be necessary.
- *Inspire:* ideally, the mantra should also stake out ground that is meaningful and relevant to as many employees as possible. Brand mantras can do more than inform and guide; they can also inspire if the brand values tap into higher-level meaning with employees as well as consumers.

Regardless of how many words make up the mantra, there will always be a level of meaning beneath the mantra that will need to be articulated. Almost any word is ambiguous enough that several interpretations are possible. Consequently, it becomes important to explain in greater detail just what is meant by each word or term in the mantra. For example, 'fun', 'family' and 'entertainment' in Disney's case could each take on meanings such that Disney felt the need to drill deeper with the mantra to provide a stronger foundation. Two or three short phrases were therefore added to clarify each of the words.

Brand mantras point out the importance of *internal branding* – making sure that members of the organization are properly aligned with the brand and what it represents.[28] Much branding literature has taken an *external* perspective, focusing on strategies and tactics that firms should take to build or manage brand equity with customers. Without question, at the heart of all marketing activity is the positioning of a brand and the essence of its meaning with consumers. In terms of strategic and tactical importance, properly positioning a brand is essential to creating a strong brand.

Equally important, however, is positioning the brand internally – that is, the manner by which the brand positioning is explained and communicated internally. With service companies especially, an up-to-date and deep understanding of the brand by employees is critical. In the past, comparatively little attention was paid to an *internal* perspective to consider what steps firms should take to be sure their employees and marketing partners appreciate and understand basic branding notions and how they can affect and help – or hurt – the equity of their particular brands. Recently, though, a number of companies have put forth initiatives to improve their internal branding.

Chapter 8 describes brand charters as a means to communicate internally and to marketing partners. Besides brand mantras, companies need to engage in continual open dialogue with their employees. Branding should be perceived as participatory. Some firms have pushed business-to-employee (B2E) schemes through corporate intranets and other means. For example, after the Ford Motor Company offered its US employees free computers to help them get online, they initiated a regular communication programme with employees, called True Blue. Walt Disney is seen as so successful at internal branding and having employees support its brand that it teaches seminars at its Disney Institute on the 'Disney style' of creativity, service and loyalty for employees from other companies.

In some cases, internal branding can both motivate employees and serve to attract customers externally. For example, to help create an expectation of trust with its customers, Midas ran an ad campaign showing its own employees as heroes. Awareness of the Midas corporate brand rose 25 percent as a result.[29] In short, internal branding is a critical management priority. Successful internal branding requires a mixture of resources and processes, all designed to inform and inspire employees to maximize their mutually beneficial contribution to brand equity.

CHAPTER REVIEW

Determining the desired brand knowledge structures involves positioning a brand in the minds of consumers. According to the customer-based brand equity model, deciding on a positioning requires determining a frame of reference (by identifying the target market and the nature of competition) and the ideal points of parity and points of difference brand associations. Determining the proper competitive frame of reference depends on understanding consumer behaviour and the consideration sets consumers adopt in making brand choices.

Points of difference are those associations unique to the brand that are also strongly held and favourably evaluated by consumers. Determining points of difference associations that are strong, favourable and unique is based on desirability and deliverability considerations, which are combined to determine the resulting anticipated levels of sales and costs that might be expected with the positioning. Points of parity, on the other hand, are those associations that may be shared with other brands. Category point of parity associations are those associations that consumers view as being necessary to be a legitimate and credible product offering within a certain category. Competitive point of parity associations are those associations designed to negate a competitor's points of difference. Deciding on these four ingredients will determine the brand positioning and dictate the desired brand knowledge structures.

A broader set of considerations is also useful for positioning, especially for a more developed brand that spans many categories. A mental map accurately portrays in detail all salient brand associations and responses for a particular target market (eg, brand users). Core brand associations are those sets of abstract associations (attributes and benefits) that characterize the five to ten most important aspects of a brand. Core brand associations can serve as an important foundation for the brand strategy. In particular, core brand associations can serve as the basis of brand positioning in terms of how they relate to points of parity and points of difference. Finally, a brand mantra is an articulation of the 'heart and soul' of the brand. Such mantras are three- to five-word phrases that capture the essence or spirit of the brand positioning and brand values. Their purpose is to ensure that all employees within the organization as well as all external marketing partners understand what the brand most fundamentally is to represent with consumers so that they can adjust their actions accordingly.

The concepts discussed in this chapter are powerful tools to guide positioning.

Once the brand positioning strategy has been determined, the actual marketing campaign to create, strengthen or maintain brand associations can be put into place. Chapters 4 to 7 describe some of the important marketing mix issues in designing supporting marketing campaigns.

Discussion questions

1. Apply the categorization model to a product category other than drinks. How do consumers make decisions whether or not to buy the product, and how do they arrive at their final brand decision? What are the implications for brand equity management for the brands in the category? How does it affect positioning, for example?

2. Pick a brand. Describe its breadth and depth of awareness.

3. Pick a category dominated by two main brands. Evaluate the positioning of each brand. Who are their target markets? What are their main points of parity and points of difference? Have they defined their positioning correctly? How might it be improved?

4. Can you think of any negatively correlated attributes and benefits other than those listed in Figure 3.6? Can you think of any other strategies to deal with negatively correlated attributes and benefits?

5. Think of one of your favourite brands. Can you come up with a brand mantra to capture its positioning?

References and notes

[1] Much of this chapter is based on Kevin Lane Keller, Brian Sternthal and Alice Tybout, 'Three questions you need to ask about your brand', *Harvard Business Review*, September 2002, 80 (9): 80–9.

[2] Phillip Kotler and Kevin Lane Keller, *Marketing Management*, 12th edn, Upper Saddle River, NJ: Prentice Hall, 2006.

[3] Chip Walker, 'How strong is your brand?', *Marketing Tools*, January/February 1995: 46–53.

[4] Chip Walker, 'How strong is your brand?', *Marketing Tools*, January/February 1995: 46–53.

[5] Russell I. Haley, 'Benefit segmentation: a decision-oriented research tool', *Journal of Marketing* July 1968, 32: 30–5.

[6] Also, the demographic specifications given may not fully reflect consumers' underlying perceptions. For example, when the Ford Mustang was introduced, the intended market segment was much younger than the ages of the customers who actually bought the car. Evidently, these consumers felt or wanted to feel younger psychologically than they really were.

[7] Ronald Frank, William Massey and Yoram Wind, *Market Segmentation*, Englewood Cliffs, NJ: Prentice Hall, 1972.

[8] Allan Baldinger and Joel Rubinson, 'Brand loyalty: the link between attitude and behavior', *Journal of Advertising Research*, November–December 1996: 22–34.

[9] A complete treatment of this material is beyond the scope of this chapter. Useful reviews can be found in any good marketing strategy text. For example, see David A. Aaker, *Strategic Market*

Management, 7th edn, New York: John Wiley, 2005, or Donald R. Lehmann and Russell S. Winer, *Product Management*, 4th edn, New York, NY: McGraw-Hill/Irwin, 2005.

[10]Teri Agins, 'As consumers find other ways to splurge, apparel hits a snag', *Wall Street Journal*, 4 February 2005: A1, A6.

[11]Stacy Kravetz, 'Baskin-Robbins scoops up a new look', *Wall Street Journal*, 4 September 1977: B1.

[12]The concepts of 'points of parity' and 'points of difference' and many of the other ideas and examples in this section were developed by Northwestern University's Brian Sternthal and refined in collaboration with Northwestern University's Alice Tybout.

[13]Patrick Barwise and Sean Meehan, *Simply Better: Winning and keeping customers by delivering what matters most*, Cambridge, MA: Harvard Business School Press, 2004.

[14]John Czepiel, *Competitive Marketing Strategy*, Englewood Cliffs, NJ: Prentice Hall, 1992.

[15]Richard Heller, 'Folk Fortune', *Forbes*, 4 September 2000: 66–9.

[16]Brian Sternthal, 'Miller Lite case', Kellogg Graduate School of Management, Northwestern University.

[17]When Miller Lite was introduced, the assumption was that the relevant motivation underlying the benefit of 'less filling' for consumers was that they could drink more beer. Consequently, Miller targeted heavy users of beer with a sizeable introductory ad campaign concentrated on mass-market sport programmes. As it turned out, the initial research showed that the market segment they attracted was more the moderate user – older and upmarket. Why? The brand promise of 'less filling' is ambiguous. To this group of consumers, 'less filling' meant that they could drink beer and stay mentally and physically agile. From Miller's standpoint, attracting this target market was an unexpected but happy outcome because it meant that there would be less cannibalization of their more mass-market High Life brand.

[18]Richard A. Melcher, 'Why Zima faded so fast', *BusinessWeek*, 10 March 1997: 110–14.

[19]David Field, 'Airline tries loftier name', *USA Today*, 10 March 1997: B7.

[20]Keith Naughton, 'Ford's "perfect storm"', *Newsweek*, 17 September 2001: 48–50.

[21]Elizabeth Jensen, 'Campbell's juice scheme: stealth health', *Wall Street Journal*, 18 April 1997: B6.

[22]Steven Gray, 'How Applebee's is making it big in small towns', *Wall Street Journal*, 2 August 2004: B1, B4.

[23]Shelly Branch, 'Irradiated food by any other name might just win over consumers', *Wall Street Journal*, 14 August 2001: B1.

[24]Abraham Maslow, *Motivation and Personality*, 2nd edn, New York: Harper & Row, 1970.

[25]Thomas J. Reynolds and Jonathan Gutman, 'Laddering theory: method, analysis and interpretation', *Journal of Advertising Research*, February/March 1988: 11–31.

[26]Marco Vriens and Frenkel Ter Hofstede, 'Linking attributes, benefits and consumer values', *Marketing Research*, Fall 2000: 3–8.

[27]For some notable exceptions, see Hamish Pringle and William Gordon, *Brand Manners: How to create the self-confident organization to live the brand*, New York: John Wiley, 2001; Thomas Gad, *4-D Branding: Cracking the corporate code of the network economy*, New York: Financial Times Prentice Hall, 2000; Nicholas Ind, *Living the Brand: How to transform every member of your organization into a brand champion*, 2nd edn, London: Kogan Page, 2004; Scott M. David and Kenneth Dunn, *Building the Brand-Driven Business: Operationalize your brand to drive profitable Growth*, San Francisco, CA: Jossey-Bass, 2002.

[28]Kevin Lane Keller, 'Brand mantras: rationale, criteria and examples', *Journal of Marketing Management*, 1999, 15: 43–51.

[29]Nikki Hopewell, 'Generating brand passion', *Marketing News*, 15 May 2005: 10.

4 Choosing brand elements to build brand equity

PREVIEW

Brand elements, sometimes called brand identities, are trademarkable devices that serve to identify and differentiate the brand. The main brand elements are names, website addresses, logos, symbols, characters, spokespeople, slogans, jingles, packages and signage. Independent of the decisions made about the product and how it is marketed, such elements can be chosen in a manner to build as much brand equity as possible. That is, according to the customer-based brand equity model, brand elements can be chosen to enhance brand awareness; facilitate the formation of strong, favourable and unique brand associations; or elicit positive brand judgements and feelings. The test of the brand-building ability of brand elements is what consumers would think or feel about the product if they only knew about its brand name, associated logo and other characteristics. A brand element that provides a positive contribution to brand equity, for example, would be one for which consumers assumed or inferred certain valued associations or responses. Figure 4.1 displays some characters that have done well internationally and Figure 4.2 lists some slogans. Can you name them all?

This chapter considers how elements can be chosen to build brand equity. After describing the general criteria for choosing such elements, it considers tactical issues for each type of brand element. The chapter concludes by addressing how a marketer should choose an optimal set of elements to build brand equity.

CRITERIA FOR CHOOSING BRAND ELEMENTS

In general, there are six criteria for choosing brand elements (as well as more specific choice considerations in each case, as shown in Figure 4.3):

1. memorability;
2. meaningfulness;
3. likeability;
4. transferability;
5. adaptability;
6. protectability.

Answers:

1. Tony the Tiger (Kellogg's Frosties); 2. Ronald McDonald (McDonald's); 3. The Michelin Man; 4. Johnnie Walker (Image courtesy of Diageo Brands B.V.); 5. Bic Boy; 6. World Wide Fund for Nature; 7. Linux; 8. American Express; 9. Nestlé

Figure 4.1 Famous brand elements (guess the brand)

1. 'The ultimate driving machine'	6. 'Vorsprung durch technik.'
2. 'Think different'	7. 'Because you're worth it.'
3. 'We try harder'	8. 'Probably the best beer in the world.'
4. 'My goodness, my____!'	9. 'Good to the last drop'
5. 'Where do you want to go today?'	10. 'All the news that's fit to print'

Answers:

1. BMW; 2. Apple; 3. Avis; 4. Guinness; 5. Microsoft; 6. Audi; 7. L'Oréal; 8. Carlsberg; 9. Maxwell House; 10. New York Times

Figure 4.2 Classic slogans

1. **Memorable**	4. **Transferable**
Easily recognized.	Within and across product categories.
Easily recalled.	Across geographic boundaries and cultures.
2. **Meaningful**	5. **Adaptable**
Descriptive.	Flexible.
Persuasive.	Can be updated.
3. **Likeable**	6. **Protectable**
Fun and interesting.	Legally.
Rich visual and verbal imagery.	Competitively.
Aesthetically pleasing.	

Figure 4.3 Criteria for choosing brand elements

The first three criteria can be characterized as brand-building or offensive-minded in nature and concern how brand equity can be built through the judicious choice of a brand element. The latter three, however, are more brand-preserving or defensive-minded and are concerned with how the equity in a brand element can be used and maintained in the face of different opportunities and constraints. The following sections briefly consider each of these general criteria.

MEMORABILITY

A necessary condition for building brand equity is achieving a high level of brand awareness. Towards that goal, brand elements can be chosen that are memorable and so aid recall or recognition in purchase or consumption settings. In other words, the intrinsic nature of certain names, symbols, logos, and the like – their semantic content, visual properties and so on – may make them more attention-getting and easy to remember and therefore contribute to brand equity. For example, naming a brand of propane gas cylinders 'Blue Rhino' and reinforcing it with a powder-blue animal mascot with a distinctive yellow flame is likely to stick in the minds of consumers.

Meaningfulness

Besides choosing brand elements to build awareness, brand elements can also be chosen whose inherent meanings enhance the formation of brand associations. Elements may take on all kinds of meaning, varying in descriptive, as well as persuasive, content. For example, Chapter 1 described how brand names could be based on people, places, animals or birds. Two important dimensions or aspects of the meaning of a brand element are the extent to which it conveys the following.

- *General information about the nature of the product category:* in terms of descriptive meaning, to what extent does the element suggest something about the product category? How likely would it be that a consumer could identify the corresponding product category or categories for the brand based on any one element? In a related question, does the brand element seem credible in the product category? In other words, is the content of an element consistent with what consumers would expect to see from a brand in that product category?
- *Specific information about particular attributes and benefits of the brand:* in terms of persuasive meaning, to what extent does the element suggest something about the particular kind of product that the brand would likely be, for example, in terms of attributes or benefits? Does it suggest something about a product ingredient or the type of person who might use the brand? The first dimension is an important determinant of brand awareness and salience; the second dimension is an important determinant of brand image and positioning.

Likeability

Associations suggested by a brand element may not always be related to the product. Thus, elements can be chosen that are rich in visual and verbal imagery and inherently fun and interesting. Independent of its memorability and meaningfulness, how aesthetically appealing do consumers find the element? Is it likeable – visually, verbally and in other ways? In other words, independent of the particular product or service, how much would consumers like the brand element? The Brand Briefing 4.1 outlines how marketing aesthetics can be applied to brand elements and branding in general.

In terms of these first three criteria, memorable, meaningful and likeable brand elements offer many advantages. Because consumers often do not examine much information in making product decisions, it is often desirable that brand elements be easily recognized and recalled and inherently descriptive and persuasive. Moreover, memorable or meaningful brand names, logos, symbols and so on reduce the burden on marketing communications to build awareness and link brand associations. The associations that arise from the likeability and appeal of the brand elements also may play a critical role in the equity of a brand, especially when few other product-related associations exist. Often, the less concrete the possible product benefits are, the more important is the creative potential of the brand name and other brand elements to capture intangible characteristics of a brand.

Transferability

The fourth general criterion concerns the transferability of the brand element – in both a product category and geographic sense. First, to what extent can the brand element add to the brand equity of new products sharing the brand elements introduced

Brand Briefing 4.1

Brand design and aesthetics

Schmitt and Simonson explore the importance and applications of 'marketing aesthetics,' a concept with many branding implications. They refer to *marketing aesthetics* as 'the marketing of sensory experiences in corporate or brand output that contributes to the organization's or brand's identity.' They approach marketing aesthetics from three perspectives: product design, communications research and spatial design. They argue that aesthetics offers tangible value to organizations by creating loyalty, allowing for premium pricing, cutting through information clutter, affording protection from competitive attacks and saving costs and increasing productivity. The following provides a brief overview to this line of thinking.

Aesthetics strategy is defined as 'the strategic planning and implementation of identity elements that provide sensory experiences and aesthetic gratification to the organization's multiple constituents'. They describe the basic rationale for this approach as follows:

> Customers do not have direct access to an organization's or a brand's culture, missions, strategies, values, to the 'private self' of the organization or the brand. However, customers do see the public face of the organization or brand – its expressions. This public face is projected through identity elements with various aesthetic styles and themes. It is never seen in its totality, but the various perceptions are integrated into overall customer impressions.

Thus, according to their approach, the styles and themes of design elements are the vehicle of how corporate expressions affect customer impressions, as follows.

Style refers to a distinctive quality or form, a manner of expression. Style is composed of primary elements, including sight (colour, shape, line, pattern and typeface), sound (loudness, pitch and metre), touch (material and texture), taste and smell. Strategic issues in style creation are whether or not to juxtapose design elements and when styles should be adapted or abandoned. Four perceptual dimensions are identified to evaluate corporate or brand identity-related styles: complexity ('minimalism' v 'ornamentalism'), representation ('realism' v 'abstraction'), perceived movement ('dynamic' v 'static') and potency ('loud/strong' v 'soft/weak'). International hotel brands (Hyatt, Four Seasons, Mandarin Oriental and Hilton) can be seen as being positioned differently on these dimensions.

The authors argue that, to be effective, styles must be combined with themes that express an organization's or brand's private self succinctly and directly. *Themes* refer to the content, meaning and projected image of an identity. Themes can provide customers with mental anchors and reference points to allow them

Brand Briefing 4.1 *continued*

to put an organization in a wider context and distinguish its position. Themes are expressed most pointedly if they are: used as prototypical expressions of an organization's core values or mission or of a brand's character; repeated and adapted over time; and developed into a system of interrelated ideas. Themes can be expressed in a variety of ways: as corporate brand names, symbols, narratives, slogans or jingles, concepts or combinations of elements. Decisions regarding themes revolve around the use of one theme or many, theme variation or isolation, integration of verbal and visual information and adapting or abandoning themes.

Source: Bernd H. Schmitt and Alex Simonson, *Marketing Aesthetics: The strategic management of brands, identity and image*, New York: Free Press, 1997.

either within the product class or across product classes? In other words, how useful is the brand element for range or category extensions? In general, the less specific the name, the more easily it can be transferred across categories. For example, Amazon connotes a massive South American river and therefore as a brand can be appropriate for a variety of different types of products, whereas Books 'R' Us would not have afforded the same flexibility.

Second, to what extent does the brand element add to brand equity across geographic boundaries and market segments? To a large extent this depends on the cultural content and linguistic qualities of the brand element. For example, an advantage of non-meaningful names (eg, Esso) is that they translate well into other languages because they have no inherent meaning. The mistakes that even top companies have made in translating their brand names, slogans and packages into other languages and cultures over the years have become legendary. Figure 4.4 lists some global branding mishaps. Companies must review all their brand elements for cultural meaning before introducing the brand into a market.

Adaptability

The fifth consideration concerns the adaptability of a brand element over time. Because of changes in consumer values and opinions, or simply because of a need to remain contemporary, elements often must be updated over time. The more adaptable and flexible the element, the easier it is to update it. For example, logos and characters can be given a different look or design to make them appear more modern and relevant.

1. When Braniff translated a slogan touting its upholstery, 'Fly in leather', it came out in Spanish as 'Fly naked.'
2. Coors put its slogan, 'Turn it loose', into Spanish, where it was read as 'Suffer from diarrhoea.'
3. US chicken magnate Frank Perdue's line, 'It takes a tough man to make a tender chicken', sounds much more interesting in Spanish: 'It takes a sexually stimulated man to make a chicken affectionate.'
4. Why Chevy Nova never sold well in Spanish-speaking countries: *No va* means 'it doesn't go' in Spanish.
5. When Pepsi started marketing its products in China, it translated the slogan, 'Pepsi brings you back to life', literally. The slogan in Chinese really meant 'Pepsi brings your ancestors back from the grave.'
6. When Coca-Cola was first sold cola in China, it named the product something that when pronounced sounded like 'Coca-Cola'. The only problem was that the characters used meant 'Bite the wax tadpole.' It later changed to a set of characters that mean 'Happiness in the mouth.'
7. Hair products company Clairol introduced the Mist Stick, a curling iron, into Germany only to find out that mist is slang for manure in German.
8. When Gerber started selling baby food in Africa, it used the US packaging with a cute baby on the label. Later it found out that, in Africa, companies routinely put pictures on the label of what's inside because most people can't read.
9. Japan's Mitsubishi Motors had to rename its Pajero model in Spanish-speaking countries because the term related to masturbation.
10. Toyota's MR2 model dropped the number in France because the combination sounded like a French swearword.

Figure 4.4 Ten global branding mishaps

Protectability

The final consideration concerns the extent to which a brand element can be protected – both in a legal and competitive sense. In terms of legal considerations, it is important to: choose elements that can be protected internationally; formally register them with the appropriate legal bodies; and vigorously defend trademarks from unauthorized competitive infringement. The necessity of legally protecting the brand is dramatized by huge sums lost each year from unauthorized use of patents, trademarks and copyrights, as described in Brand Briefing 4.2.

A closely related consideration is the extent to which the brand element is competitively protectable. Even if a brand element can be protected legally, it still may be the case that competitive actions can take away much of the brand equity provided by the brand elements themselves. If a name, package or other attribute is too easily copied, much of the uniqueness of the brand may disappear. For example, consider the once hot ice-beer category. Although Molson Ice was one of the early entries in the category, its pioneering advantage from a branding standpoint was lost when Miller Ice and what later became Bud Ice were introduced. Thus, it is important to reduce the likelihood that competitors can imitate the brand by creating a derivative based on salient prefixes or suffixes of the name, emulating the packaging's look or other actions.

Brand Briefing 4.2

The counterfeit business is booming

From Callaway golf clubs to Louis Vuitton handbags, counterfeit versions of brands are everywhere. The fakes are soaking up profits faster than multinationals can squash counterfeiting operations and they're getting tougher to distinguish from the real thing. The difference can be as subtle as lesser-quality leather in a handbag or fake batteries inside a mobile phone. And counterfeiters can produce fakes cheaply by cutting corners on safety and quality without paying for marketing, R&D and advertising.

Fakes have long thrived in places such as Hong Kong, Rio and Moscow but counterfeiting has become increasingly sophisticated and pervasive. The World Customs Organization estimates counterfeit products account for 5 percent to 7 percent of global merchandise trade, equivalent to lost sales of as much as €343 billion. And US Customs seizures of fakes grew by 46 percent in 2004, partly because counterfeiters increased exports to Western markets.

And it's not just luxury items and consumer electronics that are being copied. The World Health Organisation says up to 10 percent of medicines worldwide are counterfeited. Those drugs not only purloin pharmaceutical industry profits but also present a danger to anyone who takes them because they are manufactured under inadequate safety controls.

About two-thirds of counterfeit goods are produced in China. Other counterfeit hotspots include the Philippines, Vietnam, Russia, Ukraine, Brazil, Pakistan and Paraguay. The operations are financed by such varied sources as Middle East businessmen who invest in facilities in Asian countries for export, local Chinese entrepreneurs and criminal networks. And some legitimate licensees make fakes on the side. Those authorized licensees can then use legitimate channels to get the products to shops. Some counterfeiters mix real products with fake ones and others ship containers filled with fakes through so many ports it becomes impossible to tell where the product originated.

The replication process has also sped up as counterfeiters have honed their engineering skills and increased their speed. Chinese factories can now copy a new golf club in less than a week. And executives at a variety of companies say counterfeiters have no trouble copying holograms and other security devices intended to distinguish fakes from real products.

Experts say China is the key to stemming the counterfeiting tide. Producing counterfeit goods is as profitable as trading illegal drugs but does not carry the same risk. In many countries, convicted counterfeiters get off with a fine. Chinese authorities have ignored the problem for years, mostly because it did not hurt local industries, but, as the country's corporate interests grow and Chinese companies are hurt by the counterfeit industry, experts say the Chinese government will be more co-operative.

Brand Briefing 4.2 *continued*

Japanese company Nichia spent three years fighting court battles all over Asia to curb piracy of its white light-emitting diode. The invention brings in €1.3 billion annually but counterfeiters copied the design and have cut Nichia's market share and dropped prices for the diode. Nichia had little success in the Asian courts and decided to instead go after US companies buying the Asian knock-offs.

Other companies have also decided to target the end users, hoping that manufacturers will eventually be forced to get a licence and pay royalties. And some patent holders are beginning to get creative and target anyone in the supply chain who ignores counterfeit businesses. Louis Vuitton has worked with New York landlords to prevent the sale of counterfeit Louis Vuitton goods by tenants on a notorious counterfeit hotspot Canal Street. But since the business of counterfeiting thrives on globalization, experts say all many companies can do for now is hope to slow, not stop, the counterfeiters.

Sources: Frederik Balfour, 'Fakes', *BusinessWeek*, 7 February 2005; Thomas Kellner, 'Hit 'em where it hurts', *Forbes*, 20 June 2005; Julia Boorstin, 'Louis Vuitton tests a new way to fight the faux', *Fortune*, 16 May 2005.

OPTIONS AND TACTICS FOR BRAND ELEMENTS

The value of choosing brand elements strategically to build brand equity can be seen by considering the advantages of having chosen 'Apple' as the name for a computer. Apple was a simple but well-known word that was distinctive in the product category – factors facilitating the development of brand awareness. The meaning of the name also gave the company a 'friendly shine' and warm brand personality. Moreover, the name could be reinforced visually with a logo that could easily transfer across geographic and cultural boundaries. Finally, the name could serve as a platform for sub-brands (eg, as with the Macintosh, a common type of Apple in the USA), aiding the introduction of brand extensions.

What would an ideal brand element be like? Consider names – perhaps the most central of all brand elements. Ideally, a brand name would be easily remembered, highly suggestive of both the product class and the particular benefits that served as the basis of its positioning, inherently fun or interesting, rich with creative potential, transferable to a wide variety of product and geographic settings, enduring in meaning and relevant over time and easily protected both legally and competitively.

Unfortunately, it is difficult to choose a name – or any brand element, for that matter – that would satisfy all of these criteria. For example, as noted earlier, the more meaningful the brand name, the more likely it is that the brand name will not be transferable to other cultures because of translation problems. Moreover, names are generally less adaptable over time. Because it is so difficult to find one brand element that will satisfy all the choice criteria, several elements are typically employed. The following sections outline the main considerations for each type of brand element. The chapter concludes by discussing how to put all of this together to design a set of elements to build brand equity.

Brand names

The name is fundamentally important because it often captures the central theme or key associations of a product in a compact and economical fashion. Brand names can be an extremely effective shorthand means of communication.[1] Whereas the time it takes consumers to comprehend marketing communications can range from half a minute (for an advertisement) to potentially hours (for a sales call), the brand name can be noticed and its meaning registered or activated in memory in just a few seconds.

Because the brand name becomes so tied to the product in the minds of consumers, however, it is also the most difficult element for marketers to change. Consequently, brand names are often systematically researched before being chosen. The days when Henry Ford II could name a car the 'Edsel' after the name of a family member seem to be long gone.

Is it difficult to come up with a brand name? Ira Bachrach, a branding consultant, notes that, although there are 140,000 words in the English vocabulary, the average native English-speaker only recognizes 20,000 words. His company, NameLab, sticks to the 7,000 words that make up the vocabulary of most TV programmes and commercials. Although that may sound like a lot of choices, each year tens of thousands of brands are registered as legal trademarks. In fact, arriving at a satisfactory brand name for a product can be a painful and prolonged process. After realizing that most of the desirable brand names are already legally registered, many a frustrated executive has lamented that 'all of the good ones are taken'.

In some ways, this difficulty should not be surprising. Any parent can probably sympathize with how hard it can be to choose a name for a child, as evidenced by the thousands of babies born each year without names because their parents have not decided on – or perhaps not agreed upon – a name. It is rare that naming a product can be as easy as it was for Ford when it introduced the Taurus car. 'Taurus' was the code name given to the car during its design stage because the chief engineer's and product manager's wives were both born under that astrological sign. As luck would have it, upon closer examination, the name turned out to have a number of desirable characteristics. Consequently, it was chosen as the actual name for the car in the USA, saving thousands of dollars in research and consulting expenses.

Naming guidelines

Selecting a brand name for a product is an art and a science. This section provides guidelines for choosing a name. It focuses on developing a new name for the product; Chapter 12 considers how a company can use existing brand or company names in various ways for new products. Figure 4.5 lists the types of possible brand names according to identity experts Landor Associates. As with any brand element, names must be

1. **Descriptive**

   Describes function literally; generally unregisterable.

   Examples: Singapore Airlines, Global Crossing.

2. **Suggestive**

   Suggestive of a benefit or function.

   Examples: marchFIRST, Agilent Technologies.

3. **Compounds**

   Combination of two or more, often unexpected, words.

   Examples: Redhat, Bluetooth.

4. **Classical**

   Based on Latin, Greek or Sanskrit.

   Example: Meritor.

5. **Arbitrary**

   Real words with no obvious tie-in to company.

   Example: Apple.

6. **Fanciful**

   Coined words with no obvious meaning.

   Example: Avanade.

Figure 4.5   Landor's brand name taxonomy

chosen with the six general criteria in mind. After outlining some more specific naming criteria, this chapter describes the process by which a name should be chosen.

In general, it is believed that brand awareness is improved the extent to which brand names are chosen that are simple and easy to pronounce or spell; familiar and meaningful; and different, distinctive and unusual.[2]

Simplicity

First, to enhance brand recall, it is desirable for the brand name to be simple and easy to pronounce or spell. Simplicity reduces consumers' cognitive efforts to comprehend and process the brand name. Short names often aid recall because they are easy to encode and store in memory (eg, Crest toothpaste, Raid pest spray, Bold laundry detergent, Comfort fabric conditioner, Jiff lemon juice, Anchor butter, Sure deodorant and Bic pens). Longer names can be shortened to ease recallability. For example, over the years Chevrolet cars have become known as 'Chevy', Budweiser beer has become known as 'Bud' and Coca-Cola has also become known as 'Coke'.

Ease of pronunciation is critical to obtain valuable repeated word-of-mouth exposure that helps to build strong memory links. Pronunciation also affects entry into consideration sets and the willingness of consumers to order or request the brand orally. Rather than risk the embarrassment of mispronouncing a difficult name (as might be the case with such potentially difficult-to-pronounce names as Hyundai cars, Fruzen Gladje ice-cream, or Faconnable clothing), consumers may just avoid pronouncing it altogether.

Clearly, it is a challenge to build brand equity for a brand with a difficult-to-pronounce name because so much of the initial marketing efforts have to be devoted to simply educating consumers as to the proper way to pronounce the name. In the case of Wyborowa imported Polish vodka (pronounced vee-ba-rova), management actually resorted to running a print ad to help consumers pronounce the brand name – a key factor of consumer behaviour for success in the distilled spirits category where less self-service exists and consumers might need to ask for the brand.

Ideally, the name should have a clear, understandable and unambiguous pronunciation and meaning. The way a brand is pronounced can affect its meaning. Consumers may take away different perceptions of the brand if ambiguous pronunciation of its name results in different meanings. One study showed that certain hypothetical products that had brand names that were acceptable in both English and French (eg, Vaner, Randal and Massin) were perceived as more 'hedonic' (ie, providing much pleasure) and better liked when pronounced in French than in English.[3]

Pronunciation problems may arise from not conforming to linguistic rules. Although Honda chose the name Acura because it was associated with words connoting precision in several languages, it had trouble with consumer pronunciation of the name (pronounced AK-yur-a) in the USA.

To improve pronouncability and recallability, many marketers seek a desirable cadence and pleasant sound in their brand names.[4] For example, names may use alliteration (repetition of consonants, such as in Coleco), assonance (repetition of vowel sounds, such as in Ramada Inn), consonance (repetition of consonants with intervening vowel change, such as in Hula Hoops) or rhythm (repetition of pattern of syllable stress, such as in Prontaprint). Some words employ onomatopoeia, composed of syllables that when pronounced generate a sound strongly suggestive of the word's meaning (eg, Kachou tissues, Ping golf clubs or Schweppes carbonated drinks).

Familiarity and meaningfulness

A second consideration to enhance brand recall is that the name should be familiar and meaningful so that it is able to tap into existing knowledge structures. Brand names may be concrete or abstract in their meaning. As pointed out in Chapter 1, all types of categories of objects can be used to form a name. Because these objects exist in memory in verbal and visual form, less learning has to occur.[5] Links can be more easily formed to the object name and product, increasing memorability.[6]

Thus, when a consumer sees an ad for the first time for a car called Neon, the fact that the consumer already has the word stored in memory should make it easier to encode the product name and so improve its recallability. In fact, Chrysler chose that name for its Dodge car because it also connoted 'young, youthful and vibrant', fitting the desired image for the product.

To help create strong brand category links and aid recall, the brand name may also be chosen to suggest the product or service category (eg, Just Juice 100 percent fruit juices, Ticketmaster ticket selling service and Burger King fast food restaurants). Brand elements that are highly descriptive of the product category or its attribute and benefits, however, may be potentially quite restrictive.[7] For example, it may be difficult to introduce a soft drink extension for a brand called Just Juice!

Differentiation, distinctiveness and uniqueness

Although choosing a simple, easy to pronounce, familiar and meaningful brand name can, on the one hand, improve recallability, on the other, to improve brand recognition, it is important that names be different, distinctive and unusual. As Chapter 2 noted, recognition depends on consumers' ability to discriminate between brands and more complex brand names are more easily distinguished. Distinctive names can also facilltate the learning of intrinsic product information.[8]

The distinctiveness of a brand name is a function of its inherent uniqueness as well as its uniqueness in the context of rivals in a product category. Similarity of two names may also be defined in terms of either meaning or sound.[9] Distinctive words may be seldom-used or atypical words for the product category (eg, Apple computers), unusual combinations of real words (eg, Toys 'R' Us), or made-up words (eg, Xerox or Exxon). Even made-up names, however, have to satisfy linguistic rules and convention (eg, try to pronounce names without vowels such as Blfft, Xgpr, or Msdy!)

As with all brand choice criteria, trade-offs must be recognized. Even if a distinctive name is advantageous for brand recognition, it also has to be seen as credible and desirable in the product category. A notable exception is Smuckers jelly in the USA, which has tried to turn the handicap of its distinctive – but potentially dislikeable – name into a benefit through its slogan, 'With a name like Smuckers, it has to be good!'

Although choosing a memorable name is valuable, it is often necessary for the brand to have broader meaning to consumers than just the product category it is in. Because the brand name is a compact form of communication, the explicit and implicit meaning that consumers extract from the name can be critical. In particular, the brand name may be chosen to reinforce an important attribute or benefit association that makes up its product positioning (see Figure 4.6). Suggestive names are of course related to language, so non-native English speakers can find examples in their own markets with their own language.

PowerBook

In 1989, Apple had just introduced a heavy, ineffective portable computer that had failed in the marketplace. Needing a name for its latest portables, it turned to name consultant Lexicon. Using focus groups of users of competitive products, Lexicon began working with the terms laptop and notebook. PowerBook became the winner because it combined two things that are common but not typically used together: 'book', a small product that holds a lot of information, and 'power'. Lexicon's linguists even liked the sounds of the brand name and how it would relate to the product positioning, asserting that the 'p' in 'power' would bring to mind compactness and speed and the 'b' in 'book' would suggest dependability.[10]

ColorStay lipsticks	Lean Cuisine low-calorie frozen meals
Head & Shoulders shampoo	Mastercard credit cards
SnackWell reduced fat snacks	iPod MP3 player
DieHard car batteries	PlayStation videogame
Rollerblade inline roller skates	Motorola RZR (Razor) mobile phone
Red Bull energy drink	

Figure 4.6   Sample suggestive brand names

Besides performance-related considerations, brand names can be chosen to communicate more abstract considerations. For example, brand names may be intangible or emotion-laden to arouse certain feelings (eg, Fairy washing-up liquid, Impulse body sprays and Obsession perfumes).

A descriptive brand name should make it easier to link the reinforced attribute or benefit.[11] That is, it should be easier to communicate to consumers that a laundry detergent 'adds fresh scent' to clothes if it is given a name such as 'Blossom' than if it is given a neutral, non-suggestive name such as 'Circle'.[12] Although brand names chosen to reinforce the initial positioning of a brand may help linkage of that brand association, they may also make it harder to link new associations to the brand if it has to be repositioned.[13] For example, if a brand of laundry detergent were to be named Blossom and positioned as 'adding fresh scent', it may be more difficult to attempt to reposition the product and add a new association – for example, that the product 'fights tough stains'. Consumers may find it more difficult to accept or just too easy to forget the new positioning when the brand name continues to remind them of other product considerations.

With sufficient time and marketing, however, the restrictive nature of suggestive names sometimes can be overcome. British Airways no longer stands for airline services around the British isles. When two former Texas Instruments engineers were considering the name for their portable personal computers, they chose the name 'Compaq' because it suggested a small computer. Through subsequent introductions of 'bigger' personal computers, advertising campaigns and other marketing activity, Compaq has been able to transcend the initial positioning suggested by its name.

It must be recognized, however, that such marketing manoeuvres can be a long and expensive process. Imagine the difficulty of repositioning brands such as 'I can't believe it's not butter!' or 'Wow, your hair smells terrific!' Thus, it is important when choosing a meaningful name to consider the possible contingencies of later repositioning.

Meaningful names are not restricted to real words. Consumers can extract meaning, if they so desire, even from made-up brand names. For example, one study of computer-generated brand names containing random combinations of syllables found that 'whumies' and 'quax' were found to remind consumers of a breakfast cereal and that 'dehax' reminded them of a laundry detergent.[14] Thus, consumers were able to extract at least some product meaning from these essentially arbitrary names when instructed to do so. Nevertheless, the likelihood of consumers extracting meaning out of highly abstract names will depend on their motivation to do so. In many cases, consumers may not be so inclined.

Made-up names, however, are generally devised more systematically. Fictitious words are typically based on combinations of morphemes. A *morpheme* is the smallest linguistic unit having meaning. There are 6,000 morphemes in the English language, including real words (eg, 'man') as well as prefixes, suffixes or roots. For example, Compaq computer's name comes from a combination of two morphemes indicating 'computers and communication' and a 'small, integral object'. The use of the less common morpheme 'paq' as an ending – instead of pak, pac or pach – was an attempt to suggest something scientific and unusual. Similarly, Nissan's Sentra car is a combination of two morphemes suggesting 'central' and 'sentry'.[15] By combining carefully chosen morphemes, it is possible to construct brand names that actually have some relatively easily inferred or implicit meaning.

Characteristics	Definitions and/or examples
Phonetic devices	
Alliteration	Consonant repetition (Coca-Cola)
Assonance	Vowel repetition (BlackBerry)
Consonance	Consonant repetition with intervening vowel changes (Weight Watchers)
Masculine rhyme	Rhyme with end-of-syllable stress (Tampax)
Feminine rhyme	Unaccented syllable followed by accented syllable (American Airlines)
Weak/imperfect/slant rhyme	Vowels differ or consonants similar, not identical (Black & Decker)
Onomatopoeia	Use of syllable phonetics to resemble the object itself (Schweppes)
Clipping	Product names attenuated (Club Med, Coke)
Blending	Morphemic combination, usually with elision (Duracell, Swatch)
Initial plosives	/b/, /c-hard/, /d/, /g-hard/, /k/, /p/, /q/, /t/ (Bic)
Orthographic devices	
Unusual or incorrect spellings	Kwik-Fit, Vodafone
Abbreviations	Q8, 7 UP for Seven Up
Acronyms	Amoco
Morphologic devices	
Affixation	Post-it
Compounding	Cup-a-Soup
Semantic devices	
Metaphor	Representing something as if it were something else (Arrid); simile is included with metaphor when a name describes a likeness and not an equality (Aquafresh)
Metonymy	Application of one object or quality for another (Midas)
Synecdoche	Substitution of a part for the whole (Red Lobster)
Personification/pathetic fallacy	Humanizing the non-human or ascription of human emotions to the inanimate (Ralph Lauren)
Oxymoron	Conjunction of opposites (Portaloo)
Paranomasia	Pun and word plays (Beefeater)
Semantic appositeness	Fit of name with object (Autoglass)

Figure 4.7   Brand name linguistic characteristics

A number of linguistic issues could be raised with brand names.[16] Figure 4.7 contains an overview of different categories of linguistic characteristics, with definitions and examples. Even individual letters can contain meaning that may be useful in developing a new brand name. The letter X has become much more common in recent years (eg, ESPN's X Games, Nissan's Xterra SUV and Microsoft's Windows XP and Xbox) because X is now seen to represent 'extreme', 'on-the-edge' and 'youth' – that is, 'what's alternative, what's next and what's new'.[17] Research has shown that, in some instances, consumers prefer products with names bearing some of the letters from their name (eg, a Jonathan may exhibit a greater-than-expected preference for a product named Jonoki).[18]

Even the sounds of letters can take on meaning. For example, some words begin with phonemic elements called *plosives* (ie, the letters *b, c, d, g, k, p* and *t*), whereas others use *sibilants* (ie, sounds like *s* and soft *c*). Plosives escape from the mouth more quickly than sibilants and are hasher and more direct. Consequently, they are thought to make names more specific and less abstract and be more easily recognized and recalled.[19] On the other hand, because sibilants have a softer sound, they tend to conjure up romantic, serene images and are often found with products such as perfumes (eg, Chanel and Chloé).[20] One study found a relationship between certain characteristics of the letters of brand names and product features: as consonant hardness and vowel pitch increased in hypothetical brand names for toilet paper and household cleansers, consumer perception of the harshness of the product also increased.[21]

Brand names are not restricted to letters alone. Alphanumeric brand names contain one or more numbers in either digit form (eg, '5') or in written form (eg, 'five').[22] Alphanumeric brand names may include a mixture of letters and digits (eg, WD-40), a mixture of words and digits (eg, CK In24) or mixtures of letters or words and numbers in written form (eg, Saks Fifth Avenue). Alphanumeric brand names may also be used to designate generations or relationships in a product line in terms of particular product models (eg, BMW's 3, 5, and 7 series).

Naming procedures

Various procedures or systems have been suggested for naming products. Although some differences exist, most such systems can be seen as adopting a procedure along the following lines.

- *Define objectives:* in general, the first step in selecting a brand name is to define the branding objectives in terms of the six general criteria noted earlier. It is particularly important to define the ideal meaning that the brand should take. It is also necessary to recognize the role of the brand within the corporate branding hierarchy and how the brand should relate to other brands and products (as will be discussed in Chapter 11). In many cases, existing brand names may be used, at least in part. Finally, the role of the brand within the entire marketing programme must be understood, as well as having an in-depth description of the target market.

- *Generate names:* the second step involves generating as many names and concepts as possible. Any potential source of names can be used: company management and employees; existing or potential customers (including retailers or suppliers if relevant); ad agencies, professional name consultants or specialized computer-based naming companies; and so on. Tens, hundreds or even thousands of names may result from this step.

- *Screen initial candidates:* names now must be screened based on the branding objectives and marketing considerations identified in first step, as well as just common sense, to produce a more manageable list. For example, General Mills starts by eliminating the following.

  - Names that have unintentional double meaning.
  - Names that are unpronounceable, already in use, or too close to an existing name.
  - Names that have obvious legal complications.
  - Names that represent an obvious contradiction of the positioning.

  They next have in-depth evaluation sessions with management personnel and marketing partners to narrow the list down to a handful of names. Often, a quick-and-dirty legal search may be conducted to help screen out legal 'problem children'.

- *Study candidate names:* collect more extensive information on each of the final five to ten names. Before spending large amounts of money on consumer research, it is advisable to do an extensive international legal search. Because of the costs involved, searches are sometimes done sequentially, only testing in a new country those names that survived the legal screen from the previous one.

- *Research final candidates:* next, consumer research is often conducted to confirm management expectations as to the memorability and meaningfulness of the names. Consumer testing can take many forms. Many firms attempt to simulate the actual marketing campaign for the brand and consumers' likely purchase experiences as much as possible.[23] Thus, consumers may be shown the product and its packaging, price or promotion so that they understand the rationale for the name and how it will be used. Realistic three-dimensional packaging as well as concept boards or animated advertising may also be shown. Multiple samples of consumers may have to be surveyed depending on the target markets involved (eg, to capture differences in regional or ethnic appeal). The effects of the brand name with repeated exposure and when spoken versus when written can also be factored in.

- *Select final name:* based on all of the information collected, management can choose the name that maximizes the firm's branding and marketing objectives and then formally register the name.

In conducting the consumer research and selecting a brand name, it should be recognized that there will almost always be negative associations with one segment of consumers or another. In most cases, however, assuming these associations were not severe, they would disappear or dissipate after the onset of the initial marketing. Similarly, names often are initially disliked in part because of their lack of familiarity or, in the case of a name change, because they represent a deviation from the norm. In assessing the potential impact of a new brand name, it is important to separate these temporal considerations from more enduring effects. Here is how a new airline arrived at its name.[24]

JetBlue

Traditionally, airlines use descriptive names that evoke geographic origins (eg, British Airways, Singapore Airlines, Alitalia) or broad geographic reach (eg, Cathay Pacific). In launching an airline with a fresh concept – stylish travel for the budget-minded flier – JetBlue decided it needed an evocative name. Working with an ad agency, Merkley & Partners, and a brand consultant, Landor, a list of names was generated – Fresh Air, Taxi, Egg and It. The name Blue – suggesting peaceful clear skies – quickly became a favourite, but trademark lawyers noted that it would be impossible to protect the name without a distinctive qualifier. The first candidate, TrueBlue, went by the wayside when it became apparent that it was also the name of a car rental agency. JetBlue emerged as the best substitute and the brand was born.

Figure 4.8 lists some common naming mistakes according to the brand name consultancy, Interbrand.[25]

1. Treating naming as an afterthought.
2. Ignoring complex trademark and URL issues.
3. Keeping a brand name that is no longer relevant.
4. Ignoring that naming is not only creative, but strategic.
5. Falling into the subjectivity trap.
6. Overlooking the global implications of names.
7. Failing to effectively communicate the name internally.
8. Ending verbal communication of a brand with its name.
9. Naming when it's not very necessary.
10. Believing that naming is an easy process.

Figure 4.8 Ten sources of naming mistakes
Source: Interbrand

Website addresses (URLs)

Uniform resource locators (URLs) are used to specify locations of pages on the web and are also commonly referred to as *domain names*. Anyone wishing to own a URL must register and pay for the name with a domain registry. In recent years, as companies clamoured for space on the web, the number of URLs increased dramatically. Every three-letter combination and virtually all words in a typical English dictionary have been registered. The sheer volume of registered URLs often makes it necessary for companies to use coined words if they wish to have a website for the brand. For example, when Andersen Consulting selected a new name, it chose the coined word 'Accenture' in part because www.accenture.com had not been registered.

Another issue facing companies with regard to URLs is protection of their brands from unauthorized use in domain names.[26] To protect its brand from unauthorized use in a URL, a company can sue the current owner of the URL for copyright infringement, buy the name from the owner or register all conceivable variations of its brand as domain names ahead of time. According to Gartner, the average company on Forbes' Global 2000 list had at least 300 registered URLs in 2001. Large companies are now carefully monitoring the web for unauthorized use of their brands.

Caterpillar

Heavy machinery manufacturer Caterpillar assigned its trademark lawyer, Gene Bolmarcich, the task of protecting the company's brand online. Caterpillar has 600 registered URLs and Bolmarcich estimates that he spends 95 percent of his time protecting Caterpillar's name online. During the spring of 2000, the company reclaimed some 50 URLs by firing off cease-and-desist letters to companies registering names such as CAT that infringed Caterpillar's copyright. Caterpillar also guards against infringement overseas by registering its name in ten countries, but, Bolmarcich says, 'You can't ever fully defend yourself.'

Brand recall is critical for URLs because, at least initially, consumers must remember the address to get to the site. At the peak of the internet boom, investors paid €5.13 million for Business.com, €1.5 million for Autos.com and €752,000 for Bingo.com. Many of these 'common noun' sites failed, however, and were criticized, among other things, as being too generic in name. During this time, many firms adopted names that started with a lower-case *e* or *i* and ended in 'net', 'systems', or, especially, 'com'. Many of these names became liabilities after the internet bubble burst, forcing firms such as Internet.com to revert to a more conventional name, INTMedia Group.[27] Yahoo, however, was able to create a memorable brand and URL.

Yahoo!

Jerry Yang and David Filo named their web portal (created as a Stanford University thesis project) 'Yahoo!' after thumbing through the dictionary for words that began with 'ya', a computing acronym for 'yet another'. Filo stumbled upon '*yahoo*' which brought back fond childhood memories of his father calling him 'little yahoo'. Liking the name, they created a more complete acronym: 'Yet another hierarchical officious oracle.'

Typically, for an existing brand, the main URL is a straightforward and maybe even literal translation of the brand name (www.shell.com), although there are exceptions and variations.

Logos and symbols

Although the name is typically the central element of the brand, visual brand elements can also play a critical role in building brand equity, especially in terms of brand awareness. Logos as the graphic elements of a brand have a long history as a means to indicate origin, ownership or association. For example, families and countries have used logos for centuries to visually represent their names (eg, the Hapsburg eagle of the Austro-Hungarian Empire).

There are many types of logos, ranging from corporate names or trademarks (ie, word marks) written in a distinctive form, on the one hand, to, on the other, abstract logos, which may be unrelated to the word mark, corporate name or corporate activities.[28] Examples of brands with strong word marks (and no accompanying logo separate from the name) include Coca-Cola, Dunhill and Kit-Kat. Examples of abstract logos include the Mercedes star, Rolex crown, CBS eye, Nike swoosh and the Olympic rings. These non-word mark logos are also often called *symbols*.

Many logos fall between these two extremes. Often logos are devised as symbols to reinforce or embellish the brand meaning. Some logos are literal representations of the brand name, enhancing brand awareness (eg, the Arm & Hammer, International Committee of the Red Cross and Apple logos). Logos can be concrete or pictorial in nature (eg, the American Express centurion, the Sun-Maid raisins girl and Ralph Lauren's polo player). Certain elements of the product or company can become a symbol (eg, the Goodyear blimp, McDonald's golden arches and the Playboy bunny).

The importance of logos and symbols can be seen from the results of a study that asked 150 consumers their impressions of companies based on their names alone and also when their logos were present. As Figure 4.9 shows, the results could differ dramatically depending on the company involved. Clearly, logos have meaning and associations that change consumers' perceptions of the company.[29]

Like brand names, logos can acquire associations through their inherent meaning as well as through marketing. In terms of inherent meaning, even abstract logos can have different evaluations depending on the shapes involved. As with names,

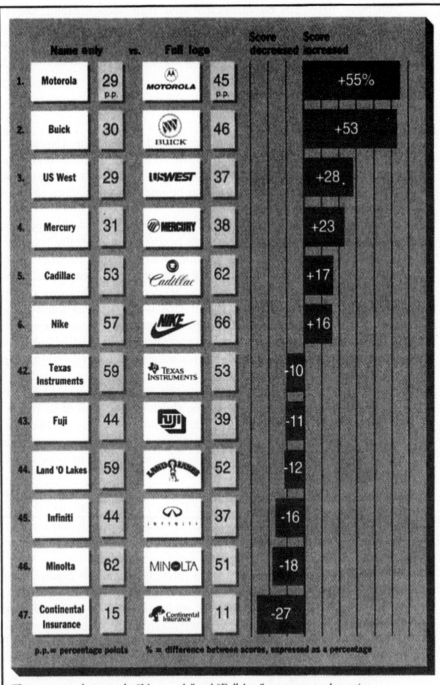

	Name only	vs.	Full logo		Score decreased	Score increased
1.	Motorola	29 p.p.	MOTOROLA	45 p.p.		+55%
2.	Buick	30	BUICK	46		+53
3.	US West	29	US WEST	37		+28
4.	Mercury	31	MERCURY	38		+23
5.	Cadillac	53	Cadillac	62		+17
6.	Nike	57	NIKE	66		+16
42.	Texas Instruments	59	TEXAS INSTRUMENTS	53	-10	
43.	Fuji	44	fuji	39	-11	
44.	Land 'O Lakes	59	LAND O LAKES	52	-12	
45.	Infiniti	44	INFINITI	37	-16	
46.	Minolta	62	MINOLTA	51	-18	
47.	Continental Insurance	15	Continental Insurance	11	-27	

p.p. = percentage points   % = difference between scores, expressed as a percentage

The percentages shown on the "Name only" and "Full logo" are average top box ratings ("agree strongly") within a 5-point rating scale on the image contribution attributes, based only on respondents who are aware of the company or brand.

Figure 4.9   Brand evaluations with and without logos: six best and worst image contributions

Source: Alvin H. Schechter, 'Measuring the value of corporate and brand logos', *Design Management Review*, Winter, 1993. Courtesy of the *Design Management Review* (Vol. 4, No. 1, Winter 1993) a publication of the Design Management Institute (www.dmi.org). Individual copies of this and other DMI *Review* articles are available for purchase at www.dmi.org/publications.

abstract logos can be distinctive and thus recognizable. Nevertheless, because abstract logos may lack the inherent meaning of a more concrete logo, one of the dangers is that consumers may not understand what the logo is intended to represent without a significant marketing initiative to explain its meaning.

Benefits

Logos and symbols are easily recognized and can be a valuable way to identify products, although a concern is how well they become linked in memory to the corresponding brand name and product to boost brand recall. That is, consumers may recognize certain symbols but be unable to link them to any specific product or brand.

Another branding advantage of logos is their versatility: because they are often non-verbal, they can be updated as needed and generally transfer well across cultures. Because logos are often abstract, without much product meaning, they can be relevant and appropriate in a range of categories. For example, brands often develop logos because their identity may be needed on a wide range of products, although perhaps in a subordinate way as a means to endorse sub-brands. Logos can allow the corporate brand to play a more explicit secondary role for these various products.

Abstract logos are often useful when the use of the full brand name is restricted. In the UK, for example, National Westminster Bank created a triangular device as a logo in part because the name itself was long and cumbersome and the logo could more easily appear as an identification device on chequebooks, literature, signs and promotional material.[30] It also uses the shortened version of its name, NatWest. Thus, logos and symbols can be particularly important in services because of their intangible, abstract nature. For example, many insurance firms use symbols of strength (eg, the stallion for Lloyds TSB), security (eg, the umbrella of Legal and General) or some combination of the two (eg, pillars of Allianz).

Finally, unlike brand names, logos can be easily changed to achieve a more contemporary look. For example, John Deere revamped its deer trademark for the first time in 32 years in 2000, making the animal appear to be leaping up rather than landing. The change was intended to 'convey a message of strength and agility with a technology edge'.[31]

In updating logos, however, it is important to make gradual changes that do not lose sight of the inherent advantages of the logo. In the 1980s, the trend for many firms was to create more abstract, stylized versions of their logos. In the process, some of the meaning, and thus equity, residing in these logos was lost. Recognizing the logo's potential contribution to brand equity, some firms in the 1990s reverted to a more traditional look for their symbols. Another trend has been to move from two-dimensional designs to three-dimensional designs with gradients and shadows. The logo designs also increasingly include versions for moving media, such as the symbol for Microsoft's Windows which waves like a flag during computer start-up or web page loading.

Regardless of the reason why, changing a logo is not cheap. According to Allen Adamson, managing director of the brand consultancy Landor Associates, creating a symbol or remaking an old one for a big brand 'usually costs €684,000'.[32]

Characters

Characters represent a special type of symbol – one that takes on human or real-life characteristics. Brand characters typically are introduced through advertising and can play a central role in these and subsequent ad campaigns and packaging designs. Like other brand elements, characters come in many forms. Some characters are animated (eg, the Michelin man, Tony the Tiger and Snap, Crackle and Pop), whereas others are live-action figures (eg, Captain Bird's Eye or Ronald McDonald). More recent examples include the M&M Sweets, Churchill bulldog, Sega's Sonic the Hedgehog and the Crazy Frog.[33]

Green Giant

One of the most powerful characters is Pillsbury's Jolly Green Giant.[34] He can be traced back to the 1920s, when the Minnesota Valley Canning Company placed a green giant on the label of a variety of sweet, large English peas as a means to circumvent trademark laws that prevented them from naming the product 'Green Giant'. Ad Agency Leo Burnett used the character in print ads beginning in 1930 and in TV ads beginning in the early 1960s. At first, TV ads featured an actor wearing green body make-up and a suit of leaves. Later, the ads moved to full animation. Creatively, the ads have been very consistent. The Green Giant is always in the background, with his features obscure and only says 'Ho-Ho-Ho'. He moves very little, doesn't walk and never leaves the 'valley'. The Green Giant has been introduced into international markets, following the same set of rules. The Little Sprout character was introduced in 1973 to bring a new look to the brand and allow more flexibility. Unlike the Green Giant, the Little Sprout is a chatterbox, often imparting product information. The Green Giant brand has enormous equity to Pillsbury and it has found that using the name and character on a product has been an effective signal to consumers that the product is 'wholesome' and 'healthy'.

Benefits

Brand characters can provide a number of brand equity benefits. Because they are often colourful and rich in imagery, they tend to attract attention. Consequently, characters can be useful for creating brand awareness. Brand characters can help brands break through the marketplace clutter as well as help to communicate a product benefit. For example, fun breakfast helped to reinforce Snap, Crackle and Pop have the product association.

Perhaps a commoner image enhancement is related to brand personality and the likeability of the brand. The human element of characters can help to create perceptions of the brand as being fun and interesting. The ability of a consumer to have a relationship with a brand may be easier when the brand has a humanistic character. As a result of the meaning and various feelings that can become attached to them, popular characters are often valuable licensing properties, providing direct revenue and additional brand exposure (see Chapter 7).

Finally, because characters do not typically have direct product meaning, they may also be transferred relatively easily across categories. For example, Aaker notes that 'the Keebler's elf identity (which combines a sense of home style baking with a touch of magic and fun) gives the brand latitude to extend into other baked goods – and perhaps even into other types of food where homemade magic and fun might be perceived as a benefit'.[35]

Cautions

There are drawbacks to using brand characters, in that they can be so well liked that they dominate other brand elements and actually *dampen* awareness.

Eveready

When Ralston Purina introduced its drumming pink bunny that 'kept going . . . and going . . . and going' in ads for their Eveready Energizer battery, many consumers were so captivated by the character that they paid little attention to the name of the brand. As a result, they often mistakenly believed that the ad was for rival Duracell. Consequently, Eveready found it necessary to add the pink bunny as a reminder to their packages, promotions and other marketing communications to create stronger brand links.

Characters often must be updated over time so that their image and personality remains relevant to the target market. Recently, Michelin launched a slimmer version of its tubby Michelin Man (whose real name is Bibendum) to mark his hundredth year. A company press release notes: 'Thinner and smiling, Bibendum will look like the leader he is, with an open and reassuring manner.' In general, the more realistic the brand character, the more important it is to keep it up to date. One advantage of fictitious or animated characters is that their appeal can be more enduring and timeless than real people. Brand Briefing 4.3 lists some guidelines from a leading consultant.

Slogans

Slogans are short phrases that communicate descriptive or persuasive information about a brand. Slogans often appear in advertising but can play an important role on packaging and in other aspects of marketing. For example, Snickers' 'Hungry? Grab a Snickers' slogan has appeared in ads and on the bars' wrapper. Slogans are powerful devices because, like names, they are an efficient, shorthand means to build brand equity. Slogans can function as useful 'hooks' or 'handles' to help consumers grasp the meaning of a brand in terms of what it is and what makes it special. They can summarize and translate the intent of a marketing campaign in a few short words or phrases. For example, State Farm Insurance's 'Like a good neighbor, State Farm is there' has been used for decades in the USA as a slogan to represent the brand's dependability and friendship. Brand Briefing 4.4 discusses Intel's strategy.

Benefits

Slogans can be devised in several ways to help build brand equity. Some slogans help to build brand awareness by playing off the brand name in some way (eg, 'My doctor said Mylanta', or 'Step up to the Mic' for Micatin). Other slogans build brand

Brand Briefing 4.3

Balance creative and strategic thinking to create great characters

Brand characters are a staple of consumer marketing but generating them and making sure they evolve is difficult. Great characters, the Pillsbury Doughboy for example, can embody a brand's story and spark enthusiasm for it. But bringing a character to life through advertising requires navigating a host of pitfalls. Character, a US company, helps create brand characters and revitalize old ones.

During three-day camps, a team from a client company learns to flesh out a new or current character through improvisational acting, discussion and reflection. According to Character president David Altschul, brand characters are unique in that they straddle the worlds of marketing and entertainment. Their function is to represent a brand, but they are in competition with characters that consumers are exposed to through television, cinema, video games and novels. Altschul emphasizes consistency across all communications and familiarizing all employees with the story behind the brand. The results of the camps are intended to equip creative directors with background and insights into the company's character that can spur ideas and approaches.

The following are some of the tips for brand characters presented at the camps.

- *Human traits are appealing:* M&Ms sweets gained more appeal once the M&M characters were given more human traits.
- *Create a life:* use a full back story to fill out the character. This ensures that the character can evolve over time and continue to connect with consumers.
- *Make them vulnerable:* even superheroes have flaws. Sidekick in Barclaycard ads makes cardowner look good and in control.
- *Imagine the long run:* General Mills' Jolly Green Giant has been around for decades. Don't get rid of older characters just to make room for new ones. Consumers can get very attached to such characters.
- *Don't ask too much:* characters with a simple task or purpose work best. Using characters for new products or other purposes can dilute the effectiveness of the character.

To be effective, brand characters have to be engaging in their own right while staying true to the brand. Most characters, though, are conceived as short-term solutions to specific problems. If the audience likes a character, companies face the challenge of turning it into an asset. At this point some companies try to freeze the character's attributes and preserve them, but Altschul cautions against this strategy, saying static characters can lose their appeal and fail to connect emotionally with consumers. Equally, however, characters that are marketed too heavily can also crash. The California Raisins met such a fate when licensing pushed them into every possible type of paraphernalia without much thought about their back story.

Brand Briefing 4.3 *continued*

Altschul maintains that viewers connect with characters whose struggles are familiar. He says the way to ensure that a brand character adds value for the long run is to address strategic questions such as: 'What is this story about?', 'What are the flaws, vulnerabilities and sources of conflict that connect the character to the brand in a deep, intrinsic way?', 'What human truth is revealed through the story that audiences can relate to?'

Altschul's company helps clients find this intersection between story and marketing by defining the essence of a brand and the character and then clarifying the connection between the two. The brand character is profiled to bring out the personality traits, behaviour and mission that may be used for future storylines. And the participants talk about how the character should look, act and interact with others to communicate the essence of the brand. The goal is to create guidelines for how the character may evolve and suggests ways the character could be used beyond traditional advertising media. Altschul suggests that companies also establish principles for the brand to stay 'in character', including ways the character can serve as conscience for the brand when making decisions such as line extensions, alliances and competitive responses.

Sources: Fara Warner, 'Brands with character', *Fast Company*, May 2004; David Altschul, 'The balancing act of building character', *Advertising Age*, 4 July 2005; www.characterweb.com

awareness even more explicitly by making strong links between the brand and the corresponding product category by combining both entities in the slogan (eg, 'If you're not wearing Dockers, you're just wearing pants'). Most important, slogans can help to reinforce the brand positioning and desired point of difference (eg, 'Nothing runs like a Deere', 'It's hard to stop a Trane' and 'Help is just around the corner. True value hardware'). For market leaders, slogans often employ 'puffery' in which the brand is praised with subjective opinions, superlatives and exaggerations (eg, Keebler's 'Uncomparably good'; Bayer's 'Bayer works wonders').

Slogans often become closely tied to advertising campaigns and can be used to summarize the descriptive or persuasive information conveyed in the ads. For example, DeBeers' 'A diamond is forever' communicates the intended message that diamonds bring eternal love and romance and never lose value. Slogans can be more expansive and more enduring, however, than just ad taglines. Campaign-specific lines may be used to help reinforce the message of a particular campaign instead of the brand slogan for a certain time. For example, through the years, Nike has used ad lines such as 'What are you getting ready for?', 'Why sport?' and 'I can' for campaigns instead of its brand slogan, 'Just do it.' Such substitutions can emphasize that the campaign represents a departure of some kind from the message conveyed by the brand slogan or just a way to give the brand slogan a rest so that it remains fresh.

Brand Briefing 4.4

Intel coming out from the inside

Intel has been very successful in brand management. Its move to brand the microprocessors inside PC computers, the Intel Inside campaign, was launched in 1991 and Intel has become one of the world strongest brands. However, the campaign's success also led to a problem: effectively, the company had two very strong logos – the corporate one with a 'dropped' e and the Intel Inside logo. Also, the company needed to communicate a broader role for its brand in consumer electronics, wireless communications and healthcare. Intel wants to create all kinds of chips and software, not just microprocessors.

The decision was taken to move to a single logo. Early in 2006, Intel launched a new brand design that involved changes to the Intel Inside logo and the original Intel 'dropped' e logo, which was created by Robert Noyce and Gordon Moore 37 years ago as they were forming their 'integrated electronics' company. The new design clearly mainatins the heritage of the old logo but keeps the 'swoosh'-like element from the Intel Inside design.

It also includes a new tagline: 'Intel. Leap ahead.' This is designed to communicate what drives Intel as a company and what Intel makes possible. '"Intel. Leap ahead." is a simple expression that declares who we are and what we do,' said Kim, then Intel's chief marketing officer. 'This is part of our heritage. Our mission at Intel has always been to find and drive the next leap ahead – in technology, in education, social responsibility, manufacturing and more – to continuously challenge the status quo. It's about using Intel technology to make life better, richer and more convenient for everyone.'

The group planned to spend €1.37 billion on marketing communications with the new look and message in 2006 (Figure 4.10).

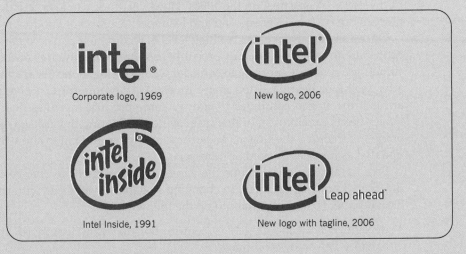

Corporate logo, 1969

New logo, 2006

Intel Inside, 1991

New logo with tagline, 2006

Figure 4.10   Intel's logos (1969–2006)

Source: Amanda Andrews, 'Intel will spend $2bn on selling new look in 2006', *The Times*, 31 December 2005; www.intel.com.

Designing slogans

Some of the most powerful slogans are those that contribute to brand equity in many ways. Slogans can play off the brand name in a way to build both awareness *and* image (eg, 'Maybe she's born with it, maybe it's Maybelline' for Maybelline cosmetics; or 'It won't let you down' for Sure deodorant). Slogans also can contain meaning that is relevant in both a product-related and non-product-related sense. For example, consider the Champion sportswear slogan, 'It takes a little more to make a Champion.' The slogan could be interpreted in terms of product performance, as meaning that Champion sportswear is made with a little extra care or with special materials, but also could be interpreted in terms of user imagery as meaning that Champion sportswear is associated with top athletes. This combination of superior product performance and aspirational user imagery is a powerful platform on which to build brand image and equity. Benetton has had an equally strong slogan on which to build brand equity ('United colours of Benetton'), but, as Brand Briefing 4.5 describes, the company has not always taken full advantage of it.

Updating slogans

Some slogans become so strongly linked to the brand that it becomes difficult to introduce new ones. Timex watches gave up trying to replace its 'Takes a licking and keeps on ticking' and returned to the tagline in its advertising, eventually changing it to 'Life is ticking.' Marketers of 7 UP tried a number of successors to its 'Uncola' slogan – including 'Freedom of choice', 'Crisp and clean and no caffeine', 'Don't you feel good about 7 UP' and 'Feels so good coming down' and the edgy 'Make 7 UP yours' – before arriving at 'The only way to go is up' in 2004.

Thus, a slogan that becomes so strongly identified with a brand can potentially box it in. Slogans can take on lives of their own and become public catchphrases, as with Remington's 'I liked it so much I bought the company' in the 1980s and Budweiser's 'Whassup?!' in the 1990s. However, there can also be a downside: such phrases can become overexposed and lose specific brand or product meaning.

Once a slogan achieves such a high level of recognition and acceptance, it may still contribute to brand equity, but probably as more of a reminder of the brand. Consumers are probably unlikely to consider what the slogan means in a thoughtful way after seeing or hearing it too many times. At the same time, a potential difficulty arises if the slogan continues to convey some product meaning that the brand no longer needs to reinforce. In this case, by not facilitating the linkage of new, desired brand associations, the slogan can become restrictive and fail to allow the brand to be updated as much as desired or necessary.

Because slogans are perhaps the easiest brand element to change, there is more flexibility in managing them. In changing slogans, however, as with changing other brand elements, it is important to do the following.

- Recognize how the slogan is contributing to brand equity, if at all, through enhanced awareness or image.
- Decide how much of this equity enhancement, if any, is still needed.
- Retain as much as possible the needed or desired equities still residing in the slogan while providing whatever twists of meaning are needed to contribute to equity in other ways.

Brand Briefing 4.5

Benetton's brand equity management

One of the world's top clothing manufacturers (with global sales of €1.64 billion), Benetton has experienced ups and downs in managing its brand equity. Benetton built a powerful brand by creating a broad range of basic, colourful clothes that appealed to a wide range of consumers. The slogan, 'United colours of Benetton', would seem to almost perfectly capture the company's desired image and positioning. It embraces both product considerations (the colourful character of the clothes) and user considerations (the diversity reflected by the people who wear the clothes), providing a strong platform for the brand. Benetton's ad campaigns reinforced this positioning by showing people from many racial backgrounds wearing a variety of clothes and products.

Benetton's campaigns switched directions, however, in the 1980s by addressing controversial social issues. Created in-house by designer Oliverio Toscani, Benetton print ads and posters featured such unusual and sometimes disturbing images as a white child wearing angel's wings alongside a black child sporting devil's horns; a priest kissing a nun; an Aids patient and his family in the hospital moments before his death; and, in an ad run only once, 56 close-up photos of male and female genitalia. In 1994, Benetton launched a €10.2 million ad campaign in newspapers and billboards in 110 countries featuring the torn and bloodied uniform of a dead Bosnian soldier. In 2000, a campaign entitled 'We, on death row' showed American death row inmates with pictures of the prisoners and details about their crimes and length of incarceration.

Critics have labelled these campaigns as gimmicky 'shock' advertising and accused Benetton of exploiting sensitive social issues to sell jumpers. One fact is evident. Although these campaigns may be appreciated by and effective with a certain market segment, they are more 'exclusive' in nature – distancing the brand from many other consumers – than the early Benetton campaigns, which were inviting and 'inclusive' in nature. Not surprisingly, the ad campaigns were not always well received by its retailers and franchise owners.

The image of the dead Bosnian soldier received an especially hostile reaction throughout Europe. In the USA, some of Benetton's more controversial ads have been rejected by the media and Benetton's US retailers commissioned their own campaign from TBWA/Chiat/Day ad agency in an attempt to create their own, more sophisticated image for the brand. After the death row ads, Sears pulled the brand from shelves of its 400 shops. Response from US consumers was equally negative: sales of Benetton products shrunk by half to €35.5 million between 1993 and 2000. By 2001, the number of Benetton shops in the USA dropped to 150 from 600 in 1987.

From 2001, Benetton's advertisements started featuring conventional images – teenagers in colourful Benetton clothing. Benetton, however, maintained that the company would still continue with its 'socially responsible' status by focusing on

Brand Briefing 4.5 *continued*

non-controversial themes like racial discrimination, poverty, child labour and Aids awareness. To that effect, in early 2003, Benetton in association with the UN's World Food Programme, launched a year-long, €10.9 million communication campaign, called Food for Life.

Sources: Leigh Gallagher, 'About face', *Forbes*, 19 March 2001; Michael McCarthy, 'Benetton in spotlight', *USA Today*, 16 February 2002: B3; George E. Belch and Michael A. Belch, 'Benetton group: evolution of communication strategy', *Advertising and Promotion: An integrated marketing communications perspective*, New York: McGraw-Hill, 2003.

In many cases, modifying a slogan may prove more fruitful than introducing a new one with a new set of meanings. For example, Dockers switched its slogan from the well-received 'Nice pants' to 'One leg at a time' in the late 1990s before reverting to the previous slogan when recognizing that too much built-up equity had been given up.

Jingles

Jingles are musical messages written around the brand. Typically composed by professional songwriters, they often have enough catchy hooks and choruses to become almost permanently registered in the minds of listeners – sometimes whether they want them to or not! During the first half of the twentieth century, when broadcast advertising was confined primarily to radio, jingles became important branding devices. Figure 4.11 lists famous US brand jingles according to an advertising trade publication.

1. You deserve a break today (McDonalds).
2. Be all that you can be (US Army).
3. Pepsi Cola hits the spot (Pepsi Cola).
4. M'm, m'm good (Campbell's).
5. See the USA in your Chevrolet (GM).
6. I wish I was an Oscar Meyer Wiener (Oscar Meyer).
7. Double your pleasure, double your fun (Wrigley's Doublemint Gum).
8. Winston tastes good like a cigarette should (Winston).
9. It's the real thing (Coca-Cola).
10. A little dab'll do ya (Brylcreem).

Figure 4.11   *Advertising Age* top ten US jingles of the twentieth century

Source: www.adage.com

Jingles can be thought of as extended musical slogans and in that sense can be classified as a brand element. Because of their musical nature, however, jingles are not nearly as transferable as other brand elements. Jingles can communicate brand benefits, but they often convey product meaning in a non-direct and abstract fashion. The potential associations that might occur for the brand from jingles are probably most likely to relate to feelings and personality and other such intangibles. Jingles are perhaps most valuable in terms of enhancing brand awareness. Often, the jingle will repeat the brand name in clever and amusing ways that allow consumers many encoding opportunities. Because of their catchy nature, consumers are also likely to mentally rehearse or repeat the jingle even after seeing or hearing the ad, providing even additional encoding opportunities and increasing memorability.

A well-known jingle can serve as a foundation for advertising for years. As an example, in the USA, the familiar 'Give me a break' jingle for KitKat bars has been sung in ads by professionals and everyday people since 1988 and has helped to propel the brand to the sixth best-selling chocolate bar. Similarly, after two decades as the centerpiece of its ad campaign, there was an uproar when the US Army switched from its 'Be all that you can be' to 'Army of one'. Finally, Intel's three-second, four-note sound signature echoes the company's slogan ('In-tel In-side'). Although seemingly simple, the first note alone is a mix of 16 sounds, including a tambourine and a hammer striking a brass pipe.[36]

Packaging

Like other brand elements, packaging has a long history. Early humans used leaves and animal skin to cover and carry food and water. Glass containers appeared in Egypt some 4,000 years ago. Later, the French emperor Napoleon awarded 12,000 francs to the winner of a contest to find a better way to preserve food, which lead to vacuum-packing.[37]

From the perspective of both the firm and consumers, packaging must achieve a number of objectives:[38]

• identify the brand;
• convey descriptive and persuasive information;
• provide protection during distribution;
• assist storage in the home;
• aid product consumption.

To achieve the marketing objectives for a brand and satisfy the desires of consumers, the aesthetic and functional components of packaging must be chosen correctly. Aesthetic considerations relate to a packaging's size and shape, material, colour, text and graphics. Innovations in printing processes now permit eye-catching and appealing graphics that convey elaborate and colourful messages on the pack at the 'moment of truth' – the point of sale.[39] Functionally, structural design is crucial. For example, innovations with food products have resulted in packs being resealable, tamperproof and more convenient to use (eg, easy to hold, easy to open or squeezable). Changes in canning have made vegetables crunchier and special wraps have extended the life of refrigerated food.[40] Despite all of the attention to food packaging, opportunities remain because consumers still report many problems. In one survey, consumers complained about packs that stick, rip or don't protect their contents. Out of frustration, some consumers were actually even doing their own repackaging at home.[41]

Benefits

Packaging can have important brand equity benefits. Often, one of the strongest associations that consumers have with a brand relates to the look of its packaging. For example, if you ask the average consumer what comes to mind when they think of Heineken beer, a common response is 'green bottle'. The packaging can become important to brand recognition. Moreover, the information conveyed or inferred from the packaging can build or reinforce valuable brand associations. Molson's beer sales increased by 40 percent in the USA in 2004 after modifying the bottle's back labels to include cheeky 'ice-breakers' for bar patrons such as 'On the rebound', 'Sure, you can have my number' and 'Fairly intimidated by your beauty.'[42]

Structural packaging innovations can create a point of difference that permits a higher margin. New packaging can also expand a market and capture new market segments.

Packaging changes can have an immediate effect on sales. For example, sales of the Heath chocolate bar increased 25 percent in the USA after its wrapper was redesigned. Similarly, Rice-A-Roni's sales increased 20 percent in the first year after a packaging change. One trend has been to make both bigger and smaller pack versions of products (as well as portions) to appeal to new market segments.[43] Jumbo products have been introduced with hot dogs, pizzas, buns, frozen dinners and beer. For example, Pillsbury's introduction of Grand biscuits – 40 percent larger than existing offerings in the USA – was the most successful new product in the company's 126-year history.

Packaging at the point of sale

Packaging design also has become more important in recent years as brand proliferation continues and advertising is seen as becoming less cost-effective. Packaging can be a means of having strong appeal on the shelf and standing out from the clutter. The importance of packaging at the point of purchase can be seen by recognizing that the average supermarket shopper may be exposed to 20,000 or more products in a shopping visit that lasts less than 30 minutes and during which many purchases may be unplanned. For many consumers, the first encounter with a brand may be on the supermarket shelf. Because few product differences exist in some categories, packaging innovations can provide at least a temporary edge on competition.

For these reasons, packaging has been seen as a particularly cost-effective way to build brand equity.[44] Along these lines, packaging is sometimes called the 'last five seconds of marketing' as well as 'permanent media' or 'the last salesman'. Wal-Mart looks at packaging critically and tests whether or not consumers understand the brand promise behind the pack within 3 seconds and up to 15 feet from the shelf. Note that consumer exposure to packaging is not restricted to the point of sale and moments of consumption, because brand packaging often can play a starring role in advertising.[45]

Packaging innovations

In mature markets especially, packaging innovations can provide a short-term sales boost. For example, the 2-litre jug bottle and the 12-pack carton helped US soft drink makers experience steady 5 percent to 7 percent growth in the 1980s. With the rate of growth of the soft drink industry slowing down to 2 percent to 3 percent in the 1990s, soft drink makers sought packaging innovations to fuel growth. As a result, Pepsi-Cola introduced the 24-pack Cube, resealable bottles, Pepsi Mini cans and the wide-mouth, 1-litre Big Slam bottle. Even the look of Pepsi's packaging, which had not changed since 1973, was updated in a €342 million global redesign, eventually arriving at blue packaging with updated graphics.

The drinks industry has been characterized by packaging innovations. Following the lead from Snapple's wide-mouth glass bottle in the USA, Arizona's iced teas and fruit drinks in oversized, pastel-coloured cans became a €205 million brand in a few years with no marketing support beyond point-of-sale and rudimentary outdoor ads, designed in-house.[46] More recently, a number of beer and wine brands introduced have aluminum bottles as a means to make their products more appealing and convenient to drink.[47]

Packaging design

For all these reasons, packaging design has been elevated in its importance and has become an integral part of product development and launch. As with the choice of a brand name, packaging design has become a more sophisticated process. In the past, packaging design was often an afterthought, and colours, materials and so forth were often chosen arbitrarily. For example, legend has it that the colour of the famous Campbell's soup can had its origins in one executive at the company liking the look of the red and white kit of an American football team!

These days, packaging designers bring artistic techniques and scientific skills to packaging design in an attempt to meet the marketing objectives for a brand. These consultants conduct detailed analyses to break down the pack into a number of elements. They decide on the optimal look and content of each element and the proper packaging hierarchy in terms of which elements should be dominant in any one pack (eg, the brand name, illustration or some other graphical element) and how the elements should relate. When brand extensions are introduced, these designers can also decide which elements should be shared across packs and which elements should differ (and how). The Brand Briefing 4.6 describes the activities of Landor Associates, a packaging design and image management firm.

Designers often refer to the 'shelf impact' of a pack – the visual effect that the pack has at the point of sale when seen in the context of other packs in the category. For example, 'bigger and brighter' packs are not always better when competitors' packs are also factored in.[48] Although some information is legally required on packaging (eg, nutrition information for food), decisions can be made about design elements to improve brand awareness and facilitate the formation of brand associations.

Perhaps one of the most important visual design elements is colour.[49] Some packaging designers believe that consumers have a 'colour vocabulary' when it comes to

Brand Briefing 4.6

Brand makeover experts: Landor Associates

Landor Associates, one of the leading image consultants and strategic designers, called the ferryboat Kalmath, anchored on Pier 5 in San Francisco, home for years. Although the firm has since moved into more spacious headquarters, Landor has retained the ferryboat as a symbol of its creativity and innovation. Landor has provided a range of services to a varied list of clients with brands such as Pepsi, FedEx, GE, Delta, Frito-Lay, Hyatt, Levi's, Japan Airlines, Lucent, Procter & Gamble, Microsoft, Cathay Pacific and LG Group.

One recent client was BP. Landor helped BP transform itself from a middle-ranking oil company to a leading global brand. When BP acquired Amoco (1998), Castrol (2000) and Arco (2000), the brand became the means for unifying clashing cultures and rallying around a vision. The new brand captured BP's strategy, represented by the slogan 'beyond petroleum', and four beliefs: performance, progression, innovation and green. Launched in July 2000, BP's Brand Driver Platform became the foundation for a brand strategy that extended from a new positioning to a new logo, redesigned service stations and everything in between – advertisements, brochures, website, tanker trucks, kiosks, employee training and rewards programmes. Landor also spent time with BP employees, engaging them with the brand and shifting their focus from products to customers.

By moving their brand to the centre of its business, BP has used it to guide strategic decisions – such as investing in renewable energy sources – and direct the daily activities of employees. By 2001, BP's sales increased 23 percent worldwide. By 2002, 65 percent of employees reported understanding how to apply brand to their job (an increase of 41 percent) and *Fortune* magazine named BP a 'most admired company'. From 2001–2005, a period when most oil and petrol companies were losing public favour, BP's brand strength increased by 27 percent. The value of its intangible assets, including brand, grew by more than €4.8 billion (a 30 percent increase). BP's ability to outperform its competitors and transcend the petrol category led it to be named one of 10 'breakaway brands' by a *Fortune*/Brand Economics study (31 October 2005).

products and expect certain types of products to have a particular look. For example, it is believed that it would be difficult to sell milk in anything but a white container. At the same time, certain brands are thought to have 'colour ownership' such that it would be difficult for other brands to use a similar look. One US design executive outlined the following brand colour palette.[50]

- *Red:* Ritz crackers, KitKat bars, Colgate toothpaste and Coca-Cola soft drinks.
- *Orange:* Orange mobile phone services, Vax carpet cleaners and RAC breakdown service.
- *Yellow:* Kodak film, Juicy Fruit chewing gum, Cheerios cereal, Lipton tea and Jiff lemons.

- *Green:* Del Monte canned fruit, Green Giant vegetables and 7 UP lemon-lime soft drink.
- *Blue:* IBM computers, Domestos bleach, Comfort fabric conditioner and Pepsi-Cola soft drinks.

Colour can affect consumers' perceptions of the product itself.[51] For example, consumers ascribe sweeter taste to orange drinks the darker the orange shade of the can or bottle.

Colour is thus a critical element of packaging. Recent years have seen a rise in the use of blue as the look or even name for companies (eg, Blue Martini, JetBlue, Bluetooth), perhaps because blue 'suggests stature and professionalism' and 'is cool, hip and relevant to technology' and therefore is a 'safe choice'.[52] Purple also came on strong as a 'funky alternative' and therefore was embraced by many new economy firms. In addition to the product inferences signalled by the colour and other packaging design elements, it is also important that any other associations conveyed by the packaging be consistent with information conveyed by marketing.

Packaging changes

Although packaging changes can be expensive, they can be cost-effective compared with other marketing communication costs. Packs are changed for a number of reasons.[53] Packaging may be upgraded to signal a higher price, to more effectively sell products through new or shifting distribution channels (eg, Kendall Oil in the USA redid its package to make it more appealing to do-it-yourselfers when it found more of its sales coming from supermarkets and D/Y shops rather than service stations) or when there is a significant product line expansion that would benefit from a common look (eg, Weight Watchers foods). Pack redesign may also accompany a product innovation to signal changes to consumers. For example, when Procter & Gamble introduced Liquid Tide laundry detergent in the USA, the company felt that the 10 percent market share that the brand achieved was helped by the addition of a well-received drip-proof spout and bottle cap design.[54]

Perhaps the commonest reason for a redesign is that the packaging looks outdated. Under these circumstances, it is important not to lose the pack's equities that have been built up. Packaging often has some unique graphic features that have achieved a high level of awareness and preference. The need to create a more contemporary look must be reconciled with the need to preserve existing pack equities. In 1997, British Airways hoped for a more international look by adding Delft pottery, Chinese calligraphy and other ethnic designs on the tail fins of many of its planes. A hostile public response forced the company to repaint their planes in 2001 with the Chatham Dockyard Union Flag, a design first used on Concorde.[55]

Packaging changes have accelerated in recent years as marketers have sought to gain an advantage wherever possible. As one Coca-Cola ad executive noted: 'There's no question the crowded marketplace has inspired companies to change their boxes more often and there's greater use of promotional packages to give the appearance that things are changing.' In making a packaging change, it is thus important to recognize its effect on the original or current customer franchise for the brand.[56] To identify or confirm key pack equities, it is often necessary to conduct consumer research (see Brand Briefing 4.7).

Brand Briefing 4.7

Inside a packaging makeover

Betty Crocker's parent company, General Mills, spent more than €684,000 and one year on making over its cake, biscuit and muffin boxes. Packaging consultants, food photographers, graphic artists, marketers and consumers were consulted. Here's how it unfolded.

- In 2002, Betty Crocker conducted focus groups to find out whether customers agreed with internal suspicions that their inconsistent packaging designs were sorely in need of a facelift. When focus group participants said that the box failed to stand out, its purple background was 'anti-Betty' and the cake 'looked fake', the company sprang into action.

- The Betty Crocker team then got to work trying to nail down what Betty, a fictional housewife, would like in a pack. The company's design consultants, Lipson Alport Glass and Associates, created more than 100 versions of Betty's red spoon logo, and handwriting analysts deconstructed dozens of versions of her signatures to go on the boxes. Twenty people at the consulting firm worked on the redesign project in a room papered with sketches.

- The firm finalized a design for the red spoon as well as colours, fonts and logos to make sure the packaging would stay consistent and be striking. As one consultant noted, the goal was to 'get that classic warm-and-homey feeling, with a soft, sunny background, evoking a kitchen'. A red box border was created for uniformity, but a wavy band was included to 'evoke the stirring of batter'.

- A team including a photographer, art director and four food stylists worked for weeks on the baking photos that would appear on the cake box covers. Cakes were baked, sliced and photographed by the dozen. Every angle, every size was discussed.

- With all the pieces in place, the new packaging was launched. In 2003, a consumer survey showed four out of five shoppers preferred the new boxes. And more than half those surveyed said they would be more likely to buy the product based on the new designs versus the old. The Betty Crocker management team was thrilled. As one marketing director commented: 'It's like seeing your best friend get a makeover. You hope it'll be fabulous, and when it is, you want to applaud.'

Sources: Michele Meyer, 'Recipe for success?', *USA Weekend Magazine*, 20 July 2003; Kate Bertrand, 'Stylish packaging acts as home décor', *BrandPackaging*, September 2004; Ted Mininni, 'True brand differentiation: not new or improved', *BrandPackaging*, April 2005.

If packaging recognition is a critical consumer success factor for the brand, however, packaging changes must be conducted carefully. If changed too significantly, consumers may not recognize the new pack.

The importance of packaging is reflected in the fact that some marketing observers refer to it as the 'fifth P' of the marketing mix. Packaging can play an important role

1. *Know your consumer:* get inside your consumer's head and heart to learn about what motivates the purchase.
2. *Take the big-picture approach:* packs that are most effective borrow ideas from a wide range of product categories. They look at all forms of packaging and put the best ideas together in unique ways.
3. *Understand that packaging aesthetics and function are both critical:* the pack has to grab consumers' attention in a sea of competing messages, but it also has to work well so that consumers will buy again.
4. *Know your distribution channels:* how do retailers view your packs? How are channels changing? Which retailers like which pack configurations?
5. *Educate management:* make sure senior management recognizes the importance of packaging.

Figure 4.12   Guidelines for creating high-impact packaging

in building brand equity directly through points of difference created by functional or aesthetic elements of the packaging or indirectly through the reinforcement of brand awareness and image. Figure 4.12 contains the recommendations of one expert on how to create packaging with high impact and Brand Briefing 4.8 reviews some academic research.[57]

Brand Briefing 4.8

The psychology of packaging

Academic Brian Wansink has conducted research studies into the consumer psychology of packaging. Here is how he approaches the topic and views some of his findings: 'Packaging can be such an important brand-building tool that it is sometimes called the "fifth P". Since it is estimated that the majority of brand choice decisions are made at the point-of-purchase, the right package can instantly catch a consumer's eye, communicate value, reinforce a brand's equity, and provide key comparison information.[58,59] The bright red and yellow colours of a Tide box can attract attention, while the black and white boxes of an Apple iPod can reinforce an exclusive, "think different" image. The slender shape of one shampoo bottle emphasizes elegance, while the squat shape of another holding the same volume leads people to think it contains less shampoo inside.'

Many managers think the pack's main purpose is to encourage purchase. For many consumer packaged goods, the pack keeps on marketing the brand and influencing consumers long after it is purchased. After it is home it can influence how a person perceives its taste and value and it can influence how much a person uses at a time and even how he or she uses it.

- *Packaging can influence taste:* our sense of taste and touch is very suggestible, and what we see on a pack can lead us to taste what we think we are going to taste.

Brand Briefing 4.8 *continued*

In one study, 181 people were sent home with nutrition bars that either claimed to contain '10 grams of protein' or '10 grams of soy protein.' In reality, both nutrition bars were identical, and neither contained any soy. Nevertheless, because many people believe soy to have a unfavourable taste, they rated the bars with 'soy' on the package as, 'grainy', 'unappealing' and 'tasteless'.[60] People often taste what they expect to taste. The right words and image on a pack can have a big influence on these expectations.

- *Packaging can influence value:* long after we have bought a product, a pack can still lead us to believe we bought it as it was a good value. First, most people believe that the bigger the pack, the better the price per weight. Even the shape of a pack can influence what we think.[61] One study found that people believe tall, narrow packs hold more of a product than short, wide packs.[62]

- *Packaging can influence consumption:* studies of 48 types of foods and personal care products[63] have shown that people pour and consume 18–32 percent more of a product as the size of the container doubles.[64] A big part of the reason why this occurs is because these larger sizes subtly suggest a higher 'consumption norm'.[65] This is so hardwired that it happens in a wide range of contexts. One study gave Chicago cinema-goers free medium or large popcorn buckets and showed that those given the larger buckets ate 45 percent more![66] Even when 14 day-old popcorn was used, people still ate 32 percent more even though they said they hated the popcorn.[67] The same thing happens at parties. US students at a party were offered snacks from either huge bowls or from twice as many half-sized bowls. Those taking from the large-bowls took and ate 53 percent more than those eating from the small bowls.[68]

- *Packaging can influence how a person uses a product:* for some mature brands, one strategy to increase use has been to encourage people to use the brand in new situations (soup for breakfast) or for new uses (bicarbonate of soda as a refrigerator deodorizer). An analysis of 26 products and 402 consumers showed that the commonest way in which consumers learned about new uses for products was from reading the pack. The study showed that twice as many people had learned about the new use from the pack as from television ads.[69] Part of the reason such on-pack suggestions are effective is they are likely to reach a person who is already favourable to the brand.

A pack can influence what we buy, but it can also influence how we use it, how much we consume and how much we enjoy it. Packaging continues to influence us long after it is purchased, and it can be an important part of what contributes to a brand's equity.

PUTTING IT ALL TOGETHER

The previous discussion highlighted considerations for brand names, URLs, logos, symbols, characters, slogans, jingles and packaging. Each of these different elements can play a role in building brand equity. Conceptually, it is necessary to 'mix and match' these elements to maximize brand equity. That is, as summarized in Figure 4.13, each brand element has strengths and weaknesses. Thus, marketers must 'mix' brand elements by choosing different ones to achieve different objectives. At the same time, marketers must 'match' the elements by making sure that certain ones are chosen to reinforce each other by shared meaning. For example, research has shown that meaningful names that are represented as logos are easier to remember than without such reinforcement.[70]

The set of brand elements can be thought of as making up the *brand identity*. The cohesiveness of the brand identity depends on the extent to which the elements are consistent. Ideally, elements would be chosen that support other brand elements and that could easily be incorporated into other aspects of the brand and marketing campaign.

Some strong brands have valuable elements that reinforce each other. For example, consider Charmin toilet tissue. Phonetically, the name itself probably conveys softness. The original brand character, Mr Whipple, and the brand slogan, 'Please

	Brand element				
Criterion	**Names and URLs**	**Logos and symbols**	**Characters**	**Slogans and jingles**	**Packaging and signs**
Memorability	Can be chosen to enhance brand recall and recognition	Generally more useful for brand recognition	Generally more useful for brand recognition	Can be chosen to enhance brand recall and recognition	Generally more useful for brand recognition
Meaningfulness	Can reinforce almost any type of association, although sometimes only indirectly	Can reinforce almost any type of association, although sometimes only indirectly	Generally more useful for non-product-related imagery and brand personality	Can convey almost any type of association explicitly	Can convey almost any type of association explicitly
Likeability	Can evoke much verbal imagery	Can provoke visual appeal	Can generate human qualities	Can evoke much verbal imagery	Can combine visual and verbal appeal
Transferability	Can be limited	Excellent	Can be limited	Can be limited	Good
Adaptability	Difficult	Can typically be redesigned	Can sometimes be redesigned	Can be modified	Can typically be redesigned
Protectability	Generally good, but with limits	Excellent	Excellent	Excellent	Can be closely copied

Figure 4.13   Critique of brand element options

don't squeeze the Charmin', used in the USA also help to reinforce the point of difference for the brand of 'softness'.

Brand names characterized by rich, visual imagery often can yield powerful logos or symbols. Wells Fargo, a large California-based bank, has a brand name rich in the heritage of the US West that can be exploited in marketing. Wells Fargo has adopted a stagecoach as a symbol and has named individual services to be thematically consistent – for example, creating investment funds called Stagecoach Funds.

CHAPTER REVIEW

Brand elements are those trademarkable devices that serve to identify and differentiate a brand. The main elements are names, URLs, logos, symbols, characters, slogans, jingles and packaging. Elements can be chosen to both enhance brand awareness and facilitate the formation of strong, favourable and unique brand associations.

In choosing and designing brand elements, six criteria are particularly important. First, elements can be chosen to be inherently memorable, both in terms of brand recall and recognition. Second, elements can be chosen to be inherently meaningful such that they convey information about the nature of the product category or particular attributes and benefits of a brand or both. The element may even reflect brand personality, user or usage imagery or feelings for the brand. Third, the information conveyed by brand elements does not necessarily have to relate to the product alone and may simply be inherently appealing. Fourth, elements can be chosen to be transferable within and across product categories (ie, to support line and brand extensions) and across geographic and cultural boundaries and market segments. Fifth, elements can be chosen to be adaptable and flexible over time. Finally, brand elements must be chosen that are legally protectable and, as much as possible, competitively defensible.

The chapter reviewed a number of considerations for each type of brand element. Because elements have different strengths and weaknesses it is important to 'mix and match' them to maximize their collective contribution to brand equity. Elements are 'mixed' by choosing different ones to achieve different objectives. Brand elements are 'matched' by designing some elements to be mutually reinforcing and to share some meaning.

Discussion questions

1. Pick a brand. Identify all of its brand elements and assess their ability to contribute to brand equity according to the choice criteria identified in this chapter.

2. What are your favorite brand characters? Do you think they contribute to brand equity in any way? How? Can you relate their effects to the customer-based brand equity model?

3. What are some other examples of slogans not listed in the chapter that make strong contributions to brand equity? Why? Can you think of any 'bad' slogans? Why do you consider them to be so?

4. Choose a pack of any supermarket product. Assess its contribution to brand equity. Justify your decisions.

5. Can you think of some general guidelines to help marketers mix and match brand elements? Can you ever have 'too many' elements? Which brand do you think does the best job of mixing and matching brand elements?

References and notes

[1] For a stimulating treatment of brand naming, see Alex Frankel, *Word Craft*, New York: Crown Publishers 2004.

[2] An excellent overview of the topic, some of which this section draws on, can be found in Kim R. Robertson, 'Strategically desirable brand name characteristics', *Journal of Consumer Marketing*, 1989, 6 (4): 61–71.

[3] Frances Leclerc, Bernd H. Schmitt, and Laurette Dube, 'Foreign branding and its effects on product perceptions and attitudes', *Journal of Marketing Research*, May 1994, 31: 263–70. See also M. V. Thakor and B. G. Pacheco, 'Foreign branding and its effect on product perceptions and attitudes: a replication and extension in a multicultural setting', *Journal of Marketing Theory and Practice*, Winter 1997: 15–30.

[4] Eric Yorkston and Geeta Menon, 'A sound idea: phonetic effects of brand names on consumer judgments', *Journal of Consumer Research*, 2004, 31 (June): 43–51; Richard R. Klink, 'Creating brand names with meaning: the use of sound symbolism', *Marketing Letters*, 2000, 11 (1): 5–20.

[5] Kim R. Robertson, 'Recall and recognition effects of brand name imagery', *Psychology and Marketing*, 1987, 4: 3–15.

[6] Robert N. Kanungo, 'Effects of fittingness, meaningfulness and product utility', *Journal of Applied Psychology*, 1968, 52: 290–5.

[7] Kevin Lane Keller, Susan Heckler and Michael J. Houston, 'The effects of brand name suggestiveness on advertising recall', *Journal of Marketing*, January 1998, 62: 48–57.

[8] Luk Warlop, S. Ratneshwar and Stijn M. J. van Osselaer, 'Distinctive brand cues and memory for product consumption experiences', *International Journal of Research in Marketing*, 2005, 22: 27–44.

[9] Daniel J. Howard, Roger A. Kerin and Charles Gengler, 'The effects of brand name similarity on brand source confusion: implications for trademark infringement', *Journal of Public Policy & Marketing*, 2000, 19 (Fall): 250–64.

[10] Alex Frankel, 'Name-o-rama', *Wired*, June 1997: 94.

[11] William L. Moore and Donald R. Lehmann, 'Effects of usage and name on perceptions of new products', *Marketing Science*, 1982, 1 (4): 351–70.

[12] Keller, Heckler and Houston, 'Effects of brand name suggestiveness on advertising recall.'

[13] Keller, Heckler and Houston, 'Effects of brand name suggestiveness on advertising recall.'

[14] Robert A. Peterson and Ivan Ross, 'How to name new brands', *Journal of Advertising Research*, December 1972, 12 (6): 29–34.

[15] Robert A. Mamis, 'Name calling', *Inc.*, July 1984.

[16]Tina M. Lowrey, L. J. Shrum and Tony M. Dubitsky, 'The relationship between brand-name linguistic characteristics and brand-name memory', *Journal of Advertising*, 2003, 32 (3): 7–17.

[17]Michael McCarthy, 'Xterra discovers extra success', *USA Today*, 26 February 2001: 4B.

[18]C. Miguel Brendl, Amitava Chattopadyhay, Brett W. Pelham and Mauricio Carvallo, 'Name letter branding: valence transfers when product specific needs are active', *Journal of Consumer Research*, 2005, 32 (December): 405–15.

[19]Bruce G. Vanden Bergh, Janay Collins, Myrna Schultz and Keith Adler, 'Sound advice on brand names', *Journalism Quarterly*, 1984, 61 (4): 835–40; Bruce G. Vanden Bergh, Keith E. Adler and Lauren Oliver, 'Use of linguistic characteristics with various brand-name styles', *Journalism Quarterly*, 1987, 65: 464–8.

[20]Daniel L. Doeden, 'How to select a brand name', *Marketing Communications*, November 1981: 58–61.

[21]Timothy B. Heath, Subimal Chatterjee and Karen Russo, 'Using the phonemes of brand names to symbolize brand attributes', in *The AMA Educator's Proceedings: Enhancing knowledge development in marketing*, eds. William Bearden and A. Parasuraman, Chicago: American Marketing Association, August 1990.

[22]Much of this passage is based on Teresa M. Paiva and Janeen Arnold Costa, 'The winning number: consumer perceptions of alpha-numeric brand names', *Journal of Marketing*, July 1993, 57: 85–98.

[23]John Murphy, *Brand Strategy*, Upper Saddle River, NJ: Prentice Hall, 1990, 79.

[24]Alex Frankel, 'The new science of naming', *Business 2.0*, December 2004, 53–5.

[25]Beth Snyder Bulik, 'Tech sector ponders: what's in a name?', *Advertising Age*, 9 May 2005: 24.

[26]Matt Hicks, 'Order out of chaos', *eWeek*, 1 July 2001.

[27]Rachel Konrad, 'Companies resurrect abandoned names, ditch ".com"', CNET News.com, 13 November 2000.

[28]John Murphy, *Brand Strategy'*.

[29]Pamela W. Henderson and Joseph A. Cote, 'Guidelines for selecting or modifying logos', *Journal of Marketing*, 1998, 62 (2): 14–30.

[30]John Murphy, *Brand Strategy'*.

[31]Michael McCarthy, 'More firms flash new badge', *USA Today*, 4 October 2000: B3.

[32]Ibid.

[33]Paul Durman, 'Crazy Frog turns into a real prince', *The Times*, 6 March 2005: Business section.

[34]Cyndee Miller, 'The Green Giant: an enduring figure lives happily ever after', *Marketing News*, 15 April 1991: 2.

[35]David A. Aaker, *Building Strong Brands*, New York: Free Press, 1996: 203.

[36]Dirk Smillie, 'Now hear this', *Forbes*, 25 December 2000: 234.

[37]Nancy Croft, 'Wrapping up sales', *Nation's Business*, October 1985: 41–2.

[38]Susan B. Bassin, 'Value-added packaging cuts through store clutter', *Marketing News*, 26 September 1988: 21.

[39]Raymond Serafin, 'Packaging becomes an art', *Advertising Age*, 12 August 1985: 66.

[40]Trish Hall, 'New packaging may soon lead to food that tastes better and is more convenient', *Wall Street Journal*, 21 April 1986: 25.

[41]'Food packages rile consumers', *Wall Street Journal*, 11 November 1987.

[42]Nate Nickerson, 'How about this beer label: "I'm in advertising!"', *Fast Company*, March 2004: 43.

[43]Eben Shapiro, 'Portions and packages grow bigger and bigger', *Wall Street Journal*, 12 October 1993: B1.

[44]Alecia Swasy, 'Sales lost their vim? Try repackaging', *Wall Street Journal*, 11 October 1989: B1.

[45]'Packaging plays starring role in TV commercials', *Marketing News*, 30 January 1987.

[46]Gerry Khermouch, 'John Ferolito, Don Vultaggio', *Brandweek*, 14 November 1995: 57.

[47]Paul Glader and Christopher Lawton, 'Beer and wine makers use fancy cans to court new fans', *Wall Street Journal*, 24 August 2004: B1–B2.

[48]For interesting discussion, see Margaret C. Campbell and Ronald C. Goodstein, 'The moderating effect of perceived risk on consumers' evaluations of product incongruity: preference for the norm', *Journal of Consumer Research*, December 2001, 28: 439–49.

[49]For an interesting application of colour to brand names, see Elizabeth G. Miller and Barbara E. Kahn, 'Shades of meaning: the effect of color and flavor names on consumer choice', *Journal of Consumer Research*, 2005, 32 (June): 86–92.

[50]Michael Purvis, president of Sidjakov, Berman and Gomez, as quoted in Carla Marinucci, 'Advertising on the store shelves', *San Francisco Examiner*, 20 October 1986: C1–C2.

[51]Lawrence L. Garber Jr, Raymond R. Burke and J. Morgan Jones, 'The role of package color in consumer purchase consideration and choice', MSI Report 00–104, Cambridge, MA: Marketing Science Institute, 2000; Ronald Alsop, 'Color grows more important in catching consumers' eyes', *Wall Street Journal*, 29 November 1984: 37.

[52]Susan Carey, 'American companies are blue and it's not just the stock market', *Wall Street Journal*, 30 August 2001: A1.

[53]Bill Abrams and David P. Garino, 'Package design gains stature as visual competition grows', *Wall Street Journal*, 14 March 1979: 48.

[54]Amy Dunkin, 'Want to wake up a tired old package? Repackage it', *Business Week*, 15 July 1985: 130–4.

[55]Melanie Wells, 'Face-lift fever', *Forbes*, 15 November 1999: 58.

[56]Garber, Burke and Jones, 'Role of package color.'

[57]James W. Peters, 'Five steps to packaging that sells', *Brand Packaging*, July/August 1999, 3 (4): 3.

[58]Peter H. Bloch, 'Seeking the ideal form: product design and consumer response', *Journal of Marketing*, 1995, 59 (3): 16–29.

[59]Peter H. Bloch, Frederick F. Brunel, T. J. Arnold, 'Individual differences in the centrality of visual product aesthetics: concept and measurement', *Journal of Consumer Research*, 2003, 29 (4): 551–65.

[60]Brian Wansink and Se-Bum Park, 'Sensory suggestiveness and labeling: do soy labels bias taste?', *Journal of Sensory Studies*, 2002, 17 (5) (November): 483–91.

[61]Valerie Folkes and Shashi Matta, 'The effects of package shape on consumers' judgment of product volume: attention as mental containment', *Journal of Consumer Research*, 2004, 31 (September): 390–401.

[62]Priya Raghubir and Aradna Krishna, 'Vital dimensions in volume perception: can the eye fool the stomach?', *Journal of Marketing Research*, 1999, 36 (August): 313–26.

[63]Valerie Folkes, Ingrid Martin and Kamal Gupta, 'When to say when: effects of supply on usage', *Journal of Consumer Research*, 1993, 20 (December): 467–77.

[64]Brian Wansink, 'Can package size accelerate usage volume?', *Journal of Marketing*, 1996, 60 (July): 1–14; Folkes, Martin and Gupta, 'When to say when'.

[65]Brian Wansink, 'Environmental factors that increase the food intake and consumption volume of unknowing consumers', *Annual Review of Nutrition*, 2004, 24: 455–79.

[66]Brian Wansink and SeaBum Park, 'At the movies: how external cues and perceived taste impact consumption volume', *Food Quality and Preference*, 2001, 12 (1) (January): 69–74.

[67]Brian Wansink and Junyong Kim, 'Bad popcorn in big buckets: portion size can influence intake as much as taste', *Journal of Nutrition Education and Behavior*, 2005.

[68]Brian Wansink and Matthew M. Cheney, 'Super bowls: serving bowl size and food consumption,' *JAMA – Journal of the American Medical Association*, 2005, 293 (14) (13 April): 1727–8.

[69]Brian Wansink and Jennifer M. Gilmore, 'New uses that revitalize old brands', *Journal of Advertising Research*, 1999, 39 (2) (April/May): 90–8.

[70]Terry L. Childers and Michael J. Houston, 'Conditions for a picture superiority effect on consumer memory', *Journal of Consumer Research,* September 1984, 11: 551–63; Kathy A. Lutz and Richard J. Lutz, 'Effects of interactive imagery on learning: application to advertising', *Journal of Applied Psychology*, 1977, 62 (4): 493–8.

5 Designing marketing campaigns to build brand equity

PREVIEW

Although judicious selection of brand elements and the resulting brand identity can make an important contribution to customer-based brand equity, the primary input comes from marketing activities related to the brand and the corresponding marketing campaigns. This chapter considers how marketing activities in general and product, pricing and distribution strategies in particular can build brand equity – that is, enhance brand awareness, improve the brand image, elicit positive brand responses and increase brand resonance. Chapter 6 considers how marketers can create integrated marketing communication campaigns to build brand equity.

In both of these chapters, the focus is on marketing activities from a branding perspective. The question is how marketing campaigns should be designed to build brand equity. This chapter also considers how the brand itself can be integrated into the marketing campaign to maximize the creation of brand equity. To obtain a broader perspective on marketing activities, however, it is necessary to consult a basic marketing management text, as well as the specific references noted in these chapters.[1] The analysis begins by considering some developments in designing marketing campaigns. After next reviewing product, pricing and channel strategies, this chapter concludes by considering the important topic of retailers' own labels in Brand Briefing 5.9.

NEW PERSPECTIVES ON MARKETING

The strategy and tactics behind marketing campaigns have changed dramatically as firms have dealt with the shifts of the 'new economy' in their external marketing environment. As outlined in Chapter 1, changes in the economic, technological, political–legal, sociocultural and competitive environments have forced marketers to embrace new approaches and philosophies. Four drivers of this new economy are:[2]

- digitalization and connectivity (through internet, intranet and mobile devices);
- disintermediation and reintermediation (via new middlemen of various sorts);

Consumers

- A substantial increase in customer power.
- Greater variety of available goods and services.
- Great amount of information about practically anything.
- Greater ease in interacting and in placing and receiving orders.
- Ability to 'chat' with others and compare notes on products and services.

Companies

- Can operate a powerful new information and sales channel with augmented geographic reach to inform and promote a company and its products.
- Can collect fuller and richer information about markets, customers, prospects and competitors.
- Can facilitate two-way communication with their customers and prospects, and improve transaction efficiency.
- Can send ads, coupons, promotion and information by e-mail to customers and prospects who give them permission.
- Can customize offerings and services to individual customers.
- Can improve purchasing, recruiting, training and internal and external communication.

Figure 5.1   Capabilities of the new economy

- customization and customerization (through tailored products and by providing customers with ingredients to make products themselves);
- industry convergence (through the blurring of industry boundaries).

These drivers, and others related to forces such as privatization and regulation, have combined to give customers and companies new capabilities (see Figure 5.1). These changes have implications for brand management. Marketers are increasingly abandoning the mass-market practices that built brand powerhouses in the 1950s, 1960s and 1970s to implement new approaches.[3] Even marketers in traditional industries are rethinking their practices. Consider Brand Briefing 5.1, which addresses how Innocent drinks found a specific recipe for its drinks – and business.

Brand Briefing 5.1

Innocent drinks: innovative and cost-effective marketing

Innocent Drinks was born 1998, when three college friends joined together to start a business. To see if their idea was working, they tried a unique form of product concept testing. The test site was a music festival in London and the stimuli £500 worth of fruit. Bins were marked 'Yes' and 'No' and a handwritten sign read: 'Do you think we should give up our jobs to make these smoothies?' By the end of the day the 'Yes' bin was overflowing with empties. The following day the founders quit their jobs to start Innocent Drinks.

Brand Briefing 5.1 *continued*

Innocent provides natural, pure juice drinks without sugar, water or concentrates. The company has 41 percent national awareness and market share grew from 14 percent to over 30 percent in four years. Its drinks are available in over 4,000 outlets, including Sainsburys, Eat, Starbucks and many independent retailers. This growth and awareness could not have been achieved without effective, creative and inexpensive marketing. Focus lies on creative communication and the less conventional, which means using every medium available to communicate with consumers.

The brand's voice is light-hearted, simple and friendly, and being 'innocent' is an important aspect to maintaining a consistent voice throughout all aspects of the brand. A key element is packaging, which is a smart representation of the brand. The labels are constantly changed and carry cute messages such as 'Separation occurs, but mummy still loves daddy'. The sampling methods are unique and a great example is the 'Cow van', complete with horns, eyelashes and a tail. When a button is pressed, the cow goes 'moo'. Other vans are covered in grass and can be made to dance. Customer care is important and if a customer is displeased or just bored they can call the Banana Phone or pop in and visit Fruit Towers. A bad smoothie means that a 'sorry smoothie' arrives the next day. These are small things with a low cost, but they make an enormous difference and add richness to the customer experience.

By being seen in so many articles, the company has had a great return on its media investments. For every £1 spent, Innocent created a multiple of 6.7 in return. Innocent's unique communications, friendly products and innovative channels to reach customers all create publicity. Internal communication and marketing is important and the company strives for motivated and engaged employees who become ambassadors for the brand. Living the brand is the key.

In summary, Innocent shows how an appealing brand and tone that is communicated creatively and consistently and that is 'lived' in all customer interactions – whether that is talking to consumers on the phone, selling in to a new outlet or driving a delivery vehicle – can deliver high market impact at relatively inexpensive marketing cost – less than £100,000.

Sources: Edvin Colyer, 9 December 2002 'Can small businesses sprout big brands?' 13 July 2007, www.brandchannel.com; Innocent Drinks website, 13 July 2007, www.innocentdrinks.com; Laura Cummings, 9 July 2003, 'Just an Innocent business?' 13 July 2007, http://news.bbc.co.uk; Lizzy Stallard, 22 March 2004, 'Innocent drinks – savvy', 13 July 2007, www.brandchannel.com; Richard Reed, 2003, 'Brand building without a budget'.

The changed marketing environment of the twenty-first century has forced marketers to alter the way they develop marketing campaigns. Integration and personalization have become increasingly crucial factors in building and maintaining strong brands as companies attempt to engage in a broad set of tightly focused activities that are meaningful to their target customers.

Integrating marketing

In today's marketplace, there are many means by which products and services and their corresponding marketing campaigns can build brand equity. Channel strategies, communication strategies, pricing strategies and other activities can all enhance or detract from brand equity. The customer-based brand equity model provides guidance on interpreting these effects. One implication of the conceptualization of customer-based brand equity is that the *manner* in which brand associations are formed does not matter – only the resulting awareness and strength, favourability and uniqueness of brand associations.

In other words, if a consumer has an equally strong and favourable brand association from Rolaids antacids to the concept 'relief' because of product experiences, reading an article, exposure to a 'problem–solution' television ad that concludes with the tagline 'Rolaids spells relief' *or* because of knowledge that Rolaids sponsors a sports award, the effect in terms of customer-based brand equity should be identical unless additional associations are created (eg, 'advertised on television') or existing associations are affected in some way (eg, 'speed or potency of effects').

Thus, from the perspective of customer-based brand equity, marketers should evaluate *all* possible means available to create knowledge structures according to effectiveness criteria as well as efficiency and cost considerations. At the centre of brand-building efforts is almost always the product or service. Other marketing activities surrounding that product, however, can be critical, as well as the manner by which the brand is integrated into these supporting activities.

Consistent with this view, Schultz, Tannenbaum and Lauterborn conceptualize one aspect of integrated marketing, integrated marketing communications, in terms of contacts.[4] They define a *contact* as any information-bearing experience that a customer or prospect has with the brand, the product category or the market that relates to the marketer's product or service. According to these authors, a person can come into contact with a brand in numerous ways:

> For example, a contact can include friends' and neighbours' comments; packaging; newspaper, magazine and television information; ways the customer or prospect is treated in a shop; where the product is shelved; and the type of signs that appear in retail establishments. And the contacts do not stop with the purchase. Contacts also consist of what friends, relatives and bosses say about a person who is using the product. Contacts include the type of customer service given with returns or enquiries or even the letters a company writes to resolve problems or to solicit additional business. All of these are customer contacts with the brand. These bits and pieces of information, experiences and relationships, created over time, influence the potential relationship among the customer, the brand and the marketer.

The bottom line is that there are many ways to build brand equity. Unfortunately, there are also many firms attempting to build brand equity. Creative and original thinking is necessary to create fresh marketing campaigns that break through the noise in the marketplace to connect with customers. Marketers are increasingly trying unconventional means of building brand equity. As just one example, consider the existence of pop-up stores – temporary stores that blend retail and event marketing.

Vacant

Cutting-edge retailer Vacant has exclusive retail concept and exhibition stores that choose to open for one month only in empty spaces in cities such as New York, London, Tokyo, Shanghai, Paris, Berlin and Stockholm, showing one-off, hard-to-find and limited edition products from established brands and emerging designers. Vacant products range from cars to boutiques. Limited quantities are available and not all products on display can be purchased. Store locations are announced by e-mail to Vacant Club members only moments before opening.[5]

Ultimately, however, creativity must not sacrifice a brand-building goal and marketing campaigns must be orchestrated in a way to provide seemlessly integrated solutions and experiences for customers that create awareness, spur demand and cultivate loyalty.

Personalized marketing

The expansion of the web and continued fragmentation of mass media has brought the need for personalized marketing into focus. Many maintain that the new economy celebrates the power of the individual consumer.[6] According to one writer: 'The worry for big brand owners is that this [individualism] is leading to a fragmentation of brands as people try to express their individuality by moving away from the mass market.'[7]

To adapt to the increased consumer desire for, and competitive forces impelling towards, personalization, marketers have embraced concepts such as experiential marketing, one-to-one marketing and permission marketing.

Experiential marketing

Experiential marketing promotes a product by not only communicating its features and benefits but also connecting it with unique and interesting experiences. One marketing commentator describes experiential marketing so: 'The idea is not to sell something, but to demonstrate how a brand can enrich a customer's life.'[8] For example, consider how American Express won the grand prize in *Adweek* magazine's 2005 Buzz Awards for branded entertainment.

American Express

A decades-long sponsor of the US Open tennis tournament in New York, American Express decided to expand its sponsorship in 2004 beyond the tennis grounds to the heart of Manhattan. As the company noted: 'American Express is always looking for ways to provide special experiences and access to our card members.' Part of the Rockefeller Center was converted into a stadium with seating in front of a 25-foot TV screen showing live matches. There were also concession stands, US Open merchandise, a replica tennis court for exhibitions and participation and events featuring past and current tennis players. Many perks were reserved for American Express cardholders, including a daily draw for courtside seats to the next evening's matches with limousine transport. The objective of the event, which drew 337,000 people, was to expand the perception of American Express as enhancing an experience, not just as a method of payment.[9]

Pine and Gilmore, pioneers of the topic, argue that we are on the threshold of the 'experience economy', an era in which all businesses must orchestrate memorable events for their customers.[10] They claim:

- if you charge for stuff, you are in the *commodity* business;
- if you charge for tangible things, you are in the *goods* business;
- if you charge for the activities you perform, you are in the *service* business;
- if you charge for the time customers spend with you, then and only then are you in the *experience* business.

Citing examples from a range of companies, they maintain that saleable experiences come in four varieties: entertainment, education, aesthetic and escapist.

Academic Bernd Schmitt underscores the importance of experiential marketing: 'The degree to which a company is able to deliver a desirable customer experience – and to use information technology, brands, and integrated marketing communication and entertainment to do so – will largely determine its success in the global marketplace of the new millennium.'[11]

Schmitt details five types of experiences – sense, feel, think, act and relate – that are becoming vital to consumers' perceptions of brands. He also describes how various 'experience providers' (such as communications, visual/verbal identity and signs, product presence, co-branding, spatial environments, electronic media and sales-people) can be used as part of a marketing campaign to create these experiences. In describing an increasingly demanding consumer, Schmitt writes: 'Customers want to be entertained, stimulated, emotionally affected and creatively challenged.' Figure 5.2 lists Schmitt's rules for successful experiential marketing. The Brand Briefing 5.2 describes how some marketers are thinking more carefully about brand scents.

One-to-one marketing

Don Peppers and Martha Rogers popularized the concept of one-to-one marketing.[12] The rationale is that consumers help to add value by providing information to marketers; marketers add value, in turn, by taking that information and generating rewarding experiences for consumers. In doing so, the firm is able to create switching costs, reduce transaction costs and maximize utility for consumers, all helping to build strong, profitable relationships. One-to-one marketing is thus based on:

- focus on individual consumers through consumer databases: 'We single out consumers';
- respond to consumer dialogue via interactivity: 'The consumer talks to us';
- customize products and services: 'We make something unique for him or her.'

Another tenet of one-to-one marketing is the importance of treating different consumers differently because of their different needs and different current as well as future value to the firm. In particular, Peppers and Rogers stress the importance of devoting more marketing effort to the most valuable consumers.

Peppers and Rogers identify brands that practice one-to-one marketing, such as Avon, Owens-Corning, Amway and Nike.[13] They note how Ritz-Carlton hotels use databases to store consumer preferences so that if a customer makes a special request in one of its hotels, it is already known when he or she stays in another. For example,

1. Experiences don't just happen; they need to be planned. In that planning process, be creative; use surprise, intrigue and, at times, provocation. Shake things up.
2. Think about the customer experience first, and then about the functional features and benefits of your brand.
3. Be obsessive about the details of the experience. Traditional satisfaction models are missing the sensory, gut feel, brain-blasting, all-body, all-feeling, all-mind 'EJ' experience. (EJ = exultate jubilate.) Let the customer delight in exultant jubilation!
4. Find the 'duck' for your brand. More than five years ago, I stayed for the first time in the Conrad Hotel in Hong Kong. In the bathroom on the rim of the bath there was a bright yellow rubber duck with a red mouth. I fell in love with the idea (and the duck) immediately. It's the one thing that I always remember when I think about the hotel – and it becomes the starting point of remembering the entire hotel experience. Every company needs to have a duck for its brand. That is, a little element that triggers, frames, summarizes and stylizes the experience.
5. Think consumption situation, not product, eg, 'grooming in the bathroom' not 'razor'; 'casual meal' not 'hot dog'; and 'travel' not 'transportation'. Move along the sociocultural dimension.
6. Strive for 'holistic experiences' that dazzle the senses, appeal to the heart, challenge the intellect, are relevant to people's lifestyles and provide relational, ie, social identity, appeal.
7. Profile and track experiential impact with the 'experiential grid.' Profile different experiences (sense, feel, think, act and relate) across experience providers (logos, ads, packaging, advertising, websites, etc.)
8. Use methodologies eclectically. Some methods may be quantitative (questionnaire analysis); others qualitative (a day in the life of the customer). Some may be verbal (focus group); others visual (digital camera techniques). Some may be conducted in artificial lab settings; others in pubs or cafe's. Anything goes! Be explorative and creative, and worry about reliability, validity and methodological sophistication later.
9. Consider how the experience changes when extending the brand – into new categories, on to the web, around the globe. Ask yourself how the brand could be leveraged in a new category, in an electronic medium, in a different culture through experiential strategies.
10. Add dynamism and 'Dionysianism' to your company and brand. Most organization and brand owners are too timid, too slow and too bureaucratic. The term 'Dionysian' is associated with the ecstatic, the passionate, the creative. Let this spirit breathe in your organization and watch how things change.

Figure 5.2   Schmitt's guidelines for experiential marketing

Source: Adapted with the permission of The Free Press, a Division of Simon & Schuster Adult Publishing Group, from EXPERIMENTAL MARKETING: How to Get Customers to Sense, Feel, Act, and Relate to Your Company and Brands by Bernd H. Schmidt. Copyright © 1999 by Bernd H. Schmidt. All rights reserved.

Brand Briefing 5.2

Making sense out of brand scents

The smell of a new car is distinctive. When Rolls-Royce customers complained in the 1990s that the new cars weren't as good as the old models, researchers tracked the problem to a surprising source: its smell. The company then recreated the aroma of a 1965 Rolls and now sprays it in all new models. So can scent be used to entice customers or to make a place a little more memorable?

Las Vegas casinos have long infused scents into gaming areas to encourage gamblers to stay longer. Now the connection between scent and shopping is being explored in more venues. Companies looking for an edge are tinkering with scent as

Brand Briefing 5.2 *continued*

a way to distinguish their brand or shop. The barrage of advertising consumers take in is heavily weighted toward visuals. Although distinctive ringtones and other sounds are used to build brand awareness, most communication appeals to only one of the five human senses: sight.

Along with research institute Millward Brown, brand expert Martin Lindstrom conducted an international study on consumer reaction to colour, smell and taste. The study concluded that, after sight, smell is the most important sense. In his analysis, Lindstrom found that 83 percent of all communication appeals to sight. He maintains that all five senses are important when building a brand. He urges companies to employ each of the five senses to amplify the company's recognition in the market. He says only 20 of the top 200 brands worldwide use all five senses.

In one test, identical pairs of running shoes were placed in separate rooms. One room was infused with a pleasant floral scent and one wasn't. Test subjects preferred the trainers in the scented room by a margin of 84 percent and even estimated the value of the shoes in the scented room higher than the ones in the unscented room.

On the heels of research like this, companies are looking to use scent to lure customers into their stores and into lingering longer. Victoria's Secret has long used feminine vanilla scents in its shops but now retailers such as the Samsung Experience concept store are also looking to distinguish themselves from competitors. But experts caution that scents aren't guaranteed to boost sales. The best scents are unobtrusive. Anything overwhelming can drive customers away. And smells should appeal to the same gender the product is trying to appeal to.

Westin Hotels developed a fragrance, White Tea, to use in its hotels' public spaces. The scent was designed to have international appeal and contribute to a subtle, relaxing ambience in the lobbies. Travellers also encounter a unique scent on Singapore Airlines through the towels passed out on all flights. The theory is that passengers will associate the subtle scent with a positive, relaxing experience.

Some brands have a built-in advantage of sensory marketing. Crayola's crayons were not designed to have a signature scent but the manufacturing process left them with a recognizable smell. Many adults connect the smell of crayons with childhood, leaving Crayola with an incidental brand element that can be very valuable. When Crayola's parent company was considering ways to stand out among the generic competition in new markets, it decided to trademark the smell.

Sources: Martin Lindstrom, 'Follow your nose to marketing evolution', *Advertising Age,* 23 May 2005; Linda Tischler, 'Smells like brand spirit', *Fast Company,* August 2005; Martin Lindstrom, 'Smelling a branding opportunity', *Brandweek,* 14 March 2005; Lucas Conley, 'Brand sense', *Fast Company,* March 2005; Maurren Morrin and S. Ratneshwar, 'Does it make sense to use scents to enhance brand memory?' *Journal of Marketing Research,* 2003, 40 (February): 10–25.

if a customer requests 'a glass of white wine with an ice cube' from room service while staying at the Ritz in one city, room service at the Ritz in another city would know to add an ice cube if the customer requested a glass of white wine there too.

Peppers and Rogers also provide an example of a localized version of one-to-one marketing. After having ordered flowers at a local florist for his or her mother, a customer might then receive a postcard 'reminding him that he had sent roses last year and that a phone call would put a beautiful arrangement on her doorstop again for her birthday this year'. Although such reminders can be helpful, marketers must not assume that customers always want to repeat their behaviours. For example, what if the flowers were a doomed, last-chance attempt to salvage a failing relationship – a reminder under such circumstances might not be so welcome!

Permission marketing

Permission marketing is the practice of marketing to consumers only after gaining their express permission. It is another tool with which companies can break through the clutter and build customer loyalty. A pioneer of the topic, Seth Godin, maintains that marketers can no longer employ 'interruption marketing' in terms of mass media campaigns featuring magazines, direct mail, billboards, radio and television commercials and the like, because consumers have come to expect – but not necessarily appreciate – these interruptions.[14] By contrast, Godin asserts, consumers appreciate receiving marketing messages they gave permission for: 'The worse the clutter gets, the more profitable your permission marketing efforts become.'

Given the number of marketing communications that bombard consumers every day, Godin argues that if marketers want to attract attention, they first need to get a consumer's permission with some kind of inducement – a free sample, a sales promotion or discount or a competition. By eliciting co-operation in this manner, marketers can *potentially* develop stronger relationships with consumers so that they want to receive more communications. Those relationships will only develop, however, if marketers respect consumers' wishes and if consumers express a willingness to become involved with a brand.[15]

Permission marketing is capturing marketers' interest because of the powerful technology that now exists. With the help of large databases and advanced software, companies can store gigabytes of customer data and process this information to send targeted, personalized marketing messages to customers.

Godin identifies five steps to effective permission marketing.

1. Offer the prospect an incentive to volunteer.
2. Offer the interested prospect a curriculum over time, teaching the consumer about the product or service being marketed.
3. Reinforce the incentive to guarantee that the prospect maintains the permission.
4. Offer additional incentives to get more permission from the consumer.
5. Over time, build on the permission to change consumer behaviour towards profits.

Godin also offers four tests of permission marketing (see Figure 5.3). According to Godin, effective permission marketing works because it is 'anticipated, personal and relevant'. For example, Columbia House – a classic permission marketer – sends its club members a monthly music selection, something members anticipate and is

- Does every marketing effort you create encourage a learning relationship with your customers? Does it invite customers to 'raise their hands' and start communicating?
- Do you have a permission database? Do you track the number of people who have given you permission to communicate with them?
- If consumers gave you permission to talk to them, would you have anything to say? Have you developed a marketing curriculum to teach people about your products?
- Once people become customers, do you work to deepen your permission to communicate with those people?

Figure 5.3   Four tests for permission marketing

Source: Adapted with the permission of Simon & Schuster Adult Publishing Group, from PERMISSION MARKETING: Turning Strangers into Friends and Friends into Customers by Seth Godin. Copyright © 1999 by Seth Godin. All rights reserved.

relevant to them. The selection is personal because it represents a category of music that the member has specified as a preference. If the member chooses not to keep the selection, he or she simply returns it. Permission marketing on the web is also typified by Amazon.com.

Amazon.com

With customer permission, Amazon uses software to track its customers' purchasing habits and can send them personalized marketing messages. Each time a customer buys something from Amazon.com, he or she can receive a follow-up e-mail containing information about other products that might interest him or her based on that purchase. For example, if a customer buys a book, Amazon might send an e-mail containing a list of titles by the same author or of titles also purchased by customers who bought the original title. With just one click, the customer can get more detailed information. Amazon also sends periodic e-mails to customers informing them of new products, offers and sales. Each message is tailored to the individual customer based on past purchases and specified preferences, according to customer wishes.

Permission marketing can be seen as developing the 'consumer dialogue' component of one-to-one marketing. One drawback to permission marketing, however, is that it presumes consumers know what they want to some extent. In many cases, consumers have undefined, ambiguous or conflicting preferences, such that it might be difficult for them to be expressed. So, it is important to recognize that consumers may need to be given guidance and assistance in forming and conveying their preferences. In that regard, 'participatory marketing' may be a more appropriate term, because marketers and consumers need to work together to find out how the firm can best satisfy consumer goals.[16]

Reconciling the new marketing approaches

These new approaches to personlization help to reinforce important marketing concepts and techniques. From a branding point of view, they are a particularly useful means of thinking how to both elicit positive brand responses and create brand resonance to build customer-based brand equity. One-to-one, permission and experiential marketing are all potentially effective means of getting consumers more actively involved with a brand.

According to the CBBE model, however, such approaches emphasize different aspects of brand equity. For example, on the one hand, one-to-one and permission marketing can be seen as particularly effective at creating stronger behavioural loyalty and attitudinal attachment. Experiential marketing, on the other hand, would seem to be particularly effective at establishing brand imagery and tapping into a variety of different feelings as well as helping to build brand communities. Despite potentially different areas of emphasis, all three approaches can be seen as a means of building stronger consumer–brand bonds.

Marketing strategies must transcend a product or service to create stronger bonds with consumers and maximize brand resonance. This broader set of activities is sometimes called *relationship marketing,* where marketers attempt to transcend the purchase exchange process with consumers to make more meaningful and richer contacts.[17] Relationship marketing attempts to provide a more holistic, personalized brand experience to create stronger consumer ties. In other words, relationship marketing attempts to expand both the depth and breadth of brand-building marketing campaigns.

One implication of these new marketing approaches is that the traditional 'marketing mix' concept and the notion of the '4 Ps' of marketing – product, price, place (or distribution) and promotion (or marketing communications) – in many cases may not fully describe modern marketing campaigns. There are many activities that do not fit neatly into one of those designations. Nevertheless, firms still have to make decisions about what exactly they are going to sell, how (and where) they are going to sell it and at what price. In other words, firms must still devise product, pricing and distribution strategies as part of their marketing campaigns. The specifics of how those strategies are set, however, have changed considerably. These topics and some of the newer developments are discussed next, with the topic of communication strategy being addressed in Chapter 6.

PRODUCT STRATEGY

The product is at the heart of brand equity because it is the primary influence on what consumers experience with a brand, what they hear about a brand from others and what the firm can tell customers about the brand in their communications. In other words, at the heart of a great brand is invariably a great product.

Designing and delivering a product or service that fully satisfies consumer needs and wants is a prerequisite for successful marketing, regardless of whether the product is a tangible good, service or organization. To create brand loyalty, consumers' experiences with the product must at least meet, if not actually surpass, their expectations. As Chapter 2 noted, numerous studies have shown that high-quality brands tend to perform better financially – for example, yielding higher returns on investment.[18]

This section considers two topics: how consumers form their opinions of the quality and value of a product, and the importance of taking a broad perspective through relationship marketing in formulating product strategy and offerings.

Perceived quality and value

Perceived quality has been defined as customers' perceptions of the overall quality or superiority of a product or service relative to another and with respect to its intended purpose. Thus, perceived quality is an overall assessment based on customer perceptions of what constitutes a quality product and how well the brand rates on those dimensions. Achieving a satisfactory level of perceived quality has become more difficult as product improvements have led to heightened consumer expectations regarding the quality of products.[19]

Much research attention has been devoted to understanding how consumers form their opinions about perceived quality. The specific attributes or benefits that become associated with favourable evaluations and perceptions of product quality vary from category to category. Nevertheless, consistent with the CBBE model from Chapter 2, research has identified the following general dimensions of product quality.[20]

- *Performance:* levels at which the primary characteristics of the product operate (eg, low, medium, high or very high).
- *Features:* secondary elements of a product that complement the primary characteristics.
- *Conformance quality:* degree to which the product meets specifications and is absent of defects.
- *Reliability:* consistency of performance over time and from purchase to purchase.
- *Durability:* expected economic life of the product.
- *Serviceability:* ease of servicing the product.
- *Style and design:* appearance or feel of quality.

Consumer beliefs along these dimensions often underlie perceptions of the quality of the product that, in turn, can influence attitudes and behaviour towards a brand.

Brand intangibles

As noted in Chapter 2, product quality depends not only on functional product performance but on broader performance considerations as well. For example, product quality may be affected by factors such as the speed, accuracy and care taken with product delivery and installation; the promptness, courtesy and helpfulness of customer service and training; and the quality of repair service.

As also pointed out in Chapter 2, brand attitudes may not necessarily be based only on product performance but may also depend on more abstract product imagery, such as the symbolism or personality reflected in the brand. These 'augmented' aspects of a product are often crucial to its equity. Finally, as noted in Chapter 3, consumer evaluations may not correspond to the perceived quality of the product and may be formed by less thoughtful decision-making, such as simple heuristics and decision rules (eg, regarding brand reputation or product characteristics such as colour or scent).

Marketers thus must take a broad, holistic approach to building brand equity. Consistent with this observation, McKinsey Consulting has put forth an approach to marketing that it has dubbed *3D marketing*.[21] 3D marketing emphasizes three product or service benefit dimensions.

1. *Functional benefits:* product and performance attributes; value; quality; etc.
2. *Process benefits:* ease of access to product information; broad product selection; simplified/assisted decision-making; convenient transactions; automatic product replenishment; etc.
3. *Relationship benefits:* value based on personalized service; strong emotional relevance; information sharing that creates value exchange; differentiated loyalty rewards; etc.

McKinsey argues that, whereas traditional marketing communicates functional benefits, in an increasingly crowded marketplace, marketers must employ experiential marketing tactics and differentiate their products or services by communicating benefits from among the other two dimensions: 'By improving the fuller customer experience, companies can keep consumers happier and hold on to them longer.'

Value chain

Consumers often combine quality perceptions with cost perceptions to arrive at an assessment of the value of a product. In considering consumer value perceptions, it is important to realize that costs are not restricted to the actual monetary price but may reflect opportunity costs of time, energy and any psychological involvement in the decision that consumers might have.[22]

From a firm's perspective, it is therefore necessary to take a broad view of value creation. Michael Porter has proposed the value chain as a strategic tool for identifying ways to create more customer value.[23] He views firms as a collection of activities that are performed to design, produce, market, deliver and support products. The value chain identifies five primary value-creating activities (inbound logistics, operations, outbound logistics, marketing and sales, and service) and four support activities that occur throughout these primary activities (firm infrastructure, human resources management, technology development and procurement). According to Porter, firms can achieve competitive advantages by improving performance and reducing costs in any or all of these value-creating activities. He also emphasizes the importance of effectively managing core business processes and cross-functional integration and co-operation.

Porter notes how firms can create competitive advantages by partnering with other members of the value chain (eg, suppliers as well as distributors) to improve the performance of the customer value-delivery system. For example, Procter & Gamble works closely with retailers such as supermarkets to ensure that P&G brands can be quickly and efficiently distributed to shops. For example, P&G created a well-staffed office near Wal-Mart's headquarters, to co-ordinate these efforts better. From a branding perspective, these activities are potentially a means of creating strong, favourable and unique brand associations that can serve as sources of brand equity.

Relationship marketing

A number of topics in this and other chapters can be related to relationship marketing. Relationship marketing is based on the premise that current customers are the key to long-term brand success.[24] The importance of customer retention can be seen from some of the benefits it provides.[25]

- Acquiring new customers can cost five times more than the costs involved in satisfying and retaining current customers.
- The average company loses 10 percent of its customers each year.
- A 5 percent reduction in the customer defection rate can increase profits by 25 percent to 85 percent, depending on the industry.
- The customer profit rate tends to increase over the life of the retained customer.

This section considers three important relationship marketing issues: mass customization, aftermarketing and loyalty schemes.

Mass customization

The concept behind mass customization, namely, making products to fit the customer's exact specifications, is an old one, but the advent of digital-age technology enables companies to offer customized products on a previously unheard-of scale. Via the internet, customers can communicate their preferences directly to a manufacturer, which can, by using a sophisticated production line, assemble the product for a price comparable to that of a non-customized item. Dell Computers is a classic example of the power of mass customization. Dell's built-to-order computers, sold directly by the company on the web or over the phone, helped make it the most successful computer manufacturer of the 1990s.

In an age defined by the pervasiveness of mass-market goods, mass customization enables consumers to distinguish themselves with even basic purchases. 'Customization addresses the need for individuality,' said an analyst with Fallon McElligott advertising. 'We seek experiences and products that have our stamp, our seal as part of the look.' For example, Nike enables customers to put their own personalized message on a pair of shoes with the NIKEiD programme. At the website, visitors can make a customized shoe by selecting the size, width and colour scheme and affixing an eight-character personal ID to their creation. Land's End also allows customization of certain trousers and shirts on its website for a better fit.

Mass customization can offer supply-side benefits too. Inventory can be reduced, saving warehouse space and the expense of keeping track of everything and of having to discount leftover merchandise.[26] Mass customization has its limitations, however, because not every product is easily customized and not every product demands customization. But even makers of expensive and production-intensive goods are looking for ways to employ mass customization. John Deere used complexity theory to provide customized tractors for commercial farmers.[27]

Mass customization is not restricted to products. It can be especially powerful with websites.[28] From 10 percent to 15 percent of respondent samples reported being interested in customizing products online across products such as greeting cards, consumer electronics, clothing and jewellery.[29]

Many service organizations such as banks are developing customer-specific services and trying to improve the personal nature of their service experience (eg, more service options, more customer-contact personnel and longer service hours). In support of these types of activities, academics Rust, Moorman and Dickson provide evidence suggesting that service firms should, on average, allocate *fewer* resources to traditional quality, productivity and efficiency controls and allocate *more* resources to service-orientated revenue expansion initiatives such as customer satisfaction, customer retention and loyalty, customer relationship management (CRM) and customer equity schemes.[30]

Aftermarketing

As with brand awareness, both purchase *and* consumption issues should be reflected in product strategies to achieve the desired brand image. Much marketing activity is devoted to finding ways to encourage trial and repeat purchases by consumers. Perhaps the strongest and potentially most favourable associations, however, result from actual product experience – what Procter & Gamble calls the 'second moment of truth' (with the first moment of truth occurring at purchase).

Unfortunately, not enough marketing attention is typically devoted to finding ways for consumers to appreciate the advantages and potential capabilities and benefits of products. Perhaps in response to this oversight, one notable trend in marketing is *aftermarketing* – that is, those marketing activities that occur after customer purchase. Innovative design, thorough testing, quality production and effective communication – through mass customization or any other means – are without question the most important considerations in enhancing product consumption experiences that build brand equity. In many cases, however, they may only be necessary and not sufficient conditions for brand success, and other means to enhance consumption experiences may need to be employed.

For example, instruction manuals for many products are too often an afterthought, put together by engineers who use overly technical terms and convoluted language.[31] As a result, consumers' initial product experiences may be frustrating or, even worse, unsuccessful. In many cases, even if consumers are able to figure out how to make the product perform its basic functions, many more advanced features – highly desirable and potentially unique to the brand – may not be appreciated by consumers.

To enhance consumers' consumption experiences, it is important to develop manuals that clearly and comprehensively describe both what the product potentially can do and how consumers can realize these product benefits. With increasing globalization, writing easy-to-use instructions has become even more important as they often require translation into many languages.[32] Manufacturers are spending more time designing and testing instructions to make them as user-friendly as possible.

To achieve these goals, user manuals increasingly may need to use multimedia (eg, employing DVD or CD-ROM technology) to graphically, succinctly and persuasively portray product functions and benefits. Intuit, makers of the Quicken personal finance management software, routinely sends researchers home with first-time buyers to check that their software is easy to install and to identify any problems that

1. Establishing and maintaining a customer information file (tracking all current, potential, inactive and past customers).
2. 'Blueprinting' customer contacts (identifying and characterizing points of interaction with customers in search of 'moments of truth').
3. Analyzing customer feedback (explore the nature of satisfaction and dissatisfaction).
4. Conducting customer satisfaction surveys (to also signal interest in customers' reactions).
5. Formulating and managing communication programmes (sending customers proprietary magazines or newsletters).
6. Hosting special customer events or programmes (celebrating relationships with the brand).
7. Identifying and reclaiming lost customers (one of the best sources for new customers).

Figure 5.4   Seven aftermarketing activities

Source: Reprinted from Terry Vavra, *Aftermarketing: How to keep customers for life through relationship marketing,* Chicago: Irwin Professional Publishers, 1995.

might arise. Corel software adopts a similar 'follow me home' innovation and also has 'pizza parties' at the company where marketing, engineering and quality assurance teams analyze market research together so that marketing was not just handing down conclusions to other departments.[33]

Aftermarketing, however, involves more than the design and communication of product instructions. As one expert in the area notes: 'The term "aftermarketing" describes a necessary new mind-set that reminds businesses of the importance of building a lasting relationship with customers, to extend their lifetimes. It also points to the crucial need to better balance the allocation of marketing funds between conquest activities (like advertising) and retention activities (like customer communication programmes).'[34] Creating stronger ties with consumers can be as simple as creating a well-designed customer service department, easily accessible by a free phone number or via the web. Examples of seven specific activities to nurture loyalty and build relationships with customers are summarized in Figure 5.4.

Aftermarketing can also involve the sale of related, complementary products that are ingredients, help to make up a system or in any other way enhance the value of the core product. Printer manufacturers such as Hewlett-Packard derive much of their revenue from high-margin postpurchase items such as ink cartridges and paper. Analysts have estimated that the average owner of a home printer spends twice as much on consumables over the lifetime of the machine as on the machine itself.[35]

Loyalty schemes

Loyalty or frequency schemes have become one popular means by which marketers can create stronger ties to customers.[36] The purpose of frequency marketing has been defined as 'identifying, maintaining and increasing the yield from a firm's "best" customers through long-term, interactive, value-added relationships'. Firms in all different kinds of industries have established loyalty schemes through mixtures of specialized services, newsletters, premiums and incentives. Often these loyalty schemes involve extensive co-branding arrangements or brand alliances.

Airline loyalty schemes

In 1981, American Airlines founded the first airline loyalty scheme, called AAdvantage. This frequent-flyer scheme rewarded the airline's top customers with free trips and upgrades based on mileage flown. By recognizing customers for their patronage and giving them incentives to bring their business to American Airlines, the airline hoped to increase loyalty among its passengers. The scheme was an instant success and other airlines quickly followed suit. These days, members can earn miles at more than 1,500 participating companies, which include 35 hotel chains representing more than 75 brands, more than 20 airlines, 8 car rental companies and 25 retail/financial companies. In addition, members can earn miles when making purchases with one of more than 60 affinity card products in 30 countries. More than 100 frequent-traveller schemes exist, but American Airlines still has the largest, with membership of over 50 million by 2005.[37]

Many businesses besides airlines have introduced loyalty schemes. In 1991, American Express started its membership rewards scheme, which gives cardholders points based on the amount they spend. The points can be redeemed for items such as airline tickets, jewellery and electronics. Also in 1991, Safeway, the third-largest grocer in the USA, started the Safeway Savings Club which earned its members discounts on certain items in stores. Within a year, the Safeway Savings Club had 1.2 million members. Starwood Hotels launched an aggressive frequent guest scheme backed by a €34.2 million ad campaign in 1999.[38] UK food retailer Tesco has taken the one-to-one approach even further and puts it at the centre of its strategy – see Chapter 8.

Loyalty schemes have been adopted by such industries because they often yield results.[39] As one marketing executive said, 'Loyalty programmes reduce defection rates and increase retention. You can win more of a customer's purchasing share.' The value created by the loyalty scheme creates switching costs for consumers, reducing price competition between brands. Some tips for building effective loyalty schemes are the following.[40]

- *Know your audience:* most loyalty marketers employ sophisticated databases and software to determine which customer segment to target with a given scheme. It is important to target customers whose purchasing behaviour can be changed by the scheme.
- *Change is good:* marketers must constantly update the scheme to attract new customers and prevent other companies in their category from developing 'me too' ones. 'Any loyalty programme that stays static will die', said one executive.
- *Listen to your best customers:* suggestions and complaints from top customers must be carefully considered, because they can lead to improvements in the scheme. Since they typically represent a large percentage of business, top customers must also receive better service and more attention.
- *Engage people:* it is important to make customers want to join the scheme. This includes making it easy to use and offering immediate rewards when customers

sign up. Once they become members, customers must be made to 'feel special, by' for example, by sending them birthday greetings, special offers or invitations to events.

Summary

The product is at the heart of brand equity. Products must be designed, manufactured, marketed, sold, delivered and serviced in a way to create a positive brand image with strong, favourable and unique brand associations; elicit positive brand responses in terms of favourable judgements and feelings; and foster greater degrees of brand resonance. Product strategy entails choosing both tangible and intangible benefits to be embodied by the product and its surrounding marketing activities that are desired by consumers as well as deliverable by the marketing campaign. A range of possible associations can become linked to the brand – some functional and performance-related and some abstract and imagery-related. Perceived quality and perceived value are particularly important brand associations that often drive consumer decisions.

Because of the importance of loyal customers, relationship marketing has become a branding priority. Consequently, consumers' actual product experiences and after-marketing activities have taken on increased importance in building customer-based brand equity. Those marketers who will be most successful at building CBBE will take the necessary steps to make sure they fully understand their customers and how they can deliver superior value before, during and after purchase.

PRICING STRATEGY

Price is the one revenue-generating element of the traditional marketing mix and price premiums are one of the most important benefits of a strong brand. This section considers the kinds of price perceptions that consumers might form and pricing strategies that the firm might adopt to build brand equity.

Consumer price perceptions

The pricing policy for a brand can create associations in consumers' minds with the relevant price tier or level for the brand in the category, as well as its corresponding price volatility or variance (in terms of the frequency or magnitude of discounts). In other words, the pricing strategy can dictate how consumers categorize the price of the brand (eg, as low-, medium- or high-priced) and how firm or flexible consumers see that price (eg, as frequently or infrequently discounted).

Consumers often rank brands according to price tiers in a category.[41] For example, Figure 5.5 shows the price tiers that resulted from a study of ice-cream.[42] In that market, as the figure shows, there was a relationship between price and quality. Within any price tier, as the figure also shows, there is a range of acceptable prices, called

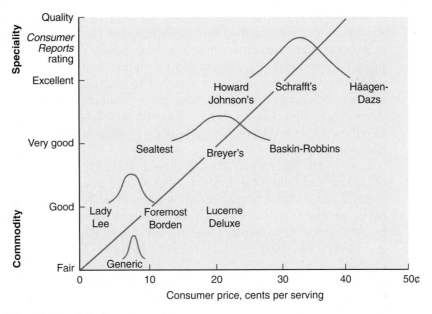

Figure 5.5 Price tiers in the ice-cream market

price bands. The price bands provide managers with some indication of the flexibility and breadth they can adopt in pricing their brands within a particular price tier. Some companies sell several brands to compete in many categories. Figure 5.6 shows clothing from Phillips Van Huesen that covers a range of prices and corresponding retail outlets.

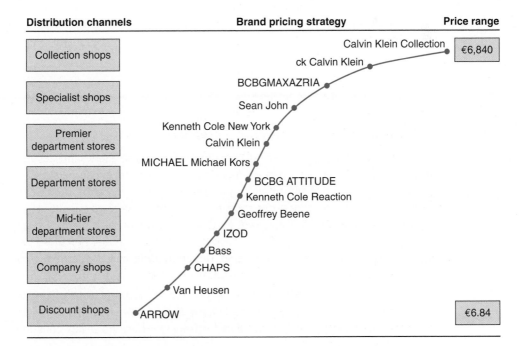

Figure 5.6 Phillips Van Heusen brand price tiers

Besides these descriptive 'mean and variance' price perceptions, consumers may have price perceptions that have more inherent product meaning. In particular, in many categories, consumers may infer the quality of a product on the basis of its price. As noted earlier, consumers may combine their perceptions of product quality with their perceptions of price to arrive at an assessment of its perceived value. Consumer associations of perceived value are often an important factor in their decisions. Accordingly, many marketers have adopted *value-based pricing strategies* – attempting to sell the right product at the right price – to address consumer wishes, as described in the next section.

Consumers' perceptions of value should obviously exceed the cost to the company of making and selling the product. As Chapter 2 pointed out, consumers are willing to pay a premium for certain brands because of what they represent. Based on tangible or intangible considerations, consumers place a value on the unique aspects of a brand that justifies a higher price in their minds. For example, at one time, Hitachi and General Electric (GE) jointly owned a factory in England that made identical televisions for the two companies. The only difference was the brand name on the television. Nevertheless, the Hitachi televisions sold for a €51.3 premium over the GE televisions. Moreover, Hitachi sold twice as many sets as GE, despite the higher price.[43] Similarly, the sparkling white wines from the Champagne region are the only true Champagnes and they generally command higher prices than sparkling wines from other areas – and then there are also differences between the individual Champagne labels.

In short, price has complex meanings and can play many roles for consumers. Brand Briefing 5.3 provides insight into how consumers perceive and process prices as part of their shopping behaviour. From a branding perspective, it is important to understand the price perceptions that consumers have for a brand. As part of this understanding, it is necessary to uncover quality and value inferences and any price premiums.

Brand Briefing 5.3

Understanding consumer price perceptions

Many economists assume that consumers are 'price takers' and accept prices at face value or as given. However, as Ofir and Winer note, consumers and customers often process price information, interpreting prices in terms of their knowledge from earlier purchasing experience, formal communications (eg, advertising), informal communications (eg, friends or family members) and point-of-sale or online information. Purchasing decisions are based on consumers' perceived prices, however, not the marketer's stated value. Understanding how consumers arrive at their perceptions of prices is thus a marketing priority.

Research has shown that surprisingly few consumers can recall prices of products accurately, although they may have fairly good knowledge of the range involved. When examining or considering an observed price, however, consumers often

Brand Briefing 5.3 *continued*

compare it with internal frames of reference (pricing information from memory) or external frames of reference (eg, a posted 'recommended retail price'). Internal reference prices occur in many types, such as the following:

- 'fair price' (what product should cost);
- typical price;
- last price;
- upper-bound price (most consumer would pay);
- lower-bound price (least consumer would pay);
- competitive prices;
- expected future price;
- usual discounted price.

when consumers evoke one or more of these frames of reference, their perceived price can vary from the stated price. Most research on reference prices has found that 'unpleasant surprises', such as when the stated price is higher than the perceived price, have a greater effect on purchase likelihood than pleasant surprises.

Consumer perceptions of prices are also affected by pricing strategies. For example, research has shown that a relatively more expensive item can be seen as less expensive by breaking the price down into smaller units (eg, a €500 annual membership is seen as more expensive than 'less than €50 a month'). Research has also shown that one reason why prices often end with the number nine (eg, €49.99) is that consumers process prices in a left-to-right manner rather than holistically or by rounding. This effect is more pronounced when a competing product's prices are numercially and psychologically closer. Even the competitive environment has been shown to affect consumer price judgements: deep discounts can lead to lower perceived prices over time than frequent, shallow discounts (high–low pricing), even if the averages are the same.

Clearly, consumer perceptions of price are complex and depend on the context.

Sources: Chezy Ofir and Russell S. Winer, 'Pricing: economic and behavioral models', in *Handbook of Marketing*, eds Bart Weitz and Robin Wensley, New York: Sage Publications, 2002: 5–86;
Peter R. Dickson and Alan G. Sawyer, 'The price knowledge and search of supermarket shoppers', *Journal of Marketing*, July 1990: 42–53; Gurumurthy Kalyanaram and Russell S. Winer, 'Empirical generalizations from reference price research', *Marketing Science*, Fall 1995: 161–9; John T. Gourville, 'Pennies-a-day: the effect of temporal reframing on transaction evaluation', *Journal of Consumer Research*, March 1998: 395–408; Mark Stiving and Russell S. Winer, 'An empirical analysis of price endings with scanner data', *Journal of Consumer Research*, June 1997: 57–68; Joseph W. Alba, Carl F. Mela, Terence A. Shimp and Joel E. Urbany, 'The effect of discount frequency and depth on consumer price judgements', *Journal of Consumer Research*, September 1999: 99–114; Manoj Thomas and Vicki Morwitz, 'Penny wise and pound foolish: the left-digit effect in price cognition', *Journal of Consumer Research*, 26 June 2005: 54–64; Eric Anderson and Duncan Simester, 'Mind your pricing cues', *Harvard Business Review*, September 2003, 81(9): 96–103; Tridib Mazumdar, S.P. Raj and Indrajit Sinha, 'Reference price research: review and propositions', *Journal of Marketing*, October 2005: 69.

Setting prices to build brand equity

Choosing a pricing strategy to build brand equity involves determining the following:

- a method or approach for how current prices will be set;
- a policy or set of guidelines for the depth and duration of promotions and discounts over time.

There are many approaches to setting prices that depend on a number of considerations. This section highlights a few of the most important issues as they relate to brand equity.[44]

Factors related to the costs of making and selling products and the relative prices of rival products are important determinants for an optimal pricing strategy. Increasingly, however, firms are placing greater importance on consumer perceptions and preferences in developing a pricing strategy. Many firms use a value-pricing approach to set prices and an everyday, low-pricing approach to determine their discount pricing policy over time. This section describes each approach in turn.

Value pricing

The objective of value pricing is to uncover the right blend of product quality, product costs and product prices that fully satisfies the needs and wants of consumers and the profit targets of the firm. As a concept, marketers have employed value pricing in various ways for years. Its increased adoption as a pricing strategy in recent years, however, is a result of an increased level of competition between brands and more demanding customers. With a more debt-burdened and cost-conscious consumer base, many firms have met with resistance to higher prices from consumers – often for the first time in their history.[45] They have learned the hard way that consumers will not pay price premiums that exceed their perceptions of the value of a brand. Perhaps the most vivid illustration of this was the episode involving a price cut for Philip Morris' leading cigarette brand, Marlboro (Brand Briefing 5.4).[46]

Two important lessons emerged from the Marlboro episode. First, strong brands can command price premiums. Once Marlboro's price difference entered a more acceptable range, consumers were willing to pay the still higher price to be able to buy Marlboro, and the sales of the brand started to increase. Second, strong brands cannot command an excessive price premium. The clear signal sent to marketers everywhere by Philip Morris' experience is that price rises without corresponding investments in the value of the brand may increase the vulnerability of the brand to lower-priced competition. In these cases, consumers may be willing to 'trade down' because they no longer can justify to themselves that the higher-priced brand is worth it. Although the Marlboro price discounts led to short-term profitability declines, they also led to regained market share that put the brand on stronger footing over the longer haul.

In this challenging new climate, several firms have been successful by adopting a value pricing strategy. For example, Carrefour and Wal-Mart have pricing strategies that have made them retailing giants. Ikea's low-cost, nice design offer has made it enormous and changed the rules of furniture retailing. Ryanair combines low fares with no frills to make a distinctly different offer – and has thereby shaken up the airline industry. Taco Bell in the USA reduced operating costs enough to lower prices for many

Brand Briefing 5.4

Marlboro's price drop

On 2 April 1993, Philip Morris dropped a bombshell in the form of a three-page announcement: 'Philip Morris USA . . . announced a major shift in business strategy designed to increase market share and grow long-term profitability in a highly price sensitive market environment.' Quoting tobacco unit president William I. Campbell, the statement continued: 'We have determined that in the current market environment caused by prolonged economic softness and depressed consumer confidence, we should take those steps necessary to grow our market share rather than pursue rapid income growth rates that might erode our leading marketplace position.'

Philip Morris announced four steps, the last of which caught the eye of marketers and Wall Street alike: a cut in the price of Marlboro (roughly 40 to 50 cents a pack), which was expected to decrease earnings in Philip Morris' most profitable unit by 40 percent. The action was justified by the results of a month-long test in Portland, Oregon, the previous December in which a 40-cent decrease in pack price had increased market share by four points.

Stock market reaction to the announcement was swift. By day's end, Philip Morris' share price had declined from $64.12 to $49.37, a 23 percent drop that represented a one-day loss of $13 billion in shareholder equity! There was a ripple effect in the stock market, with significant stock price declines for other consumer goods companies with major brands (eg, Sara Lee, Kellogg's, General Mills and Procter & Gamble). A company that took one of the biggest hits was Coca-Cola – its shareholders lost $5 billion in paper in the days following 'Black Friday'.

A number of factors probably provided the impetus for Marlboro to cut prices so dramatically. The economy certainly was still sluggish coming out of a recession. Private label or store brand cigarettes had been increasing in quality and were receiving more attention from customers and retailers.

A prime consideration suggested by many was related to Philip Morris' hefty price increases. These rises had often occurred two to three times a year such that the retail price of a pack of Marlboros more than tripled between 1980 and 1992. The 80 cents to $1 difference between premium brands and discount brands that was prevailing at that time was thought to have resulted in steady sales increases for the discount brands. The growth in sales for those brands came at the expense of Marlboro's market share, which had dropped to 22 percent and was projected to decline to 18 percent if Philip Morris had made no changes.

Although much of the popular press attempted to exploit Marlboro's actions to proclaim that 'brands were dead', nothing could have been further from the truth. In fact, a more accurate interpretation of the whole episode is that it showed that new brands were entering the scene, as evidenced by the ability of discount brands to create their own brand equity on the basis of strong consumer associations with 'value'.

Brand Briefing 5.4 *continued*

At the same time, existing brands, if properly managed, can command loyalty, enjoy price premiums and still be extremely profitable. By cutting the difference between discount cigarettes and Marlboro to roughly 40 cents, Philip Morris was able to woo back many customers. Within nine months of the price drop, its market share increased to almost 27 percent, eventually rising to almost 30 percent.

Source: Laura Zinn, 'The smoke clears at Marlboro', *BusinessWeek*, 31 January 1994: 76–7.

of the items on its menu to under 68 cents, sparking a trend in fast foods. The success of these and other firms has dramatized the potential benefits of implementing a value pricing strategy. Another convert was General Motors, although its adoption faces a tougher test.

General Motors

General Motors (GM) launched an employee pricing plan in June 2005 to clear out inventories of vehicles ahead of the new model year. The promotion was a wild success, racking up huge sales gains in the summer. At the time, GM executives said the plan's simplicity – everyone got the same low price that company employees received – would help the carmaker shift to a new pricing strategy aimed at switching consumers' focus to vehicle values instead of the size of discounts. Although the plan was extended beyond the summer, GM announced in September a transition towards 'total value promise' pricing, under which it would try to offer prices on 2006 models that, in comparison with its traditional prices, would be closer to what GM believed were the prices customers actually paid once incentives were included. The prices, however, generally would be higher than the employee prices being advertised. One GM executive noted that employee pricing was never meant to be a long-term promotion. 'Like any promotion, it has a life span,' Mr LaNeve said. 'But what we learned is: the customer is smart. They recognize a really good value when they see one and they really appreciate transparent prices.' Some industry analysts, however, felt it would be difficult for GM to wean consumers off employee pricing.[47]

As might be expected, there are a number of opinions regarding the keys to success in adopting a value-based pricing approach. In general, an effective value pricing strategy should strike the proper balance between the following:

- product design and delivery;
- product costs; and
- product prices.

In other words, the right kind of product has to be made the right way and sold at the right price. The chapter next considers issues related to each of these three areas. Brand Briefing 5.5 describes an eight-step process for making better pricing decisions.

Brand Briefing 5.5

Eight steps to better pricing

Robert J. Dolan, an academic pricing expert, describes pricing as 'managers' biggest marketing headache'. To relieve this headache, Dolan recommends that managers focus on the process of pricing rather than the results. He suggests that managers can make improvements to the pricing process by following these eight steps.

1. *Assess what value your customers place on a product or service:* rather than basing pricing decisions on product cost, companies should determine a product's value to the customer.
2. *Look for variation in the way customers value the product:* customers often vary in how and why they use the product, leading different customers to value the product differently. Companies can customize prices to take advantage of these different values.
3. *Assess customers' price sensitivity:* companies should determine the price elasticity (percent change in quantity sold given a 1 percent change in price) for its products in three areas: customer economics, customer search and usage, and the competitive situation.
4. *Identify an optimal pricing structure:* rather than a fixed price, companies can decide to offer discounts based on quantity purchased or use bundle pricing to sell a combination of products. The different pricing structures can be analyzed to determine the optimal one.
5. *Consider competitors' reactions:* to avoid price wars, companies must consider the long-term effects of price decisions in terms of the competition.
6. *Monitor prices realized at the transaction level:* though a product may have a single list price, it may have many possible final prices due to discounts and rebates. Additionally, the real net revenue from a product is affected by factors such as customer returns and damage claims. The real price of a product must account for these elements.
7. *Assess customers' emotional response:* a customer's emotional response to a price can have long-term effects that outweigh the short-term economic effect of a sale.
8. *Analyze whether the returns are worth the cost to serve:* high cost-to-serve customers do not necessarily pay high prices, just as customers who spend little do not always receive low-cost service. Where possible, companies should aim to get customers to spend in accordance with the cost of serving them.

Source: Reprinted by permission of Harvard Business Review. From 'How do you know when the price is right?' by Robert J. Dolan, September-October 1995. Copyright © 1995 by the Harvard Business School Publishing Corporation, all rights reserved.

The first key is the proper design and delivery of a product. Product value can be enhanced through many types of well-conceived and executed marketing campaigns. Proponents of value pricing point out that the concept does not mean selling stripped-down versions of products at lower prices. Consumers are willing to pay premiums when they perceive added value in products and services.

Brand Briefing 5.6 describes how Louis Vuitton Moët Hennessy (LVMH) is able to command luxury prices.

Brand Briefing 5.6

Selling luxury at Louis Vuitton Moët Hennessy

Luxury leather goods maker Louis Vuitton was established in Paris in 1855. For more than a century and a half, the company made hand-crafted luggage and other leather goods. It remained a small, family-controlled company until the 1970s, when French businessman Henry Racamier married a Vuitton heiress and rapidly expanded and diversified the business. When Racamier took over in 1977, the company had only two shops in France and had combined sales of less than €34.2 million. By the mid-1980s, the company had 95 shops across the globe and revenues topping €342 million.

In 1987, the merger of Louis Vuitton with French spirits, champagne and perfume group Moët Hennessy marked an era of consolidation in the luxury goods industry. Louis Vuitton Moët Hennessy (LVMH) instantly became the world's largest luxury goods company, raking in €2.73 billion in revenues in 1991. The company's more notable brands included Christian Dior, Givenchy, Moët & Chandon and Dom Perignon. The company continued to grow in the 1990s by acquiring a number of other luxury goods companies, including fashion label Christian Lacroix and shoe designer Berluti in 1993; TAG Heuer watchmaker in 1999; and the Donna Karan brand in 2000. This gave LVMH a portfolio of 60 luxury brands and it became the number one worldwide seller of champagne, cognac and fashion and leather goods, and the number three seller of perfumes and cosmetics. The company's revenues topped €9.2 billion in 2003.

LVMH has pursued a luxury pricing strategy, which means high mark-ups, limited availability and few, if any, markdowns. Louis Vuitton sells its products only through a global network of company-owned shops. This keeps margins high and allows the company to maintain control of its products through every step in the channel. Bernard Arnault explained, 'If you control your factory, you control your quality; if you control your distribution, you control your image.' In 2004, LVMH had a global network of 1,286 shops, a 28 percent increase over 1999. Its 284 Louis Vuitton shops and 461 Sephora locations comprise over half of the outlets in this network.

Because maintaining an upmarket image is vital to a luxury brand, LVMH devotes over 10 percent of annual sales to promotion and advertising. The company advertises its brands primarily in fashion and lifestyle publications. Some of the leading

Brand Briefing 5.6 *continued*

brands sponsor international events with luxury cachet, as Louis Vuitton does by sponsoring the America's Cup. Because image is an essential part of marketing luxury goods, LVMH is careful to evaluate every advertising and promotional opportunity for consistency with the image of its brands. As a result, the company manages a portfolio of luxury brands unparalleled in both size and sales.

But managing a portfolio of luxury brands with a slowing global economy can be challenging. LVMH has focused on its highly profitable Vuitton brand (especially in Japan) and other top brands, such as Celine women's wear, Pucci fashion, Ruinart champagne and Zenith watches. These were seen to have the most potential. The company sold other brands, such as the Lacroix couture fashion house, which was struggling.

Sources: William Echikson, 'Luxury steals back', *Fortune*, 16 January 1995; Lisa Marsh, 'LVMH thinks of Vuitton globally, acts on 5 Ave', *New York Post*, 5 December 2000; Joshua Levine, 'Liberté, fraternité – but to hell with égalité!', *Forbes*, 2 June 1997; Janet Guyon, 'The magic touch', *Fortune*, 6 September 2004: 229–36; Alessandra Galloni, 'Its closets full, LVMH decides to return to basics', *Wall Street Journal*, 8 October 2004: A1, A10.

Some companies have been able to *increase* prices by introducing new or improved 'value-added' products. In certain categories, marketers have been able to couple product innovations and improvements with higher prices that strike an acceptable balance to at least some market segments. Examples of such additions range from new flavours and bottle designs for iced teas to newly designed toothbrushes with special features such as rippled bristles and handles with tiny shock absorbers to lavishly packaged facial tissues with aroma and lotion.

When Gillette introduced the Mach III in 1998, it priced the cartridges at a 50 percent premium over its then priciest blade, SensorExcel, despite the prevailing deflationary climate. The price increase did not deter customers and Gillette reached its highest market share, 71 percent, since 1962. A Mach III extension, M3 Power, was launched in 2004 with similar premium pricing and quickly achieved market leadership in many countries. Many products have been able to combine improvements that provide consumers greater convenience with higher prices. For example, Hefty One-Zip sandwich, freezer and food storage bags, featuring 'sliding tab' technology, were able to command a 15 percent premium over the older 'tongue in groove' technology.[48]

With the advent of the web, many critics predicted that the ability of extensive, assisted online consumer searches would result in only low-cost providers surviving. The reality has been that the advantages of creating strong brand differentiation have led to price premiums for brands sold online just as much as when sold offline. For example, although undersold by numerous book and music sellers online, Amazon.com was able to maintain market leadership, eventually forcing low-priced competitors such as Books.com and others out of business.[49]

The second key to a successful value pricing strategy is to lower costs as much as possible. Meeting cost targets invariably requires additional cost savings through productivity gains, outsourcing, material substitution (less expensive or less wasteful materials), product reformulations, process changes (automation or other factory improvements) and so on.[50] As one marketing executive put it:

> The customer is only going to pay you for what he perceives as real value-added. When you look at your overhead, you've got to ask yourself if the customer is really willing to pay for that. If the answer is no, you've got to figure out how to get rid of it or you're not going to make money.[51]

For example, by investing in efficient manufacturing technology, Sara Lee was able to maintain adequate margins for years on its L'eggs women's hosiery in the USA with minimal price increases. The combination of low prices and the strong L'eggs brand image resulted in an almost 50 percent market share.[52] At the same time, cost reductions cannot sacrifice quality, effectiveness or efficiency.

> For example, when Sears fired 30 percent of their clothing buyers after buying Land's End, the remaining staff lacked the necessary merchandising experience with the Sears shops. Overcompensating for the fact that they had ordered too much for the spring season during 2003, they under-ordered for 2004. As a result, Sears shops found themselves with the wrong merchandise at the wrong time. While other retailers reported vibrant sales, Sears reported an unexpected modest sales decline.[53]

The final key to a successful value pricing strategy is to understand exactly how much value consumers perceive in the brand and thus to what extent they will pay a premium over product costs.[54] Techniques are available to estimate these consumer value perceptions (see Chapter 10). Perhaps the most straightforward approach involves directly asking consumers their perceptions of price and value.

The price suggested by estimating perceived value can often be used as a starting point in determining actual marketplace prices, adjusting by cost and competitive considerations as necessary. For example, to halt a precipitous slide in market share for its flagship 9-Lives brand, the pet products division of Heinz took a new tack in its pricing strategy. The company found from research that consumers wanted to be able to buy cat food at the price of 'four cans for a dollar', despite the fact that its cat food cost between 29 and 35 cents a can. As a result, Heinz reshaped its product packaging and redesigned its manufacturing processes to be able to hit the necessary cost, price and margin targets. Despite lower prices, profits for the brand doubled. Consumer-driven pricing strategies can thus lead to better marketing solutions.

Premium ice-cream

Facing rising costs for raw ingredients such as cream, cocoa and vanilla, US premium ice-cream makers found a subtle way to raise prices. Makers of brands such as Friendly's, Edy's and Turkey Hill quietly shrunk the size of their popular 64-ounce containers by 8 ounces (about 2 servings) but kept the price steady, resulting in a higher per ounce price by about 14 percent. The rationale for the move was that consumers paid far more attention to prices than to weights and at least some diet-orientated consumers preferred smaller quantities anyway. The new containers were the same height and weight as the old ones (just thinner), making it harder for consumers to detect differences on the shelves. Concerns that some consumers would feel cheated, however, caused some manufacturers to hold the line on their pack sizes.[55]

From a brand equity perspective, it is important that consumers find the price of the brand appropriate and reasonable given the benefits that they feel they accrue. To achieve the proper balance of perceived value, there is always tension between lowering prices on the one hand and increasing consumer perceptions of product quality on the other hand. Academics Lehmann and Winer believe that, although price reductions are more commonly employed to improve perceived value, in reality they are often more expensive than adding value through various brand-building marketing activities.[56] Their argument is that the lost revenue from a lower margin on each item sold is often much greater than the additional cost of value-added activities, primarily because many of these costs are fixed and spread over *all* the units sold, as opposed to the per unit reductions that result from lower prices.

At the same time, it should be recognized that different consumers may have different value perceptions and therefore could – and most likely should – receive different prices. Price segmentation involves setting and adjusting prices for appropriate market segments. In part because of wider adoption of the internet, firms are increasingly employing yield management principles such as those adopted by airlines to vary their prices for different market segments according to their different demand and value perceptions.[57]

Insurance companies' pricing

One of the best examples of highly individualized pricing is the insurance industry. In essence, pricing of insurance is determined from a risk-assesment perspective – where there are higher risks, the insurance company must collect more money to cover what they are likely to pay out. Therefore, insuring a car will be priced according to factors such as age, gender, address and whether or not the car will be driven by someone under 25 years of age. Also, the car models are a factor in the equation – certain brands and models are more likely to be stolen or involved in accidents than others. All of these significant factors are combined to determine what a driver will pay. The effects of this 'mathematical' approach to pricing can be dramatic. In one example, an insurance company used to have just three main pricing categories but moved on to 1,500 electronically generated price levels. 'Safe bets' now pay up to 20 percent less than the old system; high-risk drivers are penalized, however, and pay up to 20 percent more. The new pricing system, plus a drop in number of claims filed, helped to drive that company's operating income 16 percent higher in 2004 to €2.12 billion.[58]

Everyday low pricing (EDLP)

Everyday low pricing (EDLP) has received increased attention as a means of determining the nature of price discounts and promotions over time. EDLP eschews the sawtooth, whiplash pattern of alternating price increases and decreases or discounts in favour of establishing a more consistent set of 'everyday' base prices for products. In many cases, these EDLP prices are based on the value pricing considerations noted previously.

In the early 1990s, Procter & Gamble made a well-publicized conversion to EDLP (see Brand Briefing 5.7). By reducing list prices on half of its brands and eliminating many temporary discounts, P&G reported that it saved €120 million in 1991 or 10 percent of its previous year's profits. Advocates of EDLP argue that maintaining consistently low prices on major items every day helps build brand loyalty, fend off own label inroads and reduce manufacturing and inventory costs.[59]

Brand Briefing 5.7

Procter & Gamble launches value pricing

In 1991, Procter & Gamble shifted from a discount- and promotion-driven pricing strategy to an everyday low pricing strategy. There were problems with the old pricing system. First, many retailers didn't pass the discounts on to customers. Some retailers engaged in forward buying and diverting tactics – stocking up on huge quantities and selling them after the discount expired or in regions that were not even 'on deal'. Second, consumers became conditioned to buying brands only when they were discounted. Even worse, consumers were looking to private label substitutes to obtain even lower prices. To stimulate sales, the frequency and depth of discounts kept increasing until at one point, 17 percent of all products sold by P&G, on average, were on deal. Escalating discounts and deals with the trade created cost whiplashes, and the company was making 55 daily prices on 80 or so brands, which necessitated reworking every third order.

P&G's solution to these problems was to implement an EDLP strategy, although it faced challenges in making the strategy successful. First, P&G could not deliver everyday low prices without incurring everyday costs. To reduce costs, P&G implemented changes. The company cut overhead according to four simple guidelines: change the work, do more with less, eliminate work and reduce costs that cannot be passed on to consumers. P&G simplified the distribution chain to make restocking more efficient through continuous product replenishment. The company also scaled back its product portfolio by eliminating 25 percent of its stock-keeping units.

Over six years, P&G halved its coupon expenditures and cut trade promotion by a fifth. With the EDLP policy, list prices were reduced by 12–24 percent on nearly all of P&G's US brands. In their place, P&G put greater emphasis on brand-building advertising and marketing communications (increasing it by 20 percent). P&G also spent more than ever on research and development (over €684 million in 1994) and halved the time to market for new products. Moreover, P&G improved its relationships with retailers and was rated in a US survey of retailers as the consumer goods company most helpful in making retailers more efficient.

What were the results? One award-winning academic study suggested that P&G's market share decreased 16 percent. The revenue from higher prices was offset at least in part by the increased cost from greater advertising. According to the authors, the cuts in sales promotions decreased trial and penetration, as would be

Brand Briefing 5.7 *continued*

expected, but did not necessarily translate into greater behavioural loyalty from customers. When P&G encountered some difficulties in the late 1990s, it altered its value pricing strategy in some segments and reinstated selected price promotions.

Sources: Alecia Swasy, 'In a fast-paced world, Procter & Gamble sets its store in old values', *Wall Street Journal*, 21 September 1989: A1; Zachary Schiller, 'The marketing revolution at Procter & Gamble', *BusinessWeek*, 25 July 1988: 72; Bill Saporito, 'Behind the tumult at P&G', *Fortune*, 7 March 1994: 74–82; Zachary Schiller, 'Procter & Gamble hits back', *BusinessWeek*, 19 July 1993: 20–2; Zachary Schiller, 'Ed Artzt's elbow grease has P&G shining', *BusinessWeek*, 10 October 1994: 84–6; Zachary Schiller, 'Make it simple', *BusinessWeek*, 9 September 1996: 96–104; 'Executive update: value pricing plan helps push products', *Investor's Business Daily*, 30 August 1995.

For an analysis of P&G's strategy, see Kusum L. Ailawadi, Donald R. Lehmann and Scott A. Neslin, 'Market response to a major policy change in the marketing mix: learning from P&G's value pricing strategy', *Journal of Marketing*, 2001, 65(1): 71–89.

Even strict adherents of EDLP, however, see the need for price discounts over time. Well-conceived, timely sales promotions can provide important financial incentives to consumers and induce sales. As part of revenue management systems or yield management systems, many firms have been using sophisticated models and software to determine the optimal schedule for markdowns and discounts.[60] If that is the case, why do firms seek greater price stability? Manufacturers can be hurt by an overreliance on trade and consumer promotions and the resulting fluctuations in prices for several reasons.

As has been well documented, trade discounts rose considerably in past years in both breadth and depth. For example, the percentage of the total marketing communications expenditures devoted to trade promotions increased dramatically in the last few decades, from one-third to almost one-half of the budget total, and the extent of the average price discount, which previously was only 4 percent, grew to 10–15 percent.

Unfortunately, many trade promotion payments are not passed along as savings to consumers.[61] For example, although trade promotions are only supposed to result in discounts on products for a certain length of time and in a certain geographic region, that is not always the case. With *forward buying*, retailers order more product than they plan to sell during the promotional period so that they can later obtain a bigger margin by selling the remaining goods at the normal price after the promotional period has expired. With *diverting*, retailers pass along or sell the discounted products to retailers outside the designated selling area.

Although these practices may seem to benefit the retailer, critics argue that they can produce a false economy. Often overlooked are the extra expenses involved due to additional warehouse space, shipping costs and overheads. In justifying their switch to EDLP, Procter & Gamble argued that only 30 percent of its promotion discounts actually reached consumers in the form of lower prices – 35 percent was thought to be lost in the form of higher retailer costs, while another 35 percent was thought to be taken as profits by retailers. By reducing both the number of trade discounts as well as its wholesale list prices, P&G attempted to leave retailers in approximately the same net profitability position but to restore the price integrity of their brands.

From a manufacturer's perspective, these retailer practices created production complications: factories had to run overtime because of excess demand during the promotion period but had slack capacity when the promotion period ended, costing manufacturers millions. On top of it all, on the demand side, many marketers felt that the see-saw of high and low prices on products actually trained consumers to wait to buy the brand until it was discounted or on special, thus eroding its perceived value. By creating a brand association to 'discount' or 'don't pay full price', brand equity was diminished.

Summary

To build brand equity, marketers must determine strategies for setting prices and adjusting them, if at all, in the short and long run. Increasingly, these decisions will reflect consumer perceptions of value. The benefits delivered by the product and its relative advantages with respect to competitive offerings, among other factors, will determine what consumers see as a fair price. Value pricing strikes a balance between product design, product costs and product prices. Everyday low pricing is a complementary pricing approach to determine the nature of price discounts and promotions over time that maintains consistently low, value-based prices.

CHANNEL STRATEGY

The manner in which a product is sold or distributed can have a profound impact on the resulting equity and sales success of a brand. *Marketing channels* are defined as 'sets of interdependent organizations involved in the process of making a product or service available for use or consumption.'[62] Channel strategy involves the design and management of intermediaries such as wholesalers, distributors, brokers and retailers. This section considers how channel strategy can contribute to brand equity.[63]

Channel design

A number of channel types and arrangements exist. Broadly, they can be classified into direct and indirect channels. *Direct channels* involve selling through personal contacts between the company and prospective customers by mail, phone, electronic means, visits and so forth. *Indirect channels* involve selling through third-party intermediaries such as agents or broker representatives, wholesalers or distributors and retailers or dealers.

Increasingly, the best channel strategies will be those that can develop 'integrated shopping experiences' that combine physical stores, internet, telephone and catalogues. For example, consider the variety of channels through which Nike sells its products.

- *Retail:* Nike products are sold in several types of shops such as shoe, sporting goods, department and clothing shops.

- *Nike Town shops:* these shops, in prime streets in cities around the globe, offer a complete range of Nike products and push the latest fashions.
- *Niketown.com:* the e-commerce website allows consumers to buy direct.
- *Catalogue retailers:* Nike's products appear in numerous shoe, sporting goods and clothing catalogues.
- *Outlet shops:* outlet shops feature discounted Nike merchandise.
- *Speciality shops:* Nike equipment from product lines such as Nike Golf and Nike Hockey are often sold in specialised shops such as golf or hockey equipment suppliers.
- *All conditions gear (ACG) standalone shops:* The first of these shops, which sell Nike's ACG outdoor products, opened in 2000 at a US ski resort.

Much research has considered the pros and cons of these channels. Although the decision depends on the relative profitability of the options, some specific guidelines have been proposed. For example, one study for industrial products suggests that direct channels may be preferable when the following are true:[64]

- product information needs are high;
- product customization is high;
- product quality assurance is important;
- purchase lot size is important;
- logistics are important.

On the other hand, this study suggests that indirect channels may be preferable when:

- a broad assortment is essential;
- availability is critical;
- after-sales service is important.

Exceptions to these generalities exist, especially depending on the market segments involved.

It is rare that a manufacturer will use only a single channel. More likely, it will be the case that several channel types will be employed.[65] These channels must be managed carefully, as Tupperware found out.[66]

Tupperware

Tupperware pioneered the plastic food storage container business in the USA and the means by which they were sold in the 1950s. With many mothers staying at home and growth in the suburbs exploding, Tupperware parties with a local neighborhood host became a successful avenue for selling. Unfortunately, with more women entering the workforce and heightened competition from brands such as Rubbermaid, Tupperware experienced a 15 year decline in sales to close out the twentieth century. Sales only turned around with some new approaches to selling, including booths at shopping centres and a push on to the web. A subsequent decision to place products in all 1,148 Target stores, however, was a disaster. Such selling was difficult given the very different retail environment. Moreover, because the product was made more available, interest in the parties plummeted. Frustrated, many salespeople dropped out and fewer new ones were recruited. Although the products were removed from shops, the damage was done and profit plunged almost half in 2003. As one distributor commented: 'We just bit off more than we could chew.'

In designing a hybrid channel system, the risk is having too many channels (leading to conflict between channel members or a lack of support) or too few channels (resulting in market opportunities being overlooked). Therefore, in general, the goal is to maximize channel coverage and effectiveness while minimizing channel cost and conflict. John Deere, US maker of tractors as well as residential and commercial products such as mowers, was able to expand beyond its mainly rural network of more than 2,500 dealers and gain access to an additional 100,000 US customers by beginning to sell through Home Depot. In doing so, it avoided conflict by assigning dealers to handle the service for purchases made from the mass channel, ensuring that the dealers gained immediate revenue and an opportunity for future sales.[67]

Because direct and indirect channels are often used, it is worthwhile considering the brand equity implications of both routes.

Indirect channels

Although indirect channels can consist of a number of types of intermediaries, this discussion concentrates on retailers. Retailers tend to have the most visible and direct contact with customers and therefore have the greatest opportunity to affect brand equity. Retailers come in many forms. Consumers may have associations with any one retailer on the basis of a number of factors, such as product assortment, pricing and credit policy, and quality of service. Through the products and brands they stock, the means by which they sell and so on, retailers strive to create their own brand equity by establishing awareness and strong, favourable and unique associations.

At the same time, retailers can influence the equity of the brands they sell, especially in terms of the brand-related services that they can support or help to create. Moreover, the interplay between a shop's image and the brand images of the products it sells is an important one. Chapter 7 examines how the brand image of a retailer can be 'transferred' to the products it sells. That is, because of the knowledge and associations that consumers have regarding retailers, consumers infer or make certain assumptions about the products they sell, such as 'this shop only sells good-quality, high-value merchandise, so this particular product must also be good quality and high value'. Chapter 15 describes how retailers can build their own brand image and equity. This section considers how the marketing activity of retailers can directly affect the brand equity of the products they sell.

Push and pull strategies

Besides indirect means of image transfer, retailers can directly affect the equity of the brands they sell. The actions retailers take in stocking, displaying and selling products can enhance or detract from brand equity, suggesting that manufacturers must help retailers add value to brands.

Yet, at the same time, a battle has emerged between manufacturers and retailers making up their channels of distribution. Because of factors such as greater competition for shelf space between what many retailers feel are increasingly undifferentiated brands, retailers have gained in power and are now in a better position to set the terms of trade with manufacturers. Increased power means that retailers can command more frequent and lucrative trade promotions.

Increasingly, supermarket chains are demanding payments to stock a new brand in the form of cash payments for the shelf space itself (slotting allowances), introductory deals (eg, one free with three), postponed billing or extended credit (dating), payment for retailer advertising or promotion in support of the new brand and so on.[68] Even after stocking brands, retailers can later require generous trade promotions to keep them on the shelf. Outside the supermarkets, department stores are requiring that suppliers guarantee their stores' profit margin and insist on cash rebates if the guarantee is not met.[69] For all these reasons, manufacturers are vulnerable to retailers' actions.

Retailers have thus increased their power over manufacturers. One way for manufacturers to regain power is by creating strong brands through some of the brand-building tactics described in this book – for example, by selling innovative and unique products – properly priced and advertised – that consumers demand. In this way, consumers may ask or even pressure retailers to stock and promote manufacturers' products. By devoting marketing efforts to the end consumer, a manufacturer is said to employ a *pull strategy*, because consumers use their buying power and influence on retailers to 'pull' the product through the channel. Alternatively, marketers can devote their selling efforts to the channel members themselves, providing direct incentives for them to stock and sell products to the consumer. This approach is called a *push strategy*, because the manufacturer is attempting to reach the consumer by 'pushing' the product through each step of the distribution chain.

Although certain brands seem to emphasize one strategy more than another (eg, push strategies are usually associated with more selective distribution and pull strategies with broader, more intensive distribution), in general, the most successful branding strategies often blend the two. For example, when Goodyear introduced its Aquatred tyre, an all-season radial designed to provide better traction on wet roads, it was priced 10 percent higher than Goodyear's previous top-of-the line mass market tyre. Nevertheless, Goodyear was able to sell two million Aquatreds in the first two years of its introduction by combining strong merchandising support for dealers with a persuasive advertising campaign directed at consumers.[70]

Channel support

Services provided by channel members can enhance the value to consumers of purchasing and consuming a brand name product (see Figure 5.7). Although firms are increasingly attempting to provide some of the services themselves through such means as free phone numbers and websites, establishing a 'marketing partnership' with retailers may nevertheless be critical to ensure proper channel support and the execution of these various services. Two aspects of such a partnership involve retail segmentation activities and co-operative advertising campaigns.

Retail segmentation A manufacturer can initiate marketing and merchandising campaigns to assist retailers' selling efforts. One important realization in developing these strategies is that retailers have to be treated as if they were 'customers' too. Because of their different marketing capabilities and needs, retailers may need to be divided into segments or even treated individually in designing the optimal marketing

Service	Explanation
Marketing research	Gathering information necessary for planning and facilitating interactions with customers.
Communications	Developing and executing communications about the product and service.
Contact	Seeking out and interacting with prospective customers.
Matching	Shaping and fitting the product/service to the customer's requirements.
Negotiations	Reaching final agreement on price and other terms of trade.
Physical distribution	Transporting and storing goods (inventory).
Financing	Providing credit or funds to make a transaction possible.
Risk-taking	Assuming risks associated with getting the product or service from firm to customer.
Service	Developing and executing continuing relationships with customers, including maintenance and repair.

Figure 5.7   Services provided by channel members

Source: Reprinted from Donald Lehmann and Russell Winer, *Product Management*, Burr Ridge, IL: Irwin, 1994.

campaign so that they will provide the necessary brand support.[71] The following packaged goods companies customized their marketing efforts to particular retailers.[72]

- Frito-Lay developed a tailored supply chain system for its tortilla chip and potato crisp markets, enabling fast and broad distribution, fewer stock-outs and better-turning shop displays for its retail customers.
- SC Johnson has used customized market research to develop ways to help strategic retail customers.
- Scotts Miracle-Gro customizes its product lines, marketing events and supply chain for hardware co-operative channels.

Different retailers may need to be given different product mixes, special delivery systems, customized promotions or even their own branded version of the products.

For example, marketing scholar Shugan refers to *branded variants* as branded items that are not directly comparable to other items carrying the same brand name.[73] Branded variants can be found in a diverse set of durable and semi-durable goods categories.[74] Manufacturers create branded variants in many ways, including changes in colour, design, flavour, options, style, stain, motif, features and layout. Branded variants can reduce retail price competition because they make direct price comparisons by consumers difficult. Thus, different retailers may be given different items or models of the same brand to sell. Shugan and his colleagues show that as the manufacturer of a product offers more branded variants, a greater number of shops carry the product, and these shops offer higher levels of retail service for these products.[75]

Co-operative advertising One relatively neglected means of increasing channel support is through better-designed and implemented co-operative advertising campaigns. Traditionally with such advertising, a manufacturer pays for a portion of the advertising that a retailer runs to promote the manufacturer's product and its availability in the retailer's place of business. Manufacturers generally share the cost of advertising run by the retailer (usually half), up to a certain limit. To be eligible to receive co-op funds, the retailer usually must follow the manufacturer's stipulations as to the nature of brand exposure in the ad. The total funds the manufacturer provides to the retailer is usually based on a percentage of cash purchases made by the retailer from the manufacturer.[76]

The rationale behind co-operative advertising for manufacturers is that it concentrates some of the communication efforts at a local level where they may be more relevant to consumers. Unfortunately, the brand image communicated through such ads is not as tightly controlled as when a manufacturer runs its own ads, and there is a danger that the emphasis may be on the shop or on a particular sale it is running rather than on the brand. Perhaps even worse, there is also a danger that a co-op ad may communicate a message about the brand that runs counter to its desired image.

Some manufacturers are attempting to gain better control over such advertising by providing greater assistance to retailers. For example, Goodrich created an image ad for its tyres that could be recut to plug various local dealerships at the same time. US storage box maker Rubbermaid has collaborated with big retailers such as Wal-Mart and Home Depot to find approaches that achieve the best of both worlds – allowing Rubbermaid to create more awareness and loyalty for its brand while stimulating sales momentum for the retailer in the same ad.[77]

Increasingly, it would seem desirable to achieve synergy between the manufacturer's own ad campaigns for a brand and its corresponding co-op ad campaigns with retailers. The challenge in designing effective co-op ads will continue to be how to strike a balance between pushing the brand while selling the retailer at the same time. In that sense, co-operative advertising will have to live up to its name and manufacturers will have to get involved in the design and execution of retailer's campaigns rather than just handing over money or supplying generic, uninspired ads.

So, in eliciting channel support, manufacturers must be creative in how they develop marketing and merchandising campaigns aimed at the trade or any other channel members. In doing so, it is important to consider how channel activity can encourage trial purchase and communicate or demonstrate product information to build brand awareness and image and to elicit positive brand responses.

Direct channels

For some of the reasons noted previously, manufacturers may choose to sell directly to consumers. Chapter 6 describes some general issues surrounding direct marketing in terms of how it fits into the marketing communications mix. This section considers some of the brand equity issues regarding selling through direct channels.

Company-owned shops

To gain control over the selling process and build stronger relationships with customers, some manufacturers have opened their own shops.

- In December 1994, after the US Federal Trade Commission ended a 16-year ban on the jeans maker selling its own wares, Levi Strauss began to open up Original Levi's Stores in the USA and abroad, located mostly in city centres and upmarket suburban shopping centres.[78]

- Nike Town shops stock essentially all of the products Nike sells. Each location consists of a number of individual shops or pavilions that feature shoes, clothes and equipment for a different sport (eg, tennis, jogging, biking, or water sports) or different lines within a sport (eg, there might be three basketball shops and two tennis shops). Each shop develops its own concepts based on lights, music, temperature and multimedia displays.

A number of other brands have created their own stores, such as Bang & Olufsen audio equipment, OshKosh B'Gosh children's wear and Warner Bros entertainment. Dr Martens – known for its thick-soled, lace-up boots – opened a large five-storey-shop in London, trying to transform the brand into a lifestyle brand.

Company shops provide many benefits.[79] Primarily, they show off a brand and all its product varieties in a way not easily achieved through normal retail channels. For example, Nike might find its products spread all through department stores and sports stores. These products may not be displayed in a logical, co-ordinated fashion and certain product lines may not even be stocked. By opening its own stores, Nike can put its best foot forward by showing the depth, breadth and variety of its products. These types of stores can provide the added benefit of functioning as a test market to gauge consumer response to product designs, presentations and prices, allowing firms to keep their fingers on the pulse of consumers' shopping habits.

A disadvantage with company stores is that some companies lack either the skills, resources or contacts to operate as a retailer. For example, the Disney Store, started in 1987, sold exclusive Disney branded merchandise, ranging from toys and videos to collectibles and clothing, priced from €2 to €2,000. Disney viewed the stores as an extension of the 'Disney experience', referring to customers as 'guests' and employees as 'cast members'. The company struggled, however, to find the right retail formula and, after experiencing slumping sales, the chain of stores in Japan and later North America was sold to the Children's Place.

Another issue with company shops, of course, is potential conflict with existing retail channels and distributors. In many cases, however, these shops can be seen as bolstering brand image and building brand equity rather than as direct sales devices. For example, Nike views its shops as essentially advertisements and tourist attractions. Nike reports that research studies have confirmed that Nike Town stores enhanced the Nike brand image by presenting the full scope of Nike's sports and fitness lines to customers and 'educating them' on the value, quality and benefits of Nike products. The research also revealed that, although only about one in four visitors made a purchase at a Nike Town shop, 40 percent of those who did not buy during their visit eventually purchased Nike products from another retailer.

These manufacturer-owned shops can also be seen as a means of hedging bets with retailers who continue to push their own labels. With one of its main US retailers, JC Penney, pushing its own Arizona brand of jeans, Levi's can protect its brand franchise to some extent by establishing its own distribution channel. Nevertheless, many retailers and manufacturers are avoiding head-on clashes over distribution channels. Manufacturers in particular have been careful to stress that their shops are not a competitive threat to their retailers but rather 'showcases' that can help sell merchandise for any retailer carrying their brand.[80] Brand Briefing 5.8 describes some of Goodyear's channel conflict issues.

Brand Briefing 5.8

Goodyear's partnering lessons

Goodyear spent several years recovering from mistakes with the middlemen it used to distribute tyres. A well-respected brand that once managed the top tyre reseller network in the USA, Goodyear damaged its reputation through its apparent indifference to distributors. The company's prices varied from month to month and, when distributors would order tyres, often only half of the order would be filled. Distributors nationwide said it was just getting hard to do business with Goodyear and many began selling other brands instead.

Goodyear earned dealer loyalty in the 1970s and 1980s through competitive pricing, on-time deliveries and highly visible marketing in the Goodyear airship. In 1992, Goodyear announced a distribution deal with Sears, even though the company had promised dealers it would not sell through discount retailers. Then it made similar deals with Wal-Mart and Sam's Club. To increase sales, the company began to offer the big retailers bulk discounts. As a result, smaller, independent dealers had to pay as much for their tyres as customers could pay at other retailers.

Shortly after Firestone had to recall 6.5 million tyres in 2000, Goodyear dealers – instead of taking advantage of their competitor's legal and image problems – annoyed many of its distributors. Goodyear dealership owners complained of pressure to buy more tyres than they needed, uneven pricing and poor quality.

By 2004, Goodyear had 5,300 authorized dealers, about the same number as in 1994. While overall US tyre sales grew, Goodyear's replacement tyre sales slumped 14 percent. That represents of loss of about €376 million in sales.

Yet manufacturers can keep distributors happy and prevent breaks in the supply chain. Resellers often put significant amounts of money into maintaining their premises and paying sales staff. To compensate them, manufacturers can offer dealers exclusive access to new products. Goodyear followed this advice in trying to win back its dealers. It originally sold its popular Assurance tyres exclusively through authorized dealers.

Manufacturers can also stick to fixed prices when they offer products directly to consumers. If they do offer big discounts, they should offer them at discount factory outlets, where they won't confuse customers. And manufacturers can back up distributors by educating them about the products so the retail partners can shape an effective salesforce. When Mary Kay began selling its cosmetics online in 1997, it also helped its members of its direct salesforce set up their own online shops. Sharing product information and also doing good advertising contributes to distributors' success. Ultimately, companies have to share the power to make decisions with their distributors and recognize that dealers' success benefits them too. In the tyre business, dealers have captured more of the retail market and so manufacturers must keep them happy and profitable if they want the benefits of a smooth supply chain.

Source: Based on 'Giving dealers a raw deal', *Business 2.0*, December 2004.

Other means

As well as creating their own shops, some marketers – such as Adidas, Polo and Levi Strauss (with Dockers) – are attempting to open their own shops within department stores. Procter & Gamble has created informational and promotional electronic kiosks for Oil of Olay; and Diageo, seller of Smirnoff vodka and Bell's whisky, opened in-house 'drink zones' in Sainsbury and Tesco in the UK. These approaches can offer the desirable dual benefits of appeasing retailers – and perhaps even benefiting from the retailer's brand image – while at the same time allowing the firm to retain control over the design and implementation of the product presentation at the point of sale.

Finally, another channel option is to sell directly to consumers via phone, mail or electronic means. Retailers have sold their goods through catalogues for decades. Direct selling, a successful strategy for brands such as Mary Kay and Avon, is being increasingly used by many mass marketers, especially those that also sell through their own shops. These vehicles not only help to sell products but also contribute to brand equity by increasing consumer awareness of the range of products associated with a brand and increasing consumer understanding of the benefits of those products. As Chapter 6 describes, although direct marketing can be done in many ways, they all represent an opportunity to engage in a dialogue and establish a relationship with consumers.

Web strategies

One lesson from the dot-com boom and bust is the advantage of having both a 'bricks and mortar' channel and an online retail channel. In some cases, consumers are ordering from companies online and picking up the physical products at their local shop rather than having them posted.[81] The Boston Consulting Group concluded that multichannel retailers were able to acquire customers at half the cost of internet-only retailers, citing a number of advantages for the multichannel retailers.[82]

- They have market clout with suppliers.
- They have established distribution and fulfillment systems (eg, Next).
- They can cross-sell between websites and shops (eg, Marks & Spencer and Tesco).

Many of these advantages are realized by multichannel product manufacturers. Recognizing the power of integrated channels, many internet-based companies are engaging in 'physical world' activities to boost their brand. For example, Yahoo! opened a promotional store in New York and estyle.com launched a twice-yearly mail-order catalogue. Integrated channels allow consumers to shop when and how they want. For example, one research study suggested that nearly half of the most sophisticated shoppers found items they wanted online but purchased them in shops.[83] Figure 5.8 shows an analysis of the JC Penney channel mix, which reveals that its most profitable customers were those that shopped using several channels.

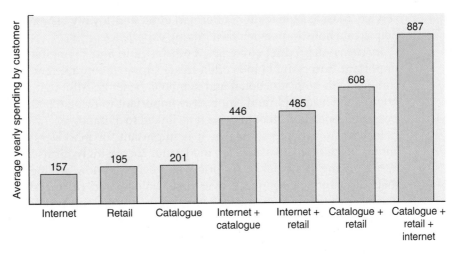

Figure 5.8   Customer channel value analysis for JC Penney stores in the USA
Source: Customer Value Analysis, Doubleclick, 2004.

Summary

Channels are the means by which firms distribute their products to consumers. A channel strategy to build brand equity involves designing and managing direct and indirect channels to build brand awareness and improve the brand image. Direct channels can enhance brand equity by allowing consumers to better understand the depth, breadth and variety of the products associated with the brand as well as any distinguishing characteristics. Indirect channels can influence brand equity through the actions taken and support given to the brand by intermediaries such as retailers and the transfer of any associations that these intermediaries might have to the brand.

Direct and indirect channels offer advantages and disadvantages that must be thoughtfully combined to both sell products in the short run as well as maintain and enhance brand equity in the long run. As is often the case with branding, the key is to mix and match channel options so they collectively achieve these goals. Thus, it is important to assess each possible channel option in terms of its direct effect on product sales and brand equity as well as its indirect effect through interactions with other channel options.

CHAPTER REVIEW

This chapter considered approaches to designing marketing campaigns as well as issues regarding the development of product, pricing and distribution strategies to build brand equity.

Relationship marketing involves activities that deepen and broaden how consumers think and act towards a brand. Experiential, one-to-one and permission marketing are all means of getting consumers more actively involved with the product or service. Mass customization, aftermarketing and loyalty schemes are also ways to help create holistic, personalized buying experiences.

In terms of product strategies, both tangible and intangible considerations are important. Successful brands often create strong, favourable and unique brand associations with both functional and symbolic benefits. Although perceived quality is often at the heart of brand equity, it is important to recognize the range of different possible associations that may become linked to a brand.

In terms of pricing strategies, it is important for marketers to understand consumer perceptions of value for the brand. Increasingly, firms are adopting value-based pricing strategies to set prices and everyday low pricing strategies to guide their discount pricing policy over time. Value-based pricing strategies attempt to balance product design and delivery, product costs and product prices. Everyday low-pricing strategies attempt to establish a stable set of 'everyday' prices and only introduce price discounts very selectively.

In terms of channel strategies, it is important to match brand and shop images to exploit secondary associations; integrate push strategies for retailers with pull strategies for consumers; and consider a range of direct and indirect distribution options.

The following chapter considers how to develop integrated marketing communication campaigns to build brand equity.

Brand Briefing 5.9

Own label strategies and responses

This appendix considers the issue of own labels or store brands. After portraying private label branding strategies, it describes how major manufacturer's brands have responded to their threat.

Own labels

Although different terms and definitions are possible, *own labels* or *private labels* can be defined as products marketed by retailers and other members of the distribution chain. They can be called *own-label brands* when they actually adopt the name of the shop itself in some way (eg, Safeway Select). Such labels should not be confused with *generics*, whose simple packaging typically provides no information as to who made the product.

Own label brands typically cost less to make and sell than the national or manufacturer brands with which they compete. Thus, the appeal to consumers of buying own-label brands often is the cost savings involved; the appeal to retailers of selling such brands is that their gross margin is often 25 percent to 30 percent – nearly twice that of national brands.

The history of own labels is one of many ups and downs. They became common in the Victorian era and, in the first half of the twentieth century, own-label brands

Brand Briefing 5.9 *continued*

were introduced. Under competitive pressure from the mass marketing practices adopted by large packaged-goods companies in the 1950s, private labels fell out of favour with consumers.

Because the appeal of own labels to consumers has been their lower cost, sales generally have been highly correlated with personal disposable income. The recession of the 1970s saw the introduction of low-cost, basic-quality and minimally packaged generic products that appealed to bargain-seeking consumers. During the subsequent economic recovery, though, the lack of perceived quality eventually hampered sales of generics and many consumers returned to national or manufacturer's brands.

To compete better, own label makers have begun improving quality and expanding the variety of their offerings to include premium products. In recognition of the power of bold graphics, supermarket chains have been careful to design attractive, upmarket packaging for their own premium branded products. Because of these and other actions, own-label sales have made inroads in new markets. Retailers value own labels for their profit margins and as a way of differentiation to drive customer loyalty. US retailer Target has introduced a stream of exclusives, such as its stylish Mossimo and Isaac Mizrahi clothing brands.[84]

Own label status

In the USA, own label goods have accounted for roughly 16 percent of supermarket revenue. In other countries, these percentages are often higher. For example, western Europe dominates the market for own labels in the supermarket, with the biggest being Switzerland at 45 percent, Germany at 30 percent, Spain at 26 percent and Belgium at 25 percent.[85]

Own labels in the UK make up over a third of sales at supermarkets, in part because the grocery industry is more concentrated. The five largest supermarket chains make up almost two-thirds of sales in the UK (but only two-fifths of sales in the USA). Two of the large UK supermarket chains are Tesco and Sainsbury.

- Tesco, with a brand slogan 'Every little helps', has several own-label brands, ranging from Value to Finest, and has its own lifestyle brands such as Organic, Free From and Healthy Living. These are positioned as 'Making life taste better.'

- Sainsbury has used its name to introduce 500 lines across fruit, vegetables, grocery and household products. Sainsbury's own-brand products are categorized into one of three quality tiers: eg, the lasagne range comprises the Basics sub-brand for 'good', the core own-label line for 'better' and the premium Taste the Difference for 'best'. Clothing and housewares were added to Sainsbury's own-brand product ranges in late 2004.

Own label appeal is widespread. In supermarkets, own label sales have always been strong in product categories such as dairy goods, vegetables and beverages.

Brand Briefing 5.9 *continued*

More recently, own labels have been successful in previously 'untouchable' categories such as cigarettes, disposable nappies and cold remedies. One study indicated that, although the 17 percent of households who shop primarily on the basis of price and are classified as 'heavy' own label buyers account for 42 percent of total own label sales, nearly one-third of all consumers regularly buy some own label goods. Sixty-eight percent of consumers interviewed by Nielsen either slightly or strongly agreed with the statement: 'Private label brands are a good alternative to other brands.'[86]

Nevertheless, some categories have not seen a strong own label presence. Many shoppers, for example, still seem unwilling to trust their hair, complexion or dental care to own brands. Own labels also have been relatively unsuccessful in categories such as biscuits, sweets, cereal, pet foods, baby food and beer.

One implication that can be drawn from this pattern of product purchases is that consumers are being more selective in what they buy, no longer choosing to buy only national brands. For less important products in particular, consumers seem to feel 'that top-of-the-line is unnecessary and good is good enough.'[87] Categories that are particularly vulnerable to own label advances are those in which there is little perceived quality difference between brands – for example, over-the-counter pain relievers, bottled water, plastic bags, kitchen towels and dairy products.

Own label branding strategy

Although the growth of own labels has been interpreted by some as a sign of a decline of brands, the opposite conclusion may in fact be more valid: own label growth could be seen in some ways as a consequence of clever branding strategies. In terms of building brand equity, the point of difference for own labels in consumers' eyes has always been 'good value', a desirable and transferable association across many product categories. As a result, own labels can be extremely broad and their name can be applied across many diverse products.

As with national brands, implementing a value-pricing strategy for such labels requires determining the right price and product offering. For example, one reported rule of thumb is that the typical 'no-name' product has to sell for at least 15 percent less than a national brand, on average, to be successful. The challenge for own labels has been to determine the appropriate product offering.

Specifically, to achieve the necessary points of parity, or even to create their own points of difference, own labels have been improving quality and as a result are aggressively positioning against even national brands. *Consumer Reports'* analysis of 65 US store brand and national brand products in 6 categories – facial tissues, paper towels, plastic bags, canned peaches, chips and yogurt – revealed that many

Brand Briefing 5.9 *continued*

own brands were at least as good as national brands and consumers could cut their costs by as much as half by switching to own brands.[88]

Many US supermarket chains have introduced their own premium brands, such as Safeway Select, Von's Royal Request and Ralph's Private Selection. For example, A&P positioned its premium Master Choice brand to fill the void between the mass market national brands and the upmarket speciality brands the chain sells. It has used the brand across a wide range of products, such as teas, pastas, sauces and salad dressings. Trader Joe's offers 2,000 own label products – a tenth of what would be found in a typical supermarket – but creates a fun, roomy atmosphere for bargain-seekers wanting the best in gourmet-style foods, health food supplements and wines.[89]

Sellers of own labels are also adopting more extensive marketing communications. For example, A&P produces a glossy Master Choice insert and uses Act Media shopping trolleys, freezer vision, instant coupon machines and television advertising in selling its America's Choice brand. Consider how Loblaws has been successful at creating its own brands.

Loblaws

Loblaws is Canada's largest food distributor. In 1978, it was the first chain in Canada to introduce generics, reflecting a carefully crafted strategy to build an image of quality and high value in six areas. By 1983, Loblaws carried over 500 generic products that accounted for 10 percent of sales. This success was due to innovative marketing, low costs and a large network of suppliers. In 1984 Loblaws chose to introduce a private label brand, President's Choice, that was designed to offer value through exceptional quality and moderate prices. These categories ranged from basic supermarket categories such as chocolate chip cookies, colas and cereals to more exotic categories such as Devonshire custard from England and gourmet Russian mustard. These products also used distinctive and attractive packaging with modern lettering and colourful labels and names ('decadent' biscuits, 'ultimate' frozen pizza and 'too good to be true' peanut butter). In terms of marketing communications, Loblaws put into place a strong promotional campaign with much in-store merchandising. Loblaws also introduced *Insider's Report*, a quarterly publication featuring its own brands and offering consumers shopping tips.[90]

Brand responses to own labels

Procter & Gamble's value pricing was one strategy to combat competitive inroads from private labels and other brands. Other brands also have been successful at fending off private labels.

Brand Briefing 5.9 *continued*

Heinz Ketchup

Heinz has retained more than half its market share in the ketchup category for years. Its ingredients for success include a distinctive, slightly sweet-tasting product; a carefully monitored price gap with competitors; and aggressive packaging, product development and promotion. For example, since 1998, it has introduced EZ Squirt Bottles, spicy flavours, a 'trap cap' that eliminates watery ooze and coloured (Blastin' Green) ketchup. 'Hipper' advertising has been used to announce the innovations and the price gap with own labels has been kept at under 20 percent.

As suggested by this example, the approach adopted by Heinz and others to stay a step ahead of own label and other competitors is to emphasize both innovation and relevance in their marketing (see Chapter 13).

To compete with own labels, a number of tactics have been adopted by marketers of major national or manufacturers' brands (see Figure 5.9). First, marketers of major brands have attempted to decrease costs and reduce prices to negate the primary point of difference of own labels and achieve a critical point of parity. In many categories, prices had crept up to a point at which price premiums over own labels were 30 percent to 50 percent, or even 100 percent. In those categories in which consumers make frequent purchases, the cost savings of 'trading down' to an own-label brand were therefore substantial. For example, before Marlboro dropped its prices, a smoker who purchased, on average, 10 packs of cigarettes a week could have saved over €342 a year by switching from a premium brand such as Marlboro that cost €1.37 a pack to an own-label brand that only cost 68 cents a pack.

In instances in which major brands and own labels are on a more equal footing with regard to price, major brands often compete well because of other favourable brand perceptions that consumers might have. For example, when StarKist cut

---

- Decrease costs.
- Cut prices.
- Increase R&D expenditures to improve products and identify product innovations.
- Increase advertising and promotion budgets.
- Eliminate stagnant brands and extensions and concentrate on fewer brands.
- Introduce discount 'fighter' brands.
- Supply private label makers.
- Track own brands' growth and compete market by market.

Figure 5.9   Major brands' responses to own labels

Brand Briefing 5.9 *continued*

prices on its tuna to only five cents higher than own labels in the USA, it was able to slice the own label share in the category in half (from 20 percent to 10 percent) because of the positive image its brand had with consumers.

Marketers of major brands have cut prices on older brands to make them more appealing. Procter & Gamble cut prices on a number of old standbys (eg, Joy washing-up liquid, Era laundry detergent, Luvs disposable nappies and Camay beauty soap) by 12 percent to 33 percent, shifting them into the middle-tier level of pricing. Similarly, Miller dropped prices on its one-time flagship Miller High Life beer by 20 percent.

It should be noted that one problem faced by marketers of brands is that it can be difficult to lower prices. Supermarkets may not pass on the wholesale price cuts they are given. Moreover, marketers may not want to alienate retailers by attacking their own brands too forcefully, especially in zero-sum categories in which their brands could be easily replaced. For example, for Luvs nappies, P&G eliminated jumbo packs, streamlined packaging designs, simplified printing and trimmed promotions, increasing retail margins from 3.3 percent to 8.6 percent as a result. Nevertheless, faced with margins on its own brand of 8–12 percent, the Safeway chain still chose to drop the Luvs brand.

Besides these various pricing moves to achieve points of parity, marketers of major brands have tried to achieve additional points of difference to combat the threat of own labels. They have increased R&D expenditures to improve products and identify innovations. They have increased advertising and promotion budgets. They have also tracked own brand growth more closely than in the past and are competing on a market-by-market basis. Marketers of major brands have also adjusted their brand portfolios. They have eliminated stagnant brands and extensions and concentrated on fewer brands. They have introduced discount 'fighter' brands that are specially designed and promoted to compete with own labels.

Marketers have also been more aggressive legally in protecting their brands. In 2005, Unilever filed a suit against global supermarket giant Ahold alleging trademark and trade dress infringement across four of its European margarine brands as well as Lipton iced tea and Bertolli olive oil. Unilever maintains that the packaging looked too similar to its own brands.[91]

One controversial move by some marketers is to supply own label makers. In the USA, for example, *Consumer Reports* reported that behind the scenes, Sara Lee, Del Monte, and Bird's Eye all supplied products – sometimes lower in quality – to be used for own labels.[92] Other marketers, however, criticize this 'if you can't beat 'em, join 'em' strategy, maintaining that these actions, if revealed, might create confusion or even reinforce a perception by consumers that all brands in a category are essentially the same.

Brand Briefing 5.9 *continued*

Future developments

Many marketers feel that the brands most endangered by the rise of own labels are second-tier brands. For example, in the USA's laundry detergent category, the success of an own label such as Wal-Mart's Ultra Clean is more likely to come at the expense of Oxydol, All or Fab rather than market leader Tide. In Britain, the average share of 52 leading brands measured fell only from 34.2 percent to 32.6 percent between 1975 and 1999 – the 'losers' were the smaller 'trade-dependent' brands that invested less in marketing and tried to compete on price with own labels.[93] Highly priced, poorly differentiated and undersupported brands are vulnerable to own label competition.

At the same time, retailers will need the quality and image that go along with well-researched, efficiently manufactured and professionally marketed major brands, if nothing else because of the wishes of consumers. When A&P let own brands soar to 35 percent of its dry grocery sales mix in the 1960s, many shoppers defected and it was forced to drop the percentage to under 20 percent as a result. Similarly, Federated Department Stores, owners of the own label wizard Macy's chain, has vowed to keep its percentage of revenue from own labels at under 20 percent.

Discussion questions

1. Have you had any experience with a brand that has done a great job with relationship marketing, permission marketing, experiential marketing or one-to-one marketing? What did the brand do? Why was it effective? Could others learn from that?

2. Think about products you own. Assess their design. Critique their aftermarketing efforts. Are you aware of all of the products' capabilities? Identify a product whose benefits you feel you are not fully capitalizing on. How might you suggest improvements?

3. Choose a product category. Profile all the brands in the category in terms of pricing strategies and perceived value. If possible, review these brands' pricing histories. Have these brands set and adjusted prices properly? What would you do differently?

4. Take a trip to a department store. Evaluate the in-store marketing. Which categories or brands seem to be receiving the biggest in-store push? What unique in-store merchandising efforts do you see?

5. Take a trip to a supermarket. Observe the extent of own label brands. In which categories do you think own labels might be successful? Why?

References and notes

[1] Philip Kotler and Kevin Lane Keller, *Marketing Management*, 12th edn, Upper Saddle River, NJ: Prentice Hall, 2006.

[2] Ibid.

[3] Greg Farrell, 'Marketers get personal', *USA Today*, 19 July 1999: B9.

[4] Don E. Schultz, Stanley I. Tannenbaum and Robert F. Lauterborn, *Integrated Marketing Communications*, Lincolnwood, IL: NTC Business Books, 1993.

[5] Bridget Finn, 'Why pop-up shops are hot', *Business 2.0*, 17 November 2004, www.trendwatching.com

[6] Christopher Locke, Rick Levine, Doc Searls and David Weinberger, *The Cluetrain Manifesto: The end of business as usual*, Cambridge, MA: Perseus Press, 2000.

[7] Richard Tomkins, 'Fallen icons', *Financial Times*, 1 February 2000.

[8] Peter Post, 'Beyond brand: the power of experience branding', *ANA/The Advertiser*, October/November 2000.

[9] www.adweek.com/buzz

[10] B. Joseph Pine and James H. Gilmore, *The Experience Economy: Work is theatre and every business a stage*, Cambridge, MA: Harvard University Press, 1999.

[11] Bernd H. Schmitt, *Experiential Marketing: How to get customers to sense, feel, think, act and relate to your company and brands*, New York: Free Press, 1999.

[12] Don Peppers and Martha Rogers, *The One to One Future: Building relationships one customer at a time*, New York: Doubleday, 1997; Don Peppers and Martha Rogers, *Enterprise One to One: Tools for competing in the interactive age*, New York: Doubleday, 1999; Don Peppers and Martha Rogers, *The One to One Fieldbook: The complete toolkit for implementing a 1 to 1 marketing program*, New York: Doubleday, 1999. For some more recent discussion from these authors, see Don Peppers and Martha Rogers, *Return on Customer: Creating maximum value from your scarcest resource*, New York: Currency Doubleday, 2005. See also, Sunil Gupta and Donald R. Lehmann, *Managing Customers as Investments: The strategic value of customers in the long run*, Cambridge, MA: Harvard Business School Press, 2005.

[13] Don Peppers and Martha Rogers, 'Welcome to the 1:1 future', *Marketing Tools*, 1 April 1994.

[14] Seth Godin, *Permission Marketing: Turning strangers into friends, and friends into customers*, New York: Simon & Schuster, 1999.

[15] Susan Fournier, Susan Dobscha and David Mick, 'Preventing the premature death of relationship marketing', *Harvard Business Review*, January–February 1998: 42–51. See also, Erwin Danneels, 'Tight-loose coupling with customers: the enactment of customer orientation', *Strategic Management Journal*, 2003, 24: 559–76.

[16] Neeli Bendapudi and Robert P. Leone, 'Psychological implications of customer participation in co-production', *Journal of Marketing*, 2003, 67 (January): 14–28.

[17] Jennifer Aaker, Susan Fournier and S. Adam Brasel, 'When good brands do bad', *Journal of Consumer Research*, 2004, 31 (June): 1–16; Pankaj Aggarwal, 'The effects of brand relationship norms on consumer attitudes and behavior', *Journal of Consumer Research*, 2004, 31 (June): 87–101; Pankaj Aggarwal and Sharmistha Law, 'Role of relationship norms in processing brand information', *Journal of Consumer Research*, 2005, 32 (December): 453–64.

[18] David A. Aaker and Robert Jacobson, 'The strategic role of product quality', *Journal of Marketing*, October 1987: 31–44.

[19] Stratford Sherman, 'How to prosper in the value decade', *Fortune*, 30 November 1992: 91.

[20]David Garvin, 'Product quality: an important strategic weapon', *Business Horizons*, May–June 1985, 27: 40–3; Philip Kotler, *Marketing Management*, 10th edn, Upper Saddle River, NJ: Prentice Hall, 1999.

[21]David Court, Tom French, Tim McGuire and Michael Partington, *Marketing in Three Dimensions: The new challenge for marketers*, New York: McKinsey & Company, 1999.

[22]Kotler and Keller, *Marketing Management,* 12th edn.

[23]Michael E. Porter, *Competitive Advantage,* New York: Free Press, 1985.

[24]Robert M. Morgan and Shelby D. Hunt, 'The commitment trust theory of relationship marketing', *Journal of Marketing*, 1994, 58 (2): 20–38.

[25]Frederick F. Reichheld, *The Loyalty Effect*, Boston, MA: Harvard Business School Press, 1996.

[26]Chris Woodyard, 'Mass production gives way to mass customization', *USA Today*, 16 February 1998: 3B.

[27]Paul Roberts, 'John Deere runs on chaos', *Fast Company*, November 1998: 164–73.

[28]Evantheia Schibsted, 'What your breakfast reveals about you', *Business 2.0,* 20 March 2001: 80.

[29]Christopher M. Kelley, 'Do your shoppers want custom products?', Forrester Research, 21 May 2003.

[30]Roland T. Rust, Christine Moorman and Peter R. Dickson, 'Getting returns from service quality: is the conventional wisdom wrong?', MSI Report 00–120, Cambridge, MA: Marketing Science Institute, 2000.

[31]Lourdes Lee Valeriano, 'Loved the present! Hated the manual!', *Wall Street Journal*, 15 December 1994: B1.

[32]Jessica Mintz, 'Using hand, grab hair. Pull.', *Wall Street Journal*, 23 December 2004: B1, B5.

[33]Jacqueline Martense, 'Get close to your customers', *Fast Company*, August 2005: 37.

[34]Terry Vavra, *Aftermarketing: How to keep customers for life through relationship marketing*, Chicago: Irwin, 1995.

[35]Lee Gomes, 'Computer-printer price drop isn't starving makers', *Wall Street Journal*, 16 August 1996.

[36]'Loyal, my brand, to thee', *Promo,* 1 October 1997; Arthur Middleton Hughes, 'How Safeway built loyalty: especially among second-tier customers', *Target Marketing*, 1 March 1999; Laura Bly, 'Frequent fliers fuel a global currency', *USA Today*, 27 April 2001.

[37]www.aa.com

[38]Christina Binkley, 'Hotels raise the ante in business-travel game', *Wall Street Journal,* 2 February 1999: B1.

[39]James L. Heskett, W. Earl Sasser Jr and Leonard A. Schlesinger, *The Service Profit Chain*, New York: Simon & Schuster, 1997.

[40]Grahame R. Dowling and Mark Uncles, 'Do customer loyalty programs really work?', *Sloan Management Review*, Summer 1997: 71–82. See also, Steven M. Shugan, 'Brand loyalty programs: are they shams?', *Marketing Science,* spring 2005, 24: 185–93.

[41]Robert C. Blattberg and Kenneth Wisniewski, 'Price-induced patterns of competition', *Marketing Science,* fall 1989, 8: 291–309.

[42]Elliot B. Ross, 'Making money with proactive pricing', *Harvard Business Review*, November–December 1984: 145–55.

[43]Norman Berry, 'Revitalizing brands', *Journal of Consumer Marketing*, 1988, 5 (3): 15–20.

[44]For a more detailed treatment of pricing strategy, see Thomas T. Nagle and Reed K. Holden, *The Strategy and Tactics of Pricing: A guide to profitable decision-making*, 3rd edn, Upper Saddle River, NJ: Prentice Hall, 2002; Kent B. Monroe, *Pricing: Making profitable decisions*, 3rd edn,

New York: McGraw-Hill/Irwin, 2002; and Robert J. Dolan and Hermann Simon, *Power Pricing*, New York: Free Press, 1997.

[45]Yumiko Ono, 'Companies find that consumers continue to resist price boosts', *Wall Street Journal*, 8 March 1994: B8.

[46]Ira Teinowitz, 'Marlboro Friday: still smoking', *Advertising Age*, 28 March 1994: 24.

[47]Lee Hawkins Jr, 'GM to end employee-pricing plan', *Wall Street Journal*, 9 September 2005: A8; Christine Tierney, 'GM extends employee discount', *Detroit News*, 26 August 2005.

[48]Dean Starkman, 'Hefty's plastic zipper bag is rapping rivals', *Wall Street Journal*, 2 February 1999: B1.

[49]Peter Coy, 'The power of smart pricing', *BusinessWeek*, 10 April 2000.

[50]Allan J. Magrath, 'Eight timeless truths about pricing', *Sales & Marketing Management*, October 1989: 78–84.

[51]Thomas J. Malott, chief of Siemens, quoted in Stratford Sherman, 'How to prosper in the value decade', *Fortune*, 30 November 1992: 90–103.

[52]Christopher Power, 'Value marketing', *BusinessWeek*, 11 November 1991: 132–40.

[53]Sandra Jones, 'How Sears came down with seasonal disorder', *Business 2.0*, July 2004: 66–7.

[54]For a discussion of customer value mapping and economic value mapping, see Gerald E. Smith and Thomas T. Nagle, 'Pricing the differential', *Marketing Magazine*, June 2005: 28–32.

[55]Bruce Mohl, 'Downsizing ice cream', *Boston Globe*, 18 April 2004.

[56]Donald Lehmann and Russell Winer, *Product Management*, Burr Ridge, IL: Irwin, 1994.

[57]Amy Cortese, 'Goodbye to fixed pricing?', *BusinessWeek*, 4 May 1998: 71–84.

[58]Adrienne Carter, 'Telling the risky from the reliable', *BusinessWeek*, 1 August 2005: 57–8.

[59]Richard Gibson, 'Broad grocery price cuts may not pay', *Wall Street Journal*, 7 May 1993: B1.

[60]Amy Merrick, 'Retailers try to get leg up on markdowns with new software', *Wall Street Journal*, 7 August 2001: A1, A6.

[61]Zachary Schiller, 'Not everyone loves a supermarket special', *BusinessWeek*, 17 February 1992: 64–6.

[62]Kotler and Keller, *Marketing Management*, 12th edn.

[63]For a more detailed treatment of channel strategy, see Anne T. Coughlan, Erin Anderson, Louis W. Stern and Adel I. El-Ansary, *Marketing Channels*, 6th edn, Upper Saddle River, NJ: Prentice Hall, 2001.

[64]V. Kasturi Rangan, Melvyn A. J. Menezes and E. P. Maier, 'Channel selection for new industrial products: a framework, method and applications', *Journal of Marketing*, July 1992, 56: 69–82.

[65]Rowland T. Moriarty and Ursula Moran, 'Managing hybrid marketing systems', *Harvard Business Review*, 1990, 68: 146–55.

[66]Rick Brooks, 'A deal with target put lid on revival at Tupperware', *Wall Street Journal*, 18 February 2004: A1, A9.

[67]Mya Frazier, 'John Deere cultivates its image', *Advertising Age*, 25 July 2005: 6.

[68]William M. Weilbacher, *Brand Marketing*, Lincolnwood, IL: NTC Business Books, 1993: 53.

[69]Laura Bird and Wendy Bounds, 'Stores' demands squeeze apparel companies', *Wall Street Journal*, 15 July 1997: B1.

[70]Farrell, 'Stuck!'.

[71]For a discussion of CRM issues with multichannel retailers, see Jacquelyn S. Thomas and Ursula Y. Sullivan, 'Managing marketing communications', *Journal of Marketing*, October 2005, 69: 239–51.

[72]Matthew Egol, Karla Martin and Leslie Moeller, 'One size fits all', *Point*, September 2005: 21–4.

[73]Steven M. Shugan, 'Branded variants', *Research in Marketing*, AMA Educators' Proceedings, Series no. 55, Chicago: American Marketing Association, 1989: 33–8.

[74]Shugan cites alarm clocks, answering machines, appliances, baby items, binoculars, dishwashers, luggage, mattresses, microwaves, sports equipment, stereos, televisions, tools and watches as examples.

[75]Mark Bergen, Shantanu Dutta and Steven M. Shugan, 'Branded variants: a retail perspective', *Journal of Marketing Research*, February 1995: 9.

[76]George E. Belch and Michael A. Belch, *Introduction to Advertising and Promotion*, Chicago: Irwin, 1995.

[77]Raju Narisetti, 'Joint marketing with retailers' spreads', *Wall Street Journal*, 24 October 1996.

[78]Bill Richards, 'Levi Strauss plans to open 200 stores in 5 years, with ending of FTC ban', *Wall Street Journal*, 22 December 1994: A2.

[79]Mary Kuntz, 'These ads have windows and walls', *BusinessWeek*, 27 February 1995: 74.

[80]Elaine Underwood, 'Store brands', *Brandweek*, 9 January 1995: 22–7.

[81]'Clicks, bricks and bargains', *The Economist*, 3 December 2005: 57–8.

[82]'The real internet revolution', *The Economist*, 21 August 1999: 53–4.

[83]Don Peppers and Martha Rogers, 'The "store" is everywhere', *Business 2.0*, 6 February 2001: 72.

[84]Lorrie Grant, 'Retailers private label brands see sales growth boom', *USAToday*, 15 April 2004.

[85]George Anderson, 'Private labels: the global view', 28 September 2005, www.retailwire.com

[86]Ibid.

[87]Chip Walker, 'What's in a name', *American Demographics*, February 1991: 54.

[88]'Battle of the brands', *Consumer Reports*, August 2005: 12–15.

[89]Irwin Speizer, 'The grocery store that shouldn't be', *Fast Company*, February 2004: 31.

[90]Mary L. Shelman and Ray A. Goldberg, 'Loblaw companies limited', Case 9–588–039, Boston, MA: Harvard Business School, 1994; Gordon H. G. McDougall and Douglas Snetsinger, 'Loblaws', in *Marketing Challenges,* 3rd edn, eds. Christopher H. Lovelock and Charles B. Weinberg, New York: McGraw-Hill, 1993: 169–85; 'President's choice continues brisk pace', *Frozen Food Age*, March 1998.

[91]Jack Neff, 'Marketers put down foot on private-label issue', *Advertising Age*, 4 April 2005: 14.

[92]'Battle of the brands'.

[93]Chris Hoyt, 'Kraft's private label lesson', *Reveries*, February 2004.

Integrating marketing communications to build brand equity

Chapter 5 described how marketing activities and product, price and distribution strategies can contribute to brand equity. This chapter considers the final and perhaps most flexible element of marketing campaigns. Marketing communications are the means by which firms attempt to inform, persuade and remind consumers – directly or indirectly – about the brands that they sell. In a sense, marketing communications represent the voice of the brand and are a means by which the brand can establish a dialogue and build relationships with consumers. Although advertising is often central to a marketing communications campaign, it is usually not the only element – or even the most important one – for building brand equity. Figure 6.1 displays some of the commonly used marketing communication options for the consumer market.

Although communication options can play various roles in the marketing campaign, one important purpose of all marketing communications is to contribute to brand equity. According to the customer-based brand equity model, marketing communications can contribute to brand equity by creating awareness of the brand; linking points of parity and points of difference associations to the brand in consumers' memory; eliciting positive brand judgements or feelings; and facilitating a stronger consumer–brand connection and brand resonance. In addition to forming the desired brand knowledge structures, marketing communications can provide incentives that elicit the differential response that makes up customer-based brand equity.

The flexibility of marketing communications lies in part with the number of different ways that they can contribute to brand equity. At the same time, brand equity provides a focus for how different marketing communication options can best be designed and implemented. Accordingly, this chapter considers how to develop marketing communication campaigns to build brand equity. The assumption is that the other elements of the marketing campaign have been put into place. Thus, the optimal brand positioning has been defined – especially in terms of the desired target market – and product, pricing and distribution decisions have been made.

The chapter begins by describing the realities of marketing communications and the changing media landscape. To provide necessary background, the main communication options are evaluated in terms of their role in contributing to brand equity and some of their main costs and benefits. The chapter concludes by considering how to employ communication options in a co-ordinated way to build brand equity. For the sake of brevity, this chapter will not consider issues such as media scheduling, budget estimation techniques and research approaches.[1]

Media advertising	**Trade promotions**
TV	Trade deals and buying allowances
Radio	Point-of-sale display allowances
Newspaper	Push money
Magazines	Contests and dealer incentives
Direct response advertising	Training programmes
Mail	Trade shows
Telephone	Co-operative advertising
Broadcast media	**Consumer promotions**
Print media	Samples
Computer-related	Coupons
Media-related	Premiums
Online advertising	Refunds and rebates
Websites	Contests and sweepstakes
Interactive	Bonus packs
	Price-offs
Place advertising	**Event marketing and sponsorship**
Billboards and posters	Sports
Cinema, airlines and lounges	Arts
Product placement	Entertainment
Point of sale	Fairs and festivals
Point-of-sale advertising	Cause-related
Shelftalkers	**Publicity and public relations**
Aisle markers	**Personal selling**
Shopping trolleys	
In-store radio or TV	

Figure 6.1   Marketing communications options

NEW MEDIA

The media environment has been changing dramatically. Traditional media such as TV, radio, magazines and newspapers seem to be losing their grip on consumers. After the dotcom crash and subsequent hangover early in the past decade marketers returned to the web with a vengance, pouring €12.3 billion into internet advertising in 2005.[2] While web advertising jumped 20 percent during this time, spending for TV ads remained flat.

The prognosis for TV advertising is not necessarily good. With more cable companies building hard-drive digital video recorders (DVRs) into digital set boxes, household penetration is rapidly growing, estimated to be in one-third of US households and one fifth of European households by 2008.[3] One survey found that almost three-quarters of users of DVRs frequently or always skip ads when watching recorded programmes. Fragmentation from the proliferation of satellite and cable channels has exacerbated the problem.

Although media rates have continued to climb, viewership and readership for some demographics such as teenagers continue to slide. The results of a Forrester Research survey of online 12- to 17-year-olds revealed that 94 percent owned a game console, two-thirds considered themselves active gamers, and more than half of males said they would rather play video games than watch TV.

Paid search services from Yahoo! and Google have become a €2 billion industry. Consumers are creating and sharing content online as consumer communities and blogs have emerged. Some 72 percent of teens exchange instant messages each day. Mobile phones are becoming a critical device for more than phone conversations.

This media landscape has forced marketers to re-evaluate how they should best communicate with consumers. As a result, the strategies behind marketing communication campaigns have been changing dramatically. Consider how Agent Provocateur has combined different communication channels to form an integrated whole (Brand Briefing 6.1).

Brand Briefing 6.1

Agent Provocateur

The first Agent Provocateur shop was opened in 1994 by Joseph Corré and Serena Rees on Broadwick Street in Soho, London. From the start, the idea was to represent more than an undergarment for women, to make a statement; a protest against a societal reflex that treated issues of sexuality and sex as tasteless and cheap. Corré and Rees wanted to design lingerie that would confirm sexy, desirable and 'erotic' as normal, sophisticated characteristics of a woman's lifestyle. As Corré and Rees said: 'A woman wearing a scrumptious pair of turquoise tulle knickers promotes in herself a sexy superhero feeling which exudes itself as a confident and positive sexuality.'

To persuade customers and consumers of its point of view, Agent Provocateur uses both mass market and relationship-building media channels to reach target groups where they are most susceptible to the racy messages. To 'liberate' women (and the men who have difficulty purchasing such items for their partners) and incite them to purchase a pair of the pricey knickers, Agent Provocateur uses high-tech experience marketing with brand entertainment to get customers in the mood.

Although the brand attracts tremendous numbers of visitors to its website (Figure 6.2), it has little effect on the success of the shops in chic streets in cities such as London, Paris, Milan and New York. In fact, the boutiques and the exclusive locations are as intricate a part of the brand's image and the promise of sophisticated, upmarket value. An absence of boutiques and mass communication would conflict with the message that lingerie and the sexuality of a woman should not be hidden out of sight and confined to the internet or mail-order catalogues. The boutique is a clear communications channel that consistently depicts the brand's essence as an all-encompassing experience of exclusive lingerie, innuendo, confident sexuality and, of course, a touch of eroticism. The website, 'viral' marketing campaigns and three-dimensional mail-order catalogues are seen as channels for extended relationships with their customers after they have left the boutique or if they are out of reach altogether.

Brand Briefing 6.1 *continued*

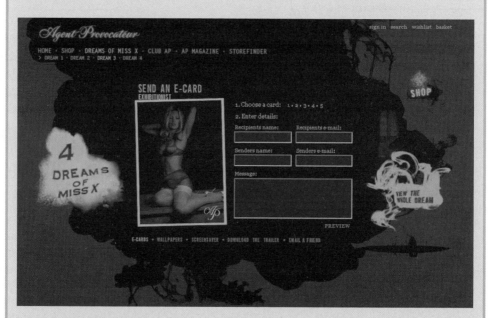

Figure 6.2   Agent Provocateur website

Agent Provocateur is also a brand that entertains its customers and consumers alike. In 1999, it launched a website featuring its lingerie worn by models in provocative poses throughout the pages of the site. It was a huge success and reached 43 million hits per month. The Agent Provocateur website serves as a virtual boutique for the well-seasoned customer and as an 'inspirational' source for the new buyer of erotic lingerie and accessories including perfume, literature, toys and films. The website is intended to emulate the boutique experience (with the virtual store assistant dressed in a short pink dress) but, at the same time, provide the customer with entertainment that will lock them to the site for a longer period of time. In December 2001, Kylie Minogue took to the virtual stage on behalf of Agent Provocateur in the erotic commercial 'Proof' in which 360 million viewers crowded cyberspace to take a peek. The company continued to launch short films and video clips in 2005 with a viral marketing campaign that included the collection called 'Exhibitionist'. In 2006 Mike Figgis, the film director, was commissioned to direct short films starring the model Kate Moss. 'The dreams of Miss X' was shown on the site and its debut generated such a response that the server crashed within two hours. The films were also rigged with viral marketing technology that provided the customer with an opportunity to interact with the video by clicking on an item and be redirected to the online shop. This is a powerful tool for Agent Provocateur in that it serves as a method of measurement in addition to its entertainment value.

Brand Briefing 6.1 *continued*

Corré takes advantage of all campaign activities as opportunities to create and encourage interest and curiosity for the brand. Corré is never shy of the media, and this seems to drive more faithful customers to his shops and sites. Agent Provocateur did well to establish itself as an 'upstart' in high society, as it seems that there is little that can harm the brand's credibility among its customer base.

Sources: www.agentprovocateur.com; www.largedesign.com; www.e-consultancy.com, 'Agent Provocateur releases first interactive viral video using coull.tv', press release, 16 November 2006.

Challenges in designing brand-building communications

The new media environment has complicated marketers' challenge to build effective and efficient marketing communication campaigns. Skillfully designed and implemented marketing communications require careful planning and a creative knack. Towards that goal, it is helpful to consider a few tools to provide some perspective.

Perhaps the simplest – but most useful way – to judge advertising or any other communication option is by its ability to achieve the desired brand knowledge structures and elicit the differential response that makes up brand equity. For example, how well does a proposed ad campaign contribute to awareness or to creating, maintaining or strengthening certain brand associations? Does sponsorship cause consumers to have more favourable brand judgements and feelings? To what extent does a promotion encourage consumers to buy more of a product? At what price premium? Along these lines, Figure 6.3 displays a simple three-step model for judging the effectiveness of advertising or any communication option to build brand equity.

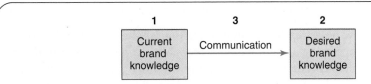

1. What is your current brand knowledge? Have you created a detailed mental map?
2. What is your desired brand knowledge? Have you defined optimal points of parity and points of difference and a brand mantra?
3. How does the communication option help the brand get from current to desired knowledge with consumers? Have you clarified the specific effects on knowledge engendered by communications?

Figure 6.3   Sample text for marketing communication effectiveness

Information processing model of communications

To provide perspective, it is helpful to consider in more depth the process by which marketing communications might affect consumers. Several models have been put forward to explain communications and the steps involved in the persuasion process – recall the discussion on the hierarchy of effects model from Brand Briefing 2.5 in Chapter 2. For example, for a person to be persuaded by any form of communication (a TV advertisement, newspaper editorial, classroom lecture, etc.), six steps must occur.[4]

1. *Exposure:* a person must see or hear the communication.
2. *Attention:* a person must notice the communication.
3. *Comprehension:* a person must understand the intended message or arguments of the communication.
4. *Yielding:* a person must respond favourably to the intended message or arguments of the communication.
5. *Intentions:* a person must plan to act in the desired manner of the communication.
6. *Behaviour:* a person must act in the desired manner of the communication.

The difficulty of creating a successful marketing communication campaign can be seen by recognizing that each of the six steps must occur for a consumer to be persuaded. If there is a breakdown or failure in any step, then communication will not result. For example, consider the potential pitfalls in launching a new advertising campaign.

- A consumer may not be exposed to an ad because the media plan missed the mark.
- A consumer may not notice an ad because of a boring and uninspired creative strategy.
- A consumer may not understand an ad because of a lack of product category knowledge or technical sophistication or because of a lack of awareness and familiarity about the brand itself.
- A consumer may fail to respond favourably and form a positive attitude because of irrelevant or unconvincing product claims.
- A consumer may fail to form a purchase intention because of a lack of an immediate perceived need.
- A consumer may fail to buy the product because of a failure to remember anything from the ad when confronted with the available brands in a shop.

To show how fragile the process is, assume there is a one in two chance of *each* of the six steps being accomplished – probably a generous assumption. The probability of all six steps occurring, assuming they are independent events, would be:

$$0.5 \times 0.5 \times 0.5 \times 0.5 \times 0.5 \times 0.5 = 1.5625 \text{ percent}$$

If the chance of each step occurring, on average, was one in ten, then the probability of all six events occurring would be 0.000001. In other words, only one in a million! No wonder advertisers sometimes lament the limited power of advertising.

One implication of the information processing model is that, to increase the odds of a successful campaign, marketers must attempt to increase the likelihood that *each* step occurs. For example, from an advertising standpoint, the ideal ad campaign would ensure the following occurred.

1. The right consumer was exposed to the right message at the right place and at the right time.
2. The creative strategy for the advertising causes the consumer to notice and attend to the ad but does not distract from the intended message.
3. The ad properly reflects the consumer's level of understanding about the product and the brand.
4. The ad correctly positions the brand in terms of desirable and deliverable points of difference and points of parity.
5. The ad motivates consumers to consider purchase of the brand.
6. The ad creates strong brand associations with all of these stored communication effects so that they can have an effect when consumers are considering making a purchase.

Clearly, marketing communication campaigns must be designed and executed carefully if they are to have the desired effects.

Role of many communications

In making the decision as to how much and what kinds of marketing communications are necessary, economic theory would suggest spending on a budget and across options according to marginal revenue and cost. For example, the communication mix would be optimally distributed so that the last penny spent on each communication option generated the same return. Because such information may be difficult to obtain, however, other models of budget allocation emphasize more observable factors such as stage of brand lifecycle, objectives and budget of the firm, product characteristics, size of budget and media strategy of competitors. These factors are typically contrasted with the different characteristics of the media.

For example, marketing communication budgets tend to be higher when there is low channel support, much change in the marketing campaign over time, many hard-to-reach customers, more complex customer decision-making, differentiated products and non-homogeneous customer needs and frequent product purchases in small quantities.[5] Personal selling tends to become a more dominant element when the brand has a high unit value, is technical in nature, requires demonstration, must be tailored to the specific needs of customers and is purchased infrequently or involves a trade-in; when the firm has a limited communications budget; and when customers are easily identified.[6]

Besides such efficiency considerations, communication options also may be chosen to reach specific market segments. For example, advertising may attempt to bring customers into the market or attract a competitor's customers to the brand, whereas promotions may attempt to reward loyal users of the brand or vice versa.

Invariably, marketers will employ many methods to achieve their goals. In doing so, they must understand how each communication option works; and understand how to assemble and integrate the best set of communications. The following section presents an overview and critique of the options from a brand-building perspective: broadcast, print, direct response, online and place advertising media; consumer and trade promotions; event marketing and sponsorship; publicity and public relations; and personal selling. Later, the chapter, will consider how these options should best be combined.

OVERVIEW OF MARKETING COMMUNICATION OPTIONS

Advertising

Advertising can be defined as any paid form of non-personal presentation and promotion of ideas, goods or services by an identified sponsor. Advertising plays an important and often controversial role in contributing to brand equity. Although advertising is a powerful means of creating strong, favourable and unique brand associations and eliciting positive judgements and feelings, it is controversial because its specific effects are difficult to quantify and predict. Nevertheless, studies have shown the potential power of advertising to affect brand sales.

For example, the American Association of Advertising Agencies has compiled a list of some of the studies demonstrating the productivity of advertising expenditures. Analyses of advertising effects using the Profit Impact of Marketing Strategy (PIMS) database of 750 consumer businesses in a variety of industries showed that firms which increased advertising during a recessionary period gained one-half to a full market share point coming out of a recession, whereas those firms who cut their advertising budget only gained two-tenths of a share point.[7]

Other studies also document the power of advertising. For example, an analysis of the effects of advertising on sales using Nielsen's single-source database of 142 packaged goods brands from 1991 to 1992 revealed that around half of the time, advertising worked. Specifically, 70 percent of the ad campaigns in the sample boosted sales immediately, although the effect was only strong in 30 percent of the cases. Forty-six percent of campaigns appeared to yield a long-term sales boost. Additional analyses revealed other interesting findings.[8]

- Increased sales could come from a single advertisement.
- 'Blitz campaigns' with concentrated exposure schedules could suffer from diminished returns, such that ads shown less frequently over a longer period of time were more effective.
- Advertising was more likely to increase both sales and profits than 'money-off' sales promotions, which almost always lost money.

Another comprehensive study of effectiveness conducted by a research supplier, Information Resources, using a different database reinforces these findings and provides additional observations as to how advertising, as well as promotion, works (Brand Briefing 6.2).[9] Finally, one meta-analysis found that advertising effectiveness had remained stable throughout the years, although it was more pronounced for new products.[10]

Brand Briefing 6.2

Understanding the effects of advertising

Information Resources Inc. (IRI) examines how advertising works. The company uses a single-source testing service, BehaviorScan, which tracks behaviour of individual households from TV sets to tills in supermarkets in test markets across the USA. Consumers who join IRI's Shoppers Hotline panel agree to have computers record when the TV set is on and to which station it is tuned; to have scanners record product codes of their purchases at supermarkets; and to use a hand-held scanner at home to record purchases at other retailers. IRI can send different commercials to different preselected homes to test the effects of advertising copy and weights. BehaviorScan can also test the effects of store features, displays, coupons and so forth.

In 1989, IRI reviewed the results of 389 research studies over 7 years and offered the following principles concerning advertising and promotion effectiveness.

- TV advertising weight alone is not enough. Only roughly half of heavy TV advertising plans have a measurable effect on sales, although when they do have an effect it is often large. The success rate is higher for new products or line extensions than for established brands.

- TV advertising is more likely to work when there are changes in copy or media strategy. Examples are a new copy strategy or an expanded target market.

- When advertising is successful in increasing sales, its effect lasts beyond the period of peak spending. Recent evidence shows that the long-term positive effects of advertising last up to two years after peak spending. Moreover, the long-term incremental sales generated are about double the incremental sales observed in the first year of an advertising spending increase.

- About 20 percent of advertising plans pay out in the short term. However, when the long-term effect of advertising is considered, it is likely that most advertising plans that show a significant effect in a split cable experiment would pay out.

- Promotions almost always have a measurable effect on sales. However, the effect is usually short term.

- Payout statistics on promotions are dismal. Roughly 16 percent of trade promotions are profitable. Furthermore, promotions' effects are often purely short term, except for new products.

- These statistics on advertising and promotion payouts show that many brands are overspending on marketing support. Many classes of spending can be reduced at an increase in profits.

- Allocating marketing funds involves a continuous search for marketing campaigns that offer the highest return on marketing revenue. Tradeoffs between advertising, trade promotions and consumer promotions can be highly profitable when based on reliable evaluation systems that measure this productivity.

Brand Briefing 6.2 *continued*

● The trend towards promotion spending is not sound from a marketing productivity standpoint. When the strategic disadvantages of promotions are included (that is, losing control to the trade and training consumers to buy only when there's a deal running), then the case is compelling for a re-evaluation of current practices and the incentive systems responsible for this trend.

Sources: Leonard M. Lodish, Magid Abraham, Stuart Kalmenson, Jeanne Livelsberger, Beth Lubetkin, Bruce Richardson and Mary Ellen Stevens, 'How TV advertising works: a meta analysis of 389 real world split cable TV advertising experiments', *Journal of Marketing Research*, May 1995: 125–239; Magid Abraham and Leonard Lodish, 'Advertising works', Information Resources Inc., 1989.

Besides these broad-based empirical studies, numerous case studies point to the power of advertising, even during difficult economic times. For example, during the summer of 2001, Home Depot in the USA found its sales surging 16 percent in the face of a sluggish economy when they invested in a heavy product push with advertising featuring paint, appliances and energy-savers such as thermostats.[11] Coca-Cola, Red Lobster, Heinz and Gillette also chose to step up their ad spending during this time and similarly experienced sales increases. These experiences echoed those of other brands that had chosen to invest in advertising during an economic recession or downturn. For example, during the 1989–1991 recession, brands such as Jif peanut butter, Bud Light beer and L'Oréal all increased US advertising expenditures and thus their market share as a result.

Given the complexity of designing advertising – the number of strategic roles it might play, the number of specific decisions involved and its complicated effect on consumers – detailed guidelines are difficult to provide. Different media have different strengths, however, and therefore are best suited to play certain roles in a campaign. Beyond that, advertising media is not the same from country to country and this is also reflected in costs. Figure 6.4 provides a breakdown of advertising costs by media in European markets, and Figure 6.5 summarizes the advantages and disadvantages of the main media. This section highlights some issues for each medium.

Television

Television is powerful medium because it allows for sight, sound and motion and reaches a broad spectrum of consumers. Virtually all European households have televisions and the average European watches TV for more than 15 hours a week. The wide reach of TV advertising translates to low cost per exposure. From a brand equity perspective, TV advertising has two particularly important strengths. First, on the one hand, it can be an effective means of vividly demonstrating product attributes and persuasively explaining their corresponding consumer benefits. Second, TV advertising can be a compelling means for dramatically portraying user and usage imagery, brand personality and other brand intangibles.

Cost per thousand (in euros) – after deduction of discounts

	Australia	Austria	Belgium	Czech Republic	Denmark	Finland	France	Germany	Greece	Hong Kong	Hungary	Italy	Japan	Latvia	Netherlands	Norway	Poland	Portugal	Romania	Russia	Slovakia	Slovenia	Spain	Sweden	Switzerland	Taiwan	Turkey	UK	USA
Television	9.9	9.8	13.5	5.6	6.9	7.5	6.9	13.8	4.0	6.9	3.5	3.7	3.4	0.9	6.2	11.3	1.6	2.8	0.5	1.8	2.7	5.3	4.2	8.2	18.2	2.8	1.8	7.0	5.5
Newspapers	8.0	8.4	17.1	4.8	8.0	9.5	26.8	6.9	14.6	1.9	18.0	10.4	5.8	3.8	16.0	8.6	4.0	2.9	2.5	5.1	2.7	13.1	11.2	15.6	33.1	1.7	6.0	4.2	15.7
Magazines	6.5	12.0	7.0	5.1	7.5	5.5	6.2	4.3	11.6	5.1	14.1	2.1	3.0	5.6	13.0	7.4	3.4	4.4	2.8	17.6	8.1	6.7	23.3	6.1	19.7	6.4	n/a	3.8	n/a
Radio	n/a	2.8	8.1	1.3	1.7	1.8	6.1	1.5	0.2	n/a	1.8	1.1	2.1	1.0	1.1	3.2	0.7	0.8	0.3	n/a	1.0	1.5	2.6	2.6	8.9	n/a	n/a	2.0	1.4
Cinema	n/a	44.1	80.9	33.7	37.5	n/a	n/a	60.1	n/a	n/a	n/a	n/a	n/a	n/a	56.3	n/a	50.1	n/a	n/a	n/a	n/a	n/a	n/a	36.7	77.7	n/a	n/a	39.9	n/a

n/a means data is not available.

Important note: This comparison is very rough and is only meant to give a feel for the different cost levels for each medium and country. Media prices vary with the purchasing power of the audience, but also in relation to how much advertising is available in the given medium, the demographics and usage habits of the audience of the media, and many other factors.

It is worth noting the differences between some countries, such as the notoriously expensive TV in Germany or the low price of TV against magazines in Spain. In considering media strategy and integrated communications, one must not only think of the media characteristics but also national differences in cost and usage to make effective campaigns.

Figure 6.4 Cost of media in different countries

Source: OMD

Medium	Advantages	Disadvantages
Television	Mass coverage. High reach. Impact of sight, sound and motion. High prestige. Low cost per exposure. Attention-getting. Favourable image.	Low selectivity. Short message life. High absolute cost. High production costs. Clutter.
Radio	Local coverage. Low cost. High frequency. Flexible. Low production costs. Well-segmented audiences.	Audio-only. Clutter. Low attention-getting capabilities. Fleeting message.
Magazines	Segmentation potential. Quality reproduction. High information content. Longevity. Many readers.	Long lead time for placement. Visual only. Lack of flexibility.
Newspapers	Wide coverage. Low cost. Short lead time for placing ads. Ads can be placed in interest sections. Timely (current ads). Reader controls exposure. Can be used for coupons.	Short life. Clutter. Low attention-getting capabilities. Poor reproduction quality. Selective reader exposure.
Direct response	High selectivity. Reader controls exposure. High information content. Opportunities for repeat exposure.	High cost per contact. Poor image (junk mail). Clutter.
Interactive	Customized and personalized. In-depth information. Can be engaging.	Unobtrusive. Often lacks emotionality.
Outdoor	Location-specific. High repetition. Easily noticed.	Short exposure time requires short ad. Poor image. Local restrictions.

Figure 6.5   Advertising media characteristics

Source: Reprinted from George E. Belch and Michael A. Belch, *Introduction to Advertising and Promotion*, 3rd edn, Homewood, IL: Irwin, 1995.

On the other hand, television advertising has its drawbacks. Because of the fleeting nature of the message and the potentially distracting creative elements often found in a TV ad, product-related messages and the brand itself can be overlooked by viewers. Moreover, the large number of ads and non-programming material creates clutter that makes it easy for consumers to ignore or forget ads. A large number of channels creates fragmentation and digital video recorders give viewers a way to avoid commercials (see Brand Briefing 6.3). Another disadvantage of TV ads is the

Brand Briefing 6.3

Have it your way in the DVR market

Digital video recorders came into widespread use when TiVo was launched in 1999 in the USA (Sky Plus is the equivalent in the UK). The company branded the gadget as a way for customers to get the television shows they wanted, when they wanted, without commercials. TiVo users buy the TiVo box and then pay €8.86 a month for a device to record and store programming. Sports fans can, for instance, stop a game and replay the action. The invention has attracted a loyal base of fans who say TiVo has altered more than their viewing habits – it has changed the way they think about television.

New technology historically has been tough to brand. TiVo succeeded in creating a niche for something new, reaching one of the ultimate benchmarks of cultural acceptance – it became a verb! To 'TiVo' something in the USA now extends to all DVRs. TiVo was the one to set expectations for the DVR category but the company has begun losing ground to competitors as other brands move in and improve on the concept, and in other countries TiVo did not get the first mover advantage it enjoyed in the USA, letting Thomson, Humax and others enter other markets (although interestingly no competitor seems to have managed to establish a brand like TiVo did in the USA).

TiVo announced in late 2004 that it would allow advertisers to put logos over their ads so the logos would be visible when viewers fast-forwarded through the ads. This tactic, some industry watchers say, contradicted TiVo's 'TV your way' philosophy. In 2005, TiVo had to deal with the departures of the company's chief executive and president, rumours of an Apple takeover and the demise of an exclusive deal with DirecTV.

After these setbacks, though, TiVo finalised a seven-year deal with Comcast that allowed the cable operator to use TiVo technology for its cable boxes. Comcast made the deal in part to capitalize on the TiVo name and its popularity with customers. Beginning in 2006, Comcast planned to offer traditional cable boxes with TiVo inside, a move that could help the cable company retain customers. The Comcast deal let TiVo move towards being more of a software component instead of a stand-alone box and allow it to spend less on its own advertising and instead dedicate resources to improving its product.

Cable companies recognize that DVRs are gaining traction. DVR service penetration will increase to 20 percent of western European digital TV homes by 2008, says Yankee Group. Forrester Research reports that DVR penetration in the USA will be even higher and reach nearly 50 percent in 2009. And if cable customers automatically get DVRs, penetration will continue to grow quickly. Consumer electronics companies and cable operators such as Sony, Samsung, LG, Panasonic, DirecTV, EchoStar, Time Warner, Cox Communications and Gemstar are jostling for position in the DVR market.

The advent of DVRs could also transform the way TV viewing data is collected. Nielsen ratings do not include households with DVRs. The growth of DVRs in homes

Brand Briefing 6.3 *continued*

makes it necessary to include them in the data or else a significant chunk of viewers will be missing from the data. But the expense of creating a measurement system that takes DVR technology into account is a deterrent.

To adapt to DVR technology, advertisers have had to come up with new formats that work with DVRs. Some advertisers have created mini-programmes, similar to cinema trailers, and other long-form advertisements that viewers can access on DVRs. Several companies offer technology to help satellite and cable operators target viewers with customized ads. Companies such as Honda and Miramax Films have already used interactive commercials that use DVD-like menus to give viewers options.

The challenge is that advertisers don't know how many people will go into the interactive ads and how far into the ad they will venture. But experimentation with interactive ads is growing and some view them as a potential venue for educational programming. One problem the ads present is that they take a long time to produce. Ultimately, executives are hoping interactive ads will be more appealing than traditional ads because viewers control them and decide when they want to watch them.

Sources: Megan Larson, 'Fast forward', *Adweek*, 4 April 2005; Allen P. Adamson, 'I love you, TiVo, now change', *Advertising Age*, 17 January 2005; Tony Case, 'Sizing up PVRs', *Brandweek*, 20 September 2004; Diane Anderson, 'Second act', *Adweek*, 4 April 2005.

high cost of production and placement, although prices vary considerably from country to country. Another problem is that the price of TV advertising has increased considerably while the proflieration of media has made the share of the prime time audience smaller. It seems to be ever harder, and more expensive, for TV to attract large and diverse audiences to single programmes.

Nevertheless, properly designed and executed TV ads can increase sales and profits. For example, over the years, one of the most consistently successful US advertisers has been Apple. Its '1984' ad for the introduction of the Macintosh computer – portraying a stark Orwellian future with a feature film look – only ran once on TV but is one of the best-known ads in the USA. In the years that followed, Apple advertising created awareness and image for a series of products, more recently with its silhouettes iPod campaign. Each year, the American Marketing Association awards 'Effies' to those brands whose advertising campaigns have had a demonstrable benefit for sales and profits. Brand Briefing 6.5 discusses now Apple won its award for an iPod campaign.

By any number of measures, the effectiveness of any one ad, on average, has diminished. For example, Video Storyboards noted that the number of viewers who reported that they paid attention to TV ads dropped significantly in the

Brand Briefing 6.4

Changing media consumption habits in Europe (2006)

A pan-European study in 2006 by the European Interactive Advertising Association (EIAA), showed some interesting facts about online habits.

- Social networking websites were used by nearly a quarter of Europeans, at least once a month.
- Europeans were spending on average over 11 hours a week online.
- Broadband penetration was up 14 percent across Europe year on year.
- About 70 percent of Europeans spent the majority of their time online for personal reasons rather than for work.
- Consumer confidence towards the internet was high with nearly half of Europeans choosing the internet as their preferred media to find what they wanted quickly.
- Europeans spent 28 percent more time on the internet in 2006 than they did in 2004.
- This extra time is not taken from other media. Radio and magazine media consumption also increased from 2004 to 2006, by 14 percent and 11 percent, respectively.

Source: EIAA Mediascope Europe Study 2006, June 2007, www.eiaa.net

Brand Briefing 6.5

iPod silhouettes campaign captures music lovers

Apple and its ad agency, TBWA/Chiat/Day Los Angeles won a Grand Effie in June 2005 for the iPod silhouettes advertising campaign and, at the European Effie awards they got a Gold Award in the IT and telecoms category and a gold award for brand integration. The Effie awards are given in recognition of the year's most effective advertising campaigns.

Apple began selling the iPod MP3 player in 2001. The device was a hit with celebrities and technical writers but many consumers were under the impression it was a sophisticated device for tech fans, rather than the average music lover. The ad agency and Apple set a goal to 'Create a campaign that extended iPod's relevance to more music lovers and told the world this wasn't just a tech gadget available to few, but was the icon that stood for a new experience with music.'

The marketing effort was designed to appeal to Mac fans as well as people who had not used Apple products in the past. The campaign ran all over the world, so the

Brand Briefing 6.5 *continued*

message had to be simple enough to work across cultures. The ads also had to portray the iPod as cool, but not so cool as to be beyond the reach of anyone who enjoyed music.

Apple wanted to establish the iPod as a universal icon of digital music. The company set a goal of increasing sales by half in the USA and a quarter in other markets. The idea behind the campaign was that the iPod was a passport to enjoying music whenever and wherever a consumer wanted. Text within the ads such as 'iPod. Welcome to the digital music revolution. 10,000 songs in your pocket. Mac or PC' told of iPod's capabilities in a simple, appealing way. And the concept of 10,000 songs was designed to appeal to consumers in markets like Japan, where other mini-disc players with less capacity crowded the market.

The top markets for digital music were picked based on their role as influencers for youth culture in their regions. Apple's campaign ran in a handful of big cities such as San Francisco and Shanghai and used them as the focus for all media spending in that market. Those cities were flooded with iPod hoardings, bus posters, print ads and TV commercials that were intended to spread the message 'iPod is everywhere.'

The television commercials featured people in silhouette listening to iPods and dancing in front of neon backgrounds. Songs in the ads included U2's 'Vertigo' and Eminem's 'Lose Yourself'. Similar images of people dancing were used for the print ads, hoardings and posters.

Three months after the start of the silhouettes campaign, iPod sales were up half over sales from the quarter before the campaign launched. In the USA, the iPod grabbed the biggest market share of all MP3 players. Duke University began giving iPods to all new students and school districts started experimenting with the devices as tools for teaching language skills. The campaign ran in 16 countries.

Sources: Jay Parsons, 'A is for Apple on iPod', *Dallas Morning News*, 6 October 2005; www.apple.com; www.effie.org, 'Apple computer: iPod silhouettes', New York Marketing Association 2008.

last decade. As a result, some marketers are rethinking their media plans. Consider how Sony Ericsson approached the US launch of its T68i camera phone in Brand Briefing 6.6.

In designing and evaluating an ad campaign, it is important to distinguish the *message strategy* or positioning of an ad (ie, what the ad attempts to convey about the brand) from its *creative strategy* (ie, how the ad expresses the brand claims). Designing effective advertising campaigns is both an art and a science: The artistic aspects relate to the creative strategy of the ad and its executional information; the scientific aspects relate to the message strategy of the ad and the brand claim information it

Brand Briefing 6.6

Sony Ericsson and the US T68i launch

In 2002, Sony Ericsson was about to launch its first Sony Ericsson-branded global product, the T68i phone. The US market posed a special challenge. The phone had many features that were new to the US market – a colour screen and a snap-on camera, as well as Bluetooth-enabled games. While it is always advantageous to have a strong product with new features, it was also a challenge to put across because understanding of these features was so low. (In other words, the campaign needed to secure responses from awareness to comprehension to intention and behaviour in one campaign – a difficult task given the information processing model shown earlier.) So seen in this way, the campaign budget was very limited in relation to its objectives. How could the campaign hope to communicate so much in a short time?

The solution was to take the product all the way to the potential customers and make people talk about it. At a reported cost of €3.42 million, Sony Ericsson hired actors to circulate, incognito, in tourist spots and bars where they would make casual conversation with people while conspicuously displaying the T68i. The actor might then ask someone to use the camera to snap his or her picture. Unless asked, the actors did not reveal they were working for Sony Ericsson.

A second element of the campaign involved the use of 'leaners' – 60 actresses and female models with extensive training in the phone's features who frequented trendy lounges and bars without telling the establishments what they were doing. One scenario was to have the actress' phone ring and the caller's picture pop up on the screen (a new feature at that time). In another scenario, two women sat at opposite ends of the bar playing an interactive version of the Battleship game on their phones.

A third part of the campaign featured 'Phone Finds', which were dummy phones left at various places around cities so that consumers could accidentally find them. The screen on the phone directed the finders to a website, where they could enter a contest to win a free phone.

The approach was the brainchild of John Maron, Sony Ericsson's US marketing director. 'That was an easy way to create a very non-invasive interesting conversation with somebody without the pressure of it feeling, like, this is a pitch,' says Maron. 'In a sense, it was for the people to just fit into the area in which they were.'

The campaign resulted in heavy media coverage, both because of the product it featured and the novel marketing techniques used. The campaign far exceeded its expectations and was a good start for the brand in the USA.

Sources: Suzanne Vranica, 'Sony Ericsson campaign uses actors to push camera-phone in real life', www.wsj.com, 31 July 2002; Scott Goodson, 'If marketing starred Bravehart', www.reveries.com, 4 September 2005; CBS News, 'Undercover marketing uncovered: hidden cameras capture salespeople secretly pitching products', 25 July 2004, www.cbsnews.com; Eric Mayne 'Ford puts focus on Fusion', Detroit News, 3 July 2005.

Define positioning to establish brand equity

Competitive frame of reference

- Nature of competition.
- Target market.

Point of parity attributes or benefits

- Necessary.
- Competitive.

Point of difference attributes or benefits

- Desirable.
- Deliverable.

Identify creative strategy to communicate positioning concept

Informational (benefit elaboration)

- Problem solution.
- Demonstration.
- Product comparison.
- Testimonial (celebrity or unknown consumer).

Transformational (imagery portrayal)

- Typical or aspirational usage situation.
- Typical or aspirational user of product.
- Brand personality and values.

Motivational ('borrowed interest' techniques)

- Humour.
- Warmth.
- Sex appeal.
- Music.
- Fear.
- Special effects.

Figure 6.6   Factors in designing effective advertising campaigns

Source: Based in part on a framework in John R. Rossiter and Larry Percy, *Advertising and Promotion Management*, 2nd edn, New York: McGraw-Hill, 1997.

contains. Thus, as Figure 6.6 describes, the main concerns in devising an advertising strategy are:

- defining the proper positioning to maximize brand equity;
- identifying the best creative strategy to communicate or convey the desired positioning.

Chapter 3 described issues with respect to positioning strategies to maximize brand equity. Creative strategies can be classified as either informational (ie, elaborating on a specific product-related attribute or benefit) or transformational (ie, portraying a specific non-product-related benefit or image).[12] These categories each encompass specific creative approaches. Regardless of which approach is taken, certain motivational or 'borrowed interest' devices are often employed to attract consumers' attention and raise their involvement. These devices include the presence of cute babies, frisky puppies, popular music, well-liked celebrities, amusing situations, provocative sex appeals or fear-inducing threats. Such techniques are thought to be necessary in the tough media environment characterized by low-involvement consumer processing and much competing ad and programming clutter.

Unfortunately, these attention-getting tactics are often *too* effective and distract from the brand or its product claims. Thus, the challenge in arriving at the best creative strategy is figuring out how to break through the clutter to gain the attention of consumers but still be able to deliver the intended message. Consider how Virgin chose to introduce its credit card in Australia.[13]

Virgin Credit Card

When the card was launched in Australia, 80 percent of the market was dominated by four banks and the rest was crowded with 300 other cards. Australians had low expectations with regard to their credit cards. Most cards charged an annual fee of at least €68.4, with interest rates of 16–18 percent, and rewards were taking longer to earn. The campaign for Virgin cards, entitled 'Plastic Surgery', was based on showing the discounts and rewards available with the card and the 12.4 percent rate of interest and lack of annual fee. The ad featured extra costs being snipped off the card. Press advertisements, online banner ads, radio, TV and direct marketing were also used. Within a week of launching the card, Virgin had 50,000 applications and after 17 months it had 400,000 customers, or 4 percent of the market.

What makes an effective TV ad? Fundamentally, a TV ad should contribute to brand equity in a demonstrable way – for example, by enhancing awareness, strengthening a key association or adding a new association or eliciting a positive consumer response. In applying the consumer information processing model, six criteria were identified as affecting the success for advertising: consumer targeting, the ad creative, consumer understanding, brand positioning, consumer motivation and ad memorability.

Although managerial judgement using criteria such as these can and should be employed in evaluating advertising, research also can play a role. Advertising strategy research is often invaluable in clarifying communication objectives, target markets and positioning options. To evaluate the effectiveness of message and creative strategies, *copy testing* is often conducted, in which a sample of consumers is exposed to candidate ads and their reactions are gauged in some manner.

Unfortunately, copy-testing results vary depending on how they are conducted. Consequently, the results of each test must be interpreted as only one possible data point that should be combined with managerial judgement and other information in evaluating the merits of an ad. Copy testing is perhaps most useful when managerial judgement reveals clear positive and negative aspects to an ad and is therefore inconclusive. In this case, copy testing may shed some light on how these various conflicting aspects collectively affect consumer processing.

Regardless, copy-testing results should not be seen as a means of making a 'go' or 'no go' decision; ideally, they should play a diagnostic role in helping to understand *how* an ad works. As an example of the potential fallibility of pretesting, consider the US TV series *Seinfeld*.

Seinfeld

In October 1989, *The Seinfeld Chronicles*, as it was called then, was shown to groups of viewers to gauge the show's potential, like most television pilot projects awaiting network approval. The show tested badly – very badly. The summary research report noted that 'no segment of the audience was eager to watch the show again.' The reaction to Seinfeld himself was 'lukewarm' because his character was seen as 'powerless, dense, and naive'. The test report also concluded that 'none of the supports [was] particularly liked and viewers felt that Jerry needed a better back-up ensemble'. Despite the weak reaction, NBC decided to go ahead with what became one of the most successful shows of the 1990s. Although they later also changed their testing methods, NBC's experience reinforces the limitations of testing and the dangers of relying on single numbers.[14]

Future prospects

In the digital era, the future of television and traditional mass market advertising is uncertain. In 2004, Procter & Gamble executive Jim Stengel gave a sobering status report to the advertising industry.[15] Stengel pointed out that, although new media were now abundant, marketers and agencies were not using or measuring them sufficiently. He noted that 90 percent of P&G's global ad spending was on TV in 1994, but one of its most successful brand launches, for Prilosec in 2003, allocated only about one-quarter of its spending to TV.

Other advertisers warn of eventually bypassing ad agencies via interactive shopping channels, CD-ROM catalogues, multimedia kiosks and online services.[16] Nevertheless, at least for some, the power of TV ads remains. As one advertising executive put it: 'Nothing competes with prime time television when it comes to communicating with a mass audience. Other mediums can't entertain and inform in the same captivating way.'

Radio

Radio is a pervasive medium: 66 percent of people in EU countries listen to radio daily, and in many cases people spend more time with radio than any other medium. Perhaps the main advantage of radio is flexibility – stations are highly targeted, ads are relatively inexpensive to produce and place, and short closings allow for quick responses. For example, radio can be used to target only the places where a brand is sold or to target people in the vicinity of particular shops.

Radio is a particularly effective medium in the morning and can complement or reinforce TV ads. Radio also enables companies to achieve a balance between broad and localized market coverage. Obvious disadvantages are a lack of visual image and the relatively passive nature of consumer processing that results. Several brands, however, have built brand equity using radio.[17]

What makes an effective radio ad?[18] Radio has been less studied than other media. Because of its low involvement nature and limited sensory options, radio advertising often must be focused. For example, the advertising pioneer David Ogilvy believes four factors are critical.[19]

1. Identify your brand early in the commercial.
2. Identify it often.
3. Promise the listener a benefit early in the commercial.
4. Repeat it often.

Nevertheless, radio ads can be extremely creative. The lack of visual images is seen by some as a positive aspect because they feel that the clever use of music, sounds, humour and other creative devices can tap into the listener's imagination in a way to create powerfully relevant and liked images.

Print

Print media offer a stark contrast to broadcast media. Most important, because of their self-paced nature, magazines and newspapers can provide detailed product information. At the same time, the static nature of the visual images in print media makes it difficult to provide dynamic presentations or demonstrations. Another disadvantage of print advertising is that it can be a passive medium.

In general, the two main print media – magazines and newspapers – have many of the same advantages and disadvantages. Magazines are particularly effective at building user and usage imagery. Magazines can also be highly engaging: one study showed that consumers were: more likely to view magazine ads as less intrusive; more truthful and more relevant than other media; and less likely to be doing other tasks.[20] Newspapers, however, are more timely and pervasive. Daily papers are read by roughly three-quarters of the population and tend to be used a lot for local (especially retailer) advertising. However, although advertisers have some flexibility in designing and placing newspaper ads, poor reproduction quality and short shelf-lives can diminish some of the possible impact of newspaper advertising as compared with magazine advertising.

Although print advertising is well suited to communicating product information, it can also effectively communicate user and usage imagery. Brands such as Carlsberg, Absolut and Guess have also created strong non-product associations through print. Some brands attempt to communicate both product benefits and user or usage imagery in their print advertising – for example, carmakers such as Mercedes, Lexus and Volvo or cosmetics makers such as L'Oréal and Revlon.

One of the longest-running print campaigns is for Absolut vodka.

Absolut

In 1980, Absolut was a tiny brand, selling 12,000 cases a year. Research conducted at that time had pointed out a number of liabilities for the brand: the name was seen as gimmicky, the bottle shape was ugly and bartenders found it hard to pour, shelf prominence was limited and there was no credibility for a vodka brand made in Sweden. Michel Roux, president of Carillon (Absolut's importer) and TBWA (Absolut's New York ad agency) decided to use the oddities of the brand – its quirky name and bottle shape – to create brand personality and communicate quality and style in a series of print ads. Each ad visually depicted the product in an unusual way and reinforced the image with a two-word headline using the brand name in a clever play on words. For example, the first ad showed the bottle prominently displayed, crowned by an angel's halo, with the headline 'Absolut Perfection' at the bottom of the page. Follow-up ads explored various themes (eg, seasonal, geographic, celebrity artists) but always attempted to portray a fashionable, sophisticated and contemporary image. By 2001, Absolut had become the leading imported vodka in the USA and the third-largest premium spirits brand in the world.

Guidelines What makes an effective print ad? Although the evaluation criteria noted earlier for television advertising basically apply, print advertising has special requirements and rules. For example, research on ads in magazines reveals that it is not uncommon for two-thirds of the readers to not even notice any particular ad, and for only 10 percent or so of the audience to read much of the copy of any one ad. Many readers only glance at the most visible elements of a print ad, making it critical that an ad communicate clearly, directly and consistently in its illustration and headline.

In judging the effectiveness of a print ad, in addition to considering the communication strategy (eg, target market, communication objectives and message strategy) the following questions should be addressed.

1. Is the message clear at a glance? Can you quickly tell what the advertisement is all about?
2. Is the benefit in the headline?
3. Does the illustration support the headline?
4. Does the first line of the copy support or explain the headline and illustration?
5. Is the ad easy to read and follow?
6. Is the product easily identified?
7. Is the brand or sponsor clearly identified?

Figure 6.7   Print ad evaluation criteria

Source: Philip Ward Burton and Scott C. Purvis, *Which Ad Pulled Best?* 5th edn, Lincolnwood, IL: NTC Business Books, 1987.

Figure 6.7 offers guidelines for print ads that can be summarized in terms of three simple criteria: clarity, consistency and branding.[21]

Direct response

In contrast to advertising in broadcast and print media, which typically communicates to consumers in a non-specific and non-directive manner, *direct response* refers to the use of mail, telephone, internet and other non-personal contact tools to communicate with or solicit a response from specific customers and prospects. Direct response can take many forms and is not restricted to solicitations by mail, telephone or even within traditional broadcast and print media.[22]

One increasingly popular means of direct marketing in the USA is infomercials.[23] An infomercial attempts to combine the 'sell' of commercials with the draw of educational information and entertainment. As such, infomercials can be thought of as a cross between a sales call and a television ad. Infomercials can vary in length but are often 30-minute video programmes that are made at the cost of €171,000 to €342,000. Some individuals have become famous with late night US channel switchers for pitching various wares. Increasingly, companies selling products that are complicated, technologically advanced or require a great deal of explanation are turning to infomercials, such as Callaway Golf, Carnival Cruises, Mercedes, Microsoft, Philips Electronics, Universal Studios and online job search site Monster.com.[24]

Guidelines   Direct marketing has consistently outgrown every media spending category since 1986. This growth is a function of technological advances (eg, the ease of setting up free phone numbers), changes in consumer behaviour (eg, increased need for convenience) and the needs of marketers (eg, the desire to avoid wasteful communications to non-target customers or customer groups). The advantage of direct response is that it facilitates the establishment of relationships with consumers by marketers.

Direct communications through newsletters, catalogues, electronic home pages and so forth allow marketers to explain to consumers developments with their brands over time, as well as allowing consumers to provide feedback to marketers as to their likes and dislikes and specific needs and wants. By learning more about customers, marketers can fine-tune marketing campaigns to offer the right products to the right customers at the right time. In fact, direct marketing is often seen as a key component of relationship marketing – an important marketing trend reviewed in Chapter 5.

As the name suggests, the goal of direct response is to elicit some type of behaviour from consumers; as such, it is easy to measure the effects of direct marketing efforts – people either respond or they do not. The disadvantages to direct response, however, are the intrusiveness and clutter involved. To implement an effective direct marketing campaign, three critical ingredients are:

- developing an up-to-date and informative list of current and potential future customers;
- putting forth the right offer in the right manner; and
- tracking the effectiveness of the marketing campaign.

To improve the effectiveness of direct marketing, marketers are embracing database marketing. Regardless of the particular means of direct marketing, marketers can potentially benefit from database marketing to create campaigns tailored for specific consumers. Marketers collect names and information from consumers regarding their attitudes and behaviour and compile it in a database. Aside from ordering products, names and information can be collected from consumers in a variety of ways – for example, by sending in a coupon, filling out a warranty card or entering a sweepstake.

Database marketing is generally thought to be more effective at helping firms to retain existing customers than to attract new ones. As a rule of thumb, many marketers believe that database marketing makes more sense the higher the price of the product and the more often it is bought. Database marketing pioneers include financial services firms and airlines. Packaged goods companies are also exploring the possible benefits of database marketing. For example, Procter & Gamble set up a database to market its Pampers disposable nappies, allowing it to send out 'individualized' birthday cards for babies and reminder letters to parents to move their child up to the next size.[25] Database management tools will become a priority to marketers as they attempt to track the lifetime value of customers.

Interactive

The end of the twentieth century was the dawn of interactive, online marketing communications. With the growth of the web, marketers scrambled to build a presence in cyberspace. The approaches that companies adopted vary widely. Reviewing all the guidelines for online marketing is beyond the scope of this text.[26] This section concentrates on two crucial online brand-building tools: websites and interactive ads.

Websites The main advantages to marketing on the web are the low cost and the level of detail and degree of customization it offers. By capitalizing on its interactive nature, marketers can construct sites that allow any consumer to choose brand information relevant to his or her needs or desires. As such, interactive marketing can help build relationships. In creating these online information sources for consumers, it is important to deliver timely and reliable information. Websites must be updated frequently and offer as much customized information as possible, especially for existing customers.

Because consumers often go online to seek information rather than be entertained, some of the more successful sites are those that are able to convey expertise in a consumer-relevant area. For example, P&G's Pampers.com and General Mills' Cheerios.com offer baby and parenting advice. Websites can store company and product information, press releases, advertising and promotional information, as well as links to partners and vendors. Many web marketers collect names and addresses for a database and conduct e-mail surveys and online focus groups.

Designing websites requires creating eye-catching pages that can sustain browsers' interest, employing the latest technology and communicating a corporate message. One top designer notes that it is important that users feel as if they have just entered a new, cohesive world, requiring that different pages and content areas within a site have consistent design elements, colours and placement. Design is crucial because, if consumers do not have a good experience, it may be difficult to entice them back.

To spread the word about their websites, advertisers adopt a number of approaches. Marketing on the web will change as its technology changes. Improved audio and video capabilities will allow adverts with more impact and advances in software that ensure secure transactions will encourage online sales. Print and broadcast ads, however, may not translate well into a high-tech media form. The challenge will be to entertain people but still communicate desired information.

Online ads A number of potential advantages exist for web advertising: It is accountable because software can track which ads went to which sales; it is non-disruptive, so it doesn't interrupt consumers; and it can target consumers so that only the most promising prospects are contacted, who could then seek as much or as little information as they desired.[27]

Unfortunately, there are disadvantages. Many consumers find it easy to ignore banner ads. From 1995 to 2001, the click-through rate for banner ads slipped from 40 percent to 0.5 percent. Too many ads were uninspired as advertisers struggled to learn how to use the medium. Efforts to create more attention through pop-up or pop-under ads that generate mini-windows, however, often infuriated consumers.

Increasingly, web ads are becoming closer to traditional advertising, as with streaming web ads. BMW created a series of made-for-the-web film using directors such as Guy Ritchie and actors such as Madonna. Ford and General Motors both created online video games to promote their cars. For example, Ford's game for its Escape small sport utility vehicle allowed players to steer the vehicle through a racecourse on the moon. Users could then e-mail the game to friends and issue a challenge to beat their score. [28]

As a manifestation of permission marketing, e-mail ads in general – often including advanced features such as personalized audio messages, colour photos and streaming video – have increased in popularity. E-mail ads often receive response rates of 20–30 percent at a cost less than that of banner ads. Tracking these response rates, marketers can fine-tune their messages. The key, as with direct advertising, is to create a good customer list. Brand Briefing 6.7 describes the growth of online ads.

Brand Briefing 6.7

More revenue and interest for online ads

Online video ads are providing advertisers with an increasingly appealing avenue for reaching consumers. Some online ads with embedded hyperlinks and pop-up windows now allow customers to interact with images instead of just watching ads. Spending on online advertising is on the rise as the technology improves and more households acquire high-speed connections.

Mitsubishi made a campaign in 2004 that was an early user of online video ads. The carmaker made TV commercials, shown for a limited time but in premium time slots, which closed with a dramatic, ambiguous scene and announced that the ending could be viewed online. The Mitsubishi site received a million visitors, more than 70 percent of whom watched the ad more than once. A significant benefit of such ads is that, because online traffic is easily tracked, companies know how long visitors stay on their site and what they view. The Mitsubishi effort yielded a big spike in sales of the saloon featured.

Innovative campaigns like Mitsubishi's also draw viewers in a valuable demographic: 18- to 34-year-olds. Young adults are spending more and more time on the web, and online ads are being created as interactive entertainment to capture them as they trawl their favourite sites. Access to that demographic is prompting companies to create their own video ads. In 2001, McDonald's spent 80 percent of its advertising budget on prime time television. In 2005, it allocated less than half its ad budget to prime-time. McDonald's shows some of its television ads online and also offers customized videos featuring stars like Beyoncé Knowles.

Video ads are far outpacing other forms of internet advertising and are expected to keep growing. One obstacle to the growth of the ads, though, is that, because many websites are not configured to support video, there is a limited number of slots. Many companies believe that the more time a consumer spends on their site, the better. For American Express, one of the attractions of using the web in this way is that it fosters a sense of community, a feeling that works well for a company promoting the benefits of membership. American Express is experimenting with advertising content in other places as well, gradually shifting its budget to new places, including the reality television series The Restaurant, where it can connect with consumers.

Video advertising is also finding a niche on mobile phones, iPods and BlackBerries. Nestlé Purina PetCare decided to explore this venue in 2005 with sound files that could be downloaded to music players and tips for pet owners with mobile devices. Purina, looking to differentiate itself in the highly competitive pet food business, decided it would be best to reach consumers via the devices they spent the most time with. Efforts like Purina's are becoming more common as digital video recorders allow television viewers to skip commercials.

Sources: Ann M. Mack, 'Buddy movies', Brandweek, 22 November 2004; Matthew Maier, 'What's next', Business 2.0, May 2005; Ronald Grover, 'Mad Ave is starry-eyed over net video', BusinessWeek, 23 May 2005; Mei Fong, 'Don't tell the kids: computer games can make you rich', Wall Street Journal, 21 May 2004; Janet Whitman, 'Even Fido is going wireless', Dow Jones, 29 June 2005.

Mobile marketing[29]

Personal digital assistants and mobile phones are playing an increasingly important role in consumers' lives, and more marketers are taking notice. Because many consumers use the gadgets for information and entertainment as well as communication, investment in mobile marketing from a range of sectors looking to tap a new revenue stream is expected to grow rapidly.

Mobile content owners are expected to concentrate on communicating with their customers, promoting personalization options like logos, ringtones and wallpapers. Broadcast media owners and publishers are looking to build interactivity into programming to establish closer relationships with audiences. Packaged goods, travel, fashion and financial services are interested in mobile marketing as a cost-effective channel for customer communications. And more companies will offer 'infotainment' content services such as news, sports and games.

Mobile phones present a unique opportunity for markets because they can be in consumers' hands at the point of sale or consumption. A US campaign for Hershey's chocolate milk at 15,000 convenience stores featured a sticker on refrigerators instructing the purchaser to text the barcode on the milk container to enter a contest. That interaction, besides promoting the brand, provided data about advertising campaigns and distribution strategies. A marketer can put different short-code keywords into calls to text the various print and electronic media, and then determine which ad medium is most effective in driving consumer awareness and interaction.

Most of these efforts would require consumer permission and opt-in; therefore, they would only be received by subscribers willing to participate. But many consumers will also receive messages from their network operator or handset without opting in. A question therefore is, how can marketers get mobile phone users to opt in? Spam is already a problem for some phone users, however, and network operators may need to initiate controls to assure consumers that they won't be inundated with mobile marketing messages. Experts say the answer lies in quality content, which could range from weather updates to downloadable coupons, and ensuring messages become more sophisticated and appealing as better data formats are adopted.

Vibes Media

Vibes Media creates text message-based marketing campaigns and has developed software that allows marketers to communicate with customers in new ways. The US company has used its live Text-2-Screen and Pix-2-Screen platforms to allow users to submit text and images that go directly to a screen behind a band at a venue. Vibes Media used this technology for a Motorola promotion in Times Square in New York on New Year's Eve and for band Green Day's concert tour. It also runs programmes in bars for clients such as Bud Light, where customers can type text into their phones and the message will be flashed on a big screen. And song requests can be texted to radio stations, letting listeners avoid the busy signal they would usually encounter on the phone.

Several years ago, the idea of mobile marketing was met with fear that marketers would alienate customers with product pitches. But creative messages that pull consumers into dialogue with the brand have evolved into an appealing way to increase brand awareness, especially when it is part of a larger campaign in other media.

Place

The last category of advertising is also often called 'non-traditional', 'alternative' or 'support' advertising because it has arisen as a way to complement more traditional advertising media. *Place advertising*, also called out-of-home advertising, is a broadly defined category that captures advertising outside traditional media. Increasingly, ads and commercials are showing up in unusual spots, sometimes as parts of experiential campaigns. The rationale often given is that, because traditional media – especially television advertising – are seen as becoming less effective, marketers are better off reaching people in other environments, such as where they work, play and, of course, shop. Some of the options available include hoardings; cinema/and airlines; product placement; and point-of-sale advertising.

Billboards and posters In 1925, Burma-Shave placed four hoardings in sequence along roads in the USA with the following slogans:

> Shave the modern way.
> Fine for the skin.
> Druggists have it.
> Burma-Shave.

The success of the campaign convinced marketers that consumers would notice and remember simple messages conveyed in 'unexpected' places. Poster sites now employ colourful, digitally produced graphics, backlighting, sounds, movement and unusual – even three-dimensional – images to attract attention. Also, they do not even necessarily have to stay in one place. Marketers can buy ad space on poster-laden trucks that are driven continuously all day in marketer-selected areas. For example, Oscar-Mayer sends six 'Wienermobiles' across the USA each year to increase brand exposure and goodwill.

Such poster ads are now showing up everywhere. Transit ads on buses, underground and commuter trains – around for years – have become a valuable way to reach working women. Street furniture (bus shelters and kiosks in public areas) has become a fast-growing area. Goodyear, whose brand-emblazoned airship enjoyed clear skies for 50 years, has been joined by Fuji, Met Life, Monster.com, Blockbuster and others in the air.

Advertisers now can buy space in stadia and arenas and on rubbish bins, bicycle racks, parking meters, airport luggage carousals, lifts, petrol pumps, the bottom of beer glasses, airline snacks and supermarket produce in the form of tiny labels on apples and bananas. Leaving no stone unturned, advertisers can even buy space above urinals, which, according to research studies, office workers visit an average of three to four times a day for four minutes a visit.[30]

Cinemas, aircraft and other places Increasingly, advertisers are placing traditional TV and print ads in unconventional places.[31] Companies such as Whittle Communication and Turner Broadcasting have tried placing TV and commercial programming in classrooms, airport lounges and other public places. Airlines now offer media-sponsored audio and video programming that accepts advertising (eg, *USA Today Sky Radio* and *National Geographic Explorer*) and include catalogues in seat pockets for mail-order companies. Today, cinema chains run ads on their screens. Although the same ads that also appear on TV or in magazines often appear in these unconventional places, many advertisers believe it is important to create specially designed ads for these out-of-home exposures.

Product placement Marketers pay large fees so that their products can make cameo appearances in films and on television, with the exact sum depending on the amount and nature of the brand exposure. This practice got a boost in 1982 in the USA when – after Mars declined an offer for use of its M&M's brand – the sales of Reese's Pieces increased 65 percent after prominently appearing in *ET: The Extraterrestrial*.[32] Placement is not restricted to films. Brand Briefing 6.8 provides more detail on product placement.

Brand Briefing 6.8

Product placement becomes more creative and more lucrative

As product placement during prime time grows steadily, advertisers have begun to employ the approach in other arenas. In video games, in the booming category of reality television and in TV programming, product placement is viewed as an effective way to reach an increasingly fragmented audience. Consider also how much global exposure can be achieved from placement in films, TV shows like *Lost* or *Sopranos*, or computer games like *World of Warcraft*.

Media research firm PQ Media found that product placement had increased an average of 16 percent a year since 1999 and projected that spending on the practice would reach €2.90 billion in 2005. Advertisers are embracing product placement because they are discouraged by the returns on traditional commercials and they are wary of viewers with digital video recorders avoiding commercials. Also, product placement enjoys a reputation as a more subtle consumer overture than commercials. Some experts warn, however, that viewers will reach a limit when it comes to accepting product placements. Too many products, especially if they are not woven smoothly into the content, will be a turn-off. An analysis by Abram Sauer has estimated that an average film from Hollywood has about 21 visible brand placements.

Formulas for structuring such deals vary. Sometimes the approach can be straightforward. Boxing equipment brand Everlast simply makes sure it is featured in films about boxing, appearing in *Requiem for a Heavyweight*, *Raging Bull*, *Ali*, *Cinderella Man*, *The Hurricane* and *Million Dollar Baby* – imagine the cumulative effect on a boxing fan of seeing all these films (which, of course, such a person would do).

When Oprah Winfrey wanted to give new cars to all members of her US studio audience in 2004, General Motors agreed to provide 275 cars, worth a total of €4.8 million, in hopes that her reputation for good taste and quality would rub off on the Pontiac G6 models. In 2005, nine brands supported Warner's teen movie *The Sisterhood of the Traveling Pants* with print campaigns, contests and e-mails to

Brand Briefing 6.8 *continued*

customers in exchange for exposure in the film. And little-known bands have watched their record sales shoot up following appearances on television shows such as Fox's *The OC* and HBO's *Six Feet Under*.

Usually those partnerships are the results of calculated negotiations. Sometimes, though, companies just get lucky. During the April 2005 Masters golf tournament, Tiger Woods sank a spectacular chip shot that put Nike's One Platinum ball in a perfect camera position. Viewers saw the Nike Swoosh symbol inch towards the hole and then hover for a full second before dropping in. Experts say Nike couldn't have choreographed a better product placement.

Product placement deals tend to be creative and more experimental than traditional advertising. For the 2003–04 season of the TV show *24*, Ford reached a deal with Fox to feature a truck and created long ads that mirrored the plot lines of the show to air at the beginning and the end of the episode. As deals like this have become commoner, advertisers have gained the clout to dictate how their products are portrayed. Set designers and prop masters rely on free product placements to meet their budgets and are therefore more willing to let advertisers weigh in on when and how their products are used.

In China, some television stations are broadcasting shows produced by advertisers as product placement vehicles. The arrangement is a boon to the advertisers, who spend much less on producing brand-centred shows than paying for pricey Chinese TV ads, and to the broadcasters, who get free programming.

Interactive, exciting and largely untapped by advertisers, video games are another relatively new channel to consumers. Video games have charged on to the advertising scene, representing a chance to reach a valuable demographic: young males. The ad industry is excited by the potential for live, in-game product placements and ads delivered to gamers who play while online. Sometimes the product placement actually increases the realism of the game – it is hard to imagine *Gran Turismo* without real car and tuning brands or *FIFA Football* without the appropriate strips and stadium advertising being present. The company behind most TV audience measurements worldwide, Nielsen, is working on ways to measure game-play behaviour so advertisers will have more data about advertising viewership.

Finally, product placement can also take place in other companies' communications, resulting in a co-branding approach. Ikea's catalogues and shops are full of example interiors, where Hewlett-Packard and Philips get to display their computers and TVs exclusively. It is not publicly known what these companies pay for the privilege, but considering the reach and exposure of Ikea's catalogues and shops, it is not likely to be a small sum.

Sources: Marc Graser, 'Product-placement spending poised to hit $4.25 billion in '05', *Advertising Age*, 4 April 2005; Geoffrey A. Fowler, 'New star on Chinese TV: product placements', *Wall Street Journal*, 2 June 2004; Ethan Smith, 'Ticket out of obscurity', *Wall Street Journal*, 2 August 2004; Abram Sauer, 'Brand cameo awards 2006', www.brandchannel.com.

Product placements can be combined with promotions to publicize a brand's entertainment tie-ins. For example, BMW complemented product placement in the James Bond film *Goldeneye* with an extensive direct mail and advertising campaign to help launch its Z3 roadster. Some firms benefit from product placement at no cost by supplying their product to the production company (eg, Nike does not pay to be in scenes but often supplies shoes, jackets and bags) or simply because of the creative demands of the storyline (eg, the central character in the film *Castaway*, played by Tom Hanks, was a FedEx pilot; as a result, the brand played a prominent role in the plot development without FedEx having to pay anything).[33] To test the effects of product placement, marketing research companies such as CinemaScore conduct viewer exit surveys to determine which brands are noticed.

Point of sale A myriad of possibilities have emerged for communicating with consumers at the point of sale. In-store advertising appears on shopping trolleys, aisles and shelves, as well as promotion options such as demonstrations, live sampling and instant coupon machines. Point-of-sale radio provides FM-style programming and commercial messages to 6,500 supermarkets and 7,900 chemists in the USA. Programming includes a store-selected music format, consumer tips and commercials. Wal-Mart TV is installed in 2,800 stores with a mixture of information and advertising.

The appeal of point-of-sale advertising lies in the fact that studies have shown that consumers in many product categories make the bulk of their buying decisions in the shop. For example, according to a study by ActMedia, which places ads in 7,000 US supermarkets, 70 percent of buying decisions are made in the shops. In-store media are designed to increase the number and nature of spontaneous and planned buying decisions.

Guidelines Non-traditional or place media present interesting options for marketers to reach consumers. Ads now can appear almost anywhere where consumers have a few spare minutes or even seconds to notice them. The main advantage of such media is that a very precise and – because of the nature of the setting involved – captive audience often can be reached in a cost-effective manner. Because out-of-home ads must be quickly processed, however, the message must be simple and direct. In fact, outdoor advertising is often called the '15-second sell.' Thus, strategically, out-of-home advertising is often more effective at enhancing awareness or reinforcing existing brand associations than at creating new ones.

The challenge with non-traditional media is demonstrating their reach and effectiveness through credible research. Another worry is consumer backlash against overcommercialization. Perhaps because of the pervasiveness of advertising, however, consumers seem to be less bothered by non-traditional media than in the past. For example, unlike Europeans, Americans resisted the notion of on-screen advertising in cinemas and videos.[34] Yet, almost half of all cinemas now run ads, albeit often bigger and more cinematic than their small-screen companions.

Consumers must be favourably affected in some way to justify the marketing expenditures for non-traditional media, and some firms offering ad placement in supermarket checkout lines, fast food restaurants and health clubs have suspended business at least in part because of a lack of consumer interest. The bottom line, however, is that there will always be room for creative ways of placing the brand in front of consumers. The possibilities are endless. For example, who could have guessed that RJR Nabisco would distribute sandals with the word *Camel* carved on their soles so beachgoers would leave 'Camel tracks' in the sand to help promote its cigarette![35]

Promotion

Sales promotions can be defined as short-term incentives to encourage trial or usage of a product or service.[36] Sales promotions can be aimed at either the trade or at consumers. Like advertising, sales promotions come in all forms. Whereas advertising typically provides consumers with a *reason* to buy, sales promotions offer consumers an *incentive* to buy. Thus, sales promotions are designed to:

- change the behaviour of retailers so that they stock a brand and support it;
- change the behaviour of consumers so they buy a brand for the first time, buy more or buy a brand earlier or more often.

Analysts maintain that the use of sales promotions grew in the 1980s and 1990s for a number of reasons. Brand management systems with quarterly evaluations were thought to encourage short-term solutions, and an increased need for accountability seemed to favour communication tools whose effects we are more quickly and easily observed than the often 'softer' perceptual effects of advertising. Economic forces worked against advertising effectiveness as ad rates rose steadily despite what was perceived as an increasingly cluttered media environment and fragmented audience. Consumers were thought to be making more in-store decisions and to be less loyal and more immune to advertising. Many mature brands were seen as less easily differentiated. On top of it all, retailers became more powerful.

For all these reasons, consumer and trade promotions were seen by some marketers as a more effective way to influence the sales than advertising. Trade promotions were especially favoured because of the necessity of securing distribution so that consumers could be given the opportunity to buy the brand if they so chose.

There clearly are advantages to sales promotions. Consumer sales promotions let manufacturers discriminate on price by effectively charging different prices to consumers who vary in their price sensitivity. Besides conveying a sense of urgency to consumers, promotions can build brand equity through information conveyed or actual product experience that helps to create strong, favourable and unique associations. Sales promotions can encourage the trade to maintain full stocks and support the manufacturer's merchandising efforts.

Equally, however, from a consumer behaviour perspective, there are disadvantages to sales promotions, such as decreased brand loyalty and increased brand switching, as well as decreased quality perceptions and increased price sensitivity. Besides inhibiting the use of franchise-building advertising or other communications, diverting marketing funds into coupons or other sales promotions sometimes led to reductions in research and development budgets and staff. Perhaps most important, widespread discounting might have led to an increased importance of price as a factor in consumer decisions, breaking down traditional loyalty patterns.

1. Type: what type of promotion should be used?
   Immediate v delayed value.
   Price cut v added value.
2. Product scope: to what pack sizes or models should the promotion apply?
   Multiple or selective.
   More or less popular.
   In-line or out-of-line.
3. Market scope: in which geographic markets should the promotion be offered?
   National or regional.
4. Timing: when should the promotion be offered and for how long?
   When to promote (in or out of season).
   When to announce (early or later).
   Duration (long or short).
   Frequency (high or low).
5. Discount rate: what explicit or implicit discount should the promotion include?
   Deep or shallow.
6. Terms: what terms of sale should be attached to the promotion?
   Tight or loose.

Figure 6.8   Issues in designing sales promotions

Source: Adapted from John A. Quelch, 'Note on sales promotion design', Teaching Note N-589–021, Boston: Harvard Business School, 1988.

Another disadvantage of sales promotions is that in some cases they may merely subsidize buyers who would have bought the brand anyway. Moreover, new consumers attracted to the brand may attribute their purchase to the promotion and not to the merits of the brand itself and, as a result, may not buy again when a promotional offer is withdrawn. Finally, retailers have come to expect and demand trade discounts. The trade may not actually provide the agreed upon merchandising and may engage in non-productive activities such as forward buying and diversion (see Chapter 5). Because of these perceived drawbacks with sales promotions, recent years have seen some shift back to other forms of communication.[37]

Promotions have many possible objectives.[38] With consumers, objectives may focus on new category users, existing category users and/or existing brand users. With the trade, objectives may centre on distribution, support, inventories or goodwill. In designing a sales promotion, John Quelch argues that six issues must be addressed (see Figure 6.8). He argues that the choices made in each of these areas will depend on factors such as the level of consumer involvement, inventory risk and franchise strength of a brand.

Consumer promotions

Consumer promotions are designed to change the choices, quantity or timing of consumers' product purchases. Although consumer sales promotions come in all forms, a distinction has been made between customer franchise-building promotions (eg, samples, demonstrations and educational material) and non-customer franchise-building promotions (eg, price-off packs, premiums, sweepstakes and refund offers).[39]

Customer franchise-building promotions are seen as enhancing the attitudes and loyalty of consumers towards a brand – in other words, those promotions that affect brand equity.

For example, sampling is seen as a way to create strong, relevant brand associations while also perhaps kick-starting word of mouth among consumers. Sampling is increasingly being done at the point of use (ie, when consumers might actually use the product) as marketers become more precise in what, where and how they deliver samples to maximize brand equity. As part of a sampling campaign in the USA, aerobics instructors at Bally's Fitness Clubs handed out Dove body wash, deodorant and face cloths to students at the end of classes before they took a shower.[40]

Thus, sales promotions are being judged by their ability to contribute to brand equity as well as generate sales. The US Promotion Marketing Association bestows 'Reggie' awards to recognize 'superior promotional thinking, creativity and execution across the full spectrum of promotional marketing'. Brand Briefing 6.9 describes an

Brand Briefing 6.9

Samsung DigitAll *Matrix* promotional campaign

Samsung's DigitAll *Matrix* campaign marked the first time the manufacturer launched a global promotional/advertising campaign linked to a blockbuster film. The breakthrough visual effects and prestige of the film resonated with Samsung's core audience of high-tech enthusiasts (aged 17 to 39): trendsetting, stylish consumers eager to own the latest gadgets. Samsung's creative focus was on the marriage of state-of-the-art technology with high fashion and enhanced experiences – traits shared with the film and the manufacturer.

The initial component of the *Matrix* campaign was Samsung's development of a themed wireless telephone, a reproduction of the hand prop created by the producers and production designer for use in the film. The custom phone also received exposure in the *Enter the Matrix* video game. The Samsung logo was also seen on the phone in the video releases of *The Matrix Reloaded* and *Enter the Matrix*. The Samsung Matrix phone was a limited edition. Samsung's development, manufacture and launch of this customized product were achieved in fewer than 12 months.

Samsung's ad creative showed the film's stars with ten flagship Samsung electronics from a variety of brand groups. (Samsung was the only promotional partner to use star likenesses in its campaigns.) Broadcast spots mirrored the look and action of the film and used actors from the film. The film's assistant director James McTeigue was retained to shoot the TV spots, which featured five products. The appearance and parameters of the campaign were reinforced across all Samsung communications channels.

Globally, participating territories were encouraged to develop relevant holistic campaigns, using the following elements: advertising (broadcast, outdoor, in-cinema, print, online banner ads, co-op print), Samsung's online microsite, POP displays,

Brand Briefing 6.9 *continued*

banners and signs, corporate film screenings, wireless marketing tie-ins (Samsung Fun Club), public relations, guerilla marketing (eg, moving vehicle advertising, building wraps, public transport).

The campaign timeline: promotional support surrounding the *Enter the Matrix* video game debut (February 2003); advertising flights, regional special events, microsite online, locally executed marketing campaigns synchronized with the release worldwide (1 April–30 June 2003). Corporate screenings in London, Brazil and Singapore surrounding the premiére helped enthuse Samsung employees and consumers. Samsung received additional branding at these events with signs on buildings, press coverage, displays and product sampling, bandit marketing and popcorn bags.

The results: 50 territories around the world participated; marketing materials created in 30 languages; €67 million media/promotional spend globally; 650+ individual creative pieces developed; one billion advertising impressions received; Samsung.com website page viewers increased 65 percent after the Samsung.com/*Matrix* microsite was opened. Traffic surpassed Samsung's previously most-popular microsite (Olympics) by 500,000 impressions.

Source: www.pmalink.org.

award-winning promotion from 2004. As reflected by this example, creativity is as critical to promotions as to advertising or any other form of marketing communications.

Promotion strategy must reflect the attitudes and behaviour of consumers. The last decade or so has seen a steady fall in the percentage of coupons redeemed by US consumers. The redemption rate was 3.5 percent in 1983, but dropped to only 0.94 percent in 2004.[41] One contributing factor is coupon 'clutter'. In 2004, marketers distributed 342 billion coupons, about 82 percent of which were loose inserts in Sunday newspapers. As a result, one area of promotional growth is in-store coupons, which marketers have increasingly turned to as redemption rates of traditional out-of-store coupons slip.

Trade promotions

Trade promotions often come in the form of financial incentives or discounts given to retailers and distributors to stock and display a product (eg, through slotting allowances, point-of-sale displays, contests and dealer incentives, training programmes, trade shows and co-operative advertising). Such promotions are typically designed to either secure shelf space and distribution for a new brand or to achieve more shelf space. Shelf and aisle positions are important because they affect the ability of the brand to catch the eye of the consumer – placing a brand on a shelf at eye level may double sales.[42]

Because of the large amount of money spent on trade promotions, there is increasing pressure to make trade promotions more effective, as suggested by the following commentary:

> Increasingly, the answer that glues the two into a workable partnership is account-specific promotions, tailored to each retailer, with budgets carved up to suit each market's demands. Manufacturers are decentralizing promotions, giving more responsibility for trade budgets to field salesmen. Big companies are setting up internal departments to implement and track these myriad local promotions; mid-size and smaller companies who can't afford the infrastructure are turning to outside services.[43]

Additionally, as noted in Chapter 5, some companies are attempting to substitute consumer-orientated promotions and advertising with that which can build the brand in a way to satisfy retailers and manufacturers. For example, since 1992, Procter & Gamble has run brand-specific TV and direct mail advertising customized for Wal-Mart, Kmart, Target and other US retailers.

Event marketing and sponsorship

Event marketing refers to public sponsorship of events or activities related to sports, art, entertainment or social causes. Although the origin of event marketing can be traced back to philanthropic activities from over a century ago, many observers identify big events in the 1980s, such as the Summer Olympics of 1984 and the Live Aid concert, as arousing marketers' interests in sponsorship.[44] According to the International Events Group, event sponsorship grew to total €16.8 billion globally in 2001 and €34.2 billion in 2006. Once employed mostly by cigarette, beer and car companies, sports marketing is now being embraced by virtually every type of company. Moreover, virtually every sport – from sled dog racing to fishing tournaments and from tractor pulls to professional beach volleyball – now receives corporate backing of some kind.[45] Brand Briefing 6.10 describes the sponsorship for the Olympic games.

Rationale

Event sponsorship provides a different kind of communication option. By becoming part of a special and personally relevant moment in consumers' lives, sponsors' involvement with events can broaden and deepen their relationship with their target market. Marketers report a number of reasons for sponsoring events.

- *To identify with a particular target market or lifestyle:* marketers can link their brands to events popular with either a select or broad group of consumers. Customers can be sought geographically, demographically, psychographically or behaviourally according to events. In particular, events can be chosen based on attendees' attitudes and usage regarding certain products or brands. Rolex is the official timekeeper of the Wimbledon tennis tournament because of the fit between the Rolex brand and the Wimbledon tournament image. Similarly, Subaru believed there was a match between skiing events and potential buyers of its four-wheel-drive vehicles.

Brand Briefing 6.10

Olympic sponsorships

In 1896, the first of the modern Olympic Games was held in Athens. Sponsorships have been a part of the games from their beginning. In 1896, Kodak bought advertising at the games. In the 1912 games in Stockholm, Sweden, some ten companies bought the rights to take photographs and sell memorabilia of the games.

Sponsorship now contributes more than 40 percent of Olympic marketing revenue. Sponsorships are very specifics. Each level of sponsorship entitles companies to different rights in various regions, category exclusivity and the use of designated Olympic images and marks. For instance, the top partner level gives exclusive marketing rights and opportunities within a designated product category. These partners can exercise these rights worldwide and they may develop campaigns with the various organizing committees of the Olympic movement. In addition to the exclusive worldwide marketing opportunities, partners receive:

- use of all Olympic imagery, as well as appropriate Olympic designations on products;
- hospitality opportunities at the games;
- direct advertising and promotional opportunities, including preferential access to Olympic broadcast advertising;
- on-site concessions/franchise and product sale/showcase opportunities;
- ambush marketing protection;
- acknowledgement of their support though a broad Olympic sponsorship recognition scheme.

In the Torino 2006 Olympic Winter games, Coca-Cola, Atos, General Electric, Kodak, Lenovo, Manulife, McDonald's, Omega, Panasonic, Samsung and Visa were the top partners. Their partner status extends to the Beijing summer games in 2008, and together the partners paid €592 million for their partnership status.

Beyond this, there are domestic sponsorship deals for each event. In Torino 2006, local deals included sponsorship, ticketing and licensing. The main sponsors were Fiat Group, Sanpaolo, Telecom/TIM and Regione Piedmonte. On the next lower level of sponsorships were the official sponsors AAMS, AES, Alfa Romeo, Alpitour, Asics, Berloni, Budweiser, Eutelsat, Fiat, Finmeccanica, Ferrovie, Dello Stato, Iveco, Jet Set, Johnson & Johnson, Kyocera Mita, Lancia and Reale Mutua Assicurazioni.

Olympic supplier schemes are designed to provide support and products required by the International Olympic Committee (IOC) for its operations. Marketing rights are more restricted than for suppliers and generally do not include direct support for the staging of the games. In Torino, DaimlerChrylser provided ground transport, Mizuno clothing for staff, Schenker freight-forwarding and customs-clearing services. Beyond these, another 30 official suppliers assisted the Torino winter games.

Brand Briefing 6.10 *continued*

Licensing deals let companies create souvenirs relating to the games, team-specific souvenirs for their own country, as well as film, computer games and other multi-media opportunities.

The Olympic Games is a huge sponsorship property in all respects – huge audience, big investments. The IOC has signed deals with half of its top sponsors for 2010 and 2012. Revenue from those deals is estimated to exceed €684 million for the first time.

However, it is difficult to calculate exactly the returns of a sponsorship. Many sponsors have stayed with the Olympics for a long time, like Coca-Cola, which has been with the games since 1928. Others, like Xerox, seem less pleased with the returns. Xerox decided not to renew its sponsorship after 2008. Other recent top-level sponsors, like Samsung, have had undeniable success with its brand in the same time period. It might well be that brands and sponsorships interact in complex ways that require careful anlysis. As Clancy and Belmont point out, some brand marketers develop sponsorship and event marketing plans by a combination of marketing tools including computer-aided analytical techniques, optimization modelling and simulated test marketing to pick the right sponsorship deals and the right ways to use them.

Sources: International Olympic Committee, www.olympic.org; Kevin Clancy and Dan Belmont, 'Are the Olympics really worth it?', *Brandweek*, 9 August 2004; Zachary M. Seward 'More Olympic gold on the way', 5 May 2007, Forbes.com.

- *To increase awareness of the company or product name:* sponsorship often offers sustained exposure to a brand, a necessary condition for building recognition. By carefully choosing sponsorship events or activities, identification with a product and thus brand recall can be enhanced. For example, cars are offered as prizes and displayed prominently in televized golf competitions.
- *To create or reinforce consumer perceptions of brand image associations:* events themselves have associations that help to create or reinforce brand associations. For example, 24 Hour Total Fitness became the sponsor of a surprise 2004 reality hit TV show, *The Biggest Loser*, about US contestants competing to lose weight. In some cases, the product itself may be used at an event, providing demonstration of its abilities. For example, Seiko has been the official timer of the Olympics for years.
- *To enhance corporate image:* sponsorship is seen as a 'soft sell' and as a way to improve perceptions that the company is likeable, prestigious and so forth. It is often hoped that consumers will credit the company for its sponsorship and favour it in product choices.
- *To create experiences and evoke feelings:* events can be included as part of an experiential marketing campaign. The feelings engendered by an exciting or rewarding event may indirectly link to the brand. Marketers can also use the web

to provide support and experiences. American Express launched its Blue card at an outdoor concert in New York featuring Sheryl Crow.

- *To express commitment to the community or on social issues:* often called cause-related marketing, these sponsorships involve corporate links with charities (see Chapter 11). For example, American Express supported more than 70 causes in 18 countries with €5.9 million in donations from 1981 to 1986, ranging from the preservation of the national bird of Norway to the protection of the Italian coastline. As another example, Colgate-Palmolive has sponsored the Starlight Foundation, which grants wishes to young people who are critically ill.
- *To entertain clients or reward employees:* many events have lavish hospitality tents and other special services or activities that are only available for sponsors and their guests. Involving clients with the event in these and other ways can engender goodwill and establish contacts. From an employee perspective, events can build participation and morale or be used as an incentive. For example, when US insurer John Hancock, as part of its Winter Olympic sponsorship in 1994, offered trips to Lillehammer, Norway, as a reward for agents who generated €68,400 in commissions, twice the number of agents qualified than in years past.
- *To permit merchandising or promotional opportunities:* many marketers tie in contests or sweepstakes, in-store merchandising and direct response or other marketing activities with their event. When Sprint sponsored the World Cup in 1994, its related activities included long-distance calling cards picturing football stars, a geography programme for Latin American schools tied to game results and discounts on long-distance calls for soccer-related businesses and local teams.[46]

Despite the potential advantages, the success of an event can be unpredictable and out of the control of the sponsor. There can be much clutter in sponsorship. Finally, although many consumers will credit sponsors for providing necessary financial assistance to make an event possible, some consumers may still resent the commercialization of events through sponsorship.

Guidelines

Developing successful event sponsorship involves choosing the appropriate events, designing the optimal exposure at those events and measuring the effects of sponsorship on brand equity.[47]

Choosing sponsorship opportunities Because of the huge amount of money involved and the number of event opportunities that exist, many marketers are becoming more strategic about the events with which they will get involved and the manner in which they will do so. As it is, the sophistication in marketing events in the USA lags behind many countries in Europe and elsewhere where restricted options have spawned greater sponsorship activity.

There are potential guidelines for choosing events (see Chapter 7). Fundamentally, the marketing objectives and communication strategy that have been defined for the brand must be met by the event. Thus, the audience delivered by the event must match the target market of the brand. Moreover, the event must have sufficient awareness, possess the desired image and be capable of creating the desired effects with that market. Of particular concern is whether consumers make favourable attributions to the sponsor for its event involvement. An 'ideal event' might be one whose audience closely matches the ideal target market, that generates much favourable attention, that is unique but not encumbered with many sponsors, that lends itself to ancillary marketing activities, and that reflects or enhances the brand or corporate image of the sponsor.

Of course, rather than linking themselves to an event, some sponsors create their own. The cable sports network ESPN created the X Games to capture youth-orientated activities (eg, in-line skating, skateboarding, bungee jumping and sky surfing) that appealed to a market segment not as easily attracted to traditional sports. Companies are also using their names to sponsor the venues that hold the events. In the USA, it has been common practice to rename stadiums after sponsors. For instance, Staples paid €68.4 million over 20 years to name the Los Angeles arena where basketball and hockey teams play and where concerts and other events are also held. This also happens in Europe, notably the new arena of the Munich soccer teams 1860 and Bayern is called the Allianz Arena, after the German insurer, and, in its deal with Arsenal, Emirates has the right to put its name on the team's shirts and the team's new stadium in London.[48] Although stadium naming rights can command high fees, it should be recognized that its direct contribution to building brand equity is primarily in creating brand recognition – not brand recall – and typically would be expected to do little for brand image except to convey a certain level of scope and size.

Designing sponsorship activities Many marketers believe it is the marketing campaign accompanying a sponsorship that determines its success. A sponsor can identify itself at an event in a number of ways, including banners, signs and programmes. For more significant and broader effect, however, sponsors typically supplement such activities with samples, prizes, advertising, retail promotions and publicity. Marketers often note that from at least two to three times the amount of the sponsorship expenditure should be spent on related marketing activities.

David D'Allesandro, former chief of John Hancock, believes the key to sponsorship is building on the event so it goes beyond calculations such as cost-per-thousand TV advertising exposures. John Hancock uses sponsorships to entertain big clients, attract new customers, inspire salespeople, recruit staff and raise employee morale. For Hancock, D'Allesandro believes the best events are either very big in scope, like the Olympics, or very localized, like a youth hockey clinic with an Olympian.

Measuring sponsorship activities There are two approaches to measuring the effects of sponsorship activities: the *supply-side* method focuses on potential exposure to the brand by assessing the extent of media coverage, and the *demand-side* method focuses on reported exposure from consumers.

Supply-side methods attempt to approximate the amount of time or space devoted to the brand in media coverage of an event. For example, the number of seconds that the brand appears on television or the column inches of press clippings covering an event that mention the brand can be estimated. This measure of potential impressions delivered by an event sponsorship is then translated into an equivalent monetary value in advertising according to the ratecard associated with advertising in the particular media.

Although supply-side exposure methods provide quantifiable measures, their validity can be questioned. The difficulty lies in the fact that equating media coverage with advertising exposure ignores the content of the respective communications that consumers receive. The advertiser uses media space and time to communicate a strategically designed message. Media coverage and telecasts only expose the brand and don't necessarily embellish its meaning in any direct way. Although some public relations professionals maintain that positive editorial coverage can be worth five to ten times the advertising equivalency value, it is rare that sponsorship affords the brand such favourable treatment. As one group of critics noted:

> Equating incidental visual and audio exposures with paid advertising time is, we feel, questionable at best. A commercial is a carefully crafted persuasive declaration of a product's virtues. It doesn't compete for attention with the actual on-camera action of a game or race. A 30-second exposure of a billboard in the background can't match the value of 30 seconds in which the product is the only star.[49]

Another measurement approach is the demand-side method, which attempts to identify the effects that sponsorship has on consumers' brand knowledge. Thus, tracking or custom surveys can explore the ability of the event sponsorship to affect awareness, attitudes or sales.

Event spectators can be identified and surveyed after the event to measure recall of the event's sponsor as well as attitudes and intentions towards the sponsor as a result. For example, a survey by DDB Needham in 1992 indicated that 22 of 37 Olympic sponsors created no connection in consumers' minds with the event.[50] A random survey of viewers who watched 10 or so hours of television coverage of the 1993 US Open tennis tournament found that only 7 percent knew who sponsored the men's singles title (Nissan's Infiniti) and only 14 percent knew who sponsored the women's singles title (Bristol-Meyer's Clairol).

Public relations and publicity

Public relations and publicity are designed to promote or protect a company's image or its individual products. Publicity refers to non-personal communications such as press releases, media interviews, press conferences, feature articles, newsletters, photographs, films and tapes. Public relations may also involve such things as annual reports, fundraising and membership drives, lobbying, special event management and public affairs.

The marketing value of public relations got a boost in 1983 when public relations firm Burson-Marsteller's handling of Johnson & Johnson's Tylenol product tampering incident was credited with helping to save the brand. Brand Briefing 11.12 provides a comprehensive account of that campaign. Around that time, politicians also discovered the power of campaign sound bites that were picked up by the press as a means of broad, cost-efficient candidate exposure.

Marketers now recognize that, although public relations is invaluable during a marketing crisis, it also needs to be a routine part of any marketing communications campaign. Even companies that primarily use advertising and promotions can benefit from well-conceived and well-executed publicity. For example, when Heinz launched its new EZ Squirt kids' condiments, an extensive PR effort resulted in 4,000 news stories and a 5 percent increase in market share before advertising began.

Buzz marketing

Occasionally, a product enters the market with little fanfare yet is still able to attract a strong customer base. Something about the product attracts a group of consumers who are eager to spread word of the product among their peers. News travels in this fashion until enough tongues are wagging to constitute a 'buzz' about the brand. Increasingly, companies are attempting to create consumer word of mouth through various techniques often called *buzz marketing*.[51]

Companies may not have the luxury of time, so they often attempt to catalyze buzz marketing for new products. One popular method is to allow consumers who are likely to influence other consumers 'discover' the product in the hopes that they will pass a positive endorsement on to their peers. To improve their image with teenage boys, Lee jeans identified 200,000 'influentials' from online communities devoted to video games and sent them short films from unknown characters who turned out to be protagonists in a video game developed by Lee. On average, these films were forwarded to about six people each.[52] Back in the real world, Piaggio USA hired a street team of models to drive its Vespa scooters around Los Angeles and talk up the brand.

Tremor

Procter & Gamble's proprietary word-of-mouth technology, Tremor, has enlisted over 250,000 teen girls who qualify as 'connectors'. A connector is defined as a person with a social network five to six times larger than the average person and with a deep propensity to talk about ideas with that network. To identify a connector, a questionnaire weeds out 90 percent of potential respondents. Connectors, who are not paid, are attracted by hearing things first and being able to communicate directly back to the company. P&G has used Tremor for its own products, such as Noxzema and Pringles, and leased it to other companies, including Coca-Cola and Dreamworks (which used Tremor subjects to name the 2004 teen film comedy, *Eurotrip*). Steve Knox, chief of the P&G unit, claims the key is creating messages that create consumer word of mouth. 'The way we phrase this to people is there's a message that the consumer wants to hear and then there's a message they want to share with their friends and those are two different messages.' He claims the biggest mistake made with word of mouth is to say, 'Here's my marketing message. Make them talk about this.' P&G signed up 500,000 mothers for a new version of Tremor for 2006.[53]

Buzz marketing works well when the marketing message appears to originate with an independent source and not with the brand. Because consumers are becoming sceptical and wary of traditional advertising, buzz marketers seek to expose consumers to their brands in a unique and innocuous fashion.[54] One approach is to enlist genuine consumers able to give authentic-seeming endorsements of the brand. An ad executive with Bates USA explained the goal of this strategy: 'Ultimately, the brand benefits because an accepted member of the social circle will always be more credible than any communication that could ever come directly from the brand.'[55]

Some criticize buzz marketing as 'a form of cultural corruption' in which marketers are creating culture at a fundamental level. Critics claim that buzz marketing's interference in consumers' lives is insidious because the pitch cannot always be detected. Another potential problem with buzz marketing is that it requires a buzz-worthy product. As one marketing expert said: 'The bad news is that [buzz marketing] only works in high-interest product categories.' In spite of these drawbacks, experts predicted that buzz marketing would retain its appeal for marketers. Said one ad executive: 'The biggest problem with buzz marketing in the next 24 months will be the glut of people trying to do it.'

Author and former marketing executive Emanuel Rosen developed the following guidelines to help marketers avoid buzz marketing pitfalls in their advertising.[56]

- *Keep it simple:* simple messages spread across social networks more easily.
- *Tell us what's new:* the message must be relevant and newsworthy for people to want to tell others about it.
- *Don't make claims you can't support:* making false claims will kill buzz or, worse, lead to negative buzz.
- *Ask customers to articulate what's special about your product or service:* if customers can explain why they like the product or service, they can then communicate this to others.
- *Start measuring buzz:* this can help determine which strategies generate the most buzz.
- *Listen to the buzz:* monitoring consumer reaction can yield insights such as how to improve the product or service.

Personal selling

Personal selling involves face-to-face interaction with one or more prospective purchasers for the purpose of making sales. Personal selling represents a communication option with pros and cons almost exactly the opposite of advertising. Specifically, the main advantages to personal selling are that a detailed, customized message can be sent to customers and that feedback can be gathered to help close the sale. Prospective customers can be identified and tailored solutions can be offered. Products often can be demonstrated with customer involvement as part of the sales pitch. Personal selling can also be beneficial after the sale to handle customer problems and ensure customer satisfaction. The main disadvantages to personal selling are the high cost involved and its lack of breadth. For many mass market products, personal selling would be cost-prohibitive.[57]

Personal selling practices have changed in recent years in recognition of the importance of achieving competitive parity or even superiority with sales and customer service. According to a *BusinessWeek* magazine cover story, 'smart selling' means focusing the entire company on its customers, including changing how salespeople are hired, trained and paid.[58] These commentators believe that the keys to better selling are to do the following.

- *Rethink training:* forget high-pressure selling. Salespeople need new skills: they must learn to become customer advocates whose detailed knowledge of their customers' businesses helps them spot sales opportunities and service problems.
- *Get everyone involved:* salespeople should no longer act alone. Everyone in a company, from product designers to plant managers and financial officers, must be a part of selling to and serving customers.

- *Inspire from the top:* chief executives and top managers must frequently and visibly lead the smart-selling charge in their companies. Having the boss call regularly on customers and lead sales training sessions is a must.
- *Change the motivation:* salespeople need constant recognition – but not in the form of commission. That can be an incentive to scoring a quick sales hit. Instead, include measures of long-term customer satisfaction when calculating pay.
- *Forge electronic links:* use computerized marketing and distribution technology to track relationships with customers, make sure the right products get to the right stores at the right times and make order-taking easy. It all adds up to high-tech intimacy.
- *Talk to your customers:* make frequent phone calls, assign a company employee to a customer's plant or drop notes to frequent shoppers. Customers like the attention and the added communication leads to better intelligence-gathering.

DEVELOPING INTEGRATED MARKETING COMMUNICATION CAMPAIGNS

The previous sections examined various communication options. This section considers how to develop an integrated marketing communication (IMC) campaign in terms of the optimal range of options that should be chosen and the relationships between those options.[59] The main theme of this discussion is that marketers should 'mix and match' communication options to build brand equity – that is, choose a variety of communication options that share common meaning and content but also offer different, complementary advantages so that the whole is greater than the sum of the parts.[60] The importance of integrating communications can be seen by the following description of the communications challenge for its Saturn car by the company's ad agency, Goodby, Silverstein & Partners.

> In being assigned the Saturn account in 2002 by General Motors, ad agency Goodby Silverstein & Partners began deciding that the main brand truth to communicate was that Saturn thought differently from other car companies and truly put 'people first' – a phrase that became the tagline. A critical part of the Saturn account was then integrating the brand voice and philosophy across all media, including TV, print, outdoor advertising, brochures, motor show handouts, retail displays, direct mail, 66 retail broadcast spots and 1,500 retail newspaper ads a year, as well as an internet site. The success in integration was seen in increased and sustained sales for Saturn vehicles in 2002–2004.[61]

This broad view of brand-building activities is especially relevant when considering marketing communications designed to improve brand awareness. As noted in Chapter 2, brand awareness is related to brand familiarity and can be viewed as a function of the number of brand-related exposures and experiences that have been accumulated by the consumer.[62] Thus, *anything* that causes the consumer to notice and pay attention to the brand can increase brand awareness, at least in terms of recognition. Obviously, the visibility of the brand in many marketing communications such as sponsorship suggests that these activities may be especially valuable for enhancing brand recognition.

To enhance brand recall, however, more intense and elaborate processing of the brand may be necessary so that stronger brand links to the product category are established to improve memory performance. Similarly, because brand associations can be created in the abstract in many ways, many possible marketing communications should be considered to create the desired brand image and knowledge structures.

Criteria for IMC campaigns

There are many ways to create IMC campaigns. A number of considerations come into play when evaluating an IMC campaign – that is, when considering responses to a set of communications across a group of consumers. This discussion assumes that the marketer has thoroughly researched the target market and fully understands who they are – their perceptions, attitudes and behaviours – and therefore knows exactly what needs to be done with them in terms of communication objectives.

In assessing the impact of an IMC campaign, the overriding goal is to create the most effective and efficient communications possible. Towards that goal, six relevant criteria can be identified:

- coverage;
- contribution;
- commonality;
- complementarity;
- versatility;
- cost.

The following sections consider each criterion in turn.

Coverage

Coverage relates to the proportion of the audience that is reached by each communication option, as well as how much overlap exists. In other words, to what extent do different communication options reach the designated target market and the same or different consumers making up that market? As Figure 6.9 shows, the unique aspects of coverage relate to the 'main effects'; the common aspects relate to the 'interaction effects'.

The unique aspect of coverage relates to the inherent communication ability of a marketing communication option, as suggested by the second criterion (ie, contribution). To the extent that there is overlap in communication options, however, marketers must decide how to optimally design a campaign to reflect the fact that consumers may already have had exposure to any particular communication option. In terms of brand knowledge, an option may either reinforce associations and strengthen linkages that are also the focus of other communication options or address other associations and linkages that are not the focus of other communication options, as suggested by the third and fourth criteria (ie, commonality and complementarity). Moreover, if less than perfect overlap exists – which is almost always the case – a communication option may be designed to reflect the fact that consumers

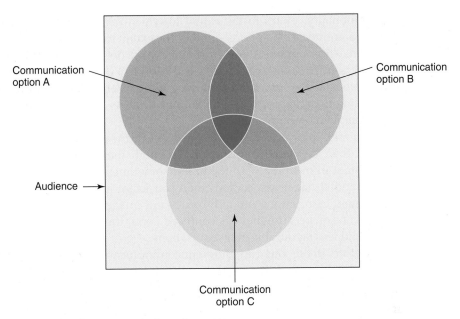

Communication option A

Communication option B

Audience

Communication option C

Figure 6.9   IMC audience communication option overlap

may or may not have seen other communication options, as suggested by the fifth criterion (ie, versatility). Finally, all of these considerations must be offset by their cost, as suggested by the sixth criterion.

Contribution

Contribution relates to the inherent ability of a marketing communication to create the desired response and communication effects in consumers *in the absence of exposure to any other communication option*. In other words, contribution relates to the 'main effects' of a marketing communication option in terms of how it affects consumers' processing of a communication and the resulting outcomes. As noted earlier, marketing communications can play many roles (eg, building awareness, enhancing image, eliciting responses, inducing sales) and the contribution of any marketing communication option will depend on how well it plays that role. Also as noted earlier, much research has considered this aspect of communications, generating conceptual guidelines and evaluation criteria in the process. Given that overlap with communication options exist, however, other factors must be considered, as follows.

Commonality

Regardless of which options are chosen, the marketing communication campaign should be co-ordinated to create a consistent and cohesive brand image in which brand associations share content and meaning. The consistency and cohesiveness of the brand image is important because the image determines how easily existing associations and responses can be recalled and how easily additional associations and responses can become linked to the brand in memory.

Commonality relates to the extent to which *common* associations are reinforced across communication options – that is, the extent to which information conveyed by communication options shares meaning. Most definitions of IMC emphasize only this criterion. For example, Burnett and Moriarty define integrated marketing communications as the 'practice of unifying all marketing communication tools – from advertising to packaging – to send target audiences a consistent, persuasive message that promotes company goals'.[63]

In general, information that is consistent in meaning is more easily learned and recalled than unrelated information – though the unexpectedness of information inconsistent in meaning with the brand sometimes can lead to more elaborate processing and stronger associations than consistent information.[64] Nevertheless, with inconsistent associations and a diffuse brand image, consumers may overlook some associations or, because they are confused about the meaning of the brand, form less strong and less favourable new associations.

Therefore, in the long run, different communication elements should be designed and combined so that they work together to create a consistent and cohesive brand image. As branding expert Larry Light states: 'The total brand experience must be a result of an integrated, focused, strategically sound, differentiated, consistent, branded marketing programme. Inconsistency, instead of integration, leads to uncertainty. Yet, uncertainty and inconsistency do seem to be the result of a lot of today's marketing practices.'[65]

Note also that there may be memory advantages to using several communication options to create positive brand images. The *encoding variability principle* in psychology argues that presenting information in varied contexts causes information to be encoded in slightly different ways. As a result, several retrieval routes are formed in memory, each of which converges on the to-be-remembered information, thereby enhancing recall.[66] In other words, different ways of learning information provide different cues for recalling information, thereby improving memory performance. Thus, the encoding variability principle suggests that an IMC campaign, by employing many communication elements, may be an effective way to create, maintain or strengthen brand associations in memory.

The more abstract the association to be created or reinforced by marketing communications, the more likely it would seem that it could be reinforced in different ways across heterogeneous communication options.[67] For example, if the desired association is 'contemporary', there may be a number of ways to make a brand seem modern and relevant. Equally, however, if the desired association is a concrete attribute (eg, 'rich chocolate taste'), it may be difficult to convey in communication options that do not permit explicit product statements (eg, sponsorship).

Finally, another commonality issue is the extent of consistency of execution – that is, the extent to which non-product-related information is conveyed in different communication options. The more co-ordinated that executional information is, the more likely it is that this information can serve as a retrieval cue to other communication effects.[68] In other words, if a symbol is established in one communication option (eg, a feather in a TV ad for a deodorant to convey mildness and softness), then it can be used in other communications to help trigger the knowledge, thoughts, feelings and images stored in memory from a previous communication.

Complementarity

Communication options are often more effective when used in tandem. *Complementarity* relates to the extent to which *different* associations and linkages are emphasized across communication options. For example, research has shown that promotions can be more effective when combined with advertising.[69] In both cases, the awareness and attitudes created by advertising campaigns can improve the success of more direct sales pitches. Thus, the ideal marketing communication campaign would ensure that the communication options chosen are mutually compensatory and reinforcing to create desired consumer knowledge structures.

Different brand associations may be most effectively established by capitalizing on those marketing communication options best suited to eliciting a particular consumer response or establishing a particular type of brand association. For example, some media are better at generating trial than engendering long-term loyalty (eg, sampling or other forms of sales promotion). As part of its 'Drivers wanted' campaign, in the USA, Volkswagen used television to introduce a storyline that it embellished on its website. Research with some industrial distributors has shown that follow-up sales efforts generate higher sales productivity when firms have already exposed customers to its products at a trade show.[70] Brand Briefing 6.12 describes how communication options may need to be explicitly tied together to capitalize on complementarity to build brand equity.

Versatility

Versatility refers to the extent that a marketing communication option is robust and effective for different consumers. There are two types of versatility: communication and consumer. The reality of any IMC campaign is that when consumers are exposed to a marketing communication, some will have been exposed to other communications for the brand, whereas other consumers will not. The ability of a marketing communication to work at two levels – communicating to consumers who have or have not seen other communications – is important. That is, some communications will not be effective unless consumers have already been exposed to other communications. For example, mass advertising or some type of awareness-creating communication is often seen as a necessary condition for personal selling. A marketing communication option is deemed robust when it achieves its desired effect *regardless* of consumers' communication history.

Besides this versatility, communication options may also be judged in terms of their broader consumer versatility – that is, in terms of how communications affect consumers who vary on measures other than their communication history, especially on brand or product knowledge or processing goals. In other words, how well does one marketing communication option inform or persuade depending on the different market segments involved? Communications directed at creating brand awareness (eg, sponsorship) may be more robust by virtue of their simplicity.

There would seem to be two ways of achieving this dual communication ability.

1. *Multiple information provision strategy:* providing different information within a communication option to appeal to different types of consumers. An important issue here is how information that is designed to appeal to one target market of

consumers will be processed by other consumers and target markets. Issues of information overload, confusion and annoyance may come into play if communications become burdened by details.

2. *Broad information provision strategy:* providing information that is rich or ambiguous enough to work regardless of consumer knowledge. The important issue is how potent or successful that information can be. By attempting to appeal to the lowest common denominator, the information may lack precision and sufficient detail to influence consumers. To be successful, consumers with disparate backgrounds will have to find information in the communication sufficiently relevant to satisfy their goals given their product or brand knowledge or communications history.

Cost

Finally, evaluations of marketing communications on all of the preceding criteria must be weighed against their cost to arrive at the most effective *and* efficient campaign.

Using IMC choice criteria

The IMC choice criteria provide guidance for designing and implementing integrated marketing communication campaigns. To do so, however, involves evaluating options, establishing priorities and tradeoffs, and executing the final design and implementation.

Evaluating communication options

Marketing communication options or communication types can be judged according to the response and communication effects that they can create as well as how they rate on the IMC choice criteria (see Figure 6.10 for a subjective macro appraisal). Different communication types and options have different strengths and weaknesses and raise different issues. Several points about the IMC choice criteria ratings are worth noting.

	TV	Print	Sales promotions	Sponsorship	Interactive
Coverage					
Breadth	+++	+	++	+++	+
Depth	+	++	++	++	+++
Contribution	+++	+++	+++	+++	+++
Commonality	+++	++	++	+	+++
Complementary	+++	+++	+++	+++	+++
Versatility	+	++	+	+	+++
Cost	+++	+++	+++	+++	+++

Figure 6.10   Macro perspectives

First, there are not necessarily any inherent differences between communication types for contribution and complementarity because each type, if properly designed, can play a critical and unique role in achieving objectives. Similarly, all marketing communications are seemingly expensive, although some differences in market prices with respect to cost per thousand can prevail. Communication types vary, however, in terms of their breadth and depth of coverage as a result of the audiences that they can deliver. Communication types also differ in terms of commonality and versatility according to the number of delivery routes involved: the more there are available with a communication type, the greater its potential commonality and versatility.

Arriving at a final mix requires, in part, decisions on priorities and tradeoffs for the IMC choice criteria.

Establishing priorities and tradeoffs

Deciding on which IMC campaign to adopt, after the various options have been profiled, will depend in part on how the choice criteria are ranked. In addition to setting priorities, decisions must be made concerning tradeoffs because the IMC choice criteria themselves are related.

Priorities will depend in part on the objectives of the communication campaign (eg, short-run v long-run concerns) and the marketing campaign in general, which, in turn, depend on a host of factors beyond the scope of this chapter. A number of possible tradeoffs can be identified with the IMC choice criteria, primarily dealing with the three factors that are concerned with overlaps in coverage.

- Commonality and complementarity will often be inversely related. The more that marketing communication options emphasize the same brand attribute or benefit, all else being equal, the less they can emphasize other attributes and benefits.
- Versatility and complementarity will also often be inversely related. The more a marketing communication campaign maximizes complementarity in content, the less critical is the versatility of any communication option. In other words, the more a communication campaign accounts for differences in consumers between communication options, the less necessary it is that any one communication is designed to appeal to different consumer groups.
- Commonality and versatility, on the other hand, do not share an obvious relationship; it may be possible, for example, to develop a sufficiently abstract message (eg, 'Brand X is contemporary') that can be effectively reinforced across multiple communication types (eg, advertising, interactive, sponsorship, promotions).

Executing final design and implementation

Once strategic guidelines are in place, executional details of each communication option must be determined, and the specific parameters of the media plan must be put in place. In terms of the former, communication options must be developed as creatively as possible to maximize the probability that they will achieve their desired objectives. In terms of the last point, decisions must be made about the concentration and continuity of the different communication options in the IMC plan. *Concentration* refers to the amount of communications that consumers receive. Consumers may be exposed to a varying amount of the same or different communications. *Continuity* refers to the distribution of those exposures in terms of how massed or diffused they are.

Brand Briefing 6.11

Audi: building prestige

A new challenge

Audi had raised its image from an average carmaker to a prestige brand with strong sales and, by 2000, was on a par with Mercedes and BMW. The brand had benefited in the late 1990s from an image of understated, private sense of prestige. But despite its sales success in the 1990s, the brand was still behind the other luxury brands, especially BMW. Audi wanted to challenge BMW for leadership, and to do this it needed to accelerate volume share growth.

Strategic solution

To sell more, the brand needed to evolve into a more public and more overt status symbol. It was not enough for a precious few to appreciate Audi's prestige. Most prestige cars are bought for outer-directed reasons – they are status symbols that gain value as more people think highly of them. Therefore to appeal to a much larger group of prestige car buyers, Audi's prestige status had to be appreciated by the general public.

The brand's tone was to move from 'understatement' to 'statement'. Its brand personality evolved from dry, witty and intellectual to bold, confident and forceful. In line with this revised strategy, the cars supplemented their strong quality and design credentials with a sportier, more aggressive, styling. Signs of change in the brand were helped by the launches of the dramatically designed TT and A2 but the real fruits of this new design philosophy were launched gradually as new versions of existing models.

Communications needed to find a way to engage this mass audience. The general concept of brand placements – events, promotions, product placements which in turn generated buzz and PR – was used to seed the idea of the brand's prestige. Advertising was then largely reserved for attracting buyers. Direct activity was deployed to convert interest into enquiries. Brand placements, advertising and direct marketing were integrated in terms of complementary roles and consistency in execution. This is summarized in Figure 6.11.

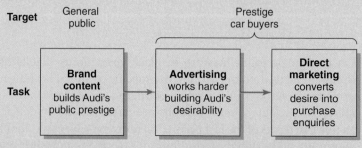

Figure 6.11

Brand Briefing 6.11 *continued*

This integrated communications campaign was planned and executed in the UK. This is how Audi planned and executed each part.

Using brand placements to build public prestige

The majority of the general public don't pay much attention to car advertising (Figure 6.12). Since most will never buy an Audi, they are even less likely to pay attention to the brand's ads.

So the Audi team had to find a way beyond advertising to engage the general public and build a sense of prestige. Appearing in the more engaging editorial space (rather than the obvious advertising space) would give the brand's message a better chance of being enthusiastically consumed by the general public; and a greater chance of becoming embedded in the public consciousness.

Brand placement also supported more targeted communications. A publicly prestigious brand is likely to command greater attention from prestige car drivers. Once brand placement has established public prestige, prestige car buyers would pay more attention to Audi's advertising and direct activity.

An understanding of what prestige meant to the general public in a broad media context was key before planning any brand placement activity. Research probed what media the general public regarded as prestigious. It fell into two categories, both of which were important. Media that was prestigious through public exposure (eg, Champions League Football on Sky) and media that was prestigious through associations with an upper class world (eg, *Yachting World* magazine).

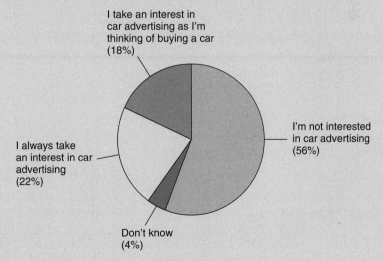

Figure 6.12   Most people don't easily engage with car advertising
Source: Hall & Partners, July 2003. Base: new car buyers.

Brand Briefing 6.11 *continued*

Those two categories were used to ensure the placements would drive both the 'public' and the 'prestige' parts of 'public prestige'.

Over time, spending on brand placements has grown (Figure 6.13).

Driving desirability among prestige car buyers

To make Audi's advertising more appealing to status-orientated prestige car buyers, advertising evolved from understated user imagery towards an overt celebration of the cars themselves. For prestige brands, the product is hero, and their tone is that of absolute confidence.

Audi's advertising became assumptive and bold, focusing on what Audi was, not what it wasn't. Different ads dramatized different elements of the cars, such as features; attitude and inspiration (Figure 6.14).

Media strategy

Audi broadened the media target from upmarket men 35+ to a broader target of all prestige car buyers (which included younger men and women). A combination of public and prestige media was used to ensure the target group saw Audi in both a public and prestige context. In TV they had an 80:20 buying strategy with 80 percent optimized to deliver big-hitting spots and 20 percent for more discreet, upmarket spots (Figure 6.15).

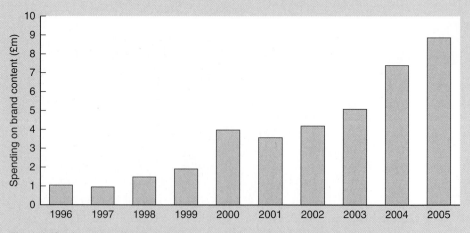

Figure 6.13   Spending on brand placements has grown

Source: Audi UK, Mediacom.

Brand Briefing 6.11 *continued*

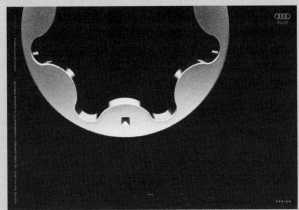

Pump: May 2002. Photographer Paul Zak

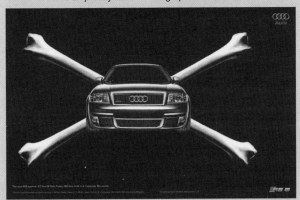

Skull and Cross Bones RS6: October 2003. Photographer Giles Revell

Quattro Sport TT: April 2005. Photographer Kulbir Thandi

Figure 6.14   Stills from Audi adverts

Brand Briefing 6.11 *continued*

	Public media	*Prestige media*
TV	Champions League Football	Southbank Show
Outdoor	Transvision, Golden Square, London Underground	Upmarket hair dressers, David Lloyd gyms
Press	Broadsheet newspapers	Magazines: *The Economist, Time, The Week*

Figure 6.15   Building public prestige through media

Direct marketing converts desire into purchase enquiries

To leverage the increased appeal generated by the brand content and advertising, direct marketing was used to convert desire into purchase enquiries. A high proportion of the budget was spent on direct marketing because its physical nature makes it possible to strongly evoke prestige associations. It was critical that each communication reflected the prestige values generated by the advertising. Paper stock weight was higher, quality materials were deployed (eg, leather and aluminium) and hi-tech formats (eg, DVDs and USB memory sticks) were incorporated.

Making the channels work together

Integration was critical given the varied audiences and channels. As 'public prestige' required the brand to have a greater weight of presence, all audiences had to see this activity as one. The choice was to integrate in the most visually obvious manner, by execution. All activities had a consistent prestigious tone; dark and moody. The well-known end-line 'Vorsprung durch Technik' was used consistently to underscore Audi's prestige.

Results

In the UK, where this communications campaign was consistently applied, the result was a 3 percentage point increase in sales growth rate. In the UK, this meant overtaking Mercedes as the second most sold premium car brand. Audi also increased its average sales price per car and the buyers were more likely to be among the richer in society – two central outcomes for a prestige brand.

Interestingly, these results were achieved even though the average marketing cost per car decreased and the incremental sales more than covered the marketing communications budget. This makes the Audi UK story a very good example of

Brand Briefing 6.11 *continued*

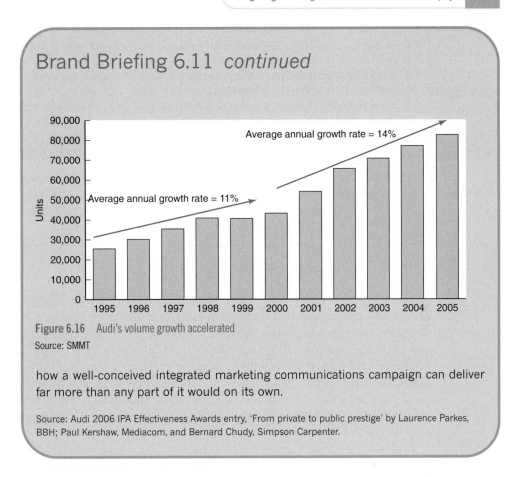

Figure 6.16   Audi's volume growth accelerated

Source: SMMT

how a well-conceived integrated marketing communications campaign can deliver far more than any part of it would on its own.

Source: Audi 2006 IPA Effectiveness Awards entry, 'From private to public prestige' by Laurence Parkes, BBH; Paul Kershaw, Mediacom, and Bernard Chudy, Simpson Carpenter.

CHAPTER REVIEW

This chapter provided conceptual frameworks and managerial guidelines for how marketing communications can be integrated to enhance brand equity. The chapter addressed this issue from the perspective of customer-based brand equity, which maintains that such equity is determined by the brand knowledge created in consumers' minds by a marketing campaign. Communication options were reviewed (broadcast, print, direct response, online and place advertising media; consumer and trade promotions; event marketing and sponsorship; publicity and public relations; and personal selling) in terms of their characteristics as well as success factors for effectiveness. The chapter also provided criteria as to how communication options should be combined.

Two implications emerge from this discussion. First, from the perspective of customer-based brand equity, all communication options should be evaluated in terms of their ability to affect brand equity. In particular, the CBBE concept provides a common denominator by which the effects of communication options can be evaluated: each option can be judged in terms of the effectiveness and efficiency by

1. *Be analytical:* use frameworks of consumer behaviour and managerial decision-making to develop well-reasoned communication campaigns.
2. *Be curious:* better understand customers by using all forms of research, and always be thinking of how you can create value for consumers.
3. *Be single-minded:* focus your message on well-defined target markets (less can be more).
4. *Be integrative:* reinforce your message through consistency and cuing across all communication options and media.
5. *Be creative:* state your message in a unique fashion; use different promotions and media to create favourable, strong and unique brand associations.
6. *Be observant:* keep track of competition, customers, channel members and employees through monitoring and tracking studies.
7. *Be patient:* take a long-term view of communication effectiveness to build and manage brand equity.
8. *Be realistic:* understand the complexities involved in marketing communications.

Figure 6.17   Marketing communications guidelines

which it affects brand awareness and by which it creates, maintains or strengthens favourable and unique brand associations. Communications options have different strengths and can accomplish different objectives. Thus, it is important to employ a mix of options, each playing a specific role in building or maintaining brand equity.

The second important insight is that the marketing communications campaign should be put together in a way such that the whole is greater than the sum of the parts. In other words, as much as possible, there should be a match between certain communication options so that the effect of any one option is enhanced by the presence of another option.

In closing, the basic message of this chapter is simple: advertisers need to evaluate marketing communication options strategically to determine how they can contribute to brand equity. To do so, advertisers need theoretical and managerial guidelines by means of which they can determine the effectiveness and efficiency of various communication options both singularly and in combination with other communication options. Figure 6.17 provides the author's philosophy concerning the design, implementation and interpretation of marketing communication strategies.

Brand Briefing 6.12

Co-ordinating media to build brand equity

In developing effective integrated marketing communications campaigns, marketing communications must sometimes be explicitly tied together to create or enhance brand equity. This section, after reviewing the nature of the problem, proposes solutions.

Factors creating weak brand links

For brand equity to be built, it is critical that the communication effects created by advertising be linked to the brand. Often, such links are difficult to create. For

Brand Briefing 6.12 *continued*

example, TV ads often do not 'brand' well; that is, weak links may exist from the communication effects created by a TV ad to knowledge about the brand in memory. The main reasons for this are: competitive clutter, ad content and structure and lack of consumer involvement. The following sections examine these factors.

Competitive clutter

Competing ads in the product category can create interference and consumer confusion as to which ad goes with which brand.[71] Chapter 4 described the ad campaign for Energizer batteries that featured a pink toy bunny that kept 'going . . . and going . . . and going'. Unfortunately, consumer research discovered that, of the people in an annual survey who named this popular commercial as their favourite of the year, 40 percent mistakenly attributed it to Eveready's main competitor, Duracell – only 60 percent correctly identified it as an Energizer ad! To exacerbate this interference problem, it is often the case that competing ads appear in the same media vehicle because they typically target the same consumers. For example, an analysis of one week of prime-time television advertising found that, of the 57 commercials that ran in an average hour, 24, or 42 percent, faced at least 1 competitor running an ad during that same time period.[72]

Ad content and structure

Factors related to the content and structure of an ad can result in weak links from the brand to communication effects created by ad exposure. For example, advertisers have a vast range of creative strategies and techniques at their disposal to improve consumer motivation and lead to greater involvement and enhanced ad processing on their part. Although these 'borrowed interest' tactics may grab consumers' attention, the resulting focus of attention and processing may be directed in a manner that does *not* create strong brand associations. For example, when the actor James Garner was advertising for Polaroid, US marketing research surveys routinely noted that many interview respondents mistakenly attributed his promotion to Kodak, its rival. Moreover, when attention-getting creative tactics are employed, the position and prominence of the brand in the ad are often downplayed. Delaying brand identification or providing few brand mentions in an ad may also raise processing intensity but result in attention being directed away from the brand. Furthermore, limited brand exposure time in the ad allows little opportunity for elaboration of existing brand knowledge, also contributing to weak brand links.[73]

Consumer involvement

In certain circumstances, consumers may not have any inherent interest in the product or service category or may lack knowledge of the specific brand (eg, in the case of a low-share brand or a market entry). The resulting decrease in consumer motivation and ability to process translates to weaker brand links. Similarly, a change in advertising strategy to target a new market segment or add a new attribute, benefit or usage association to the brand image may also fail to produce

Brand Briefing 6.12 *continued*

strong brand links because consumers cannot easily relate this new advertising information to existing brand knowledge.[74]

Strategies to strengthen communication effects

Thus, for a variety of reasons, consumers may fail to correctly identify advertising with the advertised brand or, even worse, incorrectly attribute advertising to a rival. In these cases, advertising worked in the sense that communication effects – ad claims and executional information, as well as cognitive and affective responses by consumers to that information – were stored in memory. Yet advertising failed in the sense that these communication effects were not accessible when critical brand-related decisions were made.

One common tactic to achieve ad and point-of-sale congruence and improve ad recall is to make the brand name and packaging information prominent in the ad. Unfortunately, this increase in brand emphasis means that communication effects and brand associations that can potentially affect brand evaluations are less likely to be able to be created by the ad and stored in consumer memory. In other words, although consumers are better able to recall the advertised brand with this tactic, there is *less* other information about the brand to recall. Three potentially more effective strategies are brand signatures, ad retrieval cues and media interactions, as follows.

Brand signatures

Perhaps the easiest way to increase the strength of brand links with communication effects is to create a more powerful and compelling brand signature. The *brand signature* is the manner by which the brand is identified at the conclusion of a TV or radio ad or displayed within a print ad. The signature must creatively engage the consumer and cause him or her to pay more attention to the brand itself and, as a consequence, increase the strength of brand associations created by the ad. An effective brand signature often dynamically and stylistically provides a seamless connection to the ad as a whole. For example, the US 'Got milk?' campaign always displayed that slogan in a manner fitting the ad (eg, in flames for a 'yuppie in hell' ad or in primary school print for a 'school lunchroom bully' ad). As another example, the introductory Intel Inside campaign always ended with a swirling image from which the Intel Inside logo dramatically appeared, in effect stamping the end of the ad with Intel Inside in an 'in your face' manner.

Ad retrieval cues

An effective tactic to improve consumers' motivation and ability to retrieve communication effects when making a brand-related decision is to use advertising retrieval cues. An *advertising retrieval cue* is visual or verbal information uniquely identified with an ad that is evident when consumers are making a product or service decision.

Brand Briefing 6.12 *continued*

The purpose is to maximize the probability that consumers who have seen or heard the cued ad will retrieve from long-term memory the communication effects that were stored from earlier processing of that ad. Ad retrieval cues may consist of a visual, a catchy slogan or any unique advertising element that serves as an effective reminder to consumers. For example, in an attempt to remedy a problem with mistaken attributions, Quaker Oats placed a photograph of the 'Mikey' character from its Life cereal ad in the USA on the front of the pack. More recently, Eveready featured a picture of its pink bunny character on the packaging for Energizer batteries to reduce consumer confusion with Duracell, which does actually use similar bunnies in its ads in Europe.

Ad retrieval cues can be placed in the shop (eg, on the packaging or as part of a shelf talker or some other point-of-sale device), combined with a promotion (eg, with a free-standing insert coupon), included as part of a Yellow Pages directory listing or embedded in any marketing communication option where recall of communication effects can be advantageous to marketers. By using ad retrieval cues, greater emphasis can be placed in the ad on supplying persuasive information and creating positive associations so that consumers have a reason *why* they should purchase the brand. Ad retrieval cues allow for creative freedom in ad execution because the brand and package need not be the centrepiece. The effectiveness of ad retrieval cues depends on how many communication effects are potentially retrievable and how likely these are to be retrieved from memory with only the brand as a cue, as compared with the executional information making up the ad retrieval cue. An ad retrieval cue is most effective when many communication effects are stored in memory but are only weakly associated to the brand because of one or more of the various factors noted previously.

Media interactions

Print and radio reinforcement of TV ads (in which the video and audio components of a TV ad serve as the basis for the respective types of ads) can be effective in building on communication effects from TV ad exposure and more strongly link them to the brand. Cueing a TV ad with an explicitly linked radio or print ad can create similar or even enhanced processing outcomes that can substitute for additional TV ad exposures. Moreover, a potentially useful, although rarely employed, media strategy is to run explicitly linked print or radio ads before the accompanying TV ad. The print and radio ads in this case function as teasers and increase consumer motivation to process the more complete TV ad consisting of both audio and video components.

As another strategy, combinations of TV ad excerpts within a campaign (eg, 15-second spots consisting of highlights from longer 30- or 60-second spots for those campaigns characterized by only 1 dominant ad, or umbrella ads consisting of highlights from a pool of ads for those campaigns consisting of multiple ad

Brand Briefing 6.12 *continued*

executions) and across campaigns over time (eg, including elements from past campaigns that are strongly identified with the brand) may be helpful in strengthening dormant associations and facilitating the formation of consumer evaluations of and reactions to the ads and their linkage to the brand.

TV ads over time

The rationale for these strategies is that TV ads should not be considered as discrete units that are created for a particular ad campaign and therefore run for a certain length of time before being replaced by a new campaign. Rather, TV ads should be thought of more broadly as consisting of different ingredients or pieces of information that advertisers might choose to combine in different ways over time to improve their brand-building abilities. The most important ingredients are those identifiable visual scenes, characters, symbols and verbal phrases or slogans that can serve as cues or reminders of communication effects created by a single TV ad, a campaign with several TV ads or a previous campaign.

Combining these ingredients to exploit communication effects over time offers several benefits. First, it can help to maintain the strength of unique and favourable brand associations. In particular, without such reminders, the heritage of a brand and its original associations may become weakened because the campaign is not being currently shown or a new campaign is using different creative strategies to reposition or modernize the brand. Second, it can facilitate the formation of favourable attitudes by consumers towards the advertising and brand. In other words, consumers may be likely to say, 'I like the ads for that brand.' As noted previously, such attitudes can favourably affect brand evaluations, especially for low-involvement consumer decisions.

Note that an implicit issue in this discussion is the optimal continuity to have with advertising and communication campaigns over time. Congruity theory would suggest, on the one hand, that a moderate amount of change is appropriate.[75] Too little change may not be noticed by consumers and thus have no effect. On the other hand, more dramatic changes in brand positioning may confuse consumers and result in them still continuing to think of the brand in the 'old way'. Because of strong associations in memory, consumers may either fail to incorporate new ad information into their brand knowledge structures or fail to retrieve new ad information when making later product or service decisions. In many cases, a moderate change in creative (eg, retaining the current positioning but communicating it with a new creative) may be the most effective way to maintain or enhance the strength of brand associations. If the favourability or uniqueness of brand associations are deficient in some way, however, then a more severe change in positioning emphasizing different points of parity or points of difference may be necessary.

Discussion questions

1. Pick a brand and gather all its marketing communication materials. How effectively has the brand mixed and matched marketing communications? Has it capitalized on the strengths of different media and compensated for their weaknesses at the same time? How explicitly has it integrated its communication campaign?

2. What do you see as the role of the internet for building brands? How would you evaluate the website for a brand – for example, Porsche, Ikea or Levi's?

3. From a current issue of a monthly magazine, decide which print ad you feel is the best and which ad you feel is the worst based on the criteria described in this chapter.

4. Pick up a Sunday newspaper and look at the coupon supplements. How are they building brand equity, if at all? Try to find a good example and a poor example of brand-building promotions.

5. Choose a popular event. Who sponsors it? How are they building brand equity with their sponsorship? Are they integrating the sponsorship with other marketing communications?

References and notes

[1] For a broader perspective, see a good advertising text such as George E. Belch and Michael A. Belch, *Advertising and Promotion: An integrated marketing communications perspective*, 6th edn, Homewood, IL: McGraw-Hill/Irwin, 2004; Thomas C. O'Guinn, Richard J. Seminik and Chris T. Allen, *Advertising and Integrated Brand Promotion*, 4th edn, South-Western, 2006; or John R. Rossiter and Larry Percy, *Advertising and Promotion Management,* 2nd edn, New York: McGraw-Hill/Irwin, 1997.

[2] Matthew Swibel, 'You've got ads', *Forbes*, 5 September 2005: 63–7.

[3] Paul Keegan, 'The man who can save advertising', *Business 2.0*, November 2004: 119–28.

[4] William J. McGuire, 'The nature of attitudes and attitude change', in T*he Handbook of Social Psychology*, 2nd edn, eds. G. Lindzey and E. Aronson, Reading, MA: Addison-Wesley, 1969, Vol. 3: 136–314.

[5] Thomas C. Kinnear, Kenneth L. Bernhardt and Kathleen A. Krentler, *Principles of Marketing*, 4th edn, New York: Harper Collins, 1995.

[6] Philip L. Kotler and Kevin Lane Keller, *Marketing Management*, 12th edn, Upper Saddle River, NJ: Prentice-Hall, 2006.

[7] Alexander L. Biel, 'Converting image into equity', in *Brand Equity and Advertising*, eds. David A. Aaker and Alexander L. Biel, Hillsdale, NJ: Lawrence Erlbaum Associates, 1993: 67–82.

[8] 'How to turn junk mail into a goldmine – or perhaps not', *The Economist*, 1 April 1995: 51–2.

[9] Leonard M. Lodish, Magid Abraham, Stuart Kalmenson, Jeanne Livelsberger, Beth Lubetkin, Bruce Richardson and Mary Ellen Stevens, 'How TV advertising works: a meta analysis of 389 real world split cable TV advertising experiments', *Journal of Marketing Research*, May 1995, 32: 125–39; Magid Abraham and Leonard Lodish, *Advertising Works: A study of*

advertising effectiveness and the resulting strategies and tactical implications, Chicago: Information Resources Inc., 1989.

[10]Greg Allenby and Dominique Hanssens, 'Advertising response', MSI Special Reports 2004, No. 05-200: 1–8.

[11]Lorrie Grant, 'Home Depot sales soar 16%', *USA Today,* 15 August 2001: B1.

[12]Rossiter and Percy, *Advertising and Promotion Management.*

[13]Amanda Swinburn, 'Virgin Money scoops top marketing award', *B&T,* 29 October 2004.

[14]Max Robins, 'Seinfeld aces ultimate test', *TV Guide:* 81.

[15]Jack Neff and Lisa Sanders, 'It's broken', *Advertising Age,* 16 February 2004: 1, 30.

[16]John Flinn, 'Advertising's new age', *San Francisco Chronicle,* 23 October 1994: B14.

[17]Radio Advertising Bureau 2007, 'Radio is everyone' [advertising supplement], Irving, TX: Radio Advertising Bureau.

[18]For a comprehensive overview, see Bob Schulberg, *Radio Advertising: The authoritative handbook,* Lincolnwood, IL: NTC Business Books, 1990.

[19]David Ogilvy, *Ogilvy on Advertising,* New York: Vintage Books, 1983.

[20]Magazine Publishers of America, 'How do you measure a smile?', *Advertising Age,* 26 September 2005: M6.

[21]For more discussion on these guidelines, see Philip Ward Burton and Scott C. Purvis, eds, *Which Ad Pulled Best?,* 9th edn, New York, NY: McGraw-Hill/Irwin, 2003.

[22]Julia Reed, 'Ads where you least expect them', *U.S. News and World Report,* 9 March 1987: 46.

[23]Kevin Goldman, 'P&G experiments with an infomercial', *Wall Street Journal,* 8 July 1994: B9.

[24]Jim Edwards, 'The art of the infomercial', *Brandweek,* 3 September 2001: 14–19.

[25]'How to turn junk mail into a goldmine'; Gary Levin, 'Going direct route,' *Advertising Age,* 11 November 1991, 37.

[26]See Jakki J. Mohr, Sanjit Sengupta and Stanley J. Slater, *Marketing of High-Technology Products and Innovations,* 2nd edn, Upper Saddle River, NJ: Prentice Hall, 2005; Ward Hanson, *Principles of Internet Marketing,* Cincinnati, OH: South-Western College Publishing, 1999; and Eloise Coupey, *Marketing and the Internet,* Upper Saddle River, NJ: Prentice Hall, 2001.

[27]'Banner-ad blues', *The Economist,* 24 February 2001: 63–4.

[28]Suzanne Vranica, 'GM is joining online videogame wave', *Wall Street Journal,* 26 July 2001: B11.

[29]This section is based on material from 'To boldly go fully mobile', *Marketing Week,* 27 September 2005; Adam Woods, 'Brands wait for 3G opportunity', *Revolution,* 21 June 2005; www.vibes.com

[30]Jeff Pelline, 'New commercial twist in corporate restrooms', *San Francisco Chronicle,* 6 October 1986.

[31]Chuck Stogel, 'Quest for the captive audience', *Superbrands,* 1992: 106–7.

[32]David T. Friendly, 'Selling it at the movies', *Newsweek,* 4 July 1983: 46.

[33]Joanne Lipman, 'Product placement can be free lunch', *Wall Street Journal,* 25 November 1991; John Lippman and Rick Brooks, 'Hot holiday flick pairs FedEx, Hanks', *Wall Street Journal,* 11 December 2001: B1.

[34]Scott Hume and Marcy Magiera, 'What do moviegoers think of ads?', *Advertising Age,* 23 April 1990: 4.

[35]*Consumer Reports,* December 1982: 752–5.

[36]For an excellent summary of issues related to the type, scope and tactics of sales promotions design, see John A. Quelch, 'Note on sales promotion design', teaching note N-589-021, Boston, MA: Harvard Business School, 1988.

[37]Andrew Ehrenberg and Kathy Hammond, 'The case against price-related promotions', *Admap,* June 2001.

[38]John A. Quelch, 'Note on sales promotion design'.

[39]Michael L. Ray, *Advertising and Communication Management,* Upper Saddle River, NJ: Prentice Hall, 1982.

[40]Geoffrey Fowler, 'When free samples become saviors', *Wall Street Journal*, 14 August 2001: B1.

[41]'Coupon trend reports', www.santella.com/Trends.htm

[42]Rossiter and Percy, *Advertising and Promotion Management.*

[43]Eric Hollreiser, 'Trading up from tactics to strategy in the trade game', *Brandweek*, 3 October 1994: 26–33.

[44]See Peggy Cunningham, Shirley Taylor and Carolyn Reeder, 'Event marketing: the evolution of sponsorship from philanthropy to strategic promotion', Conference on Historical Analysis & Research in Marketing, 1993: 407–25.

[45]Michael Oneal and Peter Finch, 'Nothing sells like sports', *BusinessWeek*, 31 August 1987: 48–53.

[46]Roush, 'Sports Marketer'.

[47]The Association of National Advertisers has a useful source, *Event Marketing: A management guide*, 2nd edn, www.ana.net.

[48]Eric Pfanner, 'For cash, European soccer says, "This space for rent"', *Herald Tribune*, 30 May 2005.

[49]William L. Shankin and John Kuzma, 'Buying that sporting image', *Marketing Management,* spring 1992: 65.

[50]Jim Crimmins, 'Most sponsorships waste money', *Advertising Age*, 21 June 1993: S2.

[51]Gerry Khermouch, 'Buzz marketing', *BusinessWeek*, 30 July 2001; Catherine Valenti, 'Some brands thrive without advertising', ABCNews.com, 23 August 2001.

[52]Gerry Kermouch, 'Buzz marketing'. As cited in David Godes and Dina Mayzlin, 'Firm-created word-of-mouth communication: a field-based quasi-experiment', working paper, Yale University. These researchers show how effective word-of-mouth recommendations can be created by non-loyal customers, as well as offering a scale of the breadth of a person's social network.

[53]Todd Wasserman, 'P&G buzz program Tremor moving on to mothers', *Brandweek*, 26 September 2006: 15.

[54]Mark Hughes, *Buzzmarketing*, The Woodlands, TX: Portfolio, 2005.

[55]Gerry Khermouch, 'Buzz marketing'.

[56]Emanual Rosen, *The Anatomy of Buzz*, New York: Currency, 2000.

[57]John Quelch, 'Communications policy', teaching note 5–585–021, Boston, MA: Harvard Business School, 1984.

[58]Christopher Power, 'Smart selling', *BusinessWeek*, 3 August 1992: 46–52.

[59]For a review of some academic and practitioner issues with IMC, see Prasad A. Naik, 'Integrated marketing communications: provenance, practice and principles', in *Handbook of Advertising*, eds. Gerard J. Tellis and Tim Ambler, New York: Sage, forthcoming, and Tom Duncan and Frank Mulhern eds, 'A white paper on the status, scope and future of IMC', Daniels College of Business at the University of Denver March 2004.

[60]Prasad A. Naik, Kalyan Raman and Russ Winer, 'Planning marketing-mix strategies in the presence of interactions', *Marketing Science*, 2005, 24 (10): 25–34.

[61]www.goodbysilverstein.com. For another example of IMC principles applied to automotive marketing, see Rex Briggs, R. Krishnan and Norm Borin, 'Integrated multichannel communication strategies: evaluating the return on marketing objectives – the case of the 2004 Ford F-150 launch', *Journal of Interactive Marketing*, 2005, 19 (3): 81–90.

[62]Joseph W. Alba and J. Wesley Hutchinson, 'Dimensions of consumer expertise', *Journal of Consumer Research*, March 1987, 13: 411–53.

[63] John Burnett and Sandra Moriarty, *Introduction to Marketing Communications: An integrated approach*, Upper Saddle River, NJ: Prentice Hall, 1998.

[64] Susan E. Heckler and Terry L. Childers, 'The role of expectancy and relevancy in memory for verbal and visual information: what is incongruency?', *Journal of Consumer Research*, March 1992, 18: 475–92; Michael J. Houston, Terry L. Childers and Susan E. Heckler, 'Picture-word consistency and the elaborative processing of advertisements', *Journal of Marketing Research*, November 1987, 24: 359–69; Thomas K. Srull and Robert S. Wyer, 'Person memory and judgment', *Psychological Review*, 1989, 96 (1): 58–83.

[65] Larry Light, 'Bringing research to the brand equity process', paper presented at the ARF Brand Equity Workshop, 15–16 February 1994.

[66] For example, see Daniel R. Young and Francis S. Belleza, 'Encoding variability, memory organization, and the repetition effect', *Journal of Experimental Psychology: Learning, Memory, and Cognition*, 1982, 8 (6): 545–59; and H. Rao Unnava and Robert E. Burnkrant, 'Effects of repeating varied ad executions on brand name memory', *Journal of Marketing Research*, November 1991, 28: 406–16.

[67] Michael D. Johnson, 'Consumer choice strategies for comparing noncomparable alternatives', *Journal of Consumer Research*, December 1984, 11: 741–53.

[68] Julie A. Edell and Kevin Lane Keller, 'The information processing of co-ordinated media campaigns', *Journal of Marketing Research*, May 1989, 26: 149–63; Julie Edell and Kevin Lane Keller, 'Analyzing media interactions: the effects of co-ordinated print-TV advertising campaigns', Marketing Science Institute Report No. 99-120.

[69] William T. Moran, 'Insights from pricing research', in *Pricing Practices and Strategies*, ed. E. B. Bailey, New York: The Conference Board, 1978: 7–13.

[70] Timothy M. Smith, Srinath Gopalakrishna and Paul M. Smith, 'The complementary effect of trade shows on personal selling', *International Journal of Research in Marketing*, 2004, 21 (1): 61–76.

[71] Raymond R. Burke and Thomas K. Srull, 'Competitive interference and consumer memory for advertising', *Journal of Consumer Research*, June 1988, 15: 55–68; Kevin Lane Keller, 'Memory factors in advertising: the effect of advertising retrieval cues on brand evaluations', *Journal of Consumer Research*, December 1987, 14: 316–33; Kevin Lane Keller, 'Memory and evaluations in competitive advertising environments', *Journal of Consumer Research*, March 1991, 17: 463–76; Robert J. Kent and Chris T. Allen, 'Competitive interference effects in consumer memory for advertising: the role of brand familiarity', *Journal of Marketing*, July 1994, 58: 97–105.

[72] Joe Mandese, 'Rivals' ads cluttering TV', *Advertising Age*, 14 October 1991.

[73] David Walker and Michael J. von Gonten, 'Explaining related recall outcomes: new answers from a better model', *Journal of Advertising Research*, 1989, 29: 11–21.

[74] Kevin Lane Keller, Susan Heckler and Michael J. Houston, 'The effects of brand name suggestiveness on advertising recall', *Journal of Marketing*, January 1998, 62: 48–57.

[75] Joan Meyers-Levy and Alice M. Tybout, 'Schema congruity as a basis for product evaluation', *Journal of Consumer Research*, June 1989, 16: 39–54.

7 Using secondary brand associations to build brand equity

PREVIEW

Chapters 4 to 6 described how brand equity could be built through the choice of brand elements (Chapter 4) or through marketing and product, price, distribution and marketing communication strategies (Chapters 5 and 6). This chapter considers the third means by which brand equity can be built – namely, through related or 'secondary' brand associations. That is, brands themselves may be linked to other entities that have their own knowledge structures in the minds of consumers. Because of these linkages, consumers may assume or infer that some of the associations or responses that characterize the other entities may also be true for the brand. Thus, in effect, associations are transferred from other entities to the brand. In other words, the brand essentially 'borrows' some brand knowledge and, depending on the nature of those associations and responses, perhaps brand equity from other entities.

This indirect approach to building brand equity is referred to as using *secondary brand knowledge*. Secondary brand knowledge may be important if existing associations or responses are deficient in some way. So, secondary associations can be used to create strong, favourable and unique associations or positive responses that might otherwise not be present. Secondary brand knowledge can also be an effective way of reinforcing associations and responses in a fresh way.

This chapter considers the means by which secondary brand knowledge can be created by linking the brand to the following (see Figure 7.1):

- companies;
- countries of origin or other geographic areas;
- channels of distribution;
- co-branding;
- licensing;
- celebrity endorsements;
- sporting, cultural or other events (sponsorship); and
- third-party sources (eg, awards or reviews)

As an example of the issues involved, suppose that Salomon, makers of alpine and cross-country ski bindings, ski boots and skis, decided to introduce a tennis racquet called The

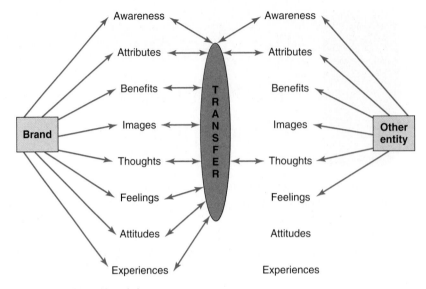

Figure 7.1   Transfer of brand knowledge

Avenger. Although the company has been selling safety bindings for skis since 1947, much of Salomon's growth was fuelled by its diversification into ski boots and the introduction of a type of ski called the monocoque. Salomon's innovative, stylish and quality products have led to strong leadership positions. In creating the marketing campaign to support the Avenger racquet, Salomon could attempt to build on secondary brand knowledge in a number of ways.

- Salomon could use associations with the corporate brand by sub-branding the product – for example, by calling it Avenger by Salomon. Consumers' evaluations of the product extension would be influenced by the extent to which consumers held favourable associations with Salomon as a company or brand because of its skiing products and felt that such knowledge was predictive of a tennis racquet that the company made.
- Salomon could try to rely on its European origins (it has its headquarters near Lake Annecy at the foot of the French Alps), although such a location would not seem to have much relevance to tennis.
- Salomon could also try to sell through upmarket, professional tennis shops and clubs in the hope that the retailers' credibility would rub off on the Avenger brand.
- Salomon could try to co-brand by identifying a strong ingredient brand for their grip, frame, or strings (eg, as Wilson did by incorporating Goodyear tyre rubber on the soles of its ProStaff Classic tennis shoes).
- Although it is doubtful that a licensed character could help, Salomon could approach one or more top professional players to endorse the racquet or could choose to become a sponsor of tennis tournaments or even the professional men's or women's tennis tournaments.
- Salomon could attempt to secure and publicize favourable ratings from third-party sources (eg, tennis magazines and websites).

CONCEPTUALIZING THE PROCESS

Linking a brand to another entity may create a set of associations between the brand and the entity as well as affect existing brand associations. Both outcomes are discussed next.[1]

Creation of brand associations

By making a connection between a brand and another entity, consumers may form a mental association between the brand and this other entity and, consequently, any or all associations, judgements, feelings and the like linked with that entity. In general, this secondary brand knowledge is most likely to affect evaluations of a product when consumers lack either the motivation or ability to judge product-related concerns.

Effects on existing brand knowledge

Linking a brand with some other entity may not only create new brand associations with the entity but may also affect existing associations. The basic mechanism involved with these indirect effects is as follows. Consumers have some knowledge of an entity. When a brand is identified as being linked with that entity, consumers may infer that some of the associations, judgements or feelings that characterize the entity may also characterize the brand. A number of theoretical mechanisms from psychology predict such an effect. For example, such reasoning by consumers could merely be a result of 'cognitive consistency' considerations – in other words, in the minds of consumers, if it is true for the entity, then it must be true for the brand.

In terms of conceptualizing this inferencing process more formally, three factors are particularly important in predicting the extent of leverage that might result from linking the brand to another entity.

1. *Awareness and knowledge of the entity:* if consumers have no knowledge of the secondary entity, there is nothing that can be transferred. Ideally, consumers would be aware of the entity, hold some strong, favourable and perhaps even unique associations regarding the entity and have good feelings about the entity.
2. *Meaningfulness of the knowledge of the entity:* given that the entity evokes potentially beneficial associations, judgements or feelings, to what extent is this knowledge relevant and meaningful for the brand? The meaningfulness of this knowledge may vary depending on the brand and product context. Some associations, judgements or feelings may seem relevant to and valuable for the brand, whereas other knowledge may seem to consumers to have little connection.
3. *Transferability of the knowledge of the entity:* assuming that some potentially useful and meaningful associations, judgements or feelings exist regarding the entity and could be transferred to the brand, to what extent will this knowledge actually become linked to the brand? Thus, an issue is the extent to which associations will in fact become strong, favourable and unique, and judgements and feelings will become positive in the context of the brand.

In other words, the questions about transferring secondary knowledge from another entity are what do consumers know about the other entity and does any of this knowledge affect what they think about the brand when it becomes linked or associated with this other entity?

Theoretically, any aspect of knowledge may be inferred from other entities about the brand (see Figure 7.1), although some types of entities are more likely to inherently create or affect certain kinds of brand knowledge than other types. For example, events may be conducive to the creation of experiences; people may be effective at bringing out feelings; other brands may be well suited to establishing particular attributes and benefits; and so on. At the same time, any one entity may be associated with many aspects of knowledge, each of which may alter brand knowledge directly or indirectly.

For example, consider the effects on knowledge of linking the brand with a cause. Identification of the brand with a cause (eg, Avon's Breast Cancer Crusade or Ronald McDonald House) could have several effects on brand knowledge. A cause marketing campaign could build awareness via recall and recognition; enhance brand image in terms of attributes such as user imagery (eg, kind and generous) and brand personality (eg, sincere); evoke feelings (eg, social approval and self-respect); establish attitudes (eg, credibility judgements such as trustworthy and likeable); and create experiences (eg, through a sense of community and participation in cause-related activities).

In general, it may be more likely for judgements or feelings to transfer from the entity than more specific associations. Many specific associations are likely to be seen as irrelevant or too strongly linked with the original entity to transfer to the brand.

The process by which knowledge such as associations from another entity can be transferred to a brand is discussed in detail in Chapter 12. As is pointed out there, the inferencing process depends on the strength of the linkage or connection in consumers' minds between the brand and other entity. The more consumers see similarities between the entity and the brand, the more likely it is that consumers will infer similar knowledge about the brand.

Guidelines

Choosing to emphasize source factors or a particular person, place or thing should be based on consumers' awareness of that entity, as well as how the associations with, judgements of or feelings for the entity might possibly become linked with the brand or affect existing brand associations. Secondary brand knowledge may be a means of creating or reinforcing an important point of difference versus competitors or a necessary or competitive point of parity.

Entities may be chosen for which consumers have some, or even a great deal of, similar associations. A *commonality* strategy makes sense when consumers have associations in memory with another entity that are congruent with desired brand associations. For example, consider a country such as New Zealand, which is known for having more sheep than people. A New Zealand sweater manufacturer that positioned its product on the basis of its 'New Zealand wool' presumably could easily establish strong and favourable brand associations because New Zealand may already mean 'wool' to many people.

However, there may be times when entities are chosen that represent a departure for the brand because there are few if any common or similar associations. Such *complementarity* strategies can be critical in terms of delivering the desired position. The challenge here is to ensure means of transferability such that the less congruent knowledge for the entity has either a direct or indirect effect on existing brand knowledge. This may require marketing campaigns that overcome initial consumer confusion or scepticism.

Even if consumers accepts an association, using secondary brand knowledge may be risky because some control of the brand image is given up. The source factors or related person, place or thing will undoubtedly have a host of other associations, of which only a smaller set will be of interest to the marketer. Managing the transfer process so that only the relevant secondary knowledge becomes linked with the brand may be difficult. Moreover, this knowledge may change over time as consumers learn more about the entity, and these new associations, judgements or feelings may or may not be advantageous for the brand. Brand Briefing 7.1 describes how secondary associations such as different sports and social sponsoring can be used to strenghten the brand. Brand Briefing 7.2 describes the David Beckham brand.

Brand Briefing 7.1

Transfer of meaning through secondary associations

This brief illustrates the process of borrowing secondary associations from another entity to strengthen a company's brand. The research methodology used in the study was the projective Brandjobs model (Figure 7.2), which is based on the most important cross-cultural human personality traits, the five-factor model (see Chapter 9 for a description of the research methodology). The research was carried out in Sweden in 2007.

The vertical dimension goes from introvert to extrovert, and the horizontal dimension from 'Getting ahead' to 'Getting along'. Combining these two dimensions results in a 'personality platform' based on human attributes. (Chapter 9 illustrates the brand personalities of some Swedish companies.) With this knowledge, correlations can be made between the personalities that characterize these companies with the personalities of nine sponsorship options that characterize various personalities and associations. The aim of the research was to develop a methodology that would help companies to choose the right sponsorship for their brands.

Figure 7.3 shows the personalities of nine sponsorship options. As described before, two strategies can be used for choosing the secondary associations that can be used to link to a brand. On one hand the *commonality* strategy makes sense when associations are sought that are congruent with desired brand associations. On the other hand, the *complementary* strategy can be used as a departure from the current position to the desired one. When the personalities of these options are

Brand Briefing 7.1 *continued*

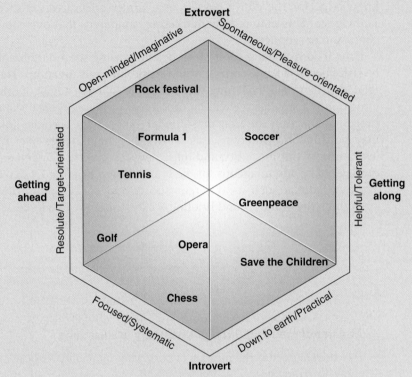

Figure 7.2   Personalities of nine different sponsorship entities (Brandjobs model research)

	H&M	BMW	IBM	Carlsberg	Ikea
Rock festival	0.78	0.38	<0	0.63	0.36
Formula 1	0.54	0.81	0.37	0.57	<0
Soccer	0.65	0.41	0.20	0.75	0.20
Greenpeace	0.10	<0	<0	0.19	0.52
Save the Children	<0	<0	<0	0.10	0.36
Opera	0.31	0.15	0.22	0.4	0.15
Chess	<0	0.10	0.82	<0	<0
Golf	0.27	0.64	0.71	0.43	<0
Tennis	0.32	0.53	0.55	0.55	<0

Figure 7.3   Correlation between brand and sponsoring activities

Brand Briefing 7.1 *continued*

analyzed for H&M (Figure 7.4) and Ikea (Figure 7.5), 'Rock festival', 'Soccer' and 'Formula 1' have commonality with the H&M personality while 'Greenpeace', 'Rock festival' and 'Save the Children' show similarities with Ikea. Chess, Golf, and Tennis would mean a departure from the current Ikea personality.

This research illustrates how a brand personality can be used to help choose the right sponsoring activity for a brand. The Brandjobs method is used to find and analyze the emotional brand personality. The personality characteristics of both the company and the secondary association from another entity have been used to see which sponsorship activities fit together, and which do not. Using a sponsorship strategy with a different personality and associations from a brand can add something new to the brand and energize the brand.

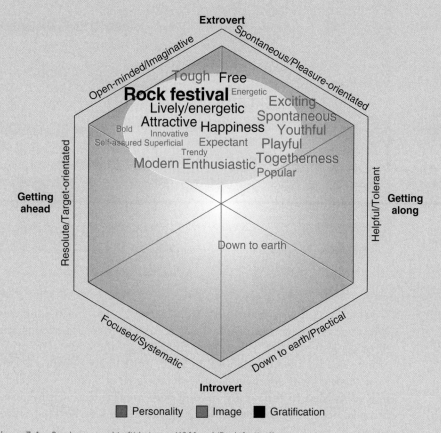

Figure 7.4   Good sponsorship fit between H&M and 'Rock festival'

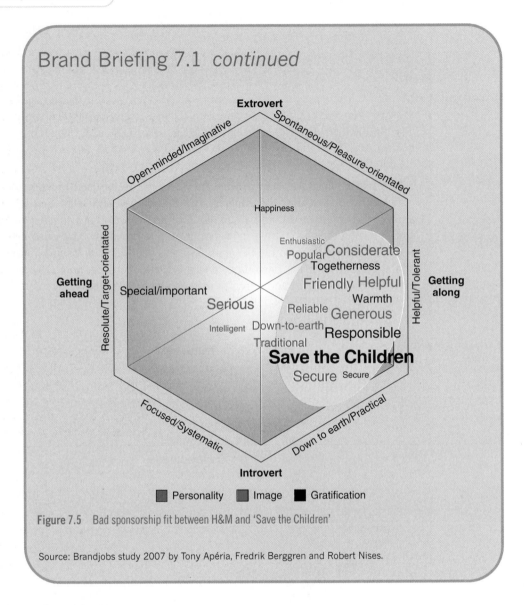

Brand Briefing 7.1 *continued*

Figure 7.5   Bad sponsorship fit between H&M and 'Save the Children'

Source: Brandjobs study 2007 by Tony Apéria, Fredrik Berggren and Robert Nises.

When Vodafone signed then Manchester United midfielder David Beckham in 2002 as an endorser, the question was at first whether or not consumers would find a fit or consistency and, if not, how much value the endorsement would add to the brand. The endorsement ended in 2005, most likely because Beckham's next club, Real Madrid, was sponsored by Vodafone's rival Siemens Mobile! When Beckham moved to Madrid the family needed help moving and settling into a new country. Initially, his wife and children were to stay in the UK. Beckham hired a personal assistant, Rebecca Loos, and she claimed to have had an affair with Beckham in the media in April 2004. This has never been admitted by David Beckham. Brand Briefing 7.2 describes the David Beckham brand in more depth.

Brand Briefing 7.2

The David Beckham brand

The football player David Beckham may be worth millions of pounds, but the David Beckham brand is worth many times more. As a footballer, Beckham will earn about €4 million for the 2007/08 season, but sponsorship deals, promotional contracts and earnings from the Beckham brand are estimated to be €13.6 million in the same period. According to *Forbes* magazine, Beckham is ranked second only to US golfer Tiger Woods as the most important sportsman of 2007.

Sports stars have become the rock stars of the age. Beckham arrived at just the right time; the world of sport was longing for a superstar while England's Premier League was establishing itself as the world's best football league, with worldwide TV coverage (Figure 7.6).

As a footballer, Beckham is known for his magic right foot and astonishing free kicks, passes and goals. But despite his success for club and country, Beckham has fought for his entire career to be recognized as a star.

The fact is that the Beckham brand was built up off the football pitch. Beckham has become known above all as a model, sex symbol and trendsetter. He's a pop star in a football kit with an enviable lifestyle and a wife who's nearly as famous – the former Spice Girl Victoria Beckham. He's a good-looking and fashion-conscious man who is known, sought out and desired by women and men the world over. In fact, many fashion experts claim that Beckham has created an interest in fashion and looks among men who previously didn't care about these subjects.

Figure 7.6   The sports brand David Beckham
Source: Rex Features

Brand Briefing 7.2 *continued*

Football was already the world's most popular sport and this fact, together with Beckham's ability to attract so many groups with varying demographics and psychographics, form a unique combination.

It's a combination that has been extremely profitable, both for football and sport in general, as well as Beckham personally, the clubs he's played for and the companies which have sponsored him. It's this combination that makes Beckham so attractive to the media and sponsors and what makes him one of the most powerful personal brands in the world.

Beckham – a Galactico, model or both?

On the pitch, Beckham has proved his worth for the clubs he has represented, but, as a brand, he has been priceless. He was the basis for Manchester United's rapid rise in popularity in South East Asia during the 1990s. And in 2003, when he became one of the so-called 'Galacticos' at Real Madrid for the princely sum of €35 million, there was much speculation that the Spanish club had bought a mannequin rather than a player. And with good reason: during four seasons with the club, Real Madrid sold €609 million worth of merchandise – an increase of 137 percent – and sold a million Beckham replica shirts in his first month at the club.

In the summer of 2007, Beckham moved to the USA to play for LA Galaxy. For the club, the league, other clubs and the sponsors, signing Beckham was a dream come true. They had the possibility of associating themselves with one of the world's most attractive people. Interest in football – and the league – in the USA increased. A bigger audience means more media coverage and therefore more sponsors, which means that all the conditions are in place. Beckham the person (not the sports star) is already known in this new market – at least as well known as the most famous stars in US sport. In research carried out by Davie Brown Entertainment, 51.9 percent of Americans knew who David Beckham was, compared with the 25 percent recognition of the basketball star Tim Duncan from the San Antonio Spurs, who was considered to be the best sportsman then competing in the USA.

The strength of the Beckham brand is reflected in his contract, which is estimated to be worth €169 million over five years. Yet, despite this outlay, it's still being seen as a lucrative deal for the club and its management group Anschutz Entertainment Group (AEG). Both AEG and Beckham receive a percentage of income from ticket sales, merchandise and sponsorship and LA Galaxy increased its sponsorship income for the 2007 season by €13.6 million. However, in autumn 2007, Beckham was not playing so much for the team because of a leg injury.

Adidas, Pepsi and Motorola

Throughout his career, brand Beckham has attracted sponsors. Multinational companies have recruited Beckham for his worldwide popularity and status, regardless

Brand Briefing 7.2 *continued*

of people's interest in football. Beckham's biggest personal sponsors are Adidas, Motorola, Pepsi and Coty, who between them pay him €13.6 million a year.

In the summer of 2003, Beckham and Adidas signed a lifetime contract estimated to be worth €2.7 million per year. In addition to this, Beckham is paid for the way in which Adidas uses his name, and even a percentage of sales. The strength of brand Beckham is illustrated by the fact that Adidas sells more Beckham-associated products than products associated with all their other sponsored sportsmen combined.

The mobile phone company Motorola (with a contract for 2006–08) uses Beckham as a global ambassador, focusing on the Asian market. In addition to the use of image rights, for which Beckham is used in advertising campaigns and point-of-sale merchandising, consumers are also offered screensavers, photos and films. Beckham also played a big role in the launch of (Moto)Red, a mobile phone created to play a part in the fight to prevent Aids in Africa.

These sponsors also see potential in Beckham's move to the USA – Adidas and Motorola have both launched TV adverts – and he has signed a contract with Walt Disney, where he will feature in the 'Year of a million dreams' campaign aimed at building interest in Disney's theme parks.

The future

Beckham himself is also thinking strategically, by creating sub-brands of himself. In 2005, he started The David Beckham Academy with the pay-off 'Live out your dreams'. The academies – in London and Los Angeles and soon opening in Asia – focus on helping young players and are sponsored by Adidas and Volkswagen.

During 2007, Beckham launched his own perfume, together with his sponsor Coty. More such products from David and his wife Victoria can be expected.

Having conquered Europe, Asia and many other parts of the football world, the USA provides exciting challenges. These include creating interest in Beckham among non-football fans and attracting more people to a game that is relatively small in America. Like Tiger Woods and Michael Jordan before him, Beckham needs to draw people to his sport, and his personality, who may not enjoy that sport. He needs to get people who have never seen him play (or seen anyone play for that matter) interested and passionate about the game. The Beckhams are regulars in the celebrity magazines, together with their Hollywood friends such as Tom Cruise and Will Smith – surely a vital element in introducing the average American to the brand of Beckham.

Sources: www.sb.se; http://news.bbc.co.uk/sport1/hi/football/6969893.stm; www.davidbeckham.com; www.davidbeckhamacademy.com; www.forbes.com/facesinthenews/2007/07/07/; www.forbes.com/2005/04/01; www.forbes.com/facesinthenews/2007/01/29; http://money.cnn.com/2007/07/05; www.askmen.com/sports/business_100/101_sports_business.htm; www.forbes.com/services/2007/07/16; www.mobiledia.com/news/47595.html.

The following sections consider some of the ways in which secondary brand knowledge can become linked to a brand.

COMPANY

The branding strategies adopted by a company that makes a product or offers a service are an important determinant of the strength of association from the brand to the company and any other existing brands. Three branding options for a new product are:

- create a new brand;
- adopt or modify an existing brand;
- combine an existing and new brand.

Existing brands may be related to the corporate brand (eg, Sony Ericsson and Nokia) or a specific product brand (eg, Sony Ericsson W900i mobile phone and Nokia N95) and may involve names, logos, symbols and so forth. To the extent that the brand is linked with another existing brand, then knowledge about the other brand may also become linked with the brand. In particular, a corporate or family brand can be a source of much brand equity. For example, as discussed in Chapter 11, a corporate brand may evoke associations with common product attributes, benefits or attitudes; people and relationships; activities and values; and corporate credibility. Brand Briefing 7.3 describes the corporate image campaign for Altoids Mints.

Brand Briefing 7.3

Altoids Mints with curiously interesting associations

In 1783, Smith Kendon, proprietor of the London firm Smith & Company, came up with the idea for an exceptionally intense mint lozenge. Originally marketed to relieve intestinal discomfort, by the 1920s, its advertising suggested that these mints could act as antidote to poisons in the stomach. This led to the start of the 'curiously strong' branding campaign that still defines the brand to this day.

The name Altoids was born out of the Latin 'alt' (to change) and the Greek 'oids' (taking the form of). Also, by the 1920s, to help protect the mints in pockets and handbags across the globe, the original cardboard box had been replaced by a distinctive metal tin. The mints are for sale in the USA, the UK, Canada and South Korea, and are a market leader in the USA. The brand was sold by Kraft to the Wrigley Company in 2004.

The 'curiously strong' branding has evolved to link with cultural experiences, such as design, art and cinema: there is an Altoids curiously strong designer award as well as an Altoids art forum, the curiously strong collection and film making through the Altoids independent cinema project.

Brand Briefing 7.3 *continued*

Figure 7.7   Marketing of the Altoid brand

Altoids have used many interactive marketing initiatives such as inviting people to send 'singing love telegrams' to friends over the internet (Figure 7.7). The 'curiously strong' phrase has also been extended to include advertising themes of homosexuality, sadomasochism and transvestism, likely to offend some groups but, equally, also likely to appeal to its target market (Figure 7.8).

Figure 7.8   Controversial press adverts for Altoids

Brand Briefing 7.3 *continued*

Figure 7.9 Rebellious image exploited through hobby projects on the web

Oddly, the Altoid tin has become a useful item for hobby projects, such as pinhole cameras, housings for small amateur radios, MP3 players, cases for the Creative Zen Micro and Apple iPod music players (Figure 7.9), tobacco or marijuana smoking devices and battery packs. Such innovations – and photos and instructions on the web about how to construct them – are brand linkages that build Altoid as an interesting, rebellious brand. Despite the curiously strong brand position it has attained, Altoids has experienced competition in the 'strong mint' market. The question some analysts have been asking is where to go from here – how can an edgy brand evolve to maintain market leadership?

Sources: www.altoids.com; www.wrigley.com; http://en.wikipedia.org/wiki/Altoids; Julie Jargon, 'Wrigley's new mints are curiously weak', *Chicago Business*, 7 January 2006; Tim Nudd, 'Altoids Sours decides that deviant sexual themes is the way to go', www.adfreak.com, 27 July 2006; www.flickr.com/groups/altoids/pool/

Using a corporate brand may not always be useful, however, depending on the awareness and image involved.

Chapter 11 considers the pros and cons of various branding strategies, including corporate and family branding strategies, and examines how different types of brand associations may potentially be linked with a product by using an existing brand to brand the new product.

Finally, it should be recognized that brands and companies are often unavoidably linked with the category and industry in which they compete, sometimes with adverse consequences. Consider the challenges faced by a brand in the oil and gas industry, which consumers generally view in a poor light. By virtue of membership of the category in which it competes, an oil company, a utility or a telecommunication company may expect to face a potentially suspicious or sceptical public *regardless* of what it does.

Research from the Reputation Institute 2007 with 60,000 consumers in 29 countries reveals that different industries have different reputations, as measured by the RepTrak Pulse index. This estimates the health of a company's overall reputation by measuring the esteem, good feeling, trust and admiration that stakeholders feel towards a company.

Some industries are seen as more trustworthy, others as more risky; some are seen as profiteers, others are seen as more giving (Figure 7.10). All companies operate in an industry context – and either suffer or benefit from the positive or negative halo around the industry. Top-rated industries are consumer products, industrial products, beverage and electrical and electronics sectors. Industries with weak reputations are telecommunications, utilities, construction/engineering, information and media, and transport and logistics. Companies in these industries face a predicament in that consumers do not trust, like or respect them. A negative context makes it challenging for individual companies to create favourable regard. The financial services

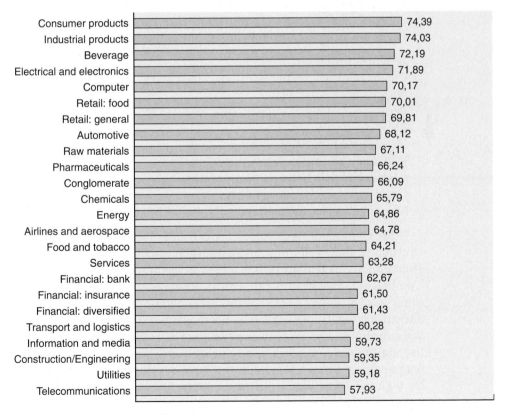

Industry	Score
Consumer products	74,39
Industrial products	74,03
Beverage	72,19
Electrical and electronics	71,89
Computer	70,17
Retail: food	70,01
Retail: general	69,81
Automotive	68,12
Raw materials	67,11
Pharmaceuticals	66,24
Conglomerate	66,09
Chemicals	65,79
Energy	64,86
Airlines and aerospace	64,78
Food and tobacco	64,21
Services	63,28
Financial: bank	62,67
Financial: insurance	61,50
Financial: diversified	61,43
Transport and logistics	60,28
Information and media	59,73
Construction/Engineering	59,35
Utilities	59,18
Telecommunications	57,93

Figure 7.10   The reputations of different industries

Source: Reputation Institute, 2007.

sector is a case in point. The different segments in the industry (banking, insurance and financial) are not highly regarded by consumers internationally, which creates challenges for companies operating in the sector.

COUNTRY OF ORIGIN AND OTHER GEOGRAPHIC AREAS

Besides the company that makes the product, the country or geographic location from which it is seen as originating may also become linked with the brand and generate secondary associations.[2] Many countries have become known for expertise in certain product categories or for conveying a particular type of image. As noted by many, the world is becoming a 'cultural bazaar' where consumers can pick and choose brands based on their beliefs about the quality of certain products from certain countries or the image that these brands or products communicate. Thus, a consumer from anywhere in the world may choose to wear Italian suits, exercise in US trainers, listen to a Japanese MP3 player, drive a German car or drink English ale. Choosing brands with strong national ties may reflect a decision to maximize product utility and communicate self-image based on what consumers believe about products from those countries.

Thus, a number of brands are able to create a point of difference in part because of consumers' identification of and beliefs about the country of origin. For example, consider the following strongly linked brands and countries:

Ikea furniture: Sweden
Chanel perfume: France
Foster's beer: Australia
Barilla pasta: Italy
BMW: Germany
Dewar's whisky: Scotland
Kikkoman soy sauce: Japan
Bertolli olive oil: Italy
Gucci shoes and handbags: Italy
Mont Blanc pens: Switzerland

Other geographic associations are possible, such as states, regions and cities. Establishing a geographic or country-of-origin association can be done in various ways. The location can actually be embedded in the brand name (eg, San Pellegrino water, Cumberland sausage or South African Airways) or combined with a brand name in some way (eg, Bailey's Irish Cream). Also, a location may become the theme in brand advertising (eg, Foster's or Coors beer). Some countries have even created advertising campaigns to promote their products. For example, 'Rums of Puerto Rico' advertise that they are only the finest-quality rums, leading to a 70 percent share of US brand sales in rums. Other countries have developed and advertised labels or seals for their products.[3] Brand Briefing 7.4 describes New Zealand's attempt to create a brand, 'The New Zealand Way.'

Because it is typically a legal necessity for the country of origin to appear visibly somewhere on the product or packaging, associations with the country of origin

Brand Briefing 7.4

Selling brands the New Zealand way

In 1991, New Zealand set out to create 'The New Zealand Way' (NZW) brand. The objective of the campaign was to build a national umbrella brand that added value to the marketing of products from New Zealand by differentiating them in international markets; raising the awareness of New Zealand's unique values and personality; and using the promotional activities of the New Zealand Tourism Board, Tradenz (a government trade development board) and manufacturers. The NZW brand was designed to position a broad range of the country's tourism and trade products and services at the forefront of world markets.

The focal point for communicating the personality and meaning of the NZW brand was to be the brand design and the campaign that was to be built around it. The three components of the NZW brand design were the brand logo, a descriptor word or short phrase (eg, quality) and the slogan, 'The New Zealand Way.' The descriptor words were to allow users of the NZW brand to customize it to suit their marketing campaigns.

The campaign included public relations, direct marketing and events in important geographic markets. By 1998, more than 170 companies were licensed to use the New Zealand Way fern brand. Goods produced by these companies accounted for more than €2.9 billion, or 20 percent, of New Zealand's foreign exchange earnings that year.

Source: http://business.newzealand.com

almost always have the potential to be created at the point of sale and to affect brand decisions there. The question really becomes one of relative emphasis and the role of country of origin or other geographic regions throughout the marketing campaign. Becoming strongly linked with a place is not without potential disadvantages. Events or actions associated with the country may colour people's perceptions. For example, strong connections with a country may pose problems if a company desires to move production elsewhere.

Waterford

Waterford Wedgwood's ornate crystal had been promoted as the ultimate in Irish handmade luxury for decades. Ads called Waterford 'the ambassador of a nation' and attributed its brilliance to 'deep, prismatic cutting that must be done entirely by skilled hands rather than machines'. Because of cost considerations, Waterford had to confront the issue of shifting production out of Ireland and using machines to make some lines. In 2003, Wedgwood decided to close two factories in England and move production from Stoke-on-Trent to Asia. Waterford was encouraged to make such a move because of consumer research in the USA – home to more than 70 percent of Waterford's crystal sales – that indicated that what mattered to its customers there was the Waterford label and not where the crystal was made. Nevertheless, many retailers worried that such a move could destroy the precious brand image that Waterford had built.

As the media landscape changes, so does the way we need to communicate to build Sweden, says the director-general of the Swedish Institute. Brand Briefing 7.5 describes the attempt to build Sweden as a modern country brand on *Second Life*.

Brand Briefing 7.5

Building Sweden as a brand on *Second Life*

The Swedish Institute (SI) is a public agency that promotes Sweden as a brand and interest in Sweden abroad. SI seeks to establish co-operation and lasting relations with other countries through active communication and cultural, educational and scientific exchanges. Its operations are carried out in co-operation with Swedish and foreign partners, as well as with embassies and consulates around the world. To achieve these goals, awareness of and interest in Sweden must first increase. One way to increase the awareness of Sweden was the inauguration of a virtual embassy in the online role-playing game *Second Life* in the spring of 2007.

'The role of the Swedish Institute is to generate goodwill and confidence in Sweden. As the media landscape changes, so does the way people gather information. It is important for us to be a part of these developments . . . It is a real pleasure to see that so much media, above all the foreign press, has recognised how progressive Sweden is. The great interest that this has generated in the media is estimated to have already paid off tenfold', said Olle Wästberg, director-general of the Swedish Institute.

Brand Briefing 7.5 *continued*

Figure 7.11   Inaguration ceremony at the Second House of Sweden on *Second Life*

The Second House of Sweden – Sweden's embassy in *Second Life* – opened its doors on 30 May 2007 (Figure 7.11). Sweden's minister for foreign affairs, Carl Bildt, cut the ribbon at an inauguration ceremony broadcast simultaneously to press conferences in Stockholm and Budapest.

The idea has generated great interest both in Sweden and abroad, according to Stefan Geens, project leader at the Swedish Institute: 'Now that we have a platform in *Second Life* to promote the culture and lifestyle of Sweden, many Swedish companies and organisations are interested in collaborating. Discussions are under way with a number of potential partners which enables SI to co-brand with other strong Swedish brands.'

Two examples: in collaboration with the Swedish Institute, the national museum in Stockholm is loaning some of its most famous works of art to the virtual embassy in *Second Life*. Since the 1880s, the museum has made loan deposits from its collections to various government bodies and museums. Today there are some 3,800 works of art that are on long loans to government premises in Sweden and Swedish embassies abroad.

Another co-branding is with the Swedish furniture retailer Ikea – which allows visitors to furnish their virtual homes in *Second Life*.

Sources: www.si.se; www.sweden.se/secondlife

Finally, the favourability of a country-of-origin association must be considered from both domestic and foreign perspectives. In the domestic market, country-of-origin perceptions may stir consumers' patriotic notions or remind them of their past. As international trade grows, consumers may view certain brands as symbolic of their cultural heritage and identity. Patriotic appeals have been the basis of marketing strategies all over the world. Patriotic appeals, however, can lack uniqueness and even be overused. For example, during the Reagan administration in the 1980s, a number of US brands in a diverse range of product categories (eg, cars, beer and clothing) used pro-USA themes in advertising, perhaps diluting the efforts of all as a result. The tragic events of 11 September 2001, raised the visibility of patriotic appeals again.

CHANNELS OF DISTRIBUTION

Chapter 5 described how members of the channels of distribution can directly affect the equity of the brands they sell by the supporting actions that they take. Because of the associations linked to shops in the minds of consumers, they can indirectly affect the brand equity of products they sell by influencing the associations inferred about these products. This section considers how shops can indirectly affect brand equity through this 'image transfer' process.

Because of associations with product assortment, pricing and credit policy, quality of service and so on, retailers have their own brand images in consumers' minds. The Brand Briefing 7.6 summarizes academic research into retailer images. Retailers create these associations through the products and brands they stock and the means by which they sell them. To more directly shape their image, many retailers advertise and promote directly to customers. The associations a shop has in the minds of

Brand Briefing 7.6

Understanding retailers' brand image dimensions

Access

The distance that consumers must travel to shop is a basic criteria in their shop choice decisions. Access is important in a consumer's assessment of total shopping costs and is especially important for retailers who wish to get a substantial share of trips by people who visit the shop to buy a few specific things and small basket shoppers who buy a few things per visit.

Atmosphere

Elements of the shop, such as colour, music and crowding, can influence consumers' perceptions, whether or not they go in, how much time they spend in it and how much money they spend. A pleasing atmosphere provides substantial hedonic utility (pleasure experience) to consumers and encourages them to visit more often, stay longer and buy more. Although atmosphere improves consumers' perceptions of the quality of merchandise, consumers also tend to associate it with higher prices. An appealing in-store atmosphere offers potential in terms of crafting a unique shop image and establishing differentiation. Even if the products and brands stocked by a

Brand Briefing 7.6 *continued*

retailer are similar to others, the ability to create a strong in-store personality and rich experiences can play a crucial role in building retailer brand equity.

Price and promotion

A retailer's price image is influenced by attributes such as average prices, how much variation there is in prices over time, the frequency and depth of promotions and where a retailer positions itself on a continuum between EDLP (everyday low price) and HILO (high–low promotional pricing). Consumers are more likely to develop a favourable price image when retailers offer frequent discounts on many products than when they offer less frequent, but steeper discounts. Further, products that have a high unit price and are purchased more frequently are more salient in determining the retailer's price image. One pricing format does not dominate another, but research has shown that large basket shoppers prefer EDLP stores while small basket shoppers prefer HILO, and it is optimal for the latter to charge an average price that is higher than the EDLP. Finally, price promotions are associated with switching shops but the effect is indirect, altering consumers' category purchase decisions while they are in the shop rather than altering their choice of which one to visit.

Cross-category assortment

Consumers' perception of the breadth of products and services offered significantly influence a retailer's image. A broad assortment can create customer value by offering convenience and ease of shopping. It is risky to extend too far too soon, but, staying too tightly coupled to an assortment and image may unnecessarily limit the retailer's range of experimentation. The logic and sequencing of a retailer's assortment policy are critical to its ability to expand its meaning and appeal to consumers over time.

Within-category assortment

Consumers' perceptions of the depth of a retailer's assortment within a product category are an important part of a shop's image and a driver of choice. As the perceived assortment of brands, flavours and sizes increases, variety-seeking consumers will perceive greater utility; consumers with uncertain future preferences will believe they have more flexibility in their choices; and, in general, it is more likely that consumers will find the item they desire. A greater number of stock-keeping units (SKUs) need not directly translate to better perceptions. Retailers often can reduce the number of SKUs substantially without damaging consumer perceptions, as long as they pay attention to the most preferred brands, the organization of the assortment and the availability of diverse product attributes.

Brand Briefing 7.6 *continued*

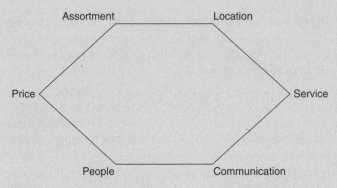

Figure 7.12   ICA's hexagon model of food retailing

ICA, a retailer with almost half of the Swedish grocery market, is part of the Dutch Ahold group and has developed a hexagon model of how shops compete in local markets (Figure 7.12). The model was developed by Mikael Hernant at ICA. When the model is used, the points on each corner are scored on a scale from 1 to 5.[4]

1. *Location:* the most important factor in the model.
2. *Assortment:* the depth and breadth of the food and non-food stocked in all categories, and how it is presented.
3. *Price:* the general price level and the intensity of price competition.
4. *People:* the 'soft' service that employees provide to the customers.
5. *Service:* the hard service, such as the number of tills, opening hours, additional services and internet delivery.
6. *Communications:* activities used to communicate with customers.

Sources: Tony Apéria, 'Brand relationship management: den varumärkesbyggande processen', doctoral thesis, Stockholm: Stockholm University, 2001; Kusum L. Ailawadi and Kevin Lane Keller, 'Understanding retail branding: conceptual insights and research priorities', *Journal of Retailing*, 2004, 80: 331–42; 'Developing parsimonious retailer equity indexes using partial least-squares analysis: a method and applications', *Journal of Retailing*, 2003, 79: 161–70.

consumers may be linked to the products they sell or affect brand associations for these products. For example, a consumer may infer certain characteristics about a product on the basis of where it is sold: 'If it is sold by Harrods, it must be of good quality and if it is sold by Aldi it must be of lower quality.' The same brand may be perceived differently depending on whether it is sold in a shop seen as prestigious and exclusive or in one seen as designed for bargain shoppers and having more mass appeal.

Shops' image associations can either benefit or hurt a brand. For many high-end brands, a natural growth strategy is to expand their customer base by tapping new channels of distribution. Such strategies can be dangerous, however, depending on how customers and retailers react. When Levi Strauss decided to expand the distribution channels in the USA for its jeans in the early 1980s to includes mass-market chains Sears and Penney's, Macy's decided to drop the brand because it felt its image had been cheapened. A brand revitalization programme in the mid-1980s brought the jeans back into the department store chain, and Levi's was careful to sub-brand its 2003 entry into discount retailers Target and Wal-Mart as Levi Strauss Signature.

Brand Briefing 7.7 describes the battle between US fashion companies Calvin Klein and Warnaco that revolved around the appropriateness of retail distribution for the Calvin Klein brand.

Brand Briefing 7.7

Calvin Klein and Warnaco's battle of the brands

From a humble start as a designer of women's coats, Calvin Klein bred a fashion empire with the help of savvy, high-image and often risqué marketing created by his in-house CRK Advertising team. Calvin Klein started the designer jeans craze in the late 1970s with ads that featured teenage actress Brooke Shields claiming that nothing came between her and her Calvins. Ads in 1985 for Obsession perfume depicted a provocative 'pseudo-orgy', and the fragrance quickly became the number two seller in the country. Klein touched off a scandal and an FBI investigation in 1995 when many of his jeans ads were labelled pornographic and exploitative because they contained revealing images of underage models. Through success and scandal, Calvin Klein remained one of the foremost names in US fashion.

Business success was fuelled in part by licensing of his name for products other than the seasonal designer clothing that made Calvin Klein a household name. For every €2,000 dress sold at Galleria Vittorio Emanuele in Milan, many more pairs of €35 jeans, €10 cotton briefs and €30 bottles of perfume bearing the CK logo passed through tills in shops across the globe. Calvin Klein and his team design the products and licensees take care of the logistics of manufacturing, distribution and retail contracts. Although licensing his name led to millions in profits, it also reduced the control Calvin Klein had over his brand.

In a move that set off a legal dispute, Calvin Klein sued licensee Warnaco in June 2000 for 'improper sales' to US discounters such as Costco and Sam's Club. Calvin Klein alleged that, by 'producing jeans and underwear expressly for downmarket discount stores', the licensee was 'cheapening' the brand. In particular, Klein found fault with Warnaco's decision to sell CK underwear to low-cost retailer JC Penney. Other Calvin Klein retail accounts, such as Dillard's and Federated department stores, were angered by this decision and threatened to halt orders of CK underwear.

Brand Briefing 7.7 *continued*

The suit claimed that Warnaco had been pushing CK merchandise into other low-cost retailers without permission.

A month after Klein's filing, Warnaco countersued, charging Calvin Klein with violating the licence agreement. Linda Wachner, chief of Warnaco, defended her company's sales to discounters by saying, '[Calvin Klein] gets a full list every year of every account and every shipment, of every dollar.' Warnaco's countersuit also accused Calvin Klein of trade libel and bad faith dealing, claiming the designer had failed to attend a design meeting for over a year.

The two sides settled as the case was going to trial in 2001, and the licence remained intact. Warnaco agreed not to sell CK jeanswear and underwear to JC Penney, but was allowed to continue selling to discount retailers Costco, Sam's Club, and BJ's at 'dramatically reduced volume'. Other terms of the settlement effectively gave Calvin Klein more control over Warnaco's dealings with the brand.

Phillips Van Heusen acquired Calvin Klein in 2003 for a deal worth €511 million that gave it the rights to the brand name, the collection business and the brand's related licensing revenue. By then Wachner had been ousted and relations between Warnaco and the new brand owners were seen to be positive.

Sources: Teri Agins, 'Calvin Klein, Warnaco settle their bitter feud', *Wall Street Journal*, 23 January 2001; Teri Agins and Rebecca Quick, 'Illegal briefs?', *Wall Street Journal*, 1 June 2000; Lisa Marsh, 'To where from eternity?' *Sunday Herald*, 28 September 2003.

CO-BRANDING

As noted previously, a new product can become linked to an existing corporate or family brand that has its own set of associations through a brand extension strategy. A brand can also use associations by linking itself to other brands from the same or a different company. *Co-branding* – also called brand bundling or brand alliances – occurs when two or more brands are combined into a joint product or are marketed together in some fashion.[5] A special case of this strategy is ingredient branding, which is discussed in the next section.[6]

Co-branding has been a way to increase the scope and influence of a brand, enter new markets, embrace new technologies, reduce costs and refresh brand image. It has become a widely used business strategy in the food, drinks, retailing, air travel and financial industries. One example of co-branding is the co-operation between Le Cordon Bleu (a French culinary academy) and Tefal (a leading French cookware manufacturer). The familiar Cordon Bleu brand helped to build awareness for the Tefal Integral product. Two other examples are the co-operation between

Mercedes-Benz and Swatch to launch a car and Intel's co-operation with computer manufacturers. Credit card companies such as Mastercard, Visa, AmEx and Diners are all veterans in co-branding. In this market, co-branding often involves three brands (eg, Shell MasterCard from Citi Cards). The basis for any co-operation is that synergy creates value for both parties, over and above the value they would expect to generate on their own. Co-branding has been around for years; for example, in the USA, Betty Crocker paired with Sunkist Growers in 1961 to market a lemon chiffon cake mix.[7] With airlines, alliances can involve a host of brands, such as Star Alliance, which includes 17 airlines. By joining any of the 17 airlines the members of the frequent flyer scheme can earn miles or points.

Brand Briefing 7.8 describes how the leading European bicycle company Cycleurope has used co-branding with Emporio Armani and Ducati to strengthen the Italian bicycle brand Bianchi.

Brand Briefing 7.8

Bianchi's co-branding with Emporio Armani and Ducati

Cycleurope, part of Grimaldi Industry, is a consolidation of companies and has evolved through acquisitions of strong bicycle brands. In the beginning, Cycleurope only had a Scandinavian presence. Today the group is the leading European bicycle maker with a turnover of €280 million (Figure 7.13).

Cycleurope has a strong brand portfolio with market-leading brands such as Bianchi (Italy), Gitane (France), Crescent (Sweden), Monark (Sweden), DBS (Norway) and Kildemoes (Denmark). Bianchi is Cycleurope's premium brand and one of the best-known bicycle brands in the world with about half of the racing market. Cycleurope wanted Bianchi to be present in all markets where the company was operating and positioned in the premium segment in each market. Bianchi was seen as the flagship in the brand portfolio.

Bianchi has a history in Italy that goes back to 1885. Bianchi stands for technology, innovation, quality and tradition. Bianchi is about giving passion to the people and the vision is to be the leading bicycle brand when it comes to quality, success in competition and setting innovative trends. Bianchi is a premium brand with a

Figure 7.13 Cycleurope logo

Brand Briefing 7.8 *continued*

certain exclusivity. Not everybody can afford it and not everybody needs it, only the passionate cyclists and the professionals.

To complement marketing for the Bianchi brand, the Cycleurope management tried to create dynamism for the brand using co-branding. The co-branding partners must be of such character that they create a special interest for the co-branded products. Under the concept 'Made in Italy' Italian co-branding partners were chosen, among them Ducati and Emporio Armani. Both these brands, like Bianchi, have a long history in Italy, both these brands are considered to be premium and very well known, but there were different strategies behind these choices. With Ducati, the purpose was to strengthen the association with road racing, while the purpose of Emporio Armani was to gain more fashion and trend associations with the Bianchi brand.

Strengthening associations through Bianchi-Ducati

Ducati could be seen as the king of motorbike racing. Both Bianchi and Ducati are in the racing segment, but in different markets – bicycles and motorcycles. The Bianchi-Ducati bicycle was made in a very limited quantity and was sold at a premium price of €5,500 only through the Ducati website (Figure 7.14). 'The purpose to co-brand with Ducati from the Bianchi side was to strengthen the current position and associations to road racing, rather than creating new associations for the Bianchi brand', said Tony Grimaldi, chief of Cycleurope.

New associations through Bianchi-Emporio Armani

Emporio Armani is a fashion brand, associated with highly respected designers and seen to be a trendsetter for clothes. The purpose behind co-branding with Emporio Armani was to create new associations, and to create design, fashion and

Figure 7.14   Co-branding Bianchi-Ducati

Brand Briefing 7.8 *continued*

Figure 7.15   Co-branding Bianchi-Emporio Armani

trend associations for the Bianchi brand. To build exclusivity and to strengthen the new associations for the Bianchi brand, Bianchi-Emporio Armani bicycles were only sold in selected Emporio Armani stores (Figure 7.15). The bicycles were launched together with the new sport collection for Emporio Armani.

'The purpose of the Bianchi-Empori Armani co-branding, from the Bianchi point of view, was foremost to gain more design associations to the Bianchi brand', said Grimaldi. The bicycle was produced in a limited quantity and sold for a premium price of €1,000.

Sources: Interview with Tony Grimaldi, chief executive, Cycleurope, 25 July 2007; Christian Sandberg, 'Brand-driven business development', thesis, Nordic Brand Academy.

Motorola co-branded an MP3-enabled phone with Apple iTunes, the ROKR, to emphasize the music player aspect of the phone. Sony Ericsson and Nokia use Carl Zeiss lenses in their phones to add credibility to their cameras (and Sony Ericsson through Sony, owns and uses the Walkman brand for mobile music players, including phones). Co-branding is also common in business-to-business settings, where companies discover that their capability might not always be in line with their credibility: co-branding can help in such situations. Cisco Systems, for instance, uses different 'relationship logos' to support its partners. The Cisco logo co-operation gives partners opportunities to demonstrate their relationship with Cisco while strengthening the Cisco brand.

Brand Briefing 7.9 describes how the chocolate bar Daim used line extensions, co-branding and ingredient branding to travel from the chocolate category to other categories such as ice-cream, cake and biscuits.

Brand Briefing 7.9

Co-branding of the Daim bar

The Daim bar was born in 1953. It has gone from a strong domestic Swedish position, as a chocolate bar, to now being an international brand covering categories such as chocolate, ice-cream, coffee, cake and biscuits. Today, Daim is the largest chocolate brand in the Nordic region and the best-selling ice-cream cone in Sweden. Since 1993, Daim has been part of Kraft Foods, which has enabled Daim to become a global brand.

Daim contains a combination of crunchy, almond-flavoured toffee and chocolate. It was clear to management that there were significant export opportunities, as well as extension opportunities for the brand. Over the years there have been changes of the packaging and the name to make the brand more consumer relevant. The name changed from Dajm to Daim in 1990, and packaging changed colour from brown to red in 1993.

Brand-driven development

The Daim management has developed the brand through line extensions within the same category; category extensions to ice-cream, cake, biscuits with brands from companies such as Unilever, McDonald's, Mandelbageriet and Bonjour); and category extensions and ingredient branding with other Kraft brands within chocolate and coffee.

Line extensions Even though the product has remained the same, Daim has developed over the years. In the beginning it was only available in 29-gram pieces. To get more shelf space, the packaging was developed to include two-pack, three-pack and five-pack variants. Then, 1998 saw the launch of a 'limited edition' Daim Orange, a strategy often used to stimulate interest in a brand. Important milestones have been the launch of Daim Double in 1971, Daim Mini in 1974, Daim individual sweets in 1992 and the return to using the strategy of limited editions in 1998.

Category extensions The first co-branded extension was ice-cream (in a family-sized tub) in 1974 with Unilever. It became a big success so it enabled a second launch in ice-cream – the Daim ice-cream cone in 1987 (also with Unilever). The McFlurry co-operation with McDonald's started in 1999, and the co-operation with Mandelbageriet for the Almondy Daim cake and Bonjour biscuits in 2001. The purpose of the alliances has been to extend the Daim brand from chocolate to other categories (chocolate is not consumed in the summer as ice-cream is). To get more shelf space in the frozen ice-cream sector, a Daim cone mini-pack was launched.

In 2001, the company's third cake was launched, combining the Daim bar with an almond cake recipe. Another cake was introduced by Almondy in 2003 using Snickers in the recipe.

Research by Stockholm University showed that the Daim ice-cream cone and McFlurry were seen as being of high quality and creating overall positive associations.

Brand Briefing 7.9 *continued*

These two products provide a sort of individual utiliaritian satisfaction. The research also indicated that there seemed to be a logical connection between ice-cream and individual confectionaries.

Category extensions and ingredient branding with other Kraft brands Kraft uses Daim for internal co-branding. Daim is used as an ingredient brand within other strong brands within chocolate and coffee. Two recent examples are linking together with Marabou and Gevalia within chocolate (Sweden) and Jacobs Cappucino coffee (Austria) and Gevalia Cappucino coffee (Sweden). The new concept Daim Inside has been developed for the ingredient strategy. This means that Daim is trying to establish a position within the coffee category. Daim is also sold at every Ikea store.

Sources: Tony Apéria, 'Brand relationship management: den varumärkesbyggande processen', doctoral thesis, Stockholm: Stockholm University, 2001; Tony Apéria, and Rolf Back, *Brand Relations Management: Bridging the gap between brand promise and brand delivery*, Sweden, Liber: 2004; Forsberg, Kennbert and Windahl, 'Varumärkesalliansers imagepåverkan på ledarvarumärket: en fallstudie av Daim och dess varumärkesallianser', Stockholm University School of Business, 2002; www.kraftfoods.com; www.qffintl.com/pdf/july_2005/6074.cfm; www.qffintl.com/pdf/july_2005/6074.cfm

Figure 7.16 summarizes the advantages and disadvantages of co-branding and licensing. The main advantage to co-branding is that a product may be uniquely and convincingly positioned by virtue of the brands involved. Co-branding can create more compelling points of difference or points of parity, or both, for the brand than might have been otherwise feasible. As a result, co-branding can generate greater sales from the existing target market as well as open up opportunities with new consumers and channels. Co-branding can reduce the cost of product introduction because two well-known images are combined, accelerating potential adoption. Co-branding also may be a valuable means of learning about consumers and how other

Advantages	Disadvantages
Borrow needed expertise.	Loss of control.
Leverage equity you don't have.	Risk of brand equity dilution.
Reduce cost of product introduction.	Negative feedback effects.
Expand brand meaning into related categories.	Lack of brand focus and clarity.
Broaden meaning.	Organizational distraction.
Increase access points.	
Source of additional revenue.	

Figure 7.16 Advantages and disadvantages of co-branding and licensing

companies approach them. In poorly differentiated categories especially, co-branding may be an important means of creating a distinctive product.

The potential disadvantages of co-branding are the risks and lack of control that arise from becoming aligned with another brand in the minds of consumers. Consumer expectations about the level of involvement and commitment with co-brands are likely to be high. Unsatisfactory performance thus could damage the brands involved. If the other brand is one that has entered into a number of co-branding arrangements, there also may be a risk of overexposure that would dilute the transfer of any association. It may also result in distraction and a lack of focus on existing brands.

Guidelines

Brand Briefing 7.10 provides insight into how consumers evaluate co-branded products. To create a strong co-brand, it is important that both brands entering the

Brand Briefing 7.10

Understanding brand alliances

Brand alliances, in which two brands are combined in some way as part of a product or some other aspect of the marketing campaign, come in all forms. Academic research has explored the effects of co-branding, ingredient branding strategies and advertising alliances.

Co-branding

Park, Jun, and Shocker compare co-brands to the notion of 'conceptual combinations' in psychology. A conceptual combination (eg, 'apartment dog') consists of a modifying concept, or 'modifier' (eg, *apartment*) and a modified concept, or 'header' (eg, *dog*). Experimentally, Park and his colleagues explored the ways that Godiva (associated with expensive, high-calorie boxed chocolates) and Slim-Fast (associated with inexpensive, low-calorie diet food) could hypothetically introduce a chocolate cake mix separately or together through a co-brand.

They found that a co-branded version of the product would be better accepted than if either brand attempted to extend individually into the cake mix category. They also found that consumers' impressions of the co-branded concept were driven by the header brand (eg, Slim-Fast chocolate cake mix by Godiva was seen as lower calorie than if the product was called Godiva chocolate cake mix by Slim-Fast; the reverse was true for associations of richness and luxury). Similarly, consumers' impressions of Slim-Fast after exposure to the co-branded concept were more likely to change when it was the header brand than when it was the modifier brand. Their findings show how carefully selected brands can be combined to overcome potential problems of negatively correlated attributes (eg, rich taste and low calories).

Brand Briefing 7.10 *continued*

Simonin and Ruth found that consumer attitudes towards a brand alliance could influence subsequent impressions of each partner's brands (such that spillover effects existed), but that these effects also depended on other factors such as product fit or compatibility and brand fit or image congruity. Brands less familiar than their partners contributed less to an alliance but experienced stronger spillover effects than their more familiar partners. Relatedly, Voss and Tansuhaj found that consumer evaluations of an unknown brand from another country were more positive when a well-known domestic brand was used in an alliance.

Levin and Levin explored the effects of dual branding, which they defined as a marketing strategy in which two brands (usually restaurants) shared the same facilities while providing consumers with the opportunity to use either one or both brands. Kumar found that introducing a co-branded extension into a product category made it less likely that a brand from the new category could turn around and introduce a counterextension into the original product category.

Ingredient branding

Desai and Keller conducted a laboratory experiment to consider how ingredient branding affected consumer acceptance of an initial line extension, as well as the ability of the brand to introduce future category extensions. Two types of line extensions, defined as brand expansions, were studied: *slot filler expansions*, in which the level of one existing product attribute changed (eg, a new type of scent in a washing powder); and *new attribute expansions*, in which a new attribute or characteristic was added to the product (eg, cough relief syrup added to sucking sweets). Two types of ingredient branding strategies were examined by branding the target attribute ingredient for the brand expansion with either a new name as a *self-branded ingredient* (eg, the washing powder with its own brand of scented bath soap) or a well-respected name as a *co-branded ingredient* (eg, washing powder with another company's scented bath soap).

The results indicated that, with slot filler expansions, although a co-branded ingredient facilitated initial expansion acceptance, a self-branded ingredient led to more favourable subsequent extension evaluations. With more dissimilar new attribute expansions, however, a co-branded ingredient led to more favourable evaluations of both the initial expansion and the subsequent extension.

Venkatesh and Mahajan derived an analytical model based on bundling and reservation price notions to help formulate optimal pricing and partner selection decisions for branded components. In an experimental application in the context of a university shop selling laptop computers, they showed that, at the bundle level, an all-brand Compaq PC with Intel 486 commanded a clear price premium over other options. The relative brand strength of Intel, however, was shown to be stronger in some sense than that of the Compaq brand.

Brand Briefing 7.10 *continued*

Advertising alliances

Samu, Krishnan and Smith showed that the effectiveness of advertising alliances for new products depended on the interactive effects of three factors: the degree of complementarity between the featured products; the type of differentiation strategy (common versus unique advertised attributes with respect to the product category); and the type of ad processing (top-down or bottom-up) that an ad evoked (eg, the explicitness of the ad headline).

Sources: Akshay R. Rao, 'Strategic brand alliances', *Journal of Brand Management*, 1997, 5 (2): 111–19; Akshay R. Rao, L. Qu and Robert W. Ruekert, 'Signaling unobservable product quality through a brand ally', *Journal of Marketing Research*, May 1999: 258–68; Allen D. Shocker, Raj K. Srivastava and Robert W. Ruekert, 'Challenges and opportunities facing brand management: an introduction to the special issue', *Journal of Marketing Research*, 1994, 31 (5): 149–58; Tom Blackett and Bob Boad, *Co-Branding: The science of alliance*, New York: St Martin's Press, 1999; C. Whan Park, Sung Youl Jun and Allan D. Shocker, 'Composite branding alliances: an investigation of extension and feedback effects', *Journal of Marketing Research*, November 1996: 453–67; Bernard L. Simonin and Julie A. Ruth, 'Is a company known by the company it keeps? Assessing the spillover effects of brand alliances on consumer brand attitudes', *Journal of Marketing Research*, 1998, 35 (2): 30–42; Kevin E. Voss and P. Tansuhaj, 'A consumer perspective on foreign market entry: building brands through brand alliances', *Journal of International Consumer Marketing*, 1999, 11 (2): 39–58; Irwin P. Levin and Aron M. Levin, 'Modeling the role of brand alliances in the assimilation of product evaluations', *Journal of Consumer Psychology*, 2000, 9 (1): 43–52; Piyush Kumar, 'The impact of cobranding on customer evaluation of brand counterextensions', *Journal of Marketing*, 2005, 69 (July): 1–18; Kalpesh Desai and Kevin Lane Keller, 'The effects of brand expansions and ingredient branding strategies on host brand extendibility', *Journal of Marketing*, January 2002, 66: 73–93; R. Venkatesh and Vijay Mahajan, 'Products with branded components: an approach for premium pricing and partner selection', *Marketing Science*, 1997, 16 (2): 146–65; Sridhar Samu, H. Shanker Krishnan and Robert E. Smith, 'Using advertising alliances for new product introduction: interactions between product complementarity and promotional strategies', *Journal of Marketing*, 1999, 63 (1): 57–74.

agreement have adequate brand awareness; sufficiently strong, favourable and unique associations; and positive consumer judgements and feelings. Thus, a necessary but not sufficient condition for co-branding success is that the two brands separately have brand equity. The most important requirement is that there is a logical fit between the brands such that the combined brand or marketing activity maximizes the advantages of the individual brands while minimizing the disadvantages.

Swatch

Eyebrows were raised when DaimlerChrysler's Mercedes-Benz unit agreed to manufacture a 'Swatchmobile', named after SMH's colourful and fashionable lines of Swatch watches.[8] Personally championed by SMH's charismatic chairman, Nicolas Hayek, the Smart Car, as it came to be known, was designed to be small (about 3 metres long) and low cost (under €7,300). The car combined the three most important features of Swatch watches – 'affordability', 'durability', and 'stylishness' – with an important feature of a Mercedes car – 'safety and security in a crash'. Critics believed the Mercedes image could suffer if the car was unsuccessful, which was a possible outcome given that many products bearing the Swatch name (eg, Swatch-branded clothes, bags, telephones, pagers and sunglasses) saw disappointing sales or were dropped altogether. Swatch sold its share of the Smart Car business to DaimlerChrysler in 1998. The Smart Car became popular in Europe, however, selling over 130,000 units in 2004. The car has not made a profit but the brand is alive and was launched in the USA in January 2008.

Besides these strategic considerations, co-branding ventures must be entered into and executed carefully. Brand Briefing 7.11 describes two criteria that define a

Brand Briefing 7.11

Co-branding and other forms of co-operation

Blackett and Russel have tried to define co-branding. According to them, it is useful to discriminate between co-branding, joint promotions, alliances and joint ventures. In its purest form, co-branding embraces a collaborative venture designed to advance the interests of the parties in a strategic fashion. The intention of the parties is to create something new which falls outside their individual areas of expertise and capability. Two criteria are used to define all these different forms of co-operative ventures. The first is the expected duration of the relationship and the second is the amount of value that can be created in the co-operation. Linking these two criteria can result in a co-operation continuum that is generally described as co-branding (Figure 7.17).

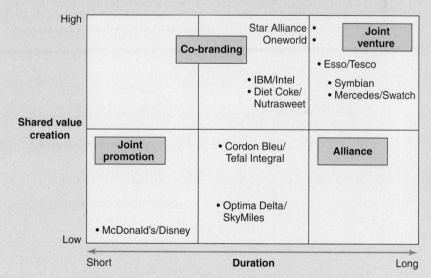

Figure 7.17   Co-branding in relation to other forms of co-operative venture

Brand Briefing 7.11 *continued*

First criterion: duration

Duration can vary from a couple of months to more than ten years. It all depends on the lifecycle of the product and the characteristics of the market. At one extreme there is the short-term joint promotion of McDonald's and Disney, which may last a couple of months while a new film is promoted. At the other extreme is the long-term joint venture between Mercedes-Benz and Swatch. In between, there are co-branding arrangements. Longer-term co-operations generally imply more extensive sharing of expertise and assets.

Second criterion: shared value creation

After examining a variety of co-operations, Blackett and Russel came to the conclusion that there was a hierarchy of types of shared value creation. They discuss four types of shared value creation (Figure 7.18):

* Reach/awareness co-branding The lowest level of co-branding occurs in situations were the parties want to increase their awareness through exposure to a partner's customer base. Many credit card companies in co-operation with other parties do this. One example is AmEx co-operation with Delta Airlines SkyMiles scheme, where members gained SkyMiles in return for money spent using the card. At this level, each of the partners gets benefits and revenue opportunities including, but not confined to, awareness.

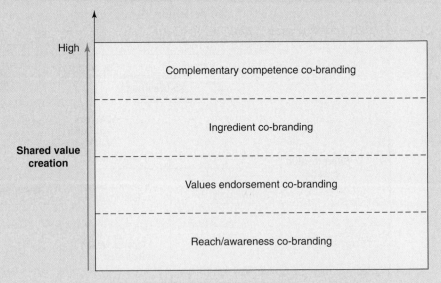

Figure 7.18 Hierarchy of types of value creation sharing in co-operative relationships

Brand Briefing 7.11 *continued*

- **Values endorsement co-branding** This level includes the endorsement of brand values and positioning. Examples are many charities that have launched co-branded affinity cards. The underlying concept for this type of co-operation is that the bank gives a portion of the transaction back to the charity as commission. There are similarities between this arrangement and sponsorships, in which the company donates to a worthy purpose in return for good publicity. The essence, of this type, is that the company wants to achieve alignment with the brand values in the customer's mind.

- **Ingredient co-branding** Here, there is an identifiable component contained in the product or the service. Some typifying examples of ingredient branding are Intel Inside and Coke Light with NutraSweet. Ingredient brands are also often used in the car industry, where manufacturers want to attach strong emotions and values to the car. The essence of this type is that the maufacturer uses and promotes branded components whose own brand image reinforces the desired attributes and values.

- **Complementary competence co-branding** At the highest level of co-branding, two complementary brands combine to produce a product that is more than the sum of the parts. Each partner relies on the other committing a selection of its skills and competences to that product. One example from the UK is the co-operation between Esso and Tesco Express that started in 1997. The intention was to develop the joint offer of supermarket products and petrol filling stations. Both parties bring their expertise, knowledge and competences from different areas to the concept. Tesco would operate the store under the Tesco Express format. In turn, Esso would operate the forecourts and sell fuel via the Tesco store. This level needs both parties to be involved in a broad commitment.

Blackett and Russel use the marriage metaphor to describe co-branding. There will be hard feelings and problems in a marriage, and there will be a need for equal contribution and investment. You have to work at the marriage to make it work. Unlike marriage, though, co-branding can be deliberately short term in nature. It all depends on the durability of the opportunity.

They conclude: 'Co-branding – like marriage – is not something to be entered into unadvisedly, lightly or wantonly; it is a very serious business enterprise involving key assets of the parties involved. The care of these assets over the course of the relationship – and beyond – must be the uppermost in the minds of the partners, and the very first item on the "heads of agreement".'

Source: Tom Blackett and Nick Russell, 'What is co-branding?', in *Co-Branding: The science of alliances*, eds. Tom Blackett and Bob Boad, London: Macmillan Business, 1999.

co-operation continuum for co-branding. Brand Briefing 7.12 describes some of DuPont's co-branding and licensing experiences. DuPont is one of the best-known and most successful ingredient brand marketers. Fundamentally, there must be the right kind of fit in values, capabilities and goals in addition to an appropriate balance of brand equity. Executionally, there must be detailed plans to legalize contracts, make financial arrangements and co-ordinate marketing. As one executive at the US brand Nabisco put it, 'Giving away your brand is a lot like giving away your child – you

Brand Briefing 7.12

Ingredient branding the DuPont way

One of the most successful ingredient brand marketers is DuPont, which was founded in the USA as a black powder manufacturer in 1802 by Frenchman E. I. duPont de Nemours. The company has introduced innovative products for use in markets ranging from clothing to aerospace. Many of its innovations, such as Lycra and Stainmaster fabrics, Teflon coating and Kevlar fibre, have become household names as ingredient brands.

Early on, DuPont learned an important branding lesson the hard way. Because it did not protect the name of its first organic chemical fibre, nylon, it could not be used as a trademark and became generic. However, by 2004, DuPont sold 30,000 products across 1,500 different product lines, and used 2,000 unique brands and 15,000 different brand registrations to support these products.

These innovations were the result of the company's massive R&D programme (€870 million spent in 2006). DuPont has 75 R&D facilities, including 35 outside the USA. These sites are staffed by nearly 2,000 scientists and researchers – including 600 with PhDs – who work to pursue science-based solutions for global markets. When the company began to focus on revitalizing its R&D in early 2000, 40 percent of its technology resources and assets were dedicated to growth; the rest supported existing products and operations. By 2005, 65 percent of the company's research was focused on growth. Dupont plans to double global investment in research and development by 2015 as it works to meet its energy sustainability goals, including investment in China.

Ingredient brands include Supro isolated soy proteins, used in food products, and RiboPrinter genetic fingerprinting technology. A question DuPont constantly confronts is whether or not to brand a product as an ingredient brand. To address this question, DuPont typically applies several criteria, both quantitative and qualitative.

● On the quantitative side, DuPont has a model that estimates the return on investment of promoting a product as an ingredient. Inputs to the model include resource allocations such as advertising and trade support, while outputs relate to favourability ratings and potential sales. The goal of the model is to determine whether or not branding an ingredient can be financially justified, especially in industrial markets.

Brand Briefing 7.12 *continued*

- On the qualitative side, DuPont assesses how an ingredient brand can help a product's positioning. If competitive and consumer analyses reveal that conveying certain associations would boost sales, DuPont is more likely to brand the ingredient. For example, one reason that DuPont launched its stain-resistant carpet fibre under the ingredient brand Stainmaster was that the company felt a 'tough' association would be highly valued in the market.

DuPont maintains that its ingredient branding strategy leads to competitive advantages, such as higher price premiums (often as much as 20 percent), enhanced brand loyalty and increased bargaining power with other members in the value chain. DuPont employs both push and pull strategies to create its ingredient brands. Consumer advertising creates consumer pull by generating interest in the brand and a willingness to request it. Extensive trade support in the form of co-operative advertising, training and promotions creates push by fostering a strong sense of loyalty to DuPont from people in the value chain. This loyalty helps DuPont negotiate favourable terms from distributors and leads to increased co-operation with new products.

One of its greatest successes is probably Lycra, the super-stretching polymer invented in DuPont labs in 1959. Generically known as spandex, Lycra got its start as an ingredient for girdles. Lycra's use has expanded steadily since its invention, from bathing suits in the 1970s to cyclists' shorts and aerobics outfits in the 1980s. More recently, nylon-Lycra bike shorts and exercise wear have became fashionable as everyday clothing, especially with young adults.

In building the brand, DuPont has applied its formula for success – one part product development and one part consumer marketing. Over the years, DuPont scientists have invented versions of Lycra that have expanded its uses. Originally too bulky for lightweight items, finer Lycra versions have been developed that can be knitted or woven into delicate fabrics and lightweight items such as tights and dresses. Mastering new and often difficult-to-make versions has made Lycra synonymous with the freedom of movement that comes from spandex. As one sportswear maker puts it: 'I wouldn't buy any spandex that wasn't from DuPont.' To reach consumers, DuPont advertises the benefits of Lycra in a print campaign with the tagline, 'Nothing moves like Lycra.' It has also teamed up with the industry trade group, Cotton Inc, to develop a 'Made with cotton and Lycra' logo for clothes tags.

The success of these efforts can be seen by the results of a DuPont study in which consumers said they would pay 20 percent more for a wool-Lycra skirt than for an all-wool version. Despite losing its original patent years ago, DuPont owns two-thirds of the worldwide spandex market with the Lycra brand.

Sources: Sasha Planting, 'DuPont company overview', www.financialmail.co.za, 17 June 2005; Monica Roman, 'How DuPont keeps 'em coming back for more', *BusinessWeek*, 20 August 1990: 68; www.chinadaily.com.cn/bizchina/2006-11/03/content_724113.htm

want to make sure everything is perfect.' The financial arrangements between brands may vary, although one common approach involves a licensing fee and royalty from the brand that is more involved in the production process. The aim is for the licensor and the licensee to benefit from these agreements as a result of the shared equity, increased awareness for the licensor and greater sales for the licensee.

More generally, brand alliances, such as with co-branding, involve a number of decision factors, such as the following.[9]

- What capabilities do you not have?
- What resource constraints are you faced with (people, time, money, etc.)?
- What growth goals or revenue needs do you have?

In assessing a joint branding opportunity, the following should be considered.

- Is it a profitable business venture?
- How does it help to maintain or strengthen brand equity?
- Is there any risk of dilution of brand equity?
- Does it offer extrinsic advantages (eg, learning opportunities)?

One of the highest-profile alliances is that of Disney and McDonalds, which had the exclusive global rights from 1996-2006 in the fast food industry to promote everything from Disney films and videos to TV shows and theme parks. McDonald's also has brand partnerships with a number of other brands, including Fisher-Price toys for its Happy Meals.

Ingredient branding

A special case of co-branding is *ingredient branding*, which involves creating brand equity for materials, components or parts that are necessarily contained within other branded products. Ingredient brands include Dolby noise reduction, Gore-Tex water-resistant fibres, Teflon non-stick coatings, Stainmaster stain-resistant fibres and Scotchgard fabrics.

From a consumer behaviour perspective, branded ingredients are often seen as a signal of quality. In a provocative study, Carpenter, Glazer and Nakamoto found that the inclusion of a branded attribute (eg, 'Alpine Class' fill for a down jacket) significantly affected consumer choices even when consumers were explicitly told that the attribute was not relevant to their decision.[10] Clearly, consumers inferred certain quality characteristics as a result of the branded ingredient.

The uniformity and predictability of ingredient brands can reduce risk and reassure consumers. As a result, ingredient brands can become industry standards to consumers such that they would not buy a product that did not contain the ingredient. In other words, ingredient brands can become a category point of parity. Consumers do not necessarily have to know exactly how the ingredient works – just that it adds value.

Ingredient branding has become more prevalent as mature brands seek cost-effective means to differentiate themselves and potential ingredient products seek to expand their sales. To illustrate the range of options for ingredient branding, consider the copy from a Singapore Airlines magazine ad, which prominently features both co-branded and self-branded ingredients in promoting one of its service offerings:

Singapore Airlines' new Raffles class: business in a class of its own

Singapore Airlines has searched the world to bring you the finest business class in the sky, see www.singaporeair.com. Top French design house, *Givenchy*, has created a cabin of contemporary elegance. And, for the ultimate in comfort, our new *Ultimo* seats from Italy are electrically controlled, offering luxurious legroom as well as personal privacy screens – a world first. In-seat laptop power is on hand for those who need to work; whereas those who prefer to relax can enjoy *KrisWorld*, your in-flight entertainment system, with over 60 entertainment options. And for the first time in the sky, you can enjoy block-buster movies with *Dolby Headphone* surround sound. In addition, our *World Gourmet Cuisine* – created by an international panel of acclaimed chefs – brings you a dining experience reminiscent of fine earth-bound restaurants, comple-mented by in-flight service even other airlines talk about.

Thus, as in this example, one product may contain a number of branded ingredients. Ingredient brands are not restricted to products and services. For example, consider how Sony, Nintendo and Microsoft set up try-out areas for their games consoles in consumer electronic shops.

Advantages and disadvantages

The pros and cons of ingredient branding are similar to those of co-branding.[11] From the perspective of the firm making and supplying the ingredient, the benefit of branding its products as ingredients is that, by creating consumer pull, greater sales can be generated at a higher margin. Additionally, there may be more stable and broader customer demand and better long-term supplier–buyer relationships. En-hanced revenues may accrue from having two revenue streams – the direct revenue from the cost of the supplied ingredients, as well as extra revenue from the royalty rights paid to display the ingredient brand.

For the manufacturer of the host product, the benefit is in using the equity from the ingredient brand to enhance its own brand equity. On the demand side, the host product may achieve access to more product categories, market segments and distri-bution channels than they otherwise could have expected. On the supply side, the host product brands may be able to share production and development costs with the ingredient supplier.

Ingredient branding is not without risks and costs. The costs of a supporting mar-keting communication campaign can be high – advertising to sales ratios for con-sumer products often surpass 5 percent – and many suppliers are relatively inexperienced at designing mass media communications that may have to contend with inattentive consumers and uncaring middlemen. As with co-branding, there is a loss of control because marketing campaigns for the supplier and manufacturer may have different objectives and may send different signals to consumers. Some manufacturers may be reluctant to become supplier-dependent or may not believe that the branded ingredient adds value, resulting in a loss of possible accounts.

Manufacturers may resent any consumer confusion as to what is the 'real brand' if the branded ingredient gains too much equity. Finally, the sustainability of the competitive advantage may be uncertain because brands that follow may benefit from consumers' increased understanding of the role of the ingredient. As a result, follower brands may not have to communicate the importance of the ingredient as much as why their particular ingredient brand is better than the pioneer or other brands.

Guidelines

Ingredient-branding schemes build brand equity in many of the same ways that conventional branding does. What are the specific requirements for ingredient branding? Brand Briefing 7.12 described the ingredient-branding efforts at DuPont, which has introduced a number of such brands. In general, four tasks must be accomplished.

1. Consumers must first perceive that the ingredient matters to the performance and success of the end product. Ideally, this intrinsic value would be easily visible or experienced.
2. Consumers must then be convinced that not all ingredient brands are the same and that this ingredient is superior. Ideally, the ingredient would have an innovation or some other substantial advantage over other options.
3. A distinctive symbol or logo must signal to consumers that the host product contains the ingredient. Ideally, the symbol or logo would function essentially as a 'seal' and would be simple and versatile – such that it could appear virtually anywhere – and credibly communicate quality and confidence to consumers.
4. Finally, a co-ordinated push and pull campaign must be put into place such that consumers understand the importance and advantages of the ingredient. Often this will involve consumer advertising and promotions and, sometimes in collaboration with manufacturers, retail merchandising and promotion. As part of the push strategy, some communication efforts may also need to be devoted to gaining the co-operation and support of manufacturers or other channel members.

LICENSING

Licensing involves contractual arrangements whereby firms can use the names, logos characters and so forth of other brands to market their own brands for a fee. Essentially, a firm is 'renting' another brand to contribute to the brand equity of its own product. Because it can be a shortcut to building brand equity, licensing has gained in popularity – North American retail sales of licensed products jumped from €2.9 billion in 1977 to €52.5 billion in 2005.[12]

Entertainment licensing has also become a big business. Licensors include film titles and logos (eg, *Harry Potter*, *Star Wars* and *Spider Man*), comic strip characters (eg, Garfield, Simpson and Peanuts characters), television and cartoon characters (eg, from *Sesame Street* and *The Simpsons*). Every summer, marketers spend millions on film tie-ins as they look for the next blockbuster franchise. Even athletes participate. US boxer George Foreman signed a €20 million-a-year licensing deal with house-wares company Salton in December 1999 to use his name on food preparation products such as the Lean Mean Low Fat Grilling Machine. Perhaps the champion of licensing is Walt Disney. Brand Briefing 7.13 describes some of its practices and strategies.

Brand Briefing 7.13

Licensing the Disney Way

The Walt Disney Company has one of the strongest brands in the world. Much of its success lies in its television, film, theme park and other entertainment ventures. These have created a host of well-loved characters and a reputation for quality entertainment. Disney Consumer Products is designed to keep the Disney name and characters fresh in consumers' minds in seven business areas.

1. *Merchandising licensing:* selectively authorizing the use of Disney characters on high-quality merchandise.
2. *Publishing:* telling the Disney story in books, magazines, comics and art.
3. *Music and audio:* playing favourite Disney songs and stories.
4. *Computer software:* programing Disney 'fun' into home computers and game systems.
5. *Educational production:* casting the characters in films for schools and libraries.
6. *The Disney Store:* bringing the Disney name to shopping centres.
7. *Catalogue marketing:* offering Disney and Disney-quality products via catalogues.

The pervasiveness of its products is staggering: in all, over three billion entertainment-based impressions of Mickey Mouse are received by children every year, equivalent to ten million impressions a day.

Disney believes that its characters appearing on quality merchandise has added greatly to their popularity. The philosophy of Walt Disney, the founder of the company, was to present his characters in toys with real play value or in high-quality merchandise that would then extend the fun of the filmed entertainment and enhance the company's reputation for excellence. The first hand-made Mickey Mouse appeared in 1930. Disney started licensing its characters for toys made by Mattel in the 1950s. Disney Licensing is now responsible for some 3,000 contracts for 16,000 products with manufacturers worldwide. Disney licenses its standard characters (Mickey, Minnie, Donald, Goofy and Pluto) and filmed entertainment (eg, theatrical releases such as *Aladdin*, *The Lion King* and *Toy Story* and TV properties such as *Duck Tales* and *Madeline*). Disney is the world's largest licensor with an estimated global retail sales of €19.3 billion for 2007.

To capitalize on the popularity of its characters, Disney has developed a family of brands for licensed products, each one featuring Mickey Mouse, Minnie Mouse or

Brand Briefing 7.13 *continued*

another character. Each brand was created for a certain age group and distribution channel. The brand combines the name and character in a logo. Each can be used in a range of product categories, including clothes and accessories, toys, home furnishings, social expressions/novelties, sporting goods and gifts.

The Artists in Licensing's Creative Resources department works with manufacturers on all aspects of product marketing, including design, prototyping, manufacturing, packaging and advertising. At each step, care is taken to ensure that the products are faithful to the look and personality of the characters. To protect and enhance the value of its brands, Disney issues standards of brand identities for Disney licensing that specify colour treatment of the logo; proper use of secondary graphic elements or trade dress (distinctive colour schemes, shapes, images, background patterns or typography) in packaging, retail signs or other communications; minimum unobstructed surrounding area; artwork reproduction procedures; use of the brand name outside the logo; and the Disney copyright notice. Disney employees interpret these guidelines, fiercely guarding the images of the characters.

One of Disney's most successful licensed characters is Winnie the Pooh. Disney has three Winnie the Pooh product lines: the familiar 'red shirt' Pooh from Disney films; the 100 Acre Collection, a more upmarket line of products that typically sell in department stores; and the Classic Pooh line based on the original illustrations from A. A. Milne's *Winnie the Pooh* books. Pooh products, which have existed since Disney's 1966 animated short *Winnie the Pooh and the Honey Tree*, have become a virtual goldmine. Between 1995 and 2004, the licensing market for Winnie the Pooh grew from €285 million to €4 billion in retail sales for Disney, and *Forbes* magazine ranks it as the second most valuable character for licensing. By comparison, Disney's other core characters – Mickey, Minnie, Goofy, Donald Duck and Pluto – grew only 20 percent over the same period. In 2001, Disney bought the rights to Winnie the Pooh and all the related characters for €248 million and no longer has to pay licensing fees to the former rights holders.

Source: Bruce Orwall, 'Disney's magic transformation?', *Wall Street Journal*, 4 October 2000.

Licensing can be lucrative for the licensor. Licensing has long been an important business strategy for designer clothes and accessories. Designers such as Donna Karan, Calvin Klein and Pierre Cardin command large royalties for the rights to use their name on merchandise such as clothing, belts, ties and luggage. Over the course of three decades, Ralph Lauren became the world's most successful designer, creating a €3.6 billion business licensing his Ralph Lauren, Double RL and Polo brands.

Guidelines

One danger is that manufacturers can get caught up in licensing a brand that is a fad and produces short-lived sales. Because of many licensing arrangements, licensed entities can become overexposed and wear out quickly as a result. Licensed merchandise sales of Barney products hit a €356 million jackpot in 1993 but faded significantly the following year before making a comeback. Sales of Izod Lacoste shirts, with their alligator crest, peaked at €329 million in 1982 but fell to €110 million in 1990 after the brand became overexposed.[13] Subsequently purchased by Phillips Van Heusen, the brand made a comeback as the result of more careful marketing.

Pokémon

Nintendo, of Kyoto, Japan, manufactures and markets home and portable video game systems. One of the most stunning creations has been the Pokémon franchise. The name, Pokémon, is short for its original name, 'Pocket Monsters'. Game Boy video games have been merchandised into anime, manga, trading cards, toys, books and other media. The Pokémon franchise also includes a mobile theme park. In 2006, the PokéPark opened in Taiwan and it was announced that it could come to the USA and Europe. Pokémon has spawned more than €10.9 billion in worldwide retail sales, while the franchise sold about 150 million games worldwide. At its peak, Nintendo's Pokémon licensing partner 4Kids Entertainment had licensed out the name to 500 companies. In 2000, the Licensing Industry Merchandisers' Association named Pokémon its licence of the year. It also won three other category awards in recognition of the brand's creative licensing and the success it was met with. Pokémon netted Nintendo licensing awards and estimated franchise revenues of €2.19 billion in 2000 alone.[14]

Firms are taking steps to protect themselves in their licensing agreements, especially those that rely on the image of their licensor.[15] For example, firms are obtaining licensing rights to a range of licensed entities – some of which are relatively enduring in nature – to diversify risk. Licensees are developing products and sales and marketing approaches so that their sales are not merely a function of the popularity of other brands. Some firms conduct marketing research to ensure the proper match of product and licensed entity or to provide more precise sales forecasts for effective inventory management.

Corporate trademark licensing, one of the fastest-growing segments, is the licensing of company names, logos or brands for use on products.[16] For example, Harley-Davidson licensed its name – synonymous with motorcycles and a certain lifestyle – to a polo shirt, gold ring and even a wine cooler. Other seemingly narrowly focused brands such as Jeep, Caterpillar, Deere and Jack Daniels have also entered a broad portfolio of licensing arrangements. Standard & Poors and Dow Jones now license their trademarks to manufacturers of financial products and to the exchanges where the products trade.

In licensing trademarks, firms may have different motivations, including generating extra revenues and profits, protecting their trademarks, increasing their exposure or enhancing their image. The profit appeal can be enticing because there are few inventory expenses, accounts receivables, manufacturing expenses and so forth. In an average deal, a licensee pays a company a royalty of about 5 percent of the wholesale price of each product, although the actual percentage can vary from 2 percent to 10 percent. As noted in Chapter 5, some firms sell licensed merchandise through their own catalogues.

As with any co-branded arrangement, however, the risk is that the product will not live up to the reputation of the brand. Inappropriate licensing can dilute brand meaning with consumers and marketing focus within the organization. When Eddie Bauer, in the midst of a retailing slump in November 2000, announced a two-year licensing deal with Compaq for special edition Compaq Presario 1400 notebooks computers sporting a distinctive trim, one industry analyst complained, 'Their business has been terribly disappointing – their entire focus should be unrelentingly on their merchandise assortment.'[17]

CELEBRITY ENDORSEMENT

Using well-known and admired people to promote products is a widespread phenomenon. Even the late US president Ronald Reagan was a celebrity endorser, pitching several products, including cigarettes, during his acting days. Some actors or actresses who refuse to endorse products in the USA are willing to do so in Japan (eg, Arnold Schwarzenegger for Aramin V-drink, Meg Ryan for Dingo cars, Leonardo DiCaprio for Suzuki Wagon, Jodie Foster for Morinaga Caffe Late and Harrison Ford for Honda Legend). Brad Pitt and Bruce Willis have done commercials overseas for a number of brands.

The rationale behind these strategies is that a famous person can draw attention to a brand and shape the perceptions of the brand by virtue of the inferences that consumers make based on their knowledge of the person. Consequently, in choosing a celebrity endorser, it is important for the celebrity to be well enough known that the awareness, image and responses for the brand may be improved.

In particular, a celebrity endorser should have a high level of visibility and a rich set of potentially useful associations, judgements and feelings.[18] Ideally, a celebrity endorser would be seen as credible in terms of expertise, trustworthiness and likeability or attractiveness, as well as having specific associations that carry potential product relevance.

Q Scores

Marketing Evaluations/TvQ conducts surveys in the USA to determine 'Q scores' for a range of entertainers and public figures. Each performer is rated on the following scale: 'one of my favourites', 'very good', 'good', 'fair', 'poor' and 'never seen or heard of before.' The sum of the 'favourite' to 'poor' ratings is 'total familiar.' The 'one of my favourites' rating is an absolute measure of appeal or popularity, since it is based on 100 percent. Because some performers would have a low 'favourite' rating, the Q score is a ratio of the 'favourite' rating to the 'familiar' score. It addresses the question, 'How appealing is he or she among those who do know him or her?' Q scores are used to reflect the potential of lesser-known personalities and provide a basis for comparison with

Rank	Performer	% of total familiar	Q score	Negative Q score
1	Tom Hanks	93	57	5
2	Mel Gibson	90	52	5
3	Bill Cosby	94	49	11
4	William Petersen	43	46	8
5	Sean Connery	87	45	8
6	Eddie Murphy	91	40	10
7	Julia Roberts	86	39	14
8	Robert de Niro	86	39	10
9	Harrison Ford	87	38	8
10	Will Smith	86	38	10
11	Jack Nicholson	82	38	11
12	Maurice Benard	18	37	23
13	Steve Martin	87	36	13
14	Jerry Orbach	44	36	8
15	Jorja Fox	39	36	9
16	Jim Carrey	92	35	16
17	George Eads	42	35	10
18	Mariska Hargitay	41	35	7
19	Anthony Lapaglia	34	35	11
20	Adam Sandler	82	34	20
21	Danny Glover	81	34	9
22	Doris Roberts	66	34	11
23	Toby Keith	59	34	19
24	Christopher Meloni	38	34	9
25	John M. Jackson	28	34	13

Figure 7.19   Q ranking of performers (among US population aged six and older)
Source: From Marketing Evaluations, Inc., Winter 2004 Performer Q Study

more established personalities. As of 2004, negative Q scores (the ratio of the 'fair' plus 'poor' ratings to the 'familiar' score) are being published as well, to reflect the proportion of the population that disliked a particular personality. Figure 7.19 gives Q scores for popular entertainers.

Potential problems

There can be problems with linking a celebrity endorser to a brand. First, celebrity endorsers can endorse so many products that they lack any specific product meaning or are just seen as opportunistic or insincere. Tennis player Anna Kournikova used her good looks to sign endorsements with a wide variety of brands, including Adidas, Berlei lingerie, Charles-Schwab, Lycos, Microsoft's XSN Sports, Multiway Sports Bra, Omega watches, Pegasus cell phones and Yonex racquets.

It can be argued that basketball player Michael Jordan lost effectiveness as an endorser when he was associated with so many brands and products, appearing in ads for Nike athletic shoes, Gatorade sports drink, Bijan fragrances, Hanes underwear, McDonald's, Ball Park Franks, Rayovac batteries, Wheaties cereal and MCI WorldCom telecommunications. He even supported his own brand in the form of Michael Jordan men's cologne and, later, the Nike subsidiary Jordan brand. Brand Briefing 7.14 describes the financial value of some contracts with endorsers.

Brand Briefing 7.14

The value of celebrity endorsers

Celebrities routinely lend their faces and personas to brands in exchange for millions. Companies hire famous athletes and actors in hopes that the celebrities' fans will also become fans of their products or services. Such endorsers can use their popularity to create positive associations for brands in the minds of consumers.

First, it should be noted that the best brand ambassadors are never the popular, great performers in their fields, but rather – at least in some countries – those who are right for the specific audience and the brand's product category. For example, *Reader's Digest's* 'European trusted brands' survey has run since 2001. For the 2006 results, research was conducted in 12 languages among 25,434 people in 14 European countries. The results identify significant differences by country as to whom and what people are most likely to trust. Although 'popular' celebrities featured at the bottom of the list in every situation in most countries, the same isn't true for 'relevant' celebrities. According to the survey, when buying a new car, people in Poland are more likely to trust the advice of a relevant celebrity than an institution (ie, motoring organization). The reverse is the case in Germany and Spain where 'relevant' celebrity ranked 15 out of 16 – only 'popular' celebrity had fewer votes.

The same variance can be seen in the media agency CIA: Mediaedge 2004 global survey, which found the following percentages for people who said they would be attracted to a placed product in a film: Mexico (53 percent), Singapore (49 percent), India (35 percent) and Hong Kong (33 percent). The USA logged a lower rating at 26 percent. None of these figures compares with The Netherlands at 9 percent and France's 8 percent, suggesting that placing for these audiences isn't worth the effort. Still, one must remember that many product placements are not obvious – as such they remain great opportunities.

Second, celebrity endorsers can carry big risks for companies, which often hire famous people as much for their clean-cut images as their professional accomplishments. Most companies conduct background checks before signing celebrities but that doesn't guard against future bad behaviour. In 1988, Anheuser-Busch built a campaign for Michelob beer around Eric Clapton's version of 'After Midnight' shortly before the singer revealed he was battling alcoholism. US basketball player Kobe

Brand Briefing 7.14 *continued*

Bryant lost millions in endorsements with McDonald's, Sprite and Nutella after he was charged with sexual assault in 2001. And in September 2005, supermodel Kate Moss was photographed using cocaine and was promptly dropped as an endorser by H&M, Chanel and Burberry. (One company, H&M, said it would honour the contract with Moss and would stand behind her since she admitted having a drug problem. Moss was going to be used in H&M ads to promote Stella McCartney's fashion range. H&M executives later changed their minds and dropped the supermodel.)

Third, risks can also work the other way around. Fidelity bank teamed up with Paul McCartney in 2005. Shortly after McCartney started endorsing Fidelity, regulators investigated the fund company over allegations that its traders accepted lavish gifts and entertainment from brokers who did business with the company.

Fourth, many consumers feel celebrities are only doing the endorsement for money and do not necessarily believe in or even use the endorsed brand. Even worse, some consumers feel that the salaries for celebrities to appear in commercials add a significant and unnecessary cost to the brand. Celebrities also can be difficult to work with and may not willingly follow the marketing direction of the brand. Tennis player Andre Agassi tried Nike's patience when – at the same time he was advertising for Nike – he appeared in commercials for the Canon EOS camera. In these ads, he looked into the camera and proclaimed 'Image is everything' – the antithesis of the 'authentic athletic performance' positioning that is the foundation of the Nike brand equity.

The following endorsement deals were reported as the largest in 2005. We leave it to you to analyze the relevance and value added to the brand – and how it affects the celebrity – from these endorsements.

> Catherine Zeta Jones: T-Mobile, €16.8 million
> Angelina Jolie: St John, €10 million
> Nicole Kidman: Chanel No 5, €10 million
> Jessica Simpson: Guthy-Renker, €6.31 million
> Gwyneth Paltrow: Estée Lauder, €5.11 million
> Charlize Theron: Dior, €5.11 million
> Julia Roberts: Gianfranco Ferré, €4.2 million
> Brad Pitt: Heineken, €3.3 million
> Scarlett Johansson: L'Oréal, €3.3 million
> Penelope Cruz: L'Oréal, €3.3 million

Sources: *Reader's Digest* 'European trusted brands' survey, www.rdtrustedbrands.com, 15 February 2006; Abram Sauer, 'Brandchannel 2004 product placement awards', www.brandchannel.com, 21 February 2005; 'The fame game: why brands want celebrities', *The Independent*, 29 July 2006; www.foxnews.com/story/0,2933,300216,00.html

Second, there must be a reasonable match between a celebrity and a product.[19] Many endorsements would seem to fail this test. Oddly, tennis star John McEnroe was the spokesperson for Bic disposable razors despite his ubiquitous two-day stubble on the tennis court. George C. Scott, an Oscar winner for his patriotic film portrayal of General Patton, seemed to be a curious choice to endorse a French Renault car. Some potentially better matches include actor Paul Hogan of *Crocodile Dundee* for Subaru's line of Out-back cars and cyclist Lance Armstrong for Bristol-Myers Squibb's cancer medicines.

Third, celebrity endorsers can get in trouble or lose popularity, diminishing their marketing value to the brand, or just fail to live up to expectations. In 2005, American Express decided to focus its US Open tennis advertising and promotion campaign on the US player Andy Roddick. The ad theme of 'Have you seen Andy's mojo?' took on new meaning, however, when Roddick tumbled out of the tournament in the first round in straight sets. Thus, linking the brand to a celebrity results in a certain lack of control; people have run into legal difficulties, personal problems or controversies of some form that diminished their marketing value (eg, as was the case with athletes Kobe Bryant, Marion Jones and O. J. Simpson, and entertainer Michael Jackson). Marion Jones, the only woman to win five medals in athletics at a single Olympics event, pleaded guilty in October 2007 to taking drugs. Even though Jones returned the five medals she won in the Sydney Olympics in 2000, the shame is not over. She faces further action from sporting bodies regarding the doping scandal.[20]

Finally, as noted in Chapter 6, celebrities may distract attention in ads such that consumers notice the stars but have trouble remembering the brand. Pepsi decided to drop Beyoncé Knowles and Britney Spears from campaigns when they felt that the Pepsi brand did not get as much promotion out of the campaigns as the singers were getting. Pepsi decided to put the spotlight back on the product with its endorsement-free follow-up, 'Pepsi. It's the cola.' After signing Céline Dion for a three-year, €10 million deal, Chrysler dumped her in the first year when commercials featuring Dion driving a Pacifica produced great sales for the singer, but not the car!

Guidelines

To overcome such problems, celebrities must be evaluated, selected and used strategically. First, it is important to choose a celebrity whose associations are relevant to the brand and likely to be transferable.

Thus, there must be a logical fit between the brand and person.[21] To reduce confusion or dilution, the celebrity ideally would not be linked to other brands. After winning Olympic gold in 1984, Mary Lou Retton appeared in commercials for so many brands that one marketing critic complained: 'I've seen more of her in the past year than I have of my mother – and I love my mother more!'[22] To broaden the appeal and reduce the risks of linking to one celebrity, some marketers have employed several.

Second, the celebrity must be used in a creative fashion that highlights the relevant associations and encourages their transfer. For example, US comedian Jerry Seinfeld's commercials for American Express used the same unflappable charm and knack for finding himself in unusual situations that he displayed on his TV show. Finally, marketing research must be undertaken to help identify potential endorser candidates and facilitate the development of the proper marketing campaign, as well as track their effectiveness.

SPORTING, CULTURAL AND OTHER EVENTS

Chapter 6 described the rationale for event marketing and sponsorship. The chapter noted that event marketing is a means of creating or reinforcing consumer perceptions of key associations. Events have their own associations that may become linked to a sponsoring brand under certain conditions.

Sponsored events can contribute to brand equity by becoming associated with the brand and improving brand awareness, adding associations or improving the strength, favourability and uniqueness of existing associations. The main means by which an event can transfer associations is by credibility. A brand may seem more likeable or perhaps even trustworthy or expert by virtue of becoming linked to an event. The extent to which this transfer takes place will depend on which events are selected and how the sponsorship deal is designed and integrated into the marketing campaign to build brand equity. Brand Briefing 7.17 discusses sponsorship strategies for the Olympics Games. Brand Briefing 7.15 describes the role event sponsorship played in building brand equity for Visa credit cards.

Brand Briefing 7.16 describes how the talented Chinese NBA star Yao Ming can be used to bridge business between the Western world and China.[23]

Brand Briefing 7.15

Event sponsorship at Visa

In 1985, Visa and MasterCard were seen as identical products that faced stiff competition from other brands, particularly American Express, which had a strong and desirable image with consumers. Visa set out to create a differentiating and enduring perception of its brand as the best payment system for all types of purchases. Visa was positioned as the brand with superior acceptance by virtue of hard-hitting comparative ads with American Express. The 'It's everywhere you want to be' campaign featured interesting, unique and prestigious locations where consumers might expect American Express to be accepted but where consumers were told to 'bring your Visa card, because they don't take American Express'. In terms of event marketing, Visa aligned itself with high-profile events (sporting events and concert tours) that did not take American Express and backed up its sponsorships with comparative advertising campaigns.

Starting in 1988, the Olympics became Visa's biggest event association. Visa's Olympic involvement has helped to reinforce its desired positioning as a high-quality, globally accepted product. Visa's sponsorship has made the brand the exclusive payment card and the official payment service for the Olympics. Visa's Olympic support and sponsorship were reinforced in many ways. Ads for the 1992 games focused on how tough the competition would be, 'but not as tough as the sellers at the ticket window if you don't have your Visa card'.

Brand Briefing 7.15 *continued*

To support Olympic fundraising, cardholder transactions were tied to Visa donations to certain Olympic teams in several countries. Visa also provided direct financial support to some athletes and teams. Since 1994, Visa's 'Olympics of the imagination' has brought schoolchildren from all over the world to the Olympics as part of an art competition tied into every winter and summer games since. The sponsorship also allows Visa's 21,000 member financial institutions to link exclusive marketing and merchandising campaigns around the games, promoting Visa products and services to cardholders and merchants worldwide.

The effect of these sponsorship and other communication efforts has been dramatic. The Athens 2004 Olympic Games and Paralympic Games generated an 87 percent consumer awareness of Visa as a sponsor, the highest of all sponsors. More importantly, research has shown that Visa is now perceived as more widely accepted than other cards and, as a result, as the card of choice for personal and family shopping, personal travel and entertainment, and even international travel, a former American Express stronghold.

Source: http://sponsorships.visa.com/olympic

Brand Briefing 7.16

Yao Ming – a bridge between China and Western markets

Shanghai-born basketball player Yao Ming has the potential to win the hearts and minds of 1.3 billion potential consumers in China (Figure 7.20). In 2004, he was unknown outside China. Now, he is set to become a real factor in trade between the Western world and China. Yao is helping McDonald's sell more hamburgers, Pepsi more soft drinks and Reebok more basketball shoes in China. McDonald's will nearly double its outlets there to 1,000 for the 2008 Olympics, says Dean Barrett, senior vice-president for global marketing: 'Yao is a tremendous global asset for us.'

The handful of big companies with Yao deals in place say they see a difference. McDonald's has even gone so far as to appoint him its 'first worldwide brand ambassador'. With Yao as its spokesman, Reebok's Fireman says he could see capturing more than a quarter of an estimated €730 million trainer business in China by 2008. The company currently does about €22 million in sales there.[24]

PepsiCo, which has an endorsement deal with Yao in China, reported sales are up almost 30 percent in a year. Richard Lee, Pepsi's Shanghai-based senior vice-president for marketing in China, says he's not sure he can attribute all of that to Yao, but he points out that Yao's persona is in keeping with Pepsi's slogan 'Dare for more.'

Brand Briefing 7.16 *continued*

Figure 7.20   Basketball player Yao Ming
Source: Rex Features

Despite this success, Yao has turned down dozens of offers. Reebok International chief executive Paul B. Fireman says Yao's handlers have done a good job of 'not rushing him out to every company, not prostituting him'. His agents, Team Yao, are mostly sticking to what may be a first in the world of sports business – a confidential, five-year marketing plan developed with the help of University of Chicago MBA students. Because of his surging popularity, Yao is ahead of schedule, and Team Yao's fear is that he will be come overexposed.

Managing Yao is a team that includes veteran US basketball agent Bill A. Duffy, former film marketer and agent Bill Sanders, University of Chicago economics professor John Huizinga and Chinese-born entrepreneur M. Erik Zhang. Sanders sees a Yao wave building that will reach its crest at the 2008 Olympics. 'The finish line is 2008. Beijing is the big day, the pinnacle of Yao's earning power. The world will be watching', says Sanders.

Team Yao's planning and patience seems to be paying off. Yao's four-year contract with the Houston Rockets is worth €13 million and he earns an estimated €11 million a year in longer-term deals with Pepsi, Reebok, Gatorade and Mcdonald's. As his

Brand Briefing 7.16 *continued*

agents strike more deals – and they say they will pick up the pace in the run-up up to the Olympics – some executives believe Yao has the potential to gross €220 million in his first 10 years in the US basketball league.

At home, Yao has done deals with China Unicom and internet company SOHU. Marketing experts say Yao could prove to be just as invaluable to Chinese companies looking to go global as to Western companies seeking business in China.

Source: 'Wow! Yao! For US brands selling in China, NBA sensation Yao Ming is one hot ticket', *BusinessWeek*, 25 October 2004.

Brand Briefing 7.17

Going for corporate gold at the Olympics

Competition at the Olympics is not restricted to athletes. Corporate sponsors also vie to maximize the return on their sponsorship investments.[26] Sponsorship is a significant part of the business side of the games. Sponsorships contributed 32 percent of the revenue of the 2004 Games. Some of the world's largest and most visible companies, including McDonald's, Coca-Cola, Visa and Kodak, spent as much as €36.5 million to sponsor the 2002 winter and 2004 summer Olympics. In 2005, Coca-Cola extended its Olympic sponsorship to 2020.

Sponsorship of the Olympics exploded with the commercial success of the 1984 summer games in Los Angeles. Many international sponsors (eg, Fuji) improved their image and increased market share. In Atlanta in 1996, top-tier 'worldwide' corporate sponsors spent €29 million for the rights to display Olympic logos in their ads and on their packaging and to secure access to tickets, hotel rooms, athletes, events and the hospitality village. Besides direct expenditures, companies spent hundreds of millions more on related marketing. Coca-Cola's total Olympic-related expenditure reportedly topped €365 million and included funding for the torch relay and a mega-retail promotion, Coke's 'red hot Olympic summer'.

Yet, Olympic sponsorship is controversial in terms of its marketing success. For example, even though Hilton was the official hotel of the 1992 summer games, only 8 percent of consumers were aware of the sponsorship just weeks after the Olympics ended. Even worse, 9 percent thought the sponsor was Holiday Inn. Similarly, Kellogg's was a 1992 sponsor, but only 20 percent of consumers named Kellogg's Corn Flakes as a brand sponsor while 35 percent named rival Wheaties. In 1996, licensees fell short of their goal of €730 million in total sales.

Brand Briefing 7.17 *continued*

In some cases, confusion may be due to ambush marketing. In ambush marketing, advertisers attempt to falsely give consumers the impression that they are sponsors by means such as running Olympic-themed ads that publicize other forms of sponsorship (for a national team or network broadcast), identifying the brand as an official supplier or using current or former Olympians as endorsers. For example, to retaliate against Visa's ads stressing exclusive Olympic acceptability, American Express ran ads that focused on its card's presence in Olympic host cities. To improve the marketing effectiveness of sponsorship, the Olympic committee has vowed to fight ambush marketing as well as to reduce the number of sponsors to avoid clutter.

Following the scandal surrounding Salt Lake City's bid for the 2002 Winter Olympics, where it was revealed that organizers gave cash and gifts to some 30 International Olympic Committee (IOC) members, many criticized the games for being overcommercialized. The scandal generated feelings of disillusionment from fans and compounded image problems resulting from drug use and poor sportsmanship. A survey conducted soon after the scandal broke revealed that 39 percent of people felt worse about the games.

To counteract these poor perceptions, the IOC launched an image campaign to promote the 2000 games. The ads, which ran in 200 countries, reflected the 'core values of the Olympic movement' by featuring footage of former Olympic champions such as Jesse Owens, as well as unsung heroes. The €110 million campaign featured web advertising, television spots, radio spots and print ads, one of which detailed how corporate sponsors contributed to the games.

The scandal caused some companies to reconsider their role in the games. An executive for Miller Brewing – which has not been a sponsor of the games – said: 'The Olympics, quite frankly, have never been more overpriced or overvalued.' Sponsorship remained a big part of the 2000 Sydney Games, but some sponsors toned down their Olympic ad blitz to seem less opportunistic and commercial. Instead of purchasing space on 50 hoardings, as the company did for the 1996 Atlanta Games, Kodak dressed 35 actors as rolls of film and had them walk around the venue. Goodyear changed the logo on its airship to display the Australian greeting 'G'day' on one side and 'Good luck' on the other. Even the brash Nike adopted a more subtle approach to advertising at the Sydney Games. When the company wrapped a 30-storey building with images of Australian athletes, it used a swoosh that measured only a few storeys.

The 2008 summer games in Beijing hold special appeal for some advertisers because they represent a connection to the burgeoning Chinese market. General Electric began its first global campaign revolving around the Beijing games in 2005. GE chose the Olympics to position the company as global and innovative to Chinese consumers. UPS also chose the Beijing games to strengthen its brand presence in

Brand Briefing 7.17 *continued*

China. UPS was a global Olympic sponsor in 1996, 1998 and 2000 but dropped out after 2000, saying its goals had been achieved. But in 2005, UPS announced it would rejoin the Olympics for 2008, this time in a limited deal that allowed the company to use the Olympic logo for marketing in China only. International and local sponsors are expected to spend a total of €730 million on the Beijing Olympics, aided partly by a nationalist spirit that drives some Chinese companies to sponsor the event.

Nevertheless, Olympic sponsorship remains controversial. Many companies believe that sponsorship yields significant benefits, creating an image of goodwill for their brand, serving as a platform to enhance awareness and communicate messages and affording numerous opportunities to reward employees and entertain clients. Others criticize the event as horribly overcommercialized, citing the Atlanta summer games as a prime example. In any case, as suggested in Chapter 6, it is clear that the success of Olympic sponsorship, like any sports sponsorship, depends in large part on how well the sponsorship is executed and incorporated into a marketing plan.

THIRD-PARTY SOURCES

Finally, it should be noted that secondary associations can be created by linking a brand to third-party sources. For example, the *Good Housekeeping* magazine seal has been seen as a mark of quality for decades (offering product replacement or refunds for defective products for up to two years after purchase). Endorsements from leading magazines (eg, *PC* magazine), organizations (eg, dental associations) and experts (eg, film critics) can improve perceptions of and attitudes towards brands.

Third-party sources may be seen as especially credible sources. As a result, they are often featured in advertising campaigns and selling efforts. Fombrun found 183 public lists in 38 countries that provide summary ratings and rankings of companies.[25] In the USA, JD Powers and Associates' customer satisfaction index helped to cultivate an image of quality for Japanese carmakers in the 1980s, with corresponding harm to the quality image of their US rivals. In the 1990s, SD power began to rank quality in other industries, such as airlines, credit cards, rental cars and phone services. The top-rated brands in these categories began to feature their awards in ad campaigns. Another example is Grey Goose vodka, which used endorsements from bartenders to drive sales in the USA.

CHAPTER REVIEW

This chapter considered the process by which other entities can help create secondary associations. Such entities include the company that makes a product, where the product is made and where it is purchased, as well as related people, places or things. By linking a brand to entities with their own set of associations, consumers may expect that some of these same associations also characterize the brand. Thus, independent of how a product is branded, the nature of the product itself and its supporting marketing campaign, brand equity can be created by 'borrowing' from other things. Creating secondary associations in this fashion may be important if the corresponding brand associations are deficient. Secondary associations may be especially valuable as a way to link favourable brand associations that can serve as points of parity or to create unique brand associations that can serve as points of difference in positioning a brand.

Eight ways to use secondary associations to build brand equity are by linking the brand to: the company making the product; the country or some other geographic location in which the product originates; retailers or other channel members who sell the product; other brands, including ingredient brands; licensed characters; famous spokespeople or endorsers; events; and third-party sources.

In general, the extent to which any of these entities can be a source of equity depends on consumer knowledge of the entity and how easily the appropriate associations or responses to the entity transfer to the brand. Global credibility or attitudinal dimensions may be more likely to transfer than specific attribute and benefit associations, although the latter can be transferred too.

Linking the brand to other entities, however, is not without risk. Some control is lost and managing the transfer process so that only the relevant secondary associations become linked to the brand may be difficult.

Discussion questions

1. Think of the country in which you live. What image might it have with consumers in other countries? Are there certain brands or products that are highly effective in using that image in global markets?

2. Pick a brand. Evaluate how it builds on secondary associations. Can you think of any ways that the brand could more effectively use secondary brand knowledge?

3. Boeing makes aircraft for commercial airlines – for example, the 727, 747, 757, 767, 777 and now the 787 jet models. Is there any way for Boeing to adopt an ingredient branding strategy with its jets? How? What would be the pros and cons?

4. After winning championships, players often complain about their lack of endorsement offers. Similarly, after every Olympics, a number of medal-winning athletes lament their lack of commercial recognition. From a branding perspective, how would you respond to the complaints of these athletes?

5. Which retailers have the strongest image and equity in your mind? Think about the brands they sell. Do they contribute to the equity of the retailer? Conversely, how does that retailer's image help the image of the brands it sells?

References and notes

[1]Kevin Lane Keller, 'Brand synthesis: the multi-dimensionality of brand knowledge', *Journal of Consumer Research*, 2003, 29 (4): 595–600.

[2]Wai-Kwan Li and Robert S. Wyer Jr, 'The role of country of origin in product evaluations: informational and standard-of-comparison effects', *Journal of Consumer Psychology*, 1994, 3 (2): 187–212.

[3]For a broader discussion of nation branding, see Philip Kotler, Somkid Jatusriptak and Suvit Maesincee, *The Marketing of Nations: A strategic approach to building national wealth*, New York: Free Press, 1997; Wally Olins, 'Branding the nation: the historical context', *Journal of Brand Management*, 2002, 9 (April): 241–48; and, for an analysis of Iceland, see Hlynur Gudjonsson, 'Nation branding', *Place Branding*, 2005, 1 (3): 283–98.

[4]Tony Apéria, 'Brand relationship management: den varumärkesbyggande processen', dissertation, Stockholm: Stockholm University, 2001.

[5]Akshay R. Rao and Robert W. Ruekert, 'Brand alliances as signals of product quality', *Sloan Management Review*, fall 1994: 87–97; Akshay R. Rao, Lu Qu and Robert W. Ruekert, 'Signalling unobservable product quality through brand ally', *Journal of Marketing Research*, May 1999, 36 (2): 258–68.

[6]Robin L. Danziger, 'Cross branding with branded ingredients: the new frontier', paper presented at the ARF Fourth Annual Advertising and Promotion Workshop, February 1992.

[7]Kim Cleland, 'Multimarketer melange an increasingly tasty option on the store shelf', *Advertising Age*, 2 May 1994: S10.

[8]www.swatch.com; Kevin Helliker, 'Can wristwatch whiz switch Swatch cachet to an automobile?', *Wall Street Journal*, 4 March 1994: A1; Audrey Choi and Margaret Studer, 'Daimler-Benz's Mercedes unit to build a car with maker of Swatch watches', *Wall Street Journal*, 23 February 1994: A14; Beth Demain Reigber, 'DaimlerChrysler smarts as BMW Mini looms', *Dow Jones Newswire*, 20 June 2001.

[9]Based in part on a talk by Nancy Bailey, 'Using licensing to build the brand', Brand Masters conference, 7 December 2000.

[10]Gregory S. Carpenter, Rashi Glazer and Kent Nakamoto, 'Meaningful brands from meaningless differentiation: the dependence on irrelevant attributes', *Journal of Marketing Research*, August 1994: 339–50. See also, Susan M. Broniarczyk and Andrew D. Gershoff, 'The reciprocal effects of brand equity and trivial attributes', *Journal of Marketing Research*, 2003, 41: 161–75.

[11]Donald G. Norris, 'Ingredient branding: a strategy option with multiple beneficiaries', *Journal of Consumer Marketing*, 1992, 9 (3): 19–31.

[12]*The Licensing Letter*, epmcom.com

[13]Teri Agins, 'Izod Lacoste gets restyled and repriced', *Wall Street Journal*, 22 July 1991: B1.

[14]James Brightman, 'Emerald shows that Pokémon can still dominate', www.gamedaily.biz, 7 June 2005.

[15]Udayan Gupta, 'Licensees learn what's in a pop-culture name: risk', *Wall Street Journal*, 8 August 1991: B2.

[16]Frank E. James, 'I'll wear the Coke pants tonight; they go well with my Harley-Davidson ring', *Wall Street Journal*, 6 June 1985: 31.

[17]Robert Berner, 'The name of the game is – the name', *BusinessWeek*, 27 November 2000: 12.

[18]Grant McCracken, 'Who is the celebrity endorsor? Cultural foundations of the endorsement process', *Journal of Consumer Research*, December 1989, 16: 310–21.

[19]Shekhar Misra and Sharon E. Beatty, 'Celebrity spokesperson and brand congruence', *Journal of Business Research*, 1990, 21: 159–73.

[20]http://sport.guardian.co.uk/athletics/story/0,,2185096,00.html

[21]Misra and Beatty, 'Celebrity spokesperson and brand congruence'.

[22]Roderick Townley, 'Is that winning smile losing its charm?', *TV Guide*, 28 June 1986: 41–2.

[23]'Wow! Yao! For US brands selling in China, NBA sensation Yao Ming is one hot ticket', *BusinessWeek*, 25 October 2005.

[24]Janet Soderstrom, 'Brand equity. It's everywhere you want to be', talk at Branding Conference, San Francisco, 26 October 1995.

[25]Charles Fombrun, 'In compilation of international corporate reputation ratings', *Corporate Reputation Review*, 2007, 10 (2): 144–52.

[26]'Wait in wings as Olympic sponsors waffle', *USA Today*, 15 March 1999; Michael McCarthy, 'Olympic ads to stress core values', *USA Today*, 20 December 1999; Bruce Horowitz, 'Sponsors scale back ad blitz', *USA Today*, 26 September 2000; Bruce Horowitz, 'Sponsors warm up a year before games', *USA Today*, 19 July 1995: 1B–2B; 'Olympic partnership', *Sports Illustrated* advertising section.

8 Developing a brand equity measurement and management system

PREVIEW

The previous six chapters have described strategies and approaches to building brand equity. The next three chapters examine what consumers know and feel about brands, how they act towards brands and how marketers can measure how well a brand is doing.

The CBBE model provides guidance as to how brand equity can be measured. Given that customer-based brand equity is defined as the differential effect that knowledge about a brand has on customer response to the marketing of that brand, there would seem to be two approaches to measuring brand equity. An indirect approach could assess potential sources of customer-based brand equity by identifying and tracking consumers' brand knowledge – the thoughts, feelings, images, perceptions and beliefs linked to the brand. A direct approach could measure customer-based brand equity by assessing the effect of brand knowledge on consumer response to different aspects of the marketing campaign.

The two approaches are complementary, and both can and should be employed by marketers. In other words, for brand equity to guide marketing decisions, marketers must fully understand the sources of brand equity, how they affect outcomes of interest (eg, sales) and how these sources and outcomes change, if at all, over time. Chapter 2 provided a framework for conceptualizing consumers' brand knowledge structures. Chapter 9 uses this information and reviews research methods to measure sources of brand equity and the customer mindset. Chapter 10 reviews research methods to measure outcomes of brand equity.

Before getting into the specifics of how to measure sources and outcomes of brand equity in those two chapters, this chapter provides some perspectives on how to think about brand equity measurement and management. Specifically, it considers how to develop and implement a brand equity measurement system. A *brand equity measurement system* is a set of research procedures designed to provide timely, accurate and actionable information on brands so marketers can make the best tactical decisions in the short run and strategic decisions in the long run. A brand equity measurement system helps to achieve a full understanding of the sources and outcomes of brand equity and how to relate the two.

The ideal system would provide complete, up-to-date and relevant information on the brand and all its competitors to the right decision-makers at the right time within an organization. Introducing a brand equity measurement system requires two critical steps: designing brand tracking studies and establishing a brand equity management system. This chapter examines these steps in detail.

Crucial to the development of such a system, however, is an understanding of how brand equity or value is created. Towards that goal, this chapter first presents the motivation for and the specific details of a model of brand equity or value creation. The brand value chain is a means by which marketers can trace the value-creation process for their brands to better understand the financial impact of their marketing expenditures and investments. Based in part on the CBBE model developed in Chapter 2, it offers a holistic, integrated approach to understanding how value is created by brands.

THE NEW ACCOUNTABILITY

Although many senior managers have embraced the marketing concept and the importance of brands, uneasiness remains over financial issues surrounding brands. Executives often struggle with questions such as: 'How strong is our brand? How can we ensure that our marketing activities create value? How do we measure that value?'

The reality of the marketing environment is that all money spent must be justified as being both effective and efficient in terms of 'return on marketing investment' (ROMI).[1] This accountability has forced marketers to address tough challenges and develop new measurement approaches.[2] But progress has been slow: a 2003 ARF-APQC study revealed that only one in five 'ROMI-achieving' companies had experienced a substantial change in the speed of decision-making due to marketing analytics, while none of the 'ROMI-aspiring' firms had done so.[3]

Complicating matters is that, depending on the industry or category, some observers believe that up to 70 percent (or even more) of marketing expenditures may be devoted to campaigns and activities that cannot be linked to short-term incremental profits, but yet can be seen as improving brand equity.[4] Measuring the long-term value of marketing in terms of its full short-term and long-term effects on consumers is crucial for assessing return on investment.

Jonathan Knowles argues that, for marketers to secure a seat in the boardroom, they must go beyond ROI measurement to address whether or not brands truly are assets that enable a business to generate superior returns over time. Along those lines, he offers the following to support his contention.[5]

- To qualify as an asset in financial terms, a brand needs to be measured in terms of its ability to generate cash flows.
- Value can only be created by changes in customer behaviour – changes in attitude do not generate cash flow.
- Brand equity needs to be measured in a way that captures the source and scale of the emotional augmentation that the brand provides to the underlying functionality of the product or service.

A comparison of studies from four countries shows that people expect something else from companies besides being profitable: Figure 8.1 shows that between 29 percent and 48 percent expect a broad social responsibility from companies. Only 2–9 percent believe that only making money should be the aim of companies.

	Norway 2005	Denmark 2004	Sweden 2005	USA 2003
Only generate profits for shareholders	9%	3%	4%	2%
Responsibility to shareholders **and** employees and customers	56%	48%	64%	52%
Shareholders, employees, customers, plus broad social responsibility	31%	48%	29%	46%

Figure 8.1 What people expect from companies
Source: Reputation Institute.

Clearly, marketers need tools and procedures that clarify and justify the value of their expenditures. The remainder of this chapter offers concepts and perspectives to help in that pursuit, beginning with the brand value chain.

THE BRAND VALUE CHAIN

The brand value chain is a structured approach to assessing the sources and outcomes of brand equity and the manner by which marketing activities create brand value.[6] The chain recognizes that many individuals within an organization can potentially affect brand equity and must be aware of relevant branding effects. Different individuals, however, make different brand-related decisions and need different types of information. Accordingly, the brand value chain provides insights to support brand managers, chief marketing officers and managing directors and chief executive officers.

Fundamentally the brand value chain assumes that the value of a brand resides with customers. Based on this insight, the model assumes that the value-creation process begins when a company invests in a marketing campaign aimed at actual or potential customers. The marketing activity associated with the campaign then affects the customer mindset with respect to the brand – what customers know and feel about the brand. This mindset, across a group of customers, results in outcomes for the brand in terms of how it performs in the marketplace – the effect of individual customer actions regarding how much and when they purchase, the price they pay and so forth. Finally, the investment community considers this market performance and other factors such as replacement cost and purchase price in acquisitions to arrive at an assessment of shareholder value in general and a value of the brand in particular.

The model also assumes that linking factors intervene between these stages. These factors determine the extent to which value created at one stage transfers or

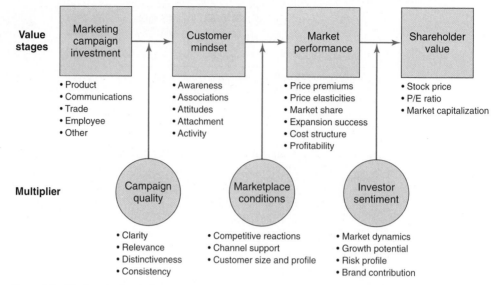

Figure 8.2   The brand value chain

'multiplies' to the next stage. Three sets of multipliers moderate the transfer between the marketing campaign and the subsequent three value stages: the campaign quality multiplier, the marketplace conditions multiplier and the investor sentiment multiplier. The brand value chain model is summarized in Figure 8.2. This section describes the model ingredients (ie, the value stages and multiplying factors) in more detail and provides examples of multiplier effects.

Value stages

Brand value creation begins with marketing activity that influences customers in a way that affects how the brand performs in the marketplace and thus how it is valued by the financial community.

Marketing campaign investment

Any marketing campaign investment that potentially can be attributed to brand value development, intentional or not, falls into this first value stage. Chapters 4 to 7 outlined many such marketing activities. Specifically, some of the bigger marketing expenditures relate to product research, development and design; trade or intermediary support; marketing communications (eg, advertising, promotion, sponsorship, direct and interactive marketing, personal selling, publicity and public relations); and employee training. The extent of the investment in a marketing campaign, however, does not guarantee success in terms of brand value creation. In the 1990s, Miller Brewing spent over €1.7 billion in measured advertising in an effort to re-establish its brand portfolio, but launched ineffective campaigns. Anheuser-Busch, Heineken and Corona were therefore able to steal key market positions and become the leading growth brands, dominating the US beer category as a result. The ability of a marketing investment to transfer or multiply down the chain will depend on qualitative aspects of the marketing campaign via the campaign quality multiplier.

Campaign quality multiplier The ability of a marketing campaign to affect the customer mindset will depend on the quality of that campaign. As outlined in earlier chapters, there are many ways to judge the quality of a campaign. Four important factors are the following.

1. *Clarity:* how understandable is the marketing campaign? Do consumers properly interpret and evaluate the meaning conveyed by brand marketing?
2. *Relevance:* how meaningful is the campaign to customers? Do consumers feel that the brand is one that should receive serious consideration?
3. *Distinctiveness:* how unique is the campaign compared with those of rivals? How creative or differentiating is the campaign?
4. *Consistency:* how cohesive and well integrated is the marketing? Do all aspects of the campaign combine to affect customers? Does the marketing campaign relate effectively to past campaign and balance continuity and change, steering the brand in the right direction?

Not surprisingly, a marketing campaign that is highly relevant to customers is likely to achieve a greater return on investment. For example, despite being outspent by such beverage brand giants as Coca-Cola, Pepsi and Budweiser, the California Milk Processor Board was able to reverse a decades-long decline in consumption of milk through a well-designed and executed 'Got milk?' campaign. On the other hand, marketers have found that expensive marketing campaigns do not necessarily produce sales. For example, brands such as Michelob, Minute Maid, 7 Up and others have seen their sales slide despite solid marketing support because of poorly targeted and delivered marketing campaigns.

Customer mindset

As described in Chapter 2, judicious marketing investment could result in a number of customer-related outcomes. Essentially, the issue is, in what ways have customers been changed as a result of the campaign? How have those changes manifested themselves in the customer mindset? Remember that the customer mindset includes everything that exists in the minds of customers with respect to a brand: thoughts, feelings, experiences, images, perceptions and beliefs. Understanding the mindset can have important implications for marketing campaigns. Brand Briefing 8.1 describes how the British supermarket Tesco redesigned its marketing on the basis of consumer research.

As will be seen in Chapter 9, many approaches and measures are available to assess value at this stage. Nevertheless, five measures have emerged from research and are also highlighted in the CBBE model as important.

1. *Brand awareness:* the extent and ease with which customers recall and recognize the brand and can identify the products and services with which it is associated.
2. *Brand associations:* the strength, favourability and uniqueness of perceived attributes and benefits for the brand. Brand associations are sources of brand value, because they are the means by which consumers feel brands satisfy their needs.

Brand Briefing 8.1

Consumer insights at Tesco

Tesco is the dominant British supermarket and is growing rapidly overseas. The company continues to deliver one of the fastest organic growth rates of any retailer, but this has not always been the case. At the beginning of the 1990s, Tesco was suffering – with falling underlying sales, slowing profit growth and investors worried about its depressed share price. To make matters worse, it was also under threat from discount food retailers entering the UK from continental Europe.

In 1997, Terry Leahy took over as chief of Tesco. He aimed to make Tesco a 'value retailer'. Leahy called the strategy he wanted to adopt 'The Tesco way.' This comprised core purpose, values, principles, goals and the balanced scorecard. One idea was to be focused on understanding the customer – both in terms of gathering knowledge and in making full use of this understanding.

Under Leahy, customer-focused initiatives were introduced. Together, they aimed to provide the best shopping experience for every customer. One important step, in February 1995, was the launch of the Clubcard, the UK's first national supermarket loyalty card scheme. The move attracted an enormous amount of media attention. There was widespread speculation that Tesco's initiative would force other leading chains to develop their own loyalty schemes. Details of customers' purchases were recorded with Clubcard points automatically awarded for every £1 spent. The points were added up quarterly, and money-off vouchers as well as product and category coupons were posted to customers' homes to be redeemed against future spending.

The cost of running the scheme was considerable. Analysts estimated the start-up costs at £10 million, in addition to the 1 percent discount on sales (an estimated £60 million 'given away' in the first year). Nevertheless, the company was convinced that this would be money well spent.

Tesco's senior management had a vision that the Clubcard would provide them with rich, self-updating information about the customer base. It would allow Tesco to gather detailed information about individual consumers' buying habits, while maintaining feedback channels through which the company could communicate directly with customers to build loyalty. The information gained from the Clubcard scheme is shared with suppliers, media companies, researchers, space planners and others who contribute to the Tesco experience. For example, one long-term supplier, MacIntosh Donald, has worked with Tesco to understand what customers want when they buy beef. It works with Tesco to understand consumer trends and makes store visits to talk to Tesco staff and customers. It has used this knowledge to develop snacking and organic products and now supplies all of Tesco's Scottish beef and lamb, employing 400 staff directly.

Other improvements were made to keep things simple for customers and employees. Systems such as electronic shelf-edge labelling all across the chain, through which

Brand Briefing 8.1 *continued*

prices could be changed from a central point; self-scanning tills; and self-service, pre-packaged products. Rewards coupons are personalized, based on data derived from previous purchases – information that helps Tesco designate customers as 'mainstream', 'finer foods', 'healthy' or 'price-sensitive'. In line with these segments, Tesco works with ranges from Value to Finest and lifestyle ranges such as Organic, Free From and Healthy Living. There are four store formats: Express, Metro, Superstore and Extra.

By the end of March 1995, five million people had joined the Clubcard scheme and Tesco recorded a 7 percent like-for-like increase in sales. Independent retail analyst AGB confirmed the impact of Clubcard on sales. It announced that, according to its monitoring system, Tesco had surged ahead of Sainsbury's for the first time to become Britain's leading retailer of packaged goods. Tesco had enjoyed a 2.1 percent increase in market share in the six months following Clubcard's launch.

One year after Clubcard's launch, it had become the UK's most popular loyalty scheme. Moreover, the Clubcard became a vital tool for understanding customers as Tesco began to exploit detailed information on their shopping habits. As well as making minor improvements to the scheme, joint marketing initiatives were set up with non-competing businesses whose customers matched the profile of the typical Tesco shopper. One of the earliest was a link-up with the travel agents LunnPoly through Thompson Holidays, which allowed Clubcard points to be redeemed for discounts on holidays. Similarly, DIY retailer B&Q joined the Tesco scheme enabling Clubcard holders to earn points for purchases made in B&Q stores.

In March 1996, the company launched *Clubcard Magazine*, produced in five versions to suit five lifestyle segments (students, younger adults without children, younger people with families, older people with children and pensioners). Each version was tailored to suit its audience, carrying targeted content, offers, promotions, competitions and advertising from suppliers, as well as information on product launches. Soon Tesco was able to boast 12 million copies being distributed every quarter. However, the most significant refinement to Clubcard, in terms of volume of trade, was the decision to extend the scheme to include points for purchases of petrol. This, together with a 'price pledge' to maintain the lowest petrol prices, resulted in a surge in petrol sales. By now, Tesco was not only UK's largest food retailer but also the fourth largest petrol retailer behind oil companies, BP, Shell and Esso. And this expansion continues: Tesco Personal Finance was launched in July 1997 through a joint venture with the Royal Bank of Scotland. Customers have a choice of 22 products and services from banking to instant car and travel insurance. Around two-thirds of the finance sales come from the Tesco stores. Tesco Mobile and Home Phone offers phone services. Internationally, Tesco has launched car insurance and credit cards in Hungary; health, home and travel insurance in Thailand; and five products in South Korea.

Brand Briefing 8.1 *continued*

Tesco also had the opportunity to study the Clubcard data in detail, relating to one of the highest-spending groups: young mothers with babies and toddlers. In January 1997, it launched its Baby Club to reflect their lifestyle. A new mother who registered for the club before the baby was born would receive a gift pack on the child's arrival and a quarterly magazine from when the baby was two months to two years old. It provided timely advice, special offers relating to the needs of a family with small children, as well as contact lists for support groups such as the National Childminding Association.

Tesco set up more clubs. In May 2001, the Baby Club was 'extended' to toddlers, with an initial target of 150,000 members. By April 2003, its membership had reached 300,000 and 2 out of 3 of its members had joined after being members of Baby Club. Other clubs included a wine club, healthy living club for organic shoppers (with 150,000 members recruited in 2003, its first year) and a kids' club.

Tesco's Clubcard scheme has over 11 million households as members and captures 85 percent of weekly sales in terms of time and products. This data is used to make multidimensional customer segmentation and tailored communications, which in 2004 meant about 4 million unique quarterly mailings with 80,000 individual combinations. The idea is to make Tesco feel more like the corner shops of England's past – that their 'local grocer' knows them.

Steve Goodroe, chief of Dunnhumby USA, which developed clubcard with Tesco, explains: 'The secret of customer relationship marketing is taking data and insights to change the way you think about your customers and your business; to move away from averages and towards customers as individuals.' Or in the words of Leahy: 'People often ask me what the secret is to our success. Well, I'll tell you: we listen carefully to the customers, and try to give them what they want.'

Sources: Tesco case study from Cranfield School of Management; Devon Wylie, 'Tesco has links with the corner shops of England's past', Seklemian/Newell, 2005, www.loyalty.vg; Doug Desjardins, 'Tesco strategies turn up competitive heat in UK', *DSN Retailing Today*, 28 February 2005; Tesco fact sheets, www.tescocorporate.com; Rhys Blakely, 'Revealed: the secret of Tesco's success', Times Online, 18 October 2004.

This case was originally written by Dr Helen Peck. It was later adapted by Chris Lawer and Simon Knox and has been expanded by the authors of this book.

3. *Brand attitudes:* overall evaluations of the brand in terms of its quality and the satisfaction it generates.
4. *Brand attachment:* how loyal a customer feels towards a brand. A strong form of attachment, *adherence,* refers to the consumer's resistance to change and the ability of a brand to withstand bad news (eg, a product or service failure). In the extreme, attachment can become *addiction.*

5. *Brand activity:* the extent to which customers use the brand, talk to others about the brand, seek out brand information, promotions and events.

A hierarchy exists in the measures of value: awareness supports associations, which drive attitudes that lead to attachment and activity. Brand value is created at this stage when customers have:

- deep, broad brand awareness;
- appropriately strong and favourable points of parity and points of difference;
- positive brand attitudes;
- intense brand attachment and loyalty; and
- a high degree of brand activity.

Creating the right customer mindset can be critical in building brand equity and value. AMD and Cyrix found that achieving performance parity with Intel's microprocessors did not reap initial benefits in 1998 when original equipment manufacturers were reluctant to adopt their chips because of their lack of a strong brand image with consumers. Moreover, success with consumers or customers may not translate into success in the marketplace unless other conditions prevail. The ability of this customer mindset to create value at the next stage depends on external factors designated as the marketplace conditions multiplier, as follows.

The *marketplace conditions multiplier* is a measure of the extent to which value created in the minds of customers affects market performance. It depends on contextual factors external to the customer. Three such factors are the following.

- *Competitive superiority:* how effective are the quantity and quality of the marketing investment of other competing brands?
- *Channel and other intermediary support:* the level of brand reinforcement and selling effort taken by marketing partners.
- *Customer size and profile:* how many and what types of customers (eg, profitable or not) are attracted to the brand.

The value created in the minds of customers will translate into favourable market performance when competitors fail to provide a significant threat, when channel members and other intermediaries provide strong support and when a sizeable number of profitable customers are attracted to the brand.

The competitive context faced by a brand can have a profound effect on its fortunes. For example, both Nike and McDonald's have benefited from the prolonged marketing woes of their main rivals, Reebok and Burger King, respectively. Both of these latter brands have suffered from numerous repositionings and management changes. On the other hand, MasterCard has had to contend for a decade with two strong, well-marketed brands in Visa and American Express and so has faced an uphill battle in gaining market share despite its well-received 'Priceless' ad campaign.

Market performance

As Chapter 2 explained, the customer mindset affects how customers react or respond in the marketplace in a six ways. The first two outcomes relate to price premiums and price elasticities. How much extra are customers willing to pay for a comparable product because of its brand? And how much does their demand increase or decrease when the price changes? A third outcome is market share, which measures the ability of a marketing campaign to drive sales. Taken together, the first three outcomes determine the direct revenue stream attributable to the brand over time. Brand value is created with higher market shares, greater price premiums and more elastic responses to price decreases and inelastic responses to price increases.

The fourth outcome is brand expansion, the success of the brand in supporting line and category extensions and product launches into related categories. Thus, this dimension captures the ability to add enhancements to the revenue stream. The fifth outcome is cost structure or, more specifically, savings in terms of the ability to reduce marketing expenditures because of the prevailing customer mindset. In other words, because customers have favourable opinions and knowledge about a brand, any aspect of the marketing campaign is likely to be more effective for the same expenditure level; alternatively, the same level of effectiveness can be achieved at a lower cost because ads are more memorable, sales calls more productive and so on. When combined, these five outcomes lead to brand profitability, the sixth outcome.

In short, brand value is created at this stage by building profitable sales volumes through a combination of these outcomes. The ability of the brand value created at this stage to reach the final stage in terms of stock market valuation again depends on external factors, this time according to the investor sentiment multiplier.

Investor sentiment multiplier The extent to which the value engendered by the market performance of a brand is manifested in shareholder value depends on contextual factors external to a brand. Financial analysts and investors consider a host of factors in arriving at their brand valuations and investment decisions, including these.

- *Market dynamics:* what are the dynamics of the financial markets as a whole (eg, interest rates, investor sentiment or supply of capital)?
- *Growth potential:* what are the growth potential or prospects for the brand and the industry in which it operates? For example, how helpful are the facilitating factors and how inhibiting are the hindering external factors that make up the firm's economic, social, physical and legal environment?
- *Risk profile:* what is the risk profile for the brand? How vulnerable is the brand likely to be to those facilitating and inhibiting factors?
- *Brand contribution:* how important is the brand as part of the firm's brand portfolio and all the brands it has?

The value of a brand is most likely to be fully reflected in shareholder value when the firm is operating in a healthy industry without environmental hindrances or barriers and when the brand contributes a significant portion of the firm's revenues and appears to have bright prospects. Obvious examples of brands that benefit from a strong market multiplier – at least for a while – were the dotcom brands. The huge premium placed on their (actually negative) market performance, however, quickly disappeared – as in some cases did the whole company!

Shareholder value

Based on information about a brand as well as many other considerations, the financial marketplace then formulates opinions and makes assessments that have direct financial implications for the brand value. Three important indicators are the stock price, the price/earnings multiple and market capitalization for a company. Research has shown that not only can strong brands deliver greater returns to stockholders but they can also do so with less risk.[7]

Starbucks

Figure 8.3 shows how Starbucks created value in its corporate brand between 1993 and 1999. Specifically, although the coffee shop chain increased its advertising budget during this time, its main investment was in market expansion and an increase in the number of outlets – and thus potential consumption opportunities for consumers. As one marketing observer noted: 'Despite its lack of national advertising, Starbucks has become a household word by turning coffee into a ubiquitous attitude product . . . and by expanding the brand beyond its traditional roots – strategically placed, extremely fragrant coffee shops – into airplanes, restaurants, hotels, supermarkets and other venues.'[8] Another commentary noted: 'Starbucks' growth has come with virtually no use of traditional media advertising; the chain has relied on in-store marketing initiatives and word of mouth to develop brand cachet.'[9] Founder Howard Schultz said: 'The marketing of Starbucks is not only what people see on the outside. The cost of internal marketing is quite high, but it is the key to our success.'[10] Because of Starbucks' superior product and service delivery, the expansion investment enhanced the customer mindset.

Figure 8.3 also displays Young & Rubicam's BrandAsset Valuator (BAV) ratings of brand strength (ie, brand relevance and differentiation) and stature (ie, brand esteem and knowledge) as perceived by consumers (see Brand Briefing 9.12). Brand strength and stature bear a strong relationship to the five dimensions of the customer mindset identified earlier. Starbucks experienced a steady improvement in consumer perceptions. This increasingly favourable customer mindset led to greater sales and a higher stock price and market capitalization.

	1993	1997	1999	2001	2003
Advertising (LNA millions)	3.73	13.48	12.24		
Number of outlets	272	1,412	2,498	4,709	8,569
BAV strength	0.59	1.5	1.8	2.4	2.2
BAV stature	2.4	6.7	10.1	13.4	13.6
Sales (revenue) (millions–net)	—	975	1,680	2,600	3,500
Stock price	2.78	4.80	6.06	9.53	16.40
Market capitalization (millions)	621	3,034	4,445	8,400	9,700

Note: BAV, BrandAsset Valuator; LNA, Leading National Advertisers.

Figure 8.3   Brand value chain analysis for Starbucks

Thus, Starbucks's investment appeared to pay clear financial dividends. Starbucks was able to create so much brand value in part because of the positive multipliers it experienced. Starbucks' campaign multiplier was positive because of the relevance and distinctiveness of its product offerings. The company also maintained great consistency. Its customer multiplier was positive because of the lack of any strong competitive reactions, the strong channel support it provided due to its retail presence and its single-minded customer focus on coffee lovers. As one research analyst said: 'It's a foregone conclusion that Starbucks owns the specialty coffee market nationally . . . . No one wants to take them head on.'[11] Another analyst noted: 'Local competition among coffee stores is intense, but Starbucks is the only one out there that has a national level of recognition and awareness.'[12] Finally, the market multiplier was equally positive due to Starbucks' corporate branding strategy and favourable financial market conditions.

Implications

According to the brand value chain, marketers create value first through shrewd investments in their marketing and then by maximizing, as much as possible, the campaign, customer and market multipliers that translate that investment into bottom-line financial benefits. The brand value chain thus provides a structured means for managers to understand where and how value is created and where to look to improve that process. Certain stages will be of greater interest to different members of the organization.

Brand and category marketing managers are likely to be comparatively more interested in the customer mindset and the effect of marketing on customers. Marketing directors are likely to be more interested in market performance and the impact of customer mindset on actual market behaviours. Finally, a managing director is likely to be comparatively more interested in shareholder value and the influence of market performance on investment decisions.

The brand value chain has a number of implications. First, value creation starts with the marketing campaign investment. Therefore, a necessary – but not sufficient – condition for value creation is well-funded, well-designed and well-implemented marketing. It is rare that marketers can get something for nothing.

Second, value creation involves more than the initial marketing investment. Each of the three multipliers can increase or decrease market value as it moves from stage to stage. In other words, value creation also involves ensuring that value transfers from stage to stage. Unfortunately, in many cases, factors that can inhibit value creation may be largely out of the hands of the marketer (eg, investors' industry sentiment). Recognizing the uncontrollable nature of these factors is important to help put in perspective the relative success or failure of a marketing campaign to create brand value. Just as sports coaches cannot be held accountable for unforeseen circumstances, such as injuries to players and financial hardships that make it difficult to attract top players, so marketers cannot necessarily be held accountable for market forces and dynamics.

Third, as is outlined in the following two chapters, the brand value chain provides a way to track value creation that can facilitate marketing research and intelligence efforts. Each of the stages and multipliers has a set of measures by which it can be assessed. In general, there are three main sources of information, and each source of information taps into one value stage and one multiplier. The first stage, the marketing campaign investment, is straightforward and can come from the marketing plan and budget. Customer mindset and the campaign quality multiplier can both be assessed by quantitative and qualitative customer research. Market performance and the marketplace conditions multiplier can both be captured through market scans and internal accounting. Finally, shareholder value and the investor sentiment multiplier can be estimated through investor analysis and interviews.

Modifications to the brand value chain can expand its relevance and applicability. First, feedback loops are possible. For example, stock prices can have an important effect on employee morale and motivation. Second, in some cases, the value creation may not occur sequentially as depicted. For example, stock analysts may react to an ad campaign for the brand – either personally or in recognition of public acceptance – and factor those reactions directly into their investment assessments. Third, some marketing activity may have only diffuse effects that are manifested over the long term. For example, cause–related or social responsibility marketing activity might affect customer or investor sentiment slowly over time. Fourth, it should be recognized that both the mean and variance of some of the measures of the brand value chain could matter. For example, in terms of the customer mindset, a niche brand may receive very high marks but only across a narrow range of customers.

BRAND AUDITS

To learn what consumers know about brands and products, marketers should conduct a brand audit to profile consumer knowledge structures. A *brand audit* is a comprehensive examination of a brand in terms of its sources of brand equity. In accounting, an audit involves a systematic inspection of accounting records involving analyses, tests and confirmations.[13] The outcome of an accounting audit is an assessment of the financial health of the firm. An outside accounting firm serves as the auditor and checks the accuracy, fairness and general acceptability of accounting records, rendering its opinion in the form of a report.

A similar concept has been suggested for marketing. A marketing audit has been defined as a 'comprehensive, systematic, independent and periodic examination of a company's – or business unit's – marketing environment, objectives, strategies and activities with a view to determining problem areas and opportunities and recommending a plan of action to improve the company's marketing performance.'[14] This has been characterized as a three-step procedure in which the first step is agreement on objectives, scope and approach; the second step is data collection; and the final step is report preparation and presentation. Thus, the marketing audit is an internally, company-focused exercise to make sure that marketing operations are efficient and effective.

A brand audit, however, is a more externally, consumer-focused exercise that involves procedures to assess the health of a brand, uncover its sources of brand equity and suggest ways to improve and exploit its equity. A brand audit requires understanding the sources of brand equity from the perspective of both the company and the consumer. From the perspective of the company, it is necessary to understand exactly what products and services are being offered to consumers and how they are marketed and branded. From the perspective of the consumer, it is necessary to dig deeply into the minds of consumers and tap their perceptions and beliefs to uncover the true meaning of brands and products.

The brand audit can be used to set a strategic direction for a brand. Are the current sources of brand equity satisfactory? Do certain brand associations need to be strengthened? Does the brand lack uniqueness? What brand opportunities exist and what are the potential challenges for brand equity? As a result of this strategic analysis, a marketing campaign can be put into place to maximize long-term brand equity. A brand audit should be conducted whenever important shifts in strategic direction are contemplated. Moreover, conducting brand audits regularly (eg, annually) allows marketers to keep their fingers on the pulse of their brands so they can be more proactively and responsively managed. As such, brand audits are useful background for managers as they set up their marketing plans.

Brand audits can have profound implications on the strategic direction for brands and their resulting performance.[15] As a result of a brand audit, luxury goods marketer Alfred Dunhill refined its classic 'English' appeal – which has been especially valuable in Asia – to also take on more of a dynamic, international flavour. In Europe, the results of a brand audit led Polaroid to decide to try to change its conventional photography image to emphasize the 'fun side' of their cameras. Polaroid learned from research that its cameras could be seen as a social stimulant and catalyst, provoking fun moments in people's lives, a theme that was picked up in advertising and which suggested the creation of new distribution strategies.

The brand audit consists of two steps: the brand inventory and the brand exploratory. Each is discussed in turn.

Brand inventory

The purpose of the *brand inventory* is to provide a comprehensive profile of how all the products and services sold by a company are marketed and branded. Profiling each product or service requires that all associated brand elements be identified as well as the supporting marketing campaign. In other words, it is necessary to catalogue the following for each product or service sold: the names, logos, symbols, characters, packaging, slogans or other trademarks used; and the inherent product attributes or characteristics of the brand and the pricing, communications, distribution policies and any other relevant marketing activity related to the brand. This information should be summarized in visual and verbal forms.

The outcome of a brand inventory should be an accurate, comprehensive and timely profile of how the products and services sold by a company are branded in terms of which elements are employed (and how) and the nature of the marketing campaign. As part of the inventory, it is also advisable to profile competitive brands, in terms of their branding and marketing efforts. Such information is useful in determining points of parity and points of difference.

Rationale

A brand inventory is a valuable first step in the brand audit for several reasons. First, it helps to suggest what consumers' perceptions may be based on. In other words, consumer associations are typically – although not always – rooted in the reality of how products and services are branded according to the particular brand elements employed and the *intended* meaning attached to them by marketing. Thus, the inventory provides information for interpreting follow-up research activity such as the brand exploratory that collects actual consumer perceptions towards the brand.

Although a brand inventory is a descriptive, useful analysis can be conducted, too, and the brand inventory may provide insight into how brand equity may be better managed. For example, the consistency of all the products or services sharing a brand name can be assessed. Are the brand elements used consistently or are there variations and versions of the brand name, logo and so forth for the same product – perhaps for no obvious reason – depending on which geographic market it is being sold in, which market segment it is aimed at? Similarly, are marketing campaigns logical and consistent across related brands? As companies expand their products geographically and into other categories, it is common for deviations – sometimes significant – to emerge in the appearance of brands and how they are marketed. An inventory should be able to reveal the extent of brand consistency.

At the same time, an inventory can reveal a lack of perceived differences between products sharing the brand name – for example, as a result of line extensions – that are designed to differ. Creating sub-brands with distinct positions is often a marketing priority, and a brand inventory may help to uncover undesirable redundancy and overlap that could lead to consumer confusion or retailer resistance.

Brand exploratory

Although the supply-side view of the brand as revealed by the brand inventory is useful, actual consumer perceptions, of course, may not reflect the perceptions that were intended to be created by a marketing campaign. Thus, the second step of the brand audit is to provide detailed information as to what consumers think of the brand by means of the brand exploratory, particularly in terms of brand awareness and the strength, favourability and uniqueness of brand associations. The *brand exploratory* is research directed at understanding what consumers think and feel about the brand and its corresponding product category to identify sources of brand equity.

Preliminary activities

First, research may already exist and be relevant. It is important to dig through archives to uncover reports that may have been forgotten, but which contain insights and answers to important questions or suggest new questions. These studies should be reviewed and summarized.

Second, it is also useful to interview staff to gain an understanding of their beliefs about consumer perceptions for the brand and its rivals. Past and current marketing managers may be able to share wisdom not necessarily captured in research. The

Free association.

Adjective ratings and checklists.

Projective techniques.

Photo sorts.

Bubble drawings.

Telling stories.

Personification exercises.

Role-playing.

Figure 8.4   Qualitative techniques

Source: Judie Lannon and Peter Cooper, 'Humanistic advertising: a holistic cultural perspective', *International Journal of Advertising*, 1983, 2: 195–213.

diversity of opinions that typically emerge from these internal interviews about the brand serves several functions – for example, increasing the likelihood that insights or ideas will be generated, as well as pointing out any inconsistencies or misconceptions that may exist internally. Although these activities may yield some useful findings and suggest certain hypotheses, they are often incomplete. As a result, additional research is often required to better understand how customers shop for and use products and services and what they think of various brands. To allow a broad range of issues to be covered and to permit issues to be pursued in depth, the brand exploratory often employs qualitative techniques. Chapter 9 reviews a number of these approaches, as summarized in Figure 8.4.

Interpreting qualitative research

In choosing qualitative techniques to include in the brand exploratory, Gardner and Levy note: 'The emphasis in such research must necessarily be given to skill in interpretation and to reaching a coherent picture of the brand. The researchers must allow their respondents sufficient self-expression so that the data are rich in complex evaluations of the brand. In this way, the consumers' thoughts and feelings are given precedence rather than the preconceptions of the researchers, although these are present too in hypothesis and questions.'[16] Levy identifies three criteria by which qualitative research can be classified and judged: direction, depth and diversity.[17] For example, any projective technique varies in terms of the nature of the stimulus information involved (eg, related to the person or the brand), the extent to which responses are more superficial and concrete in meaning versus deeper and more abstract in meaning (and thus requiring more interpretation) and how it relates to the information gathered by other techniques.

In Figure 8.4, the tasks at the top of the list (eg, free association) involve specific questions whose answers may be easier to interpret. The tasks at the bottom of the list (eg, personification exercises and role-playing) involve potentially much richer questions but answers that are also much harder to interpret. According to Levy, the more specific the question, the narrower the range of information given by the respondent. When the stimulus information in the question is open-ended and responses are freer or less constrained, the information provided tends to be greater. The more abstract and symbolic the research technique, however, the more important it is to follow up with probes and other questions that explicitly reveal the motivation and reasons behind consumers' responses.

Ideally, qualitative research conducted as part of the brand exploratory should vary in direction and depth as well as in the diversity of the techniques involved. Regardless of which techniques are employed, the challenge with qualitative research is to provide accurate interpretation – going beyond what consumers explicitly state to determine what they implicitly mean.

Conducting quantitative research

Qualitative research is suggestive, but a more definitive assessment of brand awareness and brand associations often requires a quantitative phase of research. Chapter 9 reviews quantitative approaches.

Guidelines for the quantitative phase of an exploratory are straightforward. The salient associations identified by the qualitative research phase should be assessed according to strength, favourability and uniqueness. Both specific brand beliefs and overall attitudes and behaviours should be examined to reveal potential sources and outcomes of brand equity. Additionally, the depth and breadth of awareness of the brand should be assessed by employing various cues. Typically, it is necessary to conduct similar types of research for competitors to understand their sources of brand equity and how they compare with the target brand.

Much of the discussion of qualitative and quantitative measures has concentrated on associations with the brand name element of the brand – for example, what do consumers think about the brand when given its name as a probe? Other brand elements could and should be studied because they may trigger other meanings and facets of the brand. Consumers can be asked what inferences they make about the brand on the basis of packaging, logo or other attribute alone – for example: 'What would you think about the brand on the basis of its packaging alone?' Specific aspects of the brand elements could be explored – for example, the label on the packaging or the shape of the packaging itself – to uncover their role in creating brand associations. The more it is the case that other brand elements are present and visible when consumers make brand and product decisions (eg, at the point of sale), the more important it is to employ all relevant elements as stimuli. In the process of examining other elements, it is also important to determine which one most effectively represents and symbolizes the brand as a whole.

Brand positioning and the supporting marketing campaign

The brand exploratory should uncover knowledge structures for the core brand and its competitors as well as determine the desired brand awareness and brand image and the necessary points of parity and points of difference with respect to competitors. Moving from the current brand image to the desired image typically involves decisions to add new associations, strengthen existing ones or weaken or eliminate undesirable ones in the minds of consumers. John Roberts, an Australian academic, sees the challenge in achieving the ideal positioning for a brand as being able to achieve congruence between what customers currently believe about the brand (and thus find credible), what customers will value in the brand, what the company is saying about the brand and where it would like to take the brand.

A number of managers can be part of the planning and positioning process (eg, brand, marketing research and production managers), as can relevant outside partners (eg, ad agency representatives). Once marketers have a good understanding from the brand audit of current brand knowledge structures for their target consumers and have decided on the desired brand knowledge structures for optimal positioning, additional research still may be necessary to test the viability of tactical campaigns to achieve that positioning. A number of marketing campaigns may exist that, at least on the surface, may be able to achieve the same goals, and additional research may be useful to assess their relative effectiveness and efficiency.

DESIGNING BRAND TRACKING STUDIES

The brand value chain provides an overall perspective on how brand equity or value can be created. Combined with the CBBE model, it provides guidance as to how to position a brand and how well the marketing campaign has achieved that positioning. Brand audits is a means of providing in-depth information and insights that are essential for setting long-term strategic direction for the brand. Brand audits thus are an invaluable guide to positioning a brand. In terms of more short-term tactical considerations, less-detailed brand-related information should be collected as a result of conducting tracking studies.

Tracking studies involve information collected from consumers over time. Such studies typically employ quantitative measures to provide marketers with information as to how their brands and marketing campaigns are performing. Tracking studies are a means of applying the brand value chain to understand where, how much and in what ways brand value is being created, thus offering invaluable information about how well a positioning has been achieved.

Tracking studies provide consistent baseline information to facilitate day-to-day decision-making. As more marketing activity surrounds the brand, it becomes difficult and expensive to research each marketing action.

Tracking studies provide valuable insights into the collective effects of marketing activities on the customer mindset, market outcomes and perhaps even shareholder value. Regardless of how few or how many changes are made in a marketing campaign, it is important to monitor the health of the brand and its equity so proper adjustments can be made if necessary. A tracking system can help marketers better understand a host of considerations such as category dynamics, consumer behaviour, competitive vulnerabilities and opportunities, and marketing effectiveness and efficiency.

A number of issues must be addressed in implementing a brand equity tracking system. This chapter addresses what measures should be employed in tracking studies, as well as how tracking studies should be implemented and interpreted.

What to track

Chapter 2 discussed potential measures that correspond to the customer-based brand equity model, all of which are candidates for tracking. Chapter 9 reviews quantitative measures of brand knowledge structures that also may be useful for tracking. This section provides guidelines for tracking and considers measures that may be employed in tracking. In that spirit, it should be recognized that it is usually necessary to customize tracking surveys to address issues faced by a brand. To a great extent, each brand faces a unique situation that must be reflected in questions in its tracking survey.

Product brand tracking

Tracking an individual brand involves measuring brand awareness and image. In terms of brand awareness, both recall and recognition measures should be collected. In general, awareness measures should move from general to specific questions. Thus, it may make sense to first ask consumers what brands come to mind in certain situations, to next ask for recall of brands on the basis of various product category cues and to then finish with tests of brand recognition (if necessary).

As with brand awareness, it is usually desirable that a range of measures be employed in brand tracking surveys to measure brand image, especially in terms of specific perceptions (ie, what consumers think characterizes the brand) and evaluations (ie, what the brands mean to consumers). A number of associations typically exist for a brand, depending on the richness of consumer knowledge structures, which could be tracked over time.

Given that brands often compete at the augmented product level (see Chapter 1), it is important to measure all associations that may distinguish competing brands. Thus, measures of specific, 'lower-level' associations should include all potential sources of brand equity (performance and imagery attributes and benefits). Because they often represent points of parity or points of difference, it is important to track benefit associations. To better understand any changes in benefit beliefs for a brand, however, it may be necessary to also measure the corresponding attribute beliefs that underlie those benefits. In other words, changes in descriptive attribute beliefs may help to explain changes in more evaluative benefit beliefs for a brand.

Associations that make up the potential sources of brand equity should be assessed on the basis of strength, favourability and uniqueness *in that order*. Unless associations are strong enough that they are likely to be recalled, their favourability does not matter, and unless associations are sufficiently favourable to be considerations in making a decision, uniqueness does not matter. Ideally, measures of all three dimensions would be collected, but perhaps for only certain associations and only some of the time (eg, favourability and uniqueness may only be measured once a year for three to five associations).

At the same time, it is also important to track more general, 'higher-level' judgements, feelings and other outcome-related measures. Chapter 9 outlines measures of consumers attitudes, intentions and behaviours regarding brands. After asking for their overall opinions, consumers can be asked if they have changed their attitudes, intentions or behaviour in recent weeks or months and, if so, why.

Benefit associations often determine behaviour. In that respect, Patrick LaPointe advocates four measures that he believes are largely predictive of future behaviour of prospects and customers:[18]

- functional performance of the underlying product or service;
- convenience and ease of accessing the product or service;
- brand personality; and
- pricing and value component.

Brand Briefing 8.2 provides an example of a tracking survey for McDonald's.

Brand Briefing 8.2

Sample brand tracking survey

Assume that McDonald's was interested in designing a short tracking survey to be conducted over the phone. How might it be set up? Although there are different types of questions, it might take the following form.

Interviewer: We are conducting a short phone interview concerning consumer opinions about quick-service or 'fast food' restaurant chains.

Brand awareness and usage

1. What brands of quick-service restaurant chains are you aware of?
2. At which brands of quick-service restaurant chains would you consider eating?
3. Have you eaten in a quick-service restaurant chain in the last week? Which ones?
4. If you were to eat in a quick-service restaurant tomorrow for lunch, which one would you go to?
5. What if instead it were for dinner? Where would you go?
6. Finally, what if instead it were for breakfast? Where would you go?
7. Which are your favourite quick-service restaurant chains?

We want to ask you some questions about a particular quick-service restaurant chain, McDonald's.

- Have you heard of this restaurant? [Establish familiarity.]
- Have you eaten at this restaurant? [Establish trial.]
- When I say McDonald's, what are the first associations that come to your mind? Anything else? [List all.]

Brand judgements

We are interested in your overall opinion of McDonald's.

1. How favourable is your attitude towards McDonald's?
2. How well does McDonald's satisfy your needs?

Brand Briefing 8.2 *continued*

3. How likely would you be to recommend McDonald's to others?

4. How good value is McDonald's?

5. Is McDonald's worth a premium price?

6. What do you like best about McDonald's?

7. What is most unique about McDonald's?

8. To what extent does McDonald's offer advantages that other brands cannot?

9. To what extent is McDonald's superior to other brands in the quick-service restaurant category?

10. Compared with other brands in the quick-service restaurant category, how well does McDonald's satisfy your basic needs?

We now want to ask you some questions about McDonald's as a company. Please indicate your agreement with the following statements.

McDonald's is . . .

1. Innovative
2. Knowledgeable
3. Trustworthy
4. Likeable
5. Concerned about their customers
6. Concerned about society as a whole
7. Admirable

Brand performance

We now would like to ask some specific questions about McDonald's. Please indicate your agreement with the following statements.

McDonald's . . .

1. Is convenient to eat at
2. Provides quick, efficient service
3. Has clean facilities
4. Is for the whole family
5. Has delicious food
6. Has healthy food
7. Has a varied menu
8. Has friendly, courteous staff
9. Offers fun promotions
10. Has a stylish and attractive look
11. Has high-quality food

Brand imagery

1. To what extent do people you admire and respect eat at McDonald's?

2. How much do you like people who eat at McDonald's?

3. How well do each of the following words describe McDonald's?

   Down to earth, honest, daring, up to date, reliable, successful, upper class, charming, outdoorsy

Brand Briefing 8.2 *continued*

4. Is McDonald's a restaurant that you can use in a lot of different situations?
5. To what extent does thinking of McDonald's bring back pleasant memories?
6. To what extent do you feel that you grew up with McDonald's?

Brand feelings

Does McDonald's give you a feeling of . . .

1. Warmth?
2. Fun?
3. Excitement?
4. Sense of security or confidence?
5. Social approval?
6. Self-respect?

Brand resonance

1. I consider myself loyal to McDonald's.
2. I buy McDonald's whenever I can.
3. I would go out of my way to eat at McDonald's.
4. I really love McDonald's.
5. I would really miss McDonald's if it went away.
6. McDonald's is special to me.
7. McDonald's is more than a product to me.
8. I really identify with people who eat at McDonald's.
9. I feel a deep connection with others who eat at McDonald's.
10. I really like to talk about McDonald's to others.
11. I am always interested in learning more about McDonald's.
12. I would be interested in merchandise with the McDonald's name on it.
13. I am proud to have others know I eat at McDonald's.
14. I like to visit the website for McDonald's.
15. Compared to other people, I follow news about McDonald's closely.

Corporate or family brand tracking

In the case of a family or corporate brand, additional questions may be warranted. Although many of these types of questions could be included in tracking studies for individual products for the brand, there may also be justification for tracking the corporate or family brand separately or concurrently (or both) with individual products. Besides the measures of corporate credibility identified in Chapter 2, other specific measures of corporate brand associations are possible, including some of the following (illustrated with the British Airways brand).

- How well is BA managed?
- How easy is it to do business with BA?
- How concerned is BA with its customers?
- How approachable is BA?
- How accessible is BA?
- How much do you like doing business with BA?

The actual questions used should reflect the level and nature of experience that the particular group of respondents would be likely to have had with the company.

Many companies track corporate image. For example, at one time DuPont tracked the following broad measures of corporate image.[19]

- Outstanding US companies (unaided).
- Outstanding companies on 11 attributes (unaided).
- Rating on those attributes.
- Outstanding companies in eight different industries (unaided).
- Association with those industries.
- Ratings in associated industries.
- Familiarity with products and services.
- Likelihood of investing in stock.
- Feeling about friend accepting employment.

To more fully understand what drives corporate reputation, a model (Figure 8.5) to evaluate drivers of corporate reputation was launched 2006 by the Reputation Institute, a research network established 1997 by former academics.

Interviews with the public in ten countries resulted in the following model. Trust, feeling, esteem and admiration are the central elements of a company's reputation. These four elements have therefore been placed in the inner circle of the model, constituting the actual reputation. The RepTrak model then expands these elements into 7 dimensions and 23 attributes (performance indicators), which have been established through qualitative and quantitative research as best explaining the reputation of a company.

Through statistical analysis it is possible to connect the RepTrak attributes with supportive behaviours from stakeholder groups (eg, verbal support), thus identifying what *drives* the reputation of a company. This enables a company to track, analyze and act upon its corporate reputatation among stakeholders.

When a brand is identified with many products, as with a corporate or family branding strategy, one important issue is which products the brand reminds consumers of. An important related consideration is which products are most influential in affecting consumer perceptions. To identify which products are most closely linked to the brand, consumers could be probed as to which products they associate with the brand on an unaided basis (eg, 'What products come to mind when you think of the Nike brand?') or an aided basis by listing sub-brand names (eg, 'Are you aware of Nike Air Force basketball shoes? Nike Spear React tennis apparel? Nike Air Max running shoes?'). To better understand the dynamics between the brand and its corresponding products, consumers can be probed as to their relationship ('There are

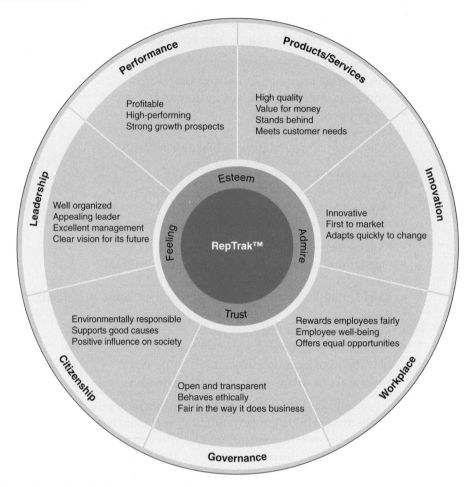

Figure 8.5 RepTrak™, Elements of corporate reputation

many different products associated with Nike. Which ones are most important to you in formulating your opinion about the brand?')

Global tracking

If tracking involves diverse geographic markets – especially if both developing and developed countries are involved – then it may be necessary to have a broader set of background measures to put the brand development in those markets in the right perspective. These brand context measures would presumably not need to be collected frequently, but could provide useful explanatory information (Figure 8.6).

How to conduct tracking studies

One question with tracking studies is, which elements of the brand should be used? In general, the brand name is always used, but, as noted in Chapter 4, it may also make sense to employ other elements, such as a logo or symbol, in probing brand structures, especially if these elements can play a visible and important role in the

Economic indicators

Gross domestic product.

Interest rates.

Unemployment.

Average pay.

Disposable income.

Home ownership and housing debt.

Exchange rates, share markets and balance of payments.

Retail

Total spent in supermarkets.

Change year on year.

Growth in house brand.

Technology

Computer at home.

DVR.

Access to and use of internet.

Phones.

PDA.

Microwaves.

Television.

Personal attitudes and values

Confidence.

Security.

Family.

Environment.

Traditional values.

Foreigners v sovereignty.

Media indicators

Media consumption: total time spent watching TV, consuming other media.

Advertising expenditure: total, by media and by product category.

Demographic profile

Population profile: age, sex, income, household size.

Geographic distribution.

Ethnic and cultural profile.

Other products and services

Transport: own car – how many.

Best description of car.

Motorbike.

Home ownership or renting.

Domestic trips overnight in past year.

International trips in past two years.

Attitude to brands and shopping

Buy on price.

Like to buy new things.

Country of origin or manufacture.

Prefer to buy things that have been advertised.

Importance of familiar brands.

Figure 8.6   Brand context measures

decision process. Conducting tracking studies also requires decisions in terms of who to track, as well as when and where to track.

Who to track

As Chapter 3 noted, several segmentation schemes can be profitably incorporated into tracking approaches. Tracking often concentrates on current customers, but it can also be informative to monitor non-users of the brand or even of the product category as a whole (eg, to suggest potential segmentation strategies). It often can be insightful to track those customers loyal to the brand versus those who are loyal to other brands or who switch brands. Among customers of the brand, it is often informative to distinguish between heavy and light users. Dividing up the market typically requires different questionnaires (or at least sections of a questionnaire) to better capture the specific issues associated with each segment.

Other types of customers can be monitored too. For example, it is often useful to track channel members and other intermediaries to understand their perceptions and actions towards the brand. Of particular interest is their image of the brand and the manner in which they feel they may be or could be helping or hurting its equity. Retailers can be asked direct questions such as, 'Do you feel that products in your shop sell faster if they have [the brand name] on it? Why?' Similarly, it also may be important to track employees (eg, salespeople) to better understand their beliefs about the brand and how they feel they are contributing to its equity or possibly could contribute to its equity. Such tracking may be especially important with service organizations, where employees play profound roles in affecting brand equity.

When and where to track

It is necessary to decide how frequently tracking information should be collected. One approach for monitoring brand associations involves continuous tracking studies, in which information is collected from consumers continually over time. The advantage is that it smooths out aberrations or unusual marketing activities or events (eg, a splashy new ad campaign or an unlikely occurrence in the marketing environment) to provide more representative baseline measures.

There is a host of ways to conduct these studies. The frequency of such tracking studies, in general, depends on the frequency of product purchase (durable goods are typically tracked less frequently because they are purchased less often) and on the consumer behaviour and marketing activity in the product category. Many companies conduct interviews with consumers every week – or even every day – and assemble the results as a rolling or moving average for monthly or quarterly reports.

Millward Brown

Marketing research tracking pioneer Millward Brown usually interviews 50 to 100 people a week and looks at the data as moving averages in its Advanced Tracking Programme. Typically, these involve short interviews (10 to 20 minutes in length, on the phone or web) covering the client brand and competitive set. Data is collected on topics as dictated by the client. Modules include: brand loyalty, brand positioning, value perceptions, awareness and response to marketing communications and in-store promotions and consumer profiles. A short (12-minute) interview for a typical consumer product administered over the phone to 50 nationally representative consumers weekly can cost roughly €171,000 annually, depending on modality.[20]

When the brand has more stable and enduring associations, tracking can be conducted less frequently. Nevertheless, even if it were the case that the marketing of a brand may not appreciably change over time, it is still important to track brands because competitive entries can change the dynamics within the market. Finally, globally, it is important to recognize the stage of the product or brand life cycle in deciding on the frequency of tracking: opinions of consumers in mature markets may not change much, whereas emerging markets may shift quickly and perhaps in unpredictable ways.

How to interpret tracking studies

For tracking measures to yield actionable insights and recommendations, they must be reliable and sensitive. One problem with many traditional measures of marketing phenomena is that they do not change much over time. Although this stability may reflect the fact that the underlying levels of brand awareness do not change much, in other cases it may be that one or more of those dimensions may have changed to some extent, but that the measures themselves are not sensitive enough to detect such subtle shifts. To develop sensitive tracking measures, it may be necessary to phrase questions in a comparative (eg, 'compared with other brands, how much . . .') or temporal (eg, 'compared with one month or one year ago, how much . . .') manner.

Another challenge in interpreting tracking studies is to decide on appropriate benchmarks. For example, what is a sufficiently high level of brand awareness? When are brand associations sufficiently strong, favourable and unique? How positive should brand judgements and feelings be? What are reasonable expectations for the amount of brand resonance? The cut-offs that are imposed must be reasonable and must properly reflect the interests of the intended internal management audience. Appropriately defined and tested targets can help management benchmark against competitors and assess the productivity of brand marketing teams.[21]

To some extent, these targets need to be driven by competitive considerations and the nature of the category. In some low-involvement categories (eg, lightbulbs), it may be difficult to carve out a distinct image, unlike higher-involvement products (eg, cars or computers). Along these lines, it may be important to allow for and monitor the number of respondents who indicate that they 'don't know' or have 'no response' with respect to the brand tracking measures: the more of these types of answers that are evident, the less consumers would seem to care.

Along these lines, Nielsen's Alastair Gordon highlights some of the reasons brand equity or health metrics have not always been helpful.

- too much focus on 'top-level' boxes or scores and indices (often too general and not prescriptive enough);
- targets that are not set at all, unattainable or inappropriate for the management level they are given to;
- treated as an independent research study and not integrated with other information such as category trends; and
- overly focused on consumer attitudes and emotional connections without a link to behaviours.

He advocates that brand health measures become more multidimensional, more directly address why consumers decide between brands and be placed in a clear 'report book' approach to understand opportunities and set appropriate targets.

One of the most important tasks in conducting brand tracking studies is to identify the determinants of brand equity.[22] Of the brand associations that can serve as sources of brand equity, which ones actually influence consumer attitudes and behaviour and create value for the brand? Marketers must identify the real value drivers – that is, those tangible and intangible points of difference that influence and determine consumers' product and brand choices. Similarly, the activities that have the most effect on brand knowledge need to be identified, especially with respect to consumer exposure to advertising and other communications. Carefully monitoring and relating key sources and outcome measures of brand equity should help to address these issues. The CBBE model and brand value chain suggest possible links and paths that can be explored.

ESTABLISHING A BRAND EQUITY MANAGEMENT SYSTEM

Tracking studies, as well as audits, can provide information concerning how to best build and measure brand equity. Nevertheless, the potential value of such research will not be realized unless structures and procedures are put into place within an organization to capitalize on the usefulness of the brand equity concept and the information that is collected. Although a brand equity measurement system does not ensure that 'good' decisions about the brand will always occur, it should increase the likelihood that they do and, if nothing else, should at least decrease the likelihood that 'bad' decisions will be made.

Embracing the concept of branding and brand equity, many firms constantly review how the concept can be best factored into the organization. Interestingly, perhaps one of the biggest threats to brand equity comes from within the organization and the fact that too many marketing managers remain on the job for only a limited time. As a result of short-term assignments, marketing managers may adopt a short-term perspective, leading to an over-reliance on quick-fix, sales-generating tactics such as line and category extensions. Because these managers lack an understanding and appreciation of the brand equity concept, some critics maintain they are running the brand 'without a licence'.

To counteract forces within an organization that may lead to ineffective long-term management of brands, internal branding has become a top priority. As part of these efforts, a brand equity management system must be put into place. Such a system is defined as a set of organizational processes designed to improve the understanding and use of the brand equity concept within a firm. As one set of commentators noted:[23]

> Implementing a brand equity management system is critical to managing one of the company's most valuable assets. It will give the company a better way to inform how to position its brands, become a living bible of what matters most for brands to succeed, enable charting brand progress towards goals, and become a tool for diagnosing and fixing a weakness that might be emerging.

Three steps should be taken to implement a brand equity management system: creating charters, assembling reports and defining responsibilities. The following subsections discuss each of these in turn. Brand Briefing 8.3 describes how the Swedish energy company Vattenfall developed a brand equity measurement and management system.

Brand equity charter

The first step in establishing a brand equity management system is to formalize the company view of brand equity into a document, the *brand equity charter*, that

Brand Briefing 8.3

Managing the Vattenfall brand

The European energy market is going through comprehensive restructuring, and the entire European market opened to competition in 2007. Swedish company Vattenfall's growth strategy started in 1997 with a vision to be a leading European energy company. The deregulation of the German electricity market in 1998 gave Vattenfall the opportunity to buy companies there and establish a European base. At the same time, Vattenfall bought two of Poland's largest electricity suppliers.

Vattenfall's core business is to produce electricity and heat. The company generates, distributes and sells electricity and heat, both to private households and industrial customers. Vattenfall was founded in Sweden almost a century ago. By 2006, the number of employees was 32,000, with sales of €13,697 million and profit €2,216 million. The State-owned Swedish company operates in Sweden, Denmark, Finland, Germany and Poland.

Vattenfall employs a monolithic brand strategy, with all operations represented by one brand. Leading is defined as being the number one for the customer, the environment and the economy. The company's mission is to enhance customers' competitiveness, environment and quality of life through being efficient and offering world-class service. As a result of internal research, three core values, openness, effectiveness and accountability, became central in the company philosophy. Besides the core values, Vattenfall developed five brand image values: empathetic, easy, partner, progressive and reliable. These values were derived from research in several markets. Vattenfall has also developed a brand promise as the internal guiding 'mantra': 'With heart and mind on your needs, we turn energy into value for life.' The brand promise is not an explicit external message. It is an internal expression capturing the spirit of the desired Vattenfall brand image that guides communications initiatives.

Vattenfall works with stakeholder, holistic brand management (as opposed to consumer brand management) to reap the business benefits of a strong brand reputation among all stakeholder groups. Stakeholder, holistic brand management means that the brand and the specific brand image attributes should be strengthened in all parts of the business, throughout the value chain and in all aspects of the communication, propositions and behaviour.

The common tool used to govern the brand platform is the Vattenfall Reputation Monitor (VRM). One of the principal outputs of the model is the 'Vattenfall Reputation Index' (VRI) that consolidates Vattenfall's reputation performance into a single measure.

The VRM enables Vattenfall to manage its corporate reputation among stakeholder groups in the four countries in which it operates: society, market, employees and capital providers. Within each stakeholder group, there are various sub-groups. The market group for instance, includes, B2C, B2B SME and B2B Large customers. All of the stakeholders are measured in the reputation monitor (Figure 8.7).

Brand Briefing 8.3 *continued*

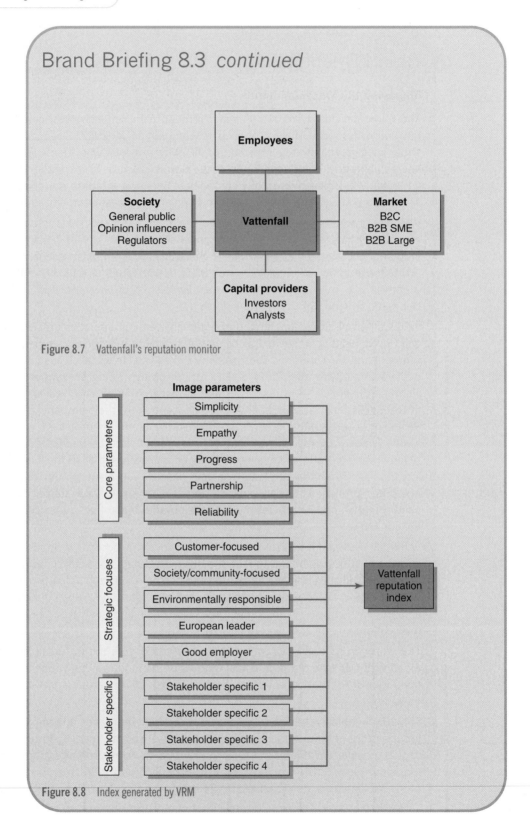

Figure 8.7   Vattenfall's reputation monitor

Figure 8.8   Index generated by VRM

Brand Briefing 8.3 *continued*

The VRM assesses how each stakeholder group rates Vattenfall and its competitors based on a set of functional and emotional image parameters and how this translates into their impression of the Vattenfall brand, captured in a stakeholder-specific VRI (Figure 8.8). The index goes from 0 to 100.

Stakeholder data are collected once a year. The VRI is expected to become a key performance indicator for Vattenfall's business, measuring across all stakeholders in each of the countries the company is present. The VRM has also been built to explain how to prioritize communications and touch point activities to improve the index. Accordingly, the VRI has also been built on statistical modelling to ensure high levels of confidence and reliability in the results.

Brand performance indicators for awareness, reputation and brand image attributes are annually set up as targets in the communication plans and evaluated in the reputation monitor.

Sources: Vattenfall Group; Stefan Nerpin, head of corporate communications, Vattenfall.

provides relevant guidelines to marketing managers within the company as well as marketing partners outside the company (eg, ad agency personnel). This document should do the following.

- Define the company's view of the brand equity concept and explain why it is important.
- Describe the scope of brands in terms of associated products and the manner in which they have been branded and marketed (as revealed by company records and the most recent brand inventory).
- Specify what the actual and desired equity is for a brand at all relevant levels of the brand hierarchy – for example, at both the corporate level and at the individual product level (see Chapter 11). Relevant associations should be defined, including those that constitute points of parity and points of difference, as well as core brand associations and the brand mantra.
- Explain how brand equity is measured in terms of the tracking study and a resulting brand equity report.
- Suggest how brand equity should be managed in terms of some general strategic guidelines (eg, stressing clarity, relevance, distinctiveness, innovativeness and consistency in marketing campaigns).
- Outline how marketing campaigns should be devised in terms of tactical guidelines (eg, ad evaluation criteria, brand name choice criteria).
- Specify the proper treatment of the brand in terms of trademark usage, packaging and communications.

Although parts of the brand equity charter may not change from year to year, it should nevertheless be updated annually to provide decision-makers with a current brand profile and to identify opportunities and potential risks. As products are introduced, brand strategies are changed and other marketing initiatives take place, they should be reflected in the brand equity charter. In-depth insights that emerge from brand audits belong in the charter.

Figure 8.9 shows the contents page for the Pillsbury brand manual. A brand with a creative brand charter is Burger King.

Burger King

As part of its brand revitalization in 2004, Burger King overhauled its marketing. In addition to introducing quirky advertising, Burger King's ad agency, Crispin Porter and Bogusky, transformed many internal aspects of the brand from the off-beat instrumental telephone 'hold' music to its employee handbook. Burger King made sure that the handbook was written to be accessible in tone and language, embracing the qualities of corporate culture the chain was trying to adopt.

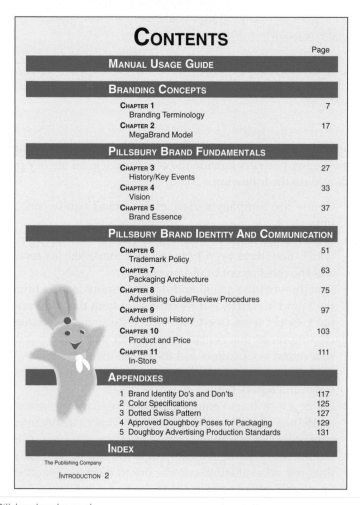

Figure 8.9 Pillsbury brand manual

Brand equity report

The second step in establishing a brand equity management system is to assemble the results of the tracking survey and other relevant performance measures into a brand equity report or scorecard to be distributed to management (monthly, quarterly or annually). Much of the information relevant to the report may exist within or be collected by the organization. Yet the information may have been presented to management in disjointed chunks such that a holistic understanding was not possible. The brand equity report attempts to integrate all these measures.[24]

The brand equity report should describe *what* is happening with a brand as well as information as to *why* it is happening. It should include all relevant internal and external measures of brand performance and sources and outcomes of brand equity.[25] In particular, one section of the report should summarize consumers' perceptions of attribute or benefit associations, preferences and reported behaviour as revealed by the tracking study. Another section of the report should include more descriptive market-level information such as:

- product shipments and movement through channels of distribution;
- retail category trends;
- relevant cost breakdowns;
- price and discount schedules where appropriate;
- sales and market share information broken down by relevant factors (eg, geographic region, type of retail account or customer);
- profit assessments.

Robert Malcolm from Diageo notes that the UK drinks group measures both input and outcome metrics and applies a complementary approach based on the GAME plan.[26]

1. *Goal:* identify key brands for the next fiscal period.
2. *Activity:* locate status on a baseline, compared with brands owned by the company or competition.
3. *Measurement:* allocate inputs with specific objectives such as changing consumer behaviour and increasing purchase intensity.
4. *Evaluation:* assess the outputs.

These measures can provide insight into the market performance component of the brand value chain. They can be compared with various frames of reference – performance last month/quarter/year – and colour coded green, yellow or red, depending on whether the trends are good, neutral or bad, respectively.

To provide feedback on marketing peformance to boards of directors, academics Gail McGovern and John Quelch advocate quarterly tracking reports of the three or four marketing or customer-related metrics that drive and predict business performance – ie, behavioural measures that are specific to the business model.[27] As an example, they note how the board of casino operator Harrah's focuses on three metrics: share of its customers' spending on gaming (share of wallet); loyalty scheme updates (an indicator of increased concentration of a customer's gaming at Harrah's); and percentage of revenue from customers visiting more than one of Harrah's 30 casinos (an indicator of cross-selling). To support tracking, Harrah's spends €34.2 million a year on a customer information system.

Similarly, Ambler and Clark offer three recommendations.[28] First, marketers must work with their finance department to develop marketing 'dashboards' and to shift metrics and forecasting responsibilities to the finance department. Second, marketers should develop with each agency a detailed brief with measurable objectives and a results-driven fee component (for agencies). Finally, marketers need to dedicate extra time to secure commitment by colleagues to their business model, strategy and metrics.

With computer technology, it has become easy for firms to place the information that makes up the brand equity report online so that it can be accessed easily. For example, MarketMind has developed a brand management database that integrates continuous consumer tracking survey data, media weight (or cost) data, warehouse sales and retail scan data and PR and editorial content.

Brand equity responsibilities

To develop a brand equity management system that will maximize long-term brand equity, organizational responsibilities and processes with respect to the brand must be defined clearly. Brands need constant, consistent nurturing to grow. Weak brands often suffer from a lack of discipline, commitment and investment. This section considers internal issues related to assigning responsibilities and duties for properly managing brand equity, as well as external issues related to the roles of marketing partners. Brand Briefing 8.4 describes principles in building a brand-driven organization.

Brand Briefing 8.4

Maximizing internal branding

Branding expert Scott Davis offers insights into what it takes to make a brand-driven organization. According to Davis, for employees to become brand advocates, they must understand what a brand is, how it is built, what their organization's brand stands for and what their role is in delivering the brand promise. He sees the process of an organization assimilating the brand into employees as going through three stages.

1. 'Hear it': how do we best get it into their hands?
2. 'Believe it': how do we best get it into their heads?
3. 'Live it': how do we best get it into their hearts?

Davis also argues that six principles should guide the brand assimilation process within an organization.

1. *Make the brand relevant:* each employee must understand and embrace the brand meaning. For example, Nordstrom empowers sales associates to approve exchanges.

Brand Briefing 8.4 *continued*

2. *Make the brand accessible:* employees must know where they can get brand knowledge and answers to their brand-related questions. For example, Ernst & Young launched 'The Branding Zone' on their intranet to provide employees with information on its branding, marketing and advertising.

3. *Reinforce the brand continuously:* the brand meaning must be reinforced with employees beyond the initial rollout of an internal branding campaign. For example, Southwest Airlines continually reinforces its brand promise of 'a symbol of freedom' through campaigns and activities with a freedom theme.

4. *Make brand education ongoing:* provide new employees with inspiring and informative training. For example, Ritz-Carlton ensures that each employee participates in an intensive orientation called 'The Gold Standard' based on principles to improve service delivery and maximize guest satisfaction.

5. *Reward on-brand behaviours:* an incentive system to reward employees for exceptional support of the brand strategy should be part of the rollout of an internal branding campaign. For example, Continental Airlines rewards employees with cash bonuses each month if the airline ranks in the top five punctual airlines.

6. *Align hiring practices:* HR and marketing must work together to develop criteria and screening procedures to ensure that new staff fit the company's culture. For example, Pret a Manger sandwich shops have such a carefully honed screen that only 20 percent of all applicants end up being hired.

Davis also emphasizes the role of senior managers in driving internal branding, noting that the managing director sets the tone and compliance with a brand-based culture and determines whether proper resources and procedures are in place.

Source: Scott Davis, 'Building a brand-driven organization', in *Kellogg on Branding*, eds. Alice M. Tybout and Tim Calkins, Hoboken, NJ: John Wiley, 2005.

Overseeing brand equity

To provide central co-ordination, a position entitled vice-president or director of strategic brand management or brand equity management should be established. That person would be responsible for overseeing the implementation of the brand equity charter and brand equity reports. He or she would ensure that product and marketing actions across divisions and geographic boundaries were performed in a way that reflects the spirit of the brand equity charter and the substance of the brand equity report. A natural place to house such duties and responsibilities is in a corporate marketing group that has a senior management reporting relationship.

Scott Bedbury, who helped direct the Nike and Starbucks brands during some of their most successful years, is emphatic about the need for 'top-down brand leadership'.[29] He advocates the addition of a chief brand officer who reports directly to the managing director and who acts in the following ways.

- Is an omnipresent conscience whose job is to champion and protect the brand – the way it looks and feels – both inside and outside the company. The role recognizes that the brand is the sum total of everything a company does and strives to ensure that all employees understand the brand and its values, creating 'brand disciples' in the process.
- Is an architect and not only helps build the brand but also plans, anticipates, researches, probes, listens and informs. Working with senior leadership, the role helps envisage not just what works best for the brand today but also what can help drive it forward.
- Determines and protects the voice of the brand by taking a long-term (two to three years) perspective. The role can be accountable for brand-critical and corporate-wide activities such as advertising, positioning, corporate design, corporate communications and consumer or market insights.

Even strong brands need to be watched carefully to prevent managers from over-confidently believing that it is acceptable to 'make one little mistake' or 'let it slide' with respect to the equity of the brand. A number of top companies (eg, Colgate-Palmolive, Canada Dry, Quaker Oats, Pillsbury, Coca-Cola and Nestlé) have created such brand equity gatekeepers for some or all of their brands at one time.[30]

Bedbury also advocates brand development reviews (full-day meetings quarterly or even half-day meetings monthly) for brands in difficult circumstances. As part of a brand development review, he suggests the following topics and activities.[31]

- *Review brand-sensitive material:* for example, brand strength monitors or tracking studies, brand audits and focus groups, as well as less formal personal observations or 'gut feelings' should all be reviewed.
- *Review the status of brand initiatives:* because brand initiatives involve strategic thrusts to either strengthen a weakness in the brand or to exploit an opportunity to grow the brand in a new direction, customer perceptions may change as a result and therefore need to be assessed.
- *Review brand-sensitive projects:* for example, evaluate advertising campaigns, corporate communications, sales meeting agendas and human resources plans (recruitment, training and retention affect the organization's ability to embrace and project brand values).
- *Review product and distribution strategies with respect to core values.*
- *Resolve brand positioning conflicts.*

Brand Briefing 8.5 contains a checklist by which firms can assess their marketing skills and performance.

One of the important roles taken by senior management is the determination of marketing budgets and where and how company resources will be allocated. It is important that a brand equity management system be able to inform and provide input to decision-makers so they can recognize the short-term and long-term ramifications of their decisions on brand equity. Decisions concerning which brands to invest in and whether or not to implement brand-building marketing campaigns or instead to

Brand Briefing 8.5

Rating a company's marketing assessment system

London Business School professor Tim Ambler has a wealth of experience in working with companies. He notes that, in his interactions, 'most companies do not have a clear picture of their own marketing performance, which may be why they cannot assess it.' To help companies evaluate if their marketing assessment system is good enough, he suggests that they ask the following ten questions – the higher the score, the better the assessment system.[32]

1. **Does the senior executive team regularly and formally assess marketing performance?**

   a. Yearly (10 points)
   b. Six-monthly (10)
   c. Quarterly (5)
   d. More often (0)
   e. Rarely (0)
   f. Never (0)

2. **What does the senior executive team understand by 'customer value'?**

   a. Don't know. We are not clear about this (0)
   b. Value of the customer to the business (as in 'customer lifetime value') (5)
   c. Value of what the company provides from the customers' point of view (10)
   d. Sometimes one, sometimes the other (10)

3. **How much time does the senior executive team give to marketing issues?**

   a. >30% (10)
   b. 20–30% (6)
   c. 10–20% (4)
   d. <10% (0)

4. **Does the business/marketing plan show the non-financial corporate goals and link them to market goals?**

   a. No/no plan (0)
   b. Corporate no, market yes (5)
   c. Yes to both (10)

5. **Does the plan show the comparison of your marketing performance with competitors or the market as a whole?**

   a. No/no plan (0)
   b. Yes, clearly (10)
   c. In between (5)

6. **What is your main marketing asset called?**

   a. Brand equity (10)
   b. Reputation (10)
   c. Other term (5)
   d. We have no term (0)

Brand Briefing 8.5 *continued*

7. **Does the senior executive team's performance review involve a quantified view of the main marketing asset and how it has changed?**
   a. Yes to both (10)
   b. Yes but only financially (brand valuation) (5)
   c. Not really (0)

8. **Has the senior executive team quantified what 'success' would look like five or ten years from now?**
   a. No (0)
   b. Yes (10)
   c. Don't know (0)

9. **Does your strategy have quantified milestones to indicate progress towards that success?**
   a. No (0)
   b. Yes (10)
   c. What strategy? (0)

10. **Are the marketing performance indicators seen by the senior executive team aligned with these milestones?**
    a. No (0)
    b. Yes, external (customers and competitors) (7)
    c. Yes, internal, (employees and innovativeness) (5)
    d. Yes, both (10)

exploit brand equity through brand extensions, reduced communication expenditures and so forth, should reflect the current and desired state of the brand as revealed through brand tracking and other measures.

Organizational design and structures

In a general sense, the marketing function must be organized in a way that optimizes brand equity. Trends in organizational design and structure reflect the recognition of the importance of the brand and the challenges of managing its equity carefully. For example, companies are embracing brand management. More industries are introducing brand managers. Often, companies have hired managers from top packaged goods companies, adopting some of the same practices as a result.

Interestingly, packaged goods companies such as Procter & Gamble continue to evolve the brand management system (see Brand Briefing 8.6). With category management, manufacturers offer retailers advice as to how to best stock their shelves. Retailers are adopting category management principles. For example, Borders asked HarperCollins to help it select which cookbooks to carry – including those published by competitors.[33] Through better optimization, one survey found that retailers reported a 14 percent sales growth from adopting category management and manufacturers reported an 8 percent hike.[34] Although manufacturers functioning as category captains can improve sales, experts caution that it is important for retailers to exercise their own insights and values to ensure their distinctiveness in the marketplace.

Brand Briefing 8.6

Category management at Procter & Gamble

Procter & Gamble, pioneers of the brand management system, and other top companies made a significant shift to incorporate category management. Previously, senior management at P&G included a handful of divisional marketing vice-presidents, who were responsible for 3 to 6 product categories and 12 to 18 brands. With the company's new category emphasis, starting in the late 1980s, a general manager was assigned to each of the 40 or so categories in which P&G competed (eg, laundry detergents, dishwashing detergents and specialized products; see Figure 8.10) and given direct profit responsibility. The duties of individual brand managers, however, were unchanged.

Although in some ways P&G's structure is counter to the trend to shrink the organization and reduce management levels, the company cites a number of advantages.

Figure 8.10   Some P&G brands

Brand Briefing 8.6 *continued*

By fostering competition between brand managers, the traditional brand manage-ment system created strong incentives to excel. These inducements came at the cost of internal co-ordination, however, because brand managers sometimes con-tested corporate resources (ad spending, manufacturing capacity, etc.) and failed to synchronize plans. Whereas a smaller share category might have been relatively neglected before (eg, in product categories such as 'hard surface cleaners'), the new scheme was designed to ensure that all categories would receive adequate resources. Thus, category management was seen as a means to provide better management of brand portfolios to increase the similarity, where appropriate, as well as the differences between brands in categories. As academic validation, Zenor provides a game theoretic analysis and empirical demonstration of the profit ad-vantages of co-ordinating prices and other marketing activities for a firm's different products and brands through category management.

Another often-cited rationale for placing more emphasis on category management is the increasing power of the trade. Because the retail trade has tended to think in terms of product categories and the profitability derived from sections of their shops, P&G felt it only made sense for it to deal with the trade along similar lines. Retailers such as Wal-Mart and regional supermarket chains such as Dominick's have embraced category management themselves as a means of defining a partic-ular product category's strategic role (eg, in terms of its ability to generate con-sumer traffic or help provide a particular image) and to address such operating issues as logistics, the role of private label products and the tradeoffs between offering product variety and avoiding inefficient duplication.

Sources: Zachary Schiller, 'The marketing revolution at Procter & Gamble', *BusinessWeek*, 25 July 1988: 72–6; Laurie Freeman, 'P&G widens power base: adds category managers', *Advertising Age*; John Byrne, 'The horizontal corporation', *BusinessWeek*, 20 December 1993: 76–81; Michael J. Zenor, 'The profit bene-fits of category management', *Journal of Marketing Research*, May 1994, 31: 202–13; Gerry Khermouch, 'Brands overboard', *Brandweek*, 22 August 1994: 25–39.

In considering the future of brand management, Hulbert, Berthon and Pitt make several observations and forecasts.[35]

- It is incumbent upon the whole organization to focus on the customer and brands will be seen as a means to that end.
- Marketing must become far more active in the initiation and driving of innovation.
- Information technology's role as a vehicle of analysis will increasingly be supple-mented by its ability to enable and maintain large-scale customer and consumer interaction and conversation.
- To be effective, the onus for ownership and management of change in brands and the brand management system will increasingly shift to senior management.

Many firms are thus attempting to redesign their marketing organizations to better reflect the challenges faced by brands. At the same time, because of changing job requirements and duties, the marketing department is disappearing from companies that are exploring other ways to conduct their marketing functions through business groups, multidisciplinary teams and so on.[36] The goal of these new schemes is to improve internal co-ordination and efficiencies as well as external focus with respect to retailers and consumers. Although these are laudable goals, clearly one of the challenges is to ensure that the equity of brands is preserved and nurtured and not neglected due to a lack of supervision. Brand Briefing 8.7 describes General Motors' struggles with the equity of its brands.

Brand Briefing 8.7

General Motors' branding challenges

General Motors' US market share dropped from 46 percent to 32 percent between 1980 and 1996. To combat this erosion, GM adopted a brand management approach, called Brandscape, whereby each of 65 car models received separate and distinct branding efforts under the direction of a different brand manager. In this system, the brand manager was responsible for vehicle style and personality, advertising, pricing, promotion and other marketing decisions. The approach enabled each model to target a specific consumer segment. For example, the Buick LeSabre was designed for 'people seeking security, comfort, safety and peace of mind'. GM indicated that the shift to brand management would enable the company to 'chase the needs of the customer' rather than 'chase the competition'.

The approach also involved establishing identities for each of GM's six car divisions: Buick, Cadillac, Chevrolet, Oldsmobile, Pontiac-GMC and Saturn. Under the old corporate structure, divisions often competed for the same customers. As a result, the distinction between divisions grew less obvious, particularly in the case of Buick, Oldsmobile and Pontiac. Brand management aimed to sharpen the contrast between divisions and reduce sales cannibalization. Between 2000 and 2006, GM planned to release a new or 'refreshed' product every 28 days, on average. The result, claimed the company, would be greater differentiation between brands.

Some criticized GM for adopting the brand management model, which was developed at packaged goods giant Procter & Gamble. 'You can't sell cars like a box of soap', said one industry expert. Another industry executive criticized the tagline for the Pontiac Bonneville by saying: '"Luxury with Attitude" sounds an awful lot like "Tide with Bleach."' Still, executives at GM insisted the packaged goods model worked with cars. 'There's a high degree of overlap between a packaged goods company and General Motors', said Jeffrey Cohen, brand manager at GMC Jimmy.

The switch to brand management was not uniform. The Oldsmobile line was intended as a brand management test piece. GM aimed to target younger consumers to reduce Oldsmobile's average buyer's age, which was 62 in 1996. The

Brand Briefing 8.7 *continued*

switch to brand management yielded models like the Oldsmobile Intrigue, a sleek sedan introduced in 1997 and backed by a €34.2 million campaign. GM significantly downplayed the Oldsmobile name on the Intrigue by only putting it on the dashboard. As a result, claimed a car industry analyst, despite the fact that 'the Intrigue is one of the best cars on the road . . . no one knows where to buy it.' Unable to attract younger buyers and drifting away from its older customer base, sales at Oldsmobile fell towards 300,000 vehicles a year, down from a million in the 1980s, and eventually the line was discontinued.

In the case of some other GM models, brand management seemed to lack enforcement. One writer cited the Cadillac Escalade as an example of 'brand management without backbone'. In 1998, Cadillac introduced the Escalade, a ritzier version of the GMC Yukon Denali. Up to that point, however, GMC had been GM's luxury truck division and Cadillac had never made a truck. Robert Zarrella, GM's North American president and champion of the brand management approach until he was relieved of his position in 2001, admitted that the Escalade introduction was not representative of brand management, but rather about 'doing something fast and making a lot of money'.

The results of the approach were not promising: market share fell to 29.5 percent in 2000. One marketing executive summarized the results of the approach by stating the company 'made almost no progress . . . in terms of changing the perception of GM brands'. Following Zarella's departure, GM began to move away from the brand management concept of separate and distinct models. In 2001, both Cadillac and Chevrolet developed advertising campaigns that focused on their umbrella brands. Additionally, GM allocated a greater percentage of its €1.9 billion annual advertising budget for overall brand marketing. 'The lesson is that divisional positioning has to be king', said John G. Middlebrook, GM's general manager for brand marketing and corporate advertising. This means that individual models and advertising will reinforce each division's positioning, such as 'American value' for Chevrolet and 'Art and science' for Cadillac.

Sources: Jeff Green, 'The carmakers "soap" sell, so far', *Brandweek*, 24 January 2000; John McElroy, 'GM's brand management might work', *Automotive Industries*, 1 September 1996; Charles Child, 'GM brand management talk is cheap', *Automotive News*, 8 March 1999; David Welch, 'Consumers to GM: you talking to me?', *BusinessWeek*, 19 June 2000; Lawrence Ulrich, 'With his departure, General Motors' chief leaves behind brand-management style', *Detroit Free Press*, 14 November 2001.

With a multiple-product, multiple-market organization, the difficulty often lies in making sure that both place and product are in balance. As one commentator noted:

As companies grow more global, they keep running into the same dilemma. . . . Is it better to be organized by product line or geography? NCR Corp., Ford Motor Co., Procter & Gamble and several others have spent fortunes transforming themselves from one to the other. But taken too far, either model can spark fresh headaches. In the product model, businesses can reap efficiencies by standardizing manufacturing, introducing products around the world faster, co-ordinating prices better and eliminating overlapping plants. Yet, companies typically find that tilting too far away from a geographic model slows their decision-making, reduces their pricing flexibility and can impair their ability to tailor products to the needs of specific customers.[37]

Like much in marketing and branding, achieving a balance is the goal to maximize the advantages and minimize the disadvantages of either approach.

Managing marketing partners

Because a brand depends on actions taken by suppliers and marketing partners, these relationships must be managed carefully. Increasingly, firms have been consolidating their marketing partnerships and reducing the number of their suppliers. This trend has been especially apparent with global advertising accounts, where some companies have placed most, if not all, of their business with one agency (eg, Colgate-Palmolive with Young & Rubicam; and American Express and IBM with Ogilvy & Mather). A number of factors affect the decision as to how many outside suppliers to hire in any one area – for example, cost efficiencies, organizational strength and creative diversification. From a branding perspective, one advantage of dealing with a single supplier such as an ad agency is greater consistency in the treatment of a brand.

Other marketing partners can also play an important role. For example, Chapter 5 described the importance of channel members and retailers in enhancing brand equity and the need for cleverly designed push campaigns.

CHAPTER REVIEW

The brand value chain is a means to tracing the value-creation process to help understand the financial impact of marketing expenditures. Taking the customer's perspective, the brand value chain assumes that the brand value-creation process begins when the firm invests in a marketing campaign aimed at actual or potential customers. Any marketing campaign investment that potentially can be attributed to brand value development falls into this category – for example, product research, development and design; trade or intermediary support; and marketing communications.

The marketing activity associated with the campaign then affects the customer mindset with respect to the brand – what customers know and feel. The customer mindset includes everything that exists in the minds of customers with respect to a brand: thoughts, feelings, experiences, images, perceptions, beliefs and attitudes. Consistent with the customer-based brand equity model, five important measures of the customer mindset are awareness, associations, attitudes, attachment and activity or experience.

The customer mindset affects how customers react or respond in a variety of ways. Six outcomes of that response are price premiums, price elasticities, market share, brand expansion, cost structure and brand profitability. Based on information about a brand, as well as many other considerations, the financial marketplace then formulates opinions and makes various assessments that affect the value of a brand. Three important indicators are the stock price, the price/earnings multiple and market capitalization for the firm.

The model also assumes that linking factors intervene between these stages. These determine the extent to which value created at one stage transfers or 'multiplies' to the next stage. Thus, there are three sets of multipliers that moderate the transfer between the marketing campaign and the subsequent three value stages: the campaign multiplier, the customer multiplier and the market multiplier.

Brand Briefing 8.8 describes' considerations that come into play when conducting positioning analysis and deciding on the desired brand image.[38] As outlined there, a brand audit is a consumer-focused exercise that involves procedures to assess the

Brand Briefing 8.8

Rolex

Brand inventory

The name of Rolex is synonymous with quality. Rolex – with its rigorous series of tests that intervene at every stage – has redefined the meaning of quality.

Rolex began when German-born Hans Wilsdorf and his brother-in-law, William Davis, founded the London-based company Wilsdorf & Davis in 1905. Wilsdorf registered the brand Rolex in 1908 and by 1910 created a timepiece that was small enough to be worn on the wrist. Rolex obtained the first official chronometer certification for a wristwatch that same year.

In 1914, a Rolex wristwatch obtained the first Kew 'A' certificate after passing the world's toughest timing test. Twelve years later, Wilsdorf developed and patented the Oyster waterproof case and screw crown. This mechanism revolutionized the watch industry as the first true protection against water, dust and dirt.

The Oyster was put to the test on 7 October 1927 when Mercedes Gleitze swam the English Channel wearing an Oyster. She emerged from her 15-hour swim with the watch functioning perfectly, much to the amazement of all. This event marked the first of a long list of 'ambassadors' Rolex uses to promote its wristwatches.

In 1931, Rolex took watches one step further by creating the Perpetual self-winding rotor mechanism. This rotor keeps the watch at an optimal tension and activates with the slightest movement of the wrist, therefore eliminating the need to wind the watch.

Rolex is a privately owned company and has been controlled by only three men in its 100-year history. André Heiniger, managing chairman of Rolex through the 1980s, stated: 'Rolex's strategy is orientated to marketing, maintaining quality, and staying out of fields where we are not prepared to compete effectively.'

Brand Briefing 8.8 *continued*

Product-related attributes

Throughout the years, Rolex timepieces have maintained the highest quality, durability and prestige on which they were founded. Each Rolex has ten unique features:

1. waterproof;
2. perpetual rotor;
3. the case back;
4. the Oyster case;
5. the winding crown;
6. the finest and purest materials;
7. quality control;
8. Rolex self-winding movement;
9. testing from the independent Controle Official Suisse des Chronometres;
10. Rolex testing.

Brand portfolio

Rolex includes three family brands of wristwatches, each with a subset of brands that define the collection (see Figure 8.11).

● The Oyster Perpetual Collection includes the 'traditional' Rolex wristwatch and has eight sub-brands that are differentiated by features and design. The Perpetual Collection targets affluent men and women.

Oyster Perpetual
- Air-King
- Perpetual
- Date
- Datejust
- Datejust Turn-O-Graph
- Day-Date
- Lady Datejust
- Lady Datejust Pearlmaster

Oyster Professional
- Explorer
- GMT-Master II
- Submariner

- Submariner Date
- Sea-Dweller 4000
- Yacht-Master
- Cosmograph Daytona

Cellini
- Cellinium
- Quartz
- Cellissima
- Classic
- Danaos
- Cestello
- Orchid
- 2005 Prince

Figure 8.11   Rolex product portfolio

Brand Briefing 8.8 *continued*

- The Oyster Professional Collection targets specific athletic and adventurer user groups through its specific features and imagery. The collection includes seven sub-brands.
- The Cellini Collection focuses on formal occasions through its elegant designs and encompasses seven sub-brands. The Cellini collection incorporates fashion and style features such as coloured leather bands and extensive use of diamonds.

In 2005, Rolex introduced the Rolex Prince, a wristwatch that was inspired by designs of the 1920s.

Brand equity drivers: communications, pricing and distribution

Rolex's brand image has been maintained through communications focused on the product's high quality, exclusive imagery, premium prices and limited distribution.

From the beginning, Rolex has displayed its high-quality products through magazine ads. In 2003, Rolex spent €22.1 million on magazine advertisements. In addition to product imagery, Rolex maintains its status imagery by aligning itself with ambassadors, sporting and cultural events and philanthropic activities.

Rolex also distinguishes itself through its pricing strategy. Prices start at about €1,710 for the basic Oyster Perpetual and can reach €136,819. Within each style, prices can vary by €1,368 – €8,209 depending on the specific materials used (eg, steel or white gold).

Rolex only sells through official dealers, of which there are about 60,000 worldwide.

Rolex has several competitors in the €29.8 billion watch and jewellery industry. However, only a few brands compete in the very high-end market.

Omega pioneered 'official sports timekeeping' with its sponsorship of the 1932 Olympic Games and has continued that marketing strategy. Consumers think of Omega as the sports watch leader and, as a result, it competes strongly with Rolex's Oyster Professional collection. Omega has worked hard to turn Rolex's points of difference into points of parity.

The Swiss watch industry made a comeback in the 1980s, aiming at younger consumers and focusing on style with the Swatch brand. A huge success, the Swiss watch industry 'demonstrated the need to communicate and evolve with the times'.

Rolex developed the Tudor Watch to protect itself from lower-end watches such as Tag Heuer, Piaget and Rado.

Brand exploratory

Customer knowledge

Rolex has used its history and tradition of excellence along with innovation to become the most powerful and recognized watchmaker. Typical consumer brand

Brand Briefing 8.8 *continued*

associations for Rolex might be 'sophisticated', 'prestigious', 'exclusive', 'powerful', 'elegant', 'snobby', 'flashy' and 'high quality'. Figure 8.12 displays a hypothetical Rolex mental map.

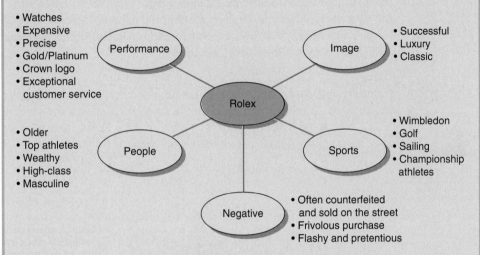

- Watches
- Expensive
- Precise
- Gold/Platinum
- Crown logo
- Exceptional customer service

Performance

Image

- Successful
- Luxury
- Classic

Rolex

- Older
- Top athletes
- Wealthy
- High-class
- Masculine

People

Sports

- Wimbledon
- Golf
- Sailing
- Championship athletes

Negative

- Often counterfeited and sold on the street
- Frivolous purchase
- Flashy and pretentious

Rolex brand mantra: Classic designs, timeless status

Figure 8.12   Rolex mental map

Sources of brand equity

Three sources of Rolex brand equity are:

- *Ambassadors:* 'In 1927, a young woman named Mercedes Gleitze swam through the icy waters of the English Channel. On her wrist was the Rolex Oyster. It marked the beginning of a long tradition: the linking of Rolex watches with exceptional individuals. . . . Rolex ambassadors have always been men and women who share Rolex's pioneering spirit: the constant pursuit of perfection.' Ambassadors fall into four categories: artists, athletes, explorers and yachtsmen. Rolex ambassadors have scaled Everest, broken the speed of sound, reached the depths of the ocean and walked on the moon.

- *Sports and culture:* Rolex sponsors elite athletic and cultural events, thus targeting very specific consumers. Some of these events include Wimbledon, Rolex Trans-Atlantic Challenge, US PGA, US Open Championship, Ryder Cup, Rolex 24 Daytona and Grand American Rolex Sports Car Series.

- *Philanthropy:* Rolex has established two philanthropic endowments.

  1. The 'Awards for Enterprise' are awarded every two years and recognize innovative work in preserving the world's natural and cultural heritage.

Brand Briefing 8.8 *continued*

2. The 'Rolex Mentor and Protégé Arts Initiative' seeks out gifted young artists and pairs them with established masters.

The customer-based brand equity pyramid (CBBE)

The customer-based brand equity pyramid for Rolex is equally strong on the left and right sides. Rolex has focused on both the superior product attributes and the imagery associated with owning and wearing a Rolex. Figure 8.13 highlights the main aspects of the Rolex CBBE pyramid.

Piracy

Counterfeiting Rolex watches has become a sophisticated industry with sales exceeding €1.2 billion a year. Counterfeit Rolexes damage the company's brand equity and present a huge risk to Rolex. In fact, Rolex dedicates extensive resources to fighting illegal use of the brand, including sponsoring the International

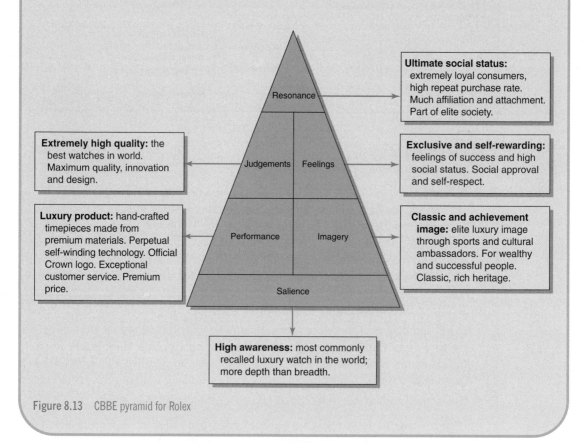

Ultimate social status: extremely loyal consumers, high repeat purchase rate. Much affiliation and attachment. Part of elite society.

Extremely high quality: the best watches in world. Maximum quality, innovation and design.

Exclusive and self-rewarding: feelings of success and high social status. Social approval and self-respect.

Luxury product: hand-crafted timepieces made from premium materials. Perpetual self-winding technology. Official Crown logo. Exceptional customer service. Premium price.

Classic and achievement image: elite luxury image through sports and cultural ambassadors. For wealthy and successful people. Classic, rich heritage.

Resonance

Judgements | Feelings

Performance | Imagery

Salience

High awareness: most commonly recalled luxury watch in the world; more depth than breadth.

Figure 8.13   CBBE pyramid for Rolex

Brand Briefing 8.8 *continued*

AntiCounterfeiting Coalition and suing companies that allow the sale of counterfeit watches.

Recommendations
The Rolex brand audit reveals a very strong brand with much equity. However, there are five areas of opportunity for Rolex.

Target women better
Women make up the majority of jewellery and watch purchases, yet Rolex's imagery campaign generally targets males and male sporting events. Rolex needs to make sure it is spending money on the right ambassadors. Rolex may want to consider more female ambassadors of elite status. Nielsen Media Research figures from 2003 show women were 35 percent of the total audience for US car racing, two percentage points more female viewers than for American football and basketball.

Along the same lines, Rolex should sponsor more female-attended sporting events. Whether ice-skating or golf, Rolex needs to get on board with the female athlete.

Introduce new designs
Research shows there is a trend towards watches with more jewels, yet the Cellini Cellisima and Orchid are the only Rolex brands that include diamonds. Rolex needs to make sure it remains a leader in style as well as functionality.

Attack the online counterfeit industry
Create an official Rolex online distribution site with which all official retailers have to link.

Understand prestige in today's world
How will prestige be defined in the twenty-first century? Will the same formula 'work' for the millennial generation as they age and move into the Rolex target market?

Justify price in terms of value
Rolex will always be high priced – how do customers justify paying more in terms of the intrinsic and extrinsic value they receive?

Sources: www.brittons-watches.co.uk; www.rolex.com; *Adweek*, 28 October 2004; *Women's Wear Daily*, July 2005; 'The advertising saga of the watch industry', *Antiquorum*, June 2002; *Watch World*, December 2004; *USA Today*, 7 February 2004;

health of the brand, uncover its sources of equity and suggest ways to improve its equity. A brand audit requires an understanding of sources of brand equity from the perspective of both the firm and the consumer. From the perspective of the firm, it is necessary to understand exactly what products and services are being offered to consumers and how they are being marketed and branded. With the consumers, it is necessary to tap their perceptions and beliefs to uncover the true meaning of brands and products.

The brand audit consists of two steps: the inventory and exploratory. The brand inventory provides a complete profile of how all the products and services sold by a company are marketed and branded. Profiling each product or service requires that the associated brand elements be identified as well as the supporting marketing campaign. The brand exploratory is a research activity directed at understanding what consumers think and feel about the brand to identify sources of brand equity.

A brand equity measurement system uses research procedures to provide timely, accurate and actionable information for marketers so they can make tactical decisions as well as long-term strategic decisions. Implementing a brand equity measurement system involves two steps: designing tracking studies and establishing an equity management system.

Brand audits help set the strategic direction for a brand. As a result of this strategic analysis, a marketing campaign can be put in place to maximize long-term brand equity. Tracking studies employing quantitative measures can then provide marketers with information as to how their brands are performing based on dimensions identified by the brand audit. Tracking studies involve information routinely collected from consumers over time and provide valuable tactical insights into the short-term effectiveness of marketing activities. Whereas brand audits measure 'where the brand has been', tracking studies measure 'where the brand is now' and whether marketing campaigns are having an effects.

Three steps must occur as part of a brand equity management system. First, the company view of brand equity should be formalized into a document, the brand equity charter. This document serves a number of purposes: it chronicles the company's philosophy with respect to brand equity; summarizes the activity and outcomes related to brand audits, brand tracking and so forth; outlines guidelines for brand strategies and tactics; and documents proper treatment of the brand. The charter should be updated annually. Second, the results of the tracking surveys and other relevant outcome measures should be assembled into a regular brand equity report for management. The report should describe *what* is happening to a brand as well as diagnostic information as to *why* it is happening. Finally, senior management must be assigned to oversee how brand equity is treated within the organization. The people in that position would be responsible for overseeing the implementation of the brand equity charter and brand equity reports to make sure that product and marketing actions across divisions and geographic boundaries are performed in a way that reflects the spirit of the charter and the substance of the report so as to maximize the long-term equity of the brand.

An alternative – albeit complementary – view of how firms should incorporate the brand equity concept into their marketing research and planning is described in Brand Briefing 8.9, which examines how ad agency Ogilvy & Mather, incorporates branding issues into its services to clients.

Brand Briefing 8.9

Managing brands at Ogilvy & Mather

Ogilvy & Mather (O&M) is one of the world's largest advertising agencies. O&M manages its clients' brands using a five-step process called *360-degree brand stewardship*. Figure 8.14 shows the principles that O&M uses to guide this process.

- We believe in brands.
- We believe companies make products but consumers own brands.
- We believe the first step in building strong brands is defining the brand/consumer relationship and articulating it in simple language.
- We believe consumers build brands the way birds build nests, from scraps and straws they chance upon.
- We believe our job is to help clients build enduring brands that become part of consumers' lives and inspire their loyalty and win their confidence.
- We believe the way to build enduring brands is to build enduring brand ideas.
- We believe brands have many constituencies who help shape the brand.
- We believe that the best way to grow a brand is by communicating effectively to all audiences at all points of contact.
- We believe in the ultimate supremacy of the brand experience.
- We believe all consumers are not created equal.
- We believe all clients are not created equal.
- We believe 360-degree brand stewardship means: creating attention-getting messages that make a promise that is consistent with and true to the brand's image and identity. And guiding actions, both big and small, that deliver on that brand promise. To every audience that brand has. At every point of contact. At all times.
- We believe that 360-degree brand stewardship ultimately leads to brand loyalty and brand profitability.
- We generate ideas and create work that sells.
- We do more than advertising.
- We value and grow specialists and organise ourselves in brand teams.
- We seek excellence in all that we do.
- We act in a media-neutral way.

Figure 8.14   360-degree brand stewardship principles

Ogilvy has a three-step process for its brand stewardship.

Phase 1: Discovery

This covers things to find out about a brand, its users and its competitive environment.

What is the essence of the brand?

Ogilvy first attempts to get to the 'DNA' of the brand using brand audits to assess what consumers think and feel. During this process, the goal is to have consumers

Brand Briefing 8.9 *continued*

tell stories and share personal histories. Ogilvy emphasizes brand-probing questions like: 'How does using the brand make you feel about yourself?'; 'What's the first thing that comes to mind when you think of this brand?'; 'What unique contribution does the brand make to your life?'; 'What personal recollections does the brand bring to mind?'

The rich personal accounts that emerge help the agency put into words the actual experience of a brand in the life of a user – what O&M calls the BrandPrint – which is the starting point for all brand-building activities. The brand essence becomes the standard against which to judge every piece of communication and behaviour.

What is the brand voice and personality?

With the BrandPrint in hand, Ogilvy can make sure the brand speaks and acts consistently – how the brand both 'talks and walks' in all communications.

What is the product behind the brand and who's buying it?

O&M also intimately learns about the product or service itself by asking questions such as: 'What does the brand do? What does it look like? What are its other physical characteristics? What are its ingredients or component parts? What is its history? Is the brand sensitive to price?' Ogilvy also collects information on consumers themselves. Who's using the product? What do they watch on TV? What do they read? What do they do for a living? What separates heavy users from light ones? Who are our loyalists and why? Are there distinct communities of users united by specific affinities other than usage?

What is the company behind the brand?

O&M also strives to fully know the company behind the brand (history, values, milestones, corporate infrastructure) by interviewing executives and employees and studying the company closely.

What is the environment in which the brand operates?

O&M recognizes that it must fully understand the market and all its different dimensions in which a brand competes.

What is the brand vision?

O&M believes great brands have a road map for the future, a galvanizing principle or course of action that everyone can get behind for the brand's growth and prosperity. For example, it maintains that IBM's vision of the technological future – e-business – has provided clear direction and inspiration for all who work for the brand.

Phase 2: strategy and planning

What challenges and opportunities face the brand?

With discovery complete, O&M assesses what the brand needs to do next, to reflect the fact that each brand is in a different situation. Where a brand stands in its

Brand Briefing 8.9 *continued*

lifecycle – the type of challenges and opportunities facing it – determines what type of creative is done, what audiences are spoken to, which media vehicles are chosen.

Who are the brand's audiences and what is their understanding of the brand?
Since a brand has many audiences or constituents that shape its image, O&M studies them and how well they understand the brand. Internal audiences, for example, need to know clearly what the brand is about if they are to deliver products and services that enhance the brand, rather than detract from it. Industry analysts and trade reporters need to know where the brand is and where it is going if they are to write about it accurately. And dealers and distributors need to treat customers in a way that is true to the brand so the sale and post-sale experiences deliver on the brand's promise. Audience assessment is often essential to the recommendations Ogilvy makes to its clients as they often find an unexpected weak spot that requires special approaches and/or funding to correct.

Where does the brand touch consumers?
At this point, the job at hand for O&M is to uncover all consumer touch points and evaluate how much effect each has in moulding images and perceptions of the brand – the who, what, when, where and how of the brand experience.

Which touchpoints are 'moments of truth'?
O&M believes some consumer touch points with the brand are more powerful than others and provide make-or-break moments for the brand or 'moments of truth'. These moments vary by brand, category and geography. Ogilvy's conviction is that, at these moments of truth, consistency of brand promise and brand behaviour are essential and energies must be focused to make sure that they delight, not disappoint, consumers.

Phase 3: Execution
How do we get it done?
Turning insight and strategy into work is where the 'rubber meets the road' for Ogilvy. Although it feels there is no blueprint for creativity, the company does use questions that drive the process and need to be answered.

What is the idea?
Unless 360-degree branding efforts are based on a 'big idea', O&M claims that they will 'pass like a ship in the night'. Besides getting to the core of the consumer/ brand relationship, it feels there is nothing more important than coming up with the big brand idea that both anchors and drives brand-building campaigns. Ogilvy notes that it's difficult to predict where the big idea will come from. Any member of the brand team – creative, account, planning or media – can spark the thought that drives a campaign.

Brand Briefing 8.9 *continued*

How does the idea inform creative efforts?
Once Ogilvy arrives at a big idea, everyone shares it. All communications (whether it's a commercial, a website, a postcard or a telemarketing script) must be created to reflect and reinforce that idea, although this does not mean all communications must look alike. Ogilvy attempts to use each communication discipline to its best advantage and always strives to remember that 360-degree communications are linked by the brand essence, brand voice, the idea and how they work together to affect attitudes and behaviours.

Where is this idea going to play out?
In an ideal world, the brand idea would play out at relevant brand intersection points, particularly at and around moments of truth (focusing on whom to talk to, in what manner and what vehicle is most relevant to their needs and most likely to get their attention and drive action). In reality, Ogilvy recognizes that it's a matter of budget, objectives and timing. Sometimes it uses all the communication and experiential vehicles at its disposal to help a brand; other times, it uses a few or just one.

How is success measured?
Success in the long term is measured by the growth and vitality of the brand. In the short term, however, there are many markers of success for O&M, depending upon the objectives of the effort. Sometimes it's market share. At other times, awareness, attitude levels and depth of brand bonding or response rates, click-through rates, pages viewed and stickiness. ROI. Lifetime value. Ultimately, Ogilvy knows it is accountable and that it is imperative that it is judged by the appropriate measures for the appropriate work

Source: Ogilvy & Mather, internal documents.

Discussion questions

1. Pick a brand. Try to do an informal brand value chain analysis. Can you trace how the brand value is created and transferred? What are the roles of the multipliers?
2. Update and supplement the brand value chain analysis for Starbucks in this chapter. What does the analysis suggest about the brand's fortunes in recent years?
3. A few years ago, Disney entered into a long-term agreement with McDonald's that included, among other things, joint promotions. From Disney's perspective and what you know about the two brands, was this the right decision? Is there any downside? Would you have wanted to conduct any research to inform the decision? What kind?

4. Consider the McDonald's tracking survey presented in Brand Briefing 8.2. What might you do differently? What questions would you change or drop? What questions might you add? How might this tracking survey differ from those used for other products?

References and notes

[1] Frederick E. Webster, Jr, Alan J. Malter and Shankar Ganesan, 'Can marketing regain its seat at the table?', *Marketing Science Institute Report No. 03-113*, Cambridge, MA, 2003. See also, Frederick E. Webster Jr, Alan J. Malter and Shankar Ganesan, 'The decline and dispersion of marketing competence', *MIT Sloan Management Review*, Summer 2005, 46 (4): 35–43.

[2] See Don E. Schultz and Heidi F. Schultz, 'Measuring brand value', in *Kellogg on Branding*, eds Alice M. Tybout and Timothy Calkins, Hoboken, NJ: John Wiley & Sons, 2005.

[3] William A. Cook and Vijay S. Talluri, 'How the pursuit of ROMI is changing marketing management', *Journal of Advertising Research*, January 2004, 44 (3): 244–54.

[4] Patrick LaPointe, *Marketing by the Dashboard Light: How to get more insight, foresight and accountability from your marketing investment*, New York: Association of National Advertisers, 2005.

[5] Jonathan Knowles, 'In search of a reliable measure of brand equity', *MarketingNPV*, July 2005, 2 (3).

[6] Kevin Lane Keller and Don Lehmann, 'How do brands create value', *Marketing Management*, May/June, 2003: 26–31. See also R. K. Srivastava, T. A. Shervani and L. Fahey, 'Market-based assets and shareholder value', *Journal of Marketing*, 1998, 62 (1): 2–18; and M. J. Epstein and R. A. Westbrook, 'Linking actions to profits in strategic decision making', *MIT Sloan Management Review*, Spring 2001: 39–49. In terms of related empirical insights, see Manoj K. Agrawal and Vithala Rao, 'An empirical comparison of consumer-based measures of brand equity', *Marketing Letters*, 1996, 7 (3): 237–47; and Walfried Lassar, Banwari Mittal and Arun Sharma, 'Measuring customer-based brand equity', *Journal of Consumer Marketing*, 1995, 12 (4): 11–19.

[7] Thomas J. Madden, Frank Fehle and Susan Fournier, 'Brands matter: an empirical demonstration of the creation of shareholder value through branding', *Journal of the Academy of Marketing Science*, 2006.

[8] Adrienne W. Fawcett, 'The marketing 100: Starbucks: Scott Bedbury', *Advertising Age*, 30 June 1997: S18.

[9] Louise Kramer, 'Brand man Bedbury departing Starbucks', *Advertising Age*, 18 May 1998: 1.

[10] Alice Z. Cuneo, 'Starbucks' word-of-mouth wonder', *Advertising Age*, 7 March 1994.

[11] Kim Murphy, 'More than coffee: a way of life', *Los Angeles Times Magazine*, 22 September 1996: 8.

[12] Seana Browder, 'Starbucks does not live by coffee alone', *BusinessWeek*, 5 August 1996: 76.

[13] Sidney Davidson, James Schindler, Clyde P. Stickney and Roman Weil, *Financial Accounting: An introduction to concepts, methods and uses*, Hinsdale, IL: Dryden Press, 1976.

[14] Phillip Kotler, William Gregor and William Rogers, 'The marketing audit comes of age', *Sloan Management Review*, winter 1977, 18 (2): 25–43.

[15] Laurel Wentz, 'Brand audits reshaping images', *Ad Age International*, September 1996: 38–41.

[16] Burleigh B. Gardner and Sidney J. Levy, 'The product and the brand', *Harvard Business Review*, March–April 1955: 33–9.

[17]Sidney J. Levy, 'Dreams, fairy tales, animals and cars', *Psychology and Marketing,* summer 1985, 2 (2): 67–81.

[18]Patrick LaPointe, *Marketing by the Dashboard Light.*

[19]John B. Frey, 'Measuring corporate reputation and its value', paper presented at the Marketing Science Conference at Duke University, 17 March 1989.

[20]Personal correspondence, Nigel Hollis.

[21]Alastair Gordon, 'Managing by metrics: practical issues and guidelines', talk at MSI Asian Marketing Conference, Singapore, July 2005.

[22]Na Woon Bong, Roger Marshall and Kevin Lane Keller, 'Measuring brand power: validating a model for optimizing brand equity', *Journal of Product and Brand Management,* 1999, 8 (3): 170–84.

[23]Joel Rubinson and Markus Pfeiffer, 'Brand performance indicators as a force for brand equity management', *Journal of Advertising Research,* June 2005: 187–97.

[24]Joel Rubinson, 'Brand strength means more than market share', paper presented at the ARF Fourth Annual Advertising and Promotion Workshop, New York, 1992.

[25]Tim Ambler, *Marketing and the Bottom Line,* 2nd edn, New York: Financial Times Prentice Hall, 2004.

[26]Rob Malcolm, 'Getting the right measure for drinks', paper presented at Marketing Science Institute Conference, *Does Marketing Measure Up? Performance metrics: practices and impacts,* London, 21–22 June 2004.

[27]Gail McGovern and John Quelch, 'Sarbox still putting the squeeze on marketing', *Advertising Age,* 19 September, 2005: 28.

[28]Tim Ambler and Bruce Clark, 'What will matter most to marketers three years from now?', paper presented at Marketing Science Institute Conference, *Does marketing measure up? performance metrics: practices and impacts,* London, 21–22 June 2004. See also Bruce H. Clark and Tim Ambler, 'Marketing performance measurement: evolution of research and practice', *International Journal of Business Performance Management,* 2001, 3, 2/3/4: 231–44, and Bruce H. Clark, Andrew Abela and Tim Ambler, 'Organizational motivation, opportunity and ability to measure marketing performance', *Journal of Strategic Marketing,* December 13 (4): 241–59.

[29]Scott Bedbury, *A New Brand World,* New York: Viking Press, 2002.

[30]Betsy Spethman, 'Companies post equity gatekeepers', *Brandweek,* 2 May 1994: 5.

[31]Bedbury, *A New Brand World.*

[32]Adapted from, Tim Ambler, *Marketing and the Bottom Line,* 2nd edn, New York: Financial Times, Prentice Hall, 2003.

[33]'Stock tips: the growing trend of category management', *Daily News,* 22 January 2003.

[34]www.cannondaleassoc.com

[35]J. M. Hulbert, P. Berthon and L. F. Pitt, 'Brand management prognostications', *Sloan Management Review,* winter 1998: 53–65.

[36]'The death of the brand manager', *The Economist,* 9 April 1994: 67–8.

[37]Joann S. Lubin, 'Place versus product: it's tough to choose a management model', *Wall Street Journal.*

[38]Philip Kotler and Kevin Lane Keller, *Marketing Management,* 12th edn, Upper Saddle River, NJ: Prentice Hall, 2006.

9 Measuring sources of brand equity: capturing the customer mindset

PREVIEW

Understanding the current and desired brand knowledge structures of consumers is vital to building and managing brand equity. As Gardner and Levy note in a classic marketing article:

> The image of a product associated with the brand may be clear-cut or relatively vague; it may be varied or simple; it may be intense or innocuous. Sometimes the notions people have about a brand do not seem very sensible or relevant to those who know what the product is 'really' like. But they all contribute to the customer's deciding whether or not the brand is 'for me'. These sets of ideas, feelings, and attitudes that consumers have about brands are crucial to them in picking and sticking to ones that seem most appropriate.[1]

Ideally, marketers would be able to construct detailed 'mental maps' of consumers to understand all their thoughts, feelings, perceptions, images, beliefs and attitudes towards a brand. These mental blueprints would then provide managers with strategic and tactical guidance to help them make brand decisions. Unfortunately, these knowledge structures are not easily measured because they reside only in consumers' minds.

Nevertheless, brand management requires a thorough understanding of the consumer. Often a simple insight into how consumers think of or use products and the particular brands in a category can result in profitable changes in the marketing campaign. As a result, many companies conduct exhaustive research studies (or brand audits, as described in Chapter 3) to learn as much as possible about consumers. Consequently, a number of detailed, sophisticated research techniques and methods have been developed to help marketers. Brand Briefing 9.1 describes the lengths to which marketers have gone in the past to learn about consumers. Much has been written on the topic of consumer behaviour. This chapter highlights some of the considerations that are critical to the measurement of brand equity.[2] Figure 9.1 outlines some considerations in understanding consumer behaviour.

According to the brand value chain, sources of brand equity arise from the customer mindset. In general, measuring sources of brand equity requires that the brand manager

Brand Briefing 9.1

Digging beneath the surface to understand consumer behaviour

Most consumer research relies on surveys to obtain consumers' reported beliefs, attitudes and behaviour. However, insights sometimes emerge from unobtrusively observing consumer behaviour rather than talking to consumers. In many instances, consumer behaviour that is observed differs from the behaviour that consumers report in surveys. For example, Hoover became suspicious when people claimed in surveys that they vacuumed their houses for an hour each week. To check, the company installed timers in certain models and exchanged them for the same models in consumers' homes. The timers showed that people actually spent only a little over *half* an hour vacuuming each week. People were exaggerating the amount. One researcher analysed household rubbish to determine the types and quantities of food that people consumed, finding that people really don't have a very good idea of how much and what types of food they eat and tend to overestimate. Similarly, much research has shown that people report that they eat healthier food than would appear to be case if you opened their cupboards.

DuPont commissioned marketing studies for its Dacron Polyester unit, which supplies filling to pillow makers and sells its own Comforel brand. One challenge: people don't give up their old pillows. Thirty seven percent of one sample described their relationship with their pillow as like 'an old married couple', and an additional 13 percent characterized it as like a 'childhood friend'. They found that people fell into distinct groups in terms of 'pillow behaviour': stackers (23 percent), plumpers (20 percent), rollers or folders (16 percent), cuddlers (16 percent) and smashers, who pound their pillows into a more comfortable shape (10 percent). Women were more likely to plump while men were more likely to fold. The prevalence of stackers led the company to sell more pillows packaged as pairs, as well as to market different levels of softness or firmness.

Much of this type of research has its roots in ethnography, the term for the study of cultures in their natural surroundings. The intent behind these observational studies is for consumers to drop their guard and provide a more realistic portrayal of who they are rather than who they would like to be. On the basis of ethnographic research that uncovered consumers' true feelings, ad campaigns have been created for a Swiss chocolatemaker with the theme, 'The true confessions of a chocaholic' (because chocolatelovers often hid stashes all though the house), for Tampax Tampons with the theme, 'More women trust their bodies to Tampax' (because teen users wanted the freedom to wear body-conscious clothes) and for Crisco shortening with the theme 'Recipe for success' (because people often baked pies and cookies in a celebratory fashion).

Sources: Jennifer Chang Coupland, 'Invisible brands: an ethnography of households and the brands in their kitchen pantries', *Journal of Consumer Research*, June 2005, 32: 106–18; John Koten, 'You aren't paranoid if you feel someone eyes you constantly', *Wall Street Journal*, 2 March 1985; Susan Warren, 'Pillow talk: stackers outnumber plumpers; don't mention drool', *Wall Street Journal*, 8 January 1998: B1.

Who buys a product or service?

Who makes the decision to buy the product?

Who influences the decision to buy the product?

How is the purchase decision made? Who assumes what role?

What does the customer buy? What needs must be satisfied?

Why do customers buy a particular brand?

Where do they go or look to buy the product or service?

When do they buy? Any seasonality factors?

What are customers' attitudes towards a product?

What social factors might influence the purchase decision?

Do customers' lifestyles influence their decisions?

How is the product perceived by customers?

How do demographic factors influence the purchase decision?

Figure 9.1   Understanding consumer behaviour

Source: George Belch and Michael Belch, *Advertising and Communication Management*, 3rd edn, Homewood, IL: Irwin, 1995.

fully understands how customers shop for and use products and services and, most important, what customers know, think and feel about brands. In particular, measuring sources of customer-based brand equity requires measuring aspects of brand awareness and image that potentially can lead to a customer response that creates brand equity. To some extent, consumer reactions to a brand may be based on their 'gestalt' knowledge. In other words, consumers may have a holistic view of brands that is difficult to divide into component parts. Yet, in many cases, consumers' perceptions of a brand can be isolated and assessed in greater detail. The remainder of this chapter describes both qualitative and quantitative approaches to identifying potential sources of brand equity – ie, to capturing the customer mindset.

Mary Goodyear uses a framework called 'Continuum of Consumerism'[3]. Goodyear describes this as a process where different markets or brand owners find themselves in different phases. Her framework shows how consumers' needs and desires are placed in focus during the development of the brand, and how consumer research needs to be adjusted to five stages of brand development. In the first two stages only cognitive research is needed. In the third stage there is a change from cognitive to conative research. She argues that product categories can differ in maturity and therefore need different research methods.

QUALITATIVE RESEARCH TECHNIQUES

As Chapter 3 noted, different types of associations can become linked to a brand. Brand Briefing 9.2 describes some of the basic ideas behind and applications of the associative network model of memory, which, as Chapter 2 noted, is a useful theoretical means of representing these associations.

Brand Briefing 9.2

Understanding consumer memory

The associative network memory model views memory as a network of nodes and connecting links. According to this model, recall or retrieval of information occurs through a concept called *spreading activation*. At any time, an information node may be a source of activation because it is either presented external information (eg, when a person reads or hears a word or phrase) or retrieves internal information being processed (eg, when a person thinks about some concept). A particular node in memory is activated, and activation spreads from that node to other nodes connected to it in memory. When the activation of a particular node exceeds a threshold level, the contents of that node are recalled. The spread of activation depends on the number and strength of the links connected to the activated node: concepts connected to the activated node whose linkages have the greatest strength will receive the most activation.

As a result of spreading activation, the strength and organization of brand associations will be important determinants of the information that can be recalled about the brand to influence consumer response and brand-related decisions. Research in psychology provides insights into some factors affecting association strength. In general, the strength of an association depends on how information is initially processed as it enters consumers' memory and where it is located. Psychologists refer to these two processes as memory *encoding* and *storage*. Encoding processes can be characterized according to the amount, or *quantity*, of processing that information receives (ie, how much a person thinks about the information) and the nature, or *quality*, of the processing that information receives (ie, the manner in which a person thinks about the information). The quantity and quality of processing are determinants of the strength of an association. Research has shown that many factors affect the quantity and quality of encoding processes, the accessibility of information from memory and the ability of consumers to recall or retrieve brand associations. Some of those factors are briefly highlighted here.

Encoding brand associations

In terms of *qualitative* considerations, the more attention is placed on the meaning of information during encoding, the stronger the resulting associations in memory will be. Thus, when a consumer actively thinks about and 'elaborates' on the significance of product or service information, stronger associations are created.

Another determinant of the strength of a newly formed association is the content, organization and strength of existing brand associations in memory.

All else being equal, it will be easier for consumers to create an association to new information when extensive, relevant knowledge structures already exist in memory. One reason why personal experiences create such strong brand associations is that information about the product is likely to be related to existing knowledge because of its self-relevance.

Brand Briefing 9.2 *continued*

In addition to congruency or consistency with existing knowledge, the ease with which information can be integrated into established knowledge structures depends on the nature of that information, in terms of characteristics such as its inherent simplicity, vividness and concreteness.

In terms of *quantitative* considerations, repeated exposure to information provides greater opportunity for processing and thus the potential for stronger associations. Recent advertising research in a field setting, however, suggests that qualitative considerations and the manner or style of consumer processing engendered by an ad are generally more important than the cumulative total of ad exposures. In other words, high levels of repetition for an uninvolving, unpersuasive ad are unlikely to have as much sales impact as lower levels of repetition for an involving, persuasive ad.

Recall of brand associations

According to the associative network memory model, the strength of a brand association increases both the likelihood that that information will be accessible and the ease with which it can be recalled by spreading activation. Accessible, recalled information is important because it can create the differential response that makes up customer-based brand equity. Recall of brand information by consumers does not depend only on the initial associative strength of that information in memory, however, but also on other considerations. Three such factors are particularly important.

First, the presence of *other* product information in memory can produce interference effects and reduce the accessibility of similar brand information in memory. In particular, the presence of other information in memory may cause the target information to be either overlooked or confused with this other information.

Second, the time since exposure to information at encoding affects the strength of a new association: the longer the time delay, the weaker the association. The time elapsed since the last exposure opportunity, however, has been generally shown to only produce gradual decay. That is, cognitive psychologists believe that memory is extremely durable, so that once information becomes stored in memory, its strength of association decays very slowly.

Third, the number and type of external retrieval cues that are available will affect memory accessibility. That is, information may be 'available' in memory (ie, potentially recallable) but may not be 'accessible' from memory (ie, able to be recalled) without the proper retrieval cues or reminders. Thus, the particular associations for a brand that are salient and come to mind depend on the context in which the brand is considered. The more cues linked to a piece of information, however, the greater the likelihood that the information can be recalled.

Brand Briefing 9.2 *continued*

Sources: John R. Anderson, *The Architecture of Cognition*, Cambridge, MA: Harvard University Press, 1983. For additional discussion, see John G. Lynch Jr and Thomas K. Srull, 'Memory and attentional factors in consumer choice: concepts and research methods', *Journal of Consumer Research*, June 1982, 9: 18–36; and Joseph W. Alba, J. Wesley Hutchinson and John G. Lynch Jr, 'Memory and decision making', in *Handbook of Consumer Theory and Research*, eds. Harold H. Kassarjian and Thomas S. Robertson, Englewood Cliffs, NJ: Prentice-Hall, 1992: 1–49; Fergus I. M. Craik and Robert S. Lockhart, 'Levels of processing: a framework for memory research', *Journal of Verbal Learning and Verbal Behavior*, 1972, 11: 671–84; Fergus I. M. Craik and Endel Tulving, 'Depth of processing and the retention of words in episodic memory', *Journal of Experimental Psychology*, 1975, 104 (3): 268–94; Robert S. Lockhart, Fergus I. M. Craik and Larry Jacoby, 'Depth of processing, recognition and recall', in *Recall and Recognition*, ed. John Brown, New York: John Wiley, 1976; Magid Abraham and Leonard Lodish, *Advertising Works: A study of advertising effectiveness and the resulting strategies and tactical implications*, Chicago: Information Resources Inc., 1989; Elizabeth F. Loftus and Gregory R. Loftus, 'On the permanence of stored information in the human brain', *American Psychologist*, May 1980, 35: 409–20.

There are also many ways to uncover the types of associations linked to the brand and their corresponding strength, favourability and uniqueness. Qualitative research is often employed to identify brand associations and sources of brand equity. *Qualitative research techniques* are relatively unstructured measurement approaches whereby a range of consumer responses is permitted. Because of the freedom afforded both researchers in their probes and consumers in their responses, qualitative research can often be useful in exploring consumer brand and product perceptions.

Ernest Dichter, one of the pioneers in consumer psychoanalytic research, applied these research principles in a study for Plymouth cars in the USA in the 1930s.[4] His research revealed the important – but overlooked – role that women played in the purchase decision. Based on his analysis, a new print ad strategy was employed that highlighted a young couple gazing admiringly at a Plymouth under the headline 'Imagine us in a car like that.' His subsequent work influenced many campaigns.[5] Some of Dichter's assertions were controversial. He argued that women used Ivory soap to wash away their sins before a date. He also equated convertibles with mistresses and suggested 'Putting a tiger in the tank' for Exxon, resulting in a long-running and successful campaign.

This section next reviews qualitative techniques that can be employed to identify sources of brand equity. Brand Briefing 9.3 describes one provocative technique, and Brand Briefing 9.4 examines some practical issues in conducting focus groups.

Free association

The simplest and often most powerful way to profile brand associations involves free association tasks whereby subjects are asked what comes to mind when they think of the brand without any more specific probe or cue than perhaps the associated product category (eg, 'What does the Rolex name mean to you?' or 'Tell me what comes to mind when you think of Rolex watches.')

Brand Briefing 9.3

Using archetype research to gain consumer insights

According to medical anthropologist G. C. Rapaille, consumers often make purchase decisions based on factors that they are aware of only subconsciously. Conventional market research typically does not elicit responses that indicate these factors, so Rapaille employs the 'archetype research' technique to uncover these hidden motivations.

Rapaille believes that children experience a significant initial exposure to an element of their world called the 'imprinting moment'. The pattern that emerges when these imprinting moments are generalized for the entire population is the archetype. The archetype is a fundamental psychological association, shared by the members of the culture, with a given cultural object. For example, the US archetype for coffee is 'home', because US children traditionally woke up to their mothers cooking breakfast and making coffee. Different cultures have dramatically different archetypes for the same objects. In France, the archetype for cheese is 'alive' because age is its most important trait. By contrast, the US archetype for cheese is 'dead'; it is wrapped in plastic ('a body-bag'), put in the refrigerator ('a morgue') and pasteurized ('scientifically dead').

Rapaille uses relaxation exercises and visualization with consumers to find the imprinting moments appropriate to the product he is researching. For example, at a focus group he will dim the lights, play soothing music and coax the subjects into a meditative state. He will then elicit stories about the product from the subjects and analyse these stories to illuminate the archetype.

One of Rapaille's projects was the Chrysler PT Cruiser. He used archetype research to arrive at the conclusion that US car buyers wanted oversized and rugged vehicles to feel safe – even intimidating – in the 'jungle out there'. These same car buyers, however, wanted the car's interior to resemble 'the Ritz-Carlton'. Based on these findings, Chrysler designers altered the PT Cruiser prototype to give it more exterior bulk and a more functional and accommodating interior. Consumers likened the PT Cruiser to a 1920s gangster car and a 1950s hot rod. The €11,700 car won accolades from the car industry, winning *Motor Trend* magazine's 2001 car of the year award. Demand for the PT Cruiser was so high that consumers paid €700 to €3,000 over the selling price at some dealerships to obtain one.

Sources: Alexandra Harrington, 'G.C. Rapaille: finding the keys in the cultural unconscious', *Response TV*, 1 September 2001; Jeffrey Ball, 'But how does it make you feel?', *Wall Street Journal*, 3 May 1999; Jack Hitt, 'Does the smell of coffee brewing remind you of your mother?', *New York Times Magazine*, 7 May 2000.

Brand Briefing 9.4

Focus group guidelines

When conducting qualitative research, consumer responses may be collected either in small groups or individually, depending on the depth and nature of the task involved. *Focus groups* are a data collection tool that gathers the opinions of six to ten people who are selected based on certain demographic, psychographic or other considerations and brought together to discuss various topics of interest at length. A professional research moderator provides questions and probes based on a discussion guide or agenda prepared by the responsible marketing managers to ensure that the right material is covered. Moderators often, however, follow and lead the discussion at times to track down some potentially useful insight as they attempt to discern the real motivations of consumers and why they are saying and doing certain things. The sessions are typically recorded and marketing managers often watch from behind one-way mirrors in the room.

Focus groups, like any research technique, can be abused if not conducted carefully. The key for marketers is to *listen*. Consumer responses must be interpreted, so it is critical that biases are eliminated. On the positive side, many insights can emerge from thoughtfully run groups. On the negative side, there are questions as to their validity, especially in today's marketing environment. Some researchers believe that consumers have been so bombarded with ads that they unconsciously (or perhaps cynically) parrot what they have heard rather than say what they think. There is also always a concern that participants are just trying to maintain their self-image and public persona or have a need to identify with the other members of the group. Participants may not be willing to admit in public – or may not even recognize – their behaviour patterns and motivations. For all these reasons, participants must feel as relaxed and at ease as possible and feel a strong obligation to speak the truth.

Focus groups may create problems. Researchers at one ad agency knew they had a problem when a fight broke out at one of their sessions. As one executive noted: 'We wondered why people always seemed grumpy and negative – people were resistant to any idea we showed them.' The problem was the room itself: cramped, stifling and forbidding. 'It was a cross between a hospital room and a police interrogation.' To fix the problem, the agency employed the Chinese practice of feng shui.

There is always the 'loud mouth' problem as well – when one highly opinionated person drowns out the rest of the group. Moreover, it may be expensive to recruit qualified subjects in the USA (€2,100 to €3,600 per group) in comparison with the less expensive costs for recruiting in Europe.

Sources: Sarah Stiansen, 'How focus groups can go astray', *Adweek*, 5 December 1988: FK 4–6; Jeffrey Kasner, 'Fistfights and feng shui', *Boston Globe*, 21 July 2001: C1–C2; Leslie Kaufman, 'Enough talk', *Newsweek*, 18 August 1997: 48–9.

The answers can be used to help marketers to clarify the range of possible associations, to form a rough mental map for the brand and assemble a brand profile.[6]

The primary purpose of free association tasks is to identify the range of possible brand associations in consumers' minds, but they may also provide some rough indication of the relative strength, favourability and uniqueness of brand associations.[7] Coding free association responses in terms of the order of elicitation – early or late in the sequence – can yield at least a rough measure of strength.[8] For example, if many consumers mention 'fast and convenient' as one of their first associations when given 'McDonald's restaurants' as a probe, then it is likely that the association is relatively strong and likely to be potentially available to affect consumer decisions. Associations later in the list, on the other hand, may be weaker. Comparing associations with those elicited for competitive brands can also provide some indication of their relative uniqueness. Finally, even favourability, to some extent, may be discerned on the basis of how associations are stated and phrased.

See Figure 9.2 for an example of a mental map for the furniture retailer Ikea.

To help understand the favourability of associations, consumers can be asked follow-up questions as to the favourability of associations they listed or, more generally, what they like best about a brand. Similarly, consumers can also be asked direct follow-up questions as to the uniqueness of associations they listed or, more generally, what they find unique about the brand. Useful questions include the following.

1. What do you like best about the brand? What are its positive aspects? What do you dislike? What are its disadvantages?
2. What do you find unique about the brand? How is it different from other brands? In what ways is it the same?

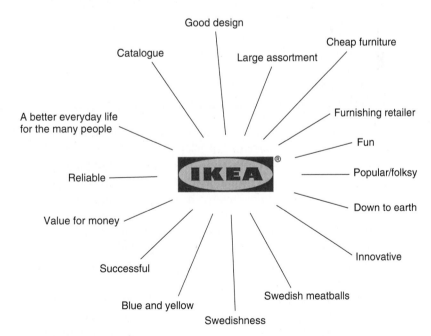

Figure 9.2   Example of a mental map

These simple, direct measures can be extremely valuable for determining core aspects of a brand image. To provide more structure and guidance, consumers can be asked follow-up questions to describe what the brand means to them in terms of 'who, what, when, where, why and how' questions such as the following.

1. Who uses the brand? What kind of person?
2. When and where do they use the brand? What types of situations?
3. Why do people use the brand? What do they get out of using it?
4. How do they use the brand? What do they use it for?

Guidelines

Two issues to consider in conducting free association tasks are how to set up the questions in terms of the types of probes and how to code and interpret the resulting data. With regard to question structure, so as not to bias results, it is best to move from more general considerations to more specific considerations, as illustrated earlier. Thus, consumers can be asked first what they think of the brand as a whole without reference to any particular category, followed by specific questions as to products and aspects of the brand image. As with many qualitative research techniques, consumers' responses to open-ended probes can be either oral or written. The advantage of oral responses is that subjects may be more spontaneous in their reporting. Figure 9.3 lists one researcher's guidelines for how to elicit brand associations from consumers.

In terms of coding the data, the protocols provided by each consumer can be divided into phrases and aggregated across consumers in categories. Because of their more focused nature, responses to specific probes and follow-up questions are naturally easier to code.

Projective techniques

Uncovering the sources of brand equity requires that consumers' brand knowledge structures be profiled accurately and completely. Unfortunately, under certain situations, consumers may feel that it would be socially unacceptable or undesirable to express their true feelings – especially to an interviewer they don't know! As a result, they may find it easier to fall back on stereotypical, pat answers that they believe would be acceptable or perhaps even expected by the interviewer.

This unwillingness or inability to reveal feelings may occur when consumers are asked about brands characterized by a preponderance of imagery associations. For example, it may be difficult for consumers to admit that a certain brand name product has prestige and enhances their self-image. As a result, consumers may instead refer to some particular product feature as the reason why they like or dislike the brand. Consumers may also find it difficult to identify and express their feelings when asked directly *even if they attempt to do so*.

For either of these reasons, an accurate portrayal of brand knowledge structures may be impossible without some rather unconventional research methods.

To understand consumers, the English qualitative researcher Wendy Gordon divides consciousness into five levels (going from A to E) and gives examples of answers and reactions from subjects in market research which may be obtained at each level

1. Include at least one visual technique (eg, moodboard technique of selecting pictures from magazines or newspapers).
2. Include at least one object-projective technique (eg, describing brand as a car, animal, fabric, vegetable, celebrity, etc.).
3. Probe for secondary associations (eg, use primary associations as stimulus words for subsequent probing, such as 'what do you associate with quality?')
4. Probe for relevant situations in which individuals have experienced the brand or drawn on knowledge about the brand.
5. Address sensory associations directly (eg, evoke product-related associations of appearance, sound, taste, smell or feel).
6. Use real stimuli when practically possible (eg, let consumers sample products or be exposed to a broad set of brand elements).
7. Use established scales for emotional and personality associations.
8. Instruct respondents to take their time and create acceptance for pauses.
9. Assure confidential treatment of responses.
10. Use person-projective techniques (eg, to mitigate censoring effects, have respondents report associations on behalf of some person or figure belonging to the same group as the respondent).
11. Validate minority associations on a subset of the majority (ensure that responses from verbal respondents are also valid for less verbal respondents by follow-up interview).
12. Criteria of salience and frequency should not be used uncritically (recognize that some words or phrases are easier to report and come to mind more quickly and that this may not always reflect the strength of brand associations).
13. Use a follow-up survey or other methods to determine relationships between strength, favourability and uniqueness of associations.
14. Elicit associations from different types of customers and from the advertising people (eg, heavy users, average users, light users and non-users).
15. Divide the sample into two and include both users and non-users (ie, avoid respondent fatigue and potential 'halo' effects).
16. Start with thorough instructions and visual techniques (verbalizations may disrupt visualizations).
17. Adapt to individual differences in response styles and response attitudes (ie, make sure that the measures fit the sample appropriately).

Figure 9.3   Guidelines for in-depth elicitation of brand associations

Source: Magne J. Supphellen, 'Understanding core brand equity: guidelines for in-depth elicitation of brand associations', *International Journal of Market Research*, 2001, 42 (3): 319–37.

(Figure 9.4).[9] If the questions are considered stupid and meaningless, level A and B answers may be given. Stereotypical answers (A) are conventional or predictable, and come automatically and with little thinking. B, games, are invented answers. When people feel attacked or threatened they can hide how they feel by, for example, joking. This can sometimes be an efficient approach to controlling a perceived intrusion. Thoughts and feelings are C. Qualitative market research can reach this level, where there is useful information on the relation between brand and consumer. Repression is D. Experienced researchers with a background in psychology may reach this level, which also can be accessed using projective techniques. E, the unconscious, is out of reach for marketing studies. However, experienced psychologists can interpret projective studies in a way that delves deeply into a consumer's mind.

Projective techniques are diagnostic tools to uncover the true opinions and feelings of consumers when they are unwilling or otherwise unable to express themselves.

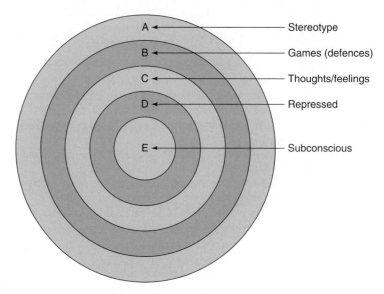

A ← Stereotype
B ← Games (defences)
C ← Thoughts/feelings
D ← Repressed
E ← Subconscious

Figure 9.4   Five levels of consciousness

The idea is that consumers are presented with an incomplete stimulus and asked to complete it or are given an ambiguous stimulus that may not make sense in and of itself and asked to make sense of it. In doing so, the argument is that consumers will reveal some of their true beliefs and feelings. Thus, projective techniques can be especially useful when deeply rooted personal motivations or personally or socially sensitive subject matters may be involved.

In psychology, a famous projective technique is the Rorschach test, in which ink blots are presented to subjects who are then asked what the ink blots remind them of. In responding, it is believed that subjects reveal certain facets of their own, perhaps subconscious, personality. Projective techniques have a long history in marketing, beginning with the motivation research of the late 1940s and 1950s.[10] A classic marketing example of projective techniques comes from an experiment exploring hidden feelings towards instant coffee conducted by Mason Haire in the late 1940s, summarized in Brand Briefing 9.5.[11] Although projective techniques do not always yield as powerful results as in that example, they often provide insights that help to assemble a more complete picture of consumers and their relationships with brands. Many kinds of projective techniques are possible. A few are highlighted here.[12]

Completion and interpretation tasks

As mentioned previously, classic projective techniques use incomplete or ambiguous stimuli to elicit consumers' thoughts and feelings. One such approach is with 'bubble exercises' based on cartoons or photos in which different people are depicted buying or using products or services. Empty bubbles, as found in cartoons, are placed in the scenes to represent the thoughts, words or actions of one or more of the participants in the scene. Consumers are then asked to figuratively 'fill in the bubble' by indicating what they believe is happening or being said in the scene. The stories and conversations told through bubble exercises and picture interpretations can be especially useful to assess user and usage imagery for a brand.

Brand Briefing 9.5

Once upon a time . . . you were what you cooked

One of the most famous applications of psychographic techniques was by Mason Haire in the 1940s. The purpose of Mason Haire's experiment was to uncover consumers' true beliefs and feelings towards Nescafé instant coffee. The impetus for the experiment was the results of a survey conducted to determine why the initial sales of Nescafé instant coffee were so disappointing. The survey asked subjects if they used instant coffee and, if not, what they disliked about it. The majority of the people who reported that they didn't like the product stated that it was because they didn't like the flavour. On the basis of consumer taste tests, however, Nescafé's management knew that consumers found the taste acceptable when they didn't know what type of coffee they were drinking. Suspecting that consumers were not expressing their true feelings, Haire designed an experiment to discover what was going on.

Haire set up two shopping lists containing the same six items. Shopping list 1 specified Maxwell House drip ground coffee, whereas Shopping list 2 specified Nescafé instant coffee, as follows.

Shopping list 1	Shopping list 2
Pound and a half of hamburgers	Pound and a half of hamburgers
2 loaves Wonder bread	2 loaves Wonder bread
Bunch of carrots	Bunch of carrots
1 can Rumford's Baking Powder	1 can Rumford's Baking Powder
Maxwell House coffee (drip ground)	Nescafé instant coffee
2 cans Del Monte peaches	2 cans Del Monte peaches
5 lbs potatoes	5 lbs potatoes

Two groups of matched subjects were each given one of the lists and asked to 'Read the shopping list. . . . Try to project yourself into the situation as far as possible until you can more or less characterize the woman who bought the groceries.' Subjects then wrote a brief description of the personality and character of that person.

After coding the responses into frequently mentioned categories, two profiles emerged.

	List 1 (Maxwell House)	List 2 (Nescafé)
Lazy	4 percent	48 percent
Fails to plan household purchases and schedules well	12 percent	48 percent
Thrifty	16 percent	4 percent
Not a good wife	0 percent	16 percent

Brand Briefing 9.5 *continued*

Haire interpreted these results as indicating that instant coffee represented a departure from homemade coffee and traditions with respect to caring for one's family. In other words, at that time, the 'labour-saving' aspect of instant coffee, rather than being an asset, was a liability in that it violated consumer traditions. Consumers were reluctant to admit this fact when asked directly but were better able to express their feelings when asked to project to another person.

The implications of the findings were clear. Based on the original survey results, the obvious positioning for instant coffee with respect to ground coffee would have been to establish a point of difference on 'convenience' and a point of parity on the basis of 'taste'. Based on the projective test findings, however, it was obvious that there also needed to be a point of parity on the basis of user imagery. As a result, a campaign was launched that promoted Nescafé as a way for housewives to free up time so they could devote time to more important household activities.

Comparison tasks

Another technique is comparison tasks in which consumers are asked to convey their impressions by comparing brands with people, countries, animals, activities, fabrics, occupations, cars, magazines, vegetables, nationalities or even other brands.[13] For example, consumers might be asked, 'If Danone yogurt were a car, which one would it be? If it were an animal, which one might it be? Looking at the people depicted in these pictures, which ones do you think would be most likely to eat Danone yogurt?' In each case, consumers could be asked a follow-up question as to why they made the comparison they did. The objects chosen to represent the brand and the reasons they were chosen can provide glimpses into the psyche of the consumer with respect to a brand. In particular, uncovering the types of associations or inferences that these choices reflect can be useful in understanding imagery associations for the brand.

For example, during the 2004 US presidential election, a random sample of undecided voters offered the following comparisons of the Republican candidate, George W. Bush, and the Democratic candidate, John Kerry, to various popular brands.

Association	Bush	Kerry
Coffee	Dunkin' Donuts	Starbucks
Technology	IBM	Apple
Car	Ford	BMW
Retailer	Kmart	Target
Fast food	McDonald's	Subway

By examining the answers to such probes, researchers may be better equipped to assemble a rich image for the brand – for example, identifying brand personality associations. Brand Briefing 9.6 outlines how a projective brand personality technique, in combination with a reputation measurement was used to gain a deeper understanding of corporate branding strategies.

Brand Briefing 9.6

A comparison of high-reputation versus low-reputation companies

In a 2007 study, researchers at the Brandjobs company explored the emotional side of a brand. Their belief was that perception of corporate image and reputation was not only based on rational judgements, but was to a large extent built on emotional aspects that are difficult to verbalize, explain or express. Their hypothesis was that it was not possible to compete using a brand that appeals to the functional and rational only. Everything rational will be copied, sooner or later. Strong brands have a corporate personality, strong relations and offer an emotional reward. The researchers' analysis focused on identifying differences on these dimensions between companies with high and low reputation (the strengths of the companies' reputations were measured by the Reputation Institute RepTrak Pulse score. The index is made up of four statements: high esteem, admiration and respect, trust and positive feeling).

Sixty-eight of the largest advertisers in Sweden were measured with the projective Brandjobs method. The aim of the research was to examine the differences in terms of image and brand personality between high- and low-reputation companies. By clustering the top ten companies and comparing them with the ten lowest companies, the intention was to get a better understanding of the symbolic and emotional description of low- and high-index companies.

The bottom ten companies were characterized by an introvert and focused/systematic brand personality. The animals used to describe these companies were: vulture, snake, snail and rhinoceros. The characteristics of the brand personality of the top companies were more extrovert and they were seen as helpful/tolerant and down to earth. The animals used to describe the top ten were: dolphin, cow and dog.

The study showed that companies with a human brand personality correlates with high reputation and supportive behaviours. The results showed that companies with a high reputation correlate with certain personality traits, relations and emotional rewards (Figure 9.5).

Sources: 'Sveriges mest djuriska företag', *Aftonbladet*, 23 June 2007; 'Dagens Industri', 22 June 2007; Tony Apéria, Fredrik Berggren and Robert Nises, *'Reputation excellence through emotional branding'*, Reputation Institute Conference, Oslo 2007.

Brand Briefing 9.6 *continued*

Bottom ten companies				Top ten companies		
Ruthless	Cold	Superficial	**Personality**	Considerate	Down to earth	Helpful
Analytical	Dominant	Systematic		Generous	Playful	Enthusiastic
Greedy	Bureaucratic	Not serious	**Image**	Competent	Reliable	Popular
Impersonal	Tactless	Unreliable		Secure	Serious	Kind
Boring		Mediocre		Traditional	Successful	Innovative
Indifferent		Submissive	**Gratification**	Happiness	Harmonic	Togetherness
Superior		Have control		Responsible	Secure	Warmth
Businesslike relation		Necessary evil	**Relation**	Helpful relation		Faithful servant
	Short-term relation				Long-term relation	
Forced relation		No relation		Deep relation	Close friend	Equal relation
Company as animal						

Figure 9.5   Characteristics of top and bottom ten companies

ZALTMAN METAPHOR ELICITATION TECHNIQUE

An interesting approach to better understanding how consumers view brands is the Zaltman Metaphor Elicitation Technique (ZMET).[14] This is based on a belief that consumers often have subconscious motives for their purchasing behaviour. 'A lot goes on in our minds that we're not aware of,' said former academic Jerry Zaltman. 'Most of what influences what we say and do occurs below the level of awareness. That's why we need new techniques to get at hidden knowledge – to get at what people don't know they know.'

To access this hidden knowledge, he developed ZMET, 'a technique for eliciting interconnected constructs that influence thought and behaviour'. The word *construct* refers to 'an abstraction created by the researcher to capture common ideas, concepts, or themes expressed by customers'. For example, the construct 'ease of use' might capture the statements 'simple to operate', 'works without hassle' and 'you don't really have to do anything'.

ZMET stems from knowledge and research from varied fields such as 'cognitive neuroscience, neurobiology, art critique, literary criticism, visual anthropology, visual sociology, semiotics . . . art therapy and psycholinguistics.' The technique is based on the idea that 'most social communication is nonverbal' and as a result two-thirds of all stimuli received by the brain are visual. Using ZMET, Zaltman teases out consumers' hidden thoughts and feelings about a particular topic, which often can be expressed best using visual metaphors. Zaltman defines a metaphor as 'a definition of one thing in terms of another, [which] people can use . . . to represent thoughts that are tacit, implicit, and unspoken'.

A ZMET study starts with participants being asked in advance to think about the research topic at hand and select a minimum of 12 images from their own sources (eg, magazines, catalogues and family photo albums) that represent their thoughts and feelings about the topic. The participants bring these images with them for a personal two-hour interview with a study administrator who uses advanced interview techniques to explore the images with the participant and reveal hidden meanings through a 'guided conversation'. Finally, the participants use a computer program to create a collage with these images that communicates their subconscious thoughts and feelings about the topic. The findings are compiled in an interactive multimedia program. The guided conversation consists of steps that include some or all of the following.

1. *Storytelling:* participants describe the content of each picture.
2. *Missed images:* participants describe the picture or pictures that he or she was unable to obtain and explain their relevance.
3. *Sorting task:* participants sort pictures into meaningful groups and provide a label or description for each group.
4. *Construct elicitation:* participants reveal basic constructs and their interconnections using images as stimuli through the Kelly repertory grid and laddering techniques (described in Chapter 3).
5. *The most representative picture:* participants indicate which picture is most representative.
6. *Opposite images:* participants indicate pictures that describe the opposite of the brand or the task that they were given.
7. *Sensory images:* participants indicate what does and does not describe the concept in terms of colour, emotion, sound, smell, taste and touch.
8. *Mental map:* after reviewing all of the constructs discussed and asking participants if the constructs are accurate representations of what was meant and if any important ideas are missing, participants create a map or causal model connecting the constructs that have been elicited.
9. *Summary image:* participants create a summary image or montage using their own images (sometimes augmented by images from an image bank) to express important issues. Digital imaging techniques may be employed to help creation of the image.
10. *Vignette:* participants put together a vignette or short video to help communicate important issues.

Once the interviews are completed, researchers identify themes or constructs, code the data and assemble a consensus map involving the most important constructs.

Quantitative analyses of the data can provide information for advertising, promotions and other marketing mix decisions. ZMET has been applied in a variety of ways, including as a means of helping understand consumers' images of brands, products and companies. Marketers can employ ZMET for a variety of consumer insight research topics. Zaltman lists several of these:

> ZMET is useful in understanding consumers' images of brands, products, and companies, brand equity, product concepts and designs, product usage and purchase experiences, life experiences, consumption context and attitudes towards business.

For example, DuPont enlisted Zaltman to research US women's attitudes towards hosiery. Conventional research yielded the conclusion that 'women mostly hated wearing pantyhose' but DuPont market researchers were not convinced that this conclusion provided a complete picture. Zaltman used ZMET with 20 subjects to uncover deeper answers to the question: 'What are your thoughts and feelings about buying and wearing pantyhose?' He discovered that women had a 'like-hate' relationship with tights; they disliked the discomfort and run-proneness of tights but liked the feel of elegance and sexiness they got from wearing them. This prompted manufacturers to include more sexy and alluring imagery in their advertising. Figure 9.6 is a consensus map that emerged from a study of lingerie.

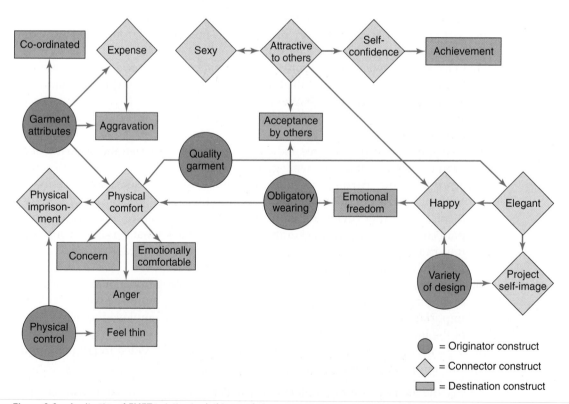

Figure 9.6   Application of ZMET to intimate clothing market

Brand personality and values

As defined in Chapter 2, brand personality is the human characteristics or traits that can be attributed to a brand.[15] Brand personality can be measured in different ways. Perhaps the simplest and most direct way is to solicit open-ended responses to a probe such as the following:

> If the brand were to come alive as a person, what would it be like? What would it do? Where would it live? What would it wear? Who would it talk to if it went to a party (and what would it talk about)?

If consumers have difficulty getting started, they can be given an example or prompt as a guide. For example, one study of Ryanair showed the following:

> Ryanair is seen as a successful, and innovative person. But we can also see the some negative characteristics such as unserious, unreliable, and unpersonal.

Other means are possible for capturing consumers' points of view. For example, consumers could be given pictures or magazines and asked to assemble a profile of the brand. These pictures could be of celebrities or anything else. Along these lines, ad agencies often conduct 'picture sorting' studies to clarify who are typical users of a brand. As Chapter 3 noted and as discussed in Brand Briefing 9.7, brand personality and user imagery may not always agree.

Brand Briefing 9.7

Brand identity and the brand identity prism

According to European branding expert Jean-Noël Kapferer, a brand's identity must precede its image. He proposes a brand identity prism with six facets that reinforce each other (Figure 9.7). The prism is widely used in Europe by practitioners. The facets can be researched qualitatively and brand strengths and weaknesses can be defined.

Kapferer argues: 'Too often, brands are examined through their component parts: the brand name, its logo, design or packaging, advertising or sponsorship, or image and name recognition, or very recently, in terms of financial brand recognition. Real brand management, however, begins much earlier, with a strategy and a consistent integrated vision. Its central concept is brand identity, not brand image. This identity must be defined and managed. It is the heart of brand management.'

The prism gives a comprehensive picture of how a brand owner wants the target group to perceive the brand's identity. The facets of the prism model are as follows.

- *Physique:* the sum of a brand's basic characteristics constitutes its physique.
- *Personality:* the brand has a personality and can with time develop character. An easy way to bestow a personality on the brand is to give it a spokesperson – human or animal.

Brand Briefing 9.7 *continued*

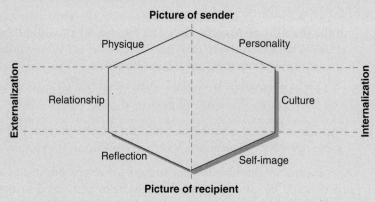

Figure 9.7 Six facets of brand identity

- *Culture:* each brand has a culture from which all products within the brand frame originate. The product is an embodiment of that culture.
- *Relationship:* a brand has relationships with its consumers and frequently offers possibilities for interpersonal exchanges. This is particularly true for brands in the service sector or retail brands.
- *Reflection:* a brand reflects its customers' image and becomes a means of identification. People are often well able to describe what type a certain brand's consumers are, and consumers can consequently use the brand to show who or what they identify themselves with. The Coca-Cola reflection is young, but older people drink it too, suggesting that the older consumer group identifies – or wishes to – with young people's values. Brand owners often create such target group reflections. The reflection thus mirrors the customers' image – not the group itself but how it is perceived.
- *Self-image:* if reflection is considered to be the target group's external reflection, the self-image is the consumer's internal mirror. We create a picture of ourselves through our attitudes to the brands we use.

It can be argued that the model illustrates that people can have connections with brands as they do with human beings. The relationship facet can on one side be seen as a parent–child relationship or a teacher–student relationship. On the other side it can seen as equal. Some examples of relationships that can exist between a brand and a consumer are the businesslike, the close friend and the short-term versus long-term.

Tony Apéria discusses the links between brand personality and reflection (reflection is often referred to as user image).[16] Brand personality can be formed by the characteristics of the people who buy or use the brand. Characteristics associated with the user are transferred to the brand and thereby provide it with personality. In some cases,

Brand Briefing 9.7 *continued*

the brand can be attributed qualities that are more advanced in the reflection. One possible explanation is that customers buy certain brands to signal who they want to be rather than who they are. If reflection governs personality, the brand owner may ask if it is possible to influence what kind of people are using the brand. An important conclusion is that it is important to communicate a flattering user image.

The concepts of physique, relationship and reflection make the visible facets. They are explicit and easy to pinpoint in conventional research. Brand personality, culture and self-image are the invisible and implicit facets. If the goal is to understand the brand in depth, it is not sufficient to investigate the explicit and visible facets of the brand. It is also necessary to examine the implicit and the invisible. The brand identity prism model is important because it describes the brand as a holistic entity, and it shows that to understand a brand in depth you need get beneath the rational to reach the more subconscious levels. The model also highlights that, in mature markets, is not enough to position the brand with its benefits, you must know all facets of the brand to be true to its identity.

Source: Jean-Noël Kapferer, *Strategic Brand Management,* London: Kogan Page, 1992.

The big five

Brand personality can be assessed more definitively through adjective checklists or ratings. Jennifer Aaker conducted academic research that provides an interesting glimpse into the personality of well-known brands, as well as a methodological means to examine the personality of any one brand.[17] Based on data involving 114 personality traits on 37 US brands by 600 people, she created a scale that reflected 5 factors (with underlying facets) of brand personality.

1. Sincerity (down to earth, honest, wholesome and cheerful).
2. Excitement (daring, spirited, imaginative and up to date).
3. Competence (reliable, intelligent and successful).
4. Sophistication (upper class and charming).
5. Ruggedness (outdoorsy and tough).

Figure 9.8 depicts the traits that make up the Aaker brand personality scale. Respondents in her study rated how descriptive each trait was for each brand according to a seven-point scale (1 = not at all descriptive; 7 = extremely descriptive); responses were then averaged to provide summary measures. Figure 9.9 lists the ratings of the 37 brands from the study on the 5 factors. Note that certain brands tended to be strong on one particular factor (eg, Hallmark with 'sincerity', Porsche with 'excitement', AT&T with 'competence', Lexus with 'sophistication', and Levi's with 'ruggedness'). Other brands (eg, Nike) were high on more than one factor. Some

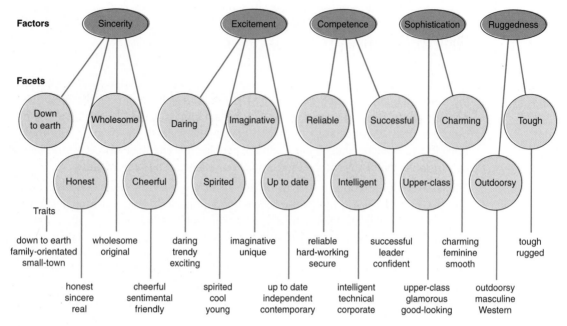

Figure 9.8   Aaker's brand personality measures in the USA

brands (eg, MCI) scored poorly on all factors. A cross-cultural study exploring the generalizability of this scale outside the USA found that three of the five factors applied in Japan and Spain, but that a 'peacefulness' dimension replaced 'ruggedness' both in Japan and Spain, and a 'passion' dimension emerged in Spain instead of 'competency'.[18] Research on brand personality in Korea revealed that two culture-specific factors emerged (passive likeableness and ascendancy), reflecting the importance of Confucian values in Korea.[19]

Experiential methods

Researchers are attempting to improve the effectiveness of qualitative approaches as well as go beyond traditional techniques to research consumers in their natural environment.[20] The rationale is that no matter how clever the research design, consumers may not be able to express their true selves as part of a formalized study. By tapping more directly into home, work or shopping behaviours, researchers may be able to elicit more meaningful responses from consumers.[21] As markets become more competitive and brand differences are threatened, any insight that helps to support a stronger brand positioning or create a stronger link to consumers is seen as indispensable (Brand Briefing 9.8).

So, researchers have been sent into consumers' homes in the morning to see how they approach their days, have given business travellers Polaroid cameras and diaries to capture their feelings when in hotel rooms and conducted 'pager studies' in which participants are instructed to write down what they're doing when they are paged.[22] Ogilvy & Mather has sent its researchers into homes with hand-held cameras to get

	AT&T	Advil	AmEx	Apple	Avon	Campbell's	Charlie	Cheerios
Sincerity	1.06	0.92	0.83	0.92	1.08	1.25	0.83	1.14
Excitement	0.91	0.72	0.83	0.95	1.03	0.87	0.96	0.77
Competence	1.15	0.95	0.99	1.07	1.01	1.01	0.77	0.88
Sophistication	0.85	0.75	0.87	0.86	1.22	0.89	1.13	0.76
Ruggedness	0.94	0.90	0.83	0.92	0.92	0.93	0.77	0.84

	CNN	Crest	Diet Coke	ESPN	Guess?	Hallmark	Hershey	IBM
Sincerity	0.99	1.09	0.94	0.99	0.88	1.27	1.11	0.89
Excitement	1.02	0.84	0.93	1.10	1.15	1.21	0.88	0.91
Competence	1.18	0.99	0.85	1.04	0.90	1.12	0.89	1.10
Sophistication	0.93	0.87	0.90	0.89	1.24	1.31	0.96	0.84
Ruggedness	1.01	0.94	0.89	1.23	1.03	0.95	0.85	0.91

	K-Mart	Kodak	Lego	Lee	Levi's	Lexus	Mattel	McDonald's
Sincerity	1.07	1.10	1.11	1.14	1.20	0.87	1.13	1.14
Excitement	0.85	0.99	1.10	1.00	1.11	1.12	1.10	0.97
Competence	0.97	1.08	1.01	0.99	1.05	1.07	1.04	1.02
Sophistication	0.78	0.96	0.87	1.09	1.13	1.27	0.90	1.02
Ruggedness	0.91	1.02	1.10	1.34	1.43	1.03	1.13	0.90

	MCI	Mercedes	Michelin	MTV	Nike	Oil of Olay	Pepsi	Porsche
Sincerity	0.81	0.84	0.96	0.70	0.98	1.00	1.02	0.71
Excitement	0.82	1.07	0.86	1.27	1.17	0.85	1.04	1.26
Competence	0.90	1.06	1.03	0.82	1.03	0.94	0.89	0.95
Sophistication	0.73	1.31	0.82	1.02	1.05	1.17	0.95	1.37
Ruggedness	0.75	0.99	1.20	0.93	1.36	0.76	0.99	1.07

	Reebok	Revlon	Saturn	Sony	Visa
Sincerity	0.94	0.96	0.96	0.87	0.90
Excitement	1.12	1.06	1.05	0.94	0.87
Competence	0.97	0.98	0.99	1.02	1.02
Sophistication	1.00	1.31	1.08	0.89	0.87
Ruggedness	1.30	0.85	1.00	0.90	0.87

Figure 9.9 Personality ratings of selected US brands

a close-up picture of how people live. Hours of footage are then condensed into documentary-like, 30-minute videos to show how people communicate and interact in real life.[23] Tetra Pak Korea sent employees out on a 'brand safari' to meet customers, instead on only relying on market research. The idea behind the safari was also to strengthen the importance of the consumer in the Tetra Pak culture. The idea is to observe consumers unobtrusively as they shop or as they consume products to capture every nuance of their behaviour.

Brand Briefing 9.8

Making the most of consumer insights

Marketers frequently emphasize the importance of consumer focus in developing products and services. Consumer research plays a significant role in uncovering information valuable to consumer-focused companies. David Taylor, founder of the Brand Gym consultancy, cautions that not all findings from consumer research can be considered insights. He defines an insight as 'a penetrating, discerning understanding that unlocks an opportunity'. An insight holds far more potential than a finding. Using Microsoft as an example, Taylor draws the contrast between the finding that 'people need to process more and more information and data' and the insight that 'information is the key to power and freedom'. This insight would seem to be able to be used by Microsoft to develop products that appeal to a larger consumer base than if the company relied solely on the finding.

Taylor developed criteria to evaluate insights.

- *Fresh:* an insight might be obvious and, in fact, overlooked or forgotten as a result. Check again.
- *Relevant:* an insight when played back to other target consumers should strike a chord.
- *Enduring:* by building on a deep understanding of consumers' beliefs and needs, a true consumer insight should have potential to remain relevant over time.
- *Inspiring:* all the team should be excited by the insight and see different but consistent applications.

Insights can come from consumer research such as focus groups, but may also come from using what Taylor describes as the 'core insight drills'. A sample of these drills follows.

- How could the brand/category do more to help improve people's lives?
- What do people really value in the category and what would they not miss?
- What conflicting needs do people have? How can these tradeoffs be solved?
- What bigger market is the brand really competing in from a consumer viewpoint? What could the brand do more of to better meet these 'higher-order' needs?
- What assumptions do people make about the market that could be challenged?
- How do people think the product works and how does it work in reality?
- How is the product used in reality? What other products are used instead of the brand, where the brand could do a better job?

These 'drills' can help companies unearth consumer insights that lead to better products and services and, ultimately, to stronger brands.

Source: David Taylor, 'Drilling for nuggets: how to use insight to inspire innovation', *Brand Strategy*, March 2000.

Marketers such as Procter & Gamble seek consumers' permission to spend time with them in their homes to see how they use and experience products. Business-to-business companies can also benefit from visits that help to cement relationships and supplement research efforts. Technology firms such as Hewlett-Packard use cross-functional customer visits as a market research tool to gain a competitive advantage. One expert on the subject, Ed McQuarrie, offers the following advice as to best practices for a customer visit.[24]

1. Use the visits you already make better by co-ordinating them with perennial questions and logging and reviewing customer profiles.
2. Take every opportunity to ask questions (eg, set aside an hour to solicit feedback).
3. Get engineers in front of customers, not just marketers.
4. Conduct scheduled visits.
5. Visit different kinds of customers.
6. Get out of the conference room.

Yahoo! has moved to 'immersion groups' where a group of four to five people talk informally with the company's product developers and even interact in work sessions to design products.[25]

Tetra Pak Korea

To speed up the innovation process in order to launch successful new products Tetra Pak Korea involved employees cross-functionally in the innovation process. In a research project in the spring of 2007 that was carried out in co-operation with researchers from Brandjobs, it used projective photos to get below the surface of the Korean consumer and understand the jobs consumers needed to get done. The photos of men and women were first validated with Korean consumers. Different kinds of projective stimuli were used in the process, photos of men, women, children, animals, feelings and relationships. Figure 9.10 shows a photo from the Brand Safari when Tetra Pak employees meet consumers face to face.

Of special importance to many companies are leading users. Many firms are using online groups of consumers to give feedback via instant messages or chat-rooms. One company with close ties to leading-edge users is Burton Snowboards.

Burton Snowboards

Burton Snowboards, saw its market share increase from 30 percent to 40 percent by focusing on one objective – providing the best equipment to the largest number of snowboarders. To accomplish this goal, Burton's research approach is to focus on the 300 professional riders worldwide, 39 of whom are on its sponsored team. Staff members talk to the riders – on the slopes or on the phone – almost every day, and riders help to design almost every Burton product (Figure 9.11). Company researchers immerse themselves in the riders' lives, watching where they shop, what they buy and what they think about the sport and the equipment. To make sure it doesn't lose touch with

Figure 9.10   Tetra Pak employees meet consumers face to face.

consumers, however, the company makes sure at least 10 of its 22 US sales representatives visit slopes at the weekend to interact with snowboarders. Moreover, at any given time, two large trailers are travelling in North America, six buses are criss-crossing Japan and four trucks are rumbling through Europe, all with the purpose of testing gear on consumers. Burton also has the eTeam – an online community of 25,000 teenagers who provide real-time feedback in exchange for free product trials.[26]

Summary

The range of qualitative research techniques is limited only by the creativity of the marketing researcher. Qualitative research answers questions such as 'What?', 'Why?' or 'How?' However, it cannot answer the question 'How many?' It is concerned with understanding.

Qualitative research also has drawbacks. The insights that emerge have to be tempered by the realization that the samples involved are often very small and may not necessarily generalize to broader populations. Moreover, given the qualitative nature of the data, there may be questions of interpretation. Different researchers examining the same results may draw different conclusions.

One example of qualitative research is projective techniques. These techniques don't guarantee access to the truth but they are ways to enable the person or group being interviewed to get in touch with their thoughts, feelings and behaviours.

Figure 9.11   Burton Snowboards

QUANTITATIVE RESEARCH TECHNIQUES

Usually, projective techniques have been used only in qualitative studies, but they can be used in quantitative studies as well. Photo-sorting techniques can accomplish this, in a quantitative manner, by using validated personality photos (as projective interviewing stimuli), representing brand personalities. This way, respondents can project their needs and perceptions through the personalities and reveal deep-lying perceptions as well as higher-level information, eg socially less acceptable items.

In the 1980s, Belgian motivation researcher J.P. Heylen developed a model with eight sectors, representing eight basic personalities that brands may have. He combined two dimensions that are recognized by modern social psychology as underlying human behaviour.

- The biological dimension from introvert repressive to extrovert expressive orientation.
- The social dimension from ego-orientation self-assertion to we-orientation affiliation.

The model was pioneering a technology in marketing research through its ability to measure in consumers' subconscious, implicit needs and corresponding brand personality perceptions – in addition to conventional explicit data. Other models based on similar projective techniques are Brandjobs from Sweden, Censydiam from Belgium and NeedScope from New Zealand.

Results from a Brandjobs study will help explain these models (Brand Briefing 9.9). Brandjobs was developed for strategic brand research with segmentation and

Brand Briefing 9.9

The quantitative projective technique Brandjobs

Brandjobs is based on a five-factor model.

- Extrovert–introvert.
- Agreeableness (to what degree one is focused on oneself or other in terms of needs, perceptions, wishes, etc).
- Conscientiousness (to what degree one is spontaneous/impulsive or strict patient).
- Openness to new experiences.
- Neuroticism–emotional stability.

In the Brandjobs platform of Figure 9.12 four of these dimensions are explicit. Vertically, is the extrovert–introvert dimension. Helpful/tolerant corresponds with agreeableness; Focused/Systematic with conscientiousness; and Open-minded/Imaginative

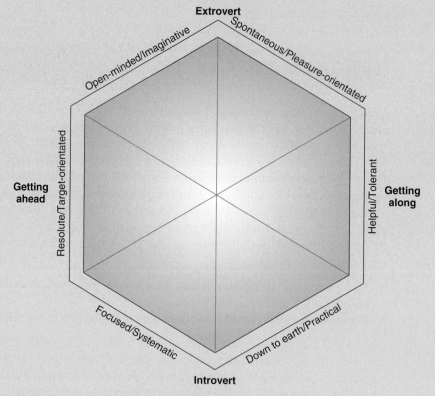

Figure 9.12 The Brandjobs platform

Brand Briefing 9.9 *continued*

with openness. The neuroticism dimension is not explicit in the model because no one wants to build neurotic brands. This dimension also corresponds to some extent with extroversion. These quantitative projective methods enable researchers to reach the underlying dynamics of the market. The validated personality photo in addition ensures that the implicit meaning of brands and attributes are accurately shown on the map. The horizontal dimension goes from 'Getting ahead' to 'Getting along'. This axis describes if the brand is used to 'get ahead' of others or how people 'get along' with other people, family, friends, groups and society. Combining the vertical and horizontal dimensions enables a personality platform to be created based on the most important human personalities.

Validated photos have been developed that give stability to the interpretation of interview answers. The subject combines test objects (brands and products) with validated photos of men or women. Figure 9.13 shows the perceptions of 68 brand

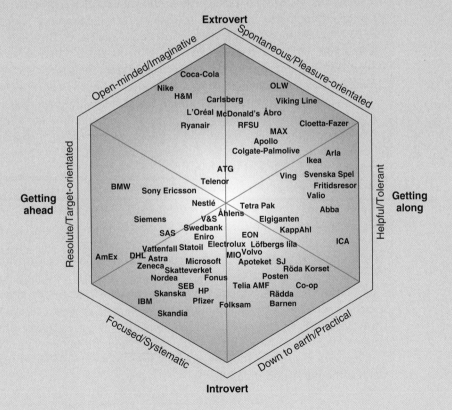

Figure 9.13   Results from 68 brands

Brand Briefing 9.9 *continued*

personalities. After combining the brand with the photo, respondents are asked to describe why the people in the photos use the brands they have been associated with.

The study covers examples from 68 of the largest advertisers in Sweden. The aim was to get a better understanding of the emotional side and the personality of these corporate brands. Rational answers are easy to measure, but the emotional side is more difficult. The perception of corporate image and reputation is not only based on rational judgements. It is to a large extent built on emotional aspects that are difficult to verbalize, explain or express. The hypothesis was that strong corporate brands have a personality, relationship and offer an emotional reward. The analysis focused on identifying differences on these dimensions between companies with high and low reputation index scores (measured with the RepTrak Pulse index).

If the corporate brand's position is in the middle of a sector, the brand has the personality of that sector. Two examples are the European banks Nordea and SEB. They are found in the sector Focused/Systematic. The closer the brand is to the map's frame, the larger the number of consumers that agree on its personality. One extremely extrovert position is shown by Coca-Cola with the Open-minded/Imaginative personality. A position close to the centre point is a sign of disagreement within the subject group. Either the brand has a vague personality, or it is a strong market leader that possesses something which attracts everyone. One example of a vague personality is shown by the Swedish retailer Åhlens. This personality is connected to all photos and as a result it ends up with a generic position in the middle of the map.

The results showed that companies on the 'Getting along' side of the platform had higher reputation and supporting behaviours than those on the 'Getting ahead' side.

Figure 9.14 shows the corporate image and brand personality of the retail fashion brand H&M. The strength of the brand's reputation was 68.8 (the RepTrak Pulse index goes between 0 and 100). The personality is Extrovert and Open-minded/Imaginative. The image is modern, trendy, youthful, innovative and successful. Some words that elaborate on the personality are self-assured, spontaneous and playful. The feelings/emotions connected to the brand are attractive and lively/energetic. The relationship that exists between the brand and the consumers is flirty, fun friend, intense and faithful servant. When respondents were asked to name the animals that they felt expressed the brand, they chose the horse and the butterfly.

Brand Briefing 9.9 *continued*

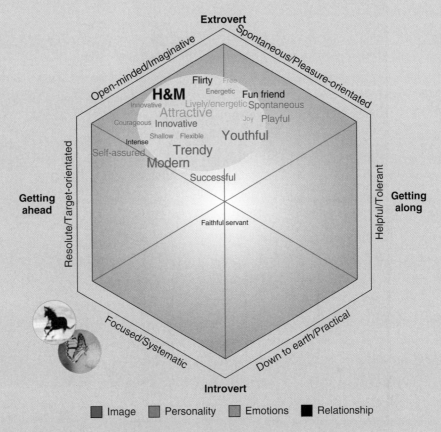

Figure 9.14   H&M's corporate image

Figure 9.15 shows the corporate image and brand personality of furniture retailer Ikea. The strength of the brand's reputation was 84.0. The image and personality of Ikea can be seen as a blueprint for a very successful global retailer with a very good reputation.

The personality is Extrovert and Helpful/Tolerant but also to a large extent Spontaneous/Pleasure-orientated. The image is popular/folksy, reliable, successful, trendy and innovative. Some words that elaborate on the personality are challenging, flexible and down to earth. The feelings/emotions connected to the brand are

Brand Briefing 9.9 *continued*

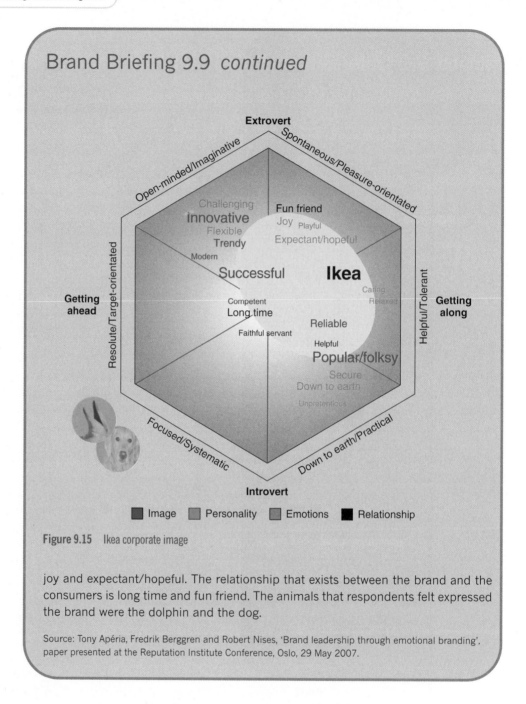

Figure 9.15   Ikea corporate image

joy and expectant/hopeful. The relationship that exists between the brand and the consumers is long time and fun friend. The animals that respondents felt expressed the brand were the dolphin and the dog.

Source: Tony Apéria, Fredrik Berggren and Robert Nises, 'Brand leadership through emotional branding', paper presented at the Reputation Institute Conference, Oslo, 29 May 2007.

positioning as well as research concerned with development of communications and design, secondary association research, brand extension and co-branding research and innovation research. (Brand Briefing 7.1 presented the results from a Brandjobs study that investigated how secondary associations could be linked to a brand.)

Online market research on the rise

Online market research is gaining credibility as a way to test advertising, conduct focus groups and gather opinions. Soliciting and collecting consumer data online can be less expensive and the data may be easier to oversee than traditional market research. But in some situations it cannot be as effective as face-to-face interviews or focus groups. Nevertheless, in 2005, companies spent more than €800 million on online market research, a 16 percent increase over 2004, according to the *Inside Research newsletter*.

The top ten countries in 2006 for online access included Iceland (86.3 percent); Australia (70.2 percent); USA (69.6 percent) and Luxembourg (68 percent).[27] Decreasing telecommunication costs have driven companies to devote more energy to online research. The migration of market research to the internet began with companies asking web users about websites but quickly expanded into other areas.

Recruitment is essential to conducting useful online marketing research. In some instances, invitations to participate in an online survey are e-mailed to a large group and recipients click on a link if they are willing to complete the survey. Other marketers rely on pop-up links to questionnaires and commission online panels of consumers who agree to participate in surveys. The best online panels make respondents feel they belong to a club where their input is valuable.

The online approach to market research has many positive aspects. Projects are unrestricted by geography, which facilitates multi-country research that can be managed from one location. This method avoids interviewer bias and ensures data is analyzed uniformly, rather than given to different researchers. Proponents say online surveys are convenient, far less intrusive than a telephone call or being intercepted on the street by an interviewer with a clipboard. Respondents may be more comfortable sitting down in their homes and therefore offer more thoughtful and honest answers, especially on sensitive issues. Online research results come back quickly and can be analyzed straight away. Administration and analysis costs plummet with online surveys.

One significant contributor to the growth of online market research is the increase of corporate pre-testing of films and advertising. Cruise company Royal Caribbean conducts online research using past customers to find out what types of cruises and which destinations they would like. Consulting companies have developed software to aid customer participation. Using such software, Danish toymaker Lego brought together 10,000 customers who responded to an e-mail invitation to participate in a new product contest.

The online brainstorming led to the creation of the 3,100-piece Star Wars Imperial Destroyer, the company's largest and most expensive set (Figure 9.16). It sold out in five weeks. The software Lego used allows consumers to rank product concepts and gives them the option to add their own ideas. The list of options is constantly shuffled and ranked according to the average scores. The highest-scoring ideas eventually percolate up to the top of the list. Proctor & Gamble solicited ideas from tens of thousands of customers for labels on Pringles Prints crisps. One of the ideas, factoids from the *Guinness Book of World Records*, was introduced in 2005.

Online research is not a perfect tool. Programing costs are higher than for traditional questionnaires. The number of people willing to take part in surveys in general is declining because of cynicism about marketing in general as well pressures

Figure 9.16   Lego used online research for a Star Wars model
Source: Rex Features

on consumers' time. This trend may creep into the online realm. If online surveys are too long, customers may opt not to finish. Also, the absence of an interviewer makes it harder to gauge if someone is being honest, especially since online surveys can attract internet junkies who crank out questionnaires by the dozen. Participants may be tempted to rush through such surveys and there is no interviewer to prod them with a follow-up question. A decreasing concern is whether online users differ from the general population, because non-internet users may have a difference perspective. Internet users may have the same attitudes as non-users on issues such as food but may differ on products like digital cameras.

An area where online research fails to measure up to focus groups is in situations where marketers want to closely document reaction to products. Although virtual focus groups may be convened with the use of web cameras, many researchers prefer face-to-face interaction for the opportunity to watch consumers' faces as they interact with products. For some research goals, such as testing the smell or feel of a product, online research is of no use. Figure 9.17 gives guidelines for conducting online surveys.

- Don't take advantage of respondents' willingness to participate. Diversity in respondents is essential to generating solid data.
- Recruit consumers and profile them when they first join a panel and then match them to projects, rather than letting them select projects.
- Engage participants in continuing conversations. For example, Bose created the Bose Information Exchange to encourage fans to discuss its technology.
- Keep questions focused. Respondents will not want to spend more than five minutes answering questions. Offer incentives if respondents need to be willing to offer in-depth answers or answer questions regularly.
- If surveying children, obtain parental consent.
- E-mail invitations are effective for a well-defined audience and web links are a good way to tease out general feedback from website visitors. It is more difficult to target particular respondent profiles using web links.
- Include the purpose of the survey and how long it should take to complete.
- Use open-ended questions.

Figure 9.17   Online survey guidelines

Sources: Allison Fass, 'Collective opinion', *Forbes*, 28 November 2005; Robin T. Peterson and Zhilin Yang, 'Web product reviews help strategy', *Marketing News*, 1 April 2004; 'Marketing research association executive director predicts dramatic growth for online marketing research in 2006 and beyond', *Business Wire*, 18 January 2006; Richard Kottler, 'Eight tips offer best practices for online MR', *Marketing News*, 1 April 2005.

Awareness

Recall that brand awareness is related to the strength of the brand in memory, as reflected by consumers' ability to identify brand elements under different conditions. Brand awareness relates to the likelihood that a brand will come to mind in different situations and the ease with which it does so given different types of cues.

Several measures of awareness of brand elements can be employed.[28] Choosing the appropriate measure depends on the relative importance of brand awareness for consumer behaviour in the category and the resulting role it plays in the success of the marketing campaign for the brand, as discussed in Chapter 2.

Brand recognition

Recognition processes require that consumers be able to discriminate a stimulus – a word, object, image or whatever – as something they have previously seen. Brand recognition relates to consumers' ability to identify the brand under a variety of circumstances and can involve identification of any of the brand elements. In the most basic recognition procedure, consumers are given individual items, visually or orally, and are asked if they have previously seen or heard of these items. To provide a more sensitive test, it is often useful to include decoys or lures – items that consumers could not possibly have seen. In addition to 'yes' or 'no' responses, consumers can be asked to rate how confident they are in their recognition of an item.

A number of additional, somewhat more subtle, recognition measures involve 'perceptually degraded' versions of the brand. In some cases, the brand element may be distorted in some way or shown for an extremely brief time. For example, brand name recognition could be tested with missing letters. Figure 9.18 tests your ability to recognize brand names with less than full information. These more subtle measures may be particularly important for brands that have a high level of recognition to provide more sensitive assessments.

A brand name with a high level of awareness will be recognized under less than ideal conditions. Consider the following list of incomplete names. Which ones do you recognize? Compare your answers with the key in the footnote.

1. D _ _ N E _
2. K O _ _ K
3. B A _ I L _ A
4. H Y _ T _
5. A D _ _ A S
6. V _ L _ O
7. L _ F T _ _ _ S A
8. M _ L _ A

9. G _ L L _ T _ _
10. Z _ _ A
11. H _ L L _ _ R K
12. M _ R C _ _ E S
13. T _ S _ O
14. L _ G _
15. N _ K _

Answers:
(1) Disney; (2) Kodak; (3) Barilla; (4) Hyatt; (5) Adidas; (6) Volvo; (7) Lufthansa; (8) Milka; (9) Gillette; (10) Zara; (11) Hallmark; (12) Mercedes; (13) Tesco; (14) Lego; (15) Nike.

Figure 9.18   Don't tell me, it's on the tip of my tongue

Brand recognition is especially important for packaging, and some marketing researchers have used creative way to assess the visibility of packaging design. As a starting point, they consider the benchmark or 'best case' of the visibility of a pack when a consumer with 20-20 vision, is face to face with a pack, at a distance of less than five feet, under ideal lighting conditions.

A question then is whether the packaging design is robust enough to be still recognizable if one or more of these four conditions is not met. Because shopping is often not conducted under 'ideal' conditions, such insights are important. For example, one research study indicated that one in six members of the population who wear glasses do not wear them when shopping in a supermarket.[29] An important question then is whether a pack is still recognizable.

Research methods using tachistoscopes (T-scopes) and eye-tracking techniques exist to test the effectiveness of packaging designs according to specific criteria.

- How a pack stands out on a shelf.
- Effect and recall of specific design elements.
- Distance at which a pack can first be identified.
- Angle at which a pack can first be identified.
- Speed with which a pack can be identified.
- Perceived pack size.
- Copy visibility and legibility.

These measures can provide more sensitive measures of recognition than simple 'yes' or 'no' tasks. By applying these direct and indirect measures of brand recognition, marketers can determine which brand elements exist in memory and, to some extent, the strength of their association. One advantage brand recognition measures have over recall measures is that they can be used in any eventuality. For example, because recognition often depends on sight, visual recognition measures can be used. It may be difficult for consumers to describe a logo or symbol in a recall task either verbally or pictorially, but much easier for them to assess the same elements visually in a recognition task.

Nevertheless, brand recognition measures only provide an approximation of *potential* recallability. To determine whether the brand elements will actually be recalled under various circumstances, measures of brand recall are necessary.

Brand recall

Brand recall relates to the ability of a consumer to identify a brand under a variety of circumstances. With brand recall, consumers must retrieve the brand element from memory when given some related probe or cue. Thus, brand recall is a more demanding memory task than brand recognition.

Different measures of brand recall are possible depending on the type of cues provided to consumers. *Unaided recall* on the basis of 'all brands' provided as a cue is likely to identify only the strongest brands. *Aided recall* uses cues to help consumer recall. One possible sequence of aided recall might use progressively narrower cues – such as product class, product category and product type labels – to provide insight into the organization of consumers' brand knowledge structures. For example, if recall of the Porsche Boxster sports car in non-German markets was of interest, recall probes could begin with 'all cars' and move to more and more narrowly defined categories such as 'sports cars,' 'European sports cars' or even 'high-performance German sports cars'. For example, consumers could be asked: 'When you think of European sports cars, which brands come to mind?'

Other types of cues may be employed. For example, consumers could be probed on the basis of product attributes (eg, 'When you think of chocolate, which brands come to mind?) or usage goals (eg, 'If you were thinking of having a healthy snack, which brands come to mind?') Often, to capture the breadth of brand recall and to assess brand salience, it may be important to examine the context of the purchase decision or consumption usage situation. For example, consumers could be probed according to purchase motivations as well as times and places when the product could be used to see which brands came to mind. The more that brands have strong associations to these non-product considerations, the more likely it is that they will be recalled when consumers are given those situational cues. Combined, measures of recall based on product attribute or category cues as well as situational or usage cues give an indication of breadth and depth of recall.

Besides being judged as correctly recalled, brand recall can be distinguished according to order, as well as latency or speed of recall. In many cases, people will recognize a brand when it is shown to them and will recall it if they are given a sufficient number of cues. Thus, potential recallability is high. The more important issue is the salience of the brand: do consumers think of the brand under the right circumstances – for example, when they could be either buying or using the product? How quickly do they think of the brand? Is it automatically or easily recalled? Is it the first brand recalled?

Corrections for guessing

Any research measure must consider the issue of consumers making up responses or guessing. That problem may be especially evident with certain types of aided awareness or recognition measures for the brand. Spurious awareness occurs when consumers erroneously claim that they recall something that they really don't and that maybe doesn't even exist. For example, one market research firm, Oxtoby-Smith, conducted a benchmark study of awareness of health and beauty products.[30] In the study, it asked consumers questions like this:

> The following is a list of denture adhesive brand names. Please answer yes if you've heard the name before and no if you haven't. Okay? Orafix? Fasteeth? Dentu-Tight? Fixodent?

Although 16 percent of the sample reported that they had heard of Dentu-Tight, there was one problem: it didn't exist! Similarly high levels of recall were reported for plausible-sounding but fictitious brands such as Four O'Clock Tea (8 percent), Leone Pasta (16 percent) and Mrs Smith's Cake Mix (31 percent). On the basis of this study, Oxtoby-Smith found that spurious awareness was around 8 percent for health and beauty products and even higher in some categories. In one case, a proposed line extension was mistakenly thought to already exist by about half of the sample (a finding that no doubt sent a message to the company that they should go ahead and introduce the product!)

The problem with spurious awareness is that it may send misleading signals about the strategic direction for a brand. For example, Oxtoby-Smith reported that one of its clients was struggling with a 5 percent market share despite the fact that 50 percent of survey respondents reported that they were aware of the brand. On the surface, it would seem that the recommended strategy would be to improve the image of the brand and attitudes towards it in some way. Upon further examination, it was determined that spurious awareness accounted for *almost half* of the survey respondents who reported brand awareness, suggesting that a more appropriate solution to the true problem would be to first build awareness to a greater degree. Marketers should be sensitive to the possibilities of misleading signals because of spurious brand awareness, especially with new brands or ones with plausible-sounding names.

Strategic implications

The advantage of aided recall measures is that they yield insight into how brand knowledge is organized in memory and what kinds of cues or reminders may be necessary for consumers to be able to retrieve the brand from memory. Understanding recall when different levels of product category specificity are used as cues is important because it has implications for how consideration sets are formed and product decisions are made by consumers.

For example, again take the case of the Porsche Boxster. Assume that recall of this particular car model was fairly low when all cars were considered but very high when European sports cars were considered. In other words, consumers strongly categorized the Porsche Boxster as a prototypical sports car but tended to think of it in only that way. If that were the case, for more consumers to entertain the possibility of buying a Boxster, it might be necessary to broaden the meaning of Porsche so that it had a stronger association with cars in general. Of course, such a strategy would run the risk of alienating existing customers who had been attracted by the 'purity' and strong identification of the Boxster as a sports car. Deciding on the appropriate strategy would depend on the relative costs and benefits of targeting the two different segments.

The important point to note is that the category structure that exists in consumers' minds – as reflected by brand recall performance – can have profound implications for consumer choice and marketing strategy, as demonstrated by Brand Briefing 9.10. The insights gleaned from measuring brand recall are also valuable for developing brand identity and integrated marketing communication campaigns, as Chapters 4 and 6 showed. For example, brand recall can be examined for each brand element to explore the extent to which any one brand element (the name, symbol, logo, etc.) suggests another brand element. In other words, is it the case that consumers are aware of all the different brand elements and understand how they relate?

In addition to obtaining a thorough understanding of brand awareness, it is important to gain a complete understanding of brand image, as covered in the following section.

Image

One vitally important aspect of the brand is its image, as reflected by the associations that consumers hold. Strong, favourable and unique associations provide the foundation for customer-based brand equity.

Brand Briefing 9.10

Understanding categorical brand recall

An experiment by Prakash Nedungadi provides a compelling demonstration of the importance of understanding the category structure that exists in consumer memory, as well as the value of strategies for increasing the recallability or accessibility of brands when choices are being made.

As a preliminary step in his study, Nedungadi examined the category structure for US fast food restaurants that existed in consumers' minds. He found that a 'major subcategory' was 'hamburger chains' and a 'minor sub-category' was 'sandwich shops'. He also found from usage and linking surveys that, within the major sub-category of national hamburger chains, a major brand was McDonald's and a minor brand was Wendy's and, within the minor sub-category of local sandwich shops, a major brand was Joe's Deli (a brand in his survey area) and a minor brand was Subway. Consistent with this reasoning, in an unaided recall and choice task, consumers were more likely to remember and select a brand from a major subcategory than from a minor sub-category and, within a sub-category, a major brand rather than a minor brand.

Nedungadi next looked at the effects of different brand 'primes' on subsequent choices of the four fast food restaurants. Brands were primed by having subjects in the experiment first answer a series of seemingly unrelated questions – including some questions about the brand to be primed – before making their brand selections. Because of this initial exposure, a target brand was 'primed' in memory and therefore potentially more accessible during the choice task. Two key findings emerged.

First, a major brand that was primed was more likely to be selected in the later choice task even though the attitudes towards the brand were no different from those of a control group. In other words, merely making the brand more accessible in memory increased the likelihood that it would be chosen *independent of any differences in brand attitude*.

Second, priming a minor brand in a minor sub-category actually benefited the *major* brand in that sub-category more. In other words, by drawing attention to the minor sub-category of sandwich shops – which could easily be overlooked – the minor brand, Subway, indirectly primed the major brand, Joe's Deli, in the sub-category. The implications of his research are that marketers must understand how consumers' memory is organized and, as much as possible, ensure that the proper cues and primes are evident to prompt brand recall.

In sum, brand recall provides insight into category structure and brand positioning in consumers' minds. Brands tend to be recalled in categorical clusters when consumers are given a general probe. Certain brands are grouped together because they share certain associations and are thus likely to cue and remind consumers of each other if one is recalled.

Sources: Prakash Nedungadi, 'Recall and consumer consideration sets: influencing choice without altering brand evaluations', *Journal of Consumer Research*, December 1990, 17: 263–76; Joseph W. Alba and J. Wesley Hutchinson, 'Dimensions of consumer expertise', *Journal of Consumer Research*, March 1987, 13: 411–54.

As noted earlier in this chapter, as well as in Chapter 2, brand associations come in many forms and can be classified in many ways. It is useful to make a distinction between lower-level considerations related to consumer perceptions of specific performance and imagery attributes and benefits versus higher-level considerations related to overall judgements, feelings and relationships. As noted in Chapter 2, there is an obvious connection between the two levels because consumers' overall responses and relationship with a brand typically depend on perceptions of attributes and benefits of that brand. This section considers some issues in measuring lower-level brand performance and imagery associations.

Beliefs are descriptive thoughts that a person holds about something (eg, a particular software package has many helpful features and menus and is easy to use).[31] Brand association beliefs are those specific attributes and benefits linked to the brand and its competitors. For example, consumers may have beliefs about Sony PlayStation video games such as 'fun and exciting', 'cool and hip', 'colourful', 'good graphic quality', 'advanced technology' and 'sometimes violent'. They may also have associations regarding the brand logo and the slogan, 'Live in your world. Play in ours.' PlayStation user imagery may be 'used by a teenager or 20-something male who is serious about playing video games, especially sports games'.

Chapter 2 provided measures to tap into performance and imagery associations. The qualitative research approaches described are useful for uncovering the different types of specific brand associations making up the brand image. To better understand their potential contribution to brand equity, the belief associations that are identified can be assessed on the basis of strength, favourability and uniqueness making up the sources of brand equity.

First, open-ended measures could be employed that tap into the strength, favourability and uniqueness of brand associations, as follows.

- What are the strongest associations you have with the brand? What comes to mind when you think of the brand? (Strength)
- What is good about the brand? What do you like about the brand? What is bad about the brand? What do you dislike about the brand? (Favourability)
- What is unique about the brand? What characteristics or features does the brand share with other brands? (Uniqueness)

To provide specific insights, these associations could be rated on scales according to strength, favourability and uniqueness, as Figure 9.19 illustrates with Lipton iced tea. (Figure 9.2 showed how degrees of strength of the associations can be represented on a mental map.)

Any potentially relevant association can and should be measured, including performance-related attributes and benefits – such as primary characteristics and supplementary features; product reliability and durability; service effectiveness, efficiency and empathy; style and design; and price – as well as imagery-related attributes and benefits related to user profiles; purchase and usage situations; brand personality and values; and history, heritage and experiences. Indirect tests also can be employed to assess the derived importance and favourability of these brand associations (eg, through multivariate regression techniques).

One methodology, brand concept maps (BCM), elicits brand association networks (brand maps) from consumers and aggregates individual maps into a consensus map.[32] With this approach, structure is added by providing survey respondents with

1. To what extent do you feel the following product characteristics are descriptive of Lipton iced tea (where 1 = strongly disagree and 7 = strongly agree)?

   _____ convenient

   _____ refreshing and thirst-quenching

   _____ real and natural

   _____ good-tasting

   _____ contemporary and relevant

   _____ used by young professionals

2. How good or bad is it for iced tea to have the following product characteristics (where 1 = very bad and 7 = very good)?

   _____ convenient

   _____ refreshing and thirst-quenching

   _____ real and natural

   _____ good-tasting

   _____ contemporary and relevant

   _____ used by young professionals

3. How unique is Lipton iced tea in terms of the following product characteristics (where 1 = not at all unique and 7 = highly unique)?

   _____ convenient

   _____ refreshing and thirst-quenching

   _____ real and natural

   _____ good-tasting

   _____ contemporary and relevant

   _____ used by young professionals

Figure 9.19   Brand association ratings in terms of strength, favourability and uniqueness

a set of brand associations that are used in the mapping stage. The mapping stage is also structured and has respondents use the brand associations provided to build an individual brand map that shows: how brand associations are linked to each other; to the brand; and how strong these linkages are. Finally, the aggregation stage is also structured as a step-by-step process for analyzing individual brand maps and uncovering the common thinking involved. Figure 9.20 displays a brand concept map for the Mayo Clinic provided by a sample of patients.

Other approaches

A more complicated quantitative technique for assessing overall brand uniqueness is multidimensional scaling, or perceptual maps. *Multidimensional scaling* (MDS) is a procedure for determining the perceived relative images of a set of objects, such as products or brands. MDS transforms consumer judgements of similarity or preference into distances represented in perceptual space. For example, if brands A and B are judged by respondents to be the most similar of a set of brands, the MDS algorithm will position brands A and B so that the distance between them in multidimensional space is smaller than the distance between any other two pairs of brands. Respondents may base their similarity between brands on any basis – tangible or intangible.[33]

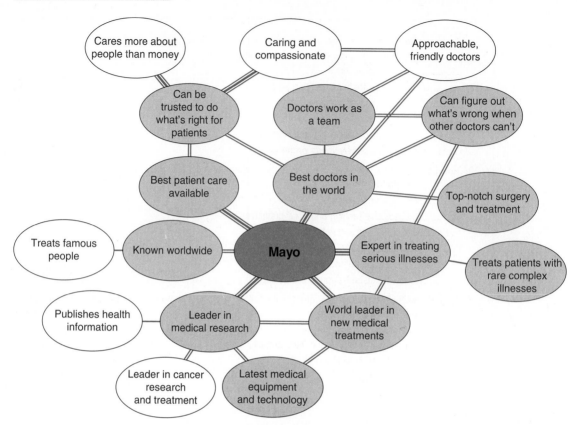

Note: N = 90 patients. The grey circles signify core associations (included on at least half of the individual maps) and the white circles signify non-core associations. The types of lines (single, double, triple) signify the intensity of the connection between brand associations.

Figure 9.20   Mayo Clinic brand concept map

European academics Jean-Noël Kapferer and Gilles Laurent have proposed a related scale to measure the brand sensitivity of a product class.[34] They characterize brand sensitivity in terms of the relationships between brands for a given consumer in a given product class, particularly with respect to comparisons between national brands versus unbranded products or private labels in that product class. The types of items in their scale are displayed in Figure 9.21. According to their approach, the strength of a brand is reflected by the number of its customers who are brand-sensitive. Brand sensitivity can be seen as a potential proxy for or measure of brand uniqueness. In other words, if consumers are not brand-sensitive for a category as a whole, it is unlikely that any one specific brand will be unique.

Brand responses

The purpose of measuring more general, higher-level considerations is to find out how consumers combine more specific, lower-level considerations about a brand in their minds to form different types of brand responses and evaluations. Chapter 2 provided examples of measures of brand judgements and feelings. Brand Briefing 9.11 provides insight into brand attitudes and judgement. Reynolds and Phillips advocate

Direct questions

Forced choice between two items

1. For PRODUCT . . .
   'I prefer to buy a well-known brand' or
   'I don't mind buying the store brand.'

Four items **measured against a Likert (five-point) scale**

1. 'When I buy a PRODUCT, I look at the brand.'
2. 'I do not choose a PRODUCT according to the brand.'
3. 'For a PRODUCT, the brand name is not that important.'
4. 'When I buy a PRODUCT, I take account of the brand.'

Indirect measures

1. A monetary measure involving three well-known brands: the last brand purchased by consumer in the product category and the first other two brands mentioned in a spontaneous brand awareness question. Would the consumer maintain his/her choice if the price differential increased by 10 percent, 25 percent, 50 percent between the chosen brand and the other two competitors?
2. A monetary measure between the last brand bought by consumer and a private label or store brand in the product category.
3. A mini-information display board choice task. Five brands and five product attributes (including brand name and price) were included in a grid and consumers were asked to choose a brand. Brand sensitivity was indicated by usage of the brand name attribute in making the choice.

Figure 9.21   Kapferer and Laurent's brand sensitivity measure

Brand Briefing 9.11

Understanding brand attitudes

There are several ways to conceptualize or model attitudes. Two such ways with clear branding implications are highlighted here. One view takes the position that consumers form attitudes because they provide a function of some kind for a person. Daniel Katz, a social psychologist, developed a functional theory of attitudes to account for the types of roles that attitudes can play. He identified four functions.

1. The *utilitarian* function deals with attitudes formed on the basis of rewards and punishments.
2. The *value-expressive* function deals with attitudes formed to express an individual's central value or self-concept.
3. The *ego-defensive* function deals with attitudes formed to protect an individual from either external threats or internal feelings of insecurity.
4. The *knowledge* function deals with attitudes formed to satisfy an individual's need for order, structure, and meaning.

Brand Briefing 9.11 *continued*

Consumers thus form attitudes towards brands to provide the function they are seeking. In this way, they might like and use certain brands because they satisfy their needs (utilitarian function), allow themselves to express their personality (value-expressive function), bolster a perceived weakness they have (ego-defensive function) or simplify decision-making (knowledge function).

Perhaps the most widely accepted approach to modelling attitudes is based on which brand attitudes are seen as a function of the associated attributes and benefits that are salient for the brand. Fishbein and Ajzen have proposed what has been probably the most influential multi-attribute model. As applied to marketing, this *expectancy-value model* views brand attitudes as a multiplicative function of:

- the salient beliefs that a consumer has about the brand (ie, the extent to which consumers think that the brand possesses certain attributes or benefits); and
- the evaluative judgement regarding those beliefs (ie, how good or bad it is that the brand possesses those attributes or benefits).

Thus, overall brand attitudes depend on the strength of association between the brand and salient attributes or benefits and the favourability of those beliefs.

According to the model, belief strength can be measured by having consumers rate the probability that the brand possesses each of the salient attributes or benefits, as follows.

How likely is it that Colgate toothpaste fights tooth decay?

Extremely unlikely   1 2 3 4 5 6 7   Extremely likely

Similarly, belief evaluations can be measured by having consumers rate the favourability of the salient attributes or benefits.

How good or bad is it that Colgate toothpaste fights tooth decay?

Very bad -3 -2 -1 0 1 2 3   Very good

Overall brand attitudes are then the sum of each attribute belief strength multiplied by its favourability. Fishbein and Ajzen also developed a theory of reasoned action to extend the multi-attribute model to include interpersonal, social effects. According to the theory, attitudes towards brands can also depend on consumers' beliefs about other people's opinions as well as consumers' motivation to comply with these other people's wishes.

Brand attitudes and judgements can vary in their strength. Attitude strength has been measured in psychology by the reaction time to evaluative queries about the attitude object: individuals who can evaluate an attitude object quickly are assumed to have a highly accessible attitude. Research has shown that attitudes formed from direct behaviour or experience are more accessible than attitudes based on information or other indirect forms of behaviour. Highly accessible brand

Brand Briefing 9.11 *continued*

attitudes are more likely to be activated spontaneously upon exposure to the brand and to guide subsequent brand choices.

Because of the embedded meaning that they contain, abstract associations such as attitudes, or even benefits to some extent, tend to be inherently more evaluative than attributes. Because of this evaluative nature, more abstract associations can be more durable and accessible in memory than the underlying attribute information. Moreover, brand attitudes may be stored and retrieved in memory separately from the underlying attribute information. In fact, academic Peter Farquhar believes that one key element of brand equity is attitude accessibility. Attitude accessibility can be measured on a computer by seeing how long it takes a consumer to indicate his or her brand evaluation ratings. Although these differences may be in microseconds, they may still be significant managerially.

Sources: Daniel Katz, 'The functional approach to the study of attitudes', *Public Opinion Quarterly*, 1960, 24: 163–204; Martin Fishbein and Icek Ajzen, *Belief, Attitude, Intention, and Behavior: An introduction to theory and research*, Reading, MA: Addison-Wesley, 1975; Icek Ajzen and Martin Fishbein, *Understanding Attitudes and Predicting Social Behavior*, Englewood Cliffs, NJ: Prentice Hall, 1980; Russell H. Fazio, David M. Sanbonmatsu, Martha C. Powell and Frank R. Kardes, 'On the automatic activation of attitudes', *Journal of Personality and Social Psychology*, February 1986, 50: 229–38; Russell H. Fazio and Mark Zanna, 'Direct experiences and attitude behavior consistency', in *Advances in Experimental Social Psychology*, Vol. 14, ed. Leonard Berkowitz, New York: Academic Press, 1981: 161–202; Ida E. Berger and Andrew A. Mitchell, 'The effect of advertising on attitude accessibility', *Journal of Consumer Research*, December 1989, 16: 280–88; Russell H. Fazio, Martha C. Powell and Carol J. Williams, 'The role of attitude accessibility in the attitude and behavior process', *Journal of Consumer Research*, December 1989, 16: 288–316; Amitava Chattopadhyay and Joseph W. Alba, 'The situational importance of recall and inference in consumer decision-making', *Journal of Consumer Research*, June 1988, 15: 1–12; John G. Lynch Jr, Howard Mamorstein and Michael Weigold, 'Choices from sets including remembered brands: use of recalled attributes and prior overall evaluations', *Journal of Consumer Research*, September 1988, 15: 169–84; Peter H. Farquhar, 'Managing brand equity', *Marketing Research*, September 1989, 1: 24–33.

a 'share-tiering' approach to measuring brand equity with four brand response constructs: relative barrier or brand price; brand quality perceptions; brand purchase loyalty; and self-report future brand purchase trend.[35]

Purchase intentions

Other measures related to brand attitudes and consideration are purchase intentions.[36] Intention measures could focus on the likelihood of buying the brand or the likelihood of switching from the brand to another. Research in psychology suggests that purchase intentions are most likely to be predictive of actual purchase when there is correspondence between the two in these categories.[37]

- Action (eg, buying for own use or to give as a gift).
- Target (eg, specific type of product and brand).

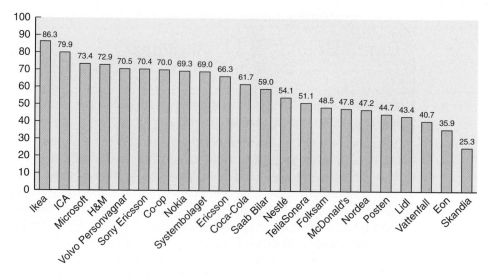

Figure 9.22   Buying intent. 'If I had the opportunity I would buy the products/services of . . .'

- Context (eg, in what type of shop based on what prices and other conditions).
- Time (eg, within a week, month or year).

In other words, when asking consumers to forecast their likely purchase of a product or a brand, it is important to specify *exactly* the circumstances involved – the purpose of the purchase, the location of the purchase, the time of the purchase and so forth. For example, consumers could be asked:

> Assume your refrigerator broke down over the next weekend and could not be inexpensively repaired. If you went to your favourite electricals shop and found all the different brands competitively priced, how likely would you be to buy an Electrolux refrigerator?'

Consumers could indicate their purchase intention on a probability scale that ranges from 0 (definitely would not buy) to 10 (definitely would buy).

The Swedish RepTrak 2006 research indicated that companies with a high reputation such as Ikea (rared at 84.9 out of 100), ICA (the market leader in food retailing 78.2), Volvo Cars (76.8), Sony Ericsson (72.7), H&M (71.8) and Microsoft (70.2) are given the highest scores regarding buying intent. At the end of the list of RepTrak 2006 companies (Figure 9.22) we found low-reputation companies such as Skandia (30.1), Lidl (35.3), Eon (41.6) and Vattenfall (47.5). Figure 9.22 indicates that companies with high reputation get high scores on buying intent.

Brand relationships

Chapter 2 characterized brand relationships in terms of resonance and offered measures on four dimensions: behavioural loyalty, attitudinal attachment, sense of community and active engagement. This section considers additional considerations with respect to those dimensions.

Behavioural loyalty and attitudinal attachment

To capture reported brand usage and behavioural loyalty, consumers could be asked questions directly. Alternatively, consumers could be asked what percentage of their last purchases in the category went to the brand (past purchase history) and what percentage of their planned next purchases will go to the brand (intended future purchases). For example, the marketers or brand managers of Fuji film might ask the following:

- Which brand of film do you usually buy?
- Which brand of film did you buy last time?
- Do you have any film on hand? Which brand?
- Which brands of film did you consider buying?
- Which brand of film will you buy next time?
- Do you expect to take pictures in the next two weeks?
- Have you taken any pictures in the last two weeks?

These types of questions can provide information on brand attitudes and usage for Fuji, including potential gaps with competitors and which other brands might be in the consideration set at the time of purchase.

These measures could be open-ended, dichotomous (forcing consumers to choose a brand) or involve multiple choice or rating scales. The answers to these types of questions also could be compared with actual measures of consumer behaviour to assess whether consumers are accurate in their predictions. For example, if 30 percent of consumers reported, on average, that they thought they would take pictures in the next two weeks, but only 15 percent of consumers reported two weeks later that they actually had taken pictures during that period, then Fuji brand managers might need to devise strategies to convert more intentions to actual behaviour.

Brand substitutability

Industry consultants Longman and Moran have developed a measure of substitutability related to brand behaviours and brand equity.[38] Their measure is based on a scale produced by the answers to two questions.

1. Which brand did you buy last time?
2. If the brand had not been available, what would you have done (ie, waited, gone to another shop or bought another brand – and, if another brand, which one)?

Based on their responses, consumers are placed into one of six segments, which are assumed to be of decreasing value for the brand.

1. People who bought your brand last time and who would have waited or gone to another shop to buy your brand.
2. People who bought your brand last time but would have accepted any other brand as a substitute.
3. People who bought your brand last time but specified a particular other brand as a substitute.
4. People who bought another brand last time but named your brand as a possible substitute.

5. People who bought another brand last time and did not name your brand as a substitute.
6. People who bought another brand last time and would have waited or gone to another shop to buy that brand.

Longman and Moran view repeat rate – how many of the people who bought a particular brand last time would buy it again this time – as a key indicator of brand equity: the higher the repeat rate, the greater the brand equity and the greater the marketing profitability; the less that people are willing to accept substitute brands, the more they are likely to buy again.

In a business-to-business setting, Narayandas advocates analyzing sales records, talking to sales teams and conducting surveys to assess where customers stand on a 'loyalty ladder'. Successively higher levels of loyalty are associated with (in ascending order):[39]

1. wanting to improve the relationship;
2. endorsing products;
3. resisting competitors' blandishments;
4. being willing to pay premiums, seeking to collaborate on product development;
5. willing to invest in partner firms.

Other brand resonance dimensions

Although attitudinal attachment may require fairly straightforward questions, both sense of community and active engagement could involve more varied measures because a more diverse set of issues may be involved. As marketing campaigns create more contact points with potential or existing customers, it will become increasingly important to assess how consumers are connecting or relating to the elements of marketing campaigns.

For example, in terms of engagement, measures could explore word-of-mouth behaviour, online behaviour and so forth. For online behaviour, measures could explore the extent of customer-initiated interactions versus firm-initiated interactions, the extent of learning and teaching by the customer versus the firm, the extent of customers teaching other customers and so on.[40] The key to such metrics is the qualitative nature of the interaction and how it reflects intensity of feelings. One mistake made by many internet firms was to put too much emphasis on 'eyeballs' and 'stickiness' – the number and duration of page views at a website, respectively. The depth of the underlying brand relationships of the customers making those visits, however, and the manner in which those relationships manifest themselves in brand-beneficial actions will typically be more important.

Fournier's brand relationship research

Susan Fournier has reframed brand personality in relationship terms.[41] Fournier views brand personality not as a set of interpersonal attributes, but as the relationship role enacted by the brand in its partnership with the consumer. She has proposed interesting ideas concerning brand equity by developing a framework for conceptualizing and understanding the relationships that consumers form with the brands they know and use.

Fournier argues that brands can and do serve as viable relationship partners and suggests a reconceptualization of the notion of brand personality within this framework. Specifically, Fournier suggests that the everyday execution of marketing mix decisions constitutes a set of behaviours enacted on the part of the brand. These actions trigger a series of inferences regarding the implicit *contract* that appears to guide the engagement of the consumer and brand and, hence, the type of relationship that is formed. Brand personality as conceptualized within this framework concerns the *relationship role* enacted by the brand in its partnership capacity. For example, if the brand expresses behaviours that signal commitment to the consumer and, further, if it sends gifts as symbols of affection, the consumer may infer a courtship or marriage-type of engagement with the brand.

Fournier identifies a typology of 15 relationship types characterizing consumers' engagement with brands (Figure 9.23). Fournier argues that this view of brand personality provides more actionable guidance to managers who wish to create and manage their brand personalities in line with marketing actions than does the trait-based view, which concerns general personality tendencies that might or might not be connected with marketing strategies and goals.

Fournier has conducted fascinating research that reframes the conceptualization and measurement of brand strength strictly in relationship terms. Here, a brand's strength is defined in terms of the strength, depth and durability of the consumer–brand relational bond using the multifaceted concept of brand relationship quality (BRQ). Extensive validation work supported a multifaceted hierarchical structure for the BRQ construct that includes six main dimensions of relationship strength, many with important sub-facets. The main facets are interdependence, self-concept connection, commitment, love/passion, intimacy and brand partner quality.

Fournier argues that these facets and their sub-facets (eg, trust within the partner quality facet or consumer-to-firm and firm-to-consumer intimacy) have superior diagnostic value over competing strength measures, and she suggests they have greater managerial utility in their application. In her experience, BRQ measures have been incorporated in brand-tracking studies, where they provide profiles of brand strength vis-à-vis competitors, useful ties to marketplace performance indicators and specific guidance for the enhancement and dilution of brand equity through managerial actions in the marketplace. Although brand relationship quality has many commonalities with brand resonance, it provides valuable additional perspectives and insights.

The main facets of brand relationship quality are as follows.

* *Interdependence:* the degree to which the brand is ingrained in the consumer's daily course of living, both behaviourally (ie, in terms of frequency, scope and strength of interactions) and cognitively (ie, in terms of longing for and preoccupation with anticipated brand interactions). Interdependence is often revealed through the presence of routinized behavioural rituals surrounding brand purchase and use and through separation anxiety experienced during periods of product deprivation. At its extremes, interdependence becomes dependency and addiction.

Relationship form	Case examples
Arranged marriage: non-voluntary union imposed by preferences of third party. Intended for long-term, exclusive commitment.	Karen's husband's preferred brands (e.g., Mop 'n Glo, Palmolive, Hellman's); Karen's Esteé Lauder, imposed through gift-giving; Jean's use of Murphy's Oil Soap as per manufacturer recommendation.
Casual friend: friendship low in affect and intimacy, characterized by infrequent or sporadic engagement and few expectations of reciprocity or reward.	Karen and her household cleaning brands.
Marriage of convenience: long-term, committed relationship precipitated by environmental influence rather than deliberate choice and governed by satisfaction rules.	Vicki's switch to regional friend's baked beans brand from favoured brand left behind; Jean's loyalty to DeMoulas salad dressing brand left behind by client at the bar.
Committed partnership: long-term, voluntarily imposed, socially supported union high in love, intimacy, trust and commitment to stay together despite adverse circumstances. Adherence to exclusivity rules expected.	Jean and virtually all her cooking, cleaning and household appliance brands; Karen and Gatorade.
Best friendship: voluntary union based on reciprocity principle, the endurance of which is ensured through continued provision of positive rewards. Characterized by revelation of true self, honesty and intimacy. Congruity in partner images and personal interests common.	Karen and Reebok running shoes; Vicki and Crest or Ivory.
Compartmentalized friendship: highly specialized, situationally confined, enduring friendship characterized by lower intimacy than other friendship forms but higher socio-emotional rewards and interdependence. Easy entry and exit.	Vicki and her stable of shampoos, perfumes and lingerie brands.
Kinship: non-voluntary union with lineage ties.	Vicki's preferences for Tetley tea or Karen's for Ban, Joy and Miracle Whip, all of which were inherited through their mothers.
Rebound relationship: union precipitated by desire to replace earlier partner, as opposed to attraction to replacement partner.	Karen's use of Comet, Gateway and Success Rice.
Childhood friendship: infrequently engaged, affective relationship reminiscent of childhood times. Yields comfort and security of past self.	Jean and Jell-O pudding.
Courtship: interim relationship state on the road to commited partnership contract.	Vicki and her Musk scent brands.

Figure 9.23   A typology of consumer–brand relationships

Relationship form	Case examples
Dependency: obsessive, highly emotional, selfish attractions cemented by feeling that the other is irreplaceable. Separation from other yields anxiety. High tolerance of other's transgressions results.	Karen and Mary Kay; Vicki and Soft 'n Dry.
Fling: short-term, time-bounded engagement of high emotional reward. Devoid of commitment and reciprocity demands.	Vicki's trial-size shampoo brands.
Enmity: intensely involving relationship characterized by negative affect and desire to inflict pain or revenge on the other.	Karen and her husband's brands, post divorce; Jean and her recommended-but-rejected brands (e.g., ham, peanut butter, sinks).
Enslavement: non-voluntary relationship union governed by desires of the relationship partner.	Karen and Southern Bell, Cable Vision. Vicki and Playtex, a bra for large-breasted women.
Secret affair: highly emotive, privately held relationship considered risky if exposed to others.	Karen and the Tootsie Pops she sneaks at work.

Figure 9.23 *Continued*

- *Self-concept connection:* the degree to which the brand delivers on important identity concerns, tasks, or themes, thereby expressing a significant part of the self-concept, both past (including nostalgic references and brand memories) and present, and personal as well as social. Grounding of the self provides feelings of comfort, connectedness, control and security. In its extreme form, self-connection reflects integration of concepts of brand and self.
- *Commitment:* dedication to continued brand association and betterment of the relationship, despite circumstances foreseen and unforeseen. Commitment includes professed faithfulness and loyalty to the other, often formalized through stated pledges and publicized intentions. Commitment is not defined solely by sunk costs and irretrievable investments that pose barriers to exit.
- *Love/passion:* affinity towards and adoration of the brand, particularly with respect to other options. The intensity of the emotional bonds joining relationship partners may range from feelings of warmth, caring and affection to those of true passion. Love includes the belief that the brand is irreplaceable and uniquely qualified as a relationship partner.
- *Intimacy:* a sense of deep familiarity with and understanding of both the essence of the brand as a partner in the relationship and the nature of the consumer–brand relationship itself. Intimacy is revealed in the presence of a strong consumer–brand relationship culture, the sharing of little-known personal details of the self, and an elaborate brand memory containing significant experiences or associations. Intimacy is a two-dimensional concept: the consumer develops intimate

knowledge of the brand, and also feels a sense of intimacy exhibited on the part of the brand towards the individual as a consumer.

- *Partner quality:* perceived partner quality involves a summary judgement of the calibre of the role enactments performed by the brand in its partnership role. Partner quality includes three components: an empathic orientation towards the other (ability of the partner to make the other feel wanted, cared for, respected, noticed and important; responsiveness to needs); a character of reliability, dependability and predictability in the brand; and trust or faith in the belief that the brand will adhere to established relationship rules and be held accountable for its actions.

COMPREHENSIVE MODELS OF CONSUMER-BASED BRAND EQUITY

The customer-based brand equity model (CBBE) presented in this text provides a comprehensive, cohesive overview of brand building and equity. Other researchers and consultants have also put forth consumer-based brand equity models that share principles with the CBBE model. Brand Briefing 9.12 presents a detailed account of arguably the most successful industry model, Young and Rubicam's Brand Asset Valuator (BAV). Other firms have introduced well-received models of brand building that provide insights into how to measure brand equity.[42]

Brand dynamics

Marketing research supplier Millward Brown's Brand Dynamics model offers a graphical way to represent the strength of the relationship consumers have with a brand. As Figure 9.24 displays, the Brand Dynamics model adopts a hierarchical approach to determine the strength of the relationship a consumer has with a

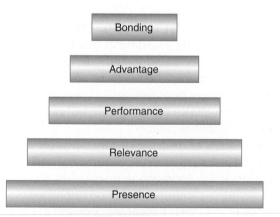

Figure 9.24   Brand Dynamics from Millward Brown

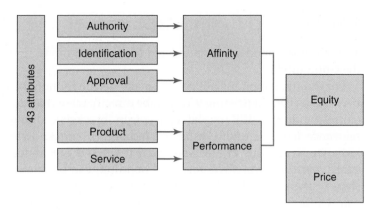

Figure 9.25   Equity Engine from Research International

brand. The five levels of the model, in ascending order of an increasingly intense relationship, are presence, relevance, performance, advantage and bonding. Consumers are placed into one of the five levels depending on their brand responses. By comparing the pattern across brands, it is easy to uncover relative strengths and weaknesess and where brands can focus their efforts to improve their loyalty relationships.

Equity engine

Another market researcher, Research International, developed the Equity Engine (Figure 9.25).[43] Its model deliniates three dimensions of brand affinity – the emotional and intangible benefits of a brand – as follows.

- *Authority:* the reputation of a brand, whether as a long-standing leader or as a pioneer in innovation.
- *Identification:* the closeness customers feel to a brand and how well they feel the brand matches their personal needs.
- *Approval:* the way a brand fits into society and the intangible status it holds for experts and friends.

The model combines affinity measures with measures of a brand's perceived functional performance to provide an assessment of overall equity. Finally, the equity measure is combined with price to provide a closer marketplace approximation of how consumers combine brand associations to make decisions.

The Equity Engine can provide diagnostic information as to what is working or not working with a brand. For example, Research International describes how an analysis of the Japanese baby food market revealed that health and nutrition were important in two ways: in terms of category membership and as a point of parity but also to provide reassurance and trust. True differentiation in this category was related to emotional issues of identification and peer acceptability, but only once the image of acceptable functional performance was firmly in place.[44]

Relationship to the CBBE model

These industry models can be related to the CBBE model and be seen as a sub-set of the CBBE model.

For example, the four pillars that make up the foundation of Young & Rubicam's BAV model (Brand Briefing 9.12) can be directly related to aspects of the CBBE model (corresponding CBBE model concept in brackets): differentiation (superiority); relevance (consideration); esteem (credibility); and knowledge (resonance). Similarly, the five stages of Millward Brown's Brand Dynamics model (presence, relevance, performance, advantage and bonding) can be related to the four ascending steps of the CBBE model (identity, meaning, responses and relationships) and specific CBBE model concepts (eg, salience, consideration, performance or quality, superiority and resonance). Finally, each of the dimensions and sub-dimensions of Research International's Equity Engine model also can be directly related to components of the CBBE model.

Thus, the CBBE model subsumes the concepts and measures from each of these industry models. At the same time, the CBBE model provides additional substance and insight. Noteworthy aspects of the CBBE model are: its emphasis on brand salience and breadth and depth of brand awareness as the foundation of brand building; its recognition of the dual nature of brands and significance of both rational and emotional considerations in brand building; and the importance it places on brand resonance as the culmination of brand building and a more meaningful way to view brand loyalty.

CHAPTER REVIEW

According to the brand value chain, sources of brand equity arise from the customer mindset. In general, measuring sources of brand equity requires that the brand manager fully understand how customers shop for and use products and services and, most important, what customers know, think and feel about brands. In particular, measuring sources of customer-based brand equity requires measuring aspects of brand awareness and brand image that potentially can lead to the differential customer response that creates brand equity.

This chapter described both qualitative and quantitative approaches to measuring consumers' brand knowledge structures and identifying potential sources of brand equity – that is, measures to capture the customer mindset. Qualitative research techniques can identify possible brand associations. Quantitative research techniques can approximate the breadth and depth of brand awareness; the strength, favourability and uniqueness of brand associations; the favourability of brand responses; and the nature of brand relationships. Because of their unstructured nature, qualitative measures are well suited to providing an in-depth glimpse of what brands and products mean to consumers. To obtain more precise and generalizable information, however, quantitative scale measures are used.

Figure 9.26 summarizes some of the measures discussed in the chapter.

Qualitative techniques

Free association.

Adjective ratings and checklists.

Projective techniques.

Photo sorts.

Bubble drawings.

Telling stories.

Personification exercises.

Role-playing.

Experiential methods.

Quantitative techniques

- Brand awareness.

   Direct and indirect measures of brand recognition.

   Aided and unaided measures of brand recall.

- Brand image.

   Open-ended and scale measures of specific brand attributes and benefits.

   Strength.

   Favourability.

   Uniqueness.

- Overall judgements and feelings.
- Overall relationship measures.

   Intensity.

   Activity.

Figure 9.26   Summary of qualitative and quantitative research methods

Brand Briefing 9.12

Young & Rubicam's Brand Asset Valuator*

Young & Rubicam's Brand Asset Valuator (BAV) is the world's largest database of consumer-derived information on brands. BAV measures brands on five measures of equity value and in terms of a broad array of perceptual dimensions. BAV provides comparative measures of the equity value of thousands of brands across hundreds of different categories, as well as a set of tools for planning brand extensions, joint branding ventures and other strategies designed to maintain brand value. BAV has also been linked to a unique set of financial analytics, which allows a brand's contribution to a company's intangible value to be determined.

Since 1993, BAV has carried out research with 500,000 consumers in 48 countries. Consumers' perceptions of 38,000 brands have been collected across 56 parameters.

BAV represents a unique brand equity research tool. Unlike most conventional surveys, respondents evaluate brands from many categories. BAV is thus able to follow global trends and to draw the broadest possible conclusions about how consumer-level brand equity is created and built – or lost. In the USA, data are collected in quarterly waves, which allows short-term trends in branding to be followed.

*This Brand Briefing includes contributions from Ed Lebar, Phil Buchler, Monika Sawicka and Ryan Barker.

Brand Briefing 9.12 *continued*

In addition to the original measures, recent BAV surveys have included greater emphasis on brand usage and future usage intent, and have also built in measures of brand loyalty.

Four Pillars

The key components of brand health in BAV are the four pillars. Each pillar is derived from various measures that relate to different aspects of consumers' brand perceptions and together trace the progression of a brand's development.

- *Differentiation:* measures the degree to which a brand is seen as different from others. This is a necessary condition for profitable brand building.
- *Relevance:* measures the breadth of a brand's appeal (the overall size of a brand's franchise) but not necessarily its profitability.
- *Esteem:* how well the brand is regarded and respected – in short, how well it's liked.
- *Knowledge:* how familiar and intimate consumers are with a brand. Interestingly, high levels of knowledge are inversely related to a brand's potential.

Leading indicators of brand health: brand strength   Differentiation (the extent to which a brand has a distinctive meaning for the consumer and is able to gain consumer choice, preference and loyalty) and relevance (which correlates with household penetration) combine to determine brand strength. These two pillars point to the brand's future value, rather than just reflecting its past.

Lagging indicators of brand health: brand stature   Esteem and knowledge together create brand stature, which is a 'report card' on a brand's past performance.

Pillar patterns   Relationships between these four dimensions – a brand's 'pillar pattern' – reveal much about a brand's current and future status. Typical pillar patterns are shown in Figure 9.27. Just after they are launched, brands show low levels on all pillars. Strong new brands tend to show higher levels of differentiation than relevance, while both esteem and knowledge are lower still. 'Leadership' brands show high levels on all four pillars. Finally, declining brands show high knowledge – evidence of past performance – relative to a lower level of esteem, and even lower relevance and differentiation.

Comparison of pillar patterns of brands – in the same or different categories – permits the diagnosis of brands' relative strengths and weaknesses, whereas tracking

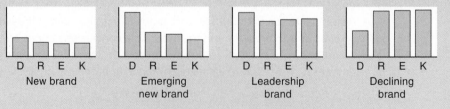

Figure 9.27   Pillar patterns

Brand Briefing 9.12 *continued*

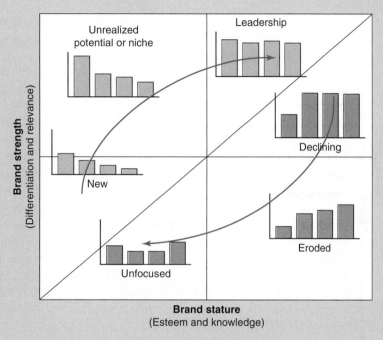

Figure 9.28   The BAV PowerGrid

changes in pillar patterns for the same brand over time traces the progress of the brand's consumer equity value.

The PowerGrid

Young & Rubicam has integrated brand strength (differentiation and relevance) and brand stature (esteem and knowledge) into a visual analytical device known as the PowerGrid (Figure 9.28). The PowerGrid depicts the stages in the cycle of brand development – each with its characteristic pillar patterns – in successive quadrants.

Brands generally begin their life in the lower left quadrant, where they first need to develop relevant differentiation and establish a reason for being.

Most often, the movement from there is 'up' into the top left quadrant. Increased differentiation, followed by relevance, initiates a growth in brand strength. These developments occur before the brand has acquired esteem or is widely known. This quadrant represents two types of brands: for brands destined for a mass target, this is the stage of emerging potential, in which the brand's growing strength must be translated into stature; specialist or narrowly targeted brands, however, tend to remain in this quadrant (when viewed from the perspective of a mass audience) and can use their strength to occupy a profitable niche. From the point of view of brand leaders, potential competitors will emerge from this quadrant.

Brand Briefing 9.12 *continued*

The upper right Leadership Quadrant is populated by brand leaders – those that have both high levels of brand strength and brand stature. Both older and relatively new brands can be in this quadrant, meaning that brand leadership is truly a function of the pillar measures, not just of longevity, and that, when properly managed, a brand can build and maintain a leadership position indefinitely. Although declining brand equity is not inevitable, brands whose strength has declined (usually driven by declining differentiation) can also be seen in this same quadrant. Brands whose strength has started to dip below the level of their stature display the first signs of weakness, which may well be masked by buoyant sales and wide penetration.

Brands that fail to maintain their brand strength – their relevant differentiation – begin to fade and move 'down' into the bottom right quadrant. These brands become vulnerable not just to existing competitors, but also to the depredations of discount price brands, and they frequently end up being drawn into heavy and continuous price promotion to defend their consumer franchise and market share. This process, if allowed to continue, takes its toll on brand stature, which also starts to decline. Figure 9.29 provides a depiction of European brands from 2005 in each of these quadrants, and Figure 9.30 shows how brand development may vary by

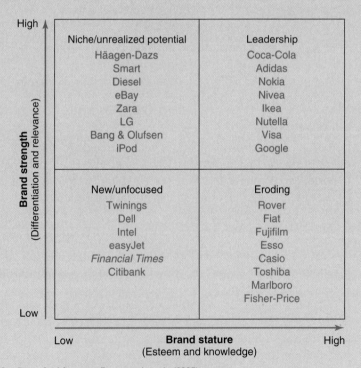

Niche/unrealized potential	**Leadership**
Häagen-Dazs	Coca-Cola
Smart	Adidas
Diesel	Nokia
eBay	Nivea
Zara	Ikea
LG	Nutella
Bang & Olufsen	Visa
iPod	Google
New/unfocused	**Eroding**
Twinings	Rover
Dell	Fiat
Intel	Fujifilm
easyJet	Esso
Financial Times	Casio
Citibank	Toshiba
	Marlboro
	Fisher-Price

Figure 9.29   PowerGrid for some European brands (2005)

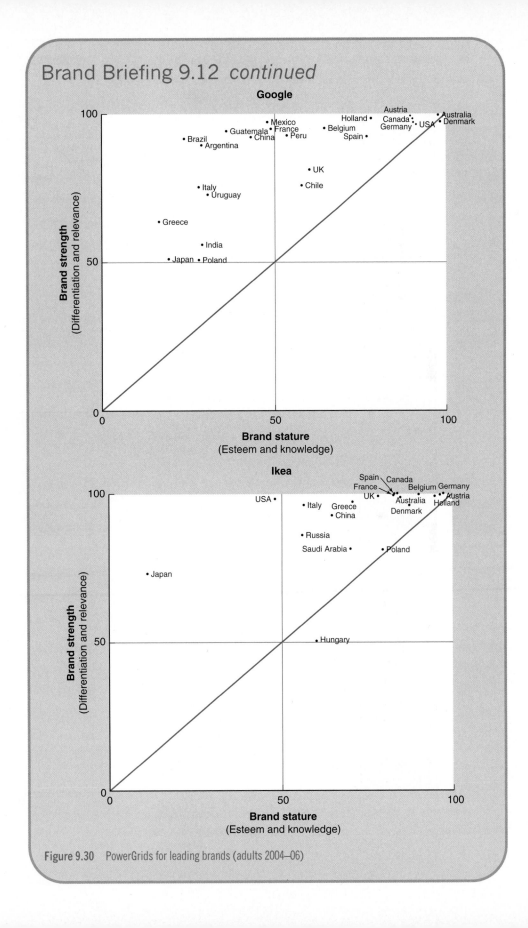

Brand Briefing 9.12 *continued*

Figure 9.30 PowerGrids for leading brands (adults 2004–06)

Brand Briefing 9.12 *continued*

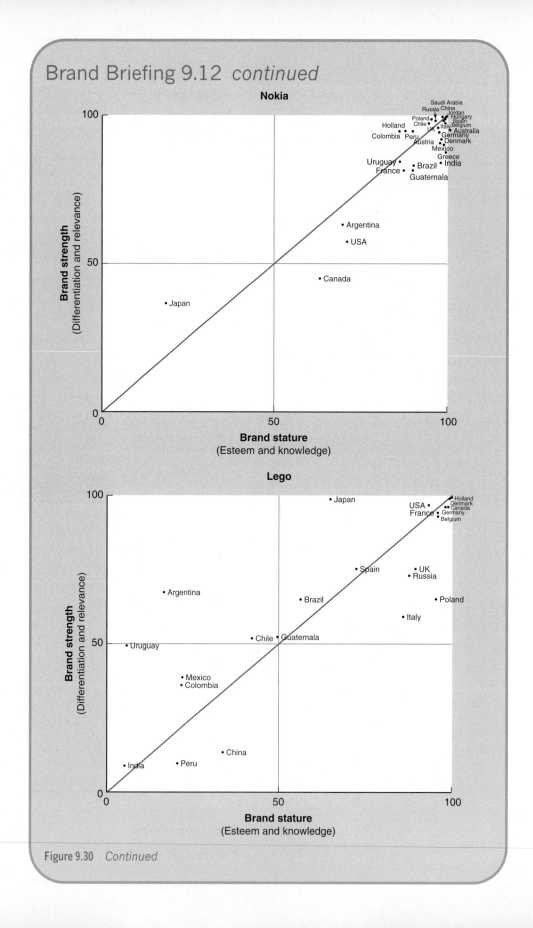

Figure 9.30   *Continued*

Brand Briefing 9.12 *continued*

Differentiation	Relevance	Esteem	Knowledge
1 Ferrari	1 National Post Office	1 Sony	1 Coca-Cola
2 Harley-Davidson	2 Sony	2 Coca-Cola	2 National Post Office
3 Porsche	3 Nokia	3 Nokia	3 Nestlé
4 Ikea	4 Duracell	4 Levi's	4 Adidas
5 Rolls-Royce	5 Coca-Cola	5 Adidas	5 Philips
6 Coca-Cola	6 Colgate	6 Duracell	6 Sony
7 Mercedes-Benz	7 Philips	7 Ferrero Rocher	7 Colgate
8 Rolex	8 Nestlé	8 BMW	8 Ferrero Rocher
9 Mon Chéri	9 Nivea	9 Nike	9 Gillette
10 Egypt	10 Adidas	10 Gillette	10 Nokia
11 Ferrero Rocher	11 Colgate-Palmolive	11 Nestlé	11 Levi's
12 BMW	12 Ferrero Rocher	12 Philips	12 Pepsi
13 Chanel	13 Milka	13 Mercedes-Benz	13 McDonald's
14 Jaguar	14 Nike	14 Nivea	14 Nivea
15 India	15 Kleenex	15 Disney	15 Kodak
16 Disney	16 Google	16 Olympic Games	16 Coke Light/Diet Coke
17 Smart	17 Levi's	17 Lego	17 Nike
18 Australia	18 Spain	18 Kodak	18 Fanta
19 Levi's	19 Kodak	19 Carte D'or (ice-cream)	19 Ford
20 Bailey's	20 Carte D'or (ice-cream)	20 Milka	20 Volkswagen

Figure 9.31   Top 20 brands in Europe

market – for example, Nokia has a much more uniform global image than, say, Lego or Google. Figure 9.31 shows the top 20 European brands in in each of these four pillars.

Brand image associations

In addition to the pillar measures, BAV measures brands against 48 brand image and brand personality attributes. Brand imagery can be analyzed in terms of all the single attributes or in terms of a reduced number of factor groupings. Because, like all BAV measures, the image attributes have been selected for their applicability to all categories, it is possible to compare the images of brands in widely differing categories. One useful technique when trying to understand a brand's positioning is to determine which other brands its image is closest to. For example, for a website or computer brand, it is helpful to know whether its image has more in common with Gap or with John Lewis.

Drivers of brand strength and stature   By analyzing the relationships between a brand's imagery on attributes and its position in the PowerGrid, it is possible to

Brand Briefing 9.12 *continued*

obtain a precise understanding of the type of imagery that drives brand strength and brand stature.

Because the BAV covers so many different categories, one of the uses of the brand image component of BAV is to examine brand *elasticity* – the ease with which a brand can be 'stretched' into a new category. According to BAV, the probability of success of such brand extensions depends on two criteria.

- *Brand profile similarity:* how similar – across all 48 attributes – is the image of the brand to the image of the brands in the target category? Does the brand have 'permission to play'? Does its image match the lowest common denominator of the target category, the imagery shared by all brands in the category and which thus represents the minimum cost of entry?
- *Does the brand have what it takes to stand out in the new category?* Although the image of the brand may have given it strong differentiation in its original category, this same imagery may not serve it so well in the new category. Does it also have necessary points of parity that would allow this differentiation to matter?

As shown in Figure 9.32, cross-analysis of these two criteria, according to Young & Rubicam, provides a clear prescription for brand extension strategies. If the brand's imagery satisfies the cost of entry for the category and also has the ability to drive differentiation, this is the clearest green light for pushing ahead.

When a brand's imagery has what it takes to create differentiation in the new category but lacks the cost of entry image characteristics, then entry into that category will not be easy, but the brand may be able to achieve an 'ambush' entry. If its differentiating

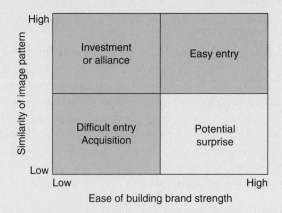

Figure 9.32   Brand elasticity

Brand Briefing 9.12 *continued*

characteristics are sufficient to overcome the barriers and gain it credibility, they will then propel it to a position of strength in the new category.

When the brand's image profile is dissimilar to the new category and its current imagery would not differentiate it in the new category, then the chances of a successful extension are low, and an entry into the category would be better accomplished via the acquisition either of a brand in the category or of one whose imagery makes it more suitable for the job.

If a brand's imagery meets the cost of entry level for the category but is lacking in drivers of differentiation, then it is clear that a successful entry can be achieved, but only with considerable investment. In this case, an option is to seek an alliance with another brand in the category: the two brands may be able to reinforce each other's strengths and jointly create a stronger presence there.

In a recent addition to the BAV, the effect on individual brands of *brand alliances* – from sweepstakes promotions to website links between brands – has been measured. The effects are various and unpredictable. For example:

- alliances between Levi's and Wal-Mart produced an improvement of the brand strength of Wal-Mart, but left Levi's virtually unchanged;
- in contrast, Levi's did benefit from an alliance with Yahoo!, growing differentiation and brand strength.

Summary

There is a lot of commonalty between the basic BAV model and the CBBE framework, as the four factors in the BAV model can be related to elements of the CBBE framework:

- BAV's knowledge relates to CBBE's brand awareness and familiarity;
- BAV's esteem relates to CBBE's favourability of brand associations;
- BAV's relevance relates to CBBE's strength of brand associations (as well as perhaps favourability);
- BAV's differentiation relates to CBBE's uniqueness of brand associations.

Note that brand awareness and familiarity are handled differently in the two approaches. The CBBE framework maintains that awareness is a necessary *first* step in building brand equity. The BAV model treats familiarity in a more affective manner – almost in a warm feeling or friendship sense – and thus sees it as the *last* step in building brand equity.

The main advantage of the BAV model is that it provides rich descriptions and profiles of many brands. It also provides focus on four dimensions. It provides a brand landscape in which marketers can see where their brands are located relative to other brands or with respect to different markets. The descriptive nature of the BAV

Brand Briefing 9.12 *continued*

model does mean, however, that there is potentially less insight as to exactly *how* a brand could rate highly on those factors. Because the measures underlying the four factors have to be relevant across many product categories, the measures (and thus the factors) tend to be abstract and not related directly to product attributes or benefits and more specific marketing concerns. Nevertheless, the BAV model represents a landmark study in terms of marketers' ability to understand what drives top brands and where their brands fit in with other brands.

Discussion questions

1. Pick a brand. Employ projective techniques to attempt to identify sources of its brand equity. Which measures work best? Why?

2. Run an experiment to see if you can replicate the Mason Haire instant coffee experiment (see Brand Briefing 9.5). Do the same attributions still hold? If not, can you replace coffee with a brand combination from another product category that would produce pronounced differences?

3. Pick a product category. Can you profile the brand personalities of the leading brands in the category using the Brandjobs personality model (see Brand Briefing 9.9)?

4. Pick a brand. How would you best profile consumers' brand knowledge structures? How would you use quantitative measures?

5. Think of your brand relationships. Can you find examples of brands that fit into Fournier's categories?

References and notes

[1]Burleigh B. Gardner and Sidney J. Levy, 'The product and the brand', *Harvard Business Review*, March–April 1955: 35.

[2]Some leading textbooks in this area are J. Paul Peter and Jerry C. Olson, *Consumer Behavior and Marketing Strategy*, 7th edn, Homewood, IL: Irwin, 2005; Wayne D. Hoyer and Deborah J. MacInnis, *Consumer Behavior*, 3rd edn, Boston: Houghton Mifflin College, 2004; and Michael R. Solomon, *Consumer Behavior: Buying, having and being*, 7th edn, Upper Saddle River, NJ: Prentice Hall, 2007.

[3]Mary Goodyear, 'Divided by a common language: diversity and deception in the world of global marketing', *Journal of the Market Research Society*, April 1996: 110–22.

[4]John Motavalli, 'Probing consumer minds', *Adweek*, 7 December 1987: 4–8.

[5]Ernest Dichter, *Handbook of Consumer Motivations*, New York: McGraw-Hill, 1964.

[6]Yvan Boivin, 'A free response approach to the measurement of brand perceptions', *International Journal of Research in Marketing*, 1986, 3: 11–17.

[7]H. Shanker Krishnan, 'Characteristics of memory associations: a consumer-based brand equity perspective', *International Journal of Research in Marketing,* October 1996: 389–405.

[8]J. Wesley Hutchinson, 'Expertise and the structure of free recall', in *Advances in Consumer Research,* Vol. 10, eds Richard P. Bagozzi and Alice M. Tybout, Ann Arbor, MI: Association of Consumer Research, 1983: 585–9.

[9]Wendy Gordon, *Goodthinking: A guide to qualitative research,* Henley-on-Thames: Admap, 1999.

[10]Sydney J. Levy, 'Dreams, fairy tales, animals and cars', *Psychology and Marketing,* 1985, 2 (2): 67–81.

[11]Mason Haire, 'Projective techniques in marketing research', *Journal of Marketing,* April 1950: 649–56. Interestingly, a follow-up study several decades later suggested that instant coffee users were no longer perceived as psychologically different from drip grind users. See Frederick E. Webster Jr and Frederick Von Pechmann, 'A replication of the "shopping list" study', *Journal of Marketing,* April 1970, 34: 61–3.

[12]Levy, 'Dreams, fairy tales'.

[13]Jeffrey Durgee and Robert Stuart, 'Advertising symbols and brand names that best represent key product meanings', *Journal of Consumer Marketing,* 1987, 4 (3): 15–24.

[14]Gerald Zaltman and Robin Higie, 'Seeing the voice of the customer: metaphor-based advertising research', *Journal of Advertising Research,* July/August 1995: 35–51; Daniel H. Pink, 'Metaphor marketing', *Fast Company,* April 1998; Gerald Zaltman, 'Metaphorically speaking', *Marketing Research,* summer 1996; www.olsonzaltman.com; Gerald Zaltman, *How Customers Think: Essential insights into the mind of the market,* Boston, MA: Harvard Business School Press, 2003; Wendy Melillo, 'Inside the consumer mind: what neuroscience can tell us about marketing', *Adweek,* 16 January 2006.

[15]For an approach to brand personality based on narrative thought processes, see Jerry Olson and Doug Allen, 'Building bonds between the brand and the customer by creating and managing brand personality', paper presented at Marketing Science Institute conference on Brand Equity and the Marketing Mix: Creating Customer Value, Tucson, AZ, 2–3 March 1995.

[16]Tony Apéria, 'Brand relationship management: den varumärkesbyggande processen', dissertations, Stockholm: Stockholm University, 2001.

[17]Aaker, 'Dimensions of brand personality.' See also Jennifer Aaker, 'The malleable self: the role of self-expression in persuasion', *Journal of Marketing Research,* 1999, 36 (2): 45–57.

[18]Jennifer L. Aaker, Veronica Benet-Martinez and Jordi Garolera, 'Consumption symbols as carriers of culture: a study of Japanese and Spanish brand personality constructs', *Journal of Personality and Social Psychology,* 2001, 81 (3): 492–508.

[19]Yongjun Sung and Spencer F. Tinkham, 'Brand personality structures in the United States and Korea: common and culture-specific factors', *Journal of Consumer Psychology,* 2005, 15 (4): 334–50.

[20]Gil Ereaut and Mike Imms, '"Bricolage"': qualitative market research redefined', *Admap,* December 2002: 16–18.

[21]Jennifer Chang Coupland, 'Invisible brands: an ethnography of households and the brands in their kitchen pantries', *Journal of Consumer Research,* 2005, 32: 106–18; Mark Ritson and Richard Elliott, 'The social uses of advertising: an ethnographic study of adolescent advertising audiences', *Journal of Consumer Research,* 1999, 26 (December): 260–77.

[22]Melanie Wells, 'New ways to get into our heads', *USA Today,* 2 March 1999: B1–B2.

[23]David Goetzel, 'O&M turns reality TV into research tool', *Advertising Age,* 10 July 2000: 6.

[24]Edward F. McQuarrie, 'Taking a road trip', *Marketing Management,* 1995, 3 (4): 9–21.

[25]David Kiley, 'Shoot the focus group', *BusinessWeek,* 14 November 2005: 120–1.

[26]Rekha Balu, 'Listen up! (it might be your customer talking)', *Fast Company*, May 2000: 304–16.

[27]www.internetworldstats.com/top25.htm

[28]Thomas K. Srull, 'Methodological techniques for the study of person memory and social cognition', in *Handbook of Social Cognition*, Vol. 2, eds Robert S. Wyer and Thomas K. Srull, Hillsdale, NJ: Lawrence Erlbaum, 1984: 1–72.

[29]Bill Abrams and David P. Garino, 'Package design gains stature as visual competition grows', *Wall Street Journal*, 6 August 1981: 25.

[30]Raymond Gordon, 'Phantom products', *Forbes*, 21 May 1984: 202–4.

[31]Philip Kotler, *Marketing Management: Analysis, planning, implementation and control*, 12 edn, Upper Saddle River, NJ: Prentice Hall, 2006.

[32]Deborah Roedder John, Barbara Loken, Kyeong-Heui Kim and Alokparna Basu Monga, 'Brand concept maps: a methodology for identifying brand association networks', Marketing Science Institute Report No. 05-112.

[33]Joseph F. Hair Jr, Rolph E. Anderson, Ronald Tatham and William C. Black, *Multivariate Data Analysis*, 4th edn, Englewood Cliffs, NJ: Prentice Hall, 1995.

[34]Jean-Noël Kapferer and Gilles Laurent, 'Consumers' brand sensitivity: a new concept for brand management', paper presented at the Annual Conference of the European Marketing Academy, 1985; Jean-Noel Kapferer and Gilles Laurent, 'Consumer brand sensitivity: a key to measuring and managing brand equity', presentation at Marketing Science Institute conference on Defining, Measuring, and Managing Brand Equity, Austin, TX, 1–3 March 1988.

[35]Thomas J. Reynolds and Carol B. Phillips, 'In search of true brand equity metrics: all market share ain't created equal', *Journal of Advertising Research*, June 2005: 171–86.

[36]J. Scott Armstrong, Vicki G. Morwitz and V. Kumar, 'Sales forecasts for existing consumer products and services: do purchase intentions contribute to accuracy?', *International Journal of Forecasting*, 2000, 16: 383–97.

[37]Icek Ajzen and Martin Fishbein, *Understanding Attitudes and Predicting Social Behavior*, Englewood Cliffs, NJ: Prentice Hall, 1980.

[38]'Longman-Moran Analytics', internal company document, unpublished.

[39]Das Narayandas, 'Building loyalty in business markets', *Harvard Business Review*, September 2005: 131–8.

[40]Vikas Mittal and Mohanbir S. Sawhney, 'Managing customer retention in the attention economy', working paper, University of Pittsburgh, 2001.

[41]Susan M. Fournier, 'Consumers and their brands: developing relationship theory in consumer research', *Journal of Consumer Research*, 1998, 24 (3): 343–73; Susan M. Fournier, 'Dimensioning brand relationships using brand relationship quality', paper presented at the Association for Consumer Research annual conference, Salt Lake City, UT, October 2000; Susan M. Fournier, Susan Dobscha and David G. Mick, 'Preventing the premature death of relationship marketing', *Harvard Business Review*, January–February: 42–51; Susan M. Fournier and Julie L. Yao, 'Reviving brand loyalty: a reconceptualization within the framework of consumer–brand relationships', *International Journal of Research in Marketing*, 1997, 14: 451–72.

[42]For a helpful review of different perspectives, see Jonathan Knowles, 'In search of a reliable measure of brand equity', *MarketingNPV*, July 2005, 2 (3).

[43]www.research-int.com

[44]Phil Sutcliffe, 'Fact or fallacy: branding realities or myths?', Research International white paper, 20 July 2000.

Measuring outcomes of brand equity: capturing market performance

Ideally, it would be possible to create a 'brand equity index' – one easily calculated number that would summarize the 'health' of a brand. But just as a thermometer provides only one indication of how healthy a person is, any one measure of brand equity provides only one indication of the health of a brand. Brand equity is complex enough that many measures are required. Having several measures increases the diagnostic power of marketing research and the likelihood that managers will better understand what is happening to their brands and, perhaps more important, why.[1]

In arguing that researchers should employ several measures of brand equity, marketing executive Richard Chay drew an interesting comparison between measuring brand equity and determining the performance of an aircraft in flight:

> The pilot of the plane has to consider a number of indicators and gauges as the plane is flown. There is the fuel gauge, the altimeter and a number of other important status indicators. All of these dials and meters tell the pilot different things about the health of the plane. There is no one gauge that summarizes everything about the plane. The plane needs the altimeter, compass, radar and the fuel gauge. As the pilot looks at the instrument cluster, he has to take all of these critical indicators into account as he flies.[2]

Chay concludes by noting that the gauges on the plane are analogous to the measures of brand equity, which are necessary to assess collectively the health of a brand.

The previous chapter described approaches for measuring brand knowledge structures and the customer mindset to be able to identify and quantify potential sources of brand equity. By applying these techniques, marketers should be able to gain a good understanding of the depth and breadth of brand awareness; the strength, favourability and uniqueness of brand associations; the nature of brand responses; and the nature of brand relationships for their brands. The customer-based brand equity (CBBE) model states that, as a consequence of creating such knowledge structures, consumers will respond more favourably to marketing activity for a brand than if the brand had not been identified to consumers. As described in Chapter 2, a product with brand equity can potentially enjoy seven customer-related benefits.

1. Be perceived differently and produce different interpretations of product performance.
2. Enjoy greater loyalty and be less vulnerable to competitive marketing actions.

3. Command larger margins and have more inelastic responses to price increases and elastic responses to price decreases.

4. Receive greater trade co-operation and support.

5. Increase marketing communication effectiveness.

6. Yield licensing opportunities.

7. Support brand extensions.

The CBBE model maintains that these benefits, and thus the value of a brand, depend on the brand knowledge and sources of brand equity. As Chapter 9 described, these individual components can be measured; however, to provide more direct estimates, their resulting value still must be estimated in some way. This chapter examines procedures to assess the effects of brand knowledge structures on these and other outcomes of interest to marketers – that is, measures that capture market performance for the brand. In doing so, marketers are able to get a much clearer picture of the value of the brand. The Brand Briefing 10.1 describes how academic researchers have explored how branding affects the consumer behaviour processes that underlie these benefits.

Brand Briefing 10.1

Understanding how brands affect consumer behaviour

Academic researchers have identified theoretical mechanisms to explain why strong brands receive a differential response from consumers. These explanations typically relate to assumptions concerning aspects of consumer behaviour in either a micro or macro sense. The mechanisms can be classified within three different stages of how brand knowledge is created and put to use by consumers: *attention and learning* – that is, the building of brand knowledge structures; *interpretation and evaluation* of marketing information or brand options – that is, the use of brand knowledge; and mechanisms that are thought to affect the *actual choice process* – that is, the application of brand knowledge. All through these stages of consumer behaviour, advantages have been documented for strong brands.

Attention and learning

Strong brands can have a memory encoding and storage advantage over unknown or weak brands in building brand awareness and image. Consumers familiar with a brand have better encoding ability and better-developed procedural knowledge. More elaborate memory structures promote the formation of linkages with new associations. Consumers can also develop a greater number of stronger links for familiar brands.

Moreover, because strong brands have better-developed brand knowledge structures in the minds of consumers, there is a greater likelihood that the links that make up this knowledge will be uniquely associated with the brand. When consumers have less-developed knowledge structures, associations may end up being stored under the product category and not the specific brand. Along those lines,

Brand Briefing 10.1 *continued*

learning can decrease for brands that are late to enter into a market because they are seen as having less novel features.

Consideration

Another advantage related to brand strength is differential inclusion of brands that are more accessible in consumers' consideration sets. The accessibility advantage for brands with more associations in a wide variety of contexts implies that strong brands are more likely to be in consumers' consideration sets. Strong brands also receive an advantage when consumers begin their search with well-known and well-regarded brands that are seen as being more likely to satisfy their needs.

Selective attention

Strong brands may find the strength of their brand affected at an involuntary level to the extent that consumers automatically encode frequency information as they are exposed to brand names, symbols, slogans and logos through marketing activity. Non-verbal information about the brand, such as symbols, slogans and logos, may be more potent or meaningful than verbal cues. Strong brands can also be given selectively more exposure, attention, comprehension and retention by consumers. Similarly, consumers may selectively allocate more attention to advertising for well-known brands.

In short, it appears that information about strong brands is more easily noticed, and the frequency of advertising of strong brands may create favourable associations even in the absence of voluntary processing of the brand information. In addition, consumers may give more selective attention to strong brands than to other brands.

Interpretation and evaluation

There is evidence for both direct and indirect mechanisms operating to create differences in how consumers interpret and evaluate brands and related marketing information.

Direct effects occur when brand-related information is input directly into the decision process. For instance, one conceptual mechanism that is moderated by differences in brand knowledge is loss aversion. With loss aversion, the losses of switching from a known brand loom larger than the potential gains from using another, lesser-known brand (eg, as the result of a price reduction). Thus, the possibility of a potential loss leads to an advantage for strong brands. Consumers may rely on the affect associated with a familiar brand to aid decision-making. The halo effects related to the positive feelings regarding a strong brand can positively bias the evaluation of advertising of the brand. Similarly, consumer confidence is another potential diagnostic cue derived from a well-developed knowledge structure. Consumer confidence is increased when consumers are more familiar in a domain. In addition, consumer confidence may lead to greater use of favourable associations

Brand Briefing 10.1 *continued*

to facilitate decision-making. In summary, consumers are likely to directly use the confidence associated with familiarity as well as affect transfer when evaluating and selecting strong brands.

Indirect effects are perhaps commoner than direct effects and are driven by uncertainty or ambiguity in the decision process. After brand information has been acquired, consumers may interpret or evaluate the information. This evaluation and enhancement may be especially critical if there are ambiguities associated with brand-related information. In general, ambiguity in making decisions favours the incumbent or stronger brand. For example, confirmation biases can lead to favourable evaluations in the presence of ambiguous information (eg, as a result of advertising). When evaluating ambiguous stimuli, the determinant of evaluative directionality is previous attitudes. With positive evaluations, cognitive evaluations should be more receptive and less critical and richer for brands with which people have more experience in more contexts. Finally, consumers may use brand names as a signal of the credibility of product claims. Thus, evaluation advantages – through more elaboration – may help strong brands to *indirectly* create even stronger and more favourable associations.

Choice

Perhaps the most frequently cited advantage for strong brands at the choice stage is the notion of brand recognition or familiarity as a choice heuristic. Essentially, when consumers have limited knowledge in a product category, the brand name may be the most accessible cue available. In addition, using a familiar brand name as a diagnostic cue is thought to be a consumer strategy for dealing with risk and uncertainty, especially when consumers have limited experience. The presence of a known brand can limit consumers' ability to detect differences in product quality across brands, even when they sample other brands. Clearly, one of the most effective mechanisms that provide advantages to strong brands is their inherent familiarity.

Source: Steven Hoeffler and Kevin Lane Keller, 'The marketing advantages of strong brands', *Journal of Brand Management*, 2003, 10 (6): 421–45.

This chapter first reviews comparative methods, which are means to assess the effects of consumer perceptions and preferences on consumer response to the marketing campaign and the specific benefits of brand equity. Next, it considers holistic methods, which attempt to come up with an estimate of the overall or summary value of a brand.[3] Some of the interplay between branding and financial considerations are included in Brand Briefing 10.4 at the end of the chapter.

COMPARATIVE METHODS

Comparative methods involve research studies or experiments that examine consumer attitudes and behaviour towards a brand to directly estimate the benefits arising from having a high level of awareness and strong, favourable and unique brand associations. There are two types of comparative methods. *Brand-based* comparative approaches use experiments in which one group of consumers responds to an element of marketing activity when it is attributed to the target brand and another group responds to that same element or activity when it is attributed to a competitive or fictitiously named brand. *Marketing-based* comparative approaches use experiments in which consumers respond to changes in elements of the marketing campaign or activity for the target brand or competitive brands.

The brand-based comparative approach holds the marketing campaign fixed and examines consumer response based on changes in brand identification, whereas the marketing-based comparative approach holds the brand fixed and examines consumer response based on changes in the marketing campaign. This section describes each of these two approaches in turn. Conjoint analysis is then described as a technique that, in effect, combines the two approaches.

Brand-based comparative approaches

As a means of measuring the outcomes of brand equity, brand-based comparative approaches hold the marketing element or activity under consideration fixed and examine consumer response based on changes in brand identification. These approaches typically employ experiments in which one group of consumers responds to questions about the product or some aspect of its marketing campaign when it is attributed to the brand and one or more groups of consumers respond to the same product or aspect of the marketing campaign when it is attributed to other brand or brands, typically a fictitiously named or unnamed version of the product or service or one or more competitive brands. Comparing the responses of the two groups provides some insights into the equity of the brand. Consumer responses may be based on beliefs, attitudes, intentions or actual behaviour.

Competitive brands can be benchmarks in brand-based comparative approaches. Although consumers may interpret marketing activity for a fictitiously named or unnamed version of the product or service in terms of their general product category knowledge (eg, by assuming prototypical product or service specifications and price, promotion and distribution strategies for the anonymous entry in the category), they may also have a particular brand, or exemplar, in mind. This exemplar may be the category leader or some other brand that consumers feel is representative of the category (eg, their most preferred brand). Inferences for any missing information may be made based on their knowledge of this particular brand in memory. Thus, it may be instructive to examine how consumers evaluate a proposed ad campaign, promotion offering or new product when it is also attributed to one or more rivals.

Applications

The classic example of the brand-based comparative approach is 'blind testing' studies in which consumers examine or use a product with or without brand identification. For example, recall the beer taste test from Chapter 2, which showed how dramatically consumers' perceptions differed depending on the presence or absence of brand identification. Thus, one natural application of the brand-based comparative approach is with product purchase or consumption, as long as the brand identification can be hidden in some way for the 'unbranded' control group. Products could be existing ones or proposed extensions. Brand-based comparative approaches are also useful to determine brand equity benefits related to price margins and premiums.

T-Mobile

Deutsche Telecom has invested much time and money in building its T-Mobile mobile communication brand. In the UK, however, the company leases its network lines to competitor Virgin Mobile. As a result, the audio quality of the signal that a T-Mobile customer receives in making a call should be identical to the audio quality of the signal for a Virgin Mobile customer. After all, the same network is being used to send the signal. Despite that fact, research has shown that Virgin Mobile customers rate their signal quality significantly higher than those of T-Mobile. The strong Virgin brand image appears to cast a halo over its service offerings, causing consumers to change their impressions of product performance.

Critique

The main advantage of a brand-based comparative approach is that, because it holds all aspects of the marketing campaign fixed for the brand, it isolates the value of a brand. Understanding exactly how knowledge of the brand affects consumer responses to prices, advertising and so forth is extremely useful in developing strategies in these areas. At the same time, an almost infinite variety of marketing activities could potentially be studied, so the totality of what is learned will depend on how many applications are examined.

Brand-based comparative methods are particularly applicable when the marketing activity under consideration represents a change from past marketing of the brand, for example, a new sales or trade promotion, ad campaign or proposed brand extension. If the activity under consideration is strongly identified with the brand (eg, an ad campaign that has been running for years), it may be difficult to attribute some aspect of the marketing campaign to a fictitiously named or unnamed version of the product or service in a believable fashion.

Thus, a crucial consideration with the brand-based comparative approach is the experimental realism that can be achieved when some aspect of a marketing campaign is attributed to a fictitiously named or unnamed version of a product or service. Some realism will need to be sacrificed to gain sufficient control for isolating the effects of brand knowledge. Detailed concept statements of the activity under consideration can be employed in situations when it may otherwise be difficult for consumers to examine or experience that element of the marketing campaign without being aware of the brand.

Thus, concept statements may be useful in assessing customer-based brand equity when consumers make some type of product evaluation or respond to a proposed price or distribution change. For example, consumers could be asked to judge a proposed product when it is either introduced by the firm as a brand extension or introduced by an unnamed firm in that product market. Similarly, consumers could be asked acceptable price ranges and shop locations for the brand name product or a hypothetical unnamed version. Nevertheless, a concern with brand-based comparative approaches is that the simulations and concept statements used may highlight those particular characteristics that are mentioned or featured and make them more salient than they would otherwise be, distorting the results.

Marketing-based comparative approaches

Marketing-based comparative approaches hold the brand fixed and examine consumers' responses based on changes in the marketing campaign.

Applications

There is a long tradition of exploring price premiums using marketing-based comparative approaches. In the mid-1950s, Edgar Pessemier developed a monetary measure of brand commitment that involved a step-by-step increase of the price difference between the brand normally purchased and another brand.[4] Pessemier plotted the percentage of consumers who switched from their usual brand as a function of price increases to reveal brand-switching and loyalty patterns. Variations of this approach have been adopted by marketing researchers to derive similar types of demand curves, and many companies now try to assess price sensitivity and thresholds for brands. For example, Intel routinely surveys computer shoppers to find out how much of a discount they would require before switching to a personal computer that did not have an Intel microprocessor in it or, conversely, what premium they would be willing to pay to buy a personal computer with an Intel chip.

Marketing-based comparative approaches can be applied in other ways. Consumers' responses to different advertising strategies, executions or media plans can be assessed through multiple test markets. For example, IRI's electronic test markets (see Brand Briefing 6.2) and other such methodologies can permit tests of advertising weights or repetition schedules as well as ad copy tests. By controlling other factors, the effects of a brand and product can be isolated. Recall from Chapter 2 how Anheuser-Busch conducted test markets that revealed its beer had such a strong image with consumers that advertising could be cut, at least in the short run, without hurting sales.

Potential brand extensions can also be explored by collecting consumer evaluations of a range of concept statements describing brand extension candidates. For example, Figure 10.1 gives the results of a consumer survey examining reactions from a survey in the late 1990s to possible extensions of the Planter's nuts brand in the USA. Contrasting those extensions of which consumers approve with those of which they disapprove provides some indication of the equity of the brand involved. In this example, the results would seem to suggest that consumers expected any Planter's

Average scale rating*	Proposed extensions
10	Peanuts
9	Snack mixes, nuts for baking
8	—
7	Pretzels, chocolate nut confectionery, caramel popcorn
6	Snack crackers, potato crisps, nutritional granola bars
5	Tortilla chips, toppings (ice-cream/dessert)
4	Lunch snack packs, dessert mixes (biscuit/cake/brownie)
3	Ice-cream/ice-cream bars, toppings (salad/vegetable)
2	Cereal, toaster pastries, oriental starters/sauces, stuffing mix, refrigerated dough, jams/jellies
1	Yogurt

*Consumers rated proposed extensions on a scale from 0 (definitely would not expect Planter's to sell it) to 10 (definitely would expect Planter's to sell it).

Figure 10.1   Reactions to proposed Planter's extensions

brand extension to be 'nut-related'. Appropriate product characteristics for a possible Planter's brand extension would seem to be 'crunchy', 'sweet', 'salty', 'spicy' and 'buttery'. In terms of where in a shop consumers would expect to find Planter's products, the snack and confectionery sections seem most likely. On the other hand, consumers do not seem to expect to find Planter's products in the breakfast food aisle, baking products section, refrigerated section or frozen food section. Consistent with these results, besides selling peanuts, mixed nuts, cashews, almonds and baking nuts, Planters now sells trail mix, peanut bars and chocolate-covered nuts.

Critique

The main advantage of the marketing-based comparative approach is the ease of implementation. Almost any proposed set of marketing actions can be compared for the brand. At the same time, the main drawback of the approach is that it may be difficult to discern whether consumer responses to changes in marketing stimuli are being caused by brand knowledge or more generic product knowledge. In other words, it may be that, for any brand in the product category, consumers would be willing or unwilling to pay certain prices, accept a particular brand extension and so forth. One way to determine whether consumers' responses are specific to the brand is to conduct similar tests of their responses with competing brands. A statistical technique well suited to doing just that is described next.

Conjoint analysis

Conjoint analysis is a survey-based multivariate technique that enables marketers to profile the consumer decision process with respect to products and brands.[5]

Specifically, by asking consumers to express preferences or make choices between carefully designed product profiles, marketing researchers can determine the trade-offs consumers are making between brand attributes and thus the importance they attach to those attributes.[6] Each profile shown to consumers is made up of a set of attribute levels. Particular attribute levels for any one profile are chosen on the basis of experimental design principles to satisfy certain mathematical properties. The value that consumers attach to each attribute level, as statistically derived by the conjoint formula, is called a *part worth*. The part worths can be used to estimate how consumers would value a new combination of the attribute levels.

In particular, one attribute that can be included is the brand name. The part worth for the 'brand name' attribute would then reflect its value. One classic study of conjoint analysis was reported by Green and Wind.[7] This study concerned consumers' evaluations of a spot-remover product. Five attributes were studied: packaging design, brand name, price, *Good Housekeeping* magazine approval and money back guarantee. Figure 10.2 contains the 18 profiles that made up the experimental design. Figure 10.3 shows the results of the statistical analyses to determine the part worths.

Applications

Conjoint analysis has a number of possible applications. Ad agency Ogilvy & Mather has used a brand/price tradeoff methodology to assess advertising effectiveness and brand value.[8] Brand/price tradeoff is a simplified version of conjoint measurement with just two variables – brand and price. Consumers are faced with simulated purchase choices between combinations of brands and prices. Each choice triggers an increase in the price of the selected brand, forcing the consumer to choose a preferred brand and paying less. In this way, consumers reveal how much their brand loyalty is worth and, conversely, which brands they would relinquish for a lower price.

Other variations and applications of conjoint analysis have been used by researchers with an interest in brand image and equity.[9] For example, Rangaswamy, Burke and Oliva use conjoint analysis to explore how brand names interact with physical product features to affect the extendability of brand names to other product categories.[10] Barich and Srinivasan apply conjoint analysis to corporate image campaigns to show how it can be used to determine the company attributes that are relevant to customers, rank the importance of those attributes, estimate the costs of making improvements (or correcting customer perceptions) and prioritize image goals so that the improvements in perceptions obtain the maximum benefit, in terms of customer value, for the resources spent.[11]

Critique

The main advantage of the conjoint approach is that it allows for different brands and different aspects of the product or marketing campaign (product composition, price, distribution outlets, etc.) to be studied simultaneously. Thus, information about consumers' responses to different marketing activities can be uncovered for both the focal and competing brands. One of the disadvantages of conjoint analysis is

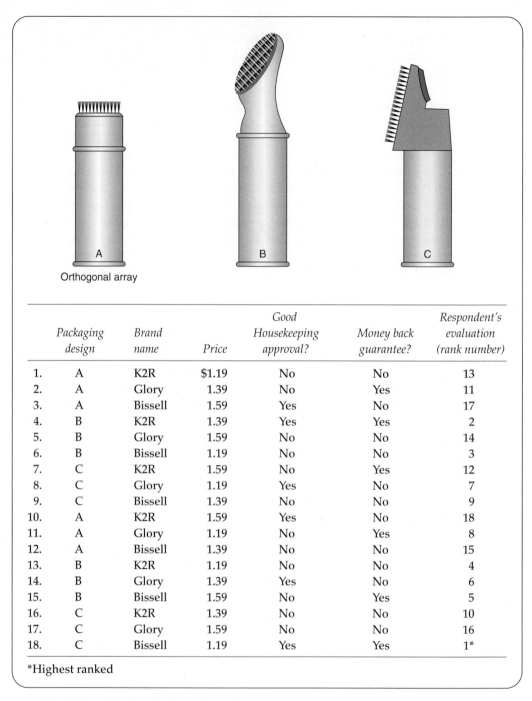

Orthogonal array

	Packaging design	Brand name	Price	Good Housekeeping approval?	Money back guarantee?	Respondent's evaluation (rank number)
1.	A	K2R	$1.19	No	No	13
2.	A	Glory	1.39	No	Yes	11
3.	A	Bissell	1.59	Yes	No	17
4.	B	K2R	1.39	Yes	Yes	2
5.	B	Glory	1.59	No	No	14
6.	B	Bissell	1.19	No	No	3
7.	C	K2R	1.59	No	Yes	12
8.	C	Glory	1.19	Yes	No	7
9.	C	Bissell	1.39	No	No	9
10.	A	K2R	1.59	Yes	No	18
11.	A	Glory	1.19	No	Yes	8
12.	A	Bissell	1.39	No	No	15
13.	B	K2R	1.19	No	No	4
14.	B	Glory	1.39	Yes	No	6
15.	B	Bissell	1.59	No	Yes	5
16.	C	K2R	1.39	No	No	10
17.	C	Glory	1.59	No	No	16
18.	C	Bissell	1.19	Yes	Yes	1*

*Highest ranked

Figure 10.2   Product profiles for conjoint analysis application

that marketing profiles may be presented to consumers that violate their expectations based on what they know about brands. Thus, if conjoint analysis is employed, care must be taken that consumers do not evaluate unrealistic product profiles or scenarios. Additionally, it can be difficult to specify and interpret brand attribute levels, although there are guidelines for its use.[12]

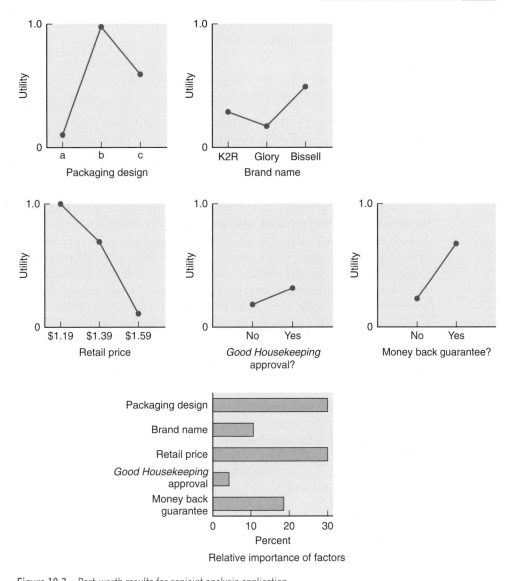

Figure 10.3   Part-worth results for conjoint analysis application

HOLISTIC METHODS

Comparative methods attempt to approximate specific benefits of brand equity. *Holistic methods* aim to place an overall value on a brand in either abstract utility terms or concrete financial terms. Thus, holistic methods attempt to 'net out' various considerations to determine the unique contribution of the brand. The *residual approach* attempts to examine the value of the brand by subtracting consumers' preferences for the brand based on physical product attributes alone from their overall brand preferences. The *valuation approach* attempts to place a financial value on brand equity for accounting purposes, mergers and acquisitions or other such reasons. This section describes these approaches.

Residual approaches

The rationale behind residual approaches is that brand equity is what remains of consumer preferences and choices after subtracting physical product effects. A tenet of these approaches is that it is possible to infer the relative valuation of brands through the observation of consumer preferences and choices *if* as many sources of measured attribute values are taken into account as possible. Specifically, researchers have defined brand equity as the incremental preference over and above that which would result for the product without brand identification. According to this view, brand equity would then be calculated by attempting to subtract preferences for objective characteristics of the physical product from overall preference.[13]

Kamakura and Russell propose a measure that employs consumer purchase histories from supermarket scanner data to estimate brand equity through a residual approach.[14] Specifically, their model attempts to explain the choices observed from a panel of consumers as a function of the shop environment (actual shelf prices, sales promotions, displays, etc.), the physical characteristics of available brands and a residual term dubbed 'brand equity'. By controlling for other aspects of the marketing mix, their approach attempts to estimate that aspect of brand preference unique to a brand. Swait, Louviere and colleagues have proposed a related approach to measuring brand equity that designs choice experiments that account for brand names, product attributes, brand image and differences in consumer socio-demographic characteristics and brand usage.[15] They define the *equalization price* as the price that equates the utility of a brand to the utilities that could be attributed to a brand in the category where no brand differentiation occurred. Equalization price can be seen as a proxy for brand equity.[16]

Srinivasan, Park and Chang have proposed a comprehensive residual methodology to measure brand equity based on the multi-attribute attitude model.[17] Their approach reveals the relative sizes of bases of brand equity by dividing brand equity into three components: brand awareness, attribute perception biases and non-attribute preference. The *attribute perception-biased component* of brand equity is the difference between subjectively perceived attribute values and objectively measured attribute values. Objectively measured attribute values can be collected from independent testing services such as the US magazine *Consumer Reports* or experts in the field. The *non-attribute preference component* of brand equity is the difference between subjectively perceived attribute values and overall preference and reflects the consumer's configural appraisal of a brand that goes beyond the assessment of the utility of individual product attributes. They also incorporate the effects of enhancing brand awareness and preference on consumer 'pull' and the brand's availability. They propose a survey procedure to collect information to estimate these perception and preference measures.

Dillon and his colleagues have presented a model for decomposing ratings of a brand on an attribute into two components: brand-specific associations (ie, features, attributes or benefits that consumers link to a brand); and general brand impressions (ie, overall impressions based on a more holistic view of a brand).[18] A variation on this approach has been proposed by Ailawadi, Lehmann and Neslin.[19] As opposed to survey data, they use retail sales data to calculate a 'revenue premium' as an estimate of brand equity by calculating the difference in revenues between a brand and a generic or private label in its same category.

Critique

Residual approaches provide a benchmark for interpreting brand equity. In particular, they may be useful for situations in which approximations of brand equity are necessary and thus may also be valuable to researchers interested in a financially orientated perspective. The disadvantage of these approaches is that they are most appropriate for brands characterized by a predominance of product-related attribute associations because they are unable to distinguish between non-product-related attribute associations. Consequently, the residual approach's diagnostic value for strategic decision-making in other cases is limited.

More generally, note that this approach takes a static view of brand equity by attempting to identify sources of consumer preferences to uncover the contribution by the brand. This approach contrasts sharply with the 'process' view advocated by the customer-based brand equity framework, as reflected by the brand-based and marketing-based comparative approaches, which stress looking at consumers' responses to the marketing of a brand and attempting to uncover the extent to which that *response* is affected by brand knowledge. Consumers' responses are defined in terms of perceptions, preferences and behaviours and, most important, with respect to a variety of marketing activities. That is, the CBBE framework goes beyond attempting to dissect consumer preferences to the product itself to assess how consumers respond to the marketing of a brand and, especially, new marketing activity supporting it.

This distinction is also relevant for the issue of 'separability' in brand valuation raised by researchers. For example, Barwise and his colleagues note that marketing efforts to create an extended or augmented product (eg, extra features or service plus other means to enhance brand value) 'raise serious problems of separating the value of the brand name and trademark from the many other elements of the 'augmented' product'.[20] According to customer-based brand equity, those efforts could affect the favourability, strength and uniqueness of various brand associations, which would, in turn, affect consumer response to *future* marketing activities. For example, imagine that a brand becomes known for providing extraordinary customer service because of certain policies and favourable advertising, publicity or word of mouth (eg, as with Nordstrom department stores or Singapore Airlines). These favourable perceptions of customer service and the favourable attitudes they engender could create customer-based brand equity by affecting consumers' responses to a price policy (eg, a willingness to pay higher prices), a new ad campaign (eg, the acceptance of an ad illustrating customer satisfaction) or a brand extension (eg, interest in trying a new retail outlet).

Valuation approaches

For many companies, the bulk of their value may be wrapped up in a brand. For example, *Forbes* magazine noted that, although PepsiCo has a net tangible book value of only €4.4 billion, it has a market value or cap of over $90 billion, with brands esti- mated as making up 70 percent of its intangible assets or more than €34.2 billion.[21] The ability to value a brand may be useful for a number of reasons.

- *Mergers and acquisitions:* both to evaluate possible purchases as well as to facilitate disposal.
- *Brand licensing:* internally for tax reasons and to third parties.
- *Fundraising:* as collateral on loans or for sale or leaseback arrangements.
- *Brand management decisions:* to allocate resources, develop brand strategy or prepare financial reports.

For example, many companies appear as attractive acquisition candidates because of the strong competitive positions of their brands and their reputation with con- sumers. Unfortunately, the value of the brand assets in many cases is largely ex- cluded from a company's balance sheet and therefore of little use in determining overall value. As one commentator put it:

> The worth of a strong brand is rarely represented fully in a company's stock price. It doesn't appear on a balance sheet. But it's the motor behind the num- bers, the fuel that drives consumers to the marketplace and helps them make choices.[22]

It has been argued that adjusting the balance sheet to reflect the true value of a com- pany's brands permits a more realistic view and allows assessment of the purchase premium to book value that might be earned from brands after acquisition. Such a calculation, however, would require estimates of capital required by brands and the expected post-acquisition return on investment (ROI) of a company.

Separating out the percentage of revenue or profits that is attributable to brand equity is difficult.[23] In the USA, there is no conventional accounting method for doing so. Thus, despite the fact that expert analysts estimate the value of the Coca-Cola name to approach €45.8 billion, it appears in the owner's books as only €17.1 *million*. Based on accounting rules, Coca-Cola's assets in 2004 had a book value of €21.4 billion, with various intangible assets assessed at €2.6 billion and a market cap of €68.4 billion. Clearly, market-based estimates of value can differ dramatically from those based on US accounting conventions.[24] In other countries, however, there has been more move- ment in the direction of attempting to capture that value. How do you calculate the financial value of a brand? This section, after providing some accounting background and historical perspective, describes the leading brand valuation approach.[25]

Accounting background

The assets of a company can be classified as either tangible or intangible. *Tangible as- sets* include property, plant and equipment; current assets (inventories, marketable securities and cash); and investments in stocks and bonds. The value of tangible as- sets can be estimated using accounting book values and reported estimates of re- placement costs. Intangible assets, on the other hand, are defined as any factors of production or specialized resources that permit the company to earn cash flows in excess of the return on tangible assets. In other words, intangible assets augment the earning power of a firm's physical assets. *Intangible assets* are typically lumped by accountants under the heading of goodwill and include things such as patents, trade-marks and licensing agreements, as well as 'softer' considerations such as the skill of management and customer relations.

In an acquisition, the goodwill item often includes a premium paid to gain control, which, in certain instances, may even exceed the value of tangible and intangible assets. Despite these intangibles being so disparate in nature, they are all swept together under the term *goodwill*. In Britain and certain other countries, it has been common to write off the goodwill element of an acquisition against reserves; tangible assets, however, are transferred straight to the acquiring company's balance sheet.

Historical perspectives

Brand valuation's recent past started with Rupert Murdoch's News Corporation, which included a valuation of some of its magazines on its balance sheets in 1984, as permitted by Australian accounting standards. The rationale was that the goodwill element of publishing acquisitions – the difference in value between net assets and the price paid – was often enormous and damaging the balance sheet. The recognition that the titles themselves contained much of the value of the acquisition was used to justify placing them on the balance sheet, improving the debt/equity ratio as a result and allowing the News Corporation to get some much-needed cash to finance buying foreign media companies.

In the UK, drinks group Grand Metropolitan was one of the first British companies to place a monetary value on the brands it owned and to put that value on its balance sheet. When Grand Met acquired Heublin distributors, Pearle eye care and Sambuca Romana liqueur in 1987, it placed the value of some of its brands – principally Smirnoff – on the balance sheet for roughly €684 million. In doing so, Grand Met used one of two methods. If a company consisted of primarily one brand, it figured that the value of the brand was 75 percent of the purchase price, whereas if the company had many brands, it used a multiple of an income figure.

British firms used brand values primarily to boost their balance sheets. By recording their brand assets, the firms maintained that they were attempting to bring their shareholder funds nearer to the market capitalization of the firm. In the UK, Rank Hovis McDougal (RHM) succeeded in putting the worth of the company's brands as a figure on the balance sheet to fight a hostile takeover bid in 1988. With the brand value information provided by Interbrand (via a method described later in this chapter), the RHM board was able to go back to investors and argue that the bid was too low and to repel it.

Accounting firms in favour of valuing brands argue that it is a way to strengthen the presentation of a company's accounts, to record hidden assets so that they are disclosed to company's shareholders, to enhance a company's shareholders' funds to improve its earnings ratios, to provide a realistic basis for management and investors to measure a company's performance and to reveal detailed information on brand strengths so that management can formulate appropriate brand strategies. In practical terms, however, recording brand value as an intangible asset is a way to increase the asset value of a firm.

Practices have varied from country to country. Brand valuations have been accepted for inclusion on the balance sheets of companies in countries such as the UK,

Australia, New Zealand, France, Sweden, Singapore and Spain. When UK group Grand Metropolitan acquired Pillsbury for €3.7 billion in January 1989, it revalued Pillsbury's intangible assets to add €1.6 billion to its intangible assets. Unlike a US company, Grand Met did not intend to write down those intangible assets (unless permanently impaired). Grand Met also adjusted its goodwill account (separate from intangible assets) by a substantial amount as a result of the Pillsbury acquisition.[26]

In the UK, Martin Sorrell improved the balance sheet of WPP by attaching brand value to its primary assets, including J. Walter Thompson Company, Ogilvy & Mather and Hill & Knowlton, stating in an annual report that:

> Intangible fixed assets comprise certain acquired separable corporate brand names. These are shown as a valuation of the incremental earnings expected to arise from the ownership of brands. The valuations have been based on the present value of notional royalty savings arising from [ownership] and on estimates of profits attributable to brand loyalty.[27]

In the USA, generally accepted accounting principles mean that placing a brand on the balance sheet would require amortization of that asset for up to 40 years. Such a charge would severely hamper profitability; as a result, companies avoid such accounting manoeuvres. However, other countries (including Canada, Germany and Japan) have gone beyond tax deductibility of brand equity to permit some or all of the goodwill arising from an acquisition to be deducted for tax purposes.

General approaches

For determining the value of a brand in an acquisition or merger, there are cost, market and income approaches.[28]

The cost approach maintains that brand equity is the amount of money that would be required to reproduce or replace the brand (including all the costs of research and development, test marketing, advertising, etc.). One criticism of approaches involving historic or replacement cost is that this rewards past performance in a way that may bear little relation to future profitability – for example, many brands with expensive introductions have been unsuccessful. Equally, for brands that have been around for decades (such as Heinz, Kellogg's and Chanel), it would be almost impossible to find out what the investment in brand development was – and largely irrelevant. Finally, it obviously is easier to estimate costs of tangible assets than intangible assets, but the latter often may lie at the heart of brand equity. Similar problems exist with a replacement cost approach – for example, the cost of replacing a brand depends a great deal on how quickly the process would take and what competitive, legal and logistical obstacles might be encountered.

According to the market approach, brand equity can be thought of as the present value of the future economic benefits to be derived by the owner of the asset. In other words, it is the amount an active market would allow such that the asset would exchange between a willing buyer and willing seller. The main problems with this approach are the lack of open market transactions for brand name assets and the fact that the uniqueness of brands makes extrapolating from one market transaction to another problematic. Brand Briefing 10.2 reviews considerations in the relationship of brand equity to the stock market.

Brand Briefing 10.2

What is a brand worth?

Brandmetrics is a 'no-frills' valuation methodology that arose from academic work in South Africa (Figure 10.4). The model is based on the premise that the definition of an asset given by accountants – ie, resources under the control of an enterprise that will generate economic benefits for the enterprise – applies to brands. The BrandMetrics model was conceived to bring two concepts together: the accounting definition of an asset and the marketing presumption that brands generate economic benefits.

Conceptualizing brand equity as the 'incremental cash flows that accrue to a branded as compared with a non-branded product', researchers set out to distinguish the financial structure of the brand that belongs to the non-branded and branded portions by using the concept of economic profit. Economic profit is understood to be the amount of after-tax, operating profit that a company earns which exceeds the cost of the capital the company has employed in operating the business.

The BrandMetrics approach therefore starts with a calculation of the economic profit on the basis that a normal company (or unbranded product) would earn no more than the cost of capital. The excess profit over and above the cost of capital is attributable to resources that must be identified. Among these are the brand and its customers. A BrandMetrics valuation requires income statement and balance sheet data for each brand being valued. Because this is not always available, accounting techniques of allocation have been adopted.

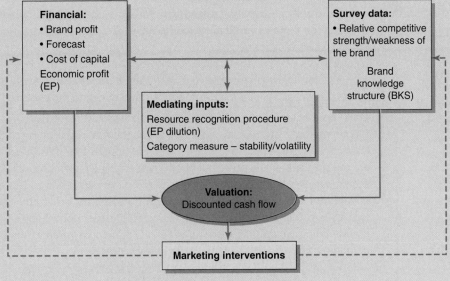

Figure 10.4   The valuation flowchart

Brand Briefing 10.2 *continued*

A technique borrowed from actuarial science is then applied to figure out what proportion of the economic profit can be ascribed to the brand. Resource recognition procedure (RRP) is based on the Delphi forecasting technique. A gathering of experts from within the company representing the functions in the firm are subjected to a three-hour session controlled by a trained facilitator. Using spreadsheets to capture and analyze the data as it comes in, the group is taken through at least four rounds of analysis.

In the first round, an exhaustive list of resources that might drive economic profit is generated and projected on a screen. Through an iterative process during which group members vote, rank and rate the resources, the list is reduced. Typically, there will be consensus on a final five to eight items. Each member then allocates 100 percent across the final resources and the scores are averaged to give a weighting to each. Finally, each member allocates a score from a scale from zero to ten to indicate the extent to which brand equity influences each resource.

The mean, weighted scores are summed to produce a percentage that, when applied to the economic profit, produces the brand premium profit (BPP) or the portion attributable to the brand. BrandMetrics does not limit the projection of the brand profits to a set number of years. Due to the algorithms that support the model, each brand is uniquely modelled to represent its relative strength in numbers of years of economic expected life. Two devices are used to calculate this.

- *Category expected life analysis:* because the ability of a brand to sustain profits is a function of the category in which it trades, BrandMetrics evaluates these according to four variables: longevity (category maturity); leadership (market share stability of volatility); barriers and churn (competitive activity); and vulnerability (external forces). Each is examined in detail and scored on a five-point scale. When multiplied, the set values behind each score produce numbers of years out of 40 for a notional dominant brand; and out of 10 for a notional marginal brand.[29] Thus, each category is defined by a number of years of economic expected life.

- *Brand knowledge structure (BKS) analysis:* consistent with the CBBE model, BKS is a function of both awareness and associations. Market research is used to establish levels of awareness and brand associations for each brand in the category. These are reduced to a single score out of 100 percent. The highest scores and the lowest scores achieved by any brand in the category are computed to represent the notional dominant and marginal brands and these scores are mathematically transformed into the years of economic expected life described above. Scores for the brands being valued are then converted by the same method thus producing a unique number of years for the brand being measured.

Each brand has a franchise run (the years closest to the base year of the valuation) and a decay phase. Thus the marketing task is to ensure that the total number of

Brand Briefing 10.2 *continued*

years never decreases and marketing objectives should be to increase the number of years in the franchise run, thus improving the brand value.

The BPP is projected into the future using the budget data for the brand and a conservative growth rate for years further into the future. These are eventually stepped down to a reasonable growth rate based on a consensus for the country's gross domestic product and inflation.

The brand value is the capitalized present value of this projection using the weighted average cost of capital (WACC) as the discount rate calculated according to corporate finance principles. It comprises a risk-free rate, a cost of debt extracted from the annual accounts, a cost of equity calculated according to the capital asset pricing model (CAPM), which uses market betas and a risk premium estimated with reference to stock market data. These are weighted according to the balance between debt and equity funding.

The third approach to determining the value of a brand, the income approach, argues that brand equity is the discounted future cash flow from the future earnings stream for the brand. Three income approaches are as follows.

1. Capitalizing royalty earnings from a brand name (when these can be defined).
2. Capitalizing the premium profits that are earned by a branded product (by comparing its performance with that of an unbranded product).
3. Capitalizing the actual profitability of a brand after allowing for the costs of maintaining it and the effects of taxation.

As a rule of thumb, Chevron's Lew Winters reports that accountants are inclined to price a brand at four to six times the annual profit realized from the sale of the product bearing the brand name to be acquired. The methodology described in the next section is largely based on an income approach.

Interbrand's brand valuation methodology

Interbrand evaluated a number of approaches in developing its brand valuation methodology. Its goal was to identify an approach that incorporated marketing, financial and legal aspects; followed fundamental accounting concepts; allowed for regular revaluation in a consistent way; and was suitable for acquired and home-grown brands.

Interbrand decided to approach the problem of brand valuation by assuming that the value of a brand, like the value of any other economic asset, was the present worth of the benefits of future ownership.[30] In other words, brand valuation is based on an assessment of what the value is today of the earnings or cash flow that the brand can be expected to generate in the future.[31]

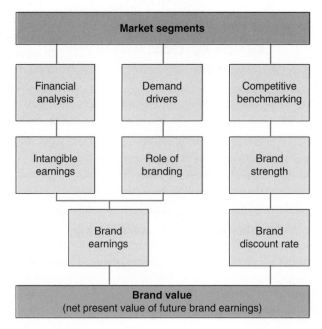

Figure 10.5   Brand valuation model

Interbrand follows a methodology that is largely based on an income approach.[32] According to Interbrand, to capture the complex value creation of a brand, the following valuation steps should be performed (Figure 10.5).[33]

1. *Market segmentation:* split the consumer market for the brand into non-overlapping and homogenous groups of consumers according to applicable criteria such as product or service, distribution channels, consumption patterns, purchase sophistication, geography, existing and new customers, etc. The brand is valued in each segment and the sum of the segment valuations constitutes the total value of the brand.
2. *Financial (role of branding) analysis:* identify and forecast revenues and 'earnings from intangibles' generated by the brand for each of the distinct segments determined in step 1. Intangible earnings are defined as: branded revenues less operating costs, applicable taxes and a charge for the capital employed. The concept is similar to the notion of economic profit.
3. *Demand (brand strength) analysis:* assess the role that the brand plays in driving demand for products and services in the markets in which it operates. The proportion of intangible earnings attributable to the brand is measured by an indicator referred to as the 'role of branding index' (RBI) by first identifying the drivers of demand for the branded business, then determining the degree to which each driver is directly influenced by the brand. The role of branding represents the percentage of intangible earnings that are generated by the brand. Brand earnings are derived by multiplying the role of branding by intangible earnings.
4. *Competitive benchmarking:* determine the competitive strengths and weaknesses of the brand. A specific brand discount rate that reflects the risk profile of its expected future earnings is derived via a 'brand strength score' (Figure 10.6). This

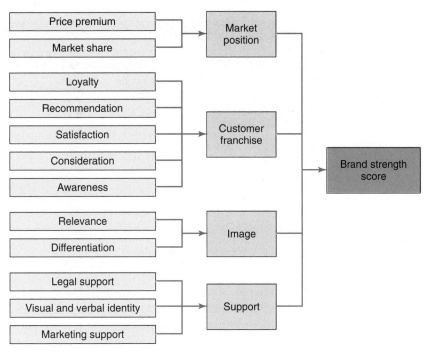

Figure 10.6   Brand strength assessment

measure comprises extensive competitive benchmarking and a structured evaluation of the brand's market, stability, leadership position, growth trend, support,
geographic footprint and legal protectability. The ideal brand would be a risk-free
asset (or government bond yield).

5. *Brand value calculation:* calculate the brand value as the net present value (NPV) of
the forecast brand earnings, discounted by the brand discount rate. The NPV calculation comprises both the forecast period and the period beyond, reflecting the
ability of brands to continue generating earnings.

According to Interbrand, the RBI index can vary considerably – on average, by industry,
from a low of 10 percent for bulk chemicals to over 80 percent for soft drinks and 90 percent for perfumes. Other observed RBI indices are hotels (30 percent), financial services
(40 percent), household appliances (55 percent) and consumer electronics (70 percent).
Figure 10.7 shows the calculation of the RBI index for a hypothetical beer brand.

Summary

Brand valuation and the 'brands on the balance sheet' are controversial subjects.[34] The
advantage of the Interbrand approach is that it is general and can be applied to almost
any brand or product. Yet even Interbrand recognizes the complexities involved:

> The valuation of brands is still a relatively new concept. There is no active mar-
> ket in brands, as there is with stocks and shares or real estate. Brand valuation
> is without question partly art and partly science. Judgement is involved just as
> it is for any other valuation method for any other asset, tangible or intangible.

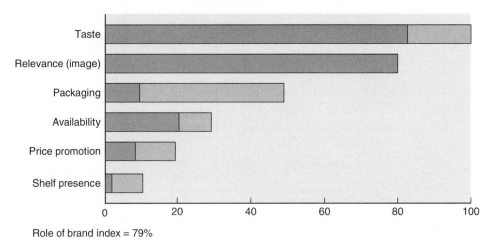

Role of brand index = 79%

Figure 10.7   Example of role of branding in the beer segment

Specialized knowledge of marketing, accounting and trademark law is required to ensure that the correct blend of professional skills is present. Any
brand valuation method has to take into account a wide variety of data, both
factual and qualitative. Skilled professional judgement is needed to arrive at
the right conclusions on the role of the brand, its strength and the underlying
stream of cash flow it generates. All of the conclusions reached need to be supported as far as possible by independent research studies.[35]

Many marketing experts, however, feel it is impossible to reduce the richness of a
brand to a single, meaningful number and that any formula is an abstraction and
arbitrary. Thus, the disadvantage of valuation approaches is that they make a host of
potentially oversimplified assumptions to arrive at one measure of brand equity. For
example, Sir Michael Perry, as chairman of Unilever, objected for philosophical
reasons:

The seemingly miraculous conjuring up of intangible asset values, as if from
nowhere, only serves to reinforce the view of the consumer sceptics, that
brands are just high prices and consumer exploitation. At Unilever, we have
consistently rejected this approach.[36]

Academic Peter Fader points out a number of limitations of valuation approaches:
they require judgemental data and thus are subjective; intangible assets are not
always synonymous with brand equity; the methods sometimes defy common sense
and lack 'face validity' (eg, IBM's brand equity bounced around from number 3 or
number 4 to as low as number 282 according to *Financial World* over just a few years);
the financial measures generally ignore or downplay investments in future equity
(eg, advertising or R&D); and the strength of the brand measures may be confused
with the strength of the company.[37]

At the heart of much of the criticism is the issue of separability. An *Economist* magazine editorial put it this way: 'Brands can be awkward to separate as assets. With
Cadbury's Dairy Milk, how much value comes from the name Cadbury? How much
from Dairy Milk? How much merely from the product's (replicable) contents or

design?'[38] To make a sports analogy, extracting brand value may be as difficult as determining the value of the coach to a team's performance.

As a result of these criticisms, the climate regarding brand valuation has changed. In 1989, Britain's Accounting Standards Committee ruled that companies could only value brands if they were acquired in a takeover and only if they were then depreciated over 20 years against profits – adopting the more conservative US practice of gradually writing off goodwill (brands and all). The International Accounting Standards Committee is also grappling with the issue.

CHAPTER REVIEW

This chapter considered two ways to measure the benefits or outcomes of brand equity: comparative methods (a means of assessing the effects of consumer perceptions and preferences on aspects of the marketing campaign) and holistic methods (attempts to come up with an estimate of the overall value of the brand). Figure 10.8 summarizes the approaches, which can be seen as complementary. In fact, understanding the particular range of benefits for a brand on the basis of comparative methods may be useful as inputs in estimating the overall value of a brand by holistic methods.

Combining these outcome measures with the measures of sources of brand equity from Chapter 9 as part of the brand value chain can provide insight into the effectiveness of marketing actions. Nevertheless, assessing the ROI of marketing activities remains a challenge.[39] Four guidelines can be offered for improving the ability to create and detect ROI from brand marketing activities.

1. *Spend wisely – focus and be creative:* to be able to measure ROI, there needs to be a return to begin with! By investing in distinctive and well-designed marketing activities, there is a greater chance that a positive and discernible ROI will ensue.

Comparative methods involve experiments that examine consumer attitudes and behaviour towards a brand to more directly assess the benefits arising from having a high level of awareness and strong, favourable and unique brand associations.

- *Brand-based comparative approaches:* experiments in which one group of consumers responds to an element of the marketing campaign when it is attributed to the brand and another group responds to that same element when it is attributed to a rival or fictitiously named brand.
- *Marketing-based comparative approaches:* experiments in which consumers respond to changes in elements of the marketing campaign for the brand or competitive brands.
- *Conjoint analysis:* a survey-based multivariate technique that enables marketers to profile the consumer buying decision process with respect to products and brands.

Holistic methods attempt to place an overall value on the brand in either abstract utility terms or financial terms. Thus, holistic methods attempt to 'net out' various considerations to determine the unique contribution of the brand.

- *Residual approach:* examines the value of a brand by subtracting consumers' preferences for the brand based on physical product attributes alone from overall brand preferences.
- *Valuation approach:* places a financial value on the brand for accounting purposes, mergers and acquisitions or other such reasons.

Figure 10.8 Measures of outcomes of brand equity

2. *Look for benchmarks – examine competitive spending levels and historical company norms:* it is important to get a feel for a market or category to understand the boundaries of what might be expected.
3. *Be strategic – apply brand equity models:* use models such as the CBBE and the brand value chain to provide discipline and a structured approach to planning, implementing and interpreting marketing activity.
4. *Be observant – track both formally and informally:* qualitative and quantitative insights can be used to understand brand performance.

Perhaps the dominant theme of this and the previous chapter has been the importance of employing several measures and research methods to capture the richness and complexity of brand equity. No matter how well conducted, single measures of brand equity run the risk of missing something important. Recall the problems encountered by Coca-Cola from its over-reliance on blind taste tests, described in Brand Briefing 1.1. In explaining the New Coke debacle, marketing consultant Randy Scruggs makes an interesting analogy concerning the effects of Coca-Cola's focus on a single measure to assess consumer response, likening it to the interpretation that someone might give when viewing a pencil head on from the end with the eraser.[40] From that perspective, a pencil might look like a disc. If one were to look through a magnifying glass – akin to Coke's 190,000 taste tests – one would be even more convinced that what one was looking at was a disc! Only if one were to look at the pencil from other angles and perspectives would it be clear that it was multidimensional. Thus, as this analogy suggests, a single measure only provides at best a one- or two-dimensional view of a brand. To extend Scruggs' analogy, measuring the volume of a pencil may reveal something about its size but would say nothing about how well the pencil writes, how comfortable it is to hold and so forth. Thus, any one measure of brand equity necessarily overlooks or distorts information.

Consistent with this view and according to the definition of customer-based brand equity, no single number or measure fully captures brand equity.[41] Rather, brand equity should be thought of as a multidimensional concept that depends on what knowledge structures are present in the minds of consumers and what actions a firm takes to capitalize on the potential offered by these knowledge structures. Thus, there are many different sources of brand equity and many possible outcomes of brand equity depending on the skill and ingenuity of the marketers involved. Different firms may be more or less able to maximize the potential value of a brand according to the type and nature of their marketing activities. Brand Briefing 10.3 describes brand acquisitions that failed. As academic Peter Fader says:

> The actual value of a brand depends on its fit with a buyer's corporate structure and other assets. If the acquiring company has manufacturing or distribution capabilities that are synergistic with the brand, then it might be worth paying a lot of money for it. Paul Feldwick, a British executive, makes the analogy between brands and properties on the Monopoly game board. You're willing to pay a lot more for Marvin Gardens if you already own Atlantic and Ventnor avenues![42]

Accordingly, the CBBE framework emphasizes the importance of employing a range of research measures to capture the potential sources and outcomes of brand

Brand Briefing 10.3

Beauty is in the eye of the beholder

Companies make acquisitions because they wish to expand their business. In making acquisitions, a company has to determine what it feels the brands are worth. In some instances, the hoped-for brand value has failed to materialize, serving as a reminder that the value of a brand is partly a function of what you do with it. The booming business environment of the 1990s has many such failures.

A classic example is the €1.16 billion acquisition of Snapple by Quaker Oats in 1994. Snapple had become a popular US brand through powerful grass roots marketing and a willingness to distribute to small outlets and corner shops. Quaker changed Snapple's ad campaign – abandoning the rotund and popular Snapple Lady – and revamped its distribution system. Quaker also changed the packaging by updating the label and putting Snapple in larger bottles, moves that did not sit well with loyal customers. The results were disastrous: Snapple began losing money and market share, allowing a host of competitors to move in. Unable to revive the foundering brand, Quaker sold the company in 1997 for €205 million to Triarc, which owned other beverages.

Another unsuccessful acquisition occurred when Quality Dining bought Bruegger's Bagels in 1996 with €97.1 million in stock. Within one year, Quality Dining agreed to sell the bagel chain back to its original owners for €34.2 million after taking a €139 million charge on the acquisition. Experts blamed an overly ambitious expansion strategy. Quality Dining planned to expand to 2,000 shops within 4 years, despite the fact that, before the acquisition, Bruegger's posted 2 consecutive annual losses due to its expansion to 339 shops. The new ownership also set the lofty goal of entering the top 60 domestic markets, which limited the amount of advertising and promotional support each market received. As Bruegger's fortunes turned, competitor Einstein/Noah Bagel overtook the company as the market leader in the USA. One franchisee commented, '[Quality Dining] would have had to stay up pretty late at night to screw up anything more than they did.'

In 1996, Wells Fargo bought First Interstate Bancorp for €8.8 billion. The acquisition failed largely because the two US banks had differing business styles. Wells Fargo focused on providing convenience for its customers, whereas First Interstate concentrated on customer service and support through its neighborhood branches. Following the merger, however, Wells Fargo alienated many First Interstate customers by failing to deliver on its promise that 'it will be business as usual' for those customers. The bigger bank lost customers' deposits, bounced good cheques, made balance errors and answered complaints slowly or not at all. Many customers closed their accounts with Wells Fargo, causing non-California account numbers to fall between 1 percent and 1.5 percent a month during 1997. The chairman and president of Wells Fargo apologized to bank customers in the 1997 annual report and admitted: 'Overall, it was a sorry experience for far too many of our customers.'

Brand Briefing 10.3 *continued*

Unfortunately for Wells Fargo, the customer exodus reduced earnings, and the bank was acquired in 1998 by Minneapolis-based Norwest.

Sources: 'Cadbury is paying Triarc $1.45 billion for Snapple unit', *Baltimore Sun*, 19 September 2000; Thomas M. Burton, 'The profit center of the bagel business has quite a big hole', *Wall Street Journal*, 6 October 1997; Jim Carlton, 'Wells Fargo discovers getting together is hard to do', *Wall Street Journal*, 21 July 1997; David Olive, 'Merger track record spotty', *Financial Post*, 15 December 1998.

equity, as the next two chapters will consider. Figure 10.9 displays a set of crucial brand equity and tracking measures according to branding expert David Aaker.[43]

Loyalty

1. Price premium
   - A pack of chocolate chip cookies from Nabisco is priced at €1.47. How much extra would you be willing to pay for Pepperidge Farm instead of Nabisco?
   - Brand Y would have to cost _____ percent less than Brand X before I would switch brands.
   - For chocolate chip cookies, would you prefer Nabisco at €1.47 or Pepperidge Farm at €1.56?

2. Satisfaction/loyalty (among those who have used the brand)
   - Considering my recent use experience, I would say I was (dissatisfied, satisfied, delighted).
   - The brand met my expectations during the last use experience.
   - Would you buy the brand at the next opportunity?
   - Would you recommend the product or service to others?
   - The brand is (the only, one of two, one of three, one of more than three) brand(s) that I buy and use.

Perceived quality and leadership

1. Perceived quality. In comparison with other brands, this brand is . . .
   - Very high quality.
   - Consistently high quality.
   - The best, one of the best, one of the worst, the worst.

2. Leadership/popularity. In comparison with other brands, this brand is . . .
   - Growing in popularity.
   - A leading brand in the category.
   - Respected for innovation.

3. Esteem. In comparison with other brands, I
   - Hold this brand in high esteem.
   - Highly respect this brand.

Figure 10.9   Aaker's measures of brand equity across products and markets

Associations and differentiation

1. Perceived value
   - The brand is good value for the money.
   - There is a reason to buy this brand over others.
2. Personality
   - This brand has a personality.
   - This brand is interesting.
   - I have a clear image of the type of person who would use the brand.
   - This brand has a rich history.
3. Organization
   - This is a brand I would trust.
   - I admire the Brand X organization.
   - I would be proud to do business with the Brand X organization.
4. Differentiation
   - This brand is different from other brands.
   - This brand is basically the same as the other brands.

Awareness

1. Brand awareness
   - Name the brands in this product class.
   - Have you heard of this brand?
   - Do you have an opinion about this brand?
   - Are you familiar with this brand?

Market behaviour

1. Market share
   - Market share based on market surveys of usage or syndicated data.
2. Price and distribution indices
   - Relative market price – the average price at which the brand was sold during the month, divided by the average price at which all brands were sold.
   - The percentage of shops carrying the brand.
   - The percentage of people who have access to the brand.

Figure 10.9   *Continued*

Brand Briefing 10.4

Branding and finance

Marketers must be able to quantify their actitivities directly or indirectly in financial terms. One topic that has received academic interest is the relationship between brand equity valuations and stock market information and performance. Another important topic is the accounting implications of branding.

Brand Briefing 10.4 *continued*

Brand equity estimates

Academics Carol Simon and Mary Sullivan have developed a technique for estimating a firm's brand equity derived from financial market estimates of brand-related profits. They define brand equity as the incremental cash flows that accrue to branded products over and above the cash flows that would result from the sale of unbranded products. To implement their approach, they begin by estimating the market value of the firm. The market value of the firm's securities are then assumed to provide an unbiased estimate of the future cash flows that are attributable to all of the firm's assets. Their methodology attempts to extract the value of a firm's brand equity from the value of the firm's other assets. The result is an estimate of brand equity based on the financial market valuation of the firm's future cash flows.

Their rationale is as follows. They assume that the financial market value of a firm is based on the aggregate earning power of both tangible and intangible assets. They also make the 'efficient market' assumption that, in a well-functioning capital market, securities prices provide the best estimate of the value of a company's assets. In other words, the financial market's valuation of the firm incorporates the expected value of future cash flows and returns.

From these premises, Simon and Sullivan derive their methodology to extract the value of brand equity from the financial market value of the firm. The total asset value of the firm is defined as the sum of the market value of common stock, preferred stock, long-term debt and short-term debt. The value of intangible assets is captured in the ratio of the market value of the firm to the replacement cost of its tangible assets. Three categories of intangible assets are defined: brand equity, non-brand factors that reduce the firm's costs relative to competitors (eg, R&D and patents) and industry-wide factors that permit monopoly profits, such as regulation. By considering factors such as the age of the brand, order of entry into the category and current and past advertising share, Simon and Sullivan then provide estimates of brand equity.

Figure 10.10 gives their estimates of brand equity for some selected food companies in the USA. According to this analysis, the high estimated brand equity of Tootsie Roll suggests that, even though it may be relatively easy to develop a 'me too' confectionery product, a considerable amount of the profits ascribed to Tootsie Roll accrue directly from its strong brand name. Simon and Sullivan conducted an in-depth analysis tracing the brand equity of Coca-Cola and Pepsi over three events in the soft drink industry from 1982 to 1986 – for example, showing how the introduction of Diet Coke increased the equity of Coca-Cola and decreased the equity of Pepsi.

Stock market reactions

Researchers have studied how the stock market reacts to the brand equity for companies and products. For example, David Aaker and Robert Jacobson examined the

Brand Briefing 10.4 *continued*

Company	Brand equity
Anheuser-Busch	35
Brown-Foreman	82
Cadbury Schweppes	44
Campbell's	31
Dreyer's Ice Cream	151
General Mills	52
Heinz	62
Kellogg's	61
Pillsbury	30
Quaker	59
Ralston Purina	40
Sara Lee	57
Seagram	73
Smucker	126
Tootsie Roll	148

Figure 10.10 Simon and Sullivan's brand equity for food product companies (as a percentage of replacement value)

association between yearly stock return and yearly brand changes (as measured by EquiTrend's perceived quality rating of brand equity) for 34 companies during the years 1989 to 1992. They also compared the accompanying changes in current-term return on investment (ROI). They found that, as expected, stock market return was positively related to changes in ROI. They also uncovered a strong positive relationship between brand equity and stock return. Firms that experienced the largest gains in brand equity saw their stock return average 30 percent. Conversely, those firms with the largest losses in brand equity saw average stock losses of 10 percent. The researchers concluded that investors can and do learn about changes in brand equity – not necessarily through EquiTrend studies (which may have little exposure to the financial community) but by learning about a company's plans and campaigns.

More recently, using data for firms in the US computer industry in the 1990s, Aaker and Jacobson found that changes in brand attitude were associated contemporaneously with stock return and led to accounting financial performance. They also found five factors (new products, product problems, competitors' actions, changes in top management and legal actions) that were associated with significant changes in brand attitudes. Awareness that did not translate into more positive attitudes, however, did little to the stock price. The authors conclude: 'So

Brand Briefing 10.4 *continued*

it's not the brands customers know, but the brands customers respect, that are ultimately successful.' Similarly, using *Financial World* estimates of brand equity, another comprehensive study found that brand equity was positively related to stock return and that this effect was incremental to other accounting variables such as the firm's net income.

Adopting an event study methodology, Vicki Lane and Robert Jacobson were able to show that stock market participants' responses to brand extension announcements, consistent with the tradeoffs inherent in brand leveraging, depend on brand attitude and familiarity. Specifically, the stock market responded most favourably to extensions of high-esteem, high-familiarity brands (eg, Coke, Norton/Symantec) and to low-esteem, low-familiarity brands (in the latter case, presumably because there was little to risk and much to gain with extensions). The stock market reaction was less favourable (and sometimes negative) for extensions of brands for which consumer familiarity was disproportionately high compared with consumer regard and to extensions of brands for which consumer regard was disproportionately high compared with familiarity. Natalie Mizik and Robert Jacobson found that the stock market reacted favourable when a firm increased its emphasis on value appropriation (ie, extracting profits in the marketplace) versus value creation (ie, innovating, producing and delievering products to the market), although certain qualifying conditions prevailed.[44]

In another event study of 58 firms that changed their names in the 1980s, Horsky and Swyngedouw found that, for most of the firms, name changes were associated with improved performance; the greatest improvement tended to occur in firms that produced industrial goods and whose performance before the change was relatively poor. Not all changes, however, were successful. They interpret the act of a name change as a signal that other measures to improve performance (eg, changes in product offerings and organizational changes) will be undertaken.

Vithala Rao and his colleagues analyzed financial performance of 113 firms over five years and found that corporate branding strategies were associated with higher values of Tobin's Q. Tobin's Q is a forward-looking measure of intangible assets and a firm's future profit potential calculated as the ratio of the market value of the firm to the replacement cost of the firm's assets. A mixed branding strategy (where a firm used corporate names for some products and individual names for others) was associated with lower values of Tobin's Q. The researchers also concluded that most firms would have been able to improve their Tobin's Q had they adopted a branding strategy different from the one suggested by examining their brand portfolios. Thomas Madden and colleagues found that strong brands not only delivered greater returns to stockholders versus a relevant market benchmark, they did so with less risk.[45]

Brand Briefing 10.4 *continued*

Accounting perspectives on brands[46]

Accountants have adopted accounting standards to allow comparability in financial information. Two organizations inform these standards: the Financial Accounting Standards Board (FASB) for the USA and London-based International Accounting Standards Board (IASB) for much of the rest of the world. The FASB and IASB have a close working arrangement and their standards are increasingly similar. Over 90 countries use the IASB standards and those that do not (eg, Japan, Hong Kong, Canada and Australia, each of whom have their own standard-setting bodies) work closely with the IASB to ensure that their financial reporting is not out of step.

Producing accounting standards or modifying existing ones is a slow process. Suggestions are received from a variety of sources and once they are on the agenda as a project, are subject to open forum discussions and research by FASB and IASB staff. Each change has to be published as an exposure draft, discussion paper and working draft. Comments are received, assessed and accommodated until a standard is deemed ready for issue. The standard is issued by the FASB under the title Statement of Financial Accounting Standards (SFAS) and by the IASB as International Financial Reporting Standards (IFRS).

Intangible assets have been a focus of attention by both bodies since the 1980s. Events between 2000 and 2005 have signalled substantial change in the restricted role given to brands as intangible assets because:

> [Investors need] better information about intangible assets because those assets are an increasingly important economic resource for many entities and are an increasing proportion of the assets acquired in many business combinations.'[47]

The FASB issued the revised SFAS 141 in June 2001. The IASB followed suit with similar amendments to the IFRS 3 in January 2005. With these directives, when company A buys company B, the difference between the purchase price and net asset value (if it exists) may no longer be ascribed solely to goodwill. The standards require accountants to account for the costs of the intangibles that make up the goodwill portion. In other words they have to work out why the premium over net asset value was paid. What was bought for that price? The task of the accountants, after the event, is to identify and value as many of these intangibles as the standard will permit them to recognize.

The standard provides detailed guidance as to which intangibles will and are likely to meet the recognition criteria. In particular, they recognize trademarks, trade names, service marks, collective marks and certification marks. Thus, brands are

Brand Briefing 10.4 *continued*

now recognized as intangible assets and must be valued at their fair value at the time of the purchase, where fair value is defined as:

'the price that would be received for an asset . . . in a current transaction between marketplace participants in the reference market . . .'[48]

Fair value is the market value of the asset, not its book value and both the FASB and IASB have issued standards on fair value measurement. Notably, the measurement of fair value: reflects the market estimate of the future discounted inflows associated with the asset; and is based on a premise that the asset is valued 'in use'. In other words, the buyer of the asset would continue to use it as it had previously been used and would operate it in conjunction with other assets in the business. The rule states that the value of a brand (or any other intangible asset) should ideally be based on a marketplace value.

Because it is hard to find comparable deals in the market, the valuations will often have to be estimates of the potential of the brand over its useful life. The potential of the brand is how much money the brand makes today; the useful life is influenced by among other things the category of the brand (soft drinks brands are more likely to maintain their value than consumer electronics, because the latter is more dependent on continuous betting on technology and products). The statement limits the accountant's choice to three valuation types: market, cost and income, as described above. It also recommends that accountants maximize the use of inputs from the market rather than from the entity itself, reducing the influence of probably subjective views. The standard also suggests that risk be accommodated through the use of a discount rate in which a risk premium is added to the risk-free rate.

So if a company is acquired, its brand will be valued and appear in the acquiring company's balance sheet as an acquired intangible asset. The buyer's brand, however, will still not be listed in the balance sheet as an asset because it is internally generated and accounting standards do not accommodate internally generated brands. Undoubtedly, the accounting boards will address this anomaly in the future.

One of the leading accounting firms, Ernst & Young, points out that any modelled calculation of the future is a prediction and not an observation. It stresses that:

users of financial reports will need clear distinctions to be made between objective and subjective figures, between realised gains and losses, gains and losses based on real market prices, and gains and losses based on hypothetical calculations.

The introduction of IFRS 3 means that, in the long run, brands will increasingly be recognized assets, with specific values assigned to them. This is a step towards increasing the accountability of branding professionals as well as getting increased

Brand Briefing 10.4 *continued*

top management focus on brand management. The treatment of brands as distinct assets is likely to have big implications for brand management.

Sources: Carol J. Simon and Mary W. Sullivan, 'Measurement and determinants of brand equity: a financial approach', *Marketing Science,* Winter 1993, 12 (1): 28–52; David A. Aaker and Robert Jacobson, 'The financial information content of perceived quality', *Journal of Marketing Research,* May 1994, 31: 191–201; David A. Aaker and Robert Jacobson, 'The value relevance of brand attitude in high-technology markets', *Journal of Marketing Research,* November 2001, 38: 485–93; M. E. Barth, M. Clement, G. Foster and R. Kasznik, 'Brand values and capital market valuation', *Review of Accounting Studies,* 1998, 3: 41–68; Vicki Lane and Robert Jacobson, 'Stock market reactions to brand extension announcements: the effects of brand attitude and familiarity', *Journal of Marketing,* January 1995, 59: 63–77; Dan Horsky and Patrick Swyngedouw, 'Does it pay to change your company's name? A stock market perspective', *Marketing Science,* Fall 1987: 320–35; Vithala, R., Rao, V. R., Manoj, K. Agrawal and Denise Dahlhoff, 'How is manifested branding strategy related to the intangible value of a corporation?', *Journal of Marketing,* October 2004, 68: 126–41; www.iasb.org; www.pwc.com; 'IFRS3: uncovering the true value of an acquisition'; 'How fair is fair value', www.kmpg.com; 'Ernst & Young Global', May 2005, www.ey.com; Afra Sajjad 'IFRS-US convergence of accounting', 18 July 2006, www.accountancy.com

Discussion questions

1. Choose a product. Conduct a branded and unbranded experiment. What do you learn about the equity of the brands in that product class?
2. Can you identify any other advantages or disadvantages of the comparative methods?
3. Pick a brand and conduct an analysis similar to that done with the Planter's brand. What do you learn about its extendability as a result?
4. What do you think of the Interbrand methodology? What do you see as its main advantages and disadvantages?
5. What do you think of Young & Rubicam's Brand Asset Valuator (see Brand Briefing 9.12)? What do you see as its main advantages and disadvantages?

References and notes

[1] C. B. Bhattacharya and Leonard M. Lodish, 'Towards a system for monitoring brand health', Marketing Science Institute Working Paper Series, July 2000, 00–111.

[2] Richard F. Chay, 'How marketing researchers can harness the power of brand equity', *Marketing Research,* 1991, 3 (2): 10–30.

[3] Peter Farquhar and Yuji Ijiri make other distinctions in classifying brand equity measurement procedures. Peter H. Farquhar, Julia W. Han and Yuji Ijiri, 'Recognizing and measuring brand assets', Marketing Science Institute Report, 1991: 91–119. They describe two broad classes of measurement approaches to brand equity: separation approaches and integration

approaches. Separation approaches view brand equity as the value added to a product. Farquhar and Ijiri categorize separation approaches into residual methods and comparative methods. Residual methods determine brand equity by what remains after subtracting physical product effects. Comparative methods determine brand equity by comparing the branded product with an unbranded product or an equivalent benchmark. Integration approaches, on the other hand, typically define brand equity as a composition of basic elements. Farquhar and Ijiri categorize integration approaches into association and valuation methods. Valuation methods measure brand equity by its cost or value as an intangible asset for a particular owner and intended use. Association methods measure brand equity in terms of the favourableness of brand evaluations, the accessibility of brand attitudes and the consistency of brand image with consumers. The previous chapter described techniques that could be considered association methods. This chapter considers techniques related to the other three categories of methods.

[4]Edgar Pessemier, 'A new way to determine buying decisions', *Journal of Marketing*, 1959, 24: 41–6.

[5]Paul E. Green and V. Srinivasan, 'Conjoint analysis in consumer research: issues and outlook', *Journal of Consumer Research*, 1978, 5: 103–23; Paul E. Green and V. Srinivasan, 'Conjoint analysis in marketing: new developments with implications for research and practice', *Journal of Marketing*, 1990, 54: 3–19.

[6]For more details see Betsy Sharkey, 'The people's choice', *Adweek*, 27 November 1989: MRC 8.

[7]Paul E. Green and Yoram Wind, 'New ways to measure consumers' judgments', *Harvard Business Review*, July–August 1975, 53: 107–11.

[8]Max Blackstone, 'Price trade-offs as a measure of brand value', *Journal of Advertising Research*, August/September 1990: RC3-RC6.

[9]For some discussion, see Jordan Louviere and Richard Johnson, 'Measuring brand image with conjoint analysis and choice models', in 'Defining, measuring and managing brand equity: a conference summary', ed. Lance Leuthesser, MSI Report 88–104, Cambridge, MA: Marketing Science Institute, 1988.

[10]Arvind Rangaswamy, Raymond R. Burke and Terence A. Oliva, 'Brand equity and the extendibility of brand names', *International Journal of Research in Marketing*, March 1993, 10: 61–75. See also Moonkyu Lee, Jonathan Lee and Wagner A. Kamakura, 'Consumer evaluations of line extensions: a conjoint approach', in *Advances in Consumer Research*, Vol. 23, Ann Arbor, MI: Association of Consumer Research, 1996: 289–95.

[11]Howard Barich and V. Srinivasan, 'Prioritizing marketing image goals under resource constraints', *Sloan Management Review*, summer 1993: 69–76.

[12]Marco Vriens and Curtis Frazier (2003), 'The hard impact of the soft touch: how to use brand positioning attributes in conjoint', *Marketing Research:* summer: 23–7.

[13]V. Srinivasan, 'Network models for estimating brand-specific effects in multi-attribute marketing models', *Management Science*, January 1979, 25: 11–21.

[14]Wagner A. Kamakura and Gary J. Russell, 'Measuring brand value with scanner data', *International Journal of Research in Marketing*, 1993, 10: 9–22.

[15]Joffre Swait, Tulin Erdem, Jordan Louviere and Chris Dubelar, 'The equalization price: a measure of consumer-perceived brand equity', *International Journal of Research in Marketing*, 1993, 10: 23–45.

[16]See also Eric L. Almquist, Ian H. Turvill and Kenneth J. Roberts, 'Combining economic analysis for breakthrough brand management', *Journal of Brand Management*, 1998, 5 (4): 272–82.

[17]V. Srinivasan, Chan Su Park and Dae Ryun Chang, 'An approach to the measurement, analysis and prediction of brand equity and its sources', *Management Science*, September 2005, 51 (9): 1433–48. See also, Chan Su Park and V. Srinivasan, 'A survey-based method for measuring and understanding brand equity and its extendability', *Journal of Marketing Research*, May 1994, 31: 271–88. See also Na Woon Bong, Roger Marshall and Kevin Lane Keller, 'Measuring brand power: validating a model for optimizing brand equity', *Journal of Product and Brand Management*, 1999, 8 (3): 170–84.

[18]William R. Dillon, Thomas J. Madden, Amna Kirmani and Soumen Mukherjee, 'Understanding what's in a brand rating: a model for assessing brand and attribute effects and their relationship to brand equity', *Journal of Marketing Research*, November 2001, 38: 415–29.

[19]Kusum Ailawadi, Donald R. Lehmann and Scott A. Neslin, 'Revenue premium as an outcome measure of brand equity', *Journal of Marketing*, 2003, 67 (4): 1–17. See also, Avi Goldfarb, Qiamg Lu and Sridhar Moorthy, 'Measuring brand equity in an equilibrium framework: a structural approach', working paper, University of Toronto, 2005.

[20]Patrick Barwise (with Christopher Higson, Andrew Likierman and Paul Marsh), 'Brands as separable assets', *Business Strategy Review,* summer 1990: 49.

[21]Oliver Hupp and Ken Powaga, 'Using consumer attitudes to value brands: evaluation of the financial value of brands', *Journal of Advertising Research*, September 2004: 225–31.

[22]Sharkey, 'The people's choice'.

[23]Joanne Lipman, 'British companies value US brand names – literally', *Wall Street Journal*, 9 February 1989: B6; Laurel Wentz, 'WPP considers brand valuation', *Advertising Age*, 16 January 1989: 24.

[24]Bernard Condon, 'Gaps in GAAP', *Forbes*, 25 January 1999: 76–80.

[25]For an excellent summary, see Jeffrey Parkhurst, 'Leveraging brand to generate value', Chapter 18, in *From Ideas to Assets*, ed. Bruce Berman, New York: John Wiley, 2002.

[26]David M. Fredricks, 'Branded assets: the issue of measurement', paper presented at the ARF Fourth Annual Advertising and Promotion Workshop, 12–13 February 1992.

[27]Quoted in 'What's a brand worth?', editorial, *Advertising Age*, 18 July 1994.

[28]Lew Winters, 'Brand equity measures: some recent advances', *Marketing Research,* December 1991: 70–3; Gordon V. Smith, *Corporate Valuation: A business and professional guide,* New York: John Wiley, 1988.

[29]The 40-year limit was chosen because it was the number of years used by the American accounting profession for the amortization of goodwill. The ten years was broadly based on estimates of product failure rates.

[30]Michael Birkin, 'Assessing brand value', in *Brand Power*, ed. Paul Stobart, Washington Square, NY: New York University Press, 1994.

[31]Simon Mottram, 'The power of the brand', paper presented at the ARF Brand Equity Conference, 15–16 February 1994.

[32]Interbrand, eds Raymond Perrier and Paul Stobark, *Brand Valuation*, 3rd edn, London: Premier Books, 1997. For some additional perspectives, see Jeffrey Parkhurst. 'Leveraging brand to generate value', Chapter 18, in *From Ideas to Assets*, ed. Bruce Berman, New York: John Wiley, 2002.

[33]Jan Lindemann, 'Brand valuation', *Pool*, 2003, 24 Autumn.

[34]For some stimulating points of view, see the special issue on brand valuation of the *Journal of Brand Management*, 1998, 5 (4).

[35]Susannah Hart and John Murphy, *Brands: The new wealth creators*, New York: New York University Press, 1998.

[36]Diane Summers, 'IBM plunges in year to foot of brand name value league', *The Financial Times*, 11 July 1994.

[37]Peter Fader, course notes, Wharton Business School, University of Pennsylvania, 1998.

[38]'On the Brandwagon', *The Economist*, 20 January 1990.

[39]Scott Davis and Jeff Smith, 'Do you know your brand ROBI?', *Management Review,* October 1998: 55–7.

[40]Randy Scruggs, letter to author, 1996.

[41]For an interesting empirical application, see Manoj K. Agarwal and Vithala Rao, 'An empirical comparison of consumer-based measures of brand equity', *Marketing Letters* 7, 1996, 3: 237–47.

[42]Fader, course notes.

[43]David A. Aaker, *Building Strong Brands,* New York: Free Press, 1996.

[44]Natalie Mizik and Robert Jacobson, 'Trading off between value creation and value appropriation: the financial implications of shifts in strategic emphasis', *Journal of Marketing*, January 2003, 67: 63–76.

[45]Thomas J. Madden, Frank Fehle and Susan M. Fournier, 'Brands matter: an empirical demonstration of the creation of shareholder value through brands', Harvard Business School working paper No. 02-098.

[46]This section is largely based on a white paper, 'The final barrier: marketing and accounting converge at the corporate finance interface', by Roger Sinclair (www.brandmetrics.com).

[47]FAS 141, Business Combinations, FASB, June 2001.

[48]Statement of Accounting Standards No. 15X, Fair Value Measurement, FASB, 21 October 2005: i.

Designing and implementing branding strategies

This chapter considers issues related to branding strategies and how brand equity can be maximized across all the brands and products that might be sold by a company. The branding strategy, or brand architecture, concerns which brand elements a firm chooses to apply across the products it sells. As noted in Chapter 2, many firms employ complex branding strategies. For example, brand names may consist of many brand name elements (eg, Toyota Camry V6 XLE) and may be applied across a range of products (eg, Toyota cars and trucks). What is the best way to characterize a branding strategy under such instances? What guidelines exist to choose the right combinations of names and other brand elements to manage brand equity across a range of products? Branding strategy is critical because it is the means by which the firm can help consumers understand its products and services and organize them in their minds.

Chapter 11 begins by describing two strategic tools. The brand–product matrix and the brand hierarchy help to characterize and formulate branding strategies by defining relationships between brands and products. The chapter next suggests guidelines as to how to design branding strategies. Finally, the chapter concludes by considering issues in implementing branding strategies, including designing the brand hierarchy and the supporting marketing campaign. Guidelines are provided concerning the number of levels of the hierarchy to use, how brands from different levels of the hierarchy can be combined, if at all, for any one particular product and how any one brand can be linked, if at all, to multiple products. Brand Briefing 11.12 devotes special attention to the topic of cause marketing.

BRAND ARCHITECTURE

The *branding strategy* reflects the number and nature of common and distinctive brand elements applied to the products sold by a company. In other words, branding strategy involves deciding which brand names, logos, symbols and so forth should be applied to which products and the nature of new and existing brand elements to be applied to new products. Some marketing commentators use the term *brand architecture* to describe branding strategies. Using the brand architecture metaphor implied by that name, a common distinction often made in branding strategies is whether a firm is or should be applying an umbrella corporate or family brand to all their products (ie, a 'branded house') or a collection of individual brands with different names (ie, a 'house of brands').

Brand architecure involves defining both brand boundaries and brand complexity. Which products should share the same brand name? How many variations of that brand name should be employed? The role of defining branding strategies and brand architecture is two-fold.

- *Clarify brand awareness:* improve consumer understanding and communicate similarities and differences between products.
- *Motivate brand image:* maximize transfer of equity to/from the brand to products to improve trial and repeat purchase.

The brand–product matrix

To characterize the product and branding strategy of a firm, one useful tool is the *brand–product matrix*, a graphical representation of all the brands and products sold. The matrix (or grid) has the brands of a firm as rows and the corresponding products as columns (see Figure 11.1).

The rows of the matrix represent *brand–product relationships* and express a brand extension strategy in terms of the number and nature of products sold as different brands. A *brand line* consists of all products – original as well as line and category extensions – sold under a particular brand. Thus, a brand line would be one row of the matrix. As Chapter 12 discusses, a potential new product extension for a brand must be judged by how effectively it leverages existing brand equity from the parent brand to the new product, as well as how effectively the extension, in turn, contributes to the equity of the parent brand.

The columns of the matrix represent *product – brand relationships* and capture the brand portfolio strategy in terms of the number and nature of brands to be marketed in each category. The *brand portfolio* is the set of all brands and brand lines that a company sells in a particular category. Thus, a brand portfolio would be one particular column of the matrix. Different brands may be designed and marketed to appeal to different market segments.

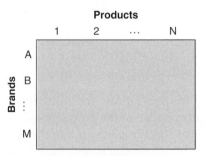

Figure 11.1   Brand–product matrix

A brand portfolio must be judged on its ability to collectively maximize brand equity: any one brand in the portfolio should not harm or decrease the equity of other brands. In other words, the optimal brand portfolio is one in which each brand maximizes equity in combination with all other brands in the portfolio. Brand Briefing 11.1 describes the design of LG Electronics' brand portfolio.

Brand Briefing 11.1

LG Electronics: building brand through fast innovation

LG Electronics was established in Korea 1958 and sells consumer electronics, home appliances and mobile communications. The company was originally named Lucky Goldstar, from which the name LG was derived. The name of the company is often accompanied by the slogan 'Life's good', which is a high order summary of its promise: that its products will make your life good.

After the name change, determined brand revitalization resulted in LG's brand reaching the level of a global contender with a tremendous rate of growth. LG aims to be a respected global electronics brand, and the financial highlights show a global consolidated sale of €32.5 billion in 2006.

LG has a vision to rank among the global top three in electronics and information technology by 2010 and, to reach that, it has adopted a growth strategy of 'Fast innovation' and 'Fast growth' based on a philosophy of 'Great company, great people'.

This strategy is also expressed in set targets. 'Fast innovation' aims to set extremely high innovation goals and secure a competitive edge, 30 percent more than the competitors can do. 'Fast innovation' means 30 percent more sales and corresponding improvement in market share, product development that is faster by 30 percent than competitors' and technology development and establishment of corporate value three years ahead of competitors. With 'fast growth' the company strives to expand its market size and earnings quickly, in the process improving the growth rate in terms of monetary value rather than quantity.

Fast innovation

The 'fast innovation' strategy is observable in the state-of-the-art mobile phones and flat-screen TVs made by LG Electronics. The company has recognized the importance of research and development as a competitive edge and devotes approximately 30 percent of its staff worldwide to these tasks.

To promote its image as an innovator, it wants to offer more attention-getting products. At the Consumer Electronics Show in Las Vegas 2005 it rolled out a €10,260, 60-inch plasma TV with a built-in digital video recorder. And it showed a stand-alone DVR with a 160-gigabyte hard drive that offered an electronic programme guide and connection to a PC, and it launched a refrigerator with a built-in LCD TV. The

Brand Briefing 11.1 *continued*

company was also the first to put both next-generation technologies, Sony's Blu-ray and Toshiba's HD-DVD, into one player. The aim in combining both these formats was to end the confusion and inconvenience of competing high-definition disc formats.

The TDR (tear-down-and-redesign) strategy is another important element in LG's approach. TDR puts focus on search for innovation in everything from design and production to marketing. The strategy aims to find new ideas from the ground up and all employees are encouraged to comply with at least one TDR activity a year, with bonuses awarded when a TDR activity is complete. In this way, management encourages change via innovation and involvement and employees are encouraged to participate. The TDR strategy has been successful in the USA, where LG has emerged as a premium brand, thereby erasing its reputation as a maker of cheap microwave ovens and air conditioners sold under the Goldstar brand.

Finally, in 2005 alone, the company won 16 innovation awards in Las Vegas and 'The design team of the year' in the Red Dot design awards.

Fast growth

LG Electronics is determined to be one of the world's top three home electronics companies by 2010. LG's three divisions – mobile phones, digital displays and appliances – strives to increase productivity by 30 percent to make this possible.

The mobile phone division makes the LG Chocolate, LG Shine and the co-branded LG Prada. In 2006, the phone division had 6.3 percent market share and sold 64 million handsets, which it aims to increase to 78 million units in 2007. Behind the success is a large design team in Korea, which has put a great focus on branding and creating stylish phones. A crucial parameter is speed of development and it is important that the company has an edge in that area. One example is when LG, together with Verizon's developed multimedia services, and to support the project, flew engineers, marketers and product development specialists to synchronize phones with servers and networks. In this case LG cut its launch cycle by a quarter.

The digital display division is growing as well, and the company has high ambitions. LG Electronics ran second worldwide in sales of plasma TVs and fifth in LCD, hopes to pass rivals such as Matsushita, Sony, Samsung, Sharp and Philips Electronics to become the leader in both categories by 2008. LG Electronics has also been successful in a venture with Philips in LCD screens, which makes them the world's top maker of liquid crystal displays for TVs. Sales of plasma TVs are expected to more than double from 877,000 in 2005 to 2 million in 2006, and sales of LCD TVs is expected to increase from 1.5 million to 4 million. The total market share in LCD and plasma TVs in 2006 was 10 percent.

Brand Briefing 11.1 *continued*

LG's transformation from low-end appliances to a high-end brand has helped this category tremendously, and not just in consumer demand: the brand appeal led to an alliance with Home Depot in the USA. The alliance has helped LG to more than double its US distribution to 3,000 outlets. That helped the brand to grow from almost no US sales in 2002 to 5.5 percent of the market for refrigerators and 5.9 percent for washing machines in the first half of 2005. This has increased global sales of LG's white goods to €7.32 billion in 2006, up from €6 billion in 2004. Most impressive is the move upmarker, which means the company has attracted consumers willing to spend more for better design and high performance. The reward is a third place in the USA after Whirlpool and Electrolux.

The success of LG illustrates that brands need to continually prove themselves through their product portfolio. In some ways, being absolutely right in terms of consumer insights is worth little if it is not taken to market fast enough. Conversely one could say that simply outpacing competitors is a strong brand message in itself. This is especially true in industries like consumer electronics and technology products, where the market takes innovation and improvement for granted. Based on this, LG spans a very broad range of products under its one brand, but is doing so based on aggressive innovation.

Sources: *Fast Thinking*, 19 July 2007, www.fastthinking.com; LG Electronics, 19 July 2007, www.lge.com; Ki Ho Park/Kistone, 24 October 2005, 'No. 21: LG Electronics', 19 July 2007; Marie-France Han and Sumeet Chatterjee, 17 May 2007, 'LG Elec to boost appliance sales, profit', 19 July 2007, www.businessweek.com; www.reuters.com; Moon Ihlwan, Cliff Edwards and Roger Crockett, 24 January 2005, 'Korea's LG: will it be the next Samsung?', 19 July 2007, www.businessweek.com; Moon Ihlwan, 30 May 2006, 'Korea: set to duel in digital TV', 19 July 2007, www.businessweek.com; Moon Ihlwan, 30 October 2006, *'Red-hot white goods'*, 19 July 2007, www.businessweek.com; Moon Ihlwan, 29 January 2007, *'The devil dials Prada on LG's new phone'*, 19 July 2007, www.businessweek.com

One final set of definitions is useful.[1] A *product line* is a group of products within a product category that are closely related because they function in a similar manner, are sold to the same customer groups, are marketed through the same type of outlets or fall within given price ranges. A product line may be composed of different brands or a single family brand or individual brand that has been extended. A *product mix* (or product assortment) is the set of all product lines and items sold. Thus, product lines represent different sets of columns in the brand–product matrix that, in total, make up the product mix. A *brand mix* (or brand assortment) is the set of all brand lines sold.

A branding strategy can be characterized according to its *breadth* (ie, in terms of brand–product relationships and brand extension strategy) and its *depth* (ie, in terms of product–brand relationships and the brand portfolio or mix). For example, a branding strategy can be seen as both deep and broad if the firm has a large number of brands, many of which have been extended into various product categories. This chapter only briefly considers the breadth of a branding strategy and brand extensions – Chapter 12 is devoted to these topics.

Breadth of a branding strategy

The breadth of a branding strategy concerns the number and nature of products linked to the brands sold by a company. A number of considerations arise concerning the product mix and which products the firm should manufacture or sell. Strategic decisions have to be made concerning how many product lines a company should carry (ie, the breadth of the product mix), as well as how many variants should be offered in each product line (ie, the depth of the product mix).

Breadth of product mix

Lehmann and Winer investigated factors affecting product category attractiveness.[2] They note three sets of factors determining the attractiveness of a product category (Figure 11.2).

- *Aggregate market factors:* characteristics describing the market. All else being equal, a category is considered attractive if it is relatively large (as measured both

Aggregate market factors
Market size.
Market growth.
Stage in product lifecycle.
Sales cyclicity.
Seasonality.
Profits.

Category factors
Threat of new entrants.
Bargaining power of buyers.
Bargaining power of suppliers.
Current category rivalry.
Pressures from substitutes.
Category capacity.

Environmental factors
Technological.
Political.
Economic.
Regulatory.
Social.

Figure 11.2   Category attractiveness criteria

in units and revenue); fast-growing (both in current and projected terms) and in the growth stage of the product lifecycle; non-cyclical and non-seasonal in sales patterns; and characterized by relatively high, steady profit margins.

- *Category factors:* structural factors affecting the category. In general, a category is considered attractive if the threat of new entrants is low (eg, due to barriers of entry from economies of scale, product differentiation, capital requirements, switching costs or distribution systems); bargaining power of buyers is low (eg, when the product bought is a small percentage of buyers' costs or is sharply differentiated or when buyers are earning high profits, lack information about competitive offerings or are unable to integrate backwards); current category rivalry is low (eg, when there are few or an imbalance of competitors in fast-growing markets); few close product substitutes exist in the eyes of consumers; and the market is operating at or near capacity.
- *Environmental factors:* external forces unrelated to the product's customers and competitors that affect marketing strategies. Technological, political, economic, regulatory and social factors will affect the prospects of a category and should be forecasted.

All of these factors relate to consumers, competition and the marketing environment and must be assessed to determine the attractiveness of a product category or market. The ultimate decision to enter such markets, however, must also take into account the firm's capabilities and abilities – its core competencies – as well as its strategic goals. The names chosen for the products to enter these markets will depend on the branding strategy adopted, as described in Chapter 12.

Xerox

When Xerox felt it had to move into office automation and computing, it chose to brand its first computers with the Xerox name. Because of the near-generic qualities of the name – synonymous with photocopying – it is perhaps not surprising that consumers balked. Print ads announcing that 'Here's a Xerox that does not even make a copy' may have raised questions in consumers' minds as to how – or even if – the computer worked. Xerox ultimately quit the personal computer business, though it carried on making monitors.

Depth of product mix

Once decisions concerning product categories and markets have been made, decisions concerning the product line strategy must also be made. Product line analysis requires a clear understanding of the market and the cost interdependencies of products.[3] Specifically, product line analysis involves examining the percentage of sales and profits contributed by each item in the product line. The ability of each item to withstand competition and address consumer needs also must be assessed. At its simplest, a product line is too short if the manager can increase long-term profits by adding items; the line is too long if the manager can increase profits by dropping items.[4] Increasing the length of the product line typically expands market coverage and therefore market share, but also increases costs. From a branding perspective, longer product lines may decrease the consistency of the associated brand image if the same brand is used.

Laura Ashley

Although a raging success in the 1980s, Laura Ashley found its sales wilting in the 1990s. The brand meant different things to different people and, unfortunately, many of these people worked at Laura Ashley! Stores in the USA and Europe offered different product lines. Designers and buyers were scattered all over the world and introduced hundreds of clothing styles, many of which clashed with the English country styles and flowery fashions for which Laura Ashley had become famous. The chain's vast range of lines – which included adult clothes, children's clothes and home furnishings – was filled with weak sellers and duplicate styles. Eighty-two percent of the company's sales came from just 22 percent of the merchandise. New management pared down the brands, eliminating 30 percent of the clothing styles and 20 percent of the home furnishing lines. They also consolidated design, buying and merchandising and took steps to create a more consistent store design and format.[5] Having lost momentum, however, Laura Ashley found itself struggling in the marketplace as a succession of 10 chief executives in 13 years attempted to re-energize the brand. In 2005, a new chief shifted the company's core focus from fashion to home furnishings and sales began to rise.

Given that product policy has been set for a firm in terms of product boundaries (ie, appropriate product categories and product lines), then the proper branding strategy must be decided upon in terms of which brand elements should be used for which products. Specifically, decisions must be made as to which products to attach to any one brand as well as how many brands to support in any one product category. The former decision concerns brand extensions and is discussed in detail in the next chapter; the latter decision concerns brand portfolios, which are addressed next. Brand Briefing 11.2 describes VF's experiences in stretching its brand name and business through strategic acquisitions.

Brand Briefing 11.2

Stretching the VF brand

The largest clothingmaker in the world, VF was founded in 1899 as Reading Glove & Mitten, but in 1919 was renamed Vanity Fair Silk Mills after its focus shifted to women's underwear. In the 1970s it expanded into jeanswear and workwear by acquiring H. D. Lee, manufacturer of Lee jeans. During the next three decades, VF acquired other brands (Figure 11.3). This narrow growth strategy served the company well, but VF's sales flattened by 2000 as expansion became difficult. As one commentator noted, 'There's only so much growth you can squeeze from dungarees and bras.' To spur growth, VF sought to stretch its brand by buying clothing companies in other categories.

Brand Briefing 11.2 *continued*

Owned brands

- *Jeanswear:* Lee, Wrangler, Timber Creek by Wrangler, Hero by Wrangler, Riders, Rustler, Brittania, Chic, Gitano, 20X, Maverick, HIS, Old Axe.
- *Underwear:* Vanity Fair, Vassarette, Bestform, Lily of France, Curvation, Gemma, Lou, Bolero, Intima Cherry, Variance, Belcor.
- *Imagewear:* Red Kap, Bulwark, Penn State Textile, Horace Small, Lee Sport, CSA, Chase Authentics, VF Solutions, E. Magrath.
- *Outdoor:* The North Face, JanSport, Eastpak, Napapijri, Kipling, Vans, Reef.
- *Sportswear:* Nautica, John Varvatos.

Licensed brands

- Tommy Hilfiger underwear, NFL Red and NFL White imagewear.

Figure 11.3   VF brand portfolio

Beginning in 2000 with its €92.3 million acquisition of the (loss-making) North Face brand of outdoor clothes and equipment, VF bought other brands in the same category. In 2004, it acquired skateboard and surf footwear label Vans, surf footwear company Reef, outfitter Napapijri, and lifestyle backpack brand Kipling for more than €273.6 million combined. It also expanded into sportswear with its €432 million acquisition of the men's sportswear brand Nautica, which also included the designer label John Varvatos. VF's size advantage and its expertise in clothing enabled it to revamp the sourcing, distribution and financial operations of each of these brands to make them more profitable. For example, The North Face posted a net loss of €68.4 million the year before it was purchased by VF; 5 years later sales nearly doubled to €342 million and operating profit margins rose by a third to 13 percent.

VF's brand expansion has been a significant contributor to its success. As stated on its website, two key points of VF's strategy are to:

- build a portfolio of strong brands that deliver great value to consumers;
- target brands to reach a variety of consumer segments across all retail channels.

These strategic moves enabled VF to achieve sales exceeding €4.1 billion and €324 in net profit in 2004, while maintaining an industry-leading 12.8 percent operating margin. As one analyst noted: 'VF has outperformed the competition because when the performance of one brand goes a little bit south, there are others that pick up the slack.'

Sources: www.vfc.com; Michael V. Copeland, 'Stitching together an apparel powerhouse', *Business 2.0*, April 2005: 52.

Depth of a branding strategy

The depth of a branding strategy concerns the number and nature of brands marketed in the product class sold. Why might a firm have several brands in the same product category? The primary reason relates to market coverage. Although multiple branding was pioneered by General Motors, Procter & Gamble is widely recognized as popularizing the practice.

The main reason for having several brands is to pursue several market segments.[6] These market segments may be based on all types of considerations – price, channels of distribution, geographic boundaries and so forth. For example, as part of a plan to upgrade Holiday Inn Worldwide, the hotel chain broke its domestic hotels into five separate chains to tap into five benefit segments: the upmarket Crowne Plaza, the traditional Holiday Inn, the budget Holiday Inn Express and the business-orientated Holiday Inn Select and Holiday Inn Suites & Rooms.[7] Each chain received different marketing treatments and emphasis. For example, Holiday Inn Express has been advertised with the humorous 'Stay smart' advertising campaign showing the brilliant feats that ordinary people could attempt after staying at the chain. Posing as scientists, doctors and even members of the rock group Kiss, these people always utter the same line when their identity and credentials are questioned, 'No, but I did stay at a Holiday Inn Express.' Marriott had adopted a similar strategy earlier, and other hotel chains have followed suit.

In many cases, brands have to be introduced because any one brand is not viewed equally favourably by all the market segments a company would like to target. Brand Briefing 11.3 outlines Volkswagen's strategy. Other reasons for introducing several brands in a category include to:[8]

- increase shelf presence and retailer dependence;
- attract consumers seeking variety who may otherwise switch to another brand;
- increase competition within the firm;
- achieve economies of scale in advertising, sales, merchandising and physical distribution.

Brand Briefing 11.3

Managing the portfolio at Volkswagen

Volkswagen has its roots in building simple cars for the masses – its main model for many years, the Beetle, became the car produced in the highest quantity in history. It was a car that put Europe on wheels, but also at its peak grabbed two-thirds of the USA's imported car market.

As people improved their standard of living, the modest Beetle had to be replaced by more comfortable and modern offers – so, from the 1970s on, VW introduced cars that became household names in their own right, such as the Golf, the Polo and the

Brand Briefing 11.3 *continued*

Passat. Then it announced unexpectedly luxurious models – a Passat with a large, luxury-type W8 engine, a people carrier, the Touareg, and a luxury saloon, the Phaeton.

The introduction of the Phaeton was a sensation in the industry. Here VW went head-to-head with Mercedes-Benz, BMW, Audi and Lexus with cars costing €50,000. To build the Phaeton, VW spent €186 million on a 'transparent factory' in Dresden – a factory with glass walls and hardwood floors.

The VW brand covers a range from the Fox to the Phaeton, ranging from €12,000 to €120,000 for a Phaeton with the biggest engine – before any extras. Yet, was the Phaeton a smart move that would ensure customers would raise their esteem for the brand? Would it mean that customers could, during their lives, grow from the more affordable models and aspire to finally affording the most luxurious model? Or was it driven by management prestige, to show that VW could make cars as well as anyone else?

The Phaeton does not look like a commercial success. It sold poorly in most markets outside Germany and the production levels were only 5,000 cars a year. Moreover, it did not seem to do much for the brand – in 2005 the brand was estimated to have lost about 12 percent of its financial value from the year before, a staggering disappointment if one expected the Phaeton and Touareg to be 'silver bullets' that would build brand equity. And the commercial success continued to hang on the more modest models. For instance, VW enjoys a very strong position in Germany, where the Fox and Polo were leading their segments in 2006 and the Golf continued to head the list of newly registered cars in Germany.

On the other hand, the move might be better understood if one looks at Volkswagen AG's portfolio. It also owns, among other brands, Bentley – and the Phaeton shares a large portion of its parts and technology with its Bentley models. And the Bentley brand management is seen as a success. So, in other words, the Phaeton might not have had to pay for itself, because a lot of its development is paid for. Moreover, the larger picture of the VW portfolio makes the Phaeton look more logical, as the Bentley Continental costs over €160,000. Suddenly, the Phaeton makes more sense both in terms of investment and the VW brand.

Still, one can wonder whether the VW brand itself has a clear strategy. In 2007, the Tiguan compact SUV was launched. The following statement was made in the annual report for 2006 and it makes us wonder what it means – that the core values of the brand at the same time are a new direction for the brand?

> Volkswagen has reinterpreted its traditional strengths under the slogan 'forward to the roots'. The Volkswagen Tiguan, a dynamic, compact SUV that will be launched on the market in 2007, represents this new direction for the brand. The perfect symbiosis of dynamic handling and comfort, versatility and all-round economy, it represents the brand's core values.

Brand Briefing 11.3 *continued*

Figure 11.4   Entrance to the Audi Car Factory, Brussels, Belgium
Source: Rex Features

Sources: 'Should Volkswagen stop for directions?', www.brandchannel.com; 'The best global brands 2005', *BusinessWeek*, 1 August 2005; Volkswagen annual reports 2004–06.

In designing a brand portfolio, marketers need to trade off market coverage and other considerations with costs and profitability. As with a product line, a portfolio is too big if profits can be increased by dropping brands; a portfolio is not big enough if profits can be increased by adding brands. In other words, any brand should be clearly differentiated and appealing to a sizeable enough marketing segment to justify its marketing and production costs. Brand lines with poorly differentiated brands are likely to be characterized by cannibalization and require pruning.[9] Brand Briefing 11.4 describes an academic approach to portfolio management.

The main principle in designing a brand portfolio is to *maximize market coverage* so no potential customers are being ignored, but to *minimize brand overlap* so brands are

Brand Briefing 11.4

Achieving the ideal brand portfolio

As brand portfolios evolve, they require more precise management focus. Periodic efforts to analyze and streamline expanding portfolios play an important role in brand management. Companies need a structured, clear-cut method for evaluating and refining their brand inventories to maximize how well they fit together and enhance each other's strengths, rather than merely how strong they are independently. This approach prevents small, niche brands that still bring value to the company from stagnating due to under-investment.

Hill, Ettenson and Tyson detail five steps to help managers decide how to allocate budgets across a portfolio. The authors recommend periodic portfolio planning, which entails an analysis of the entire brand roster that complements brand management efforts. Their portfolio planning framework allows managers to compare brands directly and offers direction both for the individual brands and the portfolio.

Understanding the portfolio

This step first requires taking an inventory of brands owned by the company. Hill, Ettenson and Tyson suggest compiling a list of all of a company's trademarks, and adding to it any partner brands. The authors recommend that the list not simply include the most prominent brands on a company's roster, since it is often the older, underused, or struggling brands that need most attention. The final list should then be updated by deleting obsolete trademarks and checking against the company's communications materials.

Assessing brand contribution

The second step requires analysis of the contribution of each brand in the inventory to the portfolio. The analysis accounts for revenues, marketing expenses and senior management time per brand and the brand's relative importance in the portfolio. The authors note that brands can have hidden benefits, such as providing leverage with trade partners or serving as a platform for a product line extension. Managers then evaluate all of these variables to rank the brands in triads according to profit and overhead.

Assessing market position

The authors assert that brands are like vectors: they have force and direction. The next step of portfolio analysis is gauging these two variables to get a sense of the health of a brand. Traction is a measure of the strength of the brand. It is determined from market research data as well as feedback from customers, suppliers and employees. Traction captures loyalty to the brand.

The momentum variable shows managers where the brand is headed. The purpose of measuring momentum is to identify problems with brands before they appear as declines in volume and market share. To determine a brand's momentum,

Brand Briefing 11.4 *continued*

managers need to interview internal and external stakeholders and ask them incisive questions to understand unspoken thoughts and feelings about the brand and its place relative to competitors. The researchers suggest managers take note of subtleties like body language to accurately capture responses.

Addressing problems and identifying opportunities

The researchers maintain that most brands fall into eight categories that are determined by their contribution to the company, current market performance and prospects. Each brand should be assigned to one of the following categories.

- *Power:* a brand that needs to be defended ferociously and deployed judiciously.
- *Sleeper:* a brand that can grow into a power brand.
- *Slider:* a valuable brand that has lost momentum, is slipping backwards and needs immediate intervention to prevent meltdown.
- *Soldier:* a solid brand that contributes quietly without the need for much management attention.
- *Black hole:* a brand that sucks up resources and may not ever pay out.
- *Rocket:* a brand that is on its way to power brand status.
- *Wallflower:* a small, underappreciated brand with very loyal customers, often underpriced and undermarketed.
- *Discard:* a brand that should have been retired years ago.

The authors contend that the most difficult brands to categorize and manage are those with low traction and contribution but high momentum. They can be either black holes or rockets and are tough to distinguish because they are often newer brands that have yet to reach their full potential. Additionally, many companies fail to funnel enough resources into power, sleeper, soldier and wallflower brands because they are spending so much time and attention on brands that should be discontinued. Soldier brands often form 60–80 percent of a portfolio. Managers should be careful to boost these brands with periodic infusions of resources.

Developing a plan for the portfolio

Managers face the challenge of maximizing the portfolio. They must allocate funds to each of the brands, knowing that, in the zero-sum game of portfolio planning, giving resources to one brand takes opportunity away from another. The options that must be considered include selling brands, repositioning brands, promoting brands and consolidating brands. Hill, Ettenson and Tyson argue that knowing when and where to invest in a brand is critical. Consequently, they recommend creating a list of brands to watch closely and establishing deadlines for decisions on the futures of

Brand Briefing 11.4 *continued*

those brands. This analysis should provide guidance for streamlining the portfolio and following up with brands that require attention. One of the most valuable aspects of the process is the investment of management time, which requires managers to engage with the brands and think strategically about the portfolio.

Sources: Sam Hill, Richard Ettenson and Dane Tyson, 'Achieving the ideal brand portfolio,' *MIT Sloan Management Review*, winter 2005. © 2005 by Massachusetts Institute of Technology. All rights reserved, Distributed by Tribune Media Services.

not competing among themselves to gain the same customer's approval. Each brand should have a distinct target market and positioning.[10] For example, beginning in 2000, Procter & Gamble sought to maximize market coverage and minimize brand overlap by pursuing organic growth from core brands, rather than introducing new brands. The company focused its innovation on core brands, which led to market-leading brand extensions such as Crest whitening products, Pamper's training nappies and Mr Clean Magic Eraser products.[11]

Besides these considerations, there are roles that brands can play as part of a brand portfolio (Figure 11.5).

Flankers

An important role for certain brands is as protective flanker or 'fighter' brands. The purpose of flanker brands is to create stronger points of parity with competitors' brands so that more important (and more profitable) flagship brands can retain their desired positioning. In particular, as noted in Chapter 5, many firms are introducing discount brands as flankers to compete with store brands and own labels and protect their higher-priced brand companions. In some cases, firms are repositioning existing brands in their portfolio to play that role. For example, the one-time

- To attract a particular market segment not currently being covered by other brands of the firm.
- To serve as a flanker and protect flagship brands.
- To serve as a cash cow and be milked for profits.
- To serve as a low-end entry-level product to attract new customers to the brand franchise.
- To serve as a high-end product to add prestige and credibility to the portfolio.
- To increase shelf presence and retailer dependence.
- To attract consumers seeking variety who may otherwise have switched to another brand.
- To increase competition within the firm.
- To yield economies of scale in advertising, sales, merchandising and physical distribution.

Figure 11.5   Possible special roles for brands in a portfolio

'champagne of bottled beer' Miller High Life beer was relegated in the 1990s to being a discount brand to protect the premium-priced Miller Genuine Draft and Miller Lite. Similarly, P&G repositioned its one time top tier Luvs nappies to serve as a price fighter against own labels and store brands to protect the Pampers brand.

In designing fighter brands, marketers must walk a fine line. Fighter brands must not be designed to be so attractive that they take sales away from their higher-priced comparison brands or referents. At the same time, if fighter brands are seen as connected to other brands in a portfolio (eg, by virtue of a common branding strategy), then fighter brands must not be designed so cheaply that they reflect poorly on these other brands.

Cash cows

Some brands may be kept around despite dwindling sales because they manage to hold on to customers and maintain their profitability with little marketing support. These 'cash cows' can be milked by capitalizing on their brand equity. For example, despite the fact that technological advances have moved much of its market to its newer razors, Gillette still sells older brands such as Trac II, Atra and Sensor because withdrawing these brands might result in customers switching to a rival, so it may be more profitable for Gillette to keep them in its portfolio.

Low-end entry-level or high-end prestige brands

Many brands introduce line extensions or variants in a category that vary in price and quality. These sub-brands build on associations with other brands while distinguishing themselves on the basis of price or quality. In this case, the end points of the brand line often play a specialized role.

The role of a relatively low-priced brand in a portfolio often may be to attract customers to the brand franchise. Retailers like to feature these traffic-builders because they often are able to 'trade up' customers to a higher-priced brand. For example, BMW introduced certain models into its 3-series in part as a means of bringing new customers into its brand franchise with the hope of later moving them up to higher-priced cars. BMW then took this approach one step further in 2004 by introducing the 1-series, which started at €16,280 in the USA and was built on the same production line as the 3-series.

The role of a relatively high-priced brand often is to add prestige and credibility to the entire portfolio. For example, one analyst argued that the real value to Chevrolet of its Corvette high-performance sports car was in 'its ability to lure curious customers into showrooms and at the same time help improve the image of other Chevrolet cars. It does not mean a hell of a lot for GM profitability, but there is no question that it is a traffic-builder.'[12] It was hoped that Corvette's technological image and prestige would cast a halo over the entire Chevrolet line.

Summary

In short, brands can play a number of roles within a portfolio based on considerations related to consumers, the competition and the company. Brands may expand coverage, provide protection or extend an image. In all portfolio decisions, the criteria are simple, even though their application can be complicated: each brand name product must have a clear role, what it is supposed to do for the firm; and well-defined positioning as to what benefits or promises it offers consumers, as encapsulated in the associations that the company would like it to own or represent in customers' minds. In that way, brands can maximize coverage and minimize overlap and so optimize the portfolio. Due to product proliferation, many firms are finding that they can cut the number of brands and product variants they offer and still profitably satisfy consumers.[13]

BRAND HIERARCHY

The brand–product matrix helps to highlight the range of products and brands sold by a firm. As described, it assumes each product is given one brand name. In many cases, a firm may want to make connections across products and brands to show consumers how these products and brands may be related. As a result, brand names are typically not restricted to one name but often consist of a combination of name elements. For example, a Dell Inspiron XPS notebook computer consists of three brand name elements, 'Dell', 'Inspiron' and 'XPS'. Some of these elements may be shared by many products; others are used on a restricted range of products. For example, whereas Dell uses its corporate name to brand many of its products, Inspiron designates a certain type of computer (ie, one that is portable as opposed to desktop), and XPS identifies a particular model of Inspiron (ie, one designed to maximize gaming performance.).

A *brand hierarchy* is a means of summarizing the branding strategy by displaying the number and nature of common and distinctive brand elements across the firm's products, revealing the explicit ordering of brand elements. By capturing the potential branding relationships between the products sold by a firm, a brand hierarchy is a useful means of portraying a firm's branding strategy. Specifically, a brand hierarchy is based on the realization that a product can be branded in different ways depending on how many new and existing brand elements are used and how they are combined for any one product. Because certain brand elements are used to make more than one brand, a hierarchy can be constructed to represent how (if at all) products are nested with other products because of their common brand elements. Some brand elements may be shared by many products (eg, Ford); other elements may be unique to certain products (eg, F-series trucks). Figure 11.6 shows a brand hierarchy for General Motors.

As with any hierarchy, moving from the top level to the bottom typically involves more entries at each succeeding level – in this case, more brands. There are different ways to define brand elements and levels of the hierarchy. Perhaps the simplest representation of possible brand elements and thus potential levels of a brand hierarchy – from top to bottom – might be as follows.

- Corporate (or company) brand (eg, Colgate-Palmolive).
- Family brand (eg, Colgate).
- Individual brand (eg, Colgate Total).
- Modifier (designating item or model) (eg, Colgate Total Whitening).

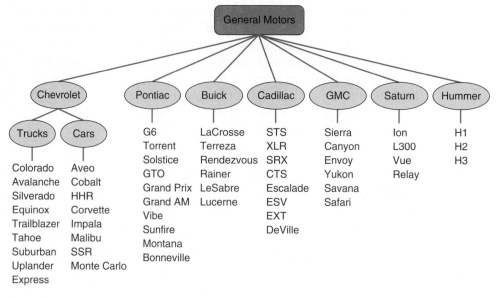

Figure 11.6   General Motors' brand hierarchy in the USA

The highest level of the hierarchy technically always involves one brand – the *corporate or company brand*. For legal reasons, the company or corporate brand is almost always present somewhere on a product or packaging, although it may be the case that the name of a company subsidiary may appear instead of the corporate name. For example, US group Fortune Brands owns many companies, such as Titleist golf balls and clubs, Footjoy golf shoes and gloves, Jim Beam whisky, Courvoisier cognac, Master Lock locks and Moen taps, but does not use its corporate name on any of its lines. For some firms, the corporate brand is virtually the only brand used (eg, as with Nokia and Ericsson). Other firms combine their corporate brand name with family brands or individual brands (eg, conglomerate Siemens' varied electrical engineering and electronics business units are branded with descriptive modifiers, such as Siemens Transportation Systems). Finally, in some cases, the company name is virtually invisible and, although technically part of the hierarchy, receives virtually no attention in the marketing campaign (eg, the V&S Group does not use its name on its Absolut vodka).

At the next level down, a *family brand* is used in more than one product category but is not necessarily the name of the company itself. For example, ConAgra's Healthy Choice family brand is used to sell packaged meats, soups, pasta sauces, breads, popcorn and ice-cream. Other examples of family brands include Seagram's Tropicana juices and PepsiCo's Gatorade. Most firms typically only support a handful of family brands. If the corporate brand is applied to a range of products, then it functions as a family brand, too, and the two levels collapse to one for those products.

An *individual brand* is restricted to essentially one product category, although it may be used for several products within the category. For example, in the 'salty snack' product class, Frito-Lay offers Fritos corn chips, Doritos tortilla chips, Lays and Ruffles potato crisps and Rold Gold pretzels. Each brand has a dominant position in its respective category within the broader salty snack product class. A *modifier* is a means of designating a specific item or model type or a particular version or configuration of the product. Land O'Lakes offers 'whipped', 'unsalted' and 'regular' versions of its butter. Yoplait yogurt comes in 'light', 'custard style' or 'natural' flavours.

Figure 11.6 is an abridged version of a hierarchy for General Motors' branding strategy for the USA in 2005. It is important to note that, as this example suggests, different levels of the hierarchy may receive different emphasis in developing a branding strategy. For example, General Motors traditionally chose to downplay its corporate name in branding its cars, although the name recently has played a more important role in its supporting marketing activities. As will be discussed later in this chapter, such shifts in emphasis are an attempt by the firm to harness the positive associations and mitigate against the poor associations of different brands in different contexts, and there are ways to place more or less emphasis on the elements that combine to make up a brand.

Akzo Nobel

A Netherlands-based maker of healthcare products, coatings, chemicals and fibres, Akzo Nobel uses a four-tier brand hierarchy based on the following rationale.[14]

- Use of the *corporate brand* only in some industrial markets for chemicals, coatings and fibres where the company name establishes a product's reputation.
- Use of the *corporate brand plus a product brand* in some industrial markets for chemicals, coatings and fibres to add value or help position a product in relation to other brands.
- Use of a *prominent product brand endorsed by the corporate brand* in some industrial markets for coating materials where the product brand is especially strong, but can still be helped by a corporate endorsement.
- Use of *only a product brand* in pharmaceuticals and some coating products where the marketing strategy makes this approach most desirable (but the corporate name might still appear on company stationery and signs).

Building equity at different hierarchy levels

Before considering how the brand hierarchy can help to formulate branding strategies, it is worthwhile first examining some issues in building brand knowledge structures – and thus brand equity – at each of the levels of the brand hierarchy.

Corporate or company brand level

For simplicity, this chapter refers to corporate and company brands interchangeably, recognizing that consumers may not necessarily draw a distinction between the two or recognize that firms may subsume multiple companies. A corporate image can be thought of as the associations that consumers have in memory with the company making the product or providing the service as a whole. Corporate image is a particularly relevant concern when the corporate or company brand plays a prominent role in a branding strategy.

More generally, some marketing experts believe that a factor increasing in importance in consumer purchase decisions is consumer perceptions of a firm's whole role in society – for example, how it treats employees, shareholders, neighbours and others. As the head of a large ad agency put it: 'The only sustainable competitive advantage any business has is its reputation.'[15] Consistent with this reasoning, a global survey of financial analysts indicated that 91 percent of the sample agreed that a company that failed to look after its reputation would meet financial difficulties. Moreover, 96 percent of the analysts responded that the chief executive's reputation was fairly, very or extremely important in influencing their ratings.[16]

Similarly, the annual 2007 RepTrak survey, carried out in 29 countries by the Reputation Institute concluded that a strong statistical correlation existed between an excellent corporate reputation and consumers' intentions to buy a company's products and services, recommend them to other people, buy a company's stock and recommend the stock to other investors.[17] Interbrand found that a strong corporate brand could improve a company's stock price by 5 percent to 7 percent in a bull market and mitigate losses in a bear market.[18] Not coincidentally, a survey by *PR Week* magazine found that almost three in four managing directors were worried about threats to their organizations' corporate reputation.[19] In justifying marketing investments, executives at Accenture maintain that a strong corporate image can also attract and motivate employees.

The realization that consumers and others may be interested in issues beyond product characteristics and associations has prompted much marketing activity to improve corporate image. A corporate image will depend on a number of factors, such as the products a company makes, the actions it takes and the manner in which it communicates with consumers. Barich and Kotler identify a host of determinants of company image (Figure 11.7).[20] As one chief executive at Johnson & Johnson observed: 'Reputations reflect behaviour you exhibit day in and day out through a hundred small things. The way you manage your reputation is by always thinking and trying to do the right thing every day.'[21] Brand Briefing 11.12 details how Johnson & Johnson managed to preserve both the reputation of the Tylenol and its own corporate reputation by responding appropriately to a product safety crisis.

Corporate brand equity can be defined as the differential response by consumers, customers, employees, other firms or any relevant constituency to the words, actions, communications, products or services provided by an identified corporate brand entity. In other words, positive corporate brand equity occurs when a relevant constituency responds more favourably to a corporate ad campaign, a corporate-branded product or service, a press release and so on than if the same offering were to be attributed to an unknown or fictitious company. Corporate brand equity occurs when relevant constituents hold strong, favourable and unique associations regarding the corporate brand in memory. A corporate brand can be a

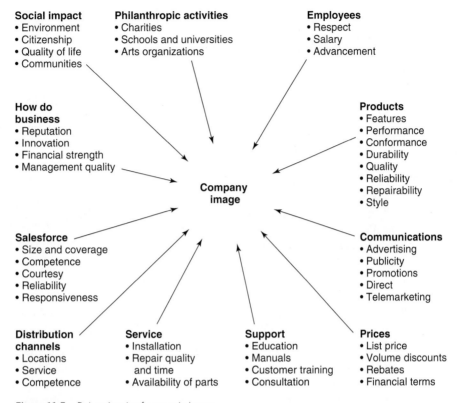

Social impact
- Environment
- Citizenship
- Quality of life
- Communities

Philanthropic activities
- Charities
- Schools and universities
- Arts organizations

Employees
- Respect
- Salary
- Advancement

How do business
- Reputation
- Innovation
- Financial strength
- Management quality

Products
- Features
- Performance
- Conformance
- Durability
- Quality
- Reliability
- Repairability
- Style

Company image

Salesforce
- Size and coverage
- Competence
- Courtesy
- Reliability
- Responsiveness

Communications
- Advertising
- Publicity
- Promotions
- Direct
- Telemarketing

Distribution channels
- Locations
- Service
- Competence

Service
- Installation
- Repair quality and time
- Availability of parts

Support
- Education
- Manuals
- Customer training
- Consultation

Prices
- List price
- Volume discounts
- Rebates
- Financial terms

Figure 11.7   Determinants of corporate image

powerful means for firms to express themselves in a way that is not tied to their specific products or services. Brand Briefing 11.5 describes one approach to defining corporate brand personality.

Brand Briefing 11.5

Corporate brand personality

Three core dimensions that a company's brand personality needs to reflect: heart, mind and body. These dimensions are composed of two personality traits each: passionate and compassionate (heart); creative and disciplined (mind); and agile and collaborative (body).

Corporate personality is defined as 'a form of brand personality specific to a corporate brand'. Brand personality is understood as 'the human characteristics or traits that can be attributed to a brand.' The authors note that, despite the fact that brand personality refers to both product brands and corporate brands, corporate brands are distinct from product brands because the former is designed to encompass

Brand Briefing 11.5 *continued*

a wider range of associations. The authors define the dimensions of corporate personality as follows.

- The 'heart' of the company is comprised of two traits: *passionate* and *compassionate*. The company must be passionate about serving its customers and competing in the market and must have compassion for employees, stakeholders and members of the communities in which it operates.
- The 'mind' of the company contains two traits: *creative* and *disciplined*. A company must be creative in serving customers and winning in the market, while adopting a disciplined approach that ensures appropriate and consistent actions across the organization.
- The 'body' of the company is made up of two traits: *agile* and *collaborative*. The company must possess the agility to react profitably to changes in the market and also employ a collaborative approach that ensures it works well with people inside and outside the company towards common goals.

A tradeoff exists between the two traits within the 'mind' dimension: 'while it is necessary to encourage and maintain creativity in the organization, this creativity must be focused to a certain degree'. To be successful, a firm must use its core capabilities and focus on its core business, instead of pursuing every opportunity that arises. This tradeoff can be managed by 'setting appropriate priorities that provide clear direction to all members of the organization as to what its business goals are and how they can be met'. One company that has blended creativity and discipline is 3M, which requires its scientists to spend 15 percent of their time researching topics of interest to them beyond their specific research role. Thus the company encourages innovative research and thinking, but ensures that this research augments its core business rather than distracts from it.

These dimensions have a multiplying effect, not merely an additive effect. For example, passion can drive creativity in an organization. In turn, creativity spurs agility, as more creative firms are able to rapidly find solutions to problems or recognize new opportunities. Additionally, discipline engenders better collaborative efforts, as guidelines and partnership principles are more readily established and followed.

It is important to build these dimensions of corporate personality traits into a brand because the corporation competing in the twenty-first century will be defined 'as much by *who* it is as *what* it does'. This contrasts with the historical case for companies where the identity of a company was based on what products and services it sold and its actions in the market. A company's employees are, in many cases, the outward face of the company that consumers see and so define 'who' it is. It is therefore necessary, the authors assert, that employees embody the personality traits that the company has established. If all employees act with a 'heart', 'mind' and 'body', the company will be better positioned to achieve success.

A corporate brand is distinct from a product brand in that it can encompass far more associations. That is, a corporate brand may evoke associations wholly different from an individual brand, which is identified only with a certain product or products. For example, a corporate brand name may be more likely to evoke associations with common products and their shared attributes or benefits; people and relationships; activities and values; and corporate credibility, as will be discussed below. These associations can have an important effect on the brand equity and market performance of individual products. For example, one research study revealed that consumers with a favourable corporate image of DuPont were likely to respond favourably to the claims made in an ad for Stainmaster carpet and so buy the product.[22]

Building and managing a strong corporate brand has additional requirements. For example, it necessitates that the firm keep a high public profile, especially in terms of influencing and shaping abstract types of associations. The chairman or managing director, if associated with a corporate brand, must be willing to maintain a public profile to help to communicate news and information, as well as perhaps provide a symbol of marketing activities. At the same time, by virtue of a more visible public profile, a firm must also be willing to be subject to more scrutiny and be more transparent in terms of its values, activities and campaigns. Corporate brands thus have to be comfortable with a high level of openness.

A corporate brand offers a host of marketing advantages, but only if corporate brand equity is carefully built and nurtured – a challenging task. Evidence is mounting for the advantages of a strong corporate brand. Many of the marketing winners in the next few years will therefore be those firms that build and manage corporate brand equity. Brand Briefing 11.6 describes a closely related concept – corporate reputation – and how it may be looked at from the perspective of consumers and other firms.[23] This chapter next considers the other three levels of the brand hierarchy.

Brand Briefing 11.6

Corporate reputations: most-admired companies in USA

The results of the RQ 2005 study of corporate reputations by Harris Interactive and the Reputation Institute demonstrated both the enduring character of corporate reputations and their ability to change quickly. According to Charles Fombrun, executive director of the Reputation Institute and co-creator of the annual RQ study, 'Corporate reputations are Janus-faced. Companies like Johnson & Johnson and Coca-Cola have consistently dominated our public rankings, whereas oil, tobacco and scandal-plagued companies have anchored the bottom of the distribution. At the same time, reputations can change quickly, with autos and pharmaceuticals taking a big hit in 2005, but technology companies like Google skyrocketing to the top of the list.'

The rated companies are determined from a sampling of 6,000 respondents who are asked to name 2 companies with the best corporate reputations in the USA and 2

Brand Briefing 11.6 *continued*

companies with the worst reputations. The open-ended nominations are summed to create a list of the 60 'most visible companies'. Some 20,000 people are then asked to rate the companies on the 20 attributes of the Harris-Fombrun Reputation Quotient, which is designed to measure corporate reputations in 6 areas: emotional appeal, product/service quality, financial performance, social responsibility, vision and leadership, and workplace environment. Here are the 2005 results.

Rank	Company
1	Johnson & Johnson
2	Coca-Cola
3	Google
4	UPS
5	3M
6	Sony
7	Microsoft
8	General Mills
9	FedEx
10	Intel

Source: Reputation Institute, 2005

Family brand level

Family brands, like corporate or company brands, are applied across product categories. The main difference is that because a family brand may be distinct from the corporate or company brand, company-level associations may be less salient. People sometimes refer to these as *range brands* or *umbrella brands*.

Family brands are used instead of corporate brands for several reasons. As products become more dissimilar, it may be harder for the corporate brand to be used and still retain any product meaning or to effectively link the disparate products. Distinct family brands, however, can be circumscribed to evoke a specific set of associations across a group of related products.[24] As with corporate brands, these associations may relate to common product attributes, benefits and attitudes and, perhaps to a lesser extent, people and relationships, campaigns and values, and corporate credibility.

Family brands thus can link common associations to many products. The cost of introducing a related new product can be lower and the likelihood of acceptance can be higher when an existing family brand is used for a new product. However, if the products linked to the family brand and their supporting marketing campaigns are not carefully considered and designed, the associations with the family brand may become weaker and less favourable. Moreover, the failure of one product may damage other products sold by the firm under the same brand by virtue of the common brand identification. These pros and cons must be assessed to determine whether a 'branded house' or 'house of brands' is the more appropriate strategy.

Individual brand level

Individual brands are restricted to essentially one product category, although there may be many product types offered on the basis of different models, package sizes, flavours and so forth. The main advantage of creating individual brands is that the brand and all its supporting marketing activity can be customized to meet the needs of a specific customer group. Thus, brand elements, as well as product design, marketing communication campaigns and pricing and distribution strategies, can all be designed to focus on a certain market. Moreover, if the brand runs into difficulty or fails, the risk to other brands and the company itself is minimized. The disadvantages of creating individual brands, however, are the difficulty, complexity and expense involved in developing separate marketing campaigns to build sufficient levels of brand equity. Chapter 12 examines the pros and cons of individual brands versus corporate or family brands in the context of considering brand extensions.

Modifier level

Regardless of whether corporate, family or individual brands are employed, it is often necessary to distinguish brands according to the types of items or models involved. Adding a modifier often can signal refinements or differences in the brand related to factors such as quality levels (eg, Johnnie Walker Red Label, Black Label, Gold Label and Blue Label whisky), attributes (eg, Wrigley's Spearmint, Doublemint and Juicy Fruit flavours of chewing gum), functions (eg, Kodak's 100-, 200-, and 400-speed 35-mm and APS films) and so forth.[25] Brand modifiers can play an important organizing role in communicating how products within a category that share the same brand name differ on one or more significant attribute or benefit dimensions. Thus, one of the uses of brand modifiers is to show how one brand variation relates to others in the brand family. As such, modifiers play an important role in ensuring market coverage within a category for the company as a whole. Modifiers help to make products more understandable and relevant to consumers or even the trade. Modifiers can even become strong trademarks if they are able to develop a unique association with the parent brand – an example being the fact that only Guinness has widget.[26]

Product descriptor

Although not a brand element per se, the product descriptor chosen for a branded product may be an important ingredient of a branding strategy. The product descriptor helps consumers understand what the product is and does and also helps to define the relevant competition in consumers' minds. In some cases, it may be hard to describe succinctly what the product is, especially in the case of a product with unusual functions.

Introducing a new product with a familiar product name may facilitate basic familiarity and comprehension but perhaps at the expense of a richer understanding of how the product is different from closely related, existing products.

Corporate image dimensions

Before considering some of the decisions needed to set up a brand hierarchy, it is worthwhile considering the types of associations that may exist at the corporate or company brand level – or perhaps even the family brand level. This section highlights some of the types of associations that are likely to be linked to a corporate brand and can potentially affect brand equity (see Figure 11.8).[27]

Common product attributes, benefits or attitudes
Quality.
Innovativeness.

People and relationships
Customer orientation.
Values and activities.
Concern with environment.
Social responsibility.

Corporate credibility
Expertise.
Trustworthiness.
Likeability.

Dimensions of the RepTrak model

The Reputation Institute research has enabled the development and improvement of the previous model of reputation analysis. Statistical analysis and focus groups have shown that a company's reputation can be optimally rated based on four questions about: admiration and respect; trust; good feelings; and esteem.

In addition, the RepTrak model (Figure 8.5) includes 23 performance indicators and the questions related to these performance indicators can help to explain a company's reputation. Companies can therefore aim to improve their reputation by working on these performance indicators.

The performance indicators are divided into seven dimensions: products and services; innovation; workplace; governance; citizenship; leadership and performance.

Figure 11.8   Corporate image associations and the RepTrak model
Source: Reputation Institute

Common product attributes, benefits or attitudes

As with individual brands, a corporate or company brand may evoke performance or imagery attribute or benefit associations as well as judgement and feeling associations. Thus, a corporate brand may evoke a strong association for consumers with a product attribute (eg, Cadbury's with 'chocolate'), type of user (eg, BMW with 'executives'), usage situation (eg, Club Med with 'fun times') or overall judgement (eg, Sony with 'quality').

If a corporate brand is linked with products across diverse categories, then some of its strongest associations are likely to be with those intangible attributes, abstract benefits or attitudes that span each of the product categories. For example, companies may be associated with products or services that solve problems (eg, Black & Decker), bring excitement and fun to certain activities (eg, Nintendo), are built with the highest quality standards (eg, Motorola), contain advanced or innovative features (eg, Rubbermaid) or represent market leadership (eg, Hertz). Two product-related corporate image associations – high quality and innovation – deserve special attention.

A *high-quality corporate image association* involves the creation of consumer perceptions that a company makes products of the highest quality. A number of organizations rate products (eg, JD consumer testing magazines and various trade publications) and companies on the basis of quality. As Chapter 2 pointed out, consumer surveys often reveal that quality is one of the most important, if not *the* most important, decision factors for consumers.

An *innovative corporate image association* involves the creation of consumer perceptions of a company as developing new and unique marketing campaigns, especially with respect to product introductions or improvements. Keller and Aaker's experiments showed how corporate image strategies – being innovative, environmentally concerned or involved in the community – could differentially affect corporate credibility and strategically benefit the firm by increasing the acceptance of brand extensions as a result.[28] Specifically, they showed how corporate images of being environmentally concerned and involved in the community affected consumer perceptions of corporate trustworthiness and likeability but not corporate expertise. Interestingly, a company with an innovative corporate image was not only seen as expert but also as trustworthy and likeable.

Being innovative is seen in part as being modern and up to date, investing in research and development, employing the most advanced manufacturing capabilities and introducing the latest products features. An image priority for many Japanese companies – from consumer products companies such as Kao to more technically orientated companies such as Canon – is to be perceived as innovative.[29] Perceived innovation is also a competitive weapon and priority for firms in other countries. Michelin ('A better way forward') describes how its commitment to the environment, security, value and driving pleasure has been driving innovation. Brand Briefing 11.7 describes how 3M has developed an innovative culture and image.

People and relationships

Corporate image associations may reflect characteristics of the employees of the company. Although this is a natural strategy for service firms such as airlines

Brand Briefing 11.7

Innovation at 3M

Minnesota Mining and Manufacturing (3M) has fostered a culture of innovation and improvisation since its very beginnings. In 1904, the company's directors were faced with a failed mining operation, but they turned the leftover grit and wastage into a revolutionary product: sandpaper. Today 3M makes more than 60,000 products, including sandpaper, adhesives, computer disks, contact lenses and optical films. Each year, 3M launches scores of products, and the company earns about 35 percent of its revenue from products introduced within the past five years. The company regularly ranks among the top ten US companies in patents received. 3M has an annual R&D budget of €684 million, which is a healthy portion of its annual €11.4 billion in sales.

3M has a long history of innovation. In addition to inventing sandpaper, the company has developed many products that were the first of their kind:

> 1925: Scotch masking tape
> 1930: Scotch transparent tape
> 1939: Reflective traffic sign
> 1956: Scotchguard fabric protector
> 1962: Tartan Track, first synthetic running track
> 1979: Thinsulate thermal insulation
> 1980: Post-it Notes
> 1985: Refastening tape for nappies
> 1995: Non-chlorofluorocarbon aerosol inhaler
> 2000: Laminating products that do not require heat

3M is able to consistently innovate in part because the company promotes a corporate environment that encourages discoveries. The following are some tactics the company uses to ensure its culture remains focused on innovation.

- 3M encourages everyone, not just engineers, to become 'product champions'. The company's '15 percent rule' allows all employees to spend up to 15 percent of their time working on projects of personal interest. Post-it Notes, masking tape and the company's microreplication technology developed as a result of 15 percent rule activities.

- Each promising idea is assigned to a multidisciplinary venture team headed by an 'executive champion'.

- 3M expects failures and uses failed products as opportunities to learn how to make products that work. Its slogan is: 'You have to kiss a lot of frogs to find a prince.'

- 3M hands out its Golden Step awards each year to the venture teams whose new products earned more than €1.37 million in US sales or €2.74 million in worldwide sales within three years of commercial introduction.

In the late 1990s, 3M struggled as sales stalled and profits fell. The company restructured, shed non-core businesses and cut its workforce. As a result, 3M saw

Brand Briefing 11.7 *continued*

record sales and income in 2000. When 3M named former General Electric executive James McNerney as its new chairman and chief executive that year, McNerney vowed he would continue to improve the company's bottom line while keeping its culture of innovation intact.

Sources: Philip Kotler and Kevin Lane Keller, *Marketing Management*, 12th edn, Upper Saddle River, NJ: Prentice-Hall, 2006; www.3m.com; 3M 2000 annual report.

(eg, Singapore Airlines), rental cars (eg, Avis), hotels (eg, Ritz-Carlton) and retailers (Asda) and manufacturing firms, others have also focused attention on their employees in communication campaigns. The rationale for such a positioning is that the traits exhibited by employees will directly or indirectly have implications for consumers concerning the products the firm makes or the services they provide.

Saturn

General Motors created a division, Saturn, that advertises itself as a 'Different kind of car company' in an attempt to build unique relationships with consumers. According to then GM chairman John Smale, Saturn's brand promise (and point of difference) was that it was the car to buy for consumers who 'want a car built, sold and serviced by people who really care – people whose No. 1 priority is to satisfy you and build and preserve a relationship with you, no matter what it takes.' The marketing campaign created associations for Saturn of it coming from a 'dedicated and caring' car company.[30]

Shops also derive brand equity from employees. For example, growing from its origins selling shoes, Seattle-based Nordstrom became one of the leading US fashion shops through a commitment to quality, value, selection and, especially, service. Legendary for its 'personalized touch' and willingness to go to extraordinary lengths to satisfy its customers, Nordstrom creates brand equity in large part through the efforts of its salespeople and the relationships they develop with customers.

Thus, a *customer-focused corporate image association* involves the creation of consumer perceptions of a company as responding to and caring about its customers. In such cases, consumers believe that their voice will be heard and that the company is not attempting to exploit them. Thus, a company seen as customer-focused is likely to be described as 'listening' to customers and having their best interests in mind. Often this philosophy is reflected throughout the marketing campaign and other communications.

Values and activities

Corporate image associations may reflect values and activities of the company that do not always directly relate to the products they sell. Brand Briefing 11.8 describes how Clif Bar remained consistent with its values. In many cases, such efforts are

Brand Briefing 11.8

Corporate values take centre stage at Clif Bar

Gary Erickson founded the Clif Bar business in 1990 in California after what he calls 'the epiphany'. Erickson was in the middle of a 175-mile bike ride and could-n't stand another bite of the bland energy bars he had brought along. He decided that he could make a better bar himself. Erickson developed his own recipe and named his company after his father, Clif. The company has grown to €68.4 million in sales and has been profitable every year.

Clif Bar's focus on health extends from products aimed at consumers with an active lifestyle to its work environment. The corporate headquarters houses a gym with personal trainers, bikes that employees can use during lunchtime and a climbing wall. Employees have the option to work longer hours and take off every other Friday. They are encouraged to use company time to volunteer for community projects. Addition-ally, Clif Bar invested in a wind farm that creates energy to offset the carbon dioxide generated by the company's manufacturing, offices and employee commuting.

As the energy bar market matured, Clif Bar began to compete against food con-glomerates with big advertising budgets. In 2000, Kraft bought competitor Balance Bar and Nestlé scooped up PowerBar. The same year, Erickson turned down a buy-out offer from a large food conglomerate, reasoning that a corporate owner would destroy the culture he had worked so hard to create. Furthermore, he didn't want to move the company and force employees to relocate. The decision to remain private has worked; profits have been rising since 1998.

In the late 1990s, Clif Bar sponsored cyclist Lance Armstrong and the US Postal Service team in the Tour de France. However, when Armstrong became more of a celebrity, PowerBar offered him €274,000 a year, 10 times what the team had been getting from Clif Bar. Clif Bar lost the sponsorship, but Erickson and Sherry O'Loughlin, a former marketing manager at Kraft and Quaker Oats whom Erickson brought in as co-chief executive, realized they needed to rely on grass roots promo-tion. They designed a campaign recognizing the support riders who help cyclists win, which drove thousands of cycling enthusiasts to the Clif Bar website.

Clif Bar prefers interacting with consumers in person, as opposed to TV ads. One of the company's primary methods is sampling in stalls at marathon finish lines, and at other events such as the opening of 'eco-friendly' hotel rooms in San Francisco. Additionally, Clif Bar wrappers tell the story of the company's founding and pro-mote the causes it supports.

In 2003, Clif Bar made a bold move and made all of its products organic. The switch required finding many new suppliers. Although costs rose 15 percent, Erickson chose not to raise prices, a decision that a corporate parent might not have backed. But Erickson felt the move was the right one considering sales of all organic prod-ucts had been growing and Clif Bar sales subsequently rose in health-food shops. The rising popularity of organic products helped offset the sales slowdown endured

Brand Briefing 11.8 *continued*

in the energy bar category as a result of the low-carb craze. Brand extensions such as the Luna bar for women and the Clif Nectar with five or fewer ingredients have also helped spur growth. By remaining committed to making healthy products and demonstrating respect for employees, consumers and the environment, Clif Bar has remained successful even as competition has intensified.

Sources: Melanie Warner, 'Clif Bar's solo climb', *Business 2.0*, December 2004; Julie Schmit, 'Raising the bar on how business gets done', *USA Today*, 14 March 2005; Gary Erickson, 'Bottom line is where you draw it', *Seattle Post Intelligencer*, 28 October 2005; www.clifbar.com.

publicized through marketing campaigns. Firms can run corporate image ad campaigns as a means of describing to consumers, employees and others the philosophy and actions of the company with respect to organizational, social, political or economic issues.

For example, a focus of many campaigns has been company communications and activities designed to address environmental issues and communicate social responsibility. A *socially responsible corporate image association* involves creation of consumer perceptions of a company as contributing to community development, supporting artistic and social activities and generally attempting to improve the welfare of society as a whole. An *environmentally concerned* association involves the creation of consumer perceptions of a company as developing marketing campaigns to protect or improve the environment and make more effective use of scarce natural resources. Below, we consider the broader issue of cause marketing in more detail.

British Airways: change for good

British Airways partnered with Unicef and developed a cause marketing campaign called Change For Good, in which travellers on British Airways flights are encouraged to donate leftover foreign currency from their travels. Since coins are difficult to exchange, the campaign targets this loose change. The scheme is simple: passengers deposit surplus currency in envelopes provided by British Airways, which collects the deposits and donates them to Unicef. British Airways advertises its campaign during an in-flight video, on the backs of seat cards and with in-flight announcements. The company also developed a television advertisement that featured a child thanking British Airways for its contribution to Unicef.

Corporate credibility

Besides all the associations noted previously, consumers may form more abstract judgements or feelings about a company. For example, as Chapter 2 described, consumers may form perceptions of the personality of a corporate brand. For example, one US utility company was described by customers as 'male, 35–40 years old, middle class, married with children, wearing a flannel shirt and khaki pants who would be reliable, competent, professional, intelligent, honest, ethical and business-oriented'. On the downside, the company was also described by these same customers as 'distant, impersonal and self-focused', suggesting an important area for improvement in its image.

A particularly important set of abstract associations with a corporate brand is corporate credibility. As defined in Chapter 2, corporate credibility is the extent to which consumers believe that a firm can design and deliver products and services that satisfy their needs and wants. Thus, corporate credibility depends on three factors.

1. *Corporate expertise:* the extent to which a company is seen as able to make and sell its products or conduct its services in a competent way.
2. *Corporate trustworthiness:* the extent to which a company is seen as motivated to be honest, dependable and sensitive to customers' needs.
3. *Corporate likeability:* the extent to which a company is seen as likeable, attractive, prestigious, dynamic and so forth.

Other characteristics can be related to these three dimensions – for example, success and leadership. Perceived brand credibility increases the likelihood of consumer consideration and choice.[31] Creating a firm with a strong and credible reputation may offer benefits beyond consumers' responses.

LL Bean

A brand seen by its customers as highly credible, US outdoors product retailer LL Bean attempts to earn consumers' trust every step of the way – providing advice, secure transactions, best-in-class delivery and easy returns and exchanges. Founded in 1912, the company backs its efforts with a 100 percent satisfaction guarantee as well as its golden rule: 'Sell good merchandise at a reasonable profit, treat your customers like human beings, and they will always come back for more.' Now a billion euro brand in sales, the company retains its roots of being passionate about the outdoors with a profound belief in honesty, product quality and customer service.

A highly credible company may be treated more favourably by government or legal officials. It also may be possible to attract better-qualified employees. Such a company may also help motivate employees. As one Shell Oil employee remarked: 'If you're really proud of where you work, I think you put a little more thought into what you did to help get them there.' A strong corporate reputation can help a firm survive a crisis and avert public outrage that could potentially depress sales, encourage strikes or block expansion plans. As academic Steve Greyser notes. 'Corporate reputation . . . can serve as a capital account of favourable attitudes to help buffer corporate trouble.' Brand Briefing 11.12 considers some marketing communication issues for handling a marketing crisis.

Summary

Many types of associations may become linked to a corporate brand that transcend physical product characteristics.[32] These intangible associations may provide valuable sources of brand equity and serve as critical points of parity or points of difference. Companies have a number of ways – indirect or direct – of creating these associations. In doing so, it is important that companies 'talk the talk' and 'walk the walk' by communicating to consumers as well as backing up their claims with campaigns that consumers can understand or experience.

DESIGNING A BRANDING STRATEGY

Given the levels of a branding hierarchy, a firm has many branding options available, depending on how each level is employed, if at all. There is no agreement on the type of strategy that should be adopted by all firms for all products. LaForet and Saunders analyzed the strategies of 20 brands sold by each of 20 of the biggest suppliers of products to Tesco and Sainsbury, Britain's two leading supermarket chains.[33] They categorized the strategies using a scheme that can be seen as a refinement of the four-level brand hierarchy described in this chapter. As Figure 11.9 shows, many approaches were employed. The authors note how companies within the same market could adopt sharply contrasting strategies, offering the following example.

> For a long time Cadbury, Mars, and Nestlé have competed in the confectionery market. They often match each other brand-for-brand but their branding strategies are quite different. While Cadbury led with the Cadbury name and colours across virtually all their products, such as Cadbury's Dairy Milk, Cadbury's Milk Tray, Cadbury's Flake, etc., Mars led with its brands such as Mars Bars, Snickers and Twix with no corporate endorsement. Until recently, Nestlé Rowntree pursued a branded approach like Mars, but now the Nestlé name has started to appear upon the once independently branded products.[34]

Branding strategy	Percentage of occurrence
Corporate dominant	
Corporate brands: corporate name used	5
House brands: subsidiary name used	11
Mixed brands	
Dual brands: two or more names given equal prominence	38.5
Endorsed brands: brand endorsed by corporate or house identity	13.5
Brand dominant	
Mono brands: single brand name used	19
Furtive brands: single brand name used and corporate identity not disclosed	13

Figure 11.9   Breakdown of brand types

Source: Sylvie LaForet and John Saunders, 'Managing brand portfolios: how the leaders do it', *Journal of Advertising Research*, September/October 1994: 64–76.

Miller adopts various strategies

Even within one firm, different branding strategies may be adopted for different products. For example, although Miller has used its name across its different beers over the years with various sub-brands (eg, Miller High Life, Miller Lite and Miller Genuine Draft), it carefully branded its no-alcohol beer substitute as Sharp's, its ice beer as Icehouse and its low-priced beer as Milwaukee's Best, with no overt Miller identification. The assumption was that the corporate family brand name would not be valued by the target market. Following its 2002 merger with South Africa Breweries to form SAB Miller, the Miller brand was not applied to any more beers from the 150 international and regional brands owned by the company.

Thus, it is important to note that *the brand hierarchy may not be symmetrical*. Because of considerations related to corporate objectives, consumer behaviour or competitive activity, there may sometimes be significant deviations in branding strategy and how the brand hierarchy is organized for different products or markets. Brand elements may receive more or less emphasis, or not be present at all, depending on the product and market. For example, in appealing to a market segment where the DuPont brand name may be more valuable, it might receive more emphasis than associated sub-brands. In appealing to a consumer market segment, a sub-brand may be more meaningful and thus receive relatively more emphasis (Figure 11.10).

How does a firm use different levels of the brand hierarchy to build brand equity? Brand elements at each level of the hierarchy may contribute to brand equity through their ability to create awareness as well as foster associations and positive responses. Therefore, the challenge in setting up the brand hierarchy and arriving at a branding strategy is to: design the proper brand hierarchy in terms of the number and nature of brand elements at each level; and design the optimal supporting marketing campaign in terms of creating the desired amount of brand awareness and type of brand associations at each level. Specifically, designing a brand hierarchy and brand strategy involves decisions related to the following.

- The number of levels of the hierarchy to use.
- Desired brand awareness and image at each level.

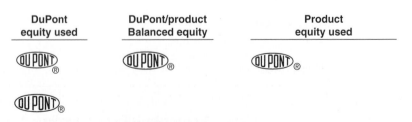

Figure 11.10   DuPont 'product-endorsed' business strategy

1. **Decide on the number of levels.**
   - *Principle of simplicity:* employ as few levels as possible.
   - *Principle of clarity:* logic and relationship of all brand elements employed must be obvious and transparent.
2. **Decide on the levels of awareness and types of associations to be created at each level.**
   - *Principle of relevance:* create abstract associations that are relevant across as many items as possible.
   - *Principle of differentiation:* differentiate between individual items and brands.
3. **Decide on how and which products to be introduced.**
   - *Principle of growth:* investments in market penetration or expansion v product development should be made according to ROI opportunities.
   - *Principle of survival:* brand extensions must achieve brand equity in their categories.
   - *Principle of synergy:* brand extensions should enhance the equity of the parent brand.
4. **Decide on how to link brands from different levels for a product.**
   - *Principle of prominence:* the relative prominence of brand elements affects perceptions of product distance and the type of image created for new products.
5. **Decide on how to link a brand across products.**
   - *Principle of commonality:* the more common elements are shared by products, the stronger the linkages.

Figure 11.11   Guidelines for brand hierarchy decisions

- How brand elements from different levels of the hierarchy are combined, if at all, for a product.
- How any one brand element is linked, if at all, to other products.

Figure 11.11 reviews these decisions in terms of five guidelines that assist the design of brand hierarchies.

Number of levels of the brand hierarchy

The first decision to make in defining a strategy is which level or levels of the branding hierarchy should be used. In general, most companies choose to use more than one level for two reasons. Each branding level used allows the firm to communicate additional, specific information. Thus, developing brands at lower levels of the hierarchy allows flexibility in communicating the uniqueness of products. At the same time, developing brands at higher levels of the hierarchy such that the brand is applied across several products is obviously an economical means of communicating common or shared information and providing synergy across the company's operations, both internally and externally.

The practice of combining an existing brand with a new brand on a product is called *sub-branding* because the subordinate brand is a means of modifying the superordinate brand. Sub-branding often combines the company or family brand name with individual brands and even model types. Extending an earlier example, ThinkPad can be seen as a sub-brand to the IBM name, with T42 as a second-level sub-brand to modify the meaning of the product. As suggested, a sub-brand, or hybrid branding, strategy offers two potential benefits in that it can facilitate access to both associations and attitudes regarding the company or family brand as a whole and, at the same time, allow specific brand beliefs. It is this latter benefit that enabled Chinese computer manufacturer Lenovo, when it purchased IBM's PC division and began selling laptops under the Lenovo brand, to retain the brand strength that had been built at the ThinkPad sub-brand level.

Sub-branding thus creates a stronger connection with the company or family brand and all the associations that come along with that. As an illustration, consider the cereal category, in which Kellogg's has adopted a sub-branding strategy whereas other manufacturers have adopted an endorsement strategy. Such strategies should have profound implications for consumers' identification of and associations with certain cereal brands. Through its sub-branding strategy and marketing activities, Kellogg's should be more effective than competitors in connecting its corporate name with its products and, as a result, possibly creating favourable associations with its corporate name.

At the same time, developing sub-brands allows the creation of brand-specific beliefs. This more detailed information can help customers better understand how products vary and which particular product may be right for them. Sub-brands also help to organize selling efforts so that salespeople and retailers have a clear picture as to how the product line is organized and how it might best be sold. For example, one of the main advantages to Nike of creating sub-brands for its basketball trainers (eg, Air Jordan, Air Flight, Air Force) has been to generate retail interest and enthusiasm.

The *principle of simplicity* is based on the need to provide the right amount of branding information to consumers – no more and no less. In general, the desired number of levels of the brand hierarchy depends on the complexity of the product line or product mix associated with a brand and thus the combination of shared and separate brand associations that the company would like to link to a product in its range.

With relatively simple products – such as lightbulbs, batteries and chewing gum – the branding strategy often consists of an individual or perhaps family brand combined with modifiers that describe differences in product features.

A company with a strong corporate brand, such as Sony or Philips, can more easily use non-descriptive alpha-numeric product names because consumers strongly identify with the parent brand. Thus, Sony has family brand names such as Cyber-Shot for its cameras, Wega for TVs and Handycams for its camcorders.[35]

For complex products – such as cars, computers or other durable goods – more levels of the hierarchy are necessary. Regardless of the complexity, it is difficult to sell a product with more than three levels of brand names without confusing consumers. In such cases, a better approach might be to introduce several brands at the same level (eg, several family brands) and expand the depth of the branding strategy.

Desired awareness and image at each hierarchy level

Once brand levels have been chosen, the question becomes: how much awareness and what types of associations are to be created for brand elements at each level? Achieving the desired level of awareness and strength, favourability and uniqueness of brand associations may take time and involve a change in consumer perceptions. Marketing campaigns must be carefully designed, implemented and evaluated. Assuming some type of sub-branding strategy is adopted involving two or more brand levels, two principles – relevance and differentiation – should guide the brand knowledge-creation process at each level.

The *principle of relevance* is based on the advantages of efficiency and economy. In general, it is desirable to create associations that are relevant to as many brands nested at the level below as possible, especially at the corporate or family brand level. The more it is the case that an association has some value in the marketing of products sold by the firm, the more efficient and economical it is to consolidate this meaning into one brand that becomes linked to all these products.[36] For example, Nike's slogan ('Just do it') reinforces a key point of difference for the brand – performance – that is relevant to most of the products it sells.

The more abstract the association, the more likely it is to be relevant in different product settings. Thus, benefit associations are likely to be extremely advantageous associations because they can cut across many product categories. Brands with strong product category and attribute associations, however, can find it difficult to create a robust enough brand image to permit extensions into new categories. For example, Blockbuster attempted to broaden its meaning from 'a place to rent videos' to 'your neighborhood entertainment centre' to create a broader brand umbrella with greater relevance to more products.

The *principle of differentiation* is based on the disadvantages of redundancy. In general, it is desirable to distinguish brands at the same level. If two brands cannot be easily distinguished, then it may be difficult for retailers to justify supporting both of them. It may also be confusing for consumers as they choose between them. For example, consider the following three Microsoft products: Media Extender, Media Connect and Windows Connect Now. On the basis of the names alone, there would seem to be potential for consumer confusion as to what the products are. Although the names are similar, the products are completely different and are, respectively: a device to make an Xbox function as a media centre; a device to deliver PC-stored content to your stereo or TV and an architecture to simplify wireless home networking.[37]

Although new products and extensions are critical to keeping a brand innovative and relevant, they must be introduced thoughtfully. Without restraint, brand variations can get out of control.[38] The typical US supermarket now stocks 40,000 items, twice as many as a few years ago, which raises the question: do consumers really need nine kinds of Kleenex tissues 16 and 72 varieties of Pantene shampoo? To control its inventory and avoid brand proliferation, Colgate-Palmolive discontinues one item for each it introduces.

Although the principle of differentiation is important at the individual brand or modifier levels, it is also valid at the family brand level. For example, one of the criticisms of marketing at General Motors is that the company has failed to distinguish between its family brands of cars. The principle of differentiation also implies that not all products should receive the same emphasis at any level of the hierarchy. An issue in designing a brand hierarchy thus concerns the relative emphasis received by products making up the brand hierarchy. If a corporate or family brand is associated with several products, which one should be the flagship product? What should represent 'the brand' to consumers? Which product do consumers think best represents or embodies the brand? Understanding these brand drivers is important in identifying sources of brand equity and therefore how to best fortify and build on the brand.

Combining brand elements from different levels

If brand elements from different levels of the hierarchy are combined for new products, it is necessary to decide how much emphasis should be given to each one. For example, if a sub-brand strategy is adopted, how much prominence should individual brands be given at the expense of the corporate or family brand?

When several brands are used, each brand element can vary in the relative emphasis it receives in the combined brand. The *prominence* of an element refers to its relative visibility compared with other brand elements. For example, the prominence depends on factors such as its order, size and appearance, as well as its semantic associations. A name is generally more prominent when it appears first, is larger and looks more distinctive. For example, assume PepsiCo has adopted a sub-branding strategy to introduce a vitamin-fortified cola, combining its corporate family brand name with a new brand name (eg, Vitacola). The Pepsi name could be made more prominent by placing it first and making it bigger: PEPSI *Vitacola*. Alternatively, the individual brand could be made more prominent by placing it first and making it bigger: Vitacola BY PEPSI.

Along these lines, Gray and Smeltzer define *corporate/product relationships* as the approach taken in communicating the relationship of products to each another and to the corporate entity. They identified five categories.[39]

1. *Single entity:* one product line or set of services is offered such that the image of the company and the product tend to be one and the same (eg, FedEx).
2. *Brand dominance:* the decision is made not to relate brand and corporate names (eg, Altria makes little connection to Philip Morris, which in turn is loosely connected at best to Marlboro and its other cigarettes).
3. *Equal dominance:* separate images are maintained for products, but each is also associated with the company. Neither the corporate nor the individual brand names dominate (eg, at the company level, General Motors with its car divisions and individual brands – Buick LeSabre, Buick Electra, Buick Riviera and so forth).
4. *Mixed dominance:* sometimes individual product brands are dominant and sometimes the corporate name is dominant. In some cases, they are used together with equal emphasis (eg, the German firm Bosch uses its corporate name on some of the products it manufactures but not on others, such as Blaupunkt radios).
5. *Corporate dominance:* the corporate name is supreme and applied across a range of product lines, and communications tend to reinforce the corporate image (eg, Xerox).

The principle of prominence states that the relative prominence of brand elements affects perceptions of product distance and the type of image created for a product. That is, the relative prominence of the brand elements determines which element or elements become the primary one(s) and which element or elements are secondary.

In general, primary elements should be chosen to convey the main product position-ing and points of difference. Secondary elements are often chosen to convey a more restricted set of associations such as points of parity or perhaps an additional point of difference. A secondary brand element may also facilitate awareness. Thus, with the Motorola RAZR mobile phone, the primary brand element – reinforced through the slender, hinged design – is the RAZR name, which reinforces the cutting-edge style that makes up the desired user and usage imagery for the phone. The Motorola name, on the other hand, is a secondary brand element that ideally conveys credibil-ity, quality and professionalism.

The relative prominence of the individual brand compared to the corporate brand should affect perceptions of product distance and the type of image created for the product. If the corporate or family brand is made more prominent, then its associa-tions are more likely to dominate. If the individual brand is made more prominent, however, then it should be easier to create a more distinctive image. In this case, the corporate or family brand is signalling to consumers that the new product is not as closely related to its other products with that name. As a result, consumers should be less likely to transfer corporate or family brand associations. At the same time, the success or failure of the product should, because of the greater perceived distance involved, be less likely to affect the image of the corporate or family brand. With a more prominent corporate or family brand, however, feedback effects are more likely to be evident. Chapter 12 discusses these issues.

To illustrate how relative prominence can affect the image of a product, assume that in the Pepsi Vitacola example given earlier, Pepsi is the more prominent element. By making the corporate and family brand prominent, the new product would take on many of the associations common to other Pepsi-branded products (eg, cola). If the Vitacola brand were more prominent, however, then the product would be likely to take on a more distinct positioning. In this case, the Pepsi name would function more for awareness and perhaps only transfer broader, more abstract associations, such as perceived quality or brand personality.

Finally, in some cases, the brand elements may not be explicitly linked at all. A brand endorsement strategy is when a brand element appears on the packaging, sign or product in some way but is not directly included as part of the brand name. Often this distinct element is the corporate brand name or logo. For example, Nestlé places its logo on almost all of its products but retains distinct brand names such as KitKat, San Pellegrino and Powerbar. As noted earlier, Kellogg's, though, adopts a sub-brand strategy with its cereals that combines the corporate name with individual brands – eg, Kellogg's Corn Flakes and Kellogg's Special K. The brand endorsement strategy presumably establishes the maximum distance between the corporate or family brand and the individual brands, suggesting it would yield the smallest trans-fer of brand associations to the new product but, at the same time, minimize the like-lihood of negative feedback.

Linking brand elements with several products

The previous discussion highlighted how different brand elements can be applied to a particular product (ie, 'vertical' aspects of the brand hierarchy). Next, the chapter con-siders how any one brand element can be linked with several products (ie, 'horizontal' aspects). There are many ways to connect a brand element with several products. The *principle of commonality* states that the more brand elements are shared by products, the stronger the linkages between the products.

The simplest way to link products is to use the brand element 'as is' across the products. Other possibilities exist if the brand, or some part of it, is adapted in some fashion to make the connection. For example, a common prefix or suffix of a brand name may be adapted for different products. Hewlett-Packard capitalized on its LaserJet computer printers with products using the 'Jet' suffix, for example, the DeskJet, PaintJet, ThinkJet and OfficeJet printers. Sony has given its portable audio equipment a 'man' suffix: Walkman personal stereos and Discman portable CD players. McDonald's has used its 'Mc' prefix to introduce Chicken McNuggets, Egg McMuffin and the McRib sandwich. Initials can sometimes be used, as with designer names such as Donna Karan's DKNY brand, Calvin Klein's CK brand and Ralph Lauren's Double RL brand.

A relationship between a brand and products can also be made with common symbols. For example, corporate brands often place their logo more prominently on their products than their name (eg, Nabisco), creating a strong brand endorsement strategy.

Nestlé

At one time, Nestlé ran advertising that attempted to create greater awareness and understanding of its corporate brand. The ads contained the slogan 'makes the very best' – a subtle variation of its well-known 'Nestlé's makes the very best chocolate' slogan – and prominently displayed a logo of a nest with a mother and two baby birds. Although the founder's name, Nestlé, in fact means 'little nest', the company's hope in using the symbol was to communicate abstract associations of warmth, family and shelter. The symbol is used on Nestlé packaging to unite a diversified set of products with vastly different names.

Finally, often it is desirable to have a logical ordering of brands in a product line to communicate how the brands are related and to simplify consumer decision-making. The relative ordering may be communicated to consumers though colours (eg, American Express offers Blue, Green, Gold, Platinum and 'Black' Centurion cards), numbers (eg, BMW offers its 3, 5 and 7 series cars) or other means. Brand Briefing 11.9 describes how Acura attempted to rename its product line to create more structure. Such a branding strategy is especially important in developing brand migration strategies for how customers should switch between the brands offered by the company (see Chapter 13).

Developing a brand architecture

In developing brand strategies, marketers must first define the relevant customer segments. How much overlap exists across segments and how much can products be cross-sold? Second, marketers must have well-defined brand positioning and equity in terms of points of parity and points of difference. The brand mantra can be crucial to helping establish product boundaries or brand 'guard rails'. A brand mantra should offer rational and emotional benefit underpinning and be sufficiently robust

Brand Briefing 11.9

Renaming the Acura brand portfolio

Honda grew from being a motorcycle manufacturer to one of the most recognized brands in the world. Recognizing that future sales growth would come from more upmarket customers, Honda set out in the 1980s to compete with European luxury cars, primarily in the USA. Deciding that the Honda image of dependable, functional and economical cars did not have the cachet to appeal to luxury carbuyers, Honda set up the Acura division – a strategy later imitated by Toyota and Nissan with their Lexus and Infiniti brands. Matching the quality, performance and luxury of the European rivals but costing thousands less, the €6,840 Acura Integra and the €13,680 Acura Legend were introduced in 1986. By the time Lexus and Infiniti entered the US market in 1989, Acura was selling 142,000 cars annually and receiving top marks in customer satisfaction.

Rapidly rising prices – due in part to a strengthening yen – and increased competition eroded sales to the point at which Acura sales in the USA barely topped 100,000 cars in 1993. With its market leadership threatened and its customer base splintering (the average Integra buyer earned €39,000 annually, or half of the average Legend owner), Honda felt it needed a dramatic marketing move. Research indicated that its Legend, Integra and Vigor sub-brand names did not communicate luxury and order in the product line as well as the alphanumeric branding scheme of BMW, Mercedes, Lexus and Infiniti. Honda decided that the strength of the brand should lie in the Acura name. Thus, despite the fact that nearly €410 million had been spent on advertising those Acura sub-brands over 8 years, Honda announced an alphanumeric branding scheme in the winter of 1995. The accompanying €68.4 million advertising campaign retained the theme, 'Some things are worth the price.'

The new 2.5 TL and 3.2 TL (for Touring Luxury) saloons, designed to replace the Vigor, were the first rebranded models available in 1995. The following year, Acura rolled out the 3.5 RL, a replacement for its top-of-the-line Legend model. At that time, Acura also introduced two cars, called the 2.2 CL and 3.0 CL, priced in the mid-$20,000 range. The CL line was positioned below the TL but above the Integra, which had been renamed the RSX. In 1997, Honda estimated that up to 21 percent of Acura owners were switching to brands that offered SUVs, so Acura introduced the SLX (later renamed the MDX) SUV. The NSX sports car retained its name.

Acura spokesperson Mike Spencer said: 'It used to be that people said they owned or drove a Legend . . . Now they say they drive an Acura, and that's what we wanted.' Acura's name awareness in 2001 was 25 percent higher than in 1996. By including almost everything as standard equipment and with competitive base prices, Acura sales rose from 142,681 in 1996 to almost 200,000 cars by 2004.

Brand Briefing 11.9 *continued*

The new strategy can also be seen in a wider context of worldwide plans for the Acura brand. Acura was introduced in China in 2006, and the plan is to use the Acura brand in the Japanese home market as well in 2008.

Sources: Takeo Fukui, speech at North American International Auto Show, 8 January 2006; Takeo Fukui, speech at 2007 Frankfurt Motor show, 11 September 2007; David Kiley, 'I'd like to buy a vowel, drivers say', *USA Today*, 9 August 2000; Mark Rechtin, 'Honda hopes new CR-V will win back defectors', *Automotive News*, 3 February 1997; Stewart Toy, 'The selling of Acura – a Honda that's not a Honda', *BusinessWeek*, 17 March 1986: 93; Fara Werner, 'Remaking of a Legend', *Brandweek*, 25 April 1994: 23–8; Neal Templin, 'Japanese luxury car makers unveiling cheaper models in bid to attract buyers', *Wall Street Journal*, 9 February 1995; T. L. Stanley and Kathy Tryer, 'Acura plays numbers game to fortify future', *Brandweek*, 20 February 1995: 3; T. L. Stanley, 'Acura rolls TL, new nameplate position with $40m in ad fuel', *Brandweek*, 20 March 1995: 4.

to permit growth, relevant in order to drive consumer and retailer interest and differentiated enough to sustain longevity. Finally, marketers must assess the brand equity implications of the brand architecture in terms of the transfer (both positive and negative) from the parent brands to individual products, as well as the feedback from the individual products to the parent brands in return.

In doing so, it is important to keep the following brand architecture guidelines in mind:

- adopt a strong customer focus;
- avoid overbranding;
- establish rules and conventions and be disciplined;
- create broad, robust brand platforms;
- selectively employ sub-brands as means of complementing and strengthening brands; and
- selectively extend brands to establish new brand equity and enhance existing brand equity.

In evaluating brand architecture, the brand portfolio and hierarchy must be assessed carefully. For a portfolio, do all brands have defined roles? Do brands collectively maximize coverage and minimize overlap? For the brand hierarchy, does the brand have extension potential? Within the category? Outside the category? Is the brand overextended?

Adjustments to the marketing campaign

When a company moves away from a simple 'single brand, single product' strategy to adopt more complex branding – perhaps involving brand extensions, several brands or many levels of the hierarchy used for any one product – adjustments may be necessary in the marketing campaign. For example, as noted earlier, different brands can play different roles and therefore require different marketing mixes. Consequently, product design, pricing policies, distribution plans and marketing campaigns may differ significantly depending on the role of the brand and its interdependencies with other brands. In general, many of the principles discussed in Chapters 5 to 7 for developing supporting marketing campaigns to build brand equity still apply. This section highlights some of the marketing communication adjustments that may be necessary with interrelated brands and products.

Assuming several levels of a branding hierarchy are employed, levels of awareness and image may be desired at each level. In particular, if a sub-brand strategy is adopted, it may make sense to create a marketing communication campaign at the corporate, company or family brand levels to complement more product-specific or individual brand marketing communication campaigns (as in Chapter 6). As part of this higher-level campaign, companies may employ the full range of marketing communication options, including advertising, public relations, promotions and sponsorship. Two useful communication strategies to build brand equity at the corporate brand or family brand level are discussed here.

Corporate image campaigns

Corporate image campaigns are designed to create associations with the corporate brand as a whole and, consequently, tend to ignore or downplay products or sub-brands.[40] As would be expected, some of the biggest spenders on these kinds of campaigns are those well-known firms that prominently use their company or corporate name in their branding strategies, such as GE, Toyota, BT, IBM, Novartis, Microsoft, Deutsche Bank, Siemens and Hewlett-Packard. Companies run these types of non-product-specific ads – especially retail and service brands that commonly use their corporate name – in part because so many products have become linked to their family or corporate brands.

Corporate image campaigns have been criticized as an ego-stroking waste of time. Moreover, because such activities may be seen as not directly related to products, they may be overlooked or ignored. One contention that can be made, however, is that a strong corporate brand can provide invaluable marketing and financial benefits by allowing the firm to express itself and embellish the meaning and associations of its products. To maximize the probability of success, however, objectives of a corporate image campaign must be clearly defined *and* results must be measured against these objectives.[41] Many objectives are possible in a corporate brand campaign.[42]

- Build awareness of the company and the nature of its business.
- Create favourable attitudes and perceptions of company credibility.
- Link beliefs that can be used by product-specific marketing.
- Make a favourable impression on the financial community.
- Motivate present employees and attract better recruits.
- Influence public opinion on issues.

In terms of building customer-based brand equity, the first three objectives are critical. A corporate campaign can enhance awareness and create a more positive image of the corporate brand that will influence consumer evaluations and increase the equity associated with products and any related sub-brands. In certain cases, however, the latter three objectives can take on greater importance.[43] Notable examples of the first three objectives – the ones most directly related to building customer-based brand equity – are as follows.

- *Building awareness of the company and the nature of its business:* Cingular Wireless launched a teaser corporate campaign to build brand recognition during the 2001 Super Bowl. Subsequently, it launched a €51.3 million ad campaign emphasizing self-expression as a means of differentiating itself from other wireless marketers.[44] In 2004, following its merger with AT&T wireless, Cingular introduced a tagline 'Raising the bar' that highlighted the company's national network coverage in the USA. Although clearly a mature brand, HP ran a corporate brand campaign themed 'Expanding possibilities' before later switching to one themed 'Invent' to emphasize its technological leadership, vision and capabilities.
- *Building company trustworthiness and credibility:* Johnson & Johnson ran a campaign to promote the trustworthiness of the corporate brand. The commercials featured many 'warm and fuzzy' shots of families. Johnson & Johnson products were not emphasized, although its baby powder, Band-Aids and Reach toothbrush products were shown in passing. The ad concluded with the words: 'Over the years, Johnson & Johnson has taken care of more families than anyone else.' Similarly, to craft an image that transcended its products, Kraft ran a campaign featuring its Kool-Aid, Philadelphia cream cheese, Post cereal and Tombstone frozen pizza brands in a single TV spot. The intent was to show that Kraft 'got the importance of family values and made the kind of food that families with values ate'.[45]
- *Creating corporate image associations that can be leveraged by product-specific marketing:* to reposition itself as more consumer-friendly, Philips Consumer Electronics launched a global corporate advertising campaign in 2004. Centred on the company's new tagline 'Sense and simplicity', which replaced the nine-year-old tagline 'Let's make things better', the ads show innovative Philips products fitting in effortlessly with users' sophisticated lifestyles. The campaign featured flagship products, such as FlatTV with Ambilight, the HDRW720 DVD recorder with built-in hard disc and the Sonicare Elite toothbrush. Philips president and chief executive Gerard Kleisterlee described the rationale for the repositioning campaign by saying: 'Our route to innovation isn't about complexity – it's about simplicity which we believe will be the new cool.'[46]

Thus, corporate image campaigns focus on characteristics or aspects of the brand as a whole. These broader image campaigns may also be employed at the family brand level.

Brand line campaigns

A second marketing communication strategy to build brand equity at the corporate brand or family brand level is a brand line campaign. *Line campaigns* emphasize the breadth of products associated with a brand. Unlike a corporate image campaign that presents the brand in abstract terms with few, if any, references to products, brand line campaigns refer to the range of products associated with a brand line.

By showing consumers the uses or benefits of the products offered by a brand, brand line ads may be particularly useful in building brand awareness, clarifying brand meaning and suggesting applications. Brand line promotions can achieve similar goals.

Even when individual brands are used, umbrella ads that encompass several brands may serve a purpose. For example, in 2004 General Mills elected to make all its cereals with 100 percent whole grains and promoted the health benefits on all product packaging and with an advertising campaign. The benefits of whole grains included lowering the risk of heart disease, certain cancers and diabetes. Because most of us not getting sufficient levels of whole grain in their diet, these benefits are a point of difference (compared with non-wholegrain competitors) shared by all General Mills brands in the category.

Using cause marketing to build brand equity

The 1980s saw the advent of cause marketing. *Cause-related* (or *cause*) marketing has been defined as: 'The process of formulating and implementing marketing activities that are characterized by an offer from the firm to contribute a specified amount to a designated cause when customers engage in revenue-providing exchanges that satisfy organizational and individual objectives.'[47] As Varadarajan and Menon also note, the distinctive feature of cause marketing is the firm's contribution to a designated cause being linked to customers engaging in revenue-producing transactions with the firm.

Many observers in the USA credit American Express for raising awareness of the benefits of cause marketing through its 1983 campaign to help restore the Statue of Liberty. Donating a small amount of money for every credit card transaction and each new card issued, American Express gave €1.16 million to the restoration. Transactions for American Express rose 30 percent, and the issuance of new cards increased by 15 percent during this period. In the next five years, American Express supported more than 70 causes in 18 countries, ranging from the preservation of the national bird of Norway to protection of the Italian coastline.

During this time, competitors followed suit: Visa created a transaction-based donation scheme to support the 1988 Olympics (see Chapter 7) and MasterCard tied use of its credit card to donations to six charities with its 'Make a difference' campaign. Other companies became involved, too, sponsoring activities such as the Special Olympics, Live Aid and Hands Across America. Despite some drop in interest during tighter economic times in the early 1990s, companies again began to look to cause marketing. For example, in its first national US media campaign for a philanthropic cause since its Statue of Liberty campaign, American Express initiated 'Charge against hunger' in 1993. The campaign, which raised €3.42 million in a year, contributed three cents to feed the hungry every time members used their American Express cards during November and December.[48] American Express also supports the arts at the local community level, publicizing its efforts with ads praising the charitable cause while underscoring the convenience of its card. In 2006, the company partnered with Bono – lead singer of the band U2 – and his Aids organization Project Red to introduce the American Express Red card, through which the company contributes 1 percent of charges made with the card to fight Aids in Africa.

ADVANTAGES OF CAUSE MARKETING

One reason for the rise in cause marketing is the positive response it elicits from consumers.[49] Cone Communications, a firm that advises companies on cause-related marketing, revealed in the results of the 1999 Cone/Roper Cause Trends Report that 80 percent of Americans have a more positive image of companies that support a cause that they care about, nearly two-thirds of Americans report that they would be likely to switch brands to one associated with a good cause and almost three-quarters of Americans approve of supporting causes as a business practice. The report also documented the positive effect on employees: 90 percent of employees felt proud of their companies' values when the companies supported a cause and 87 percent felt a strong sense of loyalty towards companies supporting causes. Not surprisingly, these positive reactions increased dramatically after the tragic terrorist attacks in September 2001. The south-east Asia tsunami in 2004 further increased public interest in companies doing cause marketing.

Cause or corporate societal marketing (CSM) campaigns offer many benefits.

- *Building brand awareness:* because of the nature of the brand exposure, CSM campaigns can be a means of improving recognition for a brand, although not necessarily recall. As with sponsorship and other indirect forms of brand-building communications, campaigns may be better suited to increasing exposure to the brand and less suited to tying the brand to specific consumption or usage situations, because it can be difficult or inappropriate to include product-related information. At the same time, exposure to the brand can be repeated or prominent as a result of the campaign, facilitating brand recognition.
- *Enhancing brand image:* CSM offers ways of creating favourable brand differentiation. Because most campaigns do not include much product-related information, they would not be expected to have much impact on more functional, performance-related considerations. On the other hand, two types of abstract or imagery-related associations can be linked to a brand via CSM: user profiles (eg, consumers may develop a positive image of brand users to which they also may aspire in terms of being kind, generous, doing good things, etc.) and personality and values (eg, CSM could clearly bolster the sincerity dimension of a brand's personality such that consumers would think of the people behind the brand as caring and genuine).
- *Establishing brand credibility:* CSM could potentially affect credibility because consumers may think of a firm that is willing to invest in CSM as caring more about customers and being more dependable than other firms, at least in a broad sense, as well as likeable for 'doing the right things'.
- *Evoking brand feelings:* two categories of brand feelings that seem particularly applicable to CSM are social approval and self-respect. In other words, CSM may help consumers to justify their self-worth to others or to themselves. To accentuate

the former feelings, campaigns may need to provide consumers with external symbols to explicitly 'advertise' or signal their affiliation to others – for example, bumper stickers, ribbons, badges and T-shirts. In the case of the latter types of feelings, CSM campaigns can give people the notion that they are doing the right thing and that they should feel good about themselves for having done so. External symbols in this case may not be as important as the creation of 'moments of internal reflection' during which consumers are able to experience these types of feelings. Communications that reinforce the positive outcomes associated with the cause campaign – and how consumer involvement contributed to that success – could help to trigger such experiences. To highlight the consumer contribution, it may be necessary to recommend certain actions or outcomes as targets for consumers (eg, have consumers donate a certain percentage of income or a designated amount).

- *Creating a sense of brand community:* a well-chosen cause can serve as a rallying point for brand users and a means for them to connect to or share experiences with other consumers or employees of the company itself. One place where communities of like-minded users exist is on the web. Marketers may be able to tap into the close-knit online groups that have been created around cause-related issues (eg, medical concerns such as Alzheimer's, cancer and autism). In some cases, the brand might even serve as the focal point or ally for these efforts. As a result of these community-building initiatives, the brand may be seen in a more positive light.

- *Eliciting brand engagement:* participating in a cause-related activity is one way of eliciting active engagement. As part of any of these activities customers may become brand evangelists and help to communicate about the brand and strengthen the brand ties of others. A CSM campaign of 'strategic volunteerism', whereby corporate personnel volunteer their time to help administer the not-for-profit activity, could be used to engage consumers with both the cause and the brand.

Perhaps the most important benefit of cause-related marketing is that, by humanizing the firm, consumers may develop a strong, unique bond that transcends normal marketplace transactions. A dramatic illustration of such benefits is with McDonald's, whose franchises have long been required to stay close to local communities and whose 206 Ronald McDonald Houses for sick children in 19 countries symbolize its 'do-good' efforts. When whole blocks of businesses were burned and looted in the south central Los Angeles riots in 1992, one McDonald's executive observed: 'We literally had people standing in front of some restaurants saying, 'No, don't throw rocks through this window – these are the good guys.' When the dust cleared, all 60 McDonald's restaurants in the area were spared.

DESIGNING CAUSE MARKETING CAMPAIGNS

Cause marketing comes in many forms.[50] Although often associated with advertising and promotional activities, it may also involve product development. For example, in the USA Dannon launched yogurts that tied in with the National Wildlife Federation and Johnson & Johnson provides the World Wildlife Fund with a cut from sales of a special line of children's toiletries.

Some firms have used cause marketing very strategically to gain a marketing advantage.[51] Brand Briefing 11.10 describes how the Body Shop adopted cause-related marketing as the essence of its brand positioning. Ben & Jerry's has created a strong association as a 'do-gooder' through various products (such as its rain forest crunch ice-cream) and its donation of 7.5 percent of its pretax profits to various causes. Toyota ran an extensive print ad campaign with the slogan 'Investing in the things we all care about' to show how it had invested in US communities. For Toyota, this campaign may go beyond cause marketing and be seen as a means of helping the brand create a vital point of parity with respect to domestic car companies on 'country of origin'.

Brand Briefing 11.10

Image management the Body Shop way

In 1976, Anita Roddick opened the first Body Shop in Brighton, a city on the south coast of England. In her first shop, Anita offered 25 natural body products. By 2005, the Body Shop had 1,900 outlets in 50 countries, many of them franchised. The company offers 400 naturally based body care products, 550 sundry items and customized care. Its colourful, fragrant products are based on natural ingredients, particularly fruits, vegetables, flowers and herbs.

Since its early days, the Body Shop tried to avoid packaging excesses for its products. Roddick asked customers to bring bottles back for refilling because the company didn't have a large number of bottles. Today, the Body Shop has made refilling and recycling of bottles an integral part of the company's environmental stewardship approach. The bottles, which were originally chosen for their simplicity and low cost, are still the primary packaging form. In addition, the Body Shop has sub-brands, almost all of which are identified with new labelling and some new packaging forms as well.

The Body Shop has attempted to avoid the 'narrow images' of 'flawless beauty' portrayed in traditional cosmetic advertising. The Body Shop has avoided advertising and relied on in-store promotions, word of mouth and public relations. Bright, colourful posters in shops announce holidays, support Aids protection or promote particular products. All over the world, Body Shop premises 'look and feel' the same. The typical outside 'look' is a dark green wooden facade with large floor-to-ceiling display windows accented with bright, colourful, catchy campaign or promotional posters. The look inside is also consistent across all stores.

The Body Shop became not only a natural body products company, but also an organization that has attempted to make a difference in the lives of humans and animals and the protection of the environment. In addition to the traditional '4 Ps' marketing mix, the Body Shop has a 'fifth P' in its marketing mix to build brand

Brand Briefing 11.10 *continued*

equity – its corporate philosophy of 'Profits with principles', also known as 'Doing good by doing well'. To this end, the Body Shop is against animal testing, tries to minimize the company's impact on the environment, engages in fair trading relationships and encourages education, awareness and community involvement among its staff.

Although initially successful, the Body Shop struggled in recent years. Look-alike products from other chains (eg, Bath and Body Works and Boots) and supermarkets (eg, Tesco and Sainsbury) chipped away at its market share, and its messages on social causes didn't seem to arouse the same passion from customers. Body Shop shops became overstocked and cluttered with a poor product mix and advertising often missed the mark.

In response to its troubles, Roddick chose to step down as head in 1998 and the firm underwent a radical makeover in a bid to cut costs and freshen its image. The firm embraced a 'masstige' positioning (mass-market combined with prestige) with relatively low-priced products sold under the banner of their prestigious brand name. Although this approach met with some success, Dame Roddick stepped down as co-chair of the board in 2002, but remained a consultant to the company. Eventually, the company agreed in early 2006 to be taken over by French cosmetics giant L'Oréal in a deal worth £652m. L'Oréal stated that it would allow the Body Shop to be run as a standalone business with Roddick continuing to provide advice.

Source: This brief is based on a brand audit conducted as part of a Stanford Business School class project by Janet Kraus, Kathy Apruzzese, Maria Nunez and Karen Reaudin.

A danger is that the promotional efforts behind a cause marketing campaign could backfire if cynical consumers question the link between the product and the cause and see the firm as being self-serving as a result. The hope is that cause marketing strikes a chord with consumers and employees, improving the image of the company and energizing these constituents to act. With near-parity products, some marketers feel that a strongly held point of difference on the basis of community involvement and concern may in some cases be the best way – and perhaps the only way – to uniquely position a product.

To gain brand equity benefits, it is important that cause marketing efforts be branded in the right way. In particular, it is important that consumers be able to make a connection between the cause and the brand. Perhaps the classic example of doing so is McDonald's, which has used its Ronald McDonald character and its identification with children. Ronald McDonald House Charities has a network of 174 charities in 32 countries. This well-branded initiative enhances McDonald's reputation as caring and concerned for customers. Two other noteworthy US causes are the following.

- *The Avon Breast Cancer Crusade:* founded in 1993, the Avon Breast Cancer Crusade is a US initiative of Avon Products. Its aim has been to provide women with access to breast cancer education and early detection screening services such as mammograms and clinical breast examinations. In the USA, Avon is the largest corporate supporter of the breast cancer cause, with some €68.4 million generated since 1993. The crusade raises funds in two ways: through the sale of special fundraising (pink ribbon) products by Avon's nearly 500,000 independent sales representatives and 3-day, 60-mile fundraising walks.[52]
- *Liz Claiborne's Women's Work campaign against domestic violence:* in 1991, at a time when domestic violence was often a taboo or hot potato issue, Liz Claiborne developed its Women's Work campaign against domestic violence. Before starting the campaign, the company had conducted research that revealed 96 percent of its customers believed that domestic violence was a problem and 91 percent of those same customers would have a positive opinion of a company that started an awareness campaign about the issue. The main fundraising event is an annual charity shopping day every October at Liz Claiborne shops across the USA. The company donates 10 percent of sales to local organizations fighting domestic violence. Liz Claiborne also contributes proceeds from the sale of products related to the campaign. Additionally, the company pays for advertising campaigns and distributes awareness posters, brochures and mailings. Over the years, Liz Claiborne has also sponsored workshops, surveys, celebrity-endorsed awareness campaigns and other events.[53]

GREEN MARKETING

A special case of cause marketing is green marketing. Concern for the environment is a trend that is reflected in the attitudes and behaviour of both consumers and companies. For example, one survey found that 83 percent of US consumers said they prefered buying environmentally safe products.[54] Another survey found that 23 percent of US consumers claimed to make purchases based on environmental considerations.[55]

Although environmental issues have long affected marketing practices, especially in Europe, their salience has increased in recent years. The Earth Day activities in the USA in April 1990 led to an explosion of 'environmentally friendly' products and marketing campaigns. A green marketing movement was born and companies tried to capitalize on consumers' perceived increased sensitivity to environmental issues. On the corporate side, marketing initiatives have been undertaken with environmental overtones. For example, Chevron's 'People do' campaign in the USA attempted to transform consumers' poor view of oil companies and their effect on the environment by describing Chevron initiatives designed to save wildlife and preserve seashores.

McDonald's has introduced environmental initiatives such as using unbleached paper for its bags and replacing polystyrene foam sandwich clamshells with paper wraps and recyclable boxes. The company received an EPA WasteWise Partner of the Year award for its waste reduction efforts, which conserved 3,200 tons of paper and cardboard by eliminating sandwich containers and replacing them with single-layer flexible sandwich wraps; eliminated 1,100 tons of cardboard materials that would have been used for shipping by switching to light drink cups and spent €243 million on recycled content products. Brand Briefing 11.11 describes other initiatives.

From a branding perspective, however, green marketing campaigns have not been entirely successful.[56] Despite reported public interest in environmental responsibility, many of these products and campaigns were unsuccessful. What obstacles did the green marketing movement encounter?

Brand Briefing 11.11

Marketing goes green

Companies see the environment as an important issue for their customers and shareholders and, therefore, their bottom lines. Research shows the environment is one of the top five issues that young people care most about. Renewable energy power systems are growing rapidly in Europe and China. Additionally, rising oil and petrol prices contribute to the need and enthusiasm for fuel-saving technologies. The following examples show how companies have capitalized on these trends by leading the way in their industries with green marketing efforts.

Despite its industrial past, General Electric views eco-friendly products as a high-growth business. In 2005, GE launched Ecomagination, a play on its US ad campaign 'Imagination at work.' The initiative included €1 billion in annual investment in research and technology into cleaner technologies and is intended to double GE's revenue from sales of products and services that provide environmental advantages and a reduction in greenhouse gas emissions to €13.7 billion in 2010. The company built an advertising campaign around Ecomagination that targeted the company's business-to-business customers, investors, employees and consumers. GE even designed a magazine to introduce Ecomagination to the children of employees.

The motor industry is also responding to concerned consumers and rising oil prices by introducing petrol-saving and emission-reducing hybrid models, but results have been mixed. The Toyota Prius accounts for about half of all hybrid sales. Toyota followed up its success with a second-generation Prius, which it marketed in the USA in a joint campaign with the Sierra Club. Though sales of hybrids have increased in the USA, they amount to only 1.2 percent of the total car market. The higher costs of purchasing a hybrid has limited mainstream zeal for the technology and most Americans would prefer not to compromise on space, power and amenities. To attract them, carmakers are introducing hybrid powertrains and hydrogen fuel cells that deliver cleaner emissions and better mileage without compromising power. Toyota is developing an improved hybrid and a consortium of BMW, DaimlerChrysler

Brand Briefing 11.11 *continued*

and General Motors engineers has developed a two-mode hybrid, which can use electric motors more efficiently than other hybrid engines.

Along with new opportunities, environmental awareness has created sometimes uneasy partnerships between companies and activist groups, as an example from Home Depot demonstrates. The company is the largest seller of timber in the world and buys almost 10 percent of Chile's wood exports, mostly from tree farms. Beginning in 1997, environmentalists protested against its wood-buying practices outside hundreds of Home Depot stores. In response, the company announced it would not buy wood that came from endangered forests and created an environmental global project manager position to oversee contracts with its suppliers. In 2003, the company led a deal between Chile's environmentalists and logging industry to protect forests. Home Depot found that working with environmental organizations was an inexpensive way to win support from customers and counter bad publicity.

Pressure from activists has resulted in companies looking at environmental risks before investing in projects in ecologically vulnerable places. Additionally, activism has prompted creativity within companies. Wal-Mart is experimenting with a prototype supermarket that is 25–30 percent more efficient and will produce up to 30 percent fewer greenhouse gas emissions. The design includes more than two dozen energy-saving and renewable materials experiments. Projects like these are garnering favourable consumer reviews, as well as effecting environmental results.

Sources: Karl Greenberg, 'Green is good', *Brandweek*, 3 January 2005; Matthew Creamer, 'GE sets aside big bucks to show off some green', *Advertising Age*, 9 May 2005; Daren Fonda, 'GE's green awakening', *Time*, August 2005; Jim Carlton, 'Once targeted by protesters, Home Depot plays green role', *Wall Street Journal*, August 2004; Beth Daley, 'Eco-products in demand, but labels can be murky', *Boston Globe*, 9 February 2005; Theresa Howard, 'Being eco-friendly can pay economically', *USA Today*, 15 August 2005; www.bp.com; Lindsay Brooke, 'Challenging Toyota's hybrid hegemony', *New York Times*, 30 April 2006.

Overexposure and lack of credibility

So many companies made environmental claims that the public became sceptical. Government investigations into some 'green' claims (eg, the degradability of bin bags) and media reports of the spotty environmental track records behind others only increased consumers' doubts. This backlash resulted in many consumers deeming environmental claims to be marketing gimmicks.

Consumer behaviour

For social trends, the underlying reality is often complex and does not match perceptions. Attitudes towards the environment are no exception. Several studies helped to put consumer attitudes towards the environment in perspective.

A 1991 US study found that the extra consumers were willing to pay for otherwise identical products in six categories (petrol, paper, plastics, aerosols, detergents and cars) that would cause one-third less pollution was 6.6 percent. One-third of the sample was not willing to pay *anything* more. The study concluded that the products needed to achieve points of parity on quality and price and credible environmental claims for green marketing to work. Another study also found that price and quality were key to green marketing strategies. Two-thirds of their sample believed that the badge of 'environmental correctness' should not result in higher prices – for example, 'environmentally safe products shouldn't have to cost more because they use natural ingredients'. The study revealed that environmental appeals were more likely to be effective for certain market segments (eg, 31–45-year-old women) and in certain product categories (eg, cleaners, detergents, fabric softeners, nappies, aerosol sprays, paints and tinned tuna).[57]

The conclusion that can be drawn from such studies is that consumers may not be willing to pay a premium for environmental benefits, although there may be certain market segments that will. Most consumers appear unwilling to give up the benefits of other options to choose green products. For example, some consumers dislike the performance, appearance or texture of recycled paper and household products. Similarly, some consumers are unwilling to give up the convenience of disposable products, such as nappies.

Poor implementation

In jumping on the green bandwagon, many firms did a poor job. Products were poorly designed in terms of their environmental worthiness, overpriced and inappropriately promoted. For example, Starch, a market researcher, surveyed thousands of magazine readers to study 300 'green' ads that appeared in 186 magazines since 1991. The analysis revealed that the main mistake with those ads that tested as 'unpersuasive' was that they forgot to emphasize 'what's in it for me' to the consumer – they failed to make the connection between what the company was doing for the environment and how it affected individual consumers. Starch's study conclusion was that firms should be specific about product benefits in their ads.[58]

Possible solutions

The environmental movement in Europe or Japan has a longer history than that in the USA. In Europe, many of Procter & Gamble's household items, including cleaners and detergents, are available in refills that come in throw-away pouches. P&G says US customers probably would not take to the pouches. In the USA, firms continue to strive to meet the wishes of consumers concerning the environmental benefits of their products, while maintaining profitability. One expert in the field offers the following recommendations.[59]

- Make your product green before being forced to.
- Communicate environmental aspects of products, especially recycled content.
- Deliver on performance and price.

- Dramatize environmental benefits.
- Stress direct, tangible benefits.
- Be consistent and thorough.

CHAPTER REVIEW

Key to managing brand equity is the branding strategy. Brand names of products often consist of a combination of names and other brand elements. A branding strategy for a company identifies which brand elements it chooses to apply across the products it sells. This chapter described two tools to help formulate branding strategies: the brand–product matrix and the brand hierarchy. Combining these tools with customer, company and competitive considerations can help a marketing manager formulate a branding strategy.

The brand–product matrix is a graphical representation of all the brands and products sold by a firm. The grid has the brands as rows and corresponding products as columns. The rows of the matrix represent brand–product relationships and capture the brand extension strategy of the firm with respect to a brand. Potential extensions must be judged by how effectively they build on brand equity for a new product, as well as how effectively the extension, in turn, contributes to the equity of the parent brand. The columns of the matrix represent product–brand relationships and capture the brand portfolio strategy in terms of the number and nature of brands to be marketed in each category.

A branding strategy can be characterized according to its breadth (ie, in terms of brand–product relationships and brand extension strategy) and its depth (ie, in terms of product–brand relationships and the brand portfolio or mix). The breadth of the branding strategy concerns the product mix and which products the firm should manufacture or sell. The chapter considered issues concerning how many different product lines the company should carry (ie, the breadth of the product mix), as well as how many variants should be offered in each product line (ie, the depth of the product mix). The depth of the branding strategy concerns the brand portfolio and the set of all brands and brand lines that a particular seller offers. A firm may offer several brands in a category to attract different – and potentially mutually exclusive – market segments. Brands also can take on very specialized roles in the portfolio: as flanker brands to protect more valuable brands, as low-end entry-level brands to expand the customer franchise, as high-end prestige brands to enhance the worth of the entire brand line or as cash cows to milk profits. Companies must be careful to understand exactly what each brand should do for the firm and, more important, what they want it to do for the customer.

A brand hierarchy is an explicit ordering of all brand names by displaying the number and nature of common and distinctive brand name elements across the firm's products. After capturing the potential branding relationships of the different products sold by the firm, a brand hierarchy is a useful way to portray graphically a firm's branding strategy. One simple representation of possible brand elements and thus potential levels of a brand hierarchy is (from top to bottom): corporate (or company) brand, family brand, individual brand and modifier.

Specific issues arise in designing the brand hierarchy. Brand elements at each level of the hierarchy may contribute to brand equity through their ability to create awareness and foster strong, unique and favourable associations. The challenge in setting up the brand hierarchy and arriving at a branding strategy is to design the proper brand hierarchy in terms of the number and nature of brand elements to use at each level and to design the optimal supporting marketing campaign in terms of creating the desired amount of brand awareness and type of brand associations at each level.

In terms of designing a brand hierarchy, the number of levels of brands that will be employed and the relative emphasis or prominence that brands at different levels will receive when combined on any one product must be defined. In general, the number of levels employed typically is two or three. One strategy to brand a product is to create a sub-brand, whereby an existing company or family brand is combined with a new individual brand. When several brand names are used, as with a sub-brand, the relative visibility of a brand element as compared with other brand elements determines its prominence. Brand visibility and prominence will depend on factors such as the order, size, colour and other aspects of the brand's appearance. To provide structure and content to the brand hierarchy, the specific means by which a brand is used across different products and, if different brands are used for different products, the relationships between those brands must be made clear to consumers.

When designing a marketing campaign, the desired awareness and image at each level of the brand hierarchy for each product must be defined. With sub-branding, the desired awareness of a brand at any level will dictate the relative prominence of the brand and the extent to which associations linked to the brand will transfer to the product. In terms of building brand equity, determining which associations to link at any one level should be based on relevance and differentiation. In general, it is desirable to create associations that are relevant to as many brands nested at the level below as possible and to distinguish brands at the same level. Corporate or family brands can establish associations that can help to differentiate the brand, such as common product attributes, benefits or attitudes; people and relationships; activities and values; and corporate credibility. A corporate image will depend on a number of factors, such as the products a company makes, the actions it takes and the manner in which it communicates to consumers. Communications may focus on the corporate brand in the abstract or on the different products making up the brand line.

Brand Briefing 11.12

Weathering a crisis: the Tylenol experience

Tylenol has been a marketing success story in the USA.[60] Introduced by McNeil Laboratories as a liquid alternative to aspirin for children, it achieved non-prescription status when McNeil was bought by Johnson & Johnson in 1959. J&J's marketing plan promoted a tablet form of the product for physicians to prescribe as a substitute

Brand Briefing 11.12 *continued*

for aspirin when allergic reactions occurred. Tylenol consists of acetaminophen, a drug as effective as aspirin in the relief of pain and fever but without the stomach irritation that often accompanies aspirin. Backed by this push, sales for the brand grew slowly but steadily over the next 15 years. By 1974, sales reached €34.2 million, or 10 percent of the analgesic market. In defending its turf from the competitive entry of Bristol-Myers' low-priced, but heavily promoted, competitor Datril, J&J recognized the value of advertising Tylenol directly to consumers.

Thanks also to the introduction of a line extension, Extra-Strength Tylenol in tablet and capsule form, the brand's market share had risen to 37 percent of the pain reliever market by 1982. As the largest brand in the history of health and beauty aids, Tylenol was used by 100 million Americans. The brand contributed 8 percent to J&J's sales but almost twice that percentage in terms of net profits. Advertising support for the brand was heavy. A €27.3 million media campaign was scheduled for 1982 that used two different messages. The 'hospital campaign' employed testimonials from people who had been given Tylenol in hospital and reported that they had grown to trust it. The ad concluded with the tagline 'Trust Tylenol – hospitals do.' The 'hidden camera' campaign showed people who had been unobtrusively filmed while describing the symptoms of their headache, trying Extra-Strength Tylenol as a solution and vowing to use it again based on its effectiveness. These ads concluded with the tagline 'Tylenol . . . the most potent pain reliever you can buy without a prescription.'

Crisis

All of this success came crashing to the ground with the news in October 1982 that seven people had died in the Chicago area after taking Extra-Strength Tylenol capsules that turned out to contain cyanide poison. Although it quickly became evident that the problem was restricted to that area and had almost certainly been the work of a deranged person outside the company, consumer confidence was shaken. Most marketing experts believed that the damage to the Tylenol brand was irreparable. For example, advertising expert Jerry Della Femina was quoted in the *New York Times* as saying, 'On one day, every single human being in the country thought that Tylenol might kill them. I don't think there are enough advertising dollars, enough marketing men, to change that . . . You'll not see the name Tylenol in any form within a year.' Tylenol's comeback from these seemingly insurmountable odds has become a classic example of how best to handle a marketing crisis.

Recovery

Within the first week of the crisis, J&J issued a worldwide alert to the medical community, set up a 24-hour freephone number, recalled and analyzed sample batches of the product, briefed the Food and Drug Administration and offered a €68,400

Brand Briefing 11.12 *continued*

reward to apprehend the culprit responsible for the tampering. In the week of 5 October, J&J began a voluntary withdrawal of the brand by buying back 31 million bottles with a retail value of €68.4 million. The company stopped advertising and all communications with the public were in the form of press releases. To monitor consumer response to the crisis, J&J started weekly tracking surveys with 1,000 respondents. Ultimately, the company spent €1 million for marketing research in the fourth quarter of 1982. The following week of 12 October, it introduced a capsule exchange offer, promoted in half-page press announcements in 150 areas across the USA, inviting the public to send in bottles of capsules to receive tablets in exchange. This offer met with poor consumer response.

During the week of 24 October, J&J made its return to TV advertising with the goals of convincing Tylenol users that they could continue to trust Tylenol products as well as encouraging the use of the tablet form until tamper-resistant packaging was available. The spokesperson for the ad was Dr Thomas N. Gates, the company's medical director, whose deep, reassuring voice exuded confidence and control. Looking calmly into the camera, he said:

> You're all aware of the recent tragic events in which Extra-Strength Tylenol capsules were criminally tampered with in limited areas after they left our factories. This act damages all of us – you the American public because you have made Tylenol a trusted part of your healthcare and we who make Tylenol because we've worked hard to earn that trust. We will now work even harder to keep it. We have voluntarily withdrawn all Tylenol capsules from the shelf. We will reintroduce capsules in tamper-resistant containers as quickly as possible. Until then, we urge all Tylenol capsule users to use the tablet form and we have offered to replace your capsules with tablets. Tylenol has had the trust of the medical profession and 100 million Americans for over 20 years. We value that trust too much to let any individual tamper with it. We want you to continue to trust Tylenol.

The heavy media schedule for this ad ensured that 85 percent of the market viewed the ad at least four times during that week.

On 11 November 1982, six weeks after the poisonings, the chairman of J&J announced during a live teleconference with 600 news reporters throughout the USA the return of Tylenol capsules to the market in a triple-seal package that was regarded as tamperproof. To get consumers to try the new packaging, a massive coupon campaign was undertaken. On 28 November 1982, 60 million coupons offering a free Tylenol product (valued up to €1.7) were distributed in Sunday newspapers. Twenty million more coupons were distributed the following Sunday. By the end of December, 30 percent of the coupons that had been issued had been redeemed. Accompanying these efforts, J&J also engaged in activities to enlist the support of retailers in the form of trade promotions and sales calls.

Brand Briefing 11.12 *continued*

Convinced that market conditions were stable enough to commence normal advertising, J&J's ad agency developed three executions using the testimony of loyal Tylenol users with the goal of convincing consumers that they could continue to use Tylenol with confidence. The first execution contained excerpts of consumers' reaction to the tampering incident, the second ad brought back a Tylenol supporter from an ad campaign run before the tampering incident to reassert her trust in Tylenol, and the third ad used the testimony of a Tylenol user who reasoned that she could still trust the product because hospitals still used it. The recall scores for two of the commercials were among the highest recorded by ASI, a marketing research firm that conducted the testing for J&J. The return to advertising was accompanied by more coupon promotional offers to consumers.

Incredibly, by February 1983, sales for Tylenol had almost fully returned to the sales levels the brand had enjoyed six months earlier. Figure 11.12 displays the Tylenol sales growth with respect to management actions during this period. Decades later, the brand is virtually a €684 million brand, with extensions into cough and cold remedies. The next largest pain reliever competitor has only half the market share of Tylenol. Clearly, J&J's handling of an extremely difficult situation was a big factor in the brand's comeback. Another important factor, however, was the equity of the brand and its strong and valuable 'trust' association built up before the incident. The feelings of trust engendered by the brand helped to

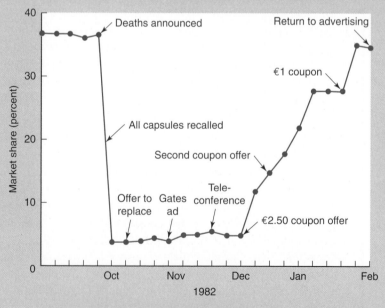

Figure 11.12 Tylenol's sales figures and management's actions

Brand Briefing 11.12 *continued*

speed the brand recovery, a fact certainly evident to J&J (note the number of times the word *trust* appears in the initial Gates ad – five times).

Crisis marketing guidelines

Not all brands have handled crises as well. Although Exxon spent millions of euros advertising its petrol and crafting its brand image in the USA, it had essentially ignored marketing its corporate identity and image. This decision came back to haunt it in the weeks following 24 March 1989. That morning, the tanker Exxon Valdez hit a reef in Prince William Sound, Alaska, resulting in some 11 million gallons of oil spilling into the waters off Alaska. The spill wreaked devastation on the fish and wildlife of some 1,300 square miles of the previously unspoiled area. Top Exxon officials declined to comment publicly for almost a week after the incident and the public statements that were eventually made sometimes appeared to contradict information from other sources (eg, regarding the severity of the spill) or assigned blame for the slow clean-up efforts to other parties, such as the US Coast Guard. Exxon received withering press coverage and was the source of countless jokes on talk shows. In frustration and anger, some of Exxon's consumers tore up their Exxon credit cards. On 3 April, ten days after the accident, Exxon's chairman ran an open letter to the public in the form of a full-page message expressing the company's concern and justifying its actions to address the situation.[61]

All marketing managers must assume that, at some point, a crisis will arise. Brands such as Nestlé (breast milk substitutes in Africa), Firestone tyres, Shell (oil platform in the North Sea) and Arla Foods (connection with drawings of the prophet Muhammad in Danish newspapers) have experienced a potentially crippling crises. In general, the more that brand equity and a strong corporate image have been established – especially with respect to corporate credibility and trustworthiness – the more likely it is that a company can weather the storm. Careful preparation and a well-managed crisis management campaign, however, are critical. Most experts would agree that the Exxon incident is a good example of how *not* to handle a crisis. As Johnson & Johnson's nearly flawless handling of the Tylenol product-tampering incident suggests, two keys to managing a crisis are that the response by the firm should be seen by consumers as both swift *and* sincere.

Swiftness

The longer it takes a firm to respond to a crisis, the more likely it is that consumers can form bad impressions as a result of unfavourable media coverage or word of mouth. Perhaps even worse, consumers may find out that they do not really like the brand that much after all and switch products. For example, Perrier was forced to halt production worldwide and recall all its bottles in February 1994 when traces of

Brand Briefing 11.12 *continued*

benzene, a carcinogen, were found in excessive quantities in the bottled water. Over the next few weeks, several explanations were offered as to how the contamination occurred, creating confusion and scepticism. Perhaps even more damaging, the product itself was off the shelves until May 1994. Despite an expensive relaunch, the brand struggled to regain lost market share and a year later found its sales less than half of what they had been. Part of the problem was that, during the time the product was unavailable, consumers and retailers found substitutes (eg, waters such as San Pellegrino). With its key 'purity' association tarnished (the brand had been advertised as the 'Earth's first soft drink' and 'It's perfect. It's Perrier.'), the brand had no compelling points of difference over these competitors.[62] Finally, compounding the problems arising from the crisis, the brand was gaining a stodgy image and was seen as much more appealing to the over-45 consumer market and much less appealing to those consumers under 25 years old. Eventually, the company was taken over by Nestlé.

Sincerity

Swift actions must also come across as sincere to consumers. The more sincere the response by the firm – in terms of public acknowledgment of the severity of the effect on consumers and the firm's willingness to take whatever steps are necessary and feasible to solve the crisis – the less likely it is that consumers will form negative views about the firm's behaviour. For example, although Gerber had established a strong image of trust with consumers, baby food is a product category characterized by an extremely high level of involvement and need for reassurance. When consumers reported finding shards of glass in some jars of its baby food, Gerber tried to reassure the public that there were no problems in its manufacturing plants but refused to withdraw products from shops. Some consumers found Gerber's response unsatisfactory because the brand's market share slumped from 66 percent to 52 percent within a couple of months. As one company official admits: 'Not pulling our baby food off the shelf gave the appearance that we aren't a caring company.'[63]

Brand crises are difficult to manage because, despite a firm's best efforts, it is difficult to maintain control. To some extent, the firm is at the mercy of public sentiment and media coverage, which it can attempt to direct and influence but sometimes can take on a life of their own. Swift and sincere words and actions, however, often can go a long way towards defusing the situation. As one commentator notes:

> No one strategy works in every crisis. There are too many variables – the news play, the marketplace, public sympathy or antipathy, whether the company cleans house as well as its image. . . Reality still counts. But simple honesty – 'We've got a problem and we're doing X, Y and Z about it' – is inevitably the last resort.[64]

Discussion questions

1. Pick a company. As completely as possible, characterize its brand portfolio and brand hierarchy. How would you improve the company's branding strategies?

2. Do you think the Nestlé corporate image campaign described in this chapter will be successful? Why or why not? What do you see as success factors for a corporate image campaign?

3. Contrast the branding strategies and brand portfolios of market leaders in two industries. For example, contrast the approach by Anheuser-Busch and its Budweiser brand with that of Kellogg's in the ready-to-eat cereal category.

4. What are some of the product strategies and communication strategies that General Motors could use to enhance the level of perceived differentiation between its divisions?

5. Consider the companies in Brand Briefing 11.6 as having strong reputations. By examining their websites, can you determine why they have such strong reputations?

References and notes

[1] Philip Kotler, *Marketing Management*, 11th edn, Upper Saddle River, NJ: Prentice Hall, 2003.

[2] Donald R. Lehmann and Russell S. Winer, 'Category attractiveness analysis', Chapter 4, and 'Market potential and forecasting', Chapter 7, in *Product Management,* Donald R. Lehmann and Russell S. Winer, Burr Ridge, IL: Irwin, 1994.

[3] Glen L. Urban and Steven H. Star, *Advanced Marketing Strategy: Phenomena, analysis and decisions,* Englewood Cliffs, NJ: Prentice Hall, 1991.

[4] Kotler, *Marketing Management*.

[5] Tara Parker-Pope, 'Laura Ashley's chief tries to spruce up company that isn't dressing for success', *Wall Street Journal*, 22 September 1995: B1.

[6] Neil A. Morgan and Lopo Leotte do Rego, 'Brand portfolio strategy and firm performance', Marketing Science Institute working paper 06-101, 2006.

[7] David Greising, 'Major reservations', *BusinessWeek*, 26 September 1994: 66.

[8] Kotler, *Marketing Management*; Patrick Barwise and Thomas Robertson, 'Brand portfolios', *European Management Journal*, September 1992, 10 (3): 277–85.

[9] For a methodological approach to assessing the extent and nature of cannibalization, see Charlotte H. Mason and George R. Milne, 'An approach for identifying cannibalization within product line extensions and multi-brand strategies', *Journal of Business Research*, 1994, 31: 163–70.

[10] Jack Trout, *Differentiate or Die: Survival in our era of killer competition,* New York: Wiley, 2000.

[11] Patricia Sellers, 'P&G: teaching an old dog new tricks', *Fortune*, 31 May: 166.

[12] Paul W. Farris, 'The Chevrolet Corvette', case UVA-M-320, Charlottesville, VA: Darden Graduate Business School Foundation, University of Virginia, 1995.

[13] Laurens M. Sloot , Dennis Fok and Peter C. Verhoef, 'The short- and long-term impact of an assortment reduction on category sales', Marketing Science Institute working paper 06-116, 2006; Jie Zhang and Aradhna Krishna, 'Brand level effects of SKU reductions', working paper, University of Michigan, 2006.

[14]Kathryn Troy, 'Managing the corporate brand', research report 1214-98-RR, New York: The Conference Board, 1998.

[15]Laurel Cutler, vice-chairman of FCB/Leber Katz Partners, a New York City advertising agency, quoted in Susan Caminit, 'The payoff from a good reputation', *Fortune*, 6 March 1995: 74.

[16]Hill and Knowlton, Return on Reputation Study, March 2006.

[17]Ny källa gällande RepTrak

[18]Jeffrey Parkhurst, 'Leveraging brand to generate value', in *From Ideas to Assets*, ed. Bruce Berman, New York, NY: John Wiley, 2002.

[19]Louis Capozzi, 'Corporate reputation: our role in sustaining and building a valuable asset', *Journal of Advertising Research*, September 2005: 290–3.

[20]Howard Barich and Philip Kotler, 'A framework for image management', *Sloan Management Review*, winter 1991: 94–104.

[21]Kate Ballen, 'America's most admired corporations', *Fortune*, 10 February 1992: 40.

[22]'DuPont: corporate advertising', case 9-593-023, Boston, MA: Harvard Business School, 1992; John B. Frey, 'Measuring corporate reputation and its value', presentation given at Marketing Science Conference, Duke University, 17 March 1989.

[23]Charles J. Fombrun, *Reputation*, Boston, MA: Harvard Business School Press, 1996.

[24]Zeynep Gurhan-Canli, 'The effect of expected variability of product quality and attribute uniqueness on family brand evaluations', *Journal of Consumer Research*, June 2003, 30: 105–14.

[25]Much of this section – including examples – is based on an article by Peter H. Farquhar, Julia Y. Han, Paul M. Herr and Yuji Ijiri, 'Strategies for leveraging master brands', *Marketing Research*, September 1992: 32–43.

[26]Ibid.

[27]For reviews of corporate images see, for example, Grahame R. Dowling, *Corporate Reputations*, Melbourne, Australia: Longman Professional, 1994; and James R. Gregory, *Marketing Corporate Image*, Lincolnwood, IL: NTC Business Books, 1991.

[28]Kevin Lane Keller and David A. Aaker, 'The effects of sequential introduction of brand extensions', *Journal of Marketing Research*, February 1992, 29: 35–50. See also T. J. Brown and P. Dacin, 'The company and the product: corporate associations and consumer product responses', *Journal of Marketing*, January 1997, 61: 68–84.

[29]Masashi Kuga, 'Kao's strategy and marketing intelligence system', *Journal of Advertising Research*, April/May 1990, 30: 20–5.

[30]John Smale, 'Smale on Saturn – don't change what's working', *Advertising Age*, 28 March 1994: S24.

[31]Tulun Erdem and Joffre Swait, 'Brand credibility, brand consideration and choice', *Journal of Consumer Research*, June 2004, 31: 191–8; Marvin E. Goldberg and Jon Hartwick, 'The effects of advertiser reputation and extremity of advertising claim on advertising effectiveness', *Journal of Consumer Research*, September 1990, 17: 172–9.

[32]Majken Schultz, Mary Jo Hatch and Mogens Holten Larsen, eds, *The Expressive Organization: Linking identity, reputation and the corporate brand*, New York: Oxford University Press, 2000; Mary Jo Hatch and Majken Schultz, 'Are the strategic stars aligned for your corporate brand?', *Harvard Business Review*, February 2001: 129–34; James Gregory, *Leveraging the Corporate Brand*, Chicago: NTC Press, 1997; Lynn B. Upshaw and Earl L. Taylor, *The Masterbrand Mandate*, New York: John Wiley, 2000.

[33]Sylvie LaForet and John Saunders, 'Managing brand portfolios: how the leaders do it', *Journal of Advertising Research*, September/October 1994: 64–76. See also Sylvie LaForet

and John Saunders, 'Managing brand portfolios: why leaders do what they do', *Journal of Advertising Research*, January/February 1999: 51–65.

[34]Ibid.

[35]Beth Snyder Bulik, 'Tech sector ponders: what's in a name?', *Advertising Age*, 9 May 2005: 24.

[36]Tulin Erdem and Baohung Sun, 'An empirical investigation of the spillover effects of advertising and sales promotions in umbrella branding', *Journal of Marketing Research*, November 2002, 39: 408–20.

[37]Beth Snyder Bulik, 'Tech sector ponders'.

[38]Emily Nelson, 'Too many choices', *Wall Street Journal*, 20 April 2001: B1, B4.

[39]Edmund Gray and Larry R. Smeltzer, 'Corporate image: an integral part of strategy', *Sloan Management Review*, summer 1985: 73–8.

[40]For a review of practices, see David W. Schumann, Jan M. Hathcote and Susan West, 'Corporate advertising in America: a review of published studies on use, measurement, and effectiveness', *Journal of Advertising*, September 1991, 20 (3): 35–56.

[41]David M. Bender, Peter Farquhar and Sanford C. Schulert, 'Growing from the top: corporate advertising nourishes the brand equity from which profits sprout', *Marketing Management*, 1996, 4 (4): 10–19; Nicholas Ind, 'An integrated approach to corporate branding', *Journal of Brand Management*, 1998, 5 (5): 323–9; Cees B. M. Van Riel, Natasha E. Stroker and Onno J. M. Maathuis, 'Measuring corporate images', *Corporate Reputation Review*, 1, no. 4 1998, 1 (4): 313–26.

[42]Gabriel J. Biehal and Daniel A. Shenin, 'Managing the brand in a corporate advertising environment', *Journal of Advertising*, 1998, 28 (2): 99–110.

[43]Mary C. Gilly and Mary Wolfinbarger, 'Advertising's second audience: employee reactions to organizational communications', MSI working paper 96–116, Cambridge, MA: Marketing Science Institute, 1996.

[44]Suzanne Vranica, 'Cingular ads shift to clear from cryptic', *Wall Street Journal*, 27 August 2001: B7.

[45]Vanessa O'Connell, 'Kraft Foods plans "umbrella" campaign', *Wall Street Journal*, 15 June 1998: B8.

[46]'Sense and simplicity: Philips is spending 80 million [euro] on a rebranding strategy that will emphasise simplicity and give consumers what they want', *ERT Weekly*, 23 September 2004.

[47]P. Rajan Varadarajan and Anil Menon, 'Cause-related marketing: a coalignment of marketing strategy and corporate philanthropy', *Journal of Marketing*, July 1988, 52: 58–74.

[48]Greg Goldin, 'Cause-related marketing grows up', *Adweek*, 17 November 1987: 20–2; Ronald Alsop, 'More firms push promotion aimed at consumers' hearts', *Wall Street Journal*, 29 August 1985: 23.

[49]Sankar Sen and C. B. Bhattacharya, 'Does doing good always lead to doing better? Consumer reactions to corporate social responsibility', *Journal of Marketing Research*, May 2001, 38: 225–43.

[50]Yumiko Ono, 'Do-good ads aim for sales that do better', *Wall Street Journal*, 2 September 1994: B8.

[51]M. Drumwright, 'Company advertising with a social dimension: the role of noneconomic criteria', *Journal of Marketing*, October 1996, 60: 71–87; A. Menon and A. Menon, 'Enviropreneurial marketing strategy: the emergence of corporate environmentalism as market strategy', *Journal of Marketing*, January 1997, 61: 51–67.

[52]Hamish Pringle and Marjorie Thompson, *Brand Spirit: How cause-related marketing builds brands*, Chichester, NY: Wiley, 1999.

[53]Ibid.

[54]Judann Dagnoli, 'Consciously green', *Advertising Age*, 19 September 1991: 14.

[55]Lawrence E. Joseph, 'The greening of American business', *Vis. A. Vis*, May 1991: 32.

[56]Joanne Lipman, 'Environmental theme hits sour notes', *Wall Street Journal*, 3 May 1990: B6.

[57]Leah Rickard, 'Natural products score big on image', *Advertising Age*, 8 August 1994: 26; Kevin Goldman, 'Survey asks which "green" ads are for real', *Wall Street Journal*; Lorne Manly, 'It doesn't pay to go green when consumers are seeing red', *Adweek*, 23 March 1992: 32–3.

[58] Ibid.

[59]Jacquelyn A. Otman, 'When it comes to green marketing, companies are finally getting it right', *Brandweek*, 17 April 1995.

[60]J. A. Deighton, 'Features of good integration: two cases and some generalizations', in *Integrated Communications: The search for surgery in communication voices*, eds J. Moore and E. Thorsen, Hillsdale, NJ: Lawrence Erlbaum Associations, 1996.

[61]Nancy Langford and Steven A. Greyser, 'Exxon: communications after Valdez', case 9–593–014, Boston, MA: Harvard Business School, 1995.

[62]Stephen A. Greyser and Norman Klein, 'The Perrier recall: a source of trouble', case 9–590–104, Boston, MA: Harvard Business School, 1990; Stephen A. Greyser and Norman Klein, 'The Perrier relaunch', case supplement 9–590–130, Boston, MA: Harvard Business School, 1990.

[63]Ronald Alsop, 'Enduring brands hold their allure by sticking close to their roots', *Wall Street Journal Centennial Edition*, 1989.

[64]Leslie Savan, 'Selling a sullied product', *San Francisco Chronicle*, 17 August 1986: 5.

12 Introducing and naming products and brand extensions

PREVIEW

Chapter 11 considered developing a corporate branding strategy. Two tools were introduced: the brand–product matrix to show the products and brands marketed by a company; and the brand hierarchy to portray relationships between brand elements. This chapter considers the role of product strategy in creating, maintaining and enhancing brand equity. Specifically, it develops guidelines for introducing and naming of products and brand extensions.

To provide some historical perspective, for years firms tended to follow the lead of Procter & Gamble, Unilever, Coca-Cola and other consumer goods marketers in avoiding introducing any products using an existing brand name. Over time, tight economic conditions, a need for growth and other factors forced firms to rethink their 'one brand–one product' policies. Recognizing the value of their brands, many firms have since decided to build on that asset by introducing a host of products under their strongest brand names.

More and more firms are seeking to build 'power' or 'mega' brands that establish a broad market with products that appeal to many customer segments, all underneath the brand umbrella. One obvious example is the Virgin brand run by Sir Richard Branson. He has recognized that the primary asset of Virgin is its brand and he is using it in different business sectors. Unilever's Dove has made forays from soap into skincare and bodycare products, backed by a 'Campaign for real beauty'. At the same time, marketers are realizing that too many product variations can be counter-productive and ill-advised brand proliferation may repel consumers.

Because of their prevalence and importance, much has been learned about best practice for managing brand extensions. The chapter describes some brand extension issues and the advantages and disadvantages of brand extensions. It then presents a model of how consumers evaluate brand extensions and offers guidelines concerning the proper means of introducing and naming products and brand extensions. The chapter concludes by summarizing academic research on brand extensions. Brand Briefing 12.14 addresses important issues with respect to line extensions.

NEW PRODUCTS AND BRAND EXTENSIONS

It is worthwhile to first consider the sources of growth for a firm. One useful perspective is offered by Ansoff's product–market expansion grid. As shown in Figure 12.1, growth strategies can be categorized according to whether they involve existing or new products and whether they target existing or new customers or markets. Brand Briefing 12.1 describes McDonald's growth strategies along these lines. Brand Briefing 12.2 explores in detail how McDonald's managed an extension into healthier food. Although existing products can be used to penetrate existing customer markets further or expand into new customer markets (the focus of Chapter 13), new products are vital to the long-term success of a firm.

As noted in Chapter 11, factors related to consumer behaviour, corporate capabilities and competitive actions affect the development of a product or market. A discussion of all of the issues involved is beyond the scope of this chapter. This section, however, addresses some brand equity implications of new products.[1]

When a firm introduces a product, it has three choices as to how to brand it.

1. It can develop a new brand, individually chosen for the product.
2. It can apply, in some way, one of its existing brands.
3. It can use a combination of a new brand with an existing brand.

A *brand extension* is when a firm uses an established brand name to introduce a new product (approaches 2 or 3). When a new brand is combined with an existing brand (approach 3), the brand extension can also be called a *sub-brand*. A brand that gives birth to a brand extension is referred to as the *parent brand*. As noted in Chapter 11, if the parent brand is already associated with several products through brand extensions, then it may also be called a *family brand*.

Brand extensions can be classified into two categories.[2]

- *Line extension:* the parent brand is used for a product that targets a new market segment within a product category served by the parent. A line extension often involves a different flavour or ingredient variety, a different form or size or a different application for the brand (eg, Head & Shoulders Dry Scalp shampoo).
- *Category extension:* the parent brand is used to enter a different product category from that served by the parent brand (eg, Swiss Army watches).

	Current products	New products
Current markets	Market penetration strategy	Product development strategy
New markets	Market development strategy	Diversification strategy

Figure 12.1   Ansoff's growth share matrix

Brand Briefing 12.1

Expanding the McDonald's brand

In the 2000s, McDonald's faced an environment where market saturation and global health concerns provided obstacles to its growth. To generate growth, the company employed a number of growth strategies in the pursuit of global brand leadership that illustrate the quadrants of the Ansoff growth matrix.

Market penetration

McDonald's found its popularity under threat following international concern about the role of fast food in poor health and obesity, highlighted by the bad publicity that came from the 2001 book *Fast Food Nation* and the 2004 film *Super Size Me*. The company posted its first quarterly loss in 2002 and, as a consequence, 'needed to look at why its customers weren't buying and recognise that they wanted better choice and healthier options'. McDonald's responded by adding healthier products and launched a 'Bag a McMeal' website that enabled users to calculate the nutritional content of any combination of its menu items. It also launched a global advertising campaign, based on the 'I'm lovin' it' tagline, which was translated into a number of languages. This campaign replaced some 20 ad platforms that had been running in different regions. In 2004, McDonald's marketing chief Larry Light lauded the campaign's success: 'The global common brand approach has been successful beyond our expectations. Since September 2003 we've had incremental visits to our stores of 2.3 million customer visits per day and that's continuing to grow.'

Market development

Though McDonald's was forced to close restaurants in some markets such as the UK and Japan as demand fell, it still pursued growth via overseas expansion, opening more than 1,200 restaurants in 2003, bringing the total to more than 30,000 restaurants in 119 countries. Some 65 percent of McDonald's revenues in 2004 came from outside the USA and its fastest-growing market in the mid-2000s was China, where the company hoped to have 1,000 locations by the 2008 Beijing Olympics. The company sought to highlight its expansive global presence with a 2006 global 'reality packaging' promotion tied to the 'I'm lovin' it' campaign, whereby customers were encouraged to participate in a 'global casting call' by submitting online a personal story and digital photo of what they loved. In 2007, 25 finalists were to be featured on cups and bags at McDonald's restaurants around the globe. McDonald's also sought to develop a new market domestically by attracting twenty-and thirty-something females to the brand with premium salads served with Newman's Own dressing and other lighter menu options and targeted marketing as part of the 'I'm lovin' it' campaign.

Product development

McDonald's extended its brand in 2001 with the opening of its McCafé, a gourmet coffee shop inspired by the success of Starbucks, in Portugal and Austria. Another

Brand Briefing 12.1 *continued*

extension is McTreat, an ice-cream and dessert shop. Additionally, McDonald's began offering specialized menu items in different countries, such as the Teriyaki Burger in Japan and Vegetable McNuggets in Britain.

The biggest product developments, however, were necessitated by the health concerns surrounding fast food. McDonald's overhauled its menu, removing 'super size' options and adding healthier options such as fresh salads, adult versions of its Happy Meals that included salad, bottled water and a pedometer to encourage exercise, and healthier versions of its children's Happy Meals. McDonald's rapidly became the number one salad brand in the USA. The revamp of its menu was coupled with other health initiatives, including its Balanced Lifestyles platform for children that promoted healthy food choices, education and physical activity and its Go Active! campaign to promote active lifestyles, which were both endorsed by Bob Greene, TV presenter Oprah Winfrey's personal trainer. This shift in focus towards healthy eating and physical activity was emphasized by McDonald's recasting of Ronald McDonald as its 'chief happiness officer', a sports enthusiast who donned a more athletic version of his yellow and red suit and snowboarded, skateboarded and juggled fruit in TV ads. Brand Briefing 12.2 explores how McDonald's managed to be successful with this crucial extension.

The fast food chain also tapped into the premium coffee trend in the USA by launching a premium roast coffee, which sold for about a third less than a cup of Starbucks coffee. Another popular product was the McGriddle breakfast sandwich.

Diversification

McDonald's diversifies its product offerings according to regional tastes. For example, when McDonald's entered India – where beef is not consumed because cows are sacred – in 1996, it introduced the Maharaja Mac made from mutton. The company also developed spicy sauces such as McMasala and McImli.

As a result of these strategies, the company's fortunes rebounded. Furthermore, the brand was credited with a 'halo effect' that was 'driving growth for the entire quick-service restaurant category'.

Sources: 'McDonald's to spend $1.5 billion to expand in Asia-Pacific region', *Wall Street Journal*, 10 April 1998; Richard Gibson and Matt Moffett, 'Why you won't find any Egg McMuffins for breakfast in Brazil', *Wall Street Journal*, 23 October 1997; Joanna Doonar, 'Life in the fast lane', *Brand Strategy*, 6 October 2004: 20; Gina Piccolo, 'Fries with that fruit?', *Los Angeles Times*, 18 July 2005: F1; Pallavi Gogoi and Michael Arndt, 'Hamburger hell', *BusinessWeek*, 3 March 2003: 104; Kate MacArthur, 'Big Mac's back', *Advertising Age*, 13 December 2004: S1; Normandy Madden, 'In China, golf and American fare', *Advertising Age*, 25 July 2005: S6.

Brand Briefing 12.2

McDonald's Salad Plus: extending the brand into a new product category

McDonald's is a power brand on a global scale. With brand-specific associations intrinsically linked with functional products such as its Big Mac and Happy Meal, McDonald's has dominated the fast food category. However, these brand-specific associations turned out, to some extent, to be a challenge to address during the beginning of 2000, when the market climate was changing. Due to changing consumer perceptions, the fast food category saw the emergence of a sub-category: healthy fast food. This was happening as McDonald's was under attack from media and opinion leaders, who pointed to McDonald's as 'the bad guy' in the face of growing obesity in society. This development put McDonald's into a vulnerable position, because it was in danger of losing brand relevance for key target groups, who value the attributes of fast food but are also health-conscious. Consumers were re-evaluating the category and the biggest challenge for McDonald's was to retain female consumers, particularly mothers.

McDonald's was under pressure to find a solution that would appeal to the more health-conscious audience and not lose momentum within the category. The solution was to extend the brand into the healthy fast food sub-category and thus remain relevant and strong in the face of the changing market. Staying an option for mothers is a strategic issue because they function as gatekeepers for the family in terms of where to eat out. This is relevant because the Happy Meal is a very important revenue generator for McDonald's. The implications from a bottom-line perspective were evident.

However, McDonald's, on a category level, was strongly associated with one product, hamburgers, so extending into a new category posed questions, particularly from a brand territory perspective. How far could McDonald's stretch its brand without losing credibility with loyal customers who love McDonald's for its core products? In this sense the mission to remain brand an option was also a brand portfolio issue. Since there is interdependence between the products in the portfolio, the extension would affect the total brand portfolio characteristics. For instance, there was a risk that poor associations would be formed around the brand extension, which could spill over into other sub-brands and products within McDonald's existing portfolio and thereby harm the parent brand. However, an efficient launch of the sub-category product could improve McDonald's brand equity and be a valuable addition to the brand portfolio. It all depended heavily on consumers' acceptance and thus the marketing communication.

Analysis indicated that McDonald's could extend into the outer zones of its brand territory, since it was a powerful brand that was well-established all over the world. McDonald's had performed many brand extensions and several that seemed further away from the core than a healthy alternative to hamburgers. For instance, McDonald's has its own children's hospitals, which have little to do with burgers.

Brand Briefing 12.2 *continued*

However, there are brand-specific associations that create explanatory links between the McDonald's brand and children's hospitals. McDonald's has always been known as a great children's restaurant, with Happy Meal, Ronald McDonald and playgrounds. Since Ronald McDonald was used as communication tool when launching the children's hospital concept, consumers could easily trace the relevance and brand fit between hamburgers and hospitals. However, it was clear that it lacked credibility in areas associated with healthy food, which arguably made the extension into the sub-category risky. McDonald's was associated with food, but almost only unhealthy food. Still, the need for a relevant alternative to the existing menu was identified.

The extension was the biggest change to the McDonald's menu since the launch of the Big Mac in 1968 – a brand extension into salads. In the spring of 2004, eight products under the sub-brand Salads Plus were introduced in the USA and Australia. This was followed by a launch in 6,000 restaurants throughout Europe the following year. The European launch kicked off in the UK and Germany – two of the biggest markets. It was followed by roll-outs in Portugal, Scandinavia, Spain, the Netherlands, Belgium, Switzerland, France, Greece, Ireland and Austria.

Figure 12.2   McDonald's Salad Plus

Brand Briefing 12.2 *continued*

What was special about the launch of Salads Plus in Europe was that it was packaged and communicated in a way that would lower the barriers to consumer acceptance for the range. Salads Plus was packaged as a concept, where the communication was aimed at women (mothers included). A paraphrase was added to the campaign, which was formulated as 'Go active'. The Go Active concept put the product brand, Salads Plus, in the centre, but at the same time highlighted the bigger picture: a healthy lifestyle is what you eat and what you do.

Moreover, to insulate the Salads Plus from limiting brand-specific associations, the Mc-prefix was omitted from the name. Hence, McDonald's had created a true sub-brand. Furthermore, because credibility was a major issue for this brand extension, endorsement branding was used in some markets, with McDonald's building on the equity of credible spokespeople. Consequently, consumers were given a compelling reason to believe. This, in a way, also prevented the extension from alienating the core consumers who came to McDonald's for its hamburgers.

Perhaps one of the most important strategic actions was a bundling arrangement, including Salads Plus and Happy Meals. This bundling created a powerful combination for mothers (and their children), tying two important target groups together. As long as mum feels comfortable with what she eats at McDonald's, she could feel even better by providing her child with something he or she loves. Thus, for health-conscious mothers, it provided a relevant reason (and even a justification) for visiting McDonald's. This should not be underestimated, since it also highlights the importance of taking on a strategic brand portfolio perspective in developing a brand extension strategy. Even if Salads Plus was successful in sheer numbers, ie unit sales, its presence in the portfolio should also be judged on the basis of its net effect on the brand associations held by mothers regarding the McDonald's brand. Even more so in their role as family gatekeepers.

The launch of Salads Plus created a platform on which McDonald's could continue to build across Europe. For instance, the Salads Plus concept has paved the way for McDonald's to launch carrots and fruit in bags, which at one time might have seemed absurd, but in the light of the salad launch, seems perfectly well-advised. However, although McDonald's managed to create added relevance through Salads Plus, it still has a long way to go to get a strong foothold in the healthy fast food category.

Sources: www.mcdonalds.com; press release 2004-04-13; press release 2004-07-29; S. Bridges, K.L. Keller and S. Sood (1997) 'Communication strategies for brand extensions: enhancing perceived fit by establishing explanatory links', *Journal of Advertising*, Winter; K. L. Keller and D. A. Aaker, 'The effects of sequential introduction of brand extensions', *Journal of Marketing Research*, February 1992, 29: 35–50; P. A. Dacin and D. C. Smith, 'The effect of brand portfolio characteristics on consumer evaluations of brand extensions', *Journal of Marketing*, May 1994, XXXI: 229–42.

Most new products are line extensions – typically 80 percent to 90 percent in any one year. Moreover, many of the most successful new products, as rated by various sources, are extensions (eg, Colgate toothpaste, Apple iPod digital music player, Starbucks coffee liqueur and Budweiser Barbecue Sauce. Budweiser's extension was voted the best extension of a food brand in the USA for 2006).[3] Nevertheless, many products introduced are new brands (eg, YouTube video hosting website and the PSP).

Brand extensions can come in all forms. One branding expert, Edward Tauber, identifies seven strategies for establishing a category – or what he calls a franchise – extension.[4]

- *Introduce the same product in a different form:* examples: Ocean Spray Cranberry Juice Mars ice-cream bars and Rice Krispies snack bars.
- *Introduce products that contain the brand's distinctive taste, ingredient or component:* examples: Philadelphia cream cheese salad dressing and Häagen-Dazs' Bailey's ice-cream.
- *Introduce companion products for the brand:* examples: Dontos dips and Duracell Durabeam torches.
- *Introduce products relevant to the customer franchise of the brand:* examples: SAGA travel insurance and Visa traveller's cheques.
- *Introduce products that capitalize on the firm's perceived expertise:* examples: Honda lawnmowers and Canon photocopiers.
- *Introduce products that reflect the brand's distinctive benefit, attribute or feature:* example: Dettol's household cleaning products and the iPhone.
- *Introduce products that capitalize on the distinctive image or prestige of the brand:* examples: Calvin Klein clothes and accessories and Porsche sunglasses.

Brand Briefing 12.3 describes how the strong bicycle brand Crescent successfully extended the brand from bicycles to prams.

Brand Briefing 12.3

Brand extensions of the bicycle brand Crescent

Crescent is a market leader for bicycles in Sweden with a 25 percent market share. The Swedish market for bicycles is fragmented with more than 100 brands. Crescent is the most well-known bicycle brand in Sweden with about 82 percent awareness and strong associations. With this strong position, Cycleurope wanted to capitalize on the brand by developing it into other areas. Qualitative and quantitative research was carried out to identify extension opportunities. It was crucial for the management to start by defining the Crescent brand personality and its associations from a consumer perspective. The second phase of the extension research analyzed the degree of credibility for 17 potential extensions.

Results of the personality study indicated that the Crescent brand was strong on two factors: competence and ruggedness. (Cycleurope was inspired by the Aaker brand personality scale when it carried out its personality research, see Chapter 9.)

Brand Briefing 12.3 *continued*

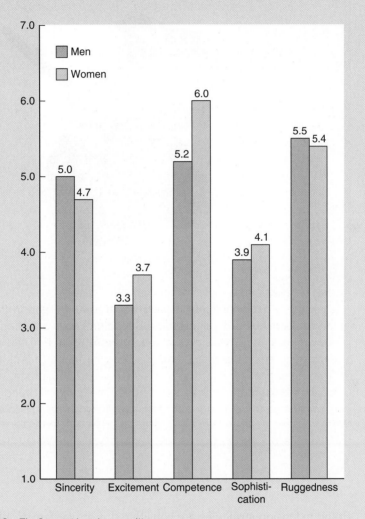

Figure 12.3   The Crescent brand personality

The consumer research also indicated that the right decision was to extend the Crescent brand into prams. The personality and the association with prams were also in line with the personality and associations with the Crescent brand. Both bicycles and prams were of high quality with a solid construction (Figure 12.4).

Brand Briefing 12.3 *continued*

Figure 12.4   Crescent pram

The rugged personality of Crescent would also fit a gap in the pram market. The market leaders, Hemmaljunga and Brio, didn't have any products suiting the consumers' desire for more robust, tough prams. Based on this research, Cycleurope decided to enter the pram market under the name Crescent – 'Baby in motion'. 'The initial goal for the first year 2007 was 2,000 prams, but shortly after the launch we raised the numbers to 10,000. The Crescent brand extension into prams is considered to be a huge success', says Tony Grimaldi, Cycleurope chief.

Sources: Interview with Tony Grimaldi, chief executive, Cycleurope, 25 July 2007; Christian Sandberg, Cycleurope, 2005–06.

Brand extension strategies are considered more systematically later in this chapter. Next, however, some of the main advantages and disadvantages of brand extensions.

ADVANTAGES OF EXTENSIONS

For most firms, the question is not whether a brand should be extended, but when, where and how. Well-planned and implemented extensions offer advantages to marketers. These advantages can be categorized as those that aid new product acceptance and those that provide feedback to the parent brand or company as whole (Figure 12.5).

Facilitate new product acceptance	Provide feedback to the parent brand and company
Improve brand image.	Clarify brand meaning.
Reduce risk perceived by customers.	Enhance the parent brand image.
Increase the probability of gaining distribution and trial.	Bring new customers into brand franchise and increase market coverage.
Increase efficiency of promotional expenditures.	Revitalize the brand.
Reduce costs of introductory and follow-up marketing campaigns.	Permit subsequent extensions.
Avoid cost of developing a new brand.	
Allow for packaging and labelling efficiencies.	
Permit consumers to seek variety.	

Figure 12.5   Advantages of brand extensions

Aid new product acceptance

The high failure rate of products is well documented. Marketing analysts estimate that perhaps only two in ten new products will be successful or maybe even as few as one. Robert McMath, who opened a collection of 75,000 once-new consumer products called the New Products Showcase and Learning Center in New York, identifies nine reasons for product failure.[5]

- The market was too small (insufficient demand for type of product).
- The product was a poor match for the company.
- The product was justified on inadequate or inaccurate marketing research or the company ignored research results.
- The company was too early or too late in researching the market (failure to capitalize on its marketing window).
- The product provided insufficient return on investment (poor profit margins and high costs).
- The product was not new or different (an idea that offered nothing new).
- The product did not go hand in hand with familiarity.
- Credibility was not confirmed on delivery.
- Consumers could not recognize the product.

Brand extensions can suffer from some of these shortcomings. Nevertheless, a product introduced as a brand extension may be more likely to succeed, at least to some degree, because it offers the advantages described in the following subsections.

Improve brand image

As Chapter 2 noted, one of the advantages of a well-known and well-liked brand is that consumers form expectations over time concerning its performance. Similarly, with a brand extension, consumers can make inferences and form expectations as to the likely composition and performance of a product based on what they already know about the brand itself and the extent to which they feel this information is relevant to the new product.[6] These inferences may improve the strength, favourability and uniqueness of the extension's brand associations. For example, when Sony introduced a new personal computer tailored for multimedia applications, Vaio, consumers may have been more likely to feel comfortable with its anticipated performance because of their experience with other Sony products than if the product had been branded by Sony as something completely new.

Reduce risk perceived by customers

One research study examining factors affecting product acceptance found that the most important factor for predicting the results of a trial of a new product was the extent to which a known family brand was involved.[7] Extensions from brands such as Tesco, Carrefour, Virgin, Philips, Nokia or others may communicate longevity and sustainability. Although corporate brands may lack specific product associations because of the breadth of products attached to their name, their reputation for being able to introduce quality products and stand behind them may be an important risk-reducer for consumers.[8] Thus, perceptions of corporate credibility – in terms of expertise and trustworthiness – can be valuable associations for brand extensions.[9] Similarly, although widely extended supermarket brands such as Findus, Weight Watchers, Green Giant and Del Monte may lack specific product meaning, they may still stand for product quality in the minds of consumers and, by reducing perceived risk, aid the adoption of brand extensions.

Increase the probability of gaining distribution and trial

Because of the potentially increased consumer demand resulting from introducing a new product as an extension, it may be easier to convince retailers to stock and promote a brand extension. For example, one study indicated that brand reputation was a key screening criteria of gatekeepers making new product decisions at supermarkets.[10]

Increase efficiency of promotional expenditures

From a marketing communications perspective, one advantage of introducing a product as a brand extension is that the introductory campaign does not have to create awareness of both the brand and the new product but instead can concentrate on the new product itself. In general, it should be easier to add a link from a brand already existing in memory to a new product than it is to first establish the brand in memory and then also link the new product to it.[11]

Research documents this extension benefit. One study of 98 consumer brands in 11 markets found that successful brand extensions spent less on advertising than did comparable new-name entries.[12] Another study found similar results, indicating that the average advertising to sales ratio for brand extensions was 10 percent, compared with 19 percent for new brands. This study identified factors moderating this extension advantage. The difference in advertising efficiency between brand extensions and new brands was shown to increase as the fit with other products affiliated with the parent brand increased, as the new product's relative price compared with that of competitors increased and as distribution intensity increased. On the other hand, the difference in advertising efficiency between brand extensions and new brands was shown to decrease when the new product was composed primarily of search attributes (ie, when product quality could be judged through visual inspection), as the new product became established in the market, and as consumers' knowledge of the new product category increased.[13]

Reduce costs of introductory and marketing campaigns

Because of these push and pull considerations in distribution and promotion, it has been estimated that a firm can save 40 percent to 80 percent on the estimated €22–36 million it can cost to launch a new supermarket product nationally in the USA. Moreover, other efficiencies can result after the launch. As one such example, when a brand becomes associated with several products, advertising can become more cost-effective for the family brand as a whole. For example, in 2001, Apple introduced the iPod portable digital music player, which quickly became the market leader and one of the company's most successful products. In subsequent years, the iPod received the majority of Apple's marketing budget and was credited with a 'halo effect' that boosted sales for the company's other products, particularly computers and software. In 2005, Apple's sales rose 68 percent from the previous year, with non-iPod products making up 61 percent of total sales and Apple computers earning 4 percent market share, up from 2.7 percent the previous year.[14]

Avoid cost of developing a new brand

As Chapter 4 indicated, developing brand elements is an art and science. To conduct the necessary consumer research and employ skilled personnel to design high-quality brand names, logos, symbols, packaging, characters and slogans can be expensive, and there is no assurance of success. As the number of available – and appealing – brand names keeps shrinking, legal conflicts are more likely to result. To avoid such conflict, a global trademark search is vital for any launch or rebranding and can cost millions. Even after a search is completed, other costs can arise. After conducting a global trademark search, PricewaterhouseCooper's consulting group spinoff Monday elected to pay a reported €4.7 million to acquire the worldwide rights to the public relations firm OneMonday trademark and domain name.[15] Monday's money was perhaps not well spent; the consulting unit was acquired and folded into the IBM brand one month after announcing the name change.

Allow for packaging and labelling efficiencies

Similar packaging and labels for extensions can result in lower production costs and, if co-ordinated properly, more prominence in shops by creating a 'poster' effect. For example, Finolus offers a variety of frozen meals in identical packaging that increases the brand's visibility when stocked together in a freezer. A similar effect is evident with other supermarket brands, such as Coca-Cola.

Permit consumers to seek variety

By offering variants within a product category, consumers who need a change – because of boredom, satiation or whatever – can switch to a different product without having to leave the brand family. Even without such motivations, by offering line extensions, customers may be encouraged to use the brand to a greater extent or in different ways than otherwise might have been the case. Moreover, to even compete in some categories, it may be necessary to have many items that together form a cohesive product line.

Suave

As an example of the benefits of expansive market coverage, consider the low-priced family brand Suave, sold by Helene Curtis in the USA. Suave includes a variety of personal care products, such as shampoo and conditioners, skin lotions and body washes, and antiperspirants and deodorants. Given the amount of brand switching and the large number of brands kept by consumers for personal care products in general and shampoos in particular, the ability of Suave to offer a full product line is a competitive advantage. By continually extending its range, Suave keeps up with trends or shifts in consumer demand.[16] Helene Curtis has adopted a 'follower' strategy: whenever a new type of product becomes successful, the company introduces a similar version under the Suave name designed to match it. Suave's advertising slogans have included: 'You don't have to spend a lot to get a lot' and 'Say yes to beautiful without paying the price.' Suave's well-defined brand image and branding strategy has resulted in high degrees of consumer loyalty and market share.

Provide feedback to the parent brand

Besides enabling acceptance of new products, brand extensions can also provide feedback to the parent brand.

Clarify brand meaning

Extensions can help to clarify the meaning of a brand to consumers and define the kinds of markets in which it competes. Thus, through brand extensions, Intersport means 'sport products', Aldi means 'inexpensive food', Cycleurope means 'bicycles', L'Oréal means 'beauty', Clairol means 'hair colouring' and Carrefour means 'hypermarkets' to consumers. Brand Briefing 12.4 shows how food retailer ICA used brand extensions to broaden its meaning to consumers.

Crayola

Crayola, known for its crayons, first sought to expand its brand into other drawing and colouring implements such as markers, pencils, paints, pens, brushes and chalk. The company then expanded into arts and crafts with Crayola Clay, Crayola Dough, Crayola Glitter Glue and Crayola Scissors. These extensions established a new brand meaning for Crayola of 'colourful crafts for kids'. In 2005, the company attempted to expand its brand meaning once again

Brand Briefing 12.4

Broadening the meaning of retailer ICA

ICA has been the leading Swedish supermarket since 1966. Since its foundation in 1917, ICA has tried to bring together retailers in co-operation. In 1964 the ICA logo was agreed upon as the symbol for the brand and 59 percent of the Swedish adult population shops in an ICA supermarket at least once a week. The turnover of the ICA group in 2006 was €8.7 billion.

Master brand level

The majority owner of ICA (60 percent) is the Dutch group Ahold, the other owner being Hakon Invest. Brand building within ICA is carried out at four levels (Figure 12.6): ICA as a master brand; sub-brands; five own labels; and, at the shop level, almost 1,400 shops. According to RepTrak Sweden, ICA had the second strongest reputation in 2006 after Ikea, and the third strongest in 2007, after Ikea and Volvo. The ICA's business is built on five values: simple, personal, safe, inspiring and modern. These values safeguard the ICA brand and its brand extensions.

ICA's sub-brand level

The retail trade in Sweden has seen a movement towards larger shops. This means that the number of ICA's Nära supermarkets (the smallest ones) decreased from 1,200 in 1998 to 743 in 2007. ICA opened hypermarkets later than its main competitor Co-op, but its Maxi ICA Hypermarkets have been successful and the number of such shops increased from 30 in 1998 to 60 in 2007.

ICA uses four formats for its supermarkets in Sweden and one format for its financial operations:

- ICA Nära (superettes): 743 small supermarkets in 2007;
- ICA Supermarket (traditional supermarkets): 460 in 2007;
- ICA Kvantum (large supermarkets): 119 in 2007;
- Maxi ICA Stormarknad (hypermarkets) 60 in and was planning more;
- ICA Banken (bank) is the name for the financial operations of ICA.

All formats have different strategies regarding outlet profile, renewal, product range, price strategy, marketing and role support.

ICA private label brand level

When ICA puts its name on its products, it guarantees the product from an environmental and ethical perspective. ICA has developed five positions for its own labels, which enables extensions of the brand within different categories.

- ICA is the umbrella brand associated with its five core values. It is this own label that carries the same name as the master brand.

Brand Briefing 12.4 *continued*

- ● ICA Gott Liv (Good Life) was launched in 2005. This brand covers healthy products in several categories.
- ● ICA I love eco is the brand that covers organic products.
- ● Skona is ICA's ecological brand for detergents, washing-up liquids, paper products and cleaners.
- ● Euro Shopper is the brand for discount products. Euro Shopper was developed co-operatively by 9 European companies in 15 countries, including Kesko, Albert Heijn, Dansk Supermarked and ICA.

The percentage of own labels is growing fast from a low number in Sweden.

The core competence of ICA is its ability to build enduring and profitable relationships with customers. This competence rests on three key components: supermarket-level branding (with three other levels: master brand, sub-brands and own brands); category management, the way ICA develops the assortment and creates profit; and customer-specific marketing. The ICA Card, launched in 1990, has enabled it to reward loyal customers and to create links between customers and individual supermarkets. It has also enabled an extension into the financial area, with the launch of the ICA Bank.

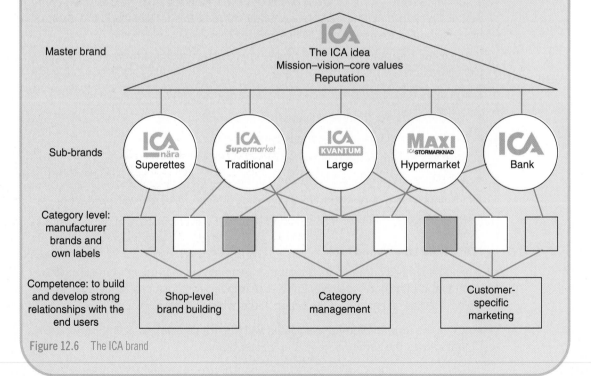

Figure 12.6   The ICA brand

Brand Briefing 12.4 *continued*

In total, ICA operates 2,250 supermarkets in Sweden, Norway and the Baltic region. In 2001, ICA received permission to start a bank in Sweden and it was launched in 2002. The ICA Bank offers various services on the Internet in about 1,400 supermarkets. The service includes bank accounts, various credit cards, loans, mortgages and insurance. Internal research indicates that ICA Bank customers are the most loyal customers.

In 2007, ICA was 'bank of the year' in Sweden. The reason it was chosen was that ICA offers easy-to-understand services at competive rates. The bank also offers a lot of outlets, co-operates with a company specializing in mortgages (SBAB) and an efficient bonus system. In 2006, ICA Bank reported its first operating profit.

According to the Swedish Quality Index, the ICA Bank has the most satisfied customers of any Swedish bank. In 2007, the bank entered into a co-operative agreement with Nordnet that allows ICA customers to trade mutual funds, equities and warrants, and to save for retirement through individual pension schemes.

Figure 12.7   The ICA Card

The enabler of the brand extension from food retail to the financial sector has been the ICA Card. Today, ICA Bank administers ICA's 3.1 million card customers. Among active customers, 1.6 million shop with their card when they shop at ICA, while the rest use their cards to accumulate bonus points.

Sources: Tony Apéria, *'Brand relationship management: den varumärkesbyggande processen'*, PhD thesis, Stockholm: Stockholm University, 2001; Tony Apéria and Rolf Back, *Brand Relations Management: Bridging the gap between brand promise and brand delivery*, Sweden: Liber, 2004; Sanna Liljestam and Hanna Wennerstein, 'ICA Banken', Stockholm University School of Business, 2004; www.ica.se; ICA group annual report 2006 and 2007; www.newsdesk.se/view/pressrelease/78320.

Brand	Original product	Extension products	New brand meaning
Weight Watchers	Fitness centres	Low-calorie foods	Weight loss and maintenance
Sunkist	Oranges	Vitamins, juices	Good health
Kellogg's	Cereal	Nutri-Grain bars, Special K bars	Healthy snacking

Figure 12.8   Expanding brand meaning through extensions

with the introduction of children's personal care products – Squeeze & Squirt Foaming Hand Soap and Body Soap. The products were designed to recall the familiar crayon packaging and were emblazoned with a character called 'Tip' that built on the equity that research revealed resided in the Crayola tip. It was not initially certain, however, whether or not the Crayola brand had permission from consumers to expand into cleaning products.

Broader brand meaning often is necessary so that firms avoid 'marketing myopia' and do not mistakenly draw narrow boundaries around their brands and either miss market opportunities or become vulnerable to rivals' strategies. Thus, as Ted Levitt pointed out, railways are not just in the 'railway' business but also the 'transportation' business.[17] In other words, railways do not necessarily compete with other railways so much as with cars and planes. Thinking more broadly about product meaning can easily result in different marketing campaigns and new product opportunities. For some brands, creating broader meaning may be the only way to expand sales (Figure 12.8).

Ocean Spray

Growers' co-operative Ocean Spray Cranberries found itself in a difficult position in the mid-2000s as Coca-Cola and PepsiCo began to expand into non-carbonated drinks, including juices. Ocean Spray contemplated selling the brand to PepsiCo, but ultimately the growers' co-op voted to remain independent. To remain competitive in the face of these giants, Ocean Spray introduced brand extensions in 2004 and 2005, including the Juice & Tea line of chilled juices, variety packs of its Craisins dried cranberries, Craisins trail mix, a sparkling red and white cranberry drink and squeezeable cranberry sauce. The brand's meaning to consumers has thus expanded from 'cranberry sauce' in the 1960s and 1970s to 'good-tasting fruit juice drinks that are good for you' in the 1980s and 1990s to 'good-tasting fruit juice drinks, snacks and innovative products'.[18]

In some cases, it is advantageous to establish related products that satisfy consumers' needs in a certain area. For example, the €26.2 billion enterprise software market is characterized by a few mega-brands (eg, Oracle and SAP) that compete in many segments with their products. Although these brands were limited to a few products at one time, they have broadened their meaning through brand extensions and acquisitions to represent 'complete business software solutions'. Similarly, many specific-purpose cleaning products have broadened out to become seen as multipurpose.

Enhance the parent brand image

According to the customer-based brand equity model, one desirable outcome of a brand extension is that it may enhance the parent brand image by strengthening an existing brand association, improving the favourability of an existing brand association, adding a new brand association or a combination of these.

One common way that a brand extension affects the parent's image is by helping to clarify its core values and associations. Core brand associations, as defined in Chapter 3, are those attributes and benefits that characterize products in the brand line and, as a result, are those with which consumers often have the strongest associations. For example, Nike has expanded from running shoes to other athletic shoes, clothing and equipment, strengthening its associations with 'peak performance' and 'sport' in the process.

Another type of association that may be improved by brand extensions is consumer perceptions of the credibility of the company. For example, one research study showed that a successful corporate brand extension led to improved perceptions of the expertise, trustworthiness and likeability of the company.[19] In the late 1990s, several firms chose to introduce online versions of their services under a separate brand name (eg, HSBC Bank chose to launch an online division called first direct). Besides having the difficulty and expense of launching a new brand, such companies also lost the opportunity to modernize the parent brand image and improve its technological credentials. In many cases, these ventures failed and their capabilities were folded back into the parent organization.

Bring new customers into the brand franchise and increase market coverage

Line extensions can benefit the parent brand by expanding market coverage, such as by offering a product benefit whose absence might have prevented consumers from trying the brand. For example, when Nurofen introduced a capsule form of its pain reliever, it was able to attract consumers who had difficulty swallowing tablets and therefore might have avoided the brand. By creating 'news' and bringing attention to the parent brand, the family brand as a whole may benefit. Snapple strove to renew its customers' interest and engagement with the brand, as well as attract new customers, with the 2004 introduction of its Snapple Lip Slicks fruit-flavoured lip balm. The brand extension served to highlight 'the wonderful attributes of Snapple – variety, flavour, smell – in a very creative, fun way'.[20] Similarly, through extensions, Tide as a family brand has managed to maintain its market leadership from the 1950s to the present.

Revitalize the brand

Sometimes brand extensions can be a means to renew interest and liking for the brand.

Old Spice

Procter & Gamble's Old Spice had to wrestle with the problem of being seen as 'your father's aftershave' to young male consumers in the USA. As one P&G

marketing executive noted: 'We recognize the need to change and bring in a new generation of young users. At the same time, we don't want to alienate the users we already have.' To revitalize the brand, a campaign backed by heavy spending was launched. New TV ads eliminated the trademark 'whistling sailor' character to show – via rapid-fire editing – active, contemporary men. On the product side, P&G put heavy support behind its fast-selling and more youthfully positioned Old Spice High Endurance personal care products (deodorant, antiperspirant, bar soap, body spray and shaving), as well as the Old Spice Red Zone family (deodorant, antiperspirant and body spray), which was launched with ads featuring an American football player, Brian Urlacher.[21]

Permit subsequent extensions

One benefit of a successful extension is that it may serve as the basis for more extensions. For example, Goodyear's introduction of its Aquatred tyres sub-brand led to the introduction of Eagle Aquatred for performance vehicles with either wider wheels or a luxury image.

Billabong

The Billabong brand was established in 1973 by Gordon Merchant, who wanted to create a brand that had 'functional products for surfers to help us better enjoy our sport'. During the 1970s and 1980s, Billabong established its brand credibility with the young Australian surfing community as a designer and producer of quality surf clothing (Figure 12.9). In the early 1980s, Billabong began to sell its products in Japan, Europe and the USA through licensees. In the late 1980s and early 1990s, the brand extended into other youth-orientated areas, such as snowboarding and skateboarding, sticking to its core brand proposition: contemporary, relevant, innovative products of consistently high quality. In 2004, the company launched a new brand called Honolua Surf, inspired by Hawaiian surf styles. As a result of its consistent growth, Billabong was ranked as the seventh most valuable brand in Australia, with an estimated value of €800 million.

Figure 12.9   Billabong

DISADVANTAGES OF BRAND EXTENSIONS

Despite their advantages, brand extensions have disadvantages (Figure 12.10).

Can confuse or frustrate consumers

As noted in Chapter 11, line extensions may confuse and perhaps even frustrate consumers as to which version of the product is 'right' for them. With 16 varieties of Coca-Cola, 35 versions of Crest toothpaste and so on, consumers can feel overwhelmed.[22] For example, one study found that consumers were more likely to make a purchase after sampling a product (and being given a coupon) when there were 6 product flavours to sample as compared to 24 flavours.[23]

In other words, in some situations, greater variety may induce shoppers to buy less. Consumers may reject extensions for tried and tested favourites or all-purpose versions that claim to supersede more specialized versions. Moreover, because of the large number of products continually being introduced, many retailers do not have enough space to stock them all. Consequently, some consumers may be disappointed when they are unable to find an advertised brand extension if a retailer is not able or is unwilling to stock it. If a firm launches extensions that consumers deem inappropriate, they may question the integrity and competence of the brand.

Brand Briefing 12.5 describes how Hugo Boss succeeded with the Boss Woman extension after initial problems.

Retailer resistance

On average, the number of consumer packaged goods stock-keeping units (SKUs) outpaces, in terms of year-on-year percentage growth, the expansion of retail shelf space. Additionally, own-brand or own-label goods rose from 15 percent to 20 percent of total supermarket sales between 1994 and 2004.[24] Many brands now come in a multitude of forms. For example, Crest toothpaste comes in 42 varieties, Head & Shoulders shampoo boasts more than 30 varieties and American Express customers

Can confuse or frustrate consumers.

Can encounter retailer resistance.

Can fail and hurt parent brand image.

Can succeed but cannibalize sales of parent brand.

Can succeed but diminish identification with any one category.

Can succeed but hurt the image of parent brand.

Can dilute brand meaning.

Can cause the company to forgo the chance develop of a new branding.

Figure 12.10   Disadvantages of brand extensions

Brand Briefing 12.5

Hugo Boss: extending into women's fashion

Hugo Boss is one of the leading international brands for men's fashion clothing. With its German heritage, Hugo Boss has always been a brand for the aspiring man, with traditional masculine values. Nevertheless, during the late 1990s its growth target demanded new revenue streams. Analysis indicated that this could be accomplished by aiming outside the traditional brand scope. Consequently, it decided to extend into the lucrative, but competitive, women's fashion market in 1998. The size of the market was tempting. At the time, sales in the women's fashion market were almost double those of men's.

The extension was to provide a powerful dual effect: the brand, Hugo Boss, would enhance the extension and the extension would subsequently enhance the brand. However, the extension strategy came with its risks. The main identified risk was the core competence of Hugo Boss as a brand – ie, it was perceived externally as being too strongly connected with manly values and its strength and expertise was seen as being in men's fashion. This was also an internal problem because the company lacked a track record in women's clothing. Given this situation, the extension strategy was not to use the main brand Boss initially, but to use the smaller and trendier brand, Hugo. Hence, the risk of diminishing the main Boss brand's equity or weakening its perceived strengths was reduced and the company was more comfortable with a discreet launch into women's fashion. Evidently, subsequent brand extension effects were sought where the initial extension, by establishing credibility in the category, would augment the succeeding extension of the main Boss brand. Everything started out fine. Hugo Woman thrived and was perceived to be a success. Boss now felt it was time to extend into women's fashion with the parent brand.

In July 1999, Hugo Boss announced the head designer for its Boss women's collection. Also, to underline the importance of the extension, a subsidiary in Milan was founded. The glamorous launch event took place in Milan during women's fashion week 2000. However, things did not go as planned. Boss Woman underperformed initially and the powerful brand did not ensure a successful extension as was predicted. The estimated financial loss was about €50 million.

Hugo Boss had underestimated the need for relevant consumer insights in women's fashion. Consequently, it failed to provide the target audience with evidence as to why a men's clothing brand would be a competent provider of clothes for women. In the face of the tough competition from established brands, Boss Woman was neither competitive nor relevant.

Furthermore, due to a lack of the right fit and style, a dilemma was created from a value-for-money perspective since the pricing was very upmarket. This issue was spurred by problems concerning quality, which also influenced the competitiveness and relevance negatively.

Brand Briefing 12.5 *continued*

Perhaps the main insight is that a brand extension requires more than a strong brand to succeed. A given extension will not be automatically enhanced by the name. On the contrary, it could be argued that the extension into women's fashion damaged the brand equity of Hugo Boss.

Given the financial losses and the risk of long-term damage to brand equity, an exit from the market might have been the obvious move. However, Hugo Boss decided to do the opposite. More management attention and marketing resources were allocated to women's fashion. The company analyzed the causes of the problems. Gradually, it developed the insights needed to take action.

The first sign of change came in February 2002, when Hugo Boss announced that Boss Woman was to be integrated into the German headquarters. This signalled restructuring, which would also solve problems with supply chain management.

More importantly, the analysis aimed to develop consumer insights. Hugo Boss conducted consumer research across Europe, which led to an in-depth understanding of the consumers' perceptions regarding fit and style. This was of paramount importance and led to changes in designs – one of the main causes identified for the previous failure. Consequently, consumers saw an increase in relevance for Boss Woman, which was vital for the turnaround.

Yet, the operational and design aspects that improved the brand's relevance were far from the only explanation. Marketing communications for Boss Woman were also altered, making the brand more interesting and relevant to target consumers. The initial strategy had tried to distance the sub-brand from its parent and the associations of traditional menswear. Although resting on a valid assumption, the strategy turned out to be flawed in this context. To create leverage, Boss Woman needed to demonstrate a solid fit in terms of brand values. This met with failure because it was distanced too far from the parent brand. Therefore, the revised strategy focused on an expression of unity with the Boss brand. The market was now seeing a powerful effect in action: the parent brand enhanced the extension and the extension enhanced the parent.

With an optimized line of clothing that focused on relevant fit and revised marketing combined with competitive value-based pricing, the break was achieved in the second half of 2003. From this point Boss Woman began to gather momentum. Today, the Boss women's collection makes about 10 percent of the group's total turnover and net sales have passed €1,495 million. In light of the initial problems, this is a remarkable achievement.

What this example shows is that many brand extensions or product innovations fail because of poor marketing strategies and execution. In fact, studies demonstrate that only 5 percent of all innovations survive. This is a daunting figure. Obviously, this is worth some thought, because many brands or products that have failed

Brand Briefing 12.5 *continued*

Figure 12.11   Boss Woman

might actually have succeeded with better marketing support. Perhaps they can even be reborn. For instance, there is an example of when Levi's launched suits, which did not work out well. What would happen if it conducted more research and analysis and tried to base its brand extension on other brand-relevant links?

Sources: www.hugoboss.com: press release 1999-07-22, press release 2002-02-28, press release 2004-04-29; K. L. Keller and D. A. Aaker, 'The effects of sequential introduction of brand extensions', *Journal of Marketing Research*, February 1992, 29: 35–50; E. M. Tauber, 'Brand leverage: strategy for growth in a cost-control world', *Journal of Advertising Research*, August/September 1988; C. W. Park, S. Milberg and R. Lawson, 'Evaluation of brand extensions: the role of product level similarity and brand concept consistency', *Journal of Consumer Research*, September 1991, (18): 185–93; D. A. Pitta and L. P. Katsanis, 'Understanding brand equity for successful brand extension', *Journal of Consumer Marketing*, 1995, 12 (12): 51–64.

can choose from 20 card types. Campbell's has introduced a number of soup lines – Condensed, 99% Fat Free, Classics and Special Choice – and offers 100 flavours.

As a result, it has become impossible for a corner shop or supermarket to offer all the varieties from all brands in any one product category. Moreover, retailers often feel that many line extensions are merely 'me too' products that duplicate existing brands and should not be stocked. Additionally, for example, Wal-Mart, for example, the biggest retailer in the USA, attempts to stock the items that sell best, dropping as many as one in five slow-moving items from its shelves annually.[25] Attacking brand proliferation, a year-long Food Marketing Institute study showed that retailers could reduce their SKUs by 5–25 percent in certain categories without hurting sales or consumer perceptions of the variety offered.[26] The 'product variety' study recommended that retailers identify duplicated and slow-moving items and eliminate them to maximize profitability.[27] Many large packaged food brands took this advice to heart and began trimming their product lines to focus on the top-selling brands. Heinz culled 40 percent of its items between 2002 and 2004, a move that yielded an operating income increase of 18 percent in 2003. General Mills reduced the number of products it sold by 20 percent in 2004 and other companies have made similar cuts.[28] Brand Briefing 12.6 summarizes one perspective on how to reduce brand proliferation and simplify marketing.

Brand Briefing 12.6

Fighting feature fatigue

Consumers face an unprecedented number of choices. Supermarkets contain more than 40,000 products, up from 7,000 products in the 1960s. Additionally, features on products continue to multiply. It is now possible to purchase a wireless device that also functions as a video game console, PDA, e-mail and internet connection, digital camera, MP3 planner and GPS system. Consumers are often overwhelmed and studies have shown that increased choice does not always yield ultimate satisfaction with a purchase. Even though a majority of participants in one study initially selected so-called 'high feature' models of a given product type, fewer than half actually preferred the high feature products in actual use. When consumers reach their threshold for comparing features, they often engage in what Yankelovich Partners calls 'one-think shopping' by choosing familiar brands that function as 'simplifiers', offering 'the shortest, most efficient path to potential satisfaction and tension release'. New features may initially help a brand stand out, but, as the product lifecycle passes, competitors copy features or bring additional features to market and consumer tastes evolve. As a consequence, 'feature fatigue' – also referred to as 'featuritis' and 'feature creep' – sets in and the brand loses its ability to differentiate.

Rust, Thompson and Hamilton recommend measures to fight feature fatigue. Their first recommendation is to seek an optimal number of features that will drive sales while delivering the ease of use that engenders long-term product loyalty. Too few features and the product will not make it into the consideration set; too many and frustrated consumers will seek alternatives. On this latter point, the authors' second recommendation is for companies to build simpler products with a greater degree of specialization for specific segments. Third, the authors suggest giving consumers help in choosing between specialized products or competing products. 'Recommendation agents' – salespeople trained to question consumers about their

Brand Briefing 12.6 *continued*

preferences – and extended product trials are two such aids. Fourth, companies can design products that do one thing very well, rather than doing many things in a middling fashion. The authors cite Apple's iPod as an example of 'how effectively a company can make sales and satisfy customers with a tightly focused solution'. Finally, the authors recommend that companies use prototypes and in-use research when developing products. This solves the product design problem, mentioned above, that many consumers prefer high feature products when making a choice but not during actual use.

In proposing a different remedy, Goffin, Northcott and Mitchell recommend that companies expand their focus beyond the technical aspects of product innovation and recognize the 'importance of innovating across the whole product (pre- and post-sales) experience'. The authors cite Hewlett-Packard as a company that went beyond product features when it became clear in 2002 that speed and performance of its low-cost inkjet printers was no longer differentiating to consumers. In response, HP developed products that gave consumers something different and desirable: the ability to print photo-quality images on a variety of surfaces. HP developed a marketing campaign that demonstrated how its digital imaging products fitted into consumers' lives and, as a result, continues to enjoy market leadership in the inkjet printer market.

More specifically, the authors adopt the Kano model (Figure 12.12) to illustrate how a company can fight feature fatigue at the concept stage of product development.

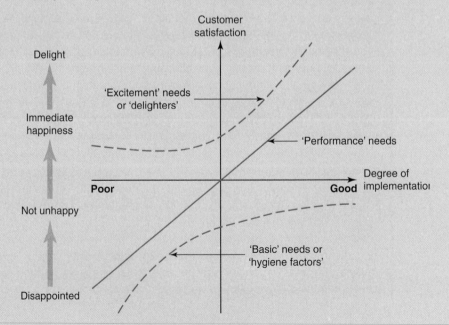

Figure 12.12   Kano model classification of product features

Brand Briefing 12.6 *continued*

As the Kano model shows, from a consumer's point of view, features fall into three categories. 'Basic' features (also called 'hygiene factors') are those without which a product would fail to be considered for purchase and are taken for granted, such as rechargeable laptop computer batteries. Providing additional performance on basic features will neither increase benefits to consumers nor raise their satisfaction. 'Performance' features, such as processor speed or screen resolution on a laptop, provide real benefits, so adding such performance features increases consumer satisfaction. 'Excitement' features (also called 'delighters') are differentiating features that 'surprise and delight customers' by providing unexpected value. The authors give the example of navigation systems in cars as an excitement feature, while warning that 'overcomplicating products can be severely damaging to brands'. A successful brand will have an optimal combination of all three types of features.

Sources: Keith Goffin et al., 'New product strategy: prevent feature fatigue!', *Critical Eye*, September–November 2005: 66; Steven M. Cristol and Peter Sealey, *Simplicity Marketing*, New York: Free Press, 2000; Sheena S. Iyengar and Barry Schwartz, 'Doing better but feeling worse: looking for the "best" job undermines satisfaction', *Psychological Science*, 2006, 17 (2): 143–50; Roland T. Rust, Deborah Viana Thompson and Rebecca W. Hamilton, 'Defeating feature fatigue', *Harvard Business Review*, February 2006: 98–107.

Can fail and hurt parent brand

The worst scenario with an extension is that not only does it fail, but it also harms the parent brand. Consider General Motors' experience with the Cadillac Cimarron.[29] This model, introduced in the early 1980s, was a 'relative' of models in other GM lines, such as the Pontiac 2000 and Chevrolet Cavalier. The target market was less affluent buyers seeking a small luxury car who wanted, but could not really afford, a full-size Cadillac. Not only was the Cadillac Cimarron unsuccessful at generating sales with this market segment, but existing Cadillac owners hated it. They felt it was inconsistent with the size and prestige image they expected from Cadillac. As a result, Cadillac sales dropped significantly in the mid-1980s. Looking back, one GM executive said:

> The decision was made purely on the basis of short-sighted profit and financial analysis, with no accounting for its effect on long-run customer loyalty or, if you will, equity. A typical financial analysis would argue that the Cimarron would rarely steal sales from Cadillac's larger cars, so any sale would be one that we wouldn't have gotten otherwise. The people who were most concerned with such long-range issues raised serious objections but the bean counters said: 'Oh no, we'll get this many dollars for every model sold.' There was no thinking about brand equity. We paid for the Cimarron down the road. Everyone now realizes that using the model to extend the name was a horrible mistake.

Even if an extension initially succeeds, by linking the brand to several products, the firm increases the risk that an unexpected problem or even tragedy with one product in the brand family can tarnish the image of some or all of the remaining products.

Audi

In 1986, the Audi 5000 suffered from a wave of bad publicity and word of mouth in the USA because it was alleged to have a 'sudden acceleration' problem that resulted in an alarming number of sometimes fatal accidents. Even though there was little evidence to support the claims (resulting in Audi, in a public relations disaster, attributing the problem to the clumsy way that Americans drove the car), Audi's US sales declined from 74,000 in 1985 to 21,000 in 1989. As might be expected, the damage was most severe for sales of the Audi 5000, but the adverse publicity also spilled over to affect the 4000 model and, to a lesser extent, the Quattro model. The Quattro might have been relatively more insulated from such repercussions because it was distanced from the 5000 by virtue of its more distinct branding and advertising strategy.[30]

Understanding when unsuccessful brand extensions may damage the parent brand is important, and this chapter later develops a conceptual model and describes some important findings to address the topic. On a more positive note, however, it should be recognized that one reason why an unsuccessful brand extension may not necessarily damage the parent brand is for the very reason that the extension may have been unsuccessful in the first place – hardly anyone may have even heard of it! Thus, the silver lining in the case when a brand extension fails as a result of an inability to secure adequate distribution or to achieve sufficient brand awareness is that the parent brand is more likely to survive unscathed. But, as will be argued below, product failures in which the extension is found to be inadequate on the basis of performance are more likely to damage parent brand perceptions than 'market' failures.

Can cannibalize sales of parent brand

Even if sales of a brand extension are high and meet targets, it is possible that this revenue may have merely resulted from consumers switching to the extension from the parent brand – in effect cannibalizing the parent brand by decreasing its sales. Line extensions are often designed to establish points of parity with current offerings competing in the parent brand category, as well as to create points of difference in other areas (eg, low-fat versions of foods). These types of line extensions may be particularly likely to result in cannibalization. Often, however, such intrabrand shifts in sales are not necessarily undesirable because they can be thought of as a form of 'pre-emptive cannibalization'. In other words, consumers might have switched to a competing brand instead of the line extension.

For example, Diet Coke's point of parity of 'good taste' and point of difference of 'low calories' undoubtedly resulted in some sales coming from traditional Coke drinkers. In fact, although US sales of Coca-Cola's cola products have held steady since 1980, sales in 1980 came from Coke alone whereas sales today also receive significant contributions from Diet Coke, Cherry Coke and decaffeinated and flavoured

Coke. Without the introduction of those extensions, however, some of Coke's sales might have gone to other soft drinks or beverages.

Can succeed but diminish identification with any one category

One risk of linking multiple products to a single brand is that the brand may not be strongly identified with any one product. Thus, brand extensions may obscure the identification of the brand with its original categories, reducing brand awareness.[31] For example, when Cadbury became linked in the UK to food products such as Smash instant potatoes, marketers of the brand may have run the risk of weakening its association with chocolate. Pepperidge Farm is a US brand that has been accused of having been extended so much (eg, into pastries, bread and snacks) that the brand has lost its original meaning as 'delicious, high-quality biscuits'.

This potential drawback has been popularized by business consultants Al Ries and Jack Trout, who in 1981 introduced the notion of the 'line extension trap'. They provide a number of examples of brands that, at the time, they believed had overextended.

Scott Paper
One such example was US-based Scott Paper, which Ries and Trout believe became overextended when its name was expanded to encompass ScotTowels paper towels, ScotTissue toilet paper, Scotties facial tissues, Scotkins and Baby Scot nappies.[32] Interestingly, in the mid-1990s, Scott decided to unify its product line by renaming ScotTowels as Scott Towels and ScotTissue as Scott Tissue, adding a common look and logo (although some distinct colours) on both packs as well as their Scott Napkins. In perhaps a risky move, Scott also decided to phase out local brand names in 80 countries where Scott garnered almost half its sales, including Andrex, its top-selling British toilet paper.[33] Scott's hope was that the advantages of brand consolidation and global branding would offset the disadvantages of losing local brand equity. Packaging was updated in 2005, keeping a unified look, and emphasis was continued on their shared 'common sense' positioning theme, as exemplified by its 'Common sense on a roll' slogan.

Some notable – and fascinating – counter-examples to these dilution effects exist, however, in terms of firms that have branded a heterogeneous set of products and still achieved a reasonable level of perceived quality in the minds of consumers for each product. As Chapter 11 noted, many Japanese and Korean firms have adopted a corporate branding strategy with a very broad product portfolio. For example, Yamaha has developed a strong reputation for motorcycles, guitars and pianos. Mitsubishi uses its name to brand a bank, cars and aircraft. Canon markets cameras, photocopiers and office equipment. Among the Korean firms, LG, Hyundai and Samsung have entered the global market with this kind of strategy. In a similar vein, the founder of Virgin Records, Sir Richard Branson, has conducted an ambitious, and perhaps risky, brand extension (see Brand Briefing 12.7). In all these cases, it seems as if the brand has been able to secure a dominant association with quality in the minds of consumers without strong product identification that might otherwise limit it.

Can succeed but hurt the image of the parent brand

If a brand extension has attribute or benefit associations that are seen as inconsistent or perhaps even as conflicting with associations for the parent, consumers may change their perceptions of the parent brand as a result. For example, when Evian licensed its brand in 2004 to Johnson & Johnson for the Affinity brand of skincare products, it risked eroding the associations with 'pure' and 'refreshing' for its water with associations more common to skincare, such as 'cleaning,' 'chemical' and 'cream'.

As another example, Chapter 4 described Miller Brewing's difficulty in creating a 'hearty' association with its US flagship Miller High Life beer in part because of its clear bottle and other factors such as its advertising heritage as the 'champagne of bottled beer'. It has often been argued that the early success of the Miller Lite light beer extension – market share soared from 9.5 percent in 1978 to 19 percent in 1986 – only exacerbated the tendency of consumers to think of Miller High Life as tasting 'watery' and not a full-bodied beer. These unfavourable perceptions were thought to have helped contribute to the sales decline of Miller High Life, whose market share slid from 21 percent to 12 percent during that same 8-year period.

Can dilute brand meaning

Potential drawbacks from a lack of identification with any one category and a weakened image may be especially evident with high-quality or prestige brands.

Gucci

In its prime, Gucci symbolized luxury, status, elegance and quality. By the 1980s, however, the label had become tarnished by sloppy manufacturing, counterfeits and even a feud between the Gucci brothers. The product line consisted of 22,000 items, distributed across all types of department stores. Not only were there too many items, but some items did not even fit the Gucci image – for example, a cheap canvas notebook with the double-G logo that was easily copied and sold on the street for €25. Sales only recovered when Gucci refocused the brand, paring the product line back to 7,000 high-end items and selling them through its own shops. The strategy helped propel Gucci to the height of the fashion business. With sales of €2.3 billion in 2004, Gucci was the world's third-biggest luxury goods company.[34]

To protect their brands from dilution, many fashion companies seeking to grow through brand extensions are forging exclusive licensing partnerships with a single retailer, such as US retailer Target's exclusive deals with Todd Oldham, Mossimo and Isaac Mizrahi. These exclusive licences enable the licensor to control inventory, avoid discounts and, most importantly, protect their brands. Nicole Miller, a fashion brand famous for cocktail gowns that can cost up to €1,825, selected Bed Bath & Beyond as its exclusive US licensing partner for its sheets and bedding.[35]

Brand Briefing 12.7

Are there any boundaries to the Virgin brand name?

Perhaps the most extensive brand extension in recent years has been undertaken by Sir Richard Branson with his Virgin brand. Branson founded the Virgin record label at the age of 21 and, in 1984, launched Virgin Atlantic Airways. Later, he made millions from the sale of his record label, his Virgin record retail chain and Virgin computer games. After licensing the Virgin name to European startup airlines who were flying the London/Athens and London/Dublin routes, Branson decided to expand the range of products carrying the Virgin brand. He has since licensed the name for use on personal computers and set up joint ventures in 1994 to market Virgin Vodka and Virgin Cola. In 1997, he took over six of the UK's rail lines and established Virgin Rail. In 1999, Branson launched Virgin Mobile, a company that provides wireless services through a partnership with Deutsche Telecom. Branson branched into e-commerce that same year with Virgin.com, a portal where consumers can purchase every product or service offered by the Virgin brand. A research study showed that the UK public voted Virgin as their most admired brand. Some 2,000 adults were asked 'which brands or companies can you think of that you really admire?' Virgin received 23 percent of the votes. Sony came second with 21 percent of votes and Tesco came third.[36]

The Virgin Group spans 3 continents and 200 companies involving such diverse products as financial services, shops, online car sales, cola, cosmetics, utilities, mobile phones, bridal shops and e-commerce ventures (see Figure 12.13). The Virgin Group employs about 50,000 people in 29 countries. Virgin had 2006 revenues of an estimated €15 billion, and Branson's personal fortune was estimated at €4.1 billion in 2004.

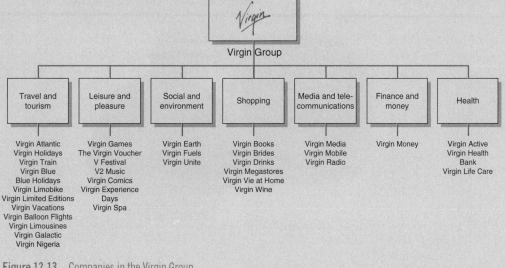

Figure 12.13 Companies in the Virgin Group

Brand Briefing 12.7 *continued*

Virgin's growth and expansion has sparked debate about Branson's seemingly undisciplined extension of the brand. One expert criticized Virgin's rapid expansion: 'Virgin makes no sense; it's completely unfocused.' When Virgin ventures are poorly received, as Virgin Cola, Virgin Vodka, Virgin PCs, Virgin Jeans, Virgin Brides and Virgin Clothing were in recent years, experts worry about the cumulative effect of these unsuccessful brands on the company's overall equity. One marketing executive illustrated the risk of launching an unsuccessful brand. 'When I'm delayed on a Virgin train I start wondering about Virgin Atlantic. Every experience of a brand counts, and negative experiences count even more.'

While extending the brand, the Virgin Group has always tried to adhere to the Virgin values: fun, value for money, quality, innovation, competitive challenge and brilliant customer service. Virgin believes in making a difference in the eyes of customers. It delivers a quality service by empowering its employees and encouraging and monitoring customer feedback to continually improve the customers' experience through innovation.

When Virgin starts a new venture, it is based on research and analysis. It reviews the industry and puts itself in the customers' shoes to see what they could make better. Fundamental questions are asked: is this an opportunity for restructuring a market and creating competitive advantage? What are the competitors doing? Is the customer confused or badly served? Is this an opportunity for building the Virgin brand? Can we add value? Will it interact with our other businesses? Is there an appropriate tradeoff between risk and reward?

Figure 12.14   Richard Branson
Source: Rex Features

Brand Briefing 12.7 *continued*

Some critics believe that Virgin consumer products will do little more than generate publicity for Virgin Airlines. They also caution about overexposure, even with the young, hip audience the Virgin brand has attracted. For example, one advertising agency executive said: 'I would imagine the risk is that the Virgin brand name can come to mean everything to everybody, which in turn means it becomes nothing to nobody.' In Branson's view, as long as a brand adds value for the consumer, then it strengthens the Virgin image: 'If the consumer benefits, I see no reason why we should be frightened about launching new products.' Among the products Branson hopes to launch are a Virgin Sports cable channel in the UK and space tourism on rocket ships with Virgin Galactic. Yet Virgin has become more disciplined about its expansion in recent years: the company only pursues new businesses if they can be projected to generate more than €110 million in sales within 3 years.

Sources: Peter Fuhrman, 'Brand-name Branson', *Forbes*, 2 January 1995: 41–2; Tara Parker Pope, 'Can the Virgin name sell cola, computers, vodka and more?', *Wall Street Journal*, 14 October 1994: B3; Miriam Jordan, 'Virgin's air chief to offer 'Unreal' Cola in Hong Kong, Japan, China by Dec. 31', *Wall Street Journal*, 23 February 1988: 36; www.virgin.com; Melanie Wells, 'Red baron', *Forbes*, 3 July 2000; Quentin Sommerville, 'High-flying brand isn't all it appears', *Scotland on Sunday*, 24 December 2000; Roger Crowe, 'Global: a brand too far?', *GlobalVue*, 28 October 1998; Raymond Snoddy, 'The moon's the limit', *The Independent*, 8 May 2006: 5; www.virgin.com.

Can cause the company to forgo the chance of developing a new brand

One easily overlooked disadvantage to brand extensions is that, by introducing a new product as a brand extension, the company loses the chance to create a new brand. For example, consider the advantages to Disney of having introduced Touchstone films, which attracted an audience interested in films with more adult themes than Disney's family-orientated releases; to Levi's of having introduced Dockers, which attracted a customer segment interested in casual trousers; and to Toyota of having introduced Lexus.

Each of these brands created associations and images and tapped into different markets from those for other brands sold by the company. Thus, introducing a product as a brand extension can have significant and potentially hidden costs in terms of lost opportunities. Moreover, there may be a loss of flexibility in the brand positioning for the extension given that it has to live up to the parent brand's promise and image. The positioning of a new brand could be introduced and updated in the most competitively advantageous way possible.

Brand Briefing 12.8 discusses the results from the most extensive study in Europe on launching products, the avoidance of launching 'me too' products and summarizes six golden rules for new products.

Brand Briefing 12.8

Launching innovative brand extensions while avoiding 'me too' products

The most extensive study on fast-moving consumer goods in Europe was carried out by Ernst & Young and Nielsen. It included 24,543 articles in 32 categories in 6 countries. The study revealed that many of the product introductions failed. The reason was lack of innovativeness. The measure of success used was the extent of a product's distribution after one year in the market. Three clear clusters were found at different levels of innovation. The study revealed that many of the new products were substitutes. Only a few new products were innovative. All new articles were classified according to the following definitions.

- *Classic innovation (1.4 percent):* a completely new product is launched when the buyer see the product as an innovation or when the product is creating a wholly new category (an example is Gillette Mach3).

- *Equity transfer (0.8 percent):* these are products from a well-known brand that are launched in new categories (for example Del Monte Sorbet. Equity transfer has the same meaning as category extension).

- *Line extension (6.1 percent):* a variant of a brand which is launched in an existing category.

- *'Me too' products (76.7 percent):* products that do not add value because similar products already exist (two examples are retailers' own brands or a variant of a taste that already exists in the assortment).

- *Seasonal/temporary (12.9 percent):* products with short lifecycles (for example, Christmas cakes or bonus packages).

- *Conversion/substitution (2.1 percent):* a product is replaced by a similar product without value being created for the consumer (for example a 5-kg pack of washing powder being replaced by a 4.5-kg one).

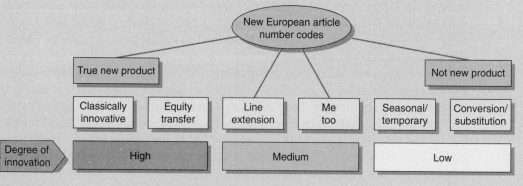

Figure 12.15   Degree of innovation model

Brand Briefing 12.8 *continued*

The first cluster, which was very uncommon, was defined as 'true new product'. The cluster had 2.2 percent of all new products and covered 'classic innovation' and 'equity transfer'. Six percent of the products in this cluster were 'stars', meaning that they achieved 90 percent distribution after a year. The second cluster was 'line extensions'. This cluster had 6.1 percent new products, of which 3 percent were stars. The third cluster was 'me too' which was the largest with 76.7 percent of all products. Only 1 percent of the products in this category were stars.

According to Ernst & Young and Nielsen, there are six rules for successful introductions.

- Genuine innovations ('classically innovative' and 'equity transfer') are unusual but necessary for success.
- Products must include a good conceptual offer, but this is not sufficient. The performance of the product has an ever greater influence on survival. In other words, if a new product does not satisfy consumers, it does not matter how good the idea was. In addition, uniqueness is only valuable if it has consumer relevance.
- The level of trial purchase is a key factor. Trials are dependent on distribution and awareness. Awareness is, in turn, dependent on advertising and distribution.
- Further success depends on endurance. This means that the brand owner should see the product as 'new' for two to three years.
- The probability of a successful launch increases if the company already has successful products in the category. The main players have a large reserve of 'credibility capital' with both consumers and retailers. This is a barrier smaller players have to overcome when launching products.
- The 'pioneer effect' is also important. The first to enter a market will gain long-term benefits. However, this advantage can not always be guaranteed because followers can challenge with better products and/or market communications.

Sources: Tony Apéria, 'Brand relationship management: den varumärkesbyggande processen', PhD thesis, Stockholm: Stockholm University, 2001; Ernst & Young/ACNielsen, *Efficient Product Introductions: The development of value-creating relationship,* Brussels and London: ECR Europe, Ernst & Young, 1999; Ernst & Young/ACNielsen, *Efficient Product Introductions: Successful innovations/failure: A fragile boundary*, Brussels and London: ECR Europe, Ernst & Young, 1999.

UNDERSTANDING HOW CONSUMERS EVALUATE BRAND EXTENSIONS

What determines whether or not a brand extension is able to capitalize on these potential advantages and avoid, or at least minimize, these potential disadvantages? Figure 12.16 lists some brand extensions. The difficulty of introducing a brand

Successful	Unsuccessful
Dove shampoo and conditioner	Campbell's tomato sauce
Vaseline Intensive Care skin lotion	MTV phone card Hello
Cadbury's hot chocolate	Harley-Davidson wine coolers
Scania Truck Gear	Hidden Valley Ranch frozen meals
Visa traveller's cheques	Bic perfumes
Colgate toothbrushes	Kleenex nappies
Mars ice-cream bars	Clorox laundry detergent
Bic disposable lighters	Levi's Tailored Classics suits
Honda lawnmowers	Fruit of the Loom laundry detergent
Porsche coffee makers	Cadbury Soap

Figure 12.16   Examples of category extensions

extension can be recognized by noting how even leading companies have failed in launching a brand extension.

This section examines how consumers evaluate brand extensions. It develops some simple conceptual notions to help a marketing manager better forecast and improve the potential odds for success of a brand extension.[37]

Managerial assumptions

In analyzing potential consumer's responses to a brand extension, it is useful to start by assuming that consumers based their evaluation only on what they know about the parent brand and the extension category before any advertising, promotion or detailed information is made available. This baseline case provides the cleanest test of the extension concept and provides managers with guidance as to whether or not to proceed with an extension concept and, if so, what type of marketing campaign might be necessary.

In evaluating a brand extension under these conditions, consumers can be expected to use their brand knowledge, as well as what they know about the category, to try to infer what the extension product might be like. For these inferences to result in favourable consumer evaluations of an extension, four assumptions must generally hold true.

- Consumers have awareness of and positive associations with the parent brand in memory. Unless there is some potentially beneficial consumer knowledge about the parent brand, it is difficult to expect consumers to form favourable expectations of an extension.[38]
- At least some of these positive associations will be evoked by the brand extension. As will be discussed shortly, a number of factors determine which parent brand associations are evoked when consumers evaluate an extension. In general, consumers are likely to infer associations similar in strength, favourability and uniqueness to those of the parent brand when the extension is seen as being similar or close in fit to the parent.

- Negative associations are not transferred from the parent brand. Ideally, any negative associations that exist for the parent brand would be left behind and not play a prominent role in the evaluation of the extension.
- Negative associations are not created by the brand extension. Finally, it must be the case that any attributes or benefits that are viewed positively – or at least neutrally – by consumers with respect to the parent brand are not seen as a negative in the extension context. Consumers must also not infer any new attribute or benefit associations that did not characterize the parent brand but which they see as a potential drawback to the extension.

The more these assumptions hold true, the more likely it is that consumers will form favourable attitudes towards an extension. The chapter next examines some factors that influence the validity of these assumptions and considers in detail how a brand extension, in turn, affects brand equity.

Brand extensions and brand equity

The success of an extension will depend on its ability to both create its own brand equity in the new category as well as contribute to the equity of the parent.

Creating extension equity

For the brand extension to create equity, it must have a sufficiently high level of awareness and achieve points of parity and points of difference. Brand awareness will depend primarily on the marketing campaign and resources devoted to spreading the word about the extension. As Chapter 11 described, it will also depend on the branding strategy: the more prominently an existing brand is used to brand an extension, the easier it should be to create awareness of and an image for the extension in memory.

Initially, creating a positive image for an extension will depend primarily on three consumer-related factors.

- How *salient* parent brand associations are in the minds of consumers in the extension context – that is, what information comes to mind about the parent when consumers think of the proposed extension and the strength of those associations.
- How *favourable* any inferred associations are in the extension context – that is, whether this information is seen as suggestive of the type of product or service that the brand extension would be and whether or not these associations would be viewed as good or bad in the extension context.
- How *unique* any inferred associations are in the extension category – that is, how these perceptions compare with those of competitors.

As with any brand, extensions must achieve desired points of parity and points of difference. Without powerful points of difference, the brand risks becoming an undistinguished 'me too' entry, vulnerable to well-positioned competitors. Parent brand associations must be seen as relevant and differentiating in the extension category.[39] Tauber refers to 'competitive leverage' as the set of advantages that a brand conveys to an extended product in the new category – that is, 'when the consumer, by simply knowing the brand, can think of important ways that they perceive that the new brand extension would be better than competing brands in the category'.[40] This appeared to be the case with the UK launch of the Dettol Easy Mop, an extension of Reckitt Benckiser's Dettol household cleaner, which leveraged the familiar brand in outselling other entrants into the category.[41]

At the same time, it is also necessary to establish points of parity. The more dissimilar the extension product is to the parent brand, the more likely it is that this will be a positioning priority. For example, when Johnson & Johnson test-marketed a brand of aspirin for babies, the product failed despite the fact that the Johnson & Johnson name is synonymous with baby products. As it turned out, parents were just as concerned with getting fevers down quickly as they were with the safety and gentleness of an aspirin – Johnson & Johnson's main point of difference and core benefit association for its baby products. Thus, the lack of a necessary point of parity association doomed the product.

Contributing to parent brand equity

To contribute to parent brand equity, an extension must strengthen or add favourable and unique associations to the parent as well as not diminish the strength, favourability or uniqueness of existing associations for the parent.[42] The effects of an extension on consumer brand knowledge will depend on four factors.

- How *compelling* the evidence is concerning the corresponding attribute or benefit association in the extension context – that is, how attention-getting and unambiguous or easily interpretable the information is concerning product performance or imagery for that association. Strong evidence is attention-getting and unambiguous. Weak evidence – whether it is less attention getting or more ambiguous – may be ignored or discounted.
- How *relevant* the extension evidence is concerning the attribute or benefit for the parent brand – that is, how much evidence on product performance or imagery in one category is seen as predictive of product performance or imagery for the brand in other categories. Evidence will only affect parent brand evaluations if consumers feel that extension performance is indicative, in some way, of the parent.
- How *consistent* the extension evidence is with the corresponding parent brand associations. Consistent extension evidence is less likely to change the evaluation of parent brand associations. Inconsistent extension evidence creates the potential for change, with the direction and extent of change depending on the relative strength and favourability of the evidence. Note that highly inconsistent extension evidence, however, may be discounted or ignored if not viewed as relevant.[43]
- How *strong* attribute or benefit associations are held in consumer memory for the parent brand – that is, how potentially easy an association might be to change.

According to these factors, feedback effects that change brand knowledge are most likely when consumers view information about the extension as equally revealing about the parent brand and when they only hold a weak and inconsistent association about the parent brand with respect to that information. The nature of the feedback will depend on the nature of the information: an unfavourable extension evaluation can lead to negative feedback, whereas a favourable extension evaluation can lead to positive feedback. Note that negative effects are not restricted to product-related performance associations. As noted earlier, if a brand has a favourable 'prestige' image association, then a vertical extension (eg, offering a new version of the product at a lower price) may be viewed disapprovingly or even resented by consumers.

Michelin

Michelin, which possesses image associations of safety and dependability, began extending its brand to licensed merchandise that sold for far less than the average Michelin tyre. The new products, developed by a new division called Michelin Lifestyle, fell into four distinct areas: accessories, such as foot pumps, floor mats and windscreen wipers; 'high-specification lifestyle products', such as cycle helmets, wetsuits and footballs; clothing and accessories featuring Michelin's brand mascot Bibendum; and safety products developed with other companies, including ear plugs, goggles and gloves. Michelin intended these brand extensions to 'enhance the value of our brand and add emotional-type values, not just functionality, and reach out to . . . a new generation that doesn't yet associate with us'. Still, Michelin Lifestyle was careful not to stretch the brand by moving into 'fragrances and other things that have some legitimacy for a lifestyle brand. There still has to be an authentic Michelin reason for everything.'[44]

Vertical brand extensions

As noted above, brand extensions can be used to expand market coverage and bring new consumers into the brand franchise. Vertical brand extensions, where the brand is extended 'up' into more premium market segments or 'down' into more value-conscious segments, are a common means of attracting new groups of consumers. The logic behind vertical extensions is that the equity of the parent brand can be transferred in either direction to appeal to consumers who otherwise would not consider the parent brand.

Vertical extensions can bring a number of the advantages of brand extensions. An upward extension can improve brand image, as a more premium version of a brand often brings with it positive associations. Extensions in either direction can permit consumer variety-seeking, revitalize the parent brand or permit subsequent extensions. Yet vertical extensions are also susceptible to many of the disadvantages of brand extensions. A vertical extension to a new price point, either higher or lower, can confuse or frustrate consumers who have learned to expect a certain price range. There is always the possibility, particularly with an upward extension, that consumers will reject the extension and the parent brand's image will suffer. Even a successful downward extension may harm the parent's image by introducing associations common to lower-priced brands, such as inferior quality or reduced service. Brand Briefing 12.9 illustrates how the Colgate brand has been used as a lever for growth and profitability in the Swedish market. More specifically the Brand Briefing show how the brand has been used in the development of two different sub-categories, toothpaste and toothbrushes, in the oral care category.

Brand Briefing 12.9

How Colgate is used as a lever for growth and profitability

Imagine that half of all toothpaste in the world comes from one brand only. Is it really possible to be so successful? In many markets, the meaning of oral care = Colgate = oral care. Colgate's global position is based on six strengths.

● A strong brand and strong products within the oral care category.

● Advanced technology.

● Clinical domination.

● Professional partnership.

● Education in oral care.

● Worldwide resources in marketing, management, and manufacturing.

In Sweden, the Colgate brand is the market leader for toothpaste. Its main competitor is Pepsodent from Unilever. The oral care category can be divided into three sub-categories: toothpaste, toothbrushes, and special products (Figure 12.17).

For many consumers, toothpaste is a basic product. Colgate-Palmolive developed the market based on consumer needs. Three segments were chosen (Figure 12.18).

● The family segment (including children's). Consumers look for a toothpaste that gives good basic protection and oral hygiene. This segment is distinguished by the lowest price.

● The therapeutic segment. Consumers look for strong protection and are very involved in oral hygiene.

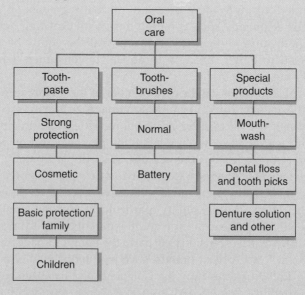

Figure 12.17   Development of the oral care category

Brand Briefing 12.9 *continued*

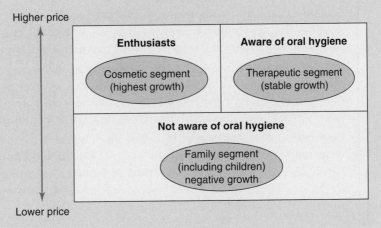

Figure 12.18   Segmentation of the toothpaste sub-category

- The cosmetic segment. Consumers are looking for beauty. This was the fastest-growing segment. This segment is distinguished by a higher price, often costing 25–30 percent more than basic toothpaste.

Colgate-Palmolive has products in all these segments. In 2007, it had a portfolio in Sweden of 14 sub-brands positioned in these segments. The first four are positioned in the family segment (with lower prices) and the next ten in the two premium segments (with higher prices).

- Colgate Blå (Blue) Mint.
- Colgate Herbal Whitening.
- Colgate Karies Kontroll (Caries Control).
- Colgate Triple Action.
- Colgate Max Fresh.
- Colgate Oxygen.
- Colgate 2in1.
- Colgate Sensation White.
- Colgate Sensitive.
- Colgate Sensitive Whitening.
- Colgate Sensitive Multiprotection.
- Colgate Tandsten Kontroll Plus Whitening.
- Colgate Total.
- Colgate Time Control.

Strategic brand management

Brand Briefing 12.9 *continued*

Colgate's goal is to be the market leader in all segments with as few products as possible. Colgate-Palmolive balances growth with a cost focus. Consumers should be offered more value at the same time as cost-effectiveness increases.

In 1998, Colgate-Palmolive launched toothbrushes in Sweden, and in the 2000 the brand was the market leader in this sub-category. Its main targets were users of premium and super premium toothbrushes who were not sensitive to price. Colgate-Palmolive also developed the market for battery toothbrushes.

Colgate-Palmolive was one of the pioneers of efficient consumer response (ECR) techniques in Europe. The company was quick to establish itself as a leading partner in ECR and category management in Europe. Colgate-Palmolive has brands strongly anchored in consumers' consciousness and has developed partnerships with retailers that guarantee distribution and availability.

Sources: Tony Apéria, 'Brand relationship management: den varumärkesbyggande processen, PhD thesis, Stockholm: Stockholm University, 2001; Tony Apéria and Rolf Back, *Brand Relations Management: Bridging the gap between brand promise and brand delivery*, Sweden: Liber, 2004.

One of the biggest risk factors of a vertical extension is that it will succeed but cannibalize sales of a parent brand. Though the extension may bring new consumers to the brand franchise, it may take customers from the parent brand. This problem is commonly experienced when brands attempt downmarket vertical extensions. For example, Philip Morris launched Marlboro Basic to compete with Monarch, a rival discount brand. This move led to massive cannibalization of the flagship Marlboro brand, Philip Morris' operating profit plummeted 46 percent and profitability fell across the tobacco industry. Similarly, at a time when it held 70 percent global market share with its Kodak Gold brand, Kodak launched the discount Kodak Funtime brand to compete with lower-priced Fuji film. Cannibalization of the Kodak Gold brand followed and Kodak found itself in a price war with Fuji that led to a significant decline in Kodak Gold's market share. While the parent brand name 'gives you the credibility to quickly gain share in the lower-end market', cannibalization is a likely outcome because, 'if you've already persuaded people that only the best products are sold under your brand, then they'll readily buy the least expensive item with that brand name'.[45]

Despite the problems inherent with vertical extensions, many companies have succeeded in extending their brands to new markets across a range of price points. For example, Marriot hotels covers a range of options above and below the mid-range Marriott parent brand, from luxury hotels and resorts under the J. W. Marriott brand to suburban hotels under Courtyard by Marriott to value hotel/motels under Fairfield Inn by Marriott. In fashion, Armani has extended from high-end Giorgio Armani and Giorgio Armani Prive' to mid-range luxury with Emporio Armani, to affordable luxury with Armani Jeans and Armani Exchange. In each of these cases, a clear differentiation exists between brands, minimizing the potential for overlap, which would bring consumer confusion and brand cannibalization. Additionally, these extensions lived up to the core promise of the parent brand, thus reducing the possibility that they would hurt the parent's image.

To avoid difficulties, companies sometimes elect to use new brand names to expand vertically. Many examples of this strategy exist, including Toyota, which expanded into the luxury category with the Lexus brand because it was convinced that the Toyota mark did not have the credibility to enter the luxury space. When it elected to move downmarket, Toyota developed the Scion brand in part to avoid reducing the strength of the Toyota image. The Gap pursued a similar expansion strategy, using the Banana Republic brand to command a 40 percent price premium that the Gap was never likely to attain, and launched Old Navy to offer 40 percent discounts. By developing unique brand names, companies pursuing vertical expansion can avoid a negative transfer of equity from a 'lower' brand to a 'higher' brand, but sacrifice to some extent the ability to transfer positive associations from existing brands to new ones. Yet when the parent brand makes no secret of its ownership of the vertical brands, as is the case with both the Gap and Toyota, some associations may be transferred because the parent acts as a 'shadow endorser' of the new brand.[46]

Brand Briefing 12.10 illustrates how Levi's has been able to expand its market coverage and attract new consumers through vertical extensions into both high-end and discount jeans.

Brand Briefing 12.10

Levi Strauss extends its brand

Levi Strauss is an iconic US brand, known for the red tab on the back pocket of its jeans. Founded in 1853 by Bavarian immigrant Levi Strauss, the company grew to become one of the world's largest clothing companies with more than €4.4 billion in revenue. During the late 1990s, though, Levi's faced declining sales and growing debt. The company's tradition of producing durable jeans became a liability for its fashion image. The San Francisco-based company remained private despite pressure to take all or part of the company public to reduce debt.

For years, market power had been shifting away from suppliers towards retailers. Mass merchants were selling about one-third of all jeans in the USA and their share of the market was growing. Additionally, the advent of discount shops made many consumers more price-sensitive. In 1999, Levi Strauss brought in a new chief, Philip Marineau, from PepsiCo. Marineau favoured increased segmentation as a way to boost sales, so Levi's adopted a segmentation strategy to convince different retailers (department stores, specialist chains, boutiques and mass merchants) to carry Levi's products (see Figure 12.19).

Brand Briefing 12.10 *continued*

Brand	Price range (€)
Levi Strauss Signature	14–17
Levi Strauss Signature Authentics	17–18
Levi's Redtab	18–37
Levi's Silvertab	18–42
Levi's Red	36–50
Levi's Capital E	51–130
Levi's Vintage	58–237

Figure 12.19   Levi's jean segments

With the segmentation strategy, Levi's brands ranged from a relatively inexpensive discount line to €110-and-up vintage designs. Levi's had already sold to US chains J. C. Penney and Sears, Roebuck and those choices had alienated some big retailers who preferred that the brand remain exclusive and slightly more upmarket. Despite concerns among management about potential reputation damage, Levi's created the Levi Strauss Signature brand to sell at mass merchants and began selling to Wal-Mart in 2003.

The Levis Strauss Signature brand carried new labels and styles manufactured from less expensive fabric. The company positioned it as a premium mass brand. Gone were the red tab and Levi's pocket stitching and logo. The Signature brand featured the Levi's name in a cursive script. Levi's priced Signature jeans at €17 – more than other mass brands but below Levi's €21 traditional brand. The new brand experienced some bumps. Wal-Mart's other jeans were priced at €11–13 and outsold the Signature brand. In response, Wal-Mart lowered the price of men's Levi Strauss Signature jeans from €17 to €14, squeezing Levi's margins. To improve margins, in 2005, the Signature line was expanded to include an Authentics collection, with more fashion-conscious fits and finishes priced at about €18 (Figure 12.19).

Initially, the strategy led to rough spots for Levi's other brands. As executives struggled to appease Wal-Mart and find the right price point for mass retailers, other parts of the business suffered. Orders from department stores slipped and sales of traditional Levi's, which had steadied leading up to the launch of the Signature brand, resumed their decline. Furthermore, a high-fashion line called Type 1, failed. In 2006, however, Wal-Mart's price-chopping move proved effective and the Signature jeans began to sell more quickly. The company also added lines of baby clothing, bags, wallets and men's khaki trousers under its Signature brand.

Around the same time, the company's expansion into premium segments began to pay off as well. Levi's began selling its premium lines, such as Levi's Capital E, to

Brand Briefing 12.10 *continued*

Bloomingdales and Barney's New York, which had not carried the brand for years, and reported strong sales. In early 2006, Levi's launched a style with a special pocket and controls for an iPod music player that sold for €146. The segmentation strategy seems to have worked. The company posted a profit in early 2006, ending an eight-year sales decline.

Sources: www.levi.com; Sandra O'Loughlin, 'Levi Strauss seeing green with Signature blues', *Brandweek*, 25 July 2005; 'In bow to retailer's new clout, Levi Strauss makes alterations', *Wall Street Journal*, 17 June 2004; Robert Guy Matthews, 'Levi Strauss bowwows a page from Shakespeare', *Wall Street Journal*, 14 January 2005; Sandra O'Loughlin, 'Dockers addresses growth by dropping "pants"', *Brandweek*, 12 September 2005; 'The original denim brand kicks off the next revolution in digital music storage', *Business Wire*, 20 January 2006; Jacques Chevron, 'Tacit messages: a lesson from Levi's', *Brandweek*, 6 February 2006; 'Strauss & Co. on the record: Phil Marineau', *San Francisco Chronicle*, 6 March 2006.

EVALUATING BRAND EXTENSION OPPORTUNITIES

Academic research and industry experience have revealed principles concerning the proper way to introduce brand extensions. Extension strategies should follow the steps in Figure 12.20. Managerial judgement and marketing research should be employed to help make *each* of these decisions.[47]

1. Define actual and desired consumer knowledge about the brand (eg, create mental map and identify sources of equity).
2. Identify possible extension candidates on basis of parent brand associations and overall similarity or fit of extension to the parent brand.
3. Evaluate the potential of the extension candidate to create equity according to the three-factor model:
   - salience of parent brand associations;
   - favourability of inferred extension associations;
   - uniqueness of inferred extension associations.
4. Evaluate extension candidate feedback effects according to the four-factor model:
   - how compelling the extension evidence is;
   - how relevant the extension evidence is;
   - how consistent the extension evidence is;
   - how strong the extension evidence is.
5. Consider possible competitive advantages as perceived by consumers and possible reactions initiated by consumers.
6. Design marketing campaign to launch extension.
7. Evaluate extension success and effects on parent brand equity.

Figure 12.20   Steps in introducing brand extensions successfully

Define actual and desired consumer knowledge about the brand

Chapter 9 examined qualitative and quantitative measures of consumer brand knowledge structures. In particular, it noted that it is critical to fully understand the depth and breadth of awareness of the parent brand and the strength, favourability and uniqueness of its associations. Moreover, before any extension decisions are contemplated, it is important that the desired knowledge structures have been fully articulated. Specifically, what is to be the basis of positioning and core benefits satisfied by the brand? Profiling actual and desired knowledge structures helps to identify possible brand extensions as well as to guide decisions concerning their likely success. In evaluating an extension, a company must understand where it would like to take the brand in the long run. Because the introduction of an extension potentially changes brand meaning, consumer response to all subsequent marketing activity may be affected (see Chapter 13).

Identify possible extension candidates

Chapter 11 described criteria related to the consumer, company and competition for choosing which products and markets a firm should enter. With respect to consumer factors, marketers should consider parent brand associations – especially as they relate to brand positioning and core benefits – and product categories that might seem to fit with that brand image in the minds of consumers.[48] Category extension candidates can be generated through brainstorming as well as consumer research. Although consumers are generally better able to react to an extension concept than to suggest one, it still may be instructive to ask consumers what products the brand should consider offering.

One or more associations can often serve as the basis of fit. Figure 12.21 displays an analysis by Ed Tauber of possible extensions of the Vaseline Intensive Care brand by recognizing the range of associations held by consumers. Consider how Lucozade was transformed in the UK through brand extensions.

Lucozade

Beecham marketed Lucozade in Britain for many years as a glucose drink to combat dehydration and other maladies of sick children. By introducing new flavours, packaging formats and so forth, Beecham was able to capitalize on the association with the brand of it being a 'fluid replenisher' to transform its meaning into that of 'a healthy sports drink for people of all ages'. Reinforced by ads featuring the British Olympic decathlete Daley Thompson, sales and profits increased dramatically. Thus, by recognizing that Lucozade did not have to be just a pharmaceutical product but could be repositioned through brand extensions and other marketing activity as a healthy and nutritious drink, Beecham was able to transform the brand.[49]

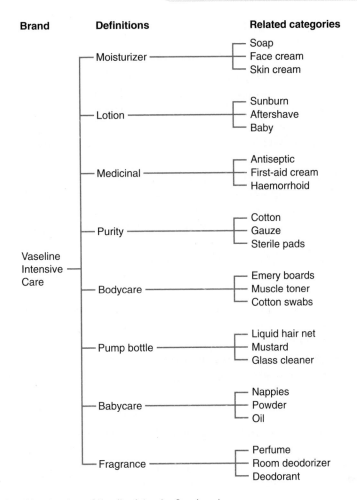

Figure 12.21 Possible extensions of Vaseline Intensive Care brand

Evaluate the potential of the extension candidate

In forecasting the success of a proposed brand extension, it is necessary to assess – through judgement and research – the likelihood that the extension would realize the advantages and avoid the disadvantages of brand extensions, as summarized in Figures 12.5 and 12.10. As with any new product, analysis of consumer, corporate and competitive factors can be useful.

Consumer factors

Evaluating the potential success of a proposed brand extension requires an assessment of its ability to achieve its own brand equity, as well as the likelihood of it affecting the equity of the parent brand. First, marketers must forecast the strength, favourability and uniqueness of *all* associations with the brand extension. In other words, what will be the salience, favourability or uniqueness of parent brand associations in the proposed extension context? Similarly, what will be the strength, favourability and uniqueness of any other inferred associations? The three-factor model of extension evaluations and four-factor model of extension feedback effects can provide guidance in studying consumer reactions.

To narrow down the list of possible extensions, consumer research is often needed (see Chapter 9). Consumers may be probed directly for their brand permission (eg, 'How well does the proposed extension fit with the parent brand?' or 'Would you expect such a new product from the parent brand?') Consumers may even be asked what products they believe are currently attached to the brand: if a majority of consumers believe a proposed extension is already being sold under the brand, then there would seem to be little risk involved in introducing it.

To understand consumers' perceptions of a proposed extension, consumer research uses open-ended associations (eg, 'What comes into your mind when you think of the brand extension?' or 'What are your first impressions on hearing that the parent brand is introducing the extension?'), as well as ratings based on reactions to concept statements.

Several pitfalls must be avoided when evaluating brand extension potential. One mistake in evaluating extension opportunities is failing to take all of consumers' brand knowledge structures into account. Often marketers focus on one or perhaps a few brand associations as a potential basis of fit and ignore other, possibly more important, associations.

Bic

By emphasizing inexpensive, disposable products, the French company Société Bic was able to create markets for non-refillable ballpoint pens in the late 1950s, disposable cigarette lighters in the early 1970s and disposable razors in the 1980s. It unsuccessfully tried the same strategy in marketing Bic perfumes in the USA and Europe in 1989. The perfumes – two for women (Nuit and Jour) and two for men (Bic for Men and Bic Sport for Men) – were packaged in quarter-ounce glass spray bottles that looked like fat cigarette lighters and sold for €3.60 each. The products were displayed on racks in plastic packages at check-out counters throughout Bic's extensive distribution channels, which included 100,000 chemists, supermarkets and other mass merchandisers. At the time, Bic described the products as extensions of its heritage – 'high quality at affordable prices, convenient to purchase and convenient to use'.[50] The brand extension was launched with a €14.6 million advertising and promotion campaign containing images of stylish people enjoying themselves with the perfume and using the tagline 'Paris in your pocket.' Nevertheless, Bic was unable to overcome its lack of cachet and negative image associations and, by failing to achieve a critical point of parity, the extension was a failure.

Another mistake in evaluating brand extensions is overlooking how literal consumers can be in evaluating brand extensions. Although consumers ultimately care about benefits, they often notice and evaluate attributes – especially concrete ones – in reacting to an extension. Brand managers, though, tend to focus on perceived benefits in predicting consumer reactions and, as a result, may overlook potentially damaging attribute associations. For example, in 1992 Bausch & Lomb introduced Bausch & Lomb Clear Choice, a colourless, alcohol-free mouthwash. This brand extension was thought to fit with Bausch & Lomb's strategy of marketing care products for 'above-the-shoulders' orifices – the eyes, ears, nose and throat – but the Bausch & Lomb name, traditionally associated with contact lenses and eyecare, was not easily transferred to mouthwash and the product was discontinued in 1995.[51]

Corporate and competitive factors

Marketers must not only take a consumer perspective in evaluating a proposed brand extension but must also take a broader corporate and competitive perspective. How effectively are the corporate assets used by the extension? How relevant are existing marketing campaigns, perceived benefits and target customers to the extension? What are the competitive advantages to the extension as perceived by consumers and possible reactions from competitors?

Too many extension products and entrenched competition can put a strain on company resources. For example, Church & Dwight in the 1980s decided to extend its Arm & Hammer bicarbonate of soda brand in the USA with its yellow box into new product categories – toothpaste, carpet deodorizer, air freshener and antiperspirant. Despite early successes, the company had one of its worst years in 1994 as earnings fell 77 percent. What happened? The market share of two of its more promising product introductions – toothpaste and laundry detergent – fell sharply when, after observing consumer acceptance of bicarbonate of soda-based products, packaged goods giants such as Procter & Gamble, Unilever and Colgate-Palmolive introduced their own baking soda versions of these products. Priced higher and with less advertising support, the market share of Arm & Hammer's products dropped. Church & Dwight management admitted that 'it was too much for a company of our size to introduce so many new products in one year' and vowed to focus on existing products in the short run.

Design marketing campaigns to launch extension

Too often, extensions are used as a shortcut to introducing a new product and insufficient attention is paid to developing a branding and marketing strategy that will maximize the equity of the extension as well as enhance the equity of the parent brand. As with a new brand, building equity for an extension requires choosing brand elements, designing the optimal marketing campaign to launch the extension and leveraging secondary associations.

Choosing brand elements

By definition, a brand extension retains one or more elements from an existing brand. Marketers should realize that extensions do not necessarily have to adopt only a brand name but can use other brand elements, too. For example, companies such as Heinz and Campbell Soup have implemented packaging designs that attempt to distinguish different line extensions or brand types but reveal their common origin.[52]

In some cases, packaging is such a critical component that it is hard to imagine an extension without the same design elements. Brands in such cases are in a dilemma because, if they choose the same type of packaging, they run the risk that the extension will not be well distinguished. On the other hand, if they choose to use different packaging, a key source of brand equity may be left behind.

Kapferer describes the experiences of Kodak when it began marketing alkaline batteries under the Ultra Life brand name in 1985. Instead of using its yellow and red colours for packaging, the battery had its own look and identity, with the Kodak name only appearing in small type. After disappointing sales, Kodak changed the packaging to give more emphasis to the Kodak name and look, with an immediate increase in sales.[53]

Thus, a brand extension can retain or modify one or more brand elements from the parent as well as adopt its own brand elements. In creating elements for an extension, the guidelines of memorability, meaningfulness, likeability, protectability, adaptability and transferability described in Chapter 4 should be followed. New brand elements are often necessary to help distinguish the extension from the parent and build its awareness and image. As Chapter 11 noted, the relative prominence of parent brand elements and extension brand elements will dictate the strength of transfer from the parent to the extension as well as the feedback to the parent brand.

Designing optimal marketing campaigns

The marketing campaigns for a brand extension must consider the guidelines in building brand equity given in Chapters 5 and 6. In terms of designing the campaign, performance and imagery associations often must be created, consumer perceptions of value must guide pricing decisions, distribution strategies must blend push and pull considerations and marketing communications must be integrated by mixing and matching communication options. Gaining retailer or intermediary acceptance is critical in an era of product proliferation.[54]

In terms of positioning a brand extension, the less similar the extension is to the parent brand, the more important it typically is to establish points of parity. The points of difference for a category extension in many cases directly follow from the points of difference for the parent brand and are easily perceived by consumers. Thus, when Nivea extended into shampoo, conditioners, deodorants, cosmetics and other beauty products, 'gentleness' presumably transferred easily. It would seem that the bigger challenge would have been to reach parity in the minds of consumers with category considerations related to glamour and how the shampoo and cosmetics made one look and feel or, in the case of deodorant, efficacy of odour protection. Thus, with category extensions, points of parity are often critical. With line extensions, however, it is often the case that a new association has to be created that can serve as an additional point of difference and help to distinguish the extension from the parent too.

For line extensions, it is important that consumers understand how the new product relates to existing products to minimize cannibalization or confusion. For example, in 2005, Anheuser-Busch launched Budweiser Select in the USA, a low-carb beer with no aftertaste positioned as an upmarker, white-collar brew. The emphasis on no aftertaste, however, drew an implicit comparison that cast other Anheuser-Busch products in a dim light and caused some consumers to abandon their usual Bud or Bud Light in favour of the new brand. As a result, nearly all of Bud Select's 1.3 percent share of supermarket sales earned in the month after its launch came at the expense of other Anheuser-Busch beers, which lost a share point.[55]

America Online, owned by Time Warner, ran into a similar problem when it extended the Netscape brand by using it to launch a low-cost, dial-up internet service provider (ISP) in 2004. At €7.30 a month, the service was priced well below the €17.50 charged for standard AOL service and offered limited features. Ironically, the Netscape service was bundled with Microsoft's Internet Explorer browser, not the latest Netscape browser. For consumers who had known Netscape as a pioneer of web browsers during the 1990s, seeing it emerge as a 'cut-rate' ISP bundled with the arch-rival browser was confusing and represented a 'low point' for the brand.[56]

Building on secondary brand associations

In general, brand extensions will often leverage the same secondary associations as the parent, although there may be instances in which competing in the extension category requires additional fortification, so linking to other entities may be desirable. A brand extension differs in that, by definition, there is always some exploitation of another brand or company. The extent to which these other associations become linked to the extension, however, depends on the branding strategy adopted and how the extension is branded. As noted earlier, the more brand elements they have in common and the more prominence they receive, the more likely it is that parent brand associations will transfer.

Evaluate extension success and effects on parent brand equity

The final step in evaluating opportunities involves assessing the extent to which an extension is able to achieve its own equity as well as contribute to the equity of the parent. Decisions have to be made concerning the introduction of a brand extension and a number of factors will affect the brand's success. To help interpret that success, brand tracking founded on the customer-based brand equity model or other measures of consumer response can be employed, centred on both the extension and the parent brand as a whole. Figure 12.22 is a checklist of 13 conceptual considerations in evaluating brand extensions. Brand Briefing 12.14 describes a perceptive analysis of line extensions by Quelch and Kenny.

In Brand Briefing 12.11 the branding expert Kapferer describes the brand territory and the differences between functional and symbolic brands regarding their ability to extend themselves.

- Does the parent brand have strong equity?
- Is there sufficient equity transfer to the extension?
- Is extension consistent with brand vision and essence?
- Is it a logical fit that will make sense to target market(s)?
- Will it create strong competitive positioning in the new category?
- Will it avoid creating negative associations in the new category?
- What implications will the extension have on brand equity?
- Does it minimize risk and dilution?
- Does it offer additional extension opportunities?
- Will extension have necessary points of parity and points of difference?
- How can the marketing campaign enhance extension equity?
- Do the organizational skills and resources required to develop the extension exist or can they be obtained?
- How should extension feedback effects to the parent brand best be managed?

Figure 12.22   Brand extension checklist

Brand Briefing 12.11

The brand territory

In consumers' minds, each brand has a legitimate territory, an area where the brand fits and which sets limits for how far it can be extended. Branding expert Kapferer distinguishes between three zones: the core (which is divided into inner and outer core), the extension zone and the forbidden zone (see Figure 12.23). The zone model of brand extension is based on Davidson. Research using traditional quantitative approaches can provide information on the inner and outer core. If information is needed on where to find the brand's extension zones, in-depth interviews or projective techniques are necessary.

- Zone 1: core. When we consider line extensions we can note that they are often relatively risk free. However, problems may arise from vertical extensions when the price is lowered.

- Zone 2: extension zone. Some brand extensions can be found within the brand's legitimate territory.

- Zone 3: forbidden zone. Some brand extensions can fall outside the brand's legitimate territory.

Kapferer suggests that not all brands lend themselves to extensions. In Figure 12.24, he exemplifies a close extension with Heinz (B), which is characterized by its know-how. Heinz can market mustard sauce as well as ketchup. The next degree of extension (C) corresponds to brand benefits. Two examples are Palmolive, which softens everything it embraces, and Bic, which simplifies things and makes them disposable and inexpensive. The next level (D) assumes that the brand is defined by its personality. The last degree of extension (E) assumes that the brand is defined by deep values.

Brand Briefing 12.11 *continued*

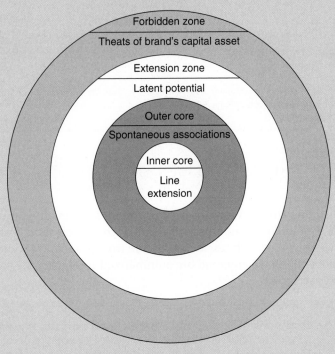

Figure 12.23   Kapferer's brand territory

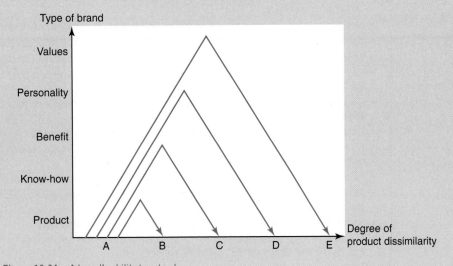

Figure 12.24   A brand's ability to extend

Brand Briefing 12.11 *continued*

One example is the Virgin brand, which spans many categories. Kapferer argues that the only way for a brand to enable brand extensions is to regard them from a higher viewpoint. This means that the brand will serve as source of inspiration and a value system.

Source: Jean-Noël Kapferer, *The New Strategic Brand Management: Creating and sustaining brand equity long term*, London: Kogan Page, 2005.

EXTENSION GUIDELINES BASED ON ACADEMIC RESEARCH

Although the previous discussion provides insight into the effects of brand extensions on brand equity, more specific guidance is necessary. Fortunately, brand extension has received much research attention from academics. Some of the important conclusions that have emerged are summarized in Figure 12.25 and described in detail in this section.[57]

- Brand extensions are successful when the parent brand is seen as having favourable associations and there is a perception of fit between the parent and the extension.
- There are many bases of fit: product-related attributes and benefits as well as non-product-related attributes and benefits related to common usage or user types.
- Depending on consumer knowledge of the product categories, perceptions of fit may be based on technical or manufacturing commonalities or more surface considerations such as necessary or situational complementarity.
- High-quality brands stretch further than average-quality brands, although both types have boundaries.
- A brand that is seen as prototypical of a product category can be difficult to extend outside the category.
- Concrete attribute associations tend to be more difficult to extend than abstract benefit associations.
- Consumers may transfer associations that are positive in the original product class but become negative in the extension context.
- Consumers may infer negative associations about an extension, perhaps even based on other inferred positive associations.
- It can be difficult to extend into a product class that is seen as easy to make.
- A successful extension can not only contribute to the parent brand image but also enable a brand to be extended even more.
- An unsuccessful extension hurts the parent brand only when there is a strong basis of fit between the two.
- An unsuccessful extension does not prevent a firm from backtracking and introducing a more similar extension.
- Vertical extensions can be difficult and often require sub-branding strategies.
- The most effective advertising strategy for an extension is one that emphasizes information about the extension (rather than reminders about the parent brand).

Figure 12.25   Brand extension guidelines based on academic research

Favourable associations

Successful brand extensions occur when the parent brand is seen as having favourable associations and there is a perception of fit between the parent brand and the extension product. To understand the process by which consumers evaluate a brand extension, many researchers have adopted a 'categorization' perspective. Categorization research has its roots in psychological research that shows that people do not deliberately and individually evaluate each new stimulus to which they are exposed, but often evaluate a stimulus in terms of whether or not it can be classified as a member of a previously defined mental category, as illustrated by the following example.

Imagine that you went to a party and found yourself in a conversation with an athletic-looking person who was casually dressed in sportswear and seemed to want to talk only about sport – what he or she read in the paper, saw on television and was involved with as a participant. You might have a mental category of a 'sport fanatic' as someone who only read the sport section of the newspaper, watched sport on television and talked sport with friends and family. As a result of this knowledge, you might quickly categorize that person as a 'sport fanatic' and your evaluation would probably depend on how you felt about sport fanatics in general. As opposed to this 'categorical processing', assume that you went up to another person at the party. This extremely pale person was dressed in an aggressive 'punk' manner yet, at the same time, also seemed to only want to talk about sport. Because of his or her appearance, this other person might not fit so neatly into your category of 'sport fanatic', so you would have to form your evaluation in a more detailed fashion, that is, by 'piecemeal processing', in which you constructed an attitude based on all the different considerations involved.

Applying categorization notions in a marketing context, it could be argued that consumers use their categorical knowledge of brands and products to simplify, structure and interpret their marketing environment.[58] For example, it has been argued that consumers see brands as categories. Over time these categories have come to be associated with attributes that are based on the attributes of the products in the brand category.[59] For example, Nivea might be associated with 'care', 'mildness', 'quality' and 'beauty' as a result of its skincare, haircare and cosmetic products.

According to a categorization perspective, if a brand were to introduce an extension that was seen as closely related or similar to the brand category, then consumers could easily transfer their attitude about the parent brand to the extension. However, if consumers were not so sure about the similarity, they might be expected to evaluate the extension in a more detailed, piecemeal fashion. In this case, the favourability of any specific associations that are inferred about the extension would be the primary determinant of extension evaluations.[60]

Thus, a categorization view considers consumers' evaluations of brand extensions to be a two-step process. First, consumers determine if in their mind there is a match between what they know about the parent brand and what they believe to be true about the extension. Second, if the match is good, consumers might be expected to transfer their parent brand attitudes to the extension. Otherwise, consumers might be more likely to evaluate the brand in a piecemeal fashion. With this latter type of processing, consumer evaluations would depend on the strength, favourability and uniqueness of salient brand associations in the extension context.

Consistent with these notions, Aaker and Keller collected consumer reactions to 20 proposed extensions from 6 well-known brands and found that both a perception of fit between the original and extension product categories and a perception of high quality for the parent brand led to more favourable extension evaluations.[61] Subsequent studies have explored whether or not these findings can be generalized to markets outside the USA. Based on an analysis of 131 brand extensions from 7 such replication studies, Bottomly and Holden concluded that this basic model could be generalized, although cross-cultural differences influenced the relative importance attached to the model's components.[62]

Thus, in general, brand extensions are more likely to be favourably evaluated by consumers if they see some bases of fit or similarity between the proposed extension and parent brand.[63] A lack of fit may condemn a potentially successful brand extension.[64]

Bases of fit

There are many bases of fit: product-related attributes and benefits, as well as non-product-related attributes and benefits related to common usage situations or user types. Any association held in memory by consumers about the parent brand may serve as a potential basis of fit. As Chapter 2 noted, many types of associations may become linked to a brand. Therefore, brand extensions may be seen as similar or close in fit to the parent in many ways. Academic researchers typically assume that similarity judgements are a function of salient shared associations between the parent brand and the extension product category. Specifically, the more common and fewer distinctive associations that exist, the greater the perception of overall similarity. These similarity judgements could be based on product-related attributes or benefits as well as non-product-related attributes or benefits.[65] Consumers may also use attributes for a prototypical brand or a particular exemplar as the standard of reference for the extension category and form their perceptions of fit with the parent brand on that basis.

To demonstrate how fit does not have to be based on product-related associations alone, Park, Milberg and Lawson have distinguished between fit based on 'product-feature similarity' (as described earlier) and 'brand concept consistency'.[66] They define brand concepts as the brand-unique image associations that arise from a particular combination of attributes, benefits and the marketing efforts used to translate these attributes into higher-order meanings (eg, high status). *Brand concept consistency* is defined in terms of how well the brand concept accommodates the extension product. The important point these researchers make is that different types of brand concepts from the same original product category may meet with varying degrees of acceptance regarding extending into the same category, even when product feature similarity is high.

The researchers distinguish between *function-orientated brands*, whose dominant associations relate to product performance (eg, Timex watches) and *prestige-orientated brands*, whose dominant associations relate to consumers' expression of self-concepts or images (eg, Rolex watches). Experimentally, they showed that the Rolex brand could more easily extend into categories such as grandfather clocks, bracelets and rings than the Timex brand. However, Timex could more easily extend into categories such as stopwatches, batteries and calculators. In the former case, there was high brand concept consistency for Rolex that overcame a lack of product feature similarity; in the latter case, there was enough product feature similarity to favour a function-orientated brand such as Timex.

Broniarczyk and Alba provide another compelling demonstration of the importance of recognizing salient brand associations. They show that a brand that may not even be as favourably evaluated as a competing brand in its category may be more successfully extended into certain categories, depending on the particular parent brand associations involved. For example, although Close-Up toothpaste was not as well liked by their sample as Crest toothpaste, a proposed Close-Up breath mint extension was evaluated more favourably than one from Crest. Alternatively, a proposed Crest toothbrush extension was evaluated more favourably than one from Close-Up. Figure 12.26 gives results from other categories.[67]

Broniarczyk and Alba also showed that a perceived lack of fit between the parent brand's product category and the proposed extension category could be overcome if key parent brand associations were salient and relevant in the extension category. For example, the US Froot Loops cereal – which has strong brand associations with 'sweet', 'flavour' and 'kids' – was better able to extend to dissimilar product categories such as lollipops and lollies than to similar product categories such as waffles and hot cereal because of the relevance of its brand associations in the dissimilar extension category. The reverse was true for Cheerios cereal, however, which had a 'healthy grain' association that was only relevant in similar extension product categories.

Thus, extension fit is more than just the number of common and distinctive brand associations between the parent brand and the extension product category.[68] These research studies and others demonstrate the importance of taking a broader perspective on categorization and fit. For example, Bridges, Keller and Sood refer to 'category coherence'. Coherent categories are those whose members 'hang together' and 'make sense'. According to these authors, to understand the rationale for a grouping of products in a brand line, a consumer needs 'explanatory links' that tie the products

Product category	Preferred brand and focal brand	Corresponding favourably evaluated extensions*
Cereal	Cheerios	Porridge; waffles
	Froot Loops	Lollipops
Soap	Camay	Moisturizer; cleansing cream
	Irish Spring	Deodorant
Computer	Apple	Video games
	IBM	Mobile phones
Beer	Coors	Wine coolers; bottled water
	Budweiser	Scotch

*The table should be interpreted as indicating that Cheerios would more successfully extend to porridge and waffles, whereas Froot Loops would more easily extend to lollipops and so on.

Figure 12.26   Role of US brand-specific associations in determining fit

together and summarize their relationship. For example, the physically dissimilar toy, bath and car seat products in the Fisher-Price product line can be united by the link 'products for children'.[69] Similarly, Schmitt and Dubé proposed that brand extensions should be viewed as conceptual combinations.[70] A conceptual combination (eg, 'apartment dog') consists of a modifying concept, or 'modifier' (eg, apartment) and a modified concept, or 'header' (eg, dog). Thus, according to this view, a proposed brand extension such as McDonald's Theme Park would be interpreted as the original brand or company name (eg, McDonald's) acting on the 'header concept' of the extension category (eg, theme parks) as a 'modifier'.

Finally, researchers have explored other, more specific, aspects of fit. Boush provides experimental data as to the context sensitivity of fit judgements.[71] Similarity judgements between pairs of product categories were found to be asymmetrical and brand name associations could reverse the direction of asymmetry. For example, more people agreed with the statement '*Time* magazine is like *Time* books' than the statement that '*Time* books are like *Time* magazine', but, without the brand names, the preferences were reversed. Smith and Andrews surveyed industrial goods marketers and found that the relationship between fit and new product evaluations was not direct but was mediated by customers' sense of certainty that a firm could provide a proposed product.[72] Zhang and Sood showed that, compared with adults, children (11- to 12-year-olds) evaluated brand extensions by relying more on surface cues (eg, brand name linguistic considerations) and less on deep cues (eg, category similarity). Finally, several researchers have shown how consumers from Western cultures judged functional brands in a more analytical fashion whereas consumers from Eastern cultures judged them more holistically.[73]

Perceptions of fit

Depending on consumer knowledge of the product categories, perceptions of fit may be based on technical or manufacturing commonalities or more surface considerations such as necessary or situational complementarity. Fit perceptions can also be based on considerations other than attributes or benefits. Taking a demand-side and supply-side perspective of consumer perceptions, Aaker and Keller showed that perceived fit between the parent brand and extension product could be related to the economic notions of perceived substitutability and complementarity in product use (from a demand-side perspective), as well as to the perceived ability of the firm to have the skills and assets necessary to make the extension product (from a supply-side perspective). Thus, Honda's perceived expertise in making engines for lawnmowers and cars may help perceptions of fit for any other machinery with small engines. Similarly, expertise with small disposable products offers opportunities for Bic. However, other extension examples have little manufacturing compatibility but greater usage complementarity – for example, Colgate's extension from toothpaste to toothbrushes or Duracell's extension from batteries to torches.

These perceptions of fit, however, may depend on how much consumers know or care about the product categories involved. As demonstrated by Muthukrishnan and Weitz, knowledgeable 'expert' consumers are more likely to use technical or manufacturing commonalities to judge fit, considering similarity in terms of technology, design and fabrication, and the materials and components used in the manufacturing process. Less knowledgeable 'novice' consumers, however, are more likely to use superficial, perceptual considerations such as common packaging, shape, colour, size and usage.[74] Specifically, they showed in their experiments that less knowledgeable consumers were more likely to see a basis of fit between tennis racquets and tennis shoes than tennis racquets and golf clubs, despite the fact that the latter actually share more manufacturing commonalities. The effects for more knowledgeable consumers, however, were reversed because they recognized the technical synergies that would be involved in manufacturing racquets and clubs. Further, Maoz and Tybout show that higher levels of involvement can lead to greater acceptance of dissimilar extensions.[75]

Broniarczyk and Alba also showed that perceptions of fit on the basis of brand-specific associations were contingent on consumers having the necessary knowledge about the parent brand. Without such knowledge, consumers again tended to rely on more superficial considerations, such as their level of awareness of the brand or their overall regard for the parent brand.[76]

High-quality brands stretch

High-quality brands stretch further than average-quality brands, although both types have boundaries. High-quality brands are often seen as more credible, expert and trustworthy. As a result, even though consumers may still believe a relatively distant extension does not really fit with the brand, they may be more willing to give a high-quality brand the benefit of the doubt. When a brand is seen as average in quality, however, such favourable source attributions may be less forthcoming and consumers may be more likely to question the ability or motives of the company involved.[77] Thus, one important benefit of building a strong brand is that it can be extended into more diverse categories.[78]

Regardless, all brands have boundaries, as a number of observers have persuasively argued by pointing out ridiculous, and even comical, hypothetical brand extension possibilities. For example, as Tauber once noted, few consumers would want shoe laces from a company famous for jelly or frozen meals from a company making washing powder!

Prototypical brands are limited

A brand that is seen as prototypical of a product category can be difficult to extend outside that category. So, if a brand is seen as representing or exemplifying a category too much, it may be difficult for consumers to think of the brand in any other way. Numerous examples exist of category leaders that have failed in introducing extensions.[79] Bayer, a brand synonymous with aspirin in the USA, ran into a stumbling block introducing the Bayer Select line of specialized non-aspirin painkillers.[80] Chiquita was unsuccessful in its attempt to move beyond its strong 'banana' association with its frozen juice bar extension.[81] Perhaps the most extreme example of this caveat is brands that lost their trademark distinctiveness and became a generic term for a category, such as Thermos and Kleenex.

To illustrate the difficulty that a prototypical brand may have in extending, consider Clorox, a brand whose name is virtually synonymous with bleach in the USA. In 1988, Clorox took on Procter & Gamble and Unilever by introducing the first bleach with detergent. After pouring €164 million into the development and distribution of its detergent products over the next three years, Clorox was only able to achieve a 3 percent market share. Despite being beaten to market, P&G's subsequently introduced Tide with Bleach was able to achieve a 17 percent market share. Reluctantly, Clorox chose to quit the market. Although a number of factors may have driven that decision, Clorox's failure can certainly be attributed in part to the fact that consumers could only think of Clorox as a bleach. On the other hand, Clorox has extended its brand into household cleaning products (eg, toilet bowl cleaners), where the bleach ingredient is seen as more relevant.

Also note that Clorox's extension failure may have also been because in a combined 'laundry detergent with bleach' product, laundry detergent is seen by consumers as the primary ingredient and bleach as secondary. As a result, a laundry detergent extension (such as Tide with Bleach) might be expected to have an advantage over a bleach extension (such as Clorox) when entering the combined laundry detergent with bleach category.[82] A similar type of interpretation might explain why US brand Aunt Jemima was successful in introducing a pancake syrup extension from its pancake mix product but why Log Cabin was less successful in introducing a pancake mix extension from its well-regarded pancake syrup product: pancake mix is seen as a more dominant ingredient than pancake syrup in breakfast pancakes. Brand Briefing 12.12 describes an interesting approach to dealing with this extendability challenge.

Concrete associations

Concrete attribute associations tend to be more difficult to extend than abstract associations. The limits to extension boundaries potentially faced by market leaders may be exacerbated by the fact that market-leading brands have strong concrete product attribute associations. In some cases, these associations may even be reinforced by their name (eg, Liquid Paper and Shredded Wheat).[83] La-Z-Boy, for example, has struggled to expand outside the narrow product line of recliners and its strong usage imagery.

The Aaker and Keller study showed that consumers dismissed a hypothetical Heineken popcorn extension as potentially tasting bad or like beer; a hypothetical Vidal Sassoon perfume extension as having an undesirably strong shampoo scent; and a hypothetical Crest chewing gum extension as tasting like toothpaste or, more generally, tasting unappealing. In each case, consumers inferred a concrete attribute association for an extension that was technically feasible even though common sense might have suggested that a manufacturer would not introduce a product with such an attribute.

More abstract associations, on the other hand, may be seen as more relevant. For example, the Aaker and Keller study also showed that the Vuarnet brand had a remarkable ability to be exported to a disparate set of product categories, for example, sportswear, watches, wallets and even skis. In these cases, complementarity may

Brand Briefing 12.12

Understanding master brands

Farquhar et al. have developed an intriguing approach to generating brand extension possibilities for prototypical brands and market leaders. They define a *master brand* as a brand so dominant in customers' minds that it 'owns' a particular association: the mention of a product attribute or category, a usage situation or a customer benefit instantly brings a master brand to mind. Examples of such master brands Coca-Cola cold drinks include Hoover vaccuum deaners, Bacardi rum, Alka-Seltzer antacid, Oxo stock cubes, Campbell's soup, Crayola crayons, Sellotape sticky tape, Philadelphia cream cheese and Vaseline petroleum jelly.

Recognizing that the exceptionally strong associations of a master brand often make it difficult to extend it directly to other product categories, they propose strategies to extend master brands *indirectly* by using master brand associations that come from different parts of the brand hierarchies. Specifically, they suggest a brand extension compass (Figure 12.27).

- *Sub-branding* introduces an element into the brand hierarchy below the level of the master brand to refine or modify its meaning (eg, DuPont Stainmaster carpet).

- *Super-branding* adds elements to a brand hierarchy above the level of the master brand, typically to suggest a product improvement (eg, Eveready Energizer batteries).

- *Brand bundling*, or 'cross-branding', fortifies a master brand through associations with other brands, including co-operative or co-branding (eg, Citibank AAdvantage Visa card).

- *Brand bridging* uses the master brand to endorse a new brand as the company attempts to move to a more distant product category (eg, T/Gel therapeutic shampoo is endorsed by Neutrogena).

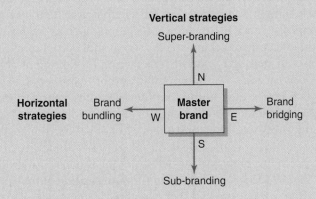

Figure 12.27   The brand extension compass

Brand Briefing 12.12 *continued*

These strategies, all of which have been discussed in earlier chapters, are suggested as ways to shield a parent or master brand by creating some distance to the extension and finding other ways to build brand equity for the extension by incorporating additional brands or brand elements. The authors note that marketing efforts can also 'stay close to home' and fortify master brands by strengthening the brand's competencies, attracting new users and developing new uses or expanding consumption among current users (see Chapter 13).

Source: Peter H. Farquhar, Julia Y. Han, Paul M. Herr and Yuji Ijiri, 'Strategies for leveraging master brands', *Marketing Research*, September 1992: 32–43.

have led to an inference that the extension would have the 'stylish' attribute associated with the Vuarnet name, and such an association was valued in the different extension contexts.

Several caveats should be noted, however, concerning the relative extendability of concrete and abstract associations. First, concrete attributes can be transferred to some product categories.[84] For example, if the parent brand has a concrete attribute that is highly valued in the extension category because it creates a distinctive taste, ingredient or component, an extension can often be successful. According to Farquhar and Herr, examples of such extensions might include Philadelphia cream cheese salad dressing, Tylenol sinus medication, Häagen-Dazs cream liqueur, Oreo biscuits and cream ice-cream and Arm & Hammer carpet deodorizer.[85]

Second, abstract associations may not always transfer easily. This second caveat emerged from a study by Bridges, Keller and Sood that examined the relative transferability of product-related brand information when it was represented either as an abstract brand association or as a concrete brand association.[86] For example, one such comparison contrasted the relative transferability of a watch characterized by dominant concrete attribute associations such as 'water-resistant quartz movements, a time-keeping mechanism encased in shockproof steel covers and shatterproof crystal' with that of a watch characterized by dominant abstract attribute associations such as 'durable'. Although these authors expected the abstract brand representation to fare better, they found that the two types of brand images extended equally well into a dissimilar product category (eg, handbags). Perhaps the most important reason for this was that consumers did not believe the abstract benefit would have the same meaning in the extension category (ie, durability does not necessarily 'transfer' because durability for a watch is not the same as durability for a handbag).

Finally, Joiner and Loken, in a demonstration of the 'inclusion effect' in a brand extension setting, showed that consumers often generalized possession of an attribute from a specific category (eg, Sony televisions) to a more general category (eg, all Sony products) more readily than they generalized the attribute from the specific category (eg, Sony televisions) to another specific category (eg, Sony bicycles). This inclusion effect was attenuated when the specific extension category increased its typicality to the general category (eg, Sony cameras versus Sony bicycles).[87]

Associations can turn bad

Consumers may transfer associations that are positive in the original product class but become negative in the extension context. Because of different consumer motivations or product usage in the extension category, a brand association may not be as highly valued as it was for the original product. For example, when Campbell's test marketed a tomato sauce with the Campbell's name, it flopped. Apparently, Campbell's strong associations with soup signalled to consumers that the sauce would be watery. To give the product more credibility, Campbell's changed the name to the Italian-sounding 'Prego' and the product has gone on to be a success.

Inferred negative associations

Consumers may infer negative associations for an extension, perhaps even based on inferred positive associations. Even if consumers transfer positive associations from the parent brand to the extension, they may still infer other negative associations. For example, the Bridges, Keller and Sood study showed that, even if consumers thought that a proposed handbag extension from a hypothetical maker of durable watches also would be durable, they often assumed that it would not be fashionable, helping to contribute to low extension evaluations.[88]

Products that are easy to make

It can be difficult to extend into a product class that is seen as easy to make. Some seemingly appropriate extensions may be dismissed because of the nature of the extension product involved. If the product is seen as comparatively easy to make – such that brand differences are hard to come by – then a high-quality brand may be seen as incongruous; alternatively, consumers may feel that the brand extension will attempt to command an unreasonable price premium and be too expensive.

For example, Aaker and Keller showed that hypothetical extensions such as Heineken popcorn, Vidal Sassoon perfume, Crest shaving cream and Häagen-Dazs cottage cheese received relatively poor marks from experimental subjects in part because all brands in the extension category were seen as being about the same in quality, suggesting that the proposed brand extension was unlikely to be superior to existing products. The failure of designers such as Bill Blass and Gloria Vanderbilt to introduce chocolates and perfume under their names may be in part a result of these perceptions of incongruity, lack of differentiation and unwarranted price premiums.

When the extension category is seen as difficult to make, on the other hand, such that brands potentially vary a great deal in quality, there is a greater opportunity for a brand extension to differentiate itself, although consumers may also be less sure as to what exactly the quality level of the extension will be.[89]

Extensions can go further

A successful extension can not only contribute to the parent brand image but also enable a brand to be extended even further. As noted earlier, a successful brand extension can change the meaning and image of a brand. An extension can help the image of the parent brand by improving the strength, favourability or uniqueness of its associations. For example, Keller and Aaker showed that when consumers did not already have strongly held attitudes, the successful introduction of a brand extension improved evaluations of a parent brand that was originally perceived to be of only average quality. Balachander and Ghose found empiricial support for a positive spillover effect from advertising of an extension on the choice of the parent brand (ie, advertising for Yoplait fat-free yogurt had a positive effect on the choice probability of its parent, Yoplait yogurt).[90] Finally, the associations that become linked to the parent brand by virtue of the extension product category may help clarify the core benefits for the brand. For example, one of Australia's leading cereal brands, Uncle Toby's, was able to broaden its meaning to be seen as a 'healthy breakfast and snack food' by introducing muesli bars and other products.

If an extension changes the image and meaning of the brand, subsequent brand extensions that otherwise might not have seemed appropriate may make more sense and be seen as a better fit. For example, Keller and Aaker showed that, by taking little steps – that is, by introducing a series of closely related but increasingly distant extensions, it may be possible for a brand to ultimately enter product categories that would have been much more difficult, or perhaps even impossible, to have entered directly.[91]

Dunhill

The Dunhill brand provides an excellent example of gradually extending a brand to transform its meaning.[92] For all practical purposes, Dunhill started as a cigarette brand that was first extended into smoking accessories (eg, pipes, pouches and lighters). After establishing itself there, the brand was extended into other high-end male accessories (eg, belts, desktop items, cufflinks, rings and clothing). Most recently, the brand was extended yet again into male fragrances and mainstream fashion items. As a result of this activity, the Dunhill brand now not only represents a leading cigarette brand but also 'luxury products and accessories for both men and women'. Said one commentator. 'It used to be all about gold cigarette cases and lighters, but Dunhill has managed to become smart without being stuffy or boring'.[93]

Boush and Loken found that distant extensions from a 'broad' brand were evaluated more favourably than from a 'narrow' brand.[94] Broad brands spanning many product categories provide strong competitive advantages.[95] Relatedly, Dacin and Smith have shown that, if the perceived quality levels of members of a brand portfolio are more uniform, then consumers tend to make higher, more confident evaluations of a proposed new extension.[96] They also showed that a firm that had demonstrated little variance in quality across a diverse set of product categories was better able to overcome perceptions of lack of extension fit. In other words, it is as if consumers in this case think, 'whatever the company does, it tends to do well'.

In an empirical study of 95 brands in 11 non-durable consumer goods categories, in terms of stages of the product category lifecycle, early-entering brand extensions did not perform as well, on average, as either early-entering new name products or late-entering brand extensions.[97] DeGraba and Sullivan provided an economic analysis to help interpret this observation.[98] They posited that the main uncertainty in introducing a product is the inability to know if it will be received by customers in a way that will allow it to be a commercial success. They further argued that this source of uncertainty can be mitigated by spending more time on development. Under such assumptions, they showed that the large spillover effects triggered by introducing a poorly received brand extension cause introducers of brand extensions to spend more time on the development process than do introducers of new name products.

Role of product fit

An unsuccessful extension hurts the parent brand only when there is a strong basis of fit between the two. The rule of thumb emerging is that an unsuccessful brand extension potentially can damage the parent brand only when there is a high degree of similarity or fit involved – for example, in the case of a failed line extension in the same category. Perceptions of quality for a parent brand in the health and beauty aids area decreased with the hypothetical introduction of a lower-quality extension in a similar product category (shampoo). Quality perceptions of the parent brand were unaffected, however, when the proposed extension was in a dissimilar product category (facial tissues).[99] Similarly, unsuccessful extensions in dissimilar product categories did not affect evaluations of the parent brand.[100] When the brand extension is further removed, it seems easier for consumers to compartmentalize the brand's products and disregard its performance in what is seen as an unrelated product category.

Other studies reinforce this conclusion. Researchers found that dilution effects were less likely to be present with flagship products and occurred with line extensions but were not always evident for more dissimilar category extensions.[101] Gürhan-Canli and Maheswaran extended the results of these studies by considering the moderating effect of consumer motivation and extension typicality.[102] In high-motivation conditions, they found that incongruent extensions were scrutinized and led to the modification of family brand evaluations, regardless of the typicality of the extensions. In low-motivation conditions, however, brand evaluations were more extreme in the context of high (versus low) typicality. Because the less typical extension was considered an exception, its impact was reduced. Consistent with these high-motivation findings, negative feedback effects were found to be present when: extensions were perceived as belonging to product categories dissimilar to those associated with the family brand; and extension attribute information was inconsistent with image beliefs associated with the family brand.[103]

In terms of individual differences, there is evidence of a negative reciprocal effect from brand extensions, especially for high need for cognition subjects.[104] Also, dilution effects were found with owners of prestige cars when low-priced extensions were introduced, but not with owners of other cars or with non-owners of either car.[105]

Finally, Morrin examined the effect of brand extensions on the strength of parent brand associations in memory. Two computer-based studies revealed that exposing consumers to brand extension information strengthened rather than weakened parent brand associations in memory, particularly for parents that were dominant in their product category. Higher fit also resulted in greater facilitation, but only for parent brands that were not dominant. Moreover, improvements in memory for the parent due to the advertised introduction of an extension was not as great as when the same level of advertising directly promoted the parent brand.[106]

Backtracking

An unsuccessful extension does not prevent a firm from backtracking and introducing a more similar extension. The Keller and Aaker study also showed that unsuccessful extensions do not necessarily prevent a company from retrenching and later introducing a more similar extension. Consider the failure of Levi's Tailored Classics. In the early 1980s, Levi's tried to introduce a Tailored Classics line of men's suits in the USA. The range was aimed at independent-thinking 'clothes horses', dubbed by research as 'classic individualists'. Although the suit was not supposed to need tailoring, to allow for the better fit necessary for these demanding consumers, Levi's designed the trousers and jackets to be sold separately. It chose to price these wool suits quite competitively and to distribute them through its department store accounts as opposed to men's outfitters where the classic individualist usually shopped. The product failed to achieve its sales goals. This failure can probably be attributed to a number of factors (eg, problems with the target market, distribution channels and product design), but perhaps the most fundamental problem was the lack of fit with the Levi's brand image and the image needed for the extension product and desired by the target market. Levi's had an informal, rugged, outdoor image that was inconsistent with the self-image of the classic individualist.

Despite the ultimate withdrawal of the product, Levi's later was able to execute one of the most successful clothing launches, Dockers trousers. As Levi's experiences with brand extensions illustrate, failure does not mean a firm will never be able to introduce extensions – certainly not for a brand with as much equity as Levi's. A failed extension does, however, create a 'perceptual boundary' in that it reveals the limits to the brand in the minds of consumers.

Vertical extensions

Vertical extensions can be difficult and often require sub-branding strategies. For market reasons or competitive considerations, it may be desirable for the firm to introduce a lower-priced version of a product. Such a product could be introduced as its own brand and function as a fighter brand or a brand could be stretched downwards. The danger with the latter extension strategy, however, is that the parent brand image could be cheapened or tarnished in some way.

As a result, firms often adopt sub-branding strategies to distinguish their lower-priced entries. For example, Gillette introduced the Good News brand in the USA for inexpensive personal care products such as disposable razors. US Airways introduced US Airways Shuttle as an inexpensive short-haul carrier to compete with no-frills Southwest Airlines. Courtyard by Marriott was a lower-priced version of the Marriott and upmarket Marriott Marquis hotel chains (Brand Briefing 12.13). Such introductions must be handled carefully – typically, the parent brand plays a secondary role.

Brand Briefing 12.13

Expanding the Marriott brand

Marriott International grew from a root beer stand started by John and Alice Marriott in Washington, DC, during the 1920s. The Marriotts added hot food to their stand and renamed their business the Hot Shoppe, which they incorporated in 1929 when they began building a regional chain of restaurants. As the number of Hot Shoppes grew, Marriott expanded into in-flight catering by serving food on Eastern, American and Capital Airlines beginning in 1937. In 1939, Hot Shoppes began a food service management business when it opened a cafeteria in the US Treasury building. The company expanded into another hospitality sector in 1957, when Hot Shoppes opened its first hotel in Virginia. Hot Shoppes, which was renamed Marriott Corporation in 1967, grew nationally and internationally by way of acquisitions and entering new categories; by 1977, sales topped €730 million.

In the pursuit of continued growth, Marriott continued to diversify its business. Marriott's 1982 acquisition of Host International made it the top US operator of airport food and beverage facilities. In the next three years, Marriott added 1,000 food service accounts by buying three food service companies. Determining that its high penetration in the traditional hotel market did not offer opportunities for growth, the company initiated a segmented marketing strategy for its hotels by introducing the moderately priced Courtyard by Marriott hotels in 1983. These hotels constituted the largest segment of the US lodging industry, a segment filled with competitors such as Holiday Inn, Ramada and Quality Inn. Research registered greatest consumer dissatisfaction with moderately priced hotels and Courtyard hotels were designed to offer travellers greater convenience and amenities, such as balconies and patios, large desks and sofas, and pools and spas.

Early success with Courtyard prompted Marriott to expand. In 1984, Marriott entered the holiday timeshare business by acquiring American Resorts Group. The following year, the company purchased Howard Johnson company, selling the hotels and retaining the restaurants. In 1987, Marriott added three market segments: Marriott Suites, full-service suites; Residence Inn, extended stay rooms for business travellers; and Fairfield Inn, an economy hotel brand. The company explained: 'There is a lot of segmentation that's going on in the hotel business. Travellers are sophisticated and have many wants and needs. In addition to that, we saw there would be a finite . . . ability to grow the traditional business.'

Marriott Corporation split into two in 1993, forming Host Marriott to own the hotel properties and Marriott International to engage in the more lucrative practice of managing them and franchising its brands. In 1995, Marriott International bought a minority stake in the Ritz-Carlton luxury hotel group (Marriott purchased the remaining share in 1998). In 1997, it expanded again by acquiring the Renaissance Hotel Group and introducing TownePlace Suites, Fairfield Suites and Marriott Executive Residences. Marriott added a new hotel brand in 1998 with the introduction of SpringHill Suites, which provide moderately priced rooms that are 25 percent

Brand Briefing 12.13 *continued*

larger than standard rooms. The following year, the company acquired corporate housing specialist ExecuStay and formed ExecuStay by Marriott. Its size and breadth enabled Marriott to recover from the travel and tourism downturn after 2001, and by 2004 Marriott's net income per share was down only 3 percent from 2000 levels and its revenue per available room was €50 per night, €15 above the industry average.

The last Hot Shoppe closed in December 1999. This closing was fitting, because the tiny restaurant in no way resembled the multinational hospitality leader it spawned. In 2004, Marriott International was the largest hotel and resort company in the USA, with 374,000 rooms in the USA, and controlled up to one-third of available rooms in some markets. It is also one of the leading hospitality companies in the world, maintaining over 2,600 operating units in 59 countries that brought in €7.3 billion in global revenues in 2004.

Sources: www.marriot.com; Kim Clark, 'Lawyers clash on timing of Marriot's plan to split', *Baltimore Sun*, 27 September 1994; Neil Henderson, 'Marriott gambles on low-cost, classy suburban motels', *Washington Post*, 18 June 1994; Neil Henderson, 'Marriott bares Courtyard plans', *Washington Post*, 12 June 1984; Elizabeth Tucker, 'Marriot's recipe for corporate growth', *Washington Post*, 1 June 1987; Paul Farhi, 'Marriott to sell 800 restaurants', *Washington Post*, 19 December 1989; Stephane Fitch, 'Soft pillows and sharp elbows', *Forbes*, 10 May 2004: 66.

An even more difficult vertical extension is an upward brand stretch.[107] In general, it is difficult to sufficiently change people's impressions of the brand to justify a significant upward extension.

Gallo

For years, US winemaker Gallo refused to put any other brand on the label of its better vintages besides Gallo. Despite repeated ad campaigns that promised that some new varietal would 'change the way you think about Gallo' (eg, as when the winery introduced White Grenache), many consumers continued to think of the brand as a relatively inexpensive jug wine.[108] In 1995, recognizing the boundaries that exist with even strong brands, Gallo spent heavily to launch the more upmarket Turning Leaf (priced at €5 to €6 a bottle), which contained no mention of the Gallo name. Several years later, it launched Gallo of Sonoma (at €7 to €22 a bottle) to compete in the premium wine segment, using the founder's grandchildren as spokespeople in an intensive push and pull campaign. With a hip, young and fun image, case sales volume tripled to 680,000 in 1999. The brand upgraded its image again in 2006, launching the

Gallo Family Vineyards umbrella brand for its high-end wines such as Gallo of Sonoma, which became a sub-brand known as Gallo Family Vineyards Sonoma Reserve. The new umbrella brand brought with it price increases of one to two dollars and 'an overall upgrade in quality'.[109]

Concern about the unwillingness of consumers to update their brand knowledge led Honda, Toyota and Nissan to introduce their luxury car models under separate marques (Acura, Lexus and Infiniti, respectively). As it turns out, product improvements to the upper ends of their brand lines since the introduction of these marques may have made it easier to bridge the gap with their brands into the luxury market.

At the same time, it is possible to use brand modifiers to signal a noticeable, although presumably not dramatic, quality improvement – for example, Ultra Dry Pampers, extra strength painkillers, or Maybelline's XXL curlpower mascara. As noted earlier, Farquhar et al. suggest this means of indirect extension, or 'super-branding,' may be less risky than direct extensions when moving a master brand upmarket.[110] They recommend veiling the master brand from the customer's view. The idea would be for the new super-brand to draw attention to itself and the merits of the product and later unveil the super-brand's link to the 'hidden master brand' to provide reassurance to consumers. They caution that a premature connection with the master brand can generate scepticism and indecision, citing as supporting evidence US lantern maker Coleman's success in introducing upmarket camping equipment first as Peak 1 and then only later making the Coleman connection.

Vertical extensions can be especially tricky for prestige brands. In such cases, firms must often maintain a balance between availability and scarcity such that people always aspire to be a customer and not feel excluded. By launching ambitious marketing campaigns with such offerings as 'How to buy a diamond' and 'Pearl authority', jewellery chain Tiffany has tried to convince buyers of the quality of its products and the fact that they are attainable. With an average retail price of goods sold of €183, Tiffany has managed to maintain its lofty image while also drawing in a wider array of customers.[111]

Comparatively little empirical academic research, however, has been conducted on this topic. In a study of the US mountain bike industry, a brand price premium was significantly positively correlated with the quality of the lowest-quality model in the product line for the lower-quality segments of the market; for the upper-quality segments of the market, a brand price premium was also significantly positively correlated with the quality of the highest-quality model in the product line. These results suggest that managers wishing to maximize the equity of their brands should offer only high-quality products, although overall profit maximization could dictate a different strategy.[112]

Kirmani, Sood and Bridges examined the 'ownership effect' whereby owners have more favourable responses than non-owners to brand extensions in the context of brand line stretches. They found that the ownership effect occurred for upward and downward stretches of non-prestige brands (eg, Acura) and for upward stretches of prestige brands (eg, Calvin Klein and BMW). For downward stretches of prestige brands, however, the ownership effect did not occur because of owners' desires to maintain brand exclusivity. In this situation, a sub-branding strategy protected owners' parent brand attitudes from dilution.[113]

Advertising strategy

The most effective advertising strategy for an extension is one that emphasizes information about the extension (rather than reminders about the parent brand). Studies have shown that the information provided about brand extensions, by triggering selective retrieval from memory, may frame decisions by consumers and influence extension evaluations. In general, the most effective strategy appears to be one that recognizes the type of information that is salient for the brand in the minds of consumers when they first consider the proposed extension and highlights additional information that would otherwise be overlooked or misinterpreted.

For example, Aaker and Keller found that reminding consumers about the quality of a parent brand did not improve evaluations for poorly rated extensions. Because the brands they studied were well known and well liked, such reminders may have been unnecessary. Elaborating briefly on specific extension attributes about which consumers were uncertain or concerned, however, did lead to more favourable evaluations. Bridges, Keller and Sood found that providing information could improve perceptions of fit in the following two cases when consumers perceived low fit between the brand and the extension.[114]

When the parent brand and the extension shared physical attributes but the parent brand image was non-product-related and based on abstract user characteristics, consumers tended to overlook an obvious explanatory link between the parent brand and extension on the basis of shared product features (eg, a tennis shoe with a high-fashion image attempting to extend to work boots was not evaluated favourably). Information that raised the salience of the physical relationship relative to distracting non-product-related associations – a 'relational' communication strategy – improved extension evaluations (eg, when subjects were told the work boots would have leather uppers similar to those used in the tennis shoes).

When the parent brand and the extension only shared non-product-related associations and the parent brand image was product-related, consumers often made negative inferences on the basis of existing associations (eg, a tennis shoe with an image of durability attempting to extend to swimsuits was seen as being unfashionable). In this case, providing information that established an explanatory link with a new, 'reassuring' association – an 'elaborational' communication strategy – improved extension evaluations (eg, when subjects were told the swimsuits would be as fashionable as the tennis shoes).[115]

Lane found that repetition of an ad that evoked primarily benefit brand associations could overcome negative perceptions of a highly incongruent brand extension. Moreover, for moderately incongruent brand extensions, even ads that evoked peripheral brand associations (eg, brand packaging or character) could improve negative extension perceptions with sufficient repetition.[116] In a similar vein, Barone, Miniard and Romeo demonstrated in experiments that positive mood primarily enhanced evaluations of extensions viewed as moderately similar (as opposed to very similar or dissimilar) to a favourably evaluated core brand.[117]

Research has also explored other aspects of extension marketing campaigns. Keller and Sood found that 'branding effects' in terms of inferences based on parent brand knowledge operated both in the absence and presence of product experience with an extension, although they were less pronounced or, in the case of an unambiguous negative experience, even non-existent.[118] In considering the effects of retailer displays, one study found that evaluations of a 'high-equity' brand could be diminished by an unfamiliar competitive brand when: a mixed display structure led consumers to believe that the competitive brand was diagnostic for judging the high-equity brand; the precedence given to one brand over another in the display made expectations about brand differences or similarities accessible; and the unfamiliar competitive brand disconfirmed these expectations.[119] McCarthy et al. showed how new brands could compete effectively with extensions if consumers were able to process favourable product information.[120]

Brand Briefing 12.14

Guidelines for profitable line extensions

In a perceptive and illuminating analysis, Quelch and Kenney argue that unchecked product line expansion can weaken a brand's image, disturb trade relations and disguise cost increases.[121] In describing the lure of line extensions, Quelch and Kenny began by noting seven factors that explain why so many companies have pursued such a strategy.

1. *Customer segmentation:* line extensions are seen as a low-cost, low-risk way to meet the needs of target market segments, which can be increasingly refined due to sophisticated marketing research, advertising media and direct marketing practices.

2. *Consumer desires:* more consumers are switching brands and making in-store purchase decisions. A full brand line can offer 'something for everyone' and attracts consumer attention.

3. *Pricing breadth:* line extensions give marketers the opportunity to offer a broader range of price points to capture a wider audience.

4. *Excess capacity:* many companies have added faster production lines without closing older ones. Such manufacturing capabilities can often be modified to produce line extensions.

5. *Short-term gain:* many managers believe line extensions offer immediate rewards with minimal risk. Similar to sales promotions, line extensions are seen as a dependable, quick fix to improve sales.

6. *Competitive intensity:* many managers also believe that extensions can expand the retail shelf space for the category or at least that amount devoted to the brand itself. Frequent line extensions are often used by major brands to raise the admission price to the category for newly branded or own label competitors and to drain the limited resources of third- and fourth-place brands.

Brand Briefing 12.14 *continued*

7. *Trade pressure:* the proliferation of retail channels – often demanding their own special versions of the brand to suit their marketing needs or to reduce price shopping by consumers – necessitates a more varied product line.

Quelch and Kenny continue by noting that, although it is easy to see why line extensions have been so widely embraced, managers are also discovering problems and risks of brand proliferation.

- *Weaker line logic:* because managers often extend a line without removing existing items, the strategic role of each item becomes muddled. As a result, retailers may fail to stock the entire line or even appropriate items. A disorganized product line may result in consumers seeking out a simple, all-purpose product as a result.

- *Lower brand loyalty:* although line extensions can help a single brand satisfy a consumer's diverse needs, they can also motivate customers to seek variety and hence indirectly encourage brand switching. If line extensions result in cannibalization, a suboptimal shift in marketing support or a blurring of image, the long-term health of the brand franchise will be weakened.

- *Underexploited ideas:* some products justify the creation of a new brand and potential long-term profits may suffer if such products are introduced as an extension.

- *Stagnant category demand:* a review of several product categories (pet food, crackers and biscuits, ketchup, coffee, shampoo and conditioner, cake mix and icing and pasta sauce) reveals that line extensions rarely expand total category demand.

- *Poorer trade relationships:* an explosion of extensions in virtually every product category has put a squeeze on shelf space. As manufacturers' credibility has declined, retailers have allocated more shelf space to their own label products. Competition between manufacturers for limited shelf space has escalated overall promotion expenditures and shifted margin to increasingly powerful retailers.

- *More competitor opportunities:* by spreading marketing efforts across a range of line extensions, some of the most popular entries in the brand line may be vulnerable to well-positioned and supported competitors.

- *Increased costs:* although marketers can correctly anticipate many of the increased costs of extensions, other possible complications may be overlooked, such as: fragmentation of the marketing effort and dilution of the brand image; increased production complexities resulting from shorter production runs and more frequent line changeovers; more errors in forecasting demand; increased

Brand Briefing 12.14 *continued*

logistics complexity; increased supplier costs; and distraction of the research and development group from product development.

- *Hidden costs:* although these increased costs may make it difficult for a line extension to increase demand enough or command a high enough margin to achieve profitability, they remain hidden for several reasons. Traditional cost accounting systems allocate overheads to items in proportion to their sales, which can overburden the high sellers and undercharge the slow movers. Moreover, because line extensions are added one at a time, it is easy to overlook broader cost considerations that may affect or be affected by the entire brand line.

Line extensions also carry inherent risks due to their contribution to the already overwhelming number of choices consumers face (see Brand Briefing 12.6) With 8 varieties of Budweiser and 35 versions of Crest already on the market, each successive line extension threatens to drive choice-saturated consumers to competing brands with fewer varieties.[122]

Quelch and Kenny conclude by offering eight directives to help marketing managers improve their product line strategies.

1. *Improve cost accounting:* study, in detail, the absolute and incremental costs associated with the production and distribution of each stockkeeping unit (SKU) from the beginning to the end of the value chain, accounting for timing of demand. Tackle underperforming SKUs and consider the incremental sales, costs and savings of adding a new one.

2. *Allocate resources to winners:* to avoid undersupporting new, up-and-coming SKUs and oversupporting those whose appeal may be weakening, use an accurate activity-based cost-accounting system combined with an annual zero-based appraisal of each unit to ensure a focused product line that optimizes the company's use of manufacturing capacity, advertising and promotion dollars, salesforce time and retail space.

3. *Research consumer behaviour:* make an effort to learn how consumers perceive and use each SKU, especially in terms of loyalty and switching patterns. Identify core items that have a long-standing appeal to loyal heavy users and other items that reinforce and expand usage among existing customers. Consider a third set of SKUs to attract new customers or to persuade multibrand users to buy more from the same line more often.

4. *Apply the line logic test:* ensure that everyone who may affect the success of the marketing campaign (eg, salespeople) is able to state in one sentence the strategic role that a given SKU plays in the brand line. Similarly, ensure

Brand Briefing 12.14 *continued*

that the consumer is able to understand quickly which SKU fits his or her needs.

5. *Co-ordinate marketing across the line:* adopt consistent and logical pricing and packaging to simplify understanding of the brand line by salespeople, trade partners, customers and others.

6. *Work with channel partners:* to improve trade relationships and new product acceptance, set up multifunctional teams to screen new product ideas and arrange in-store testing with leading trade customers to research, in advance, the sales and cost effects of adding SKUs to the brand line.

7. *Expect product-line turnover:* foster a climate in which product-line deletions are not only accepted but encouraged.

8. *Manage deletions:* if items identified as unprofitable cannot be quickly and easily restored to profitability, develop a deletion plan that addresses customers' needs while managing costs.

In related research, Reddy, Holak and Bhat studied the determinants of line extension success using data on 75 line extensions of 34 cigarette brands over 20 years (Figure 12.28).[123] Their findings reinforce many of the Quelch and Kenney conclusions, indicating that:

● line extensions of strong brands are more successful than those of weak brands;

● line extensions of symbolic brands enjoy greater market success than those of less symbolic brands;

● line extensions that receive strong advertising and promotional support are more successful than those that receive meagre support;

● line extensions entering earlier into a product sub-category are more successful than those entering later, but only if they are extensions of strong brands;

● company size and marketing competencies also play a part in an extension's success;

● earlier line extensions have helped in the market expansion of the parent brand;

● incremental sales generated by line extensions may more than compensate for the loss in sales due to cannibalization.

Despite the pitfalls of line extensions and the many considerations necessary to properly manage extensions, the allure of line extensions for companies remains

Brand Briefing 12.14 *continued*

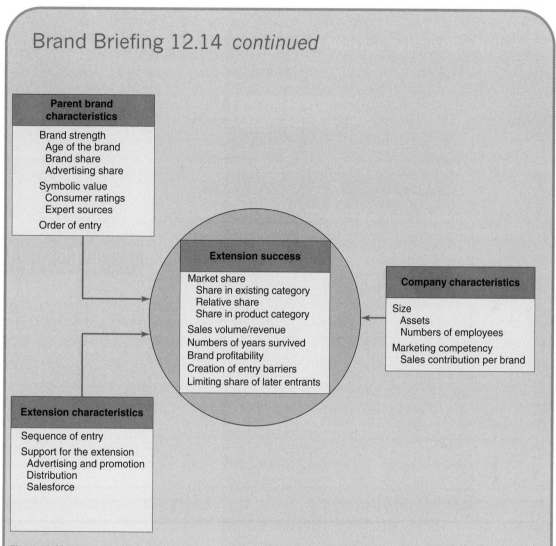

Figure 12.28   Line extension success model

strong, primarily due to the cost and risk involved in launching an entirely new brand. One report showed that line extensions take half as long to develop, cost far less to market and enjoy twice the success rate of major new brand launches (Figure 12.29). For these reasons, it comes as no surprise that, of the 1,561 new consumer packaged goods products introduced in 2004, 94 percent were line extensions or brand extensions, up from an average of 87 percent since 1995.[124]

Brand Briefing 12.14 *continued*

	Line extensions	Substantially new product
Annual sales	€17.5 million	€38.7 million
Average cost	€7.3 million	€18.2 million
Success rate	51%	26%
Average time to market	10 months	15 months
Average time to pay back investment	12 months	20 months

Cost of major product launch (€m)	
Concept screening	1.8
Concept and use test	0.7
TV commercial production	0.4
In-market test	0.9
Slotting fees	11.0
Consumer promotion	5.8
Advertising	29.2
Total	49.8

Figure 12.29   Brand launch economics

CHAPTER REVIEW

This chapter examined the role of extensions in managing brand equity. Brand extensions are when a firm uses an established brand name to introduce a new product. Brand extensions can be distinguished by whether the new product is being introduced in a product category currently served by the parent (a line extension) or in a different category (a category extension). Brand extensions can come in all forms. They offer many benefits but also can pose problems. This chapter outlined these pros and cons and offered guidelines to maximize the probability of extension success.

Assumptions regarding brand extensions are that consumers remember positive associations about the parent brand and that at least some of these positive associations will be evoked by the extension. Moreover, negative associations should not be transferred from the parent brand or created by the brand extension. The ability of the extension to establish its own equity will depend on the salience of parent brand associations in the minds of consumers in the extension context and the resulting favourability and uniqueness of any inferred associations. The ability of the extension to contribute to parent brand equity will depend on: how compelling the evidence is concerning the corresponding attribute or benefit association in the extension context; how relevant or diagnostic the extension evidence is concerning the attribute or benefit for the parent brand; and how strong existing attribute or benefit associations are held in consumer memory for the parent brand.

The chapter also outlined a process to evaluate brand extension opportunities. It was argued that extension strategies need to be considered by using managerial judgement and consumer research to systematically conduct the following steps: define actual and desired consumer knowledge about the brand; identify possible extension candidates; evaluate the potential of extension candidates; design marketing campaigns to launch extensions; and evaluate extension success and effects on parent brand equity. Finally, research findings concerning brand extensions were summarized that dealt with factors affecting the acceptance of a brand extension as well as the nature of feedback to the parent brand.

Discussion questions

1. Pick a brand extension. Use the models presented in the chapter to evaluate its ability to achieve its own equity as well as contribute to the equity of a parent brand. If you were the manager of that brand, what would you do differently?

2. Do you think a brand such as David Beckham will be able to transform its product meaning? What are the arguments for or against?

3. How successful do you predict these recently proposed extensions will be? Why?
   a. Mont Blanc (pens) and fragrances and other accessories (watches, cufflinks, sunglasses and pocket knives).
   b. Evian (water) and high-end spas.
   c. Starbucks (coffee) and film production and promotion.
   d. Trump (hotels and casinos) and vodka and mortgage services.

4. Consider the following brands, and discuss the extendability of each:[125]
   a. Harley-Davidson
   b. Red Bull
   c. Tommy Hilfiger
   d. Tesco
   e. Ryanair
   f. Barilla
   g. Grey Goose Vodka
   h. Victoria's Secret
   i. Hugo Boss
   j. Lego
   k. Harry Potter

5. There are four fake brand extensions in the following list; the other six were marketed at one point. Can you identify the fakes?[126]
   a. Ben-Gay Aspirin: pain relief that comes with a warm glow.
   b. Burberry Baby Stroller: for discriminating newborns.

c. Smith & Wesson Mountain Bikes: ride without fear.

d. Atlantic City Playing Cards: talcum-coated for easy shuffling.

e. Pond's Toothpaste: reduces the appearance of fine wines.

f. Slim Jim Beef-flavoured Throat Lozenges: for meatlovers who like to sing karaoke.

g. Frito-Lay Lemonade: a tangy, crunchy thirst quencher.

h. Cosmo Yoghurt: spoon it up, slim down those thighs.

i. Richard Simmons Sneakers: shake your cute little booty to the oldies.

j. Madonna Condoms: for men who are packing.

References and notes

[1] For a more comprehensive treatment, see Glen Urban and John Hauser, *Design and Marketing of New Products*, 2nd edn, Upper Saddle River, NJ: Prentice Hall, 1993.

[2] Peter Farquhar, 'Managing brand equity', *Marketing Research*, September 1989, 1: 24–33.

[3] 2006 TippingSprung Survey of Top Brand Extensions, third annual survey in collaboration with *Brandweek*.

[4] Edward M. Tauber, 'Brand leverage: strategy for growth in a cost controlled world', *Journal of Marketing Research*, August/September 1988, 28: 26–30.

[5] Robert M. McMath, 'The vagaries of brand equity', paper presented at the ARF Fourth Annual Advertising and Promotion Workshop, 12–13 February 1992.

[6] Byung-Do Kim and Mary W. Sullivan, 'The effect of brand experience on extension choice probabilities: an empirical analysis', working paper, University of Chicago Graduate School of Business, 1995.

[7] Henry J. Claycamp and Lucien E. Liddy, 'Prediction of new product performance: an analytical approach', *Journal of Marketing Research*, November 1969: 414–20.

[8] Kevin Lane Keller and David A. Aaker, 'The effects of sequential introduction of brand extensions', *Journal of Marketing Research*, February 1992, 29: 35–50; John Milewicz and Paul Herbig, 'Evaluating the brand extension decision using a model of reputation building', *Journal of Product & Brand Management*, 1994, 3 (1): 39–47.

[9] See also Jonlee Andrews, 'Rethinking the effect of perceived fit on customers' evaluations of new products', *Journal of the Academy of Marketing Science*, 1995, 23 (1): 4–14.

[10] David B. Montgomery, 'New product distribution: an analysis of supermarket buyer decisions', *Journal of Marketing Research*, 1978, 12 (3): 255–64.

[11] David A. Aaker and Ziv Carmon, 'The effectiveness of brand name strategies at creating brand recall', working paper, University of California at Berkeley, 1992.

[12] Mary W. Sullivan, 'Brand extensions: when to use them', *Management Science*, June 1992, 38 (6): 793–806.

[13] Daniel C. Smith, 'Brand extension and advertising efficiency: what can and cannot be expected', *Journal of Advertising Research*, November/December 1992: 11–20. See also Daniel C. Smith and C. Whan Park, 'The effects of brand extensions on market share and advertising efficiency', *Journal of Marketing Research*, August 1992, 29: 296–313.

[14] Al Ries, 'Understanding marketing psychology and the halo effect', *Advertising Age*, 17 April 2006; Mike Musgrove, 'At 30, Apple is mainstream – and a target', *Washington Post*, 7 April 2006: F1.

[15] Joff Wild, 'A trademark minefield out there', *The Financial Times*, 22 July 2002: 15.

[16]Laurie Freeman, 'Helene Curtis relies on finesse', *Advertising Age*, 14 July 1986: 2.

[17]Theodore Levitt, 'Marketing myopia', *Harvard Business Review,* July–August 1960: 45–6.

[18]Naomi Aoki, 'Beyond the bag', *Boston Globe*, 26 September 2004: E1.

[19]Keller and Aaker, 'Effects of sequential introduction of brand extensions'.

[20]Jeff Cioletti, 'It's da balm!', *Beverage World*, December 2004: 37.

[21]Kevin Goldman, 'Old Spice's familiar sailor is lost at sea', *Wall Street Journal*, 10 September 1993: B2; Jane L. Levere, 'A guy's guy tired of plain old soap? Old Spice is counting on it', *New York Times*, 1 August 2003.

[22]Barry Schwartz, *The Paradox of Choice: Why more is less*, New York: Ecco, 2004.

[23]Laura Shanahan, 'Designated shopper', *Brandweek*, 26 March 2001: 46.

[24]Robert Berner, 'There goes the Rainbow Nut Crunch', *BusinessWeek*, 19 July 2004: 38.

[25]Ibid.

[26]Ira Teinowitz and Jennifer Lawrence, 'Brand proliferation attacked', *Advertising Age*, 10 May 1993: 1, 48. The product categories studied were pasta sauce, toilet tissue, pet food, salad dressing, cereal and toothpaste.

[27]For additional support, see Peter Boatwright and Joseph C. Nunes, 'Reducing assortment: an attribute-based approach', *Journal of Marketing*, July 2001, 65: 50–63.

[28]Robert Berner, 'There goes the Rainbow Nut Crunch'.

[29]B. G. Yovovich, 'Hit and run: Cadillac's costly mistake', *Adweek's Marketing Week*, 8 August 1988: 24.

[30]Sullivan, 'Measuring image spillovers.'

[31]Maureen Morrin, 'The impact of brand extensions on parent brand memory structures and retrieval processes', *Journal of Marketing Research,* 1999, 36 (4): 517–25.

[32]Al Ries and Jack Trout, *Positioning: The battle for your mind*, New York: McGraw-Hill, 1985.

[33]Joseph Weber, 'Scott rolls out a risky strategy', *BusinessWeek*, 22 May 1995: 48.

[34]Alessandra Galloni, 'Inside out: at Gucci, Mr Polet's new design upends rules for high fashion', *Wall Street Journal*, 9 August 2005: A1.

[35]Teri Agins, 'Bringing chic to sheets', *Wall Street Journal*, 8 September 2004.

[36]www.virgin.com, 22 July 2007.

[37]For a conceptual review of brand extension literature, see Sandor Czellar, 'Consumer attitude toward brand extensions: an integrative model and research propositions', *International Journal of Research in Marketing*, 2003, 20: 97–115.

[38]Catherine W. M. Yeung and Robert S. Wyer Jr, 'Does loving a brand mean loving its products? The role of brand-elicited affect in brand extension evaluations', *Journal of Marketing Research*, November 2005, 62: 495–506.

[39]Stijn M. J. Van Osselaer and Joseph W. Alba, 'Locus of equity and brand extension', *Journal of Consumer Research,* March 2003, 29: 539–50.

[40]Edward M. Tauber, 'Brand leverage: strategy for growth in a cost-control world', *Journal of Advertising Research*, August/September 1988: 26–30.

[41]Adam Bass, 'Brand extensions: marketing in inner space', brandchannel.com

[42]Vanitha Swaminathan, Richard J. Fox and Srinivas K. Reddy, 'The impact of brand extension introduction on choice', *Journal of Marketing*, 2001, 65 (4): 1–15.

[43]B. Loken and D. Roedder John, 'Diluting brand beliefs: when do brand extensions have a negative impact?', *Journal of Marketing*, 1993, 57 (7): 71–84.

[44]Dale Buss, 'Making tracks beyond tires', *Brandweek*, 15 September 2003: 16.

[45]Claudia H. Deutsch, 'Name brands embrace some less-well-off kinfolk', *New York Times*, 24 June 2005: C7.

[46]David A. Aaker, 'Should you take your brand where the action is?', *Harvard Business Review*, September-October 1997: 135.

[47]For a description of how marketing managers make brand extension decisions in practice, see Edwin J. Nijssen and Clara Agustin, 'Brand extensions: a manager's perspective', *Journal of Brand Management*, October 2005, 13 (1): 33–49.

[48]Gillian Oakenfull, Edward Blair, Betsy Gelb and Peter Dacin, 'Measuring brand meaning', *Journal of Advertising Research*, September–October 2000: 43–53.

[49]John M. Murphy, *Brand Strategy*, New York: Prentice Hall, 1990.

[50]Andrea Rothman, 'France's Bic bets US consumers will go for perfume on the cheap', *Wall Street Journal*, 12 January 1989: B6.

[51]Seema Nayyar, 'In your face', *Brandweek*, 7 December 1992; Dave Kansas, 'Mouthwash makers see sales evaporate', *Wall Street Journal*, 1 December 1992; Jennifer Reingold, 'Above the neck', *FW*, 18 January 1994; 'Oral care products: mouthwashes', *OTC Update*, 1 September 1996.

[52]Murphy, *Brand Strategy*.

[53]Jean-Noël Kapferer, *Strategic Brand Management*, London: Kogan Page, 1992.

[54]Franziska Volckner and Henrik Sattler, 'Drivers of brand extensions success', *Journal of Marketing*, April 2006, 70: 18–34.

[55]Jim Arndorfer, 'Bud Select cannibalizes sales of sibling brands', *Advertising Age*, 11 April 2005: 3.

[56]Rob Pegoraro, 'Fast forward', *Washington Post*, 29 May 2005: F6.

[57]For a comprehensive view of the determinants of brand extension success, see Franziska Volckner and Henrik Sattler, 'Drivers of brand extensions success', *Journal of Marketing*, April 2006, 70: 18–34.

[58]Mita Sujan, 'Nature and structure of product categories', working paper, Pennsylvania State University, 1990; Joan Myers-Levy and Alice M. Tybout, 'Schema congruity as a basis for product evaluation', *Journal of Consumer Research*, June 1989, 16: 39–54.

[59]Deborah Roedder John and Barbara Loken, 'Diluting brand equity: the impact of brand extensions', *Journal of Marketing*, July 1993: 71–84.

[60]David Boush and Barbara Loken, 'A process-tracing study of brand extension evaluations', *Journal of Marketing Research*, February 1991, 28: 16–28; Cathy L. Hartman, Linda L. Price and Calvin P. Duncan, 'Consumer evaluation of franchise extension products: a categorization processing perspective', *Advances in Consumer Research*, Vol. 17, Provo, UT: Association for Consumer Research, 1990: 120–6.

[61]David A. Aaker and Kevin Lane Keller, 'Consumer evaluations of brand extensions', *Journal of Marketing*, January 1990, 54: 27–41.

[62]P. A. Bottomly and Stephen Holden, 'Do we really know how consumers evaluate brand extensions? Empirical generalizations based on secondary analysis of eight studies', *Journal of Marketing Research*, November 2001: 494–500.

[63]David Boush, Shannon Shipp, Barbara Loken, Ezra Gencturk, Susan Crockett, Ellen Kennedy, Betty Minshall, Dennis Misurell, Linda Rochford and Jon Strobel, 'Affect generalization to similar and dissimilar line extensions', *Psychology and Marketing*, fall 1987, 4: 225–41.

[64]On the other hand, applying Mandler's congruity theory, Meyers-Levy and her colleagues showed that suggested products associated with moderately incongruent brand names could be preferred over ones that were associated with either congruent or extremely incongruent brand names. They interpreted this finding in terms of the ability of moderately incongruent brand extensions to elicit more processing from consumers that could be

satisfactorily resolved (assuming consumers could identify a meaningful relationship between the brand name and the product). See J. Meyers-Levy, T. A. Louie and M. T. Curren, 'How does the congruity of brand names affect evaluations of brand name extensions?', *Journal of Applied Psychology*, 1994, 79 (1): 46–53.

[65]Deborah MacInnis and Kent Nakamoto, 'Cognitive associations and product category comparisons: the role of knowledge structures and context', working paper, University of Arizona, 1990.

[66]C. Whan Park, Sandra Milberg and Robert Lawson, 'Evaluation of brand extensions: the role of product-level similarity and brand concept consistency', *Journal of Consumer Research*, September 1991, 18: 185–93.

[67]Susan M. Broniarczyk and Joseph W. Alba, 'The importance of the brand in brand extension', *Journal of Marketing Research*, May 1994, 31: 214–28. A Crest toothbrush was later introduced as Crest Complete.

[68]T. H. A. Bijmolt, M. Wedel, R. G. M. Pieters and W. S. DeSarbo, 'Judgements of brand similarity', *International Journal of Research in Marketing*, 1998, 15: 249–68.

[69]Sheri Bridges, Kevin Lane Keller and Sanjay Sood, 'Explanatory links and the perceived fit of brand extensions: the role of dominant parent brand associations and communication strategies', *Journal of Advertising*, 2000, 29 (4): 1–11.

[70]B. H. Schmitt and L. Dubé, 'Contextualized representations of brand extensions: are feature lists or frames the basic components of consumer cognition?', *Marketing Letters*, 1992, 3 (2): 115–26.

[71]D. M. Boush, 'Brand name effects on interproduct similarity judgments', *Marketing Letters*, 1997, 8 (4): 419–27.

[72]D. C. Smith and Jonlee Andrews, 'Rethinking the effect of perceived fit on customers' evaluations of new products', *Journal of the Academy of Marketing Science*, 1995, 23 (1): 4–14.

[73]Alokparna Basu Monga and Deborah Roedder John, 'Cultural differences in brand extension evaluation: the influence of analytic versus holistic thinking', *Journal of Consumer Research*, March 2007; Yeosun Yoon and Zeynep Gürhan-Canli, 'Cross-cultural differences in brand extension evaluations: the effect of holistic and analytic processing', *Proceedings of the Society for Consumer Psychology Conference*, American Psychological Association, 2002.

[74]A. V. Muthukrishnan and Barton A. Weitz, 'Role of product knowledge in brand extensions', in *Advances in Consumer Research*, Vol. 18, eds Rebecca H. Holman and Michael R. Solomon, Provo, UT: Association for Consumer Research, 1990: 407–13.

[75]Eyal Maoz and Alice M. Tybout, 'The moderating role of involvement and differentiation in the evaluation of brand extensions', *Journal of Consumer Psychology*, 2002, 12 (2): 119–31.

[76]Broniarcysyk and Alba, 'Importance of the brand'.

[77]Keller and Aaker, 'Effects of sequential introduction of brand extensions'.

[78]See also Arvind Rangaswamy, Raymond Burke and Terence A. Oliva, 'Brand equity and the extendibility of brand names', *International Journal of Research in Marketing*, 1993, 10: 61–75.

[79]See, for example, Peter H. Farquhar and Paul M. Herr, 'The dual structure of brand associations', in *Brand Equity and Advertising: Advertising's role in building strong brands*, eds David A. Aaker and Alexander L. Biel, Hillsdale, NJ: Lawrence Erlbaum Associates, 1993: 263–77.

[80]Ian M. Lewis, 'Brand equity or why the board of directors needs marketing research', paper presented at the ARF Fifth Annual Advertising and Promotion Workshop, 1 February 1993.

[81]Stephen Phillips, 'Chiquita may be a little too ripe', *BusinessWeek*, 30 April 1990: 100.

[82]Robert D. Hof, 'A washout for Clorox?', *BusinessWeek*, 9 July 1990: 32–3; Alicia Swasy, 'P&G and Clorox wade into battle over the bleaches', *Wall Street Journal*, 16 January 1989: 5; Maria Shao, 'A bright idea that Clorox wishes it never had', *BusinessWeek*, 24 June 1991: 118–19.

[83]Peter H. Farquhar, Julia Y. Han, Paul M. Herr and Yuji Ijiri, 'Strategies for leveraging master brands', *Marketing Research,* September 1992: 32–43.

[84]P. M. Herr, P. H. Farquhar and R. H. Fazio, 'Impact of dominance and relatedness on brand extensions', *Journal of Consumer Psychology,* 1996, 5 (2): 135–59.

[85]Farquhar, Han, Herr and Ijiri, 'Strategies for leveraging master brands'.

[86]Bridges, Keller, and Sood, 'Explanatory links'.

[87]C. Joiner and B. Loken, 'The inclusion effect and category-based induction: theory and application to brand categories', *Journal of Consumer Psychology,* 1998, 7 (2): 101–29.

[88]Bridges, Keller, and Sood, 'Explanatory links'.

[89]Frank Kardes and Chris Allen, 'Perceived variability and inferences about brand extensions', in *Advances in Consumer Research*, Vol. 18, eds Rebecca H. Holman and Michael R. Solomon, Provo, UT: Association for Consumer Research, 1990: 392–8.

[90]Subramanian Balachander and Sanjoy Ghose, 'Reciprocal spillover effect: a strategic benefit of brand extensions', *Journal of Marketing*, January 2003, 67: 4–13.

[91]See also Sandy D. Jap, 'An examination of the effects of multiple brand extensions on the brand concept', in *Advances in Consumer Research*, Vol. 20, Provo, UT: Association for Consumer Research, 1993: 607–11, as well as Vanitha Swaminathan, 'Sequential brand extensions and brand choice behavior', *Journal of Business Research*, June 2003, 56: 431–42.

[92]Murphy, *Brand Strategy.*

[93]Simon Brooke, 'Spoiled goods', *Marketing*, 22 June 2005: 32.

[94]Boush and Loken, 'A process-tracing study'.

[95]Tom Meyvis and Chris Janiszewski, 'When are broader brands stronger brands? An accessibility perspective on the success of brand extensions', *Journal of Consumer Research*, September 2004, 31: 346–57.

[96]Peter Dacin and Daniel C. Smith, 'The effect of brand portfolio characteristics on consumer evaluations of brand extensions', *Journal of Marketing Research,* May 1994, 31: 229–42. See also Boush and Loken, 'A process-tracing study'; and Niraj Dawar, 'Extensions of broad brands: the role of retrieval in evaluations of fit', *Journal of Consumer Psychology*, 1996, 5 (2): 189–207.

[97]M. W. Sullivan, 'Brand extensions: when to use them', *Management Science*, 1992, 38 (6): 793–806.

[98]P. DeGraba and M. W. Sullivan, 'Spillover effects, cost savings, R&D and the use of brand extensions', *International Journal of Industrial Organization*, 1995, 13: 229–48.

[99]Deborah Roedder John and Barbara Loken, 'Diluting brand beliefs: when do brand extensions have a negative impact?', *Journal of Marketing,* summer 1993, 57: 71.

[100]Jean B. Romeo, 'The effect of negative information on the evaluation of brand extensions and the family brand', in *Advances in Consumer Research*, Vol. 18, eds Rebecca H. Holman and Michael R. Solomon, Provo, UT: Association for Consumer Research, 1990: 399–406.

[101]D. Roedder John, B. Loken and C. Joiner, 'The negative impact of extensions: can flagship products be diluted?', *Journal of Marketing*, January 1998, 62: 19–32.

[102]Z. Gürhan-Canli and D. Maheswaran, 'The effects of extensions on brand name dilution and enhancement', *Journal of Marketing Research*, 1998, 35 (11): 464–73. See also Rohini Ahluwalia

and Zeynep Gurhan-Canli, 'The effects of extensions on the family brand name: an accessi-bility-diagnosticity perspective', *Journal of Consumer Research*, December 2000, 27: 371–81.

[103]S. J. Milberg, C. W. Park and M. S. McCarthy, 'Managing negative feedback effects associ-ated with brand extensions: the impact of alternative branding strategies', *Journal of Consumer Psychology*, 1997, 6 (2): 119–40.

[104]V. R. Lane and R. Jacobson, 'Stock market reactions to brand extension announcements: the effects of brand attitude and familiarity', *Journal of Marketing*, 1995, 59 (1): 63–77.

[105]A. Kirmani, S. Sood and S. Bridges, 'The ownership effect in consumer responses to brand line stretches', *Journal of Marketing*, 1999, 63 (1): 88–101.

[106]Maureen Morrin, 'The impact of brand extensions on parent brand memory structures and retrieval processes', *Journal of Marketing Research*, 1999, 36 (4) : 517–25.

[107]For related research, see Carol M. Motely and Srinivas K. Reddy, 'Moving up or down: an investigation of repositioning strategies', working paper 93–363, University of Georgia, Athens, 1993; and Carol M. Motely, 'Vertical extensions: strategies for changing brand pres-tige', working paper, University of Georgia, Athens, 1993.

[108]Joshua Levine, 'Pride goeth before a fall', *Forbes*, 29 May 1989: 306.

[109]Jerry Shriver, 'Gallo, Kendall-Jackson uncork fresh identities', *USA Today*, 17 March 2006: 8D.

[110]Farquhar, Han, Herr and Ijiri, 'Strategies for leveraging master brands'.

[111]Lori Bongiorno, 'How Tiffany's took the tarnish off', *BusinessWeek*, 26 August 1996: 67–9.

[112]T. Randall, K. Ulrich and D. Reibstein, 'Brand equity and vertical product line extent', *Marketing Science*, 1998, 17 (4): 356–79.

[113]Kirmani, Sood and Bridges, 'The ownership effect'.

[114]See also Hyeong Min Kim, 'Evaluations of moderately typical products: the role of within- versus cross-manufacturer comparisons', *Journal of Consumer Psychology*', 16 (1): 70–8; Richard R. Klink and Daniel C. Smith, 'Threats to the external validity of brand extension research', *Journal of Marketing Research*, August 2001, 38: 326–35.

[115]Bridges, Keller and Sood, 'Explanatory links'.

[116]V. R. Lane, 'The impact of ad repetition and ad content on consumer perceptions of incongruent extensions', *Journal of Marketing*, 2000, 64 (4): 80–91. See also, Hyeong Min Kim, 'Evaluations of moderately typical products.

[117]Michael J. Barone, Paul W. Miniard and Jean B. Romeo, 'The influence of positive mood on brand extension evaluations', *Journal of Consumer Research*, 2000, 26 (3): 386–400. See also Michael J. Barone and Paul W. Miniard, 'Mood and brand extension judgments: asymmetric effects for desirable versus undesirable brands', *Journal of Consumer Psychology*, 12 (4): 283–90.

[118]Kevin Lane Keller and Sanjay Sood, 'The effects of product experience and branding strate-gies on brand evaluations', working paper, University of California, Los Angeles, 2000.

[119]L. Buchanan, C. J. Simmons and B. A. Bickart, 'Brand equity dilution: retailer display and context brand effects', *Journal of Marketing Research*, 1999, 36 (8): 345–55.

[120]Michael S. McCarthy, Timothy B. Heath and Sandra J. Milberg, 'New brands versus brand extensions, attitudes versus choice: experimental evidence for theory and practice', *Marketing Letters*, February 2001, 12: 75–90.

[121]John A. Quelch and David Kenny, 'Extend profits, not product lines', *Harvard Business Review*, September–October 1994: 153–60. See also the commentary on this article and the issue of product line management in 'The logic of line extensions', *Harvard Business Review*, November–December 1994: 53–62.

[122]'Line extensions: less is more', *Advertising Age*, 28 February 2005: 26.

[123]Srinivas K. Reddy, Susan L. Holak and Sbodh Bhat, 'To extend or not to extend: success determinants of line extensions', *Journal of Marketing Research*, May 1994, 31: 243–62. For conceptual discussion, see Kalpesh Kaushik Desai and Wayne D. Hoyer, 'Line extensions: a categorization and an information processing perspective', in *Advances in Consumer Research*, Vol. 20, Provo, UT: Association for Consumer Research, 1993: 599–606.

[124]Jack Neff, 'Small ball: marketers rely on line extensions', *Advertising Age*, 11 April 2005: 10.

[125]For additional insights into extendability of these brands, refer to Jeff Ousbourne, 'Feel the stretch', *MBA Jungle*, www.jungleonline.com

[126]The fakes are Burberry Baby Stroller, Atlantic City Playing Cards, Slim Jim Beef Jerky Throat Lozenges, Richard Simmons Sneakers. From Jeff Ousbourne, 'Feel the stretch', *MBA Jungle*, www.jungleonline.com

13 Managing brands over time

PREVIEW

As noted in Chapter 1, one of the challenges of managing brands is the many changes that have occurred in recent years. The marketing environment will continue to evolve and change, often in significant ways, in the coming years. Shifts in consumer behaviour, competitive strategies, government regulations or other aspects of the marketing environment can profoundly affect the fortunes of a brand. Besides these external forces, a company may engage in activities and changes in strategic focus or direction that may necessitate adjustments in the way its brands are marketed. Consequently, effective brand management requires proactive strategies designed to at least maintain – if not actually enhance – customer-based brand equity in the face of all of these forces.

This chapter considers how best to manage brands over time. Effective brand management requires taking a long-term view of marketing decisions. Any action taken as part of its marketing campaign has the potential to change consumer knowledge in terms of some aspect of brand awareness or brand image. These changes in consumer brand knowledge will have an indirect effect on the success of *future* marketing activities. Thus, from the perspective of customer-based brand equity, it is important to consider how the changes in brand awareness and image that could result from a particular marketing decision may help or hurt subsequent marketing decisions (Figure 13.1). For example, the frequent use of sales promotions involving temporary price cuts may create or strengthen a 'discount' association with the brand, with potentially adverse implications on customer loyalty and responses to future price changes or non-price-orientated marketing communication efforts. Unfortunately, marketers may have a particularly difficult time trying to anticipate future consumer response: if the new knowledge structures that will influence future consumer response do not exist until the short-term marketing actions occur, how can future consumer response be realistically simulated to permit accurate predictions?

The main assertion of this chapter is that brand equity must be actively managed over time by reinforcing the brand meaning and, if necessary, by making adjustments to the marketing campaign to identify new sources of brand equity. In considering these two topics, this chapter examines a number of issues, including the advantages of maintaining brand consistency, the importance of protecting sources of brand equity, tradeoffs between fortifying and leveraging brands, and possible brand revitalization strategies. Brand Briefing 13.11 considers how to change a corporate name.

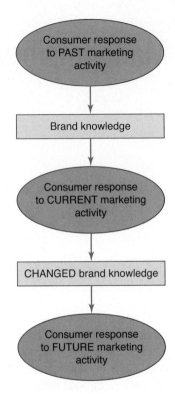

Figure 13.1   Understanding the long-term effects of marketing on brand equity

REINFORCING BRANDS

How should brand equity be reinforced over time? How can marketers make sure that consumers have the desired knowledge structures such that their brands continue to have the necessary sources of brand equity? In a general sense, brand equity is reinforced by marketing actions that consistently convey the meaning of the brand to consumers in terms of brand awareness and brand image. Questions marketers should consider are as follows.

- What products does the brand represent, what benefits does it supply and what needs does it satisfy? For example, Kellogg's has expanded from cereals into Nutri-Grain granola bars and other products, cementing its reputation as a 'maker of healthy breakfast and snack foods'.
- How does the brand make those products superior? What strong, favourable and unique brand associations exist in the minds of consumers? For example, through product development and the introduction of brand extensions, Black & Decker is now seen as offering 'innovative designs' in its small appliance products.

Both of these issues – brand meaning in terms of products, benefits and needs as well as in terms of product differentiation – depend on the firm's general approach to product development, branding strategies and other strategic concerns, as discussed in Chapters 11 and 12. This section reviews other important considerations concerning brand reinforcement.

Maintaining brand consistency

Without question, the most important consideration in reinforcing brands is the consistency of the marketing support that the brand receives, both in terms of the amount and nature of that support. Brand consistency is critical to maintaining the strength and favourability of brand associations. Brands that receive inadequate support in terms of shrinking research and development and marketing communication budgets run the risk of becoming technologically disadvantaged – or even obsolete – as well as out of date, irrelevant or forgotten.

Market leaders and failures

From the perspective of maintaining consumer loyalty, inadequate marketing support is especially dangerous when combined with price increases.

In terms of qualitative aspects of positioning, even a cursory examination of the brands that have maintained market leadership for the last 50 or 100 years or so is a testament to the advantages of staying consistent. Brands such as Armani and Coca-Cola have been remarkably consistent in their strategies once they achieved a pre-eminent market position.

Perhaps an even more compelling demonstration of the benefits of consistency is to consider the fortunes of those brands that have been inconsistent – for example, by constantly changing ad agencies.

Gateway

Like its rival Dell, Gateway achieved success in the 1990s by selling computers directly to consumers. But unlike Dell, Gateway's fortunes suffered in the 2000s as the company endured four years of falling profits between 2001 and 2004. In 2005, its stock traded below €2 a share, off from a peak of over €68.4 in 1999, and it fell out of the Fortune 500 rankings. Analysts blamed Gateway's lack of execution on its core PC business as it pursued new growth areas with a succession of strategies, such as the 1996 introduction of own-brand Gateway Country Stores, 1998's launch of internet access provision, a move into branded consumer electronics in 2002 and a 2004 merger with PC maker eMachines. Remarked one analyst: 'I've been following the company since 2000 and it's had almost as many strategies as years.'[1] Interim chief executive Rick Snyder, appointed in 2006, admitted that Gateway 'took a simple business and made it more complex than it needed to be'. Though Snyders' turnaround strategy was a simpler approach involving marketing high- and mid-range PCs to sophisticated users and capturing corporate accounts with cost-effective models, it reflected yet another change of direction.[2]

Consistency and change

Consistency does not mean, however, that marketers should avoid making changes to the marketing campaign. On the contrary, the opposite can be true: being consistent in managing brand equity may require tactical shifts and changes to maintain the strategic thrust and direction of a brand. As earlier chapters in this book described, brand awareness and brand image can be created, maintained or improved through marketing campaigns. The tactics that may be most effective for a particular brand at any one time can vary. As a consequence, prices may move up or down, product features may be added or dropped, ad campaigns may employ different creative strategies and slogans, brand extensions may be introduced or withdrawn and so on to create the same desired knowledge structures in consumers' minds. Nevertheless, despite these changes in marketing, the strategic positioning of many leading brands has remained remarkably consistent. A contributing factor to the success of these brands is that, despite tactical changes, key elements of the marketing campaign are always retained and continuity has been preserved in brand meaning over time.

In fact, many brands have kept a key creative element in their marketing communications campaigns over the years and, as a result, have created 'advertising equity'. For example, Jack Daniels whisky has stuck with rural scenes of its Tennessee home and the slogan 'Charcoal-mellowed drop by drop' for decades. Demonstrating the latent value of past advertising, recent years have seen the return of such advertising icons as Colonel Sanders for KFC, who appears in advertising and packaging focused on the restaurant's Southern roots, albeit with a thinner face and a red apron instead of a three-piece suit.[3] Dubbed *retro branding* or *retro advertising* by some marketing pundits, the tactic is a means of tying in with past advertising that was, and perhaps could still be, a source of brand equity. Most important, it may activate and strengthen brand associations that would be impossible to recreate with new advertising. From an awareness standpoint, such efforts obviously make sense. At the same time, it is important to determine whether these old advertising elements have enduring meaning with older consumers and, at the same time, can be made relevant to younger consumers. More generally, the entire marketing campaign should be examined to determine which elements are making a strong contribution to brand equity and therefore must be protected, as discussed next.

Protecting sources of brand equity

Consistency therefore should be viewed in terms of strategic direction and not necessarily the tactics employed by the marketing campaign for the brand at any one time. Unless there is some change with consumers, the competition or the company that makes the strategic positioning of the brand less powerful (eg, changes that somehow make the points of difference or points of parity for the brand less desirable or deliverable), there is likely to be little need to deviate from a successful positioning. Although brands should always look for powerful new sources of brand equity, the priority under these circumstances is to preserve and defend those sources of brand equity that already exist, as illustrated by the examples of Cascade and Intel.

While rolling out its value-pricing initiative in the USA, Procter & Gamble made a minor change in the formulation of its Cascade dishwasher powder, primarily to save costs. As a result, the product was not quite as effective as it had been under certain, albeit atypical, water conditions. After discovering the fact, one of P&G's chief competitors, Lever Brothers, began running comparative ads for its Sunlight brand that claimed: 'Sunlight fights spots better than Cascade.' Since the consumer benefit of 'virtually spotless' is a key brand association and source of brand equity for Cascade, P&G reacted swiftly. It returned Cascade to its original formula and contacted

Lever Brothers to inform that company of the change, effectively forcing it to stop running the Sunlight ads. As this episode demonstrates, P&G fiercely defends the equity of its brands, perhaps explaining why so many of its brands have had such longevity.

As another example, consider the public relations problems encountered by Intel with the 'floating decimal' problem in its Pentium microprocessors in December 1994. Although the flaw in the chip resulted in miscalculation problems in only rare instances, Intel was probably at fault – as company executives now admit – for not identifying the problem and proposing remedies to consumers sooner. Once the problem became public, Intel endured an agonizing six-week period during which the company was the focus of media criticism for its reluctance to publicize the problem and its failure to offer replacement chips. Two sources of brand equity for Intel microprocessors such as the Pentium – emphasized throughout the company's marketing campaign – are 'power' and 'safety'. Although consumers primarily think of safety in terms of upgradability, the perceptions of financial risk or other problems that might result from a potentially flawed chip should have created a sense of urgency within Intel to protect one of its prize sources of brand equity. Eventually, Intel capitulated and offered a replacement chip. Perhaps not surprisingly, only a very small percentage of consumers (an estimated 1 percent to 3 percent) actually requested a replacement, suggesting that it was Intel's stubbornness to act and not the defect per se that rankled many consumers. Although it was a painful episode, Intel maintains it learned a lot about how to manage its brand from it.

Ideally, key sources of brand equity are of enduring value. If so, these brand associations should be guarded and nurtured. Unfortunately, their value can easily be overlooked as marketers attempt to expand the meaning of their brands and add new product-related or non-product-related brand associations. The next section considers these types of tradeoffs. Brand Briefing 13.11 deals with the topic of corporate rebranding and name changes.

Fortifying versus leveraging

As Chapters 4 to 7 described, there are a number of ways to raise brand awareness and create strong, favourable and unique brand associations in consumer memory to build customer-based brand equity. In managing brand equity, it is important to recognize tradeoffs between those marketing activities that attempt to fortify and contribute to brand equity and those marketing activities that attempt to capitalize on existing brand equity to reap some financial benefit.

As noted in Chapter 2, the advantage of creating a brand with a high level of awareness and a positive brand image is that many benefits may accrue to the firm in terms of cost savings and revenue opportunities. Marketing campaigns can be designed that primarily attempt to capitalize on or perhaps even maximize these benefits – for example, by reducing advertising expenses, seeking increasingly higher price premiums or introducing brand extensions. The more that there is an attempt to realize or capitalize on brand equity benefits, however, the more likely it is that the brand and its sources of equity may become neglected and perhaps diminished. In other words, marketing actions that attempt to leverage the equity of a brand in different ways may come at the expense of other activities that may help to fortify the brand by maintaining or enhancing awareness of it and its image.

At some point, failure to fortify a brand will diminish its awareness and brand image. Without these sources of brand equity, the brand itself may not continue to yield as valuable benefits. Recall the problems encountered by Shell from inconsistent advertising support noted earlier.[4] Just as a failure to maintain a car eventually affects its performance, so too neglecting a brand, for whatever reason, can catch up with marketers.

Fine-tuning a marketing campaign

Although the tactics and marketing campaign are more likely to change than the positioning and strategic direction for a brand, tactics also should only be changed when there is evidence that they are no longer making the desired contributions to maintaining or strengthening brand equity.

Reinforcing brand meaning may depend on the nature of brand associations involved. Brand Briefing 13.1 outlines one perspective on ways to manage brand concepts. Several considerations play a particularly important role in reinforcing brand meaning in terms of product-related performance and non-product-related imagery associations, as follows.

Brand Briefing 13.1

Brand concept management (BCM)

In an award-winning academic article, C. W. Park, Bernard Jaworski and Deborah MacInnis present a normative framework termed *brand concept management* (BCM) for selecting, implementing and controlling brand image to enhance market performance. The framework consists of a sequential process of selecting, introducing, elaborating and fortifying a 'brand concept'. The brand concept guides positioning strategies, and hence the brand image, at each of these stages. The method for maintaining this concept–image linkage depends on whether the brand concept is functional, symbolic or experiential.

Specifically, the authors define a brand concept in terms of firm-selected brand meaning derived from basic consumer needs. For example, the concept for Domestos bleach is 'kills germs dead'. An important factor in influencing the selection of a brand concept is the different types of consumer needs that might prevail.

- *Functional needs:* these are defined as those that involve the search for products that solve consumption-related problems (eg, solve a current problem, prevent a potential problem, resolve conflict or restructure a frustrating situation).

Brand Briefing 13.1 *continued*

These needs are often linked to basic motivations (eg, physiological and safety needs) and are met by products with functional benefits. For example, functional benefits of a shampoo might be that it eliminates dandruff, removes greasiness, makes hair and scalp healthy and gives hair moisture and body. A brand with a *functional concept* is designed to solve externally generated consumption needs.

- *Symbolic needs:* these are defined as desires for products that meet internally generated needs for self-enhancement, role position, group membership, social approval or ego identification. Thus, consumers may value the prestige, exclusivity or fashionability of a brand because of how it relates to their self-concept. For example, symbolic benefits of a shampoo might be that it assures users that they are using a product only used by 'beautiful people' who appreciate the 'good things in life'. A brand with a *symbolic concept* is one designed to associate the individual with a desired group, role or self-image.

- *Experiential needs:* these are defined as desires for products that provide sensory pleasure, variety or cognitive stimulation. For example, experiential benefits of a shampoo might involve its scent and lather and the feelings of beauty and cleanliness from applying or using the product. A brand with an *experiential concept* aims to address these internally generated needs for stimulation or variety.

Once a broad needs-based concept has been selected, according to these researchers, it can be used to guide positioning decisions. For each of the three management stages, positioning strategies need to be implemented that enable consumers to: understand a brand image (introduction); perceive its steadily increasing value (elaboration); and generalize it to other products produced by the firm (fortification). Specifically, the *introductory stage* of BCM is a set of activities designed to establish a brand image and position in the marketplace during the period of market entry. During the elaboration stage, positioning strategies focus on enhancing the value of the brand's image so that its perceived superiority in relation to competitors can be established or sustained. At the final stage of BCM, the *fortification stage*, the aim is to link an elaborated brand image to the image of other products produced by the firm in different product classes.

Sources: C. W. Park, Bernard J. Jaworski and Deborah J. MacInnis, 'Strategic brand concept–image management',' *Journal of Marketing*, October 1986, 50: 135–45; Abraham H. Maslow, *Motivation and Personality*, 2nd edn, New York: Harper & Row, 1970; Geraldine Fennell, 'Consumer's perceptions of the product-use situations', *Journal of Marketing*, April 1978, 12: 38–47; John R. Rossiter and Larry Percy, *Advertising and Promotion Management*, New York: McGraw-Hill, 1987; Michael R. Solomon, 'The role of products as social stimuli: a symbolic interactionism perspective', *Journal of Consumer Research*, December 1983, 10: 319–29.

Product-related performance associations

For brands whose core associations are product-related performance attributes or benefits, innovation is critical to maintaining or enhancing brand equity. For example, after Timex watched brands such as Casio and Swatch gain significant market share by emphasizing digital technology and fashion (respectively) in their watches, it made innovative marketing changes. Within a short time, Timex introduced Indiglo glow-in-the dark technology, used popular models such as the Ironman in mass media advertising and launched new Timex shops to show off its products. Timex also bought the Guess and Monet brands to distribute through upmarket department stores and expand its brand portfolio. These innovations revived the brand's fortunes.[5]

For companies in categories as diverse as toys and entertainment products, personal care products and insurance, innovation is critical to success. For example, Progressive has become one of the most successful US car insurers in part due to consistent innovations in service. A pioneer in direct sales of insurance online, it was the first to offer prospective customers the ability to instantly compare price quotes from up to three other insurers. Other Progressive innovations include an accident 'concierge service' where Progressive representatives handle all aspects of the claims and repair process for its customers, and online policy management where customers can make payments and change coverage any time. See Brand Briefing 13.2 for a summary of how Gillette has built equity in its razors and blades categories through innovation.

Brand Briefing 13.2

Razor-sharp branding at Gillette

One of the strongest brands in the world is Gillette. The company owns roughly two-thirds of the US blade and razor market and even more in Europe and Latin America. In fact, more than 70 percent of its sales and profits come from overseas operations in 200 countries. Moreover, its 10 percent profit margin is substantially higher than at most packaged goods companies. How has Gillette been so successful? The company's marketing and branding practices provide a number of lessons for marketers.

Fundamentally, Gillette continually innovates to produce a demonstrably superior product. More than 40 percent of Gillette's sales in the first half of the 1990s came from new products. Gillette's credo is to 'increase spending in "growth drivers" – R&D, plants and equipment, and advertising – at least as fast as revenues go up'. As Gillette's former chief Alfred Zeien proclaimed: 'Good products come out of market research. Great products come from R&D.' Gillette spent more than 2 percent of its annual sales – €137 million – on R&D during the late 1990s, double the average for most consumer products companies. Gillette also backs its products with strong advertising and promotional support. TV ads often used a montage of

Brand Briefing 13.2 *continued*

slow-motion scenes of men shown in different roles interspersed with product shots with upbeat background music and the tagline 'The best a man can get.' Thus, Gillette's marketing can be seen as creating both strong performance and imagery associations.

The following is a history of Gillette's product innovations over 30 years.

- Trac II (1971): first twin-blade razor.
- Atra (1977): first twin-blade razor with a pivoting head.
- Good News (1976): top-selling disposable twin-blade razor.
- Atra Plus (1985): twin-blade razor with a lubricant strip.
- Sensor (1990): individually mounted twin blades.
- Sensor for Women (1992): first razor for women.
- Sensor Excel (1993): fitted with microfins that stretch skin for closer shave.
- Mach3 (1998): first triple-blade razor.
- M3 Power (2004): first disposable razor to include battery-powered vibration.
- Fusion (2006): first five-blade razor (included a single sixth blade on the top side of the cartridge).

Gillette considered the Mach3 to be the 'most important new product' in its history, and invested more than €513 million in R&D and manufacturing expenses, securing 35 patents in the process. The main advancement of the Mach3 was the triple blade, each designed to shave closer. During the launch year for the Mach3, Gillette set a marketing budget of €205 million globally and €68.4 million in the USA. The Mach3, which cost 35 percent more than the Sensor Excel, captured a stunning 35 percent of the razor market within two weeks of its launch. Mach3 surpassed the €684 million sales mark just 15 months after its debut. In 2001, Gillette released a women's version of the Mach3 called the Venus. Gillette spent €103 million on marketing for the worldwide Venus launch. In 2004, it upgraded the Mach3 by introducing the M3 Power, the first disposable razor to feature battery-powered vibration for a closer shave. A Venus version for women, called Venus Vibrance, soon followed.

Acquired by Procter & Gamble in 2005, the next year saw Gillette launch the six-bladed Fusion and Fusion Power razors. Gillette had spent €820 million on R&D since introducing Mach3 and spent more than €684 million to market the product to the world's 3.2 billion males. The payoff? A four-pack of Fusion cartridges cost double Mach3's original price.

Sources: Patricia Sellers, 'Brands, it's thrive or die', *Fortune*, 23 August 1993: 52–6; Linda Grant, 'Gillette knows shaving – and how to turn out hot new products', *Fortune*, 14 October 1996: 207–10; www.gillette.com; 'Gillette to launch massive Atra Plus advertising campaign', *PR Newswire*, 14 December 1988; William C. Symonds, 'Gillette's edge', *BusinessWeek*, 19 January 1998; Editorial, 'Gillette spends smart on Fusion', *Advertising Age*, 26 September 2005: 24.

Failure to innovate can have dire consequences. Facit was a leading Swedish company in mechanical calculators that missed the rise of electronic calculators and personal computers. Smith Corona, after struggling to sell its typewriters and word processors in a booming personal computer market, finally filed for bankruptcy. As one industry expert observed: 'Smith Corona never realized they were in the document business, not the typewriter business. If they had understood that, they would have moved into software.'[6] London Fog, a US rainwear company, found its sales slipping away to the likes of Ralph Lauren and Liz Claiborne. London Fog revamped its products and launched a bold ad campaign to try to avoid bankruptcy.[7] Maytag struggled when it focused on cost-cutting at the expense of making sought-after new products, leading retailers such as Best Buy to stop carrying the brand.[8] General Motor's Oldsmobile brand seemed to suffer from a perpetual lack of innovation and relevance.

Oldsmobile

In 1988, Oldsmobile attempted to break from its recent past with a lavish, €68.4 million ad campaign. With the theme 'This is not your father's Oldsmobile', each ad featured an icon from the 1960s – such as *Star Trek* actor William Shatner, TV game show host Monty Hall, the Beatle's Ringo Starr, astronaut Scott Carpenter and actress Priscilla Presley – paired with one of his or her children. The ads showed the celebrity parent being driven away in an Oldsmobile by his or her child. With the average age of an Oldsmobile buyer being 51, the purpose of the ads was to redefine user and usage imagery and make the brand relevant to a new market. Although the ads were among the best remembered of the year – especially among the target consumers aged 35 to 44 – sales continued to slide. Ultimately, it was withdrawn from the air. Critics faulted the campaign for drawing attention to the dowdiness of the brand's image and the fact that Oldsmobile's models really hadn't changed much. Subsequent efforts to revive the brand similarly stuttered and the brand was dropped by GM in 2004.

Thus, product innovations are critical for performance-based brands whose sources of brand equity primarily rest in product-related associations. In some cases, product advances may involve brand extensions based on a new or improved product ingredient or feature. One example is Bacardi, which recovered from a sales slide by introducing new products.

Bacardi

In the early 1990s, the increasing popularity of vodka combined with a lack of innovation in its marketing caused Bacardi to lose over 2 million cases in sales during 1991 as sales dropped to 6.4 million cases. To stop the slide, Bacardi introduced new products, beginning with a premixed drink called Bacardi Breezer. The company also introduced a lemon-flavoured rum (Bacardi Limon) in 1995 and a spiced rum (Bacardi Spice) in 1996. The company continued to develop products and, between 2001 and 2005, launched flavoured rums such as orange-seasoned Bacardi O and raspberry-flavoured Bacardi Razz, another line of premixed drinks called Bacardi Silver, premixed cocktails called Bacardi Party Drinks and a low-calorie rum called Bacardi Island Breeze. These products brought Bacardi's total revenues up to €2.4 billion and re-energized sales of the flagship rum, which grew to 8.75 million cases, in 2005.[9]

At the same time, it is important not to change products too much, especially if the brand meaning to consumers is wrapped up in a design. Recall the consumer resistance encountered by New Coke described in Chapter 1. As another example, Revlon underestimated how passionately consumers can feel about brands and how much they can resent any tampering with a product. To appeal to younger women, Revlon changed the heavy floral scent of its 30-year-old Intimate fragrance to a lighter, less sweet scent. Long-term customers protested, forcing the company to reintroduce the old formulation as 'Intimate the Original' while continuing to market the reformulated Intimate.

In making changes to a brand, it is important that loyal consumers feel that a reformulated product is a better product but not necessarily a *different* product. The timing of the announcement and introduction of a product improvement are also important: if the brand improvement is announced too soon, consumers may cease to buy existing products; if the brand improvement is announced too late, competitors may have already taken advantage of the market opportunity with their own introductions.

Non-product-related imagery associations

For brands whose core associations are non-product-related attributes and symbolic or experiential benefits, relevance in user and usage imagery is critical. Because of their intangible nature, non-product-related associations may be potentially easier to change – for example, through an advertising campaign that communicates a different type of user or usage situation. Nevertheless, ill-conceived or too-frequent repositionings can blur the image of a brand and confuse or even alienate consumers.

In categories in which advertising plays a key role in building brand equity, imagery may be an important means of differentiation. For example, in the alcoholic drinks category, millions in advertising are spent to craft an image for a brand. Consider the excellent example of brand revitalization for Johnnie Walker in Brand Briefing 13.3.

It is particularly dangerous to flip-flop between product-related performance and non-product-related imagery associations because of the fundamentally different marketing and advertising approaches each entails. Consider Heineken. Earlier ads showed simple scenes of the bottle or people peacefully drinking the beer, backed by the slogan 'Just being the best is enough.' Subsequent ads, in an attempt to make the brand more hip and contemporary, were artier – featuring a bright red star logo – and had a more prominent lifestyle component. Perhaps as a result of being too much of a departure, the ads failed to drive sales and Heineken lost its position as the leading imported beer in the USA to Corona. A new, edgy campaign from 1999, called 'It's all about the beer', was much more successful at communicating the quality message in a contemporary, humourous manner. The tagline continued into 2006, and contributed to the company's ability to regain US market share, which rose to 23 percent in 2005.[10]

Brand Briefing 13.3

Johnnie Walker: revitalizing an ageing brand

Johnnie Walker was one of the first global brands; sold in 120 countries by 1920 and now sold in 180. It's the world's biggest whisky by volume and value. Johnnie Walker is one of the world's most valuable brands, with a product range including one of the most expensive whiskies in the world.

Unfortunately, the late 1990s saw Johnnie Walker facing problems. Between 1995 and 1999 sales dropped 9.3 percent (Figure 13.2). The brand was threatened by trend-setting drinks filling expanding repertoires. Whisky was becoming 'Dad's drink'.

Johnnie Walker's brand had fragmented. The products were marketed separately, with different campaigns in different places. Between 1997 and 1999 at least 27 campaigns for Red Label and Black Label existed. Marketing was often tactical, with short-term promotional focus.

Icon brand

It was clear that fragmentation had dissipated brand strength in a category where brand is extremely important. Although the market leader in size, Johnnie Walker's brand had a fairly generic image: international and high quality. It had become two products, Red Label and Black Label. It was important that it became a great brand. Not just market leader, but a thought leader, too.

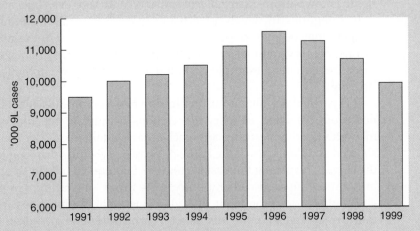

Figure 13.2   Johnnie Walker's global sales volume (1991–99)

Source: UDV pitch brief

Brand Briefing 13.3 *continued*

This meant thinking beyond 'biggest whisky', competing with Chivas Regal, Dewars and the like. It meant thinking 'icon brand', competing with other world-famous brands.

Searching for similarity, not difference

The brand's owners, Diageo, investigated how and where Johnnie Walker was drunk. After research and analysis of consumers and trends, it spotted an underlying theme: regardless of age, life stage or situation, every man shares the desire to move forward, to better himself. This innate need to progress became the universal truth that was to become the foundation of Johnnie Walker as a global brand.

Progress and Johnnie Walker

To turn this insight into a powerful brand property, the company turned to the brand's history. It was the desire to progress that had catapulted Johnnie Walker from a Kilmarnock grocery shop in the 1920s, and drove the Walker family to start global distribution in 1887.

The striding man was the strongest expression of this – originally drawn in 1908 by cartoonist Tom Browne to represent the pioneering and entrepreneurial zeal of the Walker family. It carried the strength of heritage but was inherently dynamic. Although part of the brand, the striding man had become passive. He had to change and stride forward, into the future (Figure 13.3).

Figure 13.3   The new striding man

Brand Briefing 13.3 *continued*

Figure 13.4   The brand campaign idea

Inspiring progress

The striding man forged a deep connection between the innate desire to progress and the Johnnie Walker brand. From this the campaign idea was born, with a simple but powerful exhortation to 'Keep walking' (Figure 13.4).

The 'Keep walking' global campaign

Keep walking ran in 120 countries over 6 years. Including 28 TV executions, 150 print executions, radio ads, websites, sponsorships, internal awards, consumer awards and a charitable fund. About €27.4 million is spent on media annually, although this is relatively minor compared with other global brands.

Two principles guide brand media behaviour for Johnnie Walker: reinforce stature and demonstrate pioneering spirit. Thereafter, media is managed at a local level allowing these principles to be exploited in the most appropriate way. There were two main phases: launching with focus and control; and expanding with flexibility and local sensitivity. This allowed a balance between global and local priorities.

Johnnie Walker launched its brand revitalization with 'the walk' as an expression of human progress. The same ads ran everywhere. The TV campaign was based on individual stories of personal progress; sometimes celebrities, sometimes just stories of inspiring individuals.

The campaign developed from 'personal walks' to many expressions of progress, tackling different brand needs. This helped local markets to embrace the campaign and mitigated the threat of the 'not invented here' syndrome that can dilute global campaigns.

Brand Briefing 13.3 *continued*

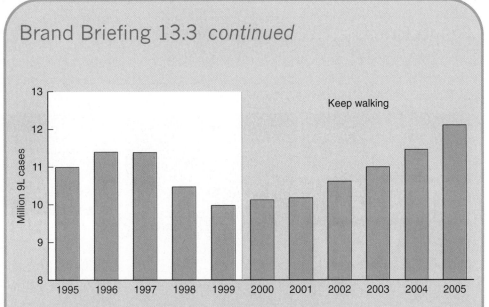

Figure 13.5   Johnnie Walker's global sales volume (1995– 2005)
Source: Impact Databank.

The reinterpretation of the brand made it come back in a spectacular way (Figure 13.5). The team behind the turnaround at Diageo and BBH, Johnnie Walker's creative agency, attributed the success to two areas.

● The campaign worked as intended with consumers, creating differentiation in the category, building an icon brand based on the values of 'progress' and branded with the striding man (Figure 13.6). As came out in research in Venezuela:

    We have to take advantage of everything we have, to enjoy everything and to give our maximum so we have no regrets when we die. We have to think we are on this earth to do something; it motivates me to be a better human being.

● The campaign worked as intended on the organization, creating belief, conviction and commitment. Rob Malcolm of Diageo summed up the results:

    Our brands are at their best when they have strong momentum – from consumers and from the organization. Beyond the obvious strength of Keep walking as a global positioning and advertising platform, it gave the organization both clear direction and confidence they could get behind. The result has been accelerated growth that even now, six years on, is still accelerating.

The team summarized their efforts like this:

    One of the secrets is looking for the things that unite; chase difference and you chase forever. Uniting behind a universal truth and a potent brand symbol can act as a strong organizational force as well as a strong consumer force. This is a

Brand Briefing 13.3 *continued*

'Quotes' 2000

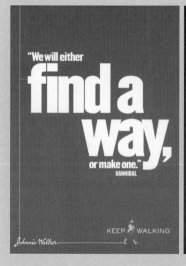
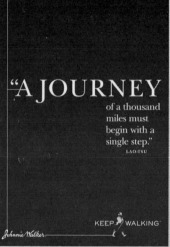

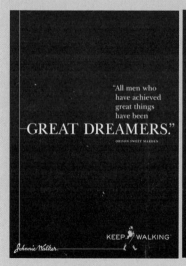

Figure 13.6   Images from the campaign in three periods

Brand Briefing 13.3 *continued*

'Icons' 2004–05

'Human' 2006–07 (photographer: Laurent Seroussi)

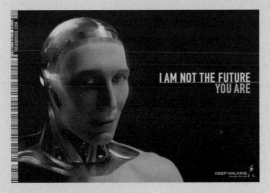

Figure 13.6   *Continued*

Brand Briefing 13.3 *continued*

Figure 13.6   *Continued*

powerful thing. Once you have it, control and flexibility are usefully wielded in equal measure. Although the world's a big place, with terrific richness and diversity, it is possible to find ways of bringing people together, and that feels like a valuable thing.

Sources: Orlando Hooper-Greenhill, BBH, 'Johnnie Walker: a walk around the world', a case study submitted to the IPA effectiveness awards in the UK; IWSR; Impact Databank; Interbrand, global brand 2001; Xtreme Information; Diageo; *Advertising Age*, 14 November 2005; valuation study, Flamingo International.

Significant repositionings may be dangerous for other reasons, too. Brand images can be extremely sticky and, once consumers form strong brand associations, they may be difficult to change. Consumers may choose to ignore or simply be unable to remember the new positioning when strong, but different, brand associations already exist in memory.[11] Club Med has attempted for years to transcend its image as a holiday romp for swingers to attract a broader cross-section of people.

For repositioning strategies to work, convincing brand claims must be presented in a compelling fashion. One brand that shifted from a primarily non-product-related image to a primarily product-related image is BMW. Uniformly decreed to be the quintessential 'yuppie' vehicle of the 1980s, sales of the brand dropped by almost half from 1986 to 1991 as new Japanese competition emerged and a backlash to the 'greed decade' set in. Convinced that high status was no longer a sufficiently desirable and sustainable position, marketing and advertising efforts switched the focus to BMW's product development and improvements, such as the responsive performance, distinctive styling and leading-edge engineering of the cars. These efforts, demonstrated in well-designed ads, helped to diminish the 'yuppie' association and, by 1995, sales had approached their earlier peak.[12]

Summary

Reinforcing brand equity requires consistency in the amount and nature of the marketing campaign for a brand. Although tactics may change, the sources of equity for the brand should be preserved and amplified where appropriate. Product innovation and relevance are paramount in maintaining continuity and expanding the meaning of the brand. Brand Briefing 13.4 describes how the British brand Burberry remade itself in the world of fashion. The chapter next considers situations in which more drastic brand actions are needed.

Brand Briefing 13.4

Remaking Burberry's image

Burberry, founded in 1856 by 21-year-old Thomas Burberry, was a veritable 'fashion disaster' in the mid-1990s. It was known to many as a stodgy throwback brand making raincoats for the middle-aged. Burberry was, in the words of one commentator, 'far off the radar screens of the fashion world'. Yet, with the help of contemporary designs and updated marketing, the brand shrugged off its staid image and became fashionable again. The company instituted a new motto – 'Never stop designing' – that encapsulated the new approach for establishing and maintaining relevance with the fickle fashion consumer.

One of Burberry's first moves to freshen its brand was to build on its classic Burberry beige 'check' pattern in a series of accessories that quickly became best-sellers, including handbags, scarves and caps. Another move was rejuvenating the check itself by using different colours, patterns, sizes and materials in designs. In its designs, Burberry was careful to maintain a balance between the contemporary and the traditional, the latter of which still resonated with modern consumers. In addition to the Burberry check, the company sought to use other iconic imagery such as its trench coat and prorsum horse insignia. The use of these brand icons reflected the fact that Burberry management felt 'the core ethos and aesthetics of the brand were relevant today because of Thomas Burberry's ingenuity and creativity'.

Another element in Burberry's turnaround was refreshing its advertising. It hired fashion photographer Mario Testino to shoot a spread featuring edgy supermodels

Brand Briefing 13.4 *continued*

such as Kate Moss wearing the iconic Burberry raincoats. The ads were credited with bringing a 'rebellious, streetwise image to the brand'. The company gave its shops a makeover as well to match the contemporary feel of the new designs. Together, Burberry's efforts turned the company's fortunes around. Between 2000 and 2004, the company recorded 5 consecutive annual revenue increases, and net profit rose 75 percent in 2004 to €111 million. One commentator summed up the company's turnaround, saying: 'Burberry appeals to a very broad market, which is why it is doing so well. But the great advertising campaigns and cool models keep the Burberry label very high-end, appealing and desirable.'

Sources: Sally Beatty, 'Plotting plaid's future', *Wall Street Journal*, 9 September 2004: B1; Mark Tungate, 'Fashion statement', *Marketing*, 27 July 2005: 28; Sharon Wright, 'The tough New Yorker who transformed a UK institution gets her reward', *The Express*, 5 August 2004: 17.

REVITALIZING BRANDS

At the beginning of the chapter, it was noted that changes in consumer tastes and preferences, the emergence of competitors or new technology or any development in the environment can potentially affect the fortunes of a brand. In virtually every product category, there are examples of once prominent and admired brands that have fallen on hard times or, in some cases, disappeared. Nevertheless, some of these brands have managed to make impressive comebacks as marketers have breathed new life into their customer franchises. Brands such as *Reader's Digest*, Coach and Bally have all seen their fortunes turned around to varying degrees in recent years. Brand Briefing 13.5 describes how Lacoste restored the status of its brand.

As these examples illustrate, brands sometimes have had to return to their roots to recapture lost sources of equity. In other cases, the meaning of the brand has had to change fundamentally to regain lost ground and recapture market leadership. Reversing a fading brand's fortunes thus requires either lost sources of brand equity to be recaptured or new sources to be identified and established. Regardless of which approach is taken, brands on the comeback trail have to make more 'revolutionary' changes than the 'evolutionary' changes to reinforce brand meaning that were described earlier in this chapter.

Often, the first place to look in turning around the fortunes of a brand is the original sources of brand equity. As Ogilvy & Mather's Norman Berry once remarked:

> The brands most likely to respond to revitalization efforts are those that have clear and relevant values that have been left dormant for a long time, have not been well expressed in the marketing and communications recently, have been

Brand Briefing 13.5

Lacoste: a brand comeback story

Lacoste, founded in France in 1933, became a style icon for its tennis-themed sportswear and is credited with selling the first polo shirt, the famed 'alligator shirt' featuring the crocodile logo. During the 1980s, when it was owned by US cereal maker General Mills, Lacoste failed to keep up with fashion trends and saw its sales drop. In response, the company cut prices and sold to discounters such as Wal-Mart and Kmart, a move that further damaged the brand's image. Lacoste continued to suffer from slow sales until 2002, when Robert Siegel, a former Levi's executive credited with creating Dockers, was brought in to oversee the relaunch of the brand in the USA. Under Siegel, Lacoste stopped selling to non-luxury retailers, prohibiting sales to places such as TK Maxx and a number of Macy's department stores. The company also regenerated its fading fashion lines by introducing tighter-fitting shirts for women, a move that increased the contribution to Lacoste's US revenues of women's wear from 7 percent to 33 percent. Lacoste went a step further and opened own-brand boutiques in fashionable shopping areas to show off its new look. As a consequence of these measures, US revenues rose more than 280 percent between 2003 and 2005.

Source: Greg Lindsay, 'The alligator's new look', *Business 2.0*, April 2006: 68–9.

violated by product problems, cost reductions, and so on. Where there is evidence that these values exist and that they were indeed a part of the brand's magnetism during healthier days, then chances of revitalization are good. If you find that the brand really does not have any strong values, chances are that the product or business strength in the past was a function simply of performance and spending characteristics and that, in fact, according to our definition, it never really became a true brand. Bringing these brands back to life is more like starting from scratch. It really isn't revitalization.[13]

In profiling brand knowledge structures to guide repositioning, it is important to accurately and completely characterize the breadth and depth of brand awareness; the strength, favourability and uniqueness of brand associations and brand responses held in consumer memory; and the nature of consumer-brand relationships. A comprehensive brand equity measurement system as outlined in Chapter 8 should be able to help reveal the status of these sources of brand equity. If not, or to provide additional insight, a special brand audit may be necessary. Of particular importance is the extent to which brand associations are still adequately functioning as points of difference or points of parity to properly position the brand. Are positive associations losing their strength or uniqueness? Have negative associations become linked to the brand – for example, because of change in the marketing environment?

Decisions must then be made as to whether to retain the same positioning or to create a new one and, if so, which positioning to adopt. The positioning considerations outlined in Chapter 3 can provide insight as to the desirability and deliverability of possible positions based on company, consumer and competitive considerations. Sometimes, the positioning is still appropriate, but the marketing campaign is the source of the problem because it is failing to deliver on it. In these instances, a 'back to basics' strategy may make sense. Brand Briefing 13.6 describes how Harley-Davidson rode a back-to-basics strategy to icon status. In other cases, however, the old positioning is just no longer viable and a 'reinvention' strategy is necessary.

Brand Briefing 13.6

Harley-Davidson Motor Company

Harley-Davidson is one of the few companies that can claim a legion of fans so dedicated that some of them get tattoos depicting the logo. Even more impressive is the fact that Harley-Davidson attracted such a loyal customer base with a minimum of advertising. Founded in 1903 in Milwaukee, Wisconsin, Harley-Davidson has twice narrowly escaped bankruptcy to become one of the most-recognized motorbike brands in the world. Among consumers throughout the world, Harley enjoys 55 percent unaided awareness. Customers are willing to endure three-year waiting lists to get their hands on a Harley.

Before the 1980s, the company relied almost exclusively on word-of-mouth endorsements and the image of its user group to sell its motorcycles. In 1983, the company established an owners club, the Harley Owners Group (HOG), which sponsored bike rallies, charity rides and other events. Every Harley owner receives free admission into the group and can sign up at the www.hog.com website. In its first year, HOG had 33,000 members. By 2001, there were more than 600,000 HOG members in more than 1,200 chapters throughout the world.

Because of financial desperation, Harley-Davidson began to license its products aggressively in the 1980s. After early errors, including the ill-advised Harley-Davidson brand of cigarettes begun in 1985 and the 'Scooter Juice' brand of wine coolers, the company licensed its name to such credible ventures as the Harley-Davidson Café chain. Other licensing agreements have led to a Harley Barbie doll, a Harley cologne, a Harley Visa card, a Ford F-150 Harley truck and even a Harley state lottery game. Harley-Davidson licensed products bring in tens of millions in revenue annually.

The company realized that the Harley leather 'uniform', while an important aspect of its core audience, was alienating potential customers. So Harley-Davidson created Harley-Davidson Motorclothes, which balanced aggressive leather riding gear with 'cuter' items such as women's underwear and baby clothes. Harley Motorclothes are a key facet of the company's general merchandise division, which saw revenues increase from €103 million in 2000 to €169 million in 2005.

Harley-Davidson continues to promote its brand with grassroots marketing. For example, most executives at the company own Harleys and often ride them with customers. This customer intimacy makes traditional advertising almost unnecessary.

Brand Briefing 13.6 *continued*

In 1996, Harley spent no money on advertising. In 1997, Harley's marketing budget was €13.6 million, only €684,000 of which went on advertising. As ever, Harley's highly visible contingent of riders provides invaluable promotions and endorsements free of cost. Additionally, many marketers seek to borrow the Harley cachet and use the bikes in other ads, giving the company free product placement.

One of the newest areas of growth for the company is women riders. The company redesigned its Sportster bike to make it more comfortable for women and it encourages women to take classes with a poster showing a woman biker and the tagline 'I am not a backrest.' In 2004, 41 percent of Learn to Ride partipants were women. After making up just 2 percent of Harley owners in the 1980s, women represented about 10 percent of Harley customers in 2004. As it attracts new buyers, the company continues to please customers and investors. In 2005, profits rose 8 percent to €656 million on sales of €3.6 billion, up 7 percent from the previous year, capping 20 consecutive years of record growth.

Sources: Bill Tucker, Terry Keenan and Daryn Kagan, 'In the money', *CNNfn*, 20 January 2000; 'Harley-Davidson extends MDI entertainment license for lotteries' hottest brand', *Business Wire*, 1 May 2001; Glenn Rifkin, 'How Harley-Davidson revs its brand', *Strategy & Business*, fourth quarter 1997; Joseph Weber, 'He really got Harley roaring', *Business Week*, 21 March 2005: 70; Rick Barrett, 'From the executive suite to the saddle', *Chicago Tribune*, 1 August 2004: CN3.

Revitalization strategies obviously involve a continuum, with 'back to basics' at one end and 'reinvention' at the other. Many revitalizations combine elements of both strategies. Finally, note that marketing failures, in which insufficient consumers are attracted to a brand, are typically much less damaging than product failures, in which the brand fails to live up to its consumer promise. In the latter case, strong, negative associations may be difficult to overcome. For example, Napster, the pioneer in internet file sharing, was forced out of business in 2002 for providing more than 60 million users with access to illegally copied digital files of songs. Given that many music fans still had a fondness for the brand from using it during its heyday, digital music company Roxio bought it in a bankruptcy auction for €3.4 million in 2002 and rebranded its Pressplay music download subscription service as Napster. The new Napster generated revenues of €15.7 million in 2006, nearly double the 2005 figure.[14]

With an understanding of the current and desired brand knowledge structures in hand, the customer-based brand equity framework again provides guidance as to how to best refresh old sources of brand equity or create new sources to achieve the intended positioning. According to the model, two approaches are possible.

1. Expand the depth or breadth of brand awareness, or both, by improving consumer recall and recognition of the brand during purchase or consumption settings.
2. Improve the strength, favourability and uniqueness of brand associations making up the brand image. This approach may involve campaigns directed at existing or new brand associations.

By enhancing brand salience and meaning in these ways, more favourable responses and greater brand resonance can result. Strategically, lost sources of brand equity can be refurbished and new sources can be established in the same ways that brand equity is created to start with: by changing brand elements, changing the supporting marketing campaign or using new secondary associations. The remainder of this section considers strategies for affecting the awareness and image of an existing brand to refresh old sources or create new sources of brand equity.

Expanding brand awareness

With a fading brand, often it is not the *depth of* brand awareness that is a problem – consumers can still recognize or recall the brand under certain circumstances. Rather, the breadth of brand awareness is the stumbling block – consumers only tend to think of the brand in very narrow ways. Therefore, as was suggested in Chapter 3, one powerful way to build brand equity is to increase the breadth of brand awareness, making sure consumers do not overlook the brand and that they will think of purchasing or consuming it in those situations in which the brand can satisfy consumers' needs and wants.

Assuming a brand has a reasonable level of consumer awareness and a positive brand image, perhaps the most appropriate starting point for creating more sources of brand equity is with ways that increase usage. In many cases, such approaches represent the path of least resistance because they do not involve potentially difficult and costly changes in brand image or positioning as much as potentially easier changes in brand salience and awareness.

Usage can be increased by either increasing the level or quantity of consumption or increasing the frequency of consumption.

In general, it is probably easier to increase the number of times a consumer uses the product than it is to change the amount used at any one time. Consumption amount is more likely to be a function of beliefs that a consumer holds as to how the product is best consumed. A possible exception to that rule is for 'impulse' consumption products whose usage increases when the product is made more available (eg, soft drinks, snacks).

Increasing frequency of use, on the other hand, involves either identifying additional or new opportunities to use the brand in the same basic way or identifying different ways to use the brand. Increasing frequency of use is a particularly attractive option for brands with large market share that are leaders in their product category.

Identifying additional or new usage opportunities

In some cases, the brand may be seen as useful only in certain places and at certain times, especially if it has strong brand associations with particular situations or user types. In general, to identify additional opportunities for consumers to use the brand more – albeit in the same basic way – a marketing campaign should be designed to include both of the following.

- Communications to consumers as to the appropriateness and advantages of using the brand more frequently in existing situations or in new situations.
- Reminders to consumers to actually use the brand as close as possible to those situations.

For many brands, increasing usage may be as simple as improving top-of-mind awareness through reminder advertising. In other cases, more creative types of retrieval cues may be necessary. These reminders may be critical because consumers often adopt 'functional fixedness' with a brand such that it can be ignored in non-traditional consumption settings.

For example, some brands are seen as only appropriate for special occasions. An effective strategy for those brands may be to redefine what it means for something to be 'special'. For example, at one time Chivas Regal ran a print ad campaign for its blended whisky with the theme 'What are you saving the Chivas for?' The ads, showing people in different scenes, included headlines such as 'Sometimes life begins when the baby-sitter arrives', 'Your Scotch and soda is only as good as your Scotch and soda' and 'If you think people might think you order Chivas to show off, maybe you're thinking too much.' For such campaigns to work, it is essential that the brand be able to retain its 'premium' brand association – a key source of equity – while consumers are convinced to adopt broader usage habits at the same time.

Another opportunity to increase frequency of use is when consumer's *perceptions* of their usage differ from the reality of their usage. For many products with relatively short lifespans, consumers may fail to replace the product in a timely manner because of a tendency to underestimate the length of productive usage.[15] One strategy to speed up product replacement is to tie the act of replacing the product to a certain holiday, event or time of year. Another strategy might be to provide consumers with better information as to either: when the product was first used or would need to be replaced; or the current level of product performance. For example, batteries offer built-in gauges that show how much power they have left, and toothbrushes have colour indicators on their brushes to indicate when they are worn.

Finally, perhaps the simplest way to increase sales is when actual use of a product is less than the optimal or recommended use. In this case, consumers must be persuaded of the merits of more regular use and hurdles to increased usage must be overcome. In terms of the latter, product designs and packaging can make the product more convenient and easier to use.

Identifying different ways to use a brand

The second approach to increasing frequency of use for a brand is to identify different applications. For example, food producers have long advertised new recipes that use their products. After years of sales declines of 3 percent to 4 percent annually, sales of Cheez-Whiz in the USA rose 35 percent when the brand was backed by a campaign promoting the product as a cheese sauce accompaniment to be used in the microwave oven.[16] Perhaps the classic example of finding applications for a product is Arm & Hammer bicarbonate of soda, whose deodorizing and cleaning properties have led to several new uses.

Other brands have taken a page from Arm & Hammer's book: Clorox has run ads stressing the many benefits of its bleach, such as how it eliminates kitchen odours; Wrigley's chewing gum has run ads touting its product as a substitute for smoking; and Tums has run ads for its antacid that promote its benefits as a calcium substitute. Coach managed to expand usage and increase frequency both for its brand and the category.

Coach

Women in the USA purchased an average of 2.4 bags in 2000, up from 1.9 in 1988, and Coach played a prominent role in this rise. Coach's strategy for growth was to fill 'usage voids' – situations where existing bag options are not appropriate – with a plethora of bag options, including evening bags, backpacks, satchels, totes, briefcases, purses and duffels. Rather than owning a few bags suitable for a limited number of uses, women were encouraged by Coach to treat handbags as 'the shoes of the twenty-first century: a way to frequently update wardrobes with different styles without shelling out for new clothes'. One gap identified by the company was summer weekend use, so Coach filled it with the introduction of the Hamptons Weekend line, which featured durable, weatherproof materials mixed with high-quality leather. Coach stores educated consumers on new uses by displaying the bags filled with beach towels and flip-flops. In the two years following its 2003 launch, the Hamptons Weekend bag sold almost 250,000 units for €27.3 million in sales.[17]

New applications may require more than just ad campaigns or merchandising approaches. Often, new uses can arise from packaging. For example, Arm & Hammer introduced a 'Fridge-Freezer Pack' (with 'freshflo vents') for its natural bicarbonate of soda that was designed to better freshen and deodorize refrigerators and freezers. Brand Briefing 13.7 describes ways to expand usage.

Improving brand image

Although changes in brand awareness are probably the easiest means of creating sources of brand equity, fundamental changes are often necessary. A new marketing campaign may be necessary to improve the strength, favourability and uniqueness of brand associations making up the brand image. As part of this repositioning – or recommitment to the existing positioning – any positive associations that have faded may need to be bolstered, any negative associations that have been created may have to be neutralized and additional positive associations may have to be created.

Repositioning a brand

In some cases, repositioning a brand requires establishing more compelling points of difference. This may simply mean reminding consumers of the virtues of a brand they have begun to take for granted. Recall how the New Coke debacle described in Chapter 1 accomplished just that in a roundabout way. Along these lines, Kellogg's Corn Flakes ran a successful ad campaign with the slogan 'Try them again for the first time.' Disneyland similarly tried to walk consumers down memory lane in 2005 ads celebrating the theme park's fiftieth anniversary. In some of these cases, a point of difference may turn out to be nostalgia and heritage rather than any product-related difference. Research has indicated that nostalgic advertising can influence consumers. One empirical study confirmed that intentionally nostalgic advertisements prompted nostalgic reflection in respondents that yielded favourable attitudes towards the advertisement and the brand.[18] Another study identified a potential

Brand Briefing 13.7

Understanding usage expansion

Academic Brian Wansink has studied marketing and branding issues associated with product consumption. Wansink describes ways to identify and communicate new usage situations. An obvious starting point is with brainstorming meetings or focus groups involving loyal or heavy users and less loyal or light users. Contrasting the preferences and behaviours of the two groups can yield insights into barriers to greater usage that must be overcome, as well as opportunities for growth. Additionally, he notes how perceptions of potentially related products and situations can be uncovered through cluster analysis or other statistical approaches.

Wansink argues that successful strategies for expansion ad campaigns are often based on clever targeting and timing. He notes how small-share brands can more affordably target users of their brands by advertising new uses on their packaging and labels. For example, Trix cereal used a side panel in the USA to note complementary products (eg, ice-cream, yogurt, trail mix, etc.) on which Trix could be sprinkled. Murphy's Oil Soap printed ideas under stickers on its spray bottles. Similarly, Roy Rogers restaurants used its paper placemats to advertise eight situations – parties, picnics, meetings and so forth – in which customers could eat take-away chicken. In terms of timing, advertising exposure ideally would coincide with situations in which brand choice has the highest likelihood of being made. For example, Campbell's schedules radio ads for its soups to be broadcast just before lunch and dinner.

Wansink defines *usage variant products* as those that have elastic demand functions because they can be easily substituted or because they are able to create their own demand when salient, such as food and household cleaning products. For such products, marketing strategies to increase consumer stockpiling (eg, promotions or changes in packaging) may increase the salience and thus use of the product. For example, larger pack sizes and price discounts, by lowering the perceived unit cost of the product, have been shown to accelerate use. Another way to increase the quantity used is to reduce the undesirable consequences of increased use. For example, a shampoo designed to be gentle enough for daily use may alleviate concerns from those consumers who believe that frequent hair washing is undesirable and therefore eliminate their tendency to conserve the amount of product they use.

Sources: Brian Wansink, 'Advertising strategies to increase usage frequency', *Journal of Marketing*, January 1996, 60 (1): 31–46; Brian Wansink and Jennifer Marie Gilmore, 'New uses that revitalize old brands', *Journal of Advertising Research*, March–April 1999: 90–8; Brian Wansink, 'Can package size accelerate usage volume?', *Journal of Marketing*, July 1996, 60 (3): 1–14; David A. Aaker, *Managing Brand Equity*, New York: Free Press, 1991.

source of nostalgic purchase behaviour called 'intergenerational influence', or the influence of a parent's purchase behaviour and brand attitudes on a child's behaviour and attitudes.[19] This study found that intergenerational influences can function as a source of brand equity, but are not felt uniformly by all mature brands. Rather, certain product categories and brands exhibit more of an 'intergenerational effect' – where parent and child share the same brand preference – than others. Categories (and corresponding brands) that exhibited the highest intergenerational effects in the USA include soup (Campbell's), ketchup (Heinz), facial tissues (Kleenex, Puffs), peanut butter (Peter Pan, Jif, Skippy), mayonnaise (Miracle Whip, Kraft, Hellman's) and pasta (Mueller, Ronzoni).

A brand may need to be repositioned to establish a point of parity on some key image dimension. A common problem for mature brands is that they must be made more contemporary by creating relevant usage situations, a more contemporary user profile or a more modern brand personality. Heritage brands may be seen as trustworthy but also boring, uninteresting and not that likeable. Updating a brand may involve a combination of new products, advertising, promotions and packaging. For example, the 170-year-old regional US beer Yuengling saw its sales almost double by introducing lighter and fuller-flavoured versions; labels that gave the beer an arty, nostalgic look; and promotions that tapped into regional pride by focusing on the brewery's history. The new image permitted higher prices and allowed the brand to gain accounts in upmarket bars and restaurants.[20]

Changing brand elements

Often, one or more brand elements must be changed to convey new information or to signal that a brand has taken on a different meaning because the product or the marketing campaign has changed. Although the name is typically the most important brand element, it is often the most difficult to change. Nevertheless, names can be dropped or changed to initials to reflect shifts in marketing strategy or to ease pronunciation and recall. Shortened names or initials also can disguise negative associations. For example, in an attempt to convey a healthier image, Kentucky Fried Chicken's name was abbreviated to KFC. The company also introduced a logo incorporating the character of Colonel Sanders to maintain tradition but modernize its appeal. Brand names may be changed for other reasons. Federal Express chose to shorten its name to FedEx and change its logo in response to what consumers called the brand.[21]

Other brand elements are easier to change and may need to be, especially if they play an important awareness or image function. Chapter 4 described how packaging, logos, characters and so forth could be modified and updated. An important point is that changes generally should be evolutionary in nature, and care should be taken to preserve the most salient aspects of the brand elements. For example, when Ramada decided it wanted to communicate a fresh, upmarket look to the public – but not lose the valuable equity it had accrued in its name – it chose to introduce a sleek new logo and signs that retained the Ramada name and bright red colour, while phasing out the Ramada Inn and Ramada Limited brands from its portfolio and spending more than a year upgrading its properties.[22] Brand Briefing 13.11 is about changing corporate names.

Entering new markets

Positioning decisions require a specification of the target market and the nature of competition to set a frame of reference. The target market or markets for a brand typically do not constitute all the segments that make up a market. In some cases, the firm may have other brands that target some segments. In other cases, however, these segments represent potential growth targets for the brand. Reaching these other segments, however, typically requires some changes or variations in marketing, especially in advertising and other communications, and the decision about whether or not to target these segments depends on a cost–benefit analysis. (Chapter 3 introduced segmentation issues and Chapter 14 considers specific issues in the context of global brands.)

To expand a brand franchise, many companies have reached out to new customer groups to build brand equity. Johnson & Johnson baby shampoo achieved greater success by promoting the gentleness and everyday applicability of its shampoo to adults.

Segmenting on the basis of demographic variables or other means and identifying neglected segments is thus one viable brand revitalization option. In some cases, just retaining customers who might move away from a brand or recapturing lost customers can be a way to increase sales. Brands such as Kellogg's Frosties cereal and Johnson & Johnson's baby oil have run ad campaigns targeting adults who presumably stopped using the product long ago. Some of these ads appeal to nostalgia or heritage. Others attempt to make the case that the product's enduring appeal is still relevant. The importance of retaining customers can be recognized by calculating their lifetime value. One US study noted that a carbuyer would spend more than €342,000 on cars during his or her lifetime, but that it costs 5 times as much to sell a car to a new customer as it does to a satisfied existing customer.[23]

Attracting a new market segment can be deceptively difficult. Gillette, Harley-Davidson and Wrangler struggled to find the right blend of products and advertising to make their brands – which have masculine images – appear relevant and appealing to women. Creating marketing campaigns to appeal to women has become a priority for makers of products from cars to computers. As described in Brand Briefing 14.11, marketers have also introduced marketing campaigns for racial groups (eg, African Americans, Asian Americans and Hispanic Americans), age groups and income groups. Attracting emerging market segments based on cultural dimensions may require different messages, creative strategies and media.[24]

Of course, one strategic option for revitalizing a fading brand is to abandon the consumer group that supported the brand in the past in favour of a new market segment.

Tommy Hilfiger

One of the hottest US fashion brands in the 1990s, Tommy Hilfiger was struggling to stay relevant by the early 2000s. Other labels such as Phat Farm, FUBU, Sean John and Ecko had drawn customers away by playing to the young, urban, hip-hop style on which Hilfiger built its 1990s success in more 'authentic' ways. Bloomingdales reduced the number of Hilfiger boutiques to 1 from 23 and Hilfiger closed all but 7 of its 44 own-brand shops in 2003. To recover,

Hilfiger cut its ties with the style that had made it popular – oversized clothes, even more oversized logos and an edgy urban aura – even going as far as removing the stylized US flag logo from much of its clothes. Hilfiger struck out in a new direction with preppy styles inspired by the sun and surf or, as a competitor described a hoarding advertising the new line: 'Pacific sunwear meets Ralph Lauren meets "From Here to Eternity."' One analyst questioned the logic of Hilfiger embracing its preppy past, asking 'Why would he try to go back to being Ralph Lauren, when that market is already saturated?'[25]

ADJUSTMENTS TO THE BRAND PORTFOLIO

Managing brand equity and the brand portfolio requires taking a long-term view. As part of this perspective, it is necessary to consider the role of brands and the relationships between brands in a portfolio over time. In particular, a brand migration strategy needs to be designed and implemented so that consumers understand how various brands in the portfolio can satisfy their needs as they potentially change over time or as the products and brands change. Managing transition is especially important in rapidly changing, technologically intensive markets. Brand Briefing 13.8 describes issues faced by Porsche.

Migration strategies

As noted in Chapter 11, brands can play special roles that help customers migrate within a portfolio. For example, entry-level brands are often critical to bringing in new customers. Ideally, brands would be organized in consumers' minds so that they at least implicitly know how they can switch between brands within a portfolio as their needs or desires change. For example, a corporate or family branding strategy in which brands are ordered in a logical way could provide a hierarchical structure in consumers' minds to aid brand migration. Carmakers are sensitive to this issue, and BMW with its numbering systems to denote higher levels of quality is a good example of such a strategy.

Finding new customers

All firms face tradeoffs in their marketing efforts between attracting new customers and retaining existing ones. In mature markets, trial is generally less important than building loyalty and retaining customers. Nevertheless, some customers inevitably leave the brand franchise – even if only due to natural causes. Consequently, it is imperative that firms develop strategies to attract new customers, especially younger ones. The marketing challenge lies in making a brand seem relevant to customers from different generations and cohort groups or lifestyles. This challenge is exacerbated when the brand has strong personality or user image associations that tie the brand to a particular consumer group.

Brand Briefing 13.8

Porsche: product development and the brand

The model most associated with German carmaker Porsche, the 911, was introduced in 1964 and continues to this day. The 911 has been updated in various ways, becoming a motoring icon. But Porsche and the 911 were not always seen as inseparable entities. Towards the end of the 1970s, the 911 was perceived as an ageing model.

In the latter half of the 1970s, Porsche launched two cars that both seem to have been conceived as successors to the 911. The 924 model, was a light, affordable front-engined sports car. In 1977, it was joined by the Porsche 928, a heavier, more luxurious car with a V8 engine. Presumably the 924 was an affordable model aimed at younger sports car-orientated buyers while the 928 was for the prestige-orientated luxury sports car customer (the main target being the USA).

These models were good cars, but they did not fit easily in the Porsche portfolio, especially with the 911. The 924 had an Audi gearbox and a Volkswagen engine, used in the Passat and even in a VW van – not the perfect image for a Porsche. The 928 was a great machine, but it was almost the opposite of the 911: water-cooled instead of air-cooled, a front engine instead of a rear engine and heavy rather than light. So even as the new models were praised for engineering and performance, the 928 even winning the European car of the year accolade in 1978, sales did not reach the levels Porsche had hoped for.

Porsche decided to keep the 911 and refine it, based on the shape and attributes that were central to its character. This saved the company, as the 911 accounted for 80 percent of sales by 1994. Still, it left the company in a difficult position with only one successful model in its line up. 'We were running into major problems and were worried about our future as an independent company', explains Andreas Schlegel from Porsche. The company responded by defining a new product strategy, optimizing its development and production processes and resolving to change its branding strategy from the ground up, introducing integrated brand management and consistent market communication.

The 928 and 924 were phased out and the Boxster was introduced in 1996. This model was made much closer to the 911 heritage, with the engine behind the driver and a light and nimble design. The new brand strategy went beyond the product line-up. For instance, dealerships were officially renamed 'Porsche Centres', which have the same silver façade and red lettering as well as a round showroom around the world. The same approach was taken in advertising, going for a global approach instead of a locally improvised position.

The Boxster helped Porsche to financial health after years of disappointing sales. From a base of only two models, the 911 and the Boxster, Porsche sold better than ever, going from 19,262 sold cars in 1995 to 88,379 in 2005.

The portfolio then became broader: from the Boxster to the Cayenne to the 911 Carrera, GT or Turbo models, the company has a car for every phase in the lives of

Brand Briefing 13.8 *continued*

its customers. It is also worth noting that the line-up gives affluent people a reason to own more than one Porsche – a Cayenne 911 or Boxster for some occasions and the large Cayenne SUV when there is family and luggage involved. Another series is about to be introduced, the Panamera, which will target 'best agers'. So Porsche has succeeded in extending its brand to performance cars of various types, and replacing its macho image with a consistent, socially accepted brand, without tarnishing its exclusive aura.

Yet there are some challenges that Porsche needs to address in the coming years. One danger Porsche faces is that massive sales of its 'not quite as upmarket' models might make the company's logo a common sight and this could make it less attractive to own the 911 flagship. Another challenge could be that the more family/mature-orientated models Cayenne and Panamera might make the brand less appealing to young customers.

Still, such challenges are 'nice problems to have' – directly an effect of increasing sales 5-fold over some 12 years. One must remember that success in branding must ultimately be judged in relation to business results.

Sources: Jorn Madslien, 'Porsche aims high in the UK market', bbc.co.uk, 26 May 2004; Jonathan Wood, *Porsche: The legend*, Bristol: Parragon, 1997; Andreas Schlegel, 'From macho brand to brand leader', speech at the Print Media Academy, Heidelberger Druckmaschinen AG, 16 November 2006.

Unfortunately, even as younger consumers age, there is no guarantee they will have the same attitudes and behave like the consumers who preceded them. In 1996, the first wave of post-war baby boomers celebrated their fiftieth birthdays and entered the 'senior, or, mature market'. Many experts forecast that this group would demand that companies embrace their own unique values in marketing their products and services. As one demographic expert says: 'Nothing could be further from the truth than saying boomers will be like their parents.' Because there can be no expectations that younger consumers will view brands and products in the same way as consumers who preceded them, strategies must be put in place to both acquire new customers and retain existing ones.

The response to the challenge of marketing across generations and cohort groups has taken all forms. Some marketers have attempted to cut loose from the past, as Tommy Hilfiger did by renouncing the urban styles it had come to embody in the 1990s. Other brands have sought to develop more inclusive marketing strategies to encompass both new and old customers.

Dove

Unilever's Dove brand was known primarily for bar soap since its introduction in 1955. Launched in the USA, it became one of Unilever's biggest global brands. As the company sought to expand the franchise, it realized Dove needed to extend beyond soap to meet the changing personal care needs of its customers, which had become more about total bodycare. Beginning in 1999, Dove introduced bodywash, facial cleansers, deodorant and, in 2003, shampoo. Dove kept its bar soap line intact and each extension emphasized Dove's moisturizing properties, so the brand broadened its appeal without alienating its core customers.[26]

Separate marketing communication campaigns

One approach to attracting a new market segment and satisfying current segments is to create separate advertising and communication campaigns. For example, Dewars launched 'Authentic' and 'Profiles' campaigns, each directed to a different segment. The 'Authentic' campaign focused on the brand heritage in terms of its product quality and Scottish roots and was focused on an older segment, including existing customers. The 'Profiles' campaign took a different tack, by profiling younger users to make the brand seem relevant and attractive to a younger audience. Media buyers then attempted to ensure that the appropriate campaign was seen by the relevant market segment.

Similar approaches have been adopted by beer companies. The increased effectiveness of targeted media makes such approaches more feasible. The drawback is the expense involved and the potential blurring of images from media overlap of target groups and if the respective ad positionings are seen as incompatible.

Brand extensions and sub-brands

Another approach to attracting new customers and keeping a brand up to date is to introduce a line extension or establish a sub-brand. These new product offerings can incorporate new technology, features and other attributes to meet the needs of new customers as well as satisfy the changing desires of existing customers. For example, in 2005, Jeep introduced the Commander, a large SUV that featured three rows of seating, an increasingly popular feature in the USA but a first for Jeep. At the same time, Jeep announced plans to launch two smaller 'crossover' vehicles that would appeal to fuel- and safety-conscious consumers reluctant to buy a full-size SUV.[27]

New distribution outlets

In some cases, attracting a new market segment may be as simple as making the product more available. For example, the sunglasses industry, which grew sales from €68.4 million in 1972 to €1.7 billion 15 years later, benefited from social and fashion trends but also a shift in distribution strategies. Sunglasses used to be sold mostly by opticians, but in the 1970s Sunglass Hut and other companies moved into shopping centres and sports shops. A leader in niche retailing, Sunglass Hut uses 2,000 high-traffic shopping and tourist destinations to reach new audiences.

Retiring brands

Because of dramatic or adverse changes in the marketing environment, some brands are just not worth saving. Their sources of brand equity may have dried up or, even worse, damaging and difficult-to-change new associations may have been created. At some point, the size of the brand franchise – no matter how loyal – fails to justify the support of the brand. In the face of such adversity, decisive management actions are necessary to bring an end to or milk the brand.

Several options are possible. A first step in retrenching a fading brand is to reduce the number of its product types (eg, pack sizes or variations). Such actions reduce the cost of supporting a brand. Under these reduced levels of support, a brand may more easily hit profit targets. If a sufficiently large and loyal enough customer base exists, marketing support can be eliminated to milk profits from these cash cows. An *orphan brand* has been defined as a once-popular brand with diminished equity that a parent company allows to decline by withdrawing marketing support. Typically, orphan brands have a customer base too small to warrant advertising and promotional expenditures. The Polaroid camera can be seen as an orphan brand. After filing for bankruptcy in 2001, the brand was bought by a private equity firm. A 2003 market research study indicated the Polaroid name was still a powerful asset, so it soon appeared on electronic devices such as TVs and DVDs in the USA. These items, which achieved distribution in Wal-Mart and Target supermarkets, generated a reported €200 million in annual sales, proving that the orphan Polaroid still had some life in it.[28]

In some cases, a brand is beyond repair. One option is to consolidate such a brand with a stronger one. For example, Procter & Gamble merged White Cloud and Charmin toilet paper in the USA, eliminating the White Cloud line in 1992. P&G also merged Solo and Bold detergents. With shelf space at a premium, brand consolidation will increasingly be seen as a way to create a stronger brand, cut costs and focus marketing.[29]

Finally, the solution may be to discontinue a product altogether. The marketplace is littered with brands that either failed to establish an adequate level of equity or found their sources of brand equity disappear because of changes in the market. Companies sometimes spin off their orphan brands when sales shrink too low. Brand Briefing 13.9 describes how the existence of orphan brands has spawned a new business model of 'orphan adopters'.

Academic Nancy Koehn explains that old brands retain some value because consumers often remember them from childhood. 'There's at least an unconscious link', says Koehn.[30] Perhaps this fact helps to explain why a US website called www.hometownfavorites.com, which offers more than 400 exotic orphan brands such as Bre'r Rabbit Molasses and My-T-Fine Pudding, has revenue approaching $1 million. As long as orphan brands remain popular with a core audience, it seems that companies are willing to sell them.[31]

Making products obsolete

How do you decide which brands to attempt to revitalize (or at least milk) and which ones to make obsolete? Beecham chose to abandon 5-Day deodorant pads, Rose Milk skincare lotion and Serutam laxative but attempted to resurrect Aqua Velva aftershave, Geritol iron and vitamin supplement and Brylcreem hairstyling

Brand Briefing 13.9

Building a business by resurrecting orphan brands

With the right marketing approach, it is possible to bring a jettisoned brand back to life. For example, in the USA, after P&G discontinued White Cloud toilet paper, Wal-Mart secured the rights to the name and used it for its own label nappies, enabling it to drop P&G's Pampers from its shelves. Recently, companies have emerged that take orphan brands and regenerate them, in effect becoming 'orphan brand adopters'.

Redox

Redox, a company headed by two former P&G executives, bought Oxydol for an estimated €4.8 million. P&G had marketed Oxydol since 1927, but the brand was stocked by only 15 percent of US stores by the time Redox purchased it. Annual sales of Oxydol had fallen from €54.7 million in 1992 to €3.4 million in 2000. While focus groups revealed that older consumers exhibited more brand loyalty and were unlikely to switch from Oxydol, consumers in their twenties wanted to buy a different detergent from their parents. Redox repositioned Oxydol as an 'extreme clean', updated the packaging by enlarging the letter X and using a green container, and launched a website (www.the-extreme-clean.com) boasting 'We're proud that Oxydol kicks some mean bootie in the washing machine.' By summer 2001, Oxydol was stocked in 70 percent of outlets in the USA. Following this success, Redox purchased Biz bleach, another orphan from P&G. The two brands combined brought in an estimated €54.7 million in 2001. Soon thereafter, a majority stake in the company was acquired by private equity firm Allied Capital for €15 million.

River West

In the USA River West, founded in 2002 by a former Kraft executive, has helped rescue six brands from the rubbish heap: Nuprin pain reliever, Metrecal diet drink, Soho soft drinks, Silkience shampoo, Structure men's clothing, Underalls underwear and Coleco video games. The company does not actually buy brands, but collects a royalty from the manufacturer based on sales. River West took Coleco, which had not survived the 1980s, and relaunched it to a gaming audience of twenty- and thirty-somethings who grew up with the brand. River West introduced hand-held and head-to-head games for Coleco, and announced plans to relaunch Colecovision, an early 1980s precursor to the Xbox and PlayStation. The brand took in an estimated €34.2 million in 2005. To revive Nuprin, River West expanded the brand's range beyond just ibuoprofen into a full-line pain medication available only in CVS chemists. These examples demonstrate how the company's business model is predicated on finding a new story to tell with the brands. 'We really don't see ourselves as a nostalgia company,' said Paul Earle, founder and president of River West. 'We can only target the heartstrings for only so long. That is not a sustainable business model.'

Sources: Steve Watkins, 'Investment firm to sell Redox brands', *Cincinnati Business Courier*, 18 October 2004; John Schmeltzer, 'Reviving the past', *Chicago Tribune*, 2 May 2006: 1.

Market prospects

- Is the rate of decline orderly and predictable?
- Are there pockets of enduring demand?
- What are the reasons for the decline? Is it temporary? Might it be reversed?

Competitive intensity

- Are there dominant competitors with unique skills or assets?
- Are there many competitors unwilling to quit or contract gracefully?
- Are customers loyal? Is there product differentiation?
- Are there price pressures?

Brand strength and organizational capabilities

- Is the brand strong? Does it enjoy high recognition and positive, meaningful associations?
- What is the market share position and trend?
- Does the business have sustainable competitive advantages with respect to key segments?
- Can the business manage a milking strategy?
- Is there synergy with other businesses?
- Does the brand fit with the firm's strategic thrust?
- What are the exit barriers?

Figure 13.7   Investment decisions in a declining industry

products. The decision to stop making a product depends on a number of factors. Aaker outlines strategic questions that can be raised when considering whether or not to invest in a fading brand (Figure 13.7).[32]

Fundamentally, the issue is the existing and latent equity of the brand. As the head of consumer packaged goods giant Unilever commented: 'If businesses aren't creating value, we shouldn't be in them. It's like having a nice garden that gets weeds. You have to clean it up, so the light and air get in to the blooms which are likely to grow the best.'[33] Brand Briefing 13.10 describes how Unilever went about culling its brand portfolio.

Brand Briefing 13.10

Brand migration at Unilever

Unilever, which was formed in 1929 by the merger of Dutch-owned Margarine Unie and the British-based Lever Brothers soap concern, owned more than 1,600 distinct brands in 2000. Some of Unilever's famed brands include Lipton tea, Ragu' pasta sauces, Bird's Eye frozen foods, Calvin Klein fragrances and Dove personal care products. Unilever also has thousands of lesser-known brands that are not strong competitors in their markets. In an effort called 'Path to growth', designed to get the most value from its brand portfolio, the company announced in 1999 its intention of eliminating three-quarters of its brands by 2003.

Brand Briefing 13.10 *continued*

Antony Burgmans, Unilever's co-chairman, described the means of reducing the brand portfolio:

> Some [brands] we will try and fold into a power brand ... Another way of doing it is just letting [a brand] fade away and see where it stops. And some may be disposed of.

The company intended to retain global brands such as Lipton, as well as its regional brands and 'local jewels' such as Persil, the leading detergent in the UK. Unilever sold brands such as Batchelors and Elizabeth Arden, delisted brands, including Blueband and Krona margarine, and merged second-tier brands such as Radion into leading brands, in this case Surf. Additionally, Unilever planned to reduce headcount by 25,000, or 10 percent of its workforce, in 5 years. The company also planned to close 100 of its 380 manufacturing sites.

While Unilever was reducing its brand portfolio, it was also making acquisitions and expanding into services. Between 1996 and 2000, the company spent more than €19.1 billion on acquisitions. In 2000, the company acquired Slim-Fast Foods and Ben & Jerry's ice-cream for a total of more than €1.7 billion. Since only 6 percent of Slim-Fast's sales came from outside North America, Unilever expected to use its global distribution network to expand the brand. Ben & Jerry's gave Unilever a super-premium ice-cream to compete against Häagen-Dazs, owned by rival General Mills' Pillsbury unit. Unilever also added a host of services in the 'health, hygiene, and indulgence sectors'. The company launched MyHome, a home-cleaning service available in the UK, and opened a chain of tea houses under the name Cha.

By the end of the first quarter in 2001, Unilever had reduced its portfolio to 900 brands and had another 250 'marked for disposal.' Unilever estimated it achieved €243 million in cost savings in 2001 from its brand reductions. Following this success, the company continued on its scheme, lowering the number of brands it owned to 400 by 2005. Yet, the company fell short of sales targets, in part because its heritage as a joint Anglo-Dutch company involved higher personnel and marketing costs, with many job functions and ad agencies overlapping. In 2003, Unilever posted €30.6 billion in sales, on a par with rival Procter & Gamble. Because Unilever employed more than twice as many people as P&G, however, its net income for the year was 45 percent lower than P&G's. Unilever launched a parallel scheme, called 'One Unilever', to remedy the duplication, streamline the agency buys and eliminate many 'contradictory local [marketing] projects'.

Sources: John Willman, 'Leaner, cleaner and healthier is the stated aim', *Financial Times*, 23 February 2000; John Thornhill, 'A bad time to be in consumer goods', *Financial Times*, 28 September 2000; 'Unilever's goal: "power brands"', *Advertising Age*, 3 January 2000; 'Unilever axes 25,000 jobs', *CNNfn*, 22 February 2000; 'Unilever sees €395m cost savings this year from brand reduction', *AFX* (UK), 9 May 2001; 'A chat with Unilever's Niall FitzGerald', *BusinessWeek Online*, 2 August 2001; Harriet Marsh, 'Unilever a year down the "path"', *Marketing*, 22 February 2001: 30; Deborah Ball, 'Despite revamp, unwieldy Unilever falls behind rivals', *Wall Street Journal*, 3 January 2005: A1.

CHAPTER REVIEW

Effective brand management requires taking a long-term view of marketing decisions. A long-term perspective of brand management recognizes that changes in the marketing campaign for a brand may, by changing consumer knowledge, affect future marketing campaigns. Additionally, a long-term view necessitates strategies designed to enhance customer-based brand equity over time in the face of changes in the marketing environment and internal changes in a company's goals and campaigns. This chapter considered how to reinforce, revitalize and cull brands and discussed managing brands over time.

Brand equity is reinforced by marketing actions that consistently convey the meaning of the brand to consumers. The most important consideration in reinforcing a brand is the consistency of the marketing support that it receives, in terms of both the amount and nature of that support. Consistency does not mean that marketers should avoid changing the marketing – in fact, tactical changes may be necessary to maintain the strategic direction of a brand. Unless there is a change in the marketing environment, however, there is little need to deviate from a successful positioning. In such cases, the critical points of parity and points of difference that represent sources of brand equity should be vigorously defended.

Reinforcing brand meaning depends on the nature of the brand association involved. For brands whose core associations are primarily product-related attributes and functional benefits, innovation in product design, manufacturing and merchandising is critical to enhancing brand equity. For brands whose core associations are primarily non-product-related attributes and symbolic or experiential benefits, relevance in user and usage imagery is critical to maintaining or enhancing brand equity. In managing brand equity, it is important to recognize the tradeoffs between those marketing activities that reinforce meaning and those that attempt to borrow from its existing brand equity to reap some financial benefit. At some point, failure to fortify the brand will diminish brand awareness and weaken its image. Without these sources of brand equity, a brand itself may not continue to yield valuable benefits. Figure 13.8 summarizes brand reinforcement strategies.

Revitalizing a brand requires either that lost sources of brand equity be recaptured or that new sources be identified and established. According to the CBBE framework, two approaches are possible: expand the depth or breadth (or both) of brand awareness by improving brand recall and recognition by consumers during purchase or consumption settings; and improve the strength, favourability and uniqueness of brand associations making up the brand image. This latter approach may involve campaigns directed at existing or new brand associations.

With a fading brand, the depth of brand awareness is often not as much of a problem as the breadth – that is, consumers tend to think of the brand in very narrow ways. Strategies to increase usage of and find new uses for the brand were reviewed. Although changing brand awareness is probably the easiest way to create sources of brand equity, a new marketing campaign often may have to be implemented to improve the strength, favourability and uniqueness of brand associations. As part of this repositioning, new markets may have to be tapped. The challenge in all of

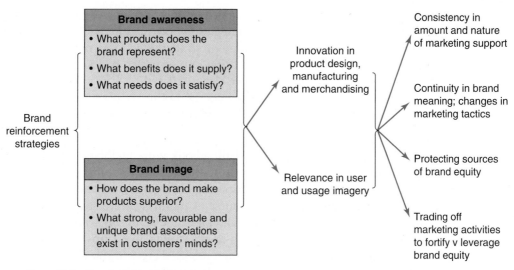

Figure 13.8 Brand reinforcement strategies

these efforts to modify brand image is to not destroy the equity that already exists. Figure 13.9 summarizes brand revitalization strategies.

As part of the long-term perspective on managing a brand portfolio, it is necessary to consider the role of brands and the relationships between brands in a portfolio over time. In particular, a migration strategy is needed to show consumers how the

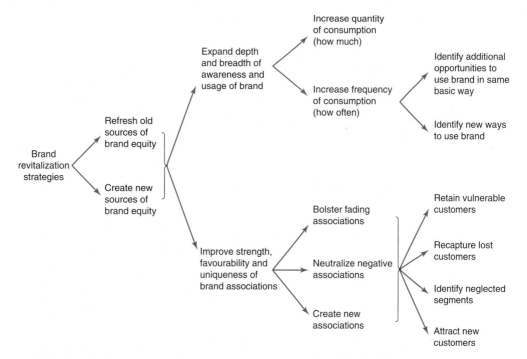

Figure 13.9 Brand revitalization strategies

brands in a portfolio can satisfy their needs as they change over time or as the products and brands themselves change. Strategies to both acquire new customers and retain existing ones were reviewed. Different strategies to stop making those products whose sources of brand equity had dried up or which had acquired damaging and difficult-to-change associations were also discussed.

In closing, the importance of the material in this chapter can be seen through the words of one marketing commentator who has an interesting view on how to think about managing brands over time:

> Brands are like ships. You could fill a book with analogies. One key common denominator is that brands, once they gain momentum, overtake agility. A brand heading in the right direction absorbs a lot of mishandling before it stops dead in the water, or goes off course. A brand heading south takes effort and time to turn around. Think through all of the similarities and you'll soon find yourself wondering why brands aren't staffed like ships. True, most brands have a captain, several admirals and assorted crew to run the engines and polish the brass. But all too few brands have a navigator whose job is to keep the ship on course towards a destination that is far over the horizon. This is especially scary when you consider your USS Brand will undergo several complete crew changeovers before reaching anything remotely resembling a safe port, and that it sails in oceans studded with the perils of changing winds, tides, and currents, to say nothing of enemy subs and icebergs appearing out of the fog.[34]

Brand Briefing 13.11

Corporate name changes

Rationale

As noted in Chapter 11, corporate brand names and corporate images can perform a variety of functions for many audiences or target markets. As these brands evolve over time, corporate names may have to be changed for a number of reasons. Hundreds of private and public companies change their names each year.

The main reason companies change their name is because of mergers and acquisitions with other businesses. In such cases, a new name may be chosen to signal different capabilities. For example, when Bell Atlantic purchased GTE in 2000, the newly merged company adopted the Verizon brand name, which combined *veritas*, the Latin word for reliability, and horizon, which was intended to signify a forward-looking attitude. In other cases, a name may be based on a combination of two corporate names. For example, when Glaxo Wellcome merged in 2000 with SmithKline Beecham, the new company became GlaxoSmithKline, and J. P. Morgan and Chase Manhattan Corporation became J. P. Morgan Chase after their 2000 merger. Finally, in some cases, the name with more potential inherent brand equity is chosen and the other name is relegated to a sub-brand role or eliminated

Brand Briefing 13.11 *continued*

altogether. For example, when Citicorp merged with Travelers, the latter name was dropped, although its familiar red umbrella symbol was retained as part of the new Citigroup look. Deciding which is the appropriate strategy depends on the existing and potential brand equity associated with each brand in the context of the newly merged business.

Another reason that corporate names may need to be changed is because of divestitures, leveraged buyouts or sale of assets. For example, when Andersen Consulting was allowed to separate from Arthur Andersen following an arbitrator's ruling in 2000, it was required to stop using the Andersen Consulting name by the end of the year. Following an extensive naming search and rebranding project, which included names solicited by Andersen Consulting employees, the firm was renamed 'Accenture' – an employee-submitted name meant to connote an 'accent on the future'. The move to a new name proved especially fortuitous when in 2002 Arthur Andersen was convicted of obstruction of justice in the wake of the Enron scandal and ceased to operate as a business. Some negative perceptions from Arthur Andersen would probably have transferred to the Andersen Consulting brand.

The corporate name may also need to be changed because of public misconceptions about the nature of the company's business. For example, Europe's third-largest food company, BSN, renamed the company after its Danone brand – a hugely successful fresh dairy products subsidiary, second only to Coca-Cola in terms of branded sales in Europe – because many consumers didn't know what the old name stood for. Moreover, BSN was used by other companies in other countries: a bank in Spain, a textile firm in the USA and a television station in Japan.[35]

Shifts in strategy may necessitate name changes. For example, US Steel changed its name to USX to play down the importance of steel in its product mix. Allegheny Airlines changed its name to USAir when it moved from a regional to a national carrier, and then later to USAirways when it wanted to be seen as an international carrier.

In addition to mergers and acquisitions, the desire to create distance from scandal can also precipitate a name change. A new name cannot repair a company's damaged reputation, though, and experts advise against making a switch in the midst of bad publicity, otherwise the stigma and suspicion will follow the new name. Philip Morris decided to change its name to get away from the association with tobacco and emphasize its range of companies, including Kraft Foods. In 2003, the company adopted the new name Altria Group. ValuJet Airlines in 1997 merged with AirTran and the new company took the AirTran name to distance itself from the crash in 1996 of a ValuJet airliner.

Brand Briefing 13.11 *continued*

Guidelines

Though name changes can yield growth opportunities, experts recommend a cautious approach to renaming. Name changes are complicated, time-consuming and expensive. They should only be undertaken when compelling marketing or financial considerations prevail and a suitable marketing campaign can be put in place. A new corporate name cannot hide product or other marketing deficiencies. Rebranding campaigns usually involve forfeiting the brand recognition and loyalty that went along with the old name. Additionally, a new name requires extensive legal and domain-name vetting to make sure the name is available and appropriate.

Once a name is chosen, the practical work of introducing it to clients, suppliers and employees begins – often with a new marketing campaign and the opportunity to work with a blank canvas. A company with little consumer exposure may spend as much as €3.42 million on research, advertising and other marketing costs (eg, signs, stationery and business cards) to change its identity, but a company with a high public profile may have to spend up to €68.4 million.[36] These factors combine to make corporate rebranding a process that demands a company's total commitment to succeed.

In changing the corporate name, the assumption is that the existing brand associations do not have the desired strength, favourability and uniqueness and that a new name can be chosen – perhaps in combination with a corporate image campaign – that better conveys the desired brand image.

Many of the issues regarding choosing brand names that were discussed in Chapter 4 are relevant in choosing or changing a corporate name. Thus, candidate names should be evaluated in terms of memorability, meaningfulness, likeability, protectability, adaptability and transferability. The importance of the name will depend on the corporate branding strategy that is adopted and the marketing objectives with respect to target markets. If the financial community is a priority, a different name may be chosen than if the consumer market is the priority. For example, if the financial community is a priority, corporate names may be changed to highlight a particular brand or company (eg, Consolidated Foods switched to Sara Lee; Castle & Cooke, switched to Dole Food Company; and United Brands switched to Chiquita Brands International). If the consumer market is the primary objective, names may be chosen to reflect or be suggestive of certain product characteristics, benefits or values.

Once a name is chosen, substantial efforts must be undertaken to sell the new name to employees, customers, suppliers, investors and the public.[37] Because of a resistance to change, reaction to a new name is almost always negative. In some cases, an especially harsh reception will cause a new name to be abandoned.

Brand Briefing 13.11 *continued*

One of the biggest name change debacles occurred with UAL, parent company of United Airlines. In 1987, UAL was no longer just an airline but a €6.1 billion business that owned Hertz car rental, as well as Westin and Hilton International hotels. It was decided that a new name was necessary to convey the identity of a travel company that offered one-stop shopping. After extensive research, the name 'Allegis' was chosen, a compound of 'allegiance' and 'aegis'. Public reaction was negative. Critics maintained that the name was difficult to pronounce, sounded pretentious and had little connection with travel services. Famed mogul Donald Trump, formerly a UAL shareholder, said the new name was 'better suited to the next world-class disease'. After 6 weeks and €4.8 million in research and promotion expenditures, the company decided to shed its car rental and hotel businesses and rename the surviving company United Airlines.[38]

Over time, though, if properly chosen and handled, names gain familiarity and acceptance. Effective implementation requires guidelines that encourage uniformity and consistency in the appearance and usage of the brand; these rules should be included as part of a revised brand charter (see Chapter 8).

Creating the UBS brand

UBS was formed in 1998 when the Union Bank of Switzerland and Swiss Bank Corporation merged. The bank struggled for recognition outside Switzerland, especially in the USA. After a period of acquiring better-known companies such as SG Warburg and PaineWebber, UBS reviewed its branding. The results showed product overlap between UBS businesses, a weak branding culture and a focus on individual employees rather than the brand.[39] In fact, a UBS representative was invited to appear on a CNBC talk show because the show hosts couldn't cope with all the UBS brands. As it turned out, on the show, even the company representative couldn't distinguish between the UBS brands.

The company worked with consultants and looked at research showing similarities between the needs of clients across parts of the business. To address these needs and reduce overlap between sub-brands, in 2003 the company adopted the UBS brand for all of its businesses. The company decided to use only the UBS letters in its name, a challenging decision because the name had no personality.[40]

So UBS launched a global brand-building effort. A new brand group was created to handle all advertising. The goal was to emphasize the bank's scope and resources, while also playing up its one-on-one client relationships. The 'You and us' campaign started in 2004, with global spending above €68.4 million. It illustrated the traditional banker–client relationship as well also the international presence of the company by using wide shots of two people in sweeping mountain settings or in airy corporate spaces. 'Could this be the world's most powerful two-person financial

Brand Briefing 13.11 *continued*

firm?' asks a voiceover or a tagline. 'You and us: UBS.' The goal was to assure customers that they could rely on the breadth and depth of the bank's offerings, whatever their financial needs.

In terms of brand recognition, the campaign worked. In 2004, UBS ranked 45 on *BusinessWeek*'s list of the top 100 global brands, its first year on the list. Additionally, awareness of the company in its target segments has risen.

Discussion questions

1. Pick a brand. Assess its efforts at managing brand equity in the past five years. What actions has it taken to be innovative and relevant? Can you suggest any changes to its marketing campaign?

2. Pick a product category. Examine the histories of the leading brands in that category over the past decade. How would you characterize their efforts at reinforcing or revitalizing brand equity?

3. Identify a fading brand. What suggestions can you offer to revitalize its brand equity? Try to apply the approaches suggested in this chapter. Which strategies would seem to work best?

4. Try to think of additional examples of brands that adopted either a 'back to basics' or 'reinvention' revitalization strategy. How well did the strategies work?

5. Conduct a review of the Unilever brand portfolio (see Brand Briefing 13.10). How successful has the company been at reducing the number of brands? What lessons are to be learned from its strategies?

References and notes

[1]Robert Levine, 'The cow in winter', *Fortune*, 17 April 2006: 55–6.

[2]Ibid.

[3]Bruce Horovitz, 'Southern finger-lickin' roots help KFC revamp', *USA Today*, 20 April 2005: 3B.

[4]For an empirical examination of the power of sustained advertising, see Cathy J. Cobb-Walgren, Cynthia A. Ruble and Naveen Donthu, 'Brand equity, brand preference and purchase intent', *Journal of Advertising*, fall 1995, 24 (3): 25–40.

[5]Chris Roush, 'At Timex, they're positively glowing', *BusinessWeek*, 12 July 1993: 141.

[6]Jonathan Auerbach, 'Smith Corona seeks protection of Chapter 11', *Wall Street Journal*, 6 July 1995: A4.

[7]Melanie Wells, 'Foggy bottom', *Forbes*, 28 May 2001: 155.

[8]Michael V. Copeland, 'Stuck in the spin cycle', *Business 2.0*, May 2005: 74.

[9]Adapted from Suein L. Hwang, 'As rivals innovate, old-line Bacardi becomes a chaser', *Wall Street Journal*, 6 July 1994: B4. See also Rich Brandes, 'Liquor holds its breath as economy teeters', *Beverage Industry*, 1 May 2001.

[10] 'Glass half full,' *Journal of Commerce*, 30 May 2005: 36A.

[11]Susan Heckler, Kevin Lane Keller and Michael J. Houston, 'The effects of brand name suggestiveness on advertising recall', *Journal of Marketing*, January 1998, 62: 48–57.

[12]Raymond Serafin, 'BMW: from yuppie-mobile to smart car of the '90s', *Advertising Age*, 3 October 1994: S2.

[13]Norman C. Berry, 'Revitalizing brands', *Journal of Consumer Marketing*, summer 1988, 5 (3): 15–20.

[14]Dawn C. Chmielewski, 'Napster posts loss despite surge in sales', *Los Angeles Times*, 9 February 2006: C1.

[15]John D. Cripps, 'Heuristics and biases in timing the replacement of durable products', *Journal of Consumer Research*, September 1994, 21: 304–18.

[16]Ronald Alsop, 'Giving fading brands a second chance', *Wall Street Journal*, 24 January 1989: B1.

[17]Ellen Byron, 'How Coach won a rich purse by inventing new uses for bags', *Wall Street Journal*, 17 November 2004: A1.

[18]Darrel D. Muehling and David E. Sprott, 'The power of reflection: an empirical examination of nostalgia advertising effects', *Journal of Advertising*, fall 2004, 33 (3): 25.

[19]Elizabeth S. Moore, William L. Wilkie and Richard J. Lutz, 'Passing the torch: intergenerational influences as a source of brand equity', *Journal of Marketing*, April 2002, 66: 2, 17.

[20]Marj Charlier, 'Yuengling's success defies convention', *Wall Street Journal*, 26 August 1993: B1.

[21]Tim Triplett, 'Generic fear to Xerox is brand equity to FedEx', *Marketing News*, 15 August 1994: 12–13.

[22]Mike Beirne, 'New logo, upscale image in at revamped Ramada', *Brandweek*, 8 November, 2004: 6.

[23]David W. Stewart, 'Advertising in a slow-growth economy', *American Demographics*, September 1994: 40–6.

[24]Ibid.

[25]Tracie Rozhon, 'Reinventing Tommy: more surf, less logo', *New York Times*, 16 March 2003: 1.

[26]Deborah Ball and Sarah Ellison, 'Two shampoos lather up for duel', *Wall Street Journal*, 28 January 2003: B7.

[27]Kathleen Kerwin, 'Can Jeep bust out of its rut?', *BusinessWeek*, 24 January 2005: 37.

[28]Peter Lattman, 'Rebound', *Forbes*, 28 March 2005: 58.

[29]Jennifer Reingold, 'Darwin goes shopping', *Financial World*, 1 September 1993: 44.

[30]Nancy F. Koehn, *Brand New: How enterpreneurs earned consumers' trust from Wedgwood to Dell*, Boston, MA: Harvard Business School Press, 2001.

[31]Betsy McKay, 'Why Coke indulges (the few) fans of Tab', *Wall Street Journal*, 13 April 2001: B1; Devon Spurgeon, 'Aurora bet it could win by fostering neglected foods', *Wall Street Journal*, 13 April 2001: B1; Jim Hopkins, 'Partners turn decrepit detergent into boffo start-up', *USA Today*, 20 June 2001: 6B; Matthew Swibel, 'Spin cycle', *Forbes*, 2 April 2001: 118.

[32]David A. Aaker, *Managing Brand Equity*, New York: Free Press, 1991.

[33]Tara Parker-Pope, 'Unilever plans a long-overdue pruning', *Wall Street Journal*, 3 September 1996: A13.

[34]Brad Morgan, 'Navigating marketing waters is a risky, learning process', *Brandweek*, 5 September 1994: 17.

[35]'BSWho?' *The Economist*, 14 May 1994: 70.

[36]Dottie Enrico, 'Companies play name-change game', *USA Today*, 28 December 1994: 4B.

[37]Amanda Bennett, 'Firms grapple to find new names as images and industries change', *Wall Street Journal*, 17 November 1986: 36.

[38]'Allegis: A $7 million name is grounded', *San Francisco Examiner*, 16 June 1987: C9.

[39]Jestyn Thirkell-White, 'UBS: brand building in a global market', *Admap*, July/August 2004.

[40]Haig Simonian, 'Three letters gain a personality', *The Financial Times*, 18 April 2005.

14 Managing brands over geographic boundaries and market segments

PREVIEW

One consideration in managing brand equity is recognizing and accounting for different types of consumers in marketing campaigns. Previous chapters have considered how and why marketers may need to create brand portfolios to satisfy different market segments and develop brand migration strategies to attract new customers and retain existing customers through brand and family lifecycles. This chapter examines the implications of differences in consumer behaviour and the existence of different types of market segments for managing brand equity. It pays particular attention to international issues and global branding strategies.

Specifically, after reviewing the rationale for taking brands into international markets, the chapter considers broader issues in developing a global brand strategy. Some of the pros and cons of developing a standardized global marketing campaign for a brand are examined. The bulk of the chapter then concentrates on strategic and tactical issues in building global customer-based brand equity, organized around the concept of the 'ten commandments of global branding.' To illustrate these guidelines, emphasis is placed on global brand pioneers such as Coca-Cola, Nestlé, Procter & Gamble and two more recent examples, Nokia and Ikea. Brand Briefing 14.11 addresses branding issues in China.

RATIONALE FOR GOING INTERNATIONAL

Many global brands have long derived much of their sales and profits from non-domestic markets: Nokia, Coca-Cola, Ikea, Shell, Electrolux, Bayer, Rolex, Marlboro, Pampers and Mercedes-Benz to name a few. Brands such as Apple, L'Oréal and Nescafé have become fixtures on the global landscape (see Brand Briefing 14.1). The successes of these brands have provided encouragement to many firms to market their brands internationally. Other forces have contributed to the interest in global marketing, too.

- Perception of slow growth and increased competition in domestic markets.
- Belief in enhanced overseas growth and profit opportunities.

Brand Briefing 14.1

L'Oréal colours the world

L'Oréal was founded in 1907 by French chemist Eugene Schueller, who developed a safe hair colour formula named 'Aureole'. L'Oréal grew to become the largest cosmetics company in the world, with more than 500 brands and 2,000 products in all sectors of the beauty business.

Recently, L'Oréal has pursued an aggressive global growth strategy, prompting one business writer to christen the company 'the United Nations of beauty'. L'Oréal has several global mega-brands. For example, Maybelline is the best-selling brand in many Asian markets, while eastern Europeans prefer L'Oréal's French brands, and African immigrants in Europe go for the American brand Dark & Lovely. At the same time, the company ensures its business remains sound at a local level by establishing national divisions. Gilles Weil, L'Oréal's head of luxury products, said: 'You have to be local and as strong as the best locals but backed by an international image and strategy.'

One of L'Oréal's success stories started with it buying the struggling US cosmetics company Maybelline in 1996. With the help of innovative product introductions, L'Oréal turned the brand into the leading make-up brand in the USA. The star product for the new Maybelline was Wondercurl, a mascara and brush that curls and thickens eyelashes. Wondercurl took off again when L'Oréal took control of Maybelline Japan in 1999. Within three months, Wondercurl captured 18 percent of the market and became Japan's leading mascara. Unit sales of Maybelline Japan rose from 5 million to 12 million within a year of the takeover.

Within national markets, L'Oréal devotes attention to customer segments. For example, in 2000 L'Oréal captured 20 percent of the €875 million US 'ethnic hair care' market with separate acquisitions of Soft Sheen Products and Carson Products. The company considered the ethnic hair care market vital because African Americans account for 30 percent of total US haircare expenditures even though they comprise only 13 percent of the population. These acquisitions added to L'Oréal's 49 percent share of the €950 million US hair colour market.

L'Oréal's next focus was China, where in 2004 it purchased the country's most popular cosmetics brand, Yue Sai, and bought bargain brand Mininurse, which had a distribution network of more than 250,000 small shops. L'Oréal also invested in a 32,000 square-foot laboratory in Pudong to develop products specific to the Chinese market, including products containing local ingredients such as ginkgo leaf and ginseng. One of the challenges in China was educating consumers about the benefits of different cosmetic products. 'In other countries women learn how to use cosmetics from the mom,' said Paolo Gasparrini, president of L'Oréal China. 'That's not the case in China. We have to substitute [for the mom].' Still, L'Oréal's Chinese sales in 2004 were up 58 percent from the previous year to €255 million.

Brand Briefing 14.1 *continued*

L'Oréal was also experiencing growth in other developing markets. In 2005, revenues rose 42 percent in Russia, 22 percent in Taiwan, 15 percent in Thailand and 13 percent in Brazil and Mexico. L'Oréal's growth helped push revenues up 6 percent to €11.8 billion in 2005, ahead of all its cosmetics competitors. As one analyst puts it: 'L'Oréal is the only real global leader in every segment of the industry.'

Sources: Richard C. Morais, 'The color of beauty', *Forbes*, 27 November 2000: 170–6; Gail Edmondson, 'L'Oréal: the beauty of global branding', *BusinessWeek*, 28 June 1999: 24; Sheridan Prasso, 'Battle for the face of China', *Fortune*, December, 2005: 156.

- Desire to reduce costs as a result of economies of scale.
- Need to diversify risk.
- Recognition of global mobility of customers.

In some product categories, the ability to establish a global profile is becoming a prerequisite for success.[1] For example, in luxury goods, where the customer base is a relatively small part of the global market, a global profile is necessary for profitability.

Ideally, the marketing campaign for a global brand would consist of a single product formulation, packaging design, advertising campaign, pricing schedule and distribution plan that would turn out to be the most effective option for each and every country. Unfortunately, such a uniform strategy is rarely best. Before considering the decisions to be made in developing a global marketing campaign, it is useful to consider some of the advantages and disadvantages for brands.

ADVANTAGES OF GLOBAL MARKETING CAMPAIGNS

A number of potential advantages have been put forth concerning the development of a global marketing campaign (Figure 14.1).[2]

In general, the more standardized the marketing campaign – that is, the less it varies from country to country – the greater the extent to which these advantages will be realized.

Economies of scale

From a supply-side or cost perspective, the advantage of a global marketing campaign is the efficiencies and lower costs that derive from higher volumes in production and distribution. The more that strong experience curve effects exist – such that the cost of making and marketing a product declines sharply with increases in cumulative

- Economies of scale in production and distribution.
- Lower marketing costs.
- Power and scope.
- Consistency in brand image.
- Ability to build on good ideas quickly and efficiently.
- Uniformity of marketing practices.

Figure 14.1   Advantages of global marketing campaigns

production – the more economies of scale in production and distribution will be realized from a global campaign.

Lower marketing costs

Another set of cost advantages can be realized from uniformity in packaging, advertising and promotion activities. In particular, the more uniform the branding strategy, the more potential cost savings should prevail. Along these lines, a global corporate branding strategy (eg, as with Philips, Samsung, Siemens, Sony, Electrolux and LG) is perhaps the most efficient means of spreading marketing costs across both products and countries.

Power and scope

A global brand profile may communicate credibility to consumers.[3] Consumers may believe that selling in many diverse markets is an indication that a manufacturer has gained expertise and acceptance. The fact that a brand is widely available may signal that the product is of high quality and convenient to use. An admired global brand can also signal social status and prestige.[4] A prominent international profile may be especially important for service brands. For example, Avis assures customers that they can receive the same high-quality service renting its cars anywhere in the world, reinforcing a benefit embodied in its slogan, 'We try harder.'

Consistency in brand image

Maintaining a common marketing platform helps to maintain the consistency of brand and company image. This consideration becomes particularly important in those markets where there is much customer mobility or where media exposure transmits images across national boundaries. For example, Gillette sells 'functional superiority' and 'an appreciation of human character and aspirations' for its razors and blades brands worldwide. Services often desire to convey a uniform image due to consumer movements. For example, American Express communicates the prestige and utility of its card and the convenience and ease of replacement of its traveller's cheques worldwide.

Ability to build on good ideas

One global marketer notes that globalization can result in increased sustainability and 'facilitate continued development of core competencies with the organization . . . in manufacturing, in R&D, in marketing, and sales, and in less talked about areas such as competitive intelligence . . . all of which enhance the company's ability to compete.'[5] Not having to develop local versions speeds up a brand's market entry process. Good ideas can be used across markets as long as the right knowledge transfer systems are put into place. IBM has a web-based communicational tool that provides instant, multimedia interaction to connect marketers. MasterCard's corporate marketing group distributes information and best practices across the organization.[6]

Uniformity of marketing practices

Finally, a standardized global marketing campaign may simplify co-ordination and provide greater control of how a brand is marketed. By keeping the core of a marketing campaign constant, greater attention can be paid to making refinements over markets and over time to improve its effectiveness.

MasterCard

MasterCard developed its 'Priceless' campaign into a 'worldwide platform'.[7] By 1998, the tagline 'The best things in life are free. For everything else, there's MasterCard' was in use in more than 30 countries. Some ads' premises were universal enough that they worked in many countries, with only language translation, such as the 'Zip' ad where the priceless moment is a man realizing his trouser zip is down before anyone else. In other cases, a locally relevant premise was used instead, with the same tagline. 'Every culture has those meaningful moments, which is why we've been able to globalize the campaign', said a creative director for McCann Erickson, which developed the campaign.[8] Sponsorships for sports with international appeal, such as World Cup football and Forumla 1 racing, increased the campaign's ability to connect with a worldwide audience. The campaign was credited with lifting brand awareness in a number of nations, driving card sales and enabling MasterCard to take market share from Visa.

Brand Briefing 14.2 describes how Nokia changed strategic focus at the start of the 1990s. This enabled it to conquer the world in mobile phones.

DISADVANTAGES OF GLOBAL MARKETING CAMPAIGNS

A number of potential disadvantages of standardized global marketing campaigns have also been raised (Figure 14.2). Perhaps the most compelling criticism is that standardized global marketing campaigns often ignore fundamental differences of various kinds across countries and cultures. Critics claim that designing one marketing

Brand Briefing 14.2

Nokia: the global leader in mobile phones

Nokia is the highest-ranked telecommunications company on the Interbrands list of global brands. According to Interbrand, Nokia is also sixth on the list of the most valuable brands (July 2005), but it is the strongest non-US brand worldwide, and its worth is put at almost €22 billion. Nokia is also number one on the Reputation Institute's list of the highest-ranking corporate reputations in China (2006). Nokia's history can be traced back to 1865 when it started making paper under the direction of engineer Fredrik Idestam. In 1967, the company became the Nokia Group and was active in many markets such as chemicals, rubber and electronics. Nokia progressed in the telecommunications field in the 1960s. Although Nokia's history is colourful it is, today, known purely as a telecommunications and mobile technology company.

In the late 1980s Nokia was a large maker of TV sets and information technology supplier. But Nokia was missing a clear brand identity because it operated in several markets. This became a problem during the recession in Finland at the beginning of the 1990s. A strategic change of course took place in 1992 with a new chief executive, Jorma Ollila, who decided it was in Nokia's best interests to concentrate on one line of business. With an eye on the future, the telecommunications industry seemed most promising. So Nokia got rid of its huge brand portfolio and chose the, then, weakest brand of the lot.

This decision took courage but today Nokia commands a third of the global mobile phone market, with a half share of the European market. Nokia's ten biggest markets are the USA, UK, Germany, China, the Arab states, India, France, Brazil and Spain, which together generate 60 percent of total sales.

When analyzing Nokia's success story, a clear feature stands out, namely innovation. Nokia fosters a culture of innovation on all levels. Nokia's units are kept small and creative, so new ideas can move forward. Innovations in Nokia can emerge from a summer trainee or a seasoned engineer. At Nokia this continuing culture of innovation is called 'renewal'. The size of Nokia has been an advantage since its re-focusing on just one business line. In the field of mobile phones the competition comes from its pricing, so high-quantity orders have offered a huge advantage for Nokia.

The decision to concentrate its activities was bold but, because of it, Nokia has become one of the strongest brands in the world.

Sources: Kirsti Lindberg-Repo, 'Asiakkaan ja brändin vuorovaikutus: miten johtaa brändin arvoprosesseja?', WSOYPro, Finland 2005; www.reputationinstitute.com

- Differences in consumer needs, wants and usage patterns for products.
- Differences in consumer response to marketing mix elements.
- Differences in brand and product development and the competitive environment.
- Differences in the legal environment.
- Differences in marketing institutions.
- Differences in administrative procedures.

Figure 14.2   Disadvantages of global marketing campaigns

campaign for all possible markets often results in unimaginative and ineffective strategies geared to the lowest common denominator. Possible differences between countries come in a host of forms, as discussed next.

Differences in consumer needs

Because of differences in cultural values, economic development and other factors, consumer behaviour with respect to many product categories is different. For example, marketing research revealed that the per capita consumption of carbonated soft drinks, beer and bottled water varies dramatically from country to country (Figure 14.3). Product strategies that work in one country may not work in another. Tupperware, which makes more than 70 percent of its annual sales outside the USA, needed to adjust its products to satisfy different consumer behaviour. In India, a plastic container paired with a spoon becomes a 'masala keeper' for spices. In Korea, stain-resistant canisters are seen as ideal for fermenting kimchi. Larger boxes are promoted as safe, airtight 'kimono keepers' in Japan.

Country	Carbonated soft drinks	Beer	Bottled water
Australia	111.8	93.0	25.3
Brazil	69.6	46.7	24.7
China	7.3	15.8	6.0
France	42.1	35.9	131.3
Germany	90.5	123.1	106.6
India	1.7	0.7	2.6
Ireland	155.2	150.8	24.1
Mexico	152.1	48.6	130.0
South Africa	53.5	55.8	1.9
USA	203.9	83.1	73.8

Figure 14.3   Per capita beverage consumption (litres)
Source: 'Drink globally', *Beverage World*, May 2003: 17.

Differences in consumer response

Consumers in different parts of the world can vary in their attitudes to marketing activity.[9] For example, countries vary in their general attitudes towards advertising itself. Research has shown that people in the USA, in general, tend to be cynical about advertising, whereas the Japanese view it much more positively. Research has also shown differences in advertising styles between the two countries: Japanese ads tend to be softer and more abstract in tone, whereas US ads tend to be richer in product information.

Price sensitivity, promotion responsiveness, sponsorship support and other activities all may differ by country. Differences in response to marketing may also be reflected in differences in consumer behaviour and decision-making. For example, in a comparative study of brand purchase intentions for Korean and US consumers, the purchase intentions of Americans were twice as likely to be affected by their product beliefs and attitudes towards the brand itself, whereas Koreans were eight times more likely to be influenced by social normative beliefs and what they felt others would think about the purchase.[10]

Brand development and the competitive environment

Products may be at different stages of their lifecycle in different countries. Moreover, the perceptions and positions of particular brands may also differ considerably between countries. Figure 14.4 shows the results of a study of leading brands in different parts of the world by Young & Rubicam with its BrandAsset Valuator (see Brand Briefing 9.12). Relatively few brands appear on all the lists, suggesting that, if nothing else, consumer perceptions of even top brands can vary significantly by region. The nature of competition may also differ. Europeans tend to have more competitors because shipping products across borders is easy. For example, US group Procter & Gamble competes in France against Italian, Swedish and Danish companies.[11]

Differences in the legal environment

Different kinds of regulatory hurdles exist in different countries. One of the challenges of developing a global ad campaign is the maze of legal restrictions. For example, at one time, laws in Venezuela, Canada and Australia stipulated that commercials had to be produced in the native country. Canada also banned prescription drug advertising on television. Poland required commercial lyrics to be sung in Polish. Sweden prohibited advertising to children. Malaysia did not allow lawyers or law firms to advertise. Advertising restrictions have been placed on the use of children in commercials in Austria, comparative ads in Singapore and product placement on public television channels in Germany. Note the challenges posed by the following example.

> At the J. Walter Thompson ad agency, executives point to a 30-second cereal commercial produced for a British TV to show how much regulations in Europe alone can sap an advert. References to iron and vitamins would have to be deleted in the Netherlands; a child wearing a Kellogg's T-shirt would be edited

Rank	USA	UK	Germany	Brazil	China	Japan 2004	France 2005
1	United States	United Kingdom	Germany	Coca-Cola	China	Tokyo Disney Land	Arté
2	Disney	Cadbury's Dairy Milk	Aldi	Jornal Nacional	Xin Wen Lian Bo	Studio Ghibli	France
3	Coca-Cola	Cadbury	Ikea	Jornal da Globo	CCTV	Doraemon	Nutella
4	Wonderful World of Disney	England	Die Olympischen Spiele	Nescau	Beijing 2008 Olympics	Mickey Mouse	Coca-Cola
5	Discovery Channel	Channel 4	Nivea	Nestlé	Coca-Cola	Uniqlo	Le TGV
6	M&M's	The pound (£)	Ritter Sport	Fantástico	Olympic Games	Disney	Levi's
7	Hallmark (card retailer)	Heinz	Günther Jauch	Ayrton Senna	Nokia	Nike	Häagen-Dazs
8	History Channel	Coca-Cola	ARD	Globo Repórter	Pepsi-Cola	Muji	Perrier
9	Dr Pepper	Dyson	Nutella	Brasil	Shanghai	Sony	Tefal
10	Hershey's	Disney	Coca-Cola	Copa do Mundo	CCTV Movie	KFC/Kentucky Fried Chicken	Ikea
11	National Geographic	Cadbury's Flake	Adidas	Rede Globo	CCTV News	Universal Studios	Carte D'or
12	US Marines	Galaxy (chocolate)	Milka	Carrefour	CCTV Sports	New York City	Canal+
13	Pringles	BBC	Maggi	O Boticário	Dove (chocolate)	Mister Donuts	Ferrero Rocher
14	Subway	Maltesers	Haribo	Sonho de Valsa	Beijing	Walt Disney Pictures	Evian
15	Oreo	BBC 1	Tempo (taschentücher)	Kibon	Jet Li	7-Eleven	M6
16	Pepsi-Cola	Cadbury's Creme Egg	Mon Chéri	McDonald's	CCTV Drama	Toys R Us	Kinder
17	Microsoft Windows	Pringles	ADAC	Brastemp	Jackie Chan	Mosburger	Bounty
18	Reese's	Olympic Games	Deutsches Rotes Kreuz	Bombeiros	Yao Ming	Honda	Haribo
19	Kraft Foods	ITV	Leibniz	Dove (sabonete)	Safeguard	McDonald's	Orangina
20	Levi's	Kellogg's Corn Flakes	Italy	Sadia	Liu Xiang	Nintendo	Hollywood (chewing gum)

Figure 14.4 Global brand rankings by country (includes products, people and countries)

out in France where children are forbidden from endorsing products on TV; and in Germany, the line 'Kellogg makes their corn flakes the best they've ever been' would be axed because of rules against making competitive claims.[12]

Although some of these laws have been or are being relaxed, legal differences still exist.

Marketing institutions differ

Marketing infrastructures may differ from country to country, making implementation of the same marketing strategy difficult. For example, channels of distribution, retail practices, media availability and media costs all may vary significantly. Foreign companies have struggled for years to break into Japan's rigid distribution system that locks out many foreign goods. China's primitive logistics – poor roads, jammed rivers and clogged railways – and inexperienced, indifferent and often corrupt middlemen present a different kind of challenge.[13] The penetration of television sets, telephones, supermarkets and so on may vary considerably, especially with respect to developing countries.

Differences in administrative procedures

In practice, it may be difficult to achieve the control necessary to implement a standardized global marketing campaign. Local offices may resist having their autonomy threatened. Local managers may suffer from the 'not invented here' syndrome and raise objections – rightly or wrongly – that the global marketing campaign misses a key feature of the local market. Local managers who feel that their autonomy has been reduced may lose motivation and feel doomed to fail.

STANDARDIZATION VERSUS CUSTOMIZATION

Given the potential pitfalls, before providing guidelines as to how to build global customer-based brand equity, it is worthwhile examining issues of standardization versus customization of brand marketing campaigns. In many ways, the fundamental issue in developing a global marketing campaign is the extent to which it should be standardized across countries because it has such a deep effect on marketing structure and processes. Brand Briefing 14.3 describes how the bicycle company Cycleurope aims to become international while balancing global and local brands.

Perhaps the biggest proponent of standardization is Levitt. In a controversial 1983 article, he argued that companies needed to learn to operate as if the world were one large market, ignoring superficial regional and national differences:

A thousand suggestive ways attest to the ubiquity of the desire for the most advanced things that the world makes and sells – goods of the best quality and reliability at the lowest price. The world's needs and desires have been irrevocably homogenised. This makes the multinational corporation obsolete and the global corporation absolute . . .

Brand Briefing 14.3

Cycleurope international branding

Since 2000, Cycleurope has been a wholly owned subsidiary of Grimaldi Industri. Cycleurope was founded in 1995 with the takeover of the majority of the shares of Monark Stiga, which was quoted on the Stockholm stock exchange. Cycleurope is a consolidation of several companies, and the company has evolved through acquisitions of local bicyclemakers. In the beginning, Cycleurope had only a Scandinavian presence. Since then, Cycleurope has evolved into a global company with its main market in Europe. In the international branding process of Cycleurope, four issues are of importance.

1. Formulating a brand management campaign.
2. Defining and communicating the corporate brand internally.
3. Global and local market segmentation and brand positioning.
4. Identifying brand and communication synergies.

Formulating a brand management campaign

The aim of Cycleurope's brand management campaign was to create a brand platform. The platform should act as a base for the company's brand management work. It should also guide the management team on all brand-related issues. The platform should help to ensure that the understanding of the brands is the same throughout the organization. Guarantees have been made that all the planning should be supported by the established platform. This has to be done before product launch and before communicating the products internally.

Brand-related issues are formulated in the *brand platform*, which contains a detailed description of a company and its brands from a brand management perspective. The contents of the platform mainly concern the executives and marketing management. To protect branding strategies from competitors, only a small part of the brand platform is chosen to be included in the *brand book*. The purpose of the brand book is to communicate the essence of a brand. The goal is that everyone internally within the organization as well as externally receives a uniform idea of what the brand stands for. The *product assortment guidelines* concern all the actual products. The purpose of these guidelines is to ensure that correct messages of the brand are communicated through products. Product assortment guidelines are for product managers (or other persons responsible for product launches) within the organization.

Defining and communicating the brand internally

Defining and communicating the corporate brand internally means creating an understanding of Cycleurope throughout the organization all over the world. The Cycleurope corporate brand contains four parts: visual identity; corporate statement; strategy; and history (Figure 14.5).

Brand Briefing 14.3 *continued*

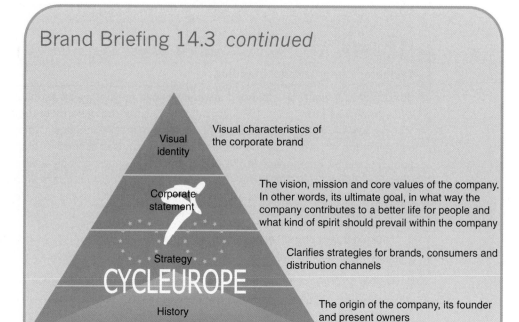

Figure 14.5   Communicating the Cycleurope brand internally

Global and local market segmentation

The market segmentation and brand positioning was designed to enable Cycleurope to act globally while being relevant locally.

- Cycleurope should take an upmarket position in all markets (countries) where it operates.

- The mega brands differ from country to country and represent strong brands that are well anchored locally.

- Affordable refers to brands that operate below the mega segment. The affordable brands also differ from market to market.

- Key account brands operate in the low-end segment. Their purpose is to compete with other bicycle companies that operate in the lowest price segment. Key account brands differ from market to market.

Cycleurope created a strong brand portfolio with local market-leading brands such as: Bianchi and Spectra (global, high-end); Legnano (Italy, affordable); Gitane (France, mega); Crescent (Sweden, mega); Monark (Sweden, affordable); DBS (Norway, mega); Kildemoes (Denmark, mega); and Everton (Denmark, affordable).

Identifying brand and communication synergies

To improve efficiency, Cycleurope should always search for simplicity, flexibility and synergies by acting as one company. The aim is to communicate easily and consistently.

Brand Briefing 14.3 *continued*

A structure of how all the brands should be described was established. The structure is the same for all Cycleurope brands, but the content differs. The brands can be described using three elements.

- *Brand profile:* the characteristics of a brand, its visual identity and brand slogan.
- *Brand statement:* the vision and mission of the brand. In other words, its ultimate goal and in what way the brand contributes to a better life for people.
- *Storytelling:* explains the origin of the brand, its founder and present owner.

All communication, verbal as well as printed, should communicate the same message. The brand platform should give the guidelines for the communication.

Sources: Christian Sandberg, 'Brand-driven business development', thesis, Nordic Brand Academy, 2007; Cycleurope corporate brand book.

But although companies customize products for particular market segments, they know that success in a world with homogenized demand requires a search for sales opportunities in similar segments across the globe in order to achieve the economies of scale necessary to compete.[14]

According to Levitt, because the world is shrinking – due to leaps in technology and communication – well-managed companies should shift their emphasis from customizing items to offering globally standardized products that are advanced, functional, reliable and low-priced for all.

Levitt's position elicited an equally strong response. One ad executive commented: 'There are about two products that lend themselves to global marketing – and one of them is Coca-Cola.' Other critics pointed out that even Coca-Cola did not standardize its marketing and noted the lack of standardization in other leading global brands, such as McDonald's and Marlboro. The experiences of these top marketers have been shared by others who found out – in many cases, the hard way – that differences in consumer behaviour prevail between countries. Many firms have been forced to tailor products and marketing campaigns to national markets as a result.

- Heinz ketchup has a slightly sweet taste in the USA but is spicier in certain European countries, where it is available in hot, Mexican and curry flavours. In the Philippines, Heinz offers a ketchup made from bananas that is dyed red. Ketchup use varies by country too. In Greece, it is poured on pasta, eggs and cuts of meat. In Japan, it is promoted as an ingredient for Western-style foods such as omelettes, sausages and pasta. Heinz has played down its US heritage in certain countries – for example, in Sweden, where ketchup is used to accompany meatballs and fishballs. In fact, Swedes thought the brand was German because of the name. In Germany, however, US themes work well and have been used in advertising.[15]

In summary, it is difficult to identify any company applying the global marketing concept in the strict sense – selling an identical brand in exactly the same way, everywhere.

Standardization and customization

Increasingly, marketers are blending global objectives with local or regional concerns. In 1999, Coca-Cola's new global marketing mantra became 'Think local. Act local' – an important twist on its old mantra, 'Think global. Act local.' Intended to get Coca-Cola back to the basics, the strategy involved hiring more local staff and allowing field managers to tailor marketing to their regions.[16] But after some 'un-Coke-like' ads began to appear and it became apparent that some localities were not ready to develop Coke's marketing entirely on their own, the 'Think local. Act local' mantra was scrapped for a hybrid strategy where a global marketing network of local executives took direction from Coke's Atlanta headquarters with room for interpretation at the local level. Brand Briefing 14.4 describes some of the history of Coca-Cola's global branding.

Brand Briefing 14.4

Coca-Cola becomes the quintessential global brand

The most recognized brand name in the world got its start in an Atlanta pharmacy, where it sold for five cents a glass. The name Coca-Cola was registered as a trademark on 31 January 1893. The drink soon became a US phenomenon; by 1895, the company had established syrup plants in Chicago, Dallas and Los Angeles.

In the 1920s, Coca-Cola pursued aggressive global branding, finding creative placements for its logo, such as on dogsleds in Canada and on the walls of bullfighting arenas in Spain. Its popularity was fuelled by colourful and persuasive advertising that cemented its image as the 'all-American' beverage. When the Vietnam war tarnished US iconography, Coca-Cola developed more globally aware advertising. In 1971, Coca-Cola ran its legendary 'I'd like to buy the world a Coke' television spot, in which a crowd of children sang the song from a hilltop in Italy. Coca-Cola's early moves into formerly restricted markets, such as China in 1978 and the Soviet Union in 1979, bolstered its image as a global company. By 1988, Coca-Cola was voted the best-known and most admired brand in the world.

Despite – or perhaps as a result of – this immense scope, Coca-Cola did not institute a uniform marketing campaign in each of its global markets. Rather, the company often tailored the flavour, packaging, price and advertising to match tastes in specific markets. For example, Coke's 'Mean Joe' Green TV ad from the USA – in which a weary football star reluctantly accepts a Coke from an admiring young fan

Brand Briefing 14.4 *continued*

and then unexpectedly tosses the kid his jersey in appreciation – was replicated in a number of regions using the same format but substituting famous athletes from those regions (eg, ads in South America used the Argentine football star Maradona, while those in Asia used the Thai player Niat). Additionally, local managers were assigned responsibility for sales and distribution of Coke products to reflect differences in consumer behaviour in their countries.

Perhaps the most standardized element of Coca-Cola is its product appearance. Coke keeps the same look and packaging everywhere (except in countries where laws dictate use of local language). The company simultaneously stresses that the brand be *relevant* and well-positioned relative to competition. In trying to stay relevant, Coca-Cola uses different advertising agencies in different countries to make the brand feel local. For example, in Australia the advertising appeals to the same 'classic, original' ideals but in a local way. Moreover, the marketing mix is designed in each country to stress that Coke is positioned positively on attributes relative to local competitive products. Hence, although Coke looks similar across the globe, its specific image may be very different, depending on what is considered 'relevant' in each country. The advantage of this approach is that Coke becomes entwined with the cultural fabric of a country, just as it has in the USA. Over time, this yields an advantage with younger generations who don't even think of Coke as an imported brand. An illustrative example that Coca-Cola recounts is of a Japanese family visiting the USA for the first time whose young son, upon passing a vending machine, joyfully exclaimed to his parents: 'Look, they have Coke here too!'

Today, Coca-Cola conducts business with more than 400 brands in 200 countries. More than 70 percent of Coca-Cola's revenues come from outside the USA, a fact that inspired Douglas Daft, when he took over as chairman and chief executive in 2000, to express his desire for Coca-Cola managers to adopt a new mantra: 'Think local. Act local.' This hyper-local focus led to missed sales targets and local advertising that, in some cases, did not fit with the Coke image, such as an Italian ad featuring naked youngsters running along a beach. So in 2002 Coke formed a 100-person team that became the 'centrepiece' of the global marketing group, setting strategy, hiring agencies, developing people and sharing best practices with the local managers. Stephen Jones, Coke's then chief marketing officer, was careful to point out that the moves did not signal a return to the days of 'Think global. Act global', instead noting: 'local markets are still accountable, but now they have guidance, process, and strategy.' With this hybrid strategy in place, Coke increased its spending on global ad campaigns in 2004 while 'boost[ing] collaboration between regions to balance global and local efforts'.

Sources: www.coca-cola.com; Betsy McKay, 'Coca-Cola restructuring effort has yet to prove effective', *Asian Wall Street Journal*, 2 March 2001; Andrew Marshall, 'Focus: can they still sell the world a Coke?', *The Independent*, 20 June 1999; Betsy McKay, 'Coke hunts for talent to re-establish its marketing might', *Wall Street Journal*, 6 March 2002: B4; Kate MacArthur, 'Coke commits $400m to fix it', *Advertising Age*, 15 November 2004: 1.

Similar to this approach, Procter & Gamble's strategy is to make global plans, re-plan for each region and execute locally. Former P&G head of marketing Robert L. Wehling made the following comments concerning the company's global marketing efforts during the 1990s:

> To us, a global brand is one that has a clear and consistent equity – or identity – with consumers across geographies. It is generally positioned the same from one country to another. It has essentially the same product formulation, deliv-ers the same benefits and uses a consistent advertising concept. That isn't to say there isn't room for local tailoring. In fact, there must be room to adapt to local needs. But where there's no justification for difference, the brand is the same in every part of the world.[17]

From these perspectives, transferring products across borders may mean consis-tent positioning for the brand, but not necessarily the same brand name and market-ing campaign in each market. Similarly, packaging may have the same overall look, but be tailored to fit the local populace and market needs. As brand consultant Robert Kahn notes: 'Global branding does not mean having the same brand every-where. It means having an overarching strategy that optimizes brand effectiveness in local, regional and international markets.' According to Kahn, one soap formula sold under different names can achieve global brand status as long as the marketing efforts are managed centrally.[18] As another example, Danone's yogurts for children are sold under a variety of names – Danonino, Danonetje, Danimals, Petit Danone – in over 30 countries, while a general manager leads a central team that co-ordinates and oversees local marketing.[19]

In short, centralized marketing strategies that preserve local customs and tradi-tions can be a boon for products sold in more than one country – even in diverse cul-tures. Fortunately, firms have improved their capabilities to tailor products and campaigns to local conditions: '[New technologies] have the important attribute of allowing customized or tailored product offerings reflecting local conditions at much lower costs. The need to standardize products worldwide is diminishing.'[20] The im-plication is that there is a decreasing concentration of activities made possible by flexible manufacturing technology, as well as an increasing ability for co-ordination made possible by advances in information systems and telecommunications.

Many good examples exist of companies that have blended standardization and customization. For example, US pizza chain Domino's tries to maintain the same deliv-ery system everywhere but has to adapt to local customs. In Kuwait, the delivery is just as likely to be made to a limousine as it is to a house; and in Japan, houses are not num-bered sequentially, making finding an address difficult. Consider how McDonald's has modified and adapted its successful formula of 'food, fun and families' overseas.

McDonald's

Although the Big Mac and Ronald McDonald appear worldwide, McDonald's customizes other aspects of its marketing campaign. It serves beer in Germany, wine in France and coconut, mango and tropical mint shakes in Hong Kong. Hamburgers are made with different meat and spices in Japan, and McSpaghetti is offered in the Philippines. McDonald's joint venture partners, who typically run the franchises abroad, take much of the responsibility for their own marketing.

Nevertheless, McDonald's commitment to product and service standardization is one reason why the retail outlets are so similar all over the world. After such a rigorous qualification process, partners come to understand and appreciate McDonald's attention to detail. As a result, most partners strictly follow the operating manual. Meticulously detailed and as thick as a phone book, the rules cover everything from how often toilet facilities should be cleaned to the temperature for frying chips.

Other notable examples of brands with differentiated global marketing strategies are Heineken and Nescafé. Although Heineken is seen as an everyday brand in the Netherlands, it is considered a 'top-shelf' brand almost everywhere else. For example, a case of Heineken costs almost twice as much in the USA as a case of the most popular US beer, Budweiser.[21] For a long time, its slogan in the UK and other countries – 'Heineken refreshes the parts other beers can't reach' – was different from its US positioning. Although advertising for Nescafé, the world's largest brand of coffee, generally stresses the taste, aroma and warmth of shared moments, the brand was positioned in Thailand as a way to relax from the pressures of daily life.[22]

GLOBAL BRAND STRATEGY

The main contention of this chapter is that, in building brand equity, it is often necessary to create different marketing campaigns to satisfy different market segments. In terms of building global customer-based brand equity, strategically it is therefore necessary to do the following.

- Identify differences in consumer behaviour (ie, how consumers purchase and use *products* and what they know and feel about *brands*) in each market.
- Adjust the branding accordingly (ie, through the choice of brand elements, the nature of the actual marketing campaign and activities and the use of secondary associations).

Note that the third way to build global brand equity, through secondary brand associations (see Chapter 7), is probably the one most likely to have to be changed. Because the various entities that may be linked to a brand may take on very different meanings in different countries, secondary associations may have to be used differently in different countries. For example, US companies such as Coca-Cola, Levi Strauss and Nike gained an important source of equity in going overseas by virtue of their US heritage, which is not much of an asset in their domestic markets. Harley-Davidson has aggressively marketed its classic American image – customized for different cultures – to generate a quarter of its sales from abroad. Brand Briefing 14.5 shows how, despite America's slipping image after the Iraq War, brands of US companies were largely unaffected.

Chapter 7 reviewed how country of origin, as in these cases, could be used to build brand equity. Thus, in developing global brands, it is important to consider how secondary associations may vary in their strength, favourability and uniqueness and may therefore play a different role in building brand equity.

Brand Briefing 14.5

US brands in the wake of war

The Iraq war, which began in March 2003, led to anti-US sentiment either worsening or emerging in many parts of the world. A global study by the Pew Research Centre for the People and the Press a year after the war began found the percentage of respondents in Europe who had a favourable view of the USA in precipitous decline. Between summer 2002 and March 2004, favourability ratings for the US fell in France and Germany by more than 20 percent. Even in Great Britain, America's strongest ally in the war, favourability towards the USA fell from 75 percent to 58 percent in March 2004. Ratings in the Middle East, while starting from a lower point, still fell. In Jordan, for example, favourability ratings dropped to 5 percent from 25 percent. The image problem was severe enough for a group of private-sector marketers, academics and companies to join forces in 2004 to combat anti-Americanism abroad by creating the Business for Diplomatic Action council.

In spite of the prevalance of hostility towards the US government, consumer research conducted since the start of the war showed that the response abroad to US brands was far milder. There were isolated attacks on US businesses, such as the burning of a KFC outlet in Pakistan that killed six employees in 2005, but US brands have not suffered, in terms of image or sales, in the same fashion as the country's image.

A joint research project by Research International and the Harvard Business School investigated how consumers valued global brands and revealed that anti-US sentiment did not influence purchase decisions regarding US-based brands. One South African respondent showed it was possible to hold opposing views on the country versus its brands, saying 'I hate the country, but I love their products.' In an interview separate from this study, a South Korean expressed a similar sentiment: 'Calling for political independence from the US is one thing, and liking American brands is another. Of course I like IBM, Dell, Microsoft, Starbucks and Coke.'

The annual survey of power brands by NOP World from 2004 showed a drop in trust and usage of US brands overseas, but only by a few percentage points on average. Between 2003 and 2004, the total percentage of consumers from 30 countries who used US brands – from a list of 15 US brands including McDonald's, Microsoft, Yahoo! and Nike – fell from 30 percent to 27 percent. The percentage of respondents who said they trusted Coca-Cola, McDonald's, Nike and Microsoft fell 3–6 percent during the same period. While these declines were 'not good news for companies that want to grow', they did not mirror the decline in attitudes towards the US government.

In fact, in some areas where anti-US sentiment was strongest, for example in France and the Middle East, US brands experienced sales growth following the war. In the consumer goods category, where boycotting was expected to have the most effect, sales in these regions rose. Coca-Cola sales in the Middle East rose by double

Brand Briefing 14.5 *continued*

digits following a small decline at the outset of the war, while sales in Europe rose 5–8 percent during the first half of 2003. Sales for McDonald's in Paris were up 8–10 percent during the same period.

One possible explanation for the disparity between the level of resentment for America the country and US brands include the global images projected by brands. Consumers buy global brands because, for example, they 'make us feel like citizens of the world and . . . somehow give us an identity.' Research by Roper has shown that consumers are more inclined to think of a brand as global, rather than as originating in a specific country. Another explanation is the fact that many of the biggest brands have large local operations that employ thousands and bring investment in local communities. For example, Coca-Cola employs 20,000 locals in its Middle Eastern operations, paying them 15 percent more on average than locally-based competitors. Procter & Gamble spent €71 million in Egypt building factories and schools and financing health education.

Sources: 'A year after Iraq war', Pew Research Centre for the People and the Press, 16 March 2004; Clay Risen, 'Re-branding America', *Boston Globe*, 13 March 2005: D1; Douglas B. Holt, John A. Quelch and Earl L. Taylor, 'How consumers value global brands', Harvard Business School Working Knowledge, 20 September 2004; 'Brands in an age of anti-Americanism', *BusinessWeek*, 4 August 2003: 69; Parija Bhatnagar, 'US brands losing lustre', *CNN Money*, 21 May 2004; Janet Guyon, 'Brand America', *Fortune*, 27 October 2003: 179; Douglas B. Holt, John A. Quelch and Earl L. Taylor, 'How consumers value global brands', Harvard Business School Working Knowledge, 20 September 2004; 'Brands in an age of anti-Americanism', *BusinessWeek*, 4 August 2003: 69; 'Regime change: brand wars in the Middle East', *The Economist*, 2 November 2002: 65.

Global customer-based brand equity

As explained in Chapter 2, to build customer-based brand equity, it is necessary to: establish breadth and depth of brand awareness; create points of parity and points of difference; elicit positive, accessible brand responses; and forge intense, active brand relationships. Achieving these four steps, in turn, involves establishing six core brand building blocks: salience, performance, imagery, judgements, feelings and resonance. In every market in which the brand is sold, consideration must be given as to how to achieve these steps and create these building blocks.

Creating brand salience

One of the most challenging aspects of building global brand equity for a widely extended, multiple-product brand is the order of product introduction. It is rare that the product rollout for a brand in new markets will duplicate the order in the home market. Often, product introductions in the domestic market are done sequentially, stretched out over a longer period of time, as compared to the near simultaneous introductions in overseas markets.

Nivea

Nivea's flagship product in its European home market has been its category leader, Nivea Creme. Although the company had introduced other skincare and personal care products, Nivea Creme was the product with the most history and heritage and reflected many of the Nivea core brand values. In Asia, however, for cultural and climate reasons, the Creme was less well received and the facial skincare sub-brand, Nivea Visage, and Creme line extension, Nivea Soft, were of greater strategic and market importance. Because these two product brands have slightly different images from the Creme brand, an important issue is what would be the effect on consumers' collective impressions of Nivea. A strong emphasis on Nivea for Men in North America raises similar questions.

Different orders of introduction can change consumer perceptions as to what a brand represents in terms of products offered, benefits supplied and needs satisfied. Thus, the breadth and depth of recall need to be examined to ensure that the proper brand salience and meaning exist along those lines.

Crafting brand image

To the extent that the composition of the product does not vary appreciably across markets, brand performance associations in terms of the basic benefits provided may not need to be that different. In other words, product functionality often will be relatively fixed across markets even if some of the specific attributes may differ. Brand imagery associations, however, may be quite different and one challenge in global marketing is to refine the brand image across diverse markets. For example, the brand's history and heritage, which may be rich and a strong competitive advantage in the home market, may be non-existent in a new market. Global research by the Reputation Institute shows that national companies often achieve higher reputation scores than international companies.[23] There seems to be an advantage for national companies. Results show that the most admired companies are often national. A desirable brand personality in one market may be less so in another. Nike's competitive, aggressive user imagery turned out to be a detriment in its introduction into European markets in the early 1990s. The company achieved greater success when it toned down its image and emphasized team concepts.

Eliciting brand responses

Brand judgements must be positive in new markets, such that consumers find the brand to be of good quality, credible, worthy of consideration and superior. Crafting the right brand image will help to accomplish these outcomes. One of the challenges in global marketing, however, is to ensure that the proper balance and type of emotional responses and brand feelings are created. Blending inner (enduring and private) and outer (immediate experiential) emotions can be difficult given cultural differences across markets.

Cultivating resonance

Finally, achieving brand resonance in new markets means that consumers must be given sufficient opportunities and incentives to buy and use the product, interact with other consumers and the company itself and learn about and experience the brand and its marketing. Clearly, interactive, online marketing can be advantageous as long as it can be designed to be accessible and relevant anywhere in the world. Nevertheless, digital efforts cannot replace grass roots marketing that helps to connect the consumer with the brand. In dealing with diverse international markets, simply exporting marketing campaigns, even with some adjustments, may be insufficient because consumers may be too much at 'arm's length'. As a result, they may not be able to develop the intense, active loyalty that characterizes brand resonance.

Global brand positioning

To capture differences in consumer behaviour and to guide efforts for revising the marketing campaign to build global customer-based brand equity, it is necessary to revisit the brand positioning in each market. Recall that developing the brand positioning in a market involves creating mental maps, defining core brand associations, identifying points of parity and points of difference and crafting a band mantra. Accordingly, in developing a global brand positioning, three sets of questions must be answered.

1. How valid is the mental map in the new market? How appropriate is the positioning? What is the existing level of awareness? How valuable are the core brand associations, points of parity and points of difference?
2. What changes need to be made to the positioning? Do any new associations need to be created? Should any existing associations not be emphasized? Do existing associations need to be modified?
3. By what means should this new mental map be created? Can the same marketing activities still be employed? What changes need to be made? What new marketing activities are necessary?

Because the brand is often at an earlier stage of development when going abroad, it will often be necessary to first establish awareness and points of parity. Once brand awareness and points of parity category considerations have been established, competitive considerations may come into the picture. In effect, a hierarchy of brand associations must be defined in a global context that defines which associations are to be held by consumers in all countries and which are to be held only in certain countries. At the same time, decisions have to be made as to how these associations should be created to account for different consumer perceptions, tastes and environments. Thus, marketers must be attuned to similarities and differences across markets.

Brand Briefing 14.6 describes how Ikea is building a leadership position in China within furniture retailing. Even though the company offered the same product range, it had to customize certain areas of communication to fit with the needs of the Chinese market.

Brand Briefing 14.6

How Ikea is building leadership in furniture retailing in China

Ikea is the world's leading furniture retailer. According to the Reputation Institute's research with 60,000 interviews in 29 countries, in 2007 Ikea had the second-best reputation in Europe, after the toy company Lego, with an index of 84.05 (out of 100).

The RepTrak Pulse measures the good feeling, trust and respect/admiration that consumers feel towards a company. The RepTrak 200 consists of the 200 companies with the world's best corporate reputations. Regionally, the RepTrak 200 is dominated by Europe (97 companies). North America comes second (44 companies), followed by Asia Pacific (41 companies) and South America (16 companies). The global top tier consists of 26 companies with RepTrak Pulse scores above 80. (Figure 14.6 lists the top 50 companies).

According to the Reputation Institute's research, the reputation of Ikea rests on five pillars: innovation, well-managed, social responsibility, leadership and financial performance. The Reputation Institute's research shows that the company is among the top five globally in these dimensions.

The vision of Ikea from its beginning has been to create a better everyday life for people. It does this by offering well-designed, functional furniture at low prices so that as many people as possible will be able to afford them.

Most of the time, beautifully designed products are created for a small part of the population – the few who can afford them. Ikea has taken a different path. It decided to side with the many. It is not difficult to manufacture expensive fine furniture. Just spend the money and let the customer pay. To manufacture beautiful, durable furniture at low prices is not so easy. It requires a different approach; finding simple solutions, scrimping and saving in every direction.

The Ikea concept began when Ingvar Kamprad (Figure 14.7), an entrepreneur from the Småland province in southern Sweden, had an innovative idea. In this part of Sweden, although the soil is thin and poor, the people have a reputation for working hard, living frugally and making the most out of limited resources. So when he started his furniture business in the 1940s, he applied the lessons he had learned in Småland. He decided to side with the many.

The name Ikea comes from the initials of Ingvar Kamprad, I and K, plus the first letters of Elmtaryd and Agunnaryd, which are the names of the farm and village where he grew up. The first Ikea shop opened in 1958. In 1965, the largest Ikea shop in the world opened in Kungens Kurva, outside Stockholm.

By 2007, there were 258 Ikea shops in 38 countries. The group owns 230 shops and employs 118,000 workers. Turnover in 2007 was €19.8 billion, with 550 million people visiting an Ikea shop every year and another 450 million visiting the website. Ikea is growing fast but the company sticks to its core idea. The growth strategy is: open 20 to 25 shops every year; raise the sales in existing outlets; and increase customer value by cutting prices. The company sees enormous opportunities because it is only operating in 38 countries so far.

Rank		RepTrak Pulse
1.	Lego (Denmark)	85.01
2.	Ikea (Sweden)	84.05
3.	Barilla (Italy)	83.53
4.	Mercadona (Spain)	83.39
5.	AP Møller-Mærsk (Denmark)	83.39
6.	Toyota (Japan)	82.79
7.	Ferrero (Italy)	82.63
8.	Petrobras (Brazil)	82.19
9.	Sberbank of Russia (Russia)	81.96
10.	Rockwool (Denmark)	81.86
11.	Michelin (France)	81.67
12.	Danfoss (Denmark)	81.45
13.	Swatch Group (Switzerland)	81.29
14.	Magnitogorsk Iron and Steel Works OAO (Russia)	81.17
15.	Kraft Foods (US)	81.07
16.	Canon (Japan)	80.82
17.	Vestas (Denmark)	80.81
18.	Danone (France)	80.68
19.	El Corte Inglés (Spain)	80.63
20.	Honda (Japan)	80.60
21.	Matsushita Electric Industrial Co. (Japan)	80.56
22.	McCain Foods (Canada)	80.43
23.	Marks & Spencer (UK)	80.19
24.	Grundfos (Denmark)	80.18
25.	United Parcel Service (UPS) (USA)	80.06
26.	Jean Coutu Group (Canada)	80.04
27.	Philips (The Netherlands)	79.82
28.	Gazprom-neft (Formerly Sybneft) (Russia)	79.59
29.	FedEx (USA)	79.39
30.	Lukoil (Russia)	79.35
31.	Vale do Rio Doce (Brazil)	79.31
32.	Novo Nordisk (Denmark)	79.09
33.	Velux (Denmark)	78.95
34.	BMW (Germany)	78.89
35.	Johnson & Johnson (USA)	78.80
36.	Deutsche Lufthansa (Germany)	78.65
37.	L'Oréal (France)	78.44
38.	Walt Disney (USA)	78.37
39.	Raiffeisen (Switzerland)	78.11
40.	Grupo Pão de Açucar (Brazil)	78.09
41.	Gazprom (Russia)	78.05
42.	Robert Bosch (Germany)	77.98
43.	Bridgestone (Japan)	77.77
44.	Nokia (Finland)	77.76
45.	Aldi (Germany)	77.75
46.	Gerdau (Brazil)	77.73
47.	Canadian Tire (Canada)	77.53
48.	Henkel (Germany)	77.34
49.	Rosneft (Russia)	77.29
50.	Luxottica (Italy)	77.26

Excellent/Top tier	above 80
Strong/Robust	70–79
Average/Moderate	60–69
Weak/Vulnerable	40–59
Poor/Lowest tier	below 40

Figure 14.6   Top 50 global companies by reputation

Brand Briefing 14.6 *continued*

Figure 14.7   Ingvar Kamprad, founder of Ikea
Source: Rex Features

The Ikea concept

Ikea customers are involved in the shopping experience. The Ikea concept relies on customers choosing, collecting, transporting and assembling the products them-selves. All products in the shops are supported by price and product information that is clearly marked on large, easy-to-read tags. This makes it easy for visitors to serve themselves. All products have names that reinforce their Swedish origin. There are, of course, knowledgeable workers available to customers when needed. Customer involvement helps keep prices low. That is the idea behind: 'You do your part. We do our part. Together we save money.'

Inside an Ikea shop, there are hundreds of inspirational displays – from realistic room settings to real-life homes, all with product combinations that provide ideas and know-how on contemporary interior design. There are up to 9,500 products offered in an Ikea shop. Many products are introduced throughout the year, accounting for 20–30 percent of the range. This gives visitors many possibilities to find solutions that best suit their needs.

The Ikea culture

A cornerstone of the Ikea brand is its strong culture. Every worker is recruited according to Ikea values. Attitude is far more important than education. New workers participate for a week in a cultural training scheme where they learn Ikea values and its origin in Småland. Kamprad's dedication to and focus of the business idea and vision manifested itself in a document that he wrote in December 1976, entitled 'A furniture dealer's testament'. The components of the testament are as follows.

● The product range: our identity.

● The Ikea spirit: a strong and living reality.

Brand Briefing 14.6 *continued*

- Profit gives us resources.
- To achieve good results with small means.
- Simplicity is a virtue.
- The different way.
- Concentration of energy: important to our success.
- To assume responsibility: a privilege.
- Most things still remain to be done. A glorious future.

The company operates very informally. This is reflected in the neat but casual dress of employees (jeans and jumpers are the norm); in the relaxed office atmosphere with practically everyone sitting in an open-plan office; and in the familiar way employees address each other. This is the norm also for the head office in Helsingborg in Sweden where everyone, including the chief executive, sits in an open room and in Leiden, Holland.

A better everyday life means getting away from status and conventions – being freer and more at ease as human beings. Cost-consciousness was another strong part of the management culture. Waste of resources is a sin at Ikea. Expensive solutions are often signs of mediocrity and an idea without a price tag is never acceptable.

Telling stories is an important part of the Ikea culture. Kamprad has personally been strongly involved in these stories. One story tells that, during his rounds of the new shop (in Hamburg), he made notes that covered 19 pages. They ranged from comments about the basic design – he felt the building had far too many angles, which added to construction costs – to the size of the price tags and the placement of posters in the store. Kamprad invited the workers to stay after work – and almost all did – so that he could thank them for their efforts. The dinner was typical Ikea style – they went first to the buffet, the managers went next and Ingvar Kamprad was among the last when only the remnants were left. After dinner, he shook hands and talked with all 150 present, finally leaving the shop after midnight. Such an experience would keep motivation high for weeks. Each worker would go home and tell his family and friends that Ingvar shook hands with him. When the store manager arrived at 6.30 the next morning, he found that Ingvar had been in the store for an hour. Although he was staying in a modest hotel, he remarked that it was probably priced €3 too high. That story will probably circulate through the company as many others do – like the one about Ingvar driving around town late at night checking hotel prices, till he found one economical enough. It's all part of the aura and the legend that surrounds him.

Brand Briefing 14.6 *continued*

Ikea in China

In 1992, Ikea started a trading office in Shanghai. The first shop opened in Shanghai in 1997, and the second in Beijing 1998. As of August 2007, Ikea has shops in Shanghai, Beijing, Guangzhou, Chengdu and Shenzhen, employing 2,500 workers. The product range offered in China is the same as elsewhere in the world. The meaning of the Ikea brand in China is modern, with a promise of the West. When Ikea opened its first shop, the perception of Ikea was of an expensive furniture retailer from the West. Since the early days, the Ikea management has been working hard at cutting prices and increasing consumer value. Today, the average price has been cut by half even though the average Chinese salary has doubled during the same period.

When Ikea opens a shop anywhere in the world, 15,000 customers on the first day is seen as a great success. In 2003, Ikea opened another shop in Shanghai and 82,000 customers came (Figure 14.8). During the day, the shop had to close several times to avoid panic and accidents (Figure 14.9). The new Shanghai shop, the first full-size shop in China, is the largest Ikea shop in Asia with its 323,000 square feet versus 86,000 square feet in the old shop. Ikea managers see people visit the shop to relax on the sofas and beds, and to escape the heat in summer. The shop communicates its Swedish origin through the colours blue and yellow, the same as the

Figure 14.8   The Ikea flagship shop in Shanghai

Brand Briefing 14.6 *continued*

Figure 14.9   Opening of the new Ikea shop in Shanghai

Swedish flag. According to many Swedish branding experts, nothing helps to build the image and reputation of Sweden as much as Ikea.

Criteria for success in China

At first, Ikea was seen as an expensive Western furniture company and the Shanghai shop still suffers from this. 'It takes long time to change the perceptions', says Ulf Smedberg, the marketing manager for China. The perceptions of customers of the newly opened shops in Guangzhou, Chengdu and Shenzhen were much better regarding price. According to Smedberg, the following actions were needed to build the brand in China.

Increase consumer value

It was necessary for Ikea to change the perception of being expensive. Ikea has been working hard to cut prices for all products. One obvious example of this is the Klippan sofa, which in 1999 had a price of €260 (RMB 2,999). In 2007 the same sofa cost €69 (RMB 795). With its new price strategy Ikea found that volume sales quadrupled and it made money (Figure 14.10). The priority has been to lower the prices and make the products available to more people, who have an income of €350 a month.

Swedishness

Swedishness is a vital part of Ikea's communications and the country is associated with a fresh, healthy way of living. This lifestyle is reflected in the choice of colours for Ikea shops and its product range. Inside the shop, a typical Swedish landscape is shown and the restaurant offers traditional Swedish meatballs. The freshness of

Brand Briefing 14.6 *continued*

Figure 14.10   Increasing consumer value

the open air is reflected in the colours and materials used in the products and the sense of space they create. In a climate that is cold and dark for much of the year, these light, bright living spaces create the sensation of summer sunshine indoors all year round. According to Smedberg, it is important and beneficial to use the Sweden origins. In the minds of Chinese people, Sweden stands for democracy, environmental friendliness, design and equal opportunities, he says. All the products have Swedish names and there is a Swedish shop. Smedberg says this origin is impossible for competitors to copy.

Consumer insights

To be successful, Ikea initiated in-depth consumer research in the homes of Chinese people to understand how they lived and what was important in their homes. Chinese people were followed for a week and interviews were carried out. Questions were asked about how they lived, what their needs were, how they slept, ate and stored their clothes. Chinese people want change, but what stops them? Consumer research points to lack of money, inspiration, tips and ideas, knowledge and confidence as some of the answers. Ikea gives Chinese people many solution ideas for how they can live a better life. Room by room, Ikea identified the problems of women and discovered how it could help them to build a better everyday life.

Positioning

Ikea's positioning in China is to sell to young professional women, and the Ikea belief is that the home is the most important place in the world. About 70 percent of Ikea's customers in China are women. The company's ambition is to be the reference for the complete home and the leader in every room. The way to do this is to distance itself from competitors and build on its strengths.

Brand Briefing 14.6 *continued*

The brand positioning for China is: Ikea will be the *reference* for the complete home by building leadership in *every room*, targeting women.

In China, women have the same level of education as men and they have the same opportunities. They are more open than men and they embrace change in the country. In recruitment, Ikea finds it easier to employ women because they find it easier to adapt to Ikea's values than men and they often are more skilled in languages. Ikea is on the side of the women in everything it does. This can also be seen as an advantage in market communications, because traditional advertising often is stereotypically male. In Ikea communications, it is women who make the decisions. Ikea is breaking with the norm and research shows that this is liked by women.

Today, Ikea has six distinct customer groups with different levels of loyalty: true loyals, happy shoppers, moderates, switchers, at risk and lost causes. One insight is that 32 percent of customers account for 85 percent of total turnover.

The Ikea catalogue

The catalogue is globally distributed free of charge once a year. In 2007, 191 million catalogues were distributed. Also in China the catalogue is a cornerstone of market communications. In China, managers found it necessary to change the catalogue concept and distribute catalogues five times a year. It took too long for the next catalogue to come, so competitors could copy Ikea concepts. This new concept is called a 'multilogue' and is now embraced globally within Ikea. Two versions of the multilogue are used. The one positioned at more high-profile customers has 136 pages, while the mass market multilogue has 64 pages. Some 50 million copies are delivered in China every year (Figure 14.11).

Figure 14.11   The 'multilogue'

Brand Briefing 14.6 *continued*

Web-based marketing communications

Research shows that 85 percent of the most important Ikea customers in China are online. This means that its site, www.ikea.com.cn, is a very important marketing tool. Smedberg explains that the website also is an important tool to 'build Swedishness'.

China is an important market for Ikea in two ways. The first is for sourcing. Today, 22 percent of Ikea's global range is produced in China. The second is the opportunities it presents as one of the world's largest markets. Ikea is well equipped to be successful in China, says Smedberg. It aims to open 25 shops in China in the next 10 years. Success will come from: home furnishings expressing confidence about life; a complete and relevant range of products that offers value for money (low price + quality + function/design); having an efficient supply chain; and having effective market communications targeting women. The ambition is to employ 10,000 workers and build a leadership position.

Sources: interviews with Ulf Smedberg, marketing manager Ikea China, 2001–2007; visits to Ikea stores in Beijing, Shanghai and Guangzhou; 'How the Swedish retailer became a global cult brand', *BusinessWeek*, European edition, 14 November 2005; www.ikea.com; www.ikea.com.cn; www.reputationinstitute.com

BUILDING GLOBAL CUSTOMER-BASED BRAND EQUITY

The previous discussion provided a perspective on some of the pros and cons of creating standardized global marketing campaigns. In designing and implementing a marketing campaign to create a strong global brand, marketers attempt to maximize the probability of realizing the advantages of a global marketing campaign while minimizing any potential disadvantages of globalization.[24] This section explores some themes or guidelines for success that have emerged in global branding, encapsulated as the 'ten commandments of global branding' (Figure 14.12).

1. Understand similarities and differences

The most fundamental guideline is to recognize that international markets can vary in terms of brand development, consumer behaviour, marketing infrastructure, competitive activity, legal restrictions and so on. As noted earlier, differences in any of these factors can have profound implications for building and managing brand equity across geographic boundaries. At the same time, many countries do not vary much in one or more of these dimensions, suggesting that differences in marketing activity may be unnecessary or ineffective. Recognition of this guideline is reflected by the fact that virtually every top global brand and company adjusts its marketing campaign in some way for some markets but holds the parameters fixed in other markets.

1. Understand similarities and differences in the global branding landscape.
2. Don't take shortcuts in building brands.
3. Establish marketing infrastructure.
4. Embrace integrated marketing communications.
5. Cultivate brand partnerships.
6. Balance standardization and customization.
7. Balance global and local control.
8. Establish operable guidelines.
9. Implement a global brand equity measurement system.
10. Leverage brand elements.

Figure 14.12   The ten commandments of global branding

Indeed, one key to global success is to recognize and take advantage of local consumer behaviour. For example, when MTV made a push for its cable channel overseas beginning in the 1990s, it initially kept much of the same programming that it played to US audiences. In most markets, however, music, film and other cultural tastes are very different, and the channel quickly learned that it needed a much greater proportion of locally relevant programming. Now, MTV International channels, such as MTV India, programme as much as 80 percent of their content in local languages and viewership has risen significantly.[25]

The experience of mobile phone operator Vodafone illustrates an interesting juxtaposition that reflects just how important consumer behaviour can be to the success or failure of any brand, even dominant brands, when entering new markets.

Vodafone

When Vodafone acquired J-Phone, the third-biggest mobile phone operator in Japan, which was known for its cutting-edge phones, in 2002, it hoped that the renamed Vodafone Japan would be a key component of its global brand strategy. Instead, Vodafone lost customers and revenues fell. The problem: 'By focusing too much on building a globally oriented brand, Vodafone failed to give Japanese consumers what they want, chiefly a wide line-up of phones with fancy features.'[26] Vodafone sought to leverage its image as a global company by offering phones that could be used anywhere, home or abroad. Yet the heaviest users, many of whom were young and not likely to go abroad, were more interested in phones with advanced features, such as video games, digital cameras, ringtones and e-mail. Japanese users also favour a broad selection of phones that is constantly updated, but Vodafone offered only 15 models compared with market leader DoCoMo's 38 and was often late with new technology. Vodafone was unable to recover from its early mistakes and in 2006 sold Vodafone Japan to Softbank, which announced plans to rename the brand Softbank Mobile.[27]

The best examples of global brands often retain a thematic consistency and alter specific elements of the marketing mix in accordance with consumer behaviour and the competitive situation in each country. An effective example of custom-tailoring the marketing mix is illustrated by Unilever's Snuggle fabric softener.

Snuggle

The product was launched in Germany in 1970 as an economy brand in a category dominated by Procter & Gamble. To counteract the negative quality inferences associated with low price, Unilever emphasized softness as the product's point of difference. The softness association was communicated through the name, Kuschelweich, which means 'enfolded in softness', and through a picture of a teddy bear on the packaging. When the product was launched in France, Unilever kept the brand positioning of economy and softness but changed the name to Cajoline, meaning softness in French. In addition, the teddy bear that had been inactive in Germany took centre stage in French advertising as the brand symbol for softness and quality. Success in France led to global expansion and, in each case, the brand name was changed to connote softness in the local language, while advertising featuring the teddy bear remained similar across global markets. By the 1990s, Unilever was marketing the fabric softener around the globe with a dozen brand names (eg, Coccolino in Italy and Mimosin in Spain), all with the same product positioning and advertising support. More importantly, the fabric softener was generally the number one or number two brand in each market.[28] Unilever continued its global expansion of the Snuggle brand by launching it in Mexico in 2003.[29]

The success of Snuggle reflects the importance of understanding similarities and differences in the branding landscape. Although marketers typically strive to keep the same brand name across markets, in this case the need for a common name was reduced since people generally do not buy fabric softener away from home. On the other hand, a common consumer desire for softness that transcended country boundaries could be effectively communicated by a teddy bear as the main character in a global ad campaign.

Developed versus developing markets

Perhaps the most basic distinction often made with global brands is between developing and developed markets (eg, India and Germany, respectively). Typically, differences in consumer behaviour, marketing infrastructure, competitive frames of reference and so on are so profoundly different that distinct marketing campaigns have to be devised for each type of market. With developing markets, often the product category itself may not be well developed, so the marketing campaign must operate at a fundamental level.

Changing landscape for global brands

Finally, it should be noted that the landscape for global brands is changing, especially with respect to younger consumers. Because of increased consumer mobility, better communication capabilities and expanding transnational entertainment options, lifestyles are fast becoming more similar across countries within sociodemographic segments than they are within countries across sociodemographic segments. Because of the growth of global media such as MTV, a teenager in Paris may have more in common with a teenager in London, New York, Sydney or almost any other city than with his or her own parents. This younger generation may be more easily influenced by trends and broader cultural movements fuelled by worldwide exposure to films, television and other media than ever before. Certainly one characteristic of this trend is that those brands that are able to tap into the global sensibilities of the youth market may be better able to adopt a standardized branding campaign and marketing strategy. Unilever uses a standard approach to market its Axe Body Spray globally based on the sex appeal that the product creates in the user.

2. Don't take shortcuts in building brands

In terms of building global customer-based brand equity, many of the tactics discussed earlier in the book apply. In particular, it is necessary to create brand awareness and a positive brand image in each country in which a brand is sold. As noted previously, the means by which sources of brand equity are created may differ, or the actual sources of brand equity themselves may vary between countries in terms of the particular attribute or benefit associations that make up the points of parity and points of difference. Nevertheless, it is critically important in each country that there exist sufficient levels of brand awareness and strong, favourable and unique brand associations to provide sources of brand equity.

The danger is that marketers will take shortcuts and fail to build the necessary sources of brand equity by inappropriately exporting marketing campaigns from other countries or markets in which a brand has established a great deal of equity. Companies have learned this the hard way. For example, in 1990, Pepsi bought the rights to bottle and sell its soft drink to German retailers. Pepsi attempted to match Coke's high prices in the market without sufficient pull from brand-building activities and merchandising and without sufficient push from a strong distribution network with the right kinds of trucks, coolers and so forth. Pepsi so alienated two German retailers, Tengelmann and Asko, that it lost distribution in those shops for a couple of years. The brand languished with a market share under 5 percent as a result and has only recently started to bounce back.[30]

Building a brand in new markets should be done from the bottom up, both strategically and tactically. Strategically, that means concentrating on building awareness first before the brand image (ie, laying the foundation for the brand). Tactically, or operationally, that means determining how to create sources of brand equity. In other words, the means by which a brand was built in one market (eg, the particular product, distribution, communication or pricing strategies and marketing activities) may not be appropriate in another market even if the same overall brand image may be desired.

Many marketing campaigns have to be adjusted because the brand is at an earlier stage of development. In some cases, rather than alter the product or the advertising to conform to local tastes, a brand will do the opposite and attempt to influence local behaviour so that it fits with the established uses of the brand. In such cases, consumer education often accompanies brand development efforts.

Kellogg's

When Kellogg's introduced its corn flakes into Brazil in 1962, cereal was eaten as a dry snack (like potato crisps) because many Brazilians did not eat breakfast. As a result, the ads focused on the family and breakfast table – much more so than in the USA. As in other Latin American countries where big breakfasts have not been part of the meal tradition, Kellogg's task was to inform consumers of the 'proper' way to eat cereal with cold milk in the morning.[31] Similarly, Kellogg's had to educate French consumers that corn flakes were meant to be eaten with cold instead of warm milk. Initial advertising showed milk being poured from transparent glass pitchers that were used for cold milk rather than opaque porcelain jugs that were used for warm milk. Similarly, a challenge to Kellogg's in increasing the relatively low per capita consumption of ready-to-eat breakfast cereals in Asia was the low consumption of milk products and the distaste with which drinking milk was held in many Asian countries. Because cereal consumption and habits vary widely between countries, Kellogg's has learned to build the brand from the bottom up in each market.

This guideline suggests a need for patience because it implies possibly backtracking in terms of brand development to engage in marketing campaigns and activities that the brand has long since moved beyond in its original markets. Although the time taken to build the brand in these other markets may be compressed because of greater financial resources and a keener understanding of effective strategies and tactics, it will still take some time. The temptation – and often mistake – is to export the current marketing campaign because it seems to 'transfer' or 'work'. Although that may be the case, the fact that a marketing campaign can meet with acceptance or even some success does not mean it is the proper marketing activity in terms of building strong sustainable global brand equity. A key to success is to understand each consumer, recognize what he or she knows or could potentially value about the brand and tailor marketing campaigns to his or her desires.

In short, one of the pitfalls that global marketers can fall into is a mistaken belief that their strong position in a domestic market can easily – or even automatically – translate into a strong position in a foreign market, especially with respect to the brand associations held by consumers. Thus, they fail to realize that, in their own country, they are building on a foundation of perhaps decades of carefully compiled associations in customers' minds. Brand Briefing 14.7 describes some of the challenges encountered by some global brands as they entered the emerging Indian market. Observing that many large companies simply diluted formulas to make less expensive products, Hindustan Lever, an Indian subsidiary of Unilever, made a substantial commitment to R&D and innovation for the Indian market. These efforts resulted in new products that were both affordable and uniquely suited to India's rural poor, including a high-quality combination soap and shampoo, that were backed by sales and marketing tactics specifically developed to reach remote and highly dispersed populations.[32]

3. Establish marketing infrastructure

A critical success factor for many brands has been their manufacturing, distribution and logistical advantages. This has involved creating a marketing infrastructure

Brand Briefing 14.7

Building brands in India

With a population of over a billion, and a growing middle class of about 300 million, India has been an attractive market for global brands since 1991, when the government relaxed restrictions on foreign investment. Yet some of the most powerful global companies have found that success at home and in other international markets by no means guarantees success in India. Motorola and Coke are just two of the numerous brands for whom growth in India proved elusive at some point.

For Motorola, India's ranking as the second fastest-growing mobile phone handset market, after China, makes it a vital place to do business. Yet in 2006, Motorola had only 6 percent of the market. Despite being priced lower than its Western competitors, Motorola did not often make it into the Indian consumer's consideration set, primarily because it had little brand awareness. Compounding this problem was the fact that the company had no distribution network, instead relying on local wireless operators, which were reluctant to push the phones because of Motorola's lack of profile. Motorola announced plans in 2006 to increase its advertising in India, admitting: 'We have a long way to go, but there's definitely momentum.'

Coke, which has a number of brands in India that give it a 50 percent market share in total, still struggled to achieve the success it had enjoyed elsewhere with its flagship Coca-Cola brand. Coke overestimated demand, came to market with prices that were too high and sizes that were too large for Indian consumers, who prefer to buy in small quantities. As a result, it endured years of losses, culminating in a €292 million write-down on the value of its Indian bottling assets in 2000. In 2003, Coke's market share was 16.5 percent, making it only the third-largest cola. To boost sales, Coke reduced the price of a 10.1-ounce bottle from 24 cents to 17 cents, and introduced a 6.8-ounce bottle for 10 cents. A new ad campaign was also introduced featuring a Bollywood star, a break with tradition at Coke, which has not used celebrities for some time. This move was indicative of the fact that 'Coke had to break a lot of its rules for India', as one former employee put it.

Though these global brands have struggled, others have succeeded by understanding Indian consumers and tailoring their offerings accordingly. Hyundai became India's second-largest carmaker by offering small, affordable and fuel-efficient cars such as the €5,112 Santro. Nokia earned 58 percent market share by selling models specially made for India, such as its 1100 phone that features a torch. Pepsi earned 24 percent market share in part because it was the first Western cola to feature Indian celebrities, including cricketer Sachin Tendulkar and actor Shahrukh Khan. LG outpaced competitors Whirlpool and Haier to €730 million in annual sales by offering refrigerators and air-conditioners that stand up better to the temperature extremes and power surges that characterize rural India. As the Indian

Brand Briefing 14.7 *continued*

market continues to grow and mature, catering to local tastes will become even more important for global brands seeking to compete there.

Sources: Om Malik, 'The new land of opportunity', *Business 2.0*, July 2004: 72; Cris Prystay, 'Branding gains respect in emerging markets', *Wall Street Journal*, 3 January 2006; Manjeet Kripalani, 'Finally, Coke gets it right', *BusinessWeek*, 10 February 2003: 47.

from scratch (if necessary), as well as adapting to capitalize on the marketing infrastructure in other countries.

Because international markets vary greatly in terms of infrastructure, companies have gone to great lengths to ensure consistency in product quality. In some cases, distribution channels have to be built from scratch. For example, after 13 years of negotiations, Nestlé was finally invited into the Heilongjiang province of China in 1987 to boost milk production. Soon thereafter, Nestlé opened a powdered milk and baby cereal plant in China. The company deemed the overburdened local trains and roads undependable to collect milk and deliver finished goods. Nestlé chose to establish its own distribution network, known as 'milk loads', between 27 villages in the region and factory collection points called 'chilling centres' where farmers could push wheelbarrows, pedal bicycles or walk to to have their milk weighed and analyzed. Production greatly increased as a result.[33] Similarly, McDonald's gets over 90 percent of its raw materials from local suppliers and will pay to create the necessary inputs if they are not locally available. Hence, investing to improve potato farms in Russia is standard practice because French fries are one of McDonald's core products and a key source of brand equity.

More often, however, companies have to adapt operations or invest in foreign partners, or both, to succeed abroad. In many cases, production and distribution are key to the success of a global marketing campaign. For example, General Motors' success in Brazil in the 1990s after years of mediocre performance can be attributed in part to its concerted efforts to develop a lean manufacturing operation and a sound dealership strategy to create the proper infrastructure.[34]

Companies often differ in their approaches to distribution and the results can be dramatic. For example, rather than leaving foreign operations in the control of fragmented local bottlers, Coca-Cola's 'anchor bottler' model resulted in the company deciding to either use only large bottlers (eg, Norway's Ringnes or Australia's Amatil) or take an equity stake in smaller bottlers to gain control of local management. On a more detailed level, Coca-Cola's intensive deployment of vending machines in Japan was vital to success in that market. Overall, Coca-Cola invested over €2.2 billion internationally from 1981 to 1993 in infrastructure and marketing. PepsiCo, however, sold off some of its bottling investments during this time. Investing in expensive ad campaigns and diversifying into restaurants and snack foods, PepsiCo's global fortunes subsequently sagged relative to Coca-Cola, resulting in

1. Select distributors. Don't let them select you.
2. Look for distributors capable of developing markets, rather than those with a few obvious customer contacts.
3. Treat local distributors as long-term partners, not temporary market-entry vehicles.
4. Support market entry by committing money, managers and proven marketing ideas.
5. From the start, maintain control over marketing strategy.
6. Make sure distributors provide you with detailed market and financial performance data.
7. Build links with national distributors at the earliest opportunity.

Figure 14.13   Seven rules for international distribution

Source: Reprinted by permission of *Harvard Business Review*. From 'Seven rules of international distribution' by David Arnold, November-December 2000. Copyright © 2000 by the Harvard Business School Publishing Corporation, all rights reserved.

renewed efforts in recent years. Figure 14.13 lists guidelines to help multinational firms maximize their control and learning from distribution partnerships in developing markets.

As in domestic markets, it is often desirable to blend push and pull strategies to build brand equity. This is certainly true in global markets and can present special challenges. Concerned about poor refrigeration in European shops, Häagen-Dazs ended up supplying thousands of free freezers to retailers across the Continent.[35] Sometimes companies have mistakenly adapted strategies that were critical factors to success, only to discover that these changes erode the brand's competitive advantage. For example, Dell initially abandoned its direct distribution strategy in Europe and instead decided to establish a network of shops. The result was a paltry 2.5 percent market share and the company lost money for the first time in 1994. Ignoring critics who said a direct distribution model would not work in Europe, Dell relaunched its personal computer line with a new management team to execute the direct model that the company had pioneered in the USA. Since then, the company has never looked back. Between 1999 and 2004, Dell's sales in Europe grew at an average rate of 19 percent annually, outpacing its competitors. By 2005, Dell had a 13 percent share of the European PC market, and the company predicted it could double or even triple that figure.[36]

4. Embrace integrated marketing communications

Some global firms have introduced extensive integrated marketing communications campaigns. Overseas markets do not have the same advertising opportunities as in the USA and Europe. As a result, Western-based marketers have had to embrace other forms of communication in those markets – such as sponsorship, promotions, public relations and merchandising – to a much greater extent.

An important consideration is that non-traditional advertising should be consistent with the brand's positioning and heritage. Disney's theme parks are not only huge profit generators (Tokyo Disneyland has been an overwhelming success with over 75 percent repeat visitors), but also serve as advertising vehicles that help solidify Disney's association with 'fun family entertainment.' eBay adopted a grass roots approach in its entry into Europe, shunning advertising just as it had done in the USA. Besides costing less, eBay's approach seemed to produce better customers: although chief competitor QXL had 50 percent more users than eBay, eBay users averaged 90 minutes a month on site compared with under 20 minutes for QXL.[37] By 2006, eBay's business in Germany, where over 20 million registered users purchased over €4.4 billion-worth of merchandise, was second only to the USA's in size.

It is common for European companies to undertake smaller, local events that can also serve a brand-building purpose. For example, Guinness has set up partnerships with entrepreneurs to develop the Irish pub concept in several countries. In 1995, some of the best pubs in Ireland joined forces with some of the best pubs in Europe in what Guinness called the 'twinning initiative'. These events had two-fold benefits in that they generated local publicity and interest as well as served to reinforce Guinness' Irish association.

To help make the quintessential Vermont brand Ben & Jerry's more locally relevant in Britain, the company ran a contest to create the 'quintessential British ice-cream flavour'. Finalists included references to royalty (eg, Cream Victoria and Queen Yum Mum), rock and roll (eg, John Lemon and Ruby Chewsday), literature (eg, Grape Expectations and Agatha Crispie) and Scottish heritage (eg, Nessie's Nectar and Choc Ness Monster). Other finalists included Minty Python, Cashew Grant and James Bomb. The winning flavour, Cool Britannia, was a play on the popular British military anthem 'Rule Britannia' and consisted of vanilla ice-cream, English strawberries and chocolate-covered Scottish shortbread.[38]

Although some companies have managed to execute their global marketing campaigns entirely with unusual forms of advertising (eg, The Body Shop), mainstream advertising options are often employed, too, suggesting that issues concerning advertising, promotion and sponsorship, among other marketing communications, need to be addressed.

Advertising

In going global, it is important to recognize that, although the brand positioning may be the same in different countries, creative strategies in advertising may have to differ. Thus, even if a basic positioning is adopted everywhere, it may need to be adapted and translated for local markets. As an example, Red Bull uses the same template for marketing to reinforce its positioning as an energy drink in any country it sells in: quirky, hand-drawn cartoon commercials extolling the fact that 'Red Bull gives you wiiiiiiings', sponsorship of action sports athletes and competitions and availability at popular nightspots. Yet Red Bull adapts this template for local 'market cells' by translating the ads into the local language, selecting locally relevant athletes and events to sponsor and targeting the trendiest nightspots where 'opinion leaders' are likely to congregate.

Different countries can be characterized as being more or less receptive to different creative styles. For example, humour is commoner in US and UK ads than, say, in German ads. Countries such as France and Italy are more tolerant of sex appeal and nudity in advertising.[39]

Camay

Procter & Gamble found that, although its US ads for Camay soap could be adapted for other countries, they turned out to be a disaster in Japan. Specifically,

Camay traditionally has been advertised as a luxury soap that makes a woman's skin feel soft and smell sweet, allowing her to feel more attractive as a result. Ads in other countries showed a beautiful woman bathing blissfully in a bathtub of suds. In ads for France, Italy and Venezuela, her husband came into the bathroom and talked to her while she was bathing. In Japan, the ads also featured a man entering the bathroom and gently touching the woman's skin and complimenting her while she bathed. Although these ads might perhaps be seen as sensual in other countries, such behaviour could be considered rude and in bad taste in Japan – even the idea of a man being in a bathroom with a woman can be seen as taboo. As a result of negative public reaction, the Japanese ad for Camay was changed to show a beautiful European-looking woman – alone – in a European-style bath.

Numerous advertising media options exist globally. Although commercial television time has been limited worldwide, the penetration of satellite and cable TV has expanded the broadcast media options. As a result, it is easier to show the same TV commercial simultaneously in many countries. Cable networks such as CNN, MTV and the Cartoon Network, Sky TV and Star TV have increased advertisers' global reach. *Fortune*, *Time*, *Newsweek* and other magazines have printed foreign editions in English for many years. Increasingly, other publishers are starting or adding local-language editions, either by licensing their trademarks to local companies, entering into joint ventures or creating wholly owned subsidiaries – for example, *Rolling Stone* with 10 editions outside the USA including mainland China, *Maxim* with 27 versions outside the UK, including Greek, and *Newsweek* in Arabic and 5 other languages.[40] French fashion title *Elle* has 35 editions targeting the same demographic group but tailored to the country where each is published.

Every country has unique media challenges and opportunities. For example, when Colgate-Palmolive decided to further penetrate the market of the 630 million or so people who live in rural India, the company had to overcome the fact that more than half of all Indian villagers are illiterate and only one-third live in households with television sets. Its solution was to create half-hour infomercials carried through the countryside in video vans.[41] To sell Tampax tampons in Mexico, Procter & Gamble created 'bonding sessions' akin to Tupperware parties led by company-designated advisers in people's homes. Although about 70 percent of women in the US, Canada and Western Europe use tampons, just 2 percent of women in most of Latin America do so. To overcome cultural inhibitors, P&G developed its unorthodox approach.[42]

Promotion and sponsorship

Chapters 6 and 7 described some of the issues in developing sponsorship schemes. It was noted that sponsorship schemes have a long tradition in many countries because of a historical lack of advertising media. Increasingly, sponsorship can now be executed globally. Entertainment and sport sponsorships can be especially effective in reaching a younger audience. For example, Nestlé has run worldwide promotional tie-ins with Disney films such as *Atlantis* and *Monsters, Inc.* Mars has become a worldwide sponsor of the World Cup and Olympics.

5. Cultivate brand partnerships

Most global brands have marketing partners in international markets, such as joint venture partners, licensees or franchisees, distributors and ad agencies.

One reason for establishing partnerships is access to distribution. For example, Guinness has used partnerships strategically to develop markets or provide expertise that the company lacked. Joint venture partners, such as with Moët Hennessy, have provided access to distribution abroad that otherwise would have been hard to achieve within the same time constraints. These partnerships have been crucial for Guinness as it expands operations into developing markets (where almost half its profits are now derived). Similarly, Lipton increased its sales by 500 percent in the first 4 years of its partnership with PepsiCo to distribute the product. Lipton adds the power of its brand to the ready-to-drink iced tea market, while PepsiCo adds its contacts in global distribution. AOL, however, struggled in Europe due to its initial failure to link up with either a media or telecommunications company.

Barwise and Robertson identify three ways to enter a new market.[43]

- By exporting existing brands into the new market (ie, introducing a 'geographic extension').
- By buying brands already sold in the new market.
- By creating an alliance with another company (eg, joint ventures, partnerships or licensing agreements).

They also identify three criteria – speed, control and investment – by which an entry strategy can be judged. There are tradeoffs between the three criteria such that no one strategy dominates (see Figure 14.14). For example, a problem with geographic extensions is speed. Because most firms do not have the financial resources and marketing experience to roll out products to a large number of countries simultaneously, global expansion can be a slow, market-by-market process. Brand acquisitions, on the other hand, can be expensive and often more difficult to control than is typically assumed. Brand alliances may offer even less control although are generally much less costly.

The choices made from these entry strategies depend in part on how the resources and objectives of the firm match up with the costs and benefits of each strategy. For example, Procter & Gamble would enter markets in categories in which it excels (eg, nappies, detergents and sanitary pads), building its infrastructure and then bringing in other categories such as personal care or healthcare. Heineken's sequential

Strategy	Speed	Control	Investment
Geographic extension	Slow	High	Medium
Brand acquisition	Fast	Medium	High
Brand alliance	Moderate	Low	Low

Figure 14.14   Evaluation criteria for market entry strategies

strategy has been different. The company enters a new market by exporting to build brand awareness and image. If the market response is satisfactory, the company will then license its brands to a local brewer in hopes of expanding volume. If that relationship is successful, Heineken may then take an equity stake or forge a joint venture. In doing so, Heineken piggybacks sales of its high-priced Heineken brand with an established local brand.[44] As a consequence of this strategy, Heineken now sells in almost 200 countries with a product portfolio of over 80 brands. With more than 110 breweries in 50 countries and export activities all over the world, Heineken is the most international brewing group.

In some countries, companies are legally required to form a partnership with a local company, as is the case in many Middle Eastern countries, or when entering certain markets, such as insurance and telecoms in India. In other cases, companies elect to establish a joint venture, a common entry strategy often seen as a fast and convenient way to enter complex foreign markets. Fuji Xerox, initially formed to give Xerox a foothold in Japan, has been highly successful and dominates the Japanese office equipment market. It even outperforms Xerox's US parent.[45]

Joint ventures have been popular in Japan, where convoluted distribution systems, tightly knit supplier relationships and close business–government co-operation have long encouraged foreign companies to link up with knowledgeable local partners. Blockbuster entered Japan with a joint venture with one of that country's best-known retailers, Den Fujita, which also runs McDonald's (Japan) and has a stake in Toys'R' Us in Japan. Blockbuster also negotiated joint ventures in France, Germany and Italy.[46] Pier 1 similarly expanded through joint ventures and licensing.[47] Pepsi has ownership positions via joint ventures and 5 outright acquisitions in 40 percent of its bottling networks outside North America.[48]

Finally, in some cases, mergers or acquisitions result from a desire to command a higher global profile. For example, US baby food maker Gerber agreed to be acquired by Swiss drugmaker Sandoz in part because of a need to establish a stronger presence in Europe and Asia, where Sandoz has a solid base.[49] Sandoz later merged with Ciba-Geigy and now is part of the Novartis group.

As these examples illustrate, different entry strategies have been adopted by different firms, by the same firm in different countries or even in combination by one firm in the same country. Brand Briefing 14.8 describes how global brand powerhouse Nestlé enters new markets. These entry strategies also may evolve over time. For example, in Australia, Coca-Cola, through its licensee Coca-Cola Amatil, not only sells its global brands such as Coke, Fanta and Sprite, but also sells local brands it has acquired such as Lift, Deep Spring and Mount Franklin. One of Coca-Cola's objectives with these acquisitions is to slowly switch demand from some of the local brands to global brands, thus capitalizing on economies of scale.

6. Balance standardization and customization

As noted earlier, one implication of the reality of similarities and differences between international markets is the need to blend local and global elements in marketing campaigns. The challenge, of course, is to determine the nature of this balance – which elements to customize or adapt and which to standardize. Customization may

Brand Briefing 14.8

Managing global Nestlé brands

For about 15 years starting in 1984, Nestlé spent more than €22 billion on acquisitions, including brands such as Carnation dairy products (USA); Perrier (France) and San Pellegrino (Italy) mineral water; Stouffer's frozen foods (USA); Rowntree confectionery (UK); Ralston Purina pet food (USA); and Buitoni-Perugina pasta and chocolate (Italy). Such acquisitions provide valuable economies of scale for Nestlé in developed markets. In less-developed markets, however, it adopts a different strategy. The company manipulates ingredients or processing technology for local conditions and then applies an appropriate brand name – for example, Nescafé coffee in some cases or a new brand, such as Bear brand condensed milk in Asia, in other cases. Nestlé strives to get into markets first and is patient – the company negotiated for more than a decade to enter China. To limit risks and simplify its efforts in new markets, Nestlé attacks with a handful of labels, selected from 11 strategic brand groups. Nestlé then concentrates its advertising and marketing money on just two or three brands.

Nestlé attempts to balance global and local control in managing its brands. Some decisions, such as branding, follow strict guidelines. The company has ten *worldwide corporate* strategic brands, including Nestlé, Nescafé, Maggi and Carnation. There are 45 strategic *worldwide product* brands, including KitKat, Coffeemate and Crunch. There are 25 *regional corporate strategic* brands, including Perugina, Findus and Stouffer's. There are 100 *regional product* brands, including Eskimo, Taster's Choice and Go-Cat. Finally, there are 700 *local strategic* brands that are important to particular countries, including Brigadeiro in Brazil.

Nestlé had used a decentralized management approach, in which most decisions apart from the worldwide and corporate brands were decided by the local managers. In 1997, after most of the acquisitions mentioned above had occurred, a new chief executive determined that Nestlé needed more formal central and regional control. The company consolidated factory management by region and combined supervision of similar products into strategic business units. Still, local managers retained the decision-making power necessary to adapt products to local tastes. For example, Nestlé continues to makes 200 varieties of Nescafé, each tuned to local palates.

Nestlé's more centralized management approach enabled the company to focus on growing its core brands at each level. From 1999 to 2003, the organic growth rate (ie, excluding acquisitions) was 5.1 percent, almost double Unilever's 2.7 percent.

Sources: Carla Rapoport, 'Nestlé's brand building machine', *Fortune*, 19 September 1994: 147–56; 'Daring, defying, to grow', *The Economist*, 7 August 2004: 55.

imply adjusting some aspect of the marketing campaign or the desired brand image or both (eg, by the creation or deletion of brand associations).

Much has been written concerning the circumstances favouring standardization over customization when designing global marketing campaigns. Some factors suggested as favouring the use of a more standardized global marketing campaign include:

- common customer needs;
- global customers and channels;
- favourable trade policies and common regulations;
- compatible technical standards;
- transferable marketing skills.

Similarly, one industry observer offered the following criteria as essential for the development of a global brand:[50]

- basic positioning and branding that can be applied globally;
- technology that can be applied globally, with local tailoring;
- capabilities for local implementation.

Reinforcing these points, Ed Meyer, the long-time head of one of the world's largest ad agencies, Grey Advertising, asserted that there are two considerations in implementing a global marketing campaign.[51] First, market development and the competitive environment must be at similar stages from country to country. New products thus often represent more promising candidates for standardization. Whereas mature products may have vastly different histories (or even positionings) in different markets, with new products perceptions have yet to be formed. For example, the 'Intel Inside' campaign has transferred relatively easily across geographic boundaries because personal computers have been relatively new to each market.

The second key consideration according to Meyer is that consumer target markets should be alike and consumers must share the same desires, needs and uses for a product. Similarly, academic Greyser claims: 'The fulcrum of global marketing rests on whether the consumer or customer segment is similar across countries seeking the same values in physical performance or psychological satisfactions or both.'[52] In other words, brand image must be relevant to consumers in both a product-related and non-product-related sense.

What types of products are difficult to sell through standardized global marketing campaigns? Many experts note that foods and beverages that have years of tradition and entrenched preferences and tastes can be particularly problematic. For example, Unilever has found that standard preferences are commoner across countries for cleaning products such as detergents and soaps than for food products. In addition, high-end products can also benefit from standardization because high quality or prestige often can be marketed similarly across countries. For example, Italian coffeemaker Illy maintains a 'one brand, one blend' strategy, offering only a single blend of espresso made of Arabica beans across the globe. As Andrea Illy, who has run his family's business since 1994, states: 'Our marketing strategy focuses on building quality consumer perceptions – no promotions, just differentiating ourselves from the competition by offering top quality, consistency and an image of excellence.'

More generally, the following types of products and brands are likely to retain a similar marketing strategy worldwide.

- High-technology products with strong functional images. Examples are televisions, DVD players, watches, computers, cameras and cars. Such products tend to be universally understood and are not typically part of the cultural heritage.
- High-image products that have strong associations with fashionability, sensuality, wealth or status. Examples are cosmetics, clothes, jewellery and alcohol. Such products can appeal to the same type of market worldwide.
- Services and business-to-business products that emphasize corporate images in their global marketing campaigns. Examples are airlines and banks.
- Retailers that sell to upper-class individuals or specialize in a salient but unfulfilled need. For example, by offering a variety of toys at affordable prices, Toys 'R' Us transformed the market by getting Europeans to buy toys for children any time of the year, not just at Christmas, and forcing competitors to level prices across countries.
- Brands positioned primarily on the basis of their country of origin. Examples include Sweden's Ikea or Australia's Foster's beer.[53]
- Products that do not need customization or other special products to be able to function properly. ITT found that standalone products such as heart pacemakers could be sold easily the same way worldwide, but that integrated products such as telecommunications equipment have to be tailored to function within local phone systems.[54]

Tradeoffs between standardization and customization and issues concerning communication and distribution strategies were outlined earlier. It is useful, however, to consider some additional issues concerning product and pricing strategies.

Product strategy

Many marketers believe that only certain products can be marketed similarly – in some places – and only after variables such as marketing mix and culture are analyzed, understood and incorporated into the marketing campaign. One reason why so many companies ran into trouble going overseas is that they unknowingly – or perhaps even deliberately – overlooked differences in consumer behaviour. Because of the relative expense and sometimes unsophisticated nature of marketing research in smaller markets, many companies chose to do without basic consumer research and put products on the shelf to see what would happen. As a result, they sometimes became aware of consumer differences only after the fact. To understand consumer preferences and avoid such mistakes, marketers may need to conduct research into local markets. For example, Japanese firms often hire local marketing experts to help design their products for local tastes.[55]

In many cases, however, research reveals that product differences are not justified for certain countries. At one time, Palmolive soap was sold globally, although with 22 fragrances, 17 packaging designs, 9 shapes and with numerous different positionings.

After marketing analyses to reap the benefits of global marketing, the company now employs just seven fragrances, one core packaging design and three shapes, all executed according to two related positionings (one for developing markets and one for developed markets).[56] Brand Briefing 14.9 describes how UPS adapted its service for Europe.

From a corporate perspective, one solution to the tradeoff between global and local brands is to sell both as part of the brand portfolio in a category. Even companies that have succeeded with global brands maintain that standardized international

---

Brand Briefing 14.9

UPS' European express

Between 1987 and 1997, United Parcel Service (UPS) of the USA spent €730 million to buy 16 delivery businesses, put brown uniforms on 25,000 Europeans and spray its brown paint on 10,000 delivery vans in the process of becoming the largest delivery company in Europe. It had to overcome obstacles along the way. French drivers were outraged that they could not have wine with lunch, British drivers protested when their dogs were banned from delivery vans, Spaniards were dismayed when they realized the brown UPS vans resembled the local hearses and Germans were shocked when brown shirts were required for the first time since 1945. UPS ultimately allowed a degree of local intepretation while standing firm on some issues of company policy, such as brown vans and uniforms and alcohol-free drivers.

Although UPS operations are basically the same, some things vary between countries: van restrictions on weekends and holidays, low bridges and tunnels, weight regulations, traffic road systems, airports and night curfews. Also, express delivery was not as popular in Europe as it was in the USA. One industry analyst said: 'Europeans are not as time-sensitive as the Americans are.'

By 1997, UPS had only 15 percent of the European parcel delivery market, sales were growing at 15 percent annually, or half the US rate, and its European operations had lost €365 million since launch. UPS lost money on intra-European express delivery, mostly because more than 90 percent of European parcel delivery is domestic.

So, UPS spent an estimated €800 between 1995 and 2000 on upgrading its European operations by purchasing vehicles, aircraft, buildings and logistics systems. Consequently, export deliveries in Europe via UPS rose at a compound annual rate of 22 percent between 1996 and 2002. By 2002, UPS employed more than 22,000 people in Europe, offered services at more than 1,200 locations and offered overnight delivery to more than 700 cities. UPS continued to grow in Europe via acquisition, buying delivery companies Stolica and Lynx in Poland and the UK, respectively, in 2005.

Sources: Adapted from Dana Milbank, 'Can Europe deliver?', *Wall Street Journal*, 30 September 1994: R15; Alan Saloman, 'Delivering a market battle', *Advertising Age*; William Echikson, 'The Continent is still a tough neighborhood for UPS', *BusinessWeek*, 29 September 1997; UPS annual reports, 2002 and 2005.

marketing campaigns work only with some products, in some places and at some times and will never totally replace brands and ads with local appeal.[57] For example, while Coca-Cola sells Coke to a growing group of consumers in Asia, it also sells local brands such as Georgia iced coffee in Japan, which outsells Coke, as well as new drinks in Japan such as Nagomi green tea and the honey-and-grapefruit drink Hachimitsu. In China, the company introduced Tian Yu Di ('heaven and earth'), a fruit juice and tea, and Yangguang ('sunshine') lemon tea, plus other flavours. In India, Coca-Cola's biggest-selling cola is Thums Up, an indigenous variant it bought in 1993. It also sells Maaza fruit-based drinks there. This combination of local and global brands enables Coca-Cola to exploit the benefits of global branding and global trends in tastes while tapping into traditional domestic markets at the same time.[58] Thus, despite the trend towards globalization, it seems that there will always be opportunities for local brands.

Pricing strategy

In designing a global pricing strategy, principles from Chapter 5 still generally apply. Thus, it is necessary to understand in each country what consumer perceptions of the value of the brand are, their willingness to pay and their elasticities with respect to price changes. Sometimes, differences in these considerations permit differences in pricing strategies. For example, brands such as Levi's, Heineken and Perrier have been able to command a much higher price outside their domestic market because they have a different brand image – and thus sources of brand equity – in other countries that consumers place more value on. In addition to such differences, distribution structures, competitive positions and tax and exchange rates all may justify differences in prices.

Unfortunately, setting very different prices for different countries is becoming more difficult.[59] Pressures for international price alignment have arisen, in part, because of the increasing numbers of legitimate imports and exports and the ability of retailers and suppliers to exploit price differences through 'grey imports' across borders. This problem is especially acute in Europe, where price differences are often large (eg, prices of identical car models may vary by 30–40 percent) and ample opportunity exists to export or shop across national boundaries.

In such cases, Hermann Simon, a German expert on pricing, recommends creating an international 'price corridor' that takes into account both the inherent differences between countries and alignment pressures. Specifically, the corridor is calculated by company headquarters and its country subsidiaries by considering market data for individual countries, price elasticities in the countries, parallel imports resulting from price differentials, currency exchange rates, costs in countries and arbitrage costs between them, and data on competition and distribution. No country is then allowed to set its price outside the corridor: Countries with lower prices have to raise them and countries with higher prices have to lower them. Another possible strategy suggested by Simon is to introduce different brands in high-price, high-income countries and in low-price, low-income countries, depending on the relative cost tradeoffs of standardization versus customization.

In Asia, many US brands command premiums over home-grown competitors because consumers in these countries associate the USA with high-quality consumer products.[60] In assessing the viability of Asian markets, it is important not to just look at average income but to also consider the distribution of incomes because of the large consumer population involved. For example, although the average annual income in India is maybe only €538, some 300 million people can still afford the same types of products that might be sold to middle-class Europeans. In China, Gillette introduced Oral-B toothbrushes at 90 cents, compared with locally produced toothbrushes sold at 19 cents. Gillette's reasoning was that, even if it only gained 10 percent of the Chinese market, it still would sell more toothbrushes there than it was selling in the USA.

7. Balance global and local control

Building brand equity in a global context must be a carefully designed and implemented process. A key decision is choosing the most appropriate organizational structure for managing global brands. In general, there are three main approaches:

- centralization at home office or headquarters;
- decentralization of decision-making to local foreign markets;
- some combination of centralization and decentralization.

In general, companies tend to adopt a combination of centralization and decentralization to balance local adaptation and global standardization.

In many, if not most, markets, the cost savings of standardization may not outweigh the revenue potential from tailoring campaigns to different groups of consumers.[61] Each aspect of the marketing campaign is a candidate for globalization. Which elements of the marketing campaign should be standardized and to what degree?[62] In a basic sense, cost and revenue considerations should be the primary considerations in deciding which elements of the marketing campaign should be adapted for which country. One approach is a mixed strategy, standardizing the 'core aspects' of the brand (those that provide its main competitive edge) but allowing local adaptation of 'secondary aspects'. According to this approach, branding, positioning and product formulation are more likely to be standardized and advertising and pricing less so; distribution is most often localized.[63]

Many global companies divide their markets into five or so regions – for example, Europe, Asia, Latin America, North America and Africa/Middle East. In considering how these markets are managed internally, a key theme is the need to balance global and local control. Coca-Cola, for example, distinguishes between local marketing activities that would appear to dilute brand equity and those that would not appear to be as efficacious as desired. Headquarters would stop the former from occurring but would not stop the latter, leaving it to a local manager's judgement as to the activity's appropriateness but also holding him or her responsible for its success. Similarly, Levi Strauss has a 'thermometer' model. Marketing elements below the 'freezing point' are fixed: 'brand soul' (described on page 745) and logos are standardized worldwide. Above the freezing point, product quality, pricing, advertising, distribution and promotions are all fluid, meaning each international division can handle the marketing mix elements as it feels appropriate.

One area of centralization is with advertising. As noted in Chapter 8, firms increasingly are shifting their advertising campaigns to agencies with global networks. Firms are making these moves to reduce costs and increase efficiency and control. Nevertheless, regional managers for both Braun and Levi Strauss have been able to bar a global campaign from being run in their area. Unilever's regional managers who seek to substitute their own campaigns, however, must produce research showing that the global plan is inappropriate. Coke and Procter & Gamble take the middle ground, developing global communications campaigns but testing them and fine-tuning them in meetings with regional managers.[64]

8. Establish operable guidelines

Brand definitions and guidelines must be established, communicated and enforced so that marketers in different regions have a good understanding of what they are expected to do and not to do. The goal is to set clear rules for how a brand should be positioned and marketed. Hence, everyone within the organization understands the brand's meaning and can translate that meaning to satisfy local consumer preferences. Brand definition and communication often revolve around two related issues. First, a document, such as a brand charter, should detail what the brand is and is not. Second, the product line should reflect only those products that are consistent with the brand definition.

Coca-Cola has a strategy document that articulates the company's strategy and how the brand positioning is manifested by marketing mix elements. This document sets out the parameters for the brand and determines how much is left to chance. Similarly, the McDonald's operating manual imposes rigorous worldwide controls (eg, the 19 steps to cook and bag chips). Nestlé ensures that branding decisions follow strict corporate guidelines.

Colgate-Palmolive

Colgate-Palmolive has been a successful global marketer because of its tight focus on marketing strategies and objectives.[65] Colgate's 'bundle books' contain, down to the smallest details, everything that Colgate knows about any given brand – and that a country or regional manager needs to know. The books describe how to market a particular product, including its attributes, formulae, ingredient sourcing information, market research, pricing positions, graphics and even advertising, public relations and point-of-sale materials. With a bundle book, a manager in any of the 200 countries and territories where Colgate sells its products can project the brand exactly like all his or her counterparts. As one executive noted: 'As the smallest among our major competitors, we are trying to make sure that we maximize our resources. By having tightly controlled brands, we can leverage across borders rapidly.'

As an example of deriving product strategy from a brand definition, consider Disney. Everyone at Disney is exposed to the Disney brand mantra, 'Fun family entertainment'. To establish global guidelines, Disney's centralized marketing group worked with members of the consumer products group for months on every product to assign them to one of three categories.

- Can be licensed without permission (eg, T-shirts).
- No licence permitted (eg, toilet paper).
- Requires validation from headquarters to license (about 20 categories – eg, air fresheners).

Internationally, Disney has noticed that the 'grey areas' grow larger and more numerous. The company also has been trying to identify which product groups may be more amenable to localizing than others. For example, films cannot be tailored for Europe because it is difficult to determine what will be attractive to those consumers. On the other hand, certain items in the Disney shops may sell well in Germany but not Japan.

Finally, for all of this to work, there must be effective lines of communication. Coca-Cola stresses the importance of having people on the ground who can manage the brand in concert with headquarters in the USA. For example, co-ordination is developed through training in headquarters; an e-mail and voicemail system is in place; and global databases are available. The goal of this integrated information system is to help local managers to tap into what constitutes 'relevance' in any particular country and then communicate those ideals to headquarters.

9. Implement a global brand equity measurement system

As suggested by the guidelines in Chapter 8, a global brand equity measurement system would provide timely, accurate and actionable information for marketers about brands so that they can make the best tactical decisions in the short run and strategic decisions in the long run in all markets. As part of this, such a system needs to be implemented so that it defines the brand equity charter in a global context, outlining how the brand positioning and resulting marketing campaign should be interpreted in different markets. With a global brand strategy template in place, brand tracking can assess the progress that is being made, especially in terms of creating the desired positioning, eliciting the proper responses and developing brand resonance.

Levi Strauss

Levi Strauss has implemented a global brand equity measurement system. Based on brand audits, Levi Strauss has defined what the 'brand soul' is for each of its brands. The brand soul is a statement of brand values and how they will be translated through marketing elements across the globe. The brand soul is described in terms of what the soul is today, what the company wants it to be in the future and how to execute and achieve that goal by means of marketing mix activity. Each territory manager helps to define what the soul is based on current knowledge and input from marketing research and advertising agencies. The brand soul is then communicated to every employee, including the receptionist, so that even the music heard while on the phone reflects the brand value in a substantive way. Marketing research in the form of brand tracking is tailored to determine how each brand is stacking up against the tenets of the brand soul in each territory. A new global marketing group was established at headquarters to handle global issues and monitor progression to the brand soul objectives in particular.

The challenge is that the marketing research infrastructure may be found lacking in many countries. When DuPont set out to implement a global tracking system for its brands, its efforts were hampered by the fact that the level of sophistication of local marketing research companies varied for the 40 primary countries in which DuPont operated.

10. Leverage brand elements

Proper design and implementation of brand elements (ie, the brand name and all related trademarked brand identifiers) can often be critical to building global brand equity. As Chapter 4 pointed out, in assembling the elements that make up a brand, an important consideration is their geographic transferability. Yet, brands have encountered resistance because of difficulty in translating their names, packaging, slogans or other elements to fit with another culture. Brand Briefing 14.10 describes some cultural differences that have been found in name memorability and recall.

Brand Briefing 14.10

Brand recall and language

Given the linguistic differences between cultures, it is not surprising that differences exist in what types of brand names are more likely to be recalled in one culture versus those in another. Studies of this issue in the cases of Chinese- and English-speaking consumers found significant differences in how they processed brand names. These studies have implications for companies looking to adapt or create brands in China.

In one study, Chinese speakers were more likely to recall names presented as brand names in visual, rather than spoken, recall, whereas English speakers were more likely to recall the names in spoken rather than visual recall, suggesting that mental representations of verbal information in Chinese are coded primarily in a visual manner, whereas verbal information in English is coded primarily in a phonological manner.

Brand Briefing 14.10 *continued*

Another study showed that a match between peripheral features of a brand name (ie, 'script' aspects, such as the type of font employed, or 'sounds' aspects, such as how the name is pronounced) and the associations or meaning of the brand resulted in more positive brand attitudes than a mismatch: Chinese native speakers were affected primarily by script matching, whereas English native speakers' attitudes were primarily affected by sound matching. These results were interpreted in terms of structural differences between logographic systems (such as Chinese, where characters stand for concepts and not sounds) and alphabetic systems (such as English, where the writing of a word is a close cue for its pronunciation) and their resulting visual and phonological representations in memory.

A related study investigated perceptions of brand names translated into Chinese. There are three types of translation for names. The first is phonetic, where Chinese characters are used that sound most like the English word. The second is semantic, where Chinese characters are chosen that approximate the meaning of the English word. The third is phono-semantic, where a translation shares similarities in meaning and sound with the English original. It is common for products in China to use 'bilingual' packaging that carries the brand name in both logographic form (ie, Chinese characters) and using the English alphabet. Typically, a pack will emphasize one name over the other by making it larger. The study found that phonetic translations were preferred if a hypothetical product emphasized the English name, while both phono-semantic and semantic translations were evaluated equally regardless of which name was emphasized.

A different study demonstrated that 'classifiers', a grammatical feature present in Chinese but not English, affected perceived similarity between objects and how words are clustered upon recall. Chinese speakers were more likely to cluster names according to a classifier than English speakers. This finding suggested that judicious selection of classifiers could influence how a brand is perceived. The study also showed that, for Chinese speakers, images in hypothetical advertisements that corresponded with a classifier present in the ad copy were preferred over images that had no correspondence.

Sources: Bernd H. Schmitt, Yigang Pan and Nader T. Tavassoli, 'Language and consumer memory: the impact of linguistic differences between Chinese and English', *Journal of Consumer Research,* 1994, 21 (12): 419–31; Nader T. Tavassoli and Yih Hwai Lee, 'The differential effect of auditory and visual advertising elements with Chineses and English', *Journal of Marketing Research,* November 2003, 40: 468–80; Yigang Pan and Bernd H. Schmitt, 'Language and brand attitudes: impact of script and sound matching in Chinese and English', *Journal of Consumer Psychology,* 1996, 5(3): 263–77, Shi Zhang, Bernd H. Schmitt and Hillary Haley, 'Language and culture: linguistic effects on consumer behaviour in international marketing research', in *Handbook of Research in International Marketing,* eds Subhash C. Jain, Northampton, MA: Edward Elgar Publishing, 2003: 228–42.

In general, non-verbal brand elements such as logos, symbols and characters are more likely to directly transfer – at least as long as their meaning is visually clear – than verbal brand elements that may need to be translated into another language. Non-verbal brand elements are more likely to be helpful in creating brand awareness than brand image, however, which may require more explicit meaning and direct statements. If the meaning of a brand element is clear visually, it can be an invaluable source of brand equity worldwide. As the saying goes: 'A picture is worth a thousand words', so it is not surprising that choosing the right brand logo, symbol or character can have a huge effect on global marketing effectiveness.

For example, the image of Ronald McDonald communicates McDonald's association with children without the need for words. Similarly, the Apple logo and the M&M characters need no translation. Other brand elements become synonymous with an association and also serve as effective communications tools without the use of words. Thus, brand logos and symbols also play an important role in global branding. The Nike swoosh connotes sport, Coke's contour bottle connotes refreshment and the Mercedes star connotes status and prestige worldwide. Perhaps the most compelling example of the importance of brand symbols is the Marlboro man.

Marlboro

In repositioning the Marlboro brand, Philip Morris created the Marlboro man, a cowboy who is almost always depicted somewhere in the Western USA among magnificent scenery deemed 'Marlboro country'. By 1975, Marlboro had become the best-selling cigarette in the USA. But the appeal of the Marlboro man extends far beyond that country. Indeed, the cowboy imagery attracts consumers from all over the world in part by capturing an image that is uniquely American. The Marlboro man has been used in 150 countries and Marlboro is the biggest-selling brand in Germany, Mexico, Switzerland, Saudi Arabia, Hong Kong, Argentina and 11 other major global markets. Marlboro is consistently ranked as one of the world's most valuable brands, due in large part to the widespread appeal of its brand character and personality.

Even non-verbal elements, however, can encounter translation problems. For example, certain colours have strong cultural meanings. Marketing campaigns using shades of green in advertising, packaging and other marketing materials ran into trouble in Malaysia, where the colour symbolizes death and disease.[66] In some cases, verbal elements can be translated into native languages without much appreciable loss in meaning. For example, Coke's 'Can't beat the feeling' slogan was translated to the equivalent of 'I feel Coke' in Japan, 'Unique sensation' in Italy and 'The feeling of life' in Chile. Germany proved a problem – no translation really worked – so the slogan was kept in English because of the relatively large bilingual audience there.

Because of a desire to standardize globally, however, many firms have attempted to create more uniform brand elements. Pursuing a global branding strategy, Mars chose to replace its Treets and Bonitos brands with the M&M brand worldwide and changed the name of its third-largest UK brand, Marathon, to the Snickers name used in the rest of Europe and the USA.[67] To create a stronger global brand, PepsiCo pulled together its dozens of company-owned brands of crisps and began to market them all abroad under a more uniform Lay's logo. The company also boosted advertising and improved quality to enhance the brand image at the same time.[68]

CHAPTER REVIEW

Increasingly, it is imperative that marketers properly define and implement a global branding strategy. A number of factors are encouraging firms to sell their products and services abroad. Some advantages of a global marketing campaign are economies of scale in production and distribution, lower marketing costs, communication of power and scope, consistency in brand image, an ability to build on ideas quickly and efficiently, and uniformity of marketing practices and thus greater competitiveness. The more standardized the marketing campaign, in general, the more these different advantages will be realized. At the same time, disadvantages of a global campaign are that it may ignore differences between countries in consumer needs, wants and usage patterns for products; consumer response to marketing mix elements; product development and the competitive environment; the legal environment; marketing institutions; and administrative procedures.

In developing a global campaign, marketers attempt to obtain as many of these advantages as possible while minimizing the disadvantages. Building global customer-based brand equity means creating brand awareness and a positive brand image in each country. Issues regarding creating a standardized marketing campaign were noted. It is difficult to identify any company applying global marketing in its strictest sense. Increasingly, marketers are blending global objectives with local or regional concerns. The means by which brand equity is built may differ from country to country or the actual sources of brand equity themselves may vary in terms of specific attribute or benefit associations. Nevertheless, there must be sufficient levels of brand awareness and strong, favourable and unique brand associations in each country in which the brand is sold to provide sources of brand equity. It is necessary to identify differences in consumer behaviour (ie, how consumers purchase and use products and what they know and feel about brands) and adjust the branding accordingly (ie, through the choice of brand elements, nature of the supporting marketing campaign and use of secondary associations).

The chapter reviewed how to modify branding to adapt to differences in consumer behaviour through product features, prices, channels and marketing campaigns. Figure 14.15 lists 'ten commandments of global branding' and questions that can be asked to help guide global brand management.

1. Understand similarities and differences in the global branding landscape.
    - Have you tried to find as many commonalities as possible between markets?
    - Have you identified what is unique about different markets?
    - Have you examined all aspects of the marketing environment (eg, stages of brand development, consumer behaviour, marketing infrastructure, competitive activity, legal restrictions)?
    - Have you reconciled these similarities and differences in the most cost-effective and brand-building manner possible?

→

Figure 14.15   Self-evaluation ratings for the ten commandments of global branding

2. Don't take shortcuts in brand building.

- Have you ensured that the brand is being built from the bottom up strategically by creating brand awareness before crafting the brand image?
- Have you ensured that the brand is being built from the bottom up tactically by determining the appropriate marketing campaigns and activities for the brand in each market given the particular strategic goals?

3. Establish marketing infrastructure.

- Have you created the appropriate marketing infrastructure – in terms of manufacturing, distribution and logistics – from scratch if necessary?
- Have you adapted to capitalize on the existing marketing infrastructure in other countries?

4. Embrace integrated marketing communications.

- Have you considered non-traditional forms of communication that go beyond conventional advertising?
- Have you ensured that all communications are integrated in each market and are consistent with the brand's desired positioning and heritage?

5. Cultivate brand partnerships.

- Have you formed partnerships with global and local partners to overcome any deficiencies in your marketing campaigns?
- Have you ensured that all partnerships avoid compromising the brand promise and do not harm brand equity in any way?

6. Balance standardization and customization.

- Have you been careful to retain elements of marketing campaigns that are relevant and add value to the brand across all markets?
- Have you sought to find local adaptations and additions that complement and supplement these global elements to achieve greater local appeal?

7. Balance global and local control.

- Have you established clear managerial guidelines as to principles and actions that all global managers must adhere to?
- Have you carefully delineated the areas in which local managers are given discretion and autonomy in their decision-making?

8. Establish operable guidelines.

- Have you explained brand management guidelines in a clear and concise fashion in a document to be used by all global marketers?
- Have you established seamless communication between headquarters and local and regional marketing organizations?

9. Implement a global brand equity measurement system.

- Do you conduct brand audits when appropriate in overseas markets?
- Have you devised a brand tracking system to provide timely, accurate and actionable information on brands in relevant markets?
- Have you established a global brand equity management system with brand equity charters, brand equity reports and brand equity overseers?

10. Leverage brand elements.

- Have you checked the relevance of brand elements to global markets?
- Have you established visual brand identities that transfer across market boundaries?

Figure 14.15   *Continued*

Brand Briefing 14.11

China's global brand ambitions

Growth at home

China, the world's most populous country with more than 1.3 billion people, was essentially closed to the world during the period between the communist overthrow of the government in 1949 until economic reforms began in 1978, culminating in China's admission to the World Trade Organisation in 2001. Since reforms began, China has industrialized at a remarkable rate and is now the world's fourth-largest economy, boasting a €77.7 billion trade surplus in 2005. The statistics are staggering: it is the world's largest garment exporter by a large margin; it is the world's largest manufacturer of consumer electronics; and it makes 80 percent of the clocks sold in the world, 50 percent of all cameras and 60 percent of all bicycles. The primary reason for China's manufacturing process is cheap labour. Manufacturing wages in China average 60 cents an hour, 95 percent lower than US averages.

China's economic boom has created opportunity for the country's citizens and companies, as well as providing a consumer base for foreign companies seeking growth. For each group, however, hurdles prevent from these opportunities being pursued fully.

A growing consumer class

Not surprisingly, China's rise to a global economic superpower enriched many of its citizens. By 2006, *BusinessWeek* estimated that 300,000 Chinese citizens were millionaires.[69] With this wealth came a new-found interest in consuming conspicuously, which precipitated a windfall for foreign luxury goods manufacturers. China went from consuming 1 percent of the world's luxury goods in 2001 to 12 percent in 2006, the third highest tally in the world. Luxury brands flocked to the mainland to cash in. By 2006, Louis Vuitton had 12 boutiques across China, Ermenegildo Zegna had more than 50 shops in a dozen cities, Rolls-Royce's Beijing outlet was one of the company's top-selling dealerships and Cartier began targeting second- and third-tier cities in search of growth. The luxury market is expected to expand even more rapidly. As China's middle class grows from 50 million in 2002 to a predicted 100 million by 2010, luxury goods brands will have a large audience. China's vast population of only children – called 'Little Emperors' for the way many are spoiled by doting parents – comprised a fifth of the population under the age of 25 in 2004 and are expected to drive demand for luxury goods.[70]

Times were not always so good, however, for China's wealthy elite. *Forbes'* 1999 survey of China's wealthiest individuals became known as the 'death list' after the government initiated a 'tax crackdown' that led to jail terms for some.[71] Attitudes have since changed and, as one wealthy film producer noted: 'We are more accepted by the media, government and society today.'[72] Yet the fact that a fortunate few have experienced an exponential increase in personal wealth belies the vast numbers of

Brand Briefing 14.11 *continued*

urban and, especially, rural poor. Rural workers earn half the average salary of urban factory workers, which is often not enough for the rural dwellers to send their children to school. Consequently, rural Chinese are migrating to cities in search of better-paying jobs, increasing urban congestion and resulting in higher unemployment. By 2010, it is predicted that half of the population will live in cities, aggravating these problems.

Despite the concerns generated by this wealth polarization, China's consumer class still has enough purchasing power to attract foreign brands.

Foreign interest

Since China began relaxing its trade policy in 1978, foreign companies have eagerly sought the Chinese consumer's *yuan* (Chinese for dollar). Coca-Cola was one of the first Western brands in China, in 1979. Through an investment of more than €730 million in joint venture bottling plants, Coke gradually expanded. Over the years, it became far more successful than Jianlibao, China's biggest domestic soft drinks maker, which saw its market share fall from 15 percent in the early 1990s to 5 percent in 2002. By 2003, Coca-Cola employed 20,000 people in China and had been profitable for 8 years.[73] FedEx also made an early move into China by buying a regional cargo airline for almost €730 million in 1989, nearly 10 years before rivals moved in. By 2006, FedEx controlled 39 percent of China–US air express delivery business.[74] Other foreign companies have also achieved considerable success in China. For example, beauty-conscious China is a €1.5 billion market for Procter & Gamble. China also accounts for more than 30 percent of international profits for Yum Brands, which owns KFC and Pizza Hut. China is the second-largest film market for Kodak, which runs more than 8,000 photo shops there. China has 126 television sets for every 100 households.[75] Additionally, some faded foreign brands have managed to remake their images in China. For example, Howard Johnson operates four- and five-star hotels in China, complete with marble floors, that have enabled the company to position itself there as an upmarket chain.

Other foreign companies have attracted Chinese consumers by buying Chinese brands and keeping the original names. For Danone, 80 percent of its sales are generated by Chinese brands.[76] It bought a local milk and vitamin drink brand Wahaha in 1996 and increased sales from 800 million bottles to 4 billion bottles within two years. It then extended Wahaha into China's largest bottled water brand, making China Danone's largest water market. In China, Danone has higher profit margins than its global average and earns more than €877 million a year.

Motorola is one of the most successful companies to enter China, yet found its market leadership besieged by local competition in the 2000s. With 300 million mobile phone users and 5 million more signing up each month in early 2004, China is by far the largest national market in the world.[77] Motorola, recognizing this potential,

Brand Briefing 14.11 *continued*

entered in the late 1980s and worked with government leaders to develop a wireless telecommunications infrastructure and related manufacturing, becoming the largest foreign investor in China's electronics industry. Unfortunately for Motorola, by 2004, the market was incredibly competitive: consumers had 800 models to choose from and young urban users typically changed phones every 8 months. Furthermore, more than 40 percent of the handset market in China had been captured by local companies such as Ningbo Bird, Nanjing Panda Electronics and TCL Mobile, many of which would not exist had it not been for Motorola's investment in China's mobile phone industry. Motorola's experience illustrates the problem of technology transfer to local companies, one of the means by which local Chinese brands grow strong locally.

Emerging local leaders

The Chinese handset manufacturers mentioned above are just one of many examples where local brands take market share from foreign heavyweights. Many Chinese consumer electronics and consumer packaged goods brands are also the market leaders at home. Haier, China's number-one appliance maker, was a €9.4 billion manufacturing giant based in Qingdao by 2005. Gome is China's top electronics retailer with over 100 shops and €1.5 billion in sales.[78] Foreign brewers were forced to regroup after forays into China were confounded by the cheaper and better-distributed market leader Tsingtao and a host of other local beers. The internet is another area where Chinese brands often rule at home. With 94 million internet users in 2005, China had the second-largest online population after the USA. In instant messaging, AOL and MSN are also-rans: a local company, Tencent, was leader in 2005, with 70 percent of the market. eBay is a distant second in online auctions to TaoBao, which ran 72 percent of the €1.24 billion of online auctions conducted in 2005.[79]

One of the reasons for the success of local brands is their superior distribution. Many Chinese firms built local distribution from the ground up, enabling them to reach millions of consumers not served by the multinationals, who initially targeted only Chinese cities. Additionally, many local brands are outspending their foreign rivals on advertising. Advertising is a battleground: with so many television sets, brands can reach many of China's billion-plus customers relatively efficiently. Of the top 10 advertisers in China in 2004, half were Chinese brands, spending a combined €1.1 billion.[80] Between 2000 and 2005, Chinese companies went from accounting for nothing to 35 percent of billings at J. Walter Thompson in China.

Perhaps no brand typifies Chinese brands' ability to win on their own turf better than Lenovo (formerly Legend), a Chinese PC manufacturer. Lenovo was started in 1984 and struggled to keep pace with foreign brands. As recently as 1997 it was losing money and market share to IBM, Hewlett-Packard and Compaq. But within

Brand Briefing 14.11 *continued*

two years it had turned its fortunes around with the help of low prices, government contracts and a vast distribution network, doubling in size between 1998 and 1999 and grabbing 15 percent market share, about twice that of its closest rival.[81] It increased its market leadership in China, which enabled it to buy IBM's PC division in 2005. In 2006, it began selling low-priced PCs bearing the Lenovo name in the USA. Lenovo's global ambitions illustrate the latest brand trend to emerge in China – that of local brands growing globally.

Locals going global

As a result of buying IBM's PC unit, Lenovo is probably the most well-known of the Chinese seeking to build brands abroad. There are many others in China, however, pursuing a similar strategy. Many observers predict that some of these brands will follow Korea's Samsung, LG and Hyundai in rising from obscurity to global prominence in a couple of decades. Appliancemaker Haier has the potential to do just that. To compete in overseas markets, Haier increased its R&D spending to 4 percent of revenues. 'In the past, we tried to design our products in Qingdao and sell them to the US and Japan,' explained chief executive Zhang Ruimin. 'They didn't meet overseas consumers' needs and didn't sell well.'[82] By 2004, Haier had 22 factories overseas and distribution through big US chains helped its foreign revenues rise to €950 million, or 13 percent of total revenues. Athletic clothing and equipment maker Li-Ning sought to build its international profile by outfitting many Chinese athletes and the Spanish basketball team for the 2004 Athens Olympics and by signing the rights to use US basketball players and logos in its marketing.[83] Other Chinese brands to set foot on foreign soil include electronics firm TCL, mobile phone maker China Kejian, networking equipment maker Huawei and Tsingtao beer.

These moves abroad are, in part, a function of the pressures facing large firms searching for revenue growth beyond an increasingly competitive domestic market. Another cause is encouragement from the Chinese government, which dictated that between 30 and 50 firms should be built into 'national champions' or 'globally competitive' companies by 2010,[84] and therefore exhorted Chinese companies 'to set up overseas operations, acquire foreign assets and transform themselves into multinational corporations'.[85] A related reason is the notion of global brand recognition as a source of national pride. One Chinese industrialist had a slogan printed on the wall of one of his factories that captured this source of Chinese companies' global aspirations: 'One who earns money in China is a winner; one who earns money overseas is a hero'.[86]

Yet the path to global brand leadership is fraught with complications. As of 2006, no Chinese brand could be considered a global brand. In fact, one advertising executive working in China argued that 'Chinese companies are light years away'

Brand Briefing 14.11 *continued*

from exporting their brands successfully.[87] Chinese companies lagged behind when it came to branding compared with global competitors, a fact Haier chief Zhang acknowledged: '[Chinese companies] started brand development very late, so we have to catch up in a very short period of time.'[88] Companies that did have an international presence, such as Haier and Lenovo, were priced as entry-level bargains, like their Korean predecessors. To buy their way to brand recognition and respect, some Chinese companies began bidding for foreign brands, as Lenovo did with IBM. Still others, like Haier, invested more heavily in R&D to bolster their images with innovation. Despite the difficulties Chinese brands encountered overseas, one consultant remained optimistic about Chinese brands one day taking their place as global brand leaders: 'Market shares will go up and down. Some Chinese companies will lose. It's a learning process. But there is no doubt that world-class Chinese brands will emerge.'[89]

Discussion questions

1. Contrast Coca-Cola's global branding strategy with Ikea's. How are they similar and how are they different? Why are they so well respected? What problems are they are facing?

2. Pick a brand marketed in more than one country. Assess the extent to which the brand is marketed on a standardized versus customized basis.

3. How aware are you of the country of origin of products you own? For which products do you care about the country of origin? Why? For those imported brands that you view positively, find out and analyze how they are marketed in their home country.

4. Pick a product category. Consider the strategies of market leaders in different countries. How are they the same and how are they different?

5. Pick a product category. How are leading brands targeting different demographic market segments?

References and notes

[1]Michael J. Thomas, Jack R. Bureau and Narsingh Saxena, 'The relevance of global branding', *Journal of Brand Management*, 1995, 2 (5): 299–307.

[2]Shaoming Zou and S. Tamer Cavusgil, 'The GMS: a broad conceptualization of global marketing strategy and its effect on firm performance', *Journal of Marketing*, October 2002, 66: 40–56.

[3]Dana L. Alden, Jan-Benedict E. M. Steenkamp and Rajeev Batra, 'Brand positioning through advertising in Asia, North America and Europe: the role of global consumer culture', *Journal of Marketing*, January 1999, 63: 75–87.

[4]Rakeev Batra, Venkatram Ramaswamy, Dana L. Alden, Jan-Benedict E. M. Steenkap and S. Ramachander, 'Effects of brand local and nonlocal origin on consumer attitudes in developing countries', *Journal of Consumer Psychology*, 2000, 9 (2): 83–95; Jan-Benedict E. M. Steenkamp, Rajeev Batra and Dana L. Alden, 'How perceived globalness creates brand value', *Journal of International Business Studies*, 2003, 34: 53–65.

[5]Ian M. Lewis, 'Key issues in globalizing brands: why there aren't any global OTC medicine brands', talk presented at the Third Annual Advertising and Promotion Workshop, Advertising Research Foundation, 5–6 February 1991.

[6]Corporate Executive Board, 'Overcoming executional challenges in global brand management', Marketing Leadership Council, Case Book, March 2001.

[7]Terry Lefton, 'The global exchange of pricelessness', *Brandweek*, November 30, 1998.

[8] Ibid.

[9]Dawar and Parker, however, show how the use of a brand name as an important signal of quality occurs in various countries. See Niraj Dawar and Philip Parker, 'Marketing universals: consumers' use of brand name, price, physical appearance and retailer reputation as signals of quality', *Journal of Marketing*, April 1994, 58: 81–95.

[10]Choi Lee and Robert T. Green, 'Cross-cultural examination of the Fishbein behavioural intentions model', *Journal of International Business Studies*, second quarter 1991: 289–305.

[11]Dennis Chase, 'A global comeback', *Advertising Age*, 20 August 1987: 142–214.

[12]Ronald Alsop, 'Countries' different ad rules are problem for global firms', *Wall Street Journal*, 27 September 1984: 33.

[13]Craig S. Smith, 'Doublemint in China: distribution isn't double the fun', *Wall Street Journal*, 5 December 1995: B1.

[14]Theodore Levitt, 'The globalization of markets', *Harvard Business Review*, May–June 1983: 92–102.

[15]Gabriella Stern, 'Heinz aims to export taste for ketchup', *Wall Street Journal*, 20 November 1992: B1.

[16]Theresa Howard, 'Coca-Cola hopes taking new path leads to success', *USA Today*, 6 March 2001: 6B.

[17]Robert L. Wehling, 'Even at P&G, only 3 brands make truly global grade so far', *Advertising Age*, 1 January 1998: 8.

[18]Shelly Branch, 'ACNielsen gives 43 brands global status', *Wall Street Journal*, 31 October 2001: B8.

[19]Frank van den Driest, 'Danone: serving up servant leadership', allaboutbranding.com, March 2006.

[20]Michael Porter, *Competitive Advantage*, New York: Free Press, 1985: 4–5.

[21]Julia Flynn, 'Heineken's battle to stay top bottle', *BusinessWeek*, 1 August 1994: 60–2.

[22]Carla Rapoport, 'Nestlé's brand-building machine', *Fortune*, 19 September 1994: 147–56.

[23]Reputation Institute and Nordic Brand Academy, internal material 2003–2007.

[24]For more information on global marketing strategies, see George S. Yip, *Total Global Strategy*, Englewood Cliffs, NJ: Prentice Hall, 1996.

[25]V. T. Bharadwaj, Gautam M. Swaroop and Ireena Vittal, 'Winning the Indian consumer', *McKinsey Quarterly Special Edition: fulfilling India's promise*, 2005.

[26]Ginny Parker, 'Going global can hit snags, Vodafone finds', *Wall Street Journal*, 16 June 2004: B1.

[27]'Softbank to change Vodafone Japan's name to Softbank Mobile', *TelecomWorldWire*, 18 May 2006.

[28]Asihish Banerjee, 'Global campaigns don't work; multinationals do', *Advertising Age*, 18 April 1994: 23.

[29]Jorge A. Monjaras, 'Unilever launches Snuggle in Mexico', *Advertising Age*, 24 February 2003: 20.

[30]Sellers, 'Pepsi opens second front'.

[31]Julie Skur Hill and Joseph M. Winski, 'Goodbye global ads', *Advertising Age*, 16 November 1987: 22.

[32]Vijay Govindarajan and Christopher Trimble, 'Serving the need of the poor – for profit', *Across the Board*, December 2001.

[33]Rapoport, 'Nestlé's brand-building machine'.

[34]Peter Fritsch and Gregory L. White, 'Even rivals concede GM has deftly steered road to success in Brazil', *Wall Street Journal*, 25 February 1999: A1, A8.

[35]Ibid.

[36]'Technology's Mr Predictable', *The Economist*, 24 September 2005.

[37]Carol Matlack, 'eBay steams into Europe', *BusinessWeek*, 6 November 2000: 116.

[38]Mark Maremont, 'They're all screaming for Häagen-Dazs', *BusinessWeek*, 4 October 1991: 121.

[39]William Wells, 'Global advertisers should pay heed to contextual variations', *Marketing News*, 13 February 1987: 18; Martin S. Roth, 'The effects of culture and socioeconomics on the performance of global brand image strategies', *Journal of Marketing Research*, May 1995, 32: 163–75.

[40]Joann S. Lublin, 'More US magazines to travel abroad', *Wall Street Journal*, 18 January 1990: B1.

[41]Miriam Jordan, 'In rural India, video vans sell toothpaste and shampoo', *Wall Street Journal*, 10 January 1996: B1, B5.

[42]Emily Nelson and Miriam Jordan, 'Seeking new markets for tampons, P&G faces cultural barrier', *Wall Street Journal*, 8 December 2000: A1, A8.

[43]Patrick Barwise and Thomas Robertson, 'Brand portfolios', *European Management Journal*, 10 September 1992, 10 (3): 277–85.

[44]Flynn, 'Heineken's battle'.

[45]David P. Hamilton, 'United it stands: Fuji Xerox is a rarity in world business: a joint venture that works', *Wall Street Journal*, 26 September 1996: R19.

[46]Gail DeGeorge, 'They don't call it Blockbuster for nothing', *BusinessWeek*, 19 October 1992: 113–14.

[47]Stephanie Anderson Forest, 'A Pier 1 in every port?', *BusinessWeek*, 31 May 1993: 81.

[48]Sellers, 'Pepsi opens second front'.

[49]Richard Gibson, 'Gerber missed the boat in quest to go global, so it turned to Sandoz', *Wall Street Journal*, 24 May 1994: A1, A4.

[50]Lewis, 'Key issues in globalizing brands'.

[51]Edward H. Meyer, 'Consumers around the world: do they have the same wants and needs?', *Management Review*, January 1985: 26–9.

[52]Stephen A. Greyser, 'Let's talk sense about global marketing', speech given to Asian Advertising Congress, Bangkok, July 1986.

[53]Rebecca Fanin, 'What agencies really think of global theory', *Marketing & Media Decisions*, December 1984: 74–82.

[54]Anders, 'Ad agencies and big concerns'.

[55]Douglas R. Sease, 'Japanese firms use US designers to tailor products to local tastes', *Wall Street Journal*, 4 March 1986: 1.

[56]Maureen Marston, 'Transferring equity across border', paper presented at the ARF Fourth Annual Advertising and Promotion Workshop, 12–13 February 1992.

[57]Lipman, 'Marketers turn sour'.

[58]Michael Flagg, 'Coca-Cola adopts local-drinks strategy in Asia', *Wall Street Journal*, 30 July 2001.

[59]Hermann Simon, 'Pricing problems in a global setting', *Marketing News*, 9 October 1995: 4.

[60]Rahul Jacob, 'Asia, where big brands are blooming', *BusinessWeek*, 23 August 1993: 55.

[61]Hubert Gatignon and Piet Vanden Abeele, 'To standardize or not to standardize: marketing mix effectiveness in Europe', *MSI Report* 95–109, Cambridge, MA: Marketing Science Institute, 1995.

[62]John A. Quelch and Edward J. Hoff, 'Customizing global marketing', *Harvard Business Review*, May–June 1986: 59–68.

[63]Hajo Riesenbeck and Anthony Freeling, 'How global are global brands?', *McKinsey Quarterly*, 4: 3–18, as referenced in Barwise and Robertson, 'Brand portfolios'. See also Dennis M. Sandler and David Shani, 'Brand globally but advertise locally? An empirical investigation', *Journal of Product & Brand Management*, 1993, 2 (2): 59–71; Gatignon and Vanden Abeele, 'To standardize or not to standardize'; Saeed Samiee and Kendall Roth, 'The influence of global marketing standardization on performance', *Journal of Marketing*, April 1992, 56: 1–17; and David M. Szymanski, Sundar G. Bharadwaj and P. Rajan Varadarajan, 'Standardization versus adaptation of international marketing strategy: an empirical investigation', *Journal of Marketing*, October 1993, 57: 1–17.

[64]Wells, 'Global campaigns'.

[65]Sharen Kindel, 'A brush with success: Colgate Palmolive company', *Hemisphere*, September 1996: 15.

[66]George E. Belch and Michael Belch, *Introduction to Advertising and Promotion Management: An integrated marketing communications perspective*, 3rd edn, Chicago, Richard Irwin, 1995.

[67]Barwise and Robertson, 'Brand portfolios'.

[68]Robert Frank, 'Potato chips to go global – or so Pepsi bets', *Wall Street Journal*, 30 November 1995: B1.

[69]Dexter Roberts and Frederik Balfour, 'To get rich is glorious', *BusinessWeek*, 6 February 2006: 46.

[70]Clay Chandler, 'Little emperors', *Fortune*, 4 October 2004: 138.

[71]Dexter Roberts and Frederik Balfour, 'To get rich is glorious'.

[72]Ibid.

[73]Leslie Chang, 'Cracking China's market', *Wall Street Journal*, 9 January 2003: B1.

[74]Dean Foust, 'Taking off like "a rocket ship"', *BusinessWeek*, 3 April 2006: 76.

[75]Russell Flannery, 'China is a big prize,' *Forbes*, 10 May 2004: 163.

[76]Leslie Chang, 'Cracking China's market', *Wall Street Journal*, 9 January 2003: B1.

[77]Ted C. Fishman, 'The Chinese century', *New York Times*, 4 July 2004: 1.

[78]Dexter Roberts, 'China's power brand', *BusinessWeek*, 8 November 2004: 77.

[79]'A behemoth kept at bay', *BusinessWeek*, 3 April 2006: 44.

[80]Frederik Balfour, 'Ad agencies unchained', *BusinessWeek*, 25 April 2005: 50.

[81]Dexter Roberts, 'How a legend lives up to its name', *BusinessWeek*, 15 February 1999.

[82]Dexter Roberts, 'China's power brands'.

[83]Deborah L. Vence, '*Not* taking care of business', *Marketing News*, 15 March 2005: 19.

[84]'The struggle of the champions', *The Economist*, 8 January 2005: 59.

[85]David Barvoza, 'Name goods in China but brand X elsewhere', *New York Times*, 29 June 2005.

[86]David Barboza, 'Some assembly needed: China as Asia's factory', *New York Times*, 9 February 2006: C1.

[87]Dexter Roberts, 'China's power brands'.

[88]Gerry Khermouch, 'Breaking into the name game', *BusinessWeek*, 7 April 2003: 54.

[89]Dexter Roberts, 'China's power brands'.

15 Closing observations

PREVIEW

This chapter provides some closing observations concerning strategic brand management. It briefly reviews the CBBE framework. Next, it highlights managerial guidelines and themes that emerged in previous chapters and summarizes success factors for branding. Following up on some of the discussion in Chapter 1, it then considers some special topics by applying the CBBE framework to strategic brand management issues for different products. The chapter concludes by considering the future of branding. Brand Briefing 15.14 presents 'The brand report card' to help managers understand and rate their brands' performance.[1]

STRATEGIC BRAND MANAGEMENT GUIDELINES

Summary of the customer-based brand equity (CBBE) framework

Strategic brand management involves the design and implementation of marketing campaigns and activities to build, measure and manage brand equity. The rationale behind the CBBE framework is to recognize the importance of the customer in the creation and management of brand equity. 'Consumers own brands and your brand is what consumers will permit you to have.' Consistent with this view, customer-based brand equity was defined in Chapter 2 as the differential effect that consumers' brand knowledge has on their response to the marketing of that brand. A brand is said to have positive customer-based brand equity when customers react more favourably to a product when the brand is identified than when it is not.

The premise of customer-based brand equity is that the power of a brand lies in the minds of consumers. More formally, brand knowledge was described in Chapter 3 in terms of an associative network memory model. Brand knowledge can be characterized in terms of two components: brand awareness and brand image.

Brand awareness is related to the strength of the brand node in memory as reflected by consumers' ability to recall or recognize the brand. Brand awareness can be characterized by depth and breadth. The depth relates to the likelihood that a brand can be recognized or recalled. The breadth relates to the variety of purchase and consumption situations in which the brand comes to mind.

Brand image is defined as consumer perceptions of and preferences for a brand, as reflected by the various types of brand associations held in consumers' memory. Although brand associations come in many forms, a useful distinction can be made between performance-related versus imagery-related attributes and benefits.

Sources of brand equity

Customer-based brand equity occurs when the consumer has a high level of awareness and familiarity with a brand and holds some strong, favourable and unique brand associations in memory. In some cases, brand awareness alone is sufficient to result in more favourable consumer responses. In other cases, brand associations play a critical role in determining the differential responses making up the brand equity. Conceptually, these three dimensions of brand associations are determined by the following.

- *Strength:* the strength of a brand association is a function of both the amount, or quantity, of processing that information initially receives as well as the nature, or quality, of that processing. The more deeply a person thinks about brand information, the stronger the resulting brand associations. Two factors facilitating the strength of association to any piece of brand information are the personal relevance of the information and the consistency with which this information is presented over time.
- *Favourability:* favourable associations for a brand are those associations that are desirable to customers and are delivered by the product and conveyed by its marketing. Associations may relate to the product or other intangible, non-product-related aspects. Not all brand associations, however, will be viewed favourably by consumers, nor will they be equally valued across different purchase or consumption situations.
- *Uniqueness:* to create the differential response that leads to customer-based brand equity, it is important to associate unique, meaningful points of difference with the brand to provide a competitive advantage and a 'reason why' consumers should buy it. For other brand associations, however, it may be sufficient that they are seen as comparable or roughly equal in favourability to competing brand associations. These associations function as points of parity in consumers' minds to establish category membership and negate potential points of difference for competitors. In other words, these associations are designed to provide consumers with 'no reason why not' to choose the brand.

Figure 15.1 summarizes these guidelines, which can provide motivation and direction in designing tactical campaigns and activities to build brand equity.

Outcomes of brand equity

Assuming that a positive brand image is created by marketing campaigns that are able to register the brand in memory and link it to strong, favourable and unique associations, a number of benefits for the brand may be realized, as follows.

- Greater loyalty.
- Less vulnerability to competitive marketing actions.

- Depth of brand awareness is determined by the ease of brand recognition and recall.
- Breadth of brand awareness is determined by the number of purchase and consumption situations in which the brand comes to mind.
- Strong brand associations are created by marketing campaigns that convey relevant information to consumers in a consistent fashion at any one point in time, as well as over time.
- Favourable brand associations are created when marketing campaigns deliver product-related and non-product-related benefits that are desired by consumers.
- Unique brand associations that are also strong and favourable create points of difference that distinguish a brand from others. Brand associations that are not unique, however, can create valuable points of parity to establish necessary category associations or to neutralize competitive points of difference.

Figure 15.1   Determinants of desired brand knowledge structures

- Less vulnerability to marketing crises.
- Larger margins.
- More inelastic consumer response to price increases.
- More elastic consumer response to price decreases.
- Greater trade co-operation and support.
- Increased marketing communication effectiveness.
- Possible licensing opportunities.
- Additional brand extension opportunities.

Tactical guidelines

The figures in Chapter 1 summarized the ingredients of the CBBE framework in terms of how to build, measure and manage brand equity. The specific themes and recommendations that were developed in subsequent chapters are as follows.

Building brand equity

Tactically, brand equity can be built through: the initial choice of the brand elements making up the brand; marketing activities and the design of the marketing campaign; and the use of secondary associations by linking the brand to other entities. Guidelines emerged in Chapters 4 to 7 for each of these three different types of approaches, as summarized in Figures 15.2 and 15.3.

A dominant theme of many of these ways to build brand equity is the importance of complementarity and consistency.

Complementarity involves choosing brand elements and marketing activities and campaigns such that the potential contribution to brand equity of one particular brand element or marketing activity compensates for the shortcomings of other elements and activities. For example, some brand elements may be designed primarily to enhance awareness (eg, through a memorable brand logo), whereas other brand elements may be designed primarily to facilitate the linkage of brand associations (eg, via a meaningful brand name or a clever slogan). Similarly, an ad campaign may be designed to create a certain point of difference association, whereas a retail promotion may be designed primarily to create a vital point of parity association. Finally,

Brand-building tools and objectives ⟶ Consumer knowledge effects ⟶ Branding benefits

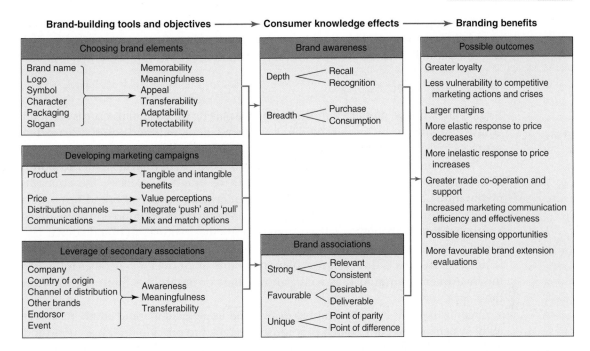

Figure 15.2   Building customer-based brand equity

other entities may be linked to the brand to exploit secondary associations and provide otherwise missing sources of brand equity or reinforce existing associations.

Thus, it is important that a varied set of brand elements and marketing activities and campaigns be put in place to create the desired level of awareness and type of image to provide necessary sources of brand equity.

At the same time, *consistency* across these elements helps to create the highest level of awareness and the strongest and most favourable associations. Consistency involves ensuring that diverse brand and marketing mix elements share a common

1. Mix and match brand elements by choosing different elements to achieve different objectives and by designing brand elements to be as mutually reinforcing as possible.
2. Ensure a high level of perceived quality and create a rich brand image by linking tangible and intangible product-related and non-product-related associations to the brand.
3. Adopt value-based pricing strategies to set prices and guide discount pricing policies over time that reflect consumers' perceptions of value and willingness to pay a premium.
4. Consider a range of direct and indirect distribution options and blend brand-building push strategies for retailers and other channel members with brand-building pull strategies for consumers.
5. Mix marketing communication options by choosing communication options based on their differential ability to affect brand awareness and create, maintain or strengthen favourable and unique brand associations. Match marketing communication options by ensuring consistency and directly reinforcing some communication options with others.
6. Build on secondary associations to compensate for otherwise missing dimensions of the marketing campaign by linking the brand to other entities such as companies, channels of distribution, other brands, characters or spokespeople or events that reinforce and augment the brand image.

Figure 15.3   Guidelines for building brand equity

core meaning, perhaps in some cases conveying the same information. For example, brand elements may be designed to convey a certain benefit association that is reinforced by a highly integrated, well-branded marketing communications campaign.

Measuring brand equity

Brand equity can be measured indirectly, by measuring the potential sources of brand equity, and directly, by measuring the possible outcomes of brand equity. Measuring sources of customer-based brand equity requires measuring aspects of brand awareness and brand image that potentially can lead to the differential customer response that creates brand equity: breadth and depth of brand awareness; the strength, favourability and uniqueness of brand associations; the nature of brand responses; and the nature of brand relationships. Measuring outcomes of brand equity involves approximating the benefits realized from creating these sources of brand equity. The brand value chain depicts this relationship more broadly by considering how marketing activity affects these sources of brand equity and how the outcomes influence the investment community, as well as how filters or multipliers intervene between the stages.

Organizationally, it is important to design and implement a brand equity measurement system as a set of research procedures designed to provide timely, accurate and actionable information for marketers so they can make the best possible tactical decisions in the short run as well as strategic decisions in the long run. Implementing a brand equity measurement system involves: conducting brand audits; designing brand tracking studies; and establishing a brand equity management system (Figure 15.4).

The dominant theme in measuring brand equity is the need to employ a full complement of research techniques and processes that capture as much as possible the richness and complexity of brand equity. Several techniques and measures are necessary to tap into all the sources and outcomes of brand equity. Simplistic approaches to measuring brand equity – for example, by attempting to estimate the equity of a brand with only one number – are fraught with error and lack diagnostic or prescriptive power.

1. Formalize the firm's view of brand equity into a document that provides guidelines to marketing managers.
2. Conduct brand inventories to profile how all of the products sold by a company are branded and marketed and conduct brand exploratories to understand what consumers think and feel about a brand as part of periodic brand audits to assess the health of brands, understand their sources of brand equity and suggest ways to improve and leverage that equity.
3. Conduct routine consumer tracking studies to provide current information as to how brands are performing with respect to the sources and outcomes of brand equity as identified by the brand audit.
4. Assemble results of tracking survey and other relevant measures into a regular brand equity report to provide descriptive information as to what is happening with a brand as well as diagnostic information as to why it is happening.
5. Establish a person or department to oversee the brand equity charter and equity reports to make sure that, as much as possible, product and marketing actions across divisions and geographic boundaries are done in a way that reflects the spirit of the charter and the substance of the report so as to maximize the long-term equity of the brand.

Figure 15.4   Guidelines for measuring brand equity

Managing brand equity

Finally, managing brand equity requires taking a long-term perspective on brands. A broad view of brand equity is critical, especially when firms are selling many products and in many markets. In such cases, brand hierarchies must be created that define common and distinct brand elements for various nested products. New product and brand extension strategies also must be designed to determine optimal brand and product portfolios. Finally, these brands and products must be effectively managed over geographic boundaries and target market segments by creating brand awareness and a positive brand image in each market in which the brand is sold.

A long-term view of brand equity is necessary because of the implications that changes in marketing campaigns and activities and the marketing environment have on consumers' brand knowledge structures and thus their response to future campaigns and activities. Managing brands over time requires reinforcing the brand meaning and adjusting the branding as needed. For brands whose equity has eroded over time, a number of revitalizing strategies are available.

Figure 15.5 highlights some concepts and Figure 15.6 highlights guidelines for managing brand equity.

1. Define brand hierarchy.
    (a) *Principle of simplicity:* employ as few levels as possible.
    (b) *Principle of clarity:* logic and relationship of all brand elements employed must be obvious and transparent.
    (c) *Principle of relevance:* create abstract associations relevant to as many products as possible.
    (d) *Principle of differentiation:* differentiate individual products and brands.
    (e) *Principle of growth:* investments in market penetration or expansion versus product development should be made according to return on investment opportunities.
    (f) *Principle of survival:* brand extensions must achieve brand equity in their categories.
    (g) *Principle of synergy:* brand extensions should enhance the equity of the parent brand.
    (h) *Principle of prominence:* adjust prominence to affect perceptions of product distance.
    (i) *Principle of commonality:* link common products through shared brand elements.

2. Define brand–product matrix
    (a) *Brand extensions:* establish new equity and enhance existing equity.
    (b) *Brand portfolio:* maximize coverage and minimize overlap.

3. Define brand equity over time
    (a) *Brand reinforcement:* innovation in product design, manufacturing and merchandising relevance in user and usage imagery.
    (b) *Brand revitalization:* 'back to basics' strategy, 'reinvention' strategy.

4. Establish brand equity over market segments
    (a) *Identify differences in consumer behaviour:* how they purchase and use products, what they know and feel about different brands.
    (b) *Adjust branding:* choice of brand elements, nature of supporting marketing campaign, leverage of secondary associations.

Figure 15.5 Concepts in managing customer-based brand equity

1. Define the brand hierarchy in terms of the number of levels and the relative prominence that brands at different levels will receive.
2. Create global associations relevant to as many brands nested at the level below in the hierarchy as possible, but sharply differentiate brands at the same level of the hierarchy.
3. Introduce brand extensions that complement the product mix of the firm, exploit parent brand associations and enhance parent brand equity.
4. Clearly establish the roles of brands in the brand portfolio, adding, deleting and modifying brands as necessary.
5. Reinforce brand equity over time through marketing actions that consistently convey the meaning of the brand in terms of what products the brand represents, what benefits it supplies, what needs it satisfies and why it is superior to competitive brands.
6. Enhance brand equity over time through innovation in product design, manufacturing and merchandising and continued relevance in user and usage imagery.
7. Identify differences in consumer behaviour in market segments and adjust the branding accordingly on a cost–benefit basis.

Figure 15.6   Guidelines for managing brand equity

The dominant themes in managing brand equity are the importance of balance in marketing activities and of making moderate levels of change in marketing over time. Without some modifications of the marketing campaign, a brand runs the risk of becoming obsolete or irrelevant to consumers. At the same time, dramatic shifts in brand strategies run the risk of confusing or alienating consumers. Thus, a consistent thread of meaning – which consumers can recognize – should run through the marketing campaign that reflects sources of equity for the brand and its core brand associations. In other words, changes in the product and how it is priced, advertised, promoted or distributed may be needed to preserve or enhance sources of brand equity over time, but these changes should illuminate and not obscure key brand associations.

Brand Briefing 15.1 describes how the global appliance company Electrolux has changed its brand strategy and philosophy to reflect the new marketing realities.

Brand Briefing 15.1

Electrolux: a global leader with a consumer focus

Electrolux is a global leader in appliances for home and professional use. The turnover of Electrolux in 2006 was €11.1 billion and the company had 59,000 employees.

Electrolux is a Swedish company founded by Axel Wenner-Gren in 1919. It was never a typical manufacturing company. From the start, its success was rooted in being close the consumer through door-to-door selling of vacuum cleaners. In 1926, the first factory outside Sweden was established. The company started its globalization strategy by buying other companies in the 1960s. In the 1980s and 1990s, Electrolux made 400 acquisitions. At the beginning of this growth period, the company

Brand Briefing 15.1 *continued*

was headed by Hans Werthén, chief executive officer from 1967 to 1974 and chairman from 1974 until 1991. The acquisition period left the company with too many brands, too many production platforms and too many employees. There was a need to focus. The brand portfolio included Zanussi and AEG and many others around the world. The corporate culture was characterized by a production and sales orientation. Electrolux then began to transform from a production-focused industrial company to an innovative, proactive, market-driven group. The culture became more characterized by product design and innovation driven by consumer insight.

Attractive products that match consumer needs and expectations are the drivers for growth and long-term profitability. Electrolux is focusing on leading the appliance industry in terms of systematic development of products based on consumer insights. Investments in building a strong, global Electrolux brand are beginning to pay off with stronger market positions and improved earnings. The formula for success comprises a continued fast pace of product development, marketing and brand building, combined with low costs for production, purchasing and distribution. This is how Electrolux will grow, says chief executive Hans Stråberg.

The Electrolux brand policy

One milestone for the company was the creation of the first brand policy in 1999. It set out four issues: focus on fewer, stronger brands; homogenous positioning for these brands in all countries and across sectors; stronger endorsement of all brands and Electrolux as the master brand; the burden of proof is local if local management wants to work with another strategy – it has to prove why its strategy is better.

The next milestone was a fresh brand policy in 2001. The new strategy said that the company should apply a branded business model. The appliance industry offers two business models. One model is to become a low-cost, high-volume producer of commodity products. The basic competitive edge here is price. The other model focuses on branding. At a board meeting in October 2001, the conclusion was that the first model was not an option for Electrolux. The branded business model was necessary to compete with companies such as Whirlpool (USA), LG and Samsung (South Korea), Bosch-Siemens (Germany), Indesit (Italy) and Haier (China). When the branded business model was chosen by the board, the company introduced a brand policy, as well as a process for brand management with common tools and principles. The company then increased its efforts towards becoming a more brand-orientated company.

The brand policy was built on six issues that the company needed to address.

1. A focus on fewer brands which will be bigger and stronger. Wherever feasible, the Electrolux brand should be one of the brands.

2. An Electrolux family of brands, where the Electrolux Group will endorse all product brands.

Brand Briefing 15.1 *continued*

3. Each brand will be positioned in a consistent manner, worldwide and across sectors.

4. The goal will be to build Electrolux as the global master brand for the consumer business. Even though it is a long-term goal, it should be implemented as soon as possible. Where the local need is proven, there can be sub-brand families for segmented offers.

5. Each sector will be responsible for a detailed evolutionary transition plan that will cover the developments for each sector for the years 2002–2004.

6. Professional sectors may continue to follow the established endorsement policy.

In the Electrolux dictionary, a brand is described as a promise to consumers and customers about what they can expect from Electrolux. This promise expresses the fundamental reason for Electrolux existing.

Stråberg's view

When Hans Stråberg was interviewed in *The Financial Times* in 2002, he said Electrolux needed fewer and stronger brands with Electrolux as the master brand. In Europe, the plan was to move from 25 to 3 brands, with 65–75 percent of sales deriving from the Electrolux name within 5 to 7 years. Typically, a local brand would at first be endorsed by the Electrolux name. In the next stage, the product might be double branded. Finally, the old brand would disappear. However, there was a danger of moving too fast and losing sales.

The starting-point, according to Stråberg, was that Electrolux had to be number one, two or three in all markets where it operated. Thereby it gained economies of scale in manufacturing and could deal with retailers from a position of strength; the enhanced visibility strengthens the company brand. The battle, he said, was to stop household appliances from being commodity products. White goods do not have to be commodity products. People are prepared to pay a premium for products that make their lives easier and more enjoyable. Attractive products provide the foundation for strong brands. Strong brands enable higher margins and greater profitability. That's why Electrolux was committed to making Electrolux a leading global brand, said Stråberg. Management decided to centralize the branding process with advertising, media, budgeting, innovation and brand tracking.

Change of culture

Management was also working internally to change the culture. Internal symbols that helped to create the desired culture were created. All managers, including the chief executives showed branding was important. There were four success factors.

1. *Innovation:* a strategy for innovative product development and attractive design was decisive for the future position of Electrolux. Consumers would spend more

Brand Briefing 15.1 *continued*

on products that better met their needs and preferences. Product innovation was therefore a key to profitable growth. So Electrolux decided to double its investment in product development to 2 percent of sales.

2. *Brand:* Electrolux was to become the global leader in the industry. In countries with strong local brands the intention was to double-brand these with the master brand to form a local platform for building the Electrolux brand. The new goal was to invest at least 2 percent of sales in brand-building activities.

3. *Staff:* to lead development in the industry, employees have to act fast and dare to do things differently. Processes and tools for attracting, developing and securing access to future leaders and competence within Electrolux were given a high priority within the company.

4. *Costs:* the company works hard on reducing costs. Among other things, it is increasing the share of purchases from low-cost countries and at the same time reducing the number of suppliers.

One important internal symbolic was the creation of a brand academy. At the launch, about 250 employees, with a background in marketing and innovation, were invited to participate in three days of education in brand management.

Another activity was the launch of an internal brand award in 1999. Every year, the best branding projects are recognized by management. The seven or eight best global projects were given the opportunity to present their branding case in a full-day session in front of the chief executive and external branding experts. Electrolux Brazil is one of the most successful countries within the group and Brazil has won the award twice. One reason for the success of Brazil is the local commitment to consumer understanding and branding.

The new strategy: thoughtful design innovator

An important part of the strategy has been consumer focus. With the brand platform 'The thoughtful design innovator', Electrolux is focusing on an outside-in perspective. Listening to the concerns and aspirations of consumers and other stakeholders is at the heart of strategy. By merging the more than 20 brands it carried in 2004 into a master brand and redefining itself as the 'thoughtful design innovator', Electrolux has taken a decisive step to reposition the group. At the January 2006 launch, Stråberg called it an 'important page in the history of our company'. Design is the foremost tool for differentiation, says Stråberg. The objective is to make our customers feel that: 'Electrolux was thinking of me when they created this product.'

Senior managers met in January 2006 to discuss the new strategy. A brand book, a blueprint for the future, called 'Thinking of you' was delivered to the 260 participants at this meeting. The message was how to shift the company from volume to value growth.

Brand Briefing 15.1 *continued*

Electrolux Brazil

Electrolux Brazil is one of the best examples of branded business success within the Group. The company has achieved outstanding results through an innovative culture that is characterized by a focus on consumer understanding, a passion for details, openness to risk-taking ideas, a strong team spirit, open and non-hierarchical communications and cross-functional small teams. There is a close link between departments such as engineering, design, prototyping and marketing. The local chief executive is obsessed with understanding consumers.

Consumer insight activities are encouraged and the culture does not allow any 'me too' products. People within the organization are looking for consumer-based differentiation in products. Of importance is the search for evidence of relevant unique selling propositions that can define the product as best in its segment. There is the key to success because these products will be sold at higher prices. Figure 15.7 shows three examples of product launches in Brazil. All the examples are innovative and differentiate themselves through design. All three were aimed at high growth and highly profitable segments. A result of Electrolux Brazil innovation has been a strong increase in volume, market share, brand strength and profitability. The refrigerator Giselle was for the highly profitable 'frost-free' segment of the market. The product scored higher on preference than the market leader Brastemp in design clinics: 71 percent preferred Giselle. Some 73 percent preferred the fabric care machine Simone in comparison with its closest competitor, and 80 percent preferred the double oven Jane.

Electrolux Brazil has been able to deliver profitable growth by living up to the brand promise. Figure 15.8 shows growth in the period 2000–06. In 2006, 5,350

Project Giselle refrigerators   Project Simone fabric care   Project Jane double oven

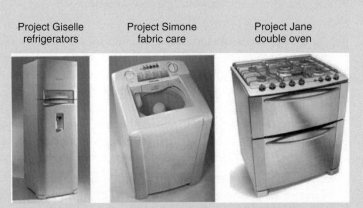

Figure 15.7   Launches by Electrolux Brazil

Brand Briefing 15.1 *continued*

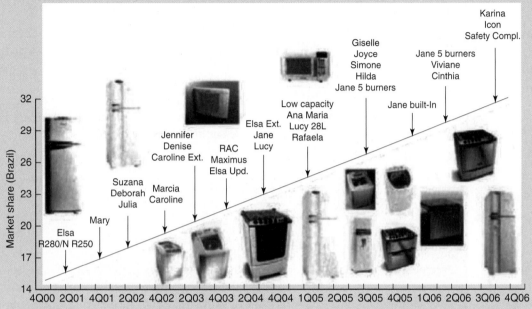

Figure 15.8   Effective execution and innovation in Brazil

employees attended a training session in delivering services. Electrolux Brazil has also been striving to deliver the best in class in point-of-sale strategies, because 70 percent of the purchase decision is made in the shop.

Sources: Electrolux annual reports, 2003–2006; Electrolux sustainablity reports, 2005–2006; Mats Rönne, interview, 27 September 2007; 'A careful clean-up to consolidate the company: Electrolux', *The Financial Times*, 5 August 2002; 'Thinking of you', Electrolux 2006, internal material.

WHAT MAKES A STRONG BRAND?

So, to create a strong brand and maximize brand equity, marketing managers must:

- understand brand meaning and market appropriate products in an appropriate manner;
- properly position a brand;
- provide superior delivery of desired benefits;

- employ a full range of complementary brand elements and supporting marketing activities;
- embrace integrated marketing communications and communicate with a consistent voice;
- measure consumers' perceptions of value and develop a pricing strategy accordingly;
- establish credibility and appropriate brand personality and imagery;
- maintain innovation and relevance for the brand;
- strategically design and implement a brand hierarchy and brand portfolio;
- implement a brand equity management system to ensure that marketing actions properly reflect the brand equity concept.

One of the most skilled brand builders is Procter & Gamble. Brand Briefing 15.2 describes how it changed marketing processes and its branding philosophy.

Brand Briefing 15.2

Reinvigorating branding at Procter & Gamble

Procter & Gamble has been a leader in marketing for about 160 years. In fact, one academic referred to the company in 2005 as 'the single greatest marketing company in the world'. Furthermore, P&G, already the world's largest consumer packaged goods company, became even larger with the €41.6 billion acquisition of Gillette in 2005. After struggling briefly at the turn of the twenty-first century, under the direction of A. G. Lafley, appointed chief executive in 2000, P&G has maintained its leadership by following four new strategies.

Renewed emphasis on R&D

Between 2001 and 2004, P&G updated all of its 200 brands. This enabled the company to increase market share in 70 percent of its businesses. The company used its R&D to develop innovative products, including the Swiffer mop, Mr Clean Magic Eraser, a battery-powered Crest SpinBrush toothbrush and teeth-whitening Crest Whitestrips. To augment such products, P&G placed renewed emphasis on design by appointing its first chief design officer in 2001 and installing a top design officer in each of its global business units. Lafley emphasized the importance of design in combination with innovation: 'When we consciously involved design at the front end – such as with Crest Whitestrips . . . and our whole line of Swiffer quick-clean products – we generated more trial, more repurchase and more sales.'

New communication approaches

While P&G increased its ad budget from 8.1 percent of sales in 2001 to 10.7 percent of sales in 2004, it also dramatically shifted 20 percent of this budget away

Brand Briefing 15.2 *continued*

from TV and towards 'media-neutral' advertising, which determines media spending without bias towards any particular medium based on precedent. When it launched the heartburn medication Prilosec OTC in 2005, 75 percent of the budget went to non-television media. In place of big television budgets, P&G pioneered 'stealth marketing' techniques such as Vocalpoint, a word-of-mouth marketing scheme that enlists 600,000 mothers, among others, to promote its brands by giving testimonials, samples and coupons to friends and neighbours. Sales in markets where Vocalpoint was used during the 2005 Dawn Direct Foam launch were double those of markets that did not use Vocalpoint.

New research approaches

P&G conducts about 10,000 consumer research projects a year, spending more than €73 million annually. The company changed its research practice under Lafley by using qualitative observational research techniques to unlock consumer insights instead of relying on quantitative analysis. Lafley referred to ethnographic research as the 'best way to create value', stating: 'If you want to understand how a lion hunts don't go to the zoo. Go to the jungle.' In keeping with this view, Lafley required that the top 50 managers at P&G visit consumers either in their homes or on shopping trips at least once a quarter.

New branding philosophy

While it did launch brands such as Swiffer, P&G began pursuing a strategy with less inherent risk: investing in 'power brands'. This strategy arose from the fact that more than 50 percent of profits and 66 percent of sales growth came from P&G's top ten global brands between 1992 and 2002. Consequently, P&G focused on building core brands from its stable, rather than adding new ones it. In some cases, as with Mr Clean, P&G went as far as resurrecting a brand and turning it into a power brand through the launch of innovative products. As another example, the company took the familiar but faded Old Spice deodorant and remade it as a performance brand, building it into the leading deodorant for men in the USA with 20 percent of the market in 2004. P&G often sought to leverage its power brands with vertical extensions into higher-margin categories, as it did with Crest Whitestrips and Mr Clean AutoDry Car Wash System, which sell for about €18 each.

Sources: 'Fast talk', *Fast Company*, June 2004: 51; Robert Berner, 'P&G has rivals in a wringer', *BusinessWeek*, 4 October 2004: 74; Mark Ritson, 'P&G's tactics point to marketing's way ahead', *Marketing*, 13 April 2005: 19; Bob Garfield, 'The chaos scenario', *Advertising Age*, 4 April 2005: 1; Nirmalya Kumar, 'Kill a brand, keep a customer', *Harvard Business Review*, December 2003: 86.

1. Failure to understand the meaning of a brand.
2. Failure to live up to the brand promise.
3. Failure to support a brand.
4. Failure to be patient with a brand.
5. Failure to control a brand.
6. Failure to balance consistency and change with a brand.
7. Failure to understand the complexity of brand equity measurement and management.

Figure 15.9   'Seven deadly sins' of brand management

Common mistakes

On the flip side of the coin, what are the common branding mistakes that prevent firms from creating strong brands? In contrast to the previous list, some of the commonest branding problems – the 'seven deadly sins of brand management' – include the following (Figure 15.9).[2]

1. *Failure to fully understand the meaning of a brand:* given that consumers 'own' brands, it is critical to understand what consumers think and feel about them and then proceed accordingly. Too often, managers convince themselves of the validity of marketing actions – for example, a brand extension, ad campaign or price hike – based on a mistaken belief about what consumers know or what marketers would like them to know. Also, managers often ignore the full range of associations – both tangible and intangible – that may characterize a brand.

2. *Failure to live up to the brand promise:* a brand should be a promise and a commitment to consumers, but too often that promise is broken. A common mistake is to set brand expectations too high and then fail to live up to them in the marketing campaign. By overpromising and not delivering, a firm is worse off in many ways than if it had not set expectations at all.

3. *Failure to support a brand adequately:* creating and maintaining brand knowledge structures requires investment. Too often, managers want to get something for nothing by building brand equity without a willingness to provide proper marketing support or, once brand equity has been built, expecting a brand to remain strong despite a lack of investment.

4. *Failure to be patient with the brand:* brand equity must be built from the ground up. Too often, managers want to take shortcuts and bypass basic branding considerations – such as achieving the necessary level of brand awareness – to concentrate on brand building.

5. *Failure to control a brand adequately:* brand equity must be understood by all employees and actions must be taken to reflect a broader corporate perspective as well as a more specific product perspective. Too often, decisions are made without a true understanding of the current and desired brand equity and without a recognition of the effect of these decisions on other brands or brand-related activities.

6. *Failure to balance consistency and change with a brand:* managing a brand necessitates striking the difficult, but crucial, balance between maintaining

continuity in marketing and implementing changes to update the product or image of a brand. Too often, managers are left behind as a result of not making adjustments in their marketing campaign to reflect changes in the marketing environment; alternatively, they may make so many changes that the brand becomes a moving target without any meaning to consumers.

7. *Failure to understand the complexity of brand equity measurement and management:* effective brand management requires discipline, creativity, focus and the ability to make hundreds of decisions. Unfortunately, marketers sometimes oversimplify the process and try to equate success in branding with one particular action or approach. By not realizing the many other actions that also have to occur, brand equity is not optimized.

Brand Briefing 15.3 describes how Carlsberg is building its brand globally.

Brand Briefing 15.3

Global branding the Carlsberg way

The main issue for Carlsberg when it comes to international branding is the trade-off between thinking global and acting local. Four issues can be highlighted.

- Ensuring consistency in brand building and using synergies across markets.
- Different life stages of the Carlsberg brand.
- Understanding cultural contexts.
- Different competitive sets.

Ensuring consistency

One important factor for ensuring consistency across markets is the creation and use of a global brand positioning document. It is crucial that management in all the markets in which Carlsberg operates have the same understanding of the brand and that they use the same guidelines for brand communications campaigns.

The same concepts and campaigns are used globally, but local executions might differ when it comes to media choice and the stress made in the messages.

Different life stages of the brand

Carlsberg has different positioning in different markets depending on the life stage of the brand, and some markets have different consumer needs. This results in two different communication foci: functional or emotional.

In the functional focus, communications stress the quality of the brand. For example, in India a slogan could be 'Carlsberg, the beer tastes good'. Emotional communication goes a step further. A conceptual slogan in some European markets could be: 'The best beer for the best moments'. In emotional communication, the emphasis is more on 'best moments' than on 'the good beer' or 'the best beer'.

Brand Briefing 15.3 *continued*

Understanding cultural contexts

Carlsberg's main slogan is 'Probably the best beer in the world'. This works well all over Western Europe but for some markets the cultural understanding could be different, so it is important to fine-tune the slogan. For example, in some Asian markets, the consumer seems to have a more literal attitude towards words and phrases and the word 'Probably' could be a sign of weakness or at least have a negative feel. In Europe, consumers seem to understand the humour behind the word 'probably' in the slogan. 'It is just a cultural thing', says Mikkel Anderssen, marketing director of international branding at Carlsberg headquarters.

So, it is important to fine-tune messages to fit the cultural understanding of a specific market.

Different competitive sets

A competitive set refers to the main competitors for Carlsberg and it is crucial to understand and monitor rivals in all the markets in which Carlsberg operates.

Carlsberg is mainly a premium brand, but, for historical reasons, Carlsberg is not a premium brand in all markets (eg, Denmark and the UK). Where this occurs, the landscape will be different and may include more 'mainstream plus' brands.

The competitive sets could be described as follows.

- *Leading international premium:* successful brands with global or wide international distribution sold at a price premium (ie, not mainstream).
- *Heineken:* globally, Heineken is the brand that Carlsberg most often finds itself competing with. However, Budweiser, Stella Artois, Corona and Beck's are also competitors.
- *Beer:* apart from those mentioned, Carlsberg considers Carlsberg's main competition to be other lager beers.
- *Local and regional premium:* these are brands that do not have global distribution but are strong in just one market (eg, Lech Premium in Poland) or across a region (eg, Tiger in Asia).

Two challenges for Carlsberg are:

- people travel more and the effect of the positioning, design and communication must be identified well;
- there are separate brand-building budgets for all markets, but it is crucial to identify synergies for cutting costs but at the same time gaining better results.

Sources: Christian Sandberg, 'Brand-driven business development', thesis, Nordic Brand Academy, 2007; Carlsberg brand book.

SPECIAL APPLICATIONS

Although conventional use of the term *product* might be seen as representing only physical items this was defined in Chapter 1 as encompassing not only physical items but also services, shops, people, organizations, places or ideas. Chapter 1 provided examples of how each of these types of products could be branded. Accordingly, the term product has been used in a broad sense and the themes and guidelines for building, measuring and managing brand equity should be appropriate for virtually all products. Nevertheless, it is worthwhile considering some specific management issues for less conventional products. This section suggests additional guidelines for six special cases: industrial and business-to-business products, high-tech products, services, retailers, small businesses and online brands.

Industrial and business-to-business products

Because industrial goods usually involve business-to-business marketing, they sometimes involve different branding practices.[3] Regardless of the type of industrial goods sold, branding guidelines can be offered (Figure 15.10). Brand Briefing 15.4 describes how Siemens attempted to create a strong industrial brand.

Adopt a corporate or family branding strategy and create a well-defined brand hierarchy. Because companies selling industrial goods are often characterized by a large and complex number of product lines and variations, it is important that a logical and well-organized brand hierarchy be devised. In particular, because of the breadth and complexity of their product mixes, companies selling industrial goods are more likely to emphasize corporate or family brands (eg, as with GE, Hewlett-Packard and IBM). In completing the brand hierarchy for industrial goods, individual brands and modifiers often take on a descriptive product meaning for clarity and differentiation. Thus, a particularly effective branding strategy for industrial goods is to create sub-brands by combining a well-known and respected corporate name with descriptive product modifiers.

Link non-product-related imagery associations. Developing supporting marketing campaigns to build brand equity for industrial goods can be different from those for consumer goods because, given the nature of the organizational buying process, product-related associations may play a relatively more important role than non-product-related associations. Industrial brands often emphasize functionality and

1. Adopt a corporate or family branding strategy and create a well-defined brand hierarchy.
2. Link non-product-related imagery associations.
3. Employ the full range of marketing communications options.
4. Leverage the equity of other companies that are customers.
5. Segment markets carefully and develop tailored branding and marketing campaigns.

Figure 15.10   Guidelines for industrial products

Brand Briefing 15.4

Business-to-business branding at Siemens

Although Siemens products have been available in the US since 1954, research indicated that only 12 percent of Americans were able to identify the company. Yet, Siemens employs over 80,000 US workers, turbines made by its Westinghouse division provide 40 percent of the country's power and more than half the cars run using Siemens parts. Though it is not a high-visibility corporation in the USA, Siemens is a household name in most of the 192 other countries in which it competes.

Siemens began its first corporate advertising campaign in the USA in 1988. But in 2000, chief executive Gerhard Schulmeyer expressed disappointment with his company's branding efforts:

> We get mad at ourselves. We haven't done the greatest job of branding. No letter could move in this country without our technology, but we never felt a need to tell the people this.

In 2001, the company set out to raise its image in the eyes of US consumers. This move represented the third step in a plan initiated in 1998 to reinvent Siemens as a high-profile brand using rival General Electric as a model. The company made the USA a primary target for advertisements that it launched in April 2001. Siemens spent €18.2 million on US media for the campaign, which was part of an estimated €365 million that the company earmarked for US marketing in 2002. The series began with teaser print ads, which were followed by television spots, that used the tagline 'Spin the globe'. These emphasized Siemens' global reach in consumer goods. Since they were aiming at increasing sales of its consumer goods, the ads featured Siemens mobile phones. One problem with the company's mobiles, however, was that they were based on European wireless standards, which were different from the dominant standard in the USA, so the company held back from mass marketing these phones until universal standards developed. Siemens' mobile phones never succeeded in competing with Nokia, Motorola, Samsung and Sony Ericsson, however, and the division was sold to Taiwan's BenQ in 2005.

The company's next focus in the USA was a campaign called 'One Siemens' designed to get the company's units to work together to win big contracts. Bundled contracts that included products and services from a number of Siemens divisions were signed to build hospitals and a sports stadium and totaled €657 million in 2004. Siemens' North America chief credited the initiative with generating half of that total, which Siemens would not have won otherwise. Still, Siemens US sales of €12 billion in 2004 were only €365 million above its 2000 sales. The company launched a new campaign in 2005 that, while consistent with its 'One Siemens' philosophy, still sought to address the recognition problems that the campaign launched in 2001 was intended to remedy. Keeping the tagline 'Spin the globe', the

Brand Briefing 15.4 *continued*

ads tried to convey Siemens' breadth by showing the company's offerings coming together to form structures such as water plants. Echoing the sentiment expressed in 2000 by Schulmeyer, Siemens' creative director said: 'Our company is ubiquitous but invisible; we're behind the scenes – that's the dilemma'.

Sources: James Cox, 'Siemens cultivates American accent', *USA Today*, 5 March 2001; Sarah Ellison, 'Siemens woos youth with new attitude', *Wall Street Journal*, 15 February 2001; Alfred Kueppers, 'Siemens's U.S. Debut Isn't Ideal', *Asian Wall Street Journal*, 19 March 2001: N1; Jack Ewing, 'Nokia, Siemens plan to join and conquer', *BusinessWeek*, 19 June 2006; Thomas Clark and Dan Roberts, 'Siemens sets a 30-month US strategy', *The Financial Times*, 29 July 2004: 25; Diane Anderson, 'Siemens engineers name recognition', *Brandweek*, 5 December 2005.

cost–benefit considerations. Nevertheless, even non-product-related associations can be useful in terms of other perceptions of the firm, such as the prestige or type of company that uses the products.

It is important that these corporate or family brands convey credibility and possess favourable global associations. Corporate credibility is often a primary risk reduction heuristic adopted by industrial buyers. For years, one source of brand equity for IBM was the fact that a marketplace perception existed that 'you'll never get fired for buying IBM'. Once that cachet faded, the brand found itself in a much more competitive situation. Creating a feeling of security for industrial buyers can thus be an important source of brand equity.

Many industrial firms distinguish themselves on the basis of the customer service they provide in addition to the quality of their products. For example, US company Premier Industrial charges up to 50 percent more than competitors for every one of the thousands of industrial parts it stocks and distributes because of its strong commitment to customer service, as exemplified by the following:

> Early one afternoon in late 1988, Premier Industrial received a call from the manager of a US Caterpillar tractor plant. A cheap electrical relay had broken down, shutting down an assembly line. A sales representative for Premier located a replacement at a warehouse halfway across the country and rushed it to a plane. By 10.30 that night, a Premier employee had delivered the part, and the line was up and running. 'You can't build tractors if you can't move the line,' remarked the Caterpillar purchasing analyst. 'They really saved us a bundle of money.'[4]

As further illustration, creative changes in customer service have allowed other companies to charge more for floor tiles or even wood. Following IBM's lead, Lucent began to shift into value-added services after losing ground in selling its telecommunications hardware opportunities.[5]

Employ a full range of marketing communication options. Another difference between industrial and consumer products is the manner by which they are sold: a different marketing communication mix exists with industrial products than with consumer products. Because of the well-defined target market and complex nature of product decisions, marketing communications tend to convey more detailed product information in a more direct way. Thus, personal selling plays an important role. At the same time, other communication options can enhance awareness or the formation of brand associations. One effective approach is to combine direct hard-sell messages with more indirect image-related messages that convey who and what the company is all about.

Leverage equity of other companies that are customers. Secondary associations can be used differently for industrial brands. For example, one common way to show credibility is to identify other companies that are customers. The challenge in communicating this endorsement through advertising, however, is ensuring that the companies used as endorsers do not distract from the message about the advertised company and its brands. Even countries can be used in an endorsement strategy. For example, Interlock – a New Zealand brand acquired by Assa Abloy that specializes in hardware for windows – has used the fact that it is the only foreign company in its industry to sell in Japan as an endorsement strategy to sell its products to firms in other countries.

Segment customers carefully and develop tailored branding and marketing campaigns. Finally, as with any brand, it is important to understand how customer segments view products and brands. For industrial goods, however, customer segments may exist within organizations as well as between organizations. Depending on the perceptions and preferences of the organizational segments involved – for example, engineers, brand or marketing managers and accountants or purchasing managers – the associations that serve as sources of brand equity may differ. It may be particularly important to achieve points of parity with these different constituencies so that points of difference can come into play. UK branding experts de Chernatony and McDonald put it this way:

> In consumer marketing, brands tend to be bought by individuals, while many people are involved in organizational purchasing. The brand marketer is faced with the challenge of not only identifying which managers are involved in the purchasing decision, but also what brand attributes are of particular concern to each of them. The various benefits of the brand, therefore, need to be communicated to all involved, stressing the relevant attributes to particular individuals. For example, the brand's reliable delivery may need to be stressed to the production manager, its low lifecycle costs to the accountant, and so on.[6]

Marketing campaigns must reflect the role of individuals in the buying centre or process initiator, influencer, purchaser, user and so on. Some individuals within the organization may be more concerned with developing a deep relationship with the company and therefore place greater value on the trustworthiness dimension and corporate credibility; other individuals may seek merely to make transactions and therefore place greater value on performance and expertise.

1. Establish brand awareness and a rich brand image.
2. Create corporate credibility associations.
3. Leverage secondary associations of quality.
4. Avoid overbranding products.
5. Selectively introduce new products as new brands and clearly identify brand extensions.

Figure 15.11 Additional guidelines for high-tech products

High-tech products

One special category of physical goods – potentially sold to both consumers and industrial customers – is 'high-tech' products. The distinguishing feature of such products is that they change rapidly because of technological innovations. It should be recognized that high-tech products are not restricted to computer- or microprocessor-related products. Technology has played an important role in branding and marketing products as diverse as razor blades and running shoes.

The short product lifecycles for high-tech products have significant branding implications (Figure 15.11). Brand Briefing 15.5 describes branding developments for Cisco, one of the most successful brands of the past decade.

Brand Briefing 15.5

Sustaining the Cisco brand

Cisco, the US networking equipment manufacturer founded in 1984, grew to be the market leader in the switchers and routers that direct traffic on the internet. As a result, the company reaped the rewards of the web boom of the late 1990s, growing from €950 million sales in 1994 to €15.6 billion in 2000. Its stock performed phenomenally, rising 100,000 percent from its 1990 listing and surpassed Microsoft in market capitalization in 2000. Cisco developed ad campaigns during this period to reinforce its central role on the internet, including one B2B effort that contained facts about the internet's growth before asking 'Are you ready?' and concluding with the tagline 'Empowering the internet generation'. A Cisco marketing executive at the time said: 'One [goal] is to make the internet relevant, and the other is to make Cisco synonymous with the internet'.

Being synonymous with the internet was a boon there, but a curse when the dot-com bubble burst. Cisco's fortunes faded as companies cut back on their investments in internet equipment. Revenue growth slowed, leading to the company posting a loss in 2001, and its market valuation declined €314 billion between March 2000 and January 2002. The company faced challenging conditions, yet

Brand Briefing 15.5 *continued*

chief executive John Chambers remained upbeat, remarking that 'Cisco does better during the tough times.'

Though the heady days of 70 percent annual growth disappeared, Cisco did survive, thanks to cost reductions and timely expansions into new networking technologies. Cisco expanded into the increasingly popular voice-over-internet market, earning 40 percent market share by 2003. It also moved into wireless internet networking by buying Linksys in 2003. To expand in its core networking business, it focused on security. As part of a global campaign based on the advantages of a secure network, Cisco sponsored the Euro 2004 football championships and ran online and television ads that used the visual metaphor of preventing a goal to reinforce the theme of security. As a result of these measures, Cisco's share of the €67.2 billion communications equipment market rose from 10 percent in 2001 to to 16 percent in 2004. Sales on the year grew 17 percent to €16 billion and net income rose 24 percent to €3.9 billion.

Cisco developed a new advertising approach in 2005, shifting the focus away from the product itself and instead emphasizing the role of Cisco in everyday life. Print ads for the US campaign featured scenes from life and the tagline 'Powered by Cisco' – for example, an image of a newborn baby with the text '8lbs 3oz. Powered by Cisco'. The ads included a 'manifesto' that concluded with a line about the internet being a 'secure, intelligent, ubiquitous network we have all built together. The network powered by Cisco. And shared by everyone'. With Cisco once again reminding consumers of its centrality to the internet – albeit with a more human tone – and financial figures again improving in 2005 to €4.4 billion in profit on sales of €18.3 billion, the company appeared to have regained its stride.

Sources: Diane Anderson, 'Cisco reboots image with $150m effort', *Brandweek*, 10 January 2005; Bradley Johnson, 'Cisco ad budget soars as it builds internet image', *Advertising Age*, 17 August 1998: 4; Andy Serwer, 'There's something about Cisco', *Fortune*, 15 May 2000: 114; John A. Byrne and Ben Elgin, 'Cisco: behind the hype', *BusinessWeek*, 21 January 2002: 54; Stephanie N. Mehta, 'Cisco fractures its own fairytale', *Fortune*, 14 May 2001: 104; Peter Burrows, 'Cisco's comeback', *BusinessWeek*, 14 November 2003: 116; Peter Burrows, 'Can Cisco settle for less than sizzling?', *BusinessWeek*, 21 February 2005: 62.

Establish brand awareness

Many high-tech companies have learned the importance of branding the hard way, as well as not relying on specifications alone to drive sales. Typically, it cannot be assumed that 'if you build a great product, they will come'. Well-designed and well-funded marketing campaigns are needed to create brand awareness and a strong brand image. In doing so, non-product-related associations concerning brand personality or other imagery may be important, especially in distinguishing near-parity products.

Create corporate credibility associations

One implication of rapid product turnover is the need to create a corporate or family brand with strong credibility associations. Because of the often complex nature of high-tech products and the continual introduction of products or modifications of existing products, consumer perceptions of the expertise and trustworthiness of the firm are particularly important. In a high-tech setting, trustworthiness also relates to consumers' perceptions of the firm's longevity and staying power. With technology companies, the chairman or managing director often is key to a brand and performs an important brand-building and communication function, in some cases as an advocate of technology.

Leverage secondary associations

Lacking the ability to judge the quality of high-tech products, consumers may use brand reputation to reduce risk. This lack of ability by consumers to judge quality also means that it may be necessary to use secondary associations to communicate product quality. Third-party endorsements from top companies, leading magazines or industry experts may help to achieve the necessary perceptions of product quality. To be able to garner these endorsements, however, will typically necessitate demonstrable differences in product performance, suggesting the importance of innovative product development.

Avoid overbranding products

One mistake made by many high-tech firms is to 'overbrand' products by using too many ingredient and endorser brands. For example, in 1995 Silicon Graphics introduced a 3D workstation, the Indigo^2 Impact, which was divided into performance categories with the following modifiers (in increasing order of performance): 'High', 'Solid', 'Killer' and 'Maximum'. Given the length of the brand name, customers used the most specific modifier as a shorthand reference for the computer. For example, customers abbreviated the 'Indigo^2 Impact Solid' to 'Solid'. By overbranding in this way, brand equity slides down the hierarchy to lower levels at the expense of the family brand or company brand. Though the company made national headlines, the Silicon Graphics master brand was not necessarily as well known as its popular Indigo sub-brands, which became problematic as successors to Indigo were introduced.

Selectively introduce new products

Another implication of the abbreviated nature of product lifecycles is the importance of brand portfolios and brand hierarchies. Several issues are relevant here. First, brand extensions are a common high-tech branding strategy. With new products continually emerging, it would be prohibitively expensive to brand them all with new names. Typically, names for new products are given modifiers from existing products – for example, alphabetical (Microsoft Windows XP), numerical (Microsoft Xbox 360), time-based (Microsoft Exchange Server 2007) or other schemes – unless they represent dramatic departures or marked product improvements for the brand, in which case a new brand name might be employed. Using a new name for a new product signals to consumers that this version is significantly different.

Thus, family brands group products. Individual items or products within those brand families must be clearly distinguished, however, and brand migration strategies must be defined that reflect product introduction strategies and consumer market trends. Other brand portfolio issues relate to the importance of retaining some brands. Too often, high-tech firms continually introduce new sub-brands, making it difficult for consumers to develop loyalty to any one brand.

Services

As noted in Chapter 1, the level of sophistication in branding services has greatly increased, as suggested by Figure 15.12. Brand Briefing 15.6 reviews how Singapore Airlines built a strong services brand.

Maximize service quality

From a branding perspective, one challenge with services is their intangible nature. One consequence of this intangibility is that consumers may have difficulty forming their quality evaluations and may end up basing those evaluations on considerations other than factors directly related to their service experience. Researchers have identified a number of aspects to service quality.[7]

- *Tangibles:* physical facilities, equipment and appearance of personnel.
- *Reliability:* ability to perform the promised service right the first time (standardized facilities and operations).
- *Responsiveness:* willingness to help customers and provide customer service.
- *Competence:* knowledge and skill of employees.
- *Trustworthiness:* believability and honesty (ability to convey trust and confidence).
- *Empathy:* caring, individualized attention.
- *Courtesy:* friendliness of customer contact.
- *Communication:* keeping customers informed in language they can understand and listening to what they say.

---

1. Maximize service quality by recognizing the myriad ways to influence consumer service perceptions.
2. Employ a full range of brand elements to enhance brand recall and signal more tangible aspects of the brand.
3. Create and communicate strong organizational associations.
4. Design corporate communication campaigns that augment consumers' service encounters and experiences.
5. Establish a brand hierarchy by creating distinct family brands or individual brands as well as meaningful ingredient brands.

Figure 15.12   Additional guidelines for services

Brand Briefing 15.6

Singapore Airlines soars

Singapore Airlines was founded in 1972 with a severe handicap compared with other airlines: the tiny island nation of Singapore had no domestic air traffic to guarantee travellers. Singapore Airlines therefore targeted the long-haul segment of the market, using Singapore's status as a business destination to build routes from North America, Europe and elsewhere in Asia. From the beginning, the airline chose to emphasize superior service to differentiate it from other carriers. It introduced the Singapore Girl, the epitome of warm and hospitable service, to entice travellers in ads, saying it was 'A great way to fly' – a tagline it retained for decades. The airline earned a reputation for 'pampering' passengers by focusing on the details of in-flight service. It was the first airline to serve hot meals and give passengers free drinks, as well as the first to provide hot towels on takeoff and landing. In 2005, first class passengers on Singapore flights received Givenchy pyjamas and Bulgari 'amenity kits'.

The company's attention to detail was also reflected in strict guidelines for what flight attendeants could wear, down to their make-up, which could be only one of two colour combinations. Singapore Airlines even experimented with standardized perfume for its attendants in the late 1990s, creating a scent called Stefan Floridian Waters. This focus on detail ensured that its customers enjoyed a consistent experience every time they encountered the brand.

Singapore Airlines also differentiated itself by leading the way in technology available on its flights. It was the first airline to offer personal video screens to passengers and the first to offer video on demand services. The age of its fleet, averaging 5.5 years, is much lower than the industry average of 13 years. Other airlines were quick to copy each innovation, so the company strove to maintain its pace of innovation to stay one step ahead of the competition. For example, the company spent more than €73 million in 2001 to equip the business class section of its planes with full-reclining SpaceBeds that moulded to passengers' body countours and, at $6^1/_2$ feet long, were billed as 'the biggest beds in business class'.

As a result of its dual focus on service and technology, Singapore Airlines has become a success story in a notoriously competitive industry, having never lost money since it started. In 2004, it was the world's most profitable airline, earning €603 million on €5.1 billion in revenues, and had a market capitalization second only to Southwest Airlines. Most importantly, Singapore Airlines remains a favourite of consumers, winning more than 500 awards since 2003, such as 'World's best international airline' from *Travel & Leisure* magazine in 2003.

Sources: Jonathan Holburt, 'Are brands becoming the export "ideology" of the 21st century?', *Advertising Age*, 13 March 2006: 24; Justin Doebele, 'The engineer', *Forbes*, 9 January 2006: 122; Greg Lindsay, 'Airworld war', *Advertising Age*, 24 October 2005: 12; Martin Lindstrom, 'Follow your nose to marketing evolution', *Advertising Age*, 23 May 2005: 136.

1. *Listening:* understand what customers really want through continuous learning about the expectations and perceptions of customers and non-customers (eg, by means of a service quality information system).
2. *Reliability:* the single most important dimension of service quality. It must be a priority.
3. *Basic service:* service companies must deliver the basics and do what they are supposed to do – keep promises, use common sense, listen to customers, keep customers informed and be determined to deliver value to customers.
4. *Service design:* develop a holistic view of the service while managing its many details.
5. *Recovery:* to satisfy customers who encounter a problem, service companies should encourage customers to complain (and make it easy for them to do so), respond quickly and personally and develop a problem resolution system.
6. *Surprising customers:* although reliability is the most important way to meet customers' service expectations, process dimensions (eg, assurance, responsiveness and empathy) are most important in exceeding customer expectations, such as by surprising customers with uncommon swiftness, grace, courtesy, competence, commitment and understanding.
7. *Fair play:* service companies must make special efforts to be fair and to demonstrate fairness to customers and employees.
8. *Teamwork:* this is what enables large organizations to deliver service with care and attentiveness by improving employees' motivation and capabilities.
9. *Employee research:* conduct research with employees to reveal why service problems occur and what companies must do to solve problems.
10. *Servant leadership:* quality service comes from inspired leadership throughout the organization, from excellent service system design, from the effective use of information and technology and from a slow-to-change, invisible, all-powerful, internal force called corporate culture.

Figure 15.13   Improving service quality

Source: Leonard L. Berry, A. Parasuraman and Valarie A. Zeithaml, 'Ten lessons for improving service quality', MSI Report 93–104, Cambridge, MA: Marketing Science Institute, 1993.

Thus, service quality perceptions depend on associations that vary in how directly they relate to the actual service experience. In terms of creating service offerings that excel, academics Berry, Parasuraman and Zeithaml offer ten recommendations for improving service quality (Figure 15.13).[8]

Employ a full range of brand elements

Intangibility also has implications for the choice of brand elements. Because service decisions and arrangements are often made away from the actual service location itself (eg, at home or at work), brand recall is critical. In such cases, an easy-to-remember and easy-to-pronounce brand name may be vital.

Because a physical product does not exist, packaging in a literal sense is not really relevant, although the physical facilities of the service provider can perhaps be seen as the external 'packaging' of a service (eg, through its signs, environmental design and reception area and clothing). Other brand elements – logos, symbols, characters and slogans – must then pick up the slack and complement the brand name to build brand awareness and image. These other elements often attempt to make the service and some of its benefits more tangible, concrete and real – for example, the 'friendly skies' of United airlines the 'bullish' nature of Merrill Lynch.

All aspects of the service delivery process can be branded. In the USA, Allied Moving Lines is concerned about the appearance of its drivers and workers, UPS has developed strong equity with the brown colour of its vans and Doubletree hotels offers freshly baked biscuits as a means of symbolizing the company's care and friendliness.

Create strong organizational associations

Organizational associations, such as perceptions about the people who make up the organization and who provide the service, are likely to be particularly important brand associations that may affect evaluations of service quality. Particularly important associations are company credibility and perceived expertise, trustworthiness and likeability.

Augment consumers' experiences

Service firms must design marketing communication and information campaigns so that consumers learn more about the brand than the information they glean from their service encounters alone. These campaigns may involve advertising and direct mail to help develop the proper brand personality. The communication campaigns should be integrated and evolve over time. Surprisingly, Citigroup walked away from a strong credibility position for its retail brand when it dropped its 'Citi never sleeps' ad campaign.

Establish a brand hierarchy

Finally, services also must consider developing a brand hierarchy and brand portfolio that permit positioning and targeting of different market segments. Classes of service can be branded vertically on the basis of price and quality. Vertical extensions often require sub-branding strategies in which the corporate name is combined with an individual brand name or modifier. In the hotel and airlines industries, brand lines and portfolios have been created by brand extensions and introductions. For example, United airlines brands its business class service as Connoisseur Class, its frequent flyer scheme as Mileage Plus, and its short-haul airlines as United Express. As another example, Hilton has introduced Hilton Garden Inns to target budget-conscious business travellers and compete with Marriott's Courtyard hotels.

Retailers

Chapters 5 and 7 reviewed issues concerning how retailers and other channel intermediaries can affect the brand equity of the products they sell as well as how they can create their own brand equity. Fundamentally, retailers create their own brand equity by establishing awareness of and associations with their product assortment (breadth and depth), pricing and credit policy, quality of service and so on. For example, Wal-Mart has become perhaps the premier US retail brand by coming to be

1. Create a brand hierarchy by branding the shop as a whole as well as individual departments, classes of service or any other aspects of the retail service or shopping experience.
2. Enhance private labels as well as manufacturers' brand equity by communicating and demonstrating their points of difference and other strong, favourable and unique brand associations.
3. Establish brand equity at all levels of the brand hierarchy by offering added value in the selection, purchase or delivery of product offerings.
4. Create multichannel shopping experiences.
5. Avoid overbranding.

Figure 15.14   Additional guidelines for retailers

seen as the low-price, high-value provider of everyday products. Consumers may form these associations in many ways, such as on the basis of personal experience, word of mouth or through advertisements or other indirect means. In building brand equity for a retailer, several guidelines are particularly relevant (Figure 15.14). Brand Briefing 15.7 describes the rise of UK retailer Tesco.

Brand Briefing 15.7

Branding success at Tesco

Tesco was the second-biggest grocery chain in the UK in the 1980s, behind the dominant Sainsbury chain. Tesco began upgrading its stores and product selection around 1983, but by 1990 the company had still been unable to take market share from Sainsbury. Tesco was still considered a 'pile it high and sell it cheap' mass-market retailer and wanted to change this perception. In a brief to its advertising agency in 1989, Tesco expressed a desire 'to develop an image campaign which will lift us out of the mould in our particular sector'.

The company's first image campaign, called 'Quest for quality', ran from 1990 to 1992. It starred British actor Dudley Moore as a Tesco employee who looked all over the globe for French free-range chickens and discovered en route other exotic products to add to the shelves. The idea was to surprise consumers with the range of high-quality goods available at Tesco. An instant success, the ad peaked at 89 percent prompted awareness in tracking studies. During the time that the campaign ran, Tesco invested heavily in the business, launching 114 initiatives that improved the shopping experience, such as baby-changing facilities and a Value product range.

Tesco then devised a campaign featuring 20 commercials, each focusing on a different initiative, that were linked by the tagline 'Every little helps'. These ads conveyed Tesco's new customer-orientated approach of always 'doing right by the customer'. Prompted awareness of these ads reached 64 percent and Tesco's revenues and market share rose steadily until it surpassed Sainsbury's as the market

Brand Briefing 15.7 *continued*

leader in 1995. Company research revealed that 1.3 million new customers started shopping at Tesco between 1990 and 1995.

Another advertising campaign that helped endear the company to customers is its Computers for Schools cause-related marketing campaign, started in 1992. It quickly became the best-known cause-related campaign in the UK, with prompted awareness levels near 50 percent. Customers receive vouchers from Tesco for every €10 spent, which they can donate to a school of their choosing. The chosen school exchanges the vouchers for computer equipment. Parent–teacher associations and school governors joined together to maximize voucher collection, which enhanced community involvement in the scheme. Tesco capitalized on the link between its brand and the Computers for Schools scheme in 1998, when the company began selling computer hardware. Since the scheme began, it has delivered almost €73 million-worth of computer equipment to schools.

In 1995, the same year it overtook Sainsbury's, Tesco introduced its frequent-shopper scheme, based on the Tesco Clubcard loyalty card. The Clubcard has been credited with driving much of Tesco's subsequent success. In addition to driving customer loyalty, the Clubcard enabled Tesco to gather reams of customer data and tailor merchandise assortments, store layouts for specific stores and customize offers to customers. The Clubcard propelled Tesco's market share rise, which reached 15 percent in 1999. In both 1998 and 1999, other British companies voted Tesco as Britain's most admired company. With the help of savvy and sustained marketing efforts, Tesco had transformed itself from an also-ran into a market leader in less than a decade.

In the following years, Tesco continued to apply its winning formula of using customer data to optimize its marketing and dominated the British retail landscape, moving beyond supermarkets to selling general merchandise. By 2005, Tesco had a 35 percent share of supermarket spending in the UK, almost twice that of its nearest competitor, and a 14 percent share of total retail sales. The company also used the same strategy to expand overseas. In 2005, Tesco had 648 stores outside the UK and was the supermarket leader in Poland, Hungary, Thailand, Ireland and Slovakia. Tesco was Britain's largest company and the fifth largest retailer in the world in 2005, after Wal-Mart, Carrefour, Home Depot and Metro. The turnover of Tesco was €50.3 billion in 2005 and its profit was €2 billion.

Sources: Ashleye Sharpe and Joanna Bamford, 'Tesco Stores Ltd', paper presented at Advertising Effectiveness Awards, 2000; Hamish Pringle and Marjorie Thompson, *Brand Spirit*, New York: John Wiley, 1999; 'The prime minister launches the 10th Tesco Computers for Schools scheme', *M2 Presswire*, 26 January 2001; Elizabeth Rigby, 'Prosperous Tesco takes retailing to a new level', *The Financial Times*, 21 September 2005: 23; Richard Fletcher, 'Leahy shrugs off talk of a "brain drain"', *The Sunday Times*, 29 January 2006: 7; Deilotte & Touche, 'Global powers of retailing – the search for sustainable growth', 2007.

Create a brand hierarchy

Establishing a brand hierarchy helps to create synergies in brand development. Retailers also must consider brand portfolio issues and whether additional shops or chains should be introduced to provide more complete market coverage. For example, Wal-Mart introduced Sam's Club in the USA to tap into the growing discount or warehouse retail market.

Similarly, individual departments can take on associations that appeal to a particular target market. For example, Nordstrom has a number of clothing departments each designed with distinct images and positions, such as t.b.d. for the latest women's trends, Brass Plum for teen girls, Encore for plus-size women and Individualist fashionable women's professional attire. These departments may be branded by the retailer or even as 'ingredient brands', designed and supported by a national manufacturer (eg, as with Polo shops in US department stores, which only sell that Ralph Lauren brand).

Enhance own labels

As a second guideline, retailers should exploit as much as possible the brand equity of the manufacturer brands they sell by communicating and demonstrating their points of difference and other brand associations. Manufacturers often employ push strategies that involve campaigns to encourage retailers to support their brands. By co-operating with and perhaps even enhancing these campaigns, retailers should be able to sell such products at higher prices and margins, generating greater profits as a result.

At the same time, there is a battle between retailers and manufacturers. Corstjens and Corstjens describe this as 'The battle for mindspace and shelf space'.[9] The retailers control the shelf space and the manufacturers build the brands and occupy the consumers' mindspace. However, as retail chains seek to build their own brands, the manufacturers' occupancy of the consumers' mindspace is being challenged.

Establish equity at all levels of the brand hierarchy

Retailers must create their own brand associations that go beyond the products they sell. Sharper Image has created a niche in the USA as a seller of creative, upmarket products and gadgets. Victoria's Secret has gained notoriety as a provider of stylish, feminine clothing. Costco and Price Club created strong discount associations.

To communicate these broader associations, retail strategies are often reflected in campaigns that focus on the advantages of shopping at the shops rather than on promotions for specific items. For example, Radio Shack in the USA advertises that it is the 'consumer-friendly' provider of electronic parts, accessories and specialized equipment through a campaign with the slogan 'You've got questions. We've got answers.'

Create multichannel shopping experiences

Increasingly, retailers are selling their wares through a variety of channels, such as shops, catalogues and websites. US chain Office Depot recognized the importance of supplementing its 800 shops in 1997 with a website and catalogue. By offering service and convenience – and not cutting its prices – Office Depot has been able to maintain its market leadership. Regardless of the channel employed, it is important that consumers have rewarding shopping experiences in searching, choosing, paying for and receiving products. In some case, these experiences may turn out to be valuable points of difference, or at least necessary points of parity, with respect to competitors.

Avoid overbranding

Finally, if a retailer is selling its own labels, it is important not to employ too many brands. Retailers are particularly susceptible to 'bottom-up branding', in which each department creates its own brands. For example, Nordstrom found itself in the position of having to support scores of brands across its different departments, sometimes with little connection between them. Recall from Chapter 5 that one advantage of shops' own brands, however, is that they often represent associations (eg, value) that transfer across categories. The greater the extent to which an abstract association (value, fashionability, etc.) can be seen as desirable and deliverable across categories, the more likely it is that efficiencies can be gained by concentrating on a few brands.

Small businesses

Building brands for a small business is a challenge because of the limited resources and budgets typically involved. Small businesses do not have the luxury of making mistakes and must design and implement marketing campaigns very carefully. Nevertheless, entrepreneurs have built brands from nothing to become powerhouse brands. Peter van Stolk launched the Jones Soda brand in the USA in 2000, marketing it as an alternative to cola with labels that looked handmade and unusual flavors such as Lemon Drop, Blue Bubblegum, Fufu Berry and MF Grape. By 2006, Jones had direct distribution through big retailers, generating €24.8 million in annual sales and was expanding into other categories such as lip balms, lollies and sweets.[10]

In general, because of limited resources, focus and consistency in marketing campaigns are critically important. To compensate for fewer funds, creativity is also paramount. Brand Briefing 15.8 contains some provocative notions on how small brands can compete with big ones. Figure 15.15 lists guidelines for small businesses. Brand Briefing 15.9 describes how Green Mountain Coffee built a strong brand.

Emphasize one or two brands

Given fewer resources, strategically it may be necessary to emphasize one or two strong brands. Along these lines, employing a corporate branding strategy can be an efficient way of building brand equity, although the focus may just be on a major family brand. For example, software developer Intuit concentrated its marketing efforts on building the Quicken brand.

Brand Briefing 15.8

How smaller can be better

Adam Morgan offers eight suggestions for small brands.

1. *Break with your immediate past:* don't be afraid to ask 'dumb' questions to challenge convention and view your brand differently.
2. *Build a 'lighthouse identity':* establish values and communicate who and why you are (eg, Apple).
3. *Assume thought leadership of the category:* break convention in terms of representation (what you say about yourself), where you say it (medium) and experience (what you do beyond talk).
4. *Create symbols of re-evaluation:* a rocket uses half of its fuel in the first mile to break loose from the gravitational pull – you may need to polarize people.
5. *Sacrifice:* focus on your target, message, reach and frequency, distribution and line extensions. Recognize that less can be more.
6. *Overcommit:* although you may do fewer things, do 'big' things when you do them.
7. *Use publicity and advertising to enter popular culture:* unconventional communications can get people talking.
8. *Be idea-centred, not consumer-centred:* sustain challenger momentum by not losing sight of what the brand is about and can be. Redefine marketing support and the centre of the company to reflect this vision.

Source: Adam Morgan, *Eating the Big Fish: How challenger brands can compete against brand leaders*, New York: John Wiley, 1999.

---

1. Emphasize one or two strong brands.
2. Focus the marketing campaign on one or two associations.
3. Employ a well-integrated set of brand elements that enhances both brand awareness and image.
4. Design creative brand-building push campaigns and consumer-involving pull campaigns that capture attention and generate demand.
5. Use as many secondary associations as possible.

Figure 15.15　Additional guidelines for small businesses

Focus on one or two key associations

Small businesses often must rely on only one or two key associations as points of difference. These associations must be consistently reinforced across the marketing campaign and over time. College Kit in the USA 'delivers products, services and

Brand Briefing 15.9

Green Mountain Coffee Roasters

Bob Stiller founded Green Mountain Coffee Roasters in 1981 when he opened a small café in the USA. According to the company, it was not long before tourists who stopped at the café asked if they could order the coffee from home. The company answered this demand by launching a mail-order business. Green Mountain sought out local customers by opening other shops. In the company's early years, it used no advertising, instead engaging in extensive sampling.

Stiller took the company public in 1993 and used the proceeds to expand the mail-order operation and open more shops. Green Mountain also invested in technological improvements for its roasting and packaging system, spending €365,000 on a system that removes air from pack of coffee and improves shelf life.

Green Mountain closed its 12 shops in 1998 to focus on the wholesale business. Wholesale customers include restaurants, convenience shops, office coffee distributors and airlines. For at-home customers, Green Mountain retained its mail-order catalogue and its Coffee Club home delivery subscription service and, in 1998, it began selling coffee and other specialized products online. In addition to 60 varieties of Green Mountain Coffee, customers can order coffee grinders, mugs, chocolates and gift baskets.

Green Mountain, which gives 5 percent of its pre-tax profits to 'socially responsible' causes, grew rapidly as its wholesale business brought it in contact with an ever-widening customer base. Between 1995 and 2000, sales increased at an average rate of 24 percent annually. In 2001, the company sold the equivalent of 10 million cups of coffee every day and maintained relationships with more than 7,000 wholesale customers. That same year, *Forbes* magazine named Stiller as its first 'entrepreneur of the year'. As demand among US consumers for organic products continued to grow, so too did Green Mountain's turnover. From 2001 to 2005, the company averaged 14 percent revenue growth, with 2005 revenues topping €117 million.

Sources: www.greenmountaincoffee.com; Luisa Kroll, 'Entrepreneur of the year: java man', *Forbes*, 29 October 2001: 142; 'Green mountain coffee, Inc. founder, president and CEO named Forbes first "entrepreneur of the year"', *Business Wire*, 16 October 2001.

marketing messages into the hands and minds of college consumers through creative, connected, sometimes outrageous and always entertaining programmes'. Thus, its key associations are 'creative', 'well-targeted' and 'marketing campaigns for college students'.

Employ a well-integrated set of brand elements

Tactically, it is important for small businesses to maximize the contributions of each of the three main ways to build brand equity. First, a distinctive, well-integrated set of brand elements should be developed that enhances both brand awareness and brand image, as suggested by the following example.

Rumba

Wall Data in the USA published connectivity software between desktop computers and various mainframes that allowed users to avoid rebooting or reconfiguring their machines. In the mid-1990s, it branded its family of software products 'Rumba' and combined that name with a symbol of a man and woman dancing cheek-to-cheek. It used the slogan 'Get connected' in advertising, promotional materials and packaging. To build awareness and image, the company even hosted rumba dance lessons at trade shows. The success of the product line permitted the later introduction of other sets of software products branded with dance themes, such as Salsa.

Brand elements should be memorable and meaningful, with as much creative potential as possible. Innovative packaging can be a substitute for ad campaigns by capturing attention at the point of sale. For example, Smartfood introduced its first product in the USA without any advertising but with unique packaging that served as a strong visual symbol on the shelf, allied to an extensive sampling campaign. Proper names or family names, which often characterize small businesses, may provide distinctiveness but suffer in terms of pronounceability, meaningfulness, memorability or other branding considerations. If these deficiencies are too great, other brand elements should be explored.

Design creative push and pull campaigns

Small businesses must design creative push and pull campaigns that capture the attention of consumers and other channel members alike. Clearly, this is a challenge on a limited budget. Unfortunately, without a strong pull campaign creating product interest, retailers may not feel enough motivation to stock and support a brand. Conversely, without a strong push campaign that convinces retailers of the merits of the product, the brand may fail to achieve adequate support or may not even be stocked. Thus, push and pull marketing campaigns ideally would be creatively designed and integrated, employing the most cost-effective tools available, to increase the visibility of the brand and get both consumers and retailers talking about the brand.

With small businesses relying on word of mouth to create brand associations, public relations and low-cost promotions and sponsorship can be an inexpensive way to enhance brand awareness and brand image (Brand Briefing 15.9). For example, Noah's Bagels reached out to the Jewish community and transplanted New Yorkers in California through well-publicized events and appearances that promoted the 'authentic' nature of the bagel chain. The US marketers of the PowerBar, a nutrient-rich, low-fat 'energy bar', used selective sponsorship of runners, cyclists and tennis players and events such as marathons to raise awareness and improve its image. Selective distribution that targets opinion leaders can also be used to implement a push strategy. For example, brands such as Perrier bottled water and Paul Mitchell and Nexus shampoo were introduced to carefully selected outlets before broadening distribution.

1. Don't forget the brand-building basics.
2. Create strong brand identity.
3. Generate strong consumer pull.
4. Selectively choose brand partnerships.
5. Maximize relationship marketing.

Figure 15.16 Additional guidelines for online brands

Use secondary associations

Finally, another way for small businesses to build brand equity is to exploit as many secondary associations as possible. Secondary associations are often a cost-effective shortcut to building brand equity. Any entity with potentially relevant associations should be considered, especially those that help to signal quality or credibility. Along those lines, to enhance perceptions of scope (ie, make the company appear 'bigger' than it really is), a website can be invaluable.

Online

Many of the guidelines for business-to-business, high-tech, retailing and small businesses may apply online, depending on the nature of the business. At the same time, other guidelines are worth reinforcing (as summarized in Figure 15.16). Brand Briefing 15.10 outlines how MySpace built one of the strongest online brands.

Brand Briefing 15.10

Making connections at MySpace

In just two years, MySpace grew from a relative latecomer as a social networking website to the dominant player in the category. Friendster, the website that launched the social networking era in August 2002, beat MySpace online by 11 months, a near-eternity in internet time. The idea behind social networking websites is deceptively simple: provide a way for web surfers to publish profiles of themselves through which to connect with old or current friends and make new ones. Whereas Friendster was unable to sustain its initial momentum, attracting fewer than a million visitors in October 2005, MySpace had more than 20 million visitors that same month.

Following on the heels of Friendster, MySpace was able to learn from the first mover's mistakes. Friendster's registered user base quickly grew to 20 million, but the company was unable to keep pace and the site was beset by technical problems. It also lacked features, not offering users the opportunity to load songs to

Brand Briefing 15.10 *continued*

stream on their profiles, start blogs, post on message boards or upload more than a handful of pictures. MySpace invested heavily in technology to keep pace with its torrid growth as well as enable users to add almost an unlimited amount of content to their pages, in particular streaming audio. This feature enabled professional and aspiring bands to build profiles and share their music with the vast audience of MySpace users. Before long, bands began launching their albums on the site, and MySpace started its own record label in 2005. MySpace also made more of an effort to tie the site into its users' real social lives, sponsoring concerts and other events.

MySpace makes its money by selling ad space. In October 2005, MySpace accounted for 10 percent of all ads viewed online. To avoid annoying its user base, it does not allow invasive pop-up ads or spyware, instead selling banner ads or promotions and allowing products and television shows to create their own MySpace accounts. This latter feature is another difference between MySpace and Friendster. Friendster initially deleted accounts not linked to a real person, barring profiles for pets and products. On MySpace, any profile that isn't offensive is welcome, and product profiles became marketing tools. For example, Disney created a *Pirates of the Caribbean* profile that attracted 70,000 'friends' on MySpace. MySpace makes upwards of €36,500 a month from brand profiles.

In July 2005, MySpace's new media business model was validated when an old media giant, News Corporation, bought MySpace's parent company, Intermix Media, for €424 million. MySpace's growth continued to accelerate; it signed up new members at a rate of 2 million a week in June 2006, pushing total registered users over 72 million. It garnered more monthly page views than any other website except Yahoo!, putting it in the internet elite. MySpace's next step was to expand into 11 countries, mostly in Europe, with a longer-term goal of entering India and China.

Sources: Jessi Hempel, 'The MySpace generation', *BusinessWeek*, 12 December 2005: 86; Allison Fass, 'Piggyback', *Forbes*, 19 June 2006; Shawn Gold interview, *Advertising Age*, 5 June 2006: S-4; Tom Braithwaite and Andrew Edgecliffe-Johnson, 'MySpace pushes for international expansion', *The Financial Times*, 20 June 2006: 28.

Don't forget the basics

With online brands, it is important to not forget brand-building basics such as establishing points of parity and points of difference. As noted in earlier chapters, one mistake of many failed dot-com brands was to be impatient and failing to build the brand from the bottom up. In research to understand online service quality, defined as the extent to which websites allow efficient and effective shopping, purchasing and delivery, one study identified 11 aspects of e-service quality: access, ease of navigation, efficiency, flexibility, reliability, personalization, security/privacy, responsiveness, assurance/trust, site aesthetics and price knowledge.[11] Land's End became a top-selling company online by treating its internet operations as a digital translation of its catalogue, ensuring that merchandise was presented properly and that excellent customer service prevailed.

Create strong brand identity

Given that consumers aren't physically confronted by brands, awareness and recall are critical. Towards that goal, choosing the right website address is a priority. With 17 million dot-com brands registered by the end of 2000, choosing the best address is difficult. URLs must be chosen with the basic brand element criteria in mind, with perhaps greater emphasis on brand recall as an objective. A simple but evocative name can be useful in that regard.

Generate strong consumer pull

An important lesson for online brands was the need to create demand offline to drive consumers online. One aspect of this strategy is to use sampling and other trial devices. For example, AOL conducted massive sampling and free giveaways of its CD-ROMs that eventually led to increased consumer adoptions. More broadly, online brands must introduce the best possible integrated marketing communication campaigns, consisting of combinations of public relations; television, radio and print advertising; sponsorship; and so on.

Choose brand partnerships

Online brands can benefit from establishing brand partners. Such linkages can drive traffic, signal credibility and help to enhance image. Partnerships must be entered selectively, however, to satisfy brand-building and profit criteria. For example, CDNOW has an active affiliate scheme with its Cosmic Credit campaign that targets low-volume, non-professional sites of music fans, but has also initiated higher-profile strategic partnerships by alliances with powerful online brands such as AOL and Excite.[12]

Maximize relationship marketing

Finally, some of the potential advantages of online brands are the customization and interactivity involved. It is especially important, then, to engage in one-to-one, participatory, experiential and other forms of relationship marketing. Creating a strong online community of the consumers and the brand, as well as perhaps other consumers, can help to achieve brand resonance. For example, one marketing executive at Yahoo! characterized its strategy by saying: 'We've really focused our marketing efforts on attracting new users and providing an experience online that makes them stay.'[13] Yahoo! attempts to make the experience as fun and entertaining as possible but also practical, useful and convenient in its range of applications. Online brokerage Ameritrade provides detailed, timely, customized financial information to its clients. Online brands can offer much potentially relevant customer information. For example, Amazon provides professional and customer reviews, purchase circles and overall sales rankings, text samples and personalized recommendations.

FUTURE BRAND PRIORITIES

The journey to understanding strategic brand management is almost over, but it is worth considering a few final questions. How will branding change in the coming years? What are the biggest branding challenges? What will make a successful 'twenty-first-century brand'? Another important question is: how will the growing interest in corporate reputation and corporate social responsibility of stakeholders other than customers affect companies' ambitions to become successful in the coming year? And then: what will happen regarding China's ambition to become a global brand powerhouse? In a general sense, the importance of branding seems unlikely to change for one critical reason: it seems highly likely that consumers will continue to value the functions provided by brands. In a more complex world, well-managed brands can simplify, communicate, reassure and provide important meaning to consumers. Using the principles reflected in the brand report card and avoiding the seven deadly sins of brand management reviewed earlier should help in the pursuit of brand management. This final section highlights important considerations in building, measuring and managing brand equity in the future and concludes by suggesting a broad theme for strategic brand management.

Building brand equity

Brand elements

In a cluttered, competitive marketplace, the elements that make up a brand will have to do more and more of the selling job. In a time-compressed marketing world, the fact that a brand name can be noticed and its meaning registered or activated in memory within just a few seconds is a tremendous asset. Creating a powerful brand with inherent marketing value to build awareness and image, as well as serve as a strong foundation to link associations, can provide a strong competitive advantage.

Although branding principles should apply in designing a twenty-first century brand, what may change are the ways to create strong brands. For example, the brand elements that are chosen will increasingly involve verbal and visual elements that creatively and dramatically help to build brand equity. Meaningful brands with creative potential will benefit from several sensory presentations. Brands have long used auditory branding devices. Film studios have always been able to take advantage of their cinematic exposure to use sight, sound and motion to present their brands (eg, Universal's spinning globe, Paramount's mountain peak and MGM's roaring lion). With increased technical abilities and improved special effects, marketers will now be able to create brand elements that come to life and capture consumer attention. Thus, the static images of brands with which marketers are used to dealing will be supplemented by multidimensional forms that play a more important role in audio and video presentations of the brand. A twenty-first century brand will consider how to take advantage of different media to customize the brand's presentation so that each brand element more effectively contributes to brand equity through enhanced awareness and image and brand elements more effectively reinforce each other so that they become more consistent and cohesive as a result.

Marketing campaigns

Strong brands will rise above other brands by better understanding the needs, wants and desires of consumers and creating marketing campaigns that surpass consumer expectations. Successful brands will have a rich but internally cohesive brand image whose associations are highly valued by consumers. Marketing campaigns will seamlessly reinforce these associations through product, pricing, distribution and communication strategies that consistently and creatively inform and remind consumers of what the brand has to offer. With these marketing campaigns, consumers will have a clear picture of what the brand represents and why it is special. Consumers will then view the brand as a 'trusted friend' and value its dependability and superiority. Marketers will engage in dialogue with consumers, listening to their product joys and frustrations and establishing a rapport and relationship that will transcend mere commercial exchanges. Marketers will develop a deep understanding of what makes their brand successful, retaining enduring core elements while modifying peripheral elements that fail to add value or unnecessarily absorb costs.

Finally, smart marketers will attempt to find ways to make sure that strong brand associations are created with all possible marketing effects. In particular, it will be necessary to carefully and imaginatively consider how the brand itself will be integrated into the marketing campaign to maximize its contribution to brand equity. In other words, the issue will not just be which brand elements are chosen to represent the brand but also how these brand elements will actually be used in the marketing campaign.

Measuring brand equity

Marketers will create formalized measurement approaches and processes that ensure they continually and exhaustively monitor their sources of brand equity and those of competitors. As part of this process, managers will develop a greater understanding of how different marketing actions affect their sources and outcomes of brand equity. Thus, marketers of successful twenty-first century brands will go beyond piecemeal research projects to devise original ways to obtain accurate, comprehensive and up-to-date information on the status of their brands. By maintaining close contact with the brand, managers will be better able to understand what makes it tick. By achieving greater accountability in marketing activities and campaigns, it will be possible for managers to put money behind the right brands at the right time and in the right ways.

Managing brand equity

It will be essential in building strong brands to align internal and external brand management. Internal brand management involves activities that ensure employees and marketing partners appreciate and understand basic branding notions and how they can affect the equity of brands. Brand management must not be perceived as a separate function within the organization but as the responsibility and obligation of all. For that to happen, however, it is important that the right structures, processes, incentives and resources are put in place – for example, through brand equity charters, reports and supervision.

Internal brand management is especially critical for a corporate brand and/or a service brand, as every employee directly or indirectly represents the brand and can therefore affect brand equity.[14] Internal brand management helps to ensure that external brand management is done properly.

External brand management involves understanding the needs, wants and desires of consumers and creating marketing campaigns for brands.

Brand Briefing 15.11

The Brand Leadership Model: bridging the gap between brand promise and brand delivery

Many branding models only illustrate brand management from an external perspective. There is a need for a holistic model that harmonizes the internal perspective with the external. The Brand Leadership Model is an eight-phase model of the brand-building process developed by Tony Apéria. The steps show how the gaps between management, employees and external stakeholders can be bridged. At the centre of the model (Figure 15.17) is brand strategy – the purpose is to connect business strategy with all brand-building activities.

1. The purpose of the first phase is to create a vision for the company.
   - Important components of the first phase are: mission, vision and organizational values.
   - Which promise does *management* want to give?
2. The second phase tries to align management's point of view with that of the employees.
   - The corporate culture should support the vision of the company.
   - Of importance is understanding the difference between espoused values and the underlying assumptions that guide employees' behaviour.
   - Which promise can *the organization* deliver?
3. The third phase involves external stakeholders, primarily customers and society.
   - Important components of the external third phase are: trends, understanding of the category, needs and image of a brand compared with its rivals. To get a thorough understanding of a brand, managers need to reach the emotional

Brand Briefing 15.11 *continued*

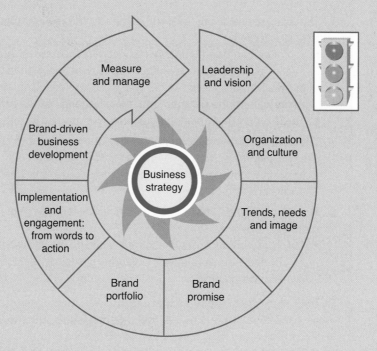

Figure 15.17 Brand Leadership Model

side of the brand. You often need projective techniques to reach the emotional and symbolic side of the brand (see presentation of the Brandjobs Model in Brand Briefing 9.9).

- Which promise does the *consumer/customer* appreciate?

4. In the fourth phase, the brand promise is defined based on management's, employees' and customers' points of view.

- There is a need to align the brand promise with delivery. A company has to deliver what it promises and needs to understand that it cannot promise anything it cannot deliver.
- Next, three questions. Which promise does the company want to give (the first phase)? Which promise can it give (the second phase)? Which promise is it allowed to give?
- The brand promise needs to align the vision and culture with the needs of external stakeholders. Gaps between these stakeholders need to be minimized.

5. The fifth phase handles how the whole brand portfolio can work together to deliver value.

- Internal as well as external roles of all brands within the brand portfolio must be defined.

Brand Briefing 15.11 *continued*

6. The sixth phase handles how the brand promise is implemented internally as well as externally.
   - Too often, the brand strategy has been defined as a document, but this is only a guide as to how to move from words to action. A brand needs to come alive. Internally there need to be brand champions who understand the brand promise, have the right attitude towards it and live the brand in their behaviour.
   - These brand champions function as role models for others.

7. The seventh phase describes how the brand is used in the brand-based business development.
   - Important components of the seventh phase are: line extensions, category extensions and co-branding.

8. Finally, the eighth phase describes how the brand needs to be measured and managed over time.
   - The most important stakeholders need to be measured. Stakeholders can be divided into employees, customers, society and others, such as media, owners and politicians.

By examining the brand in all these eight areas, management will understand what areas need to be prioritized. A traffic light system will show the areas as green, yellow or red. A red light means that corrections are urgent.

Sources: www.nordicbrandacademy.com; Tony Apéria, Fredrik Berggren and Robert Nises, 'Reputation excellence through emotional branding', Reputation Institute Conference, Oslo, 2007; James Collins and Jerry Porras, 'Building your company's vision', *Harvard Business Review*, September–October 1996; Mary Jo Hatch and Majken Scultz, 'Are the corporate stars aligned for your corporate brand?', *Harvard Business Review*, February 2001; Michael Porter, 'What is strategy?', *Harvard Business Review*, November–December 1996; Michael Porter and Mark Kramer, 'Strategy and society: the link between competitive advantage and corporate social responsibility', *Harvard Business Review*, December 2006; Edgar Schein, 'Coming to awareness of organizational culture', *Sloan Management Review*, winter 1984.

Align bottom-up and top-down management

Bottom-up brand management requires that marketing managers direct their activities so as to maximize brand equity for individual products in particular markets, with relatively little regard for other brands and products sold by the firm or for other markets in which their brands and products may be sold. Although such close, detailed brand supervision can be advantageous, creating brand equity for every product and market in this way can be expensive and difficult and, most importantly, ignores possible synergies.

Top-down brand management, however, involves marketing activities that capture the big picture and recognize synergies across products and markets to brand products accordingly. Such a top-down approach would seek to find common products and markets that could share marketing campaigns and activities and only develop separate brands and marketing activities as dictated by the consumer or competitive environment.

Unfortunately, if left unmanaged, firms tend to follow the bottom-up approach, resulting in many brands being marketed inconsistently and incompatibly. Managing brands in a top-down fashion requires centralized and co-ordinated marketing guidance and actions from high-level marketing supervisors. Particular attention must be paid to how to develop and use the corporate brand.

Both pairs of brand management activities can be mutually reinforcing: successful brands will be those that blend top-down and bottom-up as well as internal and external brand management activities. Ignoring one or more of these can put brands in peril. In avoiding this pitfall, marketers should adapt every aspect of their marketing campaigns to enhance brand equity. Such marketers will develop a deep understanding of what makes their brand successful, retaining enduring core elements while modifying peripheral elements that fail to add value or absorb unnecessary costs. Marketers of successful brands also will appreciate how their brands fit in with respect to other brands sold by the firm. They will capitalize on and judiciously exploit the potential of their brand in product development and brand extensions while at the same time recognizing its limits and boundaries.

Achieving marketing balance

These potential brand management tradeoffs suggest a broader issue and challenge with marketing and brand management. In many ways, the fundamental challenge is how to reconcile or address the many potential tradeoffs in making marketing decisions.[15] Figure 15.18 lists tradeoffs or conflicts that can occur in making strategic, tactical, financial or organizational decisions for a brand. Clearly, tradeoffs are pervasive and must be made in the context of constrained – and often limited – resources. To illustrate, recall from Chapter 3 the many negatively correlated

---

Strategic

Retaining customers v. acquiring customers
Brand expansion v. brand fortification
Product performance v. brand image
Points of parity v. points of difference

Tactical

Push v. pull
Continuity v. change
Classic v. contemporary image
Independent v. universal image

Financial

Short-run v. long-run objectives
Sales-generating v. brand-building activities
Accountable or measurable tactics v. non-measurable tactics
Quality maximization v. cost minimization

Organizational

Global v. local
Top down v. bottom up
Customization v. standardization
Internal v. external

Figure 15.18   Brand marketing tradeoffs

attributes and benefits that exist in the minds of consumers and the challenge that these relationships present for positioning.

One response is to adopt an extreme solution and maximize one of the two aspects involved with the tradeoff. Many experts advocate positions that, in effect, lead to such a singular focus. Such approaches, however, leave the brand vulnerable to the negative consequences of ignoring the other dimension.

The reality is that, for marketing success, both aspects of each tradeoff must be adequately addressed. Doing so involves achieving a more balanced marketing solution. Marketing balance occurs when marketers attempt to address all possible tradeoffs.

There are three levels of achieving marketing balance, in increasing order of potential effectiveness.

1. *Alternate:* identify and recognize the tradeoffs, but attempt to emphasize one aspect at a time and then alternate these over time so that neither is ignored. Although potentially effective, the downside of this approach is that often the firm experiences a pendulum effect. There can be a tendency to overreact to a perceived imbalance in emphasis so that an imbalance in one direction leads to a subsequent imbalance in the other direction.
2. *Divide:* split the difference and do a little of both. Again, although potentially effective, this approach may suffer if insufficient or inadequate resources are put against the two objectives such that critical mass is not achieved. Attempting to do a little of this and a little of that may lack sufficient impact.
3. *Use finesse:* try to achieve synergy between the two dimensions. Such a marketing balance is achieved by shrewdly reconciling the decision tradeoffs.

Hitting the right spot may involve some well thought out moderation and balance throughout the marketing organization and its activities. For example, marketing balance can involve strategically creative advertising that entertains and sells products. It can involve equity-building promotions such as Procter & Gamble's US promotion for Ivory soap that reinforced the attribute of 'floating' and the benefit of 'purity' while also moving product. It can involve robust brand positions such as Apple's 'The Power to be your best', which reconciled the seemingly negatively correlated benefits of 'easy to use' and 'powerful' in the minds of consumers.

Marketing balance can be more difficult to achieve than more extreme solutions in that it can involve greater discipline, care and thought. To use a golfing analogy, the golfer with the smoothest swing is often the one who hits the ball farthest and straightest. Marketing balance may not be as 'exciting' as more radical proposed solutions, but can turn out to be much more productive. Marketing balance is all about making marketing work harder, be more versatile and achieve more objectives. To realize marketing balance, it is necessary to create many meanings, responses and effects.

Marketing balance does not imply that marketers should not take chances, should not do different things or should not do things differently. It *does* imply an acceptance of the fact that marketing is multifaceted and involves many objectives, markets and activities. Marketing balance recognizes the importance of avoiding oversimplification: marketers must do many things and do them right. Fundamentally, to achieve balance, marketers must understand and address marketing tradeoffs.

Brand Briefing 15.12

David Aaker's brand equity model

One of branding's academic pioneers in the USA is David Aaker. He defines brand equity as a set of five categories of brand assets and liabilities linked to a brand, its name and symbol that add to or subtract from the value provided by a product or service to a firm or to that firm's customers or both. These categories of brand assets are: brand loyalty; brand awareness; perceived quality; brand associations; and other proprietary assets (eg, patents, trademarks and channel relationships). These assets provide various benefits and value, as shown in Figure 15.19.

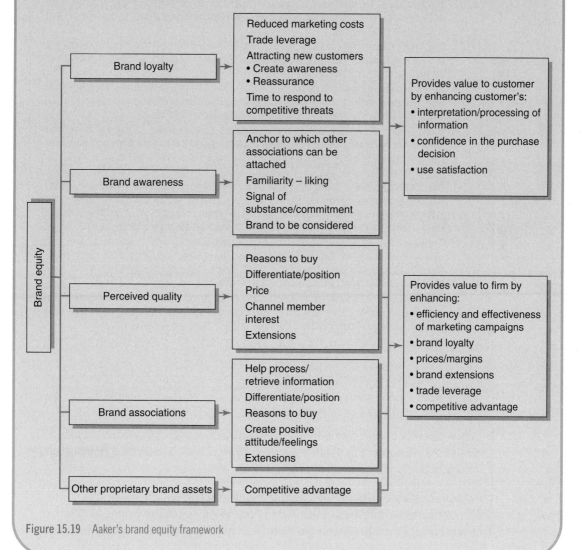

Figure 15.19   Aaker's brand equity framework

Brand Briefing 15.12 *continued*

1. *Brand identity:* have an identity for each brand. Consider the perspective of the brand-as-person, brand-as-organization and brand-as-symbol, as well as the brand-as-product. Identify the core identity. Modify the identity as needed for different market segments and products. Remember that an image is how you are perceived and an identity is how you aspire to be perceived.

2. *Value proposition:* know the value proposition for each brand that has a driver role. Consider emotional and symbolic benefits as well as functional benefits. Know how endorsing brands will provide credibility. Understand the customer–brand relationship.

3. *Brand position:* for each brand, have a position that will provide clear guidance to those implementing a communication campaign. Recall that a position is the part of the identity that is actively communicated.

4. *Execution:* execute the communication campaign so that it not only matches the identity and position but achieves brilliance and durability. Generate options and consider possibilities beyond media advertising.

5. *Consistency over time:* have as a goal a consistent identity, position and execution over time. Maintain symbols, imagery and metaphors that work. Understand and resist organizational biases towards changing the identity, position and execution.

6. *Brand system:* make sure brands in a portfolio are consistent and synergistic. Know their roles. Have or develop proven techniques to help support brand identities and positions. Exploit branded features and services. Use sub-brands to clarify and modify. Know the strategic brands.

7. *Brand leverage:* extend brands and develop co-branding campaigns only if the brand identity will be both used and reinforced. Identify range brands and, for each, develop an identity and specify how that identity will be different in disparate product contexts. If a brand is moved up or down, take care to manage the integrity of the resulting brand identity.

8. *Tracking brand equity:* track brand equity over time, including brand awareness, perceived quality, brand loyalty and especially brand associations. Have specific communication objectives. Especially note areas where the brand identity and positioning and communication objectives are not reflected in the perceptions of the brand.

9. *Brand responsibility:* have someone in charge of the brand who will create the identity and positions and co-ordinate the execution across organizational units, media and markets. Be careful when a brand is being used in a business where it is not the cornerstone.

10. *Invest in brands:* continue investing in brands even when the financial goals are not being met.

Figure 15.20   Aaker's guidelines for building strong brands

Aaker describes issues in building, measuring and managing brand equity (Figure 15.20). According to Aaker, a particularly important concept for building brand equity is brand identity. Aaker defines *brand identity* as:

> a unique set of brand associations that the brand strategist aspires to create or maintain. These associations represent what the brand stands for and imply a promise to customers from the organization members. Brand

Brand Briefing 15.12 *continued*

identity should help establish a relationship between the brand and the customer by generating a value proposition involving functional, emotional or self-expressive benefits.

Brand identity consists of 12 dimensions organized around 4 perspectives: the brand-as-product (product scope, product attributes, quality/value, uses, users, country of origin); brand-as-organization (organizational attributes, local versus global); brand-as-person (brand personality, brand–customer relationships); and brand-as-symbol (visual imagery/metaphors and brand heritage).

Brand identity structure includes a core and extended identity. The core identity – the central, timeless essence of the brand – is likely to remain constant as the brand travels to new markets and products. The extended identity includes brand identity elements organized into cohesive and meaningful groups.

A particularly important concept for managing brand equity according to Aaker is that of brand systems. Aaker emphasizes that a key to managing brands in an environment of complexity is to consider them as not just individual performers but as members of a system of brands that must support one another. He notes that the goals of the system are qualitatively different from the goals of individual brand identities and include exploiting commonalities to generate synergy, reducing brand identity damage, achieving clarity of product offerings, facilitating change and adaptation and allocating resources. Aaker also notes that many brands within a system fall into a natural hierarchy and may play different roles – for example, endorsers, drivers, strategic brands, silver bullets, branded benefits and sub-brand roles.

CHAPTER REVIEW

The challenges and complexities of the modern marketplace make efficient and effective marketing an imperative. The concept of brand equity has been put forth as a means of focusing marketing efforts. The businesses that win will be those that have marketers who successfully build, measure and manage brand equity. This final chapter reviewed guidelines to help in that endeavour. Effective brand management requires consistent actions and applications of these guidelines across all aspects of a marketing campaign. Nevertheless, to some extent, rules are made to be broken and these guidelines should be viewed only as a point of departure in the difficult process of creating a world-class brand. Each branding situation and application is unique and requires scrutiny and analysis as how best to apply, or perhaps in some cases ignore, these recommendations and guidelines. Smart marketers will capitalize on every tool at their disposal – and devise ones that are not – in their relentless pursuit of achieving brand pre-eminence. To provide further stimulation, Brand Briefings 15.11, 15.12 and 15.13 summarize ideas from brand strategists.

Brand Briefing 15.13

Scott Bedbury's eight principles

Scott Bedbury, one of the brand architects behind both the Starbucks and Nike brands in the 1990s, is a proponent of a consumercentric approach. He outlines eight principles for brand leadership.

1. Relying on brand awareness has become marketing's fool's gold.
2. You have to know it before you grow it.
3. Just because you can doesn't mean you should.
4. Transcend a product-only relationship with consumers.
5. Everything matters.
6. All brands need good parents.
7. Big doesn't have to be bad.
8. Relevance, simplicity and humanity – rather than technology – will distinguish brands in the future.

Source: From A NEW BRAND WORLD by Scott Bedbury, copyright © 2001 by Scott Bedbury. Used by permission of Viking Penguin, a division of Penguin Group (USA) Inc.

Brand Briefing 15.14

The brand report card

Choose a brand and rate it on a scale of 1 to 10 (1 = extremely poor; 10 = extremely good) for each characteristic below.[16] Create a similar report card for its competitors. Compare and contrast the results with all the relevant participants in the management of the brand. Doing so should help you identify areas that need improvement, recognize areas in which a brand excels and learn more about how a particular brand is configured.

Score

1. ____Managers understand what the brand means to consumers.

   - Are there detailed, research-driven mental maps of the target customers?
   - Is there a brand mantra?

Brand Briefing 15.14 *continued*

- Have customer-driven boundaries been defined for brand extensions and guidelines for marketing campaigns?

2. ____**The brand is properly positioned.**

- What are the necessary and competitive points of parity?
- What are the desirable and deliverable points of difference?

3. ____**Customers receive superior delivery of the benefits they value most.**

- Has an attempt been made to uncover unmet consumer needs and wants?
- Does the company focus relentlessly on maximizing customers' product and service experiences?

4. ____**The brand takes advantage of the full repertoire of branding and marketing activities available to build brand equity.**

- Has the company strategically chosen and designed its brand name, logo, symbol, slogan, packaging, signs and so forth to build brand awareness and image?
- Has it implemented integrated push and pull strategies that target intermediaries and end customers, respectively?

5. ____**Marketing and communications efforts are seamlessly integrated (or as close to it as possible). The brand communicates with one voice.**

- Have all options been considered to create brand awareness and link brand associations?
- Is there a common meaning throughout the marketing communication campaign?
- Have the unique capabilities of each communication option been exploited?
- Have brand values been preserved in communications over time?

6. ____**The brand's pricing strategy is based on consumers' perceptions of value.**

- Has the added value perceived by customers been estimated?
- Have price, cost and quality been optimized to meet or exceed consumers' expectations?

7. ____**The brand uses appropriate imagery to support its personality.**

- Has credibility been established by ensuring that the brand and the people behind it are seen as expert, trustworthy and likeable?
- Have appropriate user and usage imagery been established?
- Has the right brand personality been crafted?

Brand Briefing 15.14 *continued*

8. ____The brand is innovative and relevant.

   ● Have product improvements been made that provide greater benefits and better solutions for customers?
   ● Has it stayed up to date and in touch with customers?

9. ____For a company with several brands and products, the brand hierarchy and brand portfolio are strategically sound.

   ● For the brand hierarchy, are associations at the highest levels relevant to as many products as possible at the next lower levels and are brands well differentiated at any one level?
   ● For the brand portfolio, do the brands maximize market coverage while minimizing overlap?

10. ____The company has a system in place to monitor brand equity and performance.

   ● Is there a brand charter that defines the meaning and equity of the brand and how it should be treated?
   ● Are periodic brand audits made to assess the health of brands and to set strategic direction?
   ● Are routine tracking studies conducted to evaluate current marketing performance?
   ● Are regular brand equity reports distributed that summarize all brand-relevant research and information to assist decision-making?
   ● Have people within the organization been appointed to monitor and preserve brand equity?

Discussion questions

1. What do you think makes a strong brand? Can you add any dimension to the eight areas proposed in the Brand Leadership Model (Brand Briefing 15.11)?

2. What about deadly sins of brand management? Do you see anything missing from the list of seven in Figure 15.9?

3. Pick one of the special applications of branding and choose a representative brand within that category. How well do the five guidelines for that category apply? Can you think of others not listed?

4. What do you see as the future of branding? How will the roles of brands change? What strategies might emerge as to how to build, measure and manage brand equity? What do you see as the biggest challenges?

5. Review the tradeoffs identified as part of achieving marketing balance. Can you identify any not listed? Can you identify companies that have excelled in achieving balance for each tradeoff?

References and notes

[1] Based on Kevin Lane Keller, 'The brand report card', *Harvard Business Review*, January–February 2000: 147–57.

[2] For an application in a franchise setting, see Leyland Pitt, Julie Napoli and Rian Van Der Merwe, 'Managing the franchised brand: the franchisee's perspective', *Journal of Brand Management*, 2003, 10 (August): 411–20.

[3] Kevin Lane Keller and Frederick E. Webster, Jr, 'A roadmap for branding in industrial markets', *Journal of Brand Management*, 2004, 11 (May): 388–402.

[4] Stephen Philips and Amy Dunkin, 'King customer', *BusinessWeek*, 12 March 1990: 88–94.

[5] Daniel Lyons, 'You want fries with that?', *Forbes*, 24 May 2004: 56–7.

[6] Leslie de Chernatony and Malcom H. B. McDonald, *Creating Powerful Brands*, Oxford: Butterworth-Heinemann, 1992.

[7] A. Parasuraman, Valarie A. Zeithaml and Leonard L. Berry, 'A conceptual model of service quality and its implications for future research', *Journal of Marketing*, Fall 1985: 41–50.

[8] Leonard L. Berry, A. Parasuraman and Valarie A. Zeithaml, 'Ten lessons for improving service quality', MSI Report 93–104, Cambridge, MA: Marketing Science Institute, 1993.

[9] Judith Corstjens and Marcel Corstjens, *Store Wars: The battle for mindspace and shelf space*, Chicester: Wiley, 1995.

[10] Kate MacArthur, 'Quirky Jones Soda steps into mainstream', *Advertising Age*, 27 March 2006: 12.

[11] Valarie A. Zeithaml, Parsu Parasuraman and Arvind Malhotra, 'Understanding e-service quality', presentation made at MSI Board of Trustees Meeting, 'Marketing knowledge in the age of e-commerce', November 2000. See also Parasuraman, Zeithaml and Berry, 'A conceptual model of service quality', as well as William Boulding, Ajay Kalra and Richard Staelin, 'A dynamic process model of service quality: from expectations to behavioral intentions', *Journal of Marketing Research*, February 1993: 7–27.

[12] Donna L. Hoffman and Thomas P. Novak, 'How to acquire customers on the web', *Harvard Business Review*, May–June 2000: 179–88.

[13] Tony Apéria, 'Brand reality model: making and keeping promises', in *Marketing Broadening the Horizons*, eds Lagrosen Stefan and Svensson Göran, Lund, Sweden: Studentlitteratur, 2006.

[14] Mary Jo Hatch and Majken Scultz, 'Are the corporate stars aligned for your corporate brand?', *Harvard Business Review*, February 2001: 129–34.

[15] Kevin Lane Keller and Frederick E. Webster Jr, 'Marketing balance: finessing marketing trade-offs', working paper, Tuck School of Business, Dartmouth College, 2002.

[16] Keller, 'The brand report card'.

Index

trademarks 85, 134
corporate trademark licensing 329
traffic-builders 518
transferability 131, 133, 289
transformational advertising 67–8
Tremor 263
Tropicana 59
trustmarks 31
Tupperware 203, 703
Tylenol 82, 262, 557–62, 585

UAL 693
UBS 693–4
umbrella brands *see* family brands
Unilever 217, 654–5, 686–7, 728, 730, 739
uniqueness 54–6, 81, 104, 139–43,
603, 761
UPS 741
upward extensions 634–5
URLs 145–6
usage expansion 364, 447, 674–6, 677
USAir 110
user imagery 65

Vacant 175
valuation of brands 6–9, 354, 477–8,
479–89, 493–9
accounting standards 489, 497–9
brand premium profit (BPP) 484, 485
BrandMetrics methodology 483–5
cost approach 482
historical perspective 481–2
income approach 485
Interbrand methodology 485–9
market approach 482
resource recognition procedure
(RRP) 484
Simon and Sullivan methodology 494
stock market reactions 494–6
value chain 37–8, 183, 347–57, 387
value creation 78–9, 320–1, 349
shareholder value 354–5
value-based pricing 190, 192–9

values 531–3
Vattenfall 373–5
versatility 269–70, 271
vertical brand extensions 605, 608–9,
632, 634–5
VF 510–11
Vibes Media 248
video advertising 247
video games 251
viral marketing 225
Virgin 240–1, 567, 595, 597–9
Visa 114, 116, 335, 547
visiting customers at home 422–5
Vodafone 294, 727
Volkswagen 79, 512–14
Volvo 48

Wal-Mart 19, 158, 192, 591,
787–8
Warnaco 309–10
Waterford Wedgwood 304
websites *see* internet
Wells Fargo 491–2
Westin Hotels 178
White Cloud 684, 685
Winston 27
Women's Work campaign 552
word-of-mouth 263–4
World Wildlife Fund 25
WPP 482
Wrigley 28

X Games 261
Xerox 71, 509, 737

Yahoo! 146, 225, 425
Yamaha 595
Yao Mong 336–8
young consumers 680–3, 729
Yuengling 678

Zaltman Metaphor Elicitation
Technique (ZMET) 416–18